Operation Dragoon
Autopsy of a Battle,

the Liberation of the French Riviera
in August and September 1944

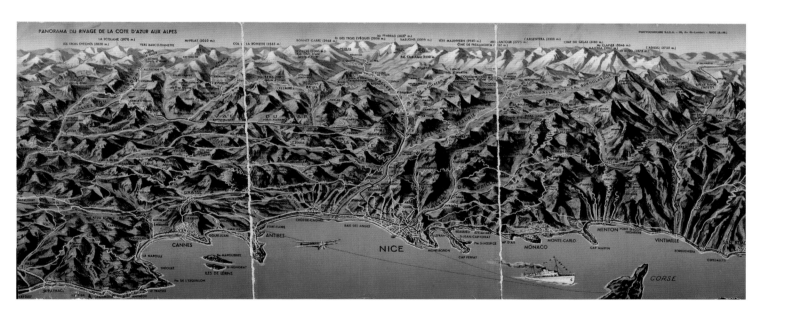

Jean-Loup Gassend

4880 Lower Valley Road • Atglen, PA 19310

Dedication

This book is dedicated to all those who were present on the
French Riviera in 1944, and particularly those who lost their
lives long before their time.

We are interested in hearing from authors with book ideas on related topics.

Published by Schiffer Publishing Ltd.
4880 Lower Valley Road
Atglen, PA 19310
Phone: (610) 593-1777
FAX: (610) 593-2002
E-mail: Info@schifferbooks.com.
Visit our web site at: www.schifferbooks.com
Please write for a free catalog.
This book may be purchased
from the publisher.
Try your bookstore first.

The author is always looking for more information,
witnesses, photos, and documents related to the
war on the French Riviera.
Contact: jean-loup@gassend.com

Table of Contents

Foreword

I have been a professional archeologist at the INRAP (National Institute of Preventive Archaeological Research) for 20 years, am specialized in the field of mortuary practices, mostly of medieval and modern times, and am particularly interested in periods of excessive mortality. My interest for these events mainly lies in the manner with which corpses were dealt with in mass graves, be it in contexts of epidemics or of inter-human violence.

It is because of this research theme that I regularly inform myself on these types of discoveries. That is how, during an investigation on the internet in 2007, I came across an excavation report concerning a World War II grave at Villeneuve-Loubet in which fourteen German soldiers had been buried simultaneously. Intrigued by this atypical discovery, it is on this occasion that I met Jean-Loup Gassend. During our numerous exchanges, he told me of his passion for World War II and for the southern France landings, and he also shared his interest for the more local history of the liberation of Villeneuve-Loubet in 1944 with me.

His work was, in part, based on the project of finding the grave of several German soldiers buried in haste in the village after the fighting that was only mentioned by a few imprecise oral accounts.

I was genuinely impressed by Jean-Loup Gassend's persistence and motivation, and by the determination that he demonstrated in order to successfully complete his task. The methods he chose (preparation, excavation, and study) illustrate the professional approach of archeologists quite well. Indeed, he first cross checked the various sources available to him (witness oral accounts, aerial photographs...) in order to precisely identify the location of burial. He then wondered about the legal framework of his intervention, and for that reason, he placed himself under the authority of the representative of the German *Volksbund*, the only organization that is authorized to take action on such war graves.

In the field, he also managed to adopt an efficient excavation strategy (photographic coverage, sketch locating the bones and the main objects, recording of the first observations) that enabled him to process the entire grave.

As is normally done in mortuary archaeology, at the end of the excavation, he made his own anthropologic study (thanks to his medical knowledge), mostly concentrating on the traumatological and pathological aspects of the discovered individuals.

To conclude his work, he made a summary of all the various data that he now presents in this captivating book, in which he places the story of the grave in the regional and historical context of the time.

Apart from the purely local value of the history of Villeneuve-Loubet, Jean-Loup Gassend's formidable work is also a good illustration of the management of bodies during certain tragic episodes of history. Indeed, with this excavation, we can observe the manner with which the living got rid of the dead, revealing the little care and attention afforded to the deceased. Above all,

it is the numerous witness accounts that Jean-Loup discovered or collected himself that sometimes enable the circumstances of death to be known and shed light on the treatment the bodies were given (looting), and detail the circumstances in which they were buried.

One of the main points of interest of the twentieth century is are the numerous sources (written or oral) that exist and that are sorely lacking for other more ancient periods. In consequence, the study of an event, as local as it may be, such as this mass grave in Villeneuve-Loubet enables us all, from very diverse sources, to better understand the reasons that contributed to it being dug and to explain certain details that archaeology alone could not have answered.

The transposition of this kind of particularly well-documented example is a major asset for the study by archaeologists of more ancient mortality crises, including those linked to war events.

Beyond these accounts about the liberation of Provence, Jean-Loup Gassend's book is also an outstanding memory work that demonstrates the value of collecting and transcribing oral accounts of the various actors in these events and of confronting them against archival documents or to available archaeological data. It is only through the confrontation of these various original sources that we can hope to correctly reconstruct the small stories of which History with a capital "H" is made.

Philippe Blanchard,
Research engineer at the INRAP (National Institute of Preventive Archéological Research), *Centre archéologique de Tours*, Indre-et-Loire, France

The wise saying that history is not what happened, but what historians say happened, does not fit this book. It is an accurate account of an important campaign where Allied and French resistance forces drove defending German forces from the parachute drop zones near le Muy, France, all the way back into Italy. The setting is picturesque Southern France, with its breathtaking views from the Maritime Alps, and yes, including the Riviera. For the paratroopers who did the fighting, it was one mountain and one mountain ridge after another, always attacking under fire, uphill. It is told by a wide variety of eyewitnesses who saw it first-hand from all angles. Remarkably, the stories fit together to make a composite, giving the reader an entertaining view of how it happened.

Howard Hensleigh, 517th Parachute Infantry Regiment.

The first time I heard of Jean-Loup Gassend was at the end of February 2012. In a letter to my brother, he asked for information and pictures of our uncle, Josef Fuchs, who had been killed in action near Grasse during the Second World War. Jean-Loup Gassend told us that he was going to write a book about the battles and other aspects of the Second World War in Provence, his native area.

I soon became enthusiastic about his work and was grateful when he offered to let me read the chapter of his book concerning our uncle and the circumstances in which he was killed. I found his way of recounting the historical facts fascinating. He interviewed not just war veterans from different countries, but also local people and relatives of those who had lost their lives.

As time went by, I received more chapters of his book – each exciting and leaving me full of interest.

What a great moment, when Jean-Loup Gassend offered to show us all the original places and scenes of action in the south of France!

In the end of August 2012 we – my husband and I – drove to Grasse and met the author. We found it deeply moving to follow him to the place where our uncle was killed, where he originally was buried – and not least to see the museum, where Jean-Loup Gassend had collected and exhibited in a very dignified manner all kinds of memorabilia from soldiers from America, Germany, and other nations who died in this area.

This book is absolutely unique. It is free of any prejudice, it is open-minded, and depicts the war as it really was: cruel and merciless. Jean-Loup Gassend's book shows how the war brought so much sadness, hardship, and misery to the people of all the countries involved. The powerful message that I can feel on every page is "War – never again!"

Dear Jean-Loup Gassend, thank you very much for sharing and for writing this book!

Stammham (Bavaria, Germany), February 2013
Maria Krieger
Niece of Josef Fuchs, a young German soldier killed in action
near Montauroux, August 15, 1944.

I served as a rifle platoon leader in B company, 509th Parachute Infantry Battalion during the invasion of Southern France beginning in August 1944. In 2010, I received an e-mail from Jean-Loup Gassend, inquiring about my battle experiences in the Riviera. This started an e-mail exchange for the next two years. He asked me about my men who were killed in combat there, and I sent him photos I had taken there in 1944. Jean-Loup also sent me current pictures of the 1944 battle sites. It brought back many memories.

I was impressed by Jean-Loup's attention to detail. He often challenged official reports that did not match the evidence. He brought me in contact with relatives of my men who were killed in combat. I learned much about the total situation in Southern France and would recommend this book to World War II history readers.

E. Mike Reuter
Veteran of the 509th Parachute Inf. Bn.

Acknowledgments

I am in debt to many people who helped or accompanied me during the writing of this book. They are too numerous to list them all here, though most contributors will find their names included within the pages of the book. Here, I will only be able to note the names of the people who were the most essential.

I wish to thank my parents, Max and Maggie Gassend, for putting up with and often actively participating in their son's outlandish hobbies; my brother Blaise Gassend for having financed much of my research in the U.S. and given much useful advice; my friends Lionel Alberti, Caroline Bouel, Sébastien Cano, Julien Fanet, Christophe Guglielmetti, Nina Kolarič, Damien Leblanc, Vincent Meyer, and Ivana Ključarić for having accompanied me during my investigations and given encouragement; Alain Endinger for being a faithful research companion; Joanna Tofilska for her irreplaceable and passionate help for my research in Poland; the countless town hall, library, and historical association workers and volunteers who helped me perform local research; Eric Miller, for believing in my project and encouraging me; Mike Constandy of Westmoreland Research for his outstanding and generous help at the U.S. National Archives; Pascal Boucard and Julien Hauser for their indispensable assistance in organizing the exhumation at Villeneuve-Loubet; veterans John DeVanie, Douglas Dillard, Dick Field, Howard Hensleigh, Bill Story, and Ed Thomas for their great assistance in putting me in contact with members of their former units; local inhabitants Jean-Pierre Battelli, Claude Bernard, Marcel Brocart, Charles Erbetta, Gustave Giordano, Denise Manaira, Manuel (of the Levens Tourism Office), Roger Monti, Bruno et François Municchi, Jacques and Alma Saussine, Max Stèque, Adèle Tacconi, and Jean Veillan for helping me find out about the history of their villages; the First Special Service Force Association; the 517th Parachute Regimental Combat Team Association; the 551st Parachute Infantry Battalion Association; the National World War II Glider Pilots Association; the Musée de la Résistance Azuréenne and Professor Jean-Louis Panicacci for so kindly opening their archives to me; Nadèje le Lédan, for allowing me to use her mother's memoires; Antonija Živcec, for helping me transcribe German interviews; Manfred Krellenberg, for his help with German navy archives; Maria Krieger for her work at the Dagneux cemetery and with the German press; Patsy McCoy and Mike Walsh for helping me learn how to research American war casualties; Ela Harari and Patricia King for their encouragements; Herwin Pingiera and Wojciech Zmyslony for helping me contact German veterans of *Reserve Division 148*; Bob Barrett for his help researching the 517th PRCT; Marion Parnell, Pierre Edouard Battarel, and Ann Ford for proofreading my manuscript and providing encouragement and suggestions; Philippe Blanchard for his advice; collectors Armand, Frédéric Brega, Didier, Laurent (two of them), Jim Pool, and Gerry Shaw; the Riviera Hash House Harriers for unknowingly bringing me to highly strategic research locations; and last but not least, Rémi Krizanaz, Ms. Smolka, and Marie Cécile Zipperling, who will recognize what help they provided. I beg the pardon of the many other people who provided great assistance, but that I may have forgotten to add to this list.

I thank the following institutions for their help and assistance: the *Archives Départementales des Alpes Maritimes*, the *Bundesarchiv*, the *Deutsche Dienststelle*, the U.S. National Archives, the *Volksbund Deutsche Kriegsgräberfürsorge*, and the Municipal Archives of Cannes, Mandelieu la Napoule, and Menton.

The following internet sites gave invaluable assistance on numerous occasions: 509thgeronimo.org, 517prct.org, archives. gov, findagrave.com, footnote.com, volksbund.de, wehrmacht-awards.com, and wwiimemorial.com.

Introduction

How an Idea was Born

I spent my teenage years living in Villeneuve-Loubet, near Nice, in southern France. I was very interested in World War II history and collected helmets and other objects I could find. My search for military objects caused me to speak with many elders, who also told me stories of what they had lived through during the war. I gradually started realizing that all these interesting local stories were much more important than the actual physical remains, and that they had, for the most part, never been documented in any way. Although every year there were celebrations for the anniversaries of the Liberation from the Germans, it was only rarely that anybody thought it useful to record the recollections of the few survivors from that period. When General Ed Thomas of the First Special Service Force came to Villeneuve-Loubet for the 60th anniversary of its liberation, I went to meet him in his hotel to tape record his recollections of the battle. He was my first interviewee. I gradually started tape recording interviews with local French elders as well, and also started doing telephone interviews with veterans of the Allied units who had fought around Nice. It became my obsession to interview everybody and anybody who may have had something interesting to say about the Liberation of the Maritime Alps in August 1944, as well as to find all documents related to this theme.

I spent most of my free time over the next six years doing taped interviews and then painstakingly transcribing them. During my conversations with the elders, I was told information that led to some surprising discoveries that will be shown in these pages. Here I present the results of my long investigation.

Theme of the Book

The intent of this book is to make an in-depth description of the infantry fighting that took place during the liberation of the French Riviera in the aftermath of the invasion of southern France on August 15, 1944. The time frame covered goes from August 15 to September 7, 1944. The boundary of the area of study is an imaginary line going through the following locations: Agay, Seillans, Andon, Toudon, Turini, and Menton. In practice, this forms the coastal strip of the Maritime Alps (the famous French Riviera), with a small portion of the Var region included.

The Maritime Alps were, for the most part, liberated by the First Airborne Task Force (FABTF). This division's actions can be separated into three phases. Phase 1, from August 15th to August 20th, was a chaotic airborne invasion, capture of the drop zones, and regrouping of forces. Phase 2, from August 21st to September 7th, was a war of movement towards the east – in other words,

through the Maritime Alps towards the Italian border. Phase 3 was after September 7th, and included static warfare in the mountains at the Italian border until the FABTF was relieved in November. The focus of this book is "phase 2," the war of movement during which most of the Maritime Alps and the eastern Var were liberated between August 21 and September 7, 1944. However, because fighting erupted in some towns within our area of study as of August 15th, we will also study certain events that occurred between August 15th and August 20th.

The entire area of study was occupied by one single German division (*Reserve Division 148*), and was then liberated by one single Allied division (the FABTF, with considerable help from the local French resistance) during the defined time period. Therefore, we will be studying the actions of two opposing forces of roughly equal strength (at least in theory) on a rather isolated front, engaged in a specific type of warfare in a well-defined time frame and location.

This study was chosen because it provides a rare opportunity to make a highly-detailed analysis of a campaign. The military units involved are clearly known and limited in number, enabling all the available archives to be searched. The number of casualties was small enough to be able to study each one of them personally. The position of the front lines changed almost every day, implying that if one knows the location an event took place, the date also automatically becomes known, and *vice versa*. A moving front also implies that the soldiers were in different and picturesque areas every day, making it much easier for their memories to register what happened and when and where. As an example, it is easier for a soldier to remember events that occurred in two different-looking villages that he was only in for one day than to remember a series of similar patrols that occurred over a period of several weeks in the same faceless forest or mountain. This is of obvious importance for a work mostly based on the recollections of witnesses of the battle.

The theme of this book was also chosen for the more simple reason: that it has never been studied in depth before. Although there are many books about Operation Dragoon and the invasion of southern France, only a few books or articles mention the advance through the French Riviera to the Italian border. These publications usually only present brief overviews of a few pages at most. This book is thus meant to fill a void that was present in the literature.

The French Resistance participated in the fighting that occurred in our area of study, and I thus made an effort to include as much information about their actions as possible. Although the artillery, aviation, and navy were also heavily involved in the fighting and played a vital role, we will not study their actions in detail in this book.

Organization of the Book

Our study starts with three introductory chapters to give the reader an idea of the atmosphere in France during the German occupation and what the night of the Allied invasion was like. The first chapter explains who the German occupiers were, what it was like to be one of them, and what it was like to live in their presence. The second chapter gives some information on how people joined the Resistance, and what it was like to be a resistance fighter. The third chapter will introduce the Allied units involved in the airborne invasion and mention some of the events that occurred on the day of the drop into France. We will then continue with the main theme of this book: detailed descriptions of the small-scale battles that took place in the towns and villages of the French Riviera. We will conclude the text with a chapter of some stories of the static mountain warfare that then followed at the Italian border.

Oral History

The backbone of this book is formed by first-hand witness accounts of the events. This book is thus mostly an oral history book. Oral accounts are known for not being the most reliable source of information, and I have therefore used a large number of more objective sources to cross check the information that was told to me by witnesses. These include more conventional sources, such as period military reports, local histories, and newspaper articles, but also more original sources, such as cemetery registers, exhumation reports, and actual excavations on the battlefields.

I found that each witness account can be broken down into two parts: 1) descriptions of events that the witness participated in himself, and 2) descriptions of events that the witness did not actually participate in, but that he found out about from other sources. The distinction between these two parts of a witness account is of the highest importance. I noted that concerning events that the witnesses participated in, the information provided was surprisingly reliable, as was confirmed by comparison with other sources. The imprecision or mistakes usually concerned numbers, ranks, and dates, the first two tending to become inflated with time. Concerning events that the witness had not participated in personally, the information was only as reliable as whatever the source of information was (various rumors); that is to say, it was often very unreliable and I usually discarded such information.

For the writing of this book, I attempted to find a large number of witnesses of all nationalities in order to be able to reconstruct events as precisely as possible. I had no difficulties locating dozens of American and Canadian veterans, as well as French civilians and résistants. However, I had the utmost difficulty locating "German" veterans (who in fact were often Polish, Czech, Slovenian, etc.), though I made every effort in my power to do so. Unfortunately, the number of German sources remains low.

When appropriate – in other words, almost always – I have given the name of the witness. However, because many of the witnesses or their families are still alive today, I have omitted their names in the few cases where their account could cause them any kind of embarrassment or problem. All witness accounts for which no reference will be given in the endnotes are interviews I made myself between 2004 and 2013. All other sources that were used, such as unpublished manuscripts, archival documents, or previously written books, will be credited. The original sources for this book were in English, French, and German. All translations were made by myself and any mistakes are my own.

Editing of Interviews

Most of the first-hand accounts that will be used in this book are interviews conducted by myself more than 60 years after the battle, with people usually over 80 years old. Some interviewees had incredibly good memories and storytelling talents. Others would barely respond to questions with more than a sentence, did the interview in a language that was not their own, or used incorrect grammar. To make these interviews readable and interesting for the average person, all of them needed to be edited. Some were only lightly edited, while others were painstakingly reconstructed from stories badly told in non-chronological order. In all cases, of course, I did not invent any of the information, and I tried to keep the accounts as true and authentic as possible.

The interviews used in the book are specially selected because they are interesting, and everything seems to indicate that they are for the most part true. However, all the interviews contain some mistakes and pieces that don't seem to fit. This is normal for any interview or type of investigation, and I purposefully left the interviews as they were, so as not to manipulate what was told to me. Sometimes interviews contain information that is downright wrong. This may seem awkward, but also serves its purpose by showing the beliefs that people had at the time, and sometimes still hold. Maybe what the witnesses say is not factually true, but what is true is that they and others believed the information to be correct at the time (and often still do today). Other times I have used accounts that are grotesquely exaggerated; these serve the purpose of illustrating just how relative "truth" is. In such cases, my opinion on the veracity of the accounts is clearly noted in the accompanying text.

Reconstruction of Events by Casualty Analysis

The conventional German archives available for the area of interest of this book are so few that no serious study can be made from them. It seemed next to impossible to know what units were sent to what locations during the events this book describes. However, I used an original approach to help solve this problem and consulted a source that previous students of the battle have ignored: the lists of German killed in action in the archive of the *Volksbund Deutsches Kriegsgräberfürsorge* (German War Graves Commission). Almost all the German soldiers who were killed in the fighting were buried in the immediate vicinity of where they were killed. They were later exhumed and identified, and this information was preserved in the archives of the *Volksbund*. I thus made a complete list of the casualties that had occurred in our area of study. The date of death and unit of the casualty often being available, I was able to reconstruct the movements of the German units on the battlefield. I was also able to precisely determine the numbers of casualties that occurred in most battles, and to compare these numbers with those that have previously been published (and that were often overestimated or purposefully exaggerated, as can be expected). I followed a similar approach for the casualties suffered by Allied units and found out with surprise that in some cases the survivors and historians of these Allied units were not at all aware of even approximately how many men had been killed in some encounters.

During the campaign, a large number of French civilians and resistance fighters were killed as well. Because these victims were not members of the military, and were thus not followed by an administration painstakingly attempting to note all casualties, making a complete list proved much more difficult than for the Allied and German soldiers. I did, however, do my best to make a complete list of resistance men who were killed. As for the civilian dead, I have only mentioned them when their death happens to be mentioned in the accounts used for this book.

I have tried to make lists that are as complete and correct as possible. However, as always with such an endeavor, there are bound to be a certain number of mistakes and omissions, and I therefore invite readers who spot any such flaws in the lists to contact me so that they can be corrected and and completed.

Battlefield Archeology and Forensics

Modern military activity produces an extraordinary amount of "pollution," mostly in the form of shell fragments, cartridge casings, and spent bullets, but also in the form of foxholes, graves, and abandoned equipment of all types. A mere few hours of fighting are normally sufficient to leave traces that can easily be located even after 70 years. In fact, a day of fighting in a remote area usually produces more artifacts than all previous and following human activity combined! When possible, the events described in this book were crosschecked by investigations at the geographical location where the events took place.

Though I myself am a medical doctor with a fair amount of experience in the field of forensic medicine and a keen interest in archaeology, I am in no way making the claim to have the methodology of a professional archeologist. However, when I did battlefield investigations, I tried to work with as much professionalism as was possible or reasonable, in order to be able to draw a maximum number of forensic and archeological conclusions that could later be shared with other researchers. I hope that any professional archeologists who may read this book will find my work interesting and performed with enough methodology that the meaning of the word "archeology" is not perverted by my use of it.

Observations on Historical Research

During my research for this text, I consulted large numbers of books that have previously been written about the war in southern France. I was shocked by the sources that some authors have used in order to draw their conclusions. The actions of the German forces, for example, are often studied using only Allied sources and reports. Needless to say, to understand the actions and frame of mind of one belligerent by using only the opinion of the opposing belligerent can be a risky work method! I also noted that numbers of casualties, whether Allied or German, were often given without any reliable source whatsoever, even though information about exact numbers of casualties is not difficult to find. Finally, some authors seem to consider that any previous publication is unquestionably trustworthy, factual, and acceptable as a reference,

when this is in fact far from always being the case. Historical facts must be proven, not simply guessed or repeated! For this book, I have attempted to use as many primary sources as possible and can only encourage others to do the same and to always (including when reading this book) keep a healthy dose of skepticism when reading the works of other scholars.

Historical Truth

Where is the exact truth in war? Does it even exist? Is anything factual? Memories become deformed, military reports contradict each other and are written triumphantly, official dates and locations of death are often wrong, men disappear never to be found again, the context in which photos are taken gets lost, archaeological deposits are incomplete, and individual witnesses only grasp tiny aspects of their environment and remember even less of it… The truth is lost the instant after it is created and occurs, even to those who were there, leaving behind only a few imprecise clues and distorted memories for those who wish to attempt to reconstruct it. Every source accessible to us is, after all, only a human-made interpretation, even if it is ourselves making that interpretation in the case of photos or archaeological results. In this book, different sources describing the same events are often put side by side, making their flaws and contradictions come unpleasantly to light, showing that no single source can even come close to recording the truth; that nothing is free of error and interpretation, nor can be trusted entirely. The real, actual truth is lost to time, never to be resurrected. I hope the numerous comparisons of sources and versions will teach the reader to become more careful and critical, but also more understanding and forgiving when interpreting historical information, or in fact any other type of information in the future.

Spirit of the Book

After all this technical talk; what is this book actually supposed to be? I hope to have created an interesting and informative history of the Liberation of the French Riviera; a history concentrated on the humans who lived (or all too often died) through the period; a history seen through the eyes of the normal people who got caught up in the turmoil of war. I have tried to design the text in order to make it accessible to any reader, and not just to fans of military history or specialist readers. I made a particular effort for each victim of the fighting to be mentioned by name, if possible with a photo, so that his or her memory will live on. These victims are those to whom this work is dedicated.

1

The Occupation of the Maritime Alps

An Introduction to the Geography of the Maritime Alps

The Maritime Alps is the "*département*" (one of the 100 administrative territories that France is divided into) at the extreme southeastern corner of France. It is bordered to the north and east by Italy, to the south by the Mediterranean Sea, to the southwest by the Var *département*, and to the northwest by the Alpes de Hautes Provence *département*. The coastal area of the Maritime Alps is known as the *Cote d'Azur*, or French Riviera, with famous towns such as Nice, Monte Carlo, Cannes, and Grasse, where many of the world's rich and famous live or have secondary residences. The vast majority of the Maritime Alps is covered by the southernmost part of the Alps: steep and isolated mountains with few roads. Only a few areas are suited for the building of cities or for agriculture, and these areas are mostly concentrated along the coast. As one goes further inland roads and towns become scarce and the terrain is mostly wild and uninhabited. The border with Italy is formed by the highest mountains in the area, which rise steeply out of the sea. The main river of the Maritime Alps is the Var (not to be confused with the Var *département*), flowing into the sea at the western border of the town of Nice. The events described in this book will mostly take place in the coastal area of the Maritime Alps and in the eastern parts of the Var *département* that borders the Maritime Alps.

The Brief History of the Maritime Alps in World War II

The Maritime Alps had a peculiar fate in World War II, quite different from that of the rest of France. In June 1940, as the French army was collapsing due to German attacks in the north of France, the Italian army performed an opportunistic surprise attack along the border of the Maritime Alps with Italy. In the next days, the Italians suffered heavy casualties and only managed a few very limited advances. However, France was forced to sign an armistice due to the actions of the German army in the north, and the French "Army of the Alps" also surrendered, though they had not actually been beaten on the battlefield.

Germany divided France into an occupied zone in the north and along the Atlantic coast and a free zone in the south. Italy was allowed to annex the few areas that it had managed to invade during the June attacks, including the town of Menton. A further 50 kilometers of French soil next to the Italian border were to be demilitarized. Thus, although the Maritime Alps were in the free zone of France, they were under partial occupation and control by the Italian army.

In November 1942, when the Allies landed in North Africa, the German army suddenly invaded the free zone of France as well. However, once again, the Maritime Alps were spared the presence of the Germans. Instead, the Maritime Alps and the neighboring *départements* were put under control of the Italian army. This had the consequence of attracting large numbers of Jews into the region, as the Italian army did not persecute them as the Germans did.

This situation did not last though, and in September 1943, following the invasion of Italy by Allied forces, the Italian army collapsed. The Italian soldiers in the Maritime Alps mostly abandoned all their military equipment and tried to cross the border back into Italy as fast as possible. The Germans swiftly sent in troops to take control of the Italian soldiers, as well as the territories they had been occupying. It was therefore only in September 1943

An Italian soldier directs traffic in the St Augustin district of Nice. It was not until September 1943 that the Maritime Alps were occupied by German forces. *Bundesarchiv, Bild 1011-027-1454-24 / Fotograf: Wolfgang Vennemann / Lizenz CC-BY-SA 3.0.*

German soldiers controlling traffic at a roadblock in the Menton area shortly after the German takeover of the Maritime Alps in September 1943. *Bundesarchiv, Bild 1011-685-00091-19A / Fotograf: Jesse.*

that the first German units finally arrived in the Maritime Alps. These troops included men of the *Division Feldherrnhalle*, who had apparently been sent to the Maritime Alps because they happened to be the first troops available for the mission.[1]

Reserve Division 148

In November 1943, *Reserve Division 148* was sent to the Maritime Alps to replace the *Division Feldherrnhalle* and take up long term occupation duties in the area. *Reserve Division 148* is the German

unit that will be mentioned regularly for the rest of this book, so we review it in detail.

For occupation duties, the Germans often used second class units that were not fit for front line service, and such was the case of *Reserve Division 148*. In fact, it was not a combat unit, but a training unit, to which soldiers were sent after only a few weeks of basic training in Germany. This enabled the Germans to occupy the Maritime Alps while wasting as little qualified human resources as possible. Experienced soldiers were sent to combat areas where they were desperately needed, while the Maritime Alps were being occupied by recruits still in training, who could, at the same time, participate in defending the area from various smaller scale threats, such as possible landings, resistance activities, and air raids. After a spending a few months with *Reserve Division 148* and completing their training, the soldiers were rotated out and sent to combat units. The division commander, 50-year-old *Generalleutnant* **Otto Fretter-Pico**, explained this in a postwar report:

> Duty: double mission: training of recruits, annihilation of enemy landings, and defense of the coast with resistance nests.
>
> Concerning the defense of the coast, because of the strength of the division, the training mission and the width of the area to defend, only securing the coast and observation was possible. Preventing a full scale landing was out of the question. (The width of each battalion's sector being 24 km.)[2]

The bulk of the division consisted of "men" born in 1926, who were 17 or 18 years old in 1944. With them were some older men, mostly over 30, who had not been drafted previously for various

Generalleutnant Fretter-Pico welcomes Generaloberst Blaskowitz on the Var River Bridge. This bridge would later become a major target for American bombers. The Var River Valley is visible in the background. Author's Collection.

St Laurent du Var, December 1943. Shortly after his arrival on the French Riviera, Generalleutnant Otto Fretter-Pico, the commander of Reserve Division 148, examines a map as he awaits an inspection by Generaloberst Blaskowitz. The Var River, the Var River Bridge, and the Mediterranean Sea are visible in the background. Author's collection.

The German army used very original and sometimes even comical paint schemes as camouflage for their bunkers. In this case, a German bunker in Antibes has been elaborately painted with fake shutters and flowers to make it look like an extension of the peaceful French villa it is built next to. Ted Rulison Collection.

This German bunker in Antibes has been painted over with a fake tree, a fake flowerpot, and a false window. Ferdinand Moscone Collection.

German coastal defenses at the Golf Juan harbor. A well-camouflaged German bunker looks out to sea while antitank walls disguised as civilian buildings obstruct the beach. Frédéric Brega Collection.

A German bunker along the coast in Nice. In this case, the word "Baths" has been painted onto the bunker to make it appear to be a public shower. Mike Reuter Collection.

This bunker in Cannes has been made to look like a gate and stone wall. MRA Collection.

In this case, the camouflage trick has been reversed, and a fake bunker has been painted around an innocent aperture in the wall of a civilian building on the coast at la Napoule. Pierre Carle Collection.

reasons, such as having a job that was important for the war effort. Most of the men came from Silesia and the Sudetenland, where *Reserve Division 148* had been formed and had its home bases. The few recruits from Germany were mostly from Bavaria. These enlisted men were under the command of experienced German officers and non-commissioned officers (NCOs) who had often been wounded on other fronts, and had then been sent to the *Reserve Division 148* to recuperate from their combat fatigue and battle wounds while passing on the lessons of their own combat experience to the recruits.

Silesia, where the majority of the enlisted men originated from, was part of the German Reich in 1944, though it was handed over to Poland after the war. Silesia has a bitter and complicated history, and its inhabitants were of mixed ethnicity. Some considered themselves completely German, while others considered themselves Polish and could not even speak German. To try to clarify things, the German authorities instituted the *Deutsches Volksliste*, a system by which residents of regions such as Silesia were classified into four categories according to how "German" they were or were not. Needless to say, the rules of classification were dubious, and in the end, many people who considered themselves Polish were also drafted into the German Army.

Furthermore, many Czech men, as well as a few Slovenians, Croatians, and men of other origins were sent to the *Reserve Division 148*. An entire battalion of Russian soldiers (*Ost Bataillon 661*) was even attached to the unit. According to what officers and NCOs of the division told Allied troops after being captured, 50% to 70% of the men in *Reserve Division 148* were "non-German."[3] These statistics are confirmed by the division's casualty lists. The consequence of this mixing of ethnicities, and of the use of large numbers of men who did not feel German, was that *Reserve Division 148* severely lacked cohesion and would be unable to put up with any real hardship when the time came. When **Uffz Rodolf Danjek** of the 6th Company of *Bataillon 372* was captured in September 1944, he went as far as to state that he "was very disgusted that he had commanded such poorly trained and disciplined troops."[4]

Order of Battle of Reserve Division 148

Reserve Division 148 consisted of two reserve infantry regiments, one reserve artillery regiment, one reserve *Füsilier* battalion, one reserve engineer battalion, and several smaller units, such as a

Young recruits of the 1st Company of Feld Ersatz Bataillon 148. 17-year-old Grenadier Friedrich Gorinschek, from Slovenia, stands first from right. He was later killed by the Resistance August 28, 1944, during the insurrection of Nice. Gorinšek Family Collection.

A typical example of a Reserve Division 148 soldier, 28-year-old Grenadier Konrad Styppa, had been a member of the Polish army before the war, but in 1944 he was sent to the Cannes area as a "German" soldier of Reserve Grenadier Bataillon 444. Konrad Styppa was killed in Cannes by Allied shelling August 17, 1944. The damage to these photos was caused by a shrapnel fragment that tore through his wallet. Styppa family Collection.

German soldiers on guard duty on the coast at Cannes. The Lérins Islands are visible to the right in the background. Archives Municipales de Cannes.

signal detachment, an anti-tank company, and various other odds and ends. Knowing the exact number of men in a unit can be very difficult, as this number usually varied greatly with time and the actual unit strength could be very different from the theoretical unit strength. This is particularly true for *Reserve Division 148*, which was constantly receiving new recruits while simultaneously shipping out soldiers who had completed their training. An official count made in July 1944 found almost 15,000 soldiers in the division, but other sources indicate that the actual number may have been much smaller. Indeed, according to declarations made by *Oberstleutnant* Hans Niedlich, who commanded one of the division's regiments, there were only about 7,000 men in *Reserve Division 148* August 15, 1944.[5]

Each reserve infantry regiment consisted of 14 companies organized into three separate battalions of four companies each, to which were added a 13th and 14th company that had specialized light artillery and anti-tank roles. The first battalion of each regiment was composed of the companies numbered 1 to 4, the second battalion companies 5 to 8, and the third battalion companies 9 to 12. Reserve companies theoretically contained approximately 200 men each, meaning that there should have been roughly 1,000 men in each battalion and 3,000 men in each reserve regiment. In reality, however, there were only about 2,000 men per regiment at the time of the Allied landing, according to *Oberstleutnant* Hans Niedlich.[6]

For the purpose of this book we will focus mainly on the infantry troops. The reader is invited to make the effort to concentrate on the names of each unit, as these unit names will continue to be mentioned regularly until the end of this book. To preserve the clarity of the text, we will later simply refer to the units as Battalions or Regiments and drop the words *Reserve* and *Infanterie* in most cases.

The infantry troops of the *Reserve Division 148* were organized in the following manner:[7]

- ***Reserve Grenadier Regiment 8***, commanded by *Oberstleutnant* Hans Niedlich, consisted of:

I: ***Reserve Grenadier Bataillon 7***, in position on the coast between Beaulieu and Motorola, with its 2nd Company in Sospel.
II: ***Reserve Jäger Bataillon 28***, in reserve in the area of la Trinité, with detachments in the Var River Valley. This unit, that was the only *Jäger*, or light infantry, battalion of the division, was used for anti-partisan sweeps and in any hotspots that appeared.
III: ***Reserve Grenadier Bataillon 164***, in position on the coast between Cros de Cagnes and Beaulieu.

- ***Reserve Grenadier Regiment 239***, commanded by *Oberst* Kurt Hahn, consisted of:

I: ***Reserve Grenadier Bataillon 327***, in reserve in the area of Mougins, with its 3rd Company in Vence. It was provided with extra vehicles in order to be mobile, and, just like *Reserve Jäger Bataillon 28*, was used in anti-partisan operations.
II: ***Reserve Grenadier Bataillon 372***, in position on the coast between Cannes and Cros de Cagnes.
III: ***Reserve Grenadier Bataillon 444***, in position on the coast between Théoule and Cannes.

- ***Ost Bataillon 661***, consisting of Russian so-called "volunteers," was attached to Regiment 239 and was stationed on the coast between Agay and Théoule.

- ***Division Füsilier Bataillon 148*** was assigned to Reserve Division 148, apparently acting as a highly mobile reconnaissance unit, at least in theory.

Reserve Artillerie Regiment 8 (consisting of *Reserve Artillerie Abteilungen 8* and *44*) and ***Reserve Pionier Bataillon 8***, which were spread out over the whole Riviera, provided the division with artillery and engineers. The other smaller units (cyclists, transmissions, transportation, etc.) that also completed the division's order of battle were usually numbered 8, 148, or 1048. The divisional headquarters was stationed in Grasse, probably to be a safe distance away from the coast in case of a landing. There were several German military hospitals in the Maritime Alps, the main two seeming to have been located in an empty summer camp in St Vallier de Thiey, and in a former clinic in Rue Bellanda, in the Cimiez district of Nice.

The main point to be noted from the disposition of the German forces is that they were virtually all concentrated in the coastal area, while almost no troops were present in the mountains above the St Vallier-

Sospel line. In other words, most of the Maritime Alps *département* was not actually occupied by German troops, and the Germans usually only ventured into these remote areas to perform patrols or specific missions.

In early August 1944, in the very days preceding the Allied invasion, it was decided that *Reserve Division 148* was to be reorganized, with the 8th and 239th Regiments each giving up one battalion in order for a third regiment to be created. This third regiment, temporarily known as *Regiment Kessler*, was to be located in the St Raphaël area. However, when the invasion occurred, *Regiment Kessler* had barely started being formed, consisting of only a HQ Company and a 13th and 14th Company. The "regiment" was quickly annihilated by the Allied forces, and we will therefore make no further mention of the unit in this book, considering how brief its existence was.[8,9]

The Soldiers of Reserve Division 148

We now read what some of the young men who were sent to *Reserve Division 148* can tell us about their experiences from the time they left Germany or Silesia. Once they arrived in Nice, they continued the training that they started in Germany, and participated in the daily routines of occupation troops, some of the more common missions being to stand guard in bunkers at the coast or on bridges, and to participate in laying minefields. **Josef Kirsner** was a German recruit from Bavaria who was sent to 11th company of *Reserve Grenadier Bataillon 164* in Nice:

In 1943, I wasn't even 17 yet and was called up by the military. In November 1943, I was inducted at Ingolstadt, near München. I contracted jaundice there and was sent to hospital. I was very lucky, because the unit I had been with was sent to Yougoslavia and then to Russia. On March 20, 1944, we were transported to France by rail, from München through Augsburg, Stuttgart, Mühlhausen, Thionville, Lyon, and Marseille. It took us six days, because the railway was always being cut by the partisans, or the Resistance, as it was called in France. On March 26, 1944, we arrived in Nice. We were very fortunate, because Nice was beautiful and it was springtime and already warm. We were sent to a large villa or winery above the town of Nice. That is where the company headquarters and the field kitchen and everything were. By foot, it was about half an hour away from Nice. I was only in that villa for six days, until April 2nd, before being sent to a course at Beaulieu, where we were quartered in a hotel called Hotel Bedford that was completely empty. I stayed there for four weeks, and I can remember that we mined the Cap Ferrat peninsula. We dug holes, then the engineers laid mines in them. On May 6th, I returned to the company in the winery above Nice for 12 days. Then, on May 18th, I was sent down to the Var Bridge, at St Laurent, to guard the bridge.

In my company, except for a couple of older men, we were all young boys, 17 and 18 years old. A lot of men were from Upper Silesia, but in fact, they were Poles who had been drafted into the German army. They could speak German, but they stuck together and spoke Polish, and I couldn't understand anything they were saying. Some had

"We were sent to a large villa or winery above the town of Nice." New recruits of Bataillon 164 in training in the garden of Villa Montana, overlooking the Var River Valley. All the recruits seem to be either teenagers or men in their mid-thirties. Josef Kirsner Collection.

Villa Montana then and as it appears today, having been transformed into a luxurious condominium. Josef Kirsner Collection. Author's Collection.

Some NCOs of Bataillon 164 in Villa Montana. Several men wear decorations, indicating that they are already battle hardened veterans. Josef Kirsner Collection.

19-year-old Grenadier Rudolf Strozyk, of the 12th Company of Bataillon 164, poses in gardens of the ultra-luxurious "Villa Ephrussi de Rothschild" on Cap Ferrat. Villefranche and the Bay of Villefranche are visible in the background. Rudolf Strozyk came from Kattowitz, and when he was later captured by the Allies, he joined the Free Polish Forces, like many other Poles of Reserve Division 148. Helena Ling Collection.

been NCOs in the Polish army. They had probably been prisoners of war, and because they had a grandfather or grandmother was German, they were conscripted into the German army, or they had volunteered for the army instead of staying in prison camps. I was from Bavaria and don't know why I ended up in that unit. There were a couple of us from München and we also stayed together. But we were young, and there were no problems between the two groups.

In St Laurent, we were quartered in a house in the middle of a big orchard that was directly beside the sea. In the orchard there were tomatoes, onions, and huge cherry trees. Eight of we soldiers lived there. We also had a bunker directly on the coast that was equipped with machine guns. The whole place was mined, but we knew where one could walk and where one could not walk. The French were not allowed in.

Our mission was to guard the Var Bridge, so that partisans wouldn't blow it up. We guarded the bridge day and night for four-hour shifts and then had eight hours off. Trucks loaded with wine, grapes, and fruit drove over the bridge into Nice to supply the city. We had to control the trucks and asked the drivers for their *Ausweiss*, "*carte d'identité*," and driver's license. They needed permits from the German *Kommandantur*. There were large tanker trucks carrying wine and we asked the drivers if they could give us some. They would go back with a pail and fill it with wine. It wasn't a problem, as they had a couple of thousand liters. When there were peaches, they would also give us a box of peaches. That is the way it was until August 30th.

In fact, I have to say that we didn't have any problems; there was no fighting, and at first it was as if there was no war going on. There was a soldier's theater in Nice, and at night we could go out into the taverns to drink coffee or a glass of wine. We were just young boys of 17 and 18. We received our pay in French money, and we paid for everything of course; we didn't steal anything. We didn't notice any great hatred from the French people. Of course, there was a war on and we weren't welcome; the French weren't happy to have Germans there occupying them.

We weren't volunteers for the German army. We had to go. Today one can't imagine what it was like at the time of the Nazis. We were afraid for our lives. If anybody did anything, he was shot. We didn't have much choice. We only heard the news on the German radio. They didn't say the truth, so we only heard what we were supposed to hear and nothing else.

Egon Fergg was another very young recruit from Bavaria, who found himself in *Reserve Pionier Bataillon 8*, the Engineer Battalion of *Reserve Division 148*. He was less than enthusiastic about being in the army:

I was called up in May, when I was 17 years old, and spent three weeks at a German barracks in Regensburg, Bavaria, where we practiced building pontoon bridges on the Danube. I was then transported by freight train to Nice, where we were supposed to receive our training. On the way from the train station in Nice to our quarters we could hear the French passers by exclaiming to each other: "But they are still kids!" We were quartered in a house called the "Ecole Normale" in St Sylvestre.

We trained in the port of Villefranche, where we practiced building pontoon bridges. We also did sports, marching, and running at the football field in Nice. We had no relations with the French civilians. We were always in our barracks in the house or on the harbor.

Our chiefs, our *Unteroffiziere*, were older. They were making us train in the heat. It was very hot and this training was not very well accepted by us, so we had bad relations with them. They didn't treat us very humanely and we didn't like it. In my group, three or four of my comrades were boys who studied theology. We didn't drink any alcohol and we didn't smoke, and our chief said: "What kind of soldiers are you? You don't smoke, you don't drink."

One time, we had to do an exercise with the gas mask at the football field. In the 40°C heat we had to put on our gasmasks to run. This was very bad treatment, so one of our comrades said to the chief: "Du Arschloch! You asshole!" We didn't say who had said it so he couldn't punish us. But when the Americans landed, the training finished abruptly and they treated us better.

Half the people came from Bavaria, Germany, and the other half came from around Kattowitz, in Upper Silesia, Poland. They could speak German, but not perfectly. They made some mistakes. Nobody was happy to be in the army and they said: "Now our country is occupied by the Russians and we have no interest to be soldiers anymore. [The Poles no doubt said this in 1945, as at the time of the southern France invasion Silesia was still firmly in the hands of the Germans.]" They were very good boys. We had a lot of fun working together.

Karl Cyron, also aged 17, was one of the rarer volunteers of *Reserve Division 148*. Although he was born in Germany, he

Rudolf Strozyk and a comrade are visibly very pleased with their surroundings in the luxurious gardens of the Villa Ephrussi de Rothschild, on Cap Ferrat. Helena Ling Collection.

"But they are still kids!" Some typical recruits of Reserve Division 148. Grenadier Georg Vogl, first from the right, is only 17 years old. His comrades all seem to be roughly the same age. All the men are equipped with older model Mauser rifles and only wear one ammunition pouch. Georg Vogl was killed in an ambush by American pathfinders of the 509th PIB at Tanneron August 17, 1944. Vogl family Collection.

18-year-old Grenadier Kaspar Fischer, of the 10th Company of Bataillon 164, poses for the camera on the Colline du Château, in Nice. The port of Nice is visible in the background. Kaspar Fischer was later to be killed in battle against the paratroopers of the 517th PIR at la Roquette sur Var August 28, 1944. Fischer Family Collection.

had spent his whole life in Hindenburg, Silesia (now Zabrze, Poland), and was an example of a Silesian who considered himself to be 100 percent German:

From March 1944 until August 1944, I was stationed in Nice as a member of the 10th Company of 164th *Ersatz Bataillon* [in fact, *Reserve Grenadier Bataillon 164*] of the 148th Infantry Division. In my train there were 800 men, almost all born in 1926. Only a few were a bit older. All of us were from Upper Silesia: Gleiwitz, Hindenburg, Beuthen, Kattowitz… A lot were from Kattowitz. It took us six days to travel from there to Nice.

It was very nice in Nice. We were recruits and spent our time training with no time off. We marched and learned how to shoot. My company commander was *Oberleutnant* Tietz, and my *Zugführer* was *Oberfeldwebel* Nava. In my Zug during training there were 60 men, and about 50 of them were from the region of Kattowitz and Gleitwitz, at the German Polish border. We called them *Volksdeutschen*. There were some people who couldn't even speak German and people who didn't want to speak it. They just had to learn the commands in German: "*Abteilung marsch, Abteilung* halt!" They weren't pleased to be soldiers, and I suspect they surrendered to the enemy at the first gun shots. I remember one guy who was called Karbowski. He had been an officer in the Polish army in 1939 and then he was with me in training. I stuck with three other *Reichsdeutschen*, and we got along well. We didn't need anybody else. We couldn't speak Polish and didn't have any contact with the Poles. There was a *Volksliste* with three classes: *Volksliste* 1 were the most German, and *Volksliste* 2 and 3 were only slightly German. I had volunteered, so was happy to be a soldier.

The Americans and English bombed the bridges and railway connections in all of France. No more supplies were coming from Germany: no equipment, no food, no ammunition, nothing. The food was bad and there was always less and less of it. When I arrived in France, we received one loaf of bread for two soldiers. After a few weeks we had to share one between four men, then six men, and in the last few weeks we received one loaf for ten men. Everyone got one slice. Imagine what that was like for 17 and 18 year olds who were still growing and needed strength.

After three or four months of training, I was sent to the coast. We stayed in Villa Fabron in Nice. There was a defensive line of bunkers near our quarters and we observed the water to see if ever the English or Canadians came. We had four-hour guard shifts, two men at a time, looking at the water to see if a submarine or boat was coming, but none ever came. Four hours of guard duty, then four hours of rest, four hours of guard duty, then four hours of rest, day and night. Each bunker had the name of a flower or plant. I was at *Stützpunkt Anemone*. There were also *Kaktus, Distel* [thistle], *Alpenveilchen* [Cyclamen], etc. I was in a 12cm mortar pit, with machine gun bunkers to the right and left.

Recruit **Josef Fröhlich**, from Troppau (now Opava, Czech Republic), was also an ethnic German and was 17 years old when he was drafted into the Wehrmacht. His experience was very similar to that of the other soldiers we have mentioned:

I was called up on March 30, 1944, in Troppau, in the mountains of Slovakia. There were lots of comrades from my region there, and lots from southern Poland, Kattowitz, Gleiwitz, and Beuthen, in Upper Silesia. They were in my company, the 3rd Company of *Füsilier Bataillon 148*. We were given uniforms, rifles, ammunition pouches, and everything a solider has, and were then loaded into a freight train. The 28th *Jäger*s were also in our train; they were all from Troppau, the *Jäger* town, my homeland. We were in the train for three weeks in freight cars, sitting down on our packs with the doors open and looking outside. When the train stopped, we got out to get fresh water for drinking,

17-year-old Grenadier Johann Meyer (at right), of the 9th Company of Bataillon 164, enjoys some free time with a comrade in the Bay of Villefranche. A practical joker has decorated their boat with a deaths head and SS runes. Johann Meyer was later to be killed in an ambush by maquisards at Porte Rouge, south of Levens, in late August 1944. Meyer Family Collection, courtesy Dr. Hartmut Pöhlmann.

then we continued on. We went to Neisse, Prague, Pilsen, Nürenberg, and Strassburg, then into the Rhône Valley to Marseille and Toulon, reaching Cannes in late April. In Cannes, the *Füsilier Bataillon* got off, but the 28th *Jäger*s continued on to Nice and we didn't see them again.

We went up to St Basile. There was a villa on a hill in the forest there north of Cannes, and we were quartered and trained there with rifles and weapons. The soldiers from southern Poland couldn't speak German very well and always spoke with each other in Polish, but I formed good friendships with them. One guy called Becker was in my company and we got along great. He always told me: "Fröhlich, du gute Kamerad! [Fröhlich, you good comrade]." They could only speak bad German, but the Germans had enlisted all of them into the reserve infantry, into my division, the 148th. When they were angry, they always said "Do pieruna [meaning 'damn it,' or more exactly, 'thunderbolt']"; it was a small swear word for them. We made good friends with them and there weren't any problems. It was good times in St Basile; we could go swimming in the sea and our elder comrades, our instructors, said: "Thank God we didn't end up in Russia and are in a nice area in southern France."

Then we were deployed in the mountains at Col d'Allos and Col du Galibier and we wound up at Vence. I turned 18 in July, and I was in Vence August 15th when the Americans landed at St Raphaël. Before that the Americans, coming from Morocco, bombed the freight station at Cannes la Bocca.

Stefan Wesoly, from Silesia, was one of the many recruits who considered himself as purely Polish:

I was conscripted in the German army in January 1944, when the Germans called up those born in 1926. But I was born in October, and in January, I was only 17 years old. After a short preparation, I was sent to southern France in a military transport sometime in March. There was an army camp in the mountains somewhere behind the town of Cannes. The Germans treated us like all the soldiers. There was no special treatment. They needed us. Most were very young as I was, and then there was another group that was over 40. There were very few in between.

After a few weeks I was sent to an observation point on the coast, also called Stützpunkt, close to the railway station of la Bocca, in the suburbs of Cannes. Our duty was to watch the sea and report if we saw any movement. All the civilians had been evacuated and the houses close to the shore were empty. We had no contact with the local population.

There were five of us at the Stützpunkt: a sergeant and four of us soldiers. Our sergeant was usually drunk. He was sleeping, and we had to watch the sea and keep quiet. We were from western Poland, which had

"Thank God we didn't end up in Russia and are in a nice area in southern France." German officers enjoy a beer in front of the famous Casino in Monte-Carlo. From left to right are Oberleutnant Barsch (CO of the 6th Company of Reserve Jäger Bataillon 28), Leutnant Boeracker, Oberleutnant Johannes Bönsch (CO of the 8th Company, Bataillon 28), Leutnant Bienek, and Oberzahlmeister Hönig. Bönsch family Collection.

been incorporated into the Reich, and we mostly spoke Polish between ourselves. We were all trying to say: "Well, how can we escape?" This was the conversation. We couldn't leave because we were always concentrated in the Stützpunkt.

Stefan Wesoly later managed to surrender to Allied troops and, like many Poles of *Reserve Division 148*, he joined a Polish unit of the British army fighting against the Germans in Italy.

Udo Taubmann was an 18 year old Bavarian also stationed in the vicinity of Cannes, with the 6th Company of *Bataillon 372*:

We arrived in March. The trip lasted six days and every train got bombed on the way to France, so in an instant we had to get off the train: "Tieffliegalarm!" Things were hard down there. We received bad food: only vegetables. We were always becoming poorer. Everything was being sent to Russia. We did training, courses on mines, shooting, always something every day. Some of us were in Cannes and were occupying bunkers. We had to guard bridges, lay mines in Cannes, and break up roads. We mined artillery positions and the coastal road in Cannes. The population wasn't happy, but those were our orders. After some time we didn't have any mines left, so we just hung up warning signs. Sometimes we waved at the girls when they were picking rose blossoms as we marched by. I also swam in the Mediterranean Sea when we had a bit of time off. I still have a picture of that. Those were the good times, down there in the salt water.

Ost Bataillon 661, consisting of Russian so-called volunteers, was no doubt the most mediocre unit in *Reserve Division 148*. Its history gives an idea of exactly how poorly motivated some soldiers of the division were. Based on the interrogation of two prisoners from *Ost Bataillon 661*, **Ivan Samorkin** and **Piotr Tichanow**, the Allies later wrote:

Ost Bataillon 661 was organized in the summer of 1942 at Volosovo, near Leningrad, from about 800 prisoners of war taken from prisoner of war camps at Volosovo, Syrlo, and Krasnoye. According to both prisoners of war, recruiting was not carried out on a volunteer basis, but Russians were selected by a group of German officers primarily on the basis of physical qualification.

Various bunkers built on the coast in the Cannes area. All of them have been painted carefully to make them blend into the scenery. MRA Collection.

See caption with top photo p 25.

Somewhere near Cannes, young soldiers of the 6th Company of Bataillon 372 pose with the tools of their trade and the infamous skull and crossbones sign that was used to mark mine fields, both real and false. Udo Taubmann Collection.

"Those were the good times, down there in the salt water." 18-year-old Grenadier Udo Taubmann, of Bataillon 372, sitting on the beach in front of the famous Carlton Hotel in Cannes and swimming in the sea with other German soldiers. Udo Taubmann Collection.

In October 1942, following a six-week training period, the battalion was sent into the southern part of the Leningrad District to guard German communication lines from Partisan attacks. Numerous desertions depleted the battalion's strength, and in October 1943, it was sent to southern France for coastal defense duty, where it occupied a sector from Théoule sur Mer to Agay.[10]

Air Raids

In the context of World War II, being stationed on the French Riviera was probably one of the best assignments a German soldier could hope to receive. The weather was nice, the troops were often quartered in luxurious houses or hotels, and as Josef Kirsner said, it was almost as if there was no war going on. However, even in this seemingly idyllic context danger was never far away, and men died almost every day. One of the most dangerous threats to the German soldiers and French civilians alike were the Allied air raids. As August 1944 approached, air raids became more and more frequent, usually targeting the railway stations in Nice and Cannes, or the important bridges on the Var river or at Anthéor. The Var Bridge in particular was like a life line through which supplies were sent to Italy, and was a favorite target. American bombers were notorious for the imprecision with which they dropped their bombs, and hundreds of civilians paid for this with their lives. The most deadly raids occured on May 26, 1944, when almost 400 civilians were killed in a single day in Nice and St Laurent du Var.[11] Being stationed in Nice, **Karl Cyron**, of *Bataillon 164*, witnessed many of these raids from a relatively safe distance:

Before the landing of August 15th, Battalion 28 had already lost about 50 men. As of April 1st, the English came from their airfields in Corsica to bomb the Var Bridge almost every day at 11 o'clock on the dot with 20 or 30 bombers. But they didn't aim properly and sometimes not a single bomb would actually hit the bridge. There were large holes everywhere in the riverbed. Battalion 28 was guarding the Var Bridge. There was one sentry at each side, and they were getting killed almost every day.

We were about three kilometers away on a hill, and we watched as the bombs fell out of the aircraft. There were flak positions on the Var; one day six aircraft were shot down at the same time and crashed into the sea. Speed boats quickly left the port in Nice to pick up those that had managed to save themselves and jumped out with their parachutes. We had to be careful of our own flak. They would fire like crazy at the airplanes, and then the fragments would come back down, all the way to Nice. We had to hide in houses, or under trees.

There was a military airport somewhere in Nice, and when I arrived in March, there were three Me 109s parked there. After a week or two, only two were left. After another couple of weeks, there was only one. By the end there were none left. When the English bombers came to attack the Var Bridge, they had fighter escorts and they shot the three Germans out of the sky.

In fact, Karl Cyron's view of the air raids was somewhat distorted by the distance from which he observed them. It was men from Battalion 164 who were guarding the Var Bridge, not men of Battalion 28, and although several soldiers did get killed in the vicinity of the bridge, the sentries did not simply stand idle waiting to die during the raids as Karl Cyron seemed to imagine. **Josef Kirsner** was one of the soldiers of *Bataillon 164* who actually was on guard duty on the western side of the Var river bridge in St Laurent:

On June 15th, the invasion of southern France began [Kirsner is obviously confusing the dates of the Normandy and Provence invasions], and it is only as of then that the Americans started attacking us with bombers almost every day. They bombed the bridge and also the little train station in St Laurent. It wasn't pretty.

There were some Italian soldiers or workers who were constantly repairing the bridge after it had been damaged in air raids so that cars and trucks could keep on using it. They had a trumpet, and whenever an air raid was coming they blew their trumpet before our own *Fliegeralarm* sounded. Beside our house in the orchard we had dug real fox holes, almost two meters deep. When there was an air raid, we ran like crazy and jumped into those holes.

At the Anthéor Bridge, two German soldiers pose with civilians who are evacuating the area because of the frequent Allied air raids. Since Anthéor was under the responsibility of Ost Bataillon 661, these two soldiers may well in fact be Russians, though they are not wearing the distinctive sleeve insignia that Russian volunteers of the German army were supposed to wear. Pierre Gautier Collection.

July 12, 1944, an American Liberator bomber flies over Villeneuve-Loubet on its way home. Smoke and dust clouds rise up from targets that have been hit in Nice and Cagnes sur Mer. The Var Valley is clearly visible in the distance. NARA.

German identification tag belonging to an antiaircraft artillery soldier recovered from the vicinity of the Var Bridge. Flak Abteilung 391 was one of the antiaircraft units stationed in the Maritime Alps. Private Collection.

It was a bit safer there than on the bridge. Once there was a train stopped in the train station at St Laurent and they bombed it. It was only a couple of hundred meters away from where our foxholes were.

We had an NCO from our company, not one from the bridge guards, but one from the headquarters villa, who was a nutcase and always checked in on us, including at night to make sure we weren't sleeping. There was a small two-man bunker on the bridge itself that had been built by the Italians. It was not reinforced with steel, and it was actually junk. The NCO told us that during air raids we were to stay on the bridge in that bunker. We thought: "The man is crazy, we are not going into that bunker, we prefer to run to our orchard." We only had 200 or 300 meters to run to our holes when there was a *Fliegalarm*. We told him: "We will not stay on the bridge because it is too dangerous! We will not use the bunker." The NCO always went into that bunker, and during one air raid a bomb landed a couple meters away from it. The bunker was torn to pieces and blown into the air, along with the

NCO, and landed in the Var river bed. We practically found nothing of him. He died in his bunker and that was the end of him. Other than that, we had no losses.

Marcel Perez, of St Laurent du Var, was a witness to the air raid mentioned by Josef Kirsner that hit a passenger train near the station in St Laurent May 26, 1944:

When I arrived at the scene, I got off my bike and saw a woman who had managed to get out of the train by herself and who Doctor Colpart was giving first aid to. A friend of mine from the Défense Passive [Civil Defense] came almost immediately. He was a farmer, a tough guy, called Lucien Bruno. We had already worked together in the past. There were still very few people there, but we decided it was best not to wait. We started by the first train car. The first wounded man we found was a German, alone in his compartment. He had a very nasty wound on his leg. In fact, his foot was almost cut off. German or not, it was out of the question to leave him there. We took a door that had been torn off the train car and used it as a stretcher. It was very heavy, but we carried it to a German outpost on the N7 [Highway Number 7]. (…)

My friend Bruno always had a small bottle of lemon balm on him, but it contained homemade *eau-de-vie* [brandy]. Since the soldier was suffering a lot, Lucien asked me if I thought a little sip would do him some good. He was a German, it is true, but he was wounded and it was a humanitarian gesture. I could only agree, and Lucien gave him the bottle, thinking he would make do with a gulp or two; but he drank the entire bottle at once. Taking the bottle back, Lucien told me: "See, he liked my lemon balm."

After transporting the German, we went back to the train, which was only 100 meters away. In the meantime, other rescuers had arrived and things were getting organized. Lucien and I went into the second car, walked down the hallway, and saw two travelers sitting face to face by the windows in the second compartment. I immediately realized that nothing could be done for them, and it shook me up terribly, because I knew both of them well. (…)

May 25, 1944, a cloud of smoke rises over Cannes as a mortally stricken American Liberator bomber crashes into the ground. MRA Collection.

Bombs dropped from Marauder aircraft hit the surroundings of the Var Bridge, where Grenadier Josef Kirsner and his colleagues of Bataillon 164 were located. St Laurent du Var is visible to the left of the Var River and Nice to the right. NARA.

St Laurent du Var: 17-year-old Grenadier Josef Kirsner and a comrade of the 11th Company of Bataillon 164 stand in front of houses that have been destroyed by American bombs that were destined for the Var River Bridge but fell off target. Note that both soldiers only wear one ammunition pouch, as was often the case within Reserve Division 148 during the Occupation. Josef Kirsner Collection.

The tragedy of May 26, 1944. American Liberator bombers fly home after targeting the St Roch railroad yards in Nice. In fact, many of the bombs fell off target, killing approximately 300 French civilians in Nice. NARA.

Lucien Bruno and I carried both their bodies to the road, after which we continued our sad work. There had not only been victims in the train. On the road, people had been killed in the cars and trucks that had stopped during the air raid. The drivers and passengers who had time to had lain down under the vehicles, but even there, some had been killed. Among them was a young man from St Laurent who had already been wounded a few weeks earlier. It was not an ordinary wound: caught in an air raid while he was crossing the Var Bridge on foot, he had lain down flat on his stomach and was hit in the kidney, not with shrapnel, but with large pebbles that had been blasted out of the river bed by the explosions. (…) On the day he died, May 26th, he was hit in the kidneys once again, but not by pebbles this time! Amongst the other dead was a taxi driver whose wife was pregnant. He was driving back from Cannes after having been requisitioned by German officers.[12]

Air raids were, of course, terrifying for the civilian population. **Josette Valaira**, from Mougins, remembers how some people panicked while they were hidden in air raid shelters:

The airplanes would fly by, and every time they flew over la Bocca they dropped bombs. We could hear them and afterwards we could see that there were fires, everything was burning down there. So we had to hold down the grandmother. She would lose her mind and cry and shout: "They are killing my children, they are killing my children, my little children!"

Such panics could have terrible consequences. **Lucette Musso**, who was a child at the time, remembered one case:

There were raids on the train station in la Bocca. Of course, some bombs fell off target. I knew a little girl, the sister of a girl who was in my class. When the bombs were falling, her mother held her in her arms so tightly that she smothered her because she was so small. She smothered her: that really shocked me.

The French Resistance

Another threat faced by the German soldiers stationed on the French Riviera was that posed by partisans, which the next chapter is dedicated to. Although the number of men who were killed by the partisans was quite small, the possibility of suddenly becoming the victim of an attack by an unseen enemy was particularly frightening to the German troops. There were bands of armed Frenchmen in the mountains in the hinterland, and in cities and villages there were informers and suppliers working for the Resistance. There were bombings of public places, sabotages, and attacks of isolated soldiers. Nothing that the Germans did could remain secret. The Germans responded to this threat with paranoia, imagining partisans, whom they called terrorists, everywhere. **Udo Taubmann** describes the situation in Cannes:

It was dangerous at night when we were on guard duty. One was very afraid to be ambushed by the terrorists. A lot of people were disappearing. Before the Americans landed, my best friend, Ewald Ripitz, from Beigheim, disappeared without a trace. His parents never found out what happened to him, but it was probably the terrorists as we called them, the partisans who took him. When I came back from the war, his father came to visit me with a bicycle from a long ways off. He wanted to know what had happened to his son, but I couldn't tell him a thing. They tried everything, but never discovered anything about their son. He just disappeared without a trace. As far as I understand it, the terrorists wanted the uniforms, and so were killing people. It was very dangerous in the area and we were not allowed to go outside on our own. Somebody who would go out by himself would not come back.

Sometimes we were engaged against partisans, but we always gave up because it was hopeless. They were up there in the mountains; they could throw grenades down and shoot at us and we were powerless to do anything against it. Once we were in a village, and all of a sudden gunfire erupted from the church. You couldn't fight the terrorists because they were always hidden, you couldn't find them. We searched for partisan nests, but it was impossible. They were all back in the mountains, and at night there would be light signals and airplanes would drop equipment, ammunition, whatever they needed.

American Liberators fly back home after an air raid on the Rague Valley Bridge in Théoule sur Mer. At the right of the picture, the city and harbor of Cannes are clearly visible. Note the two Lérins islands, off Cannes, that will be mentioned again in the next chapters. NARA.

Udo Taubmann sits at right, next to his friend Ewald Ripitz, who according to Taubmann was reported missing during the occupation period. Note the identification tag hanging from Taubmann's neck. Udo Taubmann Collection.

Several times, French civilians were shot accidentally by overzealous German soldiers who mistook them for partisans. However, being trigger happy could also have negative consequences for the Germans. **Jean-Paul Carbonel**, a resident of Cannes, was witness to a friendly fire incident during which two German patrols from two different units shot at each other one night as he was cycling home:

I was cycling down Lérins Avenue. There was a German-Polish guard at the level crossing. I passed the level crossing, kept on going down, and then I saw three Germans who came out from behind a palm tree and aimed their weapons at me. I jumped off the bike. They fired, including a burst of German *Schmeisser* submachine gun. I always got the impression that some bullets went through my hair. I found myself lying in the gutter, which was quite deep at that place, and at the same moment, another *Schmeisser* burst was fired from behind me. It passed over me and killed the three Germans that were on the road. The one who had fired behind me was *Unteroffizier* Heinrich Müller, born in Magdeburg; I found out all the details later on. I stood up and took off back home. I didn't even have time to get there when the Germans arrived. Those who had been killed were from the artillery, and needless to say, we

barely escaped with our lives. My father, mother, sister, and myself were put up against the wall, with weapons pressed against our backs. They searched the whole house, turning everything inside out, and of course they found no weapons. [In fact, several pistols were hidden in the house, hanging inside dresses in a wardrobe.]

Then the patrol from the infantry that had fired at the artillery arrived and they almost slit each other's throats. My dad was calling the police on the phone. Half an hour or 45 minutes later, the gas generator bus from the police came. One of them could speak German, so we talked things over and Müller said: "I am the one who fired." They arrested me anyways, and three days later I was interrogated by "Alice the Blonde" in Nice, at the Atlantide Hotel. She had the reputation of being most dreadful. She started interrogating me in the presence of Müller, who said: "But I am the one who shot. I was hidden behind a pillar." I hadn't even seen him; he had been behind me, hidden behind a pillar, and when they fired at me, the bullets continued on and hit his pillar. He said: "I didn't shoot first, I only fired back and I had no idea that it was a patrol from the artillery." So she said: "Ok, you can leave."

They took the three dead and brought them into the garden of the house that belonged to the Baron of Kassel. Three coffins were brought from the Cannes cemetery, and all three of them were buried there. There was a young lieutenant, a young chaplain, and a soldier who must have been around 40 or 50. Having seen them and been in the action, I can say that for years it prevented me from sleeping. At night I couldn't go to bed without seeing them in front of me.

We will go into much more detail about the Resistance in the next chapter.

Accidents

In addition to the losses caused by enemy action, the Germans lost many men due to various mishaps and diseases. When young men are sent to a foreign land, trained to be aggressive, told they are the best and given weapons and explosives, accidents are bound to happen. One NCO in **Karl Cyron**'s company was killed in such an incident:

Before the invasion, sometime in June, we already had one man killed: *Oberfeldwebel* Hoffmann. We were fishing in the sea with hand grenades because we didn't have much to eat. *Oberfeldwebel* Hoffmann used an Italian egg grenade, and it exploded immediately. It was probably a sabotaged grenade. He was a fine man, very well liked in the company. He was married and had children, and he used to talk about home. I knew him well, because every day we were given a password for the night (for example, Berlin, Danzig, Paris, or Moscow, always a different name), and he was the one who gave it to us. [*Feldwebel* Kurt Hoffmann died 28 June 1944, at the age of 29.]

The Italians had abandoned large amounts of military equipment when they had left the Maritime Alps in late 1943, and in Villeneuve-Loubet, another German soldier was victim of his curiosity when examining an abandoned grenade. An inhabitant of Villeneuve who was a teenager at the time remembered the tragic scene well:

31

A German found an Italian grenade in the Loup River and started messing around with it. He wanted to take it apart, out of curiosity. He was disassembling it and suddenly the grenade exploded. It blew up, and he found himself with his dick cut off and his balls hanging out. He had holes in him everywhere and one of his hands looked like a plate of spaghetti. It wasn't a pretty sight. He was also blinded, as it had punctured his eyes. He was still alive and they brought him to the hospital. I don't know if he made it. I don't think so, that one must have died.

Soldiers also died in vehicle accidents, and there was even an airplane crash in Cagnes sur Mer. Apparently the pilot, *Uffz* Albrecht Herbolzheimer, who had been on a training flight on a Ju 87, was flying too low and hit an obstacle. **Mme Viale** was a child next door to the crash site and remembers:

It was a little fighter that must have been doing some reconnaissance, and it crashed. A lot of Germans came to the garden to see what remains of the pilot they could find. There was a big pile of rags, and I was told: "That is the pilot." They brought over a coffin, and I saw them leaving with the coffin.

German Casualties During the Occupation

During the occupation period, almost all the German dead were buried in the civilian cemetery at Caucade, Nice. The Italians had already buried some of their dead in a corner of the cemetery, and the Germans carried on the practice. The men killed in the various air raids, partisan attacks, and accidents were buried there, as well as quite a number of dead sailors who were washed ashore. Not all the casualties were soldiers: a few were from the *Reichsbahn* (German railroads) and the Todt organization (construction workers), for example. Only a handfull of men, such as the three who were shot by Heinrich Müller in Cannes, were not buried in Nice for unknown reasons.

For this book, no attempt was made to find out the cause of death of all the soldiers who died during the Occupation. However, an exact count was made of how many Germans were buried in the Maritime Alps during the Occupation before the Allied landing. In total, between April 19, 1943, and August 14, 1944, 213 Germans were buried in the Maritime Alps: 199 were buried in Caucade Cemetery,[13] seven in Cannes, four (unconfirmed) in Grasse, one in Antibes, one in Mandelieu, and one in Menton.[14] Compared to World War II standards, these are very light casualties, but compared to today's standards, such losses for a single division in a one-year period (virtualy all the abovementioned dead were buried as of August 1943) would be considered full-scale war. As the months went by and the number of air raids and Resistance actions increased, the Germans lost more and more men. In the months of January and February 1944 for example, only 17 german soldiers were killed, whereas in June and July 1944, the number had soared to 70.

During the summer of 1944, **Karl Cyron**'s platoon from the 10th Company of *Reserve Grenadier Bataillon 164* happened to be assigned the task of being the *Ehrenzug*, or Honor Platoon of *Reserve Division 148*, which was to give military honors at Caucade Cemetery for all funerals of German soldiers:

A view of the Caucade Cemetery in Nice in early 1944. The German troops have improvised a military section in an unoccupied corner of the civilian cemetery, where they have already buried more than 50 of their dead. The causes of death were mainly linked to accidents, air raids, resistance actions, disease, and shipwrecks. The white graves visible in the foreground are those of Italian soldiers who died during the Italian occupation. Krumm family Collection.

As 1944 drew on, the German occupation troops suffered more and more casualties, forcing them to start burying their dead both in front and behind the Italian military section. Note many of the soldiers wear tropical uniforms. Karl Wickstrom Collection.

Summer 1944, the Ehrenzug, composed of men of the 10th Company of Bataillon 164, smartly march down an alley of the Caucade Cemetery, followed by comrades from the Kriegsmarine bearing coffins. The platoon is led by Feldwebel Fleischer. Grenadier Karl Cyron is clearly visible as the eighth man in the right hand column. Note that apart from Feldwebel Fleischer, none of the soldiers wear any decorations, as they have no combat experience. Karl Wickstrom Collection.

From May until July 25th, part of 10th company of *Bataillon 164* formed the Ehrenzug, and buried all the dead of the division. We had to do funerals almost every day. We buried our dead in the corner of a private cemetery and then we fired "Salut" over the graves three times: "Laden. Zur Salve hoch. Legt an. Feuer! Laden, zur Salve hoch. Feuer!" Then we marched away. Most of the men buried in the cemetery had Polish names. Once we also buried two Frenchmen who had fought for the Germans and had been shot by the French Resistance. The mother, father, sisters, and brothers were there. We also buried 14 sailors after an English submarine sunk a ship near Genoa.

The Gestapo

What we have been describing so far in this chapter concerns the regular soldiers of *Reserve Division 148*. If they had been the only Germans on the French Riviera, the presence of the German occupation forces would not have left as much of a detestable image as they did. But the acts of the German army in World War II cannot, and must not be dissociated from the Nazi philosophy and Nazi war crimes. In Nice, as elsewhere, the *Gestapo* (*Geheime Staatspolizei*, or Secret State Police) and *Sicherheit Dienst* (Security Service, or SD) mercilessly hunted down all those who had been declared undesirable by the Nazis. This category of course included Jews, but also communists, intellectuals, resistance fighters, and anybody who did not submit to the German rules. Since Nice had become a safe haven for Jews during the Italian occupation, there was no shortage of work for the *Gestapo*. It was assisted in its murderous task by French collaborationist organizations, most notably the infamous *Milice* and members of the *Parti Populaire Français* (Popular French Party, known as PPF).

Killing political enemies is understandable and follows a certain logic. However, pursuing completely innocent civilians, such as the many Jewish children who had been sent to Nice by their families in order to keep them safe, cannot be justified under any circumstances. In order to commit these criminal and despicable acts, the *Gestapo* sometimes actually recruited common law criminals who had previously served prison sentences. How ironic it is that a so-called police force was functioning with people who had sometimes been recruited straight out of prison. **Marceau Raynaud**, who was a member of the resistance, explains the methodology:

What did the Germans do? They protected thieves, criminals, pimps, and let them run free. They did not arrest them, but in exchange they had to betray French people. They received money. If they arrested a Jew, then they got a bonus.

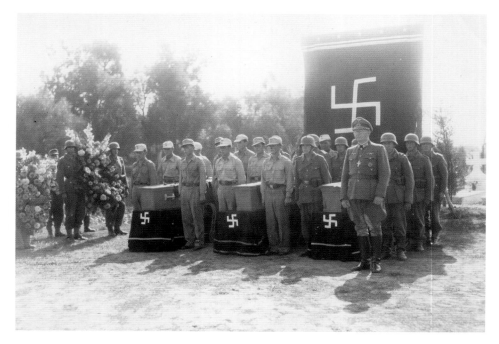

"We also buried 14 sailors after an English submarine sank a ship near Genoa." June 28, 1944, 10 sailors of Torpedoboots Flotille TA 307, whose ship was sunk June 15th and whose bodies were recovered over the following days, are buried in Caucade Cemetery. Only five of the bodies were identified. Karl Wickstrom Collection.

Surely someone with such outstanding credentials would make a fine candidate for joining the "German Police!" Indeed, **Richard Held** continued:

I speak German decently. (…) Following my 18-month prison sentence for "bread ration card trafficking," I was detained at the St Pierre prison in Marseille until July 25, 1943. Upon my release from prison, the German authorities were waiting for me on the sidewalk and brought me to the German consulate at the Prado, where I was informed that as an inhabitant of Lorraine [Lorraine was a region of France that had been annexed by Germany, meaning that its inhabitants were treated as German nationals.], I was to be repatriated to Germany. While waiting for the repatriation formalities to be concluded, which took quite a long time because my home town had been evacuated, the Germans employed me as an interpreter, and on the same day, they brought me to Mr. Panke, chief of the French Workers in Germany Employment Service, at Paradis Street in Marseille. They made me pass a quick test concerning my German language skills, and I was then ordered to stay at the disposal of Willy Bauer, chief of the Jewish Questions Service, to serve as an interpreter.[16]

The following year, **Richard Held** and Bauer ended up working in Cannes:

When I left Nice for Cannes, the chief of the *Gestapo* service in Nice, Doctor Keil, appointed me to the *Gestapo* service in Cannes, in the Jewish Questions branch, under the orders of Bauer. He gave me a German and French card with the following inscription: (…) "The French citizen Held Richard is known to our service. No measures can be undertaken against him without our approval." This card had the German stamp and Keil's signature. At the bottom was written: "Valid for one month." (…)

I normally assisted Bauer in all his operations because I was not allowed to act alone. I performed the following arrests with Bauer: the two of us arrested a Mr Bloch, who was Jewish and staying near the Gallia Hotel. He was then transferred to Nice, from where he must have been sent to Drancy in a convoy. Finally, and still in Bauer's company, I went to Mr Negri's house at 7 rue du Lac [Lac Street] to arrest him. He was not at home and later came to the *Gestapo* headquarters on his own, where he was arrested. Another time, we proceeded to search and arrest the wife of a Jewish man who had been apprehended by the PPF services of the Cavendish Hotel in Cannes. (…)

In general, Bauer and I did not make the arrests, because they were made by (…) the PPF services. These

Such criminals were given authority and the right to more or less act as they pleased, often being involved in black market affairs and corruption. One such *Gestapo* agent was Richard Held, who made the following statements about his time in the *Gestapo* after he was caught by the French police for the crimes he had participated in (see Montfleury Massacre in Chapter 7). **Richard Held**'s account describes his metamorphosis from being a petty criminal to becoming an actor of the Holocaust:

My name is Richard Louis Held. I was born in Forbach (Moselle) March 25, 1913. (…) I was sentenced to 18 months of prison by the Marseille Tribunal in 1942 for "bread ration card trafficking." In 1935, I was prosecuted for "abuse of trust and theft," but obtained a dismissal. In 1940, I was sentenced to eight months of prison by the Marseille Tribunal for "oil trafficking."[15]

Richard Held. He spoke both French and German fluently and had already been involved in criminal activities as a civilian, earning him several prison sentences. This pedigree made him attractive to the eyes of the Gestapo, so they recruited him as soon as he was released from prison. Such were the upholders of the law during the German occupation. MRA Collection.

services also performed the searches, and would advise us of the arrests. We would take charge of the prisoners and transfer them to the "Villa Montfleury." We then performed their interrogations and opened their files, after having placed seals on their apartments, for which we took the keys. The prisoners were later transferred to Nice with their files. I do not know where they were sent afterwards.[17]

The *Gestapo* had no trouble recruiting local collaborators and criminals to assist them, and a profound mistrust was created within the French population. It became difficult to know who thought what, and who was ready to turn his neighbor over to the *Gestapo* or their French collaborators. One child who grew up in this atmosphere, **Robert Centofanti**, described this mistrust:

> We were terribly afraid of the *Boches*. We constantly lived in uncertainty. People shot each other in the streets. You had to hold your tongue; you couldn't speak, because you were always afraid that what you had said might be blown out of proportion. We didn't even want to talk, because if a person had told you something good or something bad about the Germans and if the next day that person was arrested, people could have suspected that the arrest was caused by the discussion you had, by some secret that may have been said, and that you had turned him in to get an extra piece of chocolate, or an extra rationing ticket. If you heard a motor, it was automatically the Germans, because they were the only ones who had gas. So we were terribly scared.

For **Marceau Raynaud** and many others, the French collaborators were considered worse than the Germans themselves:

> The most terrible thing of all, that breaks the heart, were the Frenchmen who betrayed other Frenchmen. The Germans had the *Gestapo*; it was their political regime, they chose it that way. They terrorized the countries that they occupied, but that is what war is like. But Frenchmen who denounced other Frenchmen, now that was unacceptable.

So-called "horizontal collaboration," local French women enjoy the company of German soldiers. This incriminating photo was found abandoned on the streets of Menton after the Liberation. Louis Fiori Collection.

An inhabitant of Nice who was a child at the time described what it was like to attempt to help Jewish families, and the risks involved. He gives us a glimpse of some of the divisions that were present in French society (as well as the German forces) at the time due to the activities of the Germans:

> Before Nice was occupied by the Germans, when the Italians were still here, the French police looked for foreign Jews and put them under house arrest in the country. My parents were Protestant [The dominant religion in France is Catholicism.], so they were called upon by many Jews, and particularly German Jews who were hiding in France. They knew that in Germany the ministers were being cooperative, so they came to find my father, who acted as a kind of secretary for the minister at the Lutheran church. My father started making fake baptism certificates, but that was only a temporary solution.
>
> Then, on September 3, 1943, the Germans arrived and things changed. My parents, who, from the point of view of their opinions had been résistants at heart since 1940, were already completely in favor of the cause of Free France and of the Resistance. So they started getting organized, and from ear to mouth we got to know people who were members of networks, who provided us with fake identity cards for the people we wanted to protect.
>
> Then one day, January 9, 1944, the *Gestapo* burst into our house. We were eating, and had three Jews that my parents had helped (a Rumanian, a Pole, and a German) sitting at the table with us. The chief of this expedition, from the German Police, pounced on my father and beat him, then brought him to the bedroom, where he shot him. He left him for dead. My mother and myself were arrested,

thinking my father was dead, and were incarcerated and interrogated at the Excelsior Hotel, which was the *Gestapo* headquarters. We understood that the *Gestapo* thought we were Jews at the head of a network for helping Jews. That wasn't the case and they realized it later on.

We suspect that the person who betrayed us was a smuggler, a person that my parents were in contact with to take people to the Swiss border and smuggle them into Switzerland. Actually, we had sent several couples to Switzerland, including a Mister and Miss Wassermann, who could go to Switzerland more easily than the rest because they had relatives there. Those who went to Switzerland were usually sent to camps. The Swiss didn't mistreat them, but they were put under surveillance, whereas those who could stay with relatives or friends were accepted.

So we had accompanied the Wassermanns to the train station, where that smuggler took charge of them. We suspect that he either betrayed us or was caught himself and talked. Maybe he was captured at the Swiss border and was tortured or hustled by the Germans, I don't know. In any case, half an hour before the *Gestapo* burst into our house, a woman had come by and said: "I am coming on behalf of Mr. and Ms. Wassermann. I am also being chased after, what can you do?" My father was careful and said: "Listen Madame, it is Saturday today, you can see I am already busy, I have guests over for lunch. I will think about it. Come back on Monday and we can discuss things further." She was a woman working for the *Gestapo* who had come to see what was going on.

My mother and I stayed at the Excelsior Hotel for four days, without knowing if my father was dead or alive. We thought he was dead, since we had seen him lying motionless on the floor in the room before we were taken away. But then a friend who was part of our little resistance network walked in front of the hotel with his bicycle in one hand and a slate in the other, written on it: "Everything is going well in St Roch." We weren't allowed to look out, but I was looking through the windows anyways, and I saw him and said: "Mom, mom! Mr Beauvers just walked by!" He walked by three or four times and we understood.

In the meantime, my father had been brought to the St Roch hospital, where a nun who was pro-German took charge of him. She got my father undressed and put him on a stretcher in the hallway where there was no heating. It was in January. The nurse told her three times: "But sister…" "No, leave that man alone, he is a terrorist." Well, he survived anyway, and was then put under guard of the French police in a room that was normally used for common law prisoners who were sick or wounded. There my uncle was able to approach him.

Before the war, every winter, a German minister named Peters came to Nice to spend the winter, and he had met my father. We had found out that Minister Peters was in Paris and had been promoted to Head Chaplain of the German Army in France. My uncle went to visit him in Paris and told him about us. He replied: "But that isn't possible, what happened?" and brought my uncle see a Wehrmacht or *Gestapo* chief who said: "Listen, if you give your word of honor and if you sign a declaration saying your brother only performed humanitarian work, and never took up arms against our army, we will release him." So that is what my uncle did, of course, and anyway, it was all true. So they called Nice, and that day things changed

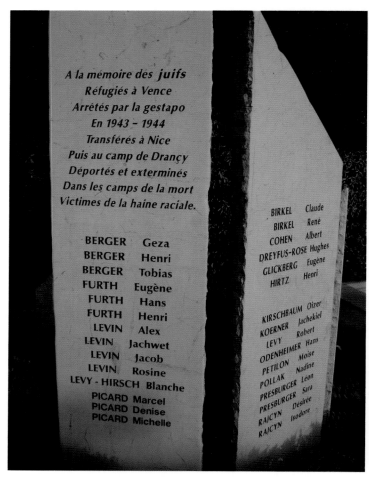

Example of a memorial dedicated to Jewish victims of the Holocaust in Vence. *Author's collection.*

for us, because they asked for a report and justifications about what had happened. Why had my father been shot, and why were my mother and I arrested?

The one who shot my father was Karl Eisenberg, a former taxi driver from Munich, Bavaria, who was a brute under Himmler's protection. At the time of the rise of Nazism in Germany, there were fights with the anti-fascists, and Eisenberg had managed to pull Himmler out of a fight with his taxi and brought him to his parents' house, where he hid him for several days. So since then, of course, Himmler had protected him. In Nice, Eisenberg was annoying all the *Gestapo* men, including the chiefs, saying: "If you bother me, I will phone Himmler, and then you will see what will happen." In the end, the Germans arrested that man themselves, because when he arrested Jews, he kept all their money for himself. Most of the time the Jews had all their valuables on them, to be able to escape or pay for hiding places. When he was arrested, that saved us. Otherwise, who knows what would have happened.

The Civilians

The presence of the German army on French soil was a huge humiliation that stains France's reputation and honor to this day. Occupations by foreign armies always cause problems, regardless of their nationality. As we have just explained, though, the presence of the German army was particularly difficult to endure because of the war crimes that were committed on an industrial scale. The Germans could organize dreaded *raffles* at any moment, when they would

"The head was gone, we found the twisted legs a bit further on; and the intestines were hanging from the electric wires." The body of Jewish Dr Richard Borger, which was found abandoned by the road at la Mescla after having been killed by the Gestapo. L'Ergot/MRA Collection.

suddenly search a street, building, or village and arrest anybody at will. The average French civilian at the time disliked the Germans, but could not do anything against them for fear of reprisals.

The civilian population not only had to put up with the Germans and their even crueler French minions, but on a daily basis they were also confronted with other problems, such as rationing, curfews, blackouts, forced labor, deportation, air raids, collaboration, black marketing, and all types of criminality. Not only food was rationed, but also fuel for vehicles, coal, cloth, tires, and virtually everything else. Old clothes had to be mended and re-mended. Shoes were made with wooden soles. The rare cars rolled on gas generators powered with wood and coal. Bicycles, which needed to be registered and for which tires were impossible to find, became the main mode of transportation. One child remembered seeing residents from the urban areas of Nice biking 15 kilometers into the country with garden hoses in places of tires in order to try to buy a few vegetables from farmers. Women had to wait in line ups for hours if they hoped to get food for their families. The quantities were always insufficient and civilians (particularly city dwellers) got used to being perpetually hungry. People became so desperate as to eat animals such as cats.

Men were often forced to work for the Germans several days per month, digging trenches or constructing fortified positions that would later be used by the Germans to hinder the Allied invasion. Under the *Service du Travail Obligatoire* (Compulsory Work Service, known as STO) laws, those who did not have an official job ran the risk of being deported to Germany to work in German factories. Many preferred to make themselves scarce or join the Resistance than to be sent to Germany.

Walking outside at night was forbidden, and freedom of any kind was severely limited. All types of smugglers and criminals thrived, as they found ways to profit from the situation. The more petty crimes were to be involved in black marketing, while more serious criminals were ready to "sell" Jews and resistance fighters to the Germans in exchange for money. A common offense was to commit a burglary under the guise of being a "German policeman." Conflicts between criminals could arise, and the *Gestapo* sometimes needed to get rid of helpers who knew a bit too much, or had become a bit too eager. Finding unidentified bodies dumped in the countryside was common, whether it was refugees who had been killed by smugglers, criminals who had been liquidated, collaborators who had been silenced, or resistance men who had been executed. In the Maritime Alps, a fashion developed during the war of blowing people's heads off with explosives to make them

unidentifiable. **Marceau Raynaud** was a young man who happened to come across such a body on the road that runs next to the Var River, north of Plan du Var:

I was in the village and somebody told us: "There's a guy who has been dynamited after the tunnel on the road after le Chaudan." We went there out of curiosity. When we got there, there was a human trunk in the trees just at the side of the road. We could see he had two bullet holes in his back. He had been killed, and then, so that his body wouldn't be recognizable, he had been dynamited. The head was gone, though we found the twisted legs a bit further on, and the intestines were hanging from the electric wires. They had crammed his backside and his mouth with explosives and then they blew him up. Maybe it was the *Gestapo*, or the *Milice*. Probably the *Gestapo*, I don't know; we never found out exactly what happened with that person. It was the first time that I was really entering the war and the events of that atrocious time period we lived through. After I saw other things, of course, but the first time it strikes you a bit.

An article was written about this incident in the *l'Ergot* newspaper after the war, explaining that the first two men who had reached the scene found a piece of meat on the road without noticing the rest of the body. Thinking the meat had been abandoned by black marketers, one of them picked it up and put it in his bag to eat it, only to throw it away again a few moments later when the rest of the body was discovered. When the police arrived, they were dismayed to see a crow dive down from the sky and fly away with the victim's right ear, as the shape of the ear could have helped identify the man. Despite this mishap, the French investigators were able to identify the shredded remains thanks to a metal ring present on the bone of one arm and that was recognized by a local surgeon who had installed the ring.[18] The body was that of Austrian Jewish medical doctor Richard Borger, who had been working forcefully as a secretary for the *Gestapo* agents at the Excelsior Hotel in Nice. It is said he was killed by Karl Eisenberg, because he knew too much about Eisenberg's corrupt activities. Borger was replaced by freshly-arrested Max Silbermann, who then worked at the *Gestapo* HQ until August 15, 1944, on which date he managed to escape thanks to the confusion caused by the Allied invasion.

Charles Erbetta was a young man living in the mountains at Touët de l'Escarène. In such rural areas, the Germans were highly suspicious of any young men, as **Charles Erbetta** soon discovered. Events like the one he describes below could of course only create intense hatred for the Germans amongst those who lived through them.

In March, they were looking for terrorists, for partisans. They weren't going into details, and they thought that there was a team of them at St Laurent, but no luck, only myself and the Tordo brothers were there. The Tordo brothers saw them coming, but I didn't. They escaped, but I got cornered like a rookie. I was with my father, but my father had seen them before I had and he said, "Be careful!" That's all he had time to say and then he hid in the stable. I was above the house, coming back down, and found

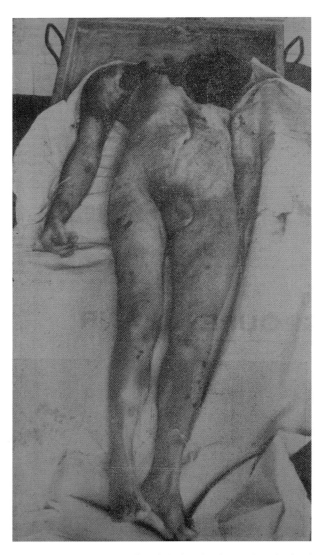

Example of another body found during the Occupation, its head blown off with explosives to prevent it from being identified. L'Ergot/MRA Collection.

Young recruits of the 6th Company of Bataillon 372 clean their rifles under the eyes of a Gefreiter. The rifles consist of older and more bulky models of the Mauser, and most of the men wear summer uniforms made of light HBT material, which was common in the French Riviera. Udo Taubmann Collection.

myself nose to nose with the Germans. They made me walk back about 20 meters with a submachine gun pressed against my stomach and were saying: "Terrorist!" But I couldn't reply. In situations like that, you are so terrified that not a word comes out. Your tongue becomes so thick that you can't speak. So they said "Raus!" But I knew their methods: when you turn your back on them they open fire, so I didn't turn around. Then one of them kicked me, and it wasn't a kick to fool around. On their boots they had a metallic heel, and that heel was always sharp because it was worn down. It cut into my thigh and I fell down like a sparrow. Then, when I was on the ground, they continued beating me. They kicked me around and then left. I don't remember anything after that. Maybe they thought I was dead, I don't know. I was lucky that they left. My father came out and picked me up and the doctor came over. He told me I had been lucky. I wasn't a pretty sight. I still have a 15cm scar from the kick. Now I am laughing about it, but back then you couldn't laugh.

Although very grave events were occurring, with people being deported or sometimes even executed in the countryside, these acts were committed by a very small minority of the German occupation force. The average German soldiers of *Reserve Division 148* were

simple draftees who tried to make the best out of a situation they had been forced into. They were not fully aware of what the *Gestapo* was doing and in any case they could not do anything about it. Most soldiers behaved correctly, but were still regarded with contempt and suspicion by the French civilians. **Marcel Guido**, a kid living near Pont du Loup, explains how he reacted to a German soldier who tried to befriend him:

A German patrol stopped at the mill in Bramafan, where I lived. Of course, the officer asked my parents if there were any *maquisards* [Resistance men] around and this and that; and he offered me some candies, which I refused. The officer sent his men away to eat a bit further on, but he stayed to talk to my mother. He told her that he had left his wife and a girl my age back home in his country, that he was in France by force, that he wasn't proud of it, and that I could accept the candies, he was giving them from the bottom of his heart. I think he said he was forced to be here because he was Polish, and to be careful of the young recruits, because they had been pumped up by Hitler and the Nazis. I took the candies but I didn't eat them. I pretended to eat them but threw them away later. It was because I was frightened; we knew what the Germans were doing all over the place, and we were afraid and that was it.

Max Stèque, a teenager living in St Cézaire, described a similar encounter and the paranoid manner with which he perceived German soldiers at the time:

I was going up the street and there was a German at the fountain eating something and he said: "Hop!" I looked at him: "Komm, komm." I thought he was calling me a cunt ["Con" in French] with his guttural accent, because I don't understand German. So I looked at him, and he insisted: "Komm, komm!" So very slowly I went nearer, and he showed me a slice of bread. They had rye bread; it was kind of like fruit cake, and there was some red jelly on it. He told me: "Gut!" Supposedly it meant "good" in German. I didn't know it, and I thought: "The bastard, he is telling me to taste ["Goute" in French] it because he wants to poison me!" Because there were still old veterans from the First World War that had conditioned us. They called the Germans "Prussians" and used to say: "Beware!

Trying to make the best of it. Obergefreiter Franz Guder (at left), of the 7th Company of Bataillon 372, relaxes with comrades in a beautiful garden, most likely in Antibes. Note the tropical uniform being worn by the man in the foreground. Franz Guder was killed in battle against the First Special Service Force at Villeneuve-Loubet August 26, 1944. Franz Guder Collection.

Never go with them! If they give you something, don't eat it, it will be poison! If you find a German lighter or pen, don't touch it, it could explode!" So we were conditioned and didn't associate with them. So I thought: "The bastard is calling me a cunt and wants to poison me!" So I was trying to tell him: "No thank you, I have already eaten, no, no." He insisted: "Gut, gut, gut!" So I took a piece as small as a nut in my mouth and then I ran to the public toilets that were a bit further on. I quickly spat the thing out, waited for the automatic flush to occur, then threw the whole piece of bread in. And I didn't swallow my saliva. I looked outside and saw the guy had left and couldn't see me anymore. I went to the public wash house and washed my mouth out thoroughly with water, then I went home by another street. You see, I was really an idiot, because it was just a guy who wanted to give me a piece of bread and jam and who was saying: "It's good."

Such language problems were not uncommon, and would have been amusing in other circumstances. **Pierre Benedetti**, a child in Fayence, remembered:

> Once the Germans went into the shop and a German wanted to buy a comb, to comb his hair. The shopkeeper asked him: "But do you want a pocket comb ["Peigne de poche"]?" But the German understood: Boche comb ["Peigne de Boche"] and got angry.

There would, of course, be infinitely more to say about the Occupation. However, the Occupation is not the theme of this book and the goal here is only to give a brief overview of it, in order to better understand and put into context the next chapters; in particular, the following chapter about the French Resistance. But before passing on to the French Resistance, let us conclude this chapter on a more positive note. This story is completely out of place compared to what we have described so far, and goes to show that war can hold unexpected surprises.

Snow White

Lorenz Rohde was the *Stabsmusikmeister* (Senior Bandmaster) of *Reserve Division 148*. Being on occupation duty on the *Côte d'Azur* would provide him with a unique career opportunity that he described years later, in an article written on the occasion of the death of *Generalleutnant* Fretter-Pico in 1967:

> When I think back on my career as a soldier and as a composer, I can only remember one person, apart from my wife, who really understood me and encouraged me: our General. We could understand each other without pronouncing any words. The first discussion that I had with the General after he took command of the division was so humane that my heart pounded, and I could hope to have received a commander who was not only good from a military point of view, but who had also opened his heart to art, and everything that was beautiful. For the leader of a military orchestra, this is a bigger matter then any outsider can realize. I was able to sit by his side repeatedly at the casino, to have conversations with this wise man. That is how something that still must seem unreal today, considering the circumstances, was able to occur. That the General not only tolerated this undertaking – which would already have been a lot – but wholeheartedly encouraged it, made our commander lovable in my eyes. You know, dear comrades, what I am talking about: my full length ballet *Snow White* that was performed under my leadership in Monte Carlo in early 1944. This is how it happened:
>
> The former German *Generalkonsul* in Monaco, Dr. Hellenthal, passed on a newspaper article to the Presidium of the State Opera that said that a German composer had written an important ballet piece. This Presidium was given my home address upon request, and I indirectly received a letter from Monaco. My joy was great to be able to report to the opera after a mere half hour drive. An agreement was reached regarding the performance of my piece. Now I needed to convince our commander that a matter which was nonessential for the war effort would keep one of his soldiers unavailable for weeks and that the war could keep on being fought just as efficiently in the meantime.
>
> Our IIa [Officer in charge of administrative matters], Major Dr. Ebersbach, brought me to the general. After listening to my presentation, he told me: "My dear Rohde, first sit down. I have a wife and children. You will bring misfortune to you and to me if anybody higher up finds out that I am letting ballets take place instead of fighting the war."
>
> This I had to admit. But then our commander saw my great distress, for which he had real understanding. He summoned his IIa and began considering how it could be made possible for Rohde to go to Monaco, without causing an event that would be destructive to the *Wehrmacht*. The IIa had the brilliant idea: Rohde would be sent to Monaco to the engineer unit, in order to take a course with them. The commander gave his consent with a laugh. He couldn't imagine then how long this course was to last.
>
> But I could partially return the favor. The General was invited to the Premier by the Presidium of the Opera. The ballet was performed, and today's Prince organized a reception in the royal loge of the theater. Between the 1st and the 2nd acts of the ballet, the General and his suite, to the insistence of the Ia [Chief of staff], Major Schulz, and the Ic [Intelligence officer], Lt Picot, were called upon for a glass of champagne in the royal loge.
>
> The former Prince held a speech about the German composer and his work, but also about the general, about whom he said friendly words. In the meantime, royal waiters distributed abundant amounts of champagne.

A scene of Lorenz Rohde's "Snow White" is played at the Monte-Carlo opera.
Gemeinschaft Ehemaliger Angehöriger der 148 ID Collection.

Stabsmusikmeister Lorenz Rohde in good company in Monte-Carlo.
Gemeinschaft Ehemaliger Angehöriger der 148 ID Collection.

Stabsmusikmeister Lorenz Rohde and Generalleutnant Fretter-Pico meet in the Monte-Carlo Opera. Author's collection.

Favorite photo themes among soldiers of Reserve Division 148 were the statues in the gardens of the villas in which they were quartered, as well as the local varieties of cactuses that must have seemed very exotic to them. Here, Gefreiter Franz Guder embraces a semi-nude statue, probably in a garden in Antibes. Franz Guder Collection.

42-year-old Gefreiter Andreas Jeck, second from right, poses with comrades of Festungs Pionier Bataillon 14 in what is apparently the Jardin des Plantes Exotiques in Monaco. Andreas Jeck was killed in a truck accident in Cannes August 15, 1944. Jeck Family Collection.

(Later, Major Schulz revealed to me that he had made a bet with Lt Picot regarding which one of them could drink the most champagne in the shortest time. Winner: Picot.)

After I pronounced a few words as a response to the Prince, the general and myself were invited to another loge to meet the sister of the Prince, Princess Antoinette. The general accepted with pleasure. He brought me with him, but then something awful happened. A German soldier who was taking pictures in the opera for a soldier's magazine followed us in without us realizing. Since this soldier was wearing a helmet, the Princess received a terrible fright. Poor her! She saw a general accompanied by an armed and helmeted soldier walk in, and probably thought that the evil Germans had something dreadful in mind. Even the photographer seemed to understand the embarrassing misunderstanding and disappeared.

After the general had talked with the Princess for a while and after she had told me a few kind words, it was time for me to return to the pedestal. But the photo business was not yet finished. The old Prince heard about the photo that had been taken and asked that it be destroyed. This was taken care of as requested.

18-year-old Grenadier Josef Klein (to the right), of the 3rd Company of Bataillon 7, poses in front of a cactus somewhere near Menton. Note that both soldiers are wearing tropical helmets, which was quite common in Reserve Division 148. Markus Bender Collection.

After the first performance of the ballet some small festivities were planned, to which the general was also invited, of course. First it was at the German *Generalkonsul* that the events were partied. Later, there was a second party to which the scene performers were also invited. There was a small ball during which the general swung his dance leg.

He only danced once, but it showed good taste that he danced with the ballerina Ludmilla Cherina, who is still shown in illustrated magazines nowadays. Dancing was not his strong point, but the ballerina told me a few days later that she found the German general "Très, très gentil [Very, very, friendly].

My engineering course was probably the most peculiar and interesting that any German soldier ever attended. I thank our general for his participation. If only there had been more commanders like him.[19]

Conclusion

The first German forces only reached the Maritime Alps in late 1943. *Reserve Division 148* was given the task of occupying the region. Most of the soldiers of this unit were inexperienced youths or older men, many of whom hardly even considered themselves German. However, the German rule was hard and strict, as elsewhere in France, and the civilian population was deprived of its freedom, safety, and many basic commodities. During the occupation period, the main war events that occurred were Allied air raids and attacks by the French Resistance. We will now pass on to Chapter 2, which is solely dedicated to the men and women of the Resistance.

2

The French Resistance

Brief Introduction to the French Resistance

France was occupied, France was humiliated, but some brave French (as well as foreign) men and women decided to do what they could to hamper the German war effort and help the Allied cause: these people formed the French Resistance. The goals of the Resistance were multiple, such as: seeking out information about the German troops and defenses, countering German propaganda by printing clandestine pamphlets, organizing illegal exfiltrations (for example, helping Jews or downed Allied airmen to escape to neutral countries), sabotaging strategic installations, training agents and guerilla fighters, executing traitors and collaborators, and collecting weapons in order be able to help the future Allied invasion. Resistance networks usually only specialized in one or two of these activities.

During the first years of the Occupation, the Resistance remained small and mainly consisted of people who kept on living their normal lives, keeping up the appearance of legality. It was only late in the war, mostly as of 1944, that actual *maquis* were formed. These consisted of groups of armed men living in the wilderness full time. The *maquis* is a type of thick and impenetrable underbrush found in southern France, and men living in this underbrush were therefore called *maquisard*s. These men formed units called *maquis*, capable of undertaking small military actions against German troops.

There were two main factors which led to the creation of *maquis* late in the war. The first was that following the creation of the STO (Compulsory Labor Service) in 1943, any unemployed men were to be sent to work in Germany. Many preferred to join the *maquis*, or at least start living clandestinely, rather than having to depart for Germany. The second factor was that, as the Allied armies approached, people began understanding that the end of the Occupation was coming and that they may be able to participate in kicking the Germans out of France. Joining the *maquis* meant abandoning legality and living in difficult conditions in the wilderness. However, the *maquis* were provided for and informed by large numbers of resistance members who had remained legal (the so-called *legaux*, or legals in English), and by a significant portion of the general population who was friendly to their cause. The *maquis* further received great help from the British Special Operations Executive (SOE), which organized airdrops of goods and infiltrated numerous specially trained agents all over France.

Resistance men needed to keep as secretive as possible. They lived in a world of false names, coded messages, and passwords and tried to know as little as possible about each other, so that in the event they were captured and tortured, they would not be able to reveal any information. The Germans brutally repressed any activities linked to the Resistance: anybody giving even the smallest help to the Resistance was risking his life, and those who were proven to be actual *résistants* were deported to concentration camps or executed if captured. It is to be noted that according to the Geneva Convention, combatants not wearing a uniform could rightfully be executed. They were not, however, to be tortured, but this of course did not prevent the *Gestapo* from doing so on a regular basis.

Because of the very nature of partisan warfare, few pictures of them were taken during the Occupation. This posed picture shows a group of resistance men from Guillaumes, an isolated mountain village that was briefly liberated in July 1944, only to be recaptured by the Germans in a costly operation a few days later. André Galtier Collection.

There were two main currents in the Resistance: the *Forces Françaises de l'Intérieur* (French Forces of the Interior, known as FFI) who politically were Gaullist, and the *Francs Tireurs Partisans Français* (Snipers and Partisans, known as FTP) who politically were communist. There was and still is animosity between these two groups. However, this sterile and fratricidal topic will be avoided as much as possible in this book, and only a few of the more comical consequences of this animosity will be mentioned. In many cases, men simply joined the resistance groups that they happened to be able to get in contact with, without being aware of any political tendencies.

The Resistance is an extremely wide and complicated topic. In particular, there were such a large number of different movements with different names that often tried to take credit for as many actions as possible, that having a proper understanding of what really occurred is next to impossible. This chapter will only provide a very brief introduction, mostly concentrated on the *maquis* that would later participate in the larger military confrontations during the liberation of the Maritime Alps and east of the Var in August 1944.

One point must be made particularly clear before continuing. Partisan warfare is forbidden by the rules of war, and because of this, certain people consider the Resistance a form of terrorism, and that Germans killed while fighting the Resistance were therefore "murdered." This simplistic and worrisome train of thought does not take into account the fact that the German armed forces did not respect the rules of war themselves. The Nazis deliberately and painstakingly hunted down and murdered millions of civilians in what is one of the darkest pages of human history. The men and women who simultaneously abandoned safety, comfort, and legality to fight these Nazis and defend their homeland deserve our admiration and respect. Rarely can a soldier (even if that soldier has no uniform) participate in something as morally right as the defense of his own village and region from the Nazi regime.

Joining the Resistance

Each person had his own personal reasons for wanting to join the Resistance. Some joined for idealistic reasons, while others had little choice, joining because they were already being tracked down by the Germans. Entering the Resistance was not always easy, and was usually done by contacting somebody who was already a member. Sometimes it was done in an indirect manner. **Jean** (who asked to remain anonymous) explains how he got recruited by the *Groupe Tartane* intelligence network in Grasse:

> At the time, it was difficult to be recruited. I had tried several times with some friends, but we had been unsuccessful. Then in November 1942, when the Germans invaded the Free Zone [Zone Libre], we heard on the radio that the French fleet had been scuttled in Toulon, and that there had been casualties. It was actually true, there had even been a lot of casualties. So with a friend, we decided: "We will celebrate a mass for the dead in Grasse, and then deposit a wreath at the War Memorial." It was like a small act of resistance. We contacted the priest, we got the mass celebrated, and then we brought a wreath to the War Memorial. André Pasqua was a police officer in Grasse in charge of keeping order. He knew us, and told us in a friendly way: "OK for the War Monument. Now disperse and we will ignore what happened." He mentioned the event to Pierazzi, saying: "There are two guys that would be interesting to have with us, because they demonstrated their patriotism."

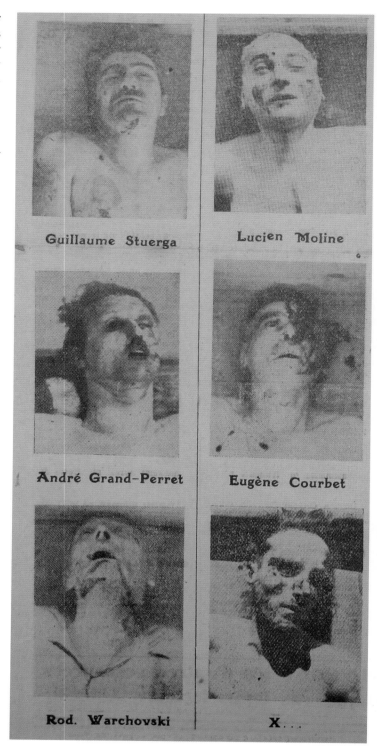

Guillaume Stuerga   Lucien Moline

André Grand-Perret   Eugène Courbet

Rod. Warchovski   X...

Becoming a member of the Résistance was an extremely risky decision. The morning of December 27, 1943, the bodies of these six resistance men, one of which was never identified, were found in various districts of Nice where they had been liquidated by the Gestapo. L'Ergot/MRA Collection.

By organizing their act of defiance and honoring the French war dead, the two had been noticed by André Pasqua, who was already a member of the network, and they were therefore subsequently recruited. **Joseph "Chambéry" Martin**, from the village of St Martin Vésubie, had been in the French Army since 1938, and had participated in the battles against the Germans in northern France in 1940. At first he remained in the French military during the Occupation, but then decided to leave:

> The commander asked me: "Why are you leaving? You will be promoted to sergeant soon. So will you stay?"

I said: "No ! I am not interested in being a German soldier in French uniform. I will go back home. I have a little bit of land and I will plant my own potatoes." But he asked me: "Martin, OK… But will you be there for the second round?" I replied: "Don't worry Sir, I will be there for the second round!"

So I was demobilized; but then there was that work service, the STO, and I was to be sent to Germany. I thought: "No! I participated in the war, I wasn't captured, I am not going to surrender myself now." So I left; I went into hiding in my village at St Martin Vésubie. With the contacts my father had, I was able to enter the Resistance. When the gendarmes [Policemen] and Germans came to my house, asking where I was, my father said: "Oh! You know, my son is a bit wild. He left and told me he was going to Germany, and I haven't had any news since."

Louis Garnero was an idealist who believed in communism and was thus a natural enemy of fascism. In 1941, he participated in a fight against French Fascists during which his eye was gouged with a knife. **Louis Garnero** explains the atmosphere in which he grew up in St Martin du Var before the war even started:

> What made me decide to join the Resistance was that, at a young age, I had already known someone who had fought in Spain in the International Brigades [during the Spanish Civil War]. He had been wounded and repatriated. He was in my village and told me about the war over there and about what the fascists did, how they would go into a village and kill everybody, including the women and children. And I also saw the famished republican refugees that they had put in camps here and there. So we kind of joined the International Brigades, five or six of us young people, and we tried to bring them food, because they were starving. We heard their stories and we decided: "We need to fight Fascism, we need to fight against it to prevent Europe from being submerged."

This type of person was naturally inclined to join the Resistance once France itself was occupied by the Germans. **Louis Garnero** continues:

> We wanted to fight. We, the young people, we couldn't go out, we couldn't move. At night you had to turn out the lights at such and such a time, you had to do

this, you had to do that. We were conditioned by the fact that our country was being occupied. We didn't accept that. We really wanted to liberate the country, we wanted to build a better world. Basically, the reason we joined was to liberate our country from the Germans.

Zézé Latil had to join the *maquis* for a more original reason. Though he had no affiliation whatsoever with the Germans, his official family name was the very Germanic-sounding Schmitzer:

> I mostly joined the Resistance because of my name. For the Germans, I was supposed to be a German who had sort of disappointed them and they wanted to take back anybody with a German-sounding name, to send us to the front. So, since my name was on their list, I took off, and fast.

Life in the Maquis

Leaving for the *maquis* meant leaving the comforts of civilization to live in the wilderness in hidden camps, where life was particularly harsh. **Joseph Tramontana** explains his departure from Callian to an FTP *maquis*:

> When you went underground, you didn't know anybody. Everything remained incognito, that was the way it was. When I left Callian to join the *maquis*, I had contacted a person I didn't know. He told me: "Go to Claviers, somebody will wait for you at the train station." I asked him: "But how will he recognize me?" So he said: "Take a newspaper, hold the newspaper in your hand, get off at the train station and wait, and somebody will come and speak to you."
>
> I arrived in Claviers, and the train left for Draguignan. I waited for a bit, and indeed, some tall guy I didn't know came towards me. When he saw I had the newspaper he said: "Ay?" I quickly understood and said: "Yes." He told me: "Don't move, someone will come and get you." I waited at the station for at least two hours, then a stranger came out of the forest and brought me to Canjuers.
>
> Those were harsh times, because when I got up there, there was practically nobody else there. There were two Spaniards, Paco and Toledo, and the other guy who had brought me from the train station and whose name I later found out was Francis Raybaud, from Bargemont. We lived in the forest for weeks. They just had a hut made of stones with a metal sheet on top and we camped there. It was hard. Where did we wash? We didn't wash! We must have stunk from far off!
>
> When you live in the forest, you have to manage to survive, you have to eat. There were lots of shepherds in Canjuers. We went to the farms to get supplies. The people suspected that we were hiding, because they knew what the Resistance was. They had sheep, and sometimes we stole sheep from them. We needed to eat. It was a strange era. I wouldn't wish today's youth to have to live through something like that, always feeling fear in your gut.

Louis "Bovis" Garnero explains his entry into one of the FTP companies that was hiding in the mountains north of Nice, and what daily life consisted of:

FTP Joseph Garnero, who joined an active maquis in spite of the fact that he only had one eye, the other having been lost to a knife during a fight with members of a French collaborationist organization. Author's Collection.

When you wanted to join the Resistance, you needed to find somebody who was already part of the Resistance. At St Martin du Var, Albertini was the guy doing that, we called him "l'Asse." Franco was the one who accompanied us, he said: "There are five of you who want to join? Then one will wait in such and such a train station, the other one in the next station, and so on. Wait at such and such a time for such and such a train, with a rose in your mouth, or a book in your hand, and this is the password." So we left, and five of us found each other together in the same train car when we arrived in Malaussène. We hadn't seen anybody, and then a guy came along and said the password. He said "Follow me," and we followed him. We climbed into the forest and that is how the days of armed resistance started.

We joined a selection camp. The selection camps were where we learned how to fight, how to manipulate weapons, and how to use explosives to blow up train tracks and bridges. That camp was commanded by a captain from the German army who had deserted. His name was Masselo, and he was our teacher. He was strict and you couldn't fool around with him. When a guy was trained, he was sent to a company to fight. We attacked convoys, blew up train tracks and bridges, or we killed those who betrayed Jews, resistance fighters, and others that the Germans were looking for.

The cook was a Czech that the Germans had conscripted and who had deserted. He was already about 50 years old and made food for us. When he called us, we would line up one behind the other. But there wasn't enough for everybody, so each day the first in line would exchange places with the last, and we would rotate. The cook calculated about how much he had, how much he could give out, and he gave us each a small ration. When we were served we sat down and ate. He would look at us, and after a while he would shout: "If you liked it, come back for seconds!" At first we believed him, but then we didn't believe him anymore. But "Le Magou" [A Jewish Medical student whose real name was Claude Mendrsisezki] always stood up and checked. He knew there was nothing left, but he was so hungry that he went

Josef Soppelsa, a German deserter who joined the FFI Groupe Morgan and who remained in Nice once the war was over. Louis Fiori Collection.

to make sure anyway. When we had cigarettes, we sat down one behind the other. The first man took one drag, then passed it on to the second. Each man took one drag and nobody took two.

We were starving to death. We ate grass, roots, anything we could find. When we could catch an animal, whether it was a cat, hare, badger, or fox, anything, we ate it. We ate grass snakes, vipers, even rats. I wasn't there when they ate rats, I was on a mission, but they ate rats three or four times in my group. The only thing we didn't eat was human flesh. Imagine being 16, 17, or 18 years old, outside in the rain and cold. When you want to eat, when you need to eat, when you feel your body needs food, it's really hard. Over there we ate anything. Cats were hard to find because even the civilians ate them. Supposedly there weren't any cats left in Nice, because everybody was hungry.

It was really, really hard. The discipline was very tough. We couldn't make any noise. We didn't have enough to eat, and one day a guy who was on guard duty saw a chamois and shot it. He got punished big time! He was almost constantly on guard duty for one month after that. He would sleep a bit, and then was back on duty. Nobody shot any more after that. If an elephant had come by we wouldn't have shot it!

We FTPs didn't get any airdrops. The AS ["Armée Secrète," or Secret Army], Combat, they all got air supplies, but we didn't because we were communists. But then one day we stole an airdrop thanks to our cook. We had found out that it was Flying Fortresses that brought in supplies and we could recognize the humming of their engines. When they came, they looked for fires. One night, the Czech cook hear the flying fortresses when he was cooking in a cave. He ran out with two or three guys and started making a fire and then they dropped the parachutes. We almost got killed because we weren't used to airdrops. We didn't know the containers came down so fast and we were all standing under them, waiting. Once we understood, we got out of the way.

As of the day we received that air drop, we had Sten guns, Colts, and lots of plastic explosive. I think that is also when the first penicillin arrived. A man also came down by parachute. He was from the Intelligence Service and we called him Roger. He was really an outstanding person. He told us: "I was supposed to be in an AS camp, but now I am with you guys instead. Well, it doesn't matter, I will train you anyway." We had been ordered to keep him with us, to not let him leave. Supposedly he was our prisoner, but he always told us: "Don't try to keep me, you are wasting your time. The day I will want to leave, I will. You don't have the capacity or the strength to keep me.

He taught us everything we needed to know about guerrilla warfare, how to fight an army. He taught us close combat, how to defend ourselves from dogs, and how to fight with knives. He was extremely strong and mastered combat terribly well. He could speak French, Patois, and Niçois [Patois and Niçois are local dialects of the Maritime Alps]. The Intelligence Service had trained him so that he could train *maquis* in France.

He taught us how to defend ourselves from dogs. A dog that had been trained by the Germans was more vulnerable than a normal dog because you knew how it would attack and that it would go for your throat. So we had learned how to protect ourselves. It wasn't difficult: you had to let the dog attack and jump at you. Then you folded your arm in front of your throat and pressed forward. The dog only bites if you pull, but if you push towards it, it can't close its mouth any more. Then it is vulnerable, and you bring it down and kill it with your knife. If you have no knife, then with the other hand you poked both its eyes out.

As can be seen, there was competition between the FTPs and the FFIs concerning the supplies that the Allies dropped by parachute. This led to some peculiar situations. **Louis Garnero** continues:

> Once I was captured by the Gaullists because we tried to steal their weapons. Our opinion was that they didn't use them enough, while we were lacking weapons. So once they caught me, it wasn't like I was going to shoot them. The friends who were with me took off, they also didn't shoot. We weren't going to start fighting between ourselves! So too bad, I stayed there and they took me prisoner. The next day they let me go, saying: "You have to tell the others to stop taking our weapons." They had plenty of weapons, but weren't doing anything with them! Well, that was what we thought. But at least they had the merit of also being part of the Resistance.

Joseph "Chambéry" Martin, the former soldier who had joined the ORA (*Organisation de Résistance de l' Armée*, or Resistance Organization of the Army, who were Gaullist. This was the real name of what Joseph Garnero referred to as the AS), was given the mission of infiltrating the FTPs to figure out what was happening with the missing parachutes. He also gives an outsider's view of the FTP:

> One day, I was given a mission. We received airdrops of material, mostly weapons and ammunition, and one time one of our airdrops was missing. We had an idea about what was going on and I was given the mission of trying

FFI Primo Eliseï, a former member of Groupe Morgan, shows a lamp he used to signal to aircraft during airdrops. Just like Joseph Garnero, Primo Eliseï only had one good eye, which didn't stop him from participating in combat operations. Author's Collection.

to join the FTPs, to spy on them and find out where they were getting their weapons from. It had to be them who were stealing from us, it wasn't the Germans. So in March 1944 I infiltrated the FTPs, and indeed, I found they had an American .30 caliber machine gun. Supposedly to join them there was a selection, and it was difficult to get in. But I got in immediately; if I had been from the *Gestapo* or the *Milice* [The *Milice* was a highly-dreaded French collaborationist organization], it would have made no difference. They welcomed me because they noticed that I had military knowledge and particularly that I knew the German MG 34 machine gun well. They had one that only fired one shot at a time. I said: "Damn it, in '39 we had taken some from the Germans, maybe I can still remember how to take it apart." I put it back together and then it worked. One of the pieces must have been set up backwards.

> The guys had to learn the "Internationale" [A famous communist song] and everything. I realized that those guys, who were all volunteers, were good guys, but had no military training, so they made stupid mistakes. They were learning the "Internationale" and I had the misfortune of saying: "It's not with the Internationale that we are going to stop the Germans. We need some military training." The chief, not knowing that I could speak Patois, turned around and asked: "Where is this guy from?" I thought: "Ouch! Maybe I spoke too much this time." I was afraid they would detect my presence. Later on, I found out that there was another mole like me. We had never been FTPs or communists, but we needed to sing with the red flag and everything.

> My mission was supposed to end August 20th, and on the 15th the Allies landed. I was at the Granges de la Brasque and was supposed to return to the ORA. I saw Lt Silves at Beuille and he told me: "So Chambery [Joseph Martin's *nom de guerre*], your mission is going to end soon?" I replied: "No Lieutenant, since I have been with the FTPs, I have made friends there and we have fought together. Anyway, we are all fighting the same enemy, so I am going to stay with them. I am much more useful over there then here. Here there are lots of officers and soldiers, while they have no military experience." So that is how I ended up being in the FTPs. I have to say, they really did a lot of work. For example, they did many more sabotage actions than the ORA. The ORA was much more about being a hidden army than about doing sabotage, whereas the FTPs did a lot of sabotage. They blew a lot of things up. In the Vésubie valley, there was a saw mill working for the Germans. They set it on fire and I participated in that.

> I immediately became a group leader, in charge of about 40 men. That's what I fought the war with. They fought, they were motivated, but they lacked training.

Marius Roquemaure joined the FTP group in the area of Claviers to get away from the Vichy-organized paramilitary service (known as the *Chantiers de Jeunesse*). His account proves that in practice, not everybody in the FTPs had communist opinions – far from it – and that not all the groups were as well organized as the ones we just described:

> My goal was to save France. That was our goal. We needed to perform actions to help liberate France and French democracy. I joined the *maquis* in Claviers because I am from Claviers. We, the young *maquisards*, had no idea whatsoever about what FTP meant. It's only later that

I found out that the FTPs were communist. I didn't know it. We had no clue, but there were political undercurrents.

We had no leaders and there wasn't much discipline, which is why a lot of *maquisards* were killed. It wasn't organized well, there was no precise leadership. The *maquisards* didn't see the risks. We were 18 and we just rushed on. At 18 you don't see the dangers, and you go and get yourself killed. We would say: "Tonight we will blow up that bridge, or we will attack that guy" and we just took off like that. Depending on the actions we did, sometimes we didn't come back to the camp and the others didn't know if we were dead or alive. There were no leaders. Everybody wanted to command, and nobody commanded.

However, in the Claviers group there were two Spaniards, Paco and Toledo, who had fought in Spain during the civil war. They were experienced in guerrilla warfare, and had a heavy influence on the fresh recruits. **Zézé Latil** remembers them:

They had been doing the same thing in Spain, so they were seasoned. They knew how to live and survive in the mountains. They mostly taught us to be discrete, to not fire a gunshot or make any noise. The first thing was silence. They had weapons, but would only use them in extreme cases. They taught us that it was best to commit suicide. There would only be noise if they had killed themselves, otherwise they wouldn't fire at anybody. They lived hidden in the forest, hidden in holes. They were used to it. They were real *maquisards*.

Joseph Tramontana was in the same group as Paco and Toledo:

They were tough guys, especially Paco. The other was a bit more fearful, but Paco! When we used a vehicle to carry weapons, he always had his plastic bomb with him, with a little wick, so that in case we got caught, he could light the wick and blow everything up, including ourselves. It was hard times, but I knew I could trust him completely. He was even a bit too fanatical and I told him: "Don't risk your life." It was a bit stupid, you had to be a bit careful. But him, he didn't care. He had fought in the war in Spain, he knew what war was about.

Marius Roquemaure also remembers the two Spaniards and their expertise in partisan warfare:

They were real *maquisards*; it was their job, they were professionals. I saw them on the road to Draguignan. They lay down in the ditch beside the road, and when the German trucks drove by, they would throw grenade after grenade into them. They managed to neutralize the trucks just between the two of them. They always did things like that at night. Some Germans were probably killed, but it was in the middle of the forest and they didn't know who had done it.

Being in the *maquis* for months at a time had a heavy effect on the men. When interviewing some of them, I felt that at the time they had accepted that the only possible outcome for them was death. They lived in a permanent state of alert, with no hope or rest to look forward to in the known future. Their commitment was much more profound than that of regular soldiers. They had decided to live beyond the boundaries and laws of regular warfare. The only two possible ways out were to be victorious or to die. Captured partisans

could expect no quarter from the Germans. **Louis Garnero**, who had joined even though he only had one eye, gives us an idea of the way he felt at the time:

What makes the strength of guerrillas is that you are used to fighting every day, every day you learned how to fight and to defend yourself. We had also become savages; believe me, we were not friendly people. Now I laugh, and I feel emotions, but back then we had no emotions anymore. We gave back what had been given to us. It was hard to kill. I don't like speaking about it, but afterwards things are good, because you feel hatred, and you have done it before. But the first time isn't easy.

Marceau Raynaud also tells about how being in the *maquis* could affect a man:

In the Resistance, the human being changes completely. You are not the same person as in civilian life. You have a certain amount of hatred, a thirst for revenge, and all that has an effect. That is why we cannot glorify ourselves for some of the things we did. For some things, if we had to do them again, we would not do them. That is why we barely talk about it. When you are officially recognized in the army, it's not the same. We were *francs-tireurs* [This untranslatable term means something along the lines of illegal-rebel-sniper]. We were, let's say, terrorists. We have to say the word as the Germans used to, we were terrorists.

We were fearless. Our morale was excellent. Sometimes we didn't eat, but it didn't matter, we were always ready. We were pumped up. We were 19, 20 years old. If I had to do it all over again, I would think it over more carefully.

Even though the Resistance did not, by definition, follow the conventional rules of war, in most cases they respected strict rules of engagement, as **Louis Ganero** explains. The purpose of all but the most extremist groups was not to kill random German soldiers:

We FTPs were not allowed to kill regular soldiers, whether Germans or others. It was forbidden, because we knew there were a lot of people who had been forcefully enlisted. The Germans took Alsatians, Poles, Czechs, everything. We said: "The German enlisted man is not at war with you." So we were not to shoot German soldiers without a reason, without them attacking us. We were allowed to kill higher ranking officers and those who had swastikas.

Marceau Raynaud, who later made presentations for high school students, goes on:

The students I make conferences for often asked the question: "But how can you be friends with the Germans now?" So I said: "It is very simple, you must not confuse the Germans with the Nazis. They have nothing to do with each other. We were fighting the regime, not the Germans. The Germans are just like me and you."

Maquis Actions

The various groups of *maquiards* were involved in several types of actions. First, they needed to find food to sustain themselves. This

A photo of men from the 8th and 27th FTPF Companies, taken in Nice after the Liberation. Raynaud Marceau stands second from right. "Cobra," a very young FTP who executed a German prisoner in Levens in August 1944, sits first from the right. Marceau Raynaud Collection.

was done with the help of the local population, and by stealing stocks of ration cards. Those who received supplies by parachute had to organize the airdrops via coded radio messages sent to England, and then be present to take delivery of the supplies and hide them somewhere. Such a task required a lot of organization. The other actions were mainly aggressive and destined to hinder the Germans and their war effort as much as possible. Typical missions were blowing up train tracks and electric pylons, attacking convoys, and killing collaborators. The men had to know the rules of subversive warfare. **Jean-Paul Carbonel**, who was living legally in Cannes but participated in some actions, explains some of the theory behind the destruction of electric pylons:

On July 14, 1944 [July 14th is the French National Day, equivalent of Independence Day in the U.S.], Francis Tonner and myself blew up the pylon that supplied what people called the electricity factory in Mougins. First we had been instructed by a man whose identifying characteristic was that he was completely disfigured, scarred and everything. We called him "Chef Sabo," "sabo" for saboteur. He gave us lessons so that we knew what to do. Needless to say, the lessons were theoretical and we didn't blow anything up. The night of July 14th, we went to that pylon with my motorcycle and placed the explosive charges. To blow up an electric pylon, whatever you do, you should not blow up all four legs, because then there is a risk that the pylon will just be shortened. You have to blow only two of the legs so that the pylon tips over, causing a break in the wires. We placed the charges, activated the detonators, and drove away on my motorcycle. On the way down to la Bocca we heard the explosion. We went to Tonner's farm, where I left the motorcycle and took a bike so that no connection

could be made in case somebody had seen us. That was one of our actions.

Louis Garnero tells us more about the proper way to blow a pylon:

We blew corner pylons, because that way, when the pylon would collapse, it would tear the wires off the next pylons, as well. By blowing a corner pylon, we did more harm than by just blowing any pylon. We found out about the electric tensions so as to cause as much damage as possible to the industry. On bridges it was the same: we put plastic charges in the angles, always in the angles because it gave more strength to the explosive. The explosives cause more damage where they find more resistance.

As one man previously put it, being a good *maquisard* also meant, to a certain extent, that one had to be a good terrorist. **Zézé Latil** explains one trick that was learned from the two Spaniards:

Sabotage everywhere. We did everything that could possibly be harmful to the Germans. We cut off roads when there were convoys and also set booby traps. We put little bombs on the road that would explode when trucks drove over them, sort of like mines. We used the primer from hunting ammunition. When the trucks drove over them it made a powerful compression, and since we put several caps, it would blow up. It was a whole system. We would make five or six of them and then we would plant them; but it was mean of us, because anybody could drive over them and be killed.

Louis Garnero tells about one mission to steal ration cards:

We did little easy missions to take ration cards. For example, we took ration cards for bread, that way the "légaux" could buy bread for us. One day, with Nini [a female resistance fighter], we went to the town hall of Gilette to get ration cards. There was a line up when we arrived and the town hall secretary was distributing tickets to everybody. We walked in and Nini said: "Resistance, we are coming to take the ration tickets." The guy pulled a revolver out on her, a tiny little thing. When Nini saw that little gun she laughed; she had a Colt in her hand and all she had to do was pull the trigger. I was standing behind her, and since she was the one who spoke the man hadn't noticed me. So I put out my hand, pinned the man's hand down, and took the revolver. Then the guy spat on me, so I slapped him. He must have been a collaborator. We didn't have orders to do anything to him, so we didn't touch him, but I still gave him a good smack. We saw that the revolver wasn't even loaded. It was a funny little thing with a cylinder, something that probably wouldn't even have killed a fly.

Not all missions worked out so well, though. **Louis Garnero** continues:

> One day, we left to blow up the train track that went from Nice to Grasse, passing by la Manda. When we went on such missions, there were always two in front acting as cover, two in the middle who were carrying the explosives, and two in the back, also for cover. We had a new guy with us who had just joined the Resistance. We were on our way, but on the Charles Albert Bridge we got unlucky. There were Germans on each side of the bridge. We were in civilian dress and they didn't know what we were doing. We walked by, and when we got to the middle of the bridge, a car stopped and a German officer stepped out and asked us for our papers. The mission leader told Cobra: "Cobra, give him your papers." That meant "bang, bang." He pulled out his gun and killed him. The new guy who was with us panicked and shot one of our men, Vidal, in the leg. We found ourselves in the middle of the bridge with Germans on both sides. In the end, we survived because on the other side of the bridge, the soldiers were Alsatians and they didn't open fire on us. They didn't move or anything. We were advancing with our submachine guns. I was carrying the wounded guy, and they told us: "We are Alsatians." We hid the wounded man and called my brother, who was a truck driver, and had a double floor under his truck to carry wounded in. He brought him to Nice, where he lost a leg.

> Before my brother arrived, we called over a medical student, Mendrsisezki, whom we called "Le Magou," and who acted as a doctor for us. He came and dressed the wound. When Le Magou left, a German patrol approached him and arrested him. They took him away and massacred him.

> When one of our guys was captured, we immediately changed camps. We knew he was going to speak. It wasn't possible not to speak. Either he would die first, or he would speak. Mendrsisezki came back. Supposedly they had attached him to a cross on an armored vehicle. I was told he was all mangled and that his eyes were poked out. We left a man behind to shoot our friend. It wasn't to prevent him from talking, we knew he had talked. It was to put an end to his torture. Gabian had decided to leave somebody behind, but he missed his shot. Later on the Germans executed him at l'Ariane.

The last part of Louis Garnero's account is actually a myth; a rumor that he heard from others at the time. The tortures faced by captured men were often wildly exaggerated after the war, when killed *résistants* were elevated to martyrdom. Nobody remembers seeing a car with a crucified man on it, and in the postmortem photo taken of Claude Mendrsisezki's body, both his eyes are clearly visible and intact. However, the myth surrounding his death does not take away the fact that he undoubtedly suffered maltreatment by the Germans before finally being executed by firing squad in the Ariane district of Nice July 22, 1944. He was 20 years old and was killed

A period photo of the village of St Jeannet, showing the steep mountains that are encountered as soon as one heads inland in the Maritime Alps. The coast was controlled by the Germans, but the Resistance was powerful in the mountainous areas. The mountains north of St Jeannet were used as a refuge by several maquis during 1944. Mike Reuter Collection.

by six bullets to the chest. As for the Alsatian soldiers mentioned by Garnero, they were in reality probably Silesians, as no traces have been found of any Alsatian enlisted men in *Reserve Division 148*.

In another similar instance, two men from the FTP Company were wounded at Gattières, then captured and brought to the prisoner's ward of the Pasteur hospital in Nice. Once again, **Louis Garnero** was part of the action:

> We had a mission leader called Gabian, in whom we had unlimited trust. Maybe he had always been lucky, but he had incredible knowledge and capacities. We were informed that our wounded men who had been captured at Gattieres, Tenerini and Calamari, were at Pasteur Hospital. Our mission chief said: "Let's go, we are going to get them out."

> We left from la Roquette sur Var, where our camp was at that time. We arrived at Pasteur, where I stayed on the

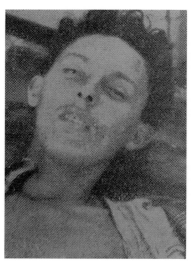

Jewish medical student Claude "le Magou" Mendrsisezki was a member of the 8th FTPF Company, where he acted as a doctor. After falling into the hands of the Germans, he was executed by firing squad July 22, 1944. L'Ergot/MRA Collection.

bottom floor as cover. Others went up to the higher floors, and Gabian went all the way to the top. When he got there, he found two French policemen guarding the wounded prisoners. There were quite a few wounded resistance men in that hospital. Gabian said: "Resistance, we are coming to liberate the prisoners." One of the policemen pulled out his gun, but he was immediately overcome, as Gabian smacked him in the head. We were used to being guerrillas and had a fair amount of know-how. The three that had climbed to the top took the guns from the policemen, and Gabian told them: "We aren't here to shoot at you guys, we don't shoot Frenchmen!" We took our two wounded, brought them down, and they left in an ambulance. They were brought to Germaine's house, which was where our wounded were looked after in Nice. She was related to Mendrsisezki. At the hospital, there were lots of political prisoners and Jews who had been tortured and the Germans brought them to the hospital to revive them, so that they could torture them some more. Everybody escaped. We opened the doors to everyone. We didn't know who they were, but they took off. I ran away on foot. After a mission, we didn't leave as a group. We split up and mingled with the crowd. In towns it was easy, since we were in civilian clothes.

Maybe two weeks later, we were on another mission in Nice. At Arson Square, Gabian said: "Look over there, the policeman. It's the guy whose gun I took. Since he is French I will give it back to him." We immediately got into position. There were two policemen and two men in plain clothes, and we positioned ourselves at each corner of the square. In our satchels we had everything we needed, submachine guns and everything. Gabian went up to the policeman and said: "Listen, I don't want you to be in trouble, I have your guns, but you will…" One of them, the one that he had hit on the head and another one in plain clothes, said: "*Gestapo*!" Gabian was a person with outstanding self control and he replied: "Yeah, *Gestapo*, and then what? You see at the corner over there?" I was holding a submachine gun. "See in this corner, and see in that corner? If you want, you will all be dead in two seconds. Now take your weapons and leave." They took their guns and left, because they were scared of us. They knew we weren't jokers, and that we had no problems with killing.

FTP leader Osiris Peragnoli, known as Gabian, who was held in very high esteem by his men because of his nerves of steel. Louis Tenerini Collection.

The details of this story have probably been enhanced with the years, however, the escape from the hospital truly did occur in these approximate circumstances, and is well documented by several sources. This case, as well as several others that will be mentioned in this chapter, were hastily classified by the French justice in September 1944, once Nice was liberated. The files regarding them remain closed to the public until 2044.[1]

It was rare for the Resistance to actually kill German soldiers. One well known case occurred at St Jeannet April 19, 1944. The 8th FTP Company, which had set up camp in a large house known as the *Château du Castelet* on the hills above St Jeannet, noticed a German vehicle approaching in the valley bellow. **Louis Tenerini** was on guard duty:

> April 19, 1944, I was on guard duty, and noticed a truck on the road down below from which armed and equipped German soldiers were coming out. They came towards us… Maybe they had noticed some smoke? (…) The Germans were climbing up towards us. We consulted each other and decided to wait for them. Our "castle" dominated the path that the Germans were using to approach us. We took up positions with our weapons, Jean Roux (an Italian army deserter) being at the machine gun.
>
> When the German got near we opened fire. They were surprised and routed. One or two of them were killed, and three were wounded, including the NCO. We kept firing as long as they were within range. We took the shoes, weapon, belt, and papers from the nearest body… he was Czech.[2]

Corrado Marcucci, another member of the FTP company, describes more details of the ambush:

> We decide that we will fire first, as soon as they are in range. The wait seems long, but they finally arrive. We can see them in the rocks down below. At the first shots fired with our "Lebel" [French World War I-era rifles] and Italian rifles, the Germans jump behind the rocks. We throw some grenades at them, but surprise! They don't explode! Jean Roux shoots down one soldier with his machine gun. Alain and Motoni get another. The enemies retreat down the hill. We approach the first dead soldier and take his papers. I don't feel proud; it is hard to kill a man in cold blood. It was our baptism of fire.
>
> We later solved the grenade question. Before being used a detonator needed to be placed inside them, but we didn't know that. The detonators were air dropped in separate packages as a safety measure.[3]

In fact, only one soldier had been killed. He was 18-year-old Johann Schmidpeter,[4] who was actually from Germany, and not Czechoslovakia, as Louis Tenerini remembers. The other members of the German patrol escaped wounded. Or course, the FTP company immediately had to evacuate their camp following this firefight. **Primo Calzoni** remembers the desperate escape towards the north, further into the mountains:

> We took the weapons of the first killed German and chased the other ones who were escaping down the hill, bounding from rock to rock. Then we left for the long walk towards Bouyon to avoid being surrounded. We were guided by two shepherds from Ascros and helped by thick

Zum ewigen Gedenken an unseren
unvergeßlichen Sohn und Bruder

Johann Schmidpeter

Bauerssohn von Rudletzholz
Soldat in einem Gren.=Rgt.

geboren am 25. Febr. 1926, gefallen am
19. April 1944. Er ruht auf dem Sol=
datenfriedhof b. Nizza, Südfrankreich.

Die Pflicht rief mich zum Krieg hinaus,
Mit Gott ging ich vom Elternhaus.
Ich dachte Euer fort und fort,
Wenn ich auch weilt' am fremden Ort.
Ich freute mich auf's Wiederseh'n,
Wenn Krieg und Sturm zu Ende geh'n
Doch anders hat's der Herr gewollt
Und hat von hier mich abgeholt.
Weiß nichts von Krieg und Erdenleid
Und bin von jeder Sorg befreit.
Drum meine Lieben, denkt stets daran:
Was Gott tut, das ist wohlgetan.

Barmherziger Jesus gib ihm die ewige Ruhe!

Brönner (Seitz) & Daentler, Eichstätt

18-year-old Grenadier Johann Schmidpeter, who was killed when he and his comrades encountered members of the 8th FTPF Company above St Jeannet. According to what his family was told, he had been shot through the head. Schmidpeter Family Collection.

fog. (…) Gigi would shout: "I can't walk anymore, I am staying here!" I would reply: "No, you will keep on!" I was carrying his bag on my back along with mine.

What a long walk it was, without food or water. We crossed the road between Bézaudun and Coursegoules at night. We needed to get out of the forest, where we couldn't see what was going on. We found a hut where we collapsed, dead tired. (…)

The shepherds had given us an old goat. Nobody wanted to kill the poor thing. I did so with an old ax. Since the Germans were after us, we didn't cook it and ate it raw, burying the head and the guts. But since the next day we had nothing to eat and the Germans had moved away, we dug the head up and boiled it in a piece of sheet metal.[5]

The FTPs had been lucky to get away from their camp at St Jeannet with no casualties, other than cases of intoxication caused by the consumption of the raw goat meat. **Louis Garnero** tells about some of the methods the Germans could use to locate resistance camps:

They came looking for us in the mountains with gliders that we called "lougi-lougi's." They could locate us because from the glider they could see that the grass was all trampled around water points. Then they would come to attack us. They either surrounded us, or attacked us by airplane.

However, using airplanes was the exception; much simpler methods were more effective, **Louis Garnero** proceeds:

There was a woman who we called the Hyena. She was from central Europe and came to villages asking inhabitants for information. She would say: "Are there any young people here? I am for the Resistance." Then they would catch us. We got attacked at la Moutette because of her and almost all got killed.

We were at la Moutette and the guy on guard duty was new. He had just arrived, was covered with tattoos and had been in the Legion, but we didn't know that. We normally immediately put the new men on guard duty, and they were often scared. He came back and told us: "There are lights coming up." So we went out and looked and said: "But those are fireflies you are seeing. It's full of fireflies here." Since he was new, we figured he was frightened. I told him: "If you see them from close up, then open fire and we will see what happens. But wait until they are at a range of 50 meters." That's how we got surrounded, because he let them come up close, he actually wasn't afraid at all. He didn't come or warn anybody, and all of a sudden we heard: "bambambam bambambam!" Afterwards we told him: "But what?" He said: "You old hands told me to let them come up to 50 meters." He explained: "I was in the Legion and participated in ambushes in Africa."

He had let them come too close and they had already surrounded us by the Duranus road. When we realized that, we hid two of our wounded in a barn. The Germans invaded our camp, but didn't manage to find them, hidden in the straw. They had found American field dressings from the airdrop, so they knew there were some wounded.

We were really done for. When the situation got desperate, we had to escape by the cliffs. There were 70 or 80 of us, and at least 1,000 of them. Me and another friend who knew the region well guided all the others, and we managed to escape by the cliffs. The Czech cook had to carry all his pots as well as his weapon, and he was 50 years old. For us, the young ones, it was alright, we were tough. When we arrived at Baou Roux, one of our guys "Le Marseillais" fell from a height of 300 or 400 meters. He must have been 17 or 18 years old. The poor guy fell because it was dark and he was really a city boy.

The FTPs went back to their camp two days later and found their two wounded still hidden in the straw. The Hyena had succeeded in her mission, but she would lose the next round, as **Louis Garnero** explains:

> We had attacked a German convoy. When we did that, we would hide on top of the cliffs that overlooked the road. We were positioned one after the other, and when the convoy would drive by and reach the last one of us, the last one would throw his Gamon bomb and then we all did the same. Nobody could get away. That time there was a taxi following the convoy that got caught up in the middle of the fire. I think the last guy didn't throw his bomb because he saw it was a French car. There was the driver and a woman inside, and we captured them and brought them with us.
>
> We were at the Breques d'Utelle. We suspected they were with the Germans, because they had been following the convoy, but we weren't sure. When we got back to the camp, somebody recognized the woman and said: "Hey, she is the one who is betraying us!" Supposedly she went to villages asking about where young people were coming to get supplies and things and then she would sell us to the Germans. She was a member of the *Gestapo*, an employee of the German army to betray people. So we said: "Oh la! She is the Hyena!" She paid. She really paid. She really got something, and we buried her up there at the Breques d'Utelle. I saw her shoes still lying on the ground maybe two years after the war.
>
> The taxi driver that was there was from Nice; I remember, it was my group's duty to guard him. He would tell me in Niçois: "I didn't do anything! Why are you keeping me here!" He saw that the women had really taken something, because she had gotten so many people tortured. He would say: "But I have three children at home who are hungry if I don't work! Release me!" We told him: "We can't release you. We will only let you go when we change camp sites." We had to be careful,

because the Germans could catch him and make him talk. I don't know what happened to him. When we changed camps we let him go. The poor guy hadn't done anything, he was just a taxi driver and was scared. He stayed with us at least two weeks, maybe more. He was hungry, but I told him: "You know, we have been hungry for a long time."

The *Gestapo* frequently sent infiltrators to try to find information on the *maquis*. **Colonel Jacques "Sapin" Lécuyer**, the commander of all resistance forces in the southeastern corner of France, explains another case where the Resistance managed to identify infiltrators:

> Around July 14th [1944], two individuals showed up in the Verdon valley at Beauvezer, where there was a control post, claiming to want to join the *Maquis*. They were not the first ones, and like all the others, they were interrogated by a little specialized commission. Their attitude was suspicious. They were asked for identification papers. Very fast (too fast!), they pulled out magnificent identity cards that were in too good a condition for the date at which they were supposed to have been issued. Additionally, the stamp, that of a police station in Nice, was not of the same color as the usual stamps from that police station. They were interrogated several times and finally admitted that they, as well as other comrades, had been sent by the *Milice* in order to determine the positions where the *Maquis* were, and where ambushes or roadblocks had been prepared, in preparation of a large scale cleaning up operation that was to occur in the following days. Aware of their guilt, they declared that they wished to redeem themselves by fighting with the *Maquis* (but it was too late!).[6]

The deaths of the Hyena and of these infiltrators brings us to one of the more controversial aspects of resistance activities: the assassination of traitors and collaborators.

Assassinations and Executions

As we have seen, the Resistance was involved in a bitter and merciless type of warfare. Their main direct enemies were not

(Continued on page 60)

The last photo of Grenadier Josef Krumm with his family. Krumm had first been assigned to border guard duty in the Pyrénées Mountains before being transferred to the 14th Company of Regiment 8 of Reserve Division 148. According to his company commander, Lt Liebich, he was killed by a gunshot fired by partisans January 31, 1944, only a few days after his arrival in southern France. Krumm Family Collection.

This impressive series of photos taken at Caucade Cemetery in Nice was sent back to Josef Krumm's family by Lt Liebich. The series allows us to observe the uniforms and faces of the soldiers and officers of Reserve Division 148. As in other photos of the division, it is notable that most of the officers and NCOs are well decorated combat veterans, whereas the enlisted men are fresh recruits with no decorations whatsoever. Krumm Family Collection.

regular German soldiers, but the *Gestapo*, French *Milice*, and all those who participated in betraying resistance fighters, Jews, and other "enemies of the state." The situation was unacceptable: French citizens were helping the Germans track down their victims, who were then sent to concentration camps and death. These collaborators needed to die. One FTP explains:

> There was the fight against the Germans, but then there was also the fight against the French. Unfortunately, there were many Frenchmen who were for Petain and who were collaborators. In France, it was the French police that arrested the most Jews, not the *Gestapo*. Obviously, when we found out about people who were selling Jews, communists, and gypsies, we, the *maquisards*, did not let those people live. No, we did not let them live. It wasn't a problem, we were at war. There were never any mistakes, because it was organized in a way that there could be no mistakes. The *légaux* warned us to beware of certain people and the information was passed on to our leadership in Marseille. They would seek out more information, and when they had the information they would say: "It's true, that person needs to be liquidated." It wasn't anybody who could just do anything; that is not true. Afterwards I heard stories, I heard nonsense, I heard lies. But never, never, never did a resistance fighter just act on his own.
>
> At one point, we found out about a smuggler who was supposedly smuggling Jews out of France. When the Jews left, they took all their valuables and gold with them, and when they got to the mountains, the smugglers killed them and took the money. When we found out about that, of course we did punitive missions that we never speak about because it is no use.
>
> We were like them, we had become savages. All we thought about was to avenge our dead. We had become evil; on the long term, combat makes you evil. But we didn't torture anybody.

Another *maquisard* remembers:

> We were mostly fighting the *Gestapo*. We killed quite a few traitors. Those people needed to be destroyed. Frenchmen who were against France! We had much more hatred for them than for the Germans. I could not accept that a Frenchman could work with the Germans and I preferred killing a Frenchman than a German.
>
> I participated in killing a *Gestapo* guy in Hyers. He had a chest of drawers that was full of bank notes. The drawers were all full of money! But we had orders never to take any money. It was an elderly person, and when they shot him I went outside in the staircase – I didn't want to see that.
>
> At Fayence we killed Colonel Perfetti. Four were killed in Mons and two in Claviers. We shot one in Draguignan. Those are actions I participated in. There were several of us looking for those people. We knew who they were. When we found them, we would take them and bring them somewhere to shoot them. The guys would say that it wasn't them; of course they weren't going to say: "We betrayed you." But we knew it, we had precise information. They tried to tell us it wasn't them, but we had proof.
>
> The two we killed in Claviers had been brought up by the St Raphaël resistance people. We never killed in the town the people were from. We always brought them somewhere else so that their bodies wouldn't be found. They were

brought up and we immediately shot them. We buried the bodies so that we wouldn't be accused of their deaths.

It was a difficult task, but no mercy could be given, as another resistant recalls:

> According to what Captain A. was saying, two girls had denounced some *maquisard*s, so we killed them at Breques d'Utelle. He made them stand in front of us and was going to shoot them, but his revolver jammed. So they turned around: "Ahhhh!" They started screaming: they hadn't expected that. So A. asked another guy: "Give me your gun," and he killed them.

Of course, during the performance of such activities mistakes were bound to happen, despite the precautions taken by the Resistance. An FTP fighter tells us about the deadly frame of mind some *maquisards* were in, and the consequences it could have:

> When we were happy, when we had performed well, the reward we were given was the right to kill. We were told: "You have 48 hours, go wherever you want and kill somebody who is fighting against us." That was our reward.
>
> That day there were six of us, as usual, and we were waiting in front of the train station to see if any fascists would come out. A fat Italian fascist came out and walked down Tiers Avenue. We followed him on the opposite sidewalk and said: "OK, when there aren't too many people, we liquidate him!" We followed him, but there were always people on the sidewalk. We reached the intersection with Gambetta Boulevard and the guy started walking up Gambetta. We were going to cross when we heard: "Hei li, hei li, hei lo…"[7] There was a company of Germans marching down the street. It was a close call for the Italian. He will never know it, if he is still alive, but it was a very close call.
>
> We went back to the train station. A car drove up and two men got out with uniforms and caps covered with stars. For us, stars meant generals, and we said: "This is going to be a good deal!" We shot them, but it was a monumental mistake, because they turned out to be two civilians, two station masters. They were on vacation, and we thought they were high ranking officers because of all the stars; they actually weren't even fighting men. It was an accident that we regret. Things like that happen in life.

The two victims of this "accident" were **Otto Huber** and **Johann Haas**. The French police report about the ensuing investigation read:

> On June 28, 1944, around 20:20, two members of the German army (railroad workers in uniform) were shot in the street, in front of 26 Boulevard du Tzarewitch in Nice. They were immediately transported to the Belvédère clinic by Mr. Chevalier and Mr. Chapon, who were the first to arrive at the scene, but they died during the transfer.
>
> On the scene of the aggression, eight 11.25mm shell casings were found, for the American "Colt." Seven or eight shots were fired. (…) The shots were probably fired from point blank range, as five bullet impacts are visible on the street around a puddle of blood.
>
> Mr. Chevalier and Mr. Chapon, directors of the "La Rochefoucault" professional formation center (…) at 45

boulevard Tzarewitch, told us that upon their arrival, the wounded were in too serious a state to be able to pronounce a word or be able to make any gestures.

One of the youths from this center, Jean Estable, aged 17, distinctly saw four young people who escaped by Primerose avenue immediately after the shots were fired. (...) According to the first results of our investigation, it seems that the perpetrators of this murder are members of the dissident groups that are currently active in the mountains north of Nice.[8]

Following this killing, the Germans cracked down on the population of Nice, publishing the following announcement in the newspapers:

On June 28th, in one of the main streets of Nice, two Germans, employed by the German railways, were killed by terrorists. In consequence:

1- The curfew for the town of Nice is advanced: it will last from 20:00 at night until 5 in the morning from July 1st to 10th;

2- The cinemas will be closed from July 1st to 14th;

3- All consumption establishments (bars, breweries, cafes) will be closed during the period July 1st to 14th, except restaurants, that are to close at 20:00.

4- The beach reserved for the French population will be closed to the public between July 1st and July 14th.[9]

This retaliation for the death of the two German railroad workers can be considered very gentle. A few days later, however, the Germans committed a much more brutal reprisal. On July 7, 1944, they hung two men, **Séraphin Torrin** and **Ange Grassi**, from the street lamps of the Avenue de la Victoire in downtown Nice, leaving them hanging for all to see. The two men were inhabitants of the village of Gattières, which had been put into the spotlight one month earlier on June 7th, when a German soldier was killed there by men of *Goupe Morgan*, the local *maquis*. FFI **Primo Elisei**, one of the *maquisards* of the group, remembers what the group leader, Georges Foata, known as Morgan, told his men about the shooting:

When I was in the *maquis*, Morgan would tell us that story. They were supposed to pick up a person coming from England at the mouth of the Var River, so a taxi driver came up from St Laurent to pick them up. Then they left, but they weren't clever, because there was an Italian army greatcoat in the car and there were Colts in the pocket of the coat. A German sergeant and some other Germans were guarding the road. Suddenly, they saw the taxi, and when they noticed the Italian greatcoat they said: "Get out." The sergeant took the coat and felt the weight of the Colts in the pocket. One of the guys always had a pistol hidden behind his back and he was standing behind, at the corner of the car. The German was talking with Morgan, and when he saw the German's eyes were riveted on Morgan, he shot him. The German fell down, so Morgan bent down and picked up the German's pistol as another German was rushing toward him with a rifle. Morgan aimed at the German, but the shot didn't go off. The pistol had jammed when it fell. So what did he do? He threw the pistol at the German's face, then jumped over the wall. Pepino, the taxi driver, jumped after Morgan, but the German fired a bullet at him from above the parapet and killed him.

Morgan broke the padlock on a shed, took a pitchfork and dressed up in some old clothes, then he left, crossing

the Var at the Pont de la Manda in front of the Germans. The others took off right and left and they all found each other again in the *maquis*.

The German who had been shot, 27-year-old Silesian *Unteroffizier* **Vinzenz Thoma** of *Reserve Jäger Bataillon 28*, died of his wounds shortly afterwards.[10] The Germans searched Gattières immediately after the shooting, but departed without any reprisals taking place. Several weeks later, however, on July 3rd, they returned to Gattières with specific information given by an informant. This time they arrested a large number of men, including local communists Séraphin Torrin and Ange Grassi. It is difficult to know exactly what transpired, as this story has been told and retold in so many different versions since the war, but it would seem that the Germans had been waiting to find appropriate victims to kill in reprisal for *Uffz* Thoma's death and Torrin and Grassi fit the profile. Both were hung publicly in the streets of Nice July 7th. The Germans purposefully forced as many civilians as possible to see the bodies. **Marceau Raynaud's** father-in-law was a bus driver:

My father-in-law was driving the bus, and they told him to make a detour to see the bodies that were hanging. It was to serve as an example: "If you kill a German, this is what is awaiting you." They terrorized us like that.

Paul Tremellat, a child from Villeneuve-Loubet, was brought all the way to Nice by his uncle to see the bodies:

My uncle had been mayor of St Jeannet before the war and was a socialist who more or less turned communist, because that is where the greatest animosity for the Germans could be found. He knew Torrin and Grassi well and they were unfortunately hung by the Germans in Nice. They left them hanging for three or four days [In fact, the bodies only hung for one day, as they were buried in Caucade Cemetery July 8th],[11] and my uncle brought me to Nice to show me what the German fascists, in other words the Nazis, were doing. He told me: "This is what the Nazis know how to do. Look what they are doing to us. Remember this for the rest of your life." And of course I did remember for the rest of my life.

Killing *maquisards* who were attacking the Germans was one thing, but leaving the bodies of these men to hang in the main street of Nice was quite another. Even the collaborationist Prefect of the Maritime Alps reported in a telegram to his superiors July 7th:

The execution was performed by hanging from lampposts at the corner of the Avenue de la Victoire and the Rue Hotel-des-Posts in Nice. I had tried intervening at the *Kommandantur* to get the location and manner of execution changed. Emotion is considerable and psychological effect negative.[12]

The only effect the execution had was to intensify the hatred of the population towards the German occupiers. To this day, Ange Grassi and Séraphin Torrin remain the most well-known symbols of German brutality in the Maritime Alps. There were, however, many other executions of *résistants* in the region during the Occupation, including several mass executions. On June 11, 1944, at St Julien du Verdon, 11 Frenchmen were killed, including several Nice high school students who had tried to join the *maquis* after the news of the Normandy landings on June 6th. The victims were let out of a

July 7, 1944, Séraphin Torrin and Ange Grassi are hung from lampposts in the main street in Nice, apparently in retaliation for the death of Unteroffizier Vinzenz Thoma of Reserve Jäger Bataillon 28, who had been mortally wounded in Gattières during a botched operation of Groupe Morgan one month earlier. MRA Collection.

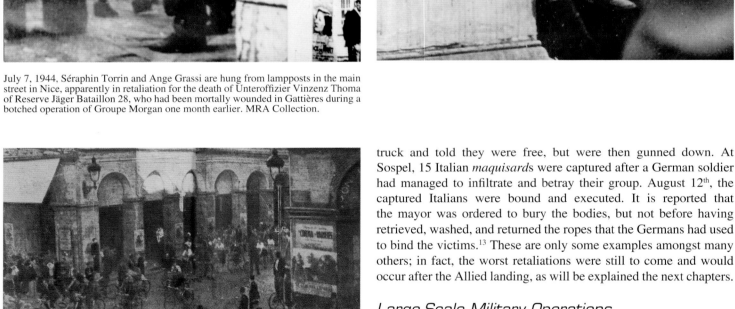

In this surreal photograph secretly taken by Groupe Lenoir, the motionless and ghostly figures of Torrin and Grassi can be seen hanging from the lampposts among the crowded Avenue de la Victoire. L'Ergot/Collection MRA.

truck and told they were free, but were then gunned down. At Sospel, 15 Italian *maquisard*s were captured after a German soldier had managed to infiltrate and betray their group. August 12th, the captured Italians were bound and executed. It is reported that the mayor was ordered to bury the bodies, but not before having retrieved, washed, and returned the ropes that the Germans had used to bind the victims.[13] These are only some examples amongst many others; in fact, the worst retaliations were still to come and would occur after the Allied landing, as will be explained the next chapters.

Large-Scale Military Operations

As we have seen, the main goal of the FTP resistance was to constantly bother and frighten the Germans as much as possible through acts of sabotage and small-scale attacks. The ORA, which the FTPs considered to be too inactive, had a different strategy. Its goal was to create a large and well organized underground army that would remain hidden until larger-scale military attacks could be performed. They attempted such a large-scale attack in mid-July 1944 in the area of Guillaumes, a remote and unpopulated zone in the northern part of the Maritime Alps.

As previously explained, the German forces were almost entirely concentrated along the coast, and capturing Guillaumes

Gilbert CAMPAN   BALDO   non identifié   GALLO   AUBÉ   GIORDAN   A. MAGNAN   R. MAGNAN   CASIMIRI   ADAM   DEMONCEAU

Eleven resistance men who were executed by the Germans at St Julien du Verdon June 11, 1944. Several of them were high school students from Nice who had been trying to join the FTPs in the wake of the news of the Normandy invasion. The execution may have been performed in St Julien as a retaliation for the death of some German soldiers in the same area. L'Ergot/MRA Collection.

had not been difficult, as no German troops were there to start with. The occupation of Guillaumes threatened a German line of communication, so troops from the two reserve battalions of *Reserve Division 148* (*Reserve Jäger Bataillon 28* and *Reserve Grenadier Regiment 327*) were sent to crush the rebellion. In short order they recaptured the rebel village, but suffered at least 15 killed in the process,[14] including *Oberleutnant* **Horst Zädow**, the company commander of the 2nd Company of *Bataillon 327*. The ORA forces had only lost two men killed, but were forced to escape back into the surrounding mountains. However, the Germans evacuated the area they had recaptured in the following days, probably because they couldn't afford to have large numbers of troops away from the coast, where a landing could occur any day.

The Guillaumes uprising demonstrates that the Resistance was not capable of winning military confrontations against the Germans, as they were too few, too disorganized, and not armed well enough. However, the Germans were just as incapable of controlling the hinterland of the Maritime Alps, because they were also too few, and their main priority was the protection of the coast. The consequence of this balance of forces is that by August 15, 1944, when the Allies finally landed, there were virtually no Germans present in the area north of the St Vallier-Levens line, and all the Germans north of this line would be captured or killed by the Resistance within two days of the landing.

Lt Friedrich Baumgaertel participated in several anti-partisan operations, including that at Guillaumes, as a member of the HQ Company of *Reserve Grenadier Bataillon 327*. He was later captured and interrogated by Allied troops, revealing very interesting information on how these operations were experienced from the point of view of the German troops, on the relations between the *Wehrmacht* soldiers and members of the *Gestapo*, and on why such heavy losses had been suffered in the fight for Guillaumes:

In mid-June 1944, by order of Kniess, a campaign was undertaken against Partisans in the area southwest of Digne. Colonel Behle was put in command of this campaign. Three battalions in all were used for the operation: one battalion was the 1st Battalion, 239th Reserve Grenadier Regiment, while the other two were from Kniess. [Lt Baumgaertel] was still administrative officer at the time and was taken along as adjutant. The campaign was carried out in cooperation with SD Marseille and with personnel of the Division Brandenburg. The sole mission of [Lt Baumgaertel's] battalion was to push through to the areas in question, surround these, and herd together the population, separating them according to sex. The SD carried out all interrogations, investigations, and trials. The troops had strict orders to confine themselves entirely to tasks of a military nature and to leave everything else to the SD. In [Lt Baumgaertel's] opinion, the success of the campaign was ridiculously small. This, he stated, was the result of a tactical error, which consisted of attacking from South and Southwest, but sending no troops to seal off escape routes in the North. This made it possible for the Partisans to escape North and Northeast.

Early in July 1944, the same error was committed during a second campaign of this nature. This operation was called Operation Panther. It was carried out by 62 Corps by order from higher HQ, under the command of Colonel Meinshausen. Two battalions were committed: 1st Battalion, 239th Reserve Grenadier Regiment under Captain Vogt; and 2nd Battalion, 8th Reserve Grenadier Regiment under Captain Beerschwenger, without success. During this Operation, 1st Battalion had heavy losses.

The second day, 2nd Company, 1st Battalion, under the command of Lt Zädow, was advancing at the point of the column near Thorame Basse. Lt Zädow, riding in one of the leading trucks, was fired upon by a MG nest while approaching a blind curve and was killed [This was in fact *Oberleutnant* Hörst Zädow, killed July 18, 1944]. During the firing, a high tension cable was broken and fell on the truck, which was loaded with 200 liters of gasoline and a large amount of ammunition. The truck exploded and many men were burned to death. The total casualties were ten dead, three severely wounded, and three wounded to a lesser degree.

Oberleutnant Bönsch, the commander of the 8th Company of Reserve Jäger Bataillon 28 and a veteran of Stalingrad, poses for the camera with several of his NCOs. It would seem that within Reserve Division 148, Reserve Jäger Bataillon 28 and Reserve Grenadier Bataillon 327 were used as a mobile intervention force whenever and wherever extra power was needed. The Jägers were involved in several bloody encounters with the Resistance, most notably in Guillaumes in July 1944. Note that all the men sport various decorations, Oberleutnant Bönsch's badge being the rather unusual Bulgarian Infantry Badge in Silver. Oberleutnant Bönsch also wears the oak leaf badge of the Jägers on his right sleeve, while his men, who were probably proud of their Jäger status, wear riding breaches. Bönsch Family Collection.

This operation took about six days. Lt Kraft was appointed as a direct aid to Colonel Meinshausen in this operation, as he had become more or less a specialist officer. He had previously been assistant administrative officer, as well as HQ commander, and leader of the 148th Reserve Division Sharp-Shooting platoon. He had often been used in connection with anti-Partisan activities.

(...)[Lt Baumgaertel], who took part in an anti-Partisan campaign, described the SD as very brutal. The ones he saw were adventurous, both young and old, who robbed and lived like kings and could afford to do anything with impunity. In anti-Partisan raids, after the troops had completed their military mission and herded the civilians together the SD arrived, interrogated and tried civilians at random, and ordered many to be shot immediately. [Lt Baumgaertel] compared SD methods with third degree methods. Orders from Germany were to shoot all partisans. The use of these crude methods was, by order, the mission of the SD. The SD was concerned with civilians only and worked a great deal in civilian clothes.

The leader of the SD in Nice was "Regierungsratsturmbannführer" Retschek [in fact spelt Retzeck], who had many Frenchmen working for him. He was known as an able man and was a very successful one. He was one of Himmler's men who was able to do what he wanted, up to and including the requisitioning of wealth and money. Later (after May 1944) Retschek was transferred from Nice to an unidentified area.

The seat of the SD in Cannes was in the Hotel Montfleury. SD officers here avoided all other officers, knowing the intense dislike for units of their type.[15]

Conclusion

As a natural reaction to the German occupation, a small number of French men and women formed resistance groups. Although active *résistants* were few and far between, they were supported by a significant proportion of the population. These resistance groups attempted to wreak maximum havoc on the Germans, and stockpiled weapons in order to be able to offer efficient help to the Allies when they would arrive. The Germans fought back bitterly and ruthlessly, executing and deporting dozens of *maquisards* in the Maritime Alps. The much-awaited Allied landing finally occurred August 15, 1944. This landing is the theme of the next chapter.

3

The Operation Dragoon Parachute Drops

The goal of this chapter is not to give a detailed description of the invasion of Southern France by Allied troops (Operation Dragoon), but simply to:

- present the Allied units that fought in the area of study.

- highlight some interesting stories that happened to the members of these units before they entered the area of study.

- give a brief overview of the airborne phase of the Allied invasion of Southern France.

Operation Dragoon

June 6, 1944, Allied forces landed in Normandy, in northern France, thus starting the liberation of the French mainland. August 15, 1944, the Normandy landing was followed by a second landing in Southern France, code named Operation Dragoon. The landing started with a parachute jump in the general area of le Muy in the early morning of August 15th by the First Airborne Task Force, followed by a seaborne invasion at sunrise in the area between Cannes and Hyères. This seaborne invasion was mainly performed by the American 3rd, 36th, and 45th Infantry Divisions and the Canadian-American First Special Service Force. Two French commando units also landed at the extreme east and west flanks of the landing zones. We will not go into details about most of these units.

The First Airborne Task Force

The First Airborne Task Force (FABTF) was a division that had been specially formed July 15, 1944, in order to perform the airborne phase of the August 15th invasion. It was made up of spare paratrooper, glider, and regular units that happened to be in Italy while the invasion was being planned. The FABTF was a very colorful and heterogeneous division, and was commanded by legendary Major General Robert T. Frederick, one of the youngest generals of the U.S. army, who had reportedly been wounded in combat no less than eight times. Virtually all the fighting that occurred in our area of study was done by units of the FABTF, and we will therefore go into a detailed description of this division. The order of battle of the FABTF was as follows (all units were American, except when specified otherwise):

There were four parachute infantry units, accompanied by supporting artillery and engineers:

- **517th Parachute Infantry Regiment** (517th PIR).
- **2nd Independent Parachute Brigade** (British), consisting of the

4th, 5th, and 6th Battalions of the Parachute Regiment and some smaller supporting units, such as the 127th Parachute Field Ambulance.
- **509th Parachute Infantry Battalion** (509th PIB).
- **551st Parachute Infantry Battalion** (551st PIB).
- **460th Parachute Field Artillery Battalion** (460th PFAB).
- **463rd Parachute Field Artillery Battalion** (463rd PFAB).
- **596th Parachute Combat Engineer Company** (PCEC).

In the days preceding the invasion, men of the 517th PIR are briefed about their future drop zone and mission. Mike Kane Collection.

The other of the units of the FABTF were to land by glider; they were:

- **550th Glider Infantry Battalion** (550th GIB).
- **64th Light Artillery Battalion** (British).
- **300th Anti-Tank Battery** (British).
- **442nd Antitank Company**.
- **602nd Field Artillery Battalion**, (602nd FAB).
- **512th Airborne Signals Company**.
- **676th Medical Collecting Company**.
- **887th Airborne Engineer Company**.
- **A Company of the 2nd Chemical Battalion**.
- **D Company of the 83rd Chemical Battalion**.
- **3rd Ordinance Medium Maintenance Company**.
- **FABTF Headquarters Company**.
- **Military Police Platoon**.

The reader should make an effort to remember what the abbreviations for these units stand for, as they will be used regularly until the end of this book. In total, there were 9,732 officers and men assigned to the FABTF on August 15, 1944, 9,089 of which were considered to be "effective." (These are the numbers cited in the FABTF's August 1944 "Summary of our operations" report. Such precise numbers are of course purely theoretical.)

The invasion was to start with an early morning jump performed by the 517th PIR, 2nd Independent Parachute Brigade, 509th PIB, 460th PFAB, 463rd PFAB, and 596th PCEC. These units were to take control of the major roads in the area of le Muy in order to prevent the Germans from reinforcing or retreating from the coastal area. The 551st PIB and the glider units were to land later in the day.

All the units of the FABTF were later to participate in the fighting in our area of study, except for the 2nd Independent Parachute Brigade and the 550th GIB. In the rest of this chapter, we will only concentrate on the major units of the FABTF that concern our study, and the 2nd Independent Parachute Brigade and 550th GIB will therefore mostly be ignored. However, three units that were not part of the FABTF and that landed by sea also fought in our zone of interest, so will therefore also be studied in detail. These units were the 141st Infantry Regiment of the 36th Infantry Division, the First Special Service Force (FSSF), and the French *Groupe Naval d'Assaut de Corse*.

History of Units of Interest

We will now take a closer look at the histories and missions of the major units of the FABTF and of the seaborne force that we are interested in.[1]

517th Parachute Regimental Combat Team

The 517th Parachute Regimental Combat Team (517th PRCT) was the name given to the team that the 517th PIR, 460 PFAB and the 596th PCEC formed. These units had been trained together and usually fought together on the battlefield. The 517th PRCT had been created in early 1943. Like all other parachute units, it contained only volunteers. These men had been especially selected and had gone through particularly tough training. They formed an aggressive and elite unit with a strong *esprit de corps*, commanded by Colonel Rupert Graves. However, the 517th was relatively inexperienced, having only been in combat in Italy for approximately ten days in June 1944. Their mission on the night of the invasion was to jump in the early morning and capture the area around le Muy and its strategic crossroads, as previously mentioned. Exceptionally, the 517th PRCT did not function entirely as a team for the invasion, as

"Chutes were passed out and fitted." August 14, 1944, at Canino airfield, Italy, the men of A Company of the 517th PIR help each other into their parachute harnesses, as they prepare to embark on their first combat jump. These photos are part of a series taken by an army photographer. More shots from the same series will be presented in the following pages. NARA/Bruce Broudy Collection.

one platoon of the 596th PCEC had been detached to the 509th PIB, which had no engineers.

The 517th PIR consisted of three battalions, each with three rifle companies and one headquarter company. The nine rifle companies were lettered A to I, and each company contained 120 to 160 men. There was also a Medical Detachment, a Service Company, and various other odds and ends, giving the 517th PIR a total strength of 2,000 men.[2] Approximately 800 more men were members of the 460th PFAB and 596th PCEC.

509th Parachute Infantry Battalion

The 509th PIB was one of the very first paratrooper units to have been formed by the U.S. Army, starting its life in 1941. By the time of Operation Dragoon, it was one of the most battle-hardened

Men of D Company of the 517th PIR pose below the nose of their Dakota aircraft. Each man wears one main parachute as well as one reserve parachute. Mike Kane Collection.

August 1944. (Once again, such precise figures, though they seem very rigorous, are in fact theoretical and prone to error, and need to be taken with a grain of salt. The FABTF August 1944 Operations Report only lists 582 "effectives" for the 551st PIB for the date of August 15th, for example.)

Glider Units

Of particular interest is the fact that of all the American glider units that participated in the invasion, only the 550th Glider Infantry Battalion was glider trained when the FABTF was formed. All the other units were trained for their glider mission in haste between July 20 and August 5, 1944, by instructors provided by the 550th GIB. The men of the 602nd PFAB were actually given the choice of volunteering for the mission (presumably because they needed some men to say behind in Italy to take care of their mules), but the men from the other units involved were apparently simply "volunteered." The most important thing the improvised glider troops learned was how to properly lash down all their equipment (such as jeeps and cannons) in the gliders, so that it would not move during the flight or landing, which could have potentially lethal consequences.

Some of the glider units had intriguing backgrounds. The 442nd Antitank Company, for example, consisted of soldiers of Japanese ancestry who had volunteered to fight in the U.S. Army, even though the U.S. was at war with Japan, and in many cases the relatives of these soldiers had been sent to internment camps in the U.S. Most of the improvised glider units were battle-hardened and had been in combat for extended periods of time. The 602nd PFAB had even landed on Kiska, Alaska, in 1943, after the island had been taken over by the Japanese. August 15, 1944, the glider troops were to land in France at le Mitant once the area had been secured by the paratroopers. Each unit was then to assist the parachute forces with their various specialized skills. According to FABTF plans, a total of 403 gliders were to be used in Operation Dragoon: 332 American Wacos and 71 British Horsas.

141st Infantry Regiment

The 141st IR was one of the three regiments that made up the 36th Infantry division. The unit was originally a Texas National Guard unit, but by August 1944, it contained men from all over the USA. It consisted of three battalions, each containing one headquarters company and four rifle companies lettered A to M (there was no J Company). By the time of Operation Dragoon the unit was highly experienced, having been involved in heavy fighting in Italy for almost one year, including at Cassino and Anzio, and having participated in two seaborne invasions. The 141st IR is of interest to us because its mission was to land on the right flank of the invasion front, in the Anthéor Cove and at Aguay, and it was then to advance east towards the city of Cannes, thus entering our area of study.

Groupe Naval d'Assaut de Corse

The *Groupe Naval d'Assaut de Corse* was a small French special forces type unit of approximately 70 men that had previously been involved in several successful commando operations along the Italian coast. The men mostly came from Corsica, Algeria, and Brittany, as Algeria and Corsica had already been liberated, while Brittany was close to England, enabling men to cross the channel and join the Allied forces during the Occupation. The *Groupe Naval d'Assaut de Corse* was the unit that landed on the extreme right flank of the seaborne invasion front, at the Pointe de l'Esquillon, in Théoule sur Mer. Its mission was to blow up the only coastal road in the area, as well as *Route Nationale* 7, in order to prevent German attack or retreat from the main landing area.

units of the U.S. Army in Europe, having been in combat since November 1942 in North Africa and Italy. Before the invasion of Southern France, it had already performed four combat jumps and fought on some of the bloodiest battlefields in Italy. To this day, the 509th remains one of the most legendary units in American military history, having performed the most combat jumps in World War II. It consisted of a single battalion of three rifle companies, each lettered A to C, plus a headquarters company. Its total strength at the time of the invasion was 700 men,[3] under the Command of Lieutenant Colonel William Yarborough. The battalion was to jump in the early morning and participate in the capture of the general area of le Muy along with the 517th PRCT.

551st Parachute Infantry Battalion

The 551st PIB was formed in 1942, had been extensively trained in the U.S., and spent several months in Panama. However, the unit had never been in combat, and this is probably why it was not assigned to jump the morning of August 15th like all the other paratrooper units of the FABTF. The 551st PIB was only to jump in the afternoon to reinforce the units that had already landed in the morning. The unit was organized in the same manner as the 509th PIB, was commanded by Colonel Wood Joerg, and 842 men were assigned to it on August 15, 1944, of which 742 participated in the parachute operation according to the 551st PIB's unit history of

First Special Service Force

The FSSF was one of the most peculiar and famous Allied units of World War II. Its main originality lies in the fact that it was made up of both Canadian and American nationals. It had been created in 1942 as a commando unit destined for a sabotage mission in Norway. Volunteers were called for from the Canadian and U.S. armies, and were then selected according to particularly strict criteria. An effort was made to attract men with experience in the use of explosives and outdoor life. Because of this, the average age of soldiers of the FSSF was greater than in other similar elite units.

The FSSF's order of battle was organized differently from regular U.S. army units, with the goal of confusing the enemy. The Force was divided into three "regiments" that actually only contained two battalions and six companies each, with only about 80 men assigned to each company. It was said that a FSSF regiment or battalion was the equivalent of a regular U.S. Army battalion or company, which was approximately true. Each company was numbered 1 to 6, with the regimental number listed after it. Thus, the 3rd Company of 2nd Regiment was called "3-2." Companies 1 to 3 formed the first battalion of their regiment, while companies 4 to 6 formed the second battalion. There were also Headquarters Detachments for each battalion and regiment, as well as a Service Company and a Medical Detachment. The unit's total strength was about 2,450 men on August 31st according to the FABTF August 1944 Operations Report, but an internal count by the FSSF August 27th only reported 1,700 men.[4]

The Forcemen, as they were called, were trained in parachuting, seaborne assault, mountain warfare, and hand to hand combat. The unit was sent to Alaska in 1943, where the Japanese had taken over several islands. In late 1943, it arrived in Italy, where it was involved in bloody but victorious fighting until Operation Dragoon. The FSSF was probably the best trained unit of its size in the whole U.S. and Canadian armies. It is said that the German troops who faced them in France in late 1944 were warned that their opponents were "treacherous, merciless, and cunning." August 15th, the FSSF was not attached to the FABTF and was assigned to capture the islands of Levent and Port-Cros, on the extreme left flak of the invasion and far out of the area of interest. However, the Force became attached to the FABTF in the following days and therefore participated in liberating the Maritime Alps. During its previous campaigns, the FSSF had been commanded by Brigadier General Frederick. However, Brigadier General Frederick had been promoted and put in command of the newly-created FABTF, and it was Colonel Edwin Walker who commanded the FSSF in France (this was the same Edwin Walker that made headlines in 1963 for having been targeted for assassination by Lee Harvey Oswald).

Quality of the Allied Units

All these units that fought in our area of study during Operation Dragoon were either highly experienced and/or highly trained units, with the highest morale and strongest *esprit de corps*. They were elite units, in which many of the men enjoyed taking risks and actually looked forward to being sent to combat. This was in stark contrast with the German *Reserve Division 148,* consisting for the most part of unmotivated recruits of mixed nationalities who had never been in combat.

The Parachute Drops of August 15, 1944

In the weeks preceding the landing, the units of the FABTF were isolated in camps in Italy, far from the front lines, in order to rest and do some final training and preparations. **Guy Carr**, of I Company of the 517th PIR, wrote in his memoir:

The paratroopers of A Company, 517th PIR, now wait for departure time next to the Dakota aircraft that will bring them to France. NARA/Bruce Broudy Collection.

"We put on our jump suits and proceeded to Service Company, where we were sprayed completely with camouflage paint from hoses." Camouflage paint is sprayed onto a soldier of the 517th PIR. Ltc George A. Sullivan Collection, courtesy Roger Sullivan.

Behind the closed doors of the S-2 and the guarded war tents, details were taking shape on maps and sand tables marked "Top Secret." Then, during the second week of August, all the men in the regiment were sent into the War Tents in small groups. We were to memorize what we saw on the sand tables and maps.

We still had no knowledge of the locations shown on the sand tables, as S-2 had reproduced only that portion of the terrain covering the area of the drop zone. We were required to etch each mountain, river, valley, power line, road, town, forest, and any other object that would be of use behind enemy lines… not on paper, but in our minds, which could not be read by any enemy.

The order soon came through to get ready. We put on our jump suits and proceeded to Service Company, where we were sprayed completely with camouflage paint from hoses. What a wild looking lot we were, as the boys with the hoses made no effort to spray only our suites, but the rest of our bodies, as well. All types of pistols and knives appeared from nowhere, and the so-called name "Butchers with big pockets" seemed appropriate. (…)

Chutes were passed out and fitted, and ammunition and "K" rations issued. Machine guns, rifles, pistols, mortars, and anything that could destroy the enemy were given a final inspection. We were also given pamphlets containing French phrases and escape kits, native currency, compasses, silk maps, and matches (this was our first clue to where we would be landing). We were given camouflage paint to be applied to our hands and faces. There were so-called artists; thus, some very interesting designs were worked up.[5]

Before the main body of a parachute unit was dropped, small, specially-trained groups of men called pathfinders had the mission of marking the drop zones. The pathfinders jumped in advance of the main force and set up radio beacons that the next planes could head towards in order to drop their loads of paratroopers as precisely as possible. In wartime, all sources of light on the ground were meticulously hidden, making it difficult for pilots to navigate and find their target areas. The mission of the pathfinders was therefore very important, and failure on their part could cause the rest of their unit to jump dozens of miles off target. Nine pathfinder teams were to jump into southern France at 3:30 on the morning of August 15th, preceding the main airborne assault by one hour. Three teams were provided by the 2nd Independent Parachute Brigade, three by the 517th PIR, and the 509th PIB, 550th GIB, and 551st PIB each provided one team. **Jim Chittenden** was a pathfinder of the 1st Independent Platoon of the 2nd Independent Parachute Brigade. This 45-man unit was to mark the drop zones in the le Muy area for the British 2nd Independent Parachute Brigade. They flew into France among a group of bombers so that the Germans would not suspect that paratroopers had been dropped:

We were split up in three sections and we dropped in three sticks. We flew into France with a flight of Mitchell bombers. Our three Dakotas dropped us and then flew on with the Mitchell bombers on a bombing raid, then came out of southern France a different way, because if on the radar the Germans would have seen three planes come in and go out again, they would have known we were there.

We were only jumping from an average of 500 feet and were down in about seven seconds. We landed at 3:20 in the morning, and the Germans didn't even know we were there. Our first person to get killed was named Eric Morley. His parachute never opened because his static line had broken. We got different reports about this. Some of them said his static line was ruptured by the acid in the batteries we carried and others said different tales. But his parachute never opened, so you can say that he was the first man killed because he went straight down.

Over the Mediterranean, we flew across the navy ships, which were sending out a Eureka beam. We got our bearing off of that. Once we passed over that ship, we flew on a certain bearing, for a certain distance of time, and they dropped us spot on the target. We were in the right place and at the right time. Our orders were to be quiet, and if we had to do anything, use your knife. Use your gun at the last minute, because we didn't want to alert anybody. This is the sort of unit we were.

"We were given camouflage paint to be applied to our hands and faces. There were so-called artists; thus, some very interesting designs were worked up" Here paratroopers of the 517th PIR show off their war paint. The American paratrooper units of the FABTF all spray painted their helmets, uniforms, and equipment as a form of improvised camouflage. The 517th, for the most part, used a mixture of spray painted green and grey-black, to which some yellow paint was sometimes added with a paintbrush, as seen in these photos. The 509th and the 551st PIBs used similar paint schemes, though the exact colors and patterns used changed from unit to unit. NARA/517prct.org/Gilles Guignard.

Jim Chittenden, of the 1st Independent Platoon, was one of the British pathfinders who spearheaded the invasion. Adrian Stevenson Collection.

We sat out by our equipment and brought the division in at approximately 6 o'clock in the morning, and at 8 o'clock we brought the gliders in. We laid the yellow silks down to mark out the landing zones for the gliders. After that, we brought supplies in and then we joined up with the division and we did any job they wanted us to do. I must say, it was a very efficient and good operation. It was one of the most successful operations ever done. The British forces did their job well. They were in the right place. We did have a part of the 5th Battalion that went astray, but it had nothing to do with us. We were on the right spot and we pulled them in, but their radar wasn't working in the plane, so they tried to break away, but a lot of their flight just followed them and they landed some 36 miles away. But it had nothing to do with us, we were on the right spot and our radars were working correctly.

Jim Chittenden's pathfinder team had been particularly successful, but this was not the case of all the pathfinder units. On the night of August 14 to 15, 1944, the area the paratroopers were supposed to jump in was covered by exceptionally thick fog, causing several pathfinder teams of the 509th PIB and 517th PIR to be dropped hopelessly off target. The entire 3rd Battalion of the 517th, along with most of the Scottish 5th Battalion, landed in the Fayence-Montauroux area, approximately 20 to 30km to the northeast of their planned drop zone. The story of these men will be described in depth in the next two chapters. As for B and C companies of the 509th PIB, they jumped approximately 30km south of their drop zone, near the coastal town of St Tropez. We will mention them further on in this text.

For the moment, we will concentrate on the men who were actually dropped close to their intended drop zones, in the region of le Muy. The essence of being a paratrooper is to feel lost behind enemy lines, and this is how most men felt as they reached the ground. The thick fog restricted vision and gave many the impression that they were over the sea as they were descending. **Bud Curtis**, of the Headquarters (HQ) of the 1st Battalion of the 517th PIR, told of his impressions of the jump in a letter written to his mother August 22nd:

We boarded C-47s in Italy (Chiteviccia [sic]) about 2:30 a.m. and had a nice pleasant ride, with no opposition at all. Most of us were asleep until almost time to jump. They woke us up and said we would be over the field in eight minutes. That was about 5:00 a.m. We stood up and hooked up. It seemed like years went by as those last minutes ticked off. I was number 13 man. The green light came on and guys began to disappear in front of me. Then there I was at the door. I had a hell of a body position. I went out the door like I was throwing a flying block with my right shoulder at somebody. I was heading down nose first when "wham," she opened and jerked me back up right. I looked up to make sure my chute was open and then I looked around. We must have jumped awfully high, because I thought I was never going to come down. There was a low fog about 100 feet off the ground and it looked just like water. I really thought my number was up for sure. I was cussing the Air Corps and all their ancestors for 17 generations back.

When I sank through the mist, I was just beginning to figure it all out when "thud," I hit the ground. I will never forget that morning. I was miles away from the jump field. Later, I found out that it was a good thing I didn't land on the jump field, as the Germans had it all ready for us with mines, machine guns, and flame throwers. All I could

Men of Company A, 517th PIR, wait under the wing of their Dakota aircraft. Note that although the uniforms and equipment of these soldiers have been spray painted for camouflage purposes, they did not use camouflage paint on their faces. NARA/ Bruce Broudy Collection.

Trooper Bud Curtis shows off all of his equipment before embarking for southern France. Curtis Family collection/517prct.org.

see was forms of trees through the fog. I cut myself out of my chute, and when I stood up I seemed to have lost my sense of balance. I fell down and rolled down the side of a mountain a few yards. I stood up again, and did the same thing again. I stood up again, took a couple of steps, and fell off a ledge about 10 feet high and about broke my neck. There was dry grass all over, and every step I took you could hear it for a mile. I decided to lay still for a while and see if I could figure out where I was. I didn't know which way to go. I heard somebody moving a little ways in front of me. I shouted the password at him, hoping it was one of our guys, but instead of getting the right answer I got a couple of bullets just over my head. I took off for a big rock and figured I would have it out with the guy, but then I heard somebody behind me. Once again, I made the mistake of hoping it was one of our guys and shouted the password to him and got my answer in hot lead. It was so foggy we couldn't see each other, but we could hear every move each of us made.

There must have been a whale of a patrol around me, and every step I took away from them I could hear them coming closer. I knew as long as it stayed foggy I could hold them off, but it began to get light, so I decided the best thing to do was make a run for it and hope they would miss. I took off, zig-zagging, and they opened up on me, but I was lucky and got to the other side of the hill and down in the valley, and there I met some of our own guys.

We climbed over another hill and came to a road and met up with most of the company. Ever since then I haven't had much trouble.[6]

Captain Robert Dalrymple, the commanding officer of the 596th PCEC, related his jump in the following terms:

I can remember when I stood in the door, in southern France, I thought: "Wow, what am I doing here?" I noticed on my watch it was 0432 on 15 August 1944, and I thought: "Well, that's two minutes late, which puts us way off the target." Actually, we were about two minutes early, but I didn't know that at the time. Well anyway, we had already had the warning light in the plane, so everybody was up and hooked up and ready to go, and I was the first out the door. We were pretty low, it seemed to me like around 800 feet. When you are leading the stick out, as soon as your chute opens, you turn yourself 180 degrees so you can see your men coming out, to make sure everybody came out. Then you had to get back and get ready to land. Well about the time I did that, we went into a little cloud bank. There was a cloud bank right down on the ground, so that was the end of that, and I swung back. I didn't know where the ground was so I had to get ready to land, and pretty soon, bang, I landed on a rock pile on the bank of the Argens River there at le Muy.

So I landed safely, and you always roll on your back, because we had an automatic 'chute release on our belly; I hit that, and then I couldn't get up! I thought: "My goodness, I am paralyzed!" But it was just a little bit of a panic, because when we jumped, we carried two canteen covers, one on each hip: one for water, of course, and the other one had three or four grenades in it. Well they were hooked in my harness, and that kept me from getting up, so I threw that off.

I said: "Well, I have got to cross this river, I know we are on the other side," and it was getting daylight pretty

quick now, so I set on down the bank and I waded across the stream, which wasn't very deep. I got up on the other bank and I turned a corner of a little building, and there was one of my men right there with his rifle on my belly. We were able to recognize each other in the twilight. There were three or four men there, so I said: "I know about what direction we have to go now because I have got the photo map in my pack." I reached down to my pack, and my pack had snapped off when I jumped. The opening shock had jerked my musette bag, which was down just on top of my

Company A, 517th troopers relax and smoke during the flight to France. NARA/Bruce Broudy Collection.

emergency 'chute, and it had snapped off. Well, there went my maps and whatever else I had in there. But anyway, I got a sense of direction because I could tell where we were from le Muy, and somehow I was able to recognize this was le Muy.

Myrle Traver was in F Co of the 517th PIR:

The night of the jump we were flying pretty high, coming in from Italy on the planes, and when we started getting close to the coast, we hit a big bank of fog and nobody could see a thing. The pilots just came to where they figured they were on land and jumped us out, because they couldn't see anything. It was one of the highest jumps we ever made, and when we were coming down we could hear what we thought were splashes in water, so we prepared for a water landing, but I found out that we were hitting woods and going down through the trees. One of

my platoon guys, Joe Martin, and me were the only two that landed there, and I could hear him. But it was foggy and in the woods, so I hollered: "Is that you, Joe?" I don't know why I said his name, I just said it, but it was him. We got out of our chutes and everything and started trying to find a road or something to gather up guys, because it was just terribly foggy, we couldn't see anything. Then we got down and we started finding a couple more guys, and then we found Colonel Graves. We stuck on this road, and we were trying to get assembled to where we could do something. We started cutting the telephone lines to disrupt all of the communications. We would cut down poles and what have you as we went along. One guy had a rifle grenade on his rifle, and we heard this "putputput," and here is a guy coming around a corner on a motorcycle. He blasted him and knocked him off the motorcycle. That's the first guy I saw killed, a German.

Cutting telephone wires was a very useful act of sabotage, but certain precautions needed to be taken to cut actual electric wires, as the paratroopers soon discovered. T5 **Dale E. Booth**, of the HQ Company of the 1st Battalion of the 517th, later wrote:

I was a member of the 517th Parachute Infantry, and **Danny Fisher** was also a member. We jumped from the same plane at about 4:30 A.M. the morning of August 15, 1944, and landed approximately five miles northeast of les Arcs, France. About 6 o'clock (A.M.), we assembled a group of 40 to 50 men and proceeded south with a French guide. At around 8 A.M., we came across some high tension wires and a captain asked Danny if he could cut the wire. He immediately went up the pole and came in contact with a high tension wire and was electrocuted. Since it was impossible to carry his body with us, we left him and proceeded to les Arcs. (...) He was in the same platoon as I was, and a very close personal friend.[7]

The officer who had given the deadly order was Capt Young. **Sgt Hoyt Kelley**, also of the 1st Battalion HQ, remembered the very poor reputation that Young had within the unit:

At the point of no return. The A Company paratroopers prepare to jump out into the great unknown. This is their first combat jump, and the tension is clearly visible on the face of PFC Chester Kochersperger. Behind him stands a trooper identified as 21-year-old Pvt Albert J. Ernst, from the Bronx, NY, who would be killed in Les Arcs in heroic circumstances the next day. NARA/Bruce Broudy Collection.

Nineteen-year-old Cpl Daniel A. Fisher, who was electrocuted soon after landing after an incompetent officer ordered him to cut down some electrical wires. Fisher Family collection/National WWII Memorial.

On the jump in southern France, [Captain Young] ordered Danny Fisher to climb an electric pole and break a line with a pick-axe. Danny, who was a sergeant, was killed by the electricity. Shortly after that event Young was shot through his helmet, possibly from the back, we've never been sure. The shot put a lot of metal flecks from his helmet into his forehead, and with all the bleeding he thought he was dying, and cried for forgiveness for Danny's death. He never came back to the outfit after that time, but became an M.P. I don't think he wanted to return to the front line.[8]

It is barely imaginable that a paratroop officer would not be aware of the deadly risks of cutting electrical wires, since such a task was one of the normal missions assigned to airborne troops. However, Captain Young was not the only officer of the 517th PIR lacking knowledge in this domain. **Claude Rickards,** of E Co of the 517th, remembered:

We were just wishing we would get there so that we could get the hell out of that thing [airplane]. That's generally what we were thinking: "I wanna get out of here!" And we couldn't get out until we got to where we were supposed to and we got the green light to jump. I guess there was some flack coming at us, but not an awful lot. And some of the guys claimed they could see tracers coming up at us. I didn't see any from where I was sitting. They had a bucket they were passing up and down the line in case you got sick, but I didn't get sick, I just sat there with my head down low, waiting for the word.

It was about 4:20 in the morning when we jumped. It was dark, and I remember the craziest thing happened when I came down – my chute stayed on top of this house, and I landed down in the walkway from the door. My chute stayed on top of the house. Boy, I got out of that chute as quick as I could, and a bunch of us got together. There were about 15 or 20 of us, and we were standing under these high tension wires. This lieutenant told this corporal to go up and cut the wires. The corporal said: "No sir, I don't have to take that order. These gloves aren't heavy enough for that." And this actually happened, and the lieutenant said: "Well, give me the damn tools, I will do it." So he went up: well, he cut the first one OK, and the second one, and he then hit the third one and the whole sky lit up and he came down. I think he died. I am pretty sure he laid there moaning and we got out of there. I think somebody stayed with him, but we had to get out of there, he was making too much noise. I can't remember much about the day of the 15th. All I know is we were getting back together; we were scattered all over hell, but most of us finally got back together anyhow.

This soldier's common sense and disobedience had saved his life. The officer who had electrocuted himself was **2nd Lt Maurice J. Miley,**[9] of the HQ Company of 2nd Battalion, 517th PIR. His manner of death is confirmed by **Erwin Scott Jr.,** of D Co of the 517th, who adds an interesting twist to the story:

We lost a lieutenant. It didn't look like a power pole to me. It barely looked like an anemic telephone pole. He told our supply sergeant to get up there and cut the wires. He looked up there and said: "I don't think I want to do it." The lieutenant said: "Well, that's an order. Get up there and do it."

"If you want those wires cut, you better get up there and do it yourself. I'm not going to do it."

"I'll have you court-martialed when I get back."

The lieutenant did climb up there and took out the wire cutters and put them on there. It was pretty high voltage of electricity and it electrocuted him. The sarg turned around and said: "Well, that's one thing I don't have to worry about."[10]

In the initial chaos of the landing, quite a few paratroopers who had the misfortune of landing near German strong points were captured, only to be released within minutes or hours once the Germans realized they were outnumbered. **Walter Perkowski**, of F Company of the 517th PIR, was one of those who briefly experienced what it was like to be a prisoner of war:

When I jumped we had a good fight. There were five of us got caught in a house and they were all wounded. I was a BAR man and I was in the back porch; I used up all my ammunition, so I went inside the house and picked up a rifle to cover one of the rooms. All the bullets were coming through, then a hand grenade came through and it blew. It stunned me, more or less, and I was captured. The German who captured me was a nice guy; he offered me a cigarette and I told him "No thanks," and he offered me a candy bar and I said, "No." I was in no mood to be eating.

The other guys were brought somewhere else and they took me to an officer. He asked me how many guys jumped. I told him 60,000, and then he hit me, grabbed hold of me, and threw me inside a trench. Mortars and shells were coming in and they pulled me out and put me and two English paratroopers in a garage and lined us against the wall. The door opened and two Germans came in with a machine gun. All of a sudden, here comes one with a bicycle and he said something to them, so they picked up the damn machine gun and the guy on the bicycle and took off and left us there. I just came out and waited for the guys to come in. The whole thing lasted about an hour or two. The other four were treated by a French doctor.

Paratroopers of the 517th PIR pose for the camera of Signal Corps photographer Sgt Irving Leibowitz. Numerous German soldiers would fall victim to paratroopers waiting in ambush by the sides of the roads. NARA.

When thinking about parachute operations, one often imagines the scenes from the movie *The Longest Day*, where paratroopers landed in the middle of groups of Germans and were gunned down before even managing to get out of their harnesses. In the drop zones of the Le Muy area, the Germans were actually far outnumbered by the paratroopers, with only a few companies of *Reserve Division 148* and *Infanterie Division 242* being concentrated in Draguignan, le Muy, and Puget sur Argens. In fact, the situation was much more frightening for the Germans than for the paratroopers, as they suddenly found themselves with their lines of communication cut off, surrounded by unknown numbers of armed enemy troops. When they left their strong points, the Germans could be attacked at any instant by paratroopers or *maquisards*. One such ambush was later to become famous among the soldiers of the 517th because of the gruesome photo that it was linked with. **Clark Archer** explains:

I arrived at Château St Roseline, the Regimental CP, at 11:00 a.m. on D-Day with Private Kellogg. We located PFC Sutton and Stephan Wierzba and were instructed to set up a road block. We moved down the slope from the CP and located the les Arcs-Trans Road. Kellogg and Wierzba were in a ditch, with Sutton to their rear on the higher ground as a lookout, and I took a position midway between them. At about 13:00, Sutton yelled, "One of ours. It's coming down Kellogg's side." Shortly thereafter, we could see the silhouette of a vehicle approaching. The car closed to within 50 yards of our position, waving their arms as if to indicate a "friendly." There was considerable reluctance to commence firing, as I did not see any visible weapons. All problems ceased as the convertible slowed down just past Kellogg's position and mine; they were Germans, there was no doubt about it. I stood up and started firing my grease gun into the driver's side door until it jammed after firing eight or nine rounds. Then Kellogg popped up and fired a full clip from

(Above photos) The graphic results of the ambush that was sprung on several German soldiers riding in a Mercedes by soldiers of the 1st Battalion of the 517th PIR near les Arcs. Ltc George A. Sullivan Collection, courtesy Roger Sullivan. Boswell Archives, originally from the Blackie Norton Collection.

his M-1 rifle. Next, Wierzba fired an "AT" grenade from his Springfield '03 rifle. The firing pin on the grenade had not been removed and subsequently it did not detonate. It did, however, hit the driver's head, splitting his skull wide open. We cut the other Germans down with small arms fire. The Germans were carrying a black canvas briefcase that contained maps. As I opened the case, I noticed that the top map was the German redeployment for the Invasion of Southern France. I put everything back in the case and rushed everything back to Headquarters. This intelligence later proved helpful in countering the German redeployment of some of their forces as the invasion was unfolding.[11]

Bill Bolin was the First Sergeant of C Co of the 517th PIR, and he later visited the scene of the ambush and drove the car back to the Regiment HQ, where it was given to Colonel Graves, the Regimental Commander of the 517th PIR:

On the way up there we came to this car, which was that Mercedes. It was full of dead Germans, about five of them. The driver was inside the car and there were two officers in the back seat, in addition to two or three others that were out on the road, who evidently had jumped out of the car. They had all been shot and killed. The driver was hit with a rifle grenade that went through his head and didn't explode because the shooter forgot to pull the pin on the grenade. I couldn't figure out what had hit that poor guy. He had a heck of a big hole in his head that went right straight through him, mostly through the ears. But he was a tough old boy; he was a sergeant, and he must have been quite a man, because he was still sitting up when we got there, though he was dead.

The front seat was all bloody from the guys that were shot. I had to sit down to drive so my back end was all bloody from that, but the company commander, Captain La Chaussee, didn't sit down. The car didn't have any top on it, and he just stood up and hung onto the windshield, waving a white handkerchief so that our own people wouldn't shoot us.

There were many such ambushes in the early morning of August 15th. Amongst the paratroopers who were involved in these firefights was a most unusual character, PFC Philip Kennamer, who had barely missed being sentenced to death in 1934 after he had shot and killed John Gorrell, a young and prominent dental student, in Tulsa, Oklahoma. Kennamer, who was himself the son of a judge, claimed he had shot Gorrell because Gorrell was planning to kidnap the girl Kennamer loved, Virginia Wilcox. The bizarre case, which also involved the suicide of a key witness and the exchange of coded messages in jail, made headlines at the time. After the trial, Kennamer was lucky to be found guilty of manslaughter only and was sentenced to 25 years in prison. He was just 19 at the time.

However, Philip Kennamer's destiny, like so many others, was unexpectedly changed by the war, and in 1943, he was paroled out of prison in order to join the army. One of the 1934 articles had described Kennamer as a boy who "had wrecked cars; he had jumped from windows, he had walked around the edge at the top of a tall building, he had discussed joining revolutions." [12] Another article told of "stunts," such as "walking around the 16th floor ledge of the Mayo Hotel and leaping from one automobile to another while travelling 50 miles an hour." [13] In other words, Kennamer was a promising paratrooper candidate, and it was as a member of the 460th PFAB that he jumped into southern France August 15th. Kennamer spent the night before the jump with his army buddy **Milton Rogers**, who later wrote:

My outfit was made up mostly of young guys, most of them right out of high school – or in some cases reform school. I was one of the older ones. Phil Kennamer, of the Oklahoma State Penitentiary (…), was three or four years older than I was, and partly due to our advanced years we had become pretty good buddies. We couldn't sleep as well as those young kids without nerves, so we sat up and talked till time to load in the planes. We were out of about everything to talk about, and finally got to religion. He said he didn't believe in God, didn't believe in much of anything.

From convict to paratrooper. PFC Philip M. Kennamer was sentenced to 25 years in jail for manslaughter in 1934, but was paroled in 1943 in order to enlist in the paratroopers. He was killed in action in Trans en Provence the morning of August 15, 1944, as a member of the 460th PFAB. Tulsa World Collection. Dominic Biello/ww2-airborne.us Collection.

I said, "You mean you think that if you get shot tomorrow it's all over?" He said, "Yep, that's what I think." [14]

After parachuting out of their aircraft, the group of men Kennamer was with got pinned down by a German machine gun near the village of Trans en Provence. Philip Kennamer and Lt Harry Moore volunteered to eliminate the opposition and rushed forward. Unfortunately, both men were gunned down by automatic fire and killed. Kennamer's buddy **Milton Rogers** wrote on:

Lt Roberts (…) came with the information that **Phil Kennamer** and **Lt Moore** had just been killed. I got down the line a ways and there they lay. Phil had a nice row of bleeding holes, maybe four or five, across his chest. It had been maybe seven or eight hours since we were talking about such matters; he then knew more about the hereafter than I did. [15]

Kennamer's obituary concluded:

"Death of soldier ends slaying story

A soldier's death in France for paratrooper Phil Kennamer has closed the book on one of the country's most publicized slayings – the 1934 Thanksgiving shooting of socially prominent John F. Gorrell.

The War Department notified Federal Judge Franklin E. Kennamer that his 28-year-old son, parolee from a 25-year manslaughter sentence in the Gorrell slaying to become a paratrooper, was killed in France 8.15.1944.

Kennamer had a leading role in a drama which received nationwide attention through a decade of trial appeals and clemency petitions.

When Kennamer last visited OK – to testify at a clemency conspiracy trial of a former ST Pardon and Parole Officer in 11.1943 – he confided to a newsman that "something just seems to tell me that I won't come back."

"I hope," the paratrooper told Managing Editor Edward D. Burks of the *Tulsa World*, "That if I die under the flag of my country, those who have condemned me will hold me differently in their memories."[16]

The inhabitants of Trans en Provence certainly hold the killer-turned-paratrooper in their memories, and his name, as well as that of Lt Moore and of French paratrooper **Jacques Debray**, who were killed at his side, are inscribed on a stone monument in their town.

The Landing as Seen by the Germans

After describing the landing from the point of view of the Allied paratroopers, it will now be interesting to view it from the German side. *Generalmajor* Ludwig Bieringer was the District Commander in *Feldkommandantur 800* (FK 800) in Draguignan, and wrote a detailed report of his memories of August 15, 1944, after the war. First, it is important to note that the invasion was not a surprise for the Germans. August 13th, **Ludwig Bieringer** attended a staff conference in Avignon, where the officers were warned:

British and American paratroopers mingle in Le Mitan. NARA.

The Commander of the Military Government area (…) informed us that the long-expected invasion on the southern coast of France was imminent and could be expected to take place as early as August 15, 44.[17]

Surprisingly, this disquieting news did not seem to alarm the German commanders, perhaps because they were already well aware that they could do nothing to change the course of events. **Bieringer** continues:

No order was issued prescribing the course of action the district commanders and their staff were to take in case of an Allied landing. The question of a timely withdrawal and transfer of the *Kommandantur* was not discussed at all (…). The District Commander, committed as the combat commander of the Marseille land front, pointed out that an effective defense of his sector was impossible with the forces he had at his disposal, which were absolutely inadequate for fighting enemy troops with up to date equipment. The only reply he received was a shrug of the shoulders.[18]

On the night of August 14th to 15th, *Generalmajor* **Bieringer** was back at *Feldkommandantur 800* in Draguignan, near which the local German army hospital and the Corps HQ were located. As the paratroopers landed and the local *maquis* took arms, he found himself surrounded by a mysterious and invisible enemy that slowly closed in on him, cutting off his communications before finally smothering his position:

15 August 44 02:00 hours. Order from Corps HQ to FK 800:

1- Enemy paratroopers jumped in the region of St Raphaël, le Muy, la Motte.
2- Alarm Company Draguignan to assemble immediately at the alarm station to attack the enemy, ascertain position of the drop zone and strength of the enemy.

The Alarm Company was composed of various static units at Draguignan (Corps Staff, motor transport company, supply company, *Feldkommandantur*). Under the command of an *Oberleutnant* from the corps staff, the company started off at 04:00 on trucks, attacked the enemy, and was routed with heavy losses in men and material.

The FK 800 had put one lieutenant and 20 men at the disposal of the Alarm Company. 50 percent of these were casualties: two men killed in action, two missing, and six wounded, among them Reserve *Leutnant* Pfannkuche, a minor casualty. The only light machine gun belonging to the FK was lost. The routed elements of the company returned at approximately noon. (…)

As of 05:00 on 15 August '44, the strong point of the FK was occupied by two machine gun and rifle squads (officials, specialists, clerks, etc.), live ammunition, hand grenades, first aid packets, etc., were distributed; files burned, and communication trenches to the corps staff situated 800m to the northeast and to the local hospital 300m to the south were secured. (…)

At noon, continuous landing operations of troop-carrying gliders in the region of le Muy and la Motte, under cover of the paratroopers who had landed there in the morning, were carried out by approximately two regiments, without any opposition from German anti-aircraft and ground defense.

(Above photos) An impressive sight. Paratroopers of the 551st PIB jump out of their aircraft, filling the sky with Nylon parachutes the afternoon of August 15, 1944. NARA.

The corps informed us that battalions of the neighboring division had been started off in the direction of the enemy air landing area. They never arrived. Nothing was heard about their fate.[19]

Indeed, on August 15th, *Reserve Division 148* sent out its *Bataillons 327* and *372* in the direction of Draguignan. As we will see in the next chapter, they ran into trouble when they reached the region of Montauroux and were never able to fulfill their mission. The *Feldkommandantur* could still have tried to escape, but fear of acting without orders prevented them from doing so:

The FK 800 could have withdrawn on that day with local actions against *maquis* formations, which, according to information from agents, had blocked the Draguignan-Grasse road early that morning. Being without a corresponding order from the OFK, I had to remain at Draguignan.[20]

This lack of initiative would cost them dearly. The next day, August 16th, the *Maquis* and paratroopers closed in for the kill. **Bieringer** found himself trying to defend his *Kommandantur* with a handful of men who were not combat troops. The situation went from bad to worse:

These shots taken through the window of a glider show the surrounding Waco gliders and Dakota aircraft. Art Helmers Collection.

The fighting spirit of the officials, specialists, and men of the FK, and their will to resist a superior enemy could not be rated very high. (...) On the invasion day, they could observe the landing of enemy airborne troops near le Muy for several consecutive hours without any chance on the part of the Germans to offer any resistance. (...)

Near the exits to the northeast, considerable movement was observed in the houses, sheds, and gardens, which were taken under our machine gun fire.

The Corps informed us that a strong patrol with guns had been started off to the city in order to ascertain what the situation was there. As we were able to observe from the FK strong point, the patrol reached as far as the first crossroad and was repulsed, leaving wounded, prisoners, and their guns behind in the hands of the *Maquis*.

The Corps further informed us that all the roads leading to the east, north, and west were blocked by the *Maquis*, and according to reports from agents, strong enemy forces were being assembled on either side of the Verdon valley.

The patrol, which on orders of the corps was sent out by the FK along the Draguignan-Fayence-Grasse road to ascertain the whereabouts of the battalions of the neighboring division (...), failed to return, as did the patrol that had started off along the road to Digne in order to repair a wire.

At noon, headed by a passenger car, several truckloads of reinforcements arrived for the *Maquis* from the direction of Brignoles-Salernes and were greeted by loud shouts of joy, which could be heard distinctly from the FK. (...) The building for the staff in the strong point was kept under continuous rifle fire by the *maquis* riflemen from their hiding places in the neighboring buildings and behind trees. (...) The FK demanded artillery fire from the Corps to be delivered on enemy positions in the outskirts of the town. Unfortunately, the range of the only gun the staff of the Corps still had at its disposal was insufficient. The first shell hit a high tension pylon, with the result that the FK remained without electricity, and as a result of this without light, radio, or drinking water. (...)

In the meantime, the gun which the *Maquis* fighters had captured from the Corps HQ had been emplaced a few hundred yards away from the FK strong point to deliver direct fire on the staff building. (...) During the day, the crew of the gun, to which one or two German artillery men had even been included by force, could be held down by our continuous machine gun fire.

By evening, cries of distress were heard from the occupying forces of the hospital that consisted of lightly wounded men with captured rifles, but without any machine guns, defending themselves against strong *Maquis* formations. The impression prevailed that the *Maquis* wanted to achieve success by taking prisoners before the arrival of Allied troops, in order to compensate for their own losses. (...) Despite being superior in numbers, the

A maquisard photographed in Draguignan a few days after the Liberation. Ted Rulison Collection.

Maquis fighters did not risk approaching the FK strong point. They limited themselves to completely encircling the strong point and, as already mentioned, kept the buildings under rifle fire.

Late in the afternoon, the Corps informed us that the Americans had reached Draguignan. At dusk, we could observe lively movement and hear the noise of motors, probably of American tanks. (…)

16 August '44, 23:00 hours. In absolute darkness, there was a sudden concentration of rifle, machine gun, submachine gun, and artillery fire on the FK strong point, causing panic among the occupying personnel. The relief parties standing in front of the staff building ran into the air raid shelter and some of the men followed. Having driven out the scared men and distributed those I could get hold of in front of the tunnel, I ordered them to occupy the space in front along the wall, the hedge row, and the spaces behind the trees. I then hastened into the command post in order to report to the Corps by phone. Despite repeated ringing, there was no reply. The wire was probably cut.

After a while, during a lull in the fighting, I heard the loud voice of Lt Pfannkuche announcing: "The Americans are in the strong point. Cease fire! The entire personnel of the strong point assemble immediately, without rifles. Hurry up! In ten minutes the enemy will open fire again."

I heard these words of Lt Pfannkuche, uttered with extreme excitement, while I was trying to get the telephone connection. I stopped immediately and hurried out. In the darkness, I could see a number of men putting down their rifles in front of the tunnel and marching away in column behind Lt Pfannkuche. After a short hesitation, I joined my men on their way into American captivity, along with my orderly, who was the only man who was remaining with me.[21]

By August 17th, the paratroopers were in control of the entire le Muy-Draguignan area. In most cases the Germans had offered little serious resistance. Le Muy, with its important road network, and les Arcs had been the scene of the most serious fighting, as can be seen by the casualty lists provided at the end of this chapter.

After his surrender, Generalmajor Bieringer is driven through Draguignan in the company of Major General Robert T. Frederick, the commanding officer of the FABTF. NARA.

The Glider Landings

The glider units were sent into southern France the morning and afternoon of August 15th, in the wake of the paratrooper units, who in the meantime were supposed to have taken control of the glider troops' landing zones. Each of the 400 gliders could transport several men or equipment, such as ammunition, jeeps, and artillery pieces. Flying in gliders was very dangerous, even more so than parachuting, as the gliders often crashed violently on landing. Pvt **Art Helmers**, of the 602nd Field Artillery Battalion, explains the atmosphere before the departure for France and the conditions of the flight and landing:

We went to an airport near Grosseto, where our tow planes and egg crates stood ready. We didn't have long to wait there, either. We had been speculating on what day we'd hit southern France, whether before or after August 15th. Well, came the night of the 14th, and it was announced that there would be a late movie. The show started about ten o'clock or ten thirty. The last few minutes before the movie began, the paratroopers marched up ahead of us, fully equipped, with guns cleaned, hand grenades ready, faces blackened, and knives sharpened. I've completely forgotten what the show was now, but I remember when the paratroopers got up and went to their planes before the show was finished.

We went to bed, but about three or a little after, the drone of plane engines woke us. They looked like Christmas trees in flight, as the red and green running lights shone on hundreds of planes from different fields gathered in formation to start their flight toward France. It was quite a feeling, lying there in a pup tent, knowing that these planes carried thousands of men who were to make a new blow against the Germans. They were to land early in the morning and, incidentally, clear the way for us when we were to come in the evening.

We spoke to the returning plane pilots, who said the landing appeared to be a smooth one, with flak practically nil. Well, we packed up our things, had a late lunch in Italy, and ate supper in France. Before taking off, we tied in all our loads, got everything lined up on the field, had some doughnuts served by the Red Cross, and climbed aboard.

I was in number 4 glider from our battery. There were eleven of us, as well as a pilot and copilot. We felt good... the pilot and his second had flak suits, we didn't have anything. We didn't have parachutes. Gliders fly quite low, and because of their gliding ability and motorless status, they have a fair chance of making *some sort* of landing if hit; no parachute needed. If they are blown apart in air, no parachute needed. The weight is carefully calculated, too, so parachutes are out.

As most of our jaunt was over water, we had life preservers, and some of the fellows from other outfits got to use them, as a couple gliders broke loose from their tow planes. We had a smooth ride. Over water the air is much less turbulent than over uneven land. We had left the field and circled until all on our flight were in formation. We then headed out and met the huge formations from the other airports, and on we went.

At 6:20 p.m., we sighted land and huge clouds of smoke from forest fires and some signs of battle. We were not shot at in our group, but some were. We crossed over mountains and went in 17 miles, to where we could see the fields we were supposed to land on. We could also

A glider pilot and co-pilot as seen from the position of the soldiers being transported within the glider. Art Helmers Collection.

Men of the 602nd FAB pose next to the Waco gliders that will carry them into southern France. Humorous inscriptions have been painted on the noses of the gliders. From left to right are, in the first photo: E. Dube and A. Hasselbring. Second photo, standing: G. Frank, W. Blummer, A. Copple, J. Forker, R. Schlub, W. Miezanek, N. Lins, Grove, and A. Baume. Sitting: J. Chiumento, Capt W. Kirby, and H. Bakawaski. Third photo: N. Lins, H. Bakawaski, D. Cardwell, J. Chiumento, and E. Dube. (Joe Banker was the name of one of the troopers, the inscription "Joe Banker's Prostitute" has no hidden philosophical or economic meaning.) Art Helmers Collection. Karl Wickstrom Collection.

see parachutes that had already landed on the fields and in bordering areas.

Now came the most important and tense moment of our ride. It was tense enough, and close enough to the time to land, that we broke up our checker game. Our pilot was a sharp, clever little guy. He had been kidding all along about landing and then chasing to a nearby German Officer School to get a pistol. Well, his job was to land us first, and he did a darned good job. Just before he pressed the release lever, he said that he'd land on the auxiliary field, not the regular one, as there were no gliders there.

With a laugh and a "Here goes!" he released us, and we were in free flight. Our speed was about 120 mph when we released, and just over 80 mph when we hit. We landed smoothly, just missing another glider by a couple feet that cut across in front of us. We had our safety belts loosened before we stopped rolling. Our glider doors jammed, and as we were kicking them open, another glider came whizzing by and took off part of the right wing, then another's wing clipped part of our tail. We piled out and hit the dirt.

There followed one of the most astonishing sights I've ever seen. Gliders by the score were descending from every direction as the tow planes flew overhead and fighter planes streaked all over the sky. The gliders coming in made a very slight "shshshsh" sound as they came in at 80 to 100mph. We got out of the open as fast as possible and under the shelter of large trees, where we wouldn't be hit.

In a few minutes, there was bedlam! The fields we had for landings were neither too big nor too good, considering the number of gliders landing. And many... very many... landed in grape arbors or orchards with a terrific rending of wood and tearing of metal. We saw gliders crash into another glider, or tear a wing off on a tree and crack up.

Surprisingly, not many men were killed or seriously wounded, considering the terrific beating the gliders took. There was one stretch of 75 yards where three gliders stood straight up on their noses. One glider had crashed head-on into a tree three feet in diameter and was a complete wreck, as you can imagine.[22]

Lt **Karl Wickstrom**, also of the 602nd FAB, had similar recollections of his trip to France:

My glider was loaded with a trailer and 12 men, six on each side. We left from the main airport in Rome. I noticed that the two glider pilots each had a parachute. I unbuckled my .45 to make it easy to draw. I decided that the 12 men and I would not be left by two pilots with chutes. It sounds bad, but I was in charge of those 12 men and that was the way I felt. Since that time, I have found out the pilots were required to carry a chute. I wish they had told me.

Our flight to southern France was over the sea. The day was beautiful and the scenery was great: just a covey of planes and gliders. When we had our two-day training, we were warned about the danger of "prop wash" [turbulence] from the plane to the gliders. The glider pilot carefully got above the prop wash to avoid danger. Sometime after we had taken off, I just happened to be looking out the window and noticed a glider go to pieces. The plane was pulling a dangling rope. I don't know, but I presume the glider pilots got caught in the prop wash. Those gliders wouldn't stand that; they were very thinly built, and so they shook until there wasn't anything left but the rope. I could see soldiers falling into the water. I imagine that from that height it was such a shock that it killed most of them. I never heard anything about it. Riding gliders into combat wasn't a good way to get your longevity pay.

I had a good session on the landing area the night before. We were to come in from the south over some trees and into a grape vineyard. The pilots didn't recognize the area. I pointed it out and we agreed. The only thing wrong with the schooling the night before is it didn't show that the grove of trees south of our landing vineyard was at least 100 feet taller than the vineyard, so when we pulled over that, the pilots had to immediately push down so they would get to the ground, because they were a hundred feet too high. Well, they pushed it down all right, but when they went over the trees it knocked off all guidance they had to the glider and the wheels, so from there on, well, we just crashed. Inside the glider, men and equipment were in fair condition. We were in southern France.

There were more of the pilots killed than anyone else in our landing because they were sitting there at the front end, and supposedly the jeeps, trailers, or the guns in the gliders just ran right over them.

Glider pilot **Milton Dank** also saw the glider break up over the sea, later remembering:

We took off from our airfield near Orbetello, Italy, and flew out over Elba and Corsica, then headed for the coast of Southern France near St Maxime. It was a glorious day, not a cloud to be seen, the water sparkling under bright sunlight. The formation was single file and took over an hour to pass a given point on the ground. My co-pilot and I alternated flying every fifteen minutes. In the jeep we were carrying, the two Japanese-American gunners were relaxed, smoking and half asleep.

My co-pilot had the control wheel and I was idly watching the planes and gliders ahead of us. Suddenly,

far ahead of us, a Waco glider climbed sharply and lost its right wing. It fell below the tow plane and broke into pieces. It was too far from us for me to see if there were any bodies in the wreckage. By the time we reached their position, only a few parts were left floating on the sea. What was responsible for the accident? Probably tow plane speed above the maximum 120 mph or a failure of the bolts that held the wing to the fuselage. There was certainly no enemy flak.

Milton Dank later wrote a book about the glider operation and interviewed some of his fellow glider pilots. One of them was able to give him more details about the crashed glider. Some gliders had gotten delayed, forcing their tow planes to fly faster to catch up:

As the gliders fly over the French coast, ships landing troops ashore are faintly visible in the distance. Art Helmers Collection.

Killed in Action

Word was received Wednesday by Sgt. and Mrs. William Kern, 1106 Troost avenue, that their son, Flight Officer William J. Kern, was killed in action on August 14 over France. Previously the Kerns had received a letter from a fellow flight officer buddie of young Kern that he had seen his glider crash as their formation of gliders were preparing to land behind the German lines in France. He related that the gliders were flying in formation and that his was the seventh behind Officer Kern's glider. He saw it suddenly dive toward the ground and crash. He intimated that Kern was killed instantly. The telegram verified his death.

Flight Officer Kern, who was 23 years old, was in the service for nearly three years and had volunteered for this almost suicidal assignment of piloting a glider plane. He was considered one of the outstanding glider pilots in the army and was highly thought of by his superior officers. He attended the local schools and was a graduate of Proviso high school.

Fifth Victory

The Review and Forrest Parker, 31 August 1944.

Soon, planes were slowing down to keep from overrunning the serials ahead of them and – worse – planes were speeding to catch up. Flight Officer "Willie" Haynes of Pawhuska, Oklahoma, watched anxiously as the airspeed needle crept higher and higher. The Waco glider was "red-lined" at 150 miles per hour; being towed above that speed meant imminent structural failure. Several times co-pilot Haynes called the Lieutenant Colonel flying the tow plane and asked him to slow down, but the speed kept increasing. When the needle moved above the "red-line," he picked up the telephone for another urgent request. At that instant the glider off his right wing disintegrated, hurling the two glider pilots into the sea.

Horrified, "Willie" Haynes watched the debris floating down, then whispered menacingly into the telephone, "Listen, you son of a bitch. I'll give you until I count to ten to slow this thing down and then I'm going to shoot your goddamn right engine out. One, two, three…"

As Willie's admiring pilot, Flight Officer Douglas Smith, told the author, "There must have been something in his voice that convinced that 'light' [Lieutenant] Colonel that he meant it, because before he reached 'eight', we were below the red-lined speed."[23]

The pilots present in the ill-fated glider were **Flight Officers William E. Kern** and **Robert Hardin**. Only Hardin's body was recovered from the sea. Several gliders were also forced to crash-land in the sea after their tug ropes snapped; however, the crews and passengers were rescued by ships without any serious injuries occurring. Doi Massato was a member of the 442nd Antitank Company, the unit composed of Americans of Japanese ancestry. They had been detached from the 442nd Infantry Regiment to serve, along with the British 300th Anti-Tank Battery, as the antitank force of the FABTF, and had then rapidly been trained to fly in gliders, as **Doi Massato** explains:

We left the 442nd about the middle of July, and we trained with gliders near Rome until August 15, 1944. We only had two glider flights, and the teacher who taught us all about the gliders said that gliders were safe because they had no motors to go wrong! We in the antitank had 57mm cannons, but we exchanged them for the British 6-pounders because 57mm guns were too big for the

gliders. Each glider would carry either a 6-pounder gun, a jeep, or ammunition. Each one was different, and then of course each glider had about six troops. In my case, I know that I went with one of the 6-pounder cannons, and there were six of us in the glider together with that cannon. It was around 4 o'clock in the afternoon when we left Italy from near Rome, and we flew over into southern France.

I know in my case I got airsick the two times that we had a short 15-minute ride in a glider, but on the day of the invasion I was not sick at all, I guess because I was all excited! As we neared the coast we experienced flack (antiaircraft guns) around the gliders. When I looked out from my glider and looked at the other gliders and saw all the flak bursts all around the gliders, it was in a sense a kind of beautiful sight. Somehow, I never got scared.

Before the flight, they showed us aerial photos of the places that we were supposed to land, and they looked like good flat football fields, all easy to land on. But when we actually got there, oh, it was completely different. Not only were there tall trees all around, but we had grape fields and hedgerows. The worst thing was that the landing areas were not that large, so all the pilots were competing with each other to find landing space. The planes that towed us let us off pretty high, maybe about 2,000 or 3,000 feet. They were actually supposed to go much lower before they released us, but I guess they got scared by the flak, so they just let us off and they high-tailed it home to Italy. The glider pilots were all left to compete for landing space, so many crashed into trees. Even when they hit the ground quite a number crashed. I know in our company we had a little less than a dozen injured, but nobody was killed.

My glider landed and crashed into one of the embankments that had been dug by the Germans and just stopped. It didn't glide in, it just stopped. The ropes that held the gun down all snapped, but the good thing was that the spades of the gun dug into the ground and stopped it from catapulting out of the glider. If it had done that, the pilot and the co-pilot would have been crushed and killed instantly. The two pilots were very lucky and none of us troopers in the glider got hurt, either.

Marvin McRoberts, of the 602nd FAB, described his glider landing in his memoir:

As our pilot was bringing in the glider I was riding in, we could see there were gliders on the ground that had landed before us. They were scattered every which way. Some were crashed for unknown reasons. I know we had been cut loose from our tow plane on the southeast side of the landing area (the field for the landing was about 1,000 yards wide and 7,000 yards long). We were to glide in for the landing north to south. The first gliders that landed that way crashed into mounds of dirt that had been placed there by the Germans. These mounds of dirt were at least six to eight feet tall and about three feet wide at the top. They crossed the field east to west, with some of the areas flooded in between. The field was also surrounded by very tall trees maybe 70 or 80 feet high.

Our pilot, seeing what had happened, kept circling to the west side, but had lost some altitude. He told us in a loud voice: "Were going to make it," then nose-dived his glider towards the ground. You have to remember that at this time we were sitting at the back, and could not see out

British soldiers stand by a damaged glider and look on as another glider prepares to land. NARA.

"We only had two glider flights, and the teacher who taught us all about the gliders said that gliders were safe because they had no motors to go wrong." At least 15 glider pilots and 10 soldiers were killed during the violent crash landings many of the gliders suffered. Here, some heavily damaged gliders are seen, including one that has completely flipped onto its back. Art Helmers Collection.

that well. All I could see were small trees and large bushes, with the large tall trees coming up fast. What this pilot did was gain speed, then pulled back his yoke wheel, clearing the trees by inches and landing as fast as he could. The grape vines helped slow us down, as there are no brakes on a glider. We stopped just short of the east side of the field. A paratrooper standing next to a GI taking motion pictures with his camera on a tripod was watching us come in. The glider that came in just south of us came in the same way and did real good until they hit some of the flooded area, flipping as the nose dug into the ground. This in turn threw

the front of the glider open. The pilot and co-pilot were thrown forward out of the glider like two peas in a pod. They were bruised and scratched up, but alive. All the GIs in that glider were killed, as the gun was pushed forward where the crew was sitting and they were crushed. We were told later, out of sixty-six gliders in two areas, only three came out whole, I was in one of the three. I still say thanks to our pilot.[24]

William E. Johnston, of the 676th Medical Collecting Company, also landed by glider, and remembered:

We got in the gliders outside of Rome and flew over into southern France. We didn't have a choice to fly in gliders and didn't like it. It was fun right at first, when you were taking training; but then, when you started in, it was one way down, and that was down! You would see holes coming in the gliders that weren't there when you left, so you realized that somebody didn't like you down below, but we still had to go down. They had sticks and stuff like that up in that grape field to tear the glider up when it landed. I think we landed 18 miles behind the German lines, at that little la Motte. The glider was torn all to pieces, but the good Lord was with us, I will put it that way. We weren't lucky, we were blessed!

All the paratroopers who witnessed the glider landing were shocked by the chaotic scene that unfolded before their eyes. **Jim Chittenden**, the British pathfinder, described the landings very simply:

If you have ever been to the sea side and seen a load of seagulls pounce on you from nowhere if someone throws a bit of bread in the air, that's what it's like when the gliders come in.

Because of the crash landings, and because people picked the gliders apart on the ground, it was reported that only 26 of the 332 Waco gliders used in the operation were able to be salvaged.[25] **Lt Edward Athey**, of H Co of the 517th PIR, lived a rather unique experience. Although he was a paratrooper, he ended up having to unexpectedly travel to France by glider for the following reasons:

It was pitch dark, and the little field that we took off from was a dirt field. Of course, on August 15th it was dry, so as the plane started up – I was the third plane off the ground – we couldn't see anything. It just became one solid dust cloud of dirt, worse than fog. And this pilot, somehow or other, pulled to the right as he was taking off, got off the runway off to the right, and finally broke through out of the dust, but he was a mile off the runway! There was a parked plane over in that area that he was heading towards, so he pulled back on the stick. He didn't have enough airspeed, but we managed to get into the air. The plane was a good 200 or 250 feet in the air, and it just nosed over, stalled out, and crashed.

It came down on the left wing and the left motor, causing a fire to start, and the tail of the plane was stuck up in the air at roughly a 70-degree angle. The door for jumping out of the plane is towards the tail, so it was 30 feet from the ground. We had to jump on that hard ground, with no parachute, to get out of the plane. That was the only way out, it just had the one door. The pilot and copilot both got out of the plane through the little bubble that was up above them that they used for taking readings and we went out through the tail. Out of the 18-man stick, they say there were five of the men and me that were walking. A couple had broken legs and two or three broken arms and cracked ribs. I only had some cuts and bruises, so I was one of the lucky ones. All I could think of was: "I don't want to stay down here in Italy, my outfit has gone to France." And that's why I went in on a glider. I had never seen a glider up close before, and I hope I never see another one up close. I made arrangements with an antitank group of the 442nd, which was the Japanese American group. My platoon sergeant had broken his jaw and half a dozen teeth in the crash. He would have gone, but I said: "No, you're not going, you're going to go back to the hospital and get your mouth worked on."

When the planes came back, they towed the gliders in and I rode in on a glider. I was there by 10:30 in the morning. The pilot managed to swing the glider around and line up with the grape lines in the vineyard and he dropped down between two rows of grapes. It took the wings off and we just roared along on the ground until we

got stopped, like a cigar. Of my outfit, of the whole combat team outfit, I was the one who landed the closest to where we were supposed to be. By noon, I had picked up a couple men from my company, but it was quite a while before I saw the company.

We will end the topic about gliders with the colorful account of **Pierre Mercier**, a French teenager living in a large estate near la Motte, the Domaine de Clastron. After seeing the first glider land, he rushed over:

> On the day of the landing, about 40 gliders landed in our grounds. The first glider landed about fifty to eighty meters away from the house. I was 15 and a half or 16 years old, and I went towards the glider and saw a gigantic black American come out with a Colt in his right hand and a bottle of Cognac in his left hand. I think the Cognac was Martel. He asked me: "Deutsch? Deutsch?" I replied: "Non, Français. French! French!" So he told me: "Drink!" But I had never drunk any alcohol before and I didn't drink. I understood they were coming from Corsica or Algeria, since they had French Cognac, so I asked: "Algeria" and he said: "Corsica, Cosica." They were arriving from Corsica.

In fact, no black troops participated in the landing, though many french witnesses swore they saw black paratroopers. This confusion was probably caused by the darkness and the camouflage paint the men were wearing on their faces, as well as the presence of Mexicans and Native Americans amongst the troops.

Saint Tropez

The soldiers of B and C Companies of the 509th PIB and of B and C Batteries, as well as some of those of D and HQ Batteries of the 463rd PFAB, had an unpleasant surprise when they reached the ground on the morning of August 15th. Indeed, the thick fog had caused them to be dropped hopelessly off target on the St Tropez peninsula, very near the coast and approximately 30km south of their intended drop zone. This mistake had tragic consequences, as an entire stick of 17 men from B Company of the 509th led by company commander Captain Ralph Miller accidentally jumped into the Mediterranean Sea. Loaded down with all their equipment, they didn't stand a chance when landing in water, and no trace of them was ever found.

These shots of the glider landings were taken by Signal Corps photographer Irving Leibowitz. NARA.

Art Helmers, of the 602nd FAB, stands next to the remains of a glider in le Mitant in August 2012. Author's Collection.

This rare color shot of landed gliders was taken a few weeks after the invasion by Dr. Ted Rulison, of the 51st Evacuation Hospital. Ted Rulison Collection.

All 17 were reported missing in action. Sergeant **Richard Fisco** was also in B Company and later wrote about how he narrowly escaped landing in the Mediterranean Sea himself:

I liked to stand in the door, looking down at the countryside on our flights. On this night we were flying over clouds, but once in a while I could see through them to the water below. We were getting close, and I turned and told the green new lieutenant, Ferris Knight, who wore a beautiful red walrus moustache and had never seen action before, that we were flying over water the last time I was able to see through the clouds. The light turned red, meaning "Stand at the door," and Lt Knight said: "Sergeant Fisco, what shall we do?" I hadn't seen an opening in the clouds in several minutes, but I knew that le Muy was only about 12 miles inland; I had no reason to think that we were not over land. Just then the light turned green and I said to the Lieutenant, "Let's get it!"

As I descended, I prepared for a water landing by slipping up into the seat of the harness and releasing the leg harness straps. This way, I could throw my arms upward and slip free and clear of the harness when I hit the water. The tops of the clouds below were solid white. As I passed through the clouds, I saw that I was indeed over water. We wore Mae West life vests, but we also carried at least a hundred pounds of arms and supplies. I screamed out to God to please bring me to land. Immediately a gust of strong, warm wind hit my back and blew me toward land. It was probably the Sirocco [The local name given to warm winds blowing up from Africa.] coming from North Africa, but as far as I was concerned, it was a breeze from Heaven. I pulled down on my two risers and slipped landwards. I landed on the steps of a villa and sprained my right ankle slightly. Since I had prepared for a water landing there were no leg harness straps to support me, and my legs buckled under me. Sergeant Harvey Sutherland of my company landed in water chest high.

Like the Avellino jump and the North Africa jump before it, this operation was one big blunder. (…) Captain Miller and sixteen men, including **First Sergeant Tony Dorsa**, drowned. They were in plane number one and had been given the green light over open water. The pilot must have been flying through dense, low fog. Captain

Captain Ralph R. Miller, Jr., Pvt Ira J. Butler, and Sgt Oscar F. Crevelling, of B Company of the 509th PIB, who all drowned when their transport aircraft accidentally dropped them while they were still over the Mediterranean Sea. Mike Reuter Collection. Candace Smith Collection. Crevelling Family Collections.

Miller was the best jumper in the battalion, having jumped hundreds of times with the riggers.[26]

As Richard Fisco mentions, **Private Harvey Sutherland** had actually landed in the sea:

I landed in the water. It was about chest high. I got myself out of the water and on to the beach. There was

From left to right: Pvt Alfred Pipino, Jr, Sgt William A. Sutherland, Pvt Julius Garcia, PFC Frank Campos, Pvt Ira J. Butler, and PFC Johnnie C. Ford. All these B Company men were on the ill-fated plane of Captain Miller, and were reported missing in action after parachuting into the sea. Mike Reuter Collection.

Men of B Company of the 509th PIB rest in the woods near St Tropez. Mike Reuter Collection.

only one trooper there. We never did find anyone else from the battalion or our own company. I had no idea where I was. We did get inland a little way to the small hill, and we figured we'd wait for daylight to get ourselves oriented.[27]

Lt Mike Reuter, of B Company of the 509th, was suspicious when he did not see land under his aircraft as the green light turned on:

We dropped into St Tropez by mistake. When we flew into that area, of course it was dark, and I was the jump master of the plane. As I looked out the door, I couldn't see anything except the clouds. I was looking for some kind of terrain feature. Then the green light went on and I still couldn't see anything, and I waited and waited, and finally somebody said: "Lieutenant, the green light is on, we gotta go." So I said: "OK, let's go." But that delay evidently put us on land, because the company commander, Captain Miller, and his whole plane went into the ocean and they all drowned.

I landed in a grape vineyard. We had those old harnesses with the clips, and I had so much stuff on that it all tightened up with the shock of coming out of the plane and I couldn't get any of these clips off. I was lying on my back and I couldn't get out of my harness, so I had to get my jump knife out of my pocket and cut my way out. Just then a shot occurred not too far away, and actually one of my men shot another one of my men at that time. He gave the password and the other kid didn't give him the counter-password and he wounded him.

Daylight occurred and we moved in there, and I joined up the other platoons on a hill overlooking St Tropez. The navy dive bombers came in and started doing some dive bombing and then we put out some coded panels to identify ourselves.

The soldier mentioned by Lt Reuter who was accidentally shot was **Pvt James Pile**, who had jumped in the same stick:

I jumped in a vineyard, and shortly after I got shot through the chest. I am not sure exactly who did it, because it was dark. It could have been one of our men, but anyway, I don't really know for sure. I was told different ways different times, but I guess there is no way I will find that out. But I know I lay there and practically passed out,

and then one of my buddies, Phil Nachefski, helped me. Of course, I was kind of weak and I threw all my equipment off, and with his help, my hand around his shoulder, we must have gone half a mile or a mile, where we had seen a signal light for us to assemble. They treated me there and then they took me up to this French home that was real close. There I passed out. As I came to, some girl was feeding me with a spoon, because of course we didn't have any blood back then. I was taken to a little hospital there in St Tropez, and then I was put on a ship.

Although far from their intended drop zone, the paratroopers showed their usual spirit of initiative and tried to make themselves as useful as possible. St Tropez was right in the middle of where the seaborne invasion was to occur, so they knew that help would be coming soon. **Lt Justin McCarthy**, of C Company, explains how the 509th PIB ended up capturing St Tropez, although doing so was not at all part of the initial plan. Thankfully, Lt McCarthy had a camera with him and took some pictures, which together with his account form a small but remarkable combat photo documentary:

We jumped in the hills near St Tropez. We organized in the morning, and Captain Walls called for me and he said: "Mac, I want you to take a patrol into town. We have been observing and we see movement in there but it looks like it's civilians. You are to go in there and get information and bring it back to me, but it's not a combat patrol; I don't want you to go in there to fight." So I took three or four guys and we went in towards St Tropez and I took my camera with me in a musette bag. Now, on the way there we saw two guys running way off in the distance. I got my binoculars out and looked, and they were Germans, but they were far away and they were running in the other direction, in toward town.

Then we went in further, and we ran into two or three civilians on the roads on the outskirts of St Tropez. Those are the ones that are in the picture with us. One of the guys that I had with me was Bailey, from Massachusetts. There are a lot of French speaking people in Massachusetts, so I always used Bailey as an interpreter. I asked him to talk to the civilians, and they told us that the Germans were pulling out and were going up to the citadel, on the hill above St Tropez. When we heard that, we said: "Well, that's what the captain wants to know." So we went back, and I told Captain Walls: "It sounds like they've pulled

"They are held up, there is a machine gun up there." C Company paratroopers carefully advance through St Tropez. Justin McCarthey Collection.

"We ran into two or three civilians on the roads on the outskirts of St Tropez." Lt McCarthey (with submachine gun) and his men pose with French civilians the morning of August 15th. Justin McCarthey Collection.

The St Tropez Citadel. Justin McCarthey Collection.

out of town and they are all up in the citadel, so at least we can go into town." He said: "All right." So then we slowly moved into St Tropez with the company.

When we went in there, there was machine gun fire from up ahead and there was another platoon ahead of us, so we were held up. I have some pictures of us in the streets. In the meantime, I sent a runner up to see what was going on and he had come back and said: "They are held up, there is a machine gun up there. They are trying to flank around it." Then later on again, they passed the word back: "We are moving up," and actually went into St Tropez. But then the Germans were up in the citadel and we were down below in the town square. There were buildings between us and the citadel so we were safe, but if we walked out to either side in those streets that looked up towards the citadel, they would shoot at us! I had men up on the roofs of the buildings and they were shooting back at the Germans in the citadel.

We were in a hotel facing the citadel, sniping at them, and Lt Mike O'Brian was up there with Sgt Joseph Buchanan. They were buddies through and through, very

good friends for years. They were in a room and **Joe Buchanan** was standing back from a window, looking up, and all of a sudden he said: "Mike! Mike! Hand me a rifle, I see one, I see one!" So Mike O'Brian handed him a rifle and he was there in the window. Then Mike said all of a sudden there was a splat, a sound like a crack, and Joe went down on the floor. Mike looked at him, and they had caught him up high in the side of the head; he said the whole side of his head was gone. He died almost instantly there. Now whether it was an aimed shot or just a lucky shot, who knows? But he was killed.

John Rimer, of B Company of the 509th, remembered a second soldier, most likely 20-year-old **Stanley Moore**, being killed in a similar fashion:

We started going through the town to see what we could get and find, and we had this real young fellow, I forget his name, who was going house to house. We kept telling him not to stick his head out the window, and when he stuck his head out the window, a sniper shot him through

PFC Stanley Moore, B Company 509th PIB, whose mother was a full blooded Cherokee, was killed in St Tropez August 15, 1944, a week before his 21st birthday. Moore Family Collection, courtesy Nancy Calhoun.

"We turned around and looked, and there we saw somebody up in the citadel window waving a big sheet on a pole." 2nd Lt Mike O'Brian leads the German prisoners out of the St Tropez citadel. Justin McCarthey Collection.

the neck and killed him. He was a real nice young kid.

Lt Justin McCarthy explains how St Tropez and its citadel finally fell to the paratroopers:

Captain Walls was new and southern France was his first combat, so I said: "I hope this new company commander doesn't decide that we are going to assault that citadel." Because there is no cover there, just short grass and little bushes. You would be a sitting duck going up that hill. But then Captain Walls called a meeting of the platoon leaders and officers, and he said: "What do you guys think?" So of course we said: "Oh! If we go up that hill Captain, that will be murder. Those Germans are masters at machine gun fire and they will mow us down like flies." He said: "It doesn't look good to me, but we know that they are landing."

When we first landed, we were getting fired on by our own ships. Of course, we weren't supposed to be there, we were supposed to be at le Muy, so our own ships threw some shells in the hills up near us. So we told the captain: "The Navy is out there. By morning, they will probably have a land party landed, with a radio, and they can direct fire. If the Germans hold the citadel, we can have the ships put heavy fire on them and even fire smoke shells so they can't see us, and then we can attack up the hill and take it. In the meantime, they may land tanks." Captain Walls agreed, he said: "Yeah, I can't see any sense in losing a lot of men going up that hill for a matter of another 12 hours." But he said: "I don't like to be in this town because we are pinned in with the water on one side of us, and if the Germans have tanks or something they can catch us in here. I think we better pull back out to the hills, up in the woods there." We said: "We agree, that's exactly what we think."

We started walking back up to the hills, and then somebody in the rear of the column said: "Hey, look." We turned around and looked, and there we saw somebody up in the citadel window waving a big sheet on a pole; a white flag. So we turned around and we went back. Captain Walls took Lt Mike O'Brian and about six guys and sent

them up there. They met the Germans at the entrance of the citadel, and they said they wanted to surrender. We marched them down, then we turned them over to the FFI unit there in St Tropez. I have a picture of them coming out of the citadel with Mike O'Brian leading them.

When we were there, they were landing Arab troops, French colonials, and they were bombed right after they landed. They set up a hospital right there in that square in St Tropez. We were down there a good part of the night helping them with the wounded.

At least two men of the 509th PIB, as well as three men of the 463rd PFAB had been killed during the fighting in and around St Tropez. Along with the 17 men of Captain Miller's stick who were dropped into the sea, this brings the total number of paratroopers killed in the St Tropez area to 22.

Casualties of the Dragoon Airborne Operation

It seems no precise casualty count has ever been made for the FABTF after Operation Dragoon, let alone a casualty count for the German troops. Adleman and Walton's book *The Champaign Campaign*, for example, mentions "434 killed, missing and wounded." Such counts are virtually useless, as no distinction is made between dead, wounded, and missing. Furthermore, this count is apparently based on a period report made August 19, 1944; in other words, when large numbers of paratroopers had not rejoined their units yet and were therefore still officially listed as missing in action. Too many authors have relied on imprecise data without actually doing research and confirming the numbers of killed by checking reliable sources, such as specific period unit casualty reports and cemetery registers.

For this book, a systematic search was made for the names of all the men of the FABTF killed or missing in action, regardless of their units (including the British units, which are all too often overlooked). Great care needed to be taken, as many sources contained false information. For example, the honor roles of both the 509th and 551st PIBs that are available online and in some books include names of men who in fact survived the war! Whenever possible, specific period documents, American Battlefield Monument Commission

A smiling Cpl Burl J. Knapp, B Company 509th, poses in St Tropez with his buddy Orthelle Cherry and with Nicole Celebonovitch, a local "FFI girl." These are sadly the last photos ever taken of Burl Knapp, as he was killed in action approximately five days later at la Napoule, August 21, 1944. Note that he is wearing a captured German belt to which he has attached his combat knife with a piece of parachute riser. Mike Reuter Collection.

Soldiers from B Company of the 509th stand in front of a St Tropez Hotel wearing their spray painted jumpsuits. August 21st, approximately five days after this photo was taken, Pvt Larry J. Ducote, standing second from right, was killed in action, while Justice F. Patrick, standing at left, was lightly wounded. Mike Reuter Collection.

and Commonwealth War Graves Commission sources were used to establish the list below, as well as the other lists presented in this book. The website findagrave.com proved very useful in finding information on some American casualties who were repatriated after the war and were otherwise very hard to research.

Between August 15 and August 19, 1944, the First Airborne Task Force and its assigned glider pilots lost a total of at least 103 men killed, missing, or mortally wounded. A list of the names of all these men is provided below. The dates of death in particular are sometimes incorrect, because they often were not recorded properly at the time, or because the date of wounding and the date of death differ. Priority has been given here to the date of wounding.

DNB=Died, non-battle, DOW=Died of Wounds, GSW=Gunshot Wound, SFW=shrapnel fragment wounds, KIA=Killed in Action, MIA=Missing in Action.

Surname	Name	Rank	Unit	Date of death or wounding	Cause of death
Allen	Glen H.	FlO	Glider crew	15.8.1944	Glider crash
Alto	Lawrence L.	FlO	95 SQ	15.8.1944	Glider crash
Andrews	Joseph	2 Lt	Glider crew	15.8.1944	Glider crash
Bell	Orman G.	FlO	10 SQ	15.8.1944	Glider crash
Billstrom	John E.	2 Lt	93 SQ	15.8.1944	Glider crash
Hardin	Robert	FlO	79 SQ	15.8.1944	Glider crash
Kern	William E.	FlO	79 SQ	15.8.1944	MIA, glider crash
Kimball	Paul R.	2 Lt	99 SQ	15.8.1944	Glider crash
La Valle	Ralph E.	FlO	84 SQ	15.8.1944	Glider crash
Leaman	Horace F.	FlO	86 SQ	15.8.1944	Glider crash
McFarland	Richard M.	FlO	7 SQ	15.8.1944	Glider crash
Sanchez	Max W.	FlO	76 SQ	15.8.1944	Glider crash
Stephens	Preston	FlO	44 SQ	15.8.1944	Glider crash
Thompson	Alfred G.	FlO	97 SQ	15.8.1944	Glider crash
Kennamer	Philip M.	PFC	C Bat 460 PFAB	15.8.1944	GSW
Moore	Harry F.	2Lt	C Bat 460 PFAB	15.8.1944	GSW
Hulshier	Allen H.	Pvt	HQ 463 PFAB	15.8.1944	
Jozefski	Chester B.	Pvt	HQ 463 PFAB	15.8.1944	
Legg	Theodor N.	PFC	D Bat 463 PFAB	15.8.1944	
Beckner	Eugene C.	T 4	B Co 509 PIB	15.8.1944	MIA over sea
Butler	Ira J.	Pvt	B Co 509 PIB	15.8.1944	MIA over sea
Campos	Frank	PFC	B Co 509 PIB	15.8.1944	MIA over sea
Crevelling	Oscar F.	Sgt	B Co 509 PIB	15.8.1944	MIA over sea
David	Robert B.	S Sgt	B Co 509 PIB	15.8.1944	MIA over sea
Dawson	Albert T.	T 5	B Co 509 PIB	15.8.1944	MIA over sea
Dorsa	Anthony J.	1 Sgt	B Co 509 PIB	15.8.1944	MIA over sea
Ford	Johnnie C.	PFC	B Co 509 PIB	15.8.1944	MIA over sea
Garcia	Julius	Pvt	B Co 509 PIB	15.8.1944	MIA over sea
Gillman	Marvin N.	T 4	B Co 509 PIB	15.8.1944	MIA over sea
Lynch	George R.	PFC	B Co 509 PIB	15.8.1944	MIA over sea
Miller	Ralph R. Jr	Capt	B Co 509 PIB	15.8.1944	MIA over sea
Pennebaker	Thomas W	Pvt	B Co 509 PIB	15.8.1944	MIA over sea
Pipino	Alfred Jr	Pvt	B Co 509 PIB	15.8.1944	MIA over sea
Potter	Leon V.	Pfc	B Co 509 PIB	15.8.1944	MIA over sea
Reid	George W.	T 5	B Co 509 PIB	15.8.1944	MIA over sea
Sutherland	William A.	Sgt	B Co 509 PIB	15.8.1944	MIA over sea
Moore	Stanley W.	PFC	B Co 509 PIB	15.8.1944	GSW
Buchanan	Joseph	Sgt	C Co 509 PIB	15.8.1944	GSW head
Kobel	Harold L.	Pvt	509 PIB	18.8.1944	DOW
Metzger	Harold D.	Cpl	C Co 509 PIB	19.8.1944	Accidental explosion
Sexton	Rex D.	PFC	509 PIB	19.8.1944	DNB
Anderson	Elmer J.	Pvt	HQ 517 PIR	15.8.1944	
Baldwin	William F.	T5	HQ1 517 PIR	16.8.1944	
Campbell	John J.	Pvt	H Co 517 PIR	18.8.1944	
Ciner	Henry A.	PFC	HQ 517 PIR	15.8.1944	
Clark	John W.	Pvt	HQ2 517 PIR	15.8.1944	
Cross	Lynwood W.	Pvt	HQ1 517 PIR	17.8.1944	
Dirkson	Vernon D.	Pvt	H Co 517 PIR	18.8.1944	GSW abdomen

Surname	Name	Rank	Unit	Date of death or wounding	Cause of death
Ernst	Albert J.	Pvt	A Co 517 PIR	16.8.1944	
Fisher	Daniel A.	Cpl	HQ1 517 PIR	15.8.1944	Electrocuted
Freeman	Harold M.	2Lt	H Co 517 PIR	16.8.1944	GSW
Gaunce	John E.	1Sgt	H Co 517 PIR	16.8.1944	GSW
Gruwell	Robert R.	Pvt	G Co 517 PIR	15.8.1944	MIA
Hathorn	Robert R.	Pvt	B Co 517 PIR	16.8.1944	
Henderson	Lowell Jr.	PFC	C Co 517 PIR	17.8.1944	
John	Frederick M.	Pvt	D Co 517 PIR	15.8.1944	
Lemen	Charles C.	Pvt	E Co 517 PIR	15.8.1944	SFW
Miley	Maurice J	2Lt	HQ2 517 PIR	15.8.1944	Electrocuted
Montgomery	Walace A.	Pvt	B Co 517 PIR	16.8.1944	
O'Brien	Joseph E.	Pvt	F Co 517 PIR	15.8.1944	
Robinson	Albert M.	2Lt	HQ2 517 PIR	17.8.1944	
Salmon	Carl G.	Pvt	C Co 517 PIR	17.8.1944?	
Scecina	George		A Co 517 PIR	16.8.1944	
Shaneyfelt	Alton L.	T4	F Co 517 PIR	15.8.1944	
Blair	Charles P.	PFC	550 GIB	18.8.1944	DOW
Dunbar	Vernon E.	PFC	550 GIB	15.8.1944	Glider crash
Florent	John L.	Pvt	550 GIB	15.8.1944	Glider crash
Klausen	Albert J.	PFC	550 GIB	15.8.1944	Glider crash
Legros	Joseph	PFC	550 GIB	15.8.1944	Glider crash
Paplatario	Anthony	1Sgt	550 GIB	16.8.1944	KIA
Sharpe	George W.	1Lt	550 GIB	15.8.1944	Glider crash
Tappen	Jerome F.	T5	550 GIB	15.8.1944	Glider crash
Yulo	Basil	PFC	550 GIB	15.8.1944	Glider crash
Funk	Jack D.		B Co 551 PIB	16.8.1944	
Wikins(ki)	Henry	Pvt	596 PCEC	15.8.1944	GSW neck
Collinson	Thomas	Pvt	A Bat 602 FAB	16.8.1944	Accidental explosion
Lencer	Rudolph M.	Sgt	A Bat 602 FAB	18.8.1944	
Barnhurst	Ira	Pvt	887 AEC	19.8.1944?	Glider crash
Brown	Douglas	Cpl	887 AEC	15.8.1944	Glider crash
Tobiassen	Reidar	Pvt	887 AEC	15.8.1944	Glider crash
Jenner	William R.	Sjt	Glider Pilot Rgt	19.8.1944	Glider crash
Calvert	Ernest	Lnc Cpl	4th Bn	15.8.1944	
Dowie	Benjamin	Pvt	4th Bn	15.8.1944	
Newell	Harry	Pvt	4th Bn	15.8.1944	
O'Flaherty	Patrick	Pvt	4th Bn	15.8.1944	
Rodger	Robert G.	Pvt	4th Bn	15.8.1944	
Stewart	Arthur C.F.	Lt	4th Bn	15.8.1944	
Burns	Gavin P.	Pvt	5th Bn Scott	15.8.1944	
Brierley	Levi	Pvt	5th Bn Scott	17.8.1944	
Davis	Charles R.	Cpl	5th Bn Scott	17.8.1944	
Fouracre	Robert G.	Pvt	5th Bn Scott	17.8.1944	
Jones	Davy J.	Pvt	5th Bn Scott	17.8.1944	
Rodgers	Herbert	Lnc Sjt	5th Bn Scott	17.8.1944	
Thomas	Gwilym J.	Cpl	6th Bn Welch	15.8.1944	
Williams	John	Cpl	6th Bn Welch	15.8.1944	

Surname	Name	Rank	Unit	Date of death or wounding	Cause of death
Stevenson	Leonard	Pvt	6th Bn Welch	17.8.1944	
Morley	Eric A.	Pvt	23rd Ind Para Bn	15.8.1944	Parachute failure
Birtles	Joseph H.	Pvt	127 Para Field Amb	15.8.1944	
Cox	Francis E.	Pvt	127 Para Field Amb	15.8.1944	
Patterson	James F.	Pvt	127 Para Field Amb	15.8.1944	
Booley	Thomas Fr.	Bmb	165th Field Reg	15.8.1944	
Debray	Jacques		1ier Btl de Choc	15.8.1944	GSW
Unknown				15/16.8.1944	Burnt

Such a detailed list can help confirm or lay to rest certain claims that have been made over the years. It is important to note that at least 30 deaths were caused by glider accidents and 18 by parachute mishaps. In other words, at least 48 out of 103, or almost half of the deadly casualties that occurred during the first four days of combat of the FABTF, were caused by landing mishaps, with gliders being particularly dangerous. Although some paratroopers were captured by the Germans during the fighting, it would seem that all these men were liberated again within hours or days. The number of men lost as prisoners is therefore very small, or perhaps even nonexistent. As a final word on the Allied casualties, veteran Charles Pugh reported in *First Airborne Task Force*, by Michel de Trez, that the body of Pvt Henry Wikins (who had changed his name from Wikinski before entering the service), of the 596th PCEC, had been mutilated by German soldiers because he was Jewish. The Individual Deceased Personnel File of Henry Wikins does not confirm this information, only stating that he died of a gunshot wound to the neck.

In the area of the intended drop zones of the FABTF (thus not including St Tropez, nor the Fayence-Montauroux area), the trace of 162 German dead can be found in the archives of the *Volksbund Deutsches Kriegsgräberfürsorge* (German War Graves Commission) for the period of the invasion. These casualties, that are listed below, officially occurred in the locations of Callas, Draguignan, Flayosc, la Motte, le Muy, les Arcs, Lorgues, Puget sur Argens, Roquebrune sur Argens, and Trans en Provence. It is important to note that this number of German killed is not directly comparable with the number of FABTF casualties, as the geographical area in which the German dead listed here occurred is smaller (St Tropez and the Fayence-Montauroux region area not included).

Many of the German dead from the drop zones were buried in the Allied cemetery in Draguignan by American Graves Registration troops. The exact locations of death for any bodies buried by the Americans is not necessarily precisely know, many being listed as having been recovered from the "vicinity of Draguignan." What exactly this vicinity encompassed is not specified, and probably depended on the mood of the soldier who was filling out the paperwork. It can, however, be excepted that many dead from the le Muy and les Arcs areas are listed in the archives has having died in the "vicinity of Draguignan."

When establishing the following list, it was, of course, not possible to properly account for German soldiers who may have died of wounds after being evacuated from the fighting area; and in a similar fashion, when a soldier is listed as having died in Draguignan, it is not possible to know whether he was actually killed there in combat, or if he in fact died of wounds in an American field hospital after having been wounded at a completely different location. Finally, although every effort was made to make this list as complete as possible, some dead undoubtedly remain unaccounted for, and the list presented here can therefore only be considered to a rough estimation of the German casualties that occurred in the drop zones at the time of the invasion.

Surname	Name	Rank	Age	Date of death or wounding	Cause of death	Unit
Cziolek	Simon	Uffz	25	17.8.1944	Callas	Leicht Art.Ers. Abt.8
Unknown				17.8.1944	Callas	
Unknown				17.8.1944	Callas	
Unknown				17.8.1944	Callas	
Unknown				17.8.1944	Callas	
Unknown				17.8.1944	Callas	
Baum	Arthur	Uffz	40	14.8.1944	Draguignan	
Filipowski	Josef	Gefr	38	8.1944	Draguignan	
Lepperhoff	Friedhelm	Flg	17	8.1944	Draguignan	
Pötzinger					Draguignan	
Scheuerling	Alfred	Uffz		15.8.1944	Draguignan	
Schroeter	Arthur	Hptm	53	15.8.1944	Draguignan	
Wanielik	Wilhelm	Ogefr	39	14.8.1944	Draguignan	
Weber	Paul		17	14.8.1944	Draguignan	
Weise	Richard	Soldat	38	13.8.1944	Draguignan	
Unknown					Draguignan	
Unknown				15.8.1944	Draguignan	
Unknown		Officer		16.8.1944	Draguignan	
Adams	Martin	Gefr	31	16.8.1944	US Draguignan	
Busch	Franz		19	15.8.1944	US Draguignan	
Chojnacki	Julian	Schütze	40	15.8.1944	US Draguignan	
Dehnel	Gotthard	Gefr	23	15.8.1944	US Draguignan	
Demmel	Johann	Ogefr	36	15.8.1944	Drag. (Le Muy)	
Dietl	Josef	Uffz	27	15.8.1944	Drag. (Le Muy)	
Dirnberger	Josef	Gefr	39	17.8.1944	US Draguignan	
Döhre	Franz	Gefr	22	18.8.1944	US Draguignan	
Ferstl	Paul		39	17.8.1944	US Draguignan	
Gröbner	Karl	Ogefr	42	17.8.1944	US Draguignan	
Grüne	Walter	Hptm	48	15.8.1944	US Draguignan	
Grunwald	Karl	Owchmst	29	15.8.1944	US Draguignan	
Hörnig	Horst	Ogefr	24	18.8.1944	US Draguignan	
Huth	Franz	Ogefr	45	15.8.1944	US Draguignan	
Jörg	Friedrich	Gren	17	16.8.1944	US Draguignan	
Kempf	Ferdinand		36	15.8.1944	Drag. (Le Muy)	
Kniep	Adolf		37	17.8.1944	US Draguignan	
Koch	Wilhelm	Uffz	42	15.8.1944	US Draguignan	
König	Eduard	Ogefr	36	17.8.1944	US Draguignan	
Kramer	Johannes	Olt	40	18.8.1944	US Draguignan	
Lackinger	Michael	Gren	32	15.8.1944	Drag. (Le Muy)	
Loibl	Georg	Funker	18	18.8.1944	US Draguignan	
Lukossek	Adolf	Ogren	18	15.8.1944	US Draguignan	
Maibach	Adolf	Ogefr	33	17.8.1944	Drag. (Les Arcs)	
Merkel	Leonhard	Gren	30	17.8.1944	US Draguignan	
Messemer	Walter	Uffz	31	18.8.1944	US Draguignan	
Naujoks	Otto	Soldat	45	18.8.1944	US Draguignan	
Nieper	Wolfgang	Oberst	49	18.8.1944	US Draguignan	

Surname	Name	Rank	Age	Date of death or wounding	Cause of death	Unit
Pahl	Otto	Uffz	43	15.8.1944	Drag. (Le Muy)	
Pirkl	Johann		17	18.8.1944	US Draguignan	
Puin	Kurt	Fwb	28	15.8.1944	Drag. (Le Muy)	
Röhsle	Josef	Stbwachmst	46	17.8.1944	US Draguignan	
Rychta	Adalbert	Gefr	35	15.8.1944	Drag. (Le Muy)	
Städtler	Ludwig	Gefr	42	15.8.1944	Drag. (Le Muy)	
Strauch	Heinrich	Gefr	40	18.8.1944	US Draguignan	
Summerer	Anton	Uffz	30	17.8.1944	US Draguignan	
Tosch	Johann	Gren	37	16.8.1944	US Draguignan	
Trojza	Edmund	Ogefr	17	17.8.1944	US Draguignan	
Valent	Josef	Sold	20	16.8.1944	US Draguignan	
Walter	Ludwig	Gefr	43	15.8.1944	Drag. (Les Arcs)	
Burghardt	Johann	Gefr	19	17.8.1944	Flayosc	
Förster	Romanus	Ogefr	42	15.8.1944	La Motte	
Haug	Friedrich	Uffz	42	15.8.1944	La Motte	
Riebs	Jakob	Gefr	42	15.8.1944	La Motte	
Rittmann	Wilhelm	Gefr	45	15.8.1944	La Motte	
Brandt	Valentin	Gefr	35	15.8.1944	Le Muy	
Dauser	Karl	Olt	36	15.8.1944	Le Muy	Pz.Jäg.Kp.1048
Eckl	Martin	Gefr	31	14.8.1944	Le Muy	
Ehrig?	Martin			15.8.1944	Le Muy	
Häfele	Wilhelm	Gefr	40	15.8.1944	Le Muy	
Hübner	Willi	Gefr	38	15.8.1944	Le Muy	
Kokott	Alfons	Soldat	31	21.8.1944	Le Muy	
Konradt	Willi	Gefr	21	16.8.1944	Le Muy	
Körber	Georg	Pio	18	15.8.1944	Le Muy	3./Res.Pi.Btl.8
Krakowski	Teophiel	Gefr	33	8.1944	Le Muy	Aufkl.Schw.1048
Kusserow	Paul		37	8.1944	Le Muy	
Mehltreter	Max	Gefr	32	18.8.1944	Le Muy	Stab.Aufkl. Schw.1048
Neumann	Herbert	Ogefr	31	8.1944	Le Muy	2./Res.Pi.Btl.8
Ott	Anton	Gefr	40	16.8.1944	Le Muy	
Schwenk	Johannes	Ogefr	37	15.8.1944	Le Muy	
Sciskala	Rudolf		39	8.1944	Le Muy	
Sobschak	Willi	Gren	40	8.1944	Le Muy	
Steiner	Johann		37	8.1944	Le Muy	
Stempfle	Lorenz	Schütze	43	8.1944	Le Muy	
Striegl	Franz	Gefr	20	16.8.1944	Le Muy	
Witzigmann	Paul	Uffz	38	16.8.1944	Le Muy	
Unknown				8.1944	Le Muy	
Unknown				8.1944	Le Muy	
Unknown				8.1944	Le Muy	
Unknown				8.1944	Le Muy	
Unknown				8.1944	Le Muy	
Unknown				8.1944	Le Muy	
Unknown				8.1944	Le Muy	

Surname	Name	Rank	Age	Date of death or wounding	Cause of death	Unit
Unknown				8.1944	Le Muy	
Frings	Josef	Ogefr	37	8.1944	Les Arcs	
Ganswindt	Franz	Uffz	31	14.8.1944	Les Arcs	
Gatermann	Heinrich	Uffz	30	16.8.1944	Les Arcs	11./Gren.Rgt.932
Lapok	Josef	Soldat	24	8.1944	Les Arcs	
Lindner	Rudi	Gefr	19	21.9.1944?	Les Arcs	
Löscher	Johannes	Soldat	19	8.1944	Les Arcs	
Marschner	Martin	Uffz	31	16.8.1944	Les Arcs	
Neurath	Jakob	Ogefr	38	14.8.1944	Les Arcs	
Prokop	Gregor	Soldat	20	8.1944	Les Arcs	
Schneider	Ludwig	Ogefr	25	16.8.1944	Les Arcs	
Trenne	Heinrich	Lt	30	16.8.1944	Les Arcs	
Unknown				8.1944	Les Arcs	
Unknown				8.1944	Les Arcs	
Unknown				8.1944	Les Arcs	
Unknown				8.1944	Les Arcs	
Unknown				8.1944	Les Arcs	
Unknown				8.1944	Les Arcs	
Unknown				8.1944	Les Arcs	
Unknown				8.1944	Les Arcs	
Unknown				8.1944	Les Arcs	
Unknown				8.1944	Les Arcs	
Unknown				8.1944	Les Arcs	
Unknown				8.1944	Les Arcs	
Unknown		Ofwb		8.1944	Les Arcs	
Unknown				8.1944	Les Arcs	
Unknown				8.1944	Les Arcs	
Unknown				8.1944	Les Arcs	
Unknown				8.1944	Les Arcs	
Unknown				8.1944	Les Arcs	
Unknown				8.1944	Les Arcs	
Unknown				8.1944	Les Arcs	
Unknown				8.1944	Les Arcs	
Unknown		Hptm		8.1944	Les Arcs	
Unknown				8.1944	Les Arcs	
Unknown				8.1944	Les Arcs	
Vocke	Max		31	15.8.1944	Lorgues	
Hanke	Ulrich	Gefr	39	16.8.1944	Puget sur Argens	
Rehfeldt	Wilhelm	Soldat	35	16.8.1944	Puget sur Argens	
Dahlhaus	Friedrich		38	16.8.1944	Roquebrune	
Gläser	Werner	Gren	19	16.8.1944	Roquebrune	
Hamburger	Fridolin		34	17.8.1944	Roquebrune	
Ketelsen	Thomas	Stbgefr	29	16.8.1944	Roquebrune	
Mysuna	Tomasz	Soldat	38	16.8.1944	Roquebrune	
Nadolny	Emil	Soldat		15.8.1944	Roquebrune	
Pettke	Edmund	Soldat	33	16.8.1944	Roquebrune	
Petzi	Fritz	Uffz	36	15.8.1944	Roquebrune	

Surname	Name	Rank	Age	Date of death or wounding	Cause of death	Unit
Reith	Paul	Gefr	18	14.8.1944	Roquebrune	
Saling	Heinrich	Lt	41	16.8.1944	Roquebrune	
Spillmann	Theodor	Ogren	19	16.8.1944	Roquebrune	
Winkler	Fritz	Uffz	37	16.8.1944	Roquebrune	11./Gren.Rgt.932
Unknown				8.1944	Roquebrune	
Unknown				8.1944	Roquebrune	
Unknown				8.1944	Roquebrune	
Unknown				8.1944	Roquebrune	
Unknown				8.1944	Roquebrune	
Unknown				16.8.1944	Roquebrune	
Unknown				16.8.1944	Roquebrune	
Unknown				16.8.1944	Roquebrune	
Unknown				16.8.1944	Roquebrune	
Undetermined					Trans en Provence	
Undetermined					Trans en Provence	
Undetermined					Trans en Provence	
Undetermined					Trans en Provence	
Undetermined					Trans en Provence	
Undetermined					Trans en Provence	
Undetermined					Trans en Provence	
Undetermined					Trans en Provence	
Unknown					Trans en Provence	
Unknown					Trans en Provence	

Conclusion

The Allied invasion of southern France was preceded by a massive drop of paratroopers of the First Airborne Task Force at 4:30 in the morning of August 15, 1944, followed by glider troops later in the day. Their intended area of action was the region of le Muy. However, due to heavy fog and bad navigation, roughly one-third of the first wave of paratroopers was dropped several dozen kilometers from their target zones, landing around St Tropez and in the Fayence-Montauroux region. The glider troops also had difficulties, with most of the gliders crashing on landing. Regardless, the airborne soldiers quickly overwhelmed the German defenders and by August 17th, the whole le Muy and Draguignan region was in Allied control. Losses had been relatively light, though at least 103 Allied soldiers of the FABTF died.

We have now finished the three introductory chapters of this book, and pass on to the first chapter about the fighting in our area of study: the Liberation of the Fayence-Montauroux region.

Collector's Corner

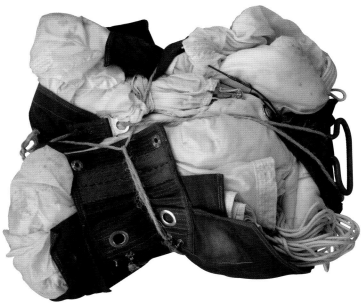

For their jump into southern France, the soldiers of the 517th PRCT were equipped with standard infantry helmets on which a rigger-modified chinstrap and chin cup had been added. The handmade chinstraps are visible on these helmets found in the Maritime Alps. Much of the equipment used by the 517th bears a typical camouflage consisting of spray painted light green and grey-black, with occasional splotches of yellow added on with a paint brush. Variations of this camouflage are visible on these specimens. Private Collections.

An American reserve parachute, as kept by a local peasant on the drop zones. At some point in time, somebody clearly became curious about the ripcord system. Private Collection.

These period photos, taken August 14th, clearly show the 517th PRCT style camouflage, as well as the rigger-made chinstraps. NARA/Bruce Broudy Collection. NARA/517prct.org.

For Operation Dragoon, the 517th PRCT not only used M-42 paratrooper jump jackets, but also regular infantry uniforms, such as M-43 field jackets and HBT jackets. Here we see an M-42 jump jacket and an HBT jacket found in the Maritime Alps, both covered with the typical 517th spray painted camouflage; of particular interest is the hand-painted Technician 4th Grade rank on the sleeve of the HBT jacket. The M-42 belonged to T5 George S. Smart, of the 460th PFAB, as is indicated by the name painted over the left breast pocket. Private Collections.

This knapsack, abandoned by a British paratrooper named Capper, bears traces of hastily applied brown camouflaged paint. Private Collection.

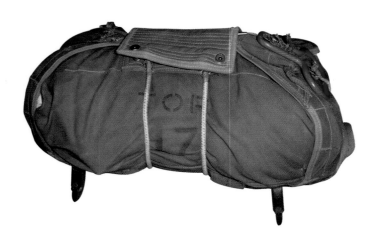

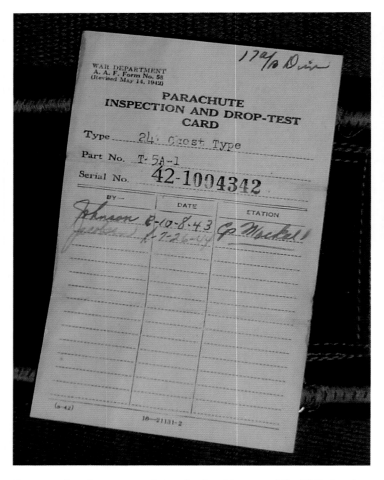

Two examples of reserve parachutes abandoned by men of the 517th. American paratroopers were equipped with two parachutes, while their British counterparts only had one, and the Americans therefore abandoned large numbers of unused reserve parachutes in their wake. These parachutes are marked with a 17, indicating they belong to the 17th Airborne Division. Inside a pocket in the parachutes, one can still find the original cards signed by the last person who folded the parachute, in order to be able to attribute responsibility in case of a parachute malfunction. In this case, one of the parachutes was last folded by an R. Johnson July 26, 1944, shortly before the invasion. Neither parachute has been unfolded since, as is proven by the presence of the seal on the rip cord system. Private Collections.

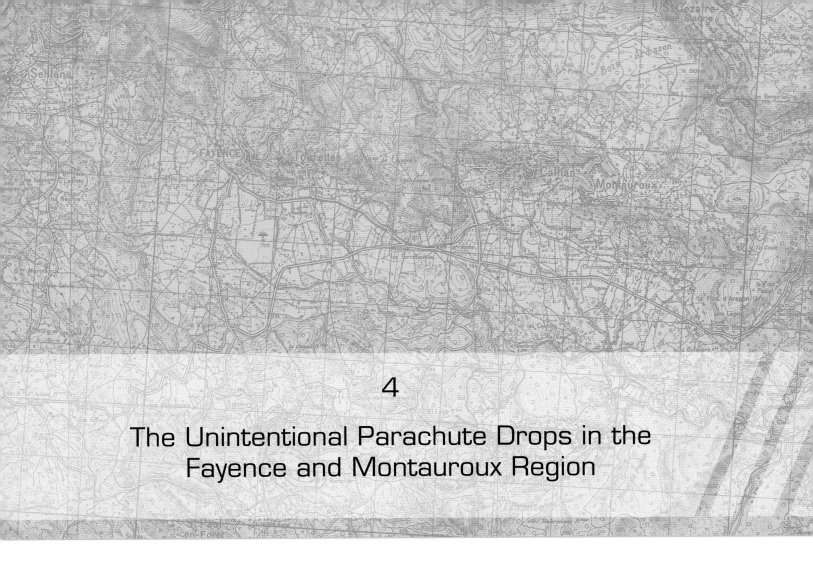

4

The Unintentional Parachute Drops in the Fayence and Montauroux Region

The Road Network Connecting the Var to the Maritime Alps

The landing of the First Airborne Task Force and the seaborne forces August 15th occurred almost exclusively in the Var *Département*, while the Maritime Alps remained completely under German control. Retreating or attacking German forces would therefore naturally have to pass from one *départment* to the other. The roads connecting the two *départements* were therefore highly strategic: if the Allies could block the roads, they could paralyze the Germans. There were only three major roads connecting the Var to the Maritime Alps in 1944:

- *Route Nationale 7* (RN7), running between Fréjus and Cannes, passing inland behind the Estérel mountains.
- *Route Départementale 6098* (D6098), also running between Fréjus and Cannes, but following the coast.
- *Route Départementale 562* (D562), running between Draguignan and Grasse and passing through the valley south of the Fayence-Montauroux area villages.

The reader should look at these roads on the map, as they are of importance to the understanding of events. As the D6098 was a coastal road, it was immediately cut off by Allied seaborne troops as they landed, and rapidly advancing American troops also managed to reach and cut off RN7 by the early hours of August 16th (these events will be described in detail in Chapter 6). As of the 16th, the D562 south of Fayence and Montauroux was therefore the only remaining line of communication for the Germans between the Var and Maritime Alps.

Introduction to the Fayence-Montauroux Area

The term "Fayence-Montauroux area" used in this chapter refers to the towns Seillan, Fayence, Tourrettes, Callian, and Montauroux. All these towns, except Fayence, that contained a small German garrison, were briefly liberated on the morning of August 15th, when paratroopers were unintentionally dropped into the area, but most of these paratroopers then quickly departed for le Muy. All these towns, except for Seillans, were then briefly reoccupied by the Germans in the following days, only to be re-liberated for good around August 20th.

The heart of the Fayence-Montauroux area is an unusually long and flat valley through which the Camiole River flows. The villages of Fayence, Tourrettes, Callian, and Montauroux are all built on the hills immediately north of the valley, providing excellent observation points from which the D562, the main Grasse-Draguignan road running through the valley, can be clearly observed. Considering that this road was the only major line of communication the Germans had left between the Var and the Maritime Alps as of August 16th, it became vital for them to control the road, as well as the villages overlooking it. Seillans, however, is built a few kilometers further west, at a distance from the D562 valley, and was therefore not as strategic. This is probably why the town was not reoccupied by the Germans after the landing had occurred, and was instead a sort of safe haven for wounded paratroopers and *maquisard*s.

Reserve Division 148's Reaction to the Invasion

Although proper sources of information about *Reserve Division 148* are lacking, it has been possible to partly reconstruct its movements

A view of Callian today, overlooking the Camiole Valley and the D562 Highway that was vital to German military movement between the Maritime Alps and the Var as of August 15, 1944. Author's Collection.

after the landing thanks to Allied reports, information about the division's casualties, and the few German sources that do exist. August 15th, *Bataillons 327, 372,* and *444,* which were stationed nearest to the invasion front in the Cannes and Antibes areas, were rushed towards the scene of the Allied landing. Part of *Bataillon 444* from Cannes was sent down RN7 towards Fréjus. *Bataillon 327* from Mougins, along with elements of *Bataillon 372,* was sent down D562 towards Draguignan; these were the battalions *Generalmajor* Bieringer referred to in the previous chapter during the siege of his *Feldkommandantur. Bataillons 7, 28,* and *164,* which were stationed further away from the invasion in the Nice and Menton areas, only reached the scene of action later on the 15th or on the 16th. *Bataillon 28* took up positions outside la Napoule, while *Bataillons 7* and *164* formed a second line of defense on the Siagne River. We will go into more details about what happened to these troops further in this text and in the next chapters.

A Landing Far Away from the Drop Zone

As we saw in the previous chapter, several groups of pathfinders were to jump into southern France one hour ahead of the main force in order to mark the drop zones and to help guide the airplanes carrying the main force into the correct area. Jim Chittenden's account explained how precisely the British pathfinders of the 1st Independent Platoon had been dropped in the le Muy area. Several of the American pathfinder teams were not at all as successful, however, with the consequence that large parts of their units were dropped completely off target, such as those who landed at St Tropez or Fayence. **Henry Filipczak**, of G Co of the 517th Parachute Infantry Regiment, explains how he became a member of the pathfinder team of the 517th PIR and why their mission August 15th turned into a complete failure:

Captain Hooper called me in one afternoon and said, "Flip," (that's what they called me) "Would you be interested in an assignment?" and I said: "Captain, whatever

you say." So he says: "Well, I would like you to become…" I am not sure he referred to it then as a pathfinder or not, but if I would be interested. I said: "Captain, anything you want me to do."

So they pulled me and another guy from the 3rd Battalion out and they took us to an airfield. For two weeks, we trained putting up panels and setting up the transponder and battery. There were 10 of us from each regiment, separated into two different squads, so that if five of us got together, hopefully we would have enough stuff that we could display the thing. So we went through this morning, noon, and night, morning, noon, and evening for two weeks. Then we got notice that we were supposed to jump the following morning and they told us to sit down and write letters to our family, which we did.

I will tell you a little bit of a thing… They brought out more beer than I had seen the whole time. So we were able to have a good time drinking beer. We didn't get loaded, but it was an unusual experience, and then we bunked down. At 2 o'clock in the morning, they woke us up and said: "Let's get ready." We got ready, and in my case they strapped a battery onto me, and all the guys had panels and stuff like that. Then we couldn't even get into the airplane, they actually had to lift us into the aircraft. We flew for I guess maybe an hour and a half and then we got the order to jump, which we did.

I understand the weather was very foggy, so the planes had to go up at a much higher altitude, and in doing so they spread us out all over. We were supposed to jump at about 900 feet, but they dropped us up so high I prepared to land about four times before I finally hit the ground, and I will use my own term, like a sad sack of shit. Eventually, after about an hour, only five of us had finally gotten together on the ground. I had the battery, but I never met up with whoever had the transponder. We never had a chance. I guess the rest of them had panels, but we couldn't have even hoped to set up panels because we were in a wooded area and panels would not have been seen from the aircraft. We didn't accomplish anything from what we were supposed to do in that jump. We had no idea where in the world we were. I don't know how far we were from the drop zone, but apparently it was miles; from what we understand, and the little I understand after the fact.

We just hung around and waited until morning, then went to a farm house. There was a Frenchmen there and he invited us in, so we went in and we slept on the floor because we were completely exhausted. Then we got up and started walking towards where we thought the main body had dropped."

According to the period after action reports, Filipczak's group landed six miles off target. The result of the inability of several of the pathfinder teams to perform their mission is that most of the 3rd

54
and

say,
lun-
tive

charged August 1945 from Er
Atlantic City, NJ.

He received the Purple
Medal w/OLC. After several
had his right foot amputatec

Henry Filipczak, of G Company of the 517th PIR, who volunteered to serve as a pathfinder shortly before the invasion. However, he and his comrades were dropped so far from the intended drop zones that they never had a chance of fulfilling their mission. Henry Filipczak Collection.

Battalion of the 517th PIR and of the 5th Scottish Battalion of the 2nd Independent Parachute Brigade, as well as elements from several other units, were dropped in the Fayence-Montauroux area, 30 kilometers away from their intended drop zones in le Muy. These paratroopers found themselves spread all over the countryside between the Siagne River and the hills overlooking Seillans! **Ralph Nelson**, of G Company of the 517th PIR, describes the preparations for the jump and the chaos 3rd Battalion of the 517th found itself in once on the ground:

We were getting ready for the next morning. We had cans of camouflage paint, green and black. We sprayed that all over ourselves and there were sand maps showing where we were supposed to go and… we never got there. Some of us landed in the woods, but I landed in a clearing at the edge of the woods. We were told to immediately get out of our parachutes when we landed and put our rifles together, which were in two pieces in a heavy bag. We were told not to get lost, but of course we were, and it was dark. We were told to look up, and if you see planes going, you go the other way. Well I looked up, and the planes were going every way! This way, that way, holy God, that was a mess! I didn't see anybody, so I started walking. Oh! I didn't get 50 feet and somebody told me to halt, so I did. Fortunately it wasn't a German, it was some of our guys. I didn't even know who they were, they were from different companies. Anyway, I say: "OK, now what?" We didn't know which way to go, so what do you think we did? We sat down and had something to eat. There was nothing else to do, and we waited. It got to be daylight, and pretty soon we could see some of our guys who were scattered here and there and all over."

Guy Carr, of I Co of the 517th, landed completely off target like the rest of the 3rd Battalion, probably in the Siagne Valley south of Le Tignet according to his description of a railroad bridge he walked on after landing:

We loaded aboard C-47s in nearly total darkness and the quivering aircraft slowly began their journey. At 0300 hours the morning of 15 August 1944, the pathfinder group made its jump, but were dropped too far away from the drop zone to set up equipment to lead the rest of us in. At 0415 hours, as we came over the coast of southern France, enemy [flak] lit the darkness time and time again. We were given the red light from the pilot and stood up and hooked up our static lines. We stood there for some five minutes, rocking back and forth, then the light turned green. As I turned into the door, I reached up and pushed the button, releasing my machine gun from under the plane's belly, then jumped out through the red exhaust flames into total darkness.

My chute had barely opened when I hit the ground. They had jumped us from an altitude of approximately 300 feet. I landed midway up a mountainside and began to roll end over end. I was completely wrapped in the chute. Finally, I came to a stop and lay there for some time in the darkness, just listening and trying to get my bearings. I heard a movement to my left and felt very helpless and afraid, as I was still tangled in the chute. I grabbed my jump knife and quietly began cutting the harness. Once free of the harness, I assembled my M-1 rifle and whispered the password, "Yellow." The answer "Two" came back to me, and I arose and walked towards the sound.

My buddy, a sergeant (later killed), was lying there all bound in his chute. He needed help to get out of the harness, as he didn't dare try to free himself. He was sure that he had come to a stop just short of a drop straight down a cliff that we later found to be a cut through the mountainside to allow railroad track passage. Finally the sergeant was on his feet, and we started down the mountain. It was still too dark to safely find our way, so we stopped and lay down until daylight. The early morning hours found us still coming down the steep slope. We finally arrived at the railroad track below and the going became easier.

It was daylight, and about 0800 hours we came to a railway bridge built high above the valley floor. We had just crossed the bridge when we saw someone coming down the railroad tracks. We both jumped into the underbrush along the tracks and waited. As the fellow came nearer, we recognized him as a civilian. We stepped out in front of him and he began jabbering in French. We let him know we wouldn't harm him, and finally, by the use of our hands, explained to him who we were. A large grin covered his face and he pointed back down the tracks. We then saw parachutes hanging from tree tops and knew that soon we would be with our outfit. I never did find my machine gun. Undoubtedly its chute never opened, or it landed some distance from me.[1]

Most of the paratroopers dropped around Fayence, Callian, and Montauroux assembled into small groups and, once they found out where they were, headed for le Muy. One of the officers who organized this migration back towards the intended drop zones was **Lt Howard Hensleigh**, of HQ Company of 3rd Battalion of the 517th PIR. With his sharp intelligence and excellent memory, he later recalled:

At the "airfield" in Italy we had seen a movie, were served Red Cross doughnuts and coffee, and were all loaded up with about 100 pounds of equipment and ammo when Mel Zais, battalion commanding officer, came to each plane and gave us encouraging words, ending with: "I will be right there with you." This had a good effect on the morale of my enlisted men of the machine gun and bazooka section of the 3rd Battalion HQ. Since I don't drink coffee those greasy doughnuts were not sitting too well in my stomach, but I thought I would need them to keep me going the extra mile after the jump.

The plane was dark and the men slept and weren't too active all the way. The C47s flew in close formation, which caused abnormal turbulence from the prop blasts of the planes ahead. We felt as though we would hit the ceiling one minute and then feel we weighed 500 pounds the next. This continued for three hours. Finally, the crew chief came back and opened the door (always on the left side). I got up and looked out, hanging onto the cable where we hooked up. I got a good look at things, but it was quite black. At first I saw water and then land. Then my stomach decided it had enough of those greasy doughnuts. I hung my head way out the door and emptied my stomach. No one in the plane knew that but me, and I surely didn't want my men to know about it, as we were going into combat.

The turbulence of the aircraft continued. We got the red light, so I gave the commands, starting with "stand up" and ending with "let's go" after the green light. Sgt Podalack and I threw out the equipment bundles and led the stick out. The prop blast was so strong that the opening shock was jarring, so hard that it tore my musette bag loose from its harness. This meant the planes were going much faster than prescribed. Since it was dark and I could not have any idea how far we were above ground, I got in the landing position immediately and very quickly hit a rock and some rough ground and said out loud softly to myself: "Well buddy, you are in France!" even if I wasn't quite sure of it.

The 3rd Battalion was scattered all over, many of us landing around the small town of Callian. I was able to locate five or six of my men almost immediately after the jump and I sent them out to go 500 yards in all directions and come back to me bringing all the equipment bundles and other parachutists that they could find, so I ended up with 20 or 30 men very quickly, and one of the men said that he had seen a house. I went to this house and pounded on the door. A lady came out on a balcony up above and asked me what was going on in French, and I said: "Américain parachutiste." She said: "Ouh là là!" and went back in the house, and it was a group of medical people who were "en vacances" [on holiday] from Paris. I put my maps out and the first map I said: "La Motte and le Muy," and then I said: "Where are we?" They replied: "Not on that map." So I pulled out another map and then they showed me that we were fairly close to Callian.

We headed out towards Callian, gathering men and equipment all the way, so that by the time I got to Callian, I must have had at least 50 or 60 paratroopers with me. At the edge of Callian, there was a man who had heard that we were coming in and he was there with what I thought was a large bottle of water. He asked me if I wanted some, and I said: "Oui," so he poured a very small amount in the glass and I said: "Encore s'il vous plait." [More please] So

he gave me about a half inch or an inch of what I thought was water, and I drank the stuff and it was "eau de vie" [brandy]: it almost burned down my throat.

In any event, we went on into Callian and by that time it was getting light, and I knew that I would need some assistance, because we were a long way away. I needed someone who knew the territory, so I asked for a guide. There was one gentleman who stepped forward and said he would do it. His wife was crying, tears were streaming down her face, and so off we went. He knew the country very well, and then very shortly we ran across Lieutenant Gibbons from H Company and some men from G Company, including Lieutenant Ridler. They were 1st lieutenants and I was a 2nd lieutenant, so I said: "Well Gibbons, these men are yours, you outrank me." So he took over the group and he said: "Hensleigh, you're my S-2; find my way back to the drop zone."

So I took four or five men, and there was an English paratroop lieutenant who was actually from South Africa who went with us. I had a couple of men from my own section, a man I knew from G Company, and we took off

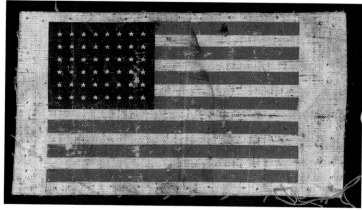

2nd Lt Howard Hensleigh and the American flag he wore sewn to his jumpsuit the night of the invasion. Howard Hensleigh Collection.

ahead of the column in order to make sure that we wouldn't run into any Germans far out. I got a bicycle some way, and I would send someone back to alert the column if there was anyone coming. There were some vehicles coming and we got off the road, let them go through us, and then shot the German drivers and so forth, and so we soon had a vehicle or two. We kept on going. Before we reached the drop zone, there was a wagon that would haul hay and a couple of horses pulling it. We put our jump casualties who had sprains and breaks on these vehicles and we kept going. Our own planes, P-47s, swooped in and dropped a bomb very close to us, even though we had thrown yellow smoke grenades out to let them know that we were American troops. One of the sergeants said: "His aim was as poor as his judgment." He missed us, so we suffered no casualties."

Lt Lud Gibbons, of I Company of the 517th PIR, found himself in almost identical circumstances:

When we jumped, we missed the drop zone by 22 miles. When we landed, we landed in trees on the side of a hill. I knew that's not where we belonged; I knew we belonged in a valley with relatively flat ground. After a little while, I located two other men and then, when daylight came, we were by the side of a path. A civilian was walking down the path and I yelled at him, and he looked over. He was surprised, of course. I waved him over and he came, and I had an English-French dictionary. I showed him in the dictionary: "Where am I?" He mentioned a name and it didn't ring a bell. I knew the names of all the areas right around where we were supposed to drop. So then I had a large scale map which I handed him, and on the dictionary it says: "Show me on this map." He looked at the map for a little bit and then pointed off the map. We were off the map. I had a small scale map, which I gave to him, and he looked at that and then he pointed to Callian. I had no idea where that was, so I made circles around the town, ever larger circles around the town of Callian until I came to an area that I recognized. And then on the map I could see that we were 22 miles away from where we belonged.

We went into the town, and I remember a few of the civilians came out of their homes to greet us, and there was a lady that handed me a glass of red wine, which was greatly appreciated. Then we assembled, and I believe there was somewhere around 100 men, but it might have been less than that. I was the ranking lieutenant, so I was in charge of getting from there to our drop zone. We looked down from Callian into the valley, and we had to go through that valley up over the next mountain, then down into the next valley, and I thought: "Well, this is going to be a hell of a mess without any armor because we have got nothing to fight armor with." We had a bazooka, which was more talk than efficiency, and we made that walk. We got started around noon, and we walked along the road until it got dark. Then we met a fellow by the name of Captain McGeever, who was an excellent officer and an excellent soldier, and he was higher ranking than I was, so he took over. The next day, we walked all day long and we finally got to where we belonged and met Colonel Zais, who was the battalion commander."

Corporal John Rupczyk, of I Company of the 517th PIR, was part of one large group of paratroopers that had landed near Seillans and then crossed through the village of Claviers on its way back to the jump zones:

Nobody said much during the flight, everybody just sat quietly. I was thinking: "Well, I wonder what the people back home are going to be thinking in the morning when they get up," because the invasion was going on. Then I was wondering if I would still be alive at noon. When we got ready to jump we were low enough I think that if that plane had its wheels down it would have been on the ground. It was low! When I jumped, I must have oscillated two or three times, then I was on the ground and my chute got caught in a small tree. I got out of the chute and I got my rifle out of the case. I started putting it together again, but the trigger housing wouldn't go in. Some guys came along and they tried to get it together and it wouldn't go, and so I had to just hold it like that. I walked around, and I saw a little shed. I ran over to that shed and my company commander was standing in the doorway of it. His name was Fastia. I said: "Where are we captain?" He says: "I don't know John, but I can tell you one thing, we are not where we are supposed to be!"

So we waited there, and when daylight came, I snapped that trigger housing right back into the rifle, there was nothing to it then. We went up 300 or 400 feet more, going through grape vineyards, and there was a house and an old French couple were there. They must have been 65 or 70 years old, and we stayed there all day. We were right by a power line, and about 5 in the afternoon the whole company got together. We followed the power line, got out onto a highway, and we started going down the road. It wasn't long before a French policeman came on a bicycle and he told us: "Don't worry, there are no Germans in Claviers," but we didn't believe him. We were young and had very little combat, but we were pretty cautious. Then, as we got in view of the town, the whole townspeople were out there: the old men were walking amongst us, giving wine to the guys; the kids were singing the French national anthem and throwing flowers on us; and the girls, who were about 16, 17 years old and older, they were walking in among us and they were kissing us. That's a nice war to fight! So we went through the town there, looking up at the roofs and the windows and everything to see if there were machine guns pointing at us, but nothing happened. We went down the road for a while, then we stopped for the night and we slept over.

Many troopers never did find out exactly where they had landed, such as **Marvin Moles**, of I Company of the 517th PIR, though according to his description, it must have been somewhere in the vicinity of Fayence and Tourrettes:

Part of the planes got off course, and I think the one that I was in was way off course. If we would have stayed in it another minute, we would probably have been in Switzerland. It was dark as a dungeon when we jumped out and our plane had started going over a mountain I think, because when I went out the door and my chute opened my feet were in the trees. If the plane had been 50 feet lower, my chute wouldn't have opened. It takes a hundred and fifty foot drop before your chute opens, so evidently the plane couldn't have been more than 300 feet up.

Of course I prepared my rifle and stuff, got it out and got it put together. But it was one dark night! I came down between the trees, but a boy came down in a tree right beside of me; he was hung up about four, five feet off the ground. Me and this boy, we got out of our chutes and found two other paratroopers and a couple of English paratroopers and we spent the next three days together.

It was still pitch dark, and we got together with the other guys and then we just kind of sat tight until daylight started, then we came out into this little old village. In this little village, the Germans had killed one of those French freedom fighters, and the French people were getting ready to bury him. They pulled the bones out of this vault and then they buried him in it. I mean, this is the very first morning now, and that's something I never saw. They got in the vault and threw out all the old bones that were in it, and they wrapped him in some blanket or something and then laid him in the vault, then slid the top back on it. So I don't know, do people do that over there? Build concrete vaults, and then if one dies, they take his bones out and put another one in later?

Then, across a hill about 500-700 yards away, a German patrol started down the road towards us and so we started shooting at them. Of course, they high-tailed it around the hill and went down another road and we never did see them anymore. We spent most of that day there; in fact, we spent that night in the village. They killed a sheep and then we chipped in the food we had. They had some of the best lamb stew I ever ate. Those people could really cook. They brought out some stuff there they called snaps [schnapps], or snoops or whatever, and they gave you a big glass of that. You drink that and man, you had to go poke your head in the water and try to cool your mouth off. It would take your breath. We had a real scrumptious dinner, then we just laid our bedrolls out and slept in the outside where they cooked the sheep and fixed dinner for us. They were great people, and I enjoyed the trip through there."

Sgt Frank Dallas, also of I Company, received a warm welcome as he reached the ground:

I landed near a farmhouse and I almost landed in a well. A French farmer came after me with a double barrel shotgun. I put my hands up in the air and showed him the American flag, and so then he started shaking hands with me. I took the parachute and threw it in the well. I don't know whether he was happy or not, but I got rid of it, then I rounded up my squad, we all got together. Then we joined the rest of the unit. We didn't have too much action right at the beginning. The next day when we got together, we started hitting small German patrols. They were bewildered because we were all over the place. We were scattered, and every time they turned around somebody got hit.

The paratroopers had landed in an area where there were almost no Germans. Neither Callian, Montauroux, nor Seillans were occupied, and there was only a small garrison of German air observation troops in Fayence. 16-year-old **Jean Veyan** lived on the hill behind Callian and was extremely impressed by the impromptu arrival of hundreds of American and British paratroopers. His experience mirrored that of the paratroopers we have just mentioned:

At midnight, a guy from the Resistance, Albert Rebufel, came and told us: "It is going to happen now, in the following hours." We couldn't hear anything and we said: "Maybe it's just a rumor?" But it was true. Around 2:30 or 3:00 in the morning, airplanes flew by at low altitude. They were so low that we could see them in the night. They must have been flying at 200 meters to be able to drop the paratroopers. The airplanes flew on towards

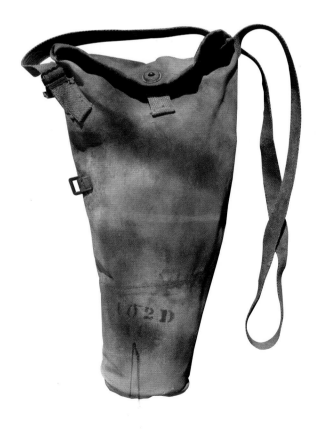

"We had cans of camouflage paint, green and black. We sprayed that all over ourselves." This gas mask bag and helmet that were abandoned by paratroopers of the 3rd Battalion, 517th PIR, after landing display the typical camouflage of the 517th. The gas mask bag has been spray painted in green and black-grey, while the helmet has only been sprayed with green, with yellow splotches added with a brush. The bad condition of the helmet is explained by the fact that it was used in a garage as a recipient for motor oil for decades after the war. Private Collections.

Fayence and I could see green and red lights coming down. I said: "They have turned on their signal lights!" But no, it was equipment parachutes that had lights on them.

Suddenly, a guy came and told us: "But there is a parachute in the olive tree just back there." We went and found an equipment parachute, full of belts of machine gun ammunition. Why had they dropped a container full of machine gun belts? We couldn't understand. The airplanes had flown by, but we didn't understand that there had been an airdrop. We couldn't see the parachutes, we could only see those lamps coming down.

I came back home and my mother was up. She said: "But didn't you come near the water tank? There were two soldiers there!" Two soldiers? What was going on? She said: " They left in that direction." I went back on the hill behind my house and I saw something shining on the ground. It was a starry night and I could see quite well. I picked the thing up and it was a pack of cigarettes. I smelled it; it smelled like American tobacco, and at the same moment I saw it was a pack of Chesterfields. I looked up and there was a pine tree covered by a parachute. It was the first American who had landed in my property and I thought: "I am going to find him, it is the Americans!" Then suddenly, I saw four or five of them lined up along a wall. One must have been an officer, because he came towards me the instant he saw me and started speaking to me in American. I couldn't understand a thing, but he kept on repeating the word "la Motte." He thought he was near la Motte, but in fact they had been dropped 30 kilometers from la Motte as the crow flies.

Later on, from my house, I could see the landscape all the way up to Fayence. All those parachutes made the woods look like flowers. There were green and red equipment parachutes (depending on the type of equipment they carried), there were camouflaged parachutes, there were parachutes of all colors, and they were everywhere.

Although the bulk of the Allied paratroopers left the Fayence-Montauroux area immediately to head for le Muy, a fair number of men who had been injured in the jump remained behind in Callian, Montauroux, Fayence, and Seillans. A handful of healthy paratroopers also stayed in the area, fighting a sort of guerrilla war against the Germans with the help of the numerous local *maquisards*. At the same time these disorganized men roamed the area, powerful German forces drove by on the D562 road, heading for or retreating from Draguignan. Over the next days, the situation in the Fayence-Montauroux area was therefore very fluid and confused. The paratroopers and *maquisards* would play a game of cat and mouse with the Germans; in which the Germans had the role of the cat. Although the Germans were more powerful, they would suffer several ambushes as well as attacks by Allied aircraft and artillery.

The Ambush Ambush

The first ambush occurred the morning of August 15th, while most of the paratroopers were still regrouping around Callian. The local resistance fighters figured that their town had now been liberated and set up an ambush at the main crossroads south of Callian, blocking the D562 road. They did not have to wait long for the first Germans to arrive in the form of a small convoy, including a bus marked with red crosses. **Jean Veyan** heard about what happened:

A group of resistance men went in the valley and fired at a German convoy. It was probably a garrison from Grasse that was going to Draguignan to fight the landing troops. They had been told: "The landing is at la Motte." The Germans were on some trucks and a bus, and they jumped down. The Germans were experienced, so the ambush didn't go well. They probably killed a few Germans, but Rebufel was wounded. He was behind a hut and a German moved off to the side and saw him. He shot Rebufel, hitting him in the shoulder with an explosive bullet. He barely survived. The Americans saved the resistance fighters, because when the Germans saw some Americans, they surrendered. They would not have surrendered to the Resistance because they were too afraid.

I know that the German bus had a big red cross on its side and that the resistance fighters realized that the men inside may have been sick; but they were armed, so they weren't 100 percent sick. They considered them to be combatants disguised as sick people. Some people said: "We shouldn't have shot at that bus." But the Resistance said: "Yes, it had a red cross on it, but inside they all had rifles." The resistance fighters opened fire on it because they saw the guys were firing at them. The guys were armed; you don't get into an ambulance with submachine guns and rifles.

Fernand Félix, an 18-year-old inhabitant of Callian, heard a similar story:

Around seven in the morning, the *maquisards* were at the crossroads beneath Callian, waiting to block the Germans. A bus with a red cross arrived full of armed Germans. A second car was following behind, but it managed to turn around and escape to Grasse and raise the alarm. There was a fight. I don't know how nobody ended up getting killed, but when the Germans saw the columns of Americans coming down from Callian, they surrendered.

PFC Louis Holzworth, of the Regimental HQ Company of the 517th PIR, was one of the paratroopers who happened to join this gunfight:

I jumped in southern France as a demolition man and I landed southeast of Callian. It was about 4 o'clock in the morning, and it was a dark night, so I couldn't see anything out the windows of the plane. Just a little bit of flak was coming up from the beach as we passed over the area. Then the pilot got a little bit worried and made a big turn, then he turned the light on and the green light came on, so we all bailed out. There were about 15 in my stick, and we were so scattered apart when we dropped that I didn't see anybody from my stick at all.

I landed in a canal with the water was up to my waist. It scared the hell out of me because I didn't know how deep it was, and I was loaded down with all my equipment, including 40 pounds of Composition C. I got over to the edge of the canal and climbed out, but everything was all wet and cold at 4 o'clock in the morning. There was a crossroad about a block away from where I landed and I heard firing, so I headed towards the firing. I got up to the roadway there and saw one of my buddies, Miller [Pvt Clyde L. Miller], laying in the middle of the road and he had his back split open where a ricochet had torn all the meat off his back. His lung was kind of exposed because he was trying hard to breath. It looked like somebody took a meat cleaver and cut open his back, because the air was coming out of his back; that's how bad he was. So I put a compress on him and I had to take off, let the medics take care of him. I joined in the fighting down by the bus. There was a bus and truck there down at the crossroad and we started shooting at the Germans and killed most of them, and a few of the rest of them surrendered.

Fernand Félix saw the captured prisoners from the bus being marched into Callian:

> They captured them and brought them up to the Penitent Chapel in Callian. They couldn't walk any more, they were crying, and the poor guys all had rosaries. They must have been thinking: "This is the end, the *maquisard*s have captured us and are going to kill us." They were exhausted, maybe they hadn't slept the night before. I remember they were walking up, sweating (it was August 15th and very hot), and they got to the town square, where there is a fountain. Some of them absolutely wanted to drink, but an FFI wanted to prevent them from doing so. But there was another guy there who had fought in the First World War and he said: "No, no, no! You let them drink. They are prisoners, you let them drink." I don't know if they were Czech or German, but there were some Germans. There was even a captain who was wounded. They locked them up in the chapel and they stayed there a day or two. They were guarded by *maquisard*s and locals. Then all those prisoners were walked up to Mons with 10 or 15 *maquisard*s.

Mons was a village located only slightly further to the north, but it was in the area under control of the Resistance and where the Germans never tried to venture after the landing. As was explained in chapter two, once the invasion started, the Germans only controlled the coastal area, and they never attempted to operate in the mountains north of the main roads and cities of the Riviera.

The ambush was mentioned by both **Capt Richard Bigler**, of the 517th Regimental HQ, and **1st Lt Kenneth B. Freund**, of the 517th Service Company, in the after action report written about the jump. There are significant discrepancies in their versions, showing how imprecise such reports can be:

> S/Sgt Allison, Tec5 Boynton joined Captain Hooper, G Co, and five men from the 3rd Battalion. A fire fight between a group of about 30 Germans that were trapped on a highway in a bus and an ambulance and elements of Service and Headquarters Company was seen to be in progress. The vehicle was destroyed, 5 enemy killed, 9 wounded, and 16 captured. Private Miller of Regimental Headquarters Company was seriously wounded in this encounter and was evacuated to Callian and hospitalized by the French.

> A French Patriot brought a message to Lt Skutnik about American soldiers and elements of the FFI engaged in a fire fight in the valley southeast of Callian at a road intersection. Lt Skutnik and M/Sgt Coil with 15 men went with the messenger and there joined the battle. Two enemy vehicles were destroyed and ten German soldiers were killed. Sixty prisoners were taken and turned over to the French for disposal.[2]

One American paratrooper, Private Robert R. Gruwell, of G Company of the 517th, had also been killed in the ambush, his sister Virginia Bunkofske later being told "about there being a 'dummy' German war ambulance and my brother being too close to it when he threw a grenade at it." Of course, it would be very interesting to know what exactly the bus with the Red Cross was: a bus transporting armed Germans, or an actual ambulance? The definite answer is brought to us by the letters that the family of

This low-quality photo shows the destroyed German ambulance as well as other ambushed vehicles at the Callian crossroads. 517 Combat Team booklet, Frédéric Brega Collection.

Pvt Robert R. Gruwell, 21, of G Company of the 517th PIR, was apparently killed by his own grenade when he tried to throw it into the German ambulance that was ambushed beneath Callian on the morning of the invasion. Virginia Bunkofske Collection.

Obergefreiter Otto Hessert, one of the Germans who had been in the bus, received in the following weeks. The first letter was written August 23rd by **Dr Wagner**, the Surgeon Major of German Field Hospital 148 in St Vallier, northeast of Callian:

Dear Ms Hessert

Your husband, *Obergefreiter* Otto Hessert, was in my field hospital for treatment, and on the 15th of this month was sent to the rear in a sanitary transport before the fighting started. On the way, the convoy came into contact with the enemy and your husband died the hero's death. Comrades recovered his body, which had several gunshot wounds, and he was buried with military honors by my men in the soldier's cemetery of St Vallier, 12km northwest of Grasse, in southern France, *Departement* Alpes Maritimes, in grave number two.

It is very painful for me, dear Ms. Hessert, to not be able to give you any more details about the hero's death of your husband. If I were to find out anything else, it would of course be my duty to inform you in the quickest manner.

For this heavy loss, I express my most heartfelt and deep sympathies. May you find comfort with the thought that your husband, faithful to his oath to the flag, gave his life for the Führer and the future of his fatherland, the *Grossdeutsches Reich.*

Heil Hitler
Yours, Dr Wagner
Surgeon Major and head doctor.[3]

Emma Hessert received a second letter, written September 12th, by *Oberleutnant* **Pusche**, her husband's company commander, which contained a few additional details:

Dear Mrs. Hessert

With these lines I will bring sorrow to your house, but it is my difficult duty to inform you that your husband has found the hero's death. I assure you and your children of my most heartfelt sympathy after this heavy loss. Unfortunately, there is not much that I can tell you about what happened to your husband. In August, he started to suffer from sciatica that became so severe that he could no longer perform his duty. I thus sent him back for treatment, and he was transferred to the field hospital in St Vallier.

Just before the southern France invasion, the hospital was evacuated further to the rear. The column that your husband was part of came into contact with American paratroopers, and while one part of the column managed to turn back, the fate of the other part of the column is not known. After a counter attack by German troops, your husband and a couple other comrades were found dead and were buried. The wound in the area of the heart leads us to believe that death occurred on the spot (…).

May God give you the strength, dear Mrs. Hessert, to deal with this hard blow from destiny. Carry your sorrow with pride, as you have sacrificed the greatest that a woman can sacrifice.

I wish all the best to you and your beloved children for the future.

Heil Hitler.
Oberleutnant Pusche.[4]

These two letters prove beyond doubt that the German ambulance was a very real ambulance transporting sick patients. The most logical interpretation of the evidence is as follows: upon finding out that the Allied invasion was imminent, the Germans decided to evacuate their field hospital in St Vallier in order to get the patients out of the danger area, and to make room in the hospital now that a large influx of wounded from the fighting could be expected. The patients were loaded in an ambulance bus and driven out on the quickest and seemingly safest evacuation route, in other words, down to Grasse and then west on the D562 highway past Callian and towards the Rhône valley. Unfortunately for the patients, they unknowingly were being sent straight into the lion's mouth! The exhaustion and despair of the German prisoners Fernand Félix saw being marched into Callian becomes more understandable! They were sick men who had been

The letter that Dr Wagner, of Reserve Division 148's St Vallier field hospital, wrote to Otto Hessert's family August 23, 1944, announcing Otto Hessert's death. This letter proves that the bus marked with a Red Cross that was ambushed by the résistants and paratroopers in Callian early August 15th was indeed an ambulance vehicle attempting to evacuate patients of the St Vallier field hospital out of the danger zone. Hessert Family Collection.

attacked and captured at the very moment when they were about to be brought to safety.

The result of this event is predictable. The French claimed that the Germans were breaking the rules of war by carrying armed men in a Red Cross vehicle (one person even claimed that the Grasse *Gestapo* was attempting to escape in the bus), while the Germans must have claimed that the ever-treacherous "terrorists" had cold-bloodedly attacked an ambulance and shot several of the patients.

This tragic and confused event had one more unexpected twist to it. Emma Hessert had organized a mass and published an obituary in memory of her dead husband, but several months later a miracle happened. Emma received a card from Otto, explaining that he was convalescing (his sciatica problems had not been solved yet) in an American prisoner of war camp. The card came as such a surprise that the local postmaster had initially refused to give it to Emma, thinking it may be fake. Otto Hessert had actually not been killed in the ambulance as had been reported. This was happy news for his wife and four kids, but how could such a mistake have occurred, and who was buried in "grave number two" in St Vallier? Otto Hessert's daughter, **Helma Schuska**, explains what her father told her upon returning home:

> He was suffering from sciatica and wrote to us that he was supposed to be sent to the hospital in Mülhausen, which was near our home, so we would be able to visit him. He was being transported in a sanitary convoy, but they were ambushed by partisans and a young German soldier who was barely 18 years old opened fire out of the Red Cross vehicle. The Germans were all very angry about that, because then of course all the partisans also opened fire and one comrade died in my father's arms; he is the one who was probably buried in that grave. The cars that were following behind all turned around and only the first vehicle was caught in the ambush. My father lay the other man down when he realized he was dead, got out of the vehicle, and took cover in the ditch beside the road and stayed hidden there until the firefight was over. He started waving a handkerchief with his right hand to say he wanted to surrender, but then he thought: "They might shoot again and ruin my right hand," so he held the handkerchief in his left hand instead. Then of course he was captured by the partisans, and they had to walk back a very long way in the mountains, and he couldn't walk properly because of his sciatica. They went back and were then handed over to the Americans and he ended up in America.

In the meantime, the body of Hessert's killed comrade had probably remained in or near the bus and started putrefying in the August heat before the Germans recovered it in the following days. According to Otto Hessert, this unknown comrade was from Kreis Germersheim, just like him, which perhaps explains why Dr Wagner's recovery team mistook the dead man for Hessert. The identity of the body became unknown once it was discovered that it was not that of Otto Hessert, and it remains unknown to this day (Apparently Hessert was never asked by authorities to help solve the mystery by giving his version of events).

The Colle Noire Ambush

After having seen the parachute operation in the morning, the inhabitants of Callian and Montauroux assumed that they were now liberated for good and organized themselves to help the Allied paratroopers. **Raymond Carbonel** was an 18-year-old living

Mitte: Otto Hessert * 1907,
Weltkrieg II, Mittelmeer 1944

OberGefreiter Otto Hessert stands between two colleagues of the Kriegsmarine. Once his family received word of his death, an obituary was published in his memory. Three months later they received a card from him, indicating that he was convalescing in an American prisoner of war camp. This card was received by Hessert's family on his eldest daughter's birthday. Hessert Family Collection.

in Montauroux, whose father had died just a few days earlier. He describes the landing and morning of August 15th as seen in Montauroux, and the reaction of the local resistance:

During the night of August 14th to 15th, around midnight, we were all awakened by the sound of aircraft engines that were sometimes close up and sometimes far away, but getting louder and louder and lasted the whole night. (…) I didn't manage to fall back to sleep, and around 6 o'clock, not being able to resist any longer, I got dressed, went down to the ground floor, and opened the front door leading to the street.

In front of me, five meters away, at the corner of Rue Neuve and Rue Eugene Second, was a strangely dressed individual (he had a camouflage suit, and I had never seen one before), wearing a helmet covered with leaves, with his face blackened (I at first thought he was a Negro) and holding a rifle in his hand.

He was an American paratrooper of the 82nd Airborne [sic]! Along with his comrades, he had been airdropped around Montauroux, Callian, and Fayence during the night… when their gliders were supposed to drop them in the vineyards of la Motte! I advanced towards him. He offered me my first American cigarette (a Chesterfield, to be precise) and told me a few words. I answered him as best I could, using all my knowledge of the English language that I had acquired in school.

Around 8 o'clock, the town crier, Mr Mari, walked down all the streets, and after a brief trumpet call made the following announcement: "All the men aged 18 to 60 must assemble in the Clos Square." This news shattered my mother, because in spite of the turmoil that was reigning in the village and the hope of imminent liberation, we could distinctly hear loud gunfire coming from the sea, and more and more airplanes were swirling in the sky. Was she to let me respond to the call and leave for the unknown eight days after losing her husband?

Our cousin Angèle Tallent then arrived. She was coming to ask my mother for advice on how to act. Should her brother Paul, my cousin who was 20, also go to Clos Square? Finally, after many hesitations, and also out of fear of what people would think of us, they decided to let us go, advising us not to get separated. I can still see the two of us: Paul had a big colored checkered shirt, blue work pants, and on his head… a big straw hat that he wore to go in the countryside. I was wearing a blue shirt, blue shorts and… sunglasses!

There were American soldiers (about 20) in the Clos Square and around 40 men, including many *résistants*, some of them with Sten submachine guns (an English weapon that was distributed to the *Maquis*), while others had revolvers or relatively old hunting rifles. All these people were bustling about, going back and forth in all directions.

After a long period of waiting, it was announced that weapons would be distributed to us and that with these weapons we were to go down into the valley to attack the Germans who were retreating towards Grasse in long convoys, and who were being bombed constantly by airplanes that were diving at la Colle Noire and enfilading the highway. We were separated into several groups, and the one that Paul and I were in was sent to the Puits crossroads [This crossroad is not in the valley, but is just east of Montauroux] (…).

We then started waiting. Airplanes were flying over us constantly with an infernal roar, forcing us to dive head first into the ditches beside the road under the illusory protection of mulberry trees that have since been cut down. Around 12 o'clock, great panic seized our group. A dozen Germans coming from the direction of Tournon on foot were spotted coming towards us about 200 meters away. Our group disintegrated, each one running away left and right to escape. What could we do with our bare fists?

Someone in charge then called us back and explained that these were Polish soldiers enlisted into the German army and quartered at Château Tournon who were simply coming to surrender as agreed upon with the local Resistance. Indeed, they had no weapons and they were sent to the town hall and treated correctly.[5]

As the afternoon wore on, with no weapons being given out, the members of Raymond Carbonel's "resistance" group took the smart decision of going home. However, in the valley below Montauroux, more serious events had taken place along the D562 highway, as Carbonel had hinted when he mentioned aircraft strafing German convoys.

Following the news of the invasion, the Germans ordered *Reserve Grenadier Bataillon 327*, which was stationed near Cannes, to counter attack towards Draguignan and come to the aid of the surrounded Germans there. Some elements of *Bataillon 372* were also involved in this operation. In the early afternoon on August 15th, the convoy *Bataillon 327* formed was driving down the D562 towards Montauroux. The soldiers had probably been informed

As soon as the invasion occurred, the inhabitants of the villages in the Fayence region took up arms, ready to battle with the Germans and assist the Allied paratroopers. Here some partisans pose for the camera in Callas. André Méglia Collection.

of the ambush against the German ambulance in the morning and were warned to watch out for *maquisard*s. Between Grasse and Montauroux, the D562 is narrow and passes through several areas suitable for ambushes. Local Frenchmen organized several actions to block the road and attack the convoy. They first tried to block the D562 by knocking an enormous rock, called the "Rocher de Siagne," onto the road. There was a small cave under the rock, forming an ideal cavity to place explosives in order to blow the rock onto the road. **Claude Bernard** lived in Montauroux and was only seven years old at the time. However, he has an excellent memory and interviewed most of the local actors of the events after the war. He explained what happened once the *Bataillon 327* convoy crossed the Siagne River:

> The convoy was attacked just after the bridge over the Siagne. The *résistants* knew that a convoy was coming. In Montauroux, people had always said: "If one day the Rocher de Siagne falls it will block the road." There is a cave under the stone, so they went there and packed it with dynamite, but just when they were going to install the detonators, the convoy arrived. So they left the dynamite in the hole and they all escaped, but one guy who was enraged by the situation took a grenade and threw it at a side car, but the grenade didn't explode. The Germans stopped because the grenade fell on the road. The *résistants* ran away and the convoy drove on, but the Germans were suspicious and knew there was a risk that they would be attacked somewhere.

A second group of *maquisard*s was waiting in ambush barely a kilometer further on. **Jean Veyan**'s father was with them, and he describes what happened:

> My father had gone to attack the Germans at the road coming from Grasse. They were hidden in a big bush. My father had been a sergeant in the army, but he was with other guys who were inexperienced. They were posted there, it was in the morning, and it was starting to get hot, so my father and one of his friends went to get some water. In the meantime, a German convoy arrived. The Germans saw the guys hiding in the bush and jumped out of their trucks and my father's friends ran away; but my father and his friend didn't know! They came back to the bush with a can of water and saw a lineup of men with guns waiting for them on a wall by the road. My father's friend said: "Urbain! The Germans! Run for your life!" What saved them is the fact that the path went into the forest and then made a turn. The shots were aimed at where the path entered the forest. They started firing and my father said: "We heard the bullets whizzing all over the place." They climbed into the forest and ended up with their pants completely torn and no more shirts, but they were alive.

A third group of Frenchmen waited for the convoy of *Bataillon 327* a few kilometers on, southeast of Montauroux, near a well known as "the Well of the Cursed," which was built alongside D562. Facing the well was the Colle Noire castle belonging to Monsieur Grosselin, which in later years would belong to famous designer Christian Dior. On the other side of the well was the local train track. After the well, the road ran in a straight line for several kilometers, with fields on either side. **Claude Bernard** explains what took place at the "Well of the Cursed":

The road was very narrow there and was surrounded by forest; the well could not be seen from the road. What happened is that a machine gun was placed further back, and Justin Ramonda and Félicien Félix were at the well. They were forward scouts who were supposed to warn the machine gun when the trucks would arrive. Unfortunately, when they saw the first truck coming the machine gun opened fire, but it must have only fired three bullets and then it jammed. The truck stopped and all the Germans jumped out right and left, and of course, like any army does when there is a point of resistance, you let it fire, you outflank it, and you wipe it out from behind. That is exactly what happened. Félicien Félix was at the well and a German soldier came and hid behind the well. The German knew the *maquisard* was on the other side, so he went around the well and found himself face to face with Félicien Félix. The German tried to fire, but the shot didn't go off. It was another twist of fate. So Félicien Félix escaped. He ran out in the open, in front of all the Germans, and they fired at him but missed. There were Germans on the train tracks and on the ballast and everything, but he managed to pass through all the bullets without being hit a single time. It was a miracle. The men on the machine gun immediately retreated as well. One guy had even brought grenades along in his school bag, to tell you that they really didn't have much equipment. He threw his school bag away and the grenades were never seen again. All the *résistants* withdrew to Montauroux, but at the well, the guy called **Ramonda** had been killed. I didn't manage to find out exactly what happened. Some people said they heard shouts and calls for help, others say they didn't hear anything.

The German convoy was stopped and they immediately spread out. They entered Colle Noire castle, which belonged to Mr Pierre Grosselin. He was there with his family and some neighbors who had come to visit one of his aunts who was ill. When Mr Grosselin heard the gunfire he told his family: "Don't run away, it would look suspicious. Stay inside and don't move." But the Germans

"If one day the Rocher de Siagne falls it will block the road." The "Rocher de la Siagne" (Siagne River Rock), standing next to the D562 highway. The morning of the landing, local partisans wanted to pack the small cavity visible at the foot of the rock with explosives, to make it collapse onto the road and block traffic. The arrival of the column of vehicles of Bataillon 327 prevented the partisans from finalizing their project. Author's Collection.

came and were very angry. They started making noise: "Hands up, and this and that." They took them outside and brought them out to the road and Mr Grosselin and his family were lined up at the side of the road.

The Germans had walked along the train tracks and found an old guy called **Auguste Perrimond** who was sitting in front of his house who had no idea what was going on. A German found him and must have felt endangered so he shot him in the head and killed him. He had just been sitting in his chair, enjoying the sunlight. He could have run away, but he didn't understand what was happening so he stayed there. So he as well as Ramonda were killed.

Mr Grosselin and his wife, friends, daughters, and sons were all lined up. Mr Grosselin could speak German, and a German officer walked by and the soldier who was guarding them asked: "What am I supposed to do with these people?" The officer replied: "When it's finished, you can shoot them." So Mr Grosselin's family asked him: "What did he say?" He answered: "Oh, it's nothing, everything is fine, don't worry." What was he supposed to tell his family? That they were going to be killed? He couldn't say anything, so he calmed them down and told them: "Don't worry, everything will be fine."

At that moment in Montauroux there was an American soldier, and my friends who were there told him: "Look, look, there are Germans." So the American looked and he

The "Well of the Cursed," built next to the D562 road. The morning of August 15th, several partisans took up position behind the well to ambush the approaching column of Bataillon 327. 20-year-old Justin Ramonda, from Montauroux, was shot and killed, while the remainder of the partisans escaped after their machine gun jammed. Author's Collection.

saw that there were indeed trucks at la Colle Noire. The American soldier took his radio and phoned somebody. In the meantime, the Germans were reorganizing, finishing off Ramonda, waiting for the soldiers who had gone off on reconnaissance to come back, and the *maquisard*s were retreating back to Montauroux. After the radio message was passed, we were there waiting to see what was going to happen. The convoy started moving on again, and at that moment we saw two airplanes in the sky: vrrroooommm! The American soldier had put a sign on the ground with bed sheets in Clos Square. It was probably to indicate a direction, or to identify himself, I am not exactly sure.

That was something marvelous, that the airplanes flew by. But then they left, and everybody was very disappointed. But in fact they flew towards Peymeinade, down into the Siagne Valley, and they came back and enfiladed the road from la Colle Noire all the way to the end. They started machine gunning like crazy and they completely shot up the convoy. So the soldiers stopped and jumped into the ditches left and right. At that moment Mr Grosselin told his family: "Run, run, don't stay here!" So they ran into the forest, but they realized that they had escaped with the Germans. The Germans were still around them, but these ones were young soldiers, they weren't bad guys who wanted to kill them. Mr Grosselin said: "Now disperse, and whatever happens, we should not get together again." So they left, two over here, two over there, so that the Germans wouldn't be able to catch them and shoot them.

The airplanes made a first low altitude pass, then came back and strafed from the opposite direction. They did two or three passes over the trucks. Needless to say everything was burning. I vaguely heard that there were 40 Germans killed.

All the people in the surrounding area witnessed the airplane attack, including **Jean Veyan**:

> In the afternoon, there was a convoy spread out on the road that had been slowed down, that had been stopped, but was still advancing towards Draguignan. I remember I was in Montauroux and two Spitfires arrived and set fire to all the trucks down in the valley. They only made two passes. They were hunting the guys down in the vineyards, because the guys were running in between the vines. A lot of people were killed there.

Udo Taubmann was a member of 6th Company of *Reserve Grenadier Bataillon 372*, which had apparently accompanied *Bataillon 327* down D562 towards Draguignan August 15, 1944. Although there is no way to certify exactly where and when the events he describes occurred because he himself did not know where he was at the time, all the details of his story indicate that he found himself in the Montauroux area August 15th. These are the memories of **Udo Taubmann** following the Allied invasion:

> We were supposed engage the paratroopers, but they had already landed and were waiting for us. We were driving through the forest and at one point we stopped. Word came from up front that there had been some men killed in the first vehicles. There were terrorists there who opened fire and then threw their weapons into a well. There should be a well there where the forest ends. At the

Josef Schwarz
Gestorben am 16. Januar 1941
nach kurzer Krankheit in einem
Lazarett im Alter von 24 Jahren.

Alois Schwarz
Gefallen am 13. März 1942
bei den Kämpfen im Osten
im 21. Lebensjahr.

Gebetsandenken an
Wolfgang Schwarz
Bauerssohn von Namsenbach
Gefreiter in einem Pionier-Batl.
Inhaber des E. K. II u. des Inf.-Sturmabz.
Gestorben am 23. April 1942
nach schwerer Verwundung
bei den Kämpfen im Osten
im Alter von 29½ Jahren.

Weinet nicht, ihr Lieben alle
Dass ich Euch so früh verliess
Dort in jener Himmelshalle
Ist ja unser Paradies.

Mein Jesus Barmherzigkeit!
Barmherziger Jesus, gib ihm die
ewige Ruhe!
Vater unser!   Ave Maria!
Buchdruckerei H. Leingärtner, Nabburg

17-year-old Grenadier Michael Schwarz, of Bataillon 327, was one of the German soldiers who was killed when his convoy was attacked by partisans and then strafed on the D562 highway south of Montauroux. Three of his four brothers had already been killed during the war. Note that his Wehrpass states he was killed in le Muy, which was probably the final destination of the convoy. Schwarz Family Collection.

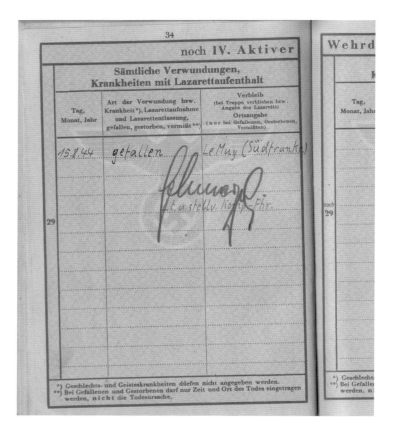

moment when we stopped, two American twin fuselage airplanes attacked us and strafed us. It had been organized by the terrorists.

The two airplanes annihilated us within five minutes. Today, I still don't know how we managed to jump out of the trucks. Nobody fired back, everyone simply looked for cover. Everything burned: the vehicles, the equipment, the field kitchen, everything. The ammunition all blew up on the trucks. They flew over us three times and destroyed everything, making us powerless. We could look up and see them firing and even see the faces of the pilots inside the airplanes.

That was our baptism of fire. It was terrible. All we had left was what we carried on our bodies. It was in the afternoon and we had to continue on foot. I was second gunner on a MG and we slowly crawled forward towards a village, firing bursts and then advancing a bit more, until we reached the village as darkness fell. That night, I was on guard duty at the edge of the village. It was pitch black and there was always shooting going on here and there. Suddenly I was hit by a burst of machine gun fire. It was dark and I don't know where the shots came from, if it was from the Americans or our own troops. I was hit three times. My left shin and heel were shot through, and I had one bullet lodged in my knee joint. I screamed, so my comrades immediately noticed me and came over to bandage me. They wanted to flee and they couldn't bring me with them, so they brought me to a French hospital in the village. I was the only soldier there, all the other comrades had left.

At one point the hospital received a radio message: it was going to be bombed and needed to be evacuated. I don't know if the message came from the Americans or

At the Well of the Cursed in August 2012, local Frenchman Claude Bernard shakes the hand of Maria Krieger, the niece of German soldier Josef Fuchs, who was killed in the area in August 1944. Author's Collection.

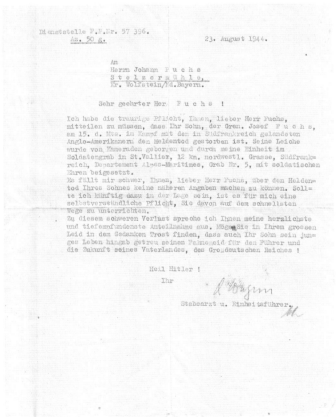

18-year-old Grenadier Josef Fuchs, of Bataillon 327, was killed in the attack of his convoy south of Montauroux. The bodies of the dead were retrieved by German soldiers in the following days and were buried near Dr Wagner's field hospital in St Vallier. The letter that Dr Wagner sent to Fuchs' father is almost identical to that he sent to Otto Hessert's family; he could not give any details about the circumstances of Fuchs' death, as he was not at the scene of action. Fuchs Family Collection.

from us. Everybody escaped and I was left lying by myself with three gunshot wounds, unable to walk. I was afraid and thought my last moments had come. Then an elderly man came, a Frenchman. He was my guardian angel, and he carried me down the stairs into a basement where there were civilians. I was so thankful, I will never forget that man. I lay in the basement for one night with the women and children. I don't know if they had been wounded by us or by the Americans. The whole basement was full and the women cried. It was horrible in there, but I was treated well. The doctors were also in the basement and were always asking me where it hurt and helping me. I can only say good things about the French.

The next morning I was separated from the civilians and brought out onto the main road near the hospital on a stretcher. There the Americans marched by for hours. I still had my watch that I had been given for my confirmation and an American came and ripped it off my arm. Then I was brought to an American field hospital. I was there for a day or two and was then loaded onto a ship. We arrived in Naples, Italy, and stayed there for a day, then I was loaded onto a hospital ship and arrived in New York.

We were afraid of the Americans; we didn't know what would happen to us if we were captured. But everything went well. I had a retained bullet in my right knee and some German doctors removed the bullet under anesthesia and fixed me up so that my knee was back in working order. But the shot in the left heel still bothers me. After half a year in Oklahoma I was called to the orderly office, and there I was given back my watch. I don't know how it was possible, and I didn't try to understand. Maybe the soldier had been seen stealing it from me and had to give it back. I don't know anything else about the incident.

The second half of Udo Taubmann's account describes events that occurred in the following days and that we have not gotten to yet. However, so as not to disrupt the continuity of his account, it has been left as a single story, instead of being separated and placed throughout the text in completely chronological order.

Some of the details previously described by Claude Bernard regarding the Colle Noire ambush can be found in the period radio communications of the 141st Infantry Regiment that, although located at the coast, was in radio contact with the isolated paratroopers at Montauroux and Callian:

> 17:35.16 August: "Parachutists still in radio contact with 2d Battalion. Road between Fayence southeast to Colle Noire heavily travelled by hostile vehicles.(…)"
>
> 11:20. 17 August: "Request air mission to bomb and strafe on road between Fayence and Tourrettes south to main highway; southeast along main highway. (…) Paratroopers are in Callian reinforced by partisans."
>
> 16:05. 17 August: "Bombing and strafing mission request on road south from Fayence was effective. Paratroopers received supplies dropped to them and report heavy troop movements from Grasse to Fayence heading along highway just south of Montauroux. (…)"
>
> 17:50. 17 August: "Message from paratroopers: yellow banner marks position to drop ammunition, batteries, and medical supplies. Marking Fayence-Mons-Montauroux with white arrows pointing to occupied enemy positions.[6]

Captain Grant Hooper, of G Company of the 517th PIR, explained in a report how some of the troopers had gotten organized in order to radio intelligence back to Allied troops:

> Cpl Allen Douglas landed near Fayence and assembled with several other parachutists on the ground. Realizing they were off the drop zone, they set up a small defense and waited for dawn. They eventually formed a mixed group of 13 men: Americans, British and Scotch. They contacted the *Maquis*, who brought them a 2300 radio they had recovered from an equipment bundle. They worked

into the frequency, took the call name, and contacted other American forces. From their positions they radioed information back to American troops, and P-47s were sent over to dive bomb and strafe. When "King Six" said they were going to bomb the town of Fayence, Cpl Douglas had them hold off until he sent a *Maquis* down into town to have the civilians evacuated, which they did promptly.[7]

Callian Battlefield Investigation

We will now see what evidence of the strafing attack on the convoy of *Bataillon 327* has been found at the location where the action occurred. Along the D562 road, one could expect to find the following types of artifacts:

- Parts of destroyed trucks.
- Pieces of damaged and burned German equipment and ammunition.
- Spent bullets and cartridge cases fired by the Allied airplanes.

18-year-old Grenadier Udo Taubmann, of the 6th Company of Bataillon 372. He was apparently wounded in the Montauroux area and fell into the hands of the American paratroopers after being treated in a civilian aid station for several days. Udo taubmann Collection.

Approximately 20 casings from .50 caliber rounds are found in a small field next to the D562 road, evidence of the strafing attacks by Allied aircraft that occurred over 60 years earlier. Private Collection.

The fields on either side of D562 have mostly been built up since the war. Several of them in Montauroux and Callian were investigated without any traces of the airplane attack on the German convoy being found. However, in one small field near the D562 bridge over the Camiole Creek, quite conclusive evidence of the strafing was discovered: approximately 20 WWII-dated spent American .50 caliber bullet casings were found evenly spread out in the field every few meters. If the cartridge cases were left by a machine gun fired by foot soldiers, they would have been found in compact groups at the locations where the gun was set up. When airplanes fire, on the other hand, the spent cartridges fall to the ground in quick succession as the aircraft advances at high speed, thus the spreading of the casings evenly over the field is consistent with a low altitude strafing. The type of ammunition (.50 caliber rounds) was the standard ammunition used by American fighter planes of the time, and therefore gives a very good hint of the nationality of the attacking fighters.

St Vallier de Thiey Battlefield Investigation

As explained in the letters written by Dr Wagner, the Surgeon Major of the field hospital in St Vallier, German forces returned to D562 in the days following August 15th and retrieved some of the bodies of their dead, bringing them back to the St Vallier hospital to be buried. It would seem that this recovery operation occurred at the latest on August 18th. The Germans buried a total of 13 bodies near their field hospital in St Vallier. These men were:[8]

Surname	Name	Rank	Age	Date of death	Burial location	Unit
Schwarz	Michael	Gren	17	15.8.1944	St Vallier	1./Res.Gren.Btl.327
Fuchs	Josef	Gren	18	15.8.1944	St Vallier	1./Res.Gren.Btl.327
Schneider	Paul	Gren	32	15.8.1944	St Vallier	1./Res.Gren.Btl.327
Jeschke	Willi	Gefr	40	15.8.1944	St Vallier	1./Res.Gren.Btl.327
Fleischer	Paul	Gren	17	15.8.1944	St Vallier	2./Res.Gren.Btl.327
Pollak	Richard		18	15.8.1944	St Vallier	2./Res.Gren.Btl.327
Synczek	Josef	Gren	21	15.8.1944	St Vallier	2./Res.Gren.Btl.327
Steinke	Franz	O Gefr	35	15.8.1944	St Vallier	2./Res.Gren.Btl.327
Bilko	Paul	Krftfahrer	21	15.8.1944	St Vallier	Kr.K.Zug 1048
Unknown (Hessert Otto)				15.8.1944	St Vallier	
Kluge	Werner	O Gren	34	17.8.1944	St Vallier	14./Pz.Jäg.Kp.239
Helms	Wilhelm	O Gefr	39	18.8.1944	St Vallier	2./28M.K.Abt
Liebetanz	Herbert	O Kan	19	18.8.1944	St Vallier	Artillery

As can be seen, eight of the casualties were from the first two companies of *Bataillon 327*, proving that elements of this unit were indeed sent towards Draguignan August 15th. Furthermore, two of the bodies are those of vehicle drivers (Bilko and Helms), which is consistent with the attack of a convoy. The official dates of death of ten of these men is August 15, 1944, while the last three died August 17th or 18th. Because of the large number of events which occurred in the Montauroux area, it is difficult to know exactly how these men died (with the exception of the unknown body, that died in the circumstances described by Otto Hessert). However, we can suspect that the ten who died August 15th were for the most part killed in the ambulance and Colle Noire ambushes. The other three probably died in other events, or may have died of wounds in the field hospital.

Dr. Wagner's men neatly buried the first 12 bodies side by side in a single mass grave about one and a half meters deep, two meters wide, and seven meters long. Digging such a grave clearly demanded an intense effort, showing the respect the German soldiers had for their dead. An additional single grave was then dug immediately beside the first grave, in which the body of Herbert Liebtanz was added, presumably because he died after the first grave had already been shut. All these bodies were recovered by the *Volksbund* in 1958, and were reburied in the German Military Cemetery of Dagneux, near Lyon.

The exhumation team retrieved the bones and identification tags of the 13 soldiers, but left behind a large number of small artifacts that then remained at the site of the temporary grave. A search of the grave site led to the discovery of these small, forgotten artifacts. The analysis of these modest remains allows us to draw a few worthwhile observations and conclusions about the circumstances in which the soldiers died and were buried:

- Approximately four bullet fragments were found, all severely deformed by impacts. One fragment could be identified as originating from a U.S. .50 caliber bullet, while a second fragment originated from a U.S. .30 caliber bullet. It seems very likely that the .50 caliber fragment is a remnant of the strafing attack and the .30 caliber fragment a remnant of the ambulance ambush, or of another attack in which U.S. paratroopers were involved.

- One spent U.S. .50 caliber casing was found buried in the grave. This is rather strange, and perhaps indicates that one German soldier may have picked up a spent casing which had fallen from the aircraft during the strafing as a souvenir, only to then be killed himself and buried with this casing still on him.

- One pair of boots, several pairs of shoes, approximately 90 tunic buttons, and numerous other buttons were found, showing that several men had not been undressed before being buried. This indicates that most probably did not die of wounds in the hospital, but were retrieved directly from the battlefield. It would have been unusual for a severely wounded patient in hospital to still be wearing his shoes and uniform.

The bodies of the German soldiers killed in the ambulance ambush and in the Colle Noire strafing attacks August 15th were recovered in the next days and buried near the German field hospital in St Vallier. The helmets of several dead soldiers have been put on their crosses, as was customarily done in the German army. Volksbund Bildarchiv.

Michael Schwarz's death card, with an imaginary depiction of his grave that was remarkably similar to his actual grave in St Vallier. Schwarz Family Collection.

Shortly after the war, German prisoners designed a neat cement grave stone for the St Vallier grave, on which all the names of the dead were recorded. Note that Otto Hessert's name is third on the stone; the Germans had mistaken a dead body for him, when he in fact was alive and well in American custody. Private Collection.

- Only one belt-ammunition pouches-bayonet-Y straps set was found. There were no helmets, gas masks, canteens, nor any other similar equipment. However, hundreds of shelter quarter buttons and loops were found. This is probably the result of the manner in which German soldiers were typically buried by their comrades: equipment was removed from the dead to be reused and the bodies were then wrapped in shelter quarters that constituted makeshift shrouds. As for the helmets, they were used as grave markers.

- Several personal objects, such as wallets, combs, a pocket watch, and pocket knives were found, showing that several men were buried with their uniforms, and that their bodies were not searched thoroughly. The fact that wallets remained is surprising, since one would expect that Frenchmen or the German burial party would have retrieved these. The unpredictability of the military situation may have prevented the French from approaching the bodies (this would also explain why they did not recover the shoes, as was normally the case), and decomposition of the bodies may explain why the burial party did not search them thoroughly. One comb is of particular interest, as it is marked "Hamburg 1937,"

creating a possible link with Wilhelm Helms, one of the men buried in the grave and who was born in Hamburg. One pocket knife was marked "Reims," a town in northern France. This was presumably a souvenir bought by one of the soldiers during a previous assignment.

- The tunic buttons found were mostly normal German army tunic buttons. About one-third of the buttons had metallic hooks behind them, indicating they originated from summer or tropical uniforms. A few tropical Navy buttons were also found, presumably belonging to Wilhelm Helms, who was in the Navy, or to the unidentified body that Otto Hessert had been confused with.

- Approximately 50 wartime German and French coins were found, as well as two coins from the Principality of Monaco. Coins from Monaco are rather rare, and we can suspect that these may have been purposefully kept by a soldier as souvenirs of his presence near the famous principality.

- One large cement grave marker was found that had been handmade by German prisoners of war after the war. Although it

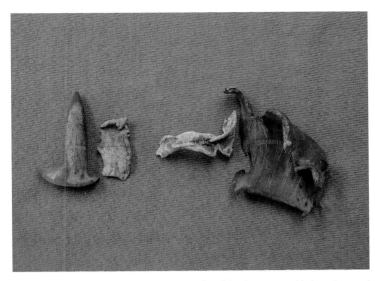

Comparison of the two largest fragments found in the grave with less damaged specimens of spent .30 and .50 caliber rounds. The characteristic crimping and grooves visible on the grave fragments identify them as also being .30 and .50 caliber rounds. Private Collection.

Bullet fragments found in the grave. Private Collection.

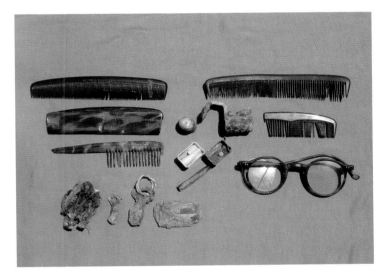

Combs, keys, razor blades, glasses, pencil sharpeners, and rifle muzzle covers. Note that one comb was made in Hamburg, the hometown of Wilhelm Helms, who was buried in the grave. Private Collection.

A bayonet and pocket knives. Note a spent American .50 caliber casing to the lower right that seems to somehow have been transported from the site of the strafing to the grave site. Private Collection.

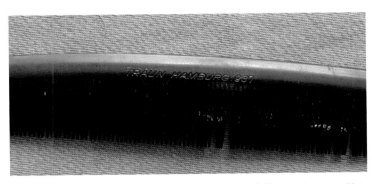

Coins from Monte-Carlo, perhaps souvenirs kept by a soldier to prove he had visited the famous principality. (See Marvin McRoberts' account in the Chapter 16.) Private Collection.

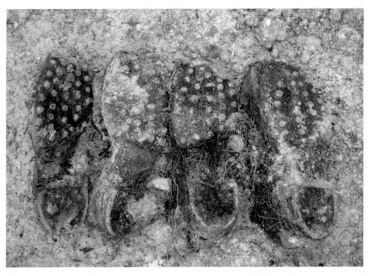

Numerous pairs of shoes, evidence that several of the dead did not die in hospital and were also not buried or pilfered by local civilians. Private Collection.

A pocket watch in a protective metal casing with a rifle muzzle cover fused to the back and remains of a rosary and of religious medallions. Private Collection.

The remains of a wallet containing wartime German coins emerges from the earth. Private Collection.

was not professional, the work was done in a very neat and tidy manner, showing once again the concern that the Germans felt for their war dead. The grave marker was made of a thickness of cement with a wire mesh sunk inside it to give the cement extra strength and prevent it from cracking. The names of the casualties are marked in the cement, including the name Otto Hessert, who actually was not killed and survived the war, as we saw previously. A grave marker for a soldier who did not actually die seems to be a rather original and rare discovery.

La Roche in Fayence

When the paratroopers jumped into the Fayence-Montauroux region the night of August 14th to 15th, the only significant German force in the entire area was a detachment of *Luftwaffe* aircraft spotters and plotters (apparently from *Flugmelde-Funk-Kompanie zbV 23*) in Fayence. This garrison was installed in a strong point at La Roche (the Rock), which consisted of two huge rocks located a few hundred meters north of Fayence. The Germans had transformed the rocks into a strong point by digging trenches and dugouts

around and between them. (La Roche was however by no means a "fortress," as some authors have written, nor a radar station, as yet others have claimed!) A small observation point was built on the top of la Roche, which dominated Fayence, the D562 highway, and all the surrounding countryside. This strategic position became the main German resistance nest for the following days. Immediately after the landing of the paratroopers, the local Resistance tried to capture la Roche. **Joseph Tramontana** was one of the men present at the botched attack:

After the landing we attacked la Roche, which dominated Fayence. In the rock there was a group of Germans, and they were using it as a kind of watch tower. But we didn't manage to kick them out. We came from behind, from the area known as le Laquet, which forms a sort of basin. They were entrenched in that rock and we couldn't get near them. There was a vineyard, then a small forest, and then we came into view of la Roche. In the forest there were bushes and pine trees, and we camouflaged ourselves in there. We couldn't go further because there was no cover. We built small shelters that we could hide in with stones.

We fired at the Germans from 200 or 300 meters away, but we couldn't see them. We would just see a helmet sticking out every now and then and we fired at the helmet. But if they saw us move, they opened fire! We had two or three wounded. I remember I had a colleague beside me who was shot through the buttocks. He must have been lying on his stomach in the vines and the bullet fired from la Roche must have just grazed his back. Since his butt must have been sticking up a bit, it entered his butt and came out his lower thigh. The poor guy was screaming with pain. I also had a cousin there who was hit in the arm by two bullets. We immediately dragged them to the road, where a Red Cross service took care of them. They had made a Red Cross camp for the wounded at le Laquet. Another guy was beside me and he was wearing an American helmet. He was hit by a bullet that dented the helmet and he was stunned, as if he had been hit in the head with a piece of bamboo. That cooled him off.

The Germans knew we were in that forest and they fired anytime anything moved. That is what war is about.

The village of Fayence. The la Roche rocks are faintly visible on the skyline to the left of town, while some buildings of Tourrettes stick out to the right. Author's Collection.

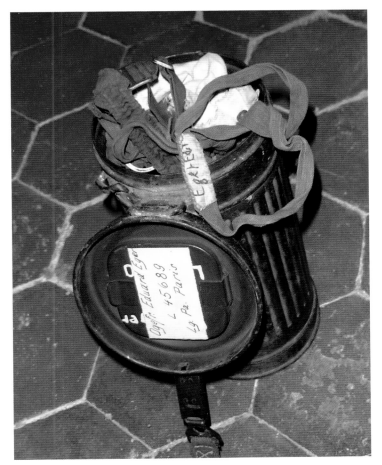

This German gas mask found in Fayence is marked as belonging to Obergefreiter Eduard Eger, from Flugmelde-Funk-Kompanie zbV 23. The presence of this air observer unit in la Roche is probably what led some authors to claim that a radar station was present in Fayence, when there were in fact only a few dugouts and trenches built around some large rocks. Private Collection.

A close-up view of the la Roche rocks that overlook Fayence and its surroundings for miles. Author's Collection.

We had cooked some chickpeas in a pot. I was holding the pot and I moved and a bullet hit the pot of chickpeas! It was better for the pot to have been hit than me. I must have been holding the pot slightly to the side. We didn't eat chick peas that night.

We took no prisoners, and as far as I know we didn't wound any Germans or anything. We didn't succeed in doing anything. They wanted to surrender to the Americans. It was actually a crazy idea, attacking a rock. A tank is what we would have needed! We could attack just like that without any cover and they would have shot us like rabbits. We should have organized ourselves better. We were badly led, the people commanding us were not military men, and we were young and fanatical. When you are young you don't realize the risks.

We stayed there two or three days, then we had to take off, because we had casualties and because we had nothing to eat. There were no supplies, no nothing, it was a big mess. Each man for himself! Sometimes somebody would go into Fayence, into the village, to try to get a bit of bread or something to eat. But Fayence was also full of Germans, so it was taking a big risk!

Just as during the Occupation, people didn't only die because of combat, but also because of random accidents. **Georges Kireeff**, from Seillans, died in such a mishap when a group of *maquisard*s attempted to drive a truck of ammunition down to Fayence from the mountains. **Félix Castelli**, who had been conscripted by the Resistance leadership in Mons, saw the truck driving off August 17th:

There were three men in the cabin, and Georges Kireeff climbed up behind on the ammunition. It was a truck that they had requisitioned somewhere and the brakes didn't work properly. It was loaded with four tons of ammunition. When they tried to slow down, they ran out of road space and the truck overturned. Those in the cabin weren't hurt, but the one who was at the back flipped over with the truck and ended up underneath it.

The memorial stone dedicated to resistance man Georges Kireeff, who was killed on the road between Fayence and Mons when the truck he was riding in overturned. Author's Collection.

No Man's Land

Once the majority of the Allied paratroopers had departed the Fayence-Montauroux area towards their intended drop zones around le Muy, the area became a sort of no man's land for the next few days. The Germans held Fayence, but elsewhere, the territory was simultaneously roamed by forces from all sides. This led to several deadly encounters, the first of which occurred August 16th at the Estoc Bridge, a few kilometers southwest of Fayence on D562. FTP fighter **Marius Roquemaure** had been wounded in the previous weeks and stayed behind, enabling him to witness what happened to his comrades:

At the period of the landing I was in Claviers, and one day they told us: "There are American troops on the road, we have to go and get them." There was a long column and we were supposed to give them directions if they needed us. We stopped maybe 300 meters before the bridge and I stayed in the car instead of meeting the column.

They went to shake their hands and realized it was a column of Germans retreating from the coast. I immediately saw it was Germans and thought: "They are going to get them!" The Germans were good at war, they had been to Russia, unlike us, who were just jokers. When they saw it was *maquisard*s, they surrounded them in an instant, captured them, and brought them to the bridge to execute them.

When they saw what was going to happen, the *maquisard*s said to each other: "Save yourselves!" and tried to escape. One fell off the bridge into a big oak tree and saved himself like that. One was wounded and walked three kilometers in the river bed holding his stomach. There was a drip of blood every meter and he died that night. The Germans shot them, but then left without trying to find anything out because they were afraid of the *Maquis*, they didn't know how many of them there were. I got back in the car and drove back to Claviers. I told everybody what had happened, saying: "They have been killed. We thought it was an American column but it was a German column."

In total, eight *maquisard*s had been surrounded by the Germans on the bridge to be executed: two were killed on the spot, four were wounded, and only two managed to escape unharmed. One of the wounded died later, as Marius Roquemaure explained. The three who died were **Jean Cabasson**, **Henri Chevalier**, and **Marius Ollivier**. The next day, another *maquisard* was killed and several others wounded when their truck met two German trucks south of Callian, where the ambulance ambush had occurred two days earlier. **Zézé Latil** was on the truck when the fire fight occurred:

We were coming from Callian, a group of men on a vehicle, to go and meet a resistance group in Claviers, but on the way we encountered two German trucks. We were face to face, and of course we machine gunned each other. Our truck was an old gas generated one with two big metal boilers at the front. Those boilers protected us by stopping most of the German discharge, otherwise we would have all been killed. The truck must have been at an angle, because all those on the right side were hit and I was lucky to be on the left side.

The Germans and we all jumped out of our vehicles and ran for cover in the fields. The Germans were experienced, and we were too young to be able to fight back. With a

The memorial stone built at the Estoc bridge, between Fayence and Callas, where three resistance men were shot by the Germans whom they had misidentified as American paratroopers. Author's Collection.

The memorial built for Maurice Astier on the D562 road. He was killed in the fire fight that ensued when a truck full of resistance men encountered a truck full of German soldiers driving in the opposite direction. Author's Collection.

group of 45 men against ten of us, it was hopeless. But our advantage was that we knew the region, so they didn't manage to get us. We disappeared into the countryside. At that age you can run fast, even when you're wounded. Three of us were severely wounded: Albert Autran, Pierre Audibert, and Maurice Astier.

As soon as the Germans got out of their truck, they got under cover and didn't move while they waited for reinforcements. They were afraid. All they wanted to do was to surrender, they didn't want to fight any more. They didn't try to chase us. They stayed on the road for a bit, checking if they had any wounded. I was observing them from a distance.

When Astier jumped off the truck, he ran maybe ten meters to behind a little wall, where he collapsed. He was shot through the groin where the femoral artery is. There was a little well there and I pulled him aside to the well, where I put a bit of water on him to refresh him because he was still talking, he didn't die right away. He just bled out. We all had military field dressings and I put the entire pack into his wound, but it didn't do anything, the blood was squirting everywhere.

It was about noon or 12:30. At 1 o'clock, I tried to find my other wounded friends. As soon as I heard them groaning, and even crying, I advanced towards them to help them. I was one of the only ones who wasn't wounded, so I was able to bring them to Callian during the night. A field hospital had been created in the town square and they were taken care of there.

Surprising as it may seem, infirmaries had been set up in Callian, Montauroux, and Fayence, where wounded from all sides were treated. Udo Taubmann, the German soldier who had been wounded one night while standing guard, was probably brought to one of these improvised hospitals. In Montauroux, **Captain Walter Plassman**, a doctor from the Medical Detachment of the 517th PIR, was in charge, and even the Germans let him take care of the wounded without bothering him, as he later explained:

We landed far from our objective, and those who could walk left to join the main forces. About six men and myself were unable to do more than hobble. One man had a fractured leg. My left knee had banged against a rock wall next to a road. With the help of two civilians, we managed to reach Montauroux, which was about one kilometer off.

I set up a casualty station in a building that had been a TB sanatorium. There were only three cots there, but people brought in mattresses. While I was there, I met a French dentist who happened to be visiting his in-laws. He was great. He managed to scrounge food and water for us. Another very helpful person was the local priest.

Things were quiet, except for a few artillery rounds that fell quite close. That night, around 1:00 A.M., about twenty-five German soldiers came into the town. They had one old truck and they were part of an engineer company. Their captain spoke some English. He said we should stay put and later they would try to evacuate us to their hospital.

The Germans remained all day. They had one wounded man with them, a gut shot. I examined him, but explained I could do nothing except give him morphine. He died a few hours later. That night, around 2:00 A.M., they pulled out, taking their dead man.[9]

Sgt John Chism set up an infirmary that worked under similar conditions in Fayence, in which one soldier of the 5th Scottish Battalion with severe stomach wounds died. This Scotsman may have been same casualty who local youth **Jean Veyan** remembered as having been wounded the morning of the jump:

> One man was killed. There was a broken branch that was sticking up like an arrow and the guy landed on it, sticking the arrow in his stomach, and died. There were also lots of men with broken limbs.

It would appear that this Scotsman (whose name I have not been able to identify, though he should be one of those included on the FABTF casualty list at the end of chapter three), as well as Private Robert R. Gruwell, who had been killed on August 15 in the ambulance ambush, are the only two Allied paratroopers to have been killed in the entire Fayence-Montauroux area. According to witnesses, Gruwell was buried in the civilian cemetery in Montauroux, but his body was never recovered after the war and he now has no known grave. Captain Walter Plassman, in Montauroux, remembered:

> Diagonally across the street from our wounded center was a Catholic church and a small cemetery. One dead soldier was brought to us by the FFI on D+1. The local priest and several others gave him a Christian burial in that small cemetery[10]

PFC Louis Holzworth, of the HQ Company of the 517th PIR, who had participated in the ambulance ambush the morning of August 15th, was one of the few paratroopers who did not walk back to le Muy, but instead stayed behind in Callian and fought with the *maquisard*s:

> I joined another group of paratroopers up near a big château west of Callian, and from there I kind of operated as a guerilla. We lived up in a hill just behind the château.

All we had was the walking wounded who got hurt on the jump staying at the château. We were going down, raiding the German vehicles that were going back and forth on the highway. We would catch an isolated one, because we didn't have that many people there, and blow them up, kill them, and destroy them. That was our mission: arrest the Germans in the rear area.

There were only about six or seven of us, so we made sure we didn't attack a big convoy. We attacked individual vehicles, and it just happened that two trucks were coming down the road, so we decided to attack them. I was working with the FFI—they had about five of them and three of us—and we came down there and hid behind the buildings by the road at the junction. As soon as they got close to us, we would open up on them and kill all we could kill. The few we didn't kill, we let the French take them away to a PW camp, or whatever they did with them. We didn't have any place to hold the prisoners, so we let the FFI take them. I shot this one guy three or four times with the carbine, then he came out with his hands up. I went over to him, turned him around, and said: "Dear God, you should be dead you know!" I let him live because he took four bullets to the upper part of the chest without hitting a vital spot. I said: "Let him live, he deserves to live." He was just a young German, about 18, so I gave him to the French and said: "Here, patch him up. I didn't kill him so let him go… let the French FFI have him," and they took him away. The carbine doesn't have the stopping action of a .45, so after that I looked around and picked up a Thompson.

As was mentioned previously, some of the paratroopers managed to get in radio contact with the 141st Infantry Regiment which had landed on the coast, and were able send important information and to ask for supplies to be dropped. The radio log of the 141st IR once again enables us to cross check the above witness accounts. The log even mentions the German ambulance that the paratroopers were using as a landmark:

> 14:00. 16 August: "(…)Paratroopers landed at 0430 on 15th. Contacted 3 companies of Germans. 15 paratroopers wounded and 3 or 4 left able bodied. They are one mile

T5 Louis Holzworth, a diehard paratrooper of the Regimental HQ Company of the 517th. He remained in Callian to fight guerrilla style with the local Resistance, which ultimately almost cost him his life. Louis Holzworth Collection.

Holzworth Demo 43

north of knocked out German ambulance on Highway 7 at crossroad [this is a mistake in interpretation by the 141st IR, the paratroopers were in fact near D562, not near the RN7].(…)"

11:10. 17 August: "2nd Battalion in contact with paratroopers. They have been reinforced by considerable group of French Partisans. Mission to be flown to them today."

11:25. 17 August: "Paratroopers have 15 wounded. They are sending patrols out to locate heavy artillery of the enemy. They will report what they find out."[11]

The paratroopers also sent back information about the German strong point in La Roche, at Fayence:

16:45. 17 August: "Request bombing mission. Paratroopers at Callian have observed an enemy concentration estimated at 400 men with tanks and guns on a mountain 800 meters north of Fayence and east of road. Desire bombing mission on mountain."[12]

One of the wounded paratroopers in the Fayence-Montauroux area was **Pvt Thomas McAvoy**, of the HQ Company of 3rd Battalion of the 517th PIR. His odyssey brings us back to the night of the jump, the reasons why they were dropped off target, and what became of the jump casualties:

August 14th, they got us together at an airport and told us: "There is a river running by this airport, everybody go down there and take a bath in the river because it will be the last one you get for a while. Tonight's the night we go to France." We come back, and they took us to a green tent that had a sand table model of our drop zone, so we could see what it looked like. They told us: "There is a house here in the corner, a road running by the house and a railroad track coming across the property. So you know positively whether you hit your drop zone if you can see that as you are coming down. We want you to congregate over there at the house." Then we went over to our last supper, they had big kettles of food for us. After we were to walk up the aluminum ladder to get on the airplane. We all had assigned seats; the people that would jump last got on the airplane first so they could get up to where their seat was. There were 23 of us. The battalion commander, Lt Col Zais, was number 1, our Regimental Surgeon, Major Vella, was number 2, and our 3rd Battalion Intelligence Officer, John Neiler, was number 3; the reason was to their importance, I believe. I will show you my importance, I was number 20! We all got on the airplane about 10 o'clock at night, and we sat there and waited for the pilot, copilot, and such to come on board whenever they were ready. The navigator got on and he could hardly walk up the center of the airplane to the cockpit. He had been drinking pretty heavy and we were all kind of alarmed about that, because we knew that we were going to rendezvous in the sky.

I don't know why the pilot didn't refuse to take the navigator, being intoxicated. It might have been that he was a friend that flew with him a lot and he knew if he turned him down for the flight he would be court marshaled and sent to prison. He took him, I believe, thinking he could sober him up during the five hours it took us to get to France. The plan was he would give us the jump signal 20 miles from the coast inside of France, and he didn't give us the jump signal until we were 50 miles in. That's terrible, missing the drop zone by 30 miles [Note: all these distances are exaggerated], and we were going crosswise on a mountain range when we got the signal to jump, so the people that were first in line dropped about 800 feet, which was just right, and I was 3rd from the last, so I jumped and it was about 400 feet off the ground. Well, it takes 300 feet for your parachute to open, so you're just flirting with death jumping that low. But it was night time, 4 o'clock in the morning, so you can't see anything and you don't know that.

My parachute opened and I slammed into a huge rock formation. That's when I broke my back, hitting that damn rock thing, but I wasn't sure how bad I was hurt. I had to get my parachute harness off and get my weapon together in case the Germans were close by. So I did that, and I noticed a guy down at a lower level than me. It was beginning to break day and I could see he had a helmet on. He saw me about the same time and he took a bead on me with his rifle and gave me the password. I had to give him the counter sign or he would shoot me! Well, I forgot the damn countersign so I just blurted out to him: "I am hurt! I am hurt, don't shoot me!" The man was Lt John Neiler and he recognized my voice. He says: "Is that you, Tom?" and I said: "Yeah." So he said: "Well, get down here with the rest of us!" and I said: "I am hurt!" So he says: "Don't play. No time to be hurt, you're in combat! Get on down here!"

I had lost the strength in my legs, I couldn't stand up. So I crawled over to the edge of the little drop off where Neiler was, and it looked like it would be about six or seven feet down. I went over the side thinking I could hold myself, let myself down easy, but I didn't have any strength to hold on so I just flopped down there and hit the ground with my feet, tipped backwards, and landed on my back. That's when I got paralyzed. I couldn't get up and my buddies had to pick me up and carry me to a farm house. Our regimental surgeon was in the same plane I was in, and when I woke up he was looking at me and he told Colonel Zais: "We are going to have to leave this guy here, he keeps passing out on us. I can't tell what his problem is without X-ray. It's some kind of back injury." So they left. He gave me a shot of morphine for my pain, then Lt Neiler,

The village of Seillans, near which Thomas McAvoy landed. The presence of mountains near the village caused many jump injuries amongst the paratroopers. Author's Collection.

who was my closest commander, came over to me and said: "Tom, let's don't be foolish. If the Germans come in here, surrender! All you're going to do is get yourself shot for nothing. They might take you to a hospital and find out what's the matter with you." He told me he would go and have to walk with the rest of them the 30 miles back to where they were supposed to land, and he would get a jeep as soon as the gliders brought them in and come back and get me. He thought he would be three to four days, and in the meantime he said: "Here is an escape packet." He gave me a little canvas bag that had five nylon maps in it, and there was 20 dollars in French money in it and a phrase booklet. You open a page and a phrase in English like: "Where is the hospital?" was the next column, and it had the same thing in Italian and the third column had the same thing in French. So you could talk to somebody that way. They would have to look up what they wanted to say and you would have to look it up.

Anyway, he left me and I went to sleep from that morphine, and I woke up two hours later and there was a middle-aged man trying to scoot me over on the bed and I scooted over so he could sit down. He could speak English, and he said he was with the French Red Cross. He wanted to know how many men were in our outfit and how many jumped, all that shit, and you don't tell somebody like that in combat if you don't know exactly who they are. So I wouldn't tell him, and I started asking him questions, and he knew more about the invasion than I did! He tells me that he would send somebody to pick me up and take me to town, and I said: "Hospital" and he says: "No, they've got doctors in town." So I went back to sleep. Four hours later I wake up and here stands a Free French guy in the *Maquis* with a British Bren machine gun across his chest. He had seen me wake up and he started smiling, he ran around to the bedside and he pointed to himself and said: "Jean," and I pointed to myself and I said: "Tom." So we knew who we were, but we couldn't speak each other's language. So I got the book out and he showed me he wanted to take me to town to the doctor.

He took me to the town of Seillans, a little French village, with his truck. It had a population of about 300, a small village, but the damn town was founded in 1059! Man I am walking through history here, and he takes me to the only tavern in town, which served as a town hall when something was happening. There were about 30 people standing out in front; they had heard he was going to bring an injured American soldier in, so they started cheering and saying things like: "Américains, liberation, liberty," and that kind of stuff. They were just happy that they were going to be liberated. Jean carried me in and set me down in the tavern, and now everybody wants to have a drink. I didn't drink, I wasn't interested in that stuff, so I gave him a sleep sign. Jean came over and picked me up, took me upstairs to a big bed in a big bedroom and laid me down, and a French doctor came right in and he spoke English. He says: "I want you to take your shirt off, your undershirt, and I want you to lay on your stomach." So they had to help me do that, and he took a needle and pricked my back with it and he said: "Do you feel that?" and I said: "Yes." So he went right up my spine and then came back down the other side, trying to find if I was paralyzed or couldn't feel it. But I was able to feel all that, and he told me that I had a very bad bruise to my back but in three weeks I would be okay.

There was a crowd of about ten people standing around my bed and the doctor called for a 16-year-old French girl. She came to the bedside and he tells her in French what he wants her to do, and then he tells me in English what he told her. He had told her that she was to massage my back every three hours that I was awake, and that it was very important, and if I had to go to the bathroom, somebody was supposed to help me go to the bathroom, bring my food to me, and that I shouldn't get out of the bed and all that. The doctor left. I never saw him again, and that girl started right away, massaging my back, and boy she did so good that I was able to recover pretty well, where I could walk in about three days.

Then every day it seemed that something was happening that involved me. The first day, in the evening, two French men came up from the tavern and took my clothes that were laying on a chair beside the bed and laid them on the bed. They said the only one word in English they knew, and it was hurry. "Hurry!" I didn't know what the hell they were talking about, so I called for Jeannette [Clariond] (the French girl) to come in. Her and her mother had an apartment right next door to the tavern where I was, so she came right in and she asked the Frenchmen what they wanted. They said: "The Germans have entered the other side of town and they are coming this way, it won't do for them to find him here. We want to take him to an old barn and put him up in the hay loft overnight." So she told me that, and let's go, get my clothes on, let's go. They took me over to that barn and I had my clothes on but no blankets and I damn near froze that night. It goes down to 40 degrees in France in the summer, in the mountains. So the next morning, by about 6 o'clock, here they come after me, got me out of that hay loft back to the tavern upstairs to my bed and there stands Jeanette with hot breakfast for me.

It was just uncanny: later on that day, a 35-year-old woman comes in, and she comes over and she does the same thing: she picks my clothes up off the chair, lays them on the bed and then gently tries to pull me out of bed. I call for Jeannette again, and she comes out there and talks to the girl in French and tries to translate for me, and she says: "That girl is so excited, I don't know what's the matter with her. She wants you to go with her, but I don't know why." And finally, she got some more guys up there, and they carried me down and we followed that girl to her apartment. Here she had a four or five-year-old little girl who had skinned her knee pretty bad and it was infected, and she wanted me to try to treat it if I could. Well somebody had found a medics kit in that area, so they had brought it in on a chair at the side of my bed and she picked that up and took it with her so when I got up there I had something to work with. I took methylaid I found in the bag and cleaned up her infected knee and that was about it, and they took me back to the tavern.

The next day, an officer from our outfit, Lt. Floyd Stott, showed up and I don't know where in the world he had come from. He came bounding up the stairs, wanting to know where the officer is up here, and I said: "There ain't no officer up here, I am the only guy up here." He said: "Well, you are impersonating an officer, I am going to get you court marshaled for that." I ask him: "Do you speak French?" He says: "No." So I told him: "These people don't speak but very little English, and how you get crossed up that I would do something like that? What advantage would I have telling somebody I was an officer?" He says: "You would get better treatment." I said: "Baloney, if I was Eisenhower himself I couldn't get better treatment than I am getting right now." He says: "I am still going to punish you!" and then damn if he don't go downstairs and tell the owner of the tavern, which was Jeannette's father: "Don't feed that guy until I tell you to, I am going to punish him," and he leaves. The tavern owner owned the whole building, and he called his daughter Jeannette down and asked her what the hell was with these people? They are trying to punish one of their own countrymen that's injured! So Jeannette asked me what was the matter and I told her he was nuts.

So the next day Jean, who had brought me there, comes to see me about 10 o'clock, and through Jeannette interpreting for him, he said that he knew a bridge that the Germans were using on a highway to get to the front lines for resupply and ammunition and material, all that stuff. Don't I think it would be a good idea to blow it up? I said: "Excellent idea Jean, go blow it up right away!" So as he leaves to blow up the bridge, he passes this goofy officer on the stairway and the officer wants to know where he is going and I say: "We just decided to blow up a bridge!" And the officer hits the ceiling again: "I am the commanding officer here, and you cannot make decisions like this!" I said: "How the hell am I supposed to know where you are to get your okay on anything? Now you just tell me what was the matter with that decision?" Well, he wouldn't backtrack at all, so I said: "You want to help? Well go down there and join them people and blow that bridge up with them!" So he did. In fact, when they got there to blow it up they had no detonators to set off the explosives, and Lt. Stott was able to rig up a grenade some way to set off the explosives and blow the bridge up.

They got the bridge blown up, and when they came back to tell me about it, damn if their truck doesn't turn over on the way back and they kill one of their men, the Free Frenchmen [Thomas McAvoy is referring to previously mentioned Georges Kireeff, who died August 17th when the truck he was riding on overturned]. Everybody in town knew the guy and they were going to have the guy's funeral the next day. So the next day, everybody in the town goes to the church, which was nearly across the street from this tavern. The American pilots started flying over the town and I saw a P-38 out my window, that twin boom outfit, and they spot all these people going to the town. They don't know if they're German or what, and damn if they don't call in artillery on the town. They hit the church, everybody in the church wants to run into their home. I had a Scotsman, I don't know where he came from, appear in my doorway and he said: "Hello Yank, anything I can do for you?" and I said: "Yeah, get me out of this building and into the basement in case they hit this building with one of them shells."

So he helped me downstairs and it wasn't a very big room: about 12 foot square, with a chest of drawers on one side of the wall, and this Scotsman starts going through those drawers to see what's in there and hello! He has found somebody's bank! It was not greens of money in it, but every drawer was full of French Francs. I think what had happened, the tavern would take their receipts like every couple of hours down there and put it in one of the drawers so in case the Germans come in, they couldn't steal their money. This Scotsman started stuffing all the money in his clothes, so I told him: "Don't go stealing their money, damn! These people have treated me so nice, and you, trying to steal their money!" He says: "Finders keepers, losers weepers." I thought: "I gotta tell this nut some kind of a story that will get him to stop," so I said: "Listen, if one of these shells goes into this building and it caves in and you and I are down in this basement, the Frenchmen are going to go after their money, and take away all these rocks that are on top of us. We will be dead, but at least they are going to report that we died down here. If they find that money on you that you are trying to steal from them, they will never tell nobody! You are going to be missing in time the rest of your life!" So he put the money back; it kind of surprised me that my story was good enough for that to happen.

Anyway, the shelling had stopped, so I told this guy: "Help me get back up to my room" and he did, and there stands Jeannette. She says: "I've got good news for you, tomorrow they are coming with a truck and they are going to take you and five or six other Americans back to the American lines." So the next day they did come, and they showed up with a German dump truck and five American paratroopers came to that spot to be picked up from the village, and they got me in the back of the dump truck. They put a huge Free French flag on a flag pole in the back so one of their guys could hold it up and the snipers would know that there were good guys in there instead of Germans, because the truck had German markings on it. So we got back to the American lines and they sent me to a young man that had the rank of Major. How in the world that boy got Major at his age I don't know, except he must have been a general's son or a general's son-in-law and he was pushing him up as fast as they could. I had to be interviewed by him because I had been behind enemy lines. He says: "What day did you get hurt? What day did you jump into France?" I said: "August 15th."
- "What day did you get hurt?"
- "August 15th."
- 'What day did you go on sick call?"
- "I didn't go on sick call."
He jumps down my throat: "What's the matter with you, dummy? Don't you people know how to go on sick

Thomas McAvoy and Jeannette Clariond pose at the Seillans fountain during a meeting many years after the war. Thomas McAvoy Collection.

call, for crying out loud? You get hurt and you expect the medical department to work big time getting you back on your feet."

So I said: "Major, what part of the story don't you understand? I am 50 miles behind the lines, who would you have me go on sick call to?"

Well, he had seen where he had put his foot in his mouth, so he says: "Dismissed," and that son of bitch put down on my record that I was alone behind the enemy lines two days instead of six.

So they sent me to the hospital, they X-rayed me, and right then they put on a body cast and I asked them: "Have you found out what's the matter?" and they said: "Yeah, you broke your back in five places." So they put me in a big green tent that held about 30 beds on each side of the aisle, and there was nobody in there. It was turning dark that night and the next morning I wake up and I look to my left and here is a German prisoner of war that's been injured. I looked to my right and the same thing, and these guys are asking me for cigarettes! The American army does not mix injured people, enemy and American, like that. I could not believe it. So then you have to get a nurse and find out what the hell is the matter, and when you need one you can't find them and if you don't need one you got one standing by your bed. So I waited 20 minutes, and finally the nurse comes walking down the aisle and I hollered at her, but she paid no attention to me. So I screamed at her. She turns around and comes back and she says: "Surely you're not an American?" I said: "Yesssss, I am an American, what the devil have you got me in here with these POWs for?" Well, she has to go see who the record shows is in bed number eight, and she comes back with two prisoners of war that they were using to do manual labor. One got on each end of my stretcher and carried me to a hospital ship that was leaving that night for Naples, Italy."

Thomas McAvoy's account is representative of what many of the other jump casualties who were left behind in the Fayence-Montauroux area experienced. Numerous details of McAvoy's story in Seillans are confirmed by the after action report about the landing written by **Captain Martin Fastia**, the commanding officer of I Company of the 517th PIR:

Second Platoon: Upon landing at the drop zone, they assembled with the rest of the company and also set up local security. Lt Stott reported to Lt Birder that he had sustained a back injury and that Cpl Boyer, Sgt Miller, and Pvt Hughes were missing. When the order came to move out, the 2nd Platoon took rear guard. After proceeding a short way, the injured men could no longer continue. Captain Fastia ordered Lt Stott to remain behind with Cpl Bailey and Privates Loeffler, Sibonga, Jerina, and Sailor. At this time, Sgt Miller and Pvt Hughes joined the platoon, and since Pvt Hughes was hurt, he also stayed behind. After obtaining all necessities, Lt Stott took charge of the group at a nearby farm house and the rest of the company moved on. Lt Stott then moved himself to a nearby hill, where he and the men dug in and put out local security.

Pvt Bennett, a platoon medic, was also left behind with Lt Stott to aid the injured men. At 1500 hours, four French Patriots approached the group. They left and later returned with a Scotch lieutenant and a truck, which the group boarded and proceeded to the town of Seillans.

There they went to a small hotel and were treated by a local doctor, after which the group rested outside of town in a barn for the night. (...)
D plus one
Lt Stott and his group (...) moved his injured men to houses throughout the town, where they were cared for by friendly villagers. Lt Stott, a French Corporal, and five Patriots boarded a truck and went to a bridge which they blew up. They saw a German truck coming in the direction of the bridge, and when the bridge was blown a falling rock from the blown bridge demolished the truck completely and killed its lone driver. (...)

D plus two
Lt Stott, with his group, was shown by the French a load of chutes, MGs, and mortars and ammo that they (the French) had collected. Pvt Bennett and 11 French patriots boarded a truck to pick up some Italian prisoners. On returning the truck turned over, killing one man [Georges Kireeff] and injuring Pvt Bennett's left arm. Lt Stott, Pvt Hughes, and a Frenchman proceeded to a nearby bridge, which they blew up. Just as the bridge blew up, Pvt Hughes had been running (for it was he who set off the charge) when his back pained him so that he fell to the ground. Just as the explosion went off, Pvt Hughes managed to throw himself over the side of the embankment, as large pieces of rock barely missed him. The time was 2300 hours. Then Lt Stott met Capt Hanna and Sgt Palmer of the Special Service Force [these two men were members of the OSS and will be mentioned in detail further on] and informed Lt Stott that Germans were in the vicinity. Lt Stott sent out a patrol, but reported back no German activity.[13]

These stories illustrate very well the "cat and mouse" situation that existed between the Germans, Allied paratroopers, and resistance fighters in the Fayence-Montauroux area.

Reoccupation by the Germans

About August 18th, the Germans started arriving in the Fayence-Montauroux area in numbers, putting an end to the "no man's land" situation, occupying Callian and Montauroux and reinforcing their garrison in Fayence. In his postwar report, *Generalleutnant* **Fretter-Pico**, commander of *Reserve Division 148*, gave an explanation of the German situation along the D562 road and why the Fayence-Montauroux area had become their main defense line:

On the evening of the 15th or on the 16th, the division received a message from *Korps* Neuling [that was in the Draguignan area] to immediately send a battalion reinforced with artillery to Draguignan. This was done, and the battalion was attacked by strong enemy forces, including tanks, approximately 8km before Draguignan. The battalion retreated back to the defense line at Fayence.[14]

The Fayence-Montauroux area had been a vital line of communication since the landing, and it was now going to become the main front line. Troops of the 141st Infantry Regiment and of the 636th Tank Destroyer Battalion (636th TDB) who had landed on the coast on the 15th were now approaching Callian from the direction of Bagnols to the south. The Germans needed to prepare the defense of Callian against these forces, and it would not do to have paratroopers and *maquisards* running loose in their midst.

Elements of *Bataillons 327* and *372*, as well as the 14th Antitank Company of *Reserve Grenadier Regiment 8*, were to take control of Callian and Montauroux and reinforce the La Roche strongpoint in Fayence. **PFC Louis Holzworth** and his desperados were still fighting a guerrilla warfare from their castle near Callian when the Germans occupied the town August 18th:

> We attacked isolated vehicles for about three days, and then all of a sudden I wake up in the morning and I see one of my buddies run up to the .50 caliber machine gun and he says: "Lou, look what's coming up the road!" There was more or less a battalion of Germans coming down the road and I told the guy: "Don't shoot, don't fire!" but he wasn't listening to me and he opened up. That road got cleared off in a hurry! I think he killed about 14 or 15 of them. So I said: "Okay listen, let's evacuate everybody and move them towards the town of Callian." We had a lot of walking wounded, broken ankles and sprained knees and stuff from the jump. So I ordered everybody to evacuate and they started heading towards the town of Callian. I stayed behind and held a rear guard action, and everybody got away but me. I was shooting down at the Germans; I killed maybe four or five coming up the side of the hill to the big wall we were hiding behind. I was firing at them, and all of a sudden a mortar goes off and slams me against the wall and puts a big hole in my right thigh. That kind of scared me, because the blood was squirting all over, as it had hit an artery. So I put a tourniquet on real fast and put my hands up to surrender, and they kept shooting at me, so I said: "I got to get inside the château." If I hadn't gotten inside the château they would probably have killed me for killing those Germans there. So I crawled over the wall, rolled down the hill to the château, and the last thing I remember was knocking on the door and then I passed out from loss of blood.
>
> I woke up and there were Germans all around me. I am lying on the cellar of the château and they were interrogating me, and I just kept saying: "Nix." The German major kicked me in the face because I lied to him. He asked me how many paratroops were in the hills and I said: "Oh, last time I counted them there was a thousand of them," and then he kicked me and knocked out a couple teeth. After that, the people in the house fed me a bowl of soup every day. They were very nice people. That was the extent of my little escapade there in southern France. The Germans held me for three or four days and then they

> finally decided to leave the area because the Americans were moving up real fast and surrounded the château. As soon as the Germans all got captured by the Americans, I made them bring all the prisoners in front of me. I was looking for that major, because my face was all bloody and my jaw was sore. I was mad. I would have killed him there if I had caught him, but he got away; he was an SS major.
>
> I got evacuated down to the beach. They operated on my leg right away because the Germans wanted to cut it off, and I said: "Nix." So I got evacuated all the way back to Italy. The morning of the jump I had stood over Miller, who was laying on the road with his back exposed from the ricochet, and I said: " Miller, I don't think you're going to make it." The funny experience was when I got evacuated off the beaches and shipped back to Italy to the hospital, I was in the same ward with Miller, and Miller's remark to me was: "Holzworth, I heard you saying that I wasn't going to make it, and here I am!"

For his actions in Callian, Louis Holzworth was awarded a well-deserved Silver Star, the citation of which read:

> For gallantry in action near Callian, France, 15 August 1944. After landing by parachute near a German supply route, Private First Class Holzworth organized and led a small group of Allied parachutists to a point from which they destroyed seven supply trucks, killing eleven of the enemy and causing many casualties. On the second day, the group was attacked by a large enemy force. Upon observing an attempt to outflank his position, Private First Class Holzworth moved to the cover of a ravine within one hundred yards of the approaching enemy. Opening fire, he killed four Germans and caused the rest to withdraw. While making his way back to his comrades, Private First Class Holzworth was seriously wounded by mortar fire. Realizing the futility of further resistance, he signaled his outnumbered comrades to retreat while he remained in position to delay the enemy. After the entire group had escaped, Private First Class Holzworth buried his weapons prior to being captured. Three days later he was freed by American troops. Private First Class Holzworth's outstanding courage is in keeping with the finest traditions of the military service.[15]

The attentive reader will have noted a certain number of discrepancies between the citation and other sources of information, as is usually the case. I have not been able to determine exactly what Château Louis Holzworth was in, because there are several châteaus (actually large houses) around Callian. However, **Jean Veyan**, from Callian, provides a good clue as to where Holzworth and his team may have been, as he seems to remember the exact same events as Holzworth:

> There was a castle called the Château Second, and from there, on the morning when the Germans were coming up the road to invade Callian, the Americans fired a complete band of machine gun ammunition at them, all 250 rounds at once. So the Germans got off the road and the Americans escaped. They delayed the Germans, since it dispersed them, but then they came up into the village.

Fernand Félix's father, an inhabitant of Callian, was involved in a similar (or perhaps the very same) action:

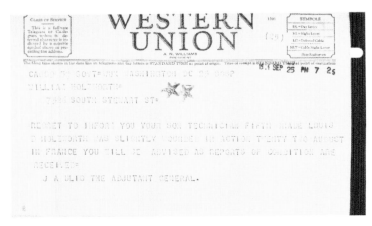

The telegram that Louis Holzworth's parents received informing them of the wounding of their son. Louis Holzworth Collection.

There was a machine gun in Callian that was being manned by First World War veterans. They were firing at the road below Callian. There was a column of 600 Germans. My father opened fire, but the Germans fired back with mortars. Because of the mortar fire, they had to escape. My father took the bolt out of the machine gun and they left.

Some of the paratroopers in Callian sent one last radio message to the 141st Infantry Regiment, noting at 18:40 on August 18th: "Group number 1 of paratroopers said they were being attacked and were smashing their radio this morning."[16] The after action report written by **Capt Richard Bigler**, of the Regimental HQ Company of the 517th PIR, also mentioned:

> Capt Hooper, S/Sgt Allison, and seven men (...) occupied the town of Callian for three days until driven out by a force of approximately 200 Germans. They then moved to Montauroux, which was held by Lt McElroy and 34 enlisted men.[17]

These period written sources help confirm what was remembered by PFC Holzworth and by the local French witnesses. As the Germans arrived, most of the inhabitants of Callian fled the area, fearing German reprisals, since the *Maquis* had been so active in the area and had even attacked an ambulance. **Jean Veyan** continues:

> Everybody was saying: "A column of Germans is coming up!" When the Americans arrived on the day of the landing, we had thought: "We are liberated, everything is over now!" But the Germans came back and all the men, and in fact the population left the villages. We left and lived in huts in the forest. There was a whole line of us escaping to go and hide in the country. We didn't have any weapons or anything and were in a clearing in the forest when a Lockheed flew over us. He flew around us twice, and the captain who was there with us, who was supposed to lead us but who was escaping like the rest of us, said: "Don't move." Luckily we didn't move; the plane flew around two or three times and dived at us to take a better look, then it left when it saw we were civilians.

When the Germans entered Callian, they found some of their wounded along with Allied wounded being cared for by the local doctor and civilians in the makeshift infirmary, and this may have helped prevent any escalation of violence. In any case, no reprisal or execution took place. The Germans were very nervous, however, because they knew they were in an area infested with partisans and lost paratroopers. **Louis Rival**, a teenager living in a large estate near the road leading up to Callian, saw the Germans searching for possible hidden enemies in the Camiole, a small local river surrounded by underbrush. (In southern France, most rivers are so small that the term creek would be more correct.):

> A group of Germans came back on foot and they inspected the inside of the house. They were probably searching for Americans who had been here for two or three days, but they didn't find them. So then they searched Camiole to see if any were hiding in the riverbed that was three-quarters dry. One young German soldier was standing in front of the kitchen window and I was in the kitchen looking at him. He was a boy who must have been one year older than me, about 18 years old,

very thin and blonde. He was standing there with all his equipment, keeping watch over the river. At one point he must have heard some footsteps and thought: "The Americans are down there." He grabbed a stick grenade that he had on his belt and lifted his arm to throw the grenade into the riverbed. At that moment he saw two of his colleagues emerging from the river. When he saw that, he was dumfounded for a second and the grenade exploded behind his head. He was killed on the spot. The other two came up, looked at him, and saw that he was dead. I don't know if they took his identification tag, I don't remember, but the poor guy stayed there for two days. For two days nobody touched him.

The Montauroux Ambush

At about the same time that they reoccupied Callian, the Germans also took possession of the nearby village of Montauroux. However, before they had retaken the town, one of their vehicles drove up towards the village on its own. Was this a reconnaissance team or a vehicle that got lost? We will probably never know, but **Raymond Carbonel** explains what happened to the vehicle on what, according to him, was August 17th, though this date cannot be verified:

> In the morning and early afternoon, the same things as the previous day occurred: lots of turmoil in the village, particularly in the Clos Square, and strafing of German convoys in the valley by Allied aircraft, since the troops that had landed on the coast still had not managed to reach us.
>
> In the late afternoon, things changed for the worst and a tragedy was narrowly avoided. Indeed, lookouts spotted a truck full of soldiers coming up towards the village by Chemin Chambarot. Immediately, a few Americans and FFIs set up a .50 caliber machine gun in the last house at the intersection of Rue Lacombe and Rue des Ecoles, on the downwards slope in the direction of the valley. Until recently, the loop hole that the weapons barrel was passed through was visible at the foot of the house's wall. (...)
>
> As soon as the truck (a Renault) was in range, the Americans and FFI opened fire. The truck stopped and

Louis Rival (at right) and Claude Bernard stand at the location where a German soldier accidentally killed himself with a grenade. The Camiole riverbed is visible to the left, while the window Louis Rival was standing in at the time is seen to the right. Author's Collection.

the Germans jumped out. All of them were shot. Eleven bodies lay on the ground once the firing ceased.

Having accomplished this act, and with the possibility of the Germans returning to the village in force, the Americans and FFI left the village. This departure was made in great confusion: a large amount of equipment, food, and cartridges were left behind. (…) They left, but the corpses of the soldiers, as well as the truck, remained in the middle of the road at the entrance of the village, and it was thus impossible for anybody arriving not to see them. Tragedy was never so near! (…) What would the reaction of German troops have been on finding the lifeless bodies of their comrades in a village where not a single combatant remained? It would probably have been very violent! Montauroux could have been changed into a field of rubble, with its houses burned and the civilian population massacred!

Luckily, a few men (not many were left in the village) with remarkable courage decided to erase all traces of the fight that had just occurred. Among them were three of my uncles, as well as Mr. Imbert, Mr. Bernard (…), and a few others. The corpses were loaded onto the truck, which was put back in working order by Mr. Bernard, and transported the bodies to the St Barthélémy ruins. There, a hole to contain the bodies was dug in great haste at the left angle of the wall. (…)

My uncles, who had not wanted me to participate in the gathering of the bodies because of my young age, asked me to act as a lookout at the corner of Rue Mirabeau and Rue Rouguière. This operation occurred without any incidents, but the last shovelfuls of earth had hardly been thrown onto the grave when German trucks transporting troops (around 30 men I believe) came into the village and stopped in the Clos Square. These Germans didn't notice anything!

We could thank Providence from the depths of our hearts… but could especially thank the anonymous brave who had – I say it loud and clear – accomplished the most heroic act of the liberation of Montauroux, that is, to have saved our village from almost certain total destruction.[18]

One of the *maquisard*s who participated in the shooting was **Marcel Guerrin**. He explains a few extra details about the shooting:

We were on guard duty. The chief's *maquis* name was Durandal, and there was Eli Gallo from Montauroux and another guy from St Cézaire whom we never saw again. We were in a shelter talking because we weren't expecting to shoot anybody, and all of a sudden that truck came along. Durandal said "Halt," and the truck stopped. Then he fired, the truck moved backwards, and as of that point everybody opened fire. We fired into the mass without aiming because they were getting out of the truck going: "Raus, Raus, Raus!"

We had an American machine gun that fired seven or eight rounds and then it jammed. The ammunition belt was made of cloth, and when we brought the gun down from the *maquis* on a truck we must have bumped it and it jammed. So we only had submachine guns left. There were Americans in the Clos Square and when they heard the shooting they came along. There was even a German who had climbed up on the wall and was going to throw a grenade. An American shot him with his rifle and the grenade exploded in his hands. The German was blown to

pieces. Nobody picked up his body, and he remained on the wall for months.

When everything was over, we went to inspect the damage. There were 11 dead in a pile, and one or two Germans had run away. There was an irrigation ditch there with a pile of Germans in it, and the water was flowing over them.

The American who was present at the scene and who shot the German who was about to throw a grenade was apparently 1st Lt McElroy, of G Company of the 517th PIR. Unfortunately, the only trace of this event that is to be found from American sources is a highly distorted and simplified version written by **Captain Grant Hooper**, commanding officer of G Company, in the after action report about the landing (In his report, Capt Hooper systematically referred to Montauroux as Callian.):

1st Lt McElroy had jumped at Callian and went patrolling to assemble other paratroopers. The column moved out while he was still patrolling through the hills. As he moved in towards Callian to rejoin the troops, he engaged the Germans in a fire fight. He killed five and was lightly wounded himself when he shot one who had pulled the pin on a grenade.[19]

Many of the locals went to see the dead Germans once they had been piled back into the truck they had arrived in. **Jean Veyan** was one of them:

I went to Montauroux and was told: "There is a truck that has just been machine gunned." I remember having seen the truck on the Church Square with the dead guys in it, with their long hair that was hanging. That disturbed me. It was a disaster.

Thirteen-year-old **Hélène Carbonel**, who lived nearby, also saw the bodies:

From left to right: Captain Grant Hooper, 1st Lt McElroy, and 2nd Lt Howard Hensleigh, all officers of the 3rd Battalion of the 517th PIR who were mentioned in this chapter. Hooper landed in St Cézaire, where he found himself completely isolated, and it was only after several days that he reached the Fayence-Montauroux area, in which McElroy had remained to fight with the FFI since August 15th. Howard Hensleigh Collection.

There was a man there and I asked him: "Jeannot, what are all the people looking at?" I was curious. He said: "It's the Germans. Do you want to see them?" I said yes, but maybe it was a mistake, because I shouldn't have looked at them. There was a tarpaulin and it had been removed, so I looked, but I left quickly because it was nauseating.

The shooting made a deep impression on **Claude Bernard**. Although his memories of it are possibly distorted because of his young age at the time, his usual blunt honesty make his description of the scene particularly worthwhile:

What I remember is a bunch of adults boiling with excitement, not paying attention to the kids anymore. I was always escaping from my parents because I was a real rascal, and I found myself going to the place where the truck was being attacked. People had said: "There is a truck coming, they are going to attack it, they are going to attack it!" I could hear the gunshots and everything, but it was in a curve, so I couldn't see them. At that moment, I have a very clear recollection: a guy came out and said: "It's all over, I killed all of them. They were morons because they were surrendering and one of them pulled out a grenade to throw it at us. The grenade exploded among them. There were some wounded, but by then they had us so worked up by not wanting to surrender that I killed them with my submachine gun." He had a Sten gun, and on the tip of the Sten were woolen versions of Nenette and Rintintin [Nenette and Rintintin were good luck symbols dating from WWI, often made into miniature good luck charms.]. I had found that guy was really the hero of the day, because he had a weapon with that decoration and he had killed all the Germans.

Everybody followed him and the truck was driven into Clos Square. We were looking and saw that it was filled with bodies, so the kids and everybody were running after the truck. We were happy, saying to each other: "The Germans, the Germans! We killed all of them!" As the truck was advancing blood was dripping out behind it. The truck stopped in Clos Square and all the kids who were there, including me, jumped onto the truck and walked on the bodies. We wanted to see the "wild beasts," you understand? And then I had a very precise memory of a young blonde soldier: he had long blonde hair, as blonde as wheat. We didn't see any people like that around us. He was really extraordinarily blonde. I am mentioning that because I later spoke to a person who told me: "I helped load the Germans into the truck and I remember one young soldier who was as blonde as wheat." I always thought that the mother of that poor blonde soldier had never seen him again.

The truck remained on the square, causing a commotion, and after a while somebody drove the truck up to the Church Square. I wanted to go there too, but they didn't let me, I was too small. So I went back to my parents and my mother held on to me, not wanting me to go. I could see people coming back down with things they had taken up there. One guy had the truck driver's ammunition pouch, for example, and you could see that it had been hit by a bullet, causing the cartridges to explode, and that is probably what had killed the guy. Another guy had a helmet and others had other things, things that I also absolutely wanted to have. My mother was holding me,

preventing me from going, but at one moment she turned her head and I ran off at full speed and went up to the church square. I remember very well all the soldiers lined up in front of the chapel with their heads towards the wall and they were naked. It was the first time in my life that I saw naked men. That had been done to make it impossible for them to be identified as German soldiers. I was there by myself and was a bit frightened.

When that was done the *Maquis* left. The Germans were down on the highway and the *résistants* said: "Lets pull out." They all left and the villagers took care of the bodies. My father, Paul Richier, Jules Court, and Raymond Carbonel dug a hole in the fortress and piled all the soldiers into that hole.

According to eight-year-old **André Christoff**, who was working in the fields below Montauroux, at least three Germans managed to escape from the scene of the ambush:

One day I was with my father and my brother, and we saw a truck of Germans going up. We knew the Americans were in the village that day, so we figured there was going to be a fight. Not even five minutes later, just as the truck reached the entrance of the village, we heard bursts of machine gun fire. We had some bullets fly over us because we were just below, approximately in the direction of the truck. The fire fight lasted for quite a while, and after a bit we saw two Germans who had escaped and who were running back down the road. At one point they stopped and knelt down, and they were looking at what was going on at the entrance of the village, where the gunfire was quieting down. Then they went on their way and disappeared. About an hour or two later, my father went up to the village, and he found a German who had both eyes gouged out.

Raymond Carbonel saw this severely wounded German being brought to Captain Walter Plassman's infirmary in Montauroux:

That afternoon, I had the first vision of the war in all its horror in front of my eyes for the first time. A cart pushed by three or four armed FFI men passed by our

"All the soldiers were lined up in front of the chapel with their heads towards the wall and they were naked." The St Barthélémy chapel, behind which the eleven German soldiers killed in the Montauroux ambush were buried. Author's Collection.

door. A young blonde German soldier was sitting on it, his hands clenched to the guardrails. He must have been about the same age as myself. He was swaying his head right and left, like a metronome, with blood dribbling off at every movement. He had no more face: his mouth, his nose, his eyes were nothing but red and bloody mush. Apparently, grenade fragments had blown off his face.

He was brought to the Prieuré [infirmary], and a few years later I found out he had been filled with morphine and that he had died during the night. It is my most atrocious memory of that period.[20]

After the war, the French Veterans Administration performed an exhumation at the site where the bodies had been buried.[21] They found 11 bodies, of which not a single one could be identified, probably because their identification tags and perhaps their clothes had been removed before burial, just as Claude Bernard claims. The French also exhumed two other unidentified German bodies from an unknown location in Montauroux. These were probably the bodies of soldiers who had died in the infirmary, such as the disfigured soldier. Because none of these 13 bodies were identified, and because the French exhumation team did not document its work properly, it has been impossible to do any research on this event from the German side. The unfortunate truckload of German soldiers simply disappeared into history once they made the mistake of driving up to the village of Montauroux on their own.

The Recapture of the Fayence-Montauroux Area by the Americans

The Germans had hardly recaptured Callian August 18th when elements of the 636th Tank Destroyer Battalion drove up the road from Bagnols, coming into view of Callian. These troops were on an advanced reconnaissance mission, and in fact they were so far advanced beyond the American lines that they were greeted to the area by friendly fire from both American artillery and aircraft! The journal of the 636th TDB noted:

The second platoon of Reconnaissance Company, while on its patrol mission, was strafed by four P-47 Thunderbolts at approximately 1200 hours (…). One armored car and two quarter tons [trucks] were destroyed, while one officer, **1st Lt Paul R. McKee** (…), was killed by machine gun fire from the planes. The Reconnaissance Platoon utilized yellow smoke prior to the second strafing, but three of the planes strafed a second time. At about 1315, the 937th Field Artillery Battalion placed fire on the Reconnaissance

44-year-old OberGefreiter Jakob Bock died in unknown circumstances in Bagnols en Forêt, where his body was found buried after the war. Presumably he was killed by partisans. His official date of death is known only as September 1944. Josefine Kaltenbach Collection.

A view of Callian (at left) and Montauroux (at right), demonstrating how the two villages dominate the Camiole Valley. Author's Collection.

Company command post, which was located in St Paul. This fire was finally brought under control and stopped after the Battalion S-2 contacted the Liaison Officer with the firing unit, who relayed the message to the Division Artillery and all artillery battalions possible, notifying them that friendly troops were in St Paul.[22]

Thirty-three-year-old Paul McKee had been working in artist Emory P. Seidel's studio in Chicago before enlisting, and considered him such a good friend that Seidel was listed as the emergency contact on McKee's dog tag and as the beneficiary for his insurance. Friendly fire accidents were very common, as we will see further on in this book. We will briefly get off the topic of Callian to mention another terrible friendly fire accident that happened at Bagnols two days later on the 20th, and was witnessed by local resident **Elianne Gouarin**:

> **Jean Raymond Dias** was ten years old and was playing, and we were sitting in front of the house. An American soldier was cleaning his rifle and the rifle started falling. The kid was right there in front of him, and when the American tried to catch his rifle, the shot went off and the kid was killed at point blank range. His mother was at the window, and when she saw her child, she started screaming. My mother immediately brought us into our house. Everybody was completely shocked that something like that had happened.

Raymond Carbonel was in German-occupied Montauroux on the 18th and tells of the artillery duels that occurred as the American units that had landed on the coast drew nearer:

> From the intensity of the gunfire coming from the sea, we could tell that the front was getting closer and that the Allied troops were not far away from us. In the village, the Germans were alert. They had a French 75mm cannon with them that they moved around the streets by hand. (…) At every halt the cannon fired two or three times, then would relocate somewhere else. On the one hand, the Germans wanted to give the impression that there were many of them and that they had artillery, and on the other hand, they wanted to avoid being detected by the Allied airplanes that were constantly flying over the village.
>
> We were lacking water at home. Since the beginning of events, the distribution of drinking water had been severely reduced due to that summer's drought and the damage inflicted by the fighting on the canal that supplied the village. In the late morning, my uncle Maurice and I went out with a can to go and fill it at the fountain. We were then caught by a bombardment. Shells were passing over our heads. (…) Metal fragments slammed onto the street and all around us. We dropped our can and ran into the hallway of the house of our friend Marcel Rouvier to take cover. (…) A young German soldier had gotten there before us! All three of us pulled our heads further down between our shoulders at every explosion. My father's friend, Mr Charles Rouvier, then came and joined us. With words, but mostly by gesture, he tried to make the young German soldier understand that it would be best for him to surrender. Finally, he understood. He shook his head negatively several times, repeating: "Nein… Nein… Offizier… Offizier…" We understood that his fear of his officer was greater than his instinctive fear. The shelling having calmed down, we went back to the

fountain to pick up our water can and the young soldier went off to his own destiny![23]

Meanwhile, in the afternoon of the 18th, plans were being made by the Americans to attack Callian and Fayence the next day. A small task force named Task Force Eitt (Named after Major Herbert Eitt, of the 141st IR) was to attack and capture both towns as of daylight on August 19th, then contact the stranded paratroopers and set up defensive positions.[24] The task force was composed mainly of B and E Companies of the 141st IR and of two platoons belonging to the Reconnaissance Company and to B Company of the 636th TDB. Small detachments of machine gunners, mortar men, and medical personnel were also provided by the 141st IR.

The next day, August 19th, Task Force Eitt advanced towards Callian against slight opposition. However, as they got near the actual village of Callian, they started encountering more determined Germans, in particular those of the 14th Antitank Company of *Reserve Grenadier Regiment 8*. One of the tank destroyers of B Company of the 636th TDB was hit by antitank fire outside Callian in the early afternoon, killing **1st Lt Robert L. Dodson**.[25] At least two civilians (**Osvald Panichi** and 64-year-old **Arthur Poulle**) were also killed by artillery fire. B and I Companies of the 141st IR then attacked the town. **Raymond Carbonel** witnessed the attack from a rooftop in Montauroux, watching through a pair of binoculars:

> On the highway in the valley there were practically no more convoys. On the other hand, an artillery duel had started between one or several German cannons that must have been located beneath Callian and American cannons that must have been hidden in the forest along the road going to Bagnols. I could distinctly hear the German cannons fire, and immediately afterwards (it must have been small caliber cannons) I would see mounds of dirt being kicked up in the fields beside the road.
>
> Suddenly, I saw groups of infantry men running out of the forest, forming skirmish lines as soon as they got out of the cover. I saw them running, then lying down when a German salvo would explode near them, then getting up and running, and so forth. At last it was the Americans who were reaching us, four days after having landed on the coast.
>
> I watched them with my binoculars until they reached the Callian-Draguignan road junction, at which point I regretfully had to stop my observation, as the neighboring house cutting off my field of vision.[26]

Lt Carl Strom was commanding B Company of the 141st IR as it entered Callian:

> I was in command of the company at the time we moved into Callian. We came in on the western side of the town and it was quite a hill up to the town itself. Sgt Gregor was going down one of the streets, and all of a sudden this German popped around the corner and shot him in the arm, then backed around the building out of sight. Of course, we immediately started taking care of Sgt Gregor and in the meantime, some of the other men went down and the Germans then were pretty much just surrendering, because they realized that we had them beaten. So when these half dozen or so Germans were brought up by our guys, why, Sgt Gregor recognized the German who had shot him. We let him give him a couple of blows, then we put him in with the rest of the prisoners. He was so mad at that German!

LT. BOBBY DODSON
. . , killed August 19 in France

Bobby, son of Mrs. Nola Mae Britt of Beeville and Eugene V. Dodson of Carrizo Springs, was born in Colorado April 1, 1921. He finished high school here and starred in the Trojan backfield, although he was perhaps the smallest (in height) of any man in any game in which he participated. He showed the fighting spirit in those games which later asserted itself on the fields of battle against the enemy and which brought high praise from his commanding officers.

He married Miss Bobby Lou Walton in Beeville on October 9, 1941, the ceremony being said in the Christian Church, of which he was a member.

Surviving, besides his wife and parents, are a brother, Eugene V. Dodson, and two nieces, Patsy Jean and Ruthy Mae Dodson, all of Bloomington.

Lt. Bobby Dodson Killed in Action In France Aug. 19

First Lieutenant Robert Louis Dodson, 23, of Beeville was killed in action in France on August 19, but the telegram announcing his death was not received here by his wife, Mrs. Bobby Lou Dodson, until a month later—September 19. No details were given.

Lt. Dodson had been in the thick of the fighting through Italy and into France, and was awarded the Silver Star for gallantry in action while serving with a tank destroyer company in Italy in the fighting there late in 1943. At that time he was a staff sergeant, but had since been promoted twice on the fields of battle.

Bobby left Beeville with the National Guard company in December, 1940, serving at Camp Bowie, Brownwood, and other camps before being sent overseas in February, 1943. He was in Africa prior to the invasion of Italy, in which he participated, and had remained there until early August, as his last letter to his wife, was sent from Italy and dated August 6. She was not aware he was in France until the telegram arrived Tuesday. He had been in the 5th Army in Italy.

23-year-old 1st Lt Robert L. Dodson, B Company, 636th TDB, from Beeville, Texas, was killed when his tank-destroyer was hit by antitank fire during the attack on Callian. Dodson Family Collection. Obituary Courtesy Shirley Garcia.

We had only the one man who was wounded and we captured about 15 to 20 Germans. I know they had one or two killed. But actually it was a piece of cake, a very easy thing, because those Germans really didn't want to fight. At one point, there I was overdoing a little scouting job on my own and I came past some bushes and two Germans jumped out with their hands up, surrendering to me. They left their rifles and stuff in the bushes. They were happy to have the opportunity to surrender at the time.

There were about four or five wounded paratroopers in the basement of one of the buildings. They had a couple of their medics there with them and some of the local people were there too, giving them first aid, feeding them, and taking care of them.

The radio communication log of the 141st IR gives good information about the attack and shows that things were tougher for I Company of the 141st than they had been for B Company and Lt Strom. The fighting in Callian ended up lasting until the next day, causing the attack on Fayence to be cancelled:

Sgt Stanley J. Gregor, B Company, 141st IR, from Belleville, Texas, was shot through the arm during the attack on Callian. Carl Strom Collection.

17:25. 19 August: "We have made contact with group number 3 of wounded paratroopers. Attack is progressing. 12 wounded paratroopers in town."

17:45. 19 August: "We are only 600 yards from the center of town. Fighting is still stiff, but we expect the town to fall fast when it does."

19:45. 19 August: "Advise commanding officer not to go for Fayence until further notice."

20:43. 19 August: "We have taken the town of Callian and are awaiting further orders."

20:50. 19 August: "From I Company: men in tall buildings are dropping grenades from buildings. We have one tank in town. Another tank is knocked out. We do not know the number of our casualties.[27]

One tank destroyer had been put out of action by a mine while approaching Callian from the west, and 23-year-old **SSgt Dudley Hudson** (I Company) was mortally wounded by a gunshot to the chest. When B Company requested contact with I Company, they received the following reply: "He will have to contact me, because it is too damn hot here with sniper fire and potato masher grenades."[28] Company I finally pulled out of the part of town that it had conquered so that it could be shelled in order to discourage the last German defenders. However, the Germans remained active, and there was still fighting going on in Callian the next morning, August 20th, when **Lt Howard Hensleigh**, of the 517th PIR, was sent there to retrieve the wounded paratroopers who had been found in town:

Early in the morning, Frank Longo and I drove to Callian in an old black French sedan furnished by Colonel Graves to get our jump casualties to the field hospital. Some of our troopers who did not join us in the march to the drop zone were in town doing a mop-up operation with the 141st Infantry Regiment. The Germans still had a few troops in town and we were shooting at each other when we got a target. So Callian was really liberated by the 141st with a little help from our troopers who remained in the area after the jump.

A Callian lady told me our jump casualties had been moved to Montauroux and a man in Callian volunteered to go with me to get me "in through a back door." The 141st IR was about to attack Montauroux, and I asked the Colonel to give me an SCR 300 radio, and that I would go into the town because our jump casualties were there and I would let him know what the situation was. His order to put artillery on it would have knocked all the roofs off the houses in Montauroux. I went in with the Frenchman. We were fired on with artillery when we were about halfway over there and got into a culvert to protect ourselves. We then went on into Montauroux and the Germans were just leaving town. We could hear their vehicles and everything. Captain Plassman, our Battalion Surgeon, was in white hospital uniform and was in charge of the small medical clinic with all of our jump casualties. There were 14 or 15 of them. He had treated some of the German casualties and they left him there without taking any of our men with them. I then called up the Colonel of the 141st and said: "You can come on into Montauroux without firing a shot and I need an ambulance to get my jump casualties off to a hospital." So they came on in, and they furnished me an ambulance and we got all the jump casualties into it and sent them off to the hospital.

August 19th, orders had come through that the 517th PIR was to advance from le Muy to relieve the 141st IR in the Fayence-Montauroux region on the 20th, so that the 141st could be pulled out of the area. Lt Howard Hensleigh's 3rd Battalion of the 517th PIR was to replace the 141st IR in Callian (which ironically the 3rd Battalion had left only five days before) in the following hours, so **Howard Hensleigh** returned to Callian in order to help flush out the last German defenders of the town:

We heard that the battalion was headed for Callian, so Longo and I did some of the cleanup work with Joe Grazzaffi, from the regimental S-2 section. A German sniper hidden in some bushes grazed a 517th lieutenant in the butt. I spotted him and Joe emptied his carbine clip on the bush. The German came out bleeding from several wounds with his hands up.

A radio message from the 141st in the early afternoon of the 20th confirms that Montauroux was found unoccupied and that there was still fighting going on in Callian over 24 hours after the attack had started:

14:32. August 20th: "A patrol entered Montauroux and found it unoccupied. Paratroopers will relieve the patrol. Callian is still occupied, but we have entered the town and are now in the process of mopping up.[29]

Another paratrooper who helped the 141st clean out the last Germans from Callian was **T5 James Bryant**. He was awarded a Silver Star, the citation (which was mistakenly dated August 21st instead of August 20th) of which read:

In the attack on Callian, Technician Bryant, an officer, and two enlisted men became separated from the main force due to heavy fire by the enemy. Sniper fire from a building severely wounded one of the enlisted men. Technician Bryant immediately charged into the building, only to be driven out again during the ensuing fight. Several grenades were thrown by one of the enemy, wounding Technician Bryant. Technician Bryant fired into the building and killed the German. He was again fired upon by two enemy soldiers, and Technician Bryant killed one with his pistol and captured the other. Using the captured soldier as a shield, he moved away from the building through intense small arms fire from the enemy in the surrounding houses. Technician Bryant returned the fire, wounding one German who screamed several times in a loud hysterical voice. The enemy, believing themselves surrounded by a superior force, immediately surrendered. Technician Bryant's gallant actions resulted in the killing of two of the enemy and the capture of one major, two lieutenants, one warrant officer, and 24 enlisted men.[30]

A radio communication from the 141st IR brings partial confirmation to this story, and indicates that the fighting in Callian finally ended on the afternoon of the 20th:

16:55. 20 August: "What shall we do with PWs and wounded? We have taken a Major, 4 Captains, and 135 PWs. We have 50 German wounded."[31]

Office of Strategic Services Actions at la Roche

Now that Callian and Montauroux had fallen, the only German force remaining in the area was the group of stubborn Germans in la Roche, at Fayence, who had resisted the *Maquis* attacks described earlier in the chapter. Since August 15th, a large number of retreating Germans had taken position in Fayence, where they were now under command of Major Paul Tornow,[32] the commanding officer of *Reserve Grenadier Bataillon 327*, the unit which had been sent towards Draguignan August 15th and had been strafed by Allied airplanes at la Colle Noire. With Callian and Montauroux in American hands and strong Resistance forces positioned north of Fayence, the defenders of la Roche were pretty much surrounded; however, they kept defending themselves during the day of August 20th.

A German helmet that was abandoned in the Fayence-Montauroux area. The helmet is covered by a chicken wire mesh that was used as a makeshift camouflage net. Such camouflage improvisations were very popular among soldiers of Reserve Division 148. Private Collection.

Task Force Eitt was supposed to have attacked Fayence on the 19th, but had not done so because of the resistance found in Callian. Now that the 517th PIR was relieving the 141st IR, it would be the responsibility of the 517th PIR to capture Fayence. Usually, the relieving of units led to a certain amount of confusion, since the new unit did not know the area yet, and this is exactly what happened when the 517th relieved the 141st. A Silver Star citation to **Lt John Neiler**, who had just been named Intelligence Officer of the 517th, explains what happened to him as he entered his newly-assigned area 20 August, unknowingly getting a bit too close to Fayence and its German defenders:

Lt Neiler had established a forward command post and had just completed the unloading of equipment and supplies when the enemy attacked the position with heavy and light machine gun and 20 millimeter antitank gunfire. Lt Neiler, after ordering everyone to take cover, and with complete disregard for his own safety, exposed himself to enemy fire to determine any possible means of escape. Leading his men to a deep ravine from which they could return to the rear area, Lt Neiler and two men returned to the evacuated position to recover the vehicles and equipment left there. While waiting for darkness, Lt Neiler observed a company of friendly troops advancing in full view and direct fire of the enemy. Again exposing himself, he rushed out into the open and warned the friendly troops in time for them to find cover before the enemy opened fire. When the enemy opened fire, Lt Neiler and his men, taking advantage of the confusion, loaded the vehicles with the equipment and supplies and drove away. Lt Neiler's courage and coolness under fire undoubtedly saved many lives and much valuable equipment.[33]

Lt Howard Hensleigh was sent off to serve as a guide to one company of the 517th PIR that had lost its way and ended up in a similar situation:

Major Paxton sent me down the road that runs west of Fayence to redirect one of the companies that got off on the wrong road. I said: "Well, you know the Germans occupy Fayence?" and he said: "Oh no, that road is clear." So I started down there, and they started firing 20mm rounds at me, so I pulled in behind a big truck. They hit the truck several times but didn't hit the car, and I crawled out of the car down into a ditch. I looked up and saw that there was a beautiful jeep sitting there. The only trouble was all the tires were flat, but the rest of it looked like it was in good shape, so I crawled up and into the jeep, and without sitting up or anything I made sure it wasn't in gear and I turned the switch. The key was right in it and the jeep started right up, so I jumped up in the seat and ran it off the embankment. The Germans were firing at me but they missed.

The 517th then attempted to find out exactly what was waiting for them in Fayence, so **1st Lt Walter Irvin** was sent out on reconnaissance. The citation of the Silver Star he received describes his action (this citation is also misdated August 21st instead of August 20th):

During an attack by his battalion on the town of Fayence, France, the advance companies came under intense enemy 20 millimeter and automatic weapons fire. These weapons were so well concealed that it was impossible to locate them. Lt Irvin, leading a patrol into town to locate the guns, had advanced only 600 yards when enemy 20 millimeter cannon fire forced them to take cover. Proceeding alone for a distance of approximately one mile under automatic enemy fire, Lt Irvin entered the town. Moving from building to building for over an hour, he succeeded in locating two enemy 20 millimeter guns, well concealed and heavily guarded by riflemen. After sketching their location, he proceeded to withdraw to his patrol, but was discovered by the enemy, who opened fire with automatic rifles and pistols. With disregard of the enemy fire, Lt Irvin returned to his patrol and then proceeded to the unit assembly area, giving the location of the enemy weapons to the artillery. At once the artillery fired on the enemy positions, knocking them out, thus making it possible for the unit to advance and capture the town.[34]

Medal citations usually present a rather exaggerated version of events, and we will soon see that Lt Irvin's actions alone were not sufficient to enable Fayence to be captured. A more realistic description of the situation in Fayence the afternoon of August 20th is made by local French medical doctor **Angelin German**, from Draguignan. He had been working with the Resistance during the Occupation and drove from Draguignan to Fayence when he found out there were many wounded there in need of evacuation:

Late on the night of August 19th, I receive a visit from messengers of the Fayence-Montauroux *Maquis*, who inform me that the American shelling has wounded many people in the village of Fayence. I decide to go and get them. To reward my team (…), which has not had a minute of rest [since August 15th] for its marvelous work, I bring them with me as well, on August 20th, at seven in the morning, in the direction of Fayence, driving on the "Route de Grasse" [the local name given to D562], hoping to give my colleagues half a day of well-deserved fresh air.

A few kilometers before Fayence, on the "Route de Grasse," we realize that the road has been cut by numerous felled trees. This action by local *maquisards* forces us to turn back. To reach Fayence, we need to drive through the village of Broves and over the pass at the Borigaille estate; in other words, reaching Fayence from the north. We thus reach the estate, where we meet one hundred or so armed *maquisards* after a long drive over very precarious paths.

A French captain who had parachuted in the previous morning has taken command. Unfortunately, he broke a leg on landing. I examine him and urgently apply a splint on his leg, advising that he should be brought to Draguignan as soon as possible for definitive treatment [This was probably Lt Tevenac, who we will say more about in the next pages]. I then inform the *maquisards* that I have come to evacuate the wounded in the village of Fayence. They call me a madman, because the village is completely occupied by a battalion of Germans with a field battery. Even so, I decide to proceed, driving extremely slowly, of course.

We approach to within 200 or 300 meters of the first houses by a dirt path. A road block has been made in the middle of the path with two carts that are blocking the way, and all along the path there are quite deep foxholes, each containing a German soldier. When they see us come they take aim, but the first one doesn't fire, and neither do the others. Maybe they had doubts because the ambulance was a German vehicle, though we had put a French flag on the right side and a Red Cross flag on the left side.

I ring the bell that all ambulances have, and we slowly bypass the road block and drive through the village, reaching the esplanade that dominates the entire region, where I know the local physician, Dr Talent, has his medical office.

We reach this position that dominates the whole area. A battery of four field cannons (Austrian 88s I believe) is firing at the Americans. There are a large number of Germans. At that moment the village doctor arrives. It is not Dr Talent, because he left on vacation a few days before the landing. It is his replacement, Dr Pendaries from Marseille, who welcomes me and brings me to several nearby garages.

The garage is filled with numerous wounded who are lying on mattresses. There are about 20 of them, including five very severe cases, in other words, with compound fractures or abdominal wounds. Among them are both civilians and German soldiers.

In accordance with my colleague, I decide to first take the most severely wounded with me. We thus install five wounded on five stretchers and we fill up all the available space in the ambulance with wounded who are less severely hit. Everything is happening as well as could be. I repeat, there are Germans among the wounded. The ambulance is ready to leave when the German officer commanding the detachment [perhaps Major Paul Tornow] arrives, forbidding us to leave.

I try to explain myself, which is difficult, since I only know a bit of German, and claim that some of the wounded are hit very severely and that they will die if they are not operated on as soon as possible. Miraculously, a woman of Polish origin who is married to a Frenchman and who is older than us, perhaps 45, arrives at that moment. She approaches and interprets for us, since she speaks German perfectly. Despite the explanations that I give and that are translated by the woman, the officer continues to refuse to let us go, because he had been instructed by his general staff never to trust *maquisard*s. They were certain that prisoners captured by the *maquisard*s would be executed, in other words "assassinated" in reprisal, just as the German soldiers had done with our companions who had been captured.

Of course, I oppose his reasoning. I assure him that the next day I will come back in person with an official certificate proving that I placed all the German wounded under the care of German doctors. The officer keeps refusing to let us leave. I thus make the following decision: I enter the officer's office that is nearby. I am dressed in white, and I inform him that I will stay there as a hostage until it is confirmed that the wounded have arrived at their proper destination.

The officer is obviously very bothered. He walks around the ambulance for a good fifteen minutes, discussing with the woman, who is named Mme Jaffard. Unfortunately time goes by, and it is already late afternoon when he finally decides to let us go.

We get back to Draguignan at nightfall. I have to add that while exiting the village from behind, we are exposed and fired on by the American artillery, which luckily misses us completely. A detail that is amusing in retrospect: Mme Cazelles, who was sitting beside me, was saying: "Ring the bell German [remember the name of the witness is Dr Angelin German]!" as if the Americans who were some 20 kilometers away could hear the sound of our alarm. I burst out laughing, but to make her happy, I ring the ambulance's bell. We got back to Draguignan without any further incidents.

The next morning, around 7 o'clock I go back to retrieve the remaining wounded. That is when I had the greatest fright of my life. On the path that we had used the previous day, loaded down with five severely wounded and a good dozen other lightly wounded, plus us five in the cabin, I see a group of American soldiers who are just finishing digging up about 50 mines: big ones, small ones, and fat anti-tank ones! None of them had exploded when we drove over them! It was another lucky day!

When I arrive in the village with my ambulance, I am told that the Germans surrendered to the Americans in the early morning, at about 5 or 6 o'clock. I am certain that Mme Jaffard played a very important role in this surrender.[35]

Indeed, in the meantime, Madame Germaine Michel-Jaffard had put the German officer into contact with an Office of Strategic Services (OSS, the precursor of the CIA) team that had convinced the Germans to surrender. To explain what happened, we will have to go back to the night of August 13-14, 1944, when OSS "Team Sceptre," consisting of Lt Walter C. Hanna (American), Lt F. Tevenac (French), and 1st Sgt Howard Palmer (American), took off from Blida, Algeria, with the mission of parachuting into the Maritime Alps, near the Italian border, in order stimulate the local resistance there. However, the airplane dropped them no less than 70 miles from their intended target, and they ended up landing in rocky hills north of Fayence, where Lt Tevenac broke his foot and Sgt Palmer sprained his leg. The small team made the best of the situation and got in touch with the local resistance groups that unsuccessfully attacked la Roche August 15th. The team later reported its opinion of the quality of the local *maquis*:

The resistance in the area was not well organized. The only things that seemed to have been done were distribution of arms by S.A.P. and the formation of local uncoordinated *Maquis*. The *Maquis* tended to accept what the resistance had to give from the point of view of "modus vivendi," but when it came to action a certain proportion would not fight.[36]

After the parachute invasion of August 15th had occurred, several lost soldiers of the 517th PIR joined up with the OSS team. As the fighting around la Roche continued, Team Sceptre exchanged several radio messages with its headquarters in Algeria (code named Spoc) describing the local situation. The contents of the messages is sometimes surprisingly nonchalant, considering the difficulties and risks that each transmission implied:

17 August. From Sceptre. "We are fighting with 200 *maquis* in area on Fayence against approximately 400 Germans with Fayence stationed in strong fortress. Also, we are attempting to block all German withdrawals (…). Germans very unhappy here. Have a prisoner who volunteered to become camp barber.

18 August. From Spoc to Sceptre. "Terrific news. You are doing exactly what is wanted. Keep Germans as unhappy as possible. Let the prisoner cut your hair but not your throat. Your signals are perfect. Congratulations and keep it up."

19 August. From Sceptre. "Withdrawal of Germans through this section becoming uncomfortable. Many on foot moving north through area Callas, Fayence, Montauroux. Trucks and troop carriers beginning to move north from Frejus up to cross roads one mile south of Fayence. (…)[37]

The report written on Team Sceptre described how they ended up meeting with Major Tornow, the commander of *Reserve Grenadier Bataillon 327*, to arrange the surrender that occurred in Fayence the morning of August 21st:

> The German soldiers in this area were demoralized – the organization was the worst the team had seen. There was no plan for withdrawal. Some of the Germans had even thrown their arms away. Some kept them only because they were afraid of the *maquis*.

> 21 August. It was thought that there were about 400 Germans [in Fayence] (…). The American army was advancing from the south at this time. That evening, the city [Fayence] was subjected to artillery fire – 80mm mortars. So Lieutenant Hanna sent a message into the city, asking the Germans to send a representative to discuss a surrender.

> In the message he had informed the Germans that they would be surrendering to American troops. Actually, the only Americans there were Lt. Hanna, his radio operator, and the parachutists they had picked up. The spot chosen for the meeting was really too near the city, since all during the meeting shells were falling all around them. However, the few Americans were spread around the rendezvous as well as possible to give the impression of numbers.

> There was some doubt as to whether the German representative would come, but at the appointed time he arrived in a Red Cross car. They presented the terms of the surrender to him and at first he was reluctant to accept them. However, after being told that his group would be wiped out if he didn't accept them, he agreed. The artillery firing was used to substantiate their bluff. The team assured him that the firing would stop when he surrendered. Actually, Lt. Hanna had no idea as to where the firing was coming from, but two of his group were sent out in an attempt to locate it.

35-year-old Major Paul Tornow, commanding officer of Reserve Grenadier Bataillon 327, who surrendered himself and approximately 200 of his men to OSS Team Sceptre and the 517th PIR in Fayence August 21, 1944. NARA.

> The German representative had been brought out by a Red Cross lady who was a resistance leader in Fayence [Germaine Michel-Jaffard]. One of the parachutists accompanied them back to the city, and it was agreed that upon his return – which would mean the safe return of the driver, too – the firing would stop. Lt Hanna added, however, that there were some groups it would be difficult to contact, so if any firing continued, it would come from these sources. Luckily, the firing ceased just about the time the parachutist returned and there was no more that night.

> In order to take 400 prisoners, Lt Hanna decided [to locate men of the 517th PIR to help take the prisoners]. Some of the group went out to try and locate some in the vicinity, but returned shortly with word that there were only 10 in a patrol and that they couldn't leave. Lt Hanna decided that if there were 10, there must be more close by, so he set out himself and found a battalion which had just arrived that day. The executive officer of the group turned out to be a friend of Lt Hanna's, so assistance was obtained immediately. He promised him a platoon, but the men were resting for the first time in several days, so he didn't alert them until 7:00. The time of the surrender had been set at 9:00, so there would be little time to spare. After the group was alerted, they started back in an old truck. Seven miles out it broke down. Lt Hanna was worried about the men he had left back at the headquarters, for they certainly couldn't carry out the surrender alone, so he and five of the group got a car and arrived at the headquarters at five minutes to nine. The white flag was up when they arrived and the Germans marched down without their weapons, which had previously been collected in one pile.

> About this time the 517th Infantry division [sic] moved in from the south, so after the prisoners were taken they were turned over to this unit. There turned out to be only about 200 in the garrison. Some of them had escaped during the night, but the group never did number as many as 400.[38]

Lt Hanna sent a triumphant radio message back to his headquarters in Algeria to announce his success:

> Amusing story. Fayence surrendered to us four hours before the unknown arrival of the 517th. We dictated terms of unconditional surrender to German C.O. in a secret rendezvous. Incredible bluff. 188 prisoners, 2 officers, over 200 weapons, 4 vehicles. Profitable evening for partisans. No casualties and no battle. Were told we saved many lives in village and in attacking group of Americans. (…)[39]

Cpl Albert Deshayes, of G Company of the 517th PIR, was one of the paratroopers who had accidentally been dropped near Fayence the night of the jump. Instead of marching off to le Muy, he had remained in the Fayence area, where he ended up meeting and joining up with the men of OSS Team Sceptre:

> After being separated from my company the morning of August 15, 1944, I started out on my own. I saw Carl Witcher and James Callahan, who were injured. I helped Carl to a farm house and sent a medic back for James, as he had back injuries. The Germans picked up Carl and held him for some two or three weeks before part of the 45th Division freed him. Striking out again, I met two French FFI Resistance fighters who said, in spite of our language barrier, that they could take me to an American officer.

After following them for some two hours, we came to a barn where I was introduced to Capt Hanna of the OSS and his partner, Howard Palmer.

This was the first time I had heard of the OSS. They assured me they had jumped about three days ahead of us and had been organizing the FFI. About the fifth day, word came to us that the German officer in command of a fort called la Roche (or "the Rock") would talk to us. We agreed to meet him at a house directly below the Rock. That same night, Capt Hanna, myself, and another American soldier were picked up from Sgt John Chism's aid station, met the German captain, and ten of his soldiers while six FFI lay in a ditch across the street. Capt Hanna did all the talking and bluffing. Part of the 460th was shelling the fort, I believe, which concerned the German Captain. He said they would surrender that night if we agreed to 1) stop the shelling, 2) treat them as POWs, and 3) a safe trip back to the rock and not to be taken prisoners by the French. Capt Hanna sent me with a French driver to take the German Captain back up the hill to the fort; the German soldiers walked. I escorted him inside the fort, and as I started to leave, he told me that I was to wait for the shelling to stop as agreed at the meeting. I was definitely not aware of this, and Capt Hanna did not have control of the artillery. Fortunately for me, the shelling stopped in about 30 minutes due to flares sent up by Capt Hanna, I believe. I joined them for a drink of wine and I felt that they were happy that for them the war was over. Some 175 Germans surrendered that night; they were supposed to stack the weapons and ammo outside the Rock and we would be there at 7 a.m. the next day. We did not know that part of the 2nd Battalion was to take Fayence the next day, August 21st, and they arrived just in time. After taking some souvenirs, we left the rest to the 2nd Battalion. (…)

On my return to France 40 years later, I learned what events led to the surrender as we were talking to the assistant mayor of Fayence and his wife. The assistant mayor talked about the day of the invasion with tears in his eyes. How word spread through the town that the hills were full of American paratroopers. A French woman, Michele Jaffard, put a white flag on a stick and marched up the hill to the Rock, which is approximately 25 feet high and would hold at least 175 men. She pleaded with the German commander to save the town from shelling, and she would get in touch with the Americans. This was the beginning of the surrender of Fayence. Germaine Michel-Jaffard died in 1973. She was written up in the French history books as a Heroine and a plaque was placed on the stone wall along the road which leads to the Rock. I wish that I would have had an opportunity to meet her. That day, 40 years later, I climbed to the top of the Rock and took some pictures. The big guns were gone, but the emplacements were still there. You can view the entire valley, the town, and every street leading up to the Rock, including the street 2nd Battalion marched up. Of course, you could see the aid station. The town and buildings were the same. I never was to see Capt Hanna again.[40]

The surrender of the Germans in Fayence marked the end of the fighting in the Fayence-Montauroux area. *Reserve Grenadier Bataillon 327* had suffered heavy losses in killed, wounded, and

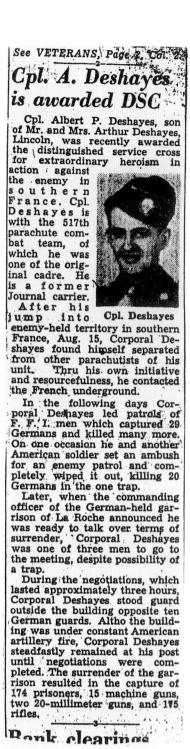

See VETERANS, Page 2, Col. 2

Cpl. A. Deshayes is awarded DSC

Cpl. Albert P. Deshayes, son of Mr. and Mrs. Arthur Deshayes, Lincoln, was recently awarded the distinguished service cross for extraordinary heroism in action against the enemy in southern France. Cpl. Deshayes is with the 517th parachute combat team, of which he was one of the original cadre. He is a former Journal carrier.

After his jump into enemy-held territory in southern France, Aug. 15, Corporal Deshayes found himself separated from other parachutists of his unit. Thru his own initiative and resourcefulness, he contacted the French underground.

In the following days Corporal Deshayes led patrols of F. F. I. men which captured 29 Germans and killed many more. On one occasion he and another American soldier set an ambush for an enemy patrol and completely wiped it out, killing 20 Germans in the one trap.

Later, when the commanding officer of the German-held garrison of La Roche announced he was ready to talk over terms of surrender, Corporal Deshayes was one of three men to go to the meeting, despite possibility of a trap.

During the negotiations, which lasted approximately three hours, Corporal Deshayes stood guard outside the building opposite ten German guards. Altho the building was under constant American artillery fire, Corporal Deshayes steadfastly remained at his post until negotiations were completed. The surrender of the garrison resulted in the capture of 174 prisoners, 15 machine guns, two 20-millimeter guns, and 175 rifles.

Cpl. Deshayes

Deshayes Family Collection.

prisoners, which included Major Paul Tornow, the battalion commander himself, who had agreed to the surrender terms given by Captain Hanna.[41] Captain Hanna and several members of his team were decorated, rewarding them for the important role they had played in the success of American operations in the area.

The Casualties

On the Allied side, the casualties of the fighting in the Fayence-Montauroux region had been rather light, with a total of only two paratroopers, two tank destroyer officers, one infantryman, and six *maquisards* being killed or mortally wounded. At least five civilians were also killed, including the mayor of Tourrettes, Mr Fleury Giraud. The Allied military and *maquis* losses were:

Surname	Name	Rank	Unit	Age	Date of death or wounding	Cause of death	Location of Death
Gruwell	Robert R.	Pvt	G Co 517 PIR	21	15.8.1944	Grenade incident	Callian
Undetermined			5th Scottish Btl		15.8.1944?	Jump injury?	Fayence
McKee	Paul R.	1Lt	Rec Co 636TD	33	18.8.1944	Friendly strafing	Callian
Dodson	Robert L.	1Lt	B Co 636TD	23	19.8.1944	Antitank fire	Callian
Hudson	Dudley W.	SSgt	I Co 141 IR	23	19.8.1944	GSW thorax	Callian

As for the German casualties, it is unfortunately not possible to make such precise estimations. Below is the list of all the bodies that were officially exhumed after the war and that are linked to the fighting in the Fayence-Montauroux area. From the dates of death and the locations of burial, it can be presumed during which incidents described in this chapter the men were killed. The location indicated is the town the men were buried in, not the town they were killed in, as that information is not known in most cases. The dates of death are also not always correct or known. As can be seen, the German losses are disproportionately large compared to the Allied losses, with at least 44 dead; this is due to the air and artillery superiority the Allies enjoyed, as well as to the highly successful ambush that occurred at Montauroux which caused the death of 11 German soldiers.

Surname	Name	Age	Date of death or wounding	Location of death
Ramonda	Justin	20	15.8.1944	Montauroux
Cabasson	Jean		16.8.1944	Estoc bridge
Chevalier	Henri		16.8.1944	Estoc bridge
Ollivier	Marius		16.8.1944	Estoc bridge
Astier	Maurice		17.8.1944	Callian
Kireeff	Georges		17.8.1944	Fayence

Surname	Name	Rank	Age	Date of death	Location of burial	Unit
Bock	Jakob	Ogefr	44	9.1944	Bagnols en Forêt	
Poppe	Robert	Lt	31	18.8.1944	Callian	Stab.Res.Div.148
Bittner	Georg	Gren	20	19.08.1944	Callian	Res.Inf.Pz.Jäg.Kp.Reg.8
Plöchl	Johann	Pio	18	19.08.1944	Callian	
Stedherm				19.08.1944	Callian	
Fröse	Walter	Kan	20	21.8.1944	Callian	
Hörl	Herbert	Gren	18	21.8.1944	Callian	
Völker	Franz	Uffz	31	21.8.1944	Callian	3./Inf.Reg.417
Zebisch	Josef	Gefr	31	21.8.1944	Callian	
Unknown					Callian	
Unknown					Callian	
Jahn	Johann	Ogefr	30	19.08.1944	Caucade	21 Flugmelde Res West Frankreich
Bahns	Johannes	Ogefr	32	15-20.8.1944	Fayence	
Müller	Albrecht		38	15-20.8.1944	Fayence	
Unknown				15-20.8.1944	Fayence	
Schwalbe	Walter	Ogefr		21.8.1944	Fayence	
Maier	Hans Georg	Lt	35		Fayence	See *Kommandant* Franzosische Riviera
Unknown					Fayence	
Unknown					Montauroux	
Unknown					Montauroux	
Unknown					Montauroux	
Unknown					Montauroux	
Unknown					Montauroux	
Unknown					Montauroux	
Unknown					Montauroux	

Surname	Name	Rank	Age	Date of death	Location of burial	Unit
Stockl					Montauroux	
Unknown					Montauroux	
Unknown					Montauroux	
Unknown					Montauroux	
Unknown					Montauroux	
Unknown					Montauroux	
Fuchs	Josef	Gren	18	15.8.1944	St Vallier	1./Res.Gren.Btl.327
Jeschke	Willi	Gefr	40	15.8.1944	St Vallier	1./Res.Gren.Btl.327
Schneider	Paul	Gren	32	15.8.1944	St Vallier	1./Res.Gren.Btl.327
Fleischer	Paul	Gren	17	15.8.1944	St Vallier	2./Res.Gren.Btl.327
Pollak	Richard		18	15.8.1944	St Vallier	2./Res.Gren.Btl.327
Schwarz	Michael	Gren	17	15.8.1944	St Vallier	1./Res.Gren.Btl.327
Synczek	Josef	Gren	21	15.8.1944	St Vallier	2./Res.Gren.Btl.327
Bilko	Paul	Krftfahrer	21	15.8.1944	St Vallier	Kr.K..Zug 1048
Steinke	Franz	O Gefr	35	15.8.1944	St Vallier	2./Res.Gren.Btl.327
Unknown				15.8.1944	St Vallier	
Kluge	Werner	O Gren	34	17.8.1944	St Vallier	14Kp Pz Jg 239
Helms	Wilhelm	O Gefr	39	18.8.1944	St Vallier	2./28M.K.Abt
Liebetanz	Herbert	O Kan	19	18.8.1944	St Vallier	Artillery

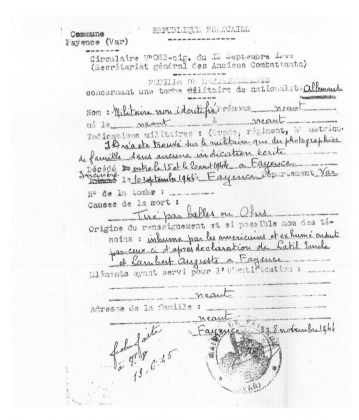

This report written by the town hall of Fayence explains that the body of a German soldier who had been killed between August 15th and August 20th was cremated September 10, 1944. The body was not identified, as only some family photographs with no written annotations were discovered on it. Ministère de la Défense et des Anciens Combattants.

This long list of dead is actually not complete. Several witnesses made the claim that many bodies were left on the D562 road after the fighting, and that these bodies had been cremated without ever being officially registered. This surprising information is confirmed by French Veterans Administration files that document three cases of bodies exhumed and cremated in Fayence in early September 1944 (These three are included in the above list.)! A paper trail remains for these three men, but apparently, no such precautions were taken for the dead that are said to have been cremated in Callian. We will now read what some of the witnesses have to say about the disposal of the bodies of the German dead in Callian. **Zézé Latil** was one of those who helped clean up the battlefield:

Lots of the inhabitants helped out in cleaning up the roads, and the few Germans that were found were cremated in the Callian Valley. A dozen Germans were doused with gasoline and burned on the spot near the Callian crossroads. Where were we supposed to bury them? Nobody wanted the bodies. The town halls and everybody didn't want to hear about it, so we had to get rid of them one way or the other, and we couldn't leave them in the fields. Some Americans had come by and taken all the identification tags, and after that, whereever there was freshly-moved earth, seeming to indicate that bodies had been buried, the bodies were all exhumed and cremated because the graves were so shallow. I know they were all cremated because I was there.

Marcel Guerrin tells of a similar story occurring slightly further down the D562 road where it passes over Camiole Creek:

We were told: "There are bodies, they need to be buried so that it won't stink." At the Camiole, there was a row of plane trees and there were a dozen dead there. They had been shot up by the air force and must have taken cover under the trees, but they got hit anyway. We went to bury them two or three days later. Only the dead guys remained on the ground, covered in worms. One guy was sitting against a tree, and he had pictures of his family in his hands. He must have been wounded and had the strength to look at the pictures of his wife and two kids.

An American officer gave us a jerry can of gasoline, so we thought: "Well, maybe they will burn." It burned slowly, but we had to bury them anyway, because then it stunk, and in August, the smell stayed impregnated in our skin. So we dragged them to the side of the road and threw a bit of earth on them so that the flies would not infest the area. It was beside the creek, so there was sand, and we threw sand on them.

It is possible that some of these bodies were later recovered, but nothing can be confirmed due to the poor notes taken by the French Veterans Administration exhumation parties. **Claude Bernard**, the disobedient child from Montauroux, also visited the battlefield once the Germans had left:

One day we tried to dig one German up, then suddenly we saw something white and we figured it must be the bones. It scared us so much that we all ran away. See, those were things that kids did, wartime kids. We were looking for trophies, for the incredible thing. We wanted to pinch their belts or whatever.

Although the fighting had ceased and the population rejoiced, the killing was not completely over yet. As in many villages, people who had collaborated with the Germans were punished.

In Montauroux, things turned particularly ugly and several people were killed; their bodies were never officially seen again. For the soldiers of the 517th PIR, the fighting was only beginning, and they were sent straight to the next battlefield a few kilometers further east at Saint Cézaire. But before moving on to Saint Cézaire, we need to examine more of the events that occurred the day of the landing, starting with the village of Tanneron.

Conclusion

The Fayence-Montauroux area unexpectedly became the focus of fighting the morning of August 15, 1944, when a large number of Allied paratroopers were accidentally dropped there due to navigational errors. The vast majority of these paratroopers rapidly left the area for their intended drop zones around le Muy. However, a few paratroopers stayed behind, and together with the *Maquis* and a team of OSS agents who had also been dropped off target, they wreaked havoc along the D562 road for the next several days. Many paratroopers who had been wounded in the drop also remained in the Fayence-Montauroux area, where they were hidden by locals or treated in improvised infirmaries.

Over the next days, D562 was used heavily by advancing and retreating German vehicles. These vehicles were strafed at least twice by Allied aircraft and were also subject to ambushes by the paratroopers and *maquisards*. August 18th, German troops of *Reserve Grenadier Battalions 327* and *372* finally took firm control of Fayence, Callian, and Montauroux, in expectation of the imminent arrival of the 141st Infantry Regiment from the south. The 141st IR, accompanied by tank destroyers, attacked Callian the very next day, securing the town on the morning of August 20th after 24 hours of fighting. The fall of Callian caused the Germans in Montauroux to retreat towards Grasse, while those in Fayence found themselves surrounded. The next day, August 21st, actions by the OSS team and by the 517th Parachute Infantry Regiment, which had relieved the 141st IR, caused the Germans remaining in Fayence to surrender, bringing an end to the fighting in the entire Fayence-Montauroux area.

Pathfinders and Forcemen in Tanneron

Tanneron is a small village built at the top of a steep hill between Cannes and the Fayence-Montauroux area. It didn't have any particular strategic importance, but unexpectedly ended up being the scene of several encounters anyhow, as will be explained. Its story is similar to that of the Fayence-Montauroux area, in the sense that the town was "liberated" once by misplaced paratroopers, then reoccupied by the Germans before being liberated for good.

The Pathfinders of the 509th Parachute Infantry Battalion

The story of Tanneron brings us back to the parachute drops of the early morning of August 15, 1944, when the pathfinder team of the 509th Parachute Infantry Battalion that was supposed to land in the le Muy area was accidentally dropped in the forest halfway between Tanneron and Montauroux instead. **Charles Petty**, one of the pathfinders, explains what happened to his team, starting from the airfield in Italy:

Fourteen paratroopers formed our pathfinder team. I, Charles Petty, was one of them, along with Armstad, Baum, Culture, DeVanie, Houghton, Justice, McGee, Sweetitz, Trzeszkowski, McDonald, Rondeau, Saiz, and our team Leader, Lt DeLeo. Our pathfinder equipment consisted of a Eureka radar device and a dozen signal lights mounted on tripod which were used to form a "T" pattern on the ground to indicate the direction of flight to pilots. McDonald was the trooper chosen to jump with the Eureka. The rest of us carried the tripod and the signal lights, in addition to our own weapons and ammunition. I, like many of us, decided to discard the reserve parachute. It would be an item less to jump with… it would serve no purpose anyhow… we were going to jump at such a low altitude! Although an order was issued for all paratroopers flying over the sea to wear a Mae West, I didn't wear one. I think we left them in the aircraft. I carried a .45, an M1 rifle, two ammo bandoliers, and many packs of Lucky Strikes in two ammo bandoliers I had sewn inside my jump jacket.

In addition to the troopers of the pathfinder team, there were two stowaways on board the airplane: Sgt Emmanuel Serano and 1st Sgt James Prettyman. Serano was the buddy of our commander, Dan DeLeo, and he had participated in the parachute raid against El Djem bridge in Tunisia and had been captured, escaped, and spent 14 months with the Italian partisan bands, raiding German installations. Somehow he showed up at the airbase where we were

training. Prettyman was not a qualified parachutist; he was attached to our team in an administrative capacity. The two sergeants begged the lieutenant to let them come along on the mission and they wouldn't take "no" for an answer. Since DeLeo couldn't give them official permission, both men decided to stow away on the airplane while DeLeo "happened" to be looking in another direction.

The airplane was in total blackout, except for a soft blue light in the ceiling of the fuselage which would give each of us a fierce appearance in our camouflage jump suits with blackened faces. Once airborne, except for the sounds of the aircraft's engine, all was quiet… nobody spoke. I looked at my buddies around me and wondered how many would live to see the sunset. Eventually some of the guys began to doze off, and I also began to feel sleepy. I finally fell asleep, and was awakened by the air corps crew chief, who was moving up and down the aisle. Moments later we neared the coast, and the crew chief shouted: "Stand in the door." DeLeo made a half turn and crouched in the exit door as the rest of us shoveled forward to close the gaps between jumpers. Our eyes were fixed on the red light in the exit door, knowing that when it changed to green it would be the signal to bail out. As we flew over the coast, the enemy's antiaircraft guns opened up on us. I expected the red light to turn green any time, but it remained red.

Suddenly, the aircraft went into a sharp turn which threw us to the side of the fuselage. It was almost impossible to stay on our feet. The crew chief hollered: "We can't make out a thing on the ground, we are going to circle out to the sea and take another crack at it!" Twice more we circled, each time drawing a barrage of flak. I remember McGee yelling: "Let's get the hell out of here," and the lieutenant shouted that he couldn't see anything out in that thick fog. On the third pass, the aircraft went into a steep glide and someone shouted: "We're going to ditch." I closed my eyes and prayed, holding tight the rosary my mother had given to me. Finally, after what seemed like an eternity, the aircraft began to level off, but the force of gravity was so great it forced us to the ground of the airplane. I grabbed the anchor line and held for dear life as the plane returned to level flight. Finally the red light went green, and I heard DeLeo shouting: "Okay, let's go," and go we did!

After my chute opened, I soon was enveloped in a dense fog. In a few seconds, I came crashing down a tree and there I hung. I was able to unhook my rifle and my pathfinder equipment and dropped them to the ground. I managed with some difficulty to reach my switchblade knife and cut loose the parachute harness. I then climbed down and found out I was in a wooded area full of tall pine trees, and was certain this was not the DZ. I called out in a low voice the password "Lafayette" but got no answer. I was alone behind enemy lines! As dawn approached, the fog began to lift, so I climbed the tree to retrieve my parachute. I wrapped it around my pathfinder equipment and hid everything in some thick underbrush nearby. As I made my way down the side of the hill, I could hear heavy artillery far off in the distance; I knew then that the invasion along the coast had begun and I immediately removed the sock covering the American flag I had sewn on the sleeve of my jacket.

By mid-morning we were six, and during the afternoon we joined up with the rest of them. We found everybody to be okay… except DeLeo, who had sustained a fractured skull when he was struck on the head by a shell fragment from the enemy's antiaircraft fire during the jump. We found that we had been dropped some 25 miles from our intended DZ.[1]

Just as several of the other pathfinder teams of the First Airborne Task Force, those of the 509th PIB had been dropped hopelessly off target, explaining why two companies of the 509th were accidentally dropped in St Tropez in the following hours, and why one entire plane load was dropped into the sea. **Pvt John DeVanie** was also a member of the pathfinder team, and the mission in southern France was to be his first combat jump:

I was in the pathfinder group, which is a group of 14 soldiers that jump behind the German lines and set up a drop zone for the rest of the soldiers. August 15, 1944, we left Rome, Italy, at about 12 p.m. or 12:30 a.m. and flew towards southern France. When the plane took off, everybody was real satisfied with the flight and everything, and as we neared the coast, the light came on for us to stand up and hook up. As we came over the coast, we received antiaircraft fire. We were standing right up next to the door of the airplane; the airplane went rocking and rolling, and we were waiting for the green light to come on so we could jump. Well, the plane turned around and went out over the water again and came back in. The second time, we got antiaircraft shells bursting all around the plane. The plane was going back and forth, everybody was trying to stand up and hold onto the static line, and the pilot went back a third time! I understand that each time he went in and out, when he went back in over the land he went more to the right than he was scheduled to arrive. The third time he went in, of course, we were anxious to get out of there. Well, the green light came on and out we went. The shock of the parachute opening knocked my helmet off. Of course it was dark, and there was kind of a misty cloud over the trees. I landed on the side of a hill and rolled down the hill, knocking the sight off my Thompson submachine gun. I had rolled up in my chute with the shroud lines wrapped around my legs and stuff and I had to cut my way out. I thought I was just on the other side of our drop zone, so I climbed, trying to get to the top of that hill. It was daylight just as I got to the top of the hill. I looked over the top and there were trucks full of Germans going down this road. Well naturally I was scared to death; I didn't know where I was and I was by myself.

Then I heard some rustling coming through the brush and I got ready to shoot, but it was one of my friends, Rene Rondeau. They just told us that this guy was going to go with us because he could speak French. Nobody else in our group could speak French, so he helped us quite a bit. We sat there, and we couldn't decide which way to go. We were scattered out a pretty good ways from each other. We

Pvt John DeVanie, one of the 14 men (plus two stowaways) who formed the pathfinder team of the 509th PIB that was accidentally dropped near Tanneron, in the hills northwest of Cannes. John DeVanie Collection.

decided to go in one direction, and luckily we ran into the rest of the group. Our Lieutenant, Dan DeLeo, had landed in a tree and had cut his forehead pretty bad, and they were getting him down out of the tree about the time we got there. We came into a house and they went and got this French underground person that told us he would lead us back. He knew the way back to the German and American lines. We buried all of our tripod, batteries, and stuff that we had right there in that area and Lt Dan DeLeo went back later on and got all of that equipment.

The pathfinders had landed between Tanneron and Montauroux, south of the D562 highway. The trucks that John DeVanie saw were probably part of the convoy of *Reserve Grenadier Bataillon 327*, which was driving towards Draguignan on D562 and that would soon be strafed at la Colle Noire. We will now see how the situation appeared from the point of view of the local French inhabitants. **Roger Alary** was a local 11-year-old boy whose second communion, planned August 15th, had to be cancelled because of the invasion. He explains what he heard about the lost pathfinders from his father:

The night of August 15th, hundreds of airplanes flew over us. We were sleeping without really sleeping. There were fishermen who had gone to fish with lamps at night. They were actually poaching, but it was because there was nothing to eat. So those fishermen heard the airplanes flying over them and then they heard strange noises in the night, and they weren't too sure what was going on. Then at dawn they heard whistling. They found that strange, and at one point they had the huge surprise of running into some soldiers. They didn't know whether they were Germans or Americans. They were camouflaged with leaves on their heads and everything. So the two groups observed each other, and the fishermen weren't armed, whereas the others were. The fisherman were good old country men who had probably never seen an American before, or not many, and they couldn't speak English, nor *vice versa*. Then finally the Americans showed their flag and said: "American, American, American!" So the people understood, and the Americans asked where they were. They had maps, so the people, including my father, showed "les Marjories" on the map. So they understood where they were, but they were actually supposed to have jumped at le Muy. They were paratroopers who had been dropped during the night. Then everybody left and went their own way.

Gilbert Graille, another local youth, also tells about the night of the jump:

I think it was the day before the landing, or maybe two days before, that an airplane made a mistake during the night and dropped 18 paratroopers at Belluny. There were tall pine trees, and they landed on them and remained hung up in the trees. At daybreak, the first inhabitants that were there heard some people calling and went to see what was going on, finding the soldiers hanging from their parachutes. The Americans immediately said: "No tedesci!" The "tedesci" were the Germans, so they were saying they weren't Germans, but Americans. So the inhabitants cut down a row of pine trees to get them down, because when you are hanging in a parachute it isn't easy to come down; they freed them that way. The locals gave food and drink to those paratroopers. They were

theoretically to get to Antibes, but they were supposed to be dropped in le Muy and they were dropped in Belluny... complete mistake. I will always remember that one of the Americans said that the day he would meet the pilot who had dropped them, there would be sparks.

Ange Merle lived near where the pathfinders had landed and the paratroopers spent one night in his house:

They arrived from Corsica and jumped at around four in the morning. There were people fishing at night, because in '44 it felt good to be able to eat a bit of fish. Those people were frightened and ran away because they didn't know what was going on, with men falling from the sky. The first person who found the Americans in the morning was August Michel. There were about 12 of them, I don't know exactly how many, but 15 at the most. One black American had landed in the water, and when cutting the ropes from his parachute he almost cut his thumb off. He was a tough guy; later on we heard that he had been killed before getting to Nice. Another one was limping; he had hurt himself a bit, but he was walking anyway. They stayed with us here in Belluny. We hosted them, but there wasn't much to feed them. We had some potatoes, and we had olive oil and wine. We even had to hold them back, because if we pulled out a bottle of wine, and there was an unlimited supply of them, the black American would drink the entire liter! We had a good time. Sometimes we have arguments in the hamlet, but when the Americans were here, there were no more arguments. Only one of them could speak French, and we spoke with the others in Italian. We understood each other in Italian because they all spoke Italian. Then they left towards Tanneron and went to join the American army around Pegomas and Cannes.

After regrouping and getting organized, the paratroopers, guided by locals, then walked to the village of Tanneron itself. August 17th, they were relaxing in Tanneron when a group of Germans was spotted approaching the village. **Lucien Graille**, Gilbert Graille's younger brother, was a couple kilometers away in a house beside the main road leading into Tanneron and tells what happened next:

My grandfather was in the house and had just had lunch, and he said: "There are soldiers down there who are coming up." So my mother said: "It's the Americans." My grandfather answered: "No, no, no. It's not the Americans, it's the Germans." The elders [WWI veterans] knew what war was, they had lived through it, so he had immediately recognized that they were Germans. He left barefoot on the road and ran up to Tanneron to warn the 16 paratroopers that nine Germans were coming towards the village. He didn't manage to make them understand that they should wait for them at the entrance of the village, so that they could wait on either side of the road and capture the Germans without firing a shot. Instead, the Americans left down the road.

The Germans were probably an isolated and retreating group of stragglers from several units. At least one of them was a member of *Reserve Grenadier Bataillon 444*, while another was from *Reserve Artillerie Regiment 8*, as we will soon see. Pathfinder **Charles Petty** explains what followed:

The Germans had patrols looking for us, but in most cases we saw them first and avoided them whenever we could. The next day, we were joined by a few members of the French underground resistance and a couple of days later we arrived at the small village of Tanneron, where we decided to rest for a few hours. Suddenly, one of our French guides shouted: "Les *Boches* sont là!" The Krauts were a half mile away, leading to the village. DeLeo quickly assembled the team, and we set up an ambush and waited for the approaching Germans. We allowed them to come within point blank range before opening fire. In two or three minutes it was all over, and the Krauts who weren't down surrendered. Serano was wounded in the leg by gunfire.[2]

Local teenager **Gilbert Vial** followed the pathfinders and saw the ambush:

We heard somebody whistling, and we asked: "What is going on?" A guy from Notre Dame de Peygros told us: "Be careful, there is a column of Germans that are marching up the road." They had shoes with metal heels that could be heard from a distance on the pavement. So what did the Americans do? They didn't chicken out, they went off on either side of the road to meet the Germans. We were 16 or 17, but seeing that stuff was interesting for us, we didn't realize the risk we were taking. Three or four Americans were kneeling on the road, and when the Germans came, the Americans challenged them. The Germans lifted their weapons, so the Americans opened fire without hesitation. One American was wounded in the knee and one or two Germans were killed.

Two German soldiers had been killed in the ambush: 17-year-old **Georg Vogl**, of *Reserve Artillerie Abteilung 44* of *Reserve Artillerie Regiment 8*, and 20-year-old **Georg Kroliczek**, of the 10th Company of *Reserve Grenadier Bataillon 444*. In fact, the ambush had been a bit more complicated than the two previous witnesses remembered. There were actually two successive firefights and Sgt Serano was not only wounded in the leg, but was also briefly captured by the Germans. Young **Lucien Graille**, whose grandfather had ran up to Tanneron to warn the Americans in the first place, explains the details of what occurred, and in particular, how his family had delayed the Germans before purposely sending them towards Tanneron so that they would fall into the ambush:

My grandfather had said: "Attract the Germans over here, show yourselves so that they come over so that I will have time to warn the Americans." So my mother, the worker we had there, my brother, and my sister all made ourselves very visible, so that the Germans would come over to see us. When they arrived, they asked us if we had anything to drink and we said: "No problem, you can have some water." We went to get pails of water at the well to fill up their canteens and everything. Their chief, who could speak a bit of French, asked my mother how to go to Grasse and if it was easier to go by St Cassien or by Pégomas. My mother said: "But going to St Cassien won't bring you to Grasse, you have to go up to Tanneron and then go down to Pégomas." He had a map and said: "But on the map it shows a road going to Grasse." He was insisting on going down to Saint Cassien, but since my mother wanted to send them towards Tanneron, she said:

"No, no, it's much further, then you have to go through Spéracèdes and everything, it's too far away; whereas this way you go down to Auribeau and then you will be right in Grasse." My mother said the road was cut, that they couldn't go because they would have to go through the valley and that it was a much longer way. The chief wasn't very convinced. He even asked us if there were any Americans here and we said there weren't. She said: "No, there are no Americans, there are only Germans here." That is why they gladly left for Tanneron.

When they got to the Peiras curve, two Americans were sent out as scouts, one on each side, and there was a fire fight, because of course the Americans didn't want to surrender and neither did the Germans, and one American was wounded. The bullet went through his leg, and in his pants he had a pack of Lucky Strike cigarettes that was shot right through the middle and the bullet went out the other side of his leg. The Germans brought the wounded American back for us to treat him, since they weren't even one kilometer away. Two Germans carried him, and I remember he was taller than them because he was a very, very tall man. They put him down and said: "Take care of him," so we disinfected the wound with what we had and bandaged him. He was gutsy, because a bullet in the leg

17-year-old Soldat Georg Vogl, who was killed when the pathfinders of the 509th PIB ambushed his group at Tanneron. His twin brother Max Vogl, had already been killed the previous month in Normandy and his father was later reported as missing in action in Poland. Vogl Family Collection.

must be painful. He thanked us, and since he had no money or anything on him, he gave us the pack of cigarettes as a souvenir. They were red Lucky Strikes, with a white circle in the middle, and the bullet had pierced the pack right through the center. I can't say that the Germans were bad, since when they brought him back they could have shot all five of us. I mean, they behaved correctly. We had sent them up to be captured and had lied to them and everything. They could very well have shot us.

The Germans had left the other American for dead, and they said: "Now we are going to get the other one who is dead beside the road." My mother told my brothers and me: "I wonder if he is really dead for good, or…" She asked the German: "Were there only two of them?" He answered: "Yes, yes, there were only two." In the meantime, the other Americans had gone back to the village and hidden there, and when the Germans returned, they didn't want to surrender of course and there was another gunfight. The Americans killed two of the Germans and the rest of them were captured. Then the Americans came back to get their wounded guy and they left with him. Mr Baptiste Setimo and Aldo Lagorio knew the region well and told them: "We will guide you back, we will show you the way." So those two local Italians guided the Americans back to their lines. They had even given them weapons and they left.

Ironically, it was Sgt Emmanuel Serano, who was not even supposed to be in combat because he had already been captured once before, who was temporarily captured again. Lucien Graille's brother **Gilbert Graille** adds a few final comments about the ambush:

The wounded man came back, walking on one foot with his arms over the shoulders of two Germans. They asked my grandmother to treat him. The American was happy to be taken care of and the Germans were happy that they had fired first. It seemed like the American wasn't even in pain, there was no hemorrhage or anything. The Germans stayed for a bit, then, when they saw he was in good hands they left. But both the Germans and the Americans were stupid. The Germans should have suspected that there were more Americans and not just two soldiers on their own like that. But they went back to Tanneron anyway and they were immediately captured when they got to the village! The American was blaming himself, because they had made a mistake and shouldn't have advanced down the road like that. They had wanted to act clever, with each going down one side of the road, but they should have waited for the Germans and ambushed them. My grandmother cut the American's pants high up on the thigh, and when his colleagues came to get him, he left with pants on one side and shorts on the other. Now we can laugh about it, but back then we weren't laughing.

Pathfinder **John DeVanie** has confused memories about the ambush, but explains how the lost paratroopers finally got back to American lines:

We didn't get back to the lines until the afternoon of the 20th. In the meantime, this guide would go ahead; he would be our lead person out there, and the next day he came running back and said: "Germans, Germans!" So we scattered out on each side of the road and they came by, and we just let them go on by. The next day we had a fire

fight with a German patrol and shot up six of them. There were three of them that surrendered whom we turned over to the French people up there. Serano got shot in the knee when we ambushed that patrol, but he was a soldier and he walked all the way back with that bullet wound. In fact, he was not supposed to even be there. He had been captured in North Africa, or somewhere along the way, and escaped two or three times, and the Germans had told him that they would kill him if they ever found him again, since he escaped. But he slipped in on our plane and jumped with us because he wanted to go back into the war.

Then on Thursday, if I remember correctly it was Thursday, we had the same situation. We heard the Germans coming and we got on each side of the path, and as they got even with us we stood up. The lead sergeant said: "Well, the war is over for us now." He could speak English as good as I could. He could speak two or three different languages, and he told us a good place to go through the German lines to get back to the American lines.

That afternoon, the American forces laid a barrage of mortars and artillery shells in on us. They thought we were all Germans. We were all scattered out in the woods there and artillery shells were blasting all the trees around us and everything. It scared the heck out of us, but our Lt Dan DeLeo went through the lines that night, like on Thursday night, to get the password, and the next afternoon, Friday, August 20th [the 20th was actually a Sunday], we went through the German lines with ten prisoners and got back to headquarters. They told us that we were going to make a push on Cannes the next morning. We thought we were going to go the rest and relaxation place (R and R), but no way.

Pathfinder **Charles Petty** explains his version of the story of how the group of paratroopers got back to the American lines in the Estérel mountains after ambushing the Germans at Tanneron:

The next day we left the village with our prisoners and heartbroken…one of our buddies (McDonald) had to be left behind. He had a bad case of fever, which turned out to be malaria. He could no longer travel with us, so we left him in the hands of a friendly French family living in the wooded area up the hill. DeLeo told him to hold on to his .45 and get rid of everything else. He was given civilian clothes, and before we left him, each of us went by his bedside and shook his hand, promising that we would come back to get him out. Along the road we stopped near a house to take a rest, and some children came out and sat with me. I gave one of the little girls one of my D-ration chocolate bars, and in return she gave me a small medallion which I attached to my dog tags. Suddenly, high explosive shells began exploding all around the immediate area. I got the little girl down in a ditch on the side of the road and there we stayed until it all stopped. I later found out that on the medallion was written: "Toi et moi, un abri pour deux," which means: "You and me, a shelter for both."… I have kept it to this days. The prisoners were told that there would be no turning back, no playing around, and I think we scared them. Later, when the GIs of an infantry division took over the prisoners, one of them gave me a little foxhole rosary, thanking me for not having killed him. I kept that little thing all through the war and it remained in the pocket of my jump jacket until today. While returning to friendly territory, Lt DeLeo organized a rescue team composed of troopers Baum, Saiz, Trzeszkowski, three British paratroopers, and a French resistance fighter by the name Mario. They made their way through enemy lines and brought McDonald back safely. By then our pathfinder team was disbanded and we all returned to our assigned units.[3]

According to Gilbert Vial, some of the wounded German prisoners were also left in Tanneron under the care of the inhabitants. As for Georg Vogl and Georg Kroliczek, the two German soldiers who had been killed in the ambush, they were both buried in the local cemetery, as **Lucien Graille** explains:

> We buried the two dead in the village cemetery. Years later people came back to retrieve them. But for a long time the helmets stayed on the crosses, as well as half the identification tag with the number on it. When people came to visit the cemetery, some of them also put flowers on the Germans' graves.

The Wounding of Lieutenant Wright

While the pathfinders had been living their adventures in Tanneron, the general front lines had approached the village from the west, and shortly after the departure of the pathfinders, Tanneron was occupied by a small German force that prepared to defend the area from the incoming Allied units. The Germans were mainly concerned with holding a roadblock on the main road that lead to both Montauroux and les Adrets, which were held by the 517th Parachute Infantry Regiment and the 2nd Independent Parachute Brigade as of August 20th. However, the 2nd Independent Parachute Brigade was then pulled out of southern France and relieved by the Canadian-American First Special Service Force (FSSF) in the early hours of August 21st. The FSSF had landed by boat on islands off Hyères the day of the invasion and had just been attached to the First Airborne Task Force (FABTF) to compensate for the departure of the 2nd Independent Parachute Brigade. It was therefore men of the 1st Regiment of the FSSF coming from les Adrets that reached les Marjories the afternoon of August 22nd, in view of the German roadblock further up the road. The FSSF was accompanied by vehicles of the 645th Tank Destroyer Battalion, which had also recently been attached to the FABTF. Young **Roger Alary**, who lived in les Marjories, describes the arrival of the Allied soldiers:

> The afternoon of the 22nd, we suddenly heard strange noises. There was a road facing our house and we saw tanks and armored vehicles approaching. There were only about 12 of them, but behind them there were hundreds and hundreds of men, marching on either side of the road with four or five meter spaces between each. They advanced and advanced, and arrived in les Marjories. At first, we didn't know if these people were Germans or Americans, but then we saw their flag and everything and we understood. A few of the officers could speak French, so they asked our parents and grandparents if there were any Germans in the area. So our fathers explained that yes, there were Germans in two places in Tanneron, where they had set up observation posts. So the Americans advanced to where those posts could be seen and fired several shots with 37mm cannons.

The handful of Germans manning the roadblocks apparently retreated, enabling the FSSF to reach the village of Tanneron itself in the late afternoon without encountering any resistance. The German forces in la Napoule, on the coast, had already retreated in the morning (see Chapter 6), rendering the mission of protecting the Tanneron road network useless. Although the Germans no longer had any plans to defend Tanneron, a group of approximately 50 Germans who were retreating from la Napoule had taken up quarters in the Château de la Verrerie, south of the village. Subsequent interrogations by the FSSF indicated that these Germans were attempting to reach Grasse without having any idea that the Allies had already advanced so far behind them, and they were very surprised when the FSSF attacked them in the early evening.[4] The Château de la Verrerie was a good bivouac for these Germans, but a very bad defensive position, as it was surrounded by hills on all sides. Remi Augier was not born at the time, but explains the story that his father repeated to him many times over the years. **Remi Augier**'s father, who was a veteran of the 1940 Battle of France, had visited the Verrerie on the afternoon of the 22nd and, having seen a large number of Germans there, he went straight to the village of Tanneron to warn the Forcemen (this was the nickname given to soldiers of the FSSF) of the German presence:

> The American soldiers were stationed in the town square, between the war monument and the town hall, and the officers were sitting at the tables of the "Hôtel des Voyageurs." My father always told me that the officer was very tall, a bit red-headed, and had a very big moustache, and my father always said he may have been Canadian. The officer took a map, unfolded it on the table, and told him: "We are here, and now you have to tell me exactly where the Germans are." My father said: "The detachment of Germans is exactly here, and to go there we should go like this and like that." Since my father knew the area well, he explained very precisely what the best way would be to get as near as possible to the Germans.
>
> So they all left; one whistle blow and a bunch of soldiers went down the Colle d'Embarque path, stopping at a place that is not very far from the Château Verrerie, and that is strategic, because it overlooks the Château. The officer told him: "I see that you have already experienced war and understand tactics well, so I am going to give

American mess tin with a soldier's name carved onto it that was left behind in Tanneron, probably by a member of the FSSF or of the 645th TDB. The identity of the original owner has not been determined, as the name "Ross" is very common, while "Jim" and "Heaven" are clearly nicknames. Private Collection.

The Verrerie Castle, south of Tanneron, in which a group of Germans retreating from the la Napoule area were bivouacking, not suspecting Allied troops were also approaching them from the north. Author's Collection.

"Then of course they all opened fire on the castle." Impacts from bullets fired by the FSSF are still visible on the window bars of Verrerie Castle to this day. Author's Collection.

you..." He took his pistol from his belt and gave it to my father, telling him: "You always stay 25 or 30 meters behind us, don't come nearer." So my father followed them. They wanted to go around the Château and surround the entire pasture, because my father had told them that there were some puddles of water at the end of the pasture where the Germans were washing themselves. My father was staying behind, but he realized that the soldiers were talking loudly, and that orders were being given loudly. It wasn't very loud, but it wasn't discreet enough.

There was a German sentry posted about 30 meters before the castle and the noise and orders must have alerted the Germans. They kept advancing for about 100 meters or so, and when they were about 80 meters away from the castle, the American officer received a bullet through the middle of the forehead that exited behind through the helmet and everything. He collapsed, wounded, and the aid men and stretcher bearers immediately went to him, but he never regained consciousness and died during the transfer to the military hospital. Then, of course, they all opened fire on the château. The Germans defended themselves, and I heard that four or five Germans were killed.

Sixteen-year-old **Gilbert Vial** was also part of the action, and has a slightly different version of events:

The American Colonel went down without any weapons to see if the Germans would surrender. I told him: "Come, I will go down with you." The two of us went down the path, and after about 150 meters I saw the pig sty beside the château. I knew the place well, but didn't think the Germans had put a sentry at the pig sty; I thought they were all together and that nobody was standing guard. The Colonel summoned the sentry. He must have told him that they were surrounded and that they could surrender, but maybe the sentry was Polish—go figure, he probably didn't even understand. I saw the sentry lift his weapon and aim at us and I wondered: "Will he shoot or not?" At the same moment, "bang," the officer was shot right in the face and fell down a meter away from me. I saw

the blood coming out and I ran back up the hill. I didn't scream or anything so that they wouldn't shoot at me. I got back up to the junction of the paths and the Americans who were there understood that it wasn't the American who had fired, so they opened fire and started throwing grenades. It was in the dry season and it set fire to the forest, and the Germans were escaping everywhere. Afterwards, I went home and I told my father and mother: "I think some Germans were killed, because I heard them screaming. One American is dead."

In fact, the "American Colonel" was Lt Allan "Spud" Wright, a Canadian from 3rd Company, 1st Regiment of the FSSF. A FSSF communication at 23:05 on the 22nd mentioned: "Lt Wright of 1st Regiment is a casualty. Reported shot in the head."[5] **Peter Cottingham**, of the HQ Detachment of 1st Regiment, explains what he heard about the incident and what actually happened to Lt Wright after being shot through the head:

During the southern France campaign, Spud Wright was leading his platoon through a pine forest west of Nice when a bunch of enemy came out of the woods with their hands up. As they were being taken prisoner, their officer appeared from the woods and shot Spud in the head. The 9mm bullet went in near his left eye and exited from the back of his skull. The officer who stupidly shot him lived about two seconds after that.

Local inhabitant Gilbert Vial indicates the path on which Lt "Spud" Wright was shot through the head August 22, 1944. Author's Collection.

From left to right: FSSF veterans Peter Cottingham, Thomas Prince, Allan "Spud" Wright, and F. Kirk. The scar from the German bullet fired at Tanneron is visible on "Spud" Wright's left temple. Peter Cottingham Collection.

Spud had vital signs of life so was sent back to hospital. They got him back on a hospital ship and he was taken to Naples, then out to the Canadian hospital in Caserta, which is a little bit north of Naples. He was there for about a month before he recovered. They tell me that he was sitting in his bed, and the nurse came in with a beer on a tray and he sat up and said "beer," and that's the first word he said.

Contrary to what the Frenchmen had thought, Spud Wright had survived his head wound and he later started a family back home in Canada, where he died in 1999 at the age of 78. Thirty-two Germans surrendered to the FSSF after the fire fight at la Verrerie, including four who were wounded. The 28 others were interrogated, revealing that 20 of them were in fact Polish. The prisoners were members of a unit of 100 men named *Kampfgruppe Zwirner* that had been formed in haste on August 14th with men from *Reserve Artillerie Regiment 8* and *Battalions 7* and *327* (Zwirner was the name of the commander of *Bataillon 164*, so perhaps this unit had been created to reinforce his battalion?). *Kampfgruppe Zwirner* then fought on the la Napoule front until it was forced to retreat towards Grasse. When the FSSF closed in on them, some of the Germans thought

that they were being attacked by partisans, as they had not been informed that the Allies were already so far inland.[6, 7]

The day after the shooting, **Gilbert Vial** and several others went back to the scene where the forest had burned down and found the bodies of four German soldiers who had died in the flames, including the body of an officer:

> Four Germans burned, and it was myself, my brother, my father, and a man named Bathélemy who went to bury them. I don't think they had been killed on the spot; they must have been wounded in the legs or something, because we saw and understood that they had dragged themselves through the woods. When we heard screams, it must have been them screaming in pain. They had suffocated and they had burned, but they weren't charred to the point to the point where you could no longer recognize that it was a human body, especially the buttons and the tags that hung around their necks were still intact. One of them was a lieutenant Colonel; he had five stripes on his shirt and only his pants were slightly burnt. He was curled up from the smoke and burns, and he had his open wallet in his hands with a picture of his wife and four kids, and before dying, or while he was waiting to be killed by the fire, we suspect he must have been looking at the photo of his wife and children. He must have been a wealthy person, because the wallet was quite sturdy and must have been quite valuable. There were papers inside it, and one of my dad's friends who didn't know how to write very well, but who had been in the First World War, had said: "See, this is his date of birth, this is his name." He was 32 years old and was the father of four children. You know, that affected us a bit. We dug holes with pickaxes and we buried them, covered them up, and put a piece of wood in the ground. The identification tags were double and we left one on the wooden stake and gave the other one to the town hall.
>
> Two or three years later, I was cutting mimosa with my brother and father and somebody came and told us: "We know that you are the ones who buried the Germans, do you still have the identification tag numbers?" In the meantime we must have handed the tags to the town hall, but we went to the spot with the people who were competent to dig up the bodies and told them: "There are two together there, and then one here and one over there." We knew where they were because we had dug the holes. The lieutenant Colonel was buried with one of his fellow soldiers and we had told them: "There, on one of those two,

Knödelseder Josef
Landwirt
29.4.26   A
Petzenberg/Ndby.
Kan.   E
Südfrankreich 9.44

18-year-old Josef Knödlseder, of Reserve Artillerie Regiment 8, was one of four German soldiers to have been killed in the fire fight at la Verrerie August 22nd. Deutsches Rotes Kreuz.

you will find a wallet." And indeed, when they removed the sand they found it, and we said: "There is a picture, probably of his wife and four children." And he brushed away some of the earth and the wallet was still intact.

Unfortunately, most of the identification tags must have been lost since the soldiers had been buried, because of the four bodies, only one was identified: that of 18-year-old **Kanonier Josef Knödlseder**, of *Reserve Artillerie Regiment 8*. The exhumation team noted, however, that one of the three unidentified bodies was that of an *Oberleutnant*. This was presumably the man who had died while looking at the photo of his wife and children. Walter Bosler, one of the German prisoners who was captured at la Verrerie August 22nd, gives a very precious hint concerning the identity of this killed officer, as he declared to his interrogators that **Lt Kuhnert**, the commander of *Kampfgruppe Zwirner*, had been killed in the fire fight.[8]

Tanneron Battlefield Investigation

An exploration was made of the path where Lt Spud Wright was shot through the head. Within meters of the place where witness Gilbert Vial said he was hit, approximately 40 U.S. WWII dated spent .30 caliber casings were found on the path and on the hill below the path. Very few other casings were found in the surrounding area. One can imagine a soldier advancing down the path to where his officer had just been shot and then opening fire at the Germans around the château. On the château itself, bullet impacts are visible on several of the metal bars that protect the ground floor windows.

Aftermath of the Liberation

The two ambushes that occurred in Tanneron led to the capture of approximately 40 Germans and the death of six others. The Allies only suffered two wounded. However, even with the Germans gone danger was ever present, and the next day, August 23rd, a jeep driven by medics and parachute riggers of the Service Company of the FSSF drove over a mine at an intersection northwest of Tanneron, killing four of its occupants. **Eugene Gutierrez**, of the Service Company, heard about the incident:

I knew a survivor of that mine blast; his name was Harold Massie, and we were very good friends. There were five or six in the jeep, and he was riding in the back and the jeep hit a land mine. It must have been a very powerful one, because with the explosion all the occupants were just blown up in the air. Some of them were killed instantly and two or three of them died about a month later from wounds. Sergeant Durham was one of those who died shortly after and Starr also died.

Massie was blown off the jeep, and he rolled down the side of the mountain, down the side of the road. He said that the sound of the mine was so loud that he momentarily couldn't hear anything, and of course he was unconscious for some time. I imagine that before aid got there it must have been at least 30 or 40 minutes, and by that time he had recouped some of his hearing. He could hear the voices of the medics that had come over but he couldn't speak. They knew that there were five people in the jeep; they accounted for four, but they had one missing and that was Massie. They started searching about the area more or less where he might have been thrown out, but they couldn't find him, so they thought he had been killed in

American .30 caliber bullet casings still visible on the surface of the ground at the location where Lt "Spud" Wright was shot. Private Collection.

action. He was really under some rocks or something, so that they couldn't see him that easily. They were about to give up when luckily somebody went lower down from the road and found him, or else he would have been lost there. They had to bring him up to the ambulance and he was in very bad shape. He had superficial shrapnel wounds on his arms and legs, but I think the worst thing was that his heart and his internal organs were damaged by the explosion. The inside of his stomach was turned almost around from the concussion and I think it tore some of the liver. He had a lot of surgeries done in his stomach to correct the condition of being thrown out of place.

Major Arthur Neesman, of the 1st Regiment HQ Detachment, reported at 14:10:

> Killed 2 enlisted men, seriously injured 3 enlisted men, and 3 other casualties. Road had been cleared by engineers.
> Killed: **Foster V. Bowden**, **Toney E. Duarte**.
> Severely wounded in action: M Sgt George E. Durham, Sgt Hugh R. Starr.
> Other casualties unknown.[9]

Hugh Starr died the next day, while **George Durham** survived until September 3rd, before finally expiring as well. The oversight of one single mine by the engineers had had tragic consequences. Tellermines were very powerful antitank mines that could completely destroy small vehicles, such as jeeps, as we will see again further on.

The war was still not quite finished at Tanneron; some French collaborators had taken refuge in an abandoned hamlet called les Gourins. When the men of the Resistance found out about this, they set out to liquidate the collaborators. Young **Roger Alary** witnessed the operation:

> The *résistants* must have heard that there were *miliciens* who were hiding in les Gourins. So one afternoon, I saw a truck with resistance men who were probably on their way to get those *miliciens*. I saw the truck coming down at full speed, and when it got to a curve it didn't manage to take the curve, and I saw it capsize into the ravine. I was astounded; it was happening about a kilometer or two away from me. The people who were onboard the truck started howling. I quickly ran and told my father, and we gathered up all the valid people from the area, so the men went to the truck and I followed them. I saw the truck in the ravine. One guy had been ejected from it and was there, but one or two others were under the truck. So dozens of people came with winches and metal bars to lift the truck up. They got them out and they were only lightly wounded. It was really extraordinary luck that none of them was severely wounded. They were scratched and torn up, but there was nothing serious. Everybody became euphoric and they came back to our hamlet.

The *miliciens* had narrowly escaped with their lives. However, this was not to last, and according to Mr Alary, they were killed in the following days.

Conclusion

The morning of August 15, 1944, the pathfinder group of the 509th Parachute Infantry Battalion was accidentally dropped in the

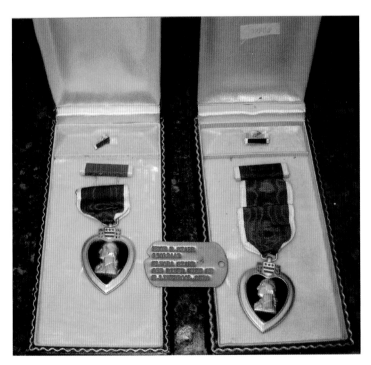

FSSF Service Company soldiers Pvt Foster V. Bowden, Pvt Toney E. Duarte, MSgt George E. Durham, and T5 Hugh R. Starr. All four men were killed or mortally wounded at Tanneron when their jeep drove over a Tellermine. Private Collection. Richmond Public Library Collection, Courtesy Linda Holmes. Private Collection. Starr Family Collection.

A poem written by Starr
and marked to his
brother.

Have you ever cowered in a hole
And heard the cannons roar?
Have you ever walked until your soul
Cried out "Oh God! No more — no more!"?

Have you ever charged on sudden death
While your buddies around you fell?
When every breath might be your last breath
Yet somehow survived the Hell?

Have you ever lain beneath the sky
While your thoughts went flying home
And well-loved scenes met your eye
From a land beyond the foam?

And you entered again the familiar door,
And friends and family met;
Back in the circle again once more
For a night, perhaps, to forget;

But then returned from peace to the strife
And din of the battle again
Where each man tries for another's life
In a world of smoke and noise, and pain?

High on a cross twixt earth and sky,
Alone in his anguish and pain,
Our Blessed Saviour did hang and die
To cleanse the world of sinful stain.

His precious Blood he freely gave
Without one thought of cost,
And this he did the world to save,
That man should not to sin be lost.

And oh! my God, since thou didst give
Thy son upon the tree
That sinners such as I might live
Oh Lord, be merciful to me!

To You I cry from the depths of sin,
As a stranger knocks upon the gate
Throw wide the door and let me in!
And do not say "Too late — too late."

A poem written by Hugh Starr in the months preceding his death. Starr Family Collection.

vicinity of Tanneron, very far from their intended drop zone of le Muy. These pathfinders remained in Tanneron, taking it easy for the next two days. On the 17th, they were warned of a group of Germans approaching Tanneron. The pathfinders ambushed the Germans, killing two of them and capturing the others. They then left Tanneron and managed to rejoin the American lines in the Estérel Mountains with the help of local Frenchmen.

Tanneron was then briefly occupied by the Germans, until it was liberated against light resistance by the First Special Service Force August 22nd. The FSSF ambushed a group of isolated and retreating Germans at the Château de la Verrerie, killing four and capturing 32 of them. The next day a jeep drove over a mine, killing or mortally wounding four of its American occupants. With Tanneron cleared out, the FSSF could advance on to Grasse. However, we must first examine the events that in the meantime had occurred further south: the seaborne invasion and the liberation of the areas of Anthéor, la Napoule, and Cannes.

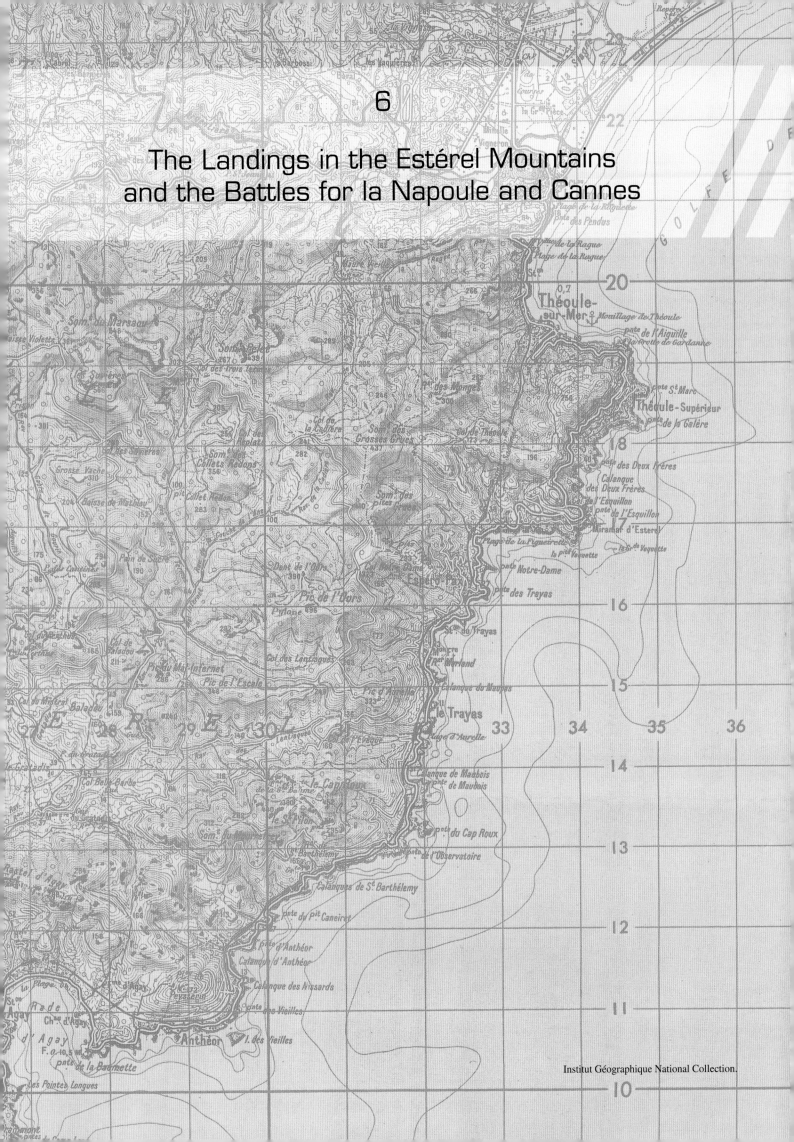

6

The Landings in the Estérel Mountains
and the Battles for la Napoule and Cannes

Institut Géographique National Collection.

Now that we have examined the landing of the airborne forces in our area of study, we pass on to the seaborne landing. We do not describe the landing operation in detail, but only analyze the extreme right wing of the invasion, where the *Groupe Naval d'Assaut de Corse* and the 141st Infantry Regiment landed west of Cannes.

Geography of the Region

The area that we will be concerned with in this chapter starts at Agay in the west, and goes all the way to Antibes to the east. To put things simply, all the western part of this area is covered by the red-colored and jagged Estérel Mountains, which rise steeply out of the sea to an altitude of up to 600 meters. At la Napoule, the land suddenly becomes very flat, particularly in the Siagne Valley west of Cannes. The terrain then rises up to form low hills to the north of Cannes and Antibes. Two main communication routes cross the area from east to west: the RN7 highway that bypasses the Estérel Mountains to the north and the D6098 road that bypasses the Estérel to the south, closely following the coast.

This photo of the men of the Groupe Naval d'Assaut de Corse was taken August 14th, the day before the landing. In his book on Operation Dragoon, historian Jacques Robichon gave this photo the following caption: "A dozen of them are represented here – Reserve Officer Auboyneau, sailors Chery, Gerard, Travers, Wissmann, Paquelet, Andreuccetti, and Second-Master Martini, all of whom would be wounded or captured a few hours later. Sub-Lieutenant Pierre Servel (in the background in the center) and Quarter-Master Jacques Guidoni (at left, near the tip of the boat) would die in the minefield of the Pointe de l'Esquillon, near le Trayas." Chaffiotte Family Collection.

The Groupe Naval d'Assaut de Corse

The French *Groupe Naval d'Assaut de Corse* was assigned the task of landing on the extreme right wing of the seaborne invasion front, in advance of the main force, at 2 o'clock in the morning on August 15, 1944. Its 67 sailors (to which at least one engineer had been attached) were to go ashore in rubber boats at the Pointe de l'Esquillon (Esquillon Point), south of the village of Théoule sur Mer, an area that was guarded by the Russian volunteers of *Ost Bataillon 661*. The mission of the French naval commandos was to blow craters in both the D6098 coastal road and the RN7 highway further inland, in order to cut off the German forces in the main landing zones further to the west. This commando-style operation, performed by an elite and experienced unit, ended in complete and tragic failure when the landing area, contrary to what had been reported, turned out to be heavily mined. The commanding officer of the *Groupe Navale d'Assaut de Corse*, **Commander Roland Seriot**, wrote a report of the operation shortly afterwards in which he described the landing in detail, including the difficult process of approaching the hostile coast without being spotted:

The badge of the Groupe Naval d'Assaut de Corse. Frédéric Brega Collection.

The operation entrusted to the *Groupe Naval d'Assaut de Corse* consisted of landing 60 to 75 men in between le Trayas and Théoule, with the mission of performing demolitions on the following roads at daylight:

- inland road between Cannes and Fréjus
- coastal road between Cannes and St Raphaël

The goal being the protection of the right flank of the main landing.

I had given the first of these missions to a detachment of 42 men under the command of Lieutenant Commander Marche, and the second to a detachment of 25 men under Lieutenant Letonturier.

I had decided to personally guide these detachments to land, assisted by a petty officer of my group, but then to return to the PTs [Patrol Torpedo boats] that had brought us in as soon as they had reached land, in order to join up with the rest of my group, which was preparing an operation. (…)

Departure from Bastia on the 14th at 18:00. Calm sea – no wind – bright night – light fog.

Stopped 1,500 meters off the point at 0035 and gave the order to put the rubbers [rubber boats] to sea; before the order is executed, a flare is fired from Cannes: stopped putting the rubbers to sea and advance slowly towards the south after the appearance of two vessels seeming to come out of Cannes; recognized that these two vessels are moving south two miles from the coast at approximately 10 knots. Returned to the landing point.

01:15 – Stopped 1,800 meters off the point. At that moment, a flare is fired from the same direction as earlier on. Gave the order to put the rubbers to sea anyway.

01:20 – I leave the 306, heading for land.

01:40 – I reach land: recognize the coast perfectly, see

a small fire halfway up hill that must be a German outpost at the spot where intelligence indicates there are three automatic weapons; it is also from there that the enemy actions described further on seem to be coming from.

01:50 – find the planed landing point that is very convenient (small 15-meter pebble beach, accessible slopes). But I am afraid that the rubbers that are coming in now and were attracted towards the left will not see my light signal; as a consequence, I go back out of the bay and call the rubbers with the red flash; the radio doesn't work (jamming).

02:00 – Spotted the rubbers that are coming towards me and reach me very fast, took command of them to guide them, still using the red flash; at that moment, a burst of submachine gun fire is fired, seeming to originate from the fire mentioned previously; very soon afterwards a red flare is fired from the same spot.

Very soon after that a white flare is fired, still from the same spot, towards the rubber boats.

This flare malfunctions and quickly falls into the water between the German outpost and the rubbers; no shots are fired. It would seem that the Germans were blinded by their flare and did not see the rubbers, the presence of which they had only suspected.

02:10 – The four rubbers of Commander Marche have entered the cove at the tip of which the beach is, 50 meters away. I turn and go back out to sea, searching for the three rubbers of Lieutenant Letonturier. I spot them immediately, heading a bit too far to the left and I call them with the flash, they correct their course and take the direction of the cove and head into it.

I turn again and head out to sea towards the PT; indeed, I have left it 50 minutes ago and my absence is only supposed to last one hour. (…)

A modern view of the "Calanque des Deux Frères" at the "Pointe de l'Esquillon," south of Théoule sur Mer, where the 67 commandos of the Groupe Naval d'Assaut de Corse landed in the early hours of August 15, 1944. Note the rugged terrain and the road overlooking the coast that the sailors were to render unusable. Author's Collection.

02:40 – Spotted the PT (that sees my signals).

02:45 – Re-embark onto the PT. I have been gone for one hour and 25 minutes.

From 02:20, when the submachine gun burst and flares were fired until 02:50, at which time the PT left out to sea, neither me, nor especially the PT, have observed any reactions from land. It thus seems that the Germans have had a false alert and were tranquilized, having seen nothing after firing their white flare.[2]

Engineer Mechanic Lucien Chaffiotte picks up the story from there in a romanced version of events that he wrote for the 20th anniversary of the landing:

At 23:30, August 14th, our speedboats stopped 1,500 meters south of Le Trayas, west of Cannes. The putting to sea of our rubber boats was delayed by the firing of some flares, but soon enough the complete group landed at the Pointe de l'Esquillon. It was five to midnight.

Our success seemed certain, as always. We were proud to be the first to reconquer the soil of our country. Everything was calm, the night was deep. In spite of the weight of their ammunition and explosives, the men were cheerfully climbing up the cove.

Alas! We didn't know that the Germans had mined this part of the coast a few days earlier. The first road we were to reach was approximately 200 meters away. The progression was rapid and silent. The officer leading the column, ORIC [Interpreter and Code Reserve Officer] Auboyneau, had already covered about a hundred meters when he tripped a mine and was severely wounded. Two men were killed at his sides.

In the first minutes of a battle, before the action starts, anxiety, often even fear, grips the fighter's heart. Cold-bloodedly crossing a minefield without any detecting equipment was an ordeal that demanded perfectly balanced nerves. Clinging on to this French earth that we had departed four years earlier, we refused to retreat. Pinned down by explosions, we wanted to vanquish.

We continued our progression. The distance separating us from the road was slowly decreasing. Death was striking constantly. Mines were exploding on all sides. We held our ranks and the progression continued. Treasures of heroism were spent until daylight, but we never reached the road. The Lieutenant Commander commanding the unit died an atrocious death, exploding on what was probably the last mine less than 20 meters from the objective. The nightmare ended with the first rays of sunlight.[2]

At the mercy of the Germans who were watching them from the road, and having suffered almost 50 percent casualties, the sailors were forced to surrender. One of the very few who managed to escape the inferno without being wounded or surrendering was **Henri Nannini:**

Inland there were explosions all over the place because the mines were connected to each other, so when one would blow up, it would set off other ones. We had four officers, two of whom (Commandant **Marche** and **Lieutenant Servel**) were killed. Up above, the Germans had turned on a spotlight and told the survivors to surrender. Chaffiotte gave himself up to the Germans with about 15 others.

As far as I was concerned, I barely set foot into the mined area because I was one of the last men to climb up, and when I saw the explosions I didn't insist. I figured the whole thing was over and that there was no point of me going in to get myself blown up and possibly captured, so I turned back, along with several others. We returned to the beach and swam away. An English ship picked us up and brought us back to Calvi. There were about seven of us who managed to get away, while the others were either wounded or captured.

This photo, taken shortly after the landing, shows a German mine field warning sign on the "Pointe de l'Esquillon." The French sailors landed in the inlet visible at the left of the photo. Ted Rulison Collection.

Meanwhile, most of the other commandos remained behind in the minefield. **Sailor Jean Campana**, who was severely wounded, tells of his experience of the landing:

We remained in Calvi for a month doing training, and on the 14th, the day before the landing, they brought us to Bastia. At Bastia there were speedboats, and we took them to go and land at the Pointe de l'Esquillon. We were supposed to blow some bridges to prevent German tanks from going to where the troops were going to land.

We had already put a rubber dinghy in the water when the Germans fired some flares and saw the speedboats. They started shooting at us, so the speedboats escaped. The boats had two motors, a diesel engine and an electric engine that made no noise, so we moved away and then the speedboats put on the electric engine and we followed the coast and returned to the spot. This time the Germans didn't see us, so we put the dinghies in the water, landed, and climbed up. We walked for quite a while. We even saw the Germans; they weren't far off and we could hear them talking. There was a cannon with a lit candle at the tip of it. We went through and then we suddenly entered a minefield.

Theoretically, there weren't supposed to be any mines. It was said that the Germans had laid them that very day, on the 14th. I think they found out we were going to land, because otherwise no mines were supposed to be there. There was a soldier from the army with us [**Marius Arzalier**] who had a special device for detecting mines. He was walking up front and didn't notice that there were mines. He is the first one who blew up and was killed. After that it didn't last long; we blew up on the mines and then it was a massacre. I think there were 27 of us, and out of 27 there were a dozen killed, and those who were not killed were wounded. Commander Marche was killed right next to me. I was wounded when I stepped on a mine. The Germans fired at us, but a dozen of our men managed to get away. They hid here and there, and a few days later they joined up with the Americans.

I was the most severely wounded. I had a perforated lung, kidney, arm, and leg. The Germans came to see us

Sergent-Chef Marius Arzalier, aged 29, from the French 71st Colonial Engineer Battalion, was apparently responsible for detecting any potential mines in the landing zone of the Groupe Naval d'Assaut de Corse. However, he was one of the first men to step on a mine and was killed. Josette Bigot Collection.

and gave us a bit of first aid, but they left us there; they didn't care, they figured we were done for. If I am still alive today, it's because I didn't have any hemorrhage. Some of them would have only been lightly wounded if it wasn't for the fact they were bleeding. There was a lieutenant who had been shot high up in the leg. He lasted two or three days and then died because he lost all his blood. One guy, **Quartier Maitre Chef Guidoni**, from Moltifao, was shot in the throat. It was nothing, but he bled out because nobody picked him up. He had no blood left and died five or six meters away from me. I was urinating blood and was breathing through my chest where the fragment had entered; it was making a rustling sound because my lung was perforated. Some blood was coming out, but there was no hemorrhage. If I had a hemorrhage I would have died. The first day I was conscious, but then I wasn't conscious anymore. We had vitamins that would make your hunger go away. I know I ate a few, but I can't remember how many. I stayed out four days before the Americans arrived.

When the Americans came by they found me. They gave me an injection and it seemed to me like my strength was coming back, but then they said: "Finnish" and they left. When I understood "Finnish" I thought: "I am dead." But two hours later they came back with two German prisoners and a stretcher and they brought me up and evacuated me. There were perhaps two or three hundred meters to get to the road. It was very steep, with rocks and everything, so the guy at the back had to carry the stretcher above his head and the guy in front was down on his knees. On the road there was a tank. They put me behind the tank and there was shooting going on all over, so they brought me behind the hill. Back there, there was no more danger and they put me in an ambulance and brought me to a field hospital made with tents. There were several other wounded and they operated on me there. I stayed there for a few days and then they sent me to St Raphaël.

Back home they had received my duffel bag and everything as if I was dead. At St Raphaël, there was a ship that came in, I still remember the name *Chasseur 53*. On the pier the people told them: "There are some sailors in the maternity." So they came to see me. *Chasseur 53* was leaving for Ajaccio that night, so I wrote a quick note that I gave to them. When they reached Ajaccio they posted my letter, and when it reached my parents' home, my parents said: "But then he isn't dead!"'"

In fact, Jean Campana was picked up by the Americans after "only" one day, as we will see later, but his perception of time was understandably clouded by the circumstances. **Commander Roland Seriot** went to visit his wounded men at the hospital in St Raphaël and was able to obtain a detailed description of the landing from them, which he summarized in his report:

Sixty-seven officers, petty officers, quartermasters, and sailors participated in this assault. Among these, ten men, including two officers and two petty officers, were killed shortly after landing. Seventeen men, including two officers, are lying wounded at the St Raphaël hospital and I have only been able to see them for two hours. Twelve men are safe and sound in St Raphaël. The balance of the men, in other words 28, are reported missing, explaining why my report will be brief and incomplete. (…)

August 18th, I visited the hospital in St Raphaël, where I had found out that some of my wounded were. I interrogated Lieutenant Letonturier and ORIC Auboyneau, who are both being treated, as well as 15 other non-commissioned officers or men who participated in the operation, and it is from them that I got the following information.

The seven rubber boats land at the correct spot that I had just identified. The landing takes place correctly and quite slowly, because climbing up the hill is quite difficult. Reserve Officer Auboyneau, as planned, takes the head of the column that is to leave first (the Marche detachment that is to blow the inland road), while Lieutenant Letonturier takes care of unloading the demolition equipment he will have to use from his rubbers.

Around 02:50, halfway between the sea and the coastal road, ORIC Auboyneau steps on a mine that wounds sailors Campana and Andreossetti; a liaison is established soon afterwards between Auboyneau and Commander Marche, who is in the middle of his column, by sailor Bertrand, who while advancing causes two mines to explode without being wounded. The decision is made by Commander Marche to leave Auboyneau where he is with one man and continue the advance.

At that moment, lower down and to the left, Sub-Lieutenant Servel (Letonturier group) blows up on a mine and is killed, along with **Second-Master Corlou** and **Quartermaster Cacaud**; sailors Wismann, Freymouth, Gerard, Ben Stali, and Crety are wounded in succession, either while trying to establish liaisons or while trying to aid wounded comrades.

Around 4 o'clock, Lieutenant Letonturier trips a mine that wounds him lightly and kills **sailor Guilcher**. Very soon afterwards, in the vicinity of Lieutenant Letonturier, sailors Marchetti, Boisard, and Dourous are wounded by mines. **Dourous** would die at daylight.

Around 04:30, more mine explosions. There is no more hope of executing either of the missions. Through one of the German-speaking men, conversations are started between Engineer Mechanic Chaffiotte and the Germans who are on the road, submachine guns in hand: nine men are killed, 17 are wounded, and the others are pinned down, causing mines to explode as soon as they move.

Commander Marche, however, declares that he is going to head into the woods and try to get back to our lines; he stands up, advances, and blows up almost instantaneously, mortally wounded and agonizing; ten minutes later he will stand up again, advance, and almost immediately fall down the cliff, where his body was later discovered.

Daylight comes, and conversations resume between the Germans and Chaffiotte, the only officer who is not wounded. The Germans talk of coming by sea and indicating a path that is clear of mines by which the wounded will be able to be evacuated.

08:30, the Germans declare that they cannot come by sea and that they will open fire on everybody if the French do not extract themselves from the minefield on their own.

Lieutenant Letonturier is only 50 meters away from the road; on his hands and knees, he tries to reach the road, but when he is 15 meters away from it, he sets off a mine, suffering a fractured leg.

As a consequence of this, Engineer Mechanic Chaffiotte tries to extract himself from the minefield by sea. He manages to reach it safely and is followed by all the able-bodied men and those with minor wounds who can walk; but the hill is too steep to be able to carry wounded men down, so it is decided that they will be retrieved later from above.

Pierre Servel, Albert Corlou, and Henri Guilcher, three former inhabitants of Brittany, were among the 11 men killed in the mine field at the "Pointe de l'Esquillon" August 15, 1944. Henri Guilcher came from the island of Sein, where most of the fit male population had sailed to England to join De Gaulle and the Free French Forces in June 1940. Amélie Jacquin Collection, Courtesy Hervé Minjon. Corlou Family Collection, Courtesy Joseph Le Goc. Clet Le Coz Collection.

As soon as the group of able-bodied and lightly wounded men has reached an area that is not mined, they are captured. Most are sent to Théoule, including Engineer Mechanic Chaffiotte. The wounded and six able-bodied men are put in a house overlooking the minefield; the Germans authorize sailors Benard and Bertrand to retrieve the wounded who are still in the minefield, under the condition that they will also bring back two pistols.

At 16:30, are now remaining in the minefield only the [original text missing] advance of the American troops.

As I write these lines, I am made aware that six men of the other column of prisoners have escaped and rejoined our lines.

According to information received from Lieutenant Boju of the *Groupe Naval d'Assaut*, who was in contact with the 36th Division, this very dense minefield, located in a very steep area, was only laid by the Germans August 1st, according to some, or August 11th according to others. I have ordered Lieutenant Boju to make a very careful investigation among the civilian population and amongst the German prisoners to clarify this point. (…)[3]

of local resistance men from the Cannes area attacked the column of French prisoners on the afternoon of August 15th, succeeding in liberating several of them. This daring operation will be explained in detail in the next chapter. A total of 11 Frenchmen were killed in the botched landing: ten sailors plus the army soldier mentioned by Campana. They were:

Surname	Name	Rank	Age	Date of death	Location of death
Arzalier	Marius	Sgt Chf Inf Col	29	15.8.1944	Théoule
Braconnier	Henri	Matl Can	20	15.8.1944	Théoule
Cacaud	René	Qrt Mtr Mnvr	24	15.8.1944	Théoule
Corlou	Albert	2 Mtr Fsl	23	15.8.1944	Théoule
Dourous	Pierre	Matl Fsl	20	15.8.1944	Théoule
Fichefeux	Pierre	2 Mtr Mnvr	33	15.8.1944	Théoule
Guidoni	Jacques	Qrt Mtr Can	28	15.8.1944	Théoule
Guilcher	Henri	Matl Gbr	23	15.8.1944	Théoule
Marche	Gérard	Capt Corvette	39	15.8.1944	Théoule
Mignot	Georges	Matl Fsl	22	15.8.1944	Théoule
Servel	Pierre	Ensgn Vaisseau	24	15.8.1944	Théoule

As mentioned by Commander Seriot at the end of his report, the terrible failure of this mission was partially mitigated when a group

In this letter sent to the family of sailor Achille Nasica, the French Navy is requesting to be informed of what German prison camp he is being held in, in order to be able to send him food and supplies. Nasica Family Collection.

The Landing in the Anthéor Cove

Appart from the French commandos, it was the 141st Infantry Regiment that was to land on the right flank of the seaborne invasion force, where it was to hit two different beaches at 8:00 in the morning, take control of the Agay area, then push inland north into the Estérel Mountains and east along the coast. The 1st Battalion of the 141st IR was to land at Anthéor Cove, code named Blue Beach, where it was to blow a railroad bridge that overlooked the beach, then advance east down the D6098 coastal road (that the French commandos had failed to crater) towards Cannes and establish a defensive line between Théoule and la Napoule. The 2nd and 3rd Battalions were to land slightly more to the west at le Dramont, on Green Beach, and capture Agay. The 2nd Battalion was then to push inland through the Estérel Mountains in order to establish several roadblocks on the RN7. The 3rd Battalion's mission was to proceed

Survivors of the Groupe Naval d'Assaut de Corse reunited at the "Pointe de l'Esquillon" every August 15th for many years after the war, to commemorate the sacrifice of their comrades. Denise Benard Collection.

into the Estérel Mountains between the 1ˢᵗ and 2ⁿᵈ Battalion to take control of the high ground. This operation would cut two of the three main routes of communication the Germans had between the Var and the Maritime Alps (the remaining one being the D562 road between Grasse and Draguignan, passing through the Fayence-Montauroux area, that were mentioned in Chapters 3 and 4). In more general terms, the 141ˢᵗ IR was to protect the right wing of the invasion front. We will concentrate mainly on the landing of the 1ˢᵗ Battalion, as it occurred nearest to our area of study, and will not go into details about the landing of the 2ⁿᵈ and 3ʳᵈ Battalions at Agay.

Anthéor Cove was a tiny inlet with a strip of beach less than 100 meters long, with rock formations on which the Germans had constructed pill boxes projecting into the sea on either side. The area between Agay and Théoule was defended by *Ost Battalion 661*, made up of poorly-motivated Russian volunteers. *Generalleutnant* Fretter-Pico had presumably assigned the defense of the Estérel to them, as with its coastline of jagged rocks, the Estérel seemed to be one of the more unlikely locations in his section of the coast for a landing to occur. Some soldiers of other German units, such as the neighboring *Reserve Division 242*, were also present at Agay August 15ᵗʰ. The defenders, both Russians and Germans, only put up very weak resistance to the landing. The hardest fighting occurred at Anthéor Cove, where C Company of the 141ˢᵗ IR was to lead the assault of the 1ˢᵗ Battalion. **1ˢᵗ Lt William Everett**, of C Co, was in the very first wave that hit the beach:

I was with Company C. We had a mission on Blue Beach, which was the beach on the extreme right at Anthéor. The rest of the battalion had to stay out until we had reduced all the resistance there. Ours was the only company that actually had to fight. H-hour was 8 o'clock. Blue Beach is a small bay; it was completely surrounded with pill boxes and entrenchments, and had the Navy not done such an excellent job, why, we could have never made it. There was only a small beach there, only fit for a few LCVPs at a time. Actually, our company consisted of five boat teams in what we used to call LCVP (Landing Craft Vehicle Personnel). They carried mainly personnel. Each boat team usually consisted of about one officer and 20 to 25 men carrying specialized equipment: flame throwers, Bangalore torpedoes, hollow charges, shaped charges, and all those things that initial assault troops need to reduce beach defenses. My men were experienced, battle-hardened soldiers; they had fought all the way through Italy, and they were veterans of Anzio, Cassino, and Rome.

Our mission required that we enter that bay and make a landing. I was the executive officer of the company at the time. The commanding officer was Lt Martin Tully. We came in five boats: three in front and two behind. Lt Tully was in boat four, and I was in boat five. We almost simultaneously hit the beach. Thank God for the Navy: their heavy bombardment and rocket fire had kept the pill boxes buttoned up. They had been salvoing approximately every three minutes, and after the last salvo we made a

"Blue Beach" and the Anthéor bridge as they appeared shortly before the invasion, ravaged by the numerous air raids that had previously been launched against the bridge. The beach itself is so small that it is for the most part hidden by the bridge, yet the entire 1ˢᵗ Battalion of the 141ˢᵗ IR would land here August 15, 1944. NARA.

The Anthéor Bridge, as it appeared in the days after the invasion. MRA Collection.

high-speed run into the little bay and landed. There was a period the Germans didn't know what was going on, and when they opened up their embrasures, we were ashore and among them. We were able to reduce them. We received some very heavy machine gun fire at this time. Lt Tulley was struck as he exited his boat and actually fell back into the boat that brought him in. This made me company commander. As the LCVPs started to withdraw, the Germans took them under fire and they sank two.

We all had specific missions. My mission was to go directly ahead up the hill. There was a seven or eight arch railroad bridge, and we had to blow a hole in it if it had not already been hit by naval gunfire or the bombardment. Fortunately, it had been hit. We kept right on up there; there was a battery of 40mm up there, and we took it very quickly. The fighting was very, very intense. I lost one of my section sergeants, **Sgt Bill Griffitts**. On the left hand side somebody threw a grenade, and it went in one of the bunkers, which must have been an ammunition bunker, because everything blew up on that side. The people on our right, Lt Dorschel and his team, had some heavy fighting in some pill boxes right there where the highway circles the bay. When the fighting stopped, we had captured close to 100 Germans and killed a few, God knows how many.

Paul Duffy was also in C Company and explains his version of the landing:

We were the first ones in. The LCVP that I was on hit the ground, the ramp went down, and I was the third man off of it. The two other LCVPs came in to our left. In fact, the gate on the one on the complete left flank went down before it got close enough to land and the LCVP sank. We cleared across the road and then went to the high ground, which was more stones than anything else. Then we sat there and looked back, and we really didn't have any action at all there. We did lose one man [Sgt William Griffitts], but that was his own fault, he went on the back side of a hill and he was cleaning his machine gun and he got shot and killed by a German that was off to our right flank.

The later assault waves nevertheless kept on running into trouble, as **Jack Wilson**, of D Company, remembers:

Our operation was set for August 15th at 8 a.m. We were on a barge called a Higgins boat [this was another name given to the LCVP] that was made of plywood. There were five small boats deployed from the ships at a time, each circling around until their time to go in to shore. Its crew consisted of two sailors: one to run the motor and one to drop the ramp. We were the 7th "wave," and pulled in on what was named Blue Beach, a narrow cove that had an adjoining strip of land. I was to be first off the boat, so I was sitting next to the ramp with my back to that strip of land. As we neared the beach, I noticed dozens of bullet

holes in the plywood, about ten inches above the heads of those sitting across from me, and knew there were bullet holes above my head, too.

The boat hit something and the operator stopped. The second sailor dropped the ramp and was immediately hit and killed by a burst of machine gun fire; I had to step over him to get out of the boat. The water was a little over my waist, with bullets hitting all around me. I really thought that this was it and that I'd never get to the beach. Holding my rifle over my head with my left hand and the Bangalore over my head with the right, I felt a slight sting in the hand holding the Bangalore and noticed blood running down my arm. If that bullet had hit the torpedo instead of my hand, it would have been over for me and several of the fellows behind me. Hearing the motor of a slow, low-flying airplane, I looked up and saw a Kingfisher pontoon plane, one that was launched from the deck of our destroyers. Inside the plane, the pilot and a gunner saw the machine gun that was shooting at us. They opened up on him, and whether they took it out or not I don't know, but most of us made it onto the beach. As soon as I hit the beach there were five or six strands of barbed wire. I slid the Bangalore under it, lit the fuse, and rolled back. Usually in a situation such as this the barbed wire was mined, but it wasn't this time.[4]

Arlis Sizemore was also in D Company of the 141st IR:

I was in the 7th wave. I think that cove where we went in was only about 80 yards wide. When those boats hit the beach, the door in front falls down. There was a machine gun that was just cutting across the top of that boat. We were lying down in the bottom, but the driver and the guy that ran the ramp got hit. We all went out of there as fast as we could go. One of my ammunition bearers [**Pvt William Benter**] behind me raised up just a little too high to put his ammunition on his shoulder and he got hit right in the neck and it killed him. He just fell off out of the boat into the water.

26-year-old veteran Sgt William C. Griffitts, of C Company of the 141st IR, who was shot and killed by a sniper after the landing on "Blue Beach" without having ever even seen his recently-born son. Griffitts Family Collection.

Pvt Sayre Hillerson, of C Company, who was apparently wounded during the attack on "Blue Beach," and later died of his wounds while being evacuated back towards Italy. Hillerson Family Collection.

Edward Stoermer, of the 1st Battalion HQ Company, remembered:

I was in the 1st Battalion of the 141st, and we landed in a small bay at the extreme right hand edge of the whole invasion. The road goes right down along the ocean there, and right on the other side of the road was this big monstrous railroad bridge. I had my pack and carbine and everything, and then I had to carry a mine detector to shore as well. I also had one round of 81mm mortar ammunition strapped to my pack in the front.

I got off of an LST onto one of those LCVPs, and I think I was in the 3rd wave to land. I thought the LCVPs were made of steel and I would be kind of protected, but I noticed that they were made out of plywood, and I thought: "A lot of good that will do me." There was a medic with us and he was crouched down there, too, but his stretcher was standing straight up and he got the end of it shot off. So we made sure that we were crouching down in there as much as we could. Then there was some kind of little ships, but they shot off big rockets which I didn't even know the Americans had. They shot them off towards the beach and behind us there was a big battleship of some sort, and when it would fire the shells went right over our heads, sounding like a freight train going right over the top of us.

Of course, we were told to get off of the boat as fast as we could when it hit the shore. They hit what I thought was the shore and they dropped the front down. I was the first guy and I went charging off of there, but the boat had hit a sandbar about eight or ten feet out, so I immediately fell down in the water and just kind of sloshed to shore. There was a big bomb hole right in the middle of this little beach, and there were a couple of guys in there; I ran down in there, but they told me to get out, that I had to get off the beach. So I ran down a little bit and there was another hole that had some barbed wire all twisted around it. I tried to crawl in the hole and got stuck, so one of my buddies who was behind me grabbed me by the feet and dragged me back out of it. The Germans were shooting at us from behind with machine guns out on the point of this bay. I remember seeing the sand spurt from where their bullets were hitting, but they didn't come too close to me.

They still kept yelling at us to get off the beach, so then I ran up over the road and around the base of the big columns of this railroad bridge; it was dug out, so I was able to dive into one of those and that's basically where I stayed until our rifle companies worked their way around out to that point. I guess the Germans either surrendered or were killed, I don't know which. In my platoon, Ronald Wright, the guy who had pulled me out of the barbed wire, was shot bad enough that they put him back on an empty LCVP and took him back to the ship.

We will end the description of the landing at Anthéor Cove with a text written by **Lt Carl Strom**, the commanding officer of B Company:

August 15th, we arrived before dawn off the coast of France with a large escort (...) which commenced

Comparison of a prewar postcard of Anthéor with a picture of the same area taken shortly after the landing. The numerous air raids that targeted the bridge during the Occupation and the final navy shelling of August 15th have burned away the vegetation and destroyed several of the houses. Vogl Family Collection. Ted Rulison Collection.

firing at the German defensive positions on the coast. As we boarded our landing craft, rocket ships sent up a seemingly unending barrage of rockets at targets on shore. As we neared the shore, the naval ships let up their fire. We could see the damage they had done to the possible German positions and it was terrific. C Company landed ahead of us and, as I jumped into the water, my good friend, Bernie Meier [There is no officer named Bernie Meier listed as being a casualty on August 15th.], CO of C Company, was standing waist deep in the water. He had been shot in the leg. I told him I would help him aboard our LCI [Landing Craft Infantry], but he said: "No, get your men ashore as quickly as possible." We rushed ashore, thankfully with no casualties. With C Company moving inland with little resistance, the Germans were apparently pulling back or out.

Moving under the railroad bridge spanning the beach, we went inland about 400 yards. On our left, on the crest of a low hill, we could see barbed wire. Moving up to it, we could see that this was a well prepared German defensive position; however, we could see no enemy troops. We considered blowing a path through the barbed wire with the

The Anthéor Cove as it appears today. Author's Collection.

Bangalore torpedoes, but we noticed a high hill immediately behind the position. We decided to move around to the back of that hill and see if we could gain a position on the top, overlooking the German position. We did this and, after setting up our machine guns to provide covering fire, attacked down the hill into the position. There was no opposition, and about 20 Germans came out of a dugout with their hands in the air. The location overlooked the bay where we had landed. If they had put up any resistance during out trip ashore, we would surely have suffered major casualties. As it was, these proved to be second line troops who had been impressed into the German army. The German officers and non-commissioned officers had all fled. They were very glad to see us. We sent a sergeant and three men with the prisoners to the road along the beach to find a prisoner collecting point and turn them over. There were three 80mm mortars set up and we disabled them.[5]

The 1st Battalion of the 141st IR had quickly taken control of Anthéor Cove. Meanwhile, the 2nd and 3rd Battalions of the 141st did the same at Green Beach at le Dramont, where the Germans offered virtually no resistance at all, as **PFC George Hemker**, of E Company, remembers:

We landed in a little bay on the 15th, and we were the first ones to hit the beach on that particular spot. But we practically walked on the beach and walked off. In other words, we didn't have any resistance there. The Germans had some bunkers, and they stayed in their bunkers because of the heavy rocket fire. We had rockets coming in, landing right in front of us as we hit the beach, so they didn't have time to take any defensive positions, they just came out of their bunkers, lay down, and gave up. We took about 15 prisoners.

T5 Eugene Johnson, a medic who was accompanying G Company, remembers an interesting encounter with a German soldier behind Green Beach:

The resistance on the beach wasn't that heavy. I think we had two or three enemy machine guns trained in our

direction and there were a few artillery shells coming over, but no heavy resistance. Now inland, no more than a quarter of a mile, we started hitting pretty heavy resistance. I was walking through this open place by myself and a German soldier hollered at me in German. I couldn't understand him, but one of the people in our platoon understood him and he hollered and told me: "Johnson, he's telling you you're in a minefield." I got warned by the enemy not to keep going in that minefield, so I turned around and went back and took another route.

Within a few hours, the American troops from Green and Blue Beaches linked up, capturing Agay and most of its defenders. In total, seven men from the 141st IR were killed August 15th, four of which were from the 1st Battalion, which had suffered the heaviest casualties at Anthéor. The names of the killed were:

Surname	Name	Rank	Unit	Age
Foster	Albert S.	PFC	HQ1 141 IR	26
Griffitts	William C.	Sgt	C Co 141 IR	26
Hillerson	Sayre	Pvt	C Co 141 IR	
Benter	William C.	Pvt	D Co 141 IR	24
Hessong	Arthur J.	PFC	E Co 141 IR	24
Chesunas	Charles	PFC	AT Co 141 IR	32
Petras	Adolph	T/Sgt	K Co 141 IR	25

If the losses were no heavier, it was probably mainly due to the fact that the defenders were for the most part non-Germans from *Ost Bataillon 661*, who had only put up a token resistance. The German troops had only suffered eight killed: four at Anthéor and four at Agay, according to what can be found in the archives of the *Volksbund*. Only two of the dead were later identified:

Surname	Name	Rank	Age	Date of death	Location of burial
Unknown				8.1944	Agay
Reiniger	Franz	Gefr	24	14.8.1944	Agay
Klann	Erich	Gren	18	14.8.1944	Agay
Unknown				8.1944	Agay
Unknown				8.1944	Anthéor
Unknown				8.1944	Anthéor
Unknown				15.8.1944	Anthéor
Unknown				15.8.1944	Anthéor

Although the Germans only had a few men killed, they lost a large number of prisoners. Being in the HQ Company of the 1st Battalion of the 141st IR, **Edward Stoermer** participated in the processing of these prisoners:

After things quieted down, they started bringing the German prisoners back to us and we searched them and put them on the LCVPs. They had their knife, fork, and spoon sets that we took away from them, and they used to have these all these beat up kind of rough-looking pocket

Arthur Hessong, Charles Chesunas, and Adolph Petras, the only three men of the 2ⁿᵈ and 3ʳᵈ Battalions of the 141ˢᵗ IR to be killed the first day of the invasion of southern France. One of Arthur Hessong's brothers had already been killed in June 1944 during the Normandy invasion. Hessong Family Collection. Patricia King Collection. Shiner Gazette Collection, Courtesy Paula Pekar.

watches. Later on, we found out it was some kind of a little case that they put their watch in to keep the sand and stuff out of it. But we didn't take any of those things; we just took any French money that they had and that was about it. We kept the money and then, about two days later, there wasn't anything for us to do but wait until they [higher ups] told us to do something, so the guys were up at a house playing poker. There wasn't that much money I don't think, just whatever some of the Germans had with them. We didn't know what it was worth, or if it was worth anything at all.

The Advance East Towards Cannes

After having cleaned up the beach at Anthéor, the 1ˢᵗ Battalion of the 141ˢᵗ IR headed east towards Cannes with C Company, led by **Lt William Everett**, following the coastal road, while the other companies progressed through the hills further inland:

In the meantime, after we had reduced most of the resistance, the rest of the battalion landed and passed through us, heading inland and to the left towards Cap Dramont. The units that landed on our left had managed to get some armor ashore, so we were joined by some Sherman tanks and M-10 tank destroyers. We began to reassemble around 12:00, and started up the road that goes along the sea, right along the cliffs toward Cannes. The paratroopers had jumped ahead of us the night before, back up around le Muy and Draguignan, so the Germans were pretty confused at this time. We were quite happy, because we had expected a lot more resistance than we actually hit. They had some kind of weird troops there. I believe they had some Indo-Chinese mixed in with regular troops. They weren't as good troops as we had fought in Italy, for instance. Some of them didn't look to me like they were front line troops.

These "weird troops" were of course the Russian "volunteers" of *Ost Bataillon 661*. Meanwhile, **Lt Carl Strom**'s B Company headed into the mountains north of the coastal road:

We immediately moved out east (...) into the mountains along the coast. Company A was on our left, attacking through the mountains, and Company C was on our right, attacking along the coastal highway. We ran into a couple of isolated pockets of resistance, but nothing that

held us up for very long. At one point, atop an outcropping of the mountain, we spotted the entrance to a cave several feet below us. Moving down, we found several Germans hiding there. They came out with their hands above their heads, again happy to surrender. Unfortunately, in climbing down the cliff, one of our men fell and was badly injured, our only casualty the first day ashore. We again sent three men, with Germans carrying our injured man on a stretcher, to the collecting area. Unfortunately, we later learned the injured man had died of his injuries (...). We continued east across the mountains parallel to the highway until dark before receiving orders to stop for the night. We spent the night on the side of a steep hill. I was dog tired, lay down with my feet propped up against a bush to keep me from rolling down the hill, and slept like a dog. During the night a German patrol came through our position, and our men had a brief fire fight with them. Fortunately no one got hurt. I was so totally exhausted that I completely slept through the action. [6]

The sinking of Landing Ship Tank 282

As **Lt William Everett**, of C Company of the 141ˢᵗ IR, advanced down the D6098 coastal road towards Cannes late on the 15ᵗʰ, he powerlessly witnessed what would turn into one of the most serious setbacks suffered by the landing force the day of the invasion:

As we were proceeding up the road, just about dusk we spotted two JU 88s coming. I guess they were at about 5,000 or 6,000 feet, no higher, coming parallel to the coast, heading towards the transport area and the beaches. They had radio control bombs and they launched one. Since we saw them, I yelled at the navy ground control radiomen to warn the ships that they were coming. I don't know if they got the warning or not, but the JU 88s launched a guided bomb and struck one of the LSTs going into Camel beach. It had one of our artillery regiments on it and they really sank it. When nightfall came, we just stopped and held our position there. That was the first day.

It was LST (Landing Ship Tank) 282, which was transporting soldiers from several artillery units, that was hit by the German remote controlled bomb. The stricken LST sank off Green Beach, where the 2ⁿᵈ and 3ʳᵈ Battalions of the 141ˢᵗ IR had landed in the morning. The official report concerning the sinking of LST 282, written by its skipper **Lt Lawrence Gilbert**, read:

The Executive Officer reported what appeared to be a single rocket fired from the plane at the beach. Upon examination with binoculars, directly under a twin-engine, twin-rudder plane, the object was apparently motionless. The object began to move ahead of the plane and downward on the same course as the plane until its elevation was approximately 25 degrees. At this point, it turned approximately 90 degrees to starboard and apparently headed for LST 282. Bright red flame and white smoke were seen coming from the tail of the object, which resembled a miniature plane. The speed of the object was exceedingly fast. The Captain told the Gunnery Officer it was a radio controlled bomb and to open fire. The number one forty millimeter located on the bow opened fire. The bomb came in across the starboard side at an elevation of approximately fifty feet. It appeared to be about to cross the ship, when suddenly it turned about 45 degrees to port and dove into the ship. An explosion followed immediately. Several guns in the forward battery had opened fire on the bomb and plane just an instant or so before the bomb dove. The bomb apparently hit a few feet forward of the superstructure, to the left of the center line, penetrating the main deck and exploding below. All guns that could bear were firing after the bomb hit until the plane was well out of range.[7]

Navy officer **Hans Bergner**, who was aboard LST 282, later wrote:

We spotted two planes coming in from over the land, far away off the starboard bow. We were talking back and forth about what the planes might be. Suddenly, there were three planes instead of two, and the third one appeared smaller and, we assumed, farther away. The reason it looked farther away was that it was not a plane, but a small radio-controlled glider bomb. It had been launched unseen from a Dornier 215. It headed initially toward the transport area, then turned at a right angle and dived right onto LST-282. We got a few shots off with the ship's guns, but they were well astern of this bomb, which was probably moving at several hundred miles an hour.

It hit right in front of our ship's wheelhouse and went into the main engine room, where it exploded. Pete was killed instantly, blown from the conn down onto the main deck. My first conscious memory is of being on the main deck, rather than on the elevated gun tub. Whether I was knocked down by the concussion or jumped because of fear, I don't really know. I looked back at the conn and could see that it was all crumpled. There was no sign of life. Flames were starting. The next 10 to 20 minutes were terrible. The Long Tom artillery ammunition began cooking off and exploding, as did the ammunition in the ship's own magazines.

There never was any formal order to abandon ship, but people saw the obvious and jumped overboard. I tried to warn some soldiers to stay on board, because we had been taught in midshipman school not to leave the ship until directed, because conditions might be even worse in the water. But soldiers get nervous on board ship, where there are no foxholes, so they said to me "F___ you," and off they went.

The first lieutenant had the bow doors halfway open when the bomb hit and all power failed. The bow ramp was still closed, and all the troops manning their vehicles on the tank deck would have been trapped. The rear cables of a large cargo elevator on the main deck were parted, however, causing the rear portion of the elevator to fall onto trucks in the tank deck. That formed a ramp from the tank deck to the main deck. Many injured soldiers, some with their uniforms on fire, scrambled up that ramp to safety. It was similar to the way red ants escape from an ant hole when someone pours in gasoline.

By now the ship had moved to within about half a mile of the beach. Lieutenant Gilbert, the skipper, got the Navy Cross for his actions that night, and he deserved it. He ordered hard left rudder, which kept the exploding LST-282 from moving in among the LSTs already lined up on the beach. As it was, we careened off the port and eventually ran aground on some rocks in front of a beautiful resort home.

In addition to his ship handling, the skipper rescued a signalman, George Heckman, who had a badly broken leg. He carried Heckman down three flights from the bridge to the water's edge, and there someone else took over and began pulling him ashore. Then the captain went back and got the engineer officer, Edward Durkee, who was unconscious and had a back full of shrapnel. The captain secured him to the rudder post with his life belt. Both were later recovered in an unconscious condition by rescue craft. The skipper himself had been wounded severely, so he did those rescues with one arm.

The last people who left the ship swam ahead, trying to beat the hulk ashore. The engines had stopped running as soon as the bomb exploded, but momentum continued to carry the ship toward shore. I myself finally jumped off the port bow. I think I let myself down to the anchor so I wouldn't have to jump so far. In midshipman school I was a non-swimmer, and had to go to swimming class when the other guys went to physical education. All I had learned during my youth in the Texas hill country was dog paddling in various creeks. But I beat that LST ashore. I had an inflatable life belt around my waist and it worked well. The Army had criticized those belts after so many men were lost in Exercise Tiger, claiming that men were pitched forward, forcing their faces into the water. I have to say that my life belt was effective when it came to the test.

When we got ashore, we got behind a large rock on the beach. As the ship got closer, the good swimmers went out and helped the wounded men get ashore. We dragged them behind the rock, because we were afraid the exploding ammunition might send shrapnel into us. Eventually, when we couldn't find any more shipmates or army men, we went up a road to Green Beach.[8]

One of the foot soldiers on LST 282 was T5 Amos Wolfgong, of the 36th Field Artillery Battalion. **Amos Wolfgong** managed to survive the attack, even though he did not know how to swim:

We were off shore, waiting to take our turn to hit the beach, and I saw two planes up the coast a ways to the north. One looked like it was on fire. We were in a command car, and I said to my buddies: "I see a plane on fire up there." So I crawled out and stood on the side of the command car so I could see it better. I saw this one plane, it looked like a plane, making a circle of fire and smoke in the sky. Just then I noticed it had separated from the other plane, and the other plane I recognized was a Ju 88. Well, I was standing there, pointing this out to my buddies. This plane had wings on it and a fuselage and so forth, and it had a jet engine on the back of it with fire flying out of it to force it through the air, and it was coming at a terrific speed.

It came right at us; I could see it right below me just for a moment and that's the last I can remember, because it exploded. I was knocked unconscious and thrown forward on the ship. Later on I began to come to, and I was underneath a 40mm antiaircraft gun. I got myself up on my feet again and I didn't seem to be hurt. By that time the ship was on fire, and it was loaded with large artillery ammunition that was exploding. I can remember one man walking up to me; he had his clothes all burned off and blood running down him, and he wanted me to help him blow up his life preserver that he had. So I led

The remains of LST 282, which took fire after being hit by a German remote-controlled bomb late on the afternoon of August 15th. The damage inflicted by the bomb blast is clearly visible at the back of the ship. The Gregg and Michelle Philipson Collection.

him over to the side of the ship where they were letting some of the soldiers down on lifeboats. Then I went to the side, and there was a big post there with the chain from the anchor wrapped around it. I laid down on the deck to avoid the pieces of the ship that were blowing past me, and then finally a sailor who had survived dropped the anchor. This chain began flying around and I had to move. This sailor took most of his clothes off and he said: "Come over here, there's a hammock hanging on the side. You can go down it." I had told him, I guess, that I could not swim.

I had all my equipment on me and it was quite heavy: wool clothes and jacket, as well as an ammunition belt and heavy shoes. My helmet had blown off in the blast, so I didn't have it. I started down the hammock that hung there part way down. I got so far down and then, not knowing how to swim in water, I didn't want to let go. Finally, the sailor came sliding down this hammock and straddled on my head. My shoulders and handholds didn't hold anymore and we went down into the water, way down, because there was no bottom. We were quite a ways out. I came up and out and I didn't see him anymore. Then I started swinging my arms like I had seen swimmers doing, and I just went a little ways, because I had heard years before that when a ship goes down it takes on water, and it would draw you right into the hole. So I started going the opposite direction from the ship.

It was getting kind of dark, and I didn't know which way the shore was. I did not go but a short distance and there, standing directly in front of me, was the man we know as Jesus, in a purple robe, holding his arm and hand down to me. I could not go in that direction any more or I would have struck him with my hand. His spirit took control of me and turned me in another direction, as I had been going out to sea. I went possibly 180 degrees, from what I can remember, and started towards the shore. It was quite a long ways—150 yards, 200 yards, something like that. I came to a big rock sticking up out of the water and I set down on there to rest a little. Then, while I was sitting there, this sailor that came down the hammock with me came along and said: "Come on, you can reach bottom here." So I slid off the rock, but there was no bottom. I came back up again and kept on going towards shore. I probably only had 100 yards yet and I made it to shore.

I went up a road that ran along the beach and there was a little barn. It was dark of course, and there were a couple of other GIs that went in ahead of me. I crawled in there and made a hole in the hay bales, then covered myself up because I had no protection with me. My rifle, everything was lost. I fell asleep, and the next morning, I was right by the wall of the barn and I could hear a GI's voice saying: "This is K Company, infantry." That woke me up, so I looked out through the crack of the barn and I saw a GI with his rifle going up through a little gulley in the brush, and I knew it would probably be safe to come down out of there. I came back down and out, and I thanked God that I wasn't hurt bad, just skinned up a little bit. I don't know how it happened, but some 20 GIs were lost in the explosion and fire, and I am still surviving.

The sunken LST 282. Walter Eldredge Collection.

The Fighting Outside la Napoule

While the 1st Battalion of the 141st IR had been heading down the coastal road towards Cannes on August 15th, the 2nd Battalion had managed to advance very rapidly through the Estérel Mountains, meeting no resistance, and had already reached their objective (the RN7 highway) by the night of August 15th to 16th. The roadblocks they immediately set up on this important line of communication surprised the Germans during the night, as **PFC George Hemker** of E Company remembers:

> We reached a highway about ten miles inland at just about dark time on the 15th, and then they told us to block off the road. The highway kind of went over a high hill there, and we were right on top of it. The hill was really a lot of gravel, in other words stone, so we couldn't dig a hole. We found places to take cover under some big rocks. During the night, we took out a couple of trucks that were coming through there; in fact, they were driving through with their lights on for a little bit, as they didn't think we were so far inland. One truck that was hit during the night was carrying fuel and it made a tremendous explosion; the fuel was on fire and it was all over the road. In the morning, there was some kind of vehicle carrying quite a few Germans, and we stopped the vehicle with a little antitank cannon we had there.
>
> Then about noon we got into a battle. They had several truck loads coming through there; they were running down the highway, and I got wounded by a piece of shrapnel in the hand. I think it was from a grenade, because there were a lot of grenades flying back and forth. I noticed the blood running off my hand and the medic we had there happened to go by and I said: "You want to put a bandage on this?" And he says: "We gotta get you back and make sure we get that shrapnel out of there." So they sent me all the way back to Italy.

By the early morning of August 16th, the 2nd Battalion of the 141st IR had set up four roadblocks at strategic positions on the RN7 highway. The easternmost block was only located three

kilometers west of la Napoule, near the hamlet of le Tremblant. As George Hemker explained, the Germans immediately tried to take back control of the vital RN7. The men who counterattacked the American positions were no longer from the badly mauled and mediocre *Ost Bataillon 661*, but from the more aggressive and fresh *Reserve Jäger Bataillon 28*, which had just arrived from Nice. However, the Silesian recruits of *Bataillon 28* were also no match for the veteran soldiers of the 141st IR and the German counter attack failed, as the 141st reported in one of its communications:

> 15:00. August 16th: "New enemy identifications: 2nd Battalion, 8th *Jäger* Regiment, 164th Division [This in fact refers to *Bataillon 28*, the correct and complete identification of which was *Reserve Jäger Bataillon 28*, 2nd Battalion of *Reserve Grenadier Regiment 8*, *Reserve Division 148*], newly arrived from Nice to counter attack this morning at approximately 0900 hours, but was dispersed by artillery and small arms fire by our 2nd Battalion. Enemy's plan of attack was for three companies abreast to attack along and to the west of Route number 7 out of Cannes supported by the 8th Company on the high ground (…). Troops appeared green—easily put to route. However, small groups cut off the route to Company "F."[9]

The 141st had one man killed in the fighting, **PFC Eugene Obenrader**, of E Company. The Germans had lost several men of *Bataillon 28*, including the commander of the 7th Company, *Oberleutnant* **Georg Seidel**. After this failed counterattack, it would seem that Battalion 28 was thereafter content with holding defensive positions facing the advanced positions of the 1st and 2nd Battalions of the 141st IR outside la Napoule and launching only minor local attacks in the following days. The front would now remain stable at le Tremblant until August 21st. Meanwhile, on August 16th, C Company of the 141st IR continued advancing

31-year-old Unteroffizier Ludwig Ernst, of the 10th Company of Bataillon 444, was killed in the first unexpected encounters with the 2nd Battalion of the 141st IR on the RN7 Highway August 16th. His body and that of a soldier who could not be identified were recovered from a shallow forest grave along the RN7 a few kilometers west of la Napoule in 1958. Deutsches Rotes Kreuz.

27-year-old Feldwebel Paul Lingansch (left), one of the Silesians from Reserve Jäger Bataillon 28 who was killed August 16, 1944. His family, which was forced to move out of Silesia after the war, was not informed of his death until April 1961. Lingansch Family Collection.

27-year-old Jäger Reinhold Götz (right), of Jäger Bataillon 28, from Trinksaifen, in Bohemia, was reported missing in the le Tremblant area August 17, 1944. His company commander wrote to his mother: "I certainly hope that your son, who fulfilled his duty in a scrupulously soldierly manner, has been made prisoner by the Americans, and that you will be informed by the Red Cross in the foreseeable future." In fact, his family never heard any news of him again until this book was being prepared in 2013. Although Reinhold Götz's body was recovered in la Napoule and identified in 1958, his family was never informed of this by the German authorities, as Trinksaifen had in the meantime become part of Czechoslovakia, and the Deutsche Dienststelle is not permitted to actively contact the next of kin of soldiers outside the borders of Germany. Kloc Family Collection.

"We got on a highway that ran parallel with the beach and headed toward the Resort City of Cannes." The scenic coastal highway leading from Anthéor to Cannes that C Company of the 141st IR followed August 15 and 16, 1944, running into slight German resistance. Author's Collection.

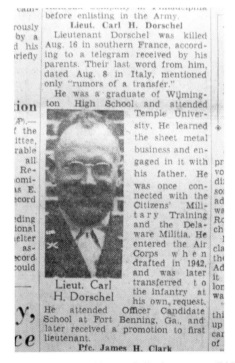

Every Evening, Delaware Historical Society Collection, courtesy Ed Richi.

northeast down the coastal highway until it reached its objective, the Rague Valley, located between Théoule and la Napoule. On the way there they found some of the wounded French commandos of *Groupe Naval d'Assaut de Corse* that the Germans had left behind before pulling out. **Lt William Everett**, who was leading C Company as it advanced towards la Napoule, remembered:

> The next day, we proceeded along the road towards Cannes. We came across some French commandos that had landed the night before and had stumbled into a minefield. When I saw some of them that had been wounded I yelled for our aid men and medical men, who came up and started helping them. We passed them back by vehicle for further medical attention. We didn't have any chance to really talk to them, all we kept hearing was everybody screaming over the radio: "Keep going, keep going, keep going!" They were not with you, but they were telling you to keep going.
>
> I had a navy fire control party with me that controlled the fire of the cruisers, battleships, and destroyers. When we hit any resistance, I would just back up and let them fire. We had no real problem; we overcame the resistance, except as we approached Napoule. The road goes around a little promontory there. Right as we went around the bend, one of my officers, Lt Dorschel, came up, and we hit some resistance, and unfortunately a sniper killed him. So that left me with only two other officers. We pulled back, then attacked and overcame the roadblock there. Then we proceeded, going down the road all that day to a position where they stopped us right outside of Cannes [In fact, outside la Napoule at the Rague Valley.]. The tanks pulled up with us and we went into a defensive position to hold the right flank of the beachhead. We took some German

positions there, pill boxes and so forth. From the sea, the land comes up very steeply to the highway and then goes up very steeply. I put a little command post around the curve in the garage in back of a house and I commanded the troops from there.

Jack Wilson, of D Company of the 141st IR, describes more details of the advance down the coastal road August 16th:

> We got on a highway that ran parallel with the beach and headed toward the resort city of Cannes. At this time, other than sporadic sniper fire, we encountered little resistance. I don't recall which company we were attached to at the time, but one day I was walking beside a fellow when someone in back of us spoke to him. He stopped, turned around to answer, and then, letting out a moan, he fell to the ground. He had been shot between the shoulder blades, and the wound looked like he'd been shot with a shotgun at close range. The sniper

PFC. EDGAR BEEMAN DIES OF WOUNDS

Central School Graduate Injured in France; Veteran of Italy *1944*

Oriskany, Sept. 14—Mrs. Edna Beeman, Utica St., received word from the War Department yesterday, that her son, Pfc. Edgar F. Beeman died of wounds received in France.

Pfc. Beeman, 22, attended Oriskany Central School, and was graduated with the class of 1940. While in school, he was a member of the school band and the Oriskany Village Band. He attended St. Stephen's Church.

Before his induction into the Army on Dec. 1, 1942, he had been employed at the Savage Arms Corp., Utica and the Union Fork and Hoe Co., Rome.

He received his basic training at Camp Phillips, Kansas and Camp Forest, Tennessee, and at one time was stationed at Fort Meade, Maryland. Pfc. Beeman left for overseas duty about Oct. 1, 1943 with the 36th Division, 141st Infantry. He took part in the battle of Italy and was wounded there, before being sent to France.

Oriskany, Sept. 13—Mrs. Edna Beeman has received word from the War Department that her son, Pfc. Edgar Beeman was wounded in France.

PFC Edgar Beeman, of C Company of the 141st IR, was mortally wounded in action August 16, 1944. Oneida County Historical Society Collection, courtesy Ed DeSanctis.

This incredible relic, a Russian PPSh submachine gun, was found hidden in a tree next to the coastal road between Théoule and le Trayas in the 1970s. The weapon, which was presumably abandoned by a Russian soldier of Ost Bataillon 661, became firmly embedded within the wood of the tree over the years. Private Collection.

The view from the "Sommet des Grosses Grues," near which the 3rd Battalion of the 141st IR encountered some resistance August 16, 1944. The towns of la Napoule and Cannes are visible in the background. Author's Collection.

had used a wooden bullet that explodes upon impact and was against international law to be used. In the commotion, someone said he thought he knew approximately where the sniper was located and offered to go find him. Another fellow and myself went with him and we fanned out, running in a zigzag course toward where we thought he was located. We got about halfway there when the sniper stood up with his hands in the air, surrendering. We shook him down for any other weapons, and finding the wooden bullets on him, we all three shot him. We returned to our group and showed the bullets to the lieutenant in charge, who said that he would have shot him too if he had been there. The wounded had been moved out when we got back, and I've wondered about him throughout the years, and if he survived.

As we continued along the highway towards Cannes, other than a few snipers, we had little resistance and no more wooden bullets. Continuing through many beautiful villas along this route, we found that almost everything had been booby-trapped, and we had been warned to be watchful and keep hands off. One particular villa was very pretty, surrounded by a stone fence with an arched gate. On the gate was a large bell for visitors to ring. I just happened to look back and saw one of my men reaching up to grab the rope. I yelled at him and reminded him of the dangers of booby-traps. He jerked his hand back, looked inside the bell, and yelled back that the damned thing was booby-trapped. I reported this to the lieutenant so it would be taken care of.[10]

The story of the wooden bullets mentioned by Jack Wilson is one of the typical WWII myths repeated by American veterans. The Germans did indeed have wooden bullets, however, these bullets were used as blanks for training and were incapable of inflicting a wound, as they disintegrated immediately when fired. What the wounded soldier had actually been shot with or why the sniper would have had wooden bullets on him remains a mystery.

While the 1st Battalion of the 141st had been following the coastal road, the 3rd Battalion had advanced in the mountains overlooking the coast. Near the "Sommet des Grosses Grues," in the hills north of le Trayas, it got into some skirmishes with what were probably remnants of *Ost Bataillon 661*. Two men from L Company, **PFCs Thurman Edwards** and **Willard Meek**, were killed in these encounters August 16th, and a third man, **Pvt Thomas Sheehan**, was mortally wounded in the head on the 17th. **PFC Thaddeus Gosik**, a machine gunner in L Company, was wounded in one fire fight:

> The Germans had a delaying action; they wanted to stop us for a little while. All the riflemen were hugging the ground, so they told the machine guns to get up on the hill. Anyhow, I put a rock in front of my head and my hand was sticking out, and I will be darned if a ricochet didn't hit my hand. When you get hit, it doesn't hurt. I didn't even know I was hit until the blood started running, and that's what put me in the hospital.

L Company also encountered mortar fire, wounding **PFC Clarence Jansen**, who later wrote:

The second day, August 16th, we were heavily hit by mortar fire. I was hit by shrapnel on my right leg, just above the ankle. The force knocked me to the ground. I called the medic and he took me to the "under construction" field hospital. They in turn sent me to a hospital ship anchored off shore, and a few days later I arrived at the 36th General Hospital in Naples. By the time they worked on my wound gangrene had set in, and there was a possibility they would have to amputate my leg below the knee. But with the use of the new medicine being used ("Penicillin") and excellent doctor and nurse care, my leg was saved, and I returned to my unit September 29, 1944.

PFC John Boyce, also of L Company, remembers a group of prisoners captured after one encounter:

There was a hill coming off the coast, and we were fighting on the north side of the mountain. We had a good fire fight somewhere in that territory and we captured maybe 30 German soldiers. As I remember it, after we captured these German soldiers, we lined them up and someone tried to ask them some questions. None of us could speak any German so we didn't get very far, and they were put in a line and forced to march back towards the coastline. I was at the back of the line, marching these guys back south, and I was amazed at how old the German prisoners looked. Of course I was 18 at the time, and most of us were just a bunch of wild Indians at 18. They were probably in their thirties or forties or something, and we were amazed at how old they were, so I said to one of the Germans, or I pointed to him to say: "Hey, let me take the pack that's on your back." He was obviously having trouble, so I took the backpack and carried it as we were marching them away, so he gave me a cigarette case, a nice shiny thing with a spread eagle sitting on the German Nazi swastika. Well, I just shoved it in my pocket, which was absolutely the stupidest thing to do, because if you are going to get caught the next day, you don't want to have some German equipment in your pocket.

The traces of seven German casualties exist for the area between Blue Beach and la Napoule. All of them were killed in the general vicinity of le Trayas, which is also presumably where 1st Lt Dorschel and the German sniper described by Jack Wilson were shot. These German casualties are listed below, along with their official dates of death:

23-year-old PFC Willard E. Meek, of L Company of the 141st IR, who was killed in action in the Estérel Mountains August 16, 1944, along with PFC Thurman H. Edwards. Meek Family Collection, courtesy William Casteel of the Newcomerstown Historical Society.

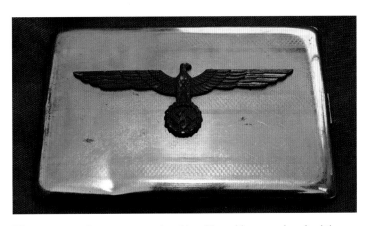

"He gave me a cigarette case, a nice shiny thing with a spread eagle sitting on the German Nazi swastika." The cigarette case that was given to John Boyce, of L Company of the 141st IR, by a German prisoner in the Estérel Mountains. John Boyce Collection.

By the afternoon of August 16th, C Company of the 141st IR had, as per plan, established a defensive line at the Rague Valley, between Théoule sur Mer and la Napoule. In front of them lay a cove spanned by a railroad bridge. Across the cove was Hill 84, which had a castle built on it and was occupied by the German soldiers of *Reserve Jäger Bataillion 28*. The men of C Company were positioned on the hill facing Hill 84, and the Rague Valley between these two hills formed the front lines. Just as in le Tremblant, in the area of action of the 141st IR's 2nd Battalion, the front would remain stable at the Rague Valley until August 21st. The 141st was fulfilling its mission of blocking the two local highways and protecting the right flank of the Allied invasion. Now that both the 141st IR and *Bataillon 28* were content to remain in defensive positions, the fighting over the next days consisted mostly of artillery attacks. German coastal batteries in Cannes repeatedly shelled the positions of the 1st Battalion, causing more casualties than the landing itself. **Jack Wilson** remembers this deadly artillery fire landing on D Company's positions:

Surname	Name	Rank	Age	Date of death	Unit	Location of burial
Nemoikin	Iwan		23	8.1944	Ost.Btl.661	Le Trayas
Unknown		Ufwb		15.8.1944		Le Trayas
Hümmer	Otto	Schütze	21	16.8.1944		Drag. (Le Trayas)
Krassa	Georg	Uffz	38	16.8.1944		Le Trayas
Krumpill	Roman		18	16.8.1944		Le Trayas
Pollin	Kurt	Fwb	22	16.8.1944		Le Trayas
Unknown				16/17.8.1944		Le Trayas

The railroad tunnel that crosses under the mountain west of Théoule sur Mer. This tunnel was used as a shelter by the American soldiers, while the tracks were used as a shortcut. This attracted heavy German artillery fire that inflicted more casualties than the actual landing had caused. Author's Collection.

"The Germans were using large coastal guns, firing mostly white phosphorus shells at us." These shots taken shortly after the Liberation of Cannes show camouflaged German bunkers and cannons that, according to the reports of the 141st IR, were used to fire on the American positions in Théoule. Damage inflicted by Allied naval counter battery fire is visible on the bunkers. MRA Collection. Traverso Collection/Archives Municipales de Cannes.

be lingering at the tunnel's mouth and along the train tracks. Their deadly artillery fire killed several soldiers from A Company, at least two of which were then buried in the gravel directly beside the tracks. It was unusual for American casualties to be buried elsewhere than in U.S. Army cemeteries, and as these two bodies had not been processed by American graves registration teams, they were officially listed as missing in action until they were recovered by the 48th Quarter Master Graves Registration Company in October 1944. On August 16th and 17th, in total, the 141st IR had 15 men killed or mortally wounded, mostly due to artillery fire. A Company suffered the heaviest casualties, with eight of its men being killed, including Samuel Braff, the elder brother of Ruby Braff, who was later to become a famous jazz trumpeter. These losses are summarized below:

I thought we'd be fighting for the city of Cannes, but we left and headed inland. Before long, we found a railroad track going inland and started walking it. We didn't get very far until we came under heavy artillery fire from the Germans. They were using large coastal guns, firing mostly white phosphorus shells at us. If you were hit by white phosphorus, it would burn until you could smother it out. We used mud to smother it. There was a railroad tunnel ahead, and we made a run for it and stayed in it for a while. We looked like we had slept in a coal bin. All train engines used coal then, and the tunnels were loaded with coal dust. You could always tell who had been in the tunnel.[11]

The railroad tunnel mentioned by Jack Wilson not only provided the Americans with shelter, it also provided them with a shortcut between Théoule and le Trayas, since it passed straight under the mountains, instead of detouring along the coast as the road did. The German artillerymen in Cannes were probably well aware of this, and predicted that many American soldiers would

Surname	Name	Rank	Unit	Age	Date of death
Brookshier	Vivan F.	PFC	A Co 141IR	22	16.8.1944
Carvalho	Joseph	PFC	A Co 141IR	30	16.8.1944
Cross	Roderick S.	PFC	A Co 141IR	28	16.8.1944
Henderson	William B.	PFC	A Co 141IR		16.8.1944
Strassburg	Alton W.	PFC	A Co 141IR	20	16.8.1944
Beeman	Edgar F.	PFC	C Co 141IR	22	16.8.1944
Dorschel	Carl H.	1Lt	C Co 141IR	31	16.8.1944
Obenrader	Eugene E.	PFC	E Co 141IR	19	16.8.1944
Edwards	Thurman H.	PFC	L Co 141IR		16.8.1944
Meek	Willard E.	PFC	L Co 141IR	23	16.8.1944
Braff	Samuel	Pvt	A Co 141IR	29	17.8.1944
Hosey	Carl O.	PFC	A Co 141IR	24	17.8.1944
Nichols	William E.	PFC	A Co 141IR		17.8.1944
Dunlap	George H. IV	Pvt	B Co 141 IR	32	17.8.1944
Sheehan	Thomas L.	Pvt	L Co 141IR	19	17.8.1944

Carvalho Killed

Private First Class Joseph Carvalho, AUS, infantryman, who has been reported missing in action in France since Aug. 16, is now listed as killed on that date, the War Department has advised his wife, Mrs. Edna (Regan) Carvalho of 73 Nashua Street. He has been overseas approximately six months.

Inducted Sept. 3, 1943, Private Carvalho trained at Camp Wheeler, Ga., and Fort Meade, Md. He left the United States last February, took part in the fighting in Italy and subsequently participated in the invasion of Southern France.

Private First Class Carvalho leaves, in addition to his wife, his mother, Mrs. Mary Carvalho of 239 Chace Street, Somerset; three sisters, Mrs. Virginia Burns, Mrs. Mary Medeiros and Miss Evelyn Carvalho, all of Somerset; four brothers, John, with the Merchant Marine; Private Francis, stationed in Colorado; Sergeant Manuel, fighting in France, and Antone of Somerset. *11-20-44*

PFC Carvalho

PFCs Alton W. Strassburg and William E. Nichols, from A Company of the 141st IR, who were killed August 16 and 17, 1944, probably by German artillery fire. Strassburg Family Collection. Sheffield Public Library Collection, courtesy Betty Dyar.

Lunenburg Man Listed Missing In Italian Area

1944

LUNENBURG, Sept. 12—Pvt. Roderick S. Cross is missing in action in Italy, according to a war department notification received by his parents, Mr. and Mrs. Ernest W. Cross, of Highland street, and his wife, Mrs. Elsie (Brewster) Cross, of Skowhegan, Me.

Pvt. Cross, who has been serving in the army for the past three years and seven months, has been stationed overseas since January. He entered the service at Camp Edwards and was later sent to Saco, Me., where he served for over a year. He received further training at Fort Dix, N. J., and at Camp Patrick Henry, Va.

Nicholas Chronicle
Richwood Weekly Newspaper 1-6-1949

Services Planned For Carl Hosey

Funeral services for Carl Hosey, 34, who was killed in action in France in 1944, will be conducted Sunday, January 16 at 1:30 p. m. at the First Baptist church.

Hosey went into the service in February 1943 and was serving with the 141st Infantry division at the time of his death.

Rev. I. E. Gregger, pastor of the Methodist church will conduct the services and military rites will be administered by the Bert B. Hickman Post, American Legion.

Survivors include his father, Luther Hosey; five brothers, Edward Willard, Eugene, Durr and Clarence. Also surviving are three sisters; Mrs. Pearl Collins, Mrs. Exie Stewart and Mrs. Clarence McClung.

Simons Funeral Home is in charge of the arrangements.

Pvt George H. Dunlap IV, B Company 141st IR, the son of a rich businessman from Mobile County, Alabama, died of wounds August 17th, after having apparently injured himself falling down a cliff, as explained by Lt Carl Strom. Erik Overbey Collection, University of South Alabama Archives, courtesy Sarah McLeod.

In response to the German artillery fire, the Allied fleet shelled the German coastal batteries in Cannes and on the Lérins Islands, just off Cannes, several times during the following days. The shelling of the bunkers on the mainland at Cannes caused several German casualties, though it also killed numerous French civilians. According to **Jean-Paul Carbonel**, who was involved with the Resistance in Cannes, the Germans had in fact not yet had time to install cannons in their bunkers on the Lérins Islands, though the naval shelling also produce some results there:

> On the Island of St Margueritte there was a bunker that didn't have any cannon in it. The *Emile Bertin* was circling off Cannes, firing salvos, and it fired one salvo onto that bunker. A shell entered through the aperture and exploded inside, killing a German soldier who should have been safe, being inside the bunker. At night, they brought him back and unloaded him at Palm Beach, then brought him to a funeral home vehicle with a cart. He was covered with a tarpaulin, but you could tell that there was a person underneath. It seems to me that the soldier had a Polish name.

PFC Joseph Carvalho, PFC Roderick S. Cross, PFC Carl O. Hosey, and Pvt Samuel Braff, of A Company of the 141st IR, were all killed by artillery fire near the train tracks in Théoule sur Mer August 16th and 17th. All four were temporarily buried in the gravel beside the tracks or in nearby properties. Samuel Braff's brother Reuben "Ruby" Braff was later to become a world famous jazz trumpeter. Carvalho Family Collection. Fall River Public Library Collection, courtesy Kathryn Kulpa. Lunenburg Public Library Collection, courtesy Amy Sadkin. Susan Atran Collection.

Lt William Everett describes what the situation was like for the men from C Company of the 141st IR during the few days of static warfare, facing Hill 84 outside la Napoule:

> For the next couple of days we were quite busy. There was some sniper fire there constantly; you couldn't move around. Every once in a while we would fire some mortars over there to keep them quiet. The Germans mounted a number of counter attacks, but we had the assistance of the navy gunfire, which was fantastically accurate. We stopped

A bunker damaged by Allied naval gunfire as it appears today on St Honorat Island. Author's Collection.

> I don't know how many counter attacks, including one night attack. They tried to come around and flank us, but that was almost impossible, because it was like a cove there, and we had platoons up above us in the hills dug in good defensive positions. I lost another officer there at la Napoule; he may have broken an ankle or something and I had to evacuate him, so that left me with just one other officer.
>
> General Dahlquist came to la Napoule and he wanted to see the positions, so I said: "OK, I will take you out to some of the positions that are on the other side of the road towards the water." He had a bunch of flunkies and aides with him, and I said: "Follow me." I ran across the road and jumped over the wall on the other side. When he followed me a sniper took a crack at him, and when he got down next to me he said: "You really fooled me. That's an old soldier's trick; he probably lined up on you and took a crack at me. On the way back, I will go first."
>
> I think about the second or third day I was trying to get some sleep, and some French officers came up and they said to me: "Why aren't you going into Cannes?" I said: "My orders are to do just what I am doing. You want to go into Cannes? Help yourself." We would watch the coastal guns open up on the destroyers. They would rush in toward Cannes, turn about, make a smoke screen, and the Germans would fire at them and when they did, the heavy cruisers would really let them have it. They shut them down real quick. It was interesting to see the navy in actual exchange of fire with coastal batteries.

View of an abandoned German coastal gun at Théoule sur Mer. The Rague Valley, which formed the front lines from August 16th to 21st, is visible in the background. Just left of the barrel of the gun is la Napoule Castle, built on Hill 84, which was defended by the German soldiers of Bataillon 28. Further to the left is the railroad bridge that crosses over the Rague Valley towards Théoule and the houses in which C Company of the 141st IR had taken up defensive positions. The village of la Napoule is visible in the background to the right of the gun barrel. Ted Rullison Collection.

Jäger Josef Ritzka, aged 18, who was killed on Hill 84 August 17, 1944. www.hultschiner-soldaten.de

Some of our engineers had mined part of the railroad bridge that crossed the little inlet there. On about the third night there we had a night attack. I was sleeping on a door, and I woke up with these tracers flying by the front door of the garage. I went out to counter whatever was going on; I was heading out towards the bridge and I heard somebody yelling "Fire in the hole!" so I ducked behind a tank that had pulled up there. When they set off the explosives the concussion really knocked the hell out of me and a lot of the men, but it didn't do much damage to the bridge. We held that position until we were relieved by some paratroopers.

By midday August 17th, the 1st Battalion of the 141st IR reported having captured up to 1,100 prisoners since the landing on August 15th. These prisoners were probably mostly men of *Ost Bataillon 661*, as well as men of *Bataillons 28* and *444*. It seems that *Ost Bataillon 661* was more or less completely annihilated by the 141st IR, with most of its Russian volunteers surrendering. *Bataillon 444* had been stationed in the Cannes area on the day of the invasion and lost some men who had been sent down the RN7 highway towards Fréjus. An idea how poor the motivation of the soldiers of *Ost Bataillon 661* was is given by one of the radio communications of the 141st IR:

12:16. 17 August: "Former Russian officer who has just been captured located 11 gun positions and gave much information on enemy around Cannes."[12]

Arlis Sizemore, of D Company, remembers the surrender of some of the Germans (or were they Russians?) in the Estérel hills:

We were near Cannes, and it was up on a hill there. I was on guard duty that night, and I heard something down the hill below there making a noise. I called the CP, and he said: "Oh, just throw a hand grenade down there and you won't give away your position." So I did; I threw a hand grenade, and next morning there was a bunch of Germans down in there who gave up.

Estérel Mountains Battlefield Investigation

One elder Frenchman who was interviewed regarding the events that occurred in the Estérel Mountains spoke about a specific location where the Germans had, according to him, "unsewn their badges" and gotten rid of them during the period of fighting. Throwing away insignia and badges was typical behavior of surrendering German soldiers, particularly in cases when soldiers wanted to attempt to conceal their identities. When the exact location the witness had mentioned was visited an incredibly intact site was found, with

"They set off the explosives, but it didn't do much damage to the bridge." This photo of the Rague Valley Bridge taken shortly after the fighting shows that the destruction was more successful than remembered by Lt Everett. MRA Collection.

A view of the positions of C Company of the 141st IR, as seen from the German positions in la Napoule Castle. The railroad bridge mentioned by Lt Everett is visible to the left. Pierre Carle Collection.

A German gas mask canister also lies on the surface of the ground. Private Collection.

numerous items still lying directly on the surface of the ground. A search of an area roughly 100 meters in diameter revealed the following artifacts:

- Five identification tags, two of which were still lying on the ground after more than 60 years. All the tags bore the markings of the 1st Company of *Ost Bataillon 661*: "1/Ost-Btl/Russ/661". Only one tag was intact, while the four others had been broken in half, as was often done by surrendering German soldiers.
- One German wound badge in black. This badge was awarded to soldiers having been wounded in combat once.
- One pocket watch.
- Two German tunic buttons that were found close together. These were perhaps torn off a tunic when the wearer tore off his shoulder boards.
- Remains of several gas masks, three grenades, one gas mask box, one mess tin, and ammunition pouches.
- Approximately one hundred spent cartridge casings (The witness had explained that when he first reached the area in 1944, he had found weapons and ammunition abandoned on the ground, so he had fired a large number of shots for fun). Most of the casings were from WWII-era German 7.92mm cartridges, with a few American .30 caliber casings mixed in. One very interesting WWII-era Russian 7.62x25mm casing was also found, proving that some of the Russian volunteers in the Estérel had been equipped with captured Russian weapons, such as the PPSh submachine gun.

These finds seem to indicate that some Russian volunteers of *Ost Bataillon 661* decided to surrender in the aftermath of the landing, but were worried about what might happen to them if their captors found out that they were Russians, and thus traitors to the Allied cause. Before surrendering, they therefore decided to get rid of their telltale identification tags and their badges that identified them as regular German army soldiers. Perhaps their plan was to try to make the Americans believe they were simply Russian prisoners of war being used by the German army for manual labor, as was often the case? One can wonder why one soldier would also have thrown away his pocket watch. Maybe he thought that this sign of wealth would betray his true identity? Or maybe he preferred to throw his watch away, rather than take the risk of it being confiscated by an American soldier? In any case, the efforts the Russian soldiers went through to hide their identity was in vain, as the Americans were perfectly aware of who they actually were, as is proven by period 141st IR radio communications. The Russian volunteers' effort did, however, provide us with valuable archeological evidence of the presence of *Ost Bataillon 661* in the Estérel Mountains at the time of the Allied invasion.

An incredibly intact archeological site. Two identification tags of soldiers of Ost Bataillon 661, both broken into two pieces, lie on the surface of the ground where they were thrown away over 65 years earlier. Private Collection.

The most significant finds made at the Estérel Moutain surrender site. Five identification tags belonging to members of Ost Bataillon 661, a pocket watch, a spent Russian submachine gun round casing, two German uniform buttons, and one German wound badge. Private Collection.

Friendly Fire Incident Near le Tremblant, August 20, 1944

The 141st IR held its positions outside la Napoule until August 20th, on which day it was relieved by the 509th and 551st Parachute Infantry Battalions. The 141st's stay was for the most part uneventful, apart from the German artillery. August 17th, the 1st and 3rd Battalions, minus C Company, were even pulled out of the Estérel front and sent to the Bagnols en Forêt and Callian areas (As explained in Chapter 4). C Company and the 2nd Battalion, which remained in the vicinity of la Napoule, lost no more men on either August 18th or 19th. However, the units luck turned just before it was relieved August 20th, when American artillery accidentally fired on the positions of G Company along the RN7 highway outside le Tremblant. **T5 Eugene Johnson**, who was a medic attached to G Company, was one of those wounded that day, and he explains the circumstances:

I was the head ranking medic in the company, and James Chesshire and I were good friends, so I stayed with James Chesshire's platoon in G Company, 141st Infantry. I think it was something like five or six days after we had invaded southern France. We had pushed the Germans back pretty good and we must have been 10 to 15 miles inland, maybe a little further than that. James, his platoon, and I were on the side of this mountain that had overgrowth on it, and I was laying in the edge of the overgrowth, watching the Germans down below in a French house with a pair of field glasses. I was watching them, and they would put on what looked like a woolen night robe over their uniform and go out to a well and get water. I was surprised they would use that, but I think the reason they did was so that we would think it was civilians down there and there wouldn't be anything coming in on them. I was watching them do that, and every once and a while I would go back to where James was to tell him about it, and I would come back and watch them a little bit more down at that farm house.

So anyway, I quit doing that and came back to James. We had one of those stoves you pump up during combat to make a little coffee or hot chocolate, or something like that. So we did that, and when I was pumping that stove up to light it, all at once we got a heavy barrage of machine gun fire, rifle fire, and heavy artillery. It was coming down heavy and I felt something hot on my leg, like someone stuck a lit cigarette on my right thigh. I knew I was hit, but I didn't realize it was that bad. I got up and I was bloody all over; blood was gushing out of my right thigh, so I knew I was hurt. I had a foxhole maybe ten paces away, so I got in my foxhole and a little Spanish boy came and pulled my belt off, made a tourniquet out of it, and stopped the bleeding. I believe there were five or seven killed in this incident, I am not sure how many, but I know it was a large number killed and several wounded. It almost got that whole platoon. I always thought that the Germans spotted me with those field glasses up there, because I am sure some of them had field glasses and were watching too.

31-year-old Jäger Fritz Weber, of the 7th Company of Bataillon 28, was killed by shell fragment wounds to both legs on the RN7 a few kilometers west of le Tremblant, officially on August 18th. When he was exhumed from a shallow grave by the road in 1958, he still had motorcyclist glasses and vehicle keys on him. Weber Family Collection.

The remains of an American foxhole in the hills overlooking le Tremblant and the RN7 in 2011. Author's Collection.

Sgt James Chesshire, of G Company, who had been preparing coffee with Eugene Johnson when the artillery hit, remembered:

We were in a wooded area, and there was a little town down the road from us, I don't know what the name of it was. Gene [Eugene Johnson] and I were making a pot of coffee, and we had one of those little gasoline stoves you can pump up; we didn't hear any shells come in because of the noise of the stove squealing. Some of the guys may have heard them, but Gene and I couldn't and they landed right on top of us. One guy, a squad leader named Gabriel [**Joseph Gabrus**], was killed, and my Lieutenant, Lt Apperbe [**Lt Henry Apperman**], died on the way to the hospital, I think. He was a Jew who escaped from Germany back in '39 the way I heard it, and he went to one of our officer candidate schools and got to be an officer. I lost him at the same time I lost Gabriel, and Johnson was also hurt. I don't know if Johnson knows that it was friendly artillery or not. I told him once, but I don't think he believed me.

I was wounded slightly but not seriously; it sort of burned my backside a little bit. I thought it was powder burns, so once I got the dead and wounded taken care of I went to the medic. He said: "Let me see." So I showed him my backside, and it was just sort of fine shrapnel. He used tweezers to pick the shrapnel out of me and I went on. I didn't turn in to hospital or anything.

Meanwhile, a more severely wounded **Eugene Johnson** was being evacuated towards the 2nd Battalion aid station in Fréjus, along with Lt Henry Apperman:

By that time, someone had called a litter jeep to come up on the side of the mountain. I think the Lieutenant and I were probably the worst two wounded, so they sent us back to a hospital. The road was all bombed out from airplane bombing and artillery, and it wasn't a very good ride, being wounded. The best I remember, it took a good 12 hours to get back to that little hospital. I don't see how the Lieutenant lived that long, because he got hit by a large piece of shrapnel in his stomach and his intestines were up on his chest. But he and I talked several times in that ambulance going down, and it was amazing to me that he could even talk, but he did. He was a brave young Lieutenant, I gotta tell you that, because not once did he act like he was frightened or scared or anything. He was assigned to us just before we made the invasion, so he was very new there, and a hell of a nice fellow. He died that night, and it was due to lack of attention really, because when we got back it was supposed to be a hospital, but the hospital hadn't had time to come and set up there and it was just a make-do thing. It was no more than a 15 by 20 tent with a dirt floor, two medical chests, and a litter right on top of them, and that is what they used to operated on me. There wasn't anything that was sterilized, it couldn't have been. When you start operating on somebody, you're supposed to be in a sterile situation, but anyway, that was an emergency and it had to be done, so they did the best they could.

I came to from the operation the next morning at about 4 o'clock, and they said they took a whole bunch of shrapnel and one bullet out of me. I looked at the bullet very closely, and it could have been a detonator out of an artillery shell too. They told me that they had made arrangements for a boat to meet just at sun-up down on the beach… We were right at the beach, and they were going to pick me up and put me on a hospital ship and take me back to Italy, where they had better facilities. The next morning, they had me down at daylight and the landing craft came in and picked me up and carried me back to the hospital ship.

It's only about a two or three-day round trip from southern France into Naples, Italy. When I got back there, I was having chills and fever, and my thigh had swollen up about twice as big as it should be. They found out I had

29-year-old Sgt Joseph Gabrus, G Company 141st IR, from Glenn Cove, NY, who was killed outside le Tremblant August 20, 1944. His nephew remembers: "Uncle Joe was in a trench in Southern France, cleaning his rifle, when he was hit by an artillery burst. Sadly it was friendly fire. A U.S. Artillery burst. He was taken by ambulance. While in the ambulance, a member of the medical corps was with him. The soldier was Joe's friend and also from Glen Cove, Tony Forigone. Tony told my family while in the ambulance Uncle Joe said to him 'They got me this time' and died. The family priest spoke to my grandmother; he said it would be easier on her if he was buried with his buddies in France. That would have been what he would have wanted. My grandmother was not in good health at the time and agreed it would cause her too much more pain. She agreed it would be best. Uncle Joe is buried in southern France at the Rhone Military Cemetery." Gabrus Family Collection.

29-year-old 2nd Lt Henry Apperman, G Company 141st IR. He was an Austrian Jew who had emigrated to the U.S. in 1938; his birth name was actually Heinrich Appermann. He was mortally wounded by friendly artillery fire outside le Tremblant August 20, 1944. Apperman Family Collection.

gangrene in it after those operation conditions, so they were going to take my leg off. But I could still feel something in my leg and I told them that, and they said they would X-ray it. So they did, and they came back and said: "Well yeah, you're right, there is something in there. There is more than one piece, too. We are going to start operating on you right now." So they gave me a sedative and rolled me into the operating room, and then, when I woke up a few hours later, they had another box of shrapnel they had got out of me. They said they felt they had got it all, but they didn't; I found out I still have three pieces in there. My leg healed up pretty good in about a month I guess, and I went back to my old outfit, G Company, 2nd Battalion, 141st Infantry, 36th Infantry Division.

The 141st IR's journal simply noted at 1430, August 20th: "Our artillery fired several short rounds—killed one man and wounded 14." [13] This, of course, did not take into account Lt Apperman, who did not die immediately. The two victims of this "friendly fire" incident were:

Surname	Name	Rank	Unit	Age	Date of death
Apperman	Henry	2Lt	G Co 141IR	29	20.8.1944
Gabrus	Joseph	Sgt	G Co 141IR	29	20.8.1944

A few hours after this unfortunate shelling, the 141st Infantry Regiment was relieved by the 551st Parachute Infantry Battalion at le Tremblant and by the 509th Parachute Infantry Battalion at Théoule.

The Fighting at la Napoule as Seen from the German Side

As soon as the location of the Allied invasion was known to the Germans, several battalions of *Reserve Division 148* converged towards the Estérel Mountains. According to *Grenadier* Josef Fröhlich, of the 3rd Company of *Füsilier Bataillon 148*, his unit, was one of the first to reach the front following the landing, having been sent to fight off the Americans at St Raphaël. Though St Raphaël is slightly outside the geographical area of study of this book, **Josef Fröhlich**'s account is still included here, as accounts from German soldiers are so hard to come by:

August 15th, when the Americans landed, we were up in Vence, a small town in the mountains near Grasse. In the afternoon, we left Vence on foot and went past the freight station in Cannes la Bocca and on to St Raphaël. Then the Americans shot our company to pieces with their battleships. When a battleship fired, first there was a flame, then smoke, and then the 45 centimeter shells came, making a "howowowow" sound; then they landed on us. There was a fruit plantation where we were, and the shells made holes that were so big you could have put a bus in them. We thought that the world was going under. In my company there were a lot of men killed and a lot of prisoners.

The Americans were 150 meters away from us. We didn't fire a shot, as we had little ammunition and no replenishment. They fired at us with the small rifles that they had, but they didn't have any luck and didn't hit me. It's all about luck. We couldn't defend ourselves, there weren't enough of us and it was no use. We stayed in St Raphaël one

18-year-old Grenadier Josef Fröhlich, one of the members of Füsilier Bataillon 148 who was lucky enough to survive the fighting at St Raphaël unscathed. Josef Fröhlich Collection.

day, then we ran back to the outskirts of Cannes and then to Nice. There were only 12 or 15 men left over from the entire company. We were very lucky and didn't receive a scratch; the others had been wounded, and whoever was wounded and couldn't walk remained behind in St Raphaël.

With the RN7 cut off by the 141st IR during the night of August 15th to 16th, one wonders how Josef Fröhlich's *Füsilier* unit traveled back from the St Raphaël area. Perhaps they followed secondary roads north of RN7, or perhaps Joseph Fröhlich was misinformed about the location where the *Füsiliers* had been engaged? At least two other German battalions were also rushed to the Estérel front August 15th. As mentioned previously, *Reserve Jäger Bataillon 28* departed Nice to reinforce and hold the front lines facing the 141st IR outside la Napoule, and most of *Reserve Grenadier Bataillon 164* (it seems that the 11th company stayed behind to guard the Var Bridge) also left Nice for la Napoule, where they were apparently put into second line positions behind *Bataillon* 28. *Grenadier* Karl Cyron was a member of the 10th Company of *Bataillon 164* and tells of his experiences, starting from being in Nice on the night of August 14th. Some of the statements in his account are clearly incorrect, but these mistakes probably reflect the opinions and beliefs that **Karl Cyron** and his comrades held true at the time, and for that reason they are just as interesting as the correct facts:

The first day of August 1944, I was sent to an NCO course in Nice. For 14 days I went to the NCO course, and on the night of August 14th, we were supposed to get our first time off. Then, around 10 or 11 o'clock, red flares were fired into the air along the whole Mediterranean coast, which signified: "*Alarmstufe 1* - level 1 alert, the English fleet has departed from Corsica." The night off was cancelled, and we had to prepare for battle.

At 2 o'clock August 15th, the English shelled the coastal defenses heavily for hours with 100 or 200 ships. When the firing stopped the landing craft came forth; they landed everywhere between Cannes and St Raphaël, but they didn't push inland, because the coast was occupied by German troops. I heard that on the afternoon of the same day, Canadian paratroopers landed by parachute and glider between Cannes, Grasse, and Fréjus. But all the land behind the coast was mined and they landed in minefields and blew up. They suffered terrible casualties and many dead.

In the morning, in the hills near the [Caucade] cemetery, the entire battalion was assembled. We were loaded onto trucks and private buses and transported

22-year-old OberGefreiter Kaspar Peschen, of the 2nd Battery of Flak Abteilung 391, was killed by shell fire in Nice the day of the invasion. Peschen Family Collection.

towards Cannes, but our group only got halfway there, because the bus broke down five or ten kilometers before Grasse. Actually, the bus driver, a Frenchman, did not want to drive us all the way to Cannes and simulated engine trouble. He worked at the motor for one hour. I don't know what he was doing, but in any case, it wasn't going well and he said he had to go to the repair station, so we all got out. He disappeared and we never saw him again. It was in the evening, and we set up tents to sleep in. That night it rained heavily. It was the only rain I experienced in southern France. The next day, the rain had stopped and we marched towards Cannes. We had to carry all the equipment, weapons, and ammunition with us. The platoon of 30 men was spread out over 300 or 400 meters. English *Jabos* [fighter bombers] flew over us often. Someone would shout the order: "*Fliegerdeckung* [take cover]" and we would hide in the trees. We arrived in Cannes at 3:00 or 4:00 the afternoon of the 16th.

We got divided into groups, were assigned an area, and received orders to dig in. We were on a hill overlooking Cannes and its port, near the Cannes Grasse highway. It was difficult to dig in, because in August the earth was so dry that it was as hard as cement. It was 35 or 40 degrees. I wandered around and found a hoe in a shed. Everybody wanted to borrow it to dig. I made a nice deep hole big enough to sleep in under a bush, to be protected from the sun.

During the first days, the English only occupied the coast between the coastal road and the sea. They didn't go any further inland than the first houses. [This information is absolutely false, but actually is what many of the German soldiers thought at the time, such as those captured at Tanneron by the FSSF, who thought they were being attacked by partisans, because nobody had told them the Allies had advanced far inland already.] We didn't fire at them because they were so far away. I didn't see any soldiers in front of me, only the artillery. We lay on the hill, observing Cannes. The entire sea was covered with ships, it was indescribable! English fighter planes flew along the coast and shot at anything that moved. The English dominated us; they had good equipment and lots of it. After a day or two they destroyed all our artillery, and we had no tanks. We had great difficulties with supplies; nothing was arriving at the front. It was very hot and we had nothing to eat or drink, but we were lucky there were orchards and vineyards in the area, so we stole things to eat. We ate grapes day after day.

Most of the time we couldn't get out of our holes, because there was an artillery spotter flying above us, observing everything. He was directing the naval fire very precisely, giving away our positions. The English were working hard trying to destroy us. The cruisers and destroyers fired at us day and night with the heaviest caliber guns. The trees by the road had no more leaves left on them. The English fired so well that they would fire artillery at a single person who would show himself. The English only bombed the countryside, though, not houses, so during the day we tried to go back and hide in sheds or houses, knowing that the English wouldn't bomb them. At night we moved back into our positions.

The afternoon of the 19th, the English unloaded tanks into the port of Cannes. [Karl Cyron is obviously confused here, as the port of Cannes remained in German hands until August 24th. It was probably the tank destroyers at

The shrapnel-torn wallet and photos of 28-year-old Grenadier Konrad Styppa, of Bataillon 444, who died in la Napoule August 16th. Konrad Styppa had previously been a soldier in the Polish army, as explained in Chapter 1. The woman in the photo is his wife, with his two children. Styppa Family Collection.

18-year-old Grenadier Johann Manietzki was in the 10th Company of Bataillon 164, just like Karl Cyron. Johann Manietzki was transported to Nice after being wounded in the left thigh by a shell fragment. He expired during treatment the afternoon of August 19th and was buried in Caucade Cemetery. Manietzki Family Collection.

Théoule that he could see from his hill.] We could observe it well from our hill, and our leaders decided that all the roads needed to be mined. We were surprised that it was only after four days they noticed we should mine the roads. It should have already been done long before. We received the order to go forward with the engineers to help lay mines. We were assembled and sent back a kilometer or two to join the engineer unit. Each man from my platoon received a Tellermine, for tanks. I didn't have to carry any because I was a second gunner on the MG and already carried boxes of ammunition.

At 2300, the platoon departed towards the front, walking one behind the other. I was always at the back of the column because I was small, measuring 1m56 [5' 3"]. It was pitch black, you couldn't see your own hand in front of your eyes. We then came under heavy fire. An English cruiser was firing 21cm shells across the road and they were landing closer and closer. The shells always came in salvos of 12 at a time, because the cruisers had four turrets with three guns each. 20 or 30 seconds would pass and then the next salvo would come, then the next.

It was now 1 o'clock, and we were approaching a large bridge going over a small river. *Unteroffizier* Oczko gave the order: "Get up, go, go!" The head of the column ran forwards and most got across the bridge. I was the second to last man of our group of 30, with a *Gefreiter* behind me. The other 28 had run across the bridge through the fire, but we two didn't make it. We were still at the start of the bridge when a shell exploded directly beside the *Gefreiter*, tearing off his right leg. I was hit by a shell fragment in the right hand and severely wounded. I think that the fire from the English boats was directed by the French Resistance, because they knew exactly where we were. The English had already sent them radios in the previous months and years so that the resistance fighters could direct their fire properly. Strangely, after the last shell landed beside us, wounding us, the shelling stopped. The resistance fighters surely gave the order not to fire any more, as far as I understand. [According to his military file, Carl Cyron was wounded in the right hand by shell fragments on a bridge north of la Napoule August 20th. This was probably the bridge where the RN7 highway crosses the Siagne River,

A portrait photo of 17-year-old Karl Cyron that he took in Italy while convalescing from his hand wound received August 19th on a bridge at la Napoule. Note that he is wearing a tropical uniform that was issued to him before the invasion. Karl Cyron Collection.

24-year-old Unteroffizier Herbert Oczko, of the 10th Company of Bataillon 164, was killed August 20, 1944, when a shell landed directly in the fox hole he had taken cover in. He was buried on Hill 84, but his body has never been recovered, or was not identified when it was later found. In any case, he has no known grave. Oczko Family Collection.

an obligatory point of passage, and thus a good target for interdiction fire by Allied artillery.]

Unteroffizier Oczko and my comrades bandaged me up to stop the bleeding. They unfastened my backpack and belt and took my rifle. I had to leave all my belongings on that bridge, including my assault pack with 50 pictures taken in southern France, and I never saw them again. One man came back with me 100 meters and then I ran back towards Cannes by myself, alone in the darkness. I passed some other German soldiers and they guided me, telling me where to go. Then I found a few houses and knocked on the doors. After knocking at three or four doors, an old woman came out. I said in French: "Je suis allemande soldate." "Oui, oui." She brought me a few houses further down, where our troops had set up a dressing station in a large living room. I thanked her: "Merci Madame!" There were already 10 or 20 comrades lying there wounded. In the morning, when the sun was up, some sanitary vehicles came and we were all loaded in to be brought to Nice. At the Var River the bridge was destroyed, so we had to drive over a wooden bridge that had been built with large planks. As we crossed the river, I saw an English *Jabo* through the window. It was coming towards us and I thought: "This is the end." But when he saw there was a Red Cross on our truck he broke off and flew away without shooting.

We weren't unloaded at the hospital in Nice. We just stayed there for a couple hours and then were sent back through Monaco and Ventimigla, to San Remo, Italy. The severely wounded were quickly sent out of the fighting area. There was a wounded artillery soldier next to me in the truck. He said the naval fire, guided by spotter planes, had completely destroyed the German artillery after one or two days. In the area of Cannes, there wasn't a single cannon left over. [We will see later on that there were in fact enough cannons left over around Cannes to cause some serious trouble for the Americans on the 21st and 22nd.]

In the hospital in San Remo, there were hundreds and hundreds of wounded. The hospital was full and men were lying on the floors in the hallways. Most had abdominal wounds or head wounds. They screamed because they were in severe pain. At first they wanted to amputate my hand, but in the end it healed well thanks to my young age. Of

course, there is still a scar and the fingers are still stiff today. I met the *Gefreiter* whose leg had been torn off. He arrived later, because his wound was so severe that he couldn't be transported. The last time I saw him he was lying in bed at the hospital. I think he survived.

I met other wounded comrades from Battalion 164 in San Remo. They told me that our beloved *Unteroffizier* Oczko had been killed. During an attack by the English artillery, he and another soldier from my platoon had jumped into a foxhole for protection. A shell landed exactly in the hole and both of them were torn to shreds. It was terrible. [According to his military file, *Uffz* **Herbert Oczko** was killed August 20th on Hill 84, facing the positions of C Company of the 141st IR. It is not known if Hill 84 was where the men from *Bataillon 164* were positioned, or if they had only temporarily taken refuge there after laying their antitank mines at the front lines.]

Most of our NCOs were not friendly, but Oczko was a very friendly man and an incredibly good *Gruppenführer*. He was a good comrade. He came from Oppeln and was already married. During the time when I was a recruit, he was the head of the kitchen at Villa Fabron, taking care of the *Gulaschkanon*, as we called it. We were together for six months.

I was also told that *Oberfeldwebel* Fleisher's 3rd Platoon from our company, a complete platoon of 30 men, gave itself up. They advanced too quickly and the Canadians moved in behind them and surrounded them, closing the sack. They couldn't get back anymore so they had to raise their hands and surrender. *Feldwebel* Fleischer had been a soldier since 1939. He had been in Russia for three years, was very experienced, and had iron on his chest: the Iron Cross First Class, Wound Badge, and the Close Combat Clasp. I think he had been seriously wounded in the leg and that is why he was sent to France. He was very strict and the men in his platoon did not like him. [A picture showing *Feldwebel* Fleischer leading his *Ehrenzug* in the Caucade Cemetery is presented in Chapter 1.]

It is clear from both Josef Fröhlich's and Karl Cyron's accounts that the Allied naval artillery was the source of very severe problems for the German troops who were fighting back the invasion. Thus, during the night of August 20th to 21st, the German navy attempted an attack against the Allied fleet, sending out three torpedo boats of *22.U-Jagdflottille*, which was based in ports in northwestern Italy. Luckily, the German navy archives have preserved a very detailed report of the German torpedo boats' catastrophic attack written by the group's leader, **Oberleutnant Börner**, who was onboard RA 259:

Report about the encounter of the RA-Group of RA 259, 255, 251 with enemy destroyers on 20/21.8.1944.

(...) Mission: RA-boats [*Räumboot Ausland*: foreign-built minesweepers] to depart from Monaco at 2130, to be reinforced with R-boats [*Räumboot*: minesweepers] in front of Nice at 2230, then RA-Boats to advance to observation positions off of the Lérins Islands and R-boats to make reconnaissance between Nice and Antibes. At 0230, meeting of the R- and RA-boats in the gulf of Juan, return together to Nice; R-boats to continue on to Menton. The departure was delayed by one hour because of torpedo regulations. Out of Monaco at 2230. Meeting in front of Nice at 2330. At 0035, the gulf of St Juan [sic] was reached; RA-boats let the R-boats turn back.

0055: RA boats advanced in line formation: number 259 (group leader), 255, 251, out of the gulf of Juan at 220 degrees, 5 knots per hour, to occupy the observation positions off the Lerins Islands.

0116: Before reaching the positions, alarm (...), a shadow ahead to port.

My order: "Stop the engines!"

The boats remain halted, in order to let the target come nearer. Radio communications forbidden because of risk of detection, but communication by megaphone possible. Target identified as an enemy destroyer with two smokestacks; out of torpedo range, it turns towards the boats. At approximately 4,000 meters, the destroyer turns to starboard and signals with three red flashes - - - [The letter W in Morse code].

0124: At this moment, fire order: "RA 259 and 255, fire both torpedoes, distance 4,000 meters." RA 251 was in an unfavorable firing position, and besides, four torpedoes seemed to me to be sufficient.

RA 259 immediately maneuvered to destroy the target, going at the lowest speed in order to make as little noise as possible. RA 251 also started its engines. At the same instant we started our engines, the destroyer briefly blinded the next RA-boat in line with a spotlight before opening fire with its heavy weapons, its shots landing near all the boats in succession.

RA 259 never got the target into its sights, as the destroyer changed courses twice. The commander could not set his targeting mechanism fast enough and the boat was difficult to maneuver. RA 251 didn't fire any torpedoes, as it was in a bad firing position.

RA 255 waited for the most favorable moment to fire and did not need to change course to take aim. The commander let the target sail into his sights and fired one torpedo that passed in front of the target as the enemy suddenly started going full engines astern. Apparently it had seen the torpedo's trajectory, as the water was

phosphorescing strongly. All RA-boats broke off to port due to the heavy fire, travelling at utmost power and laying smoke screens. RA 259 and 251 left towards Cap Antibes. RA 255 was hit in the rudder controls and started travelling in circles. During the shooting the emergency rudder was put to use, but the boat suddenly came under fire from a second destroyer with four smokestacks that was coming from the west at high speed. Both destroyers fired in turn. The destroyer with four smokestacks continued on towards Cap Antibes at high speed in pursuit of the other two RA-boats.

With the emergency rudder and engine maneuvers, it was not possible to keep RA 255 on course, so it stopped in order to let the enemy pass by and fire its second torpedo.

0140: Because this was made impossible by counter maneuvers, the boat attempted to ram the enemy. In doing so, it was hit several times with light flak weapons that succeeded in starting fires aboard. It then received a direct hit with intermediate-sized artillery in the stern, flinging the commander and part of the crew overboard. The rest of the crew jumped into the water.

0147: The stern disappeared under the surface. After another hit amidships the boat sank immediately. The destroyer remained 100 meters away during the demise of the RA-boat, circling the spot where it had sunk numerous times, illuminating the area with spotlights and trying to pick up the swimmers. It approached the castaways up to within five meters, then started off again and fired at the coast with 4 centimeter cannons. The crew of RA 255 gathered around their commander in the water and all did their best not to be captured. The men remained calm and dived under water several times. Together with the wounded, they swam towards the St Marguerite Islands, which they reached after four hours. From there, the crew was transported to Cannes by an army motorboat the next day and then on to Nice with a truck.

RA 259: As the enemy fire concentrated on RA 255, RA 259 turned to starboard, then saw a destroyer coming from astern that immediately opened fire with all weapons from a distance of about 3,000 meters. Chased by the spotlights and intermediate fire of the destroyer, the RA-boat turned back to port and followed RA 251, laying a smoke screen on the way, as RA 251's smoke generator was out of order. Numerous shells landed in the smoke cloud. During the shooting, the destroyer continued on towards Cap Antibes, probably to cut off the escape route towards Nice. Following a zigzag course, both boats thus attempted to reach the Gulf of Juan.

0150: The RA boats lost sight of each other in the middle of the gulf and went towards land separately. The destroyer ceased firing simultaneously.

0300: RA 259 attempted to contact the la Garoupe outpost to find out if the destroyer was still in front of the bay. The attempt failed, so I gave the order to steer towards Cap Antibes, so as to reach it at 0330 and then to sail towards Nice at maximum speed, as I had to assume that the boat would be spotted and destroyed by the enemy at daylight.

0445: We reached the tip of Cap Antibes and left at top speed. About five minutes later, the boat was fired on with 4 centimeter cannons from astern. The course was immediately changed to port. No enemy was visible, but one could see the flashes of the naval artillery in the direction of the Cap, further out to sea. The shells were landing close to the boat, so once again, we zigzagged away and laid a smoke screen. The enemy was recognized as a destroyer again, closing onto us with a northeastern course and firing heavily with its light and intermediate weapons. The shells were landing in the smoke cloud once again. Soon afterwards, a second destroyer came past the Cap and started firing at the other destroyer before laying its fire onto RA 259. The RA-boat's smoke canisters were empty and the shells were now landing nearby, though no hits were scored. Shortly after 0500 the fire decreased, as the enemy had lost us.

I was forced to abandon my plan of bringing the boat close to shore and trying to reach Nice by following the coast, because the destroyers were coming ever nearer and daylight would come in half an hour. Upon my order, the boat was thus run onto the beach and the crew sent ashore equipped with handheld weapons. On the order of the commander, one NCO and three men carefully advanced across the five-meter wide beach to the road beyond to search for a path that was free of mines. This was easy, as one could step on the rocks that were lying about everywhere. The boat was taking on water in the engine room. I saw that the radio had been destroyed and that all the documents had been retrieved and then went ashore myself. Army outposts were nowhere to be seen, so a patrol was immediately sent out, discovering the next outpost 500 meters away. While coming ashore, the boat's commander strayed off the path and stepped on a Stockmine that blew off his right foot. The leg was bandaged at once and a vehicle to transport the commander was requested from the outpost. There was not enough time remaining to retrieve the 2 centimeter weapons, as at 0600, the two destroyers opened fire again from a distance of about 3,000 meters, scoring a direct hit that completely tore the RA-boat apart. Both destroyers then sailed off to the west. The crew, which had taken cover during the shooting, was driven to Nice in a truck once I had assured myself that the boat was completely destroyed.

RA 251: Due to the enemy fire, the boat was hit by numerous splinters that killed *Matrosenobergefreiter* **Büddemann** and severely wounded *Maschinenobergefreiter* Krieger and *Maschinengefreiter* **Dahmen**. *Maschinengefreiter* Dahmen later died of his wounds at the hospital in Nice.

In the middle of the Gulf of Juan, RA 259, which until then had been zigzagging behind and laying a smoke screen, was lost from sight. The boat thus headed straight north towards the coast and anchored, in order to attempt to reach Nice shortly before dawn. A party of six men under the command of the *Oberfähnrich* [Senior Officer Cadet] was put ashore along with the wounded in order to link up with the army, get the wounded evacuated, and to contact the la Garoupe outpost. Contact was not established with the la Garoupe outpost, but instead, it was found out from the army outpost that there were three destroyers present in front of the bay. The commander therefore decided to carefully run the boat onto the beach and to camouflage it, in the hope of breaking through the next night.

24- and 20-year-old Obergefreiters Friedrich Büddemann and Heinrich Dahmen, of 22 U.Jagdflottille, were crewmembers onboard the torpedo ship RA 251, which attempted an attack on the Allied navy in the vicinity of the Lérins Islands during the night of August 20th to 21st. In the early hours of the 21st, the RA 251 was hit by Allied fire, and upon seeing its escape route towards Nice cut off by Allied vessels, it took refuge in Golf Juan. Büddemann, who was killed by the Allied fire, was buried in Vallauris. Dahmen, who had been wounded, was evacuated to the German field hospital in Cimiez, where he died the next day. August 22nd, with their escape route still cut off, the crew of the RA 251 was forced to scuttle its ship in Golf Juan because of the impending German retreat out of the Cannes region. Stadtarchiv Dortmund Collection, courtesy Dieter Knippschild. Dahmen Family Collection.

For the night of 21/22.8.44, the orders were: "RA 251, break through if possible or prepare to blow the boat up the next day."

No breakthrough was attempted, as at least three enemy ships were present in front of the bay at all times.

The next day, August 22nd, the entire area of Antibes was evacuated by the German troops. Therefore, RA 251 was blown in the evening as per orders. Artillery guns and secret items were destroyed because no more vehicles were available for transportation and the crew was forced to go to Nice on foot.

Between the time they came ashore and their transport to Nice, all three crews were looked after by the army soldiers, who everywhere tended to the sea people with exemplary comradeship.

Dead:
RA 251: *Mtr.Ob.Gfr.* Büddemann (killed in action), *Masch.Grf.* Dahmen (died in hospital).

Wounded:
RA 259: *Ob.Strm.* Schleich
RA 255: *Masch.Mt.* Harms, *Masch.Gfr.* Plöhm, *Fk.O.Gf.* Küper, *Mtr.O.Gfr.* Ewald.
RA 251: *Masch.O.Gfr.* Krieger.

Missing:
RA 255: *Btsmt* Lindemann, *Masch.O.Gfr.* Wegen, *Mtr.O.Gfr.* Achatz, *Mtr.O.Gfr.* Gerhold, *Mtr. Gfr.* Böckler.

Amongst whom are probably in captivity (according to the crew): *Masch.Gfr.* Wegen, *Mtr.O.Gfr.* Gerhold.[14]

As in most of the encounters that followed the invasion, the overwhelming material superiority of the Allies was enough to overcome any German initiative. Of the five missing men, only **Willi Wegen** and **Heinz Gerhold** were permanently listed as missing; the other three were presumably captured. Heinrich Dahmen died of wounds August 22nd in the main German hospital in Nice, at the south end of Bellanda Avenue in the Cimiez district.

The hospital at Bellanda Avenue was a permanent structure that the Germans had already been using during the occupation period. The soldiers who died at the hospital were brought to the Caucade Cemetery to be buried until August 19th. As of August 20th, presumably in order save time and resources, the Germans started burying their dead in a park located a couple hundred meters from the hospital, in front of the Cimiez Monastery. There were also major German military hospitals in St Vallier and Sanremo. The St Vallier hospital, previously mentioned in Chapter 4, only saw limited use after the invasion due to its proximity to the battlefields. The Sanremo hospital, on the other hand, seems to have been the main evacuation hospital for the Maritime Alps as of the start of the invasion. Several dressing stations, such as the one described by Karl Cyron in Cannes, were also improvised nearer to the front lines after the invasion started. One of these was located in Valbonne, in a bar on the main square of the village. The local population was shocked by the sight of the wounded, as **Madame Voegeli** remembers:

The landing had occurred at Cannes, so the Germans were retreating. They stopped in Valbonne, and they had made a hospital in the "Brasserie des Arcades" on the town square. They had put a big Red Cross flag on the roof of the house and would arrive in the square in trucks coming from the coast, all those with missing legs, the wounded in the stretchers, and they operated on them there. I was still very young at the time and was very frightened. The stretchers were full of blood. We kids would see all that blood when they flipped the stretchers over on the square.

Madame Chasseloup, another local youth, also remembers:

The Germans were occupying the village and had installed a field hospital where they treated the wounded. They needed to be amputated. As a child, seeing them carrying the limbs they had amputated shocked me.

Three young soldiers who had been wounded in the Cannes area died in the Valbonne field hospital and were buried in the local cemetery. They were:

Surname	Name	Rank	Age	Date of death	Wounded or died in	Unit
Drzisga	Otto	Gren	18	18.8.1944	Le Cannet	1./Res.Art. Abt.44
Cinader	Johann	Gren	17	20.8.1944	Legamet	7./Res.Jäg. Btl.28
Fiedler	Hubert	*Jäger*	18	23.8.1944	HVPl Valbonne	8./Res.Jäg. Btl.28

From the day of the invasion until August 27th, 21 German soldiers were buried in the Caucade cemetery or in Cimiez Park. Most of these men had been wounded at the front, often at Cannes and la Napoule, and had died during transport or treatment. A few of them were killed in or near Nice and their bodies had been brought back to Nice, instead of being buried at the scene of death or in the nearest cemetery, as was almost always the case as of August 15th. Indeed, it would seem that an order was issued as of the moment of the invasion to bury all the dead at the closest practical location, which is what was done in most cases. Between August 15th and 27th, a total of 10 men were buried in the Caucade Cemetery and 11 in the Cimiez Park. Their names were:

Caucade Cemetery Burials from August 15 to 27, 1944:

Surname	Name	Rank	Age	Date of death	Wounded or died in	Unit
Dürr	Willi	Stbsgefr	29	15.8.1944	Grasse	
Peschen	Kaspar	Ogefr	22	15.8.1944	Nice?	2./Flak.Abt.391
Bohl	Paul	OT Mann	39	16.8.1944	Nice?	Todt
Seidel	Georg	Olt	43	16.8.1944	Mandelieu	7./Res.Jäg.Btl.28
Korte	Josef	Stbsgefr	27	18.8.1944	DOW Nice	1./Flak.Abt.391
Uschold	Josef	Sold	18	18.8.1944	Bei Carras 15km N Nice	3./Res.Pi.Btl.8

Surname	Name	Rank	Age	Date of death	Wounded or died in	Unit
Herold	Richard	Ofwb	30	19.8.1944	DOW Nice	Fest Pio II/14
Jahn	Johann	Ogefr	30	19.8.1944	St Vallier	21 Flugmelde Res. West Frankreich
Manietzki	Johann	Gren	18	19.8.1944	La Napoule	10./Res.Gren. Btl.164
Knirsch	Franz	Uffz	36	23.8.1944	Cannes	Res.Gren.Btl.444

Cimiez Park Burials from August 15 to 27, 1944:

Surname	Name	Rank	Age	Date of death	Wounded or died in	Unit
Jasper	Theodor	Ogefr	31	20.8.1944	Nice?	Stab.Res.Gren. Rgt.239
Sikora	Zdenko	*Jäger*	18	20.8.1944	HVPl Nizza	6./Res.Jäg.Btl.28
Römmen	Matthias	Ogefr	24	21.8.1944	SW Mandelieu	8./Res.Jäg.Btl.28
Dahmen	Heinrich	Ogefr	20	22.8.1944	HVPl Nizza	22.U-Jagdflotille
Meyer-Detring	Klaus	Olt	35	22.8.1944	Le Tremblant	7./Res.Jäg.Btl.28
Kuchenmeister	Max	Ogefr	22	23.8.1944	San Remo	Kriegmarine
Podbarschek	Franz	Sold	18	23.8.1944	Mandelieu	2./Res.Pi.Btl.8
Szafranek	Richard	*Jäger*	18	23.8.1944		5./Res.Jäg.Btl.28
Muschiol	Anton	Gren	29	24.8.1944	Nice?	12./Res.Gren. Btl.444
Reh Dr.	Fritz	Lt	34	27.8.1944	Eze	Heeres.Art. Abt.1191
Zipperer	Hermann	Gren	18	27.8.1944	DOW Nice	1./Res.Gren. Btl.327

A further seven men were also buried in the Sanremo cemetery between August 15th and August 27th, though it is not at all clear how many of them were actually wounded in the fighting in the Maritime Alps. These men were:

Surname	Name	Rank	Age	Date of death	Buried in	Unit
Abasan?	Abas	Leg		16.8.1944?	Sanremo	Ost.Btl.661?
Undetermined	Ost	Ogefr		16.8.1944?	Sanremo	Ost.Btl.661?
Egle	Paul	Lt	30	16.8.1944	Sanremo	
Zangerl	Josef	*Jäger*	36	16.8.1944	Sanremo	
Fischer	Leopold	Hptgefr		23.8.1944	Sanremo	
Zihrnel?	Jean			8.1944	Sanremo	
Undetermined				8.1944	Sanremo	

39-year-old Paul Bohl, a member of the Todt Organization that was responsible for construction work for the Wehrmacht, was buried in Caudade Cemetery after dying in Nice August 16th. Bohl Family Collection.

Generalleutnant Otto Fretter-Pico photographed in unknown locations in August 1944. In the first shot he shakes hands with Rittmeister Liebich. In the second shot he is sitting next to Division Adjutant Major Dr. Ebersbach as he listens to Obergefreiter Bialowons, who is holding a map. Author's Collection. Gemeinschaft Ehemaliger Angehöriger der 148 ID Collection.

The First Airborne Task Force Takes Over the Front

August 20, 1944, the First Airborne Task Force was ordered to take over the right wing of the Allied bridgehead in the area from la Napoule to Fayence. As was explained in previous chapters, the 517th Parachute Regimental Combat Team and the First Special Service Force took up positions around Fayence and Tanneron, while the 509th and 551st Parachute Infantry Battalions relieved the 141st IR in the la Napoule area. The 509th PIB replaced C Company of the 141st IR in their positions facing Hill 84 and its castle, while the 551st PIB replaced the 2nd Battalion of the 141st IR in the hills west of le Tremblant, along the RN7 highway. The front had been stable in both these last two locations since August 16th, but this was soon to change, as the FABTF received the following orders as of 20:00 August 20th:

(2) Establish and hold defensive flank along the general line Fayence-la Napoule; protect army right (east) flank.
(3) Reconnoiter the general line Seranon-Grasse-Cannes.[15]

The FABTF was commanded by the legendary Major General Robert T. Frederick, one of the youngest generals in the entire U.S. Army, who had reportedly been wounded in combat eight times. He had previously commanded the FSSF and was a man who was used to planning aggressive and daring attacks, not to holding defensive lines. Over the following days, his units would do much more than simply "reconnoiter" in the direction of Cannes and Grasse. Starting on the 21st, all his units would advance east in a series of small but aggressive attacks until reaching positions at or near the Italian border. This may have been due to Major General Frederick deciding to take liberties

with his interpretation of the orders. It is also possible that Frederick received verbal orders giving him more freedom of action than the written orders quoted above. In any case, it seems like the Allied commanders appreciated Frederick's actions, as once he captured Cannes and Grasse on the 24th, new orders were issued the next day to advance east:

(1) Seize and hold the West bank of the Var in zone.
(2) Protect the right (East) flank of Seventh Army along the general line: Larche Pass (incl)--Toudon--West bank of the Var River to its mouth.
(3) Reconnoiter to Nice.[16]

The Allied invasion caused *Reserve Division 148* to find itself completely cut off from all other German units in France. Because of its isolated position east of the Allied bridgehead, *Reserve Division 148* was relieved from its attachment to the German 19th Army in France and was instead put under control of the Ligurian Army Corps (*Armee Abteilung Ligurien*) in Italy. August 20th, *Generalleutnant* Fretter-Pico received the following orders for his division in the Maritime Alps:

148th Reserve Division to defend area around Grasse as long as possible without running risk of annihilation.

Then to withdraw with main forces via Nice, Breil, Cuneo to take over new sector with left boundary coast at Menton, right boundary Embrun, Chianale-Varaita valley. If situation allows, groups to be pulled back fighting into Tinée and Var Valleys as far as Larche-Condamine to bar a possible Allied outflanking thrust across Maddalena Pass….

At 0900 August 19th, leaving strong rear guards in contact with Allies, main body 148 Division to withdraw from evening 19th onward first to east bank of the Var sector and to start from there movement ordered into new sector. In no circumstances to let Allies push them back by outflanking movement to north.[17]

In short, the Germans were to resist as long as possible, but to pull back whenever the Allied pressure became too strong in order to avoid unnecessary losses. In the meantime, reinforcements could be brought over from Italy and defensive positions could be prepared at the Franco-Italian border. In a postwar document, *Generalleutnant* **Fretter-Pico** gave further details on how he planned his retreat:

Because the division was only 20% mobile due to the fact that it was a training division, and because, in accordance with the orders given by the 19th Army, it was caught up in the fighting on the defense line from St Vallier to St Cézaire - Fayence - Bagnoles - les Adrets - St Jean-Théoule, the instructions given by the Ligurian Army Corps could only be performed in steps by establishing successive defense lines:

    a- St Vallier - St Cézaire - Siagne Valley.
    b- Gourdon - Loup Valley.
    c- St Jeannet - Cagnes Valley.
    d- La Roquette -Var Valley.
    e- Col de Braus - Col de Segra - Mont Ours - Pic de Baudon - La Turbie - Cap d'Ail.[18]

These were indeed the main defense lines that the Germans would establish during their retreat, not moving back until they were given an energetic push by the FABTF or the Resistance; or until they decided that they were ready to pull back. As of August 20th, the Allies were thus told to "reconnoiter" forward, while the Germans were told to resist temporarily without risking serious casualties. The consequence of these rather complementary orders is that over the next two weeks, the German retreat orders were often given almost simultaneously to Allied attack orders. The opposing forces sometimes moved in coordination like dance partners, with the Germans retreating shortly before the arrival of the Allies. However, when the coordination between the German retreat and the Allied attack was off by even just a few hours, sharp and deadly encounters occurred.

The rest of this book will consist of the analysis of the fighting that occurred at each of the defense lines mentioned above by *Generalleutnant* Fretter-Pico. In each case, the Germans selected excellent defensive positions located on steep ridges or along rivers and that controlled the local roads and bridges. The Germans also laid numerous mines, cratered the main roads, and blew almost every bridge of the French Riviera in order to slow the Allied advance.

The German Defenses at la Napoule

The Siagne River reaches the sea at the village of la Napoule, thus making la Napoule part of the Siagne River defense line mentioned by *Generalleutnant* Fretter-Pico. Furthermore, Hill 84 and the neighboring Hills 105 and 131 are the last heights west of Cannes before the terrain becomes flat, making them the last good defensive positions the Germans had available before Cannes. *Reserve Jäger Bataillon 28* had taken up positions in these hills after their unsuccessful counter attack down the RN7 highway August 16th.

Bataillon 28 seems to have organized itself in the following manner (based on analysis of where their casualties were buried and on information given in letters received by families of casualties): the 5th Company held the left wing on Hill 84, facing the 509th PIB; the 6th Company, under *Oberleutnant* Barsch, held Hill 105 in the center, facing the 551st PIB; and the 7th Company, commanded by *Oberleutnant* Meyer-Detring since *Oberleutnant* Seidel's death August 16th, was on the RN7 highway at le Tremblant, also facing the 551st PIB. The 8th Company (heavy weapons company), under *Oberleutnant* Bönsch, was in support in the hills on the right flank of the battalion. Put more simply, the companies were disposed by ascending order, according to their number, from left to right (or from south to north). We will first describe the battles in the Hill 84 area that the 509th PIB was involved in, then review the encounters of the 551st PIB at Hill 105 and le Tremblant, and finish with the final advances of the 509th into Cannes.

The Attack of Hill 84 by the 509th Parachute Infantry Battalion

The 509th PIB relieved C Company of the 141st IR in front of Hill 84 (known to the men of the 509th as "Castle Hill") on the afternoon of August 20th, and plans were made to attack Hill 84 and its castle the very next morning, on the 21st. The men of the 509th were positioned on the hill directly south of Hill 84. Between the two hills was the steep and rocky Rague Ravine, which had formed the front lines since August 16th. **Lieutenant Justin McCarthy,** of C Company of the 509th, was the platoon leader of the platoon that was to spearhead the attack:

We moved the whole battalion onto a hill looking across a small valley. They brought up the heavy machine guns, everybody was up there, and then they told us that we were going to attack a castle. C Company was the assault company, and A and B companies were to support us with fire from the ridge. C Company was to attack across the valley and up the other side to attack the castle. My platoon, the 3rd platoon of C Company, was going to be the assault platoon. So immediately after daylight the following morning, we started down from the top of the hill into the valley. We immediately drew fire from the other side, from the castle and the area around the castle, where the enemy was dug in. They fired on us, and in the meantime, our people covered them with fire. The machine gun platoon had brought up .50 caliber machine guns, and they opened fire on the area and so on and so forth, with mortars and everything. In other words, our people were putting a lot of fire on the hill there and it kept the Germans pretty well under cover. They couldn't fire too accurately for any length of time because of the firepower our people were putting on them.

As we attacked down the hill, somebody was firing at me. I thought it was probably a sniper and he was out to get me. When I was zigzagging he was staying right with me, firing very close to me, so I figured that maybe if he saw he hit me, he would leave me alone. So I made believe I was hit and

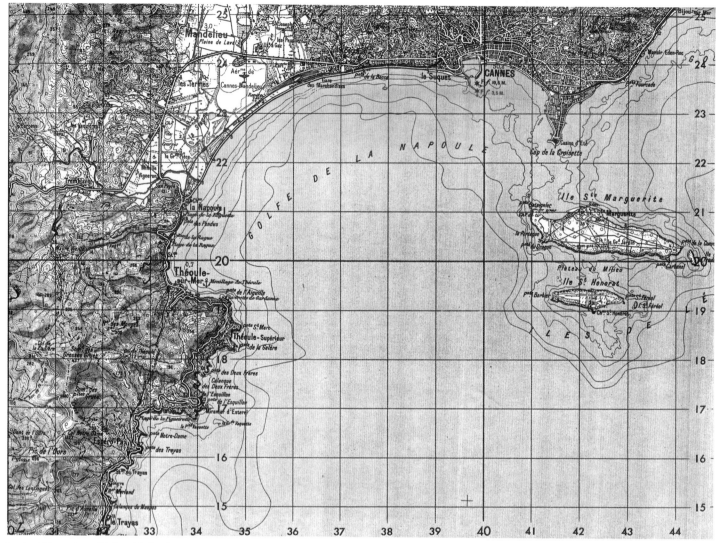

Institut Géographique National Collection.

tumbled down, then laid on the ground for a while until he stopped, so that he would move his fire to somebody else. Joe Hernandez was my runner and he always stayed near me. He saw that I was hit and he came running up to help me and I said to him: "Joe, I am not hit; I am just trying to get that sniper off me." Joe said: "OK!" and then he went on with the rest of the guys. The sniper, I guess, saw that he had got me and left me alone. Then I got up and rejoined the platoon, and we assaulted across the valley and moved up the hill on the opposite side. By the time we got up near the castle, we weren't getting fired on at all; I think they had given up. I had a couple of guys with me, and we immediately entered the castle and cleared the basement there, going room to room and around and that. There was still light fire going on outside, and finally they came in and said the area was cleared.

We have a regular military procedure when you take ground like that: redistribute ammunition, check for casualties, and check for enemy casualties, and we followed the routine. We started looking around for them. They had emplacements dug into the rocks there and we found maybe six or eight German dead. We also must have captured

The Rague Valley, located between la Napoule and Théoule, with Hill 84, also known as Castle Hill, to the left. This valley formed the front lines between August 16 and 21, 1944, with the 5th Company of Reserve Jäger Bataillon 28 holding Castle Hill, faced by the 141st IR and later the 509th PIB on the opposite hill. The 509th PIB, led by C Company's 3rd Platoon, finally attacked through the Rague Valley August 21st, seizing the castle. When B Company followed, it came under fire from remaining German snipers and was shelled heavily with mortars and artillery. A total of 13 paratroopers died during the battle. Author's Collection.

The castle as it appears nowadays. Author's Collection.

After the fighting, abandoned German equipment litters the path leading to the castle. Pierre Carle Collection.

15 or 20 prisoners in the castle. I had a couple Polish fellows that spoke fluent Polish in my platoon and a lot of the prisoners that we took there were Poles. My guys were able to converse with the prisoners and talk to them, and they were not happy. In other words, the Poles were very happy to be taken prisoner. They were not like some of those Nazis who were really "fight to the death." My guys were interpreting for me, and it sounded like the Poles were forced into the German army and that most of the time the Germans used them as laborers. But then, when things got tough, the Germans turned around and they sent the Poles down there and told them they were going to use them just like infantry, and the Poles weren't happy with it. Of course they did fire on us, because we had some men wounded there, but after we took them prisoner, some of these Poles showed us they still had all their ammunition and said: "You notice I never fired my rifle?" Some of them said: "I was shooting up in the air; I wasn't shooting at the people." The sergeant was a German, and they said: "To please the sergeant, I had to fire; but I wasn't shooting at anybody." That's the story they told. We took them and they went to the battalion in the rear. They must have had a prisoner of war camp somewhere for them.

As would often be the case during the battles against *Reserve Division 148*, the poor motivation of the many Polish soldiers undermined the efficiency of the German defense and helped save many lives. **Lt McCarthy**'s runner, Joe Hernandez, was one of those who was wounded in the attack:

In the attack on that castle, Joe Hernandez got hit by his own grenade. I talked to him after it happened, but he was confused himself. It sounded like the pin had come out of the grenade and he didn't know it. I said: "But what happened, Joe? Did somebody shoot you and knock it out of your hand?" He said: "I don't know. One minute, Mac, I was in the ditch. There were Germans just a little ways from me, we saw helmets there, walking down the ditch. I took the grenade out, I was watching the top of the helmets, and all of a sudden the grenade went off." He actually had it in his hand when it went off. Now it mangled his hand, I know that, and he also got fragments in the chest, and he was in the hospital for quite some time. From what he said, it was in a ditch right around the castle.

In our company we had a David, a couple of Davis and Davies, and one of them with the name Davies or Davis [**Sgt Roy W. David**] was also killed there. I believe he was hit badly in the head with a shell fragment. I don't remember seeing him, but Captain Tomasik came in and told me that Davis had died.

Sgt Ray Donavan, also of C Company of the 509th, was targeted by a sniper on the way down the hill during the initial attack, just like Lt McCarthy had been:

The next morning, C Company was ordered to assault the castle area and the high ground immediately north. We were to move out at dawn, and would receive supporting fire from A Company and Headquarters Company, which had .50 caliber machine guns to provide overhead support. We jumped off at dawn (...). As we went down off the hill, a sniper started to pick on me; after several close calls I dove behind a rock and hoped that he would take his sights off me.

My platoon was getting ahead of me, so I peered over the rock to check their status. At that moment, this same sniper hit the rock. Slivers of rock flew into my eyes. It didn't bother me too much at the time, and I knew I needed to catch up with my platoon, so I took off on the run. I caught up to the platoon at the bottom of the hill.

The overhead supporting fire was very heavy. We started up the next hill to assault the castle area when one of my good friends and squad leaders, **Sergeant Gerald Tilney**, was killed in action. My platoon continued the attack on the area north of the castle, while the third platoon attacked the actual castle. As we neared the top of the hill, the supporting fire from Headquarters and A Company ceased; we made the final assault on the hill and the enemy withdrew. We gained the high ground overlooking the castle and the third platoon captured the castle area proper. The Company Command Post was set up in the castle and we went into defensive status.

A German patrol approached our lines a couple hours later. Sergeant Graber began to fire on the approaching patrol. They were apparently just establishing whether or not we had taken up a defensive posture and were immediately repulsed when fired upon by Sergeant Graber's squad. At the time, Lieutenant Sammons, who was our new company commander, was at company headquarters awaiting further orders. He heard the firing, and returning to investigate, came upon me. I thought I was losing my eyesight, because my vision was becoming very clouded. Sammons called a medic, who washed my eyes out. The medic suggested that I rest in a nearby cave. The next morning my eyes were completely covered with matter and I couldn't see at all.

28-year-old Sgt Gerald K. Tilney, of C Company 509th PIB, was shot and killed while attempting to eliminate left over German snipers in the vicinity of la Napoule Castle. Robert A. Garner Collection, courtesy Diane Moore and the Crawfordsville District Public Library.

Example of a German foxhole dug on Castle Hill, overlooking the Rague Valley. According to a witness, this foxhole had been used as a temporary grave for a German soldier, and indeed, several buttons, a coin, and the remains of a shoe were found within it. Private Collection.

After two days in the cave, the medic came back and cleaned out my eyes with rubbing alcohol or something. I was moved out of the cave and could see quite well again. During that day, my vision came back completely.[19]

S/Sgt William Davis, of the 3rd Platoon of C Company, witnessed the incident in which Sergeant Gerald Tilney was killed:

We had a number of casualties. My radio operator, Joe Hernandez, was a casualty; he got injured, and one of the sergeants in the 2nd Platoon was killed by a sniper. The sniper was either in a tree or some kind of a rack behind a tree. He was up high on our left, and he injured several people and then he killed the sergeant. But then they saw the flashes of his gun, somebody zeroed in and said: "Hey, there he is!" and everybody kind of cut loose on him and knocked him out of there. I saw him fall down to the ground.

Sgt Gerald Tilney was a veteran of the 509th who had fought with them since their campaigns in Sicily. He was posthumously awarded the Silver Star for his actions at the castle:

For gallantry in action near la Napoule, France, August 21, 1944. Sergeant Tilney's company attacked a wooded hill where the enemy was firmly entrenched. The brush surrounding the hill was infested with enemy snipers who were inflicting casualties and successfully harassing the advancing troops. One platoon of the company fought its way to the top of the hill, only to be denied complete possession of their objective by sniper fire. Sergeant Tilney volunteered to locate and eliminate the snipers in order that the platoon could complete its mission. Knowing that he could best locate the snipers by attracting their fire, Sergeant Tilney, with complete disregard for his own safety, advanced from bush to bush, firing his Tommy gun at every spot likely to conceal an enemy. The enemy snipers were forced to cease firing at the platoon and concentrate their fire on Sergeant Tilney. Sergeant Tilney's platoon, during the diversion of fire, was able to move and eliminate all enemy activity in the area. Although Sergeant Tilney was fatally wounded as a result of this action, his unselfish act served as an inspiration to the members of his platoon and regiment. His courage and devotion

18-year-old Jäger Lothar Link, of the 5th Company of Reserve Jäger Bataillon 28, was one of the German defenders who was killed and later buried at the castle. Statni Okresni Archiv Bruntal Collection, courtesy Branislav Martinek.

Paratroopers of B Company, 509th PIB, rest along the western wall of the Agecroft Castle after the attack that cost the lives of six men from their company, plus one of the medics assigned to them. From left to right: Sgt Lloyd G. Van Guilder, Pvt General. S. Madden, Pvt William J. Powell, Pvt Robert N. Powell, Tom Stoner, and medic PFC Howard J. Maxwell. Mike Reuter Collection.

to duty are in keeping with the highest traditions of the military service. (…)[20]

While C Company was securing the castle, B Company in turn attacked down the ravine towards Hill 84. The Germans on the hill in the area west of the castle were now fully alert, and B Company ran into much more trouble than C Company had. **Lt Mike Reuter** was leading the 3rd Platoon of B Company of the 509th PIB:

In that attack we were in reserve, and we were following the rest of the people down that ravine. There was kind of a ravine that went down and into the big ravine. It was supposed to be done in the dark, but things got delayed, which is very common in battle, and we were exposed in the daylight to this ridge with German snipers, and they started firing at my platoon. I tried to get the column to move ahead, but the unit ahead of us had stopped and we couldn't move forward, because it was a narrow trail going through this kind of gulley. The bullets were bouncing off the rocks there, and of course a couple men were killed there, I guess, and a couple wounded. My scout (his name was Stewart) was standing right next to me when he was wounded in the arm.

The snipers were picking off my men there, so I decided that I would go up to the top of that ridge and see what I could do about it. Luckily, there were a lot of bushes and everything, and I apparently moved in between these snipers, got to the top of the ridge, and they kind of discovered I was there. A potato masher went over from the other side and exploded fairly close to me, so I threw a grenade over on the other side, and then someone with a Schmeisser machine gun opened up behind me. He couldn't see me, but he knew I was there and he was firing into the ground fairly close to me. Then I think that they got concerned that we were probably behind them and they got off the hill and left.

In the meantime, everything had moved forward at the bottom of this gulch, and when I came down, why, my platoon was gone. So I followed them up, and they were up there by the castle and they had just stopped a small counterattack and killed several Germans. One of my men had an antitank grenade on his rifle. He hit one of the Germans right in the chest. It disintegrated the man. I wasn't there at the time, but my men told me they thought these Germans that attacked were on drugs or something. They were yelling wildly, and it was kind of an insane attack. It was unorganized, and they just kept coming wildly in to attack the castle, and that's when my men shot them down.

Then I was with my platoon; I have a couple pictures taken after the engagement, sitting there by the edge of the castle. We were very tired at that time and also very thirsty. It was a very hot day. When our canteens were empty, we drank bottles of German seltzer water, which did not seem to quench our thirst.

Sgt Richard Fisco was in a platoon of B Company that was hit particularly hard during the attack, mostly due to the fact that it was under the command of a new and inexperienced lieutenant:

The first battle against rear guard action was for the Chateau de la Napoule. We passed through St Raphaël, climbed a 400-meter mountain, descended, and then ascended up into the enemy positions. We attacked down

22-year-old Cpl Burl J. Knapp, of B Company 509th PIB, who was picked off and killed by German snipers during the attack on la Napoule Castle August 21st. Knapp Family Collection. Richard Baranowski Way Library Collection, courtesy Jane Kelly.

25-year-old T5 Victor A. Osburn, a medic assigned to B Company of the 509th, was killed by a gunshot wound to the back, according to his burial report. Osburn Family Collection. Upshur County Historical Society Collection, courtesy Noel Tenney.

the bald slope into machine gun and small mortar fire, probably 40mm. My two machine gunners, Luksis [in fact probably **PFC Arthur Lundquist**] and **Knapp**, took off to the left and began to set up the machine gun right out in the open. I yelled out to them: "Bring that gun back, we're still attacking." They paid no attention and set the gun up 150 feet away. Snipers killed them immediately.

The unit in front of us was holding us up. Lt Knight turned to me and said: "Sergeant Fisco, what do you think we should do?" "Continue right through them," I answered. The other unit was now under the cover of the forest, only about 20 yards away. "I will have to get permission to move ahead," he said. I called the remainder of the platoon behind me to protect themselves by piling stones around. I surrounded myself with small boulders and lay down on my left side with my Tommy gun in my right hand, cradled over my right hip. One small mortar had been firing repeatedly from a very close distance. I could hear it fire and then hear the shells land. Then I heard one round go off and said to myself: "If I get over this one, I got the war made." I felt the pressure wave that preceded the shell. It landed on our Canadian radio man [probably **PFC George Hemsworth**], about six feet away from my head. His legs below the knees were still standing there, but the rest of him was gone. The shrapnel shattered the stock of my Tommy gun. One piece of shrapnel went half ay through the barrel, but I wasn't hurt.

Finally, the lieutenant told me that I could move ahead. I called to the men to move out. No one moved. I went back to find **Victor Osburn**, the medic, with his intestines on top of him. John Rimer was wounded. Between the dead and the wounded, I lost about a third of my platoon. That's when I started smoking cigars.[21]

Just like Sgt Gerald Tilney, Medic **T5 Victor Osburn** was awarded a posthumous Silver Star for his actions in the valley facing Hill 84:

> The infantry company to which Technician Osburn was attached as a medical aid man was attacking a wooded ridge. The route of approach to this ridge was through a deep, rock-bound valley. The enemy engaged the company as it attacked, and covered the entire length of the valley with machine gun and artillery fire. The fire from snipers in well-concealed positions was very effective, and it was impossible to advance or withdraw. Disregarding the dangers involved, Technician Osburn worked tirelessly through the entire morning, going from one wounded soldier to another, exposing himself time and again to enemy sniper and machine gun fire. During the afternoon, he located three wounded and removed them to a place of safety. Then, despite the repeated pleas from his comrades to be more careful, he attempted to aid another wounded soldier, and in so doing was himself mortally wounded. Technician Osburn's splendid example of courage, devotion to duty, and utter disregard for his own safety when going to the aid of his comrades inspired his company to maintain its attack until the enemy was overcome.[22]

PFC John Rimer was one of the B Company men who was wounded during the attack. He tells us about his recollections of that day, starting from the night before the attack:

> The night before we made the advancement, we were shelled just about all night with the "Screaming Mimis," the rockets. Those rockets were coming through there, just chopping trees down like they were toothpicks. You could see the fire coming out the tail of them. I was on outpost

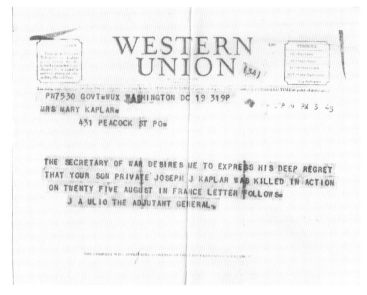

B Company men PFC Joseph L. Zadlo (top left), Pvt Joseph J. Kaplar, and PFC Ralph V. Hirales (top right), aged 24, who were all killed during the attack on the castle. Zadlo Family Collection. Kaplar Family Collection. Hirales Family Collection, courtesy Benoit Senne.

that night and I dug a hole, and all night long something was crawling on me; it was ants, and there was no way I could come out of that hole because of the shelling that they were giving us.

I got up the next morning and saw that I had dug my foxhole in a bed of ants. I don't even remember eating breakfast or anything because we didn't have any food; all we had were a few of those round, hard crackers. We made it over the hill and started down, and we were in a ravine. Now, the whole time when I was in the service training and training other people, we were told to stay out of what you can call a ravine, or a draw. They always told us to stay out of them damn things, but we went down there, and we were perfect targets for the Germans up on the side of that hill. We were almost to the bottom, then our lead people got pinned down by a machine gun and we had to stop. We couldn't keep on going, because we would then be in the line of fire, but we started taking sniper fire.

That ravine was basically all stone. The Germans would shoot down, and naturally it would ricochet until it would come to a stop or hit somebody. All around me you could hear guys crying, hollering out from being shot. I gathered up three men that were going back a little bit to see if we could find the snipers. As I was going up a hill, a sniper stepped out from behind a tree, and he saw me before I saw him and loaded on me. I got hit in my right hip, in my butt, and twice through my arm. My rifle was also shot to pieces. I don't know where the other fellows were, they were supposed to be in behind me. I rolled back down the hill, dropped off the bank, and fell back down into the ravine where I had started from.

When I rolled back down the hill, the guys wanted to know if they could help me and I said: "No, because whoever shot me is still up there and if you come out where I am he will probably shoot you, too." I unzipped my jumpsuit, and I saw that I had a big hole in my hip and I knew I was going to die. I took my first aid kit, got the bandage out of it, and stuffed it down into the hole where I had been shot. Then I took my morphine needle out of my first aid kit and stuck it in my arm. Before I gave myself the morphine, the Germans were shooting at us with the 88s, and naturally, I was kind of leery of being hit again. The 88s would shut down, then we had a little stinky 60mm mortar, and our men would shoot every so often with that 60mm. I was just cussing to myself about those mortars firing, because every time they fired, the Germans would shoot with the 88s and shells were hitting all around me. But after I gave myself the morphine I couldn't care less, because if you ever shot yourself with morphine, it will put you out of this world. You don't have any cares. I slept all day right out in the sun.

I laid there from early in the morning until late in the afternoon, I guess probably 12 hours. Somebody came by and wanted to know if I could walk. I told him: "Hell no! I can't walk!" So then they walked off and left me. Now this is something I don't know for sure, but then I think a couple of Germans came out there and picked me up. I can't swear to that. They had to be Polish or some of the others that were fighting in front of the Germans. They carried me back over the hill and loaded me into a jeep, and the next thing I knew, I was in the makeshift hospital there. Then I must have passed out again, because I don't remember anything until I got on the ship. I stayed out until I got into another hospital in Italy (the 37th Hospital).

Two weeks later I woke up. I was in hospital August, September, and October. Then they shipped me back to Kennedy General Hospital in the United States. I stayed there until the 29th, and I was discharged with a big hole in me still. But after it was all over with, I was glad that I was shot and going home.

Company A of the 509th PIB, which had been firing into the German positions to support B and C Companies while they attacked, also suffered some casualties, as **Lt John Frazier** noted:

At 0612 hours, A Company opened fire on Castle Ridge, while C Company started their move up to the ridge. At 1000 hours, Lieutenant Frazier was ordered to move his platoon to the left flank of A Company to the high ground for security. They came under heavy shelling that denied them the use of the ridge. Crosby, Leyden, and Thompson were hit trying to move up there. The platoon had to take cover below, using rocks.[23]

PFC Warren Boehmke, of A Company of the 509th, witnessed the battle for the castle from the opposite hill and remembers a very interesting event occurring that day:

At the last hill before you go into the lowlands going towards Cannes, the Germans were on one side of the hill and we were on the other side. They were pretty well dug in there, and we got to the point where there was a lot of shooting and a lot of action going on. They were shooting at us and we were shooting at them, and they were killing us and we were killing them. They would attack us, they would get stopped, then we would try to take them and they stopped us. There was a battle going on all day long, then finally they came out with a white flag, and they came over and said that they wanted to retrieve their wounded. So we ended up going down into the valley, where there were dead and wounded Germans and wounded Americans, and surprisingly, we were exchanging cigarettes, candy bars, and stuff like they were friends of ours for life. Then they got their wounded out, we got ours out, went back, and started shooting at each other again.

No other sources mention this truce, except perhaps John Rimer, who thought that he had been picked up by German prisoners after spending the day lying wounded in the valley. Perhaps the white flag that Warren Boehmke had seen had in fact been waived by Germans surrendering?

Pvt John DeVanie had been with the pathfinders of the Headquarters Company of the 509th PIB who were lost at Tanneron for five days, but had then crossed back to the American lines just in time for the battle on Hill 84. Once the Americans had taken complete control of the hill, the Germans continued spraying the area with artillery fire. **John DeVanie** was sent on a mission to try to find out where this deadly German shell fire was coming from:

We got back to the American lines at about 5 P.M., August 20th. We had made it back to our outfit, and they told us that first thing the next morning, we were going to make a push on Cannes. I spent that night in a street, wrapped up in a blanket, and it was pretty chilly. The next morning that big push was made on Cannes. When we started up toward the castle, we got small arms fire and they said it was snipers. But then one guy yelled out that he got the sniper and for us to go on. We had to go down the side of this hill and back up the hill towards the castle. We made it up to the castle under sniper fire and got inside. The American forces had occupied that castle just before I got there and made the headquarters in it. Then they told us that B Company was being pinned down by some artillery, and they had no idea where it was or what it was, so they assigned three of us to go up on this hill and reconnoiter to find out what they were doing down there and radio back.

They strapped a roll of wire on my back to unspool up this hill so we could radio back. On the way up there I stumbled over two dead Germans that were laying right there in the path going up to this hill. We found a little alcove on the top of the mountain that we got down in. We started looking over the side, and lo and behold, there were two railroad guns down at the bottom of this hill. They would shoot one and then move it backwards, and they would shoot another one and move it forward so that no one could pinpoint their location.

20-year-old Pvt David G. Bloyd, of A Company, and 32-year-old Pvt Larry J. Ducote, of B Company, who were both killed in the fighting August 21st and temporarily buried beside the train tracks at the Théoule sur Mer train station. Moundsville-Marshall County Public Library Collection, courtesy Catherine Feryok. Mike Reuter Collection.

Private Frank J. Sweetitz, one of John DeVanie's fellow pathfinders from the HQ Company of the 509th, was killed August 21st by a gunshot wound to the head, according to his burial report. Frank Sweetitz was born in Austria and had emigrated to the U.S. during his childhood. He was 31 years old at the time of his death. Dragoset Family Collection, courtesy Bill Dragoset.

Our objective was to radio back out to the ships in the harbor, to pinpoint where these railroad guns were, and they started laying a barrage of 16-inch shells around the railroad guns. Well, as we were doing this, the Germans evidently saw the glint on our binoculars; they spotted us up on top of this hill and started laying a barrage of artillery and mortar shells up towards us. Just before we got hit we saw one of the 16-inch shells hit one of these big German railroad guns and demolish it. So we did accomplish our mission, but then everything went black.

I found out later it was a mortar shell that landed right in between the three of us. We were real close together in that foxhole, and it killed one of our buddies and wounded me and Marion McGee. One of my friends saw us being blown out of that hole, and of course that ended my war career there. I was out for about two days after that. I woke up on a hospital ship; I didn't have any clothes, no weapons or anything else. They sent me down to Naples, Italy, to a field hospital. I was wounded bad enough to where they flew me back to the United States for an operation and stuff. I had been hit in the leg, back, arm, neck, and head by shrapnel, and there is still a piece in my head and four pieces in between my lungs. It did a lot of damage to the rest of my body, and I spent some 13 months in the hospital. Then I got a discharge from the hospital in September 1945.

The presence of a 170mm German railroad gun in the area north of la Napoule is mentioned in a FSSF communication at 8 A.M., August 22nd, and an inhabitant of Mougins confirmed that a railroad gun had taken position in a tunnel on the Cannes-Grasse railroad line. August 21st was a rather catastrophic day for the 509th PIB, in particular for B Company. Approximately 13 men were killed and many more wounded. The exact number of dead is difficult to ascertain, as the casualty lists of the 509th are incomplete and messy. In fact, all of the B and C Company men who were killed August 21st are officially listed as having died August 25th, although several were buried at Draguignan Cemetery on the 23rd! These mistakes in the dates of death are probably due to a mix-up in the paperwork at some point in the administrative process. In any case, witness accounts and period documents, such as medal citations and burial reports, indicate that most if not all of the following 13 men of the 509th were killed August 21st:

Pvt Leonard R. Haller, aged 21, of Company C of the 509th, was reported as missing in action for three months before his body was finally discovered in the underbrush of the Rague Valley at la Napoule. His official date of death (August 19th) is clearly wrong, as the 509th had not even reached la Napoule yet at the time. Five Rivers Public Library Collection, courtesy Nancy Moore.

Although these losses can be considered heavy for a single day of combat, the unit history was rather optimistic, stating:

At 0500 on 21 August, our artillery and mortars opened up with a terrific barrage on the enemy-held heights to the south of la Napoule. At 0600, C Company made the principal assault, attacking with two platoons abreast; one in support on the left, Company B, made a secondary attack to secure C Company's left flank. Mortar and machine gun fire support from our light machine guns and mortar platoons was furnished until C Company's advance masked the fire. The objective was in our hands by 12 hours. B Company ran into intense machine gun fire and was grenaded heavily by the enemy from positions among the rocks, but advanced and held fast. 61 German prisoners were taken during this action. Many enemy were killed and wounded. Our own casualties were relatively light.[24]

Surname	Name	Rank	Unit	Age	Probable date of death	Official date of death
Osburn	Victor A.	T5 Med	HQ Co 509 PIB	25	21.8.1944	21.8.1944
Sweetitz	Frank J.	Pvt	HQ Co 509 PIB	31	21.8.1944	21.8.1944
Bloyd	David G.	Pvt	A Co 509 PIB	20	21.8.1944	21.8.1944
Ducote	Larry J.	Pvt	B Co 509 PIB	32	21.8.1944	25.8.1944
Hemsworth	George P.	PFC	B Co 509 PIB	23	21.8.1944	25.8.1944
Hirales	Ralph V.	PFC	B Co 509 PIB	24	21.8.1944	25.8.1944
Kaplar	Joseph J.	Pvt	B Co 509 PIB	20	21.8.1944	25.8.1944
Knapp	Burl J.	Cpl	B Co 509 PIB	22	21.8.1944	25.8.1944
Lundquist	Arthur E.	PFC	B Co 509 PIB	19	21.8.1944	25.8.1944
David	Roy W.	Sgt	C Co 509 PIB	23	21.8.1944	25.8.1944
Haller	Leonard R.	Pvt	C Co 509 PIB	21	21.8.1944	19.8.1944
Tilney	Gerald K.	Sgt	C Co 509 PIB	28	21.8.1944	25.8.1944
Zadlo	Joseph L.	PFC	C Co 509 PIB		21.8.1944	25.8.1944

This photo, titled by its author as "Planning the attack on la Napoule," was probably taken August 22nd in the vicinity of la Napoule Castle. From left to right are Lt Harry S. Lieber of the Machine Gun Platoon, Capt Edmond J. Tomasik of the HQ Company, Battalion Executive Officer Maj John N. Apperson, and Capt Victor E. Garrett of the 463rd PFAB. This is the last photo ever taken of Major Apperson, as he would be killed later the same day, along with two other officers when their jeep drove over an antitank mine. Mike Reuter Collection.

Such histories are sometimes written days after the event, or by people who were not actually present at the front lines. Furthermore, unit histories tend to be written in a way that glorifies the unit in question, with the actual facts often becoming clouded in the process. For these reasons, it is wise to always seek several independent sources of information before drawing any conclusions. An actual message sent by the 509th at 2000 hours on August 21st tells a very different story, and is in direct contradiction with some of what is written in the official history, giving a more truthful impression of the situation following the attack:

> At 1700, B and C Companies moved up and captured hill. (…) Company B lost two platoons, of which all but six are missing. (…) Have no contact with 551st on left. Casualties high due to heavy artillery during day. Have few maps. Ammunition running low. 80 prisoners of war taken during assault on hill.[25]

The Germans had suffered at least five to ten killed in the castle area, three of which were buried within the castle grounds. However, the German losses are impossible to evaluate with precision due to dates of death being missing in numerous cases and to casualty lists that are probably incomplete. The total German losses for the whole la Napoule area will be presented at the end of this chapter.

The Capture of Hill 131 and of the Village of la Napoule

The 509th already planned to attack the next hill, Hill 131 (locally known as San Peyre), the very next morning, August 22nd. Company A, which had been in reserve during the Castle Hill fighting, would now lead the way. This attack went much better than the previous one to capture the castle, though there were casualties, as **Lt John Frazier** noted:

> At 2000 hours made a recon along Castle Ridge with company CO "Bud" Siegel for an attack the next day on hill San Peyre. We were shelled twice on the recon. Returned to my platoon at 2300 hours and issued the attack order. 0300 hours Aug. 22 we moved up to the line of departure. (…) The coordination was bad; we moved too fast, resulting in our receiving our own battalion's mortar fire, killing **First Sergeant Tommy Crane** and wounding Barney C. Jones of the Second Platoon. We gained our objective at about 0730 hours.[26]

If one is to trust the official dates of death, a second A Company paratrooper, **Pvt Robert E. Davison**, was also killed that day, while the company's commanding officer, **Captain Ernest "Bud" Siegel**, was wounded, recalling:

Chapter 6

We had a hill there, and they could see us right there. They had been on the hill and we chased them off. They killed a couple of our men first, and then I was sending my company in to push them off the hill down into the valley and climb the hill. When I got in front of this hill they must have seen me. I never saw the Germans fire an 88 at one person, but they did; and that was me, and I got hit in the shoulder. I was evacuated to Naples by navy hospital ship.

After capturing Hill 131, the 509th also cleared the last Germans out of the nearby village of la Napoule. The Germans apparently put up no resistance, as their casualties were extremely light, with only one German soldier being confirmed dead in the area on the 22nd. With the capture of fresh territory came a new threat posed by the many mines the Germans (including Karl Cyron's platoon) had laid during the previous days to help cover their retreat. The 509th suffered a severe blow by these treacherous weapons on the 22nd, when three officers, including the battalion's executive officer and one of its intelligence officers, were killed in bizarre circumstances described by **Captain Bud Siegel**:

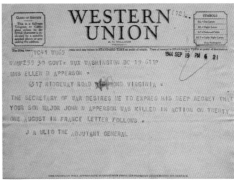

39-year-old Major John N. Apperson had only just recently been appointed Battalion Executive Officer of the 509th PIB when he was killed in action. Valentine Richmond History Center Collection. Cynthia Batty Collection.

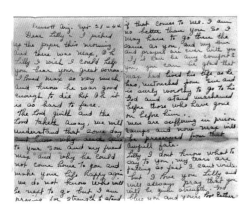

31-year-old Lt Lee Max Webb had been a Mormon preacher in Germany before the war, where he had learned German. In the army, he thus served as a linguist before volunteering for parachute duty. He had presumably been attached to the 509th to help interrogate German prisoners at the time of his death. Webb Family Collection, courtesy Gretchen Guice.

23-year-old Canadian-born West Point graduate Lt Hubert J. Fiander had recently been assigned to the 509th in the role of Intelligence Officer when he was killed. His father had disappeared in a shipping accident before his birth and his stepfather, uncle, and brother were later also all killed in similar shipping mishaps. West Point Academy Collection, courtesy Jim Pool. Gloucester Archives Collection, courtesy Sarah Dunlap.

199

509th PIB medical officers Capt Roy E. Baze and Capt Alfred J. Kelly pose in front of their makeshift "mobile hospital," consisting of a German truck that had been captured in St Tropez. The photo was probably taken in the vicinity of la Napoule Castle. Note that the truck has been Americanized by the addition of a white star above the cabin. Captain Baze was freshly assigned to the 509th before the jump into France and was killed by a mine within a day or two of this photo being taken. Mike Reuter Collection.

We had gotten the wrong kind of money in our escape kits. When you go on a mission, they give you an escape kit that has pills that can keep you awake, a file that you can put up your behind, and money. They had given us Italian money instead of French money. Major Apperson wanted to collect all the Italian money and take it to the Finance Officer, exchange it for Francs, and then give it back to the men. He was overage and green, but he was a nice guy, so you felt sorry for him. I explained to him: "Don't bother changing the money, these fellows have been with us in Africa and they know what to do with money." But he went ahead with it and tried to collect it all to take the Finance Officer and get the proper money. He had Lieutenant Fialia [**Lt Hubert Fiander**] with him, who was a West Pointer. He was driving and **Apperson** was with him, and they hit a Tellermine and it blew the jeep to pieces. They were both killed, and the money was spread all over the road and all the guys picked it up.

The third officer who was killed in the jeep was **Lt Lee Webb**, a linguist from the 2680th Military Intelligence Company (some period documents also list him as being in the headquarters of the 509th or the headquarters of the FABTF) who had parachuted into France with the FABTF. One of the 509th PIB's surgeons, **Captain Roy Baze,** commented on the incident in a letter home to his father that day: "The good Lord has certainly looked after your son. I went over a road three times today, evacuating patients; later, three officers

drove over the same road and were killed."[27] Unfortunately, Captain Baze's luck was not to last, as we will soon see. The Germans had infested the area with mines and another vehicle drove over one near the castle, luckily with less severe consequences, as **Lt Justin McCarthy** remembered:

The following day, one of the other companies was down the ridge from us. There was a road going down to where they were. They were bringing rations in there with a truck and they thought it was fired on by a light artillery weapon. They wanted the rations taken out of that truck and put in another truck, but it was under observation by the enemy, and they were afraid that if they sent another truck out there the Germans might fire on the second truck. Captain Tomasik wanted an officer to go out there with them, so I volunteered, and I went out with them and looked at that vehicle. As soon as I looked at it I said: "That was not hit by a shell, that was a mine." So they brought another truck out and they took the rations out of there and the new truck wasn't fired on. It was a mine that took the left front wheel of the truck off.

In total, five paratroopers had been killed in the vicinity of la Napoule on the 22nd (once again, there are discrepancies in the official dates of death and the dates reported on the burial files of the three officers killed by the mine); they were:

Surname	Name	Rank	Unit	Age	Probable date of death	Official date of death
Apperson	John N.	Maj	HQ Co 509 PIB	39	22.8.1944	21.8.1944
Fiander	Hubert J.	1Lt	HQ Co 509 PIB	23	22.8.1944	21.8.1944
Crane	Thomas J.	1Sgt	A Co 509 PIB	23	22.8.1944	22.8.1944
Davison	Robert E.	Pvt	A Co 509 PIB		22.8.1944	22.8.1944
Webb	Lee M.	1Lt	2680 Intel Co	31	22.8.1944	21.8.1944

One civilian in la Napoule, **Pierre Carle**, visited the battlefield and the Castle on Hill 84 a few days after the fighting:

My father owned a hotel. The Germans had requisitioned his cooking utensils to use them in the castle, so I went up to try to retrieve the cooking utensils, because my father was very fond of them. When I arrived at the castle, I was rather surprised because I saw, as far as I remember, the bodies of about 20 Germans lying on the ground there. It was in the middle of August and it stank, the bodies were black, and I didn't have the courage to go to the kitchen to get the utensils. The next day, I thought I would go back. So I returned, and was surprised to see the bodies were still there, but that they had been plundered. Their boots were gone, and I saw that the inside pockets of their tunics had been searched. There must have been visitors who were more interested than I had been and who had found, I don't know, maybe a bit of money? At least they found some boots. The people who plundered the bodies had guts, because with the state the bodies were in after having lain there in the sun for eight or ten days, it required a lot to plunder them and take their boots and all. Those Germans were buried in the castle, and later on they were unearthed and brought back, because each one had a cross with the identification tag on the cross.

At the exit of la Napoule, people were always complaining about an extremely bad smell, and we wondered where it could be coming from. It was a German who had literally been cut in half by a shell; one half of his body had been blasted into a tree and stayed stuck in the top of the tree, while the other half remained at the bottom. The lower part of the body had been buried, but nobody had noticed the other part in the tree. We noticed it later and then took it down to bury it with the rest of the body.

On the Allied side, the spectacle after the battle was barely nicer. Two paratroopers were buried beside the train tracks in Théoule, and the body of Leonard Haller, of C Company of the 509th, remained forgotten in the Rague Valley for over three months before it was finally discovered by a local Frenchman. The army sent Criminal Investigations Department agents **Silas Frazer** and **F.J. Sullivan** to investigate the find. The agents reported:

November 1, 1944, the undersigned were assigned to investigate the report of Maréchal Nonce Moracciole, Chef de Gendarmerie, Cannes, France, that a civilian, Ange Mansanti, (...) reported finding the corpse of a soldier, allegedly American, on 30 October 1944 at "Vallon de la Rague" (...). Accompanied by Moracciole, Mansanti, and Major John C. Montgomery (...), U.S. Army Medical Corps, the undersigned, on November 1, 1944, visited the place in question. There, about 200 feet high in the hills, among the shrubbery, was the corpse of what appeared to be an American paratrooper. The body was in an advanced state of decomposition, with the face decayed beyond any point of recognition. The hands were also in an advanced state of decay. The corpse was dressed in the familiar fatigue dress of a paratrooper: a camouflaged helmet with the initial "C" in adhesive tape at the back was beside the body; two unexpended hand grenades were nearby; as was an opened box of "K" rations. According to the medical opinion of Major Montgomery, the corpse was probably eight to twelve weeks old.

Major Montgomery arranged, in the presence of the undersigned, to remove the identification ("dog") tags from the upper part of the body. These tags were enclosed in adhesive tape and attached to a chain. The tags bore the inscription: Leonard R. Haller 35750995 T43-44A P.

The tags were handed over to the undersigned by this officer. In the vicinity of where the corpse was found there is a stream. Near this stream were American helmets, flares, hand grenades, used bandages, a syrette, a large bomb (...). Also present were canteen cups, torn clothing, pistol belts, trench knives, and shovels. To all appearances, this spot was a combat rendezvous. (...)

From the facts reported above, it is concluded that:

A) The identity of the corpse is that of an American soldier named Leonard R. Haller (...)

B) His death does not appear from the evidence to be the result of a criminal act.[28]

Having captured la Napoule and Hill 131, the 509th was now ready to advance on Cannes itself. The Siagne River formed the last natural obstacle before reaching the outskirts of the city. However, before telling of the river crossing, we must first go back in time to August 20th and 21st in order to describe the fighting that the 551st PIB was involved in along the RN7 highway, a couple kilometers to the northwest of Castle Hill and the 509th.

After burning the body of a killed German soldier in a vain attempt to get rid of its smell, the local gamekeeper, accompanied by civilians, flips the body into a shallow grave at la Napoule Castle. Hill 131, also known as the San Peire, is visible in the background. Pierre Carle Collection.

The bridge at the mouth of the Siagne River that was blown by the Germans as they retreated. Hill 131 is visible to the right of the photo. MRA Collection.

The 551ˢᵗ Parachute Infantry Battalion at Hill 105

In the afternoon of August 20ᵗʰ, the 551ˢᵗ PIB relieved the 2ⁿᵈ Battalion of the 141ˢᵗ IR in the hills west of Hill 105 and le Tremblant, along the RN7 highway. Facing them were the soldiers of the 6ᵗʰ and 7ᵗʰ Companies of *Reserve Jäger Battalion 28*. The 551ˢᵗ had jumped into southern France the afternoon of August 15ᵗʰ, after the other paratrooper units had already secured the landing zones. They had only been involved in light fighting since the landing and had lost only one man killed between August 15ᵗʰ and August 19ᵗʰ. Therefore, arriving in the le Tremblant area was their first experience holding a front line and can be considered their true baptism of fire. **Sgt Douglas Dillard** describes the circumstances under which the paratroopers relieved the 2ⁿᵈ Battalion of the 141ˢᵗ IR:

I was the communications sergeant in A Company of the 551ˢᵗ Battalion, and as a result, I was with the command group of the company, normally along with the company commander when the company was operating. We left the Draguigan area to move over to replace the elements of the 36ᵗʰ Division that were holding a line east of Draguignan.

We moved up in a convoy that was really not what one would normally think of a military convoy, because there was a combination of our people walking, of German trucks that had been captured, French trucks that the Resistance had made available, and motorcycles. So someone described us as a very irregular looking group of soldiers being transported in all that mix-up of different types of transportation. It created a lot of noise, there was a lot of dust, and we also felt there were observers in the area that were reporting via radio or other means to the German artillery positions.

The first afternoon was very scary, because we were making what is known as a daylight relief of a front line unit. Whenever that is done, the enemy certainly is aware of it. They know that there is activity going on, and if there is activity, it means people are out of their foxholes and they are vulnerable to either artillery or mortar fire. That aroused the Germans' attention and they decided they would go ahead and give us a good wallowing with artillery fire.

From my own personal experience, as we moved along the road, the shells started landing right on the road.

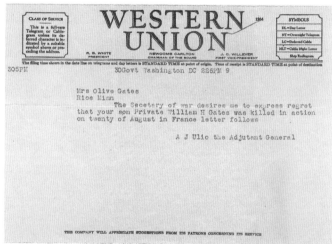

24-year-old Pvt William H. Gates, of the HQ Company of the 551ˢᵗ PIB, was killed by artillery fire immediately after reaching the Hill 105 area outside le Tremblant. Along with the personal belongings sent back to his family was a wallet decorated with a paratrooper badge. Gates Family Collection.

I think the first casualty that I remember seeing directly was one guy, I believe it was **Gates**, that had been hit and practically blown apart all over the road in front of us. So you're walking by there and you thought: "My God, is this going to happen to me?" It was a real moral problem for most of us to walk by and see that, because when it happened, you're right there by him.

As we approached the position, the artillery was coming in hot and heavy, so we had to spot a foxhole that the troops of the 36th Division had dug or begin to dig our own. I had a team of two radio operators that operated the radio for the company to communicate with battalion, so I made sure they were together in one foxhole and I got in the foxhole next to them. Of course, I was in the hole by myself that night with all that artillery raining down, so I wasn't a very happy person. I thought "number one, I would never do that again. If I am going to jump in a hole, I am going to find somebody to jump in a hole with." That was lesson learned number one. The concern is that you could be hit and bleed to death and nobody would know it.

SSgt Charlie Fairlamb, of the HQ Company of the 551st, remembers some of the more comical aspects of the relief:

We had got some transportation and were moving up to relieve elements of the 36th Division. I don't know where we got the trucks, and there weren't many, so the guys were crowded on. We got to rolling and it had been pretty dry, so there was a lot of dust. We had just got to where the 36th was in position when the Germans started shelling us, having seen all the dust, so we all bailed out and landed in the ditch alongside the road. I think it was either Carl Bagby or C.M. Wood (he was a big guy with a southern drawl in the mortar platoon). Anyway, he found himself a foxhole and jumped in. A couple of minutes later, here comes this GI running like crazy down the hill from the 36th, and when he got to the foxhole he said: "Hey, fella, you're in my foxhole" and our guy said: "Bud, you just been relieved."[29]

Cpl Jim Aikman, of the HQ Company, also remembers the fight to find a good foxhole as the paratroopers relieved the men of the 141st IR:

One time we were being shelled after relieving the 36th Division. The 36th had built some pretty dandy shelters, and Jim Heffernan found a nice big foxhole and he went in there. Then Glen Slucter dove in, and right then I came flying in there, too. Then Glen told Jim: "Well Heffernan, there's not room enough in here for all of us. You have to leave." Jim said: "Wait a minute. I was here first. If anybody leaves, it's going to be you." Nobody left.[30]

Charlie Fairlamb continues:

One of the first casualties I saw on Hill 105 [In the minds of the soldiers of the 551st, every hill in the area was called Hill 105. In fact, they were in the hills west of Hill 105, as Charlie Fairlamb indicates later in the text.] was a rifleman. We had just got there, and he was running down the road toward us, hopping on one foot and hollering: "I am going home! I am going home!" He was so happy, but I doubt that he made it home, because it took more than that.

We dug in on the rim of the hill facing Hill 105, looking across the valley. There was a steep bank in front of us, really steep, but we dug in a shallow foxhole anyway. That night, the Germans shelled us with searching and traversing fire, and you could see these explosions coming up the hill, and they kept right on coming. I was in phone communication with the mortars in our rear, on the other side of the hill, and this one shell hit real close to our foxhole and then there was a little silence, and I found I had no more contact with the mortars. I looked around, and here this medic came running down the hill just like it was

Paratroopers of the 551st PIB, apparently taken as they move into the Hill 105 area. From left to right are Flavian Hook, PFC Sidney Black, Sgt Donald Anderson, and Cpl Joe Cicchinelli. Joe Cicchinelli Collection, courtesy Pascal Hainaut.

23-year-old PFC William C. Lawson, of the HQ Company of the 551st, was mortally wounded by shrapnel in the legs shortly after reaching the Hill 105 area. Emporia Library Collection, courtesy Emma Sundberg.

Sunday afternoon, running for all he was worth. I could just make out his silhouette, carrying his bag. He came to my foxhole and said: "Jesus Christ! I thought you were killed!" He had come down to help. The medics always felt like they couldn't get hit, they had a lot of guts.[31]

Unfortunately not all the men were so lucky, and during the first afternoon, several men of the HQ Company were hit in their newly-occupied positions, as **Sgt Don Garriges**, also of HQ Company, remembers:

> When the shells began striking our area, about all we could do was keep as close to the ground as possible. I was only a few feet away from a fellow trooper, **Bill Lawson**, when he was struck by shrapnel and had his legs nearly severed at the thigh. I called for the medics, and soon two corpsmen crawled up and carried him back down the hillside. I heard he died a short time later.[32]

Cpl Jim Aikman was also present when PFC William C. Lawson was mortally wounded:

> The whole 551st was under pretty heavy artillery and machine gun fire. Our ammunition carriers had a good foxhole dug in beneath some large pines and I was there with them when one shell came in and hit a tree top. The pine needles and bark hit me in the back and I thought I had been struck by shrapnel, it stung that bad. Then I heard one of the carriers moaning, and he had both legs nearly cut off.[33]

Sgt Perry I. Ellis, of the HQ Company, was mortally hit in similar circumstances. **SSgt Leo Urban** was with him at the time:

> We were up on Hill 105, firing down into the next valley. That's where **Perry Ellis** got hit. He was a mortar sergeant. We were both up on the observation post directing fire from a foxhole and were facing each other when an artillery tree burst got him in the abdomen with a piece of shrapnel. It missed me and got him. They sent him

Perry Ellis
GENERAL COURSE
Pet Hate—Frederick Elrick
South Jr. High 1; Stamp Club 2;
Scrub Football 1; Printers Club 3, 4;
Vice Pres. 3; President 4.

25-year-old Sgt Perry I. Ellis, of the HQ Company of the 551st, was mortally wounded shortly after reaching the Hill 105 area August 20th. He died September 10th in a hospital in Italy. Central Forsyth County Public Library Collection, courtesy Fam Brownlee Jr.

back to the hospital, and a couple weeks later he was seen by George Rickard in Rome, at the hospital there. (…) He said that when he saw Ellis his hair had turned white. Ellis died there at the hospital.[34]

Perry Ellis survived almost 20 days, only dying September 10th. Abdominal wounds are slow to heal and are particularly prone to infection, which may be the reason why he died so many days after being wounded. During their first hours on the front lines, one man of the 551st was killed and at least six wounded, including two mortally. About these casualties, the medical personnel of the 551st later reported:

> At about 1730 hours on August 20, 1944, the forward section of the aid station (…) received one minor casualty and one dead, which were evacuated to the rear section of the aid station. At approximately 1945 hours, one lacerated skull injury with avulsed brain tissue and one severe laceration of both thighs with extensive loss of muscle tissue and shock were received in the forward section of the aid station. They were given first aid and a large amount of plasma and evacuated directly by captured ambulance to the 11th Evacuation Hospital.[35]

The arrival in the Hill 105 area and the ensuing casualties were a shock for the men of the 551st. The atmosphere during that first night on the front line, and the slight paranoia of some of the men of the 551st that ensued, is best described by **Sgt Don Thompson** from A Company:

> Just at dusk, we got word to secure and hold our area for the night, so I was moving my men to good positions on our perimeter. SSgt Jim Stevens, our platoon sergeant, came crawling over to our position then to say that Captain Dalton wanted to see me right away.
>
> I went with him towards the enemy-held area, to where the captain had taken over a German dugout. As we got close, Jim told me the password was "Kid," and that I had better use it when I approached the dugout or I would get my head blown off. I was thinking what an appropriate password it was, because I was just a kid (I was under the enlistment age when I came in the Army, so my folks had to sign their consent).
>
> Well, Jim showed me about where the dugout was, it was pitch dark, and I crawled up there and gave the password but got no answer. So I dropped down in there and suddenly, I felt a .45 pistol against the side of my head. It was Captain Dalton and he was taking no chances. He said: "Are you alone? Are there Germans with you? Are you captured?" Well, he had heard Jim and me talking out there and figured maybe I had been taken.
>
> Then he told me that a gap had developed between our battalion and the British Parachute Brigade on our flank, and the Germans were moving in there and might try to surround and annihilate us in the morning. The Colonel needed to make contact with the brigade so we could close the gap, and I was to take seven of my men through the German lines, find the British Brigade, and give them our position and get theirs. The captain took out a map, and by the light of a flashlight showed me where we were, then I put the map in my boot. He said: "You have to be back before daybreak, so that will give you seven or eight hours. Do you understand your mission?" I told him I did. We shook hands and saluted.

I crawled back to my platoon and got the men that the captain and I had agreed on: Cpl John Collins, Cpl Schultz, Joe Cicchinelli, PFC Jack Simpson, Rogers "Arky" Moore, Jim Dunn, and George Smith. We spaced ourselves about 50 feet apart and moved very carefully through the German positions in absolute darkness. When we had gone about three miles, we heard a heavy vehicle approaching us on the road we were paralleling, and I decided we would stop it, and if it was German we would capture it, but maybe it was one of the British vehicles.

Well, it turned out to be British, and after a near skirmish when they thought for a few moments that we were English-speaking Germans, we got squared away and they took us to their command post.

Their Colonel was mad because we had penetrated about 200 yards inside their perimeter without being discovered. Their command post was in a large, old brick building. They had captured about 50 Germans and they were all tied up and lying on the floor inside, so when we went in we were stumbling over all those bodies in the dark. Finally, we got to a door and entered an inside room where they had a light, and we exchanged information. The English Colonel said the reason for the gap was that our battalion had moved too fast the previous two days, but I was to tell Captain Dalton that the brigade would start closing the gap in the morning. [In fact, the 551st was holding positions that had been static since August 16th. As for the British Brigade, this was their last night on the front and the FSSF started relieving them early the next morning, August 21st.]

We moved very carefully back through the German lines, going a few yards, stopping and listening, then moving a few yards more. All the time we could hear German machine gun fire. At one point, George Smith said: "Sarg, I'd rather be back at Fort Benning doing pushups." A little later, we were aware of the Germans attacking the perimeter of the English brigade and could hear the German officers and non-coms shouting orders. That was at 0205, when I was checking the time. At 0315, Joe Cicchinelli made contact with our own perimeter, and around 0330 I reported back to the captain.

The first thing he said was: "Did we lose any men?" When I told him we all made it back I saw tears running down his cheeks. That tough old soldier of steel had a big, tender heart for his men.[36]

One soldier from **Sgt Douglas Dillard**'s radio team in A Company was killed in his foxhole during the night:

During the night, there were skirmishes, as I recall, between our position and German patrols operating forward of our position. One of my runners was an American Indian named Yellowrobe. What happened, unfortunately, is Yellowrobe started digging a foxhole over on the forward slope of the hill we were occupying, and he was exposed to the German positions more. He probably was up too high, he should have been down a little lower so that there was no silhouette. During the night, in receiving machine gun fire from the Germans, he was critically wounded. As a matter of fact, he was almost cut in half at the waist by the machine gun fire while he was trying to dig in on the forward slope of that hill.

The next morning, the company commander called me over and he said: "Sergeant, we've got some wounded

A paratrooper of the 551st (above) sits in a shallow foxhole in the Hill 105 area. No deeper holes could be dug in the rocky ground. What seems to be the RN7 highway is faintly visible in the background. Pictured below is the same area from a distance today. Joe Cicchinelli Collection. Author's Collection.

up here and dead, and I want you to move them down to the road so the grave registration people can pick them up." So I went over to the position where **Yellowrobe** was and he was leaning over in his foxhole. We removed his body, put him on a shelter half, and four of us carried the body down to the road.

Four men of the 551st had been killed or mortally wounded August 20th and during the night; they were:

Surname	Name	Rank	Age	Unit	Date of death
Ellis	Perry I.	Sgt	25	HQ 551 PIB	20.8.1944
Gates	William H.	Pvt	24	HQ 551 PIB	20.8.1944
Lawson	William C.	Pfc	23	HQ 551 PIB	20.8.1944
Yellowrobe	Alvin J.	Pfc	19	A Co 551 PIB	21.8.1944

The next morning, August 21st, the front was calmer, and no more men were killed by artillery fire. However, Battalion Commander Colonel Joerg ordered the 551st to attack east that afternoon as part of the general push forward of the FABTF. Company A was to take Hill 105.8, south of the RN7, with B Company in support, while C Company was to attack Hill 78, just north of the RN7. Company C's attack is described in the unit history:

Company C prepared for attack at 1700 on Hill 78. At 1910 hours moved to attack, advancing under heavy enemy mortar fire, machine guns and rifles. The German riflemen opening up from our left flank wounded 8 men. Unable to obtain mortar and artillery support, the company withdrew and reorganized on defense line.[37]

In the meantime, A Company's attack on Hill 105.8 had been more successful, and the hill was captured with no deadly casualties occurring:

> Company A received order to attack Hill 105.8. Launched attack at 1800. Encountered enemy outpost while moving on objective. Killed 3 Germans and captured 4. Moved on to objective and went into position under fire.[38]

Sgt Martin Kangas, of the HQ Company light machine gun platoon, may have been involved in this attack (Because the fighting on Hill 105 lasted for two days, it is difficult to know if Sgt Kangas is actually referring to actions that occurred on the 21st, the 22nd, or both.) and remembers:

> We assaulted a hill outside of Cannes and there was quite a fire fight. A German came out of his foxhole; I saw him pop up and he had a rifle grenade on the end of his rifle. He let that thing go and I thought I was going to get hit right between the eyes, but it settled down and floated right between my feet. Before I had a chance to fire, I think half a dozen other guys mowed him down. The grenade went off, but it didn't do anything to my feet. I think I had

a little piece of rock split my finger. I didn't even bother to have it patched up. Our mortars really laid them out; they did devastating work, and when we finally made it to the top, there were dead Germans all over the place; the Germans counterattacked right away, too.

> We tried to dig in, and oh boy, we had small arms fire coming right back at us again. All we were doing was scooping pebbles and whatnot, trying to get a little bit of cover. They pressed the cooks in for ammunition carriers, and one of them was working for Ray Little. We called this guy "Duck Legs" because of the way he walked. He came paddling across that ridge with a couple boxes of machine gun ammunition and we hollered: "Hey, Duck Legs, get down you damn fool, get down! You're going to get yourself killed up there!" and he called back: "What's the matter? Is somebody shooting at us?" It was really popping hot and heavy.

> While we were up on that ridge, the Germans were using a big gun somewhere. When they would cut loose with that thing it would blow out a half acre of timber. Man, that was devastating. The good part about it was that most of the rounds went right on over and only a few hit the top.[39]

The rounds that passed over the hill were not lost for everybody, as we will see very shortly. Company B, which had been held in reserve during the attacks, was now sent forward to support A Company. On its way, it needed to pass through a valley west of Hill 105. During its passage through the valley, B Company was hit heavily by German artillery, as **PFC George Kane** explains:

> We were on Hill 105, and **Louis Tenute** was killed by a short round from our own mortars. They were firing from a road down below us on to a target on the other side of our hill. We moved out on attack then and it was a strange situation; it was sunny and late in the afternoon, and we didn't walk along the bottom of that draw, but went on the two sides of it, and then we received a lot of fire so we stopped. I was sitting there with this friend, J.D. Smith, and we were mixing up cocoa and we were saying something like: "Look, here we are at war, we are spectators at a war." We could see the shells coming in, and we were just calmly sitting there because we didn't have orders to do anything else. Later on we got down in the draw, but that was after dark. I got hit and the medic told me to stay there.

> All through the night those guns slowly walked shells up and down that draw, up and down. The close ones—I could tell when they were going to be real close—would sound like they were coming in the back of your neck. I was hit one more time that night. I got hit once in the leg and once in the hip. I just got one Purple Heart.[40]

The shelling that had started as an interesting spectacle for the men of B Company on their second day at the front lines turned into one of their worst experiences of the war as they entered the draw west of hill 105. **PFC Richard Field**, of B Company, remembers how the shelling started:

> It was at night time, and we were advancing down towards Cannes. We weren't being really noisy, but we were also not making any great effort at being very quiet. We weren't talking or anything like that, but you could

A wounded medic of the 551st in the Hill 105 area. Note the German belt and pistol at his feet. Joe Cicchinelli Collection.

hear us, and so I am sure the Germans could hear us moving along. Then there was an unusual thing: we could see tracer fire going overhead as we advanced. We found out later that the Germans were using tracer fire to mark our advance so that the artillery would be able to zero in on us. They knew exactly where we were. We got down into this gulley at the side of this hill and that's when the artillery started. At first we heard the whistling, incoming you know, and everybody hit the deck. But then it just continued and we were scattered out and very exposed.

PFC Ben Goodman, of B Company, also remembers the German observers:

We were going down this draw, we were going to attack, and all of a sudden some flares went up, and then we got bombed. Some artillery came in and we took a lot of damage. They knew we were coming, they had it planned. There was a German up in a tree, I saw him, and he was directing the artillery. It was horrible. They kept shelling us and shelling us. They must have shelled us for at least an hour. We just hunkered on the ground, and some guys were hit, some guys were not. B Company was over there and we lost maybe ten men all together.

SSgt Joe Kosowski, of B Company, was also caught in the middle of the deadly artillery barrage:

Hill 105. I was in a ravine right in the middle of a dried-up creek, digging as deep as I could get, right down into the bank of that creek. The shells were really coming in, they were hitting us with the 88s. You could hear them, zip – bang, coming right in there. There were a few lads in our platoon that got it. One lad was always taking his helmet off, he wore that little beanie hat and we were always telling him to put his helmet on. Well, he had his head shot off.[41]

Lt Dick Mascuch was with the 3rd Platoon of B Company, which was lucky to be in the back of the column where the shelling wasn't as bad:

We were ordered to move through a draw that the Germans had zeroed in with artillery and the battalion took quite a beating. It was our first baptism of fire. We were just moving along in a column and we came under this pretty intense artillery fire. Of course, everybody hit the ground and tried to dig in, which was almost impossible. We had trained in North Carolina, which has very sandy soil, so you could dig a foxhole as big as a garage in a matter of minutes. In France, they had about two inches of soil and then solid rock. I remember, every time a shell would come in it would get very quiet and then the shell would go off. After a little wait, you would hear somebody start to dig and pretty soon everybody would be starting to dig and you could hear the entrenching tools hitting the rocks. Then another shell would come in, everything would get real quiet again, and everybody hit the ground. When a shell would go off, you would hear the shrapnel doing a sound like "bzzzzt" and then hit a tree with a big "thunk.'

I got hit, but not bad. I was lying down there and one shell went off and a piece of shrapnel went up my sleeve and burned me. I had a dirty uniform, so it got real infected.

A couple days later I went to a medic and said: "You got a band-aid?" and the guy put a band-aid on it and he says: "How did you get that?" I told him, so the medic wrote me up for a Purple Heart, and I knew there was a point system to get you home, so I took it.

Richard Field was caught in the thickest of the shelling and continues his account of that terrible night:

There was some huge artillery. When the smaller ones came in they kind of whistled, but the huge ones, the big ones, they would make a "wof wof wof wof," and when they hit, it would raise you right off the ground. I mean, there was that much of an explosion. I understand they used some railroad cannons also. These railroad cars, they would wheel them back in the tunnel and then wheel them out when they shot them, then put them back in the tunnel so they were protected.

We started scrambling around to find cover and that's how we found a dry stream bed that we got in. It was all rocks and you couldn't even dig down in it, but it was a little bit depressed, and we finally got down in that for a little bit of protection. But we were helpless, entirely helpless. There was nothing to shoot back at, there was no small arms fire, there were no Germans attacking us with infantry. It was just heavy artillery and it's a helpless feeling because all you can do is duck for cover and try to protect yourself as much as you can. There was one guy that was lying very close to me and a shell went off. It tore the top of his head right off and his brains and stuff splattered on me. You can't imagine what that's like. It's a terrible thing. How the shell missed me, I don't know, because it threw shrapnel all over. When his brain splattered on me, I didn't realize it until I got up out of there, then my jumpsuit was all messed up and everything, and of course he was dead. The whole top of his head was gone.

I remember Lt Hecq saying: "I wonder how many atheists there are here tonight?" because everybody was praying. I thought that was pretty profound that he said something like that in the middle of all this. It was a terrible night. I don't know how many men were killed, but it was terribly heavy shelling. When somebody is wounded—and I have seen different men wounded—most of the time, the first thing they say is: "Mama." They want mama. And I remember one guy, when he was wounded, he yelled: "Mama, mama!"

Obviously, it felt like it lasted an eternity, but it didn't really in actual time. I think it lasted an hour or an hour and a half, something like that. We were pinned down and we were entirely helpless. I was a scout for my squad and I found a little feeder gulley that emptied down into this dry stream. We worked our way up and got out of there, and there was a road around the back of a mountain. Some of the wounded had been carried up there. There was one fellow named Bucky Nannis, and he was laying there; at the back of his head you could see his brains. [It would seem that T4 Irving "Bucky" Nannis was actually wounded on the previous day, August 20th, when the 551st PIB reached the Hill 105 area, and is the "lacerated skull injury with avulsed brain tissue" mentioned in the previously quoted medical report.] His back was all torn apart and I figured he was dead. About 40 years later, we had a reunion in New Orleans and he came. He had been in a wheel chair ever since then and he had a male nurse with him, but he came to that reunion. That was a very emotional thing also, because we didn't realize that he had even lived. I

Drew Pearson Cited Local Vet Helping Hemoplegics

One of the two severely wounded combat veterans who received nation-wide publicity last week-end in Drew Pearson's Washington Merry-go-round column, which is a regular Sunday Sun feature, is a local man it was learned during the past week.

Irving "Bucky" Nannis, son of Mr. and Mrs. Samuel Nannis, 10 Hillside ave., this city, and Tony Diglio of New Haven, Conn., were cited by Pearson last Sunday when he said that the "veterans, doomed to life in wheel chairs, descended on Capitol Hill and single-handed moved cumbersome legislative machinery into action."

Patients at the Veterans Administration's Cushing General Hospital, Framingham, the veterans are hemoplegics — victims of combat brain injuries which cause paralysis similar to that resulting from the spinal cord injuries of the paraplegics.

With only some 25 victims of the condition in the entire country the local war hero and his companion went to Washington May 24th in an effort to help their crippled "buddies." They pooled their resources to hire an attendant to make the trip with them, and payed all their own expenses. They went to the capitol by car and then hitched their two wheel-chairs into a "train" with one attendant pushing them on the rounds of Capitol Hill. At the Senate building they sent in cards and the senators came out to see them. Their action in "invading" the capitol brought results when Senator Morse of Oregon who filed a bill in their behalf, S. 1938, while they waited. They also received the promises of Senators Pepper and Taft that they would support the bill.

At the House building, the combat veterans visited the office of Congresswoman Edith N. Rogers, but she was out at the time. They then contacted Congressman Olin Teague of Texas, who promised to file a bill in the House before they were out of the building.

In his nationally-read column, Pearson said that "When Congress passed the law providing housing for paraplegics it was generally assumed that all wheel-chair veterans would be covered, but V. A. lawyers ruled the legis-

IRVING NANNIS

lation was confined to just one type of paralysis. A separate law would be required to help the hemoplegics."

As Pearson described it, "Armed with the facts, stout hearts and their wheel-chairs, Bucky and Tony went into action. Within three hours they had sold Senator Wayne Morse on the justice of their cause and he introduced the necessary bill. More support came from Taft of Ohio, Humphrey of Minnesota and others, until the two veterans, on leaving Washington, remarked:

"'It makes you really proud of our democracy when you think that the most powerful government in the world would pause and listen to two strangers in wheel-chairs'."

Nannis entered the U. S. Army in February of 1942 and was assigned to the 82nd Airborne. In August of 1944, during the invasion of Southern France, he sustained severe wounds. Last summer he was discharged from the service.

Irving "Buckey" Nannis, who received a penetrating brain injury in the Hill 105 area that caused him to become hemiplegic and had difficulty walking for the rest of his life. His handicap did not prevent him from holding a job, getting married, and having three daughters. He passed away in 1999 at age 75. Shelley Rossitto Collection.

don't know how he did live, because you could actually see his brain matter in the back of his head.

A very, very bad and a terrible thing that I remember about that is the next morning, we had to go back down in this dry creek bed where we were and carry out our dead. We used the dead guy's shelter halves and laid them out on the ground and just wrapped the shelter half around them and used that to carry them out of there. It was difficult, because it was on the side of a hill and we had to scramble up and then go back down and get some more. I was a 19-year-old kid, and to have to put up with something like that, it was just not natural. It was a very traumatic thing to have happen. I still have nightmares and dreams about things that happened, especially that night. I will never ever forget that night and the next day. It was terrible.

One of the other men who was caught in the thickest of the shelling was **Sgt Emory Albritton**, of the B Company mortar squad:

We went up this hill, before Cannes, in a frontal attack. There was a lot of firing in both directions, and then we came back off the hill and went up a deep draw on the left side. It was a dry creek bed, and by then it was dark.

The artillery was as heavy as you can possibly imagine. What they did was, they were traversing up and down that draw and they were getting a lot of the guys. A dud landed right near me and I stuck my hand out and touched the nose and got burned good. Everett Debarr was right in front of me, and all at once a shell exploded right by us and he took all the shrapnel. He had big holes in his back, so I figured he was a goner. They were using a lot of white phosphorus and it was almost like daytime; there were a lot of small fires burning around the area and I think Lt Hecq got some phosphorous in the face. People were moaning and groaning all around.

Anyway, I had noticed a sort of ledge above us, a bunch of rocks higher up. I asked Debarr if he was all right, but all he could do was groan, so I got hold of him (he was one of the bigger guys in the company (…)), and he was mumbling: "Help me, help me." Then the two of us sort of climbed up and staggered up there, in all the artillery, and took cover the best we could. The artillery finally let up, and soon I heard hobnailed boots passing right below us as the Krauts came into the area.

When it finally got light, I looked down on the darndest mess you ever saw. The bodies of Company B's 2nd Platoon were strewn all over the area. Across the draw was a German machine gun with a three man crew and a couple ammunition bearers. I had given Debarr a shot of morphine to keep him quiet so the Germans wouldn't hear us, although he was tough as nails. After I had sized up the situation, I said to Debarr: "Look, I can leave you here and try to get up the mountain, or I can take you and try to get back to our lines." He just mumbled, so I started carrying him out. I just got him up on my shoulder and started down the hill towards the Germans. I came very close to them and they were watching us, but they did not stop us. As we went past, one of them saluted me and I nodded my head. I remember seeing **Max Williams** dead there, on the ground. He was a tough nut; I think he was from Indiana. I counted about 16 bodies, but some of them may have been just wounded. I kept working my way along and I was asking myself: "My God, where is Company B?"

Finally, I heard someone shout "Halt!" and it was F.M. [Field Manual] Reed. He damn near shot me; he thought

I was a German coming up that draw. There was an aid station right there on the side of the mountain with guys on stretchers all over the place. I had been shot through the chest that night and it wasn't bad, but I was bleeding some. I guess it was Doc Chalkley that laid me down on a stretcher.

The next thing I knew, I woke up in a tent and there were dead bodies all around me. I was on a table, and a guy named Dave Smith from our company was on my left. [Albritton is confusing names, as Dave Smith in fact died over a month later in different circumstances.] He had both arms blown off and he was dead. Another dead guy was on my right. About then I heard some guy outside say: "All the guys in here are stiffs." And I said: "Up your ass, we aren't all stiffs!" By mistake they had put me in the wrong damned tent. That was in a field hospital, not in our battalion aid station. I was strapped down and couldn't even move.

So they took me out of there, gave me a transfusion, and sent me back to the hospital in Naples via C-47. At that hospital I had Irving "Bucky" Nannis on my left and James Arness (…) on my right. [This was the same James Arness who was later to become a movie star.] (…) Bucky Nannis was paralyzed from the waist down and he still is.[42]

The person who Emory Albritton referred to as "Doc Chalkley" was **Captain Jud Chalkley**, the battalion's Second Surgeon, who spent the night of August 21st to 22nd treating the casualties of the shelling:

Our casualties were very heavy in the engagement above Cannes. The Germans hit us hard with artillery and mortars, and Batt [Captain John Battenfield] and I worked all night patching up the casualties. Batt was about 100 yards back. Jack Affleck worked very hard that night, dragging the casualties back up the hill to Batt's station, while I worked forward. We would have five or six guys there, we would get them moved back, and here would come five or six more, and some dead. It went on all night long, and we may have had as many as fifty seriously wounded that one night.[43]

Often the numbers of casualties become exaggerated in the memories of the men who lived through these tragic events. The unit history of the 551st PIB provides more factual information on the casualties:

Company B was caught in artillery barrage which opened as soon as the company entered the valley. The barrage lasted until 2300. Casualties: 8 dead, 14 wounded. Company B withdrew from canyon at 2300 and returned to former defensive positions.

By 0700, August 22, 1944, approximately 25 moderate to very severe wounds had been treated and evacuated by the aid station.[44]

Louis Tenute, who had been wounded by friendly fire, later died of his wounds, bringing the total number of dead for the afternoon and night of August 21st to nine:

Corp. Deming Is Killed in Action

Surname	Name	Rank	Unit	Age	Date of death
Billman	Lewis R.	T5	B Co 551 PIB	23	21.8.1944
Deming	James W.	T5	B Co 551 PIB	21	21.8.1944
Dennis	William E.	PFC	B Co 551 PIB	22	21.8.1944
Fields	Warren B.	Pvt	B Co 551 PIB	29	21.8.1944
Parks	Leon W.	Pvt	B Co 551 PIB	19	21.8.1944
Sepulveda	Ramon M.	Pvt	B Co 551 PIB	25	21.8.1944
Tenute	Louis J.	Pvt	B Co 551 PIB	21	21.8.1944
Williams	Max G.	Cpl	B Co 551 PIB	26	21.8.1944
Wright	William J.	Pvt	B Co 551 PIB	20	21.8.1944

Five of the eight paratroopers of B Company of the 551st PIB who were killed by artillery fire near Hill 105 August 21, 1944: 23-year-old T5 Lewis R. Billman, 21-year-old T5 James W. Deming, 22-year-old PFC William E. Dennis (middle left), 19-year-old Pvt Leon W. Parks (lower right), and 20-year-old Pvt William J. Wright (lower left). Billman Family Collection. New York State Historical Association Research Library Collection, Courtesy Sarah Wilcox. Lawrenceburg Public Library Collection, courtesy Joyce Baer. Jeanne Ward Collection. Cambria County Library Collection, courtesy Esther Vorhauer.

The next day, August 22nd, the 551st PIB was able to move back onto Hill 78, and to seize the rest of Hill 105 against no resistance. The 551st was not to participate in any more major encounters over the next few days and did not suffer any more casualties. The German troops facing them had apparently pulled out, probably because of the American successes on Hill 105 and because the 509th PIB, in the meantime, had captured Hill 131 and the village of la Napoule. These advances placed the Germans in the le Tremblant area at risk

The body of a killed German soldier lies on the ground along with abandoned German equipment in the vicinity of le Tremblant. Joe Cicchinelli Collection, courtesy Pascal Hainaut.

A farmhouse next to the RN7 highway at le Tremblant. The walls still bear witness to the artillery fire of August 1944. Author's Collection.

of being surrounded. The paratroopers advanced into new positions along the RN7 and observed the aftermath of the fighting, as **Lt Dick Durkee**, of A Company of the 551st, remembered:

> As we went down through the valley, there were bodies lying all over the area; people with their foot blown off or their head blown off or whatever, so evidently the shelling had been effective.[45]

Joe Chiccinelli of B Company has a similar memory of Hill 105: "There were dead Germans all around. Me and another guy tried to dig a foxhole deeper, and there was a dead German right under us." A small creek, the Riou de l'Argentière, flowed just in front of the newly-won positions, and the men were able to bathe and wash in it, though **Sgt Don Garrigues** made an unpleasant discovery in the process:

> That evening, we established new positions on a rocky ridge overlooking a valley which had a small creek running through it. The prospects of a swim and a chance to wash off some of the war's dirt and grime appealed to several of us and we took off down the hillside, across the little valley to the creek and jumped in. It was stagnant and that didn't bother us, but after we got out I saw the bloated corpse of a dead German floating nearby.[46]

All these accounts show that the German soldiers of the 6th and 7th Companies of *Reserve Jäger Bataillon 28* had also suffered heavily during the advances of the 551st on August 21st and 22nd. Five *Jäger*s were buried in a mass grave on top of Hill 105:

Surname	Name	Rank	Age	Date of death	Unit
Olschenka	Erich	*Jäger*	17	21.8.1944	6./Res.Jäg. Btl.28
Schuster	Leopold	*Jäger*	20	21.8.1944	Res.Jäg. Btl.28
Strzoda	Herbert	*Jäger*	18	21.8.1944	Res.Jäg. Btl.28
Weimann	Paul	O Gefr	26	21.8.1944	6./Res.Jäg. Btl.28
Böhm	Gustav	*Jäger*	17	8.1944	Res.Jäg. Btl.28

Several other Germans had also been killed around le Tremblant and Hill 105, but an exact number cannot be established due to incomplete data regarding the bodies that were later recovered there. The 7th Company of *Reserve Jäger Bataillon 28*, which had been fighting in the la Napoule area since August 16th, was hit particularly hard. August 22nd, some of its soldiers who had been captured reported that they had suffered 70 percent losses, mostly due to the Allied artillery.[47] The company commander of the 7th Company, *Oberleutnant* Georg Seidel, had already been killed August 16th, and his replacement, 35-year-old *Oberleutnant* **Klaus Meyer-Detring**, was mortally wounded in the neck shortly after reaching the front to take his place on the 21st. Because of these two consecutive losses and the heavy casualties that had occurred, the 7th Company would be led by a simple NCO for the rest of the month of August.[48] *Oberleutnant* **Johann Bönsch**, the company commander of the 8th Company of *Bataillon 28*, wrote a letter to *Oberleutnant* Meyer-Detring's wife to announce his death. The letter also gives some insight into the fighting in the Hill 105 and le Tremblant area as seen from the German side:

> September 17, 1944
> Dear Ms Meyer-Detring!
>
> As one of the few remaining comrades, I have the difficult duty of informing you that your husband, *Oblt* Meyer-Detring, was severely wounded August 22nd 1944 near le Tremblant, northwest of Cannes, and that he died of his wounds the same day at 21:00 in the *Hauptverbandplatz* [main dressing station] in Nice. His hero's grave is located in the Nice-Caucade soldier's cemetery.
>
> I had worked with Meyer-Detring since Metz, in 1942. At first we were in the same company, but when I returned from Stalingrad he was in the 5th Company of *Reserve Jäger Bataillon 28* under *Hptm.* Müller. Later, when the 7th Company was created, he took command of it until shortly before the invasion, when he became a staff officer in our division. However, his replacement, *Oblt* Seidel, was killed in the first battles near le Tremblant (…) and Meyer-Detring wanted to return to his old company. This wish was granted, and *Oblt* Meyer-Detring returned to his men August 21st. The men were all overjoyed. His company was positioned to my left, so I was in continuous contact. In the afternoon hours, the Americans broke through our positions after a violent artillery barrage. During the counterattack, your husband was severely wounded at the head of his company. (…)

The victims that we have had to give in this battle have made us harder. Our belief and our belief in the final victory has grown stronger. We want to fight in order to fulfill the legacy of the fallen.

In thankful reverence and with deepest sympathies, I greet you with

Heil Hitler!

Dr Bönsch"[49]

Often there are discrepancies in the exact dates, and the official telegram that Meyer-Detring's wife received noted August 21st, not the 22nd, as the date of his wounding. August 21st indeed seems more probable, based on the previously-mentioned American sources, and it is therefore likely that *Olt* Bönsch was mistaken when he wrote August 22nd as the date of wounding in his letter.

Another soldier who was killed in the area was *Uffz* **Gerhard Schiffhorst**, of 5th Company of *Bataillon 28*. He is officially listed as missing in action since August 21, 1944, in the la Napoule area, so his exact location of death is not known. However, he died somewhere in the zone of action of the 551st or 509th PIBs. In 1962, upon realizing that Schiffhorst was still listed as missing in action, his platoon leader, **Josef Bartsch**, sent a letter to Schifforst's wife, explaining the circumstances of his death. Accounts from the German side are so difficult to find that even such brief letters are precious and help us understand how tough the situation was for the German soldiers:

> Dear Ms Schiffhorst, I used to be your husband's platoon leader.
>
> Now I will explain to you how everything happened. As of August 20th, we were operating in the St Raphaël-Cannes area. We had occupied a hill. On August 22nd, the *Amis* [Americans] were pushing forward on our right and left, forcing us to pull back. We reached a bunker in which we felt that we were temporarily safe. After a short period of time, we saw that the *Amis* were closing in on the bunker and we decided to retreat even further. Your husband stayed behind in this bunker with four or five other men. Unfortunately, our escape did not work out and we were captured shortly afterwards. About one hour later, the soldiers who had stayed with your husband arrived and they told us that your husband had been killed by a hand grenade.
>
> I myself did not see his body. That is all I can tell you about the whereabouts of your husband.[50]

There are bunkers on the eastern slopes of both Hill 105 and Hill 131, making it difficult to know which hill the action described

35-year-old Oberleutnant Klaus Meyer-Detring was put in command of the 7th Company of Reserve Jäger Bataillon 28 after the death of its original commander, Oberleutnant Georg Seidel, August 16th. Meyer-Detring was mortally wounded in the neck shortly after reaching the front at le Tremblant August 21st. Meyer-Detring Family Collection.

30-year-old Unteroffizier Gerhard Schiffhorst, of the 5th Company of Bataillon 28, was killed in the la Napoule area August 21 or 22, 1944. He has been listed as missing in action ever since, most likely because his body was not identified when it was discovered. Schiffhorst Family Collection.

by *Uffz* Bartsch may have occurred on. However, the following note in the 551st PIB's unit history about Hill 105 on August 22nd can serve as a hint: "Company A sent out a patrol, captured pillbox and took 16 prisoners."[51] Marius Pasero, who lived right at the foot of Hill 105, had hidden in a cave with his family when fighting erupted, and was then evacuated to Fréjus, presumably by troops of the 141st IR. When **Marius Pasero** returned to his home after the battle, he found his house looted and discovered the body of a killed German, who may well have been Gerhard Schiffhorst, near the bunker below Hill 105:

> We didn't stay in Fréjus long; our area was liberated so then we came back home. But there was nothing left, everything had been looted; some people had come into our house. My mother had left in a rush and left money on the staircase; of course it had disappeared. People had taken clothes. I recognized my cap, a brand new cap that I had bought, on a guy's head at la Napoule. I never said anything to him, but I knew the guy. He was wearing my cap. We had chickens, and the Americans had eaten all of them, only the feathers were left.
>
> In the field in front of the bunker, a German soldier had been killed; well, in fact he had most likely been wounded, because he was lying on the ground with a blanket under his head. It was probably his friends who had put a blanket under his head and then left him there because they couldn't do anything, so he died. He stayed there for eight or ten days, and you can imagine he became all swollen. Afterwards, a team from the town hall came, dug a hole, turned him over into it and buried him there. [This soldier was not identified when he was later exhumed, and considering the description, it may have been the body of Gerhard Schiffhorst.]
>
> The Americans had dug holes on the crest. They had left everything behind: food, telephones, everything. There were unopened tin cans, boxes of cigarettes, boxes of corned beef, beans, stuff like that.
>
> One night, maybe two days after we came back, a German must have heard us speaking and he must have been hiding somewhere, so he came out to see us. We asked him where he was coming from. My cousin could speak German, and he explained that the German had been hiding for two or three days and eating out of tin cans that he found. So we told him: "Well, we will bring you to the Americans." But he didn't want to, he preferred to be killed then to go to the Americans. But we brought him up to the road and a jeep just happened to drive by. The Americans gave him a cigarette and brought him to St Raphaël. I suspect that the German must have been happy afterwards.

One of the other locals who returned after the fighting and observed the mayhem around le Tremblant was **Pierre Carle**:

> The night of August 14th, we took refuge in a small valley in the mountains because they were shelling all over the place before the landing. So we all went up there. My father had prepared everything, and we had a little tent to be protected. All the inhabitants of the district were living in that valley, and luckily, there was little bit of water flowing in it. From time to time we went back down because we needed to get something in our homes. We would see the Germans in trenches who were waiting for the Americans

and they would let us go by. By the way, some people didn't waste their time and they looted the empty villas; and it wasn't the Germans who did it, it was locals.
>
> August 23rd, the Americans reached la Napoule, and on the 24th, they were in Mandelieu. But on the morning of the 24th, they were not in Mandelieu yet, so I went down to see what was happening. There were no more Germans or anything, and at the gas station at the entrance of Mandelieu there were about 50 bicycles on the ground. Everybody was taking bicycles; some of them still even had weapons on them. There was something remarkable in front of the gas station that I regretted not taking. On the sidewalk there was a little remote controlled tank [this was a remote controlled Goliath tank, packed with explosives]. It is the only one I ever saw, and I don't know who took it. It was a very rare item. There was a bunker on the side of the road, and the remote controlled tank had been taken out of the bunker. Maybe they tried to use it, I don't know. No American cars or tanks had arrived there, so they must have become despaired and sabotaged it, I think. It was an item to be kept.
>
> When I found the bikes, I took one. The Americans were not in Mandelieu yet, they were still at the foot of the Estérel, so I took my bike and went to see the American lines. From the gas station, all the way to the foot of the Estérel, the road was covered with bodies, bikes, rifles, and all sorts of things. There were tunics, and some of them had thrown away their helmets. But what disturbed me the most was at the curve in the road before reaching the Estérel: there was a little Peugeot with impacts in the windshield and four dead Germans officers collapsed inside it. They must have driven around the curve and been killed through the windshield. They were black from sitting in the sun for several days. It disturbed me to see four Germans in the car, blackened, still sitting down, each shot through the head. It was frightening to see.
>
> The Americans were on the other side, at the houses of le Tremblant. They were not advancing, even though we were telling them: "You know, there are no Germans left." They were waiting for their orders, and rightly so.

The Advance to Cannes

We now return to the activities of the 509th PIB. The 509th had already captured Castle Hill on the 21st and Hill 131 and la Napoule on the 22nd. The last remaining natural defensive position before Cannes was now the Siagne River, on the western bank of which the paratroopers took up position on the 23rd. Elements of A Company were sent across the river to establish a new defense line along the RN7 highway in an area called St Cassien, just north of the Cannes airstrip, on the outskirts of la Bocca. **Lt John Frazier**, one of those sent across the Siagne, wrote:

> The morning of the 23rd, we were ordered to move forward to establish a line on river east of San Peyre [Hill 131]. Moved out in order. Took up positions, with my 2nd Platoon to coordinate fire with the other two platoons. Orders came down for my 2nd Platoon and 3rd Platoon to attack St Cassien to secure a hill for an outpost of one squad from C Company. We were supposed to have a heavy shelling from the Navy on St Cassien; it never came.[52]

Some of the A Company men who crossed the Siagne River and patrolled the far side of it met up with French resistance brothers Francis and Fernand Tonner. Fernand Tonner's future wife, **Amable Tonner**, was present that day and remembers witnessing the arrival of these first Americans:

It was August 23ʳᵈ, it must have been four in the afternoon and it was very hot. There were large umbrella pines and we were in the shade. My mother must have been sewing, and I was doing some embroidery to spend the time. Suddenly we heard some noise. We turned around and saw Francis coming, along with a submachine gun. I was surprised, and at first thought he had been arrested by the Germans; I didn't realize they were Americans. Seeing our fear, Francis said: "Don't be afraid, these are the first Americans who have just arrived, we connected up with them." The Americans sat down near us in the shade to relax and Francis sat down beside us and said: "Dont worry, it's the Liberation, it will be over soon." They must have stayed half an hour; then an order suddenly came to pull back, so they left. My husband Fernand looked at his brother and said: "I am coming with you." But Francis replied: "No, dad is alone on the farm, go back and help him, then we will see." That is how Francis saved his brother's life.

Francis left with the Americans and then we didn't see anything else. But as of 8 o'clock in the evening, we heard very intense artillery fire that lasted for at least an hour. Some people said the Americans had been spotted because they had patrolled around the district with their helmets and everything. The Germans had surely seen them with binoculars.

The advance on the eastern bank of the Siagne River unexpectedly turned into a violent engagement when the Germans counterattacked and pushed the paratroopers back in the area north of the Cannes airstrip, where the RN7 crosses over the Béal (a creek flowing rougly parallel to the Siagne). Lt Harry Lieber, of the HQ Company of the 509ᵗʰ, was responsible for a .50 caliber machine gun platoon, to which several men and machine guns of the 463ʳᵈ PFAB were temporarily attached at the time. **Lt Harry Lieber** and his men were present when the German attack took place:

This was the 23ʳᵈ, when Jack Darden moved across the bridge. Down the road, the Germans opened up with antitank guns and small arms fire. I followed Darden across the bridge with my platoon. The Germans started a counterattack down the road, forcing Darden to halt. He was hit twice but hung in there, directing his men.

Fearing a flank attack, and to get good enfilade fire on the German columns, I left Sgt Chuck Holmes with part of the platoon and two 50s on the right side of the road and took Corporal Cook's squad of 30s and two 50s to the left side. When I got the guns set up, we opened fire on the Germans attacking down the road. We were able to break up that sortie. Unfortunately, the German artillery spotter was able to pick up our muzzle blasts and started registering in. I was with a .50 caliber crew right on the roadside and we received a direct hit. Most of the gun crew and a medic [probably **Lee Polson** or **Clarence Bergeman**] were killed. I was hit bad and yelled over to Chuck Holmes to send over a medic fast. I received no answer from him, which riled me, but I later learned that he had also been hit hard. That was Chuck's fourth or fifth time being wounded in action.

21-year-old PFC Clarence Bergeman, a medic in the 509ᵗʰ, was killed by a shell fragment wound to the forehead August 23ʳᵈ. John Stoer Collection.

Three of the paratroopers of A Company of the 509ᵗʰ PIB who were among the 10 American soldiers killed in the vicinity of Béal Bridge, outside Cannes, August 23ʳᵈ: 28-year-old Sgt Stanley Beatham, Jr (left), 23-year-old Pvt Donald F. Griffin (upper right), and 20-year-old Pvt James E. White (lower right). Lincoln Historical Society Collection, courtesy Jeanette King and Bob Richford. Rhinelander District Library Collection, courtesy Ed Hughes. White Family Collection.

By that time Lieutenant Darden's platoon had pulled back to the river and Corporal Cook's squad had pulled in from the left flank, and together they swam the wounded across. The bridge was denied us by antitank gun and small arms fire. I was put under the bridge for protection while the rest were being evacuated. The ambulance could not reach us because of the blown out bridges.

Out of the night came Henry Klisiewicz, the machine gun platoon medic. He had been busy tying up and evacuating the wounded on Chuck's side. He finished tying me up, then carried me piggy back to the aid station, which was a long ways back. On the way we met Chuck Holmes, whose arm was in a sling, but he had stayed to get the platoon in defensive position before going to the aid station.[53]

Orthelle Cherry, a medic detached to A Company, later sent a letter to the sister of his buddy, William Rogge, describing how Rogge had been killed in the encounter:

Dear Mrs Schwebke

This is not the first time I've received letters like yours, and I wish I could write saying different that what I have to. Yes, Bill, your brother, was killed August 23, 1944, in a small French town a few miles before we got to Cannes. I was with him, so I know just what happened, and therefore I will tell you everything. (...)

We went on an attack of some strong points August 23, and while we were getting ready Bill said to me: "Stick close, because I think I'll be needing you before the day's over." Of course, all the guys kid me like that because they like the feeling of a "Doc" alongside them. Well, first Bill was hit in his left arm by small arms fire, but it wasn't bad, and he didn't go back to the rear like he should have.

I fixed his arm, and that's when he left his mortar and started using his rifle. We came to an open space of 30 or 40 yards that was covered by a Jerry antitank gun. There were already two dead soldiers laying in the open space and when we started across, the gun opened up again. Bill had only a few feet to go and he would have been safe in the ditch, but they got him and he didn't have a chance to live. He never knew what hit him.

Let me tell you this – your brother, Bill, died a real soldier. I hope I never have to part ways over here, but if I do, I hope it's the same way. (...) Two hours after they finished our attack, I went back and saw them carry Bill away. I didn't want to look but I couldn't help it. He looked just like he was sleeping after a tired day's work.[54]

Several of the men previously mentioned in Lt Lieber's account were awarded Silver Stars for their actions in the battle at St Cassien and at the RN7 bridge over the Siagne, the citations of which provide more details about what occurred. Company A's **Lt Kenneth Shaker**'s citation read:

For gallantry in action near San Cassine, France, on 21 August 1944. [Note the mistake in the spelling of St Cassien,

21-year-old PFC William A. Rogge, who was first shot through the arm and then killed by shrapnel fragments during the fighting outside Cannes. This photograph shows the typical camouflaged helmets and uniforms that paratroopers of the 509th wore in Italy. Also note he is wearing a pistol, two grenades, and a trench knife. William Rogge originally had two brothers and two sisters, but both brothers had already died of appendicitis and pneumonia at the time of Rogge's death at Cannes. Gloria Klinner Collection.

as well as yet another mistake in the date, which was actually August 23rd.] Lieutenant Shaker, under intense mortar and small arms fire and direct fire from two antitank guns, assembled survivors of a platoon dispersed by fierce enemy fire. With this small group he formed a defense around a former enemy strong point and held off an attacking force of over fifty men in a five-hour battle. Through the action, First Lieutenant Shaker repeatedly exposed himself to full view of the enemy in order to go to each position, encouraging his men and helping the wounded.[55]

Company A's **Lt Jack Darden** and Medic **Henry Klisiewicz**, who were mentioned by Lt Lieber, were also both awarded Silver Stars:

On 23 August, a platoon commanded by Lieutenant Dardevn, while holding a bridgehead, was subjected to heavy artillery fire, causing many casualties among his platoon. Lieutenant Darden, although wounded, refused to be evacuated and remained to direct the removal of the wounded to a place of safety and to regroup the remaining members of his platoon and personally direct the repulsing of an enemy attack.

The infantry platoon to which Private First Class Klisiewicz was attached as a medical aid man had been subjected to heavy artillery and machine gun fire and was forced to withdraw. The only route of withdrawal was along a road under direct enemy observation and fire. Private First Class Klisiewicz, knowing that the enemy could overrun the position at any time, volunteered to remain with the wounded. Although constantly exposed to enemy fire, Private First Class Klisiewicz moved from one wounded soldier to another, administering first aid, and successfully evacuated four of his comrades along the heavily-shelled road to a place of comparative safety. Again exposing himself to enemy fire, he moved far in advance of his own troops and located an officer who was seriously wounded [Probably Lt Lieber]. As the wounded officer was unable to walk, Private First Class Klisiewicz, after administering first aid, placed the wounded officer on his back and carried him a distance of over four hundred yards along the shell-beaten road to a point where other aid men completed the evacuation.[56]

The evacuation of the wounded across the Siagne was made in particularly difficult conditions. **PFC Hyman Perlo** (who later became known for his role with the Washington Bullets basketball team), **Cpl Russel Cook**, and **PFC George Bell**, of HQ and A Companies, were also all awarded the Silver Star. Below is a quote from Hyman Perlo's citation, though Russel Cook and George Bell were given identical ones:

A machine gun platoon of his battalion was subjected to an intense enemy barrage of heavy artillery and mortar fire, causing many casualties within the platoon. The problem of evacuating the wounded was difficult, as the only route to the rear was across a river ten feet in depth, and the only bridge in the area had been destroyed by the enemy. Realizing the necessity of getting the wounded to an aid station with the least possible delay, Private First Class Perlo and three of his comrades volunteered to attempt crossing the river with the wounded soldiers. By alternately swimming and carrying their wounded comrades, they successfully evacuated five seriously wounded soldiers. The work of evacuating these wounded covered a period of one and one half hours, during which time they were under direct enemy observation and were subjected to intense enemy heavy artillery fire. The courageous and voluntary actions on the part of Private First Class Perlo greatly assisted in saving the lives of his wounded comrades.[57]

One of the 509th PIB's surgeons, **Captain Roy Baze,** also came to the bridge over the Béal to help evacuate the wounded, earning him the Distinguished Service Cross, the second highest gallantry award existing for American soldiers:

> August 23, 1944, the enemy counter attacked the heights in the vicinity of *** [sic], taken that day by Company "C" of the battalion. The assault, supported by self-propelled artillery, was of the greatest intensity near a creek and bridge in this area, and casualties were occurring rapidly. On his way to render urgently needed medical aid to this sector, Captain Baze was halted at a demolished bridge half a mile below the area under assault and warned not to proceed any further, as the enemy

Pvt John J. Hay, aged 30, of D Battery of the 463rd PFAB, and his colleague George Ruell were temporarily attached to A Company of the 509th as machine gunners and were both killed during the attack outside Cannes. Katherine Frattarola Collection.

UST 26, 1945.   THE DAILY

Beyond *the* Call *of* Duty—

An artist's representation of Capt Roy Baze's actions at the Siagne Bridge that earned him a Distinguished Service Cross. Ellen O'Hara Collection.

was on the road leading to that area and subjecting it to heavy artillery fire. Determined to aid the wounded men, Captain Baze placed a litter on his shoulder and, taking the Red Cross flag from his jeep, crossed the river below the demolished bridge and proceeded the half mile to his objective, despite intermittent artillery and intense mortar and small arms fire. Reaching the bridge on the far bank, he swam the deep creek to the other side, took command of the situation, treated the wounded, restored morale and order, and directed and assisted in the evacuation. Not until five hours later – after another hazardous trip down the road and repeated crossings of the creek to assure the safe evacuation of all wounded – did Captain Baze leave the sector under assault.[58]

Approximately eight paratroopers of the 509th PIB and two of the 463rd PFAB (Once again, there are some inconsistencies in the exact dates of death, with several men being officially listed as killed in action on the 24th.) had been killed or mortally wounded in the engagement at the RN7 bridge over the Béal; they were:

Surname	Name	Rank	Unit	Age	Date of death
Bergeman	Clarence	PFC Med	HQ Co 509 PIB	21	23.8.1944
Cooper	William C.	Cpl	HQ Co 509 PIB	26	23.8.1944
Crosby	James H.	Pvt	HQ Co 509 PIB	24	23.8.1944
Polson	Lee W.	T5 Med	HQ Co 509 PIB	23	23.8.1944
Beatham	Stanley Jr.	Sgt	A Co 509 PIB	25	23.8.1944
Griffin	Donald F.	Pvt	A Co 509 PIB	23	23.8.1944
Rogge	William A.	PFC	A Co 509 PIB	21	23.8.1944
White	James E.	Pvt	A Co 509 PIB	20	23.8.1944
Hay	John J.	Pvt	D Bat 463 PFAB	30	23.8.1944
Ruell	George P.	PFC	D Bat 463 PFAB	20	23.8.1944

Three local French resistance men who had come to guide the Americans or provide them with intelligence were also killed by the German artillery fire. One of them was **Francis Tonner**, mentioned previously, who was killed along with his friend, **Henri Bergia**. **Janvier Passero** (nicknamed Kiké), from la Napoule, had also come to offer help and was killed. **Paulette Mollo**, a neighbor of Janvier Passero, went searching for him when she found out that he had gone into the battle zone and had still not returned several hours later:

I took my bike, and when I reached the airstrip, I started seeing bodies on *Route Nationale 7*. I got off the bike. The road was all smashed, with lots of holes and stones. There had been hard fighting. Big Dodge trucks were driving very slowly behind me. I overtook them, and on either side of the road, and even in the middle of the road, I saw dead people: men, soldiers. There were Frenchmen, as well as Germans and Americans. Some bodies were torn to shreds, others were missing an arm or a leg. I even saw a boot with a foot inside it; that shook me up a bit. And other bodies were intact. I didn't look at everything because it was atrocious. I remember it very well, I think it will stay in my head forever. At least ten Americans must have died there. American soldiers were there with bags with zippers, and they were putting the dead soldiers in the bags and writing their names on them.

I was still looking for Janvier Passero, and I looked and looked. Suddenly I recognized his jacket and his foot. He was lying on his back, I can still see it today. I said: "My God! Kiké!" I lifted his jacket and saw that he had been wounded all over his left side by fragments. He must have died immediately. I searched for his papers and things and a French policeman said: "*Mademoiselle*, do you know him?" I replied: "Yes, I know him, but I am looking for his papers." He said: "We have taken them already. We are bringing the bodies to Draguignan." "And why is that" "That is the way it is" I didn't try to understand; when

he said that I stopped looking and I told him: "He is my neighbor. We were waiting for him because he had been gone for at least two hours." The policeman said: "Oh, there was a skirmish."

Although Janvier Passero and Henri Bergia's bodies were found immediately, there seemed to be no trace of Francis Tonner. All his family knew was that he had last been seen near the bridge with the American soldiers and the other resistance men, including Marius Mascarello. Several weeks passed before the details of Francis Tonner's tragic death became known, as his sister-in-law **Amable Tonner** explains:

The next morning, we started coming out and looking around. There was no more noise, and Fernand came and said: "We haven't heard anything from my brother." All Marius Mascarello ever said was that he had been wounded by the first shell and had called out: "Francis, Francis," because he was hiding in a tree trunk just beside him and Francis didn't answer. Many Americans had been killed, but the Americans didn't say anything, they just came the next morning and picked everything up and erased everything. There were bits of torn flesh, of human debris.

The Tonners were sure that Francis had been wounded, because they searched for him in all the hospitals for at least three or four weeks. There were field hospitals, and it was said that they sometimes evacuated people very far away from the front. So for a long time we wondered if he was in some hospital. Since we knew the family, every day we came to visit his poor mother, who was crying. One afternoon, we were there with several other people, trying to comfort her. She was prostrate on a chair because her son meant everything to her; it was really, really hard. Suddenly we heard a cry, a terrible cry of sorrow. We turned around and saw a man speaking to Fernand, and Fernand had collapsed, holding something in his hands. We didn't dare move or do anything. Finally, someone went nearer. That man had gone to the area of the bridge and had found the back pocket of Francis' pants hanging in a tree. The back pocket was cut out and still buttoned shut with his wallet in it.

As of that day there was no more doubt, we thought: "He has been blown to pieces." Then it was made official by the town hall, and so there was a funeral one month later. On the day of the funeral a peasant said that he had

French resistance fighter Francis Tonner was one of three Frenchmen to be killed alongside the American paratroopers in the Siagne River encounter. Tonner Family Collection.

Marius Mascarello, still recovering from wounds received August 23rd at the sides of Francis Tonner and Henri Bergia, inaugurates a monument to his fallen comrades. Tonner Family Collection.

found a leg with Francis' shoe on it and that he had buried it. Maybe he thought he was doing the right thing. So they went and dug up the leg and put it in the coffin.

At least nine German soldiers were also killed in the Cannes area on the 23rd, probably by Allied artillery in most cases. One of these soldiers who died was 36-year-old *Unteroffizier* **Franz Knirsch**, of *Reserve Grenadier Bataillon 444*. When his wife asked for details about his death, **Walter Lindenthal**, one of Knirsch's comrades, wrote her a letter that gives a glimpse of the fighting as seen by the Germans:

> December 17, 1944
> Dear Ms Knirsch !
>
> (…) On the day when your beloved husband was wounded, the battle was occurring in the afternoon, and I was in the same area, but not in his immediate vicinity, because each one of us had his own mission. When I found out that my friend had been wounded by shell fragments, I immediately inquired as to his location and condition. A comrade from his group who is still assigned to me was near him when he was wounded, and a friend of Franz's and mine, namely *Uffz* Arndt, who has been severely wounded recently and is in the hospital, gave first aid to your beloved husband.
>
> Your beloved husband was in a foxhole with another man from his group when the shell landed. His comrade was mortally hit and your husband was wounded by a fragment in the thigh. Comrades from his group were aware of what happened right away and called *Uffz* Arndt, who was nearby. After applying a field dressing, he immediately carried him back on a makeshift stretcher. As comrade Arndt told me himself, your husband was fully conscious and was in almost no pain after the dressing had been applied. He greeted me and told me that he would write me as soon as things would get better.
>
> Dear Ms Knirsch, you can see by his own words that your dear husband was feeling strong and did not

himself believe that his end had come. He was loaded into the ambulance and brought from Cannes to Nice, where he died in transport during the night. He wanted to inform his beloved family himself from the hospital, but unfortunately, fate decided otherwise and did not give him the time to do so. (…)[59]

Franz Knirsch was buried in the Caucade cemetery in Nice. Further north, in Mougins, on the hills overlooking the Cannes airstrip and the Siagne valley, three soldiers of the 6th Company of *Bataillon 28* (the men who had previously defended Hill 105) were also killed by an Allied shell. The victims were **Stefan Woznicka**, **Lothar Siegert**, and **Josef Krautschneider**, all aged 17 or 18. A local French girl, **Denise Manaira**, was nearby when they died and explains:

> We were living across from the Pibonson estate. There was a little airplane flying above us all the time, and we would say: "The little plane is there again." It would spot was supposed to be spotted, and then the navy would fire. There was shelling occurring all over the place, so we didn't go out much. The Germans came to occupy the Pibonson estate August 17th or 18th. In those days, the estate had a big swimming pool that had been built long ago and they occupied the place. It must have been mostly officers who were there, because they were installed on the patio around the pool and were sunbathing. Late one morning the little plane must have spotted them; a boat fired, and three soldiers were caught in the explosion and blown to pieces. Apparently, it wasn't a pretty sight in the villa. At least one of them was killed in the house, because from what people observed later on, there was still flesh hanging from the chandeliers, with maggots falling down.
>
> We had one hour of freedom per day, and were outside the house taking some fresh air when we saw soldiers walk by carrying sheets. They had put the bodies in the sheets and somebody, maybe my grandfather, had watched them and saw them digging holes. My grandfather said: "This time there has been some damage!" and we saw the other soldiers carrying the sheets down and they buried them at the foot of the olive trees right in the angle of the roads. I think it was one of their principles to always bury people at the angle of two roads. They set up wooden crosses with names. People said that according to the names, it was young Polish guys, about 18 years old. They took the bodies away several years later.

Another local youth, **Laurent Brignone,** was present when the three bodies were exhumed in 1952:

36-year-old Unteroffizier Franz Knirsch, of Bataillon 444, was wounded by Allied artillery in Cannes August 23, 1944, and died during his evacuation to Nice, where he was buried in Caucade Cemetery. This photo of him was taken at the shooting stand in Cannes during the Occupation. Knirsch Family Collection.

18-year-old Jäger Josef Krautschneider, of the 6th Company of Reserve Jäger Bataillon 28, was one of the three soldiers to be killed by Allied naval gunfire in the Pibonson estate, in Mougins, on August 23, 1944. Rosina Krieg Collection.

I was about nine years old when they came to dig up those dead. They weren't buried very deep, and I think they were buried one beside the other, and not all on top of one another They put all the bones in packages and there were three packages, since there were three bodies. Then those people started cleaning the bones because there was a water tank nearby, and I went and helped them to clean a skull. You can imagine what happened when my mother saw me doing that. She yelled at me; she was very Catholic that had shocked her.

Mougins Battlefield Investigation

The bodies of the three soldiers were exhumed by French workers in 1952 and reburied temporarily in the village cemetery of Mougins. However, the workers left many small artifacts behind at the exhumation site, thus enabling us to compare the witness account of Denise Manaira with actual physical evidence. According to *Mme* Manaira, three 18-year-old Polish soldiers were killed and severely maimed by a shell, and were then buried under an olive tree at a crossroads.

Three bodies were indeed recovered under an olive tree at the nearby crossroad. The grave measured roughly two meters by two meters for a depth of about 60 centimeters. The bodies were identified as being 17-year-old Stefan Woznicka from Silesia, 18-year-old Lothar Siegert from Dresden, and 18-year-old Josef Krautschneider from Bohemia. Their bones presented multiple fractures consistent with multiple shrapnel wounds. The most noteworthy artifacts discovered at the site were:

- Two bent fragments of an aluminum German identification tag. Both fragments seemed to originate from a single half of one single ID tag that had been cut in half by a shell fragment. The following inscriptions were visible on the tag: "1???? B 1./ Gre??????461."

Lothar Siegert's ID tag inscriptions are listed in his military file as being 12289 1./Gren.Ers.Btl.461. The other two soldiers had tags with inscriptions that were incompatible with the recovered tag, indicating that the recovered tag must have belonged to Siegert. The type of damage to the ID tag fragments shows that Lothar Siegert was killed by shrapnel. If an item as small as an ID tag was hit by a fragment, it is likely that Siegert was also hit by a large number of other shell fragments elsewhere on his body.

- One leather wallet decorated with German wartime insignia, including the cockades and oak leaves from a German army visor cap, as well as two aluminum rank pips. X-rays of this wallet showed that it contained several coins. The wallet was hit by one projectile that travelled through the front portion of the wallet, from top to

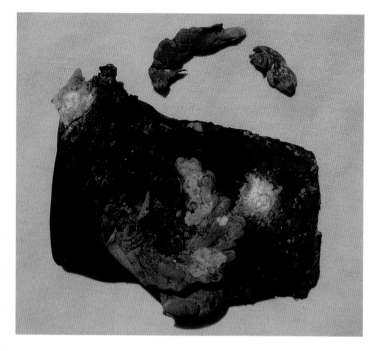

This wallet, which has been decorated with German wartime military badges, was pierced by a piece of shrapnel from the shell that killed the soldier. The drawing shows what the wallet would have looked like at the time, before being damaged. Private Collection.

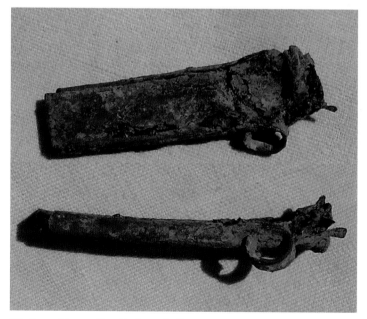

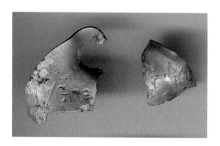

Remains of the shredded identification tag of 18-year-old Jäger Lothar Siegert, demonstrating the violence of the event in which he was killed. Private Collection.

Clip from a Mauser rifle with shrapnel still embedded in one end. Private Collection.

bottom, damaging the oak leaves decoration, as well as the wallet's metallic opening catch. The projectile cut the oak leaves into three fragments, all of which were recovered. On the X-ray of the wallet, it can be seen that some of the coins in the wallet were bent by the projectile. The irregular look of the damage to the leather and oak leaf decoration gives the impression that the damage was caused by a shrapnel fragment.

- One Mauser rifle clip for five cartridges. The clip was hit at one extremity by a shrapnel fragment that bent the clip and stayed embedded in it.

- Four iron fragments that appeared to be shrapnel from a large caliber shell, though they could have another origin, their poor condition rendering identification difficult. Two copper fragments that fit together also seem to be pieces of a shell fuze, but have not been identified with certainty.

- Four French wartime coins, ten German tunic buttons, 22 varied buttons of German origin (including one button that seems to have been damaged by shrapnel), and various metallic buckles from German equipment.

We can conclude by noting that a significant proportion of small-sized artifacts found at the former grave site bear traces of shrapnel damage, seeming to indicate that the soldiers themselves were also hit by a large number of fragments. For this to occur, the soldiers would have had to be near the seat of the explosion, making it likely that some of them would have been severely maimed. The story told by period witness Denise Manaira and the conclusions drawn from the analysis of the recovered artifacts are therefore compatible and similar.

Paratroopers from C Company; 509th PIB, joyfully pose for the camera as they approach Cannes. Justin McCarthey Collection.

Company B troopers PFC William J. Kambrick, Pvt Walter Nizinski, and Pvt Albert Paperella relax on a bench on the outskirts of Cannes. Mike Reuter Collection.

Entry into Cannes

The battle at St Cassien on the 23rd was to be the last resistance the Germans would offer in the la Napoule-Cannes area. During the night of August 23rd to 24th, the Germans pulled out of Cannes, retreating all the way to their next planned defensive line at the Loup River, roughly 15 kilometers further northeast. The unit history of the 509th PIB notes:

We were now in a position to advance on Cannes itself. Throughout the night of 23 August, our engineers and demolitions platoon worked on a ford over the Siagne, the bridge having been blown up by the retreating Germans. During the morning of 24 August, A Company's patrols pushed on towards the outskirts of Cannes. They returned with the information that the enemy had withdrawn from the city. Our engineers were experiencing considerable difficulty with the crossing of the Siagne River due to the soft bottom and mines. Our entry into Cannes was thus delayed until 1700 24 August.[60]

Jean-Paul Carbonel was one of the many locals who wanted to warn the Americans that the Germans were gone and that Cannes was now free. He drove towards the Siagne on his motorcycle with another local:

The first Americans I saw were in the ditch in front of the airfield, on the left side of the RN7. There were three of them, and

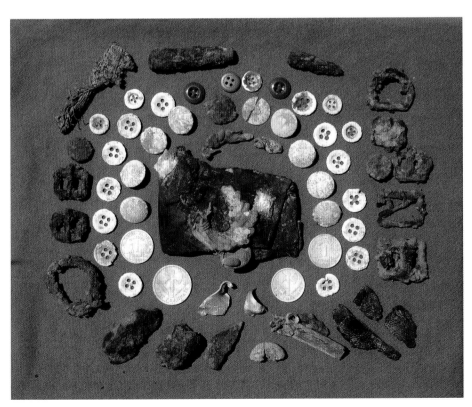

All the items found at the Mougins grave site. Private Collection.

when we arrived on the motorcycle we didn't see them at all; they were well camouflaged in the ditch and we just stumbled across them. If they had been Germans we would have been dead. They immediately asked us if we had German weapons.

The American paratroopers were known for their strong interest in souvenirs, particularly German pistols. **Jean-Paul Carbonel** then drove on to the Siagne River Bridge:

> We reached the bridge at the Siagne that had been blown at the same time as Mr Vahanian, who was the big resistance leader in Cannes, with his Fiat Balilla. The Americans were on the other side, and since there was less than 50 centimeters of water in the Siagne, an American tank [In fact, a tank-destroyer from B Company, 645th Tank Destroyer Battalion that had just been attached to the 509th.] crossed the river and wanted to climb up the other side. A man who must have been the owner of the field shouted to them that there were mines, but they refused to listen. The tank advanced, so we quickly moved back and a mine exploded and cut the treads on the front left hand side. Later, we found the pieces of an antitank plate mine [Tellermine] in the sand. The tank behind it sent out a cable and they pulled the tank out of the way. At that moment, some Americans came with metal detectors and they removed all the mines. Afterwards, the whole column crossed and climbed onto the RN7 and they followed us into la Bocca.

The Germans had heavily mined the area, as had already been proven on the 22nd, when Major Apperson and Lieutenants Fiander and Webb were killed in their jeep, and once again on the 23rd, when four men from the First Special Service Force were killed in Tanneron. Unfortunately, **Captain Roy Baze**, the brave new surgeon of the 509th PIR who had thanked "the good Lord" for his luck in a letter home two days earlier, was killed somewhere outside Cannes on the 24th when his jeep, which was clearly marked as being a medical vehicle, rolled over yet another Tellermine. **Captain Jud Chalkley**, surgeon of the 551st PIB, happened to drive by the scene:

> Then we were going along the road to Cannes, and the Germans had mined all the roads. I had gone on ahead to scout out a place for the aid station and was trying to stay in the tracks of the preceding vehicles as carefully as possible. Behind me, driving another medical jeep, was a fine young surgeon who was with the 509th Battalion. He hit a land mine, and when I drove back the next day

there was the wreckage, and parts of his body hanging in a nearby tree. He was from Paul's Valley, Oklahoma, and but for the grace of God, it would have been me up there. I looked at his tire tracks and they had gone right where mine had, except for a slight deviation in the place where the mine was laid.[61]

Captain Baze's fellow doctor in the 509th, **Captain Alfred Kelly**, wrote a letter of condolence to Baze's wife and child, explaining how he had died and summarizing the previous days of action at St Tropez, Hill 84, and the Siagne River:

> Dear Mrs Baze:
>
> Your husband, Capt. Roy E. Baze, was killed almost instantly when a mine exploded under the jeep he was driving. The man with him in the jeep, the assistant driver, was badly shaken up, but escaped death almost miraculously. The Lord just saw fit to take the doc at this time. This occurred the morning after the doctor had performed a marvelous feat of bravery and courageous action in evacuation of wounded from this same area, which was on the outskirts of Cannes. Doc Baze, in his characteristically dauntless manner, had himself taken a litter on his shoulder and, with a red cross flag, walked up a road under artillery and small arms fire to reach some wounded men and get them evacuated. For this a citation has gone in for the Distinguished Service Cross. The day before he had just as fearlessly tramped over a wooded ridge, looking for wounded that might have been left behind. It so happened that the enemy had just pulled back, but this was not known at the time, and for all we knew, enemy snipers were still lurking throughout the hillside, as they had been for most of the day.
>
> There are other stories of Doc Baze, one of which I know. It was at St. Tropez, when he landed with a force of paratroops. The fight was thick, but that didn't daunt Capt. Baze. He helped get evacuation going, and when there were no facilities set up for taking care of the wounded,

American jeeps cross the Siagne River on a makeshift bridge in the days following the Liberation. Pierre Carle Collection.

34-year-old Capt Roy E. Baze, medical officer of the 509th PIB, who was killed by an antitank mine on the outskirts of Cannes August 24, 1944. Ellen O'Hara Collection.

A sad sight: the jeep of Dr. Roy Baze, clearly marked with Geneva crosses, has been blown apart by an antitank mine that seems to have detonated under the left rear wheel of the vehicle. The man riding with Dr. Baze miraculously survived the blast. Justin McCarthey Collection.

he himself located a French hospital and began operating on the wounded. I recall him telling me about it later, how he performed an abdominal operation and resected part of the intestines in one case. This is major surgery, and the doc was doing everything from getting the men off the battlefield to General Hospital surgery, a feat few doctors would tackle even if the opportunity or situation presented itself. But Doc Baze did. He never could do enough for the boys. A few days before his death, I saw him putting on plaster casts after doing excellent debridement on compound fractures and ragged wounds. This is difficult to do in a forward aid station, and to set up sterile technique is laborious. But he did it. He had worked in a station hospital before and knew that such good operative care, when done promptly after the casualty occurred, meant shorter convalescence and better chances for the men for complete recovery.

We all thought a lot of Doc Baze and miss him. He was a top-notch doctor and they don't come any better. (…) Let me know if I can be of any further help in any way. God bless you and yours, and do not lose Faith in His guidance.

Sincerely
Alfred J. Kelly, Capt.,M.C.[62]

It was a pity that such a talented surgeon and so many years of training and experience were eliminated in an instant by a faceless weapon such as a mine. The 509th would not suffer any more killed during the fighting along the coast over the next 10 days. However, they had paid a very dire price for the capture of la Napoule and Cannes, with at least 26 men killed or mortally wounded, including the battalion executive officer, one intelligence officer and one surgeon!

Mines are a particularly treacherous weapon that do not differentiate between friend and foe or military and civilian. This was tragically and ironically demonstrated on the 24th in Biot. On the same day Captain Baze was killed in his jeep near Cannes, two German soldiers retreating out of the village of Biot were killed by a mine laid by their own engineer troops earlier in the day. Local inhabitant **Raymond Ghera** was a witness to the accident south of Biot:

The Germans had started making holes in the asphalt early in the morning to lay mines. They were big antitank mines, and then they covered them up with gravel so you couldn't see them. Later on in the day, some other Germans started leaving from Biot, where they were quartered, and the ones who were coming down from Biot didn't know about the mines. They had requisitioned Mr Govi, the woodworker, and his truck. A first car drove by without touching the mines, then two minutes later Mr Govi's truck came with a sergeant in the passenger seat and two soldiers behind. On the way up the hill, the truck broke down right in the middle of the road. It was a coal-powered truck, and coal-powered vehicles don't work all the time, so the two soldiers got out in order to push it. Just then the truck moved back a bit and one wheel went over the mine. The mine exploded and the two soldiers who had gotten out of the truck were badly wounded. The explosion was very powerful; all the rendering on the nearby chapel wall fell off, and the wheels of the truck were blown into a field.

I heard the explosion, so I understood it was the mines and ran over. Everybody ran over and we saw that the mine had caught the guys in the stomach. There were intestines hanging in the trees, but the soldiers didn't die immediately. We carried them to a house and laid them down, and there they took out their papers and said: "We are Polish." Dr Carpentier arrived at that moment and gave them each an injection so that they wouldn't suffer. The sergeant who had been sitting in front was stunned. He had been wounded by a few small fragments, but it was superficial. He was frightened, he didn't move; we took his pistol and everything and he didn't say a thing, he let himself be captured. We handed him over to the Americans when they arrived. Mr Govi was lucky and was not wounded at all.

The two soldiers did not survive for long and were then buried in the local cemetery. They were:

Name	Surname	Rank	Age	Date of death	Location	Unit
Kirchner	Hermann	Kan	36	24.8.1944	Biot	Artillery
Laske	Robert	Stbs Gefr	30	24.8.1944	Biot	Res.Art. Abt.44

After the final difficulties due to the blown bridge on the Siagne River and the mines, men from A Company of the 509th finally and triumphantly rode into Cannes on tank destroyers of the 645th TDB at five in the afternoon, August 24th. The paratroopers were welcomed by a hysterical crowd of French civilians. The unit history noted:

To make the entry into the city as impressive as possible, considering our ragged condition and lack of transportation, we loaded as many paratroopers as we could onto the backs of the tank destroyers. (…) We passed along streets lined

With a momentary lull in the fighting, troopers of the 509th discover a taste for luxury as they reach Cannes. Mike Reuter Collection.

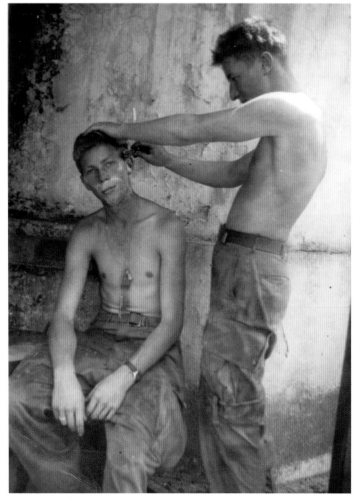

Before entering Cannes, Pvt Robert N. Powell gets a shave from Edward J. Lejkowski so as to appear tidy as they triumphantly enter the city. Mike Reuter Collection.

with wildly cheering people, some crying openly, some throwing flowers into our vehicles. It was a welcome such as we had never before received in our two years of fighting.[63]

Warren Boehmke, of A Company, recalled the entry into Cannes:

Normally, if you poked up your head or something, somebody, a sniper would be shooting at you, and that didn't happen that day. So we waited a couple hours and finally somebody decided to go over and find out, and there were no Germans there, they must have pulled out overnight. In fact, the people were coming down the road from Cannes and saying: "When are you going to come and liberate us?" But anyway, we started going towards Cannes and the tank that we were with broke down. So the Free French were coming down the road and saying: "When are you coming, when are you coming?" We said: "As soon as we get the tank running." Then we finally got it running, we got into town there, and boy, we had a hell of a greeting, with the people all standing there and cheering. It was very, very impressive.

The Free French were chasing the Germans, and we got there and the town was wide open. They were waiting for us to come in and re-liberate them; they had already done that. They had cleared off the town. I have to say, at that time the French were very heroic at what they were doing, and they were behind us 100 percent and they did all the right things.

Then we started going through the town, checking house to house to clear out any Germans around. I walked into one house – I think it was Ali Kahn's place, I am not real sure, but that's what I was told. So we got in there and then I walked into one of the rooms, opened the door, and there were two kids, Germans, about 12 or 14-years-old, sitting behind a machine gun aimed at me. They looked at me and they were scared to death, and they got up, held up their hands and surrendered. If they had opened that thing up there, they would have blown my brains out, but nothing happened and I took them back. That's who Hitler was recruiting at the end, there were a lot of kids.

Warren Boehmke is slightly exaggerating the young ages of the soldiers, who were in fact probably at least 17. However, some of them did look extremely young, as was noted by local woman **Paulette Mollo**:

The Americans arrived and there was a group of very young German soldiers. My mother had gone and asked them how old they were and told them: "I am a mother, a *Mutter*. The war is finished now and you will return to your mother, your *Mutter*, you will go and see her." And they asked them their ages. One was 15, another was going to turn 16! They were all 15 and 16. Those boys were crying because they couldn't take it any longer. They were as thin as nails. My father and some people had prepared some drinks for the Americans, but they let the Germans drink first! The Americans gave them a biscuit and a drink. They felt sorry for them and said: "They are kids."

After passing through Cannes, the 509th drove all the way to Antibes, where it arrived without incident late in the day, August 24th. All the Germans in the area had retreated, and the few remaining ones had been captured or killed by the French. In the meantime, the 551st advanced to Mougins, which had also been evacuated by the Germans.

While some Allied soldiers, such as Warren Boehmke, were very admiring of the Free French, others did not share these feelings. One such soldier was **Lt Dick Spencer**, of the 517th PIR.

August 24th, paratroopers of A Company of the 509th Parachute Infantry Battalion triumphantly ride into Cannes on the tank destroyers of the 645th Tank-Destroyer Battalion. Archives Municipales de Cannes.

Paratroopers of the 509th PIB enter Cannes to the cheers of the local population. Archives Municipales de Cannes.

Paratroopers and resistance fighters enter Cannes on a tank destroyer. Mike Reuter Collection.

Although he was not in Cannes, he expresses feelings about the Resistance that were shared by many Allied soldiers (and by many true resistance fighters) who liberated the French Riviera:

> They were a bit like our teenagers today. They were carried away by the excitement of the whole thing. Sure, a bunch would show up when we came to the edge of a town; they'd go through the town with us, getting garlands of flowers and kissing all the girls. But at the other edge of the town they'd turn around and go back in while we went on.[64]

There is a lot of truth in Dick Spencer's observation. As soon as the Allies approached a town, the number of local resistance members was suddenly be multiplied tenfold. As the Germans escaped in the face of the approaching Allies, the French would come out and shoot at or capture the last Germans, after which some would make grandiloquent claims about how the town had liberated itself on its own. The difficult fighting the Allies had put up with before reaching the town was ignored, as was the fighting that would occur beyond the town. Such claims that towns had liberated themselves without any help from the Allies are incorrect and unfounded. France was occupied for several years, and if any towns were able to suddenly "liberate themselves" in August 1944, it was only because the Allied landing had finally occurred. Of course, the average resistance fighter or French civilian understood that such claims were false or exaggerated, but some resistance men with an interest in a future local political career, or with an overdeveloped ego, manipulated events to fit their agenda.

Regardless of the exaggerated claims made by some, and of the sudden appearance of hundreds of new resistance men just as the German army was disappearing, there was a very real and active Resistance before and after the Allied landing that did take action against the Germans, and that provided the Allies with substantial help at a very dire price. These men encouraged Polish soldiers to surrender, crossed the lines to provide the Allies with intelligence, guided the Allies through unfamiliar terrain, sabotaged German installations, and attacked and killed isolated groups of Germans, to mention only a few of their activities. The image and reputation of this real Resistance was tarnished by the actions of various parasites and last-minute "*maquisards*," such as those Dick Spencer was referring to. In the next chapter, we will therefore describe some of what occurred in Cannes between the day of the landing and the arrival of the first American soldiers in order to better understand the magnitude of the sacrifices made by the local French Resistance and civilian population.

After driving through Cannes, the 509th PIB continued straight on to Antibes without meeting any German resistance. In Antibes, the paratroopers were once again cheered by the local population before taking up defensive positions east of the town. Ferdinand Moscone Collection.

The Casualties

Between August 15 and August 24, 1944, a total of at least 111 German soldiers were killed, mortally wounded, or reported missing and never heard of since in the areas of Agay, Anthéor, Théoule, les Adrets, la Napoule, Mandelieu, Cannes, le Cannet, Mougins, Pégomas, la Roquette sur Siagne, Valauris, Antibes, and Biot. Most of these casualties belonged to *Reserve Jäger Bataillon 28*, *Reserve Grenadier Bataillons 444* and *164* and to *Ost Bataillon 661*. In the same area, the Allied forces lost at least 77 men from the following units: the *Groupe Naval d'Assault de Corse*, 141st IR, 463rd PFAB, 509th PIB, 551st PIB, and the 2680th Military Intelligence Company. All the Allied casualties have been listed day by day previously in the chapter.

Following is the list of 111 German casualties of which a trace exists in the archives of the *Volksbund*. Day by day lists of casualties were not made in this chapter because too many men are unknown, or have unknown dates of death. Some of the dead were buried directly on the battlefield, while others were buried next to the hospitals in which they died in Nice, Cannes, le Cannet, and Valbonne. A few were even recovered by the American troops and buried in the Allied cemetery in Draguignan. Three men on this list are in fact missing in action in la Napoule and their bodies were never found. Their names have been inserted in place of three unknown bodies that were exhumed in la Napoule. Also included are the names of two sailors who were reported missing at sea August 21st.

Surname	Name	Rank	Age	Date of death	Killed or wounded in	Buried in	Unit
Unknown				8.1944		Agay	
Reiniger	Heinz	Gefr	24	14.8.1944		Agay	
Klann	Erich	Gren	18	14.8.1944		Agay	
Unknown						Agay	
Unknown				8.1944		Anthéor	
Unknown				8.1944		Anthéor	
Unknown				15.8.1944		Anthéor	
Unknown				15.8.1944		Anthéor	
Friede	Walter	Gefr	18	15.8.1944		Antibes	7 Alarm Flak 308
Habicht	Alfred	Uffz		15.8.1944		Antibes	7 Alarm Flak 308
Heckelmann	Lorenz	Gren	18	16.8.1944		Antibes	7./Res.Gren.Btl.372
Buffen	Lars			24.8.1944		Antibes	
Krapp	Willy					Antibes	
Kirchner	Hermann	Kan	36	24.8.1944		Biot	Artillery
Laske	Robert	Stbs Gefr	30	24.8.1944		Biot	Art.Abt.44
Unknown						Biot	
Bergmann	Karl	Lt	33	17.8.1944		Cannes	
Döring	Edwin	Ogefr		17.8.1944		Cannes	
Klöditz	Willy	Uffz	23	17.8.1944		Cannes	13./Heeresküsten Art.Rgt.1291
Ammer	Alfred	Zollass	50	18.8.1944		Cannes	Zoll
Aurmer	Kurt			18.8.1944		Cannes	
Scheffczyk	Viktor	Gefr	34	19.8.1944	Cannes	Cannes	HAKA Cannes
Kubitzky	Günter	Gren	18	23.8.1944		Cannes	
Medwed	Anton	Gren	17	23.8.1944	Cannes hospital	Cannes	
Novok	Eduard		17	23.8.1944		Cannes	9./Res.Gren.Btl.444
Unknown				23.8.1944		Cannes	
Griesberger	Adolf	Uffz	37	15.8.1944	La Napoule	US Draguignan	
Ingold	Friedrich	Ogefr	24	15.8.1944	La Napoule	US Draguignan	
Karwatzski	Alfred	Fwb	34	15.8.1944	La Napoule	US Draguignan	
Tkocz	Reinhold		19	16.8.1944	La Napoule	US Draguignan	
Jeck	Andreas	Gefr	42	15.8.1944	Cannes	Grasse	1./Fest.Pi-Stab 14
Oelschlegel	Hans	Stbs Gefr	45	16.8.1944	Pégomas	Grasse	Stab.Res.Div.148
Metzger	Georg	*Jäger*	18	15.8.1944	Pont du Riou	La Napoule	Res.Jäg.Btl.28
Czech	Erich	*Jäger*	28	16.8.1944	Le Tremblant	La Napoule	Res.Jäg.Btl.28
Falkus	Eduard	*Jäger*	17	16.8.1944	Le Tremblant	La Napoule	Res.Jäg.Btl.28
Lingansch	Paul	Fwb	27	16.8.1944		La Napoule	Res.Jäg.Btl.28
Niesporek	Franz	*Jäger*	17	16.8.1944		La Napoule	Res.Jäg.Btl.28
Drischel	Helmuth	Gren	17	17.8.1944		La Napoule	
Götz	Reinhold	*Jäger*	27	17.8.1944	Le Tremblant	La Napoule	Res.Jäg.Btl.28
Janus	Josef	*Jäger*	18	17.8.1944	Hill 93	La Napoule	5./Res.Jäg.Btl.28
Ritzka	Josef	*Jäger*	18	17.8.1944		La Napoule	5./Res.Jäg.Btl.28
Janise	Franz	Gren	17	18.8.1944	Le Tremblant	La Napoule	Res I Gesch Kp 239
Graca	August	*Jäger*	18	20.8.1944	RN7 highway	La Napoule	7./Res.Jäg.Btl.28
Oczko	Herbert	Uffz	24	20.8.1944	Hill 84	MIA	10./Res.Gren.Btl.164
Poller	Franz	Gren	17	20.8.1944	Hill 84	La Napoule	10./Res.Gren.Btl.164
Thieme	Hans	Uffz	34	20.8.1944	Hill 84	MIA	10./Res.Gren.Btl.164

Surname	Name	Rank	Age	Date of death	Killed or wounded in	Buried in	Unit
Cisek	Johann	*Jäger*	18	21.8.1944		La Napoule	Res.Jäg.Btl.28
Link	Lothar	*Jäger*	18	21.8.1944	Hill 84	La Napoule	5./Res.Jäg.Btl.28
Nowrotek	Alois	*Jäger*	27	21.8.1944	Pont du Riou	La Napoule	7./Res.Jäg.Btl.28
Olschenka	Erich	*Jäger*	17	21.8.1944	Hill 105	La Napoule	6./Res.Jäg.Btl.28
Schiffhorst	Gerhard	Uffz	30	21.8.1944	La Napoule	MIA	5./Res.Jäg.Btl.28
Schuster	Leopold	*Jäger*		21.8.1944	Hill 105	La Napoule	Res.Jäg.Btl.28
Skrzydolski	Adam	*Jäger*	18	21.8.1944	La Napoule	La Napoule	Res.Jäg.Btl.28
Strzoda	Herbert	*Jäger*	18	21.8.1944	Hill 105	La Napoule	Res.Jäg.Btl.28
Wall	Arthur	*Jäger*	18	21.8.1944	Le Tremblant	La Napoule	6./Res.Jäg.Btl.28
Weimann	Paul	Ogefr	26	21.8.1944	Hill 105	La Napoule	6./Res.Jäg.Btl.28
Wrodarczyk	Viktor	*Jäger*	17	21.8.1944		La Napoule	5./Res.Jäg.Btl.28
Bartsch	Heinz	Uffz	25	22.8.1944	Road to Cannes	La Napoule	
Konsek	August	Gren	18	28.8.1944?		La Napoule	
Böhm	Gustav	*Jäger*	17	8.1944	Hill 105	La Napoule	Res.Jäg.Btl.28
Fischer	Herbert	*Jäger*	18	8.1944		La Napoule	Res.Jäg.Btl.28
Glomb	Alfred	Ogren	24			La Napoule	
Gübler ?						La Napoule	
Niergond ?	Anton					La Napoule	
Seifert ?	Rudolf					La Napoule	
Unknown						La Napoule	
Unknown						La Napoule	
Unknown						La Napoule	
Unknown						La Napoule	
Unknown						La Napoule	
Unknown						La Napoule	
Unknown						La Napoule	
Unknown						La Napoule	
Neuwirth	Franz	Gren	18	15.8.1944	Cannes	Le Cannet	12./Res.Gren.Btl.444
Rodoschek	Anton	Gren	18	15.8.1944		Le Cannet	
Styppa	Konrad	Gren	28	17.8.1944	Le Cannet	Le Cannet	10./Res.Gren.Btl.444
Kritner	Erich	Sold		18.8.1944		Les Adrets	
Weber	Fritz	*Jäger*	31	18.8.1944	Bei Mandelieu	RN7-les Adrets	7./Res.Jäg.Btl.28
Ludwig	Ernst	Uffz	31	8.1944	Bei Frejus	RN7-les Adrets	10./Res.Gren.Btl.444
Unknown						RN7-les Adrets	
Unknown						RN7-les Adrets	
Nemoikin	Iwan		23	8.1944		Le Trayas	Ost.Btl.661
Unknown				15.8.1944		Le Trayas	
Hümmer	Otto	Schütze	21	16.8.1944	Le Trayas	US Draguignan	
Krassa	Georg	Uffz	38	16.8.1944		Le Trayas	
Krumpill	Roman		18	16.8.1944		Le Trayas	
Pollin	Kurt	Fwb	22	16.8.1944		Le Trayas	
Unknown				16.8.1944		Le Trayas	
Häusig	Karl	Uffz		22.8.1944	Plan Sarrain	Mouans Sartoux	Stab.Res.Gren.Btl.327
Krautschneider	Josef	*Jäger*	18	23.08.1944	Mougins	Mougins	6./Res.Jäg.Btl.28
Siegert	Lothar	*Jäger*	18	23.8.1944	Mougins	Mougins	Res.Jäg.Btl.28
Woznicka	Stefan	*Jäger*	17	23.8.1944	Mougins	Mougins	6./Res.Jäg.Btl.28
Seidel	Georg	Olt	43	16.8.1944	Mandelieu	Nice-Caucade	7./Res.Jäg.Btl.28

Surname	Name	Rank	Age	Date of death	Killed or wounded in	Buried in	Unit
Manietzki	Johann	Gren	18	19.8.1944	La Napoule	Nice-Caucade	10./Res.Gren.Btl.164
Knirsch	Franz	Uffz	36	23.8.1944	Cannes	Nice-Caucade	Res.Gren.Btl.444
Sikora	Zdenko	*Jäger*	18	20.8.1944	HVPl Nizza	Nice-Cimiez	6./Res.Jäg.Btl.28
Römmen	Matthias	Ogefr	24	21.8.1944	SW Mandelieu	Nice-Cimiez	8./Res.Jäg.Btl.28
Dahmen	Heinrich	Ogefr	20	22.8.1944	Golf Juan Bay	Nice-Cimiez	22.U-Jagdflotille
Meyer-Detring	Klaus	Olt	35	22.8.1944	Le Tremblant	Nice-Cimiez	7./Res.Jäg.Btl.28
Podbarschek	Franz	Sold	18	23.8.1944	Mandelieu	Nice-Cimiez	2./Res.Pi.Btl.8
Szafranek	Richard	*Jäger*	18	23.8.1944		Nice-Cimiez	5./Res.Jäg.Btl.28
Muschiol	Anton	Gren	29	24.8.1944		Nice-Cimiez	12./Res.Gren.Btl.444
Sowka	Gerhard	Pio	17	15.8.1944	Pégomas Bridge	Pégomas	
Unknown						RN7-Tanneron	
Drzisga	Otto	Gren	18	18.8.1944	Le Cannet	Valbonne	1./Res.Art.Abt.44
Cinader	Johann	Gren	17	20.8.1944	Legamet	Valbonne	7./Res.Jäg.Btl.28
Fiedler	Hubert	*Jäger*	18	23.8.1944	HVPl Valbonne	Valbonne	8./Res.Jäg.Btl.28
Büddemann	Friedrich	Ogefr	24	21.8.1944	Golf Juan Bay	Vallauris	22.U-Jagdflotille
Kube	Paul	Okan	37	16.8.1944	Les Termes	Undetermined	
Gerhold	Heinz	Ogefr	20	21.8.1944	Golf Juan Bay	Missing at sea	22.U-Jagdflotille
Willi	Wegen	Hpt Gefr	23	21.8.1944	Golf Juan Bay	Missing at sea	22.U-Jagdflotille

Conclusion

The very first troops to land near Cannes early on August 15, 1944, were the 67 French naval commandos of the *Groupe Naval d'Assaut de Corse*, who had the mission of cutting off the coastal road in Théoule and the RN7 further inland. However, their mission turned to disaster when the location they landed at turned out to be heavily mined: 11 men were killed and almost all the survivors were either wounded or captured.

The 141st Infantry Regiment landed in the Estérel Mountains at Anthéor and Agay a few hours later. By the afternoon of August 16th, they had crossed through the Estérel and set up road blocks on both the coastal road and the RN7 highway outside la Napoule. Initial losses during the landing were very light, however, casualties increased August 16th and 17th, when the Germans shelled the American positions heavily. After August 16th, the 141st IR did not advance any further east, as its mission was simply to protect the right flank of the invasion. The 141st lost a total of 24 men killed in the Estérel area.

The 509th and 551st Parachute Infantry Battalions were ordered to relieve the 141st IR outside la Napoule August 20th. The next day, both units successfully attacked the objectives directly to their fronts however, both suffered heavy casualties, with at least 26 American paratroopers killed August 20th and 21st in the vicinities of Hill 84 and Hill 105. The 509th then led the advance for the next three days, finally entering Cannes on the 24th. On the way, 16 more paratroopers of the 509th PIB, 463rd Parachute Field Artillery Battalion, and 2680th Military Intelligence Company were killed. The German forces had pulled back all the way to the Loup River, so the 509th was immediately able to cross through Cannes and Antibes and take up position on the Brague River without meeting any further opposition. A total of 42 paratroopers were killed in Théoule, la Napoule, and Cannes between August 20th and 24th.

Pvt Justus F. Patrick and Pvt Clifton R. Mullen make friends with a local female in Antibes. Mike Reuter Collection.

7

Resistance Activities in the Cannes Region

After having made an in-depth analysis of the infantry battles in the region of la Napoule that led to the liberation of the cities of Cannes and Antibes in the previous chapter, we will now describe some of the events that occurred in Cannes before the arrival of the American troops. As we will see, although the Americans had the main role in ousting the Germans from the area, the French population did not simply sit idle.

The Liberation of the Prisoners of the Groupe Naval d'Assaut de Corse

Early on the morning of August 15th, the French *Groupe Naval d'Assaut de Corse* landed at Théoule sur Mer, only located about ten kilometers from downtown Cannes. As was explained in the previous chapter, this French commando group of 67 men landed in a minefield, causing the death of eleven of them and forcing the survivors to surrender. Those who were uninjured were directed towards Grasse, while the wounded were left behind at Théoule. Several of the prisoners that were being marched to Grasse under German escort were liberated in a daring operation performed by local resistance men led by Francis Tonner. Francis Tonner and his brother Fernand both lived in a farm on the western outskirts of Cannes. Fernand Tonner's future wife, **Amable Tonner**, explains how the escape took place:

One day around noon, somebody came to the farm and told them: "There is a column of French prisoners guarded by four Germans going towards Grasse. There are about 20 of them. Maybe we should do something to liberate them." Francis and Fernand were alone at the farm. Fernand was 19 years old and adored his brother, so he always obeyed him and listened to everything he said. Francis told him: "We will try to find two or three friends and see if we can liberate them." And just like that they left on their bikes to St Jean, where they met one of their best friends, Barberis, and they found another named Lucien Albis and there was a third named Giordanengo, I think, whom I didn't know. [In fact, the team was made up of Raymond Barberis, Lucien Albi, Pierre Borghese, and the Tonner brothers.] They all left on their bicycles to the Route de Grasse. There is a chapel after Auribeau, Notre Dame de Valcluse, and they hid there while they waited for the prisoners to arrive. They waited and saw that there were only four Germans, so they thought they wouldn't put up much resistance. They each had a pistol in their pockets, that's all they had, and they were in shirtsleeves

and trousers, as it was August and very hot. I am giving that detail as it is important.

They intercepted the column on a curve, but unfortunately the Germans defended themselves body and soul. Some of the Frenchmen lay down on the ground, saying: "The war is over for us, we won't move," and others tried to follow the movement. Francis and two others got separated and left through the hills towards the Estérel, while Fernand and Barberis remained behind and fought hand to hand with two Germans. Raymond Barberis managed to disengage at once and escape into the hill, but Fernand was tackled by a German who hit him in the head and ankle with a stone, and Fernand also wounded the German with a stone, so the German finally let go. It is because he was lightly dressed, whereas the German was carrying all his gear, that Fernand managed to free himself.

They climbed up the hill that was facing them, but the German got up and started shooting at them. Since they knew the area, they took some roundabout paths to try to escape. Fernand couldn't walk anymore because his ankle was injured, so they stopped and an old lady provided shelter for them in a small shed, saying: "Get inside children, and don't move." Then, at nightfall, they left for la Bocca. In the meantime, Francis and the other two left in the opposite direction with the prisoners. They managed to meet up with the most advanced American forces and handed over the prisoners.

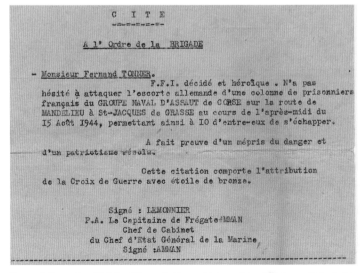

Fernand Tonner's official military citation, which explains that he participated in freeing ten captured French sailors from the Germans. Tonner Family Collection.

Twenty-five years after the operation, a journalist interviewed three of the surviving participants (Francis Tonner, Pierre Borghese, and Raymond Barberis) in order to write a detailed article about the escape. It must be kept in mind when reading it, that such articles were usually written in a rather patriotic manner, so they should be taken with a grain of salt:

The group of five men, pedaling in single file, crosses the Siagne a first time, reaches the road at Capitou, but the Germans and their prisoners have already passed. They will have to cross the Siagne again before spotting the tail of the column. As they were riding, they established their plan of attack.

Two go up ahead: Francis Tonner and Raymond Barberis. The three others will take care of the *Feldwebels* who are at the back. The first two cyclists overtake the column. There are indeed only three Germans guarding the French sailors, who are exhausted and still traumatized by the terrible night they have just lived trough. A few hundred meters further on, far ahead of the column, one of the cyclists dismounts and cusses. Simulating a flat tire, he flips over his bike at the side of the road. His friend also dismounts, sets his bike at the side of the road, and joins him. The two of them start working on the faulty machine.

And when the lead German reaches them, the three other cyclists have in the meantime reached the two Germans at the back of the column. The synchronism of the operation has been perfect. Three pistols are simultaneously pointed at the Germans, who are armed with submachine guns. Francis Tonner did not have time to assemble his Sten... but the surprise does not have the planned effect.

"We thought," admit Barberis and Borghese, "that when we threatened them with our weapons, the Germans would not offer any resistance. We were mistaken. They were diehards. With pistols on their backs, they preferred to die!..." Raymond Barberis shoots one... Another escapes. The third uses his submachine gun butt to give a blow to Fernand Tonner, who grabs hold of him. The two fall to the ground, holding onto each other tightly in a fight to the death. The German grabs a stone that Fernand manages to rip from his hands. And with the same stone, he smashes the soldier's skull...

The attack only lasted a few seconds. As soon as they start the "hold up," the *résistants* shout to the sailors to escape. Eleven of them escape, accompanied by Francis Tonner. The rest of them, who are exhausted and do not react, no longer have the strength to escape. Everyone abandons the bicycles (that bear license plates with the names of their true owners) and disperse, except for the escaped sailors, who Francis Tonner will lead all the way to Tanneron, through the forest, to the farm of Mr Jacques de Chaudens, a Swiss citizen, who will hide them until the arrival of the 1st Battalion of the 151st RA [sic].

A few minutes after the attack, some trucks filled with Germans arrived from nearby Pégomas. The gunshots had been heard from the village. Only about 15 traumatized prisoners remained behind, overwhelmed with tiredness and heat, as well as the corpses of two *Boches*.[1]

A local woman named Giordanengo was credited with having warned the column of prisoners of the impending attack to free them. Approximately ten of the *Groupe Navale d'Assaut de Corse*

prisoners managed to escape during this highly successful operation, their exact number depending on the source consulted. It is unclear if any German soldiers were actually killed in the attack. No perfect matches were found, but either or both of the two following men may possibly have been killed or mortally wounded in the operation: *Stabsgefreiter* **Willi Dürr** was buried in the Caucade Cemetery in Nice after having reportedly been killed in Grasse August 15th; and *Stabsgefreiter* **Hans Oelschlegel**, of the *Reserve Division 148* headquarters, was buried in Grasse after reportedly having been killed in Pégomas on the 16th. As we have seen in the previous chapter, Francis Tonner was unfortunately killed by a shell a few days later, on August 23rd, while accompanying the first U.S. paratroopers across the Siagne River. He was a true hero of the Resistance.

The Villa Montfleury Massacre

With the Allies having landed only a few kilometers away from Cannes August 15th, the local branch of the *Gestapo* received orders to evacuate their local headquarters in the Villa Montfleury. As the young recruits of *Bataillons 28* and *164* were rushed towards Cannes to join *Bataillon 444* and *Ost Bataillon 661* in their deadly battle against the invading force, the *Gestapo* men who had been terrorizing the local population now prepared to escape like rats. We will let one of these menial characters, **Richard Held**, whom we already presented in Chapter 1, explain the circumstances of their departure from the Villa Montfleury, in the basement of which a dozen civilian prisoners were being held (Helds account is the interrogation report made by the French police after he was captured at a later date.):

During the night of August 14th to 15th, the Allied landing occurred on the coasts of Provence. This was confirmed during the morning of August 15th. The same day at about 3 P.M., Moser, who was the chief of the *Gestapo* in Cannes, called us, as well as all the other agents, to his office, where he told us that he had just received orders to retreat to Nice.

As far as I was concerned, I returned to my home to prepare my personal luggage with my mistress. I came back to the *Gestapo* headquarters around 4 P.M. My mistress accompanied me. I noticed that the following people were also present: Moser, and his mistress Hélène; Bauer; Wirges and his wife, Bilhartz; three *Feldgendarmes* [Military Police] and their driver; and the *Gestapo* driver Barthelemy. I noticed that certain documents and files were being destroyed in the villa. It was mostly Moser who was taking care of doing so.

Willi Bauer, a member of the Cannes Gestapo who participated in the execution of the Villa Montfleury prisoners. MRA Collection.

Around 7 P.M., we all joined in the dining room for diner. The following people participated in this meal: Moser and his mistress Helene; Bauer; Bilhartz; three *Feldgendarmes*; and myself and my mistress, for a total of nine. Wirges was serving us. He and his wife ate in the kitchen. We had a hearty meal of canned foods and cold meat accompanied by Wine of the Rhine.

During the meal, we spoke about our retreat to Nice and the day's events, but no mention was made of the fate of the prisoners locked in the cells in the basement of the villa. [These were civilian prisoners who had nothing to do with the French commandos mentioned previously.] The meal lasted about 45 minutes.[2]

After the meal, most of the men departed, leaving behind only Held, Moser, Bauer, the three *Feldgendarmes*, and their driver and PPF man Paul Malaguti. **Richard Held** continues:

I entered the villa with Moser and Bauer. Moser said: "We need to liberate one prisoner, the Czech woman." All three of us went down into the basement. (…) Moser told me to assemble all the prisoners in cell number 2. He himself opened cell numbers 3 and 4 and Bauer opened cell number 1 as I myself opened cell number 2. I translated Moser's orders into French and told the prisoners: "All of you go into cell number 2 and form a line, we are going to count you." All the prisoners entered cell number 2, except the Czech woman who, on Moser's orders, stayed in her cell, number 3 I think. When all the prisoners were in cell number 2 (there were 11 of them), I closed the cell door and fetched the Czech woman in her cell. In accordance with Moser's instructions, I liberated her myself by accompanying her to the entrance of the villa, on the ground floor, where I opened the door and told her she was free to go.

At that moment I returned to the basement, where I found Moser and Bauer in the hallway in front of cell number 2, which was closed. (…) Moser and Bauer had their service pistols. I myself was in possession of an 8mm automatic revolver of Belgian manufacture loaded with seven bullets.(…) Moser told me that he had received orders to execute the prisoners before leaving Cannes. I must say that when I accompanied the Czech woman, I suspected that the other prisoners were going to be executed, because otherwise Moser would have liberated all of them at the same time or made arrangements for their transfer.

All three of us entered cell number 2 and Moser gave the following orders, which I translated into French: "All of you come back to the room at the back." The prisoners thus all came out of cell number 2 one after the other and went towards the back room, preceded by Moser. Bauer stayed in cell number 2. I was at the entrance of this cell. When the second to last prisoner (a man), the last one being Mademoiselle Conchita, walked past me, I was preparing to follow along and was looking out towards the hallway. At that moment I heard a gunshot fired in cell number 2. I turned around and saw that this gunshot had been fired by Bauer on Mademoiselle Conchita, who was screaming and holding on to Bauer. She fell to the ground, making Bauer bend forward. It is at that moment, and taking advantage of my movement, that the last prisoner, who I later found out was Mr Negri, managed to escape. I arrived next to Bauer as he fired a second shot into Mademoiselle Conchita, who was on the floor. I then took my pistol. Several shots were fired in the hallway, in which I heard the sounds of a precipitated escape. Bauer and I rushed to the door of cell number 2, where I saw several prisoners running towards the grilled door that closed the hallway. Seeing that some prisoners were going to escape, I emptied the entire clip of my pistol into them, in other words, seven bullets. Bauer did the same. As for Moser, he was firing from the back of the hallway and into cell number 4. All the prisoners fell

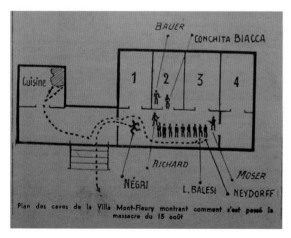

A plan of the basements of Villa Montfleury. L'Ergot/MRA Collection.

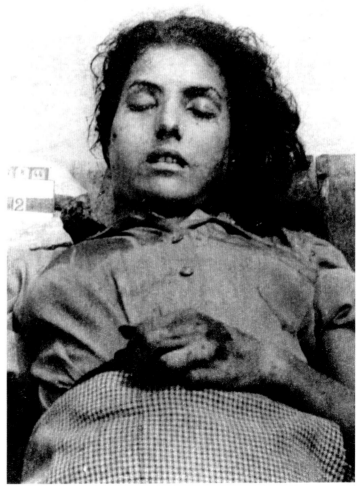

"Bauer pointed his gun at the back of the young woman's neck and fired." Conchita Biacca, who was pregnant at the time, was the first person to be shot in what would later become known as the Montfleury Massacre. Archives Municipales de Cannes.

one after the other as we fired. I cannot say precisely how many I hit because these events occurred extremely fast. In my opinion I killed two prisoners.

As I was firing the seven bullets of my clip into the prisoners, I felt pain in my left foot. I didn't pay attention to it at the time, and it was only later that I understood a bullet had gone through my foot. In fact, I am wearing the same pants as on that day and you can see the entrance and exit holes in the cloth yourself.

As soon as all the prisoners were on the ground, I climbed to the ground floor of the villa to bandage my foot. Bauer and Moser stayed a few more minutes before joining me. I didn't hear any more gunshots. To get out of the hallway, I had to step over the bodies and go through the door that was only partly open because it was blocked by the bodies.[3]

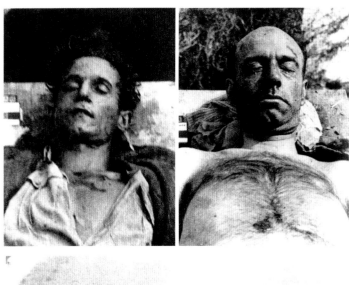

Their mission accomplished, the *Gestapo* men drove off towards Italy that very night. In the basement of the Villa Montfleury, eight prisoners lay dead. The only female victim, Conchita Biacca, had been pregnant at the time she was shot and killed. However, thanks to the very amateurish way in which the execution was performed, two of the prisoners (Louis Balesi and Marcel Neydorff) survived the shooting, lying wounded among the bodies of their dead companions. Additionally, a third prisoner, Edouard Negri, managed to escape before the shooting started, as Richard Held explained above.

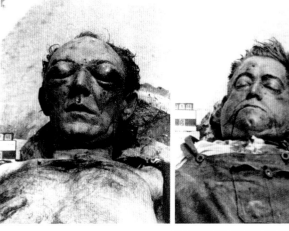

One of the three survivors, 39-year-old **Louis Balesi,** later described his plight in the *l'Ergot* newspaper (which often contained insider information from the police). It is extremely interesting to compare his version of the execution with that of Richard Held:

Surname	Name	Date of death	Location of death
Albertini	Jean	15.8.1944	Cannes Montfleury
Biacca	Conchita	15.8.1944	Cannes Montfleury
Biny	Gustave	15.8.1944	Cannes Montfleury
Chalmette	Pierre	15.8.1944	Cannes Montfleury
Froidurot	Alfred	15.8.1944	Cannes Montfleury
Krengel	Georges	15.8.1944	Cannes Montfleury
Martini	Marius	15.8.1944	Cannes Montfleury
Séguran	Hippolyte	15.8.1944	Cannes Montfleury

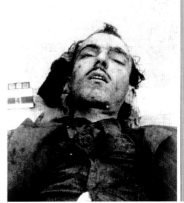
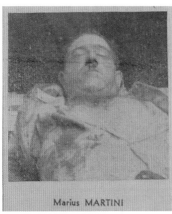

Marius MARTINI

"As many comrades," Louis Balesi tells us, "I was a member of a resistance group, the *Groupe Tartane* to be precise. On the morning of August 9th, a man from the *Gestapo* in plainclothes presented himself at my house. After having performed a careful search with no results, he brought me to Cannes, where I was imprisoned in the villa Montfleury.

In the basement of this German policeman's haunt, which had been converted to prison cells, I found my brother-in-law Hippolyte Seguran, laborer in Cagnes sur Mer, married and a father of three; my friend Marius Martini, customs officer arrested in Vence; and other members of my group: Gustave Biny, Alfred Froidurot, and Marcel Neydorff. The other prisoners, who had also been arrested recently, were a young girl (Conchita Biacca)

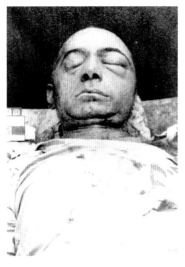

Postmortem photos taken of the other unfortunate victims of the Montfleury Massacre by the Cannes Police: Jean Albertini, Gustave Biny, Pierre Chalmette, Alfred Froidurot, Georges Krengel, Marius Martini, and Hippolyte Seguran. Archives Municipales de Cannes.

and four patriots: Jean-Francois Albertini, George Krengel, Pierre Chalmette, and Negri, whom I did not know.

I was subjected to several harsh interrogations. The questions were asked by Moser and Willy Bauer in German and were translated by Richard Held, who, when we took too long to reply, would punch us. During the interrogations, two radios were blasting constantly to cover the sound of our voices and of our cries. For food, we had two plates of soup and 30 grams of bread per day.

During the night of August 14th to 15th, we were awakened by the rumble of cannon fire. Large caliber naval artillery was firing constantly to the west, in the Estérel and the Maures. The window panes of the villa rattled, the walls shook. The Allies had landed, it was certain. The agitation that overcame the *Boches* in the villa confirmed our hypothesis.

What was going to happen to us? "We will be set free" said the optimists. "They will kill us" said the pessimists. We could hear airplanes flying by. The cannon fire intensified. Dusk came.

At half past eight, there was the sound of footsteps on the stairs leading to the basement. The chief of the Cannes *Gestapo*, Moser, and his two lieutenants, Willy Bauer and Richard Held, appeared in civilian dress, their faces tense, an evil glow in their eyes, each with an unholstered gun in

his belt. Moser, after having liberated a female prisoner, made the remaining 11 prisoners, who were spread out in four cells, assemble in cell number 2, where I was. He didn't say a word to us. The three *Boches* now had their pistols in hand.

We were all standing up, more and more worried. Moser exited cell number 2, walked down the hallway that all the cells opened into, to the end, and with gun in hand, he placed himself in front of the door to cell number 4, which he opened, and was by far the biggest.

"Send all the prisoners here!" shouted Moser to his henchmen. (…) Richard, with his back to the partially-open door that separated the hallway from the other parts of the basement (…), was standing at the door of cell number 2, with gun in hand. In the cell was Willy Bauer, pointing his gun at us. This is how things happened (in spite of the speed of the scene, each image is carved into my memory indelibly): one after another we exited cell number 2 in single file, going from the door Richard was guarding to the one Moser was guarding.

Ten of us had evacuated cell number 2 and were walking down the hallway between cell 2 and 4 when the 11th prisoner, Miss Conchita Biacca, passed in front of Willy Bauer to exit cell number 2. At that moment, Bauer pointed his gun at the back of the young woman's neck and fired. Horribly wounded, Conchita Biacca threw herself on her executioner, clinging onto him and making him fall down. To free himself, Bauer pressed the trigger again while calling for help. Richard abandoned his post at the door of cell number 2 and rushed to Bauer's help, thus freeing the entrance door to the hallway.

Our friend Negri, who had been the last to exit cell number 2 just before Miss Biacca, did not hesitate. The nine other prisoners were between him and Moser's gun at the other end of the hallway. Negri rushed for the door, got past it, and bounded up the stairs. A few bullets whistled past his ears, as Moser was firing at him. But he was already at the ground floor, crossing the garden and reaching the street, where he met an individual shouting "Police!" Negri just ran off even faster. The other man, who was probably (…) PPF Malaguti, emptied his pistol in the direction of the escapee, but in vain.

Of course, I only found out about these details later on, when I met Negri again. Logically, I should never have seen him again, since I was "put to death" by the Germans. Enraged, Moser and Bauer opened fire on us, the nine unfortunate captives who were in the hallway. Richard, who had been wounded in the foot by a ricochet bullet, had gone upstairs to bandage himself.

A few atrocious seconds followed: the nine prisoners, shrieking and crying, fell on top of one another. I had received a bullet in the chest, slightly below the heart. By chance I fell onto one of the mattresses that cluttered the hallway and I instinctively rolled myself into it. Moser and Bauer, stepping over the bodies, were firing *coups de grace* at will. They fired mine through the mattress. The bullet passed below my nose without hitting me. I had remained fully conscious and took care to play dead, only starting to breathe again once the two assassins had left the basement.

I had my watch and matches. I waited for it to be midnight, and since I could hear no more noise, except that of the artillery, I decided to go out, displacing the bodies that were piled in my way. As I opened the door to the

Crime scene photograph of the Montfleury basements taken by the Cannes Police shortly after the execution. Archives Municipales de Cannes.

"By chance I fell onto one of the mattresses that cluttered the hallway and I instinctively rolled myself into it." Crime scene photograph of the basement taken shortly after the execution. Archives Municipales de Cannes.

villa, I saw Moser outside, leaning on his car. "Halt!" he shouted. I quickly closed the door, through which he fired three shots. But I had already dived back into the basement. Not in the part where the bodies were, but near the kitchen, in the boiler room, where I buried myself in a pile of coal.

At two in the morning I left my hiding place. I found a small door leading to the garden. Proceeding in slow steps, for my wound was starting to be very painful and I had lost a lot of blood, I reached the Villa Corsica, barefoot, without a shirt or hat, where a friend, Mr Gularmi, gave me hospitality. The next day, I went to another friend's, Mr Miale (…), and stayed there, treating myself on my own until the liberation. After that, I spent three months in treatment. And now, as you can see, I am feeling quite good for a man who, after all, was "put to death" by the *Gestapo*.[4]

The execution later became known as the Montfleury Villa Massacre. Richard Held was executed for his participation in the shooting. However, as a final sickening twist to this tragedy, a word must be said about 17-year-old Paul Malaguti, the PPF Frenchman who is said to have fired at Negri as he escaped the villa. Malaguti was condemned to death after the Liberation, but was pardoned after serving in the Foreign Legion. He later became a politician in the French extreme right, close to Jean-Marie le Pen, who has been condemned several times for revisionist statements. Paul Malaguti died of cancer in 1996.[5]

The Surrender of Polish Soldiers

With the front remaining stable in the region of la Napoule for several days, Cannes found itself in the awkward situation of being the rear of the German front lines for almost ten days. The city was regularly shelled by Allied warships, causing the death of several German soldiers as well as, reportedly, 14 civilians.[6] The Germans were nervous, as **Jean-Pierre Carbonel** recalls, and kept a tight grip on the situation:

There was a group of Germans armed to the teeth and in civilian dress who patrolled around town in a car.

They had removed all the doors from the car in order to be able to jump out faster. One evening, there was a group of young people in front of the Notre Dame des Pins church and they came along. In an instant, they all jumped out with submachine guns and controlled us. They saw that we were harmless youths, but in fact, our eyes were wide open and when we had to do something, we would do it. They told us: "Come on, don't stand around, get out of here." We said: "But it is not curfew time yet." But they made us leave.

The main leaders of the local resistance groups were Stephan Vahanian and Ange-Marie Miniconi. Two of Miniconi's men were executed by the Germans August 18th. A third resistance man, **Casimir Barbier**, was last seen being carried away by the Germans to the Château de la Bocca and has been missing ever since. When some skeletons were found during construction in Cannes in 2009, Barbier's sisters thought one of them might be their brother, but the bones turned out to be from an older time period.[7]

Surname	Name	Age	Date of Death	Location of death
Berrone	Gabriel		18.8.1944	Cannes
Costa	Charles/ Clément		18.8.1944	Cannes
Barbier	Casimir	23		Cannes

The risks of attempting anything against the Germans were still great, even though the Allied armies were only a few kilometers away. However, the Resistance made particular efforts to convince Polish soldiers within the German army to surrender. Such activities were of course dangerous for both parties, as the French could be set up by real Germans pretending to be Polish, while the Polish were afraid that if they surrendered to the Resistance, they might end up being executed or recaptured by the Germans. This did not deter many French resistance members, as well as regular civilians, from helping Polish deserters by hiding them and giving them civilian clothes. **Jean-Paul Carbonel** was one of those:

During the eight or ten days of fighting, there were Polish soldiers who wanted to surrender. We had a man, Nicolas Separovitch, who was Serbo-Croat or something like that and could speak five languages, so he wrote texts in German and Polish. Then my sister, following instructions of the AS 24 [The local resistance branch], spent two or three days and nights retyping the texts on a typewriter. We distributed the copies of the text, particularly in la Bocca, to the few Germans whom we trusted. They then passed them on to their colleagues, and in fact, a lot of them surrendered to the resistance thanks to that paper that they used as a safe conduct. The message spread by word of mouth, and when one had the pamphlet, two or three would come to surrender together.

Jean Paul Carbonel was directly involved in hiding three such deserters:

Nicolas Separovitch lived in the same district as I and had spent a lot of time chatting up some soldiers. When the landing occurred, we took three Poles and hid them in the greenhouses of the Lenza property. They could communicate with each other and could escape by the train tracks if necessary. We kept them hidden in the glasshouses, and when Cannes was liberated, they came out and we gave them civilian clothes. Since it was my father who had organized the scheme, I got to keep all the equipment of the soldier named Kuhla. After the war, Mr Lenza or one of his family members wrote to the Polish embassy to ask what had happened to those three soldiers that he had hidden. The embassy replied that they had all returned to Poland and that everything was fine.

After the landing, **Pierre Carle** and his family were hiding in the hills north of la Napoule to avoid the Allied shelling, and where they met some potential German army deserters:

We had taken refuge in Mandelieu, and beside us there was an empty field that the Germans had built a bunker in using tree trunks, and they lived inside it. We often ran into them, and since my mother was Swiss she could speak German, and she would speak with those young Germans since we were just a few meters away from each other. So my mother talked to them and we were in good relations with them, but we could feel that their morale was low. Some of them weren't afraid of saying: "The end is coming, things aren't going well for us." And very few of them were actually German; they were all young Poles or Yugoslavs, and they only wanted one thing, and that was to get away as soon as possible.

In the following days, **Pierre Carle** was involved in leading a group of similar soldiers up to Tanneron so that they could cross the lines and surrender to the Americans:

We stayed there ten days. But we young people were bored and we couldn't just stay there all the time. So we would climb to the top of the hill, and sometimes I went

back home to get a blanket or something. And one day I met people who may have been part of the Resistance, I am not sure. There was a German battery located at the old race track that had a view of the Estérel mountains and the paths in the Estérel. The paths led to Agay, where the Americans had landed, and the batteries were directed towards those Americans. There were some Polish people who lived in the area or who were refugees in France, and a Polish woman spoke to some Polish soldiers from that battery and managed to convince them to desert. She explained the situation to them carefully, saying that it was a disaster and that it was in their best interest to surrender. They must have known some people from the Resistance because myself and two friends, one of which was Janvier Passero, were asked to bring them to Tanneron, where the Americans already were.

We organized to meet one day and I think about ten Poles came. Of course, we gave them civilian clothes and I remember we gave them old pairs of pants that were all torn at the knees and underneath you could see their green German underpants. They kept their German shoes because we couldn't find any shoes, and we gave them old shirts and that was enough. They also kept their German musette bags, probably because they had a few personal items they wanted to bring with them.

So we left Mandelieu and started going into the hills. At first we were careful and were looking around. We were in front and the Poles were behind. We crossed through a peach orchard and Janvier Passero took some peaches and put them in his bag. It later saved his life, because he had a gun at the bottom of the bag. I had a little pistol that the resistance people had given to me and I had put it in my back pocket.

We kept on climbing up towards Tanneron, and after a while we didn't worry about the Poles anymore, they were behind us and we were walking peacefully without worrying about anything. We were no longer looking around us to see if there were any Germans or Americans. In fact, the Poles noticed that we weren't being very careful. We were at home; we sort of felt like we were the masters, it was the liberation, and we were acting tough, whereas the Poles had been under German rule for quite a while and they were afraid of them, so they were being

Jean-Paul Carbonel, with the helmet of one of the Polish deserters named Kuhla that he helped to hide. The name Kuhla is still faintly visible on the liner of the helmet. Author's Collection.

Pierre Carle (at left) and his brothers, photographed in la Napoule with abandoned military equipment in the months following the Liberation. Pierre Carle Collection.

much more careful. We were going towards the rendezvous spot where the Poles were supposed to be picked up, and all of a sudden we were surrounded by a German patrol: "Terrorists! Terrorists!" The Poles, who had been a few meters behind us, understood. They had been suspicious and they took off, and I never saw them again, while we stayed there surrounded by Germans.

They brought us to a road and lined us up against an embankment. We stood there with our hands in the air and they said: "Terrorist, terrorist, terrorist!" From the little we could understand from each other, we told them: "No, we live here." Janvier Passero had his hands up and they looked in his musette bag, where they saw the peaches but they didn't see the gun. As for myself, as soon as we were caught, I threw my gun into a bush with dexterity that I didn't even suspect I possessed, because of course they patted us down to see if we had any weapons. So we managed not to get into trouble because of the guns.

We saw that the Germans were exhausted: they were unshaven and must have been short of water. It was in the middle of August and they were very worried about their fate. After a while, some locals came from the other side of the valley, thinking that the Germans that were guarding us were the Poles that we were bringing to the American lines. The locals came closer, and when they were 20 meters away they realized that wasn't the case at all, and that it was the Germans who were holding us back with submachine guns. So the locals also found themselves prisoners as well, but that reassured the Germans, because they realized that we were not resistance fighters and that we were not dangerous, so they let us go. We walked away, but the Germans called us back after we had gone 20 meters; however, they just wanted to ask about where they were on the map.

The Americans were not very far off, and we went and warned them that there was a German patrol. Supposedly those Germans resisted until they were all exterminated, even though they didn't seem vindictive when we saw them. The Poles probably surrendered to the Americans later on, but in a more cautious way.

Pierre Carle's opinion that these Germans were killed is probably based on the story of the Germans who were ambushed and captured by the pathfinders of the 509th PIB in Tanneron August 17th (See Chapter 5). **Jean-Paul Carbonel** also took the risk of crossing over the lines in the same area a few days later with his motorcycle to offer help to the Americans, but was disappointed by the reception he was given:

Three days before the Liberation I crossed the lines at Auribeau and went all the way to Fréjus. We weren't really welcomed by the Americans, to tell the truth; they basically told us: "What the hell are you doing here? We don't give a damn about you." Some of them could speak French and one or two of them were friendly, but the others almost considered us as spies, and wondered why we had come over to see them, so I returned to Cannes.

This is only one of the numerous examples of the profound misunderstanding that sometimes existed between the Resistance and the Allied forces as mentioned in the previous chapter, and will be mentioned again several times in this book.

Daily Life Between the Landing and the Liberation

During the few days between the landing and the Liberation, the French civilians lived under constant threat of Allied artillery and aircraft. A curfew was declared by the Germans, who blew up strategic (and not so strategic) structures, such as the ports of Cannes and Antibes. Disinformation was rife, and every day there were new rumors and counter rumors regarding the American advance and German intentions. Of course, food was scarce and electricity was cut frequently. Cannes resident **Amélie Mougins** held a diary during those days, a few extracts of which we will review to get a feel for the conditions the civilians were living in:

Tuesday August 15, 1944
6 A.M. Large airplanes are in the sky. They are troop transport aircraft. At 6:30, the telephone is cut off. At 8 A.M., it is announced the landing has occurred. Constant shelling between 8 and 11 o'clock. (…) Around 4 P.M., the port is blown up. Violent explosions. (…) Starting from 8 P.M. until 10:30 P.M., there is constant bombing either by airplanes or by the navy. We spend the night in the shelter.

Wednesday August 16, 1944
Calm morning. Shelling at 11 A.M. The cannons in the bunkers at la Croisette [The coastal road in Cannes.] fire: the navy fires back = shelter. First rumor: the Allies are at la Bocca and should be arriving any moment. In the morning the radio announces: "We have taken the port of Cannes." But we don't see anything. Calm afternoon. Rumor: American patrols are in the streets of Cannes. Unfortunately…. Not yet. The English radio announces that Cannes is captured. False. Not yet!

Thursday August 17, 1944
Shelling around 8 A.M. The navy is firing on Palm Beach. [This was in response to the bunkers in Palm Beach shelling the positions of the 141st IR at Théoule.] Big shelling around 11 A.M. Lots of damage in the vicinity. All afternoon there is bombing by the navy and by the airplanes. At 8 P.M., numerous airplanes dive bomb la Corne d'Or and Palm Beach. We stay in the hallway, not having time to get to the shelter. Frightful noise. The whole house vibrates. Windows broken. (…) The bombing destroyed a pylon. No more electricity, no more radio. (…)

Saturday August 19th
5:30 A.M. We rested in spite of the gunfire, in spite of the airplanes. One gets used to danger! The cannon fire stopped, but the airplanes are still here. 1 P.M. Morning was calm, except for the constant buzzing of the aircraft that never stops. (…)We still know nothing of what is going on, with no telephone and no radio. (…)

Monday August 21, 1944
(…) Here, with Emil's stock of food we are holding out, but in town people are miserable. A soup distribution is organized. There was a ration of 100 grams of bread per day, but we have not gotten any for three days. We accept all deprivations, all sacrifices, as long as the liberation comes fast. It is 10 o'clock. While I write, numerous airplanes fly above us. They are surely inspecting the earth, observing for the moment, in preparation for the next attack. (…)

August 15, 1944: only hours after the beginning of the Allied invasion, the Germans blew the port of Cannes. Frédéric Brega Collection.

236

A rare color photograph of the port of Cannes after being blown by the Germans. The large pink building in the background is the "Palais des Festivals," where world famous actors now meet yearly during the Cannes Film Festival. Ted Rulison Collection.

The proximity of battle did not prevent regular accidents from occurring. 42-year-old Gefreiter Andreas Jeck (right), of Festungs-Pionier Bataillon 14, was involved in a truck accident in Cannes August 15th and died of his injuries a few hours later. His body was buried in Grasse. In a similar manner, 50-year-old Zollassistent Alfred Ammer (left) died in Cannes August 18th due to reasons unrelated to the fighting. Jeck Family Collection. Ammer Family Collection.

Tuesday August 22, 1944

(…) 9:30 A.M. Intense shelling nearby. The most recent news is that bombs fell on le Suquet, on the Forville market (…). There are a few dead and some wounded. (…) Since morning, several airplanes are flying over the city without a minute's interruption. The buzzing of the engines above our heads becomes tiresome. The explosion of shells has a metallic sound to it that exasperates the nerves. Our eardrums are tired. We spent an hour in the shelter, but have come back to the fresh air. We are sick of living underground. (…)[8]

Ferdinand Moscone, a local civilian in Antibes, took similar notes during the period of fighting, and gives us some details about the curfew and the destruction of the port of Antibes:

Thursday August 17th

(…) The hours we are allowed in the streets are the following: from 6 A.M. to 9 A.M., from 11 A.M. to 2 P.M., and from 6 P.M. to 8 P.M.

Around 6 P.M. it is announced that the Germans are going to blow up the port at 7 P.M. We decide to hide in our basements.

We unhook all the frames, take off the glass doors, open the ones that cannot be removed, and carry down fragile items.

7 P.M.: nothing happens.

It seems that the dynamiting has been postponed. We will be warned by bugle one hour before it will be done. We eat in the basement and peacefully go to bed.

Friday August 18th

Around 2:30 A.M., we are awakened by the bugler in the streets. It is a false alarm, because by 4 nothing has happened. (…)

Saturday August 19th

Around 1:30 A.M., we are suddenly awakened by the sound of a car and piercing whistle blows. We also hear shouts in which we seem to make out the word "port."

At 0:55, we hear the first explosions. They occur three or four at a time at 19 or 20 minute intervals. They are violent, but do not manage to shake the building, only the metallic curtains vibrate. We count 40 explosions and it lasts until 6 A.M.

At 7, we go back to the surface and go towards the port, where many early rising spectators are going to inspect the damage. The Boulevard d'Aiguillon is a frightening spectacle of desolation. It is covered in earth, stones, glass,

The port of Antibes after being blown by the retreating Germans. Fort Carré, a renaissance period fort built by famous French military architect Vauban, is visible in the background, dominating the bay. Ferdinand Moscone Collection.

and metal debris, as well as numerous pieces of sheet metal from the airplane hangars (…). The electric and phone wires are hanging miserably. (…) The inside walls of some buildings collapsed. (…) The port is in an appalling state, but apparently it is not enough, because the Germans evacuate the area again and set off even more explosions. We count 20 more mines that finish off this "good work." (…)[9]

The Death of Unteroffizier Karl Häusig

As the days passed and the Allies drew nearer, the resistance not only became more active, but also less careful. Many people who had in fact never been *résistants* attempted last minute acts of bravado against the Germans in order to try to be remembered as "heroes of the Liberation." One such action in Plan Sarrain, north of la Napoule and only a few kilometers from the American lines, degenerated tragically August 22nd. Local youth **Pierre Esposito**'s father was a witness:

Some *maquisard*s had taken refuge in the hamlet [of Plan Sarrain]. There was a German soldier in the village square and one resistance guy tried to soften him up by offering him a glass of wine and saying: "Here, have some of our local wine, it is good." The German didn't want it, but after a while he took the glass. When he was drinking, "bang," the *maquisard* shot him. He wanted to take the German's gun, but had to kill him to do so. There were other Germans and they started shooting, and the *maquisard*s did the same, shooting two more Germans. They were only wounded, but they died later, I think. My father was 50 meters away, pretending to cut wood and looking at what was happening. When the Germans started shooting, some bullets passed between his legs and he was wounded by stone fragments.

The Germans took the entire village hostage and assembled everybody, including the women and children. We thought they were going to shoot everybody. Three *maquisard*s were found coming up to the village. They arrested them, and since they were armed they put them aside and they were executed immediately. In the meantime, the priest had arrived and had explained that the war was finished and that it was senseless to kill the *maquisard*s. He even said: "Take me as a hostage, I will sacrifice myself for them." One of the *maquisard*s named Traband had a Catholic German facing him and the German listened to the priest and only shot him in the shoulder. He didn't want to kill him, and after, when they were fired the *coup de grace*, he fired beside him. When the Germans left, the *maquisard* escaped and ran away through the forest and happened to stumble upon some more Germans who were camping. They all shot at him again when they saw him running through the woods, but they missed him and he went to his village at Auribeau.

36-year-old José Thomas, one of the two local résistants executed by the Germans in reprisal for the death of Unteroffizier Karl Häusig. Ville de Mouans Sartoux, Service des Archives.

"The Germans took the entire village hostage and assembled everybody, including the women and children." This photo was reenacted by the civilians after the departure of the Germans. These five grateful men also later erected a monument to the "Savior of Men" at the spot where they had been held hostage. Pierre Esposito Collection.

The Germans took the hostages and made them dig a hole for the dead German by the road. We put the two *maquisards* who had been executed in a trench and buried them just like that. Later we put them in the cemetery. After the Liberation there was a ceremony, and the *maquisard* who had shot the German came along, but everybody knew that the entire village had almost been executed because of him. My uncle told him: "If I had a gun, I would shoot you." The other guy pointed his gun at my uncle in front of everyone and said: "You are a traitor. But if I kill you, I will get arrested and go to prison, so it isn't worth it." The guy left for Africa afterwards. There were two or three of them that were *maquisard*s, but in order to take money for themselves.

The German soldier whose useless killing had initiated the whole event was *Unteroffizier* Karl Häusig, of the headquarters of *Reserve Grenadier Bataillon 327*. He was 28 years old and had

two children. The two *maquisard*s who were executed were **Josef Pallanca** and **José Thomas** (36 years old and also father of two children). The man who miraculously escaped the execution alive was Paul Traband. **Father Jaensen**, the priest who had intervened to try to save the three *maquisard*s, later wrote the following lines about the execution:

> Six soldiers lined up in front of them, commanded by a *Feldwebel*. The three Frenchmen asked not to be blindfolded; with a calm voice they said: "Vive la France [Long live France]" and the rifles crackled.[10]

The first Allied troops arrived in Plan Sarrain the very next day.

The German Withdrawal from Cannes and Antibes

August 23rd, the last battle in the Cannes area occurred at the RN7 bridge over the Béal, as described in the previous chapter. The next morning, the inhabitants of the area of Cannes and Antibes found the Germans had pulled out overnight, with only stragglers remaning behind. In the period between the German departure and the arrival of the Allies in the afternoon, the Resistance took control of the area. In Cannes, **Amélie Mougins** wrote the following in her diary:

Thursday, 24th of August 1944
We wake up at 5:30 A.M. We hear noises in the distance.
    7:30 A.M. Daniel arrives, saying that the FFI are in control of Cannes.
    8 A.M. Noelie is here. She confirms what Daniel says. In all directions we hear: "We are liberated... We are liberated..." We cannot believe it. Yet, every new person who arrives (...) says: "The Allies are here." Cannes is liberated.
    We go out on reconnaissance. In rue d'Antibes, where the crowd is moving about, people call out to each other and hug each other. We assault the shops that are selling flags. The houses are decorated with flags, everybody wears tricolor cockades and the Allied colors. Suddenly a rumor spreads: all the flags must be taken down, there is still danger. The Allies will only arrive in the afternoon.
    3 P.M. We are in the rue d'Antibes again. A loudspeaker announces: "No more German counterattacks now being feared, pull out the flags and wait for the Allies." (...) The

One of the numerous bridges in the Cannes area that was blown by the Germans in their retreat. Virtually not a single bridge was left standing on the French Riviera by early September 1944. Archives Municipales de Cannes.

sidewalks are swarming with people: the police are having difficulty preventing the crowd from reaching the street. We wait and wait. We find out that the FFIs are starting the *épuration* [Literally a "purge" or "purification" that occurred in almost all French towns after the Liberation to get rid of collaborators]; arrests are made. Some names are passed around.

6 P.M. Finally shouts, hurrahs: the first American armored vehicles arrive. It is madness. The crowd howls with joy. The armored vehicles are loaded with rather tired looking soldiers. We hang on to the tanks so much that we practically prevent them from driving through. There are shouts of: "Vive la France," "Vive l'Amérique," etc, etc… The sight of this demonstration is incredible. (…) Our chests dilate. We can breathe… Free, we are free at last.[11]

It would seem that not one single German soldier was killed in Cannes on August 24th. A fair number of German stragglers did, however, surrender to the Resistance before the arrival of the first American paratroopers. **Jean-Pierre Carbonel** was involved in accepting the surrender of one such group, which may be the same group that created the counter attack fears mentioned by Amélie Mougins:

Miniconi [a prominent resistance leader in Cannes] told me: "Supposedly there is a column of Germans coming down to Cannes. Go and see if it is true or not." I left with a friend of my father's who had a German grenade. I was forced to tell him that there was no detonator in the grenade. He had a 6.35 pistol with pearl handles and I had a 7.65 pistol, and in the meantime I had picked up a Carcano rifle. We left by motorcycle towards Mougins, going slowly, and there was nobody. We got to the electricity factory and there is a double "S" in the road. We passed the first "S," and at the second "S" we found ourselves in the midst of 30 or so Germans. Needless to say, they could have killed us just like that if they had wanted to. So we talked and they had come to surrender. They were the column of Germans that was coming back towards Cannes. They all had their rifles, but without bolts. Since I was a group leader, I took the German column and we left: me in front on the motorcycle and my henchman following behind. I told them: "Walk right in the middle of the road, otherwise an imbecile might start shooting." We went down to the

Palace of Justice in Cannes and there they were officially registered as prisoners of war.

A larger number of German soldiers remained in Antibes and Biot than in Cannes on August 24th, as these two towns were located further east and nearer to the next German defensive line on the Loup River. The coastal bridges over the Brague River, between Antibes and Villeneuve-Loubet, were supposed to be blown by the Germans, but the Resistance managed to take control in time to prevent this from occurring. Local resistance leader **Commandant "Gustel" Verine** wrote a memoir about the liberation of Antibes (written in the third person, in typical military style), in which he described the departure of the last Germans and the fighting at the Brague River Bridges:

Over the past 48 hours, the morale of the enemy has been low. German troop movements are always made at night and are always made towards the Var River. Discipline has slackened considerably. Isolated soldiers seize bicycles and carts to carry their gear and escape towards Nice. But the equivalent of three companies of Germans are still quartered around the Altana, in the Terriers forest. German soldiers are still holding the bunkers of the Cap d'Antibes, the Saramarter, the Sarrazine, etc…[12]

On the morning of the 24th, the *résistants* took control of Antibes, to the great satisfaction of the population. Things mostly went well, except at the bridges over the Brague, where one German soldier had to be killed before his comrades accepted surrender. Later on in the day, the Germans attempted a counterattack towards the bridges, probably in order to fulfill the mission of blowing them. **Gustel** continues:

At that moment, any fears seemed unfounded. The town was covered in flags and the population was rejoicing to be liberated. At the FFI command post, we were calmly getting things organized when alarming information reached Gustel. Successive and trustworthy information indicated a counterattack by the Germans towards Antibes and Biot. A column of *Miliciens* and soldiers coming from Cannes by the RN7 highway was preparing to reoccupy the Biot train station and the bridges over the Brague [The bridges and train station are all at the same location.], probably in order to destroy them before pulling out again.

Gustel immediately sent all the available armed FFI men towards the points that were threatened. (…) At the same time, Gustel sent messengers towards Cannes to ask for help from the FFI commander of that town and with the mission of meeting the Americans, if possible, to inform them that there were no Germans until the Brague River. (…) Before continuing the description of the events that followed, we must first come back in time to know what had occurred.

At 2 P.M., a truck loaded with *Miliciens* coming from Nice at full speed almost drove over the mines that had been put on the RN7 in front of the train station. It turned back before FFI Barone, from Biot, who was watching over the area, managed to intervene. All he could do was warn four other FFI comrades and two Gendarmes, as well as the command post at Antibes.

These patriots got into position, and when half an hour later a strong German patrol that was itself preceded by enemy elements showed up (…), it was received

L 29

The miserable remains of the Cap d'Antibes lighthouse that was destroyed by the retreating Germans. Frédéric Brega Collection.

with gunfire. The Germans also opened fire with their submachine guns and a few of them reoccupied a bunker because FFI reinforcements were arriving constantly.

The reinforcements were very badly armed and formed into three groups that surge forwards. With courage and boldness, and in spite of the casualties they suffer, they not only managed to push back the counterattack, but they threw the enemy back towards Villeneuve-Loubet. The enemy that took refuge in the bunker are surrounded. They surrendered after one of them was killed. On our side we had the deaths of two comrades to deplore: **Albert** and **Daver**. Four other comrades had been wounded: Rigel, Blanc?, Ferrari, and Gastine, who only accepted to stop fighting after his second wound.

Nevertheless, the situation is still dangerous. A truck full of German soldiers suddenly appears. It is immediately welcomed with intensive rifle fire and turns around and zigzags back towards the enemy bunker at the Deux Rives. While one group brings the prisoners and our wounded back towards Antibes, another group consisting mainly of gendarmes and policemen is left to watch over the scene of the fighting.[13]

The Deux-Rives was the next resistance point of the Germans, near the Loup River, and will be described in detail in Chapter 10. Two FFI men and two Germans were killed in the fighting at the Brague River Bridges. Two more Germans were killed by one of their own mines near Biot, as explained in the previous chapter. August 24th, the Germans therefore lost a total of four men killed

in the entire area spanning from Cannes to Biot. These FFI and German losses are summarized below (All the German killed were already included in the casualty list presented on pages 226-228.):

Surname	Name	Date of death	Location of death
Albert	Marius	24.8.1944	Biot Pont de Brague
Daver	Josef-Charles	24.8.1944	Biot Pont de Brague

Surname	Name	Rank	Age	Date of death	Location of burial
Buffen	Lars			24.8.1944	Antibes
Krapp	Willy			24.8.1944?	Antibes
Kirchner	Hermann	Kan	36	24.8.1944	Biot
Laske	Robert	Stbs Gefr	30	24.8.1944	Biot

We now revisit the day of the 24th in Antibes, as it was seen by a civilian, **Ferdinand Moscone**:

Thursday August 24th:
(…) 10 A.M.: Rumor has it that the FFI have occupied the post office and public buildings. Many young people with armbands or FTPF badges, armed with pistols, submachine guns, and grenades, are in the streets. Cars

The monument built for Marius Albert and Joseph-Charles Daver, who died while fighting back a German patrol at the Brague River Bridge, in Biot, August 24th, shortly before the arrival of American troops. Author's Collection.

The paratroopers of the 509th reach Antibes late August 24th, where they will take up defensive positions for the next few days. Ferdinand Moscone Collection.

A French Gendarme, Sgt Prince, of B Company of the 509th, and local children stand guard in front of the Antibes Gendarmerie, where some German soldiers are being held. Mike Reuter Collection.

After the heavy fighting they were involved in at la Napoule, paratroopers of B Company of the 509th take it easy in Antibes and Biot for a few days. From left to right: Edward J. Lejkowski, Pvt Albert S. Marzullo, Principe, and Pvt Justus F. Patrick. Mike Reuter Collection.

6:30 P.M: I hear noise on the route de Nice. Somebody shouts: "They are coming." I rush to the Pont du Marseillais just in time to see three American tanks loaded with soldiers arrive, so I take pictures of them. There is a frenzy, the people are crying and hugging each other. Many trucks follow and stop. The Americans are madly applauded.[14]

The Americans who arrived in Antibes were the same men of the 509th Parachute Infantry Battalion who had just driven through Cannes. After suffering at least 26 killed in the fighting at la Napoule during the previous four days, the 509th PIB had suddenly advanced 15 kilometers in a few hours against no resistance whatsoever. This was because the Germans had retreated, but also because the Resistance had taken control of Cannes and Antibes and made sure that no traps and ambushes were left along the road. The American column finally stopped in Antibes and the paratroopers took up positions at the Brague River, where the *maquisard*s had been fighting the German counterattacks earlier in the day. The front would remain static at the Brague River bridges until the 26th, as will be explained further on.

Conclusion

The Cannes and Antibes region was liberated by the soldiers of the 509th Parachute Infantry Battalion August 24, 1944, after the Germans

and motorcycles are going up and down the streets of the city. Flags are being pulled out from everywhere. In the blink of an eye, Antibes is covered with flags.

Around 11 A.M., numerous volunteers leave towards the Brague to attack a small German bunker. The FFI reach their goal, killing one German soldier and capturing three others. Unfortunately, we deplore the death of Charles Daver. There are a few wounded.

pulled out following the heavy fighting that had occurred over the previous four days. At least 42 American paratroopers had been killed at the gates of Cannes since August 20th, however, the French civilians and resistance fighters had not simply stood idle, and they also paid a heavy price for the liberation of their towns. Eight resistance prisoners were executed by the *Gestapo* in Cannes on the day of the Allied landing. Over the following two weeks and until the liberation, at least a dozen more resistance fighters would be executed or killed in combat in the general region of Cannes and Antibes. Furthermore, the shell fire of the Allied fleet caused numerous casualties among civilians. The Resistance gave valuable help to the Allies by providing them with intelligence, by helping and encouraging German defectors, by serving as guides, and by attacking isolated groups of German soldiers. The local population could therefore take pride in having played an active role in its own liberation.

A Word of Caution

In 1979, in his book *The Resistance to the Nazis in the South of France & the Story of its Heroic Leader Ange-Marie Miniconi*, British historian Peter Leslie made the claim that Colonel Schneider, the German officer in command of Cannes, had been ordered to blow all the hotels of the famous Promenade de la Croisette, on the Cannes seafront. Supposedly, local resistance leader Ange-Marie Miniconi managed to meet up with Schneider, convincing him not to blow up the hotels in exchange for which Schneider and his men would be given safe passage out of Cannes. Colonel Schneider then deactivated the detonation system that, following the sewers of the town, connected his HQ to all the beach front hotels that were packed with explosives and ready to be blown. According to Peter Leslie, Colonel Schneider was executed by the Germans for having negotiated with the Resistance in the following days.

It is notable that Peter Leslie does not give one single source to back these claims. Furthermore, no such story is mentioned in any documents written shortly after the Liberation, such as in local newspapers or in Honoré Isnard's booklet *Les Derniers Jours de l'Occupation et la Libération du Port et de la Ville de Cannes*. Mr Leslie seems confused about certain basic facts concerning the liberation of Cannes, even going as far as to believe that the town was liberated by the 141st Infantry Regiment! During my investigations for this book, no evidence was found of any Colonel Schneider having been executed (admittedly, any research is made considerably more difficult because of how common the name Schneider is), and no inhabitants of the Cannes area, including a person who had worked in the hotel business, knew about any hotels of the Croisette being packed with explosives. Similarly, no paratroopers of the 509th Parachute Infantry Battalion, who had visited the hotels very promptly after liberating the town have, to my knowledge, ever made mention of any explosives.

Considering the lack of sources, evidence, and witnesses (not to mention the doubtful description of the detonation system and the uselessness of the supposed mission), the whole Colonel Schneider story seems extremely unlikely.

Similar unproven claims have been made about an SS Colonel being shot and killed by resistance man Joseph le Fou, in the town of Nice, in the days before the Liberation. The burden of proof lies with the person making the assertion. If these officers existed and were killed, what were their names, where were they buried, and where is the evidence of their death? In Chapter 13 can be found the story of *Oberstleutnant* Hans Niedlich, who, like Colonel Schneider and the SS Colonel, was "killed" by historians multiple times, although he had in fact survived the war.

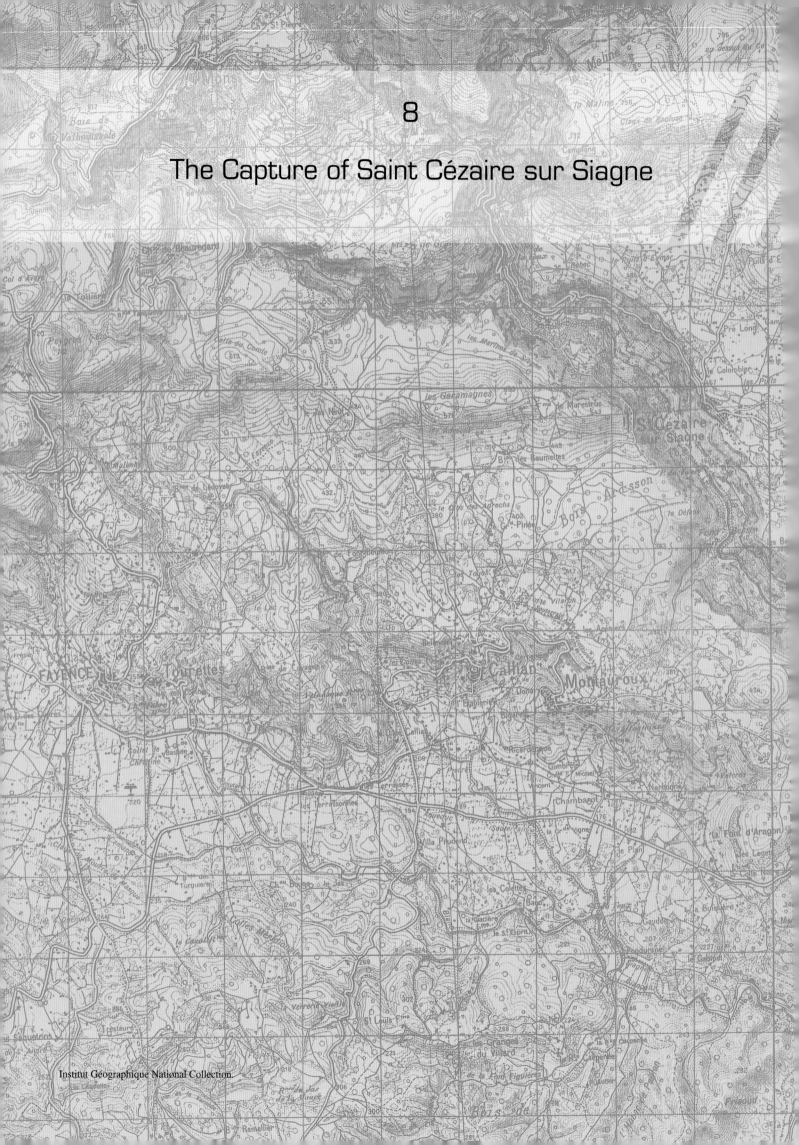

8

The Capture of Saint Cézaire sur Siagne

In chapter four, we described the liberation of the Fayence-Montauroux area by the 517th Parachute Infantry Regiment, the 141st Infantry Regiment, the French Resistance, and Captain Hanna's Office of Strategic Services (OSS) team. The last Germans had surrendered in Fayence the morning of August 21st. The next town that was on the path of the 517th PIR towards the east was St Cézaire sur Siagne, a small village built on a cliff on the east bank of the Siagne River, overlooking the Siagne Valley over many miles. The Siagne River Valley itself is approximately 300 meters deep with steep sides, and in the vicinity of St Cézaire it is crossed by only one small road that is clearly visible from the village. All these factors made St Cézaire an almost ideal defensive position for the Germans.

The Night of the Landing

As St Cézaire is rather remote, the Germans had only occasionally visited it during the occupation period, and there were therefore no Germans in town on the night of the Allied invasion. A few Allied paratroopers who were dropped particularly far off target landed on the western side of the Siagne Valley, where the inhabitants could see their parachutes in the trees the next morning. Local inhabitant **Marcelle Ardisson** remembers the morning of the invasion:

The morning of August 15th, I woke up at about 4 o'clock in the morning, and we could hear shelling over there in the Estérel: "Oh my God," I said, "they are coming!" So we were all happy. Then there were also paratroopers on the other side of the Siagne, we could see the parachutes. My God, everybody was boiling with excitement. Then some people met an Englishman who had gotten lost, and afterwards there was also a Captain, we called him Captain Grant. So they were picked up and brought into a house in the country to hide them, because there were still Germans around.

These two lost paratroopers, who had actually landed on the east side of the Siagne River, must have been among those dropped the furthest off target of the entire First Airborne Task Force. One of them was a Brit named Thomas and the other was Captain Grand Hooper, the commander of G Company of the 517th PIR. **Capt Grand Hooper** explained why he had landed so far from the rest of his company (that had already been dropped dozens of kilometers from its planned drop zone) in an after action report he wrote shortly afterwards:

Capt. G.A. Hooper, commander of Company G, had come in with the lead plane in the Company flight, and had not received the pre-planned warning the crew chief was supposed to signal to prepare the men to jump. When the signal came, Capt. Hooper was still working with a damaged harness on his own chute, but helped get the door load out and get his stick of men on the way. It was several seconds before the captain was ready to jump,

Capt Grand A. Hooper, the commanding officer of G Company of the 517th PIR, jumped out of his C-47 a few moments after the rest of his stick due to a technical mishap with his harness. This delay caused him to land in the vicinity of St Cézaire, completely isolated from any other Allied soldiers, with the exception of a British paratrooper named Thomas. Both men were hidden for a few days by the locals before being driven to the Fayence-Montauroux area by the Resistance. As can be seen by this photo, the two paratroopers were the number one tourist attraction of St Cézaire for the few days they stayed. Standing from left to right: Lucienne Mouton, Mr Chovot, Thomas, Mr Fernand, Capt Grand Hooper, Mme Chovot, Gaston Delucy, George Durante, and Henri Laugier. Sitting: Honnoré Dozole, Marcelle Ardisson, Mme Van Sentey, Mr Courbin, Marinette, Marise Laugier, and Robert Rossi. Marcelle Ardisson Collection.

but he bailed out as soon as he had his harness adjusted. He landed northwest of Grasse, approximately 40 miles from the drop zone, but contacted members of the French *Maquis*, who led him through the enemy lines to rejoin his outfit four days later.[1]

Captain Hooper and his British companion, after trailing into St Cézaire, were sheltered by the family of **Yvonne Bonhomme**, who remembered:

> One was an American called Captain Brandt who had landed in les Veyans. He had been here for about two days and then an Englishman named Thomas came out of the woods and walked into the village, so we brought him to the captain. We were afraid, since they were in the village, so my father said: "Damn it! The poor guys, we have to put them somewhere." We had a house on the road to St Vallier, so we took them up there to hide them. We didn't have anything to feed them because of the war time rationing, so people gave us things for them to eat.
>
> The American was a tall, strong, handsome man, whereas the Brit was much smaller and skinny. The two of them didn't speak too much, and you could tell that they didn't like each other very much. They just stayed a few days, then the *maquisard*s from the Var came to get them with a small car and they rejoined their army. They had written their names on the chimney in the house where we were hiding them. and when they left they said they would write to us. But you can imagine, maybe they were killed, who knows.

Ironically, hardly had Captain Hooper rejoined G Company and his men when he would have to return to St Cézaire to attack the village, as we will see later on.

Occupation by the Germans

In the days following the landing, St Cézaire was occupied by the Germans, probably as a measure to contain the paratroopers who had dropped in the Fayence-Callian area, but probably also because St Cézaire was part of the Siagne River defensive line that the Germans planned on defending. The soldiers that moved into St Cézaire were members of the 1st and 2nd Companies of *Reserve Grenadier Bataillon 7*, which had previously been stationed on the coast in the Monte-Carlo and Menton area. Upon arrival, the Germans started organizing their defensive positions. Mines were laid after a hairpin curve on the only road that crossed the Siagne Valley, leading to Callian and Mons. Foxholes were built with stones on the cliff north of the village that overlooked the valley and the road. All paths leading to the village were mined. The village formed the border between the zone controlled by the Germans and that controlled by the Resistance. All the area west and north of St Cézaire, in particular the village of Mons, was controlled by the *Maquis*, while Grasse and St Vallier to the east and northeast were firmly in German hands. As we saw in chapter four, the opposing forces were fighting for control of the Fayence-Montauroux area to the southeast.

Office of Strategic Services Action at Saint Cézaire

The first action occurred in St Cézaire the morning of August 21st, when a car departed from Resistance-controlled Mons, descended into the Siagne Valley, then headed up to the village. The vehicle was driven by resistance man Léon Roux, from Fayence, with Lt Walter

W. Taylor of the United States Marine Corps (USMC) and Office of Strategic Services (OSS) as his passenger. Lt Walter Taylor was not an average "Jarhead," but a 31-year-old archeologist who had enlisted in the USMC when the war started.[2] As they approached St Cézaire, the team ran headlong into the roadblock and mines that the Germans had prepared at the hairpin curve leading into town. **Lt Walter Taylor** later wrote a detailed report explaining why he and Roux had recklessly driven straight into a German strongpoint on their own:

> I was the Operations Officer of the OSS intelligence team for the 36th Division (Capt Justin Greene, Chief, Sgt (Michael?) Sweeny, USMC, assigned). [The 141st IR was part of the 36th ID and was fighting in Callian on the 20th, as explained in chapter four.] On D+5 we were behind the German lines, ahead of the Recon outfits that we passed on the road, to get information as to the intentions of the German division that was in Grasse and obviously intending to move; we wanted to know which way, to the attack or in retreat. That afternoon, we got to the town of Le Mons [sic], where there was a *Jedburgh* and a French Major of Marines attacking the local power house where the Germans had holed up. While Capt. Greene screened and selected an agent to go into Grasse, I went with some resistance fighters to look over the land and make plans for our trip. After we got back and we liberated a Citroën from beneath a hay stack, Capt Greene and Sgt Sweeney left to catch the headquarters of the 36th. I was to stay behind with the agent and the Citroën, accomplish the mission of taking him in and waiting and then taking him out, and then we were to get to the 36th as fast as we could. The agent had been leading the Resistance fight against the Germans ever since the landing and was absolutely exhausted, falling asleep time and time again while we were briefing him. I did not want to take him, but there seemed to be none other as competent ("when awake," as I put it). At dawn the next morning, the agent and I (after changing a flat tire) headed for the town of St. Cézaire, which was declared to be in the hands of the Resistance and where I was to let the agent down and wait for his return from Grasse. However, during the night, due to Allied pressure on Draguignan and Fayence, what evidently was a company of Germans had taken up positions in St Cézaire. On approaching the dead-still town by the steep and winding road, we ran into a roadblock of land mines; we both thought it was Resistance, and the agent took my carbine and jumped out of the car to walk toward the line of mines. He lasted just about ten feet beyond the car and died with a bullet through his head. I still thought it was the trigger-happy Resistance but started to get out of there . . . even faster when I finally saw a German forage cap behind some bushes above the road. But the car jammed against the outer coping, and a German jumped down on the road in front of me and threw a grenade under the car. I tried to get out of the right door and luckily did not, because I would have been completely exposed to the rifle fire from the high cliff on that side above the car. The grenade exploded and I was splashed unconscious on the road. When I came to, I was surrounded.
>
> It might be interesting to note that when I have thought about the incident of my capture, I have always pictured us as coming down a long hill and seeing, across a wooded stream valley, the site of the roadblock with men in uniform

scurrying about and climbing the cliff embankment. I have always blamed myself for thinking them to be Resistance and not recognizing them as Germans… and thus causing our trouble and the death of the agent. However, after years of trying, in 1963 I returned to the scene and found that the reality was quite different from my image, that the road did not go down the opposite side of the valley, that there were no trees, that the actual site of the roadblock is completely invisible from any part of the road until one is within about 20 yards; in other words, I could not possibly have seen men, of whatever persuasion, scurrying or been aware of the block! Strange tricks a (guilty) conscience can play. Anyway, after all these years I am finally free of my guilt! A marvelous feeling!

The grenade had shredded my left thumb and put ten or a dozen pieces of metal in my left leg (six of which at last count remain). I was taken to company headquarters, then to see the intelligence officer (of the battalion?); there I got some attention from a Major-Doctor. By car through strafing to Grasse, during which ride I got rid of a laundry list written on the back of a 2677th Hdq. Company (the cover for the OSS) letterhead: with my good hand I got it out of my pocket and stuffed it between the seat cushions (the company officer had returned it and my dog tags and map to me…[sic]!). In Grasse, I was interrogated, but finally managed to puke all over the interrogator, after which he left me alone. That night, they tried to move me with my *Feldwebel* guard out of Grasse eastward, but the wood-burning car broke down and we bummed a ride back to Grasse. The next day, with another vehicle, we left again. To Ventimiglia by night; I was brought into the operating room and some of the larger and more surface grenade splinters were removed by a doctor (civilian) and the sisters of the convent. That night, I had a violent serum reaction (I cannot take horse serum and told them so… but?). Next day to Genoa, where the Germans left me and a Czech prisoner alone on the top floor of a HDQ

building during a humdinger of an air raid. We had been almost continuously strafed along the coast road… each time the Germans left me in the car in the middle of the highway; after getting out on my own a couple times, I just said to hell with it and stayed put. Next night, at a regular German hospital in Alexandria, I was again interrogated, this time by a Major, who retreated and was never seen again after I had stuck my stinking hand under his narrow Prussian nose; he took all my papers with him and no one to my knowledge has ever seen them since… this was a good thing, about the only good thing that I did which had been learned in OSS schools. That night in Alexandria, I was delirious for most of the night. Next day or the second day, out by train for a long trip up into the Brenner Pass, then back out again to Verona for a day or two; then to Mantua for a somewhat longer stay; finally, by another train through the Brenner, Innsbruck to Bad… something (Bad Tolz?), then to Munich and Freising. By the time I got to Freising my wounds were pretty far gone with infection and I had a huge rash of carbuncles… which kept coming back until nearly the end of my captivity. After about two months in hospital, out to the Convalescent camp in Moosburg; after that, into the Transient camp. Towards the end of the latter, about early February, I was interrogated again: it was obvious that they were puzzled by me and also that they had no papers on me… nothing but my dog tags and two civilian pictures of my wife and me and my wife and child. I had heard that the Naval Camp was pretty good, and so when they asked me where I would rather go (yes, they did!), I told them I would rather go to the Naval Camp as a Marine then to the *Luftwaffe* Camp as a parachutist.[3]

Walter Taylor's account has brought us far from St Cézaire, but since he is one of the very few American soldiers who was captured in the Maritime Alps area, it is interesting to see the itinerary he followed. After the war, Walter Taylor returned to his archaeology, becoming a professor at Southern Illinois University, and authoring many papers and several books before dying in 1997. His work *A study of Archaeology* is still mentioned in archaeology textbooks to this day. Walter Taylor would probably have been amused to know that I was searching the area of his wounding in St Cézaire to find possible "archaeological" traces of the event.

August 21st, local 13-year-old Max Stèque witnessed the events in which Léon Roux was killed and Lt Taylor captured from his house in the northern part of town, very near the German roadblock and defensive positions. Though **Max Stèque** was young at the time, his excellent memory and blunt honesty make his observations particularly noteworthy, and his accounts will therefore be used often in this chapter:

The *Boches* were living here in my grandfather's garage, which was being used as a warehouse and contained wheelbarrows and construction tools. They had put a cannon on one side of the house and an M2 [MG 42] machine gun behind an electricity transformer. It was during the month of August, it was very hot, and all the windows were open. One morning two days before the liberation we heard rifle shots, then a short burst of machine gun fire, and then an explosion.

Actually, a car in which there was a man named Roux and an American officer had come from Fayence to see what was in the village. They had to be crazy; didn't they

The memorial stone that stands beside the road leading to St Cézaire where Léon Roux was shot and Lt Walter Taylor was wounded. Author's Collection.

The road leading to St Cézaire: Léon Roux was killed and Lt Walter W. Taylor wounded and captured after driving past the hairpin curve visible in the center of the picture. At the top left, Max Stèque's house and the electricity transformer where the Germans had emplaced a machine gun are visible. Mairie de St Cézaire Collection.

know there were *Boches* in town? They actually drove up in an open car and the *Boches* were waiting for them. When they saw an American uniform they shot them. The rifle fire we had heard was a team firing their Mausers, the burst was the M2 at the transformer, and the explosion had been a grenade. Roux was killed on the spot and the American officer was wounded.

I was in the street and my uncle told me: "Come back into the house!" But I entered one door and went straight back out another, because I was curious. I saw two Germans coming up the road, and a guy who was holding onto the shoulders of the Germans and jumping on one leg. I saw they were going to take the path that passed just under my balcony. I went back into my house, and when I got to the balcony, they walked by two meters below me. That is when I saw the guy jumping on one leg was in an American uniform and he had stripes. I think they were inverted Vs, but I am not sure. I think he was a Lieutenant. He was wounded: his leg was all limp and swinging around, and his pants looked like they had been dipped in blood. I thought: "The guy's leg must be completely smashed." They brought him to the German command post that was in front of the wash house.

The other guy who was dead (Roux) was still down there on the road, and with a friend called Jeannot, we went to Rue Mistral, from where we could partially see him from 200 meters away. We were saying: "Look, we can see the dead man, we can see the dead man! The *Boches* killed him, can you believe that?" We were happy to look at the dead guy from far off. There were Germans walking up and down who were also going to look at the man they had killed. Suddenly, there was a huge explosion and we saw a ball of smoke. The smoke dissipated in less than a minute, and from 200 meters away, we saw that there were what looked like about 20 dark stones on the road. We were happy, because the blast from the explosion had displaced the dead man's body towards the middle of the road and now we could see the whole body. Then two Germans arrived, one of which was pushing one of

my uncle's wheelbarrows. They picked up all those pieces of stuff on the road and put them in the wheelbarrow, then came back up. We didn't know anything about what happened after that.

The wheelbarrow was brought back to Max Stèque's garage, which the Germans were using as quarters. It was not until two days later, once the village had been liberated, that **Max Stèque** found out what the "dark stones" the Germans had picked off the road after the explosion and put into his uncle's wheelbarrow actually were:

On the morning of the Liberation, I got to where my kitchen is now, and the metal curtain was open by about a meter. I thought: "The *Boches* were here yesterday, let's see what is inside." I went in. I could smell something funny and I saw there was wheelbarrow filled with coal dust beside the door. I bent down towards a shelf because I saw a little flat box with German writing on it, and as I bent forward some flies flew off the wheelbarrow. I noticed that there were some hairs sticking out from the spot that the flies had just taken off from, so I pinched one of the hairs and pulled on it. I pulled out a piece of head with hair still on it; it was completely crushed, and I could see an ear that was blackened by coal dust. And that is when I understood what had happened with the wheelbarrow.

This is the explanation: the pieces that the Germans had picked off the road were actually a *Boche* who had gone to see the dead man and who had blown up on their own mines; they had mined the road, though we didn't know it. It was a Tellermine, with 12 kilograms [in fact 5.5 kilograms] of explosives in it, so the poor guy was blown to pieces. Then they sent guys down to pick up the pieces, and when they got back to the house they put coal dust in the wheelbarrow and left it there. And I found him two days later by discovering that piece of head. When I went out into the street, I saw my uncle and told him: "There is a dead guy in the wheelbarrow." He told the gamekeeper: "Qu'il est couillon ce petit. What a dummy this kid is."

Once again, mines had proven how treacherous they could be, even to their own people. The German soldier who had blown up on a Tellermine while examining the body of Léon Roux at the hairpin curve, and whose remains Max Stèque found in a wheelbarrow in his house, was 31-year-old *Obergefreiter* **Ernst Härtel**, of the 1st Company of *Reserve Grenadier Battalion 7*. Later on, **Max Stèque** was also able to observe the gory details of what happened to Léon Roux's body:

Roux had been killed on the road, and round noon the Germans brought him up to the intersection, also with a wheelbarrow, and they just left him there all afternoon in the sun. In August, in the heat, the guy had become swollen; he was enormous in that wheelbarrow. So I, being curious, wanted to walk down the sidewalk to see the dead

man, but a German came out, showed me the street and said to me, though not in a mean way: "Raus!" He didn't want me to go and look at the dead man, but I had time to see that there were swarms of flies buzzing around him, glinting in the sunlight. There were lots of them! In the evening, the Germans authorized us to bury the deceased. The carpenter had made a coffin, and they put the guy in the coffin, covered him with a sheet, and the local civilians went to bury Roux. The *Boches* weren't pleased at all, because the street was full of people accompanying the coffin, which meant that we were in cahoots with the terrorists; but they didn't say anything to us. We buried him in the earth at the cemetery, but we didn't even know what his name was.

At the time of the funeral, the identity of Léon Roux's body was not actually known, and it had to be exhumed after the Liberation to be identified by his family. Once again, **Max Stèque**'s curiosity got the best of him and he managed to witness the exhumation:

It was only about two weeks later that the family came to recognize the body and we found out that his name was Léon Roux and he was from Fayence. The grave digger, Joseph Raybaud, was one of my uncle's workmen. He only dug graves from time to time because people didn't die every day. I knew him well and I asked him: "Where are you going?" He said: "I am going to dig up the guy who died on the road. Do you want to come with me? It won't be pretty." But I went with him anyway.

We got to the coffin, which was still intact of course, but it was just a roughly-made coffin. With the corner of the shovel, he forced on it to pop the lid off. It wasn't even screwed shut; it was just closed with small nails. The cover came off and what I saw has stayed with me ever since: a black human shape, a dreadful smell, and masses of flies. Imagine if you put a thick layer of dead flies in a coffin and then lay a body into them. It looked like the guy was embedded in flies. It stunk!

The explanation is very simple: all those flies that had been buzzing around him for hours had laid their eggs on the body. When they buried him there was air in the coffin, the maggots became flies, the flies were born, and then they suffocated and formed those masses of flies that were around him. It was an atrocious sight. The body was completely black. There was a sheet over him that had also become black, because the body was in complete decomposition. It was all rotten, all liquid. Then I left, because the grave digger told me: "The family is going to arrive, it would be best if you left." Afterwards, he told me that they had recognized him by his shirt, because he had a shirt with stripes on it.

Obergefreiter Ernst Härtel, aged 31, and the letter that Lt Georg Stein, the commander of the 1ˢᵗ Company of Reserve Grenadier Bataillon 7, sent to his father. Lt Stein explained that Härtel had been killed for "The Führer, the people and the Fatherland" by stepping on a mine, and that his body had been buried in a cemetery in Grasse (which was incorrect). Erna Engler Collection.

The Battle for St Cézaire

Let us now return to August 21st. On that day, while Léon Roux and Lt Taylor were getting killed and wounded, respectively, the 517th Parachute Infantry Regiment was capturing the last Germans of the Fayence-Montauroux area at La Roche, in Fayence. The next day, the 517th PIR advanced towards the Siagne River Valley and arrived in view of St Cézaire. The men of the 517th were absolutely unaware of Lt Taylor's botched reconnaissance mission from the previous day, and were at first also under the impression that the town was unoccupied by Germans. The regimental commander, **Colonel Rupert D. Graves**, described the departure from Callian and the arrival at the Siagne River in a postwar publication:

> Twelve miles farther on [after Callian] was the town of St Cézaire, situated at the peak of a very formidable looking hill overlooking a long, narrow valley. To approach the town over anything but a steep, precipitous slope would involve many miles of circuitous travel over roadless terrain. No enemy was encountered on the way to St Cézaire, and from an observation post, it looked as if the town was deserted. One company of the 3rd Battalion was ordered to cross the ravine and attack the town frontally, while another company cut around and hit the town from the other side. The attack was to start at 7 P.M. During the afternoon, Cato [Lt Col Raymond Cato, Commander of the 460th Pack Field Artillery Battalion] ranged his artillery in, and as the advance on the town started we could see Germans rushing from the buildings to positions overlooking the ravine.[4]

Company G, under the command of Captain Grand Hooper, was to attack St Cézaire, with I Company in support. However, before going into more details about the actual attack, let us see what the effects of Cato "ranging his artillery in" had in town. As always, **Max Stèque** remembers the events with precision:

It started quite early. There was a first explosion and my uncle said: "Quick, let's go to Melchior's basement." Melchior had two vaulted basements and had told the locals: "If something happens, come to my basement, it is solid." So we quickly left for Melchior's. At the angle of the street we heard a whistling sound and my uncle pushed me; I fell down onto the sidewalk and he lay down on me. We heard a huge explosion because a shell had hit the house 30 meters away from us, across the street from the house we had just come out of. I remember my uncle saying: "They are dead." He thought my two aunts had followed us out into the street, but they actually had not come out yet, and we were 50 centimeters past the critical point. Some fragments had hit the road and the front of the house.

They then reached Melchior's basement, but **Max Stèque**'s uncle went back out after hearing that a woman had just been killed:

He went to see what was going on and then was not coming back. When he did come back he had blood on his hand, and we thought he was wounded, but he said: "Me and the gamekeeper just picked up Santoro's wife. She was killed by one of the first shells we heard. She received a fragment in her neck that cut her carotid and she bled out like a rabbit." She had been killed on her balcony while hanging out her laundry. She was the only victim of the shelling of St Cézaire. It was the Americans who were firing at us.

The woman who had been killed was **Cézarine Santoro**. There were actually some other "victims" of the shelling, but they were thankfully not human, as local resident **Marcel Raybaud** remembers. The presence of the Germans had forced his parents-in-law to move all their chickens into a henhouse that a neighbor lent them:

A view of St Cézaire from the north. The village is visible to the left, overlooking the Siagne River Valley. The 517th PIR reached the area from the right side of the picture, coming from Callian. As can be seen, St Cézaire and the Siagne Valley represented a formidable defensive position to be overcome. Author's Collection.

A shell landed right in the henhouse. Out of 15 chickens only one was left alive. So the whole street was eating chicken for two weeks afterwards.

In the meantime, G Company of the 517th had started crossing through the Siagne Valley, following the only road, and was now approaching St Cézaire. They had apparently underestimated the German defenses and several men were shot in quick succession as they neared the town. **Elsworth Harger**, of G Company, witnessed this fire fight, and though his recollection of it is not very well written, it is the only firsthand account describing the initial fire fight that seems to exist:

We sure climbed a long way up the "back side." As I recall, we lost at least three good men near the top. Two were killed instantly, and a third died while being treated by the medic—Nolan, I believe. I was next to top this ledge and had one leg cocked to push me through when Lt MacElroy shouted "I see him" and killed him. This German soldier was an expert sharpshooter. He killed the first two troopers instantly with a shot in the head, and I believe the third man, a Mexican American [**PFC Hector H. Colo**], was shot in the chest area.[5] [In fact, Hector Colo had been shot through the upper left thigh, near the groin, probably severing his femoral artery.] While Nolan was working to save him, this sniper fired and just creased both breast muscles, breaking his dog tag chain, then a second shot barely creased one wrist. I truly believe he was only annoying Nolan, knowing he was a medic, and had no intention of seriously hurting him. Nolan should have been decorated for his determination to stay on the job despite being harassed by the sniper!

A group of G Company soldiers had been caught by surprise as they advanced and had paid heavily in consequence. **Staff Sergeant Nello Arterburn**, of G Company, mentioned the event in a letter he sent home to his wife:

I've seen many of them get killed, I won't name any of them because you wouldn't know them, except one. You remember Goswick, don't you, the one that drove the car for us when we got married? He got shot in the back; when he fell, he said: "They got me," and the same day in about an hour they got four of my men.[6]

J. B. Hampton

PFCs Jesse O. Goswick (below left), J.B. Hampton, and Charles F. Stanford; three of the four G Company men who were killed outside St Cézaire. Goswick Family Collection/517prct.org. Hampton Family Collection, courtesy Tony Burriss and Catherine Edwards. Joe Simpson Collection. Venango County Historical Society Collection; courtesy Marianne S. Battista.

The four men from G Company who were killed were:

Surname	Name	Rank	Unit	Age	Date of death	Location of death	Official cause of death
Colo	Hector H.	PFC	G Co 517 PIR	19	22.8.1944	St Cézaire	GSW L thigh
Goswick	Jesse O.	PFC	G Co 517 PIR		22.8.1944	St Cézaire	
Hampton	J B	PFC	G Co 517 PIR	20	22.8.1944	St Cézaire	GSW R side
Stanford	Charles F.	PFC	G Co 517 PIR	30	22.8.1944	St Cézaire	SFW forehead

William Bowers, of G Company, attempted to approach the German positions to investigate further and barely escaped with his life:

August 1944, somewhere in the Maritime Alps, advancing upwards towards a town on a zigzagging snake-like road with cutout shoulders on the left and drop-off into terraced vineyards on the right, we were stopped by mortar and machine gun fire. I dropped on the left side of the road into a shallow drainage ditch. I have always disliked a one-sided show, so after a while I started crawling up the ditch to see where the shooting was coming from. As I came to the switch back to the right, while I heard nothing (the speed of light is much faster than the speed of sound), I saw either dust or smoke from the machine gun barrel muzzle as it was fired. I immediately dropped flat and the bullets passed over me. I waited a little, then fired four times where I saw the dust, then flattened out. Soon the machine gun fired again and the bullets passed over again, but much closer. I hesitated, then fired three times and was answered by a rifle shot. Something slapped me hard on my left thigh and I thought I was wounded, but reached back and found no blood. Must have been a piece of rock chipped off by the bullet. Now I knew I was dealing with two of them. I removed the clip with one bullet remaining so that my friends would think I had a bullet ready to fire. I put a full clip in and fired three times, then removed the remaining five bullets and inserted another full clip. Since I was firing up hill, I raised my rear sight and waited. There was another rifle shot and the bullet just barely passed over me. I felt the next shot they took would probably kill me.

During this last exchange of shots, I remembered the advice a WWII veteran had given me on my last furlough. He said: "Billy, remember all you have been taught during training, but keep a 'Goose-Creek trick' up your sleeve." With my sight raised and a full clip installed, I took my turn and fired three times, hesitated to give them time to raise up to shoot, then fired four more times while moving my shots around to cover their position. I dropped flat again and waited for the shot that would kill me, realizing I would not hear the sound of it. After a while, I realized enough time had passed for their shot and began to think I would live.

I told Lieutenant Ridler "if they shot again they would open me up from one end to the other." He said that as soon as the artillery barrage came over to quickly cross to his side, and I did! I fired two of my rifle grenades like a mortar to where I believed they were located. We kind of slept on the road that night, and the next morning, Lieutenant Ridler told me that he had sent somebody out to check and they found two of my adversaries. The advice my WWI friend gave me worked.[7]

G Company's attack had been stalled as the men took cover from the deadly German fire. I Company, which had been held in reserve, was thus ordered to cut directly through the Siagne Valley to attack in support of G Company. They were led by Captain Fastia, whose reputation amongst his men was very poor (he was relieved of his command shortly afterwards). **Pvt Marvin Moles**, of I company, remembers the attack:

G Company got pinned down on that mountain and we went right up to them. I think they killed two or three of our guys and wounded a few. I was in the 2nd platoon, and Captain Fastia was up next to the first platoon; when the firing started, he came running back down, knocking us right and left like pin balls, saying: "Go get 'em boys, go get 'em!" That rascal was something else. He went down

there and got in the back of the line, and then, after all the shooting was over, he came on up. But that's about the way his life was.

I don't know how many Germans were there, but they sure were shooting at us; it sounded like a hornet's nest. G Company was pinned down, and we went right up over them. I think a sniper must have been shooting, because I came up on this boy from G company. He was lying down under a rock, and he said: "Get down, you can't go up through there!" and I said: "Well, I ain't got time to stop, I have to keep going!" But then a bullet came right beside my face. I felt the heat of it as it went by me, the air was just plain hot. It must have been a hairbreadth from my head. So I guess it was just the good Lord didn't intend for me to die. The way the bullet came, I am sure it was a sniper.

Milton Rogers was a forward observer in C Battery of the 460th PFAB and accompanied I Company during its progression towards St Cézaire. He describes the type of terrain the paratroopers faced during their climb through the Siagne Valley and the intensity of the German fire in particularly good detail:

There was an attack on a little town on top of a terraced hill. We in America can't conceive of the shortage of land in Europe. This hill had stone walls built about four feet high, and then the dirt leveled off—sort of level—for six or eight feet, and another wall built. There were olive trees planted on the flat places.

Why an attack in the late afternoon I never figured out. Some things are just not meant to be understood in this life. The *Boche* had some mortars up on the top and they knew how to use them. There was a trail zigzagged up the hill, with breaks in the walls and steps, not in a straight line like a stair, but staggered. The *Boche*, who had time to practice, dropped a mortar shell on each flat place on that hillside. They were good.

Lt. Freestone and I were separated from our communication guys in the confusion. We were maybe halfway up the hill when the shells started dropping. We got a ways off the trail, not far enough, and were lying down maybe eight to ten feet apart, close to the uphill wall for our shelf. The shell that landed on the shelf above us killed a man, and the shell on the shelf below us killed a man. I hardly believe this myself, but it happened. The shell that fell on our shelf lit between us. It probably would

"A bullet came right beside my face, I felt the hot air from it as it went by me. It must have been a hairbreadth from my head." 21-year-old Pvt Marvin D. Moles, who barely missed being shot during the attack on St Cézaire. Marvin Moles Collection.

have killed or seriously wounded us both, except for one thing. It was a dud. It didn't explode.[8]

Luckily, many of the mortar shells the Germans fired on that day did not explode. However, **Pvt Richard Sailor**, of I company, was killed by a mortar shell on the way up, as his fellow trooper **Walter Ammermon** remembers:

We were on the way up to the town and we were getting mortar fire, but a lot of them were duds; we could hear them clank but there was no explosion. I had one guy killed right behind me. He was an arm's distance from me, right square behind me, and was wounded in the chest and the stomach by one of the mortars. He was moaning at first, so I gave him a shot with one of those little morphine syrettes to ease his pain. I was wondering if maybe I did wrong by giving it to him when he was wounded in the stomach, but the medic said: "No, he got it so bad he wouldn't have lived anyway." He was an Indian boy and we called him Chief.

Several other men from G and I Companies were wounded by mortars, one of which was **Pvt Joe Mackiewicz**, of I Company:

I was wounded at St Cézaire along with Tony Esparza as we were advancing up a terraced slope. The Germans were throwing mortar and artillery fire at us at the time. From St Cézaire, I was sent to a military hospital in Naples, Italy. I was mostly on cloud nine during this trip, so I don't remember much of the trip back to Naples. The doctors removed some shrapnel from my lower back and butt. The doctor told me that I would probably have some trouble with my back and left leg and that I may look forward to a full recovery, but that it would come back to haunt me in my later years, which it has.

Major Forrest Paxton, commanding officer of the 3rd Battalion of the 517th, was awarded a Silver Star for his actions at St Cézaire, the citation of which details the conditions faced during the attack:

Pvt. Richard
Sailor
White Earth

Pvt Richard Sailor, of I Company, was killed by a mortar shell while climbing up the steep terraced valley towards St Cézaire. Richard Sailor was a full-blooded Ojibwe Indian, whose father had been wounded and gassed in France during WWI. Their traditional Ojibwe name was "Be-gay," meaning Partridge, but the father had been forced to take the name "Sailor" upon enlisting in the U.S. army in WWI. Becker County Historical Society and Museum Collection, courtesy Amy Degerstrom.

During the attack on St Cézaire, France, the unit commanded by Lieutenant Colonel Paxton [he had been promoted in the meantime] was forced to cover difficult terrain, it being necessary to descend a steep gorge and crawl up a steep, precipitous slope to reach the enemy. The leading companies were pinned to the ground by intense enemy small arms and mortar fire. Lieutenant Colonel Paxton, exposing himself to intense enemy fire and displaying great physical endurance, courage, and leadership, made his way to the leading companies, encouraging individuals and units to advance and close with the enemy. The enemy, being in a superior position, inflicted many casualties, and Lieutenant Colonel Paxton made his way among them, encouraging them to keep under cover."

Some men of the 3rd Battalion later commented that Paxton had received the medal for simply "being there"... but at least he was actually up front with his men. **PFC Guy Carr**, of I Company, was among the men who tried to break the stalemate by aggressively attacking the Germans. He later wrote his memories of the battle:

We were now nearing the foothills of the Maritime Alps, and the fighting was becoming more and more intense. The terrain was more rugged, and the villages and towns were built on mountain crests, causing our forces to attack up the slopes directly into the enemy positions. The Germans had complete advantage of the high ground throughout this area. This was a great disadvantage to any forces attempting to capture the enemy while the high ground was in their possession. You had to move up the hill or mountain and face what was known as "plunging fire." (…)

"G" Company and my Company "I" were moving single file up a trail, heading toward the base of a hill upon which stood the village of St Cézaire. We encountered a rock wall (about four feet high) just to our right. German mortars started slamming into our column, and one shell landed in front of me. It exploded and blew one fellow completely over the wall. The concussion was so bad that he never had a chance to survive. Another fellow was knocked down by the blast and when he got up he looked around, quite dazed, and said: "My God, I must have been hit by a ton of s—t."

We finally approached the foot of the hill and "G" Company started up the slopes, but were trapped by fire from everything the Germans had to offer. They were really pinned down and could not move at all. My company started up the slope under murderous fire from the enemy. We finally fought our way beyond "G" Company, and every foot progressed up that hill was Hell. It was terraced with rock walls that were about four feet high. We had to climb over the walls, then crawl about 20 feet just to be confronted with another wall.

We spent all day long on the side of that hill under constant mortar, machine-gun, burp-gun [submachine gun], and grenade fire. Just prior to sundown, our two companies had nearly reached the top. Somehow another trooper and I became separated from the rest of the company, and foolhardy as he was, said, "Let's take this God damned town." The two of us proceeded towards the town under cover of brush and rocks. There were more rock formations about 100 yards from the town, and the German troops were using the rocks as their defensive line.

The two of us were in a real predicament here. We would take turns standing up and giving them Hell with our M-1 rifles, and how either of us kept from getting hit, I'll never know. I often think back to that day and say to myself: "What a damn fool you were to even attempt such an outlandish, crazy thing as that." I was, however, awarded the Bronze Star Medal (which I received some thirty years later). We were still continuing our method of advancement when our companies came up the hill and surged into St Cézaire.[10]

It was **Sgt Franck Dallas**, an excellent soldier of I Company, who finally managed to turn the tide of the battle by single-handedly sneaking through the German defense line and opening fire on them from behind:

I keep living it over and over again. We were attacking, I Company in the lead, G Company behind us, and when we started going up the hill we received mortar fire and small arms fire from machine guns and rifles. They had us pinned down and a few of my men were wounded. We were lucky that some of the mortar rounds were duds because they landed right in the middle of the platoon.

I took off across the field and got to the bottom of the terraces, and the Germans were about 30 feet above me. They were throwing concussion hand grenades from the top and one of the grenades rolled me over. They must have thought I was dead, but I got up and found a path which went to the left and behind them. When I popped up I didn't realize I was behind them. Then I finally realized and I started picking them off one by one as they were shooting down at my men coming up the hill. I had enough cover and could see them, and I would go from place to place. It reminded me of a turkey shoot. I killed seven, just shooting them from behind. They didn't know where it was coming from.

Then they saw where I was and four came after me. I would shoot one and run around and shoot another one, and I finally got rid of those four, too. They couldn't see me long enough to get a bead on me. After the 11th, which included a machine gun, I heard mortars firing. I destroyed the mortar by throwing their own grenades in the tube; that got rid of that. I got rid of everyone that was on top of that hill.

I know there's one thing I will never forget. There was a German who was sitting wounded. He wasn't wounded from me, he was wounded from one of our shells or something that hit him. He was holding on to his guts and his rifle wasn't very far from him. He pointed to his rifle; he wanted his rifle, I guess to shoot himself, but I wouldn't trust putting a rifle in his hands. So I took a potato masher and I put the string in one hand, put the potato masher in the other hand, and I told him to wait until I was a distance before he pulled it. And he pulled it, and I was 40 yards away when it blew up. He killed himself because he was dying a slow and painful death. I never mentioned that to many people.

Then we came up, and we took the hill and set up defenses. I received the French *Croix de Guerre* with the Bronze Palm and the Silver Star. After that I took a patrol into St Cézaire. There was Sgt Castonguay, myself, and Minano. We went into two or three of the houses, and Castonguay spoke fluent French, as he was French Canadian. They told him there were five Germans down in the basement, and we captured them and turned them over. They didn't want to fight, they gave up to start off with.

Sgt Dallas's story may seem difficult to believe, but it was confirmed by the other men of his unit and by the fact that he received the Silver Star. Only the exact number of German soldiers he killed seems overestimated, as in fact only nine Germans were later found dead on the battlefield, as we will soon see, and according to other witness accounts, he alone was not responsible for the death of all nine of them. Because **Frank Dallas**'s officer was killed in the following months, he did not receive his Silver Star until 1997, the citation of which read:

On 27 August 1944 [the date is incorrect], while moving toward a German defensive position, while serving in Company I, 3rd Battalion 517th Parachute Infantry Regiment in the town of St. Cézaire. Company I's 2nd Platoon became pinned down under heavy machine gun and mortar fire. Staff Sergeant Dallas, a Squad Leader in 2nd Platoon, suddenly dashed across an opening that was under heavy small arms fire and mortar attack. He successfully crossed the opening and reached the base of the cliff. He then climbed the 35-foot cliff and found himself behind the German positions and line of fire. Using his rifle, he quickly killed five enemy soldiers before they could determine from where they were taking fire. He continued across the German line of fire and killed six more enemy soldiers with his rifle and knocked out the machine gun and mortar replacements with hand grenades. His actions cleared the way for the remainder of the company to join him on the top of the cliff and complete their attack. Staff Sergeant Dallas's voluntary act and selfless concern for his fellow soldiers reflect great credit on himself, his unit, and the Army of the United States.

Betet in christlicher Liebe
für meinen drittältesten Sohn u. unsern lieben Bruder
Klemens Feldkamp.

Der liebe Verstorbene war geboren zu Schöppingen am 28. Sept. 1926. Nach 17 jähr. Ungewißheit erhielten wir jetzt die schmerzliche Nachricht, daß er auf dem Ehrenfriedhof Dagneux (Frankreich) zur letzten Ruhe gebettet ist. Möge er nun mit seinem Vater und seinen beiden Brüdern den ewigen Frieden gefunden haben und mit Ihnen im Himmel vereint sein.

17-year-old Grenadier Klemens Feldkamp, who was killed at St Cézaire. Klemens came from a family of eight children that had moved to Silesia in 1937. The three eldest brothers, including Klemens, were enlisted into the army and all three were killed. Their father was later deported by the Russians and died in Siberia. Feldkamp Family Collection.

It must have been about half a mile from where they started shooting at us from the top of the village to when we came out into the village. Somehow Frank Dallas got around behind the Germans. He climbed his way up the bank and he got around behind them and started shooting them from behind, I think. Old Frank, he said: "I shot 'em all twice: one time to knock 'em down and the next shot to keep 'em down." He is a character.

I just kept going up the hill, so when we got to the little old village, the Germans had darn gone. I guess we had run them all out. I think we had lost five men, and about 18 or 20 were wounded, but I think we left a whole sack full of Germans dead, and of course, I don't know how many were wounded. Whenever they left, they took the wounded with them. Then we went on in the little old village and spent the night.

Although most of the soldiers killed at St Cézaire were Silesians, some of them were true diehards, nonetheless. Frank Dallas's method of verifying that the soldiers he had shot actually were dead by shooting them a second time was not just an extravagant precaution, as is proven by the recollection of I Company's **Corporal John Rupczyk**:

We started up the mountain, and when we got maybe almost halfway up they started shooting at us with machine guns and mortars. They were throwing a lot of mortar shells, but a lot of those were duds, so you've got a lot of shells still sitting in the ground up there someplace. We had this Indian fellow that was with us in another platoon, so he was 300 or 400 feet away from me and all I heard is that he got killed, I didn't see what happened. So we started up the hill; one or two guys would jump over these terraces and the machine guns would keep on shooting, then somebody else would get up there and go. This was probably about three o'clock in the afternoon, and then we got up to maybe 150 feet from the top of the mountain and we called our artillery in. They shot I don't know how many rounds, but they hit the top of that hill an awful lot with artillery shells and that is where the German soldiers were.

Finally, around 6 or 6:30, we made it to the top. I had two guys with me that I had picked up going up the hill: one guy had an M1 rifle, the other one had a little carbine, and I had a Tommy gun. The three of us started to walk around up there and it was kind of dark already, then all of a sudden there were two explosions probably eight or ten feet away from us. I didn't know what the heck it was so I hit the ground, and I saw these two guys fall over the terrace and I thought they were dead. I got up and ran forward, and got to what looked like a big rosebush and I dropped down behind that. I laid there for a little while and it was getting kind of late, so I stood up, jumped around that rosebush, and I jumped right over a dead German. I thought he was dead; I went a little ways and then all of a sudden I happened to think about what a Polish soldier told me in Italy: "Never go past a dead German. You make sure he is dead. A lot of American boys paid the price for that at Cassino."

So then I stopped and I stood there. I looked at the German and he was a young guy, just about like me, and then here come the two guys I thought were dead. One came around and I told him: "Shoot that guy, make sure he is dead." So he shot at the German but missed him, then

33-year-old Grenadier Alois Matlok, who was killed at St Cézaire, pictured with his wife and two daughters. He had managed to keep out of the army until 1943, before finally being called up, despite protests from the company he worked for in Silesia. Matlok Family Collection.

Private Marvin Moles, of I Company, describes the end of the battle from where he was:

We fought like grizzlies going up the mountain, and it was just from one tree to another. The password was "Yellow" and "Three," I believe. If you couldn't see somebody, you would holler: "Yellow" and then of course the guy on the other side would say "Three." Or if he said "Yellow," you would say "Three." We had this one old sergeant, Sergeant Bordfiel, he was a great big old guy. He was about 35, and he had been in the army all of his life, I guess. He was going up through the woods there hollering: "Yellow... Three... Yellow... Three." He was saying both sides of the password and he had a real deep bear-toned voice, and it sounded funny. We all teased him about it the next day, but he chewed us all out.

he stepped over him and came over and sat down by me. We both sat there beside the German, looking at him, and he was laying on his side, facing us. It wasn't long before the other guy came along and he sat down with us, and all three of us were looking at this German. Then one of them said: "Well, we gotta get ready to get going" so I told him: "You had better shoot this guy, make sure he is dead." So the guy shot the German in the belly and he started to scream, and so then the other guy also shot him. I think now that we probably should have taken him prisoner, but when you are fighting you do things a lot different. This German was just a kid, so he probably wasn't quite sure of himself, but if I would have went along, he would have shot me. By that time we had the whole company together and we stayed on the mountain top all through the night, and in the morning we started to go to town.

Colonel Rupert Graves, who had been viewing the battle from the other side of the valley, noticed that the German resistance collapsed suddenly, presumably as Sgt Dallas infiltrated the German positions:

It looked as though Company I was going to have a tough time scaling the steep and long approaches to the town, as already mortar fire was beginning to fall. However, they kept on climbing and most of the mortar fire seemed to land in back of them. As they approached the top, German machine gun fire could be heard for a while, and then suddenly died out. Darkness now had fallen, and the advancing troops could no longer be seen. Finally the message came back that the town had fallen…[11]

During the fighting, the French inhabitants of St Cézaire were hiding in their basements, but several of them who looked outside, such as **Marcel Raybaud**, noted that some German soldiers (in fact probably Poles) were not interested in fighting at all:

There were German army recruits who were refusing to fight, they wanted to surrender. With my own eyes, I saw an officer with a pistol at the fountain in the town square, pointing his gun at soldiers in the old village. He was firing at the young soldiers who were trying to retreat. It was almost like in a western movie. He was preventing the young ones from retreating or leaving. When we saw that he was firing and understood what was going on, we got out of there.

Then we don't know what happened, but all the Germans retreated in no time. People slowly started going out and we saw that the Americans were nearby. The next morning, we realized that there had been some killed. If I remember correctly 11 Germans were killed here, and seven or eight Americans.

Max Stèque was hiding in a basement from which he could hear the sounds of the fighting. He describes the night, and the arrival of U.S. forces into the village the next morning:

During the night they were fighting behind the wall, they were 30 meters away from us. We could hear shouts, gunfire, explosions, like grenades exploding, maybe mortars, rifle shots, and every now and then shouts, guttural shouts like orders. We could hear everything.

In the morning, at daylight, the owner of the house said: "Its calm outside, I am going to take care of the mule." Then

we saw him come back immediately and he told us: "Soun aqui. They are here." I asked: "But who is here?" He answered: "The Americans." The street was full of Americans, big tall unshaven guys with beards, covered in gear.

They signaled to us that they wanted to eat. Melchior gave them Eau de Vie [Brandy], but they didn't like it, they weren't used to it; but they did like wine. They gladly accepted anything we gave to them, like tomatoes, and we gave them what we had. They asked for bread, but we didn't even have any for ourselves. Then a woman came along with a bunch of chickens in each hand. A shell had landed on her henhouse and it had killed all the chickens. So she gave us some and we had chicken for lunch.

The taste that American paratroopers in southern France had for tomatoes is almost legendary among the local inhabitants, and the gourmet Frenchmen were shocked to see the Americans "bite into them as if they were apples." **Marcel Raybaud** describes his impressions of the first Americans:

Very early the next morning, soldiers were walking by, but they were not coming into town. Only a few officers and men came into the village. They came from all kinds of countries. I know I found two of them, and one of them asked me for tomatoes. To give me his nationality he was telling me: "Me ruski, me ruski!" so he was Russian. I gave him two or three tomatoes. They were crazy about fresh fruits and vegetables because they were sick of eating canned food. They would eat them with an eagerness that was unthinkable!

Marcelle Ardisson recalls the arrival of the paratroopers from the point of view of a female inhabitant:

One morning we heard: "They are here." I took off running, and in the middle of the road there was a tall American. I jumped onto him and kissed him and he didn't budge. We were so happy! They kept on arriving during the whole day and we hugged them. Everybody gave them crates of peaches and tomatoes and everything. They, who had been eating canned food for so long, ate the tomatoes just like that. We put fruits out on our doorsteps so that they could make the best of them.

In the afternoon they were at the hotel. They gave their canned food because the cook didn't have enough to feed all those men. With a friend we were in the kitchen washing up. Every now and then an American soldier came in to speak to us, but we didn't understand what he said, so we kissed him and that was that.

The **Bonhommes**, who had helped hide the two misplaced paratroopers on D-day, had the pleasure of seeing Captain Grand Hooper returning to St Cézaire safe and sound at the head of G Company:

When the Americans arrived by the Siagne road, we went there with Dad, and we met Captain Brandt. He was leading his men and coming into the village.

The Aftermath of the Battle

The morning after the battle, **Colonel Rupert Graves** went to examine the battlefield where he had lost five men and where Frank Dallas had shot up the Germans from behind:

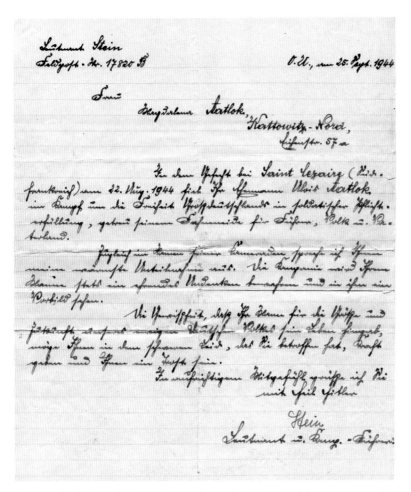

The letter that Lt Georg Stein sent back to the family of Alois Matlok, announcing that he had been killed in combat. The letter contains no factual information, apart from the date and location of death. It is, however, notable that the company commander was able to know anything at all after the violent American attack. Interestingly, the letter has been written by a person with very neat handwriting, and was then only signed by Lt Stein, whose own less fancy handwriting is visible in the previously shown Ernst Härtel letter. Matlok Family Collection.

Frank Dallas remembers Colonel Graves' visit to the site of his Silver Star earning exploits:

The next day, the commanding officer of the 517th and the general, First Allied Airborne Army, were looking at the way I came up. They looked at the bodies, and they took their wallets to get information or find out what unit they were from. They were young soldiers, they weren't old ones. They asked me a question: "Why did I put two holes in each one?" I told them: "I made a mistake one time in Italy of shooting a guy and then walking away. I thought the guy was dead and he wasn't. So I just put two shots in each one.

Marvin Moles remembers the case of one particular German soldier who had been shot and who was noticed during the battlefield inspection:

It was a pretty rough battle, but I think we made it out pretty good really, considering the terrain as it was. As we went on up, this one German was running McQuaid around one of those hedgerows. The way those hedgerows were made, they had holes in them where you could go around them. McQuaid started around this hedgerow and this German came around the other end of it and he shot at McQuaid and missed him. So McQuaid went around the hedgerow, he got behind the German as he was going around the other side, and he shot at the German and he missed. The German would shoot at McQuaid as he turned around one corner, and then as McQuaid came around the other corner he would shoot at the German as he went around. They were just going around, around and around that place. So finally McQuaid hollered for somebody to help him, and I think it was Frank Dallas who shot the

Early the next morning everything looked pretty rosy. Company I had scaled the cliffs in the face of enemy fire and killed the German gunners in their positions. Many of them were still lying around in the rocky field near the town. They were young Nazis from a reconnaissance battalion that had been sent to hold the town. Most of them looked to be about 18 or 19-years-old. However, these were the best of the German army, rabid Nazis, and as ordered had held their positions until killed.[12]

Colonel Graves was almost correct regarding the age of the soldiers; in fact, most of them were not "18 or 19," but 17 or 18. They were not from a reconnaissance battalion, but from *Reserve Grenadier Bataillon 7*. Below is a list of all the Germans who were found dead after the liberation of St Cézaire, including Ernst Härtel, who had blown up on a mine on the 21st after the ambush on Walter Taylor and Léon Roux. In the case of Alfred Flögel, it is not clear whether the date of death of August 20th is in fact correct or not. If it is, then he may have been killed at the hydroelectric plant located halfway between Mons and St Cézaire, where Lt Taylor claimed that an attack took place on the 20th. All the bodies were buried in one mass grave, as will be described further on.

Surname	Name	Rank	Age	Date of death	Location of death	Unit
Flögel	Alfred	Uffz	18	20.08.1944	St Cézaire	1./Res.Gren. Btl.7
Härtel	Ernst	Ogefr	31	21.08.1944	St Cézaire	1./Res.Gren. Btl.7
Feldkamp	Klemens	Gren	17	22.08.1944	St Cézaire	1./Res.Gren. Btl.7
Himmel	Heinrich	Gren	18	22.08.1944	St Cézaire	
Matlok	Alois	Gren	33	22.08.1944	St Cézaire	1./Res.Gren. Btl.7
Peukert	Fritz	Gren	18	22.08.1944	St Cézaire	
Raschke	Gerhard	Gren	17	22.08.1944	St Cézaire	
Stumpe	Helmut	Gren	17	22.08.1944	St Cézaire	2./Res.Gren. Btl.7
Unknown				22.08.1944	St Cézaire	
Unknown				22.08.1944	St Cézaire	

German. The guy was lying there dead and McQuaid went up there and emptied two more clips in him. That would have been 16 rounds.

The next morning, one of the battalion commanders went down there looking around where the battle was, and he came upon that German with all those bullet holes in him. I don't know, but McQuaid must have shot him all in the face and head. The commander came back and he jumped all over every one of us. He said: "It only takes one bullet to kill a man. You don't have to shoot enough in him to blow him away. He had enough holes in him to make a sieve out of him."

The American Dead

American casualties were usually very rapidly regrouped and evacuated from the battlefield to be buried in the American cemetery that had been created in Draguignan following the invasion. However, over the next couple days, the inhabitants of St Cézaire found two American bodies on the battlefield, along with leftovers from the battle. **Max Stèque** observed all this in extreme detail, of course:

In the path there were at least seven or eight American soldiers' kits, in other words a bag, ammunition pouches, the U.S. carbine, and little knives with a leather sheath. Then there were puddles of blood and little tubes with a needle to do blood transfusions or whatever. There were also quite a few bloody field dressings. They must have given first aid to the wounded before taking them away.

The Americans had left two dead. One was in the Chemin des Tirraces, and it was Linzi with his cart and some Americans who went to pick him up. With the doctor's son, who was called Bernard, we were following the group, as we were curious. We got to within 30 meters of the dead guy, who was lying at the side of the road, and I thought he was black. His face was all black on one side and we couldn't see the other side properly. With their hands they signaled us to stay where we were, not letting us come closer. Then they loaded him onto the cart, covered

Woodrow Wilson McQuaid, a killer on the battlefield but an uncontrollable drunk when off the lines, was one of the most famous enlisted men of the 517th PIR. Marvin Moles remembered: "He would give almost his whole pay check for a tube of morphine. He would shoot himself with it, then I guess he would get high as a kite. I don't know what it does to you, but anyway, he would walk up to the biggest guy around, stand beside him, and he would catch him not looking, and he would just haul loose and knock him cold. He was crazy! His face was all beat up, it looked like somebody had walked over him with hobnailed boots. He was a fighter, though, he wasn't scared of nothing." Marvin Moles Collection, Baton Rouge, Louisiana, newspaper, courtesy Lindy Bartels.

(caption within photo:) Woodrow McQuaid, and Cecil Gurley, both of Jackson, were arraigned in police court today on charges of violating the anti-narcotic laws in connection with possession of marijuana seed or plants. Both entered pleas of innocence. McQuaid was held under bond of $300 and Gurley under bond of $500.

him with American ponchos, and brought him back to the village. One American, a big tall funny guy, saw we two kids following them, so he took Bernard by the shoulders and sat him down beside the dead man, actually I think he sat him on the dead man. Then he brought me up and I was sitting against the dead man's legs. At one point one of them uncovered the body a bit and I saw that he was blond. He had a hole in his forehead and had bled; the blood had blackened in the sun and from far off he had looked like a Negro. But he was blond, with slightly curly hair. A good looking guy, and he was dead. We got all the way to the entrance of the village, then there were some Americans who wanted to see their dead buddy so they made me get off.

None of the five American that had been killed was blond, but since Jesse Goswick and Charles Stanford were the more fair-skinned of the lot, it is presumably the body of either one of them that Max Stèque saw being transported in a cart. The first body had been easy to find, however, the second left over body, that of Richard Sailor, was located far down in the Siagne Valley, where the mortars had killed him, and was therefore only rediscovered a couple days after the fighting[13] by **Max Stèque**'s uncle:

Then there was another dead guy down beside the Siagne Canal, because the Americans didn't know where to go, so they crossed through the valley, but the MG2s [MG42s] up on the cliff were spraying the whole area and one guy was hit by a bullet that entered his neck and exited on the left side of the abdomen. [In fact, Sailor was killed by multiple shrapnel wounds to the chest and left leg, according to his burial report.[14] However, the interpretation of gunshot and shrapnel wounds on a clothed body is virtually impossible, explaining Stèque's confusion.] My father-in-law had a garden down at the Siagne and badgers were eating his grapes, so he had set traps to catch them, and he thought: "I have to go down and see if I caught any badgers." There was a kind of short cut in the path that went by a rowan tree, and he saw a dead American, a big black guy lying dead at the foot of the tree. So he looked and he saw that he had a bottle of rum sticking out of his pocket. A bottle of rum was worth a fortune at the time.

My father-in-law was of Italian descent, and he would tell me the story like this: "When I saw the American, I saw he had a bottle of rum that was still almost full. So I took it and was going to have a drink, but then I thought: 'What if a German put poisoned rum there on purpose? You never know.' So I took the bottle and went up, and then I met Carlo going with two goats and I figured: "Oh, but Carlo is much older than me, and his two daughters are already married; whereas my daughters are still going to school. It would be better for him to try the rum." So I told him: "Here, have a drink." He drank it and he found it good. Then I followed him for 200 meters, and when I saw that he didn't have any pain in the stomach, well then I didn't give him any more." The bastard had used Carlo as a guinea pig. Then my father-in-law told everybody: "There is a dead guy down by the canal" and the Americans went to get him. They carried him back on a stretcher. He was already starting to putrefy and swell.

Richard Sailor was buried in the American cemetery at Draguignan August 26th, two days after his fellow paratroopers killed in St Cézaire had been laid to rest.[15]

The German Prisoner of War

Another surprise was waiting for the local inhabitants down in the Siagne Valley. **Max Stèque** continues:

> People had gardens beside the Siagne because of the food rationing. There was an Italian guy called Bianco who went to water his beans just below the village. Since the Germans were gone he had nothing to fear. He was putting water between the rows of beans, and when it would get to the end of one row, he would pass on to the next row, but he saw that the water wasn't getting to the end of the row. He thought: "What is going on? It is plugged!" So he went forward and suddenly had the fear of his life when a German soldier came out; but he had his hands up and told him: "Kamerad, Kamerad."

> It was a *Boche* who had understood that everything was over, so he had deserted and managed to get down in the valley. He wanted to surrender to the Americans, so Bianco brought him back to the village. He understood that he wasn't dangerous, but to act tough, when they reached one of the entrances of the village, what we call the Roman Door, Bianco told the *Boche* to put his hands behind his back and he walked behind him with a pitch fork. He was a hero who had made a prisoner. They sat that little *Boche* down against the fountain and he looked like he was about 16-years-old, blond and frail, with a skinny and very pale face.

> Us kids were there, and for us he was nothing but a dirty *Boche*! The Americans were all around him, but the one who was responsible for him was dark-skinned, a mulatto with a big Colt passed under his belt, so we were telling him: "You have to kill him, you have to kill him!" On the wall there was a placard representing Torrin and Grassi, some *résistants* from Nice who had been tortured by the *Gestapo* and hung at the Avenue de la Victoire [see chapter 1]. That poster was put up all over the village, so we were saying: "They are going to hang him from the chestnut tree in front of Santorro's house, just like Torrin and Grassi!" We were waiting for it to happen and telling the American: "Hey! Him there! Bang, bang! Hang him!" and we showed him the poster. So the American was laughing and finally, to please us kids, he took his gun and put it on the German's forehead and went: "bannnggg!" The guy's ass sprang this high off the ground. Then after a while we asked him for more, so he put the gun on the back of his neck and went: "bang!" And us little sadistic bastards were happy. We would have wanted him to kill him, that would have been nice!

> Then Madame Beck arrived, who had been married to a Jew who was arrested. She spoke Alsatian and the prisoner explained that he had surrendered and all that. So she explained to the villagers that he had deserted the German army and that he wanted to surrender to the Americans. She said: "He is asking for something to eat because he is famished." So somebody went to get tomatoes and gave them to him. Then there was no more "bang bang." Finally, the Americans came to get him and they probably brought him to their command post to interrogate him. Of course they didn't hang him, he was a prisoner of war.

Luckily, not all the inhabitants of St Cézaire were "little sadists," as **Yvonne Bonhomme** remembers:

> One man went to his garden down at the Siagne and he found a young German hidden in his beans, but really very young. I will remember the poor guy my whole life. He couldn't understand French and found himself surrounded by French people who were enemies. They brought him to the village and he was sitting under a tree. He had blue eyes and must have been something like 24 or 25. He looked like a hunted animal. The poor guy was there, looking at everybody, he was probably frightened since he couldn't understand what we were saying.

The Burial of the German Dead

The German soldiers who were killed on the cliffs above the Siagne had remained on the battlefield after they were visited by the American officers. Some French civilians (and probably also some American soldiers) had also, and as always, "visited" the battlefield, and Yvonne Bonhomme noted that "Some people had come during the night and stolen their boots." The mayor of St Cézaire, **François Laugier,** later wrote:

> Nine German soldiers killed on the battlefield by the Allied troops during the fighting for the liberation of the territory of St Cézaire were buried in a mass grave in the cemetery of the village, where they remain. When the bodies were discovered, their clothes seemed to have been searched through and none of the witnesses can remember if they were still wearing their metal tags. The tragic circumstances of the time had not enabled their identification. (…) I have the metallic tag of another German soldier who blew up on the same date and whose body was completely pulverized.[16]

Corporal John Rupczyk remembered that it was the German prisoners who were tasked with retrieving the bodies and burying them:

> There were maybe eight or nine prisoners that we took, and the next day they sent the batch of prisoners into that hill and they had to pick up the dead soldiers. They took them some place in town and buried them. But one soldier, I think a shell landed right on him because it just blew him to pieces and his whole body was in a wheelbarrow. People told us they were Hitler Youth, they were all young kids just about, but they fought us just as hard as they could. They gave us a good fight there.

Max Stèque was of course present when the bodies of the Germans were buried:

> Linzi had a small cart and a mule, and he was acting as a hearse. There were three of us kids, I remember, and we saw Linzi going by with his cart, and I heard him telling another guy in Provencal: "I am going to pick up the *Boches* at the cliff." So we followed along, but they said: "Hey you kids, you aren't coming." But we followed from a distance, and when we got to the cliffs Linzi said: "There is one." Indeed, a German had made a little wall of stones in front of himself to be protected, his Mauser was resting on the rocks, pointing slightly upwards, and he was lying on it, so we could only see his helmet. He had been shot in the head or face, because he was covered in blood, and he was lying dead on his weapon. He was the only one I actually saw dead there. The others were further on, but

we didn't see them because they kicked us out. "We told you kids not to come, now get out of here!"

They loaded the men—I think there were seven of them who had been killed at the edge of the cliff—onto the cart. Then they covered them up with a tarpaulin. But the cart was full, so there were feet, legs, and arms sticking out. I remember those yellow, pale feet. They had no boots, all of them had been removed. They brought the cart to the cemetery and some people went to look, and a few of us kids followed along and watched from behind the chapel. They had made the little German prisoner and another German prisoner that they had brought along dig a hole and we could see them pick up the bodies, one holding under the armpits, the other by the feet, and tossing them into the hole at random. They were all piled one on top of the other.

They threw them in one over the other, and the little prisoner poured in the contents of the wheelbarrow that was all disgusting, with stinking juice, and then they closed up the hole. There is always left over earth after a hole is closed, and it made an elongated mound on top. Two weeks later, we kids were still going there and saying: "The *Boches* are here." And we would spit on the grave because we were so hateful. "Dirty *Boches*!" and we would urinate on the grave. Little idiots! I was 13-years-old, some were 14. Oh, we couldn't stand the *Boches*. That was the way it happened.

Years later, a German ethnologist came and they exhumed the bodies. Thanks to him, they probably managed to reconstruct the skeletons, separate them, and bring them back to the families. But considering how jumbled up they were, it is possible that the families received the remains of three guys at the same time. They were all mixed up, so when they got down to where the bones were, it must have been difficult.

Max Stèque was correct; the exhumation team had difficulties separating the bodies because of the disorderly way in which they had been buried. Eight bodies were so commingled that their bones could no longer be individualized, and these eight were once again reburied in a mass grave at the German Military Cemetery of Dagneux.

The Shaving of Women

In most freshly liberated French villages, women who had relationships with German or Italian soldiers were shaved and humiliated in public. These shavings were normally not performed by any real resistance fighters, but were acts of last minute "resistance fighters" who had not had the courage to fight the Germans and found it easier to attack defenseless women once the Germans were far away. These shavings disgusted and shocked most Allied soldiers. Often, French witnesses of the period prefer not to mention the shavings, for they feel ashamed and guilty that this occurred. However, **Max Stèque** remembers the shavings that occurred in St Cézaire with his usual unadulterated honesty:

There were people that we called the *réfractaires*, who were too afraid to join the *maquis* but who were hiding so as not to go to the STO. That was really something. The day after the Liberation, one of them shaved four women. He was an avenger of wrongdoings. He was a brave man to do that, really a tough guy. All the poor women of Italian descent who had supposedly slept with the Italians were shaved. Maybe it was true, but they hadn't denounced anybody. The populace of imbeciles was in the street, including many who had been made cuckolds by the Italians, as well as a few kids. We were there, waiting for them to come out. The poor women came out with their hair in their hands and a bald head, and the rest of us were laughing.

The next day at the town square there was a small placard on the wall at the corner of the steeple, and there were people laughing. The names of all the women who were said to have slept with the Italians were written on it. Because the four they had shaved were coalmen's daughters, poor defenseless devils, while good ladies from the village had gotten out of it, their names were on the poster. The people were making fun of them: "Oh! Can you imagine that!" Then one of them who was laughing a lot and making fun of the others found the name of one of his family members on the poster, so then he got angry and tore everything off the wall!

Ferdinand Koblas and the Leftover Mines

The Germans had left many mines behind them around St Cézaire, including powerful antitank Tellermines that had blown Ernst Härtel to shreds the 21st. One of these mines was to cast a dark shadow over the joy of being liberated. We will let our storyteller **Max Stèque** explain what happened August 28, 1944, six days after the Liberation:

In the FTP camp [in Clavier], there was a young Czechoslovakian named **Ferdinand Koblas**. He had been forced into the German army and had managed to desert, because of course he was against the Germans, and he wound up in our region, where he joined the communist *maquis*, the FTP. Koblas had a few notions about mines because he had been in the German army, and a few days after the liberation he decided to get rid of the mines that had been laid in three or four paths around here. He had a guy from St Cézaire named **Edmond Roux** with him, who was 22-years-old; another guy called **Antoine Colmars**, from Nice, who had ended up in the *maquis* here; and there was another guy, Marcel Martinetti, who was only 18. He was the youngest, so he had stayed hidden behind a wall. That is what saved him.

The mines had been laid in a rush and could be seen easily. Martinetti told me that once Roux had seen Koblas take out several mines, he told him: "It's not difficult, I see how you are doing it, now I will take out the next one." Koblas told him: "Okay." He hadn't thought that they might be booby trapped. Roux did exactly what Koblas had done: he unscrewed the plate, then the fuse, and then he lifted up the mine. Martinetti told me: "At that moment I saw a thin wire under the mine, and Koblas saw it and told him: "Kaputt!" As he said kaput: "bang" they blew up... Roux and Comars were killed and Koblas was disemboweled, his guts were hanging out.

I was in a property we had in the country when the mine blew up. I was walking on a thick wall that separated two properties. There was a wild peach tree, with peaches that were starting to redden. I remember I was feeling one to find out if it was good when I heard a huge explosion that made me drop the peach. The ground shook, even though the explosion was one kilometer away. At the exit of the village I saw a crowd. I went there and it was Koblas, the Czechoslovakian, lying on a stretcher, asking for something to drink. The village doctor, Grimaldi, was there and told us: "You can give him whatever you want, he is done for." His bowels were shredded. They put him in a car anyway and wanted to bring him to the Military Hospital in Draguignan, but when they got to the other side of the valley, on the Route de Callian, he died and they brought him back.

They put the three bodies in the town hall, under some sheets, and two FTPs were standing guard in front. Nobody was allowed in, but since there was a back door to the town hall, the doctor's son, Bernard, and I took advantage of it and came in by the back. I just had time to see some bloody sheets when Roux's father arrived. They didn't want to let him in, but he had insisted on seeing his son. He lifted the sheet and underneath it was like butchery meat. The trunk was intact, but of the head, only a small piece remained at the back with some hair on it; there were no more limbs, he was torn to shreds. His father started howling like a beast. He kissed the little piece of hair, he cried and screamed, and then he needed to be accompanied back home. I still have that in my head.

22-year-old Edmond Roux, who was killed when a booby-trapped Tellermine he was handling detonated. Yvonne Bonhomme Collection.

The monument that has been erected at the site of the mine explosion. Author's Collection.

They were lying on the ground in the town hall, covered in bloody sheets. Colmars was cut in half, with his bowels protruding and only a stump near the back bone still holding him together. Roux was in pieces: there was a piece of his chest, a few pieces of leg, and then nothing else. Only Koblas was still intact, but his guts were hanging out, covered in blood, and one arm flayed with the bones visible.

The death of the three men was very traumatizing for the village, and those who were there still remember that day very well. **Marcel Raybaud** had run to the scene after hearing the explosion:

Koblas had had the strength to go and sit on the wall. When I got there he was holding his stomach and he told me: "Marcel kaputt. Marcel kaputt." Colmars received a small fragment right in the forehead; there was a small hole with a bit of brain coming out. Roux was blown to pieces. I found a piece of his head that I recognized from the curly hair. Monsieur Raybaud found a piece of tibia three or four days later. We put everything we could find together and brought it to the town hall. The people who had taken care of that had tried to form a body, but he was torn apart.

Yvonne Bonhomme also went towards the site of the explosion:

Martinetti was leaning against a wall. He couldn't breathe anymore and couldn't go any further, and he was saying: "They are all dead. They are all dead." The next day my father picked up some pieces of toes in the field. He told me: "There were pieces everywhere." When Roux's father arrived and wanted to see his son, he grabbed the piece of hair. The people around him held his arms to prevent him from touching the body.

Ferdinand Koblas was buried in the village cemetery, as **Max Stèque** explains:

They buried Koblas in the cemetery, and he stayed there for years. His grave sort of belonged to the village; it was always looked after and had flowers on it. Roux's mother went to the cemetery every day to see her son's grave, and she always gave flowers to Koblas at the same time she gave them to her son. Once Koblas' family came, they were of course received by the mayor and they had gone to see his grave at the cemetery. I think the mayor also invited them to a restaurant; well, they were welcomed fittingly. When they left they weren't happy, but they were surprised to see how much gratitude the village had for him.

Ferdinand Koblas was later declared "Mort pour la France (Died for France)," and his name was inscribed on the village war memorial, a touching end for someone who had once been a member of the German army. Interestingly, in his house that some Germans had been quartered in during their stay in St Cézaire, Max Stèque found a small box of German ZZ42 fuzes that could be used to booby trap Tellermines. He noted that only one ZZ42 fuze was missing from the box, perhaps the one that had been used to booby trap the mine that had killed Koblas and his two French helpers? An elderly woman, Mme Torino, also had the misfortune of stepping on a mine at St Cézaire. Luckily for her it was a smaller antipersonnel mine and she escaped with only minor injuries to her legs. Marcel Raybaud added an interesting detail: "Women were not undressed like they are nowadays. She had a long skirt, which probably gave her a bit of protection. But her legs and knees were burned."

The Siagne Front as Seen by the Commander of Reserve Grenadier Bataillon 7

The German unit that bore the brunt of the attack on St Cézaire was the 1st Company of *Reserve Grenadier Bataillon 7*, commanded by *Oberleutnant* Stein. *Oberleutnant* Stein unfortunately did not mention any details whatsoever about the battle in the letters he sent to the families of his soldiers who had been killed in the fighting. However, Major Karl-Ernst Schmidt, the commander of *Reserve Grenadier Bataillon 7*, wrote a short memoir after the war, in which he briefly mentioned the activities of his battalion on the Siagne River in very general terms. **Major Schmidt**'s account starts on the day of the Allied landing, when his battalion was still stationed on the coast east of Nice, and therefore also reviews some of what has been described in the previous chapters:

At the crack of dawn on August 15, 1944, the Anglo-American invasion of the Mediterranean coast started under the customary hellfire. Since the port of St Raphaël, at the mouth of the Argens River, was the kernel of the section of coast between Cannes and Hyères, it was chosen as the landing spot. The enemy's intentions of using the Rhône Valley for an advance north were quickly made clear. To make this happen, it was also to be suspected that the enemy would build a front to the east, in the Maritime Alps, at least to protect his supply lines, or perhaps even to make a thrust over the Maritime Alps' mountain passes into the Po Valley. The mission of preventing the latter possibility, or rather of delaying the former, was mostly incumbent upon our division. *Grenadier Regiment 281* (*Oberst* Kessler), which had just started its deployment to its new area, fell victim to the initial blow of the invasion [see Regiment Kessler history in Chapter 1]. (...) A battalion of our division which was to seal off the area west of Grasse surrendered [see the surrender of *Bataillon 327* at Fayence in Chapter 4], and its mission therefore became my responsibility. My battalion was detached from the *Füsilier* battalion, transported by wood-burning vehicle and deployed in the area west of Grasse. It soon succeeded in capturing advanced enemy reconnaissance patrols and finding out valuable information about our opponents. Our delaying operation, which continued at Cap Martin, Mont Agel, and Sospel, ended when we reached the Maginot Line constructions.[17]

The "enemy reconnaissance patrols" (plural) that were captured undoubtedly refers to Lt Walter Taylor, who was as far as is known the only Allied soldier to be captured in the entire area. Walter Taylor and Léon Roux had literally driven right into the German positions, so his capture can hardly be considered a prowess on the part of the *Grenadiers*. Furthermore, considering Taylor's description of the event and the fact that he was not even a member of the FABTF, it seems highly unlikely that he provided any worthwhile information whatsoever to his captors. Major Schmidt therefore exaggerates both the nature and the effects of the capture of one American officer, but he, on the other hand, says absolutely nothing about the actual fighting that occurred, and in which his battalion suffered rather heavy casualties. (Not just in St Cézaire, but also the next day in Grasse, where several dozen of his men surrendered, as will be explained in the next chapter.) Schmidt's text is written in typical military fashion, exaggerating the positive events and minimizing the negative ones, and is only of limited interest, since it is so brief. However, as it is one of the only German documents that seems to exist on the fighting at the Siagne, it was worth viewing it before concluding this chapter.

Conclusion

St Cézaire was part of the German Siagne River defensive line. Soldiers from the 1st and 2nd Companies of *Reserve Grenadier Bataillon 7* moved into the village shortly after the Allied landing. The liberation of the town was made by G and I Companies of the 517th Parachute Infantry Regiment on the afternoon of August 22, 1944. The fighting and its aftermath cost a total of 20 lives: five American paratroopers, ten German infantry men, three French partisans, one German deserter, and one civilian. The next day, the 517th moved on to St Vallier, from which the Germans had already retreated.

Generalleutnant Otto Fretter-Pico, commander of Reserve Division 148, and Major Karl-Ernst Schmidt, the commander of Reserve Grenadier Bataillon 7. Author's Collection.

9

The Liberation of Grasse and its Region

A description of the battles that occurred in the southern (La Napoule) and northern (St Cézaire) parts of the Siagne River German defensive line was made in the previous chapters. We now continue with the study of the attack that was made in the center of the Siagne line, at Peymeinade and Grasse.

The D562 highway linking Draguignan to Grasse was one of the main roads the Germans needed to defend in order to slow the Allied advance. This road crosses the Siagne at le Tignet, then goes through Peymeinade and Grasse. These towns did not present as good defensive positions as la Napoule or St Cézaire: there were no particularly strategic hills or outstanding fields of fire, and any strongpoint could be outflanked by foot troops without much difficulty. This may be the reason why the Germans were not simply concentrated along the Siagne River and had organized a more in-depth defense system, spread out between the Siagne and Grasse. Infantry men that were probably members of the 4th Company of *Reserve Grenadier Battalion 7* were sent into the hills overlooking the Siagne at le Tignet, and a lethal 88mm cannon manned by Flak troops was installed above a curve of the D562 between Peymeinade and Grasse, at a location from which it could enfilade the road over a long distance. *Generalleutnant* Fretter Pico and the headquarters of *Reserve Division 148*, which had so far been quartered in Grasse, had in the meantime retreated, first to Vence, then to St Paul.

The D562 bridge over the Siagne, which the Montauroux area Resistance would have liked to destroy August 15th to prevent German counterattacks on the landing zones, was now blown by the Germans to cover their retreat. At the same time, the Germans also destroyed the railroad bridge over the Siagne that had been designed by Gustave Eiffel, of Eiffel tower fame.

Guiding the Allies

Before getting into the actual advance of the Allies across the Siagne, we will read the account of a resistance man of the *Réseau Tartane*, in Grasse, who was ordered to cross the lines to serve as a guide to the Allied troops. Since this man wished to remain anonymous, we will simply call him **Jean**:

On the 19th or 20th, I was arrested for a stupid reason. I had taken a bike to get some food, and there was a little blue, white, and red [French] flag of the "Touring Club de France" on it. I was arrested by two French *miliciens* who said: "You are being provocative with the flag." They brought me to the entrance of their camp, but then, because the Germans were already starting to leave, they were forced to do something else and brought me to the German *Kommandantur*. I stayed there for an hour or an hour and a half, then asked the interpreter there: "What am I supposed to do?" They were packing up their archives, so he told me to leave.

Circulating was very dangerous for resistance men, as was proven when a resistant named **Roland Thibaud** was killed in Magagnosc, near Grasse, on the 21st. After his misadventure, **Jean** and his fellow resistance member, Raymond Dupont, were ordered by their commander to cross the lines and meet up with the Allies. The itinerary they followed would bring them into the resistance controlled regions north of Grasse, in which the Germans no longer dared to venture:

Pierazzi told us: "You will leave and go to the *maquis* in Thorenc, and then you will go to St Raphaël to put yourselves at the disposal of the Americans to guide

them." We took our bikes and reached the first German barrage. Dupont had a fireman's card with a tricolor stripe on it, so he showed it to them and said: "Police" and we went on. We arrived at le Tignet, and after the church there is a hairpin curve. After passing the curve we saw a German patrol of 30 or 40 men marching on either side of the road in front of us heading towards St Cézaire. We slowly turned around, left our bikes in front of the church, and we went to Thorenc by foot through the fields.

We spent the night in Thorenc, and the next day we went to Mons, where we met the first Americans. They asked us to guide them to St Cézaire, but being "dumb and disciplined" we told them: "No, we can't, we regret but we must go to St Raphaël." There was an inhabitant of Mons named Roux who told them: "I can bring you to St Cézaire." Lucky thing we didn't go, because they left and blew up on a mine and all died! [These were of course Lt Walter Taylor and Léon Roux, who were extensively mentioned in Chapter 8.]

After further adventures, during which the two would-be guides were given a very official looking pass by local resistance leader Rodolphe, they finally met up with some Americans who could bring them from Mons to St Raphaël in their car. **Jean** continues:

There were at least three Americans: the driver, the guy sitting beside him, and there was another guy standing on the rear bumper with a machine gun on the hood of the car. I have always wondered how he managed to hang on. One of the wheels on the car was flat, but the Americans said: "We don't have time" and we drove to St Raphaël just like that, on the rim. The driver was taking the curves like a madman, and I don't know how the guy on the back managed not to fall off. We arrived in St Raphaël, and I admit I have some memory lapses because I was so tired, as we had very little sleep. The Americans had coffee and we hadn't drunk any coffee for four years, so we drank coffee to stay awake. Early the next morning, we helped load jerry cans onto a truck that had come back and then we got on. Then I don't know what happened, I must have been sleeping, but we arrived at the American headquarters in a little chateau before Fayence with a Colonel in command

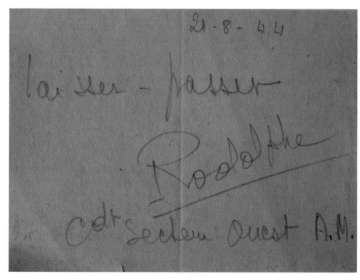

The "official pass" – in fact, a mere scribble on a loose sheet of paper given to Jean and Raymond Dupont by local resistance commander Rodolphe – allowing them to move freely through resistance-held territory northwest of Grasse. Private Collection.

and everything. The good thing about the Americans was that the commander was never very far off. There was an advance, and they dropped us off with the Americans a bit before the Siagne Bridge.

Raymond Dupond and Jean were dropped off at the Siagne River the morning of August 23rd. The First Special Service Force had crossed the river during the previous night and was advancing towards Grasse at the time.

Crossing the Siagne

Late in the evening of August 22nd, the 3rd Regiment of the FSSF had crossed the Sigane River, shortly after the 517th Parachute Infantry Regiment had attacked St Cézaire a few kilometers further north. 3rd Regiment had succeeded in crossing the Siagne against what was described as "slight opposition" in the after action report.[1] However, this slight opposition had caused the death of two forcemen, one Canadian and one American, as well as the death of one German soldier. The victims were:

Surname	Name	Rank	Unit	Age	Date of death	Location of death
Brown	Frank S Jr	Pvt	1 - 3 FSSF	20	23.8.1944	Les Veyans
Granger	Renaldo	Sgt	5 - 3 FSSF	25	22.8.1944	Les Veyans

Surname	Name	Rank	Age	Date of Death	Location of Death	Buried in	Unit
Temel	Johann	Gren	18	22.8.1944	Peymeinade	Grasse	4./Res. Gren.Btl.7

The crossing of the Siagne was briefly described by the FSSF journal:

0200. 23 Aug. (…) 3rd Regiment received machine gun and small arms fire on high ground north of le Tignet. 20mm gun and aircraft gun gave harassing fire. Began at 222400B [22 August at 24:00] and ceased at approximately 230200B August 1944. Casualties: 2 killed, 1 wounded and one evacuated (sick).[2]

The families of Allied casualties often only received shockingly few details about how their relative was killed. In many cases, a brief telegram announcing the date of death was all the next of kin ever found out, with nothing regarding the location or the cause of death. In contrast, as we have already seen in the previous chapters, the German families were often told factual details about how and where the soldier had died. Luckily, Renaldo Granger's sister sent a letter to Renaldo's buddies, asking for more information. She received a reply from **Lieutenant Robert I. Smith** that detailed the circumstances of how Renaldo Granger was mortally wounded in the Siagne area:

We were in Southern France at the time, and the company had the assignment of leading the battalion to a new area in support of another group. Your brother was the lead scout, and the terrain was very rugged and steep, which made the task very difficult, as it was in the late evening. We were halfway up a large hill, traveling single file, when I heard some rifle shots and two loud explosions. I was four men behind Renaldo and the explosion was big enough to knock me down. We were in a minefield and Renaldo and his platoon commander were hit. We had to work our way into the minefield to get them out, and it was close to twenty minutes before we had him on the stretcher and started down the

As usual, the Germans had blown all the bridges before retreating from the Siagne Valley. Here the remains of the railroad bride of the former Grasse-Draguignan railway line are visible as they appear today. Author's Collection.

Pvt. Brown Is Listed as Killed In Action

20-year-old Pvt Frank S. Brown, Jr., of 1-3 of the FSSF, was apparently killed on the road leading up from the Siagne River towards Grasse. Old Colony Historical Society Collection, courtesy Jane Hennedy.

hill to the aid station. He was weak from loss of blood, but very strong in spirit. Renaldo and I had a standing joke that I asked him about at that time. Before I joined the 5th Company, I knew Renaldo on the Anzio beachhead. We had quite a few cows on the farm, and one of the calves turned up missing one day, but after close checking I found it at Renaldo's farm. [There were many abandoned farms near the front lines at the Anzio beachhead in Italy, thus some soldiers took to milking or slaughtering cows, searching for fresh eggs, etc.] I later found that he had sold the cow, and I always insisted that half the money was legally mine. I was checking the bandages on him and talking about the cow. The last thing he said to me was: "Come back to the hospital and see me Lieutenant and I will give you your share of the money." It took an hour to get to the aid station, and he passed away soon after arrival. Plasma was given before he reached the aid station, but he had lost too much blood initially.

Renaldo was a favorite of all the boys and generally thought of as a real fellow. As a soldier and a scout, he was one of the best in the force. He never showed personal fear, and his judgment in tight situations was always correct. I sincerely hope that I can make a trip to Canada to see the people who have lost their boys over there. I will let you know in advance and will be able to tell you so much more in conversation.[3]

Artillery Duel at Peymeinade

The crossing of the Siagne and the liberation of le Tignet had been done without too much difficulty during the night of the 22nd to the 23rd, and the FSSF continued down the D562 road towards Grasse. They would meet the most serious resistance east of Peymeinade, at a location known as St Marc. The Germans had installed an 88mm cannon in a position that overlooked and enfiladed the D562. It was manned by a crew of *Luftwaffe* Flak soldiers (probably from *Flak Abteilung 391*) and was attached to a half-tracked tow vehicle (*Sonderkraftfahrzeug*) driven by truck drivers who had been "borrowed" from the *Kriegsmarine*. The area surrounding the cannon was guarded by a 20mm cannon, as well as machine guns and infantry men.

88mm cannons were powerful antiaircraft guns that the Germans also regularly used against ground targets. The cannon's precision and the velocity with which it fired made it a formidable weapon, capable of destroying Allied tanks from hundreds and even thousands of meters away. The 88 at Peymeinade had at least 13 victory rings painted on its barrel, indicating that it was credited with the destruction of 13 Allied aircraft or vehicles. This impressive record shows that the cannon crew was probably highly experienced, unlike the average soldier of *Reserve Division 148*. However, the cannon never got a chance to show its full potential, as French civilians had seen it and informed the advancing forcemen of its presence long before it got the chance of ambushing them. Charles Gandiglio, a 10-year-old living on the outskirts of Peymeinade, found himself in the middle of the action after the arrival of the first forcemen of 1st Regiment. **Charles Gandiglio**'s excellent memory has produced the following account of August 23rd as seen from Peymeinade:

The morning of August 23, 1944, I was watching over the cows as I often did, sitting in front of the door at la Grange Neuve. It was about eight in the morning, and I saw a guy appear with a helmet covered in vegetation; then a second one appeared, then a third, and a fourth and a

It is with deep regret that we hear that Paratrooper Renaldo Granger, son of Mr .and Mrs. Gee Granger, has died of wounds received in France. Our heartfelt sympathy goes out to his wife, mother and father and all other relatives.

One of the last pictures of 25-year-old Sergeant Renaldo Granger, of 5-3 of the FSSF, with his wife Ruth. The couple had two children who both died in infancy. Deanna Petri Collection.

fifth. I called my mother, saying: "Mama, the Germans are still here." We hadn't seen them for a week and we figured there would be trouble, because if the Germans were still here, then the Americans weren't going to arrive yet. The soldiers came to the farm, where we had a barn for the sheep, a thing for the pigs, a stable for the cows... They went everywhere, and with a big kick on the door would go inside with submachine guns, look around, then go back out. My mother had come out, but they didn't speak or anything. They didn't go into the house, they looked at us without saying a word, then disappeared into the countryside behind the house. So we said: "Well, the Germans are still here." The Germans we usually had around didn't look mean at all. They had their rifles, the famous Mauser, and a bayonet, but that was it; they often didn't even have helmets. But those ones were covered in grenades and things and really looked like mad men. It was impressive.

Those guys disappeared who knows where, then seven or eight minutes passed and a guy in blue overalls came along. So I called my mother again, telling her: "There is a *maquisard* coming." So she said: "A *maquisard* with the Germans?" The guy calmly came along with no weapons or anything and he asked: "Do you have any Germans around here?" My mother told him: "Yes, there are some." He was quite surprised. "Five of them just went by five minutes ago." He answered with a big smile: "But those weren't Germans, those were Americans!"

My mother took me in her arms. We were very shocked by the Americans' behavior. It was almost disappointing, because we had been expecting smiling people with flags, that we would welcome with open arms. Instead, we had those five guys that we had mistaken for enemies. We had been waiting for them for months and months, but not like that. It was really disappointing. We said: "But it isn't possible, the American people aren't like that!" They had given the impression of being barbarians, equipped the way they were, and mean, with their faces blackened. Back in those days we had never seen people with makeup on their faces, so we didn't know if they were black or white. They seemed to be a cross between man and beast, it was really impressive.

The guy in blue went back 100 meters, then made big gestures, and three or four minutes later, 60 or 80 men arrived, coming from the Siagne Valley. At the end of the convoy were my father and one of the workers from the farm, because the worker had Italian shorts and an Italian forage cap. Everybody dressed in whatever could be salvaged, so he had those Italian shorts and the forage cap. The first thing the Americans did when they arrived in the area where my father and the worker were working was to crawl up to them and train their guns on them, thinking that they were soldiers. But afterwards they understood they were farmers.

With the guy in blue acting as an interpreter, an officer asked us if there was anything important in Peymeinade. My father told him: "When the kid went to get bred yesterday, he found out that a big cannon towed by a half track had just been set up at the entrance of the de Boutigny property, as well as a machine gun." This seemed to interest the officer greatly, and he made all his men sit down in the shade of the two big hackberries in front of the farm.

In the meantime, the officer asked the guy in blue if we could bring them something to drink. Me and my sister left with pails to the well that was less than 150 meters away and emptied it to the sand. We were bringing the water and pouring it into their helmets. They had come from the Siagne, which is a 200-meter climb, and in the August heat and with everything they were carrying, it was infernal. That is why they threw lots of things away that my father found later: bazooka rockets, helmets, and even clothes.

My sister and I were running back to the well as fast as we could with the empty pails to bring them water. The officer didn't like that, because it seemed like something abnormal that could arouse the attention of Germans that could be on the hills facing us. So he told the guy in blue to tell us not to run: "Don't go too fast, just carry normally." They drank everything we gave them and in exchange we got chewing gum, biscuits, cigarettes, and all kinds of stuff. That is when we discovered chewing gum, which

we had never seen before. We hadn't seen any candies for months, or even years. At that point, we started to go back to our first impression of what liberators could be like, compared to the first five that we had seen. But today I can understand that those first guys were tense, because they didn't know if somebody might point a rifle out at them through a window.

Then the officer asked us if there was a point on the hill from where Peymeinade could been seen. My father said: "We will go to such and such a place that dominates the whole valley." We went there with the officer, the man in blue, and two or three soldiers, including a radioman. We had a perfect view of the Peymeinade valley and could locate the cannon in front of the de Boutigny property. A tripod was deployed, on which the officer installed a large set of binoculars. He made a long observation, then everybody got to look into them except me, because I was too short to reach up to their level. Seeing this, the officer picked me up by the shoulders and lifted me to the height of the binoculars so that I could see in them. I was very impressed, never having looked into a pair of binoculars before. It was an extraordinary screen. It seemed like the Germans were right there, a few meters away from us, when they were actually one kilometer away. In spite of branches that had been set up as camouflage, we could see movement around the canon. The Germans were there, in defensive positions. As for the machine gun, it was hidden in a bush and could not be seen, but we indicated its position to the officer.

At that moment, the officer called the radioman and sent a message to la Colle Noir. After five minutes, we heard the sound of tank tracks coming down the Siagne Valley. [The Cannon Company of the FSSF was equipped with four halftracks with 75mm cannons mounted on them. Two of them, which had just barely arrived in southern France, were involved at Peymeinade.] The bridges were out so they forded the river, and it must have been about noon by the time they got to the Val du Tignet. When they got there, the Americans knew what to expect, and suddenly the first German shell tore through the air and exploded in the olive trees to the right of the road. Several more shots followed, hitting to the right and left of the road the two tanks were coming on. At that point one of the tanks turned towards us while the other one started firing back. Apparently it was acting as a diversion, because it was firing randomly towards the cannon, with the shells landing at least 100 meters above and 100 meters to the left of the cannon without ever hitting it. The second tank advanced towards us to a certain point, and then took a path going down into an olive grove. It took a few minutes to get set up and then it started firing. The first shell landed 100 meters right of the canon and demolished the wall of a house. The second shell landed 50 meters to the left in one of de Boutigny's oak trees. The third shot was the right one and scored a direct hit on the halftrack towing the canon that was loaded with shells. A huge explosion followed, shaking the whole valley. That seemed to sound the death knell of the German resistance in the area. There was still some machine gun fire for a few minutes, then a relative calm set in.

Then the American officer made a phone call. Apparently the cannon had been destroyed, so for them the day had started pretty well and had ended pretty well.

The German halftrack and 88mm flak cannon that were destroyed by the Cannon Company of the FSSF east of Peymeinade near the De Boutigny house August 23rd. The cannon has multiple victory rings painted around its barrel, indicating that it had been involved in the destruction of many Allied targets in the past. The shell fired by a FSSF halftrack landed in the German halftrack, apparently setting off ammunition that was stocked within it. The resulting explosion killed four crewmembers and caused the remaining Germans to retreat towards Grasse. De Boutigny Family Collection, courtesy Charles Gandiglio.

He divided his company in two: one part went down Chemin du Candéou, while the other part left by Avenue de Peygros. They slowly advanced; there was a bit of firing going on right and left, and that is how one German who was behind a hut must have ben killed. The result was that four Germans were killed at the cannon, plus the one who was lying in the gutter. Unfortunately a gendarme was also killed at the crossroads that led up to the cannon, and two civilians were killed by a shell in front of the Peymeinade war memorial, which was really the pinnacle of bad luck.

The gendarme had come on a motorcycle. There were two of them on it, and we were later told that they had come to contact the Americans. The two of them arrived on their motorcycle, and when they got to the small train station, there was a German machine gun on the opposite embankment about 50 meters away. They got hit by a burst of machine gun fire and both of them fell down in front of the station. One gendarme named Van Schoorisse was killed on the spot, and the other one was hit by a bullet that cut his ear and scalp. The crossing keeper and his wife were in the station with their shutters closed; but when they heard the gunfire they opened their shutters a bit without making too much noise. They saw the Germans who came

19-year-old Grenadier Josef Rein, who was killed on the road beneath the 88mm cannon. Rein Family Collection.

and turned the bodies over with their feet, and for them, the guys were dead, they didn't fire a *coup de grace* at either one. One was dead and the other one had a huge wound on his head, but in the end he survived.

One of our workers, Frattini, the one who had been wearing the Italian shorts and the Italian cap, told the American officer: "I want to join up with you." So they loaded him up with cartridges, but didn't give him any weapon. For two months we didn't see him. He was an adventurer with no family or wife, and one day he came back to the farm just like he had left.

The names of the two civilians and of the gendarme who were killed during the fighting are listed below:

Surname	Name	Date of death	Location of death
Bouge	Paul	23.8.1944	Peymeinade
Philipe	Honoré	23.8.1944	Peymeinade
Van Schoorisse	Antoine	23.8.1944	Peymeinade

Four Germans were killed at their 88mm cannon when it was hit, and a fifth, mentioned by Charles Gandiglio, was killed on the D562 below the cannon. These five soldiers were all buried side by side in a field near the cannon.

Surname	Name	Rank	Age	Date of death	Location of death	Buried in	Unit
Foitzik	Vincent	Ogefr	23	23.8.1944	Peymeinade	Peymeinade	Flak
Rein	Josef	Gren	19	23.8.1944	Peymeinade	Peymeinade	Infantry
Strunk	Johann	Ogefr	37	23.8.1944	Peymeinade	Peymeinade	Haffenkpt. San Remo
Unknown				23.8.1944	Peymeinade	Peymeinade	
Unknown				23.8.1944	Peymeinade	Peymeinade	

Johann Strunk was a *Kriegsmarine* truck driver who had had the misfortune of being temporarily assigned to driving the halftrack towing the *Luftwaffe* 88mm Flak cannon. His family received a letter explaining the circumstances of his death and enabling a comparison with Charles Gandiglio's account of the battle. The letter was written by *Oberleutnant* **Georg Weis** August 31, 1944:

Dear Ms Strunk

As the company commander of your husband, *Krf. Ob.Gefr.* [*Kraftfahrer Obergefreiter* or "truck driver Corporal"] Johann Strunk, I have the sad duty of informing you, dear Misses Strunk, of the hero's death of your husband for the Führer and the Fatherland.

After the invasion of southern France by the enemy, our dear Strunk, as well as another comrade, were ordered to join a Flak battle group as drivers, and he performed exemplarily. On 23.8.1944, an encounter occurred between Paymaynade [sic] and Grasse, and the battery was fired upon. One shell exploded immediately beside the cannon, and your dear husband sought shelter in the shell hole because experience shows that two hits rarely occur at the same spot. However, against all expectations, a second shell landed in the same spot. At 15.45, our dear *Krf.Ob.Gefr.* Strunk lost his young life.

The news of the hero's death of your husband shook me deeply, because comrade Strunk was one of my most dependable soldiers and was always ready for action. (…)[4]

The details provided in this letter (as well as in other letters sent back to families of German soldiers that are shown elsewhere in this book) prove that the German forces, although they were retreating and suffering heavily from desertions and combat casualties, were still well organized and functioning as cohesive units.

Unfortunately, I have found no detailed account of the encounter by the Allies. It seems that one halftrack from the FSSF created a diversion by firing from a position from which it could not hit nor be hit by the 88mm cannon, therefore providing the second halftrack with the opportunity of moving into a good firing position from which it destroyed the 88. The after action report noted briefly:

1st Regiment's attack through St Marc resulted in the capture of 39 prisoners of war and the destruction of an ammunition dump and one 88mm gun in the area.[5]

Claude Bernard tells us a comical detail he heard about the arrival of the very first forcemen in Peymeinade:

My grandfather had dug a hole along the canal and covered it with wood and everything to be protected. When there was firing going on, they all hid in that hole. I wasn't there, but my cousin and uncle were and the priest was with them. At one point there was a lull, so they left the hole, and to their great astonishment, there was an American soldier with his pants down. He had not seen them in the hole and my female cousin who had gone out said: "Oh! Look, the man is doing a poo!" So a hand was immediately put in front of my cousin's eyes and the priest

37-year-old Kriegsmarine Obergefreiter Johann Strunk with his wife and children. His family had hoped that his job as a navy truck driver far from any fronts would keep him safe. Unfortunately, he was killed at Peymeinade next to the halftrack he had been assigned to. His only brother, who was married to his wife's sister, was killed in Russia a few weeks later. Strunk Family Collection.

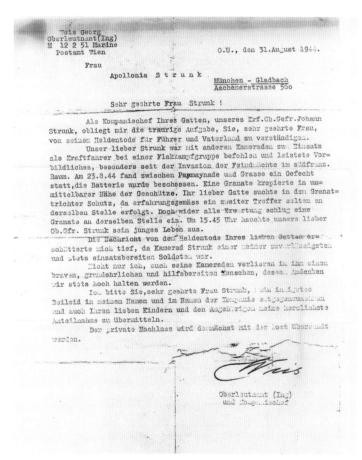

The letter that Johann Strunk's wife received announcing his death. Strunk Family Collection.

went out to hide the spectacle. The American dressed back up but was annoyed, because if there had been a German soldier in the hole he could have been killed.

Jean, the *Groupe Tartane résistant* who had crossed through the lines to St Raphaël, was now accompanying the Americans through the Peymeinade area. **Jean**'s account starts on the morning of the 23rd, when he and his comrade, Raymond Dupont, started guiding the Americans towards Grasse after being dropped off at the Siagne River:

The trucks dropped us off with the Americans a bit before the Siagne Bridge, which did not exist anymore. I don't know why the Germans blew it up; it was pointless because it was summertime, and the vehicles could ford the river with no problem. We left on foot with the Americans. We met gendarme *Adjudant* Blanchis, from Grasse, whom we knew well, and he told the Americans: "Aren't you ashamed of yourselves? You are letting these two brave young men walk in front with no weapons! They have to be armed." So the Americans gave us two carbines from soldiers who had been killed and told us: "It works like this and like that," and then we continued on towards Grasse. When we got to Peymeinade, there was a German machine gun on a hill that was firing, and in fact, there was one dead American in the middle of the road. [This was probably **Pvt Frank S. Brown**, of 1-3 FSSF, who had been killed during the night.] The Americans didn't put themselves through a lot of trouble: they halted and called the cannon vehicle they had with them: bang, bang, bang! And when nobody was left over: "OK, let's go on!" That is what they did the whole way long every time there was some resistance. They didn't take too many risks, and they were right not to do so. Some Germans had put their ammunition next to their cannon. Bang, everything blew up, and they were killed and then remained buried there.

The four German soldiers who had been killed in the immediate vicinity of the cannon, as well as a fifth soldier who had been killed a couple hundred meters further south, were buried in the garden of the de Boutigny property by Monsieur de Boutigny's gardener. **Robert Guérin**, a teenager who lived in Grasse, went to examine the cannon the day after the battle when the bodies were still lying nearby:

We found out that there had been some fighting on the Route de Draguignan. One or two Germans had been killed on the Route de Peymeinade, guys who were left there to delay the Americans and who were pretty much sacrificed. They knew very well that they could either surrender or be killed.

Then there was a large cannon with a huge halftrack, and a shell landed right on the ammunition crates and there was an enormous explosion that killed all the men who were around the cannon. I saw them lying on the ground. One still had his helmet on, so they were in combat position. One was lying against a wall, it seemed like he had dragged himself to the wall. One had his mouth open and his two front teeth were missing. I thought: "Damn, the poor guy." Another had flies that were eating his eyes. One of them must have been shaving, because he was half shaved and there was a piece of mirror in the branch of a tree. And there was one who had eaten tomatoes: a shell fragment had slit his belly open and there was a tomato in his stomach.

They were a bunch of poor devils, and then I saw some atrocious things. There was some sort of so-called resistance fighter, who became a resistance fighter the day after the liberation. The day before he would never have touched them. He turned one body over with his feet and the body burped up some air. They quickly took his boots off. They were body looters, taking everything they had: weapons, helmets, and all those things. Then the bodies stayed to dry in the sun for a day or two, and then somebody buried them.

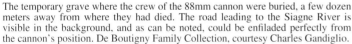

The temporary grave where the crew of the 88mm cannon were buried, a few dozen meters away from where they had died. The road leading to the Siagne River is visible in the background, and as can be noted, could be enfiladed perfectly from the cannon's position. De Boutigny Family Collection, courtesy Charles Gandiglio.

This button from a tropical Kriegsmarine uniform was found at the site of the temporary grave in Peymeinade where Johann Strunk and his comrades from the Lufwaffe were buried. Presumably, the button belonged to Johann Strunk and comes from one of his tropical uniforms, such as the one he is wearing in this photo. Private Collection. Strunk Family Collection.

One particular character in Peymeinade became famous for his German boots, as **Charles Gandiglio** remembers:

I saw a guy, in fact everybody saw him, who was a bit out of touch and who had a pair of German boots after the Liberation. He took pleasure walking on the heals: clic, clac, clic, clac, and everybody said: "The Germans kept their boots on their feet, those who lost them are those who lost their lives." It's true that they had boots that were quite pleasant to look at, all made of leather and everything, while we were walking around in wooden clogs.

A German button stamped with an anchor was found at the site where the bodies of the five German soldiers were buried and later exhumed. Because Johann Strunk was apparently the only *Kriegsmarine* soldier to be killed in Peymeinade, it can be assumed that this button was his.

German soldiers were often overtaken by the rapid Allied advance, and they then remained stranded behind the lines for a few days, hoping to rejoin their units, or being too afraid to surrender. Several days after the Liberation, **Charles Gandiglio** witnessed the surrender of two such German "holdouts":

Eight days later, we were in a vineyard. It was in the afternoon and was extremely hot as usual, and we heard some shouting near the path and we saw a white thing moving around above the embankment of the road. My father asked: "What is that thing over there?" and we then saw two Germans come out of the depths of the forest with a branch with a white handkerchief on it. It was impossible to communicate, but they had their hands up as if to say they were surrendering. So my father told them: "OK, that's nice, but what am I supposed to do with you?" It's funny, because if my father had taken his pitchfork and brought the two of them to Peymeinade, he would have received a medal.

My father said: "Listen, what do you want me to say to you? I will give you a glass of water, that's all I can do." The water was from the tank and wasn't very clean, but they were so thirsty that they drank it up. Then he told them: "Take the path down there and go to Peymeinade." We don't know what happened to them after that. They probably surrendered. They must have stayed hidden in the forest for eight days, thinking: "At least this way we will survive."

We have now dwelled into the aftermath of the fighting at Peymeinade, but at the time there was no pause for the forcemen. As soon as the German 88mm cannon was destroyed, they immediately continued their advance towards Grasse, planning to attack the town during the night.

The Liberation of Grasse

The FSSF plan of attack for Grasse was a pincer movement, in which the 1st Regiment, coming from Peymeinade, would approach the city from the south, while the 2nd Regiment would attack from the north. The attack was performed during the night of August 23rd to 24th. Most of the Germans who remained in Grasse were members of the 1st and 2nd Companies of *Reserve Grenadier Battalion 7*, which had been defending St Cézaire 24 hours earlier. The FSSF sent the following message about the German defenses of Grasse to the FABTF command at 10:10 p.m. on the 23rd:

> Only 2 companies fighting a delaying action in front of Grasse. The strength is 120 men. They are now withdrawing disorganized towards Nice. The 148th Infantry Division is going to reorganize then. We have taken about 44 prisoners of war from the 1st and 2nd companies of the 8th *Grenadier* Regiment. (…) Everything is under control. The enemy is being liquidated.[6]

In fact, it would seem that the Germans had decided to pull out without defending the town, and that the German troops that were still present in Grasse had either not had time to escape or wanted to surrender. In any case, the town was barely defended, and was captured without any Allied soldiers getting killed. A few Germans did, however, try to fight, as is evidenced by the citation for the Silver Star that **Sergeant Roe Rapp**, of 4-1 of the FSSF, was awarded:

> The platoon to which Sergeant Rapp was assigned was spearheading an attack. The advance of the platoon was halted by heavy enemy machine gun fire from the left and direct front. Sergeant Rapp and four men were ordered forward to silence one definitely located gun. Upon advancing a short distance, Sergeant Rapp discovered that instead of one gun in his path, there were seven. Deciding that the only chance of overcoming such resistance would be to rush the positions, Sergeant Rapp and the four men rose to their feet and, rapidly firing their weapons, rushed the nearest gun. The fire killed one gunner, wounded two crew men, and caused five of the enemy to surrender. The crews of the other enemy guns, seeing this, abandoned their weapons and fled in complete disorder, only to be captured later by the remainder of the platoon.[7]

In total, only one German was killed in Grasse: 31-year-old *Wachtmeister* **Hermann Münzel**, of the 3rd Battery of *Flak Abteilung 391*, who was killed by a gunshot wound to the head. Resistance man **Jean** and his friend, Raymond Dupont, were serving as guides to 4-1 of the FSSF as it entered Grasse:

> We continued all the way to Grasse. We didn't follow the road, but went through the back yards of houses, climbing over walls. Then we divided into two groups: Raymond went with one team, and I went with another. I ended up on the Route de Cannes. So I told the Americans: "We will take this little path and pass underneath the

hermann Münzel
Wachtmeister in einem Flakkampftrupp
Inhaber des EK II, des Flakkampfabzeichens
und anderer Kriegsauszeichnungen.

31-year-old Wachtmeister Hermann Münzel, of Flak Abteilung 391, who was buried in Grasse after suffering a fatal gunshot wound to the head somewhere in the vicinity August 23rd. Stadtarchiv Koblenz Collection, courtesy Peter Kleber.

barracks." The barracks were occupied by the Germans at the time. We went up the path and there was a house. I knocked on the door and one of my uncles came to open the door and was surprised to see his nephew accompanied by all those American soldiers, with their helmets daubed with black paint. I asked him: "Are there still Germans in the barracks?" He said he didn't know, so I told the Americans: "I don't know." It was nighttime, so the Americans said: "OK, we will wait for daylight and see what happens tomorrow morning." The next morning, we saw the Germans had left and that the city of Grasse was thus liberated. There were prisoners, but they weren't really Germans; they were Poles who had surrendered. In fact, they immediately lifted their arms and said: "Me not German, me Polish." They were a bit frightened; there was so much hatred after those four years of occupation and of fear that the guys preferred to surrender to regular troops, because regular troops apply the rules of war, whereas with the FFI... you never know.

> The Americans didn't want to let us go. At the time I could speak a bit of English that I had learned at school and told them: "Both of us are natives of Grasse, let us enjoy the pleasure of the Liberation." So they let us go and we went up to Grasse to celebrate the Liberation."

Major Gerry McFadden, commanding officer of the 2nd Battalion of 1st Regiment of the FSSF, only remembers encountering one German willing to fight in Grasse:

> A German got away in a car. I would imagine he was somebody of authority that was to find out if the city was still without opposition. He fired, but he didn't get anybody. I think he was emptying his gun and getting ready to run. He went down through the bottom and disappeared on us. We didn't chase him, because we didn't know which way he had gone.

2nd Regiment, coming in from the north, seems to have run into slightly more serious resistance, as they reported at 5:15 a.m.:

3 casualties: Captain Olson [Eino Olson, the Intelligence Officer of 2ⁿᵈ Regiment] severely wounded in action in the arm; 2 enlisted men wounded and one Frenchman shot in head. Sent to Force medics.[8]

It is unclear how many of these casualties were actually due to the Germans and how many were due to friendly fire, though. **Sgt Jack Knight**, of the HQ detachment of 2ⁿᵈ Regiment, remembers how one of the casualties occurred:

When we were going into Grasse, a Free French patrol mistook us for the enemy and opened fire on us, and one of my buddies was shot with an American .45 that was in the hands of one of the FFI. I was able to get to the man that was doing the shooting before the gun smoke had even cleared. I just jumped on him and pinned him down, and before I let him loose, I assured him that we were friends, we weren't enemy. I think it was an honest mistake. I brought the weapon that I took from the underground fellow home with me. It still had all the blueing on it. My own .45 was shiny as a Ford bumper.

Grasse was captured without any further casualties occurring, and over 50 German prisoners were taken. As elsewhere in the Maritime Alps, the poor motivation of many of *Reserve Division 148*'s enlisted men had severely undermined the unit's combat efficiency. Major Holt, of 2ⁿᵈ Regiment, even noted: "Picked up 35 prisoners of war. Some are Poles that were fighting against the Germans."[9] **Claude Cauvin**, a 16-year-old inhabitant of Grasse, explains the liberation of his town as seen from the inside:

In the last 24 hours everything had sped up: public buildings occupied by the Germans and convoys on the roads around Grasse were strafed. Warships finally appeared on the sea, as their presence could be detected by the flashes from their guns that were methodically shelling objectives that were probably above Grasse, the salvoes passing over the house. I can still remember the noise they produced, similar to that of a train. There were also numerous forest fires, the smoke and ashes of which darkened the atmosphere.

August 23ʳᵈ, in the morning, the ammunition depot at the Bois-Murés exploded and burned the entire day. I could watch all that from the terraces of my property as if it were a spectacle. Everything was getting closer. Finally nighttime came, bringing somewhat of a lull with it. There were still a few gunshots, then silence came along with the darkness. We had closed all the shutters of the house. Through the cracks of those in my room I noticed that the machine gun that the Germans had installed at the corner of the wall in the afternoon, facing the Route de St Jacques, had disappeared, as well as its crew.

Then came August 24ᵗʰ. Curious as one can be at that age, I got up early without warning my parents and, reassured by the strange silence, I went out and jumped over the wall into the street after seeing that the fortified chicane had been abandoned. As of that point, I discovered the remains of military activity: abandoned helmets, clips, bullet casings, equipment, even a bayonet, the only visible weapon. The street was completely deserted (…). Continuing my exploration, I went towards the terraced field under the hospital, where I discovered trenches that had been dug and were filled with all kinds of miscellaneous items mixed in with equipment: newspapers, magazines, bottles, etc…

At one point I lifted my head and stopped cold. A soldier was standing a few steps away from me. I knew

SSgt Albert Schober, of 6-1 of the FSSF, poses in Grasse with a civilian and comrades who are tasting a sample of the local wine. Robert Schober Collection.

German uniforms well enough to know that he was not a German. It was not his clothes that struck me, but the fact that he seemed not to have any weapon, apart from a solid stick that he was holding in his hand and using as a cane. He was alone, we were standing face to face, and I was probably the most surprised of the two of us. He started speaking, but my school knowledge of the English language did not help. He continued speaking, and I finally managed to distinguish the word "bath," repeated several times and accompanied by meaningful mimics. I concluded that he wanted to wash; indeed, his clothes were dusty and stained and his face was covered in dust. Without thinking, I signaled him to follow me and brought him home, where my parents took care of him. I never saw him again.

I went back into the street, where the show was starting, first with the arrival of a vehicle of which only the wheels were visible, because it was covered with crates, packs, and camouflage nets. There were four men on it, and as it stopped I also signaled them to follow me and brought them home.

René Ghio, a child living in Grasse, wrote a very good description of the day of the Liberation as seen through the eyes of a child. He was awakened by his father the morning of August 24th:

"This is it! This is it, we are liberated, the Americans have arrived during the night," says my father, shaking me.

"Really Dad, they are here?" I make a leap from the bed and run to the window.

The sun is already up, today is the 24th. I feel a bit guilty to have fallen asleep and to not have been up at the moment the Americans arrived, which I had been waiting for so long for.

"Come and see what I brought back," he says.

When I reach the garden, I think my father will stop working in the trains and will open a bicycle shop.

"There are already six of them," he tells me very proudly, "and I am going to get some more. I also found musette bags full of food."

He leaves again to search for more bicycles.

I open a musette bag. It contains various things. On top there is a round box made of orange Bakelite that is full of butter; in some paper there is some black bread that is very hard but good. I take out my knife and start spreading butter as I search through the musette. On top there is a shaving kit, then letters and a medal; I feel a bit embarrassed, as if I had stolen.

With my slice of bread in hand, I run down the path towards the road to get into the thick of the event. I heard my mother shouting at me to come back. Surprise at the end of the path: the antitank pyramids that were in place last night are nothing but a shapeless mass mixed in with broken barbed wire entanglements. There is activity at the crossroads: groups of FFIs are talking with their submachine guns slung over their shoulders. A car with a tricolor flag stops. There are also small kaki cars and big trucks carrying American soldiers, as well as some sort of tank with a big metal blade on its front. It easily pushes away the pyramids and piles them at the side of the road. I am fascinated, because I have never seen such a powerful vehicle; now it is attacking the wall of the chicane that is blocking the road. (…)

I see Gérard's house in the greenery at the end of the path.(…)

"Don't move," says a voice behind me, and I am lifted from the ground.

A guy that I did not see coming puts me back down two meters further. He has a big smile. The guy lifted me up with a single hand, and I am impressed. He shows me something in the grass.

"Be careful! Bang! Bang!"

Shit! Lemon grenades as we call them. (…) I look at the soldier, and he has a friendly face. I am with one of our liberators, and I examine him from head to toe. He doesn't look very military, except for his ammunition pouches and a tiny rifle.

"American?" I ask him.

"No, Canadian, and I speak French just like you." He laughs and puts his finger on a red plane tree leaf sewn to his sleeve. (…)

We go onto the terrace below the house. Three other soldiers are resting in the grass. The Canadian tells me that his name is Jimmy, and the others greet me. They are American and speak to me in American, it is funny.

"Chewing gum, good?" Asks one guy, giving me something that is to be chewed. It is the first time I see that and hear that name. I chew away, and am quite proud to act like the soldiers.

It is only then that I see about 10 German soldiers with no weapons sitting in the grass a bit further on under some olive trees, probably some prisoners. I explain to Jimmy

"The soldier laughs and puts his finger on a red plane tree leaf sewn to his sleeve." The famous spearhead badge worn by members of the First Special Service Force, this particular example was kept by Norm Smith, of the HQ Detachment of 1st Regiment. Author's Collection.

that I want to go home. The Americans get up, take their weapons, and along with the prisoners we cross the field towards the road. We find several small kaki cars parked beside the road. Almost all the traffic is going towards town. The Canadian stops a truck that is travelling empty back towards Peymeinade and makes all the German soldiers climb in. The Canadian brings me to a jeep, that is how he calls his car. We climb in. Between the two seats there is a big machine gun mounted. There is no windscreen, and it is really nice, the air comes straight into our faces. I climb into the back with the three others. I can't believe it. We slowly drive towards town. The four guys laugh constantly, it really feels nice; I think, "I haven't seen anybody laughing like that for years." I am very proud to be in there. If my friends could see me. I feel like I am one of the liberators.

We drive towards Grasse. We see lots of people with FFI or FTP armbands. We wonder where they are coming from and where they were during the occupation. We pass cars on which the *maquisard*s have painted "FFI" on the doors, with a blue, white, and red flag. On the sidewalks, the girls in their summer dresses laugh with the soldiers.

It is really a celebration. There are garlands on the houses, tricolored flags at the windows, a few hastily made American flags and British flags. (…) The soldiers have given me a bag of candy. They distribute some to the kids and I do the same thing with the bag they gave me. They also give out American cigarettes. Two old men come toward us with outspread hands, laughing and shouting like after a game: "We won! We won!" If I had tomatoes, I would throw them at their faces.[10]

Grasse was one of the cities best remembered by the Allied soldiers because of the warm welcome they received, and also because the city smelled so good: Grasse was the world's perfume capital. **Private Art Helmers**, of the 602nd Field Artillery Battalion, was one of the soldiers who drove through the town the day of its liberation:

The people along our ride between Grasse and Valbonne were cheering wildly for us as we moved along. Our vehicle was a captured truck that had been taken from the British, probably at Dunkirk, and now had come back into Allied hands. Since the truck was camouflaged in the noticeable German manner the people stared at first, half fearing that we were Germans retreating. Their stares gave way to succeeding waves of recognition, laughter, cheers, and a not-too-subdued hysteria. Flowers were showering upon us, strewn in our path and waved high in the air.

The towns or cities were out in force, while the farmers working in their fields dropped their tools and rushed to the fences as their families quickly followed suit, yelling and waving. Children old enough to know what was happening would wave to us, while the women would wave the hands of their smaller ones.

We were proud and pleased to be the recipients of such spontaneous and well-meant enthusiasm. We were touched, too, by the thought behind this joy; the thought that no more must they worry about the *Gestapo*, SS, or one of the more common German army gangs. These people were free and were glad to be able to show it. No conquering or liberating army could ever have been so well received, so earnestly wished for. Had we been walking, we no doubt would have received the same "fate" our comrades did, as they were kissed, wined, and dined when possible. Each time we stopped, we had to keep the people out of our way. They crowded around to speak to us, to ask us infinite numbers of questions and give us their ideas.[11]

Lt Karl Wickstrom, also of the 602nd FAB, had similar fond memories of Grasse:

Grasse had a barrel of wine in the square for all the Special Service Force troops. I was the first jeep in town. The people felt like we were the rescuers of France. There might have been a thousand troops south of us or north of us, going around there, but they just saw us, so they kept giving us things. They gave me this one bottle, about a quarter or half a gallon, and so, as I was riding out of town, just a few minutes later, I started saying: "Let's see, what should I keep of this," because I had to keep the space; o I smelled it, it was kind of a sweet smell, and I tasted it, and it had kind of a sweet taste, and so I just tossed it over the ditch. I always told my wife, I maybe threw away half a gallon of Channel n°5. But I don't know what I threw away, something they thought was pretty good I guess, if they gave it to me. You had to separate what was good for you, or not good for you.

Major Gerry McFadden, of the 1st Regiment of the FSSF, remembers the deleterious effect that these gifts had on one of his men:

When we were in Grasse, the people were very generous with the wine. As we walked down the main

Howard Williams, of 6-2 of the FSSF, poses with local "demoiselles" in Grasse. Warren MacPhie Collection.

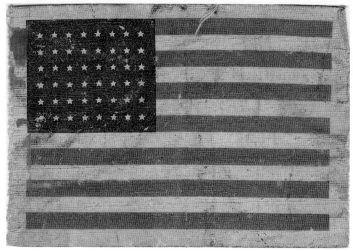

Lt Karl Wickstrom, of the 602nd PFAB, poses with joyful inhabitants of Grasse August 24th. Note that although he was not a paratrooper, he is wearing a paratrooper jump suit (with a broken zipper). The American flag visible on the left shoulder of his jumpsuit is the same one as presented here. Karl Wickstrom Collection.

street, everybody was handing a bottle of wine to us. We had a native Indian from the States, a big, hefty guy, 220 pounds maybe, and a great sergeant. The funny part of it was, somebody handed him a bottle of wine and I remember I just happened to notice. I stopped and looked, and here is this sergeant drinking the whole bottle of wine in one gulp—glup, glup, glup, glup, all the way down. He threw the bottle away, and he said: "Boy, that tasted good!" And after that we had trouble with him. He got a short circuit, and he was seeing Germans at the corner. He had a Tommy gun and fired all his ammunition around, almost hitting some of our own men. Finally, I had to tell them to get six big men, and they teased him, cornered him, and then jumped on him and beat the hell out of him, and he was knocked out. Then I got some wire or rope from my jeep and roped him tight and threw him in the back of the jeep and said: "Leave him there!" I was mad at him, he just almost killed us. He stayed there overnight, and the next morning, when I went to look at him, he was there. His eyes were open but he couldn't move, and he said: "What happened?" I told him that he was a bad boy, and he said: "I don't remember a thing." So they unwound him and he went around and apologized to all the fellows and said: "I will never take another bottle of wine. I could have killed you." So that was a little episode in Grasse.

Advancing to the Loup River

After liberating Grasse the morning of August 24th, the men of the FABTF took no time to relax, continuing straight on towards the east. Since the Germans had now retreated to their next defensive line at the Loup River, the Allies met virtually no opposition on the way. The FSSF reached the areas of Roquefort les Pins, la Colle sur Loup, Mougins, Valbonne, and Biot by nightfall, capturing approximately 40 prisoners on the way. At Valbonne, the 3rd Regiment of the FSSF and a detachment of B Battery of the 602nd FAB ran into a few German stragglers. **Art Helmers**, of the 602nd, was in a jeep that had unknowingly gotten ahead of the infantry and therefore found himself at the heart of the action:

We were moving eastward, and sometimes moving across the front, you came to a place where you didn't see any infantry and you figured they were ahead of you. Very often they'd pulled off the road, possibly to eat, possibly to regroup, or to just take a break. So I was with the first gun crew—that's a jeep pulling the 75 howitzer—and as we pulled into a town, which I believe was Valbonne, we saw the Germans 100 yards to the right, on the other side of the square. They were absolutely totally surprised, because we were well ahead of our own infantry.

We quickly turned into the first road, hopped out of the jeep, and the Germans started to run. We quickly set the gun up, and the gunner Corporal said: "To hell with the sight, I will just sight down the tube." There was no sense bothering with the sight, so we opened the tube and he sighted down the barrel of the gun and decided what he wanted to fire on. At this point, the Germans were 150 yards or so away, weaving through the buildings, and some of them had started to run up the slope behind the town to get out of the way. He sighted down the barrel, and we loaded the gun and fired. He sighted down the barrel again, we loaded the gun again, and fired at the retreating Germans as they ran out of the town, up the side of the hill. We fired three times, and two other guns behind jeeps pulled into town and moved into the roads near us. But by the time they got set up, the Germans had left the town and the rest of them were going over the hills. We did not go over to see about wounded or injured, because at that point some of the infantry showed up, so we stopped firing and hooked up our gun again and waited until the infantry had come through before a decision was made as to what we would do next.

Two young Germans were killed in Valbonne; the rest either surrendered or escaped. **Madame Voegeli**, a local child, remembers the arrival of the Allied troops and the capture of two German prisoners:

When the Americans came, they arrived in jeeps from the direction of the Route de Grasse. There was a field on the right side before reaching Valbonne and they stopped there with the jeeps. We kids went to pick flowers to give to them. The Americans were looking for two Germans who were hiding in a hut in the forest. They found them and brought them back to where the jeeps were and made them get down on their knees. So the Germans were crying and showing their wallets with pictures of their wives and children. I was also crying, because I felt sorry for them.

The two Germans who had been killed were buried in the local cemetery next to their three comrades who had died in the Valbonne field hospital over the previous days. They were:

Name	Surname	Rank	Age	Date of death	Location of death	Unit
Lesch	Helmut	Gren	17	24.8.1944	Valbonne	Inf.Pz.Jg. Ers.Kp.
Rauch	Hans	Sold	18	24.8.1944	Valbonne	

The FSSF continued advancing east to the Loup River area, reaching Villeneuve-Loubet and la Colle at nightfall, where serious resistance was encountered, obliging the FSSF to stop its progression. The encounters that occurred on the Loup will be the theme of the next chapter.

The 517th Parachute Infantry Regiment's Advance to the Var River

The 517th PIR had crossed Grasse shortly after its liberation by the FSSF, and as the FSSF advanced towards the southern part of the Loup River, the 517th advanced towards the northern sector, with a patrol from the 3rd Battalion reaching Bar sur Loup the afternoon of August 24th. From Bar, the paratroopers could see a large railroad bridge over the Loup that the Germans had not yet blown, but the patrol was incapable of preventing the Germans from destroying the bridge. **William Webb**, of the HQ Company of the 3rd Battalion of the 517th, was there:

The railroad bridge at Pont du Loup that the Germans blew August 24, 1944, just before the arrival of the paratroopers of the 517th PIR. Howard Hensleigh Collection.

The remains of the bridge at Pont du Loup as they appear today. Author's Collection.

We started a route march to keep the Germans from blowing a railroad bridge. All of a sudden they called for a wire man. I was a wire man, with a real wire and a phone up front. I went up front and Captain McGeever was sitting there, leaning up against a half wall around this city. Upon seeing me, the captain asked: "Where is your piece?"

"Back on the truck," I replied.

"Where is your helmet?"

I replied: "Back with my rifle."

Captain McGeever retorted: "Doggone, Webb, you're not much help here, put the phone right here."

As I put the phone in, he was leaning over the wall with his 03 with telescopic sights on it, and it looked like about 700 yards to the bridge. There was a German running from the German side out there; I think he was trying to set some of the charges, and the captain fired and knocked the German off the bridge. He said: "Did you see that shot, Webb?" The machine gunner started shooting about that time, but his tracers were hitting halfway down the hill and I said: "The machine gunner got him captain." He says: "Webb, you're no good to me here, why don't you just get out of here." So I told him: "Well, do you want me to salute when I leave?" We never saluted up front, of course. He said: "Webb, you're in enough trouble already. I will catch up with you later on." So I put the phone in and left. Captain McGeever was one of the finest people I ever knew, but he got killed about three days later. [Captain Joseph McGeever was killed near Col de Braus September 11, 1944.] The Germans blew up the bridge after he knocked that man off of it.

No trace of any German soldier being killed at Pont du Loup has been found in the *Volksbund* archives, and the locals also do not remember the death of any German. Perhaps the German simply lay down after hearing McGeever's bullet fly past him and escaped later on?

Over the next two days, the FSSF and 509th PIB would face a fair amount of resistance along the Loup River defense line, and their advance was therefore halted until August 27th. In the meantime, however, the 517th simply outflanked the northernmost German positions, entering the high mountains that were under Resistance control. Facing no German opposition, the 517th was able to advance east very quickly. On the 24th, after the bridge at Pont du Loup had been blown, the 517th PRCT crossed the Loup River and followed its valley northwards up to Courmes. On the 25th, they reached Coursegoules, Bézaudun, and le Broc. On the 26th, when other FABTF units were still fighting at the Loup River, the 517th was far ahead and was already able to reach the Var River at Carros. **Marcel Guido**, a kid living in the Loup River Valley, vividly remembers the passage of the American troops:

The Americans arrived by the Loup Valley. They were the shock troops, and they walked up the gorges towards Courmes, St Barnabé, and Coursegoules. They unwound a telephone wire along the whole way. We kids from the area were eight years old, and we followed them because we were finding all kinds of stuff. There were candies, chewing gum, and ration boxes, but also weapons: grenades, clips for Thompsons, and bayonets. It was the stuff they threw away all along the path, because they were loaded down like mules. They had half kilogram tin cans attached in strings from their belts and were walking like that, with grenades everywhere.

An American bayonet that young Marcel Guido found abandoned between Pont du Loup and Courmes in 1944. It has been spray painted in green paint, like most of the equipment used by the soldiers of the 517th PIR. Private Collection.

This camouflaged 517th PRCT-modified helmet was recovered at Pont du Loup by a local youth in 1944. A laundry mark (last four digits of the Army Service Number) painted inside the helmet identify it as apparently having belonged to I Company soldier Charles R. Smith, from North Carolina. Frédéric Brega Collection.

We had a vegetable garden, and the officers had come and told my mother: "If the guys come and steal something, don't say anything, because they are all…" *Legionaires*… Or I don't know what they were. "They might do something bad. Just let them do it and we will come back and pay you back." They came once or twice and took a few tomatoes, but nothing bad happened."

Paulette Blanc lived in Courmes, one of the tiny mountain villages that the 517th PIR marched through on its trek towards the Var River:

Somebody said: "The Americans are here," so a whole team of us rushed down to see them in the fields, children in front and parents behind. We found them resting with all their weapons. I think some people brought them a bottle of wine, but they didn't seem to like wine very much. They would have preferred Coca-Cola, if that even existed. Anyway, we gave what we had, which wasn't much. They only had canned food, and there were tomatoes and onions in the gardens, and they had even pulled out the onions but then thrown them away.

They had two young guys with them, two small Czech prisoners they had captured. So the people started booing them, but then the Americans said: "No, no, no! They are not Germans, they are Czech." They requisitioned a mare and loaded it with weapons, and the owner of the mare went up to Coursegoules with them.

Paratroopers from I Company of the 517th reach the remote mountain village of Courmes on their way towards Coursegoules. In the group photo, Pvt Marvin Moles recognized himself as the person standing third from the right. These two snapshots were taken by Mademoiselle Paulette Blanc. Mairie de Courmes Collection, courtesy Paul Sicard.

This helmet is one of the items abandoned by the American paratroopers during their brief visit to Courmes. The helmet was kept by local teenager Adolphe Euzière and bears all the characteristics of a helmet of the 517th PRCT: a rigger-made improvised chinstrap and the typical green and grey-black spray painted camouflage. Adolphe Euzière carved his name and the date August 24th into the side of the helmet. Upon inspection, it was found that the original American owner of the helmet had also carved his name, Moles, into the paint of the helmet in two places. Marvin Moles, of I Company, was contacted in 2004 and then returned to France to see his helmet and visit Courmes once again 60 years after he had participated in its liberation. Author's Collection.

In 2004, Marvin Moles meets the Sicard brothers and Mademoiselle Paulette Blanc in Courmes. Mlle Blanc had taken the original snapshot of Marvin Moles and his I Company buddies in Courmes in 1944. Diane Lynch Collection.

Some historians have commented on how slow the advance of the FABTF through the French Riviera was. Indeed, taking two weeks to advance about 80 kilometers may seem slow compared to the lightning advances that were made by armored columns, such as Task Force Butler, on other nearby fronts. However, such analyses do not take into account the fact that the FABTF was advancing on foot, through a zone that was heavily mined and in which almost every existing bridge had been destroyed. Furthermore, the terrain was often hilly, if not downright mountainous, the roads were winding, and the Germans were still well organized and setting up strong resistance points.

The movements of the 517th from August 22nd to 26th are a good example of how stressful the advance to the east actually was for the soldiers. Late on the 22nd, they had crossed the Siagne Valley (250 meters down then up) and had to overcome a German strongpoint at Saint Cézaire (altitude 400 meters), where five paratroopers were killed. The next day, they moved on to St Vallier (altitude 650 meters), which was heavily mined. Then, on the 24th, they marched down to Grasse and on to Pont du Loup (altitude 200 meters), where they encountered the Germans again and where all bridges had been blown. On the 25th they were in Coursegoules (altitude 1,000 meters), and on the 26th, they reached the Var River, at almost sea level, after hiking through the mountains.

For the fit young troopers who participated in this march, there was nothing "slow" about their advance through minefields and rivers and up and down steep mountains. When the 517th PIR finally reached the Var River on the 26th, it was far in advance of the other FABTF units. We will go into more details about its arrival at the Var in Chapter 12, but we must first examine the events that were slowing down the rest of the FABTF at the Loup River.

Conclusion

The town of Grasse was defended by a series of small strongpoints located between the Siagne River and Grasse itself. The most notable of these was an 88mm cannon positioned east of Peymeinade. The First Special Service Force crossed the Siagne River during the night of August 22nd to 23rd, suffering two killed, and it was then able to rapidly close in on Grasse, destroying the 88mm cannon at Peymeinade in the process. Grasse itself fell like a ripe fruit early on the 24th, and several dozen soldiers of the 1st and 2nd Companies of *Reserve Grenadier Battalion 7*, which had previously fought at St Cézaire, were captured. The FSSF and the 517th Parachute Infantry Regiment immediately pushed on towards the east after Grasse had fallen. The FSSF advanced all the way to the Loup River, where it ran into the next German defense line late August 24th. The 517th PIR was meanwhile able to cut through the mountains without encountering any resistance until it reached the Var River on the 26th.

10

Crossing the Loup River at Villeneuve-Loubet and la Colle sur Loup

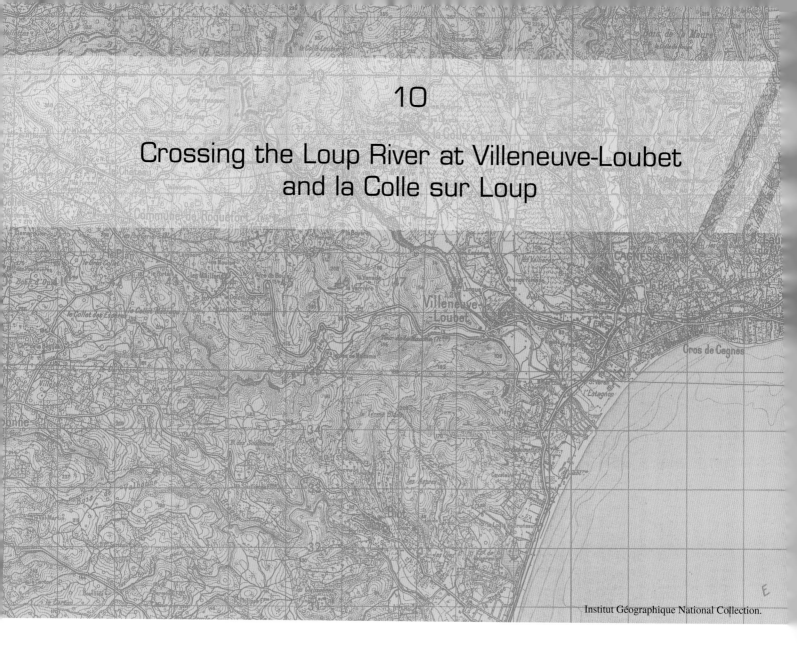

Institut Géographique National Collection.

In the chapters six through nine, we have examined the battles that occurred to cross the Siagne River. After serious fighting in the area of la Napoule for three days, and some sharp encounters at Peymeinade and St Cézaire, the First Airborne Task Force was able to suddenly advance at high speed along the main roads all the way to the Loup River, late on August 24th. 2nd Regiment of the First Special Service Force reached the Loup River near Villeneuve-Loubet, where they met resistance, while the 517th Parachute Infantry Regiment reached it at Pont du Loup. The 509th Parachute Infantry Battalion remained safely at the Brague River, only advancing to the Loup on the 26th, where they also encountered resistance. We will start the chapter by studying the fighting the FSSF was involved in at Villeneuve-Loubet and la Colle, and will then pass on to the actions of the 509th on the coast at Villeneuve-Loubet.

Advancing to the Loup River

The Loup River was the next planned German line of defense after the Siagne River. This line of defense was outposted by German soldiers of *Reserve Grenadier Bataillon 372*, with the 7th Company in Villeneuve-Loubet, 6th Company in la Colle sur Loup, 8th Company in support, and men from 5th Company apparently present in both Villeneuve and la Colle. The 14th Company of *Reserve Grenadier Regiment 239* provided antitank cannons and crews. In the days preceding the arrival of the Allied troops, the Germans

readied themselves for battle. At la Colle, the bridge was prepared for demolition and the Germans took up strategic positions in the countryside around the bridge on the east side of the Loup River.

Villeneuve-Loubet was not a very good defensive point, as it could be outflanked very easily. However, the village itself could be defended quite well, as it formed a compact mass on a hill dominated by a medieval castle. The Château de Villeneuve, as the castle was known, was surrounded by a partial moat, a large park, and several concentric walls. The Germans set up camp in the castle grounds, though inexplicably they did not enter the actual castle, although it would have provided them with excellent protection and fields of fire. They also blew the bridge over the Loup River, dug foxholes nearby, and set up cannons that enfiladed the bridge area. The inhabitants were ordered to leave the doors of their houses open so that the Germans could enter the houses if necessary.

The castle was inhabited by the Marquis de Panisse-Passis and his family. The Marquis' daughter, Elisabeth de Vanssay, wrote a day-by-day account of the liberation of Villeneuve that provides us with outstandingly detailed information on what was happening in the castle. On the 24th, **Elisabeth de Vanssay** described the German preparations and the general situation in Villeneuve:

Thursday August 24th. The night has been quite calm. The radio announces that Rumania is surrendering. A few moments later, Gallo comes to warn us that the Germans are

282

asking the inhabitants to open their windows because they are going to blow up the bridge over the Loup. We quickly open everything… we wait… but nothing happens…

At 11:30, Jeannot comes from Cagnes, telling us that a bugler was announcing that there was an alarm and that the population needed to get into shelters because the Americans were at Roquefort and were closing in on us.

At noon, the bridge has still not been blown. On the other hand, an observation aircraft flies over us at very low altitude for about three quarters of an hour. We are all on edge!

Suddenly a huge explosion: an ammunition depot is exploding on the coast.

Around eleven: great excitement in the house, as two German officers have just arrived to visit the tower. They don't say much, but seem morally and physically exhausted.

We found out later that their batteries were installed under St Paul, and that they had come to "take a fix." (…)

At six thirty there is a formidable "bang"; it is the bridge over the Loup blowing up.

Soon after, a young Pole enters the courtyard and seems to be looking for something. He tells us that he is searching for a place to hide, because himself, his officer, and his comrades are planning to go "Kamerad" when the English arrive. Very slowly we get him to clear off, but who knows if he won't come back, since "these gentlemen" have given the order to leave all the doors open. (…)

Three warships are reported to be facing us near the coast. Will the battle be tonight… at dawn... when? A suitcase is ready for the battle wounded. It is now dark, the atmosphere is calm.[1]

Foxholes built by the Germans on Aspre de Redon Hill, just west of Villeneuve. As usual, the Germans had carefully chosen their defensive positions: in this case the road leading down to Villeneuve from Roquefort and Grasse can be perfectly observed and enfiladed from the foxholes. Author's Collection.

In spite of the "calm atmosphere" and unbeknownst to Elisabeth de Vanssay, the Germans were waiting for the Allies in ambush on the west side of the Loup River, three kilometers outside Villeneuve, on Aspre de Redon Hill. They had been unable to dig in because the ground was solid rock, but they had made "foxholes" out of piled-up stones, overlooking and enfilading a long straightaway in the main road coming from Roquefort and Grasse. From this well selected spot they were waiting, ready to open fire on the first Allied troops that would come down the road from Grasse.

2nd Regiment of the FSSF had participated in liberating Grasse in the early hours of August 24th, after which it proceeded down the road towards Villeneuve-Loubet, which it reached at dusk. After advancing so many kilometers during the day without meeting any resistance, the forcemen were probably not as careful as they usually would have been, and as they reached Aspre de Redon Hill, they fell into the ambush that the Germans had prepared for them. **Sergeant John Hankes**, of 5-2 (the reader is reminded that 5-2 means 5th Company, 2nd Regiment, FSSF), was in the group spearheading the advance:

We got to Grasse and then down to Villeneuve-Loubet. It was night and dark as hell. We were probably about a mile out of town and I sent a scout out ahead, I think his name was Parker. He reported back that everything looked okay. He no sooner got back and apparently, the Germans saw him and started to mortar us pretty good. They had already figured out just where to go with those mortars ahead of time. We lost Captain Hubbard, he lost an eye [In fact, Captain Hubbard had lost an eye on a previous occasion, and it was Anthony Schiarizza who lost an eye August 24th.], and we lost several other fellows. To my knowledge none were killed, but there were several others wounded.

The German ambush had been very successful, their mortar attack having wounded no less than 16 forcemen.[2] **Morris Lazzarus**, also of 5-2, was in a platoon that was almost wiped out:

We were walking down the road towards Villeneuve-Loubet. It was early evening, I think, as it was getting dark. Then we got off to the side of the road so we wouldn't be that easy a target and a shell came in, and I think everybody in the platoon except me got injured. Nobody got killed on that. This one shell came in and knocked them all out. I guess I was so small they couldn't hit me. One of the guys I remember, Tony Schiarizza, from Peterborough, he lost an eye and he was sent back home. He was the major injury, he and one other member. The medics came along and evacuated the guys, all of them except maybe three or four of us. I think we continued on with another platoon.

Lt William Story, of 4-2, was following down the road:

We were on both sides of the road, heading towards Villeneuve-Loubet, and all of a sudden mortars started to come in before we got fully down the road into the community. I have recollection of a mortar round hitting the road and that's where the casualties occurred. We split to the side of the road and stayed in the drainage ditches, seeking as much protection as we could until it finished. It didn't go on very long. I had a couple men wounded, but they just went back to the aid station, got patched up, and came back. The wounds weren't serious, as it was small shrapnel.

Then we came under very intense artillery fire that was largely directed towards a hilltop to our left. I recall turning the platoon over to one of my sergeants and going up to talk to the battalion commander, Stan Waters, who was a personal friend, as well as being battalion commander. Stan and I were right up under the crest of that hill there, on the reverse slope from where the shells were hitting, and the shrapnel was whizzing over our heads; but we weren't bothered at all. We were trying to figure out who was doing the firing. We thought initially, from the trajectory, that it was the supporting naval ships off the coast, but a check with the forward observers knocked that out. The regimental commander wasn't sure what was going on, so we waited that out. We finally figured out it was probably a couple of German 88s. They thought they had us in ambush and that we were on the forward side of the hill. But we were not; we hadn't moved off the road, except to escape the shrapnel from the mortar rounds that came in. But they were darn close! It struck me that they were busy expending their ammunition before taking off down the road. They were definitely doing rear guard stuff. Their responsibility was to slow us down and they did that briefly. They slowed us down a few hours, because we weren't willing to take casualties if we didn't have to.

No sources, neither Allied, French, nor German, provide any information on the artillery barrage mentioned by Lt Story. In the face of this unexpected resistance, the FSSF pulled back towards Roquefort les Pins. **Major Edward Thomas**, commanding the 1st Battalion of 2nd Regiment, remembers:

The route of approach first came to a ridge [Aspre de Redon Hill], then to the Loup River, before reaching the bottom of the village. Pretty imposing terrain prospect for an attack. We went all the way on the road down through Roquefort. I think we bivouacked there all day long. I guess it was in the afternoon or early evening we started off to Villeneuve-Loubet. I had a jeep with a trailer, our only battalion vehicle, and I had the heavier weapons put on this jeep to save the men. We also had with us a shore fire control party from the Navy, because there were destroyers off shore that were giving us artillery support. At some point we were ordered into Villeneuve-Loubet. On the battle plan it was to be a night attack. Second battalion was to lead the way into the town and my battalion was to make a left flanking movement. The attack was begun in the early night, I would say.

At the time the 2nd battalion had begun their attack, I was in a big culvert under the road. My company commanders and I got into it so we could get the flashlights on the maps to decide how we were going to do this flanking, and then we got orders to pull back! The attack had already been started and it was a stupid order. Once you get an attack started you don't want to kill it. But we pulled back, and the explanation at the time was we had gotten too far out in front. Now, since that time there has been another explanation on the order; maybe it was a confused order. It is certain that order should never have been given. If you are going to give it, give it before the attack starts! We pulled back and spent the day there [in front of Aspre de Redon Hill]. Actually, there was some machine gun harassing fire from the town. A bullet hit my aid man and I tried to give him morphine out of his

kit. I was not familiar with the morphine and I was trying to punch it into his leg with the cover over it. Finally I discovered it needed to be removed before it would go in. We spent the day there, and the Germans all prepared for us to make the attack the next night.

The after action report of 2nd Regiment confirms all the previous accounts, as it recorded:

While moving toward Villeneuve-Loubet during the night 24-25, encountered machine gun, small arms, and mortar fire on high ground (…); our casualties: 16. Ordered to withdraw (…) due to change in plans.[3]

August 24th thus ended rather unsuccessfully for the 2nd Regiment. It had fallen into an ambush and was forced to pull back and set camp west of Aspre de Redon Hill, where it spent the night. **Sgt Warren MacPhie**, of 6-2, remembers the harsh conditions under which he and his comrades spent that night. The shelling was hard enough to make some of the forcemen lose their nerve:

We came down from Grasse, and we were just outside Villeneuve-Loubet on the side of a hill at the back of Villeneuve-Loubet. We got shelled badly through the night, and I think it was the American battleships out in the ocean that were shelling us, not the Germans. There was a lot of bramble weed on that hill, very sharp thorny stuff, and there was one officer who had been with the Rangers through North Africa and his nerves were pretty bad. He was pretty well shell shocked. He was trying to dig in with his bare hands on that hillside, through those brambly things with needles, and he just tore his hands all to pieces. The next morning, his hands were like two pieces of meat. I was in a shell hole with a guy from California by the name of Valeria, and he was also an ex-Ranger who had been in North Africa. He was due for repatriation back to the United States the next day and he kept saying: "I'll never make it, I'll never make it, I am never gonna get back to the States," but he did leave the next morning, and I have never heard of him since.

August 25, 1944, at Villeneuve-Loubet and la Colle sur Loup

The next day, August 25th, was mostly characterized by shelling: the Germans shelled the FSSF positions outside Villeneuve, while the American artillery and Allied navy shelled the Germans in Villeneuve. Mr Ghio, an inhabitant of Grasse, needed to go to Nice urgently to fulfill a mission for the Resistance, and to do so, he crossed the lines at Villeneuve-Loubet early on the 25th. **Mr Ghio**'s account of the crossing of the lines provides interesting information on the positions and attitudes of the Allied and German soldiers; it also describes what the terms "front lines" and "no man's land" actually meant in the context of mobile warfare:

At dawn, I wanted to cross Roquefort to reach the Loup River, but we were stopped at the start of the slope. (…) There was probably resistance along the river. We could hear gunfire coming from the valley. We turned around and went to my sister's house near the main road."[4]

After eating breakfast at his sister's house, **Monsieur Ghio** again tried to cross the lines:

After finishing our meal, we went back in the direction of Villeneuve-Loubet, following the road. When we reached the plain, there was another roadblock with American soldiers and an FFI from Grasse whom I knew. He advised us not to go any further, because the road as well as the fields to the left and right were mined. He said we needed to wait for demining teams to come. I told him that was not possible due to the importance of our mission and asked to see the commander of the advanced post. (…) The FFI spoke English and was there to act as an interpreter (…). He told us that the commander would let us through at our own risk. We advanced through the field on the right of the road, but we didn't feel safe at all and expected an explosion at any moment. 500 meters before Villeneuve, we met a few German soldiers behind an embankment. They were surprised to see civilians who seemed to be out on a stroll. One soldier took aim at us, but then let us by without saying anything. The Villeneuve Bridge having been blown, we followed the river, walking through vegetable gardens. A bit further on there were sandbanks, and we were able to cross the Loup.

After reaching Villeneuve, Mr Ghio was able to continue on to Nice. 2nd Regiment of the FSSF was planning to attack Villeneuve-Loubet at nightfall on the 25th. During the afternoon, Captain Adna Underhill took his 2nd Company of 2nd Regiment over the hills south of Aspre de Redon, from where he could clearly see the town of Villeneuve and its castle, and support the night attack if necessary. **Elisabeth de Vanssay** noted the conditions in the castle:

Friday, August 25th (…) I was taking care of my goats and Madame Bertant was walking her dogs when we heard a piercing whistling sound, then two, then three… It was shells passing overhead. Coming from where? Going where? We didn't know anything, but the fact was that they were not exploding very far away. (…)

The shells kept on passing for quite a while, but we were able to eat in the weapons room anyway. *Monsieur* and *Madame* Bertant then took refuge at the entrance of the basement, while father and mother went to rest in their room.

I go up to see them, and mother tells me that five warships are cruising in front of the coast, facing us. I take the binoculars: they are shelling Cap Ferrat and I watch them for a good while; one could see the shot being fired and the shell exploding on the Cap a few instants later. We found out later that they were American ships, among which was the French ship *George Leygues*.

Father was still sleeping and mother was going to lie down when I tell her: "It seems like one of them is getting into position to fire on us." I had not finished my sentence when I saw a shot go off and… land near the water tank facing us. These shots are repeated several times in a row, this time on Vaugrenier, then on la Madone and finally… a formidable "bang" startles us; a shell had just landed at the Gate of the Virgin: they were firing at us.[5]

Elisabeth de Vanssay would probably have been very surprised if she had known that forcemen were already present on the hills she was observing. In fact, the first shell that she saw fall near the water tank on the hill facing the castle had almost landed amongst the men of Captain Underhill's 2nd Company. **Adna Underhill** later wrote a book about his time in the FSSF, in which he vividly

remembers almost being hit by the navy fire as he advanced over the hills towards Villeneuve (Unfortunately, in his book Underhill changed the names of all the characters involved.):

Langly [In fact Underhill.] took Second Company on a flanking movement to the wooded hill southwest of town, where they could deliver flanking fire from the high ground and would also be in a position to assault from that side. En route, traveling in a large circle, they could look out over the Mediterranean and the town of Antibes nestled on its shore. Offshore were several cruisers and destroyers. Higgins pointed to the ships and turned to Jimmy Old Coyote: "It looks like we've got something bigger than Cannon Company's 75s if we need 'em."

The company had just swung back toward the hill that was their designated position when one of the cruisers opened fire on the town. The first two rounds struck the hillside Second Company had been about to occupy. While Langly checked with Regiment to make sure there was no mix up, Old Coyote replied to Higgins' earlier remark. "When they teach those sailors to shoot cannon, there's nothing between them and their target but nice flat water. Here, they've got to figure how to shoot over or around these fucking mountains." (…) In the present case, the navy was able to raise their fire and still shell Jerry's positions, and Second Company was able to deploy but held their fire.[6]

Men from the 2nd Company also discovered that some French civilians had taken refuge from the shelling in a cave in the small and isolated Cireuil Valley, at the foot of the hill the forcemen had just taken position on. **Raymond Giraud** was one of the children hiding in the cave and describes what life was like there, starting his account on the 24th:

We had hardly reached our camp when a German soldier tumbled down the cliff with a musette bag full of biscuits, saying: "Pologna. German with machine gun tac tac tac tac. Kamerad kaput and me here." He was a Pole forcefully enlisted into the German army and was deserting. My father hid him against a rock, and nowadays, 45 years later, his initials are still visible on a fallen tree. He must have had the fright of his life, because that night shells were exploding constantly. I forgot to say that my mother was absent until nightfall for the following reason: my sister had begged her to go to the village to get her little statue of the Virgin and my mother had listened to her. What an exemplary mother! But maybe that Virgin saved our lives. That night [August 24th to 25th], the Cireuil Valley received a downpour of shell fragments. The Germans, perched on the heights of St Paul and la Colle, having seen the exodus of civilians and having perhaps thought that they were Allied troops, opened fire, and believe me, it wasn't a piece of cake. My grandfather, Marius, told me: "My little one, when the shell whistles, it means it is going over you, but if it cracks, then beware, it is bad." He had been in the trenches for four years at Verdun and the Chemin des Dames, he had been gassed and wounded, and he knew the problematic by heart. At daybreak a shell exploded very near us, with the result that my sister was wounded in the heal and my mother in the knee. A 250-gram fragment hit above my head, near mother's ear, making her deaf for a month. Another fragment went through the mattress that was protecting *Monsieur* Bellessime and grazed his calf, wounding him lightly before ending up in his suitcase. Only about 20 people were wounded that day, including (…) Bruno Fornazier, who was badly hit in the legs. But in those painful moments the pinnacle of luck was reached when one shell entered the cave, passing between the legs of *Madame* Marquise de Castelane, pardon that detail, and failing to explode. If it had, there would have been at least 50 killed.

In the morning, during a lull, I lifted my head and saw a soldier covered in black on a rock. In 1943, the hills around Villeneuve had burned. "Dad, there is a soldier." "Where?" "Up there." My father said: "Camarades Francais," and following my father's advice, I repeated "Camarade Francais" as I lifted my arms. The soldier, a real giant, jumped down with a Colt in his hands, saying: "American Canadian." With gestures he asked my father for something to drink while pointing his .45 at him. Once my father tasted the water, he drank at least two liters. Since he didn't speak French, he left and brought back a Canadian named Ernest Léger who could speak French perfectly. [Ernest Léger was one of Captain Underhill's

The small cave in the Cireuil Valley, outside Villeneuve, in which several local families took refuge during the fighting between August 24th and 27th. The inhabitants later put up a plaque in recognition of the protection offered them by the Virgin Mary after a shell that landed directly in the cave failed to explode. Author's Collection.

Quebeckers from 2-2.] My father turned over the Polish prisoner to him, who would supposedly be put in more comfortable camps than German prisoners.[7]

Most of the inhabitants of Villeneuve were hiding in their basements, but some had found cover in another cave known as the Baou Trouca (meaning "the rock with the hole" in Provencal), on the eastern side of Aspre de Redon Hill. One of the evacuees who was hiding there was 8-year-old **Louis Giordano**:

The German authorities had ordered us to evacuate the village; in other words, to abandon our houses and leave everything open. Of course there was a big panic, and my parents and I took refuge at the Baou Trouca. The Baou Trouca is a rock that is perforated from right to left; originally it was to let water from a canal through.

Louis' elder brother **Gustave Giordano**, who was also in the cave, continues the story:

There were about 50 of us in there, lying head to feet. Since it was for irrigation there was still some water inside, so the elders had cut some branches and we slept on the branches. We ate whatever we could. Everybody was sharing then, there were no rich people or poor people. There was even a man from Cagnes who had come with us. He didn't know where to go and said: "I am coming with you guys." "Come in, there is room, we will work something out"

As August 25th wore on, the Americans shelled the Loup River line in preparation for their night attack, making life in the Baou Trouca rather uncomfortable. **Gustave Giordano** goes on:

The village could not be seen anymore, as it was enveloped in thick smoke that was accompanied by a strong smell of burned powder that irritated our throats. During the whole day we stayed huddled up against each other, like hunted beasts in their burrows, comforting the women and consoling or trying to distract the frightened children.

There was a woman who I will always remember. Every time we would hear a mortar come and explode on the rocks above us she would say: "Let me out of here, I want to go outside! In here we are all going to die! We are all going to die!" Suddenly my father told her: "*Madame* Galafard, if you want to go out, now is the time, because it has calmed down a little." Just as she went out a shell went off. She came back in and she didn't say a thing anymore. Another woman had a pillow with her and she was never letting go of it. My father asked her: "What are you doing with that pillow, Tata Adèle?" She answered: "You know, I am keeping it as a souvenir." She had put all her money in it, but she wouldn't tell us. We could hear the sound of crumpled paper inside it. She sold fruits and vegetables, and must have had a few savings and didn't want to leave them in her house, since everything had to be left open. In spite of everything, two or three people made us laugh. We needed a bit of humor, because some people were scared, especially those who already understood what war was, who had already seen things like that during the First World War. Everybody was scared; some didn't show it, but they were as frightened as the others.

The tower of the castle of Villeuve was hit and damaged during the shelling, and the damage has been left unrepaired to this day to serve as a reminder of the horrors of war. However, there has been a certain amount of controversy in Villeneuve about whether it was an American or German shell that caused the damage. The official version known by the inhabitants of the castle is that a shell fired by the navy caused the damage, and this version is confirmed by **Monsieur Travaca**, who was on the heights above la Colle, from where he could see both the castle and the ships at sea:

> I still remember the day when the Villeneuve castle's tower got damaged as if it was now. There was a boat on the sea, the *Jean Bart*. We saw the shot being fired and landing on the castle, demolishing the corner of the tower. Can you imagine that? We were up there, watching the sea, and we saw the shot being fired, then landing on the Chateau de Villeneuve. It demolished the corner and it is still demolished today.

Apart from the Navy, the American fire that was landing on Villeneuve on the afternoon of August 25th was provided by the 602nd Field Artillery Battalion's 75mm cannons, the 937th FAB's 155mm cannons, and the very precise and powerful 2-inch mortars of the 2nd Chemical Battalion. In the late afternoon, B Battery of the 602nd FAB took up positions at les Terres Blanches, south of Roquefort and very near the FSSF advanced positions. In fact, it was too close and quickly came under mortar fire, forcing it to retreat, as **Pvt Art Helmers** remembers:

[We] moved on past fire-swept land to the small town of Roquefort les Pins, which was seemingly a small, quiet sort of place. We moved through in silence, rather a forbidding silence. Our gun position was located among orchard trees and small beds of vegetables. Ahead of us was the brow of a hill, beyond which the lands sloped to the river 1,200 yards away. On our left, one half mile away, a wind-fanned forest fire burned fiercely. It was between five and six as we prepared our positions. Some of us foraged in the surrounding grounds for grapes, tomatoes, onions, and the like.

Suddenly, a shell burst interrupted all thought and action. Quickly followed by a second, third, and more, we realized they were enemy mortar rounds. We received a fire mission and fired closer than we had at any time since Mintunro, 1,400 yards. [The 602nd FAB had previously fought in Italy.] As we fired, the mortars swung closer, but because of the hill they had no observation and the hits were off to the side. Darkness settled in a weird light; the light of the forest fire creeping closer, and the occasional burst of a shell. With darkness, we received our first "retreat" order. We packed up in darkness and moved back as more and more shells landed closer.[8]

The 602nd FAB did not suffer any casualties, however, 11-year-old **Jeannine Muller**, who lived nearby, was killed by mortar fragments shortly afterwards. Not far from the positions the 602nd had evacuated at les Terres Blanches was the bridge outside the village of la Colle. The 1st Battalion of the FSSF had reached this bridge outside la Colle at the same time the 602nd had arrived at Roquefort late on the 25th. The forcemen found the bridge already blown by the Germans and ran into mortar fire just like the 602nd had. 1st Regiment of the FSSF reported at 19:45:

The tower of Villeneuve Castle bearing the damage inflicted by an Allied navy shell fired August 25, 1944. Elisabeth de Vanssay. Le Siège de Villeneuve. Nadèje le Lédan Collection.

11-year-old Jeannine Muller, who was killed by a German shell in Roquefort les Pins. Author's Collection.

1st Battalion 1st Regiment has 19 prisoners of war on the road to the command post. Prisoners are believed to be Polish from the 239th *Grenadiers*. They were captured at bridge la Colle. Our casualties one killed and one wounded by enemy artillery and mortar fire.[9]

At 20:42, probably after a preliminary interrogation of the prisoners, 1st Regiment added:

148th German Division are holding the area opposite us. They are to hold as long as possible and then evacuate to southeast. If that is impossible then they are to evacuate to the northeast through St Paul. Regiment is located in town on other side of river. 5th Company is located on east and 6th Company on the extreme right boundary guarding bridge. They are all Polish. Our 1st Battalion is in a good position, but are receiving heavy enemy artillery fire. We have a detail on bridge and we control the bridge area.

The heavy artillery fire mentioned in the report had killed one soldier as the 1st Battalion reached the bridge, and a second soldier was killed early in the night. These two men were:

Surname	Name	Rank	Age	Unit	Date of death	Location of death
Bartow	Clifford H	Pfc	32	2-1 FSSF	25.8.1944	Roquefort/La Colle
Ladd	Walter L	T4		1-1 FSSF	26.8.1944	Roquefort/La Colle

As for the Germans, they also lost two men, both probably killed by artillery fire:

Surname	Name	Rank	Age	Date of death	Location of death	Unit
Kadrmann	Karl	Gefr	33	24.8.1944	La Colle	8./Res. Gren. Btl.372
Maizen	Vinzent	Gren	18	25.8.1944	La Colle	6./Res. Gren. Btl.372

T4 Walter L. Ladd was one of two forcemen of 1st Regiment of the FSSF to be killed by German shells in the vicinity of the la Colle sur Loup Bridge during the night of August 25th to 26th. Private Collection.

Jean, the resistance man from the *Groupe Tartane* who had helped guide the FSSF into Grasse, was with them once again at Roquefort. Captain Geoffrey Jones, an OSS officer who had jumped into southern France just before the invasion and had in the meantime become an Intelligence Officer with the FABTF, set up his quarters in Grasse. After enjoying the liberation of Grasse, **Jean** reported to Captain Jones's office for a new assignment and he was sent down to Roquefort with two other Grasse inhabitants to make himself useful:

We spent the night at Roquefort les Pins with the Americans. When we got there we saw a body on the road. The Americans had made a sort of camp there. There was one tall American who had two pistols with pearly grips in his belt and he was drawing them like a cowboy. In fact, his friends were having fun with him: they would put a carbine in his back and he would draw his pistols with terrifying speed. I remember the Americans had loaded a terribly heavy ration box onto my back and we had brought it to the forward outposts to resupply the guys.

Jean then attempted to sleep in a building with some forcemen while the Germans pounded the area with artillery:

We could hear the noise of mortars and cannons all night, and the Americans told us: "We are staying here, we won't move, we will wait." In the room next to us there was a soldier who was crying and sobbing, so after an hour or two, with the English that still remained with me from high school, I asked: "But what happened to him? Is he severely wounded?" "No, no, no. He isn't wounded, he is shocked." A mortar shell had probably landed near him and he had not been physically wounded, but he was shocked. So with the cannon fire on one hand and him crying beside us on the other, we didn't manage to sleep the whole night.

The Attack on Villeneuve-Loubet during the Night of August 25th to 26th

While 1st Regiment was getting mauled by artillery fire at la Colle and Roquefort, 2nd Regiment was planning to attack the village of Villeneuve-Loubet the night of August 25th to 26th. The 5th and 6th Companies of 2nd Regiment were to perform the attack, with 4th Company in reserve. Fortunately, a few local civilians had decided to cross the lines during the day to provide the Allied soldiers with information and serve as guides. One of these locals was **Paul "Lolo" Fournier**:

I was 17 and a half when, on August 25, 1944, rumors were circulating that the U.S. troops were in the vicinity of Roquefort… and that they have had encounters with the Germans around le Jas de Madame (…). I left on my own by the Route Nationale 85 to go to meet them with a spade over my shoulder.

Stopped by the Germans in front of la Vacherie farm, I tell them that I live in Jas De Madame; they let me go by. Further on, in front of la Vanade, I see soldiers moving… I get closer. There, hidden in the bushes are the first U.S. infantrymen. I am immediately brought to la Vanade where, with an interpreter, they tell me that the previous day they had a serious encounter with the Germans (…). They ask me many questions and tell me that there are two other inhabitants of Villeneuve-Loubet nearby. I think they are L. Murolo and G. Tremellat. They ask me to go back to the village to try to bring back people that they can use as guides. Okay. Armed with a Colt .45, and my pockets full of chewing gum and chocolates, I go back to Villeneuve, following the crest of Aspre de Redon Hill. At the village, I try to recruit a few guys and tell them that I am sent by the U.S. troops and am supposed to find some guides.

Gustave Giordano remembers Paul Fournier's visit to the Baou Trouca cave, where several families were hiding:

Lolo Fournier came down from the forest one afternoon and came to see us. He said: "I am coming to see you because the Americans are asking for help, they want people to guide them to the town hall." But nobody wanted to go. Some people were with their wives, others were with their families, so we said: "You know, we can't move. We have the kids here and everything." So he replied: "It doesn't matter. If you aren't coming, you aren't coming." His pockets were full of chewing gum and cigarettes. I didn't smoke, but he gave me a pack of chewing gum and I was delighted. He also had a Colt, and I said: "Aren't you afraid? If the Germans find you they will kill you." But he wasn't afraid at all and said: "If the Germans come, we will burn them!" Then he left, but he warned us that the Americans would be coming for us.

Paul Fournier did finally manage to locate a few men who were willing to cross the lines with him to help guide the Allies during the imminent attack:

Misters Bardana, Ardouin, and Clar agreed to follow me back to la Vanade. (...) Mister Bardana, who could speak perfect English, explained our arrival, asked for by Captain Gold. It was around 4 o'clock; they offered us food… Nightfall came around 9 o'clock, and the sections prepared to progress towards the village. Several columns formed, with us as guides. We took Aspre Redon Hill.

The night attack of the 2nd Regiment of the FSSF on Villeneuve had now started. The troops set out over Aspre de Redon and into the forest, guided by local Frenchmen who were familiar with all the paths and hills of the area. Apparently the plan was the following: the 6th Company was to outflank Villeneuve by the north and attack the castle and village from behind, while the 5th Company would attack frontally in the area of the bridge and village. The best description of the advance is provided by the Silver Star citation of **Captain Larry Piette**, commander of 6th Company:

During the night of 25 August 1944, the 6th Company, under Captain Piette, led a battalion attack on the town of Villeneuve-Loubet, France. On a dark cloudy night, the 6th Company stole across an enemy-held ridge; waded across a stream from which all bridges had been blown by German engineers; and filtered silently into the town of Villeneuve-Loubet. The enemy garrison, unsuspecting and secure, gave no sign that they suspected the presence of our troops. Under the cover of the remaining hours of darkness, Captain Piette disposed his company with great skill and sagacity, planning to strike at dawn.[10]

The Capture of Château de Villeneuve

Part of 6th Company, guided by Marius Bardana, managed to cross the Loup River, outflank the German defenses, and get all the way to the rear entrance of the castle without firing a shot. **Warren MacPhie**, a Canadian mortar man in 6th Company, remembers:

We took off just before daybreak from the side of that hill, going towards Villeneuve. There was a river down there that we crossed. I think we had to walk through it, it wasn't that deep I don't believe. But anyway, we crossed there, then the platoon I was in went up to the castle. We came up a hill, kind of a rise at the back, and at the top of that there were two machine gun nests, and I think the Germans were asleep when we hit them. We surprised them. They were sitting there with machine guns and they never fired or anything. They were kids, probably 16 or 17, so as soon as we walked up to them in the dark they put their hands in the air and we took them prisoner. They were scared to death. I think there were six or seven in each machine gun position, and the last I saw of them we sent somebody back with them, to the rear. Then we just went in the back door of the castle. There was nobody in the castle as far as I know.

It may seem incredible that some of the German defenders were actually sleeping, but several of the other soldiers who were there, such as **Charles Chory**, confirm the story:

We marched all night, and we took up a position right outside the castle. We captured this guy, I think a boy, 15 years old. We woke him up in his sleep.

The anachronistic situation in which a modern era elite unit captured a medieval castle inhabited by a *Marquis* and his family is best described by **Albert Poirier**, a French Canadian soldier in 6th Company:

From up where we were coming from, we needed to cross a small river, but there was no water in it, it was dry. There was a Mister Maurice [probably Marius Bardana] who was guiding us because it was dark. He guided us and was very good; thanks to Maurice, we got directly to the gates of the castle. The gate was shut, so he showed me how to ring the doorbell. I rang, but nobody replied. It was about two in the morning, so the lieutenant who was with us said: "Well, we will sleep here and go back tomorrow morning." After that Maurice disappeared and I didn't see him again, and we lay down and slept until four.

At 4 o'clock we got up, and since I was French Canadian and could speak French, I went to ring the doorbell and that woke up the *marquis*. After a little while he came out with a long frock coat and he opened his doors and said: "I know where a group of Germans are sleeping." About 20 Germans were sleeping peacefully on the castle grounds and we woke them up. They were a bit surprised to be woken up with rifles and didn't offer any resistance. They simply said: "Tedesci [Tedesci means "German" in Italian]" and pointed towards the sergeant. There was one sergeant there: "He is Tedesci and the rest of us are Polish." It gave me a funny impression. They seemed rather happy and smiling... The war was over for them. There was one German who was a sergeant and a nice boy, because I spoke to him. He showed me his wallet, and he was a married man with one or two kids, because he had portraits of his children. They were very proud to be captured by the Americans because at least they were alive.

Kenneth Keddy, also of 6th Company, was among the first men to enter the castle and confirms Albert Poirier's story:

It was somewhere around midnight, and the French underground took us right into the castle. In the morning, when it was coming daylight, we went out around the outskirts, where they told us the Germans were dug in, and we took them all prisoners. We didn't have to fire a shot. We just went down and they were all pretty well sleeping. They never realized anything was going on I guess, and there was nothing to it. There was nothing to it at all, I don't think anybody even got hurt as far as I know, not with the bunch I was with, anyway. So it was pretty easy, thank God it was. The underground told us pretty well where to go, they knew where they were, and everything worked out 100 percent.

Of course, there was the big thing about the German Luger, the revolver. After they had got them all prisoner, I was down there last, so I thought: "Well, nothing going on, I will have a look around and see if I can find one." And while I was looking I came up against a slit trench about three feet deep, and there was a guy lying there sound asleep. He was stretched right out and he had his uniform all on and everything, lying there. And I, of course, held my rifle; I held it right down and hollered at him, and he pulled his arms up by his eyes and wiped his eyes, and when he looked and saw it was me, why, boy, he came right up out of there! I don't think he even put his hands down to push himself up, he just seemed to come up like there was a hydraulic lift under him. He came out and I took him out with the rest of them. We got them all prisoners.

We walked right into the castle and went right in and sat down with the people there. They said there were eight foot walls around it or something like that? I know it was big, golly.

Elisabeth de Vanssay, the *marquis'* daughter, described the capture of the castle as seen from within in her journal. Although she never exchanged notes with Albert Poirier or Kenneth Keddy, her account is strikingly similar:

Everybody sleeps in the basement except the nun, who prefers to stay in the weapons room. (…) We are shelled all night. The shells are landing very near us; in the basement we are quivering with fear. The night is frightening and it is impossible to sleep. Stephanie is extremely excited. Will we get out of this basement alive or dead? That is the question that each of us asks themselves anxiously.

Towards morning, we manage to doze off a bit when we hear Gallo, who had gone out to see what was going on, shout through the cellar window: "Madame la Marquise, les Anglais sont là [Madame la Marquise, the English are here]." In the basement we all leap up to "see the English" in spite of father's moderations. I reach the draw bridge with him a few seconds later: some Canadians are there, and we shake the hands of those nearest to us. It was Saturday, August 26, 1944, at six thirty in the morning.

The drawbridge of Villeneuve Castle that a detachment of 6-2 managed to reach without firing a shot at 6 o'clock in the morning, August 26th. Vincent Meyer Collection.

The Canadian spoke French and told us that they reached the village last night, but that we should all return indoors because they were going to do some firing. Everybody's face is glowing with joy and relief; they all think that everything is over. In his enthusiasm, Gallo brings the horses back to the stable.

I am personally less joyful, because it seems to me that it is not "really finished" yet. Maybe it is just a crazy intuition, I hope so. They all make fun of me, finding me ridiculous. While mother goes to put on some makeup, father, Gallo, and Kyrel go with the Americans to capture the Germans who are in the park and surrender. Mother wants me to dress up, but I don't feel like it.

The first Canadians have come in. I speak with them; they are very calm and don't seem at all like men who are at war. The first one I talk to is very young and admits that they are all very weary, and that war does not amuse them one bit. In the meantime, others climb up in the tower and "have fun" shooting at the remaining Germans with machine guns.[11]

Of course, it was not simply to "have fun" that the forcemen were firing at the Germans outside! On the main road that passed near the castle, German soldiers of the 14th *Infanterie Panzerjäger Kompanie* (Antitank Company) of *Reserve Grenadier Regiment 239* had set up two 75mm cannons that enfiladed the bridge over the Loup. The tower of the castle being visible from one of the gun positions, the Germans opened fire on it when they realized that the castle was in Allied hands. **Albert Poirier** was part of this action:

After the *Marquis* came and opened the door for us, part of the regiment went into the castle grounds. I climbed up into the tower with Captain Piette and some others. When we got up there, there were some German soldiers way down there who fired a shell that demolished part of the corner of the tower. They could see the tower and we could see their cannon outside the castle grounds on the road leading to the castle. We didn't have any rifles that were powerful enough to fire on them, so I said: "There is a BAR down there, we should bring it up to fire at them." Captain Piette said: "Go and get it immediately!" So I went to fetch the BAR, and the major used it to fire at the cannon. It must have hit one of the men, and all the others took off at once when they realized they were under fire. So they left the cannon there and that was the end. They only fired one shell.

I don't know if they repaired the castle, but the *marquis* said he would not repair his tower that had been damaged. He told me: "I will not get it fixed to show that the Germans fired at it." [As said previously, the major damage to the tower was in fact probably caused by a shell fired by the Allied fleet, while the smaller German shells only caused minor damage to it. In any case, it is certain that numerous shells struck the tower during the 48 hours of fighting.]

Captain Larry Piette, of 6-2, remembered a slightly exaggerated version of this action. His account is correct, except for the fact that there were no Germans in the castle, let alone any dead ones:

> We made it into the castle and to the top. It was right out of the storybooks. My men were putting dead Germans up on the parapets and shooting off of the parapets just like [in] the movies. They were actually propping the dead men up to make the Germans think we had a big force. We could see everything from up there. The Germans couldn't elevate their guns that high. The guys were saying, "Gee, this is fun," and were shooting the German gun crews just like they were on the rifle range. You tell a story like that, they're not going to believe it.[12]

As for the second German cannon, which was not visible from the tower, it was attacked by a few forcemen who climbed over the castle wall in order to get a good shot at it. The story of the two cannons became quite well known among the inhabitants of Villeneuve, and **Boris Anchisi**, who lived nearby, heard the following version:

> The Germans had disposed cannons: one near the entrance of the tunnel, and one at the first curve on the way down, which was to stop anybody from crossing the bridge that had been partially blown up. The cannon at the tunnel was firing straight ahead, because that's where the Americans were coming from. But in the end, the Americans went further north, and went up into the castle and the tower. From the tower they could look down on everything. There were three or four Germans around the cannon at the tunnel and the Americans liquidated them with sniper rifles. The cannon that was right after the curve on the way down to Villeneuve-Loubet and enfiladed the bridge and road was not visible from the castle, so the snipers couldn't get those soldiers. There is a place where

the first castle wall is very low and can be easily jumped over, and there was a garden below that, and below that was the cannon. One or two Americans went down and killed the cannon's crew. It must have happened about simultaneously with the ones that got shot from the castle at the entrance of the tunnel.

Kenneth Keddy, of 6-2, also climbed up into the tower of the castle, apparently once the German cannon crews had already been scattered:

> I was up at the top of the tower. There were other fellows down in the tower a ways, in one of those slit places, where they laid down and were watching the front. But I went right to the top of the tower, and there was a truck coming up one of the streets down through there somewhere, and I fired a shot at it. I don't know where I hit it, but it stopped and the guy jumped out and took off, so I didn't hurt anybody anyway. I will never forget it. Just like it happened yesterday.

Incredibly, the forcemen had managed to seize the castle without suffering any casualties and while capturing or killing quite a number of Germans. It was a huge mistake on the part of the Germans not to have defended the castle more vigorously.

The Capture of the village of Villeneuve-Loubet

Although the forcemen now held the high ground, the Germans down in the village itself were offering more serious resistance. Now that we have seen how one column managed to capture the castle, we will describe in detail how a second group of forcemen attacked and captured the village. **Gustave Giordano** was still in the Baou Trouca cave with other civilians when he saw the first forcemen approaching before daylight:

> When the Americans first arrived, they were following the little canal. I was second in line in the Baou Trouca, with a lumberjack called Toto beside me. He was afraid of nothing, but he was sleeping. I wasn't sleeping and had a good ear, and suddenly I heard somebody walking in the canal. So I touched him and he asked: "What?" I told him: "Toto, Toto, somebody is coming!" "Where? Where is somebody coming?" "Shhtt! Be quiet, somebody is coming, I heard footsteps." We could see silhouettes in the darkness and it was the Americans. Bardana or Fournier had sent them, saying: "You follow the canal for 500 or 600 meters and you will find a tunnel; there are lots of inhabitants of Villeneuve in there." When they got to the Baou Trouca they came forward, shining a flashlight at the ground: "French? French?" So I said: "Yes, yes, we are French." And it was the Americans, so then we were happy!

> There was a German who had climbed into a mulberry tree in a field on the other side of the river. Monsieur Clar had cooked potatoes for us, for the kids and grannies and grandpas; but each time he lit a fire, bang! The German would fire at us. He fired several times, but luckily he never hit us. But then when the Americans arrived, of course it wasn't the same anymore, and we told them: "Beware, there is a German in the mulberry tree over there, he has been shooting at us every night." "Wait!" They slowly crossed the river (there was no water in it) and climbed up

"The guys were saying: 'Gee, this is fun' and were shooting the German gun crews just like they were on the rifle range." This German soldier lying dead on the road near the mouth of the tunnel is apparently a member of the cannon crew that was shot at by forcemen who had climbed to the top of the castle tower. The fact that the soldier is not wearing a belt seems to confirm that he was indeed part of a cannon crew and was not an infantryman. The soldier appears to have been hit in the left temple. In the first photo, F.K. Robinson, of 6-2, poses with the body, while the identity of the forceman in the second photo is not known. It was common for Allied soldiers to pose with the bodies of enemies they had killed; however, for two different soldiers to have posed with the same body is a rare occurrence. The location where the photo was taken has changed little, as even the plane tree is still intact. Author's Collection, courtesy Gordon Orr.

The Baou Trouca was a simple tunnel pierced through a large rock to allow passage for a small canal. This space, which is less than a meter and a half in height, became the refuge for several dozen inhabitants during the shelling. Author's Collection.

the embankment. From the embankment to the tree there were maybe 50 or 60 meters. Suddenly we heard a burst of machine gun fire: trrrrrr! They got him!

Then the Americans came back. There was a Mr Villecrose who worked at the bank, and the Americans had asked us if anybody could speak English, so he said: "I work at the bank, I speak a bit of English." He immediately put us at ease and translated everything the Americans were saying. He said: "Don't move, don't get out yet, they are just hardly arriving." They wanted somebody to accompany them to cross the river and go to the town hall. I would have liked to go, but my father didn't want me to, as I was only 15. So Mr Clar, the one who had been cooking for us, said: "I will go with you." They went down, and when they got to the plane trees, the Germans were on the other side. Just when they were going to cross the river: trrrrrr! The Germans opened fire, but they didn't hit anybody! All the shots hit in front of them. So then of course they came back, and after that there was fighting everywhere. It smelled like smoke, it smelled like fire, it smelled like everything.

Louis Fanti, a local teenager, was hiding in a basement in the village and remembers seeing the first "Americans":

The whole family was in the basement, and just at dawn I saw a bunch of guys go by. I could only see their legs, and there were lots of them. I went up and opened the door, but one of the Americans signaled to me: "Fermez! Fermez! [Close the door]" Oh! And they could speak French, too! It was the Canadians who were going up the street to get to the castle. They fought the whole night. It was like one can imagine: gunshots, bursts of machine gun fire, we could here all that, and also a bunch of flashes of mortar shells landing. It was war.

Joseph Macocco was also hiding in the basement of his house in the village and was confused when the first forcemen arrived:

We were hiding under our house. It was strange when the Americans arrived. To say "yes," the Americans say

"yeah." So we were down there and we heard "Ja, Ja, Ja." So we said: "That's it, the *Boches* are coming back." I also heard people speaking Italian, because there were a lot of Italians in the American army, and then we heard: "Ja, ja, ja." It made such a mixture, I couldn't understand the situation at all, so we stayed in our hole. But then we realized when they came in, we saw they were Americans. But that "ja" has stayed engraved in my memory. At that moment, we weren't acting proud!

Staff Sergeant John Dawson, of 6-2, was among the forcemen who participated in the fighting in the village:

Our biggest scrap was at Villeneuve-Loubet. We forded the river, and as we came into town in the early morning, it looked like another of those occasions when the Germans had pulled out on us. We started down a street which had houses on one side and an open park on the other. Frenchmen came out of their houses in considerable numbers to see the Americans or relieve their bladders, the second seeming to preoccupy them most, for there was a solid rank of peeing Frenchmen. About that time, some fire started coming from some cleverly camouflaged foxholes. They were designed to cover the river, and the Jerries were as surprised as we were, and though we had two or three wounded, they had let too many of us get too close. They were grenaded out fast. But this was only the first of many engagements that day.[13]

One German soldier who was killed in the Bartocchi house is particularly well remembered by the inhabitants of Villeneuve. **Gustave Giordano** explains:

There was a garage with a cart inside it, and one German had the idea of hiding under the cart with a machine gun, firing towards the town hall. Every time he would see somebody walk by he would fire with the machine gun. But Lolo Fournier's father told the Americans: "You know, there is a German over there firing at us every time we cross the street." He brought them there from behind, where there was a staircase. The German didn't notice because a board from the cart was in the way, and they machine gunned him under the cart and killed him.

Captain Larry Piette's Silver Star citation provides extra details about the trouble that the forcemen encountered when capturing the village of Villeneuve:

At first light the attack commenced. Captain Piette personally accompanied the platoon that had the mission of clearing the lower streets of the town, while the other two platoons carried out their missions. The street-clearing platoon ran into heavy and accurate small arms fire from the well-prepared positions and numerically superior enemy. Captain Piette, immediately sensing the seriousness of the situation, secured a platoon from the reserve company and proceeded to lead it to the scene of action. On the way, the platoon officer was shot down and mortally wounded.[14]

The officer who was mortally wounded was **Lt Ross Samuel**, of 4-2. **Harold Johnson**, also of 4-2, was near him when he got shot:

We were going to enter this town, and there was a bridge across this creak. Lt Samuel went across there, and then there was a sniper someplace and he got him in the left leg, just above the knee. It was a dum-dum; in other words, a wooden bullet, which is supposed to be illegal. [Dumdum bullets are in fact not made of wood, and the wound was probably caused by a regular bullet fragmenting when it hit Lt Samuel's femur.] A regular bullet would have gone right through, but this, when it went in, you could almost have stuck your fist in where it came out above his knee; it made a pretty big hole.

The sniper was up in a wooded area, and a couple guys happened to be facing that direction and they saw the smoke from the rifle. They fired into there, and there was no more fire from up in that wooded area, so they apparently got him. Samuel had walked a little way across the bridge, and then he got hit and of course came back, and we took him over to the medics right away. Then we went on into town. I don't know if it was the shock or what, I've seen them get hit worse than that, but then I heard that he died. We never liked hearing that, of course. We liked him very well. He was a very nice guy. I didn't think he should have died."

22-year-old Canadian Lt Ross L. Samuel, of 4-2, was shot through the leg and mortally wounded during the attack on the village of Villeneuve. His mother had already died earlier in 1944. Ross Samuel had two brothers, one of whom remained at home with the father, while the other was serving in the air force. When the father and remaining brother returned home from the memorial mass held for Ross' death, they found out that the third brother had just been reported missing in action over the North Sea. He remains missing to this day. Samuel Family Collection.

Captain Piette's citation read on:

> Captain Piette, with absolute disregard for his own safety, led [Lt Samuel's] platoon to join his other platoon. Here, with great skill he organized the attack that broke up the German defenses. Time and again, Captain Piette exposed himself to the intense small arms fire to encourage and employ his men so that, following his inspirational example of fearlessness and courage, the men quickly stormed and seized the enemy positions, capturing 40 prisoners of war and killing or wounding 25 others.[15]

Some of the prisoners were evacuated to the rear along an itinerary that passed next to the Baou Trouca cave, where some civilians were still hiding. **Gustave Giordano** remembers:

> A bunch of German prisoners came down the opposite riverbank with Americans behind them with submachine guns. I remember Charles Luciano said: "I am going to beat one of them up! I am going to kill one of the bastards!" "But don't be stupid!" He went over there and kicked one of the Germans in the ass, lifting him high off the ground! An American said: "Hey, calm down, they are prisoners." He couldn't bear the sight of them, he spat on them and everything. A bit further on, other prisoners were carrying a wounded Canadian on a stretcher.

Concerning the wounded, **Louis Fanti** adds:

> There must have been some Canadians wounded, but they were evacuated immediately. As for the German wounded, they were brought to the town hall. They were lying there on stretchers with blankets on them, and Doctor Lefebvre and his wife were treating them.

There had also apparently been a fire fight outside Villeneuve, on the road leading into town, in which Canadian soldier **Ross Orr**, of 5-2, was involved, receiving a Distinguished Service Cross for his actions:

> When the only route for urgently needed supplies was cut off by three enemy machine guns emplaced along the road, Staff Sergeant Orr, without orders, elected to remove this obstacle. After selecting three men to provide covering fire, he approached alone, within seventy-five yards of the first gun. Armed with a sub-machine gun, he jumped into the middle of the road and demanded surrender. The enemy gunner immediately opened fire on him, but Staff Sergeant Orr stood his ground and seriously wounded both of the crew by effective fire. Under continued assault by this four-man team, the other two machine gun crews finally surrendered and the road was opened to desperately needed supplies.[16]

Lt George Parnell, who was commanding a detachment of the 887th Airborne Engineer Company in Villeneuve, had apparently run into what was apparently the same group of Germans the night before while investigating mines that had been placed on the road to Villeneuve. He wrote about the incident in a letter to his wife August 26th:

> Last night myself and three of my men moved in on a town with the infantry during the initial assault. A minefield and a blown bridge had been reported and I had to make a reconnaissance. The infantry took to the hills,

which was no good for me, as work was on the road, so my men and I took off down the road, about two miles from the furthest outpost. I rode down in my jeep with a free French partisan to tell me when I approached the minefield. This was about 11 p.m. I stopped about 200 yards from the minefield and walked the rest of the way. I had just spotted the mines laid across the road and reached down to inspect them, planning to blow them out, when we heard someone cough directly across from us in the brush. We hit the ground just as someone fired point blank at us. We withdrew back to the jeep, but when I got there one man was missing. I waited for about 10 minutes, then finally decided to send one man and the jeep back to report while I and the other lad set up the machine gun I carried on the jeep. We lay there about an hour, and believe me, I sure was glad when the man who I didn't know about came down the road and joined us. He had just stayed on the ground when we were fired on. The jeep didn't return, so I decided to withdraw on foot. This morning I went back, this time with some infantry, and 500 yards from where we had been that night we took eight prisoners. My men had taken six prior to that. Gosh, they are all children, 18-19 years old, and not German either: Poles, Checks [sic]. It's pitiful, they are only kids. [17]

The German Counterattacks at Villeneuve-Loubet

Both the village of Villeneuve-Loubet and its castle had quickly fallen into Allied hands. The Germans had offered only moderate resistance, but surprisingly, they would now mount several costly counterattacks in order to recapture the ground that they had let go so easily. We now return to the castle, in which **Elisabeth de Vanssay** wrote:

More and more Canadians arrive and rush to the well, they are dying of thirst. Mother makes "real" coffee for them and they gulp it down like ordinary glasses of water: they don't know about rationing.

They tell us that they are coming from St Tropez, conquering the ground step by step. They are exhausted. They reached Villeneuve under Bardana's guidance, who indicated what path they should follow since Roquefort. But less than 45 minutes after they arrived, the shooting started up again even more vigorously. This time, it is the castle itself that is being targeted by the Germans, for they have just realized that the Canadians have installed an observation post in the tower and are occupying the entire castle.

The officer in command, Lt Craford [Lt William Crawford, of 6-2], is wounded on the doorstep, along with two of his men. We transport him into the weapons room and with difficulty manage to get the nun to come and treat him (…). He is wounded in the throat and leg and is bleeding heavily, but is incredibly gutsy. To sustain himself, he swallows three big bowls of coffee and one bowl of wine; he does not want to lie down as we advise him to, and a few moments later we find him standing up, commanding his men in the battle that was now really starting.

The worst phase of the ordeal was now starting for us, too. We were being bombed by the batteries of la Colle, St Paul, and Vence, as well as by a mobile mortar that was moving about on the road at the Grange Rimade and then taking refuge in the tunnel after each shot! Villeneuve, occupied by the Canadians, was transformed into a fortress and the Germans were assaulting it.

It was about nine thirty in the morning when the situation suddenly deteriorated. The German fire intensified. It is war in the castle, shells are whistling in all directions and hitting the tower and the walls… All of us inhabitants of Villeneuve have taken refuge in the basement and the Americans have forbidden us to come back up, because they have installed a mortar in front of the door; and furthermore, one would be risking his life, because fragments are raining down from all directions. In the basement, Stephanie becomes hysterical and has a fit of tears. [18]

Warren MacPhie, of 6-2, had set up his mortar in the castle tower, but the German shelling forced him to abandon his position:

We went into the castle. I was mortar sergeant, and we set the mortar up on the tower of the castle. We had the high ground. When we would see activity, we would fire a shell into it. But of course they spotted where we were firing from and they started to fire back. They zeroed in and we had to get the hell out of there, because they were going to knock us down. We had no protection; we were in the wide open on top of the tower.

In the meantime, men of the 887th Airborne Engineer Company under Lt George Parnell had started working on the blown bridge over the Loup under the German artillery fire. **Lt Parnell** reported on the day's actions in a letter to his wife:

I've lost some of my best men. I can't lose the ones I wouldn't miss, but it's to be expected. (…) Today I tried clearing some mines at a bypass I have to put in, as the bridge is blown, and was caught by artillery fire, which had us pinned to the ground for several hours. Another squad of mine on another hill was caught by mortar fire. The men so far have been splendid. They haven't had a change of socks in over a week now and have had only the canned rations. [19]

What Lt Parnell did not mention specifically to his wife, probably so as not to worry her, was that one of his men, 31-year-old **PFC Cecil Fitzgerald**, had been killed by the German artillery fire near the bridge in Villeneuve. At 12:50, **Major Holt**, of the HQ Detachment of 2nd Regiment of the FSSF, reported the death: "Heavy enemy artillery. One enlisted man killed by river by 105mm shell."[20] **Gustave Giordano** also gives a few extra details on Cecil Fitzgerald's death: "He was going to get water in the river and wanted to cross the field. Bang! He caught a shell fragment in the head."

Meanwhile, back at Roquefort, the men of B Battery of the 602nd FAB were hard at work providing counter battery and supporting fire to the forcemen in Villeneuve, as **Pvt Art Helmers** remembers:

Daylight came and we got set for trouble, which came quickly! We fired missions in all directions, from far left to far right. One of our OPs [observation post] was at a castle in Villeneuve-Loubet. Surrounded on all sides, we fired in support of them to keep the Germans from overrunning the place until our infantry could retake the it. We had a hot time! The Jerries fired over us and short of us. They had a counterattack that gave us a real workout for a while. [21]

31-year-old PFC Cecil M. Fitzgerald, of the 887ᵗʰ Airborne Engineer Company, was killed by shrapnel fragments to the head and back near Villeneuve Bridge the morning of August 26ᵗʰ. Ken Nelson Collection.

This plane tree located near Villeneuve Bridge still bears the scars of a German artillery shell that hit it August 26, 1944, in the form of a large hole. Author's Collection.

Kanonier **Alfons Wiesniewski** was killed near his battery south of Vence by the Allied counter battery fire. A second German soldier named **Richard Kamussella** may also have been killed in Vence August 26ᵗʰ, but this cannot be confirmed because his exact date of death is not known. Both men were buried in Vence. Unfortunately, the Allied artillery also killed one young Frenchman in Vence, as well as at least five other civilians in la Colle and Cagnes sur Mer. These victims are listed below:

Surname	Name	Age	Date of death	Location of death
Caula	Mr	74	26.8.1944	Cagnes sur Mer
Davit	David	59	26.8.1944	La Colle sur Loup
Lambert	Jean	32	26.8.1944	La Colle sur Loup
Manuali	Adamo	69	26.8.1944	La Colle sur Loup
Salvatico	Marguerite	50	26.8.1944	La Colle sur Loup
Mario	August	24	26.8.1944	Vence

Joseph Maccoco explains how his 74-year-old grandfather, **Monsieur Caula**, was killed east of Villeneuve castle:

> The American ships were aiming at Villeneuve castle, so there were shells landing all over the place. My grandfather was with some farmers in a shelter, and unfortunately he got sick of sitting with them and wanted to go home. When he left, a shell landed right beside him and his stomach was torn apart. The others were safe because they were in the shelter.

The same **Joseph Macocco**, who was 18 at the time, decided to convince some Germans to the east of the castle to surrender:

> The Americans were at Villeneuve-Loubet and the Germans were still at the tunnel, towards Cagnes, and behind the tunnel, in a field that my parents owned. The tunnel was full of Germans with materiel. They were nicely hidden in there, and I asked a neighbor if he wanted to come and make them prisoner with me. I told him: "Come on, let's go and block them." In my little head I thought: "We can each go to one side of it." I don't know how we could have done it... You would have to be crazy to dare try to do something like that. Fittingly, he said I was crazy and ran away. He was five years older then me, so was a bit smarter then me.
>
> Since I ended up alone, I didn't feel like going to the tunnel and I got the idea of going to my parents' field instead. Lucky thing we didn't go to the tunnel or we would have been killed, and I wouldn't be here to tell you about it. I went straight to my parents' field by walking past the castle walls, under the eyes of the Germans with machine guns who were waiting for the Americans. [In fact, the castle was already in Allied hands as we know, but the soldiers Joseph Macocco saw may have been forcemen.] There were two or three of them on every machine gun every 10 meters. The Germans watched me go by; they didn't know what I was going to do, but to do something like that, you have to be irresponsible. If they had fired I would have been finished, I would have been one extra body.

296

Auguste Mario
tué le 26 août 1944

24-year-old French civilian August Mario was killed by an Allied shell that was firing back at German batteries located in Vence. Anne Verots-Guilbaud Collection.

When I reached my parents' field, I saw about 35 Germans who were lined up in front of a ditch. There was a big tough guy, an officer, and he is the one who met me. I proposed to him to surrender, and as an answer, he pulled out his pistol and held me at gunpoint for perhaps half an hour. He kept telling me: "Raus!" and I was clowning around, trying to make myself be understood with hand signs. I was not amusing him at all, and I don't know how he managed not to pull the trigger. Luckily the American ships were bombing us at that time and every time shells landed, everyone dived into the ditch and that acted as an interlude. They were shelling the castle, but the shells were landing all over the countryside where we were, cutting trees in half. We could see the branches exploding.

Every time the shelling calmed down a bit, we would get up again and the same act would start over again. I couldn't speak German, of course, so I was signaling them to surrender and saying: "Americans over there, so you prisoners." Only the officer was against me; the others weren't opening their mouths. I think they were Polish and they weren't saying a thing; they were the sheep. It is the officer who held them all back and prevented them from coming with me. The German, the real German, would not surrender.

There were several waves of shelling, and since they refused to surrender, I returned to the village. When I got to my district I met Jean Carlo. I told him what the situation was and proposed for him to come with me and he came immediately. The Americans were no longer firing, things had calmed down. When I reached the field with Carlo, I don't think the officer pulled his gun out this time, and the fact that there were two of us must have pressured the Germans, because this time they came with us almost immediately. In the meantime, they must have thought hard and must have told themselves: "They aren't crazy. We are surrounded, the firing is coming from over there. We are trapped!" So they all surrendered and came along; there were 35 of them. But we were lucky that they were Poles, because if they had all been Germans they would have buried us over there.

We went back up to the castle, but instead of walking past the walls, we went into the castle grounds by the main door, with all the guys following us. There were Germans all over the place, but nobody said anything to us, we went through without any trouble. Then we brought them to my district at St George, in front of the Bartocchi house. The Germans were all lined up and my mother took a picture of them, then the people from the town hall took all the Germans away. With Carlo, we always said there were 35 of them. As of then I didn't take care of them anymore. The Germans having left, we went to have fun. We were 18 or 18 and a half years old and were completely careless. We almost got a walloping from our parents because they had been looking for us all over the place.

Joseph Macocco's story may seem hard to believe, but it is known in Villeneuve, and is confirmed by several period FSSF reports. The surrender occurred around noon, and the number of prisoners is considered to be 36 or 38, depending on the report. It was noted in the summary of enemy action: "38 prisoners of war were surrendered to the FFI in Villeneuve-Loubet by a Polish NCO and turned over to 2nd Regt, FSSF, upon entering the town."[22] These men were mostly from the 2nd and 3rd Companies of *Reserve Grenadier Bataillon 327*, and had been on their way to St Paul, according to what they told their interrogators.[23] Perhaps they were not aware that Villeneuve had been captured and were surprised to find themselves almost at the front lines? In any case, the men of *Bataillon 372* who were holding the area around Villeneuve were not ready to surrender as easily. **Charles Chory**, of 6-2, was stationed outside the castle and met some determined German soldiers who had probably been ordered to find out where the Allied positions were:

I was outside the castle a long time; in fact, they forgot the four of us out there. We had a gun set down facing the road, because we heard they might be coming up. That's when a German came up to the side. He was only about 25, 30 yards away, that's how close he was. I told him: "Halt," and he looked at me. He saw me with a gun on him and he stepped back and went away. I went to shoot him, but would you believe my gun wouldn't go off, and he ran away? My gun was a Johnson light machine gun, and it had a long magazine with 20 rounds that got pinched, so it wouldn't feed the bullets.

Then I sent one of the guys where the German had come up, right behind a tree. I said: "Watch it, watch this guy, he might come back." And he did come back, about 10 or 15 minutes later. He was talking to somebody and I said to the guy: "Don't shoot him yet, maybe somebody else is coming up." But in fact he shot him right away and the German dropped his rifle and ran. There was another one behind him and they both ran away, but I think this guy was wounded badly. That was late in the morning, probably noon time. After this happened, we all went inside the castle.

We will now return to what was happening in the meantime within the castle, with **Elisabeth de Vanssay**'s description of events as witnessed from the basement of the castle:

The Americans who are not fighting come and rest on our mattresses. There are a dozen of them taking turns while the others are fighting, or simply lying down on the floor. They are so exhausted that they sleep deeply in spite of the infernal noise of the shells, machine guns, and grenades. Each time a shell exploded on the castle, we could hear it collapsing. One shell had just exploded in front of the basement window: we were covered with plaster and suffocating dust, and the logs that father had put as protection were pulverized. We were all extremely frightened; as for the soldiers, they hardly even woke up. "If it goes on like this for long," said father, "there will be nothing left of the castle!"

Around noon there is a bit of a lull. Mother makes us go up to peel vegetables to make soup for the Canadians, but they have invaded the kitchen, and it is in an incredible mess! Oh! They sure knew how to cook! An advantage they have over us is that everything is bathing in grease: everywhere we look there is bacon, cheese, butter… and potatoes stolen from Gallo![24]

Morris Lazzarus, of 5-2, remembers the excitement and curiosity of being in a medieval castle, feelings probably shared by many of the other forcemen who had grown up on farms during the Great Depression:

We had a free run of the castle and we could do whatever we wanted. It was a great castle, I will tell you, a real classy place. I was very impressed. There were some nice pictures on the wall and the bedrooms were the finest silks. It was interesting. I wasn't brought up in one. They had some beautiful bedrooms and there were guys lying on those beautiful beds. I guess they hadn't washed.

Elisabeth de Vanssay continues:

In the meantime, there is still artillery fire that seems to be increasing in intensity again. Indeed, soon after she went up, I see mother hurrying back to the basement, abandoning all the food to the Canadians. It is impossible to eat, and nobody is hungry anyway… Gallo arrives, saying that there are fires in the park and that it is impossible to go and extinguish them because there is too much gunfire. (…)

The whole day is spent in the basement with shells whistling and exploding all over. The Germans are resisting, and have even mounted a counter attack. Riva is in a terrible state: she is frightened, frightened for her

children, and particularly for Jeannot, who is walking about the castle as an act of bravado; the Canadians have spread about in it and are firing out all the windows with machine guns, with the shutters closed.[25]

The Germans were now launching serious counterattacks on the castle, particularly from a wooded hill to the south of it. **Sgt Jack Knight**, of the HQ Detachment of 2nd Regiment, was in the castle when some of these attacks occurred:

Villeneuve-Loubet was hard fought for, and then it was probably the strongest counterattacks we had in all of south France. I remember a fellow by the name of Harold Webb during the counterattack, who just sat calmly on a large stuffed chair in front of a slit in the castle wall, and he had a fairly narrow vision of a little wooded area. He just sat there, and when a German patrol showed up, he would fire at them and he would calmly say: "I sure scared that guy, did you see him jump into the bush?" As bad as anything got, we never allowed ourselves to think that we had killed anybody. We scared them, and caused them to run, and caused them to retreat and hide in the bushes and stuff like that, but we didn't really admit having killed even our enemy.

Morris Lazzarus, of 5-2, also participated in sniping at the approaching Germans:

I was on the second floor of the castle in a bedroom, looking out the window toward the road that came up to the castle. About 200 yards away, I saw some people coming out of the ditch and crossing the road, but they looked like they were in civilian dress, so I didn't open fire on them. As I was standing there, John Hankes came up behind me, grabbed my rifle, and took a couple pot shots over my head. That I remember vividly, because when you shoot over a

Forcemen rest in the courtyard of the castle that is covered in debris. This photo was probably taken August 27th, once the fighting was over. Elisabeth de Vanssay. Le Siège de Villeneuve. Nadèje le Lédan Collection.

Villeneuve-Loubet and its castle as seen from the south, in the area from which the Germans were counterattacking. Elisabeth de Vanssay. Le Siège de Villeneuve. Nadèje le Lédan Collection.

guy's head, the resonance in your ears almost deafens you. He says: "Those aren't civilians; those are soldiers crossing the road. What the hell are you doing? You're supposed to be shooting at 'em!" And when he did that I took my rifle back, and then I started shooting at them.

Although some of the soldiers may have wished that their bullets would only scare the enemy off, several of the counterattacking Germans were of course killed or wounded. **Josette Gatti** lived in the area of the counterattack, and her father decided to check out their house during the afternoon:

Dad was very attached to our house, so he went back up into the garden to see if the house had been damaged. Of course, the Americans who were in the castle fired at dad, thinking he was a German. All the windows had been broken and all that, because there was heavy shelling, but other than that the house was intact. Then he found a German who had been wounded down in the garden who was moaning. I don't think he survived. But I don't think he was actually German; Dad had told me he was Polish, because there were also Poles in the German army.

While most of the forcemen were beating back the counterattacks from the relative safety of the castle, a few men were also outside the castle, fighting fiercely. One of these was **PFC Henry Blackman**, of 6-2, who earned a Silver Star that day, the citation of which read:

Private First Class Blackman's company had moved into a defensive position which had been subjected to enemy counter-attacks during the entire day. Private First Class Blackman and two other men were placed on outpost duty along a likely avenue of approach for the enemy. Armed with a submachine gun and grenades, he was assigned the specific mission of driving off any enemy that attempted to approach the position from a nearby wooded area. Several enemy soldiers approached unobserved along a winding path and threw hand grenades into the outpost position. With complete disregard for his own personal safety, Private First Class Blackman ran through intense small arms fire, recovered the grenades, and threw them back among the enemy troops. Then, noticing that the enemy was massing for a counterattack, he engaged them with his submachine gun and so disorganized them that they broke and retreated. Shortly thereafter, Private First Class Blackman was seriously wounded by enemy mortar fire which had been brought to bear on his outpost in an effort to wipe it out.[26]

Sergeant Ross Orr, of 5-2, who had already forced several Germans to surrender outside Villeneuve earlier on, continued the actions that would earn him the Distinguished Service Cross once he got to the castle:

The Fifth Company occupied a castle on a hilltop (…) and Sergeant Orr immediately organized the area against counter-attack. The enemy, two hundred strong, strove continuously and fiercely to dislodge his group from this stronghold. In the face of death defying circumstances, Sergeant Orr, with his submachine gun, put an enemy machine gun which was covering an approaching enemy demolition party out of action. The demolition party was dispersed with severe losses by rifle fire and hand grenades

effectively used under Sergeant Orr's direction. In another similar counterattack, Sergeant Orr fired his submachine gun from a blazing barn into an attacking enemy formation. This attack was broken up and resulted in heavy losses to the enemy.[27]

The FSSF after action reports give a few more details about the counterattacks:

Two enemy counter-attacks of company strength against a Company of 2nd Regiment entrenched in the Fort (…) at Villeneuve-Loubet during the afternoon were repulsed with heavy casualties inflicted by our artillery, mortar, and small arms fire. The attacks, mainly mortar and hand grenade, were made in strength of 60-80 men. (…) An estimated 150 enemy wounded and 50 killed were incurred by SSF troops, mainly 2nd Regiment, in the Villeneuve-Loubet sector. On the slopes over the river (…), an estimated 30 dead were accounted for by sniper fire. In a hospital set up in a civilian residence on the la Colle-Villeneuve turnpike, the Germans treated 72 wounded from artillery and fighting in that area before pulling out at 22:00 on 26 August 1944.[28]

As was virtually always the case in Allied after action reports, the estimated number of German casualties is exaggerated, as we will see later on. One French girl who was hiding in a shelter southeast of Villeneuve in the area the German counterattacks were originating from witnessed a particularly tragic event:

We were hiding in a shelter, and the Americans on the other side saw some smoke, so they opened fire. They fired 30 shells and we were half suffocated. Then it stopped for a while and a young guy said: "I am getting out of here, I don't want to be buried alive." He ran off and was hit by a shell fragment. We stayed behind and 30 more shells were fired at the shelter. We were covered in dust and earth, and when it stopped we waited for a bit; then we all left, to escape. We were walking down the path and we saw a Pole who was with the Germans who wanted to surrender, and was running towards Villeneuve holding a stick with a piece of white cloth on it. Then a German officer came out and shot him in the back so that he would not surrender. He fell down. We didn't stick around; we left, we were too afraid. There were a dozen of us walking in single file, trying not to make any noise. Lucky thing the officer who shot the guy in the back was in front of us, because every time we saw a German, we would hide out of fear he would shoot at us. Then we went on into the reeds at the side of the river. In the reeds there were Germans crouching down on their knees, waiting with their guns. We crossed the Loup and the Americans were on the other side.

This shocking information about a German officer shooting one of his own men finds partial confirmation in the prisoner of war interrogations of German soldiers of *Bataillon 372* captured in Villeneuve and la Colle, which stated: "5th Company NCOs threatened to shoot any man attempting to desert"[29] and "One prisoner of war from 8th Company was fired upon by his officer when he deserted his machine gun position."[30] The German counterattacks had been repulsed successfully. **Elisabeth de Vanssay**, who had spent the afternoon hiding in the basement of the castle, noted:

In the evening there is a short lull; it seems that the *Boches* have been pushed back. There are less shells coming in because the Canadians managed to destroy the large mobile mortar that was firing at us. They had not managed to do so up until now because every time they had spotted its position and ranged in, the mortar displaced and everything had to be started over again. It was firing from the Villeneuve road, then would enter the tunnel and come out on the route de la Colle a few instants later. It finally became silent in the evening: the only crewmember had killed himself, since he had run out of ammunition and was the only one left who was resisting.[31]

What Elisabeth de Vanssay heard about the mortar was probably misrepresented, and it seems highly doubtful that any German would have killed himself in such a situation. The Allied reports do, however, confirm the presence of a self-propelled gun on the road between Villeneuve and la Colle,[32] as well as a violent explosion in the tunnel, apparently due to the destruction of some ammunition.[33] While the men positioned in and around the castle had been repulsing the counterattacks, some deadly gunshots had also been fired down in the village. **Lt William Story** commanded a platoon of 4-2 that had been held in reserve during the attack on Villeneuve, but that had moved into the village after it was captured:

Our company had the task on our arrival in Villeneuve-Loubet to defend the road along the river that had been shelled and mortared the night before on the way to Villeneuve-Loubet. I remember slogging into town and being ordered to set my platoon in a defensive position to await possible counterattacks. As we initially marched into town, we found no enemy troops in our area and relaxed. We came up and branched to the left, taking the road that went down alongside the river. A man came out of his house as we moved further into the countryside and offered what I thought was water. It turned out to be *eau de vie*, and I almost gagged before passing the bottle back to my non-drinking sergeant. He quickly passed it back to his men after warning them it wasn't water. We thanked the gentleman for his hospitality, even though all of us wished it had been plain water, for our canteens were dry.

We were ordered to turn back on that road and set up our night defensive line just shy of the outskirts of Villeneuve, to hold the left flank. Sadly, that afternoon, a friend of mine from 6th Company by the name of Schmidt, a Canadian from Elmira, Ontario, was coming from the castle when a German NCO with a Schmeisser fired upward through the bars of a basement window and hit Schmidt in the thigh, severing his main femoral artery. Somebody told me that the rest of the boys were so angry that they just returned the fire and that they got the German. Medics brought Schmidt and laid him on the grass near an auto repair garage where I had my platoon headquarters. The medics couldn't stop the bleeding and enlisted the help of a local doctor. He was among the citizenry who clustered about the area along with my men and others in that brief time. He too was unable to stop the bleeding and poor Schmidt died right before our eyes as the blood poured out.

Our men were so upset that they were unable to do anything that they momentarily turned their anger on the civilian doctor. Since I was the only officer there at the moment, I told the men to knock it off and their anger subsided. We covered Schmidt's body with a poncho and

passed word to our regimental staff that he had died and where his body could be found, and he stayed there until at least the next day. Jim Pringle had been the Sergeant Major of 6th Company, 2nd Regiment, until he was commissioned; and until he was commissioned he and Schmitty had been very close friends. When he saw Schmitty's body the next morning, he broke down and cried. We had covered the body with ponchos, but the flies had still gotten in there. When Jim pulled the ponchos off, seeing the flies just broke him up. That's one thing I remember out of that Villeneuve-Loubet incident. I've never forgotten it.

Sgt Floyd Schmidt was 24 years old at the time of his death and was an only son. The garage beside which he died was the Bartocchi house, which **Jospeh Macocco** lived in, and who remembered seeing Schmidt: "There was a wounded American beside our house. He was wounded in the thigh and blood was pouring out. It was impressive to see all that blood." **Sgt Jack Knight** also remembered seeing Schmidt's body:

I moved from the fortress to downtown two or three times, because that's where we were collecting prisoners, in a sort of a garage. I happened to be there at the particular time that a friend of mine was brought in on a stretcher. I pulled the shroud back and determined he was dead. Of course, the prisoners had been mislead about us killing prisoners, and they just moved back into the corner and stacked up like a bunch of scared sheep. These Axis prisoners that were in that building, they just were so sure

24-year-old Sgt Floyd S. Schmidt, from 6-2, was shot in the leg and mortally wounded in the village of Villeneuve during the afternoon of August 26th. He was an only child. Private Collection.

that I was going to turn on them. Well, I took a chance on being killed by prisoners several times, rather than mow them down. I was criticized, especially on two occasions, for not doing away with a prisoner and putting myself in personal danger to avoid out and out breaching the Geneva Convention and killing them.

The French physician who had attempted to stop Schmidt from bleeding out was the local doctor named Lefebvre. He and his wife had spent the day treating the wounded of all nationalities at the town hall. **John Dawson**, of 6-2, also remembers his presence, as well as a darker aspect of the Allied presence:

> The town's M.D., Dr Lefebvre, was very active as the day wore on, patching up our wounded. I don't recall where our medics were, but he was with our company, and I imagine the townspeople acted as stretcher bearers to get the casualties back. Anyhow, as dusk approached and we expected a counterattack, my platoon was holed up in and around the Doc's house. He and his wife were giving us wine and brandy, the full V.I.P. treatment. A bit later they turned sour and sullen, scarcely speaking. I had quite a time getting the story from them, but they finally told me their house had been looted. I was embarrassed. It seemed too dirty after the events of the afternoon, and besides, with a probable counterattack coming up, it was best to be on good terms with your sawbones.
>
> I called the guys together, told them what had happened, and said no charges would be made if the stuff reappeared in a certain room in ten minutes. It did, and the doc and his wife were pleased.[34]

The Allied soldiers were facing death everyday to liberate a country that was not their own, and some considered it their right to "liberate" items from civilians and prisoners of war, including such objects as jewelry and civilian vehicles. To the French civilians and German prisoners, this was simple theft; however, they usually put up with it without too much fuss, considering the circumstances. The orders that had been given to the FABTF were however extremely clear regarding such matters:

> In accordance with paragraph 79, Rules of Land Warfare, rigid discipline will be exercised for security of personal effects of prisoners. (…) All personnel are warned that taking for personal purposes money, watches, rings, fountain pens, insignia, or any other property of prisoners of war, in addition to being a violation of the Geneva Prisoner of War Convention of 1929, is a criminal act, amounting, according to the circumstances, to larceny or robbery in violation of Article of War 93. (…)
>
> Unit commanders will issue instructions for the maintenance of proper relations with the civil population. It should be impressed on each member of our units that their individual conduct will influence both the immediate and postwar attitude toward our country. (…) Upon entry in cities and towns, the strictest discipline will be maintained.[35]

We now return to the basement of the castle, where **Elisabeth de Vanssay** was surprised to see some of the forcemen exchanging "liberated" jewelry before the Germans mounted yet another counterattack during the night:

Our morale was doing better, first because there was less shooting, and second because there is something funny in all situations. We saw four Canadians come down to the basement and sit down around our only candle to converse with us, simultaneously throwing us some cigarettes, candies, chocolates, and chewing gum. Then they started cleaning their cartridges, "In order," they said, "for them to slide better to kill the *Boche*." And finally, a sinister thing, they took all sorts of items out of their pockets: rings, watches, money. It was their war booty that they had taken from the German prisoners and they started sharing it out among themselves. Under the candlelight, it felt like we were in the haunt of Ali Baba and the forty thieves. In the meantime, the Canadian artillery was pounding the *Boches*; the shells were whistling right by us, but we were no longer afraid, for we knew they were not aimed at us.

A bit before the charming "thieves" meeting, the Lieutenant who was in command had come to visit us. He related to us that his unit was arriving from Italy, that they had landed in St Raphael, and that they had come all the way here, gradually breaking up all resistance. He added: "In fact, the only place where we are really meeting any resistance is in Villeneuve-Loubet." He personally did not like war and went as far as to tell us: "If I had a child, I would prefer to kill him than to send him off to fight. Don't complain," he went on, "if there is a bit of destruction here; if you went to Italy there is not a stone left standing."

Before he left us I interpreted for father and mother, to ask him if in spite of the fighting it may be possible to bring the animals that had stupidly been brought to the stable back within the castle walls, because they would be safer. He told me "yes," but didn't do anything, and all were killed or burned. (…)

One of the buildings around the castle that was set on fire during the fighting. Elisabeth de Vanssay. Le Siège de Villeneuve. Nadèje le Lédan Collection.

There is less artillery fire as we prepare to go to sleep. (…) Shells started raining down on us again, and we found out the next day when everything was finished that the Germans had launched a counterattack. They managed to penetrate all the way into the yard. There the grenade fight had been terrible, but the Canadians managed to prevail. However, before pulling out, the Germans had thrown an incendiary grenade into the hayloft above the stable, which had started burning.[36]

Sgt Jack Knight remembers the fire:

We took position in the castle and they counterattacked us there. In order to try to get repossession of the place, they burned all of the buildings that surrounded the stone fence of the fortress. They were quite sure that this fire they started was going to burn us out. Well, they may just as well have yelled: "Yankee go home!" as we weren't about to withdraw under the influence of a little bit of fire. I don't even remember us making any attempt to put the fires out.

Morris Lazzarus, of 5-2, adds:

They just made the one attempt to take it back. They set fire to a barn. I think they were going to burn us out, but nothing happened, the fire didn't take hold.

Warren MacPhie, of 6-2, may have been one of the soldiers hiding in the basement with the inhabitants of the castle that Elisabeth de Vanssay described:

I was inside the castle with seven or eight of us, maybe more. Then somebody went to go out and we found out that we couldn't get out. We only had phone connection with our people, and they said that the Germans were back and had captured the ground around the castle again. We spent the night down in the basement of the castle. It's kind of a dungeon down underneath the castle. We got relieved the next morning around 8 or 9 o'clock.

During the night, the German forces finally departed from the Villeneuve-Loubet area for good. The interrogation report of some prisoners who were captured during the night of August 26th to 27th provides interesting insight on the situation of the German forces:

Two prisoners of war (…) stated that the enemy was assembling to leave Villeneuve, going to Menton. Prisoners of war also stated that they had 12 casualties yesterday, three dead and nine wounded. Prisoners of war are from 5th Company, 372nd Battalion. (…) Prisoners of war

18-year-old Grenadier Reinhard Swobodnik, of the 7th Company of Bataillon 372, is officially listed as being killed northeast of Antibes August 27th. In fact, he was probably killed during the fighting in Villeneuve-Loubet. Deutsches Rotes Kreuz.

report that 5th Company, 372nd Battalion is down to 30 men in strength. They were assembling to evacuate in woods near Villeneuve. Stated they had no food or ammunition.[37]

The fighting at Villeneuve on the 26th had cost the lives of two Canadians and one American soldier that were previously mentioned, while a further dozen men had been wounded.[38] After the Germans withdrew from the area, 14 bodies of German soldiers were found dead in the vicinity of Villeneuve, while a 15th soldier who was probably killed in the Villeneuve area (his location of death was recorded by the German army as being "northeast of Antibes") was evacuated by the Germans and buried in Castillon. These German casualties are summarized below:

Surname	Name	Rank	Age	Official date of death	Officially died in	Buried in	Unit
Forberger	Otto	Gren	19	26.8.1944	Cagnes sur mer	Villeneuve	5./Res.Gren. Btl.372
Ficker	Franz	Ogefr	34	26.8.1944	Villeneuve	Villeneuve	7./Res.Gren. Btl.372
Foks	Gerhard	Gren	17	26.8.1944	Villeneuve	Villeneuve	7./Res.Gren. Btl.372
Gnielczyk	Franz	Gren	23	26.8.1944	Villeneuve	Villeneuve	7./Res.Gren. Btl.372
Lössl	Josef	Gren	35	26.8.1944	Villeneuve	Villeneuve	7./Res.Gren. Btl.372
Mertin	Otto	Gren	22	26.8.1944	Villeneuve	Villeneuve	7./Res.Gren. Btl.372
Pilch	Hubert	Gren	17	26.8.1926	Villeneuve	Villeneuve	7./Res.Gren. Btl.372
Krzyzowski	Josef	Gren	19	29.8.1944	Villeneuve	Villeneuve	14./Inf.Pz.Jg. Kp. 239
Unknown				26.8.1944		Villeneuve	
Unknown				26.8.1944		Villeneuve	
Unknown				26.8.1944		Villeneuve	
Unknown				26.8.1944		Villeneuve	
Unknown				26.8.1944		Villeneuve	
Unknown				26.8.1944		Villeneuve	
Swobodnik	Reinhard	Gren	18	27.8.1944	NE Antibes	Castillon	7./Res.Gren. Btl.372

The Liberation of la Colle sur Loup

Meanwhile, at la Colle sur Loup, a few kilometers north of Villeneuve, the Germans had also mounted a counterattack during the day before pulling out on the night of August 26ᵗʰ to 27ᵗʰ. There had been several skirmishes and patrols on Hill 212, which overlooked the destroyed bridge over the Loup. Though four soldiers had been killed on the 24ᵗʰ and 25ᵗʰ, there were apparently no men killed on either side on the 26ᵗʰ and 27ᵗʰ, although many Germans were captured. The following is a brief description of the events at la Colle made by 1ˢᵗ Regiment of the FSSF late on August 26ᵗʰ:

> A patrol to Hill 212 at 05:00 captured three prisoners of war, followed by an enemy counterattack (…). Counterattacking force retreated in disorder in the face of artillery defensive fire and small arms fire. Captured five prisoners of war at 18:50 (…) and one swimming in creek .(…) We received heavy caliber fire and mortar fire throughout the day. Our casualties one killed [This was Walter Ladd, mentioned earlier on as having died on the 25ᵗʰ], seven wounded.[39]

The interrogation of the captured soldiers revealed some information about what had been happening on the German side:

> 6ᵗʰ Company prisoners stated that withdrawal orders were issued on the night of 25 August and then cancelled. Orders were issued for the withdrawal on the night of 26 August, but one platoon was left on Hill 212 (…) to fight a delaying action. Prisoners of war state that approximately 20 men of the platoon retreated when our patrol advanced up the hill. The balance of the platoon was captured. (…)
> Three prisoners of war from 6ᵗʰ Company, Reserve Grenadier Battalion 372, were captured early in the morning of 27 August by 1ˢᵗ Regiment FSSF on Hill 212 and one prisoner of war from 8ᵗʰ Company, Reserve Grenadier Battalion 372, deserted from machine gun position. (…) Prisoners of war from 6ᵗʰ Company had been sent back to Hill 212 to try and locate a squad which had become lost after losing its map. Prisoner of war from 8ᵗʰ Company was fired upon by his officer when he deserted his machine gun position.[40]

By the morning of the 27ᵗʰ, the Germans facing the FSSF were gone and the forcemen proceeded into la Colle. I have only managed to find a few first-hand accounts concerning la Colle: one is that of the *Groupe Tartane* resistance man Jean, who was still acting as a guide for 1ˢᵗ Regiment of the FSSF. At some point **Jean** was sent out on reconnaissance near the blown bridge over the Loup River outside la Colle:

> We reached la Colle sur Loup, where the Germans had blown up the bridge, and there were three of us Frenchmen from Grasse and one *résistant* from la Colle, so we told the Americans: "We will go and see under the remains of the bridge and see how hard it is to get through." We were young and had no military training, and we set out like four imbeciles. We went under the bridge and heard "bang!" What had happened? The guy from la Colle was wounded in the leg and the rest of us got away with being hit by small fragments. We didn't know if it was a mortar shell or what. In the end, we understood it was a mine. But then we had to go back, carrying the wounded guy. I think that was one of the biggest frights of my life, because on the way back we were wondering if we might step on another mine. We couldn't know, but we managed to get back without any further trouble. My two friends exaggerated their wounds. We had been hit by small fragments, really nothing, but there were young girls there who called themselves nurses, who were supposedly treating the wounded, and my friends took advantage of the situation to get pampered a bit.

Experienced soldiers would have known that areas such as a blown bridge or a cratered road would probably be infested with mines, as bypassing these obstacles would be the first thing untrained men, such as Jean and his three companions, would do. **Jean** goes on about the disappointing character of the FFI man from la Colle who was supposed to guide them:

> He was a phony, just like so many other "*résistants* of the last hour*,*" unfortunately. He was a phony, because if you don't know, you should say: "I don't know." He wanted to act cocky and almost got us all killed! I saw him again back in Grasse. There were hotels that had been requisitioned for the wounded, and I saw that guy who had been wounded behind the knee coming down the avenue. He had put on Lieutenant stripes. That was the resistance for you…

Another brief first-hand account about la Colle sur Loup is made by **René Ghio**, whose father had crossed through the lines at Villeneuve on the 25ᵗʰ to go to Nice to perform a mission for the resistance and later returned to Grasse, crossing the lines at la Colle:

> We left in the direction of la Colle sur Loup, Soon after (…) we met the first American soldiers, walking in two columns (…). The officers told us to beware of mines. There were lots of people near the Loup. That is where fighting was occurring yesterday and last night in order to slow down the advance of the American troops. That is also where we saw the first American and Canadian dead. There was even one wounded Frenchman.[41]

Interestingly, the town of Tourrettes sur Loup, to the north of la Colle sur Loup, seems to have been completely ignored by the

The remains of the bridge at la Colle sur Loup. A new bridge was constructed close by after the war, leaving the old bridge untouched. Author's Collection.

Oberst Kurt Hahn, commanding officer of Reserve Grenadier Regiment 239; Generalleutnant Otto Fretter-Pico, commanding officer of Reserve Division 148; and Hauptmann Becherer of the artillery study a map in the dining room of the famous Colombe d'Or Hotel in St Paul, August 25 or 26, 1944. Fretter-Pico had apparently taken up quarters in St Paul late on the 24th, arriving from Vence, and left early on the 27th. The FSSF reached the Colombe d'Or shortly afterwards, prompting Colonel Burhans to later note in his book The First Special Service Force, A War History of the North Americans: "Colonel Walker and staff signed the register immediately following the signatures of Major General Fretter-Pico and staff, 148th Division, who had checked out hurriedly the previous evening." Author's Collection.

Allied units. The 517th Parachute Infantry Regiment had bypassed Tourrettes by the north, while the FSSF had passed south ot it. The result is that one day, probably August 27th, the 512th Airborne Signal Company walked into town, thinking the place had already been liberated:

> A team from the wire section, constructing and rehabilitating a commercial circuit between Grasse and Vence, contacted an isolated enemy force in the town of Tourrettes. The wire crew was forced to abandon the wire line because of insufficient personnel and weapons. Approximately 20 enemy were in the town.[42]

The local partisans also apparently ran into the same Germans, as on the morning of the 27th, the FSSF reported: "French partisans reported a fight between French and Germans in Tourrettes. There are approximately 20 Germans in town."[43] It would seem that no casualties resulted from these encounters, and the small German force probably surrendered or pulled out shortly afterwards. The 512th Airborne Signals Company had, however, lost a man August 24th. **Pvt Joseph J. Tully**, who was 22 years old, had died of injuries after falling off a pole.

The German soldiers of Reserve Grenadier Bataillon 372 at Villeneuve-Loubet and la Colle sur Loup

It has unfortunately not been possible to find any first-hand accounts of German soldiers who fought at Villeneuve-Loubet or la Colle sur Loup. The only information about them is provided by the interrogations of prisoners made by the Allies. Such interrogation reports are written in a very messy manner and often contradict each other, but they give a good idea of the atmosphere in *Reserve Grenadier Bataillon 372*. Below is a compilation of extracts of several reports concerning both Villeneuve and la Colle:

Prisoners of war were mainly from Reserve Grenadier Battalion 372, 239th Regiment. (…)

All prisoners of war are willing talkers and 3rd class troops, except "cadre" personnel, which are excellently trained and of pure German origin. (…)

The 372nd Grenadier Battalion, now fighting a delaying action in the Vence-Cagnes sector, will withdraw at 22:00 on August 26th to the Var River. If necessary, they will fight on the west side of the Var or east side and then withdraw to Menton to join the division. (…)

Food is hard to obtain due to limited transportation. Prisoners of war state 80-90% of the personnel are non-German in this battalion. Ages average from 17-19 years old and 35-45 years old. (…)

Desertion on the part of Poles, Czechs, and some Germans continues. Three men of a machine gun section deserted with machine guns and ammunition to join our forces. A searching party sent out to locate the former also came to our lines. (…)

5th Company NCOs threatened to shoot any man attempting to desert. (…)

It has been suggested by a prisoner of war formerly an officer that propaganda leaflets be dropped in the Polish language, as at least 50% of enemy personnel do not speak any other language but Polish.(…)

Prisoner of war from 327th Battalion stated that his company and adjoining companies were to cover the retreat of the 148th Division. The assembly point for these units is believed to be in the vicinity of Menton. (…)

In a hospital set up in a civilian residence on the la Colle-Villeneuve turnpike, the Germans treated 72 wounded from artillery and fighting in that area before pulling out at 22:00 on August 26th. (…)

Civilians at les Esperes report that during the period 26-27 August, when Special Service Force supporting artillery heavily shelled German installations near the town, the officers' quarters flew a Red Cross flag, but an aid station 300 yards away had no marking whatever. (…)

Prisoners of war were told that heavy fighting was raging around St Lo five days ago. One Yugoslav prisoner of war stated he overheard officers and NCOs discussing the possibility of the Germans using gas when the Allies neared the German border. (…)[44]

The Aftermath of the Fighting in Villeneuve-Loubet

The fighting along the Loup River was now over, but a few interesting events were still to occur in Villeneuve. We will start the description of the aftermath of the battle with **Elisabeth de Vanssay**'s writings on what happened in the castle:

Sunday, August 27th.
Calm has returned for good. The Germans have been pushed back. There is still artillery fire, but it is no longer landing on us, it is destined for the Var River. We all leave the basement. Only a devastated *Monsieur* Bertant remains in it with his dogs. (…)

[The Delands] say that *Madame* Bertant's house has received a direct hit by a shell and is burning. *Madame* Bertant is extremely worried, and without saying anything to *Monsieur* Bertant, she takes off with three soldiers to see what is really happening in her home, and she obliges

Soldiers of the 7th Company of Reserve Grenadier Bataillon 372 posing for the camera in the months preceding the invasion. The soldier with a cross inked onto him is Grenadier Franz Gnielczyk, aged 23. The soldier standing at the left has been recognized by siblings as being Grenadier Otto Mertin, aged 22. Both men were Polish coal miners who were killed at Villeneuve-Loubet August 26th. The soldier eating at Mertin's right may be Alois Wühr, who we will mention further on. Anna Łuszczyńska Collection.

three German soldiers who are hiding in the debris to surrender. When she arrives, she summons them in German to surrender… a few seconds later, one of Stephanie's white aprons hanging from a stick appears at a window. In the meantime, her house burns down like a torch: she comes back to the castle despaired. Poor *Monsieur* Bertant doesn't know anything, but he is demoralized nonetheless.

At her house, *Madame* Bertant has found her servant "Sardoux" and "Minico" the cobbler. She brings them back to the castle without realizing that "Minico" was taking advantage of the situation to come into the castle to spy. The Canadians, who do not want any strangers among them, arrest them immediately and send them to Grasse. To vindicate themselves they tell them: "It is the Marquise who is ordering your arrest."

What a terrible mess our poor castle was in: no more roofs, the drainpipes are dangling, the mosaics of the courtyard are hidden under mounds of debris, and exhausted soldiers are lying everywhere and anywhere. In the middle of all this, the so-called FFI arrive, asking the Canadians for weapons. They all had very trustworthy faces. We had to be very careful because of the possibility of looting.[45]

Unfortunately, **Sgt Jack Knight**, of the HQ Detachment of 2nd Regiment, confirms that some looting occurred:

The marquis determined that some of the crown jewels had gone missing. There was a Captain Bennett there, and even though I wasn't a commissioned officer, I assisted him on the board of enquiry, and we couldn't determine that any of our people had been involved in such an escapade to steal some of the crown jewels. Of course, the whole thing incensed me pretty badly, and I think on the report that I briefly wrote, I couldn't think that he was using good sense to blame our people who were there about two days total, when there had been French forces moving in and out of his castle for two and a half years; and German troops had been moving in and out of there. Fascists and the whole scum of the Axis people had been utilizing this place to come in and out of at will. Sorry, I thought it was some lack of judgment.

Contrary to what Jack Knight thought, no other troops other than the FSSF ever actually came into the castle. On a more pleasant note, **Thomas O'brien** and **John Hankes**, of 5-2, can confirm the detail about soldiers sleeping "everywhere and anywhere":

We stayed in the castle for a few days, and then went on our way to the Italian border. Incidentally, while in the castle, I slept in a four-poster canopied bed which I presumed was the count's. It was a welcome change, having slept on the ground for the past week.

Our company (5th Company) took over the castle, and I believe we only stayed there for five days. It was very nice, as we had never seen anything like this before. In the castle we used the kitchen and I believe some beds. I remember being in the kitchen, we used to cook down there. I know that there was horse meat there, but I can't remember how we did get that horse. We ate some of that down there in the kitchen.

Warren MacPhie, of 6-2, explains where the mysterious horse meat came from:

There were a bunch of nuns who lived in there, and there was a big white horse in the barn inside the castle, and I think it was a fellow from Minneapolis who said to the nuns they had nothing to eat: "Would you like me to butcher that horse, and leave it hanging for you to eat?" and they said yes. So before we left there in the morning, he did. He killed it, skinned it, fixed it all up, quartered it, and had it all hung up there for them to eat. Then we left, and that was the end of that.

We now let **Elisabeth de Vanssay** continue her story. She also remembers the horse and the chaos the forcemen made of the kitchen, as well as some other colorful details:

In the yard in front of the stable, Marius Pellegrin was taking our poor horse, which had been wounded during the battle and was then asphyxiated in the flames, to be butchered. Since it was in perfect health, father decided to distribute its meat to the population of Villeneuve for free.

The kitchen is also a mess. There are about 20 Canadians in it lazing around or preparing grub. For our lunch we have been given a bit of grease and are making French fries. As Anna and I were preparing them and putting them in a dish to stay warn, the Canadians were taking entire handfuls from us and enjoying them.

For the occasion, we had invited Lieutenant Bennett [Lt William Bennett, of 5-2], who had taken command after Lieutenant Crawford's wounding, with the siege of Villeneuve having earned him his Captain bars. He was polite, pleasant, and not too savage for an American [Bennett was in fact a Canadian from Toronto]. It was the dinner of the "Liberation."

After lunch, Colonel Moore [The commander of the 2nd Battalion of the 2nd Regiment, FSSF.] came to see his men. We offered him drinks, then all of us climbed up to the top of the tower to raise the colors.

Here, a delicate question needed to be resolved: two of the "brilliant liberators of the land" who were combatants of the last second and notorious communists were implying that the Allied colors should be raised, including, of course, the Soviet "banner!"

It would have been the death blow for our old seigniorial dwelling. Luckily, under the southern suns, everything solves itself: only one flag existed in our home, the tricolor one.

Opening the march in the arms of Lt Bennett [Elisabeth de Vanssay had been severely wounded in an air raid at the Var bridge in the previous months.], it is with great joy that we saw the French colors spread open in the sunlight.[46]

The German Dead at Villeneuve-Loubet

As the inhabitants of the castle joyfully hoisted the French flag at the top of Chateau de Villeneuve under the brilliant sunlight, the bodies of the German soldiers who had been killed in the battle remained sprawled on the ground where death had struck them, the burning August sun accelerating their decomposition. Several dead Germans were lying on the road near the castle where they had set up their 75mm cannons. One of the local kids remembers: "We saw killed Germans on the road going up to the tunnel. They were lying on the ground with flies on them, but we didn't look because my father was telling us to move on." **François Baldini** was another of the local children who saw the dead Germans at the mouth of the tunnel:

"Would you like me to butcher that horse and leave it hanging for you to eat?" A forceman butchers the marquis' horse that was smothered in the fire in one of the barns that surrounded the castle. Author's Collection.

The day after the Liberation of Villeneuve, residents of the castle pose with two Allied officers in front of the well in the courtyard of the castle. Standing from left to right: Anna Roatta, Rina Gallo, Jean Gallo, Lt Col Robert Moore (commanding officer of the 2nd Battalion of 2nd Regiment of the FSSF), Capt Bill Bennett (of 5-2), and the Marquis de Panisse Passis. Kneeling: Maryse, Pellegrin, and Jeannot. Elisabeth de Vanssay. Le Siège de Villeneuve. Nadèje le Lédan Collection.

The French flag once again floats over the tower of Villeneuve Castle, on which the damage caused by the battle has still not been repaired to this day. Elisabeth de Vanssay. Le Siège de Villeneuve. Nadèje le Lédan Collection. Vincent Meyer Collection.

When we reached Villeneuve, there were Germans at the foot of the plane trees. One of them had been shot in the head, but maybe that had been a *coup de grace*. [This is probably the same killed German visible on the previously shown period photo taken by the forcemen.] There were flies on his face and everything. I remember he was wearing leather straps, and I was thinking: "What nice leather straps." I didn't want to take them, but I bent down to touch them and a woman there told me: "Don't take them from him!" I wasn't intending to undress a poor soldier.

The respect for the property of the dead did not last long, of course, as **Madame Viale**, from Cagnes sur Mer, explains:

At the Liberation, I was worried about my cousins in Villeneuve, so my father took his bike and went to see them to reassure me. When he got back he told us: "I was at the tunnel and saw lots of dead Germans on the way down to Villeneuve. They were all dressed, but when I went back an hour and a half or two later they had nothing left on them: no more boots, no more weapons, nothing, they were naked.

On a path leading towards the woods southeast of the castle and tunnel, from where the Germans had been counterattacking, 13-year-old **Noël Giordano** found more German dead:

I was going down the path on my own and I saw a machine gun on a tripod with three or four dead Germans lying around it. So I looked, and I saw that one of them had a rank insignia and was wearing a pair of binoculars around his neck. I wanted to take them, but the strap was passing under him and I was afraid, so I was looking to see how I could take them. Just then, some FFI arrived and they pushed me away, saying: "Get out of here! You don't have any business being here!" Then one of them turned the German over, took the binoculars, and put them around his neck. Then they left.

Unfortunately, as we have seen with some of the previous accounts, most of the FFI only appeared once the Germans were long gone; and they were not very popular among the population. **Gustave Giordano** remembers:

You know, there weren't many FFIs. Do you know when they did come out? When all the Germans were gone, then they came out of the houses. When the storm had passed, they all came out. Then there were armbands here and armbands there. But then, when they were recruiting in Nice to join the army to go to Germany, only five or six people joined up. Fauda, Fournier, Granel, and Carlo joined up and left. The others didn't go.

Gustave Giordano also witnessed a particularly outlandish case of a body of a killed German being pilfered:

There was fighting for 48 hours and a lot of Germans were killed. In the Espères Forest, there were a great deal of them because it was high ground, so they were all up there. They were already starting to decompose. One good old timer told me: "Damn, look at the boots on the one over there!" He must have been an officer and had a pair of boots. So he said: "Too bad, I am going to take those boots. I am bare foot and he has those nice boots." I told him: "Are you crazy, can't you see he is dead?" There were huge hornets taking meat off the bodies. They were completely swollen, with their belts pressing into their stomachs. It was August and extremely hot. He went to pull off the boots, but the leg and everything came off with it, and it stank. So we ran away. We said: "Do what you want, take them, but we aren't staying here!" In the end he left them there.

Taking boots and shoes was fair game, for many of the locals only had very bad shoes themselves, or sometimes no shoes at all. Under such circumstances, there was simply no logic in burying a perfectly good pair of quality German army shoes. However, other types of pilfering could be much more sinister, as former local youth **Paul Tremellat** explains:

People were even saying that so and so, who I know but whose name I will not say, had taken the gold teeth and the watches of the unfortunate dead German soldiers. It was repeated so much at the time that it must have been at least partly true.

Exactly when the bodies were finally buried is not known. The only hint of a possible time line is found in the FSSF journal, with the following message transmitted the morning of August 28th:

> From Lt Simms, 2nd Regiment. Leading French civilian wants permission to bury German dead in Villeneuve-Loubet, but has no set up for identification. Suggest one of our men go with him with a work detail of French to do the job.[47]

What resulted from this message is not clear, but in the end, nothing was apparently ever done to identify the bodies. In any case, before being buried, the bodies were all regrouped in an abandoned sand pit, where the local kids were able to look at them. Eight-year-old **Louis Giordano** was one of them:

> The sand pit and its silos formed a sort of stockroom and the German soldiers were brought there. As far as I heard, there were 14 of them. Obviously it was forbidden for us kids to go there, but the more it was forbidden, the more curious we were to know what was there, so we escaped from our parents to see. The soldiers were covered with military blankets and shelter quarters, and of course there were flies and bees that were coming to take pieces of flesh. It was quite impressive. Afterward, all those soldiers were transported in a cart and buried near the Mardaric Creek; I don't know if they are still there.

Louis Fanti was another local youth who went to look at the bodies:

> At the time I was 15 years old, and a friend and I went to see all those dead people. They were in a sand pit that had a cement floor and they were stored there. It wasn't a pretty sight, because it was right in the month of August, and with the heat their heads had become enormous. They had been dead for two or three days and they were lying there, rotting. It was appalling, it was horrible, that is the truth. I tried to count them, but at one place there was quite a high pile of them in which I didn't manage to count them. Then there were two here, three more there, another a bit further on; and when I tried to count them, the guy I was with said: "There are 30 of them," but I don't know if he was informed or not.
>
> I saw one who was 17 years old. I remember that, because in the end he was just one year older than me. His body wasn't damaged. We could see that he was very young. He was a real German, very, very blond, and didn't have a helmet. He was the one who was found in Pascal's garage, who had been killed from up on the rocks. Supposedly that idiot died shouting: "Long live Hitler." [This was the German who had been shot while hiding under a cart in front of Pascal Bartocchi's garage. Being under the cart had protected him from the sunlight and may have slowed down the decomposition process, explaining why he "wasn't damaged."] It was unfortunate to see him… Well, it was unfortunate for the others as well, but we didn't really feel sorry for them, because they hadn't done us any good. At the time, there were still survivors from the First World War, and for them the Germans were the plague!

In the end, a long hole was dug next to the Mardaric, a small creek flowing into the Loup from the west, and all the bodies were buried there. **Louis Fanti** goes on:

The exact location of the grave as it appeared in the 2000s. The area was overgrown with thorny bramble and littered with modern day trash. Absolutely nothing indicated that 14 soldiers lay buried there; in fact, this photo was taken more or less randomly, and it was only realized later that it happened to depict the location of the grave. Author's Collection.

> They requisitioned all the local Italians and foreigners and told them: "You have to come and dig a hole at such and such a place and bury the Germans in the hole." We could see them passing on the road with a cart with three or four bodies on it.

No direct witnesses of the burial left any exact accounts of what they did, however, all the survivors of the time, such as **Gustave Giordano**, tell the same version as Louis Fanti:

> They made the Italian immigrants, as we called them at the time, cart the dead. But some people also volunteered to do it. The Germans were all buried beside the Mardaric on a cart. They would tip up the cart and drop them into the hole. I don't know what became of them.

Villeneuve-Loubet Battlefield Investigation: the Exhumation of the Mass Grave of German Soldiers

The bodies of most of the German soldiers killed in the Maritime Alps were located and exhumed by the *Volksbund* in 1958. However, in several of the accounts presented above, concerning the killed Germans, the witnesses expressed uncertainty about what happened to the bodies. This is because, surprisingly, the bodies of these Germans had in fact still not been retrieved at the time I was interviewing witnesses in the early 2000s. Most of the elders in Villeneuve that I talked to did not even express any doubts; they simply and honestly told me that the bodies were still buried beside the Mardaric Creek.

I therefore set out to find these bodies, as I suspected they were still reported as missing in action. Finding them would also provide a rare opportunity to exhume the bodies carefully, and to study them in order to discover a large amount of historical, forensic, and archaeological data about who these soldiers were, how many of them there were, how they had been killed, and how they had been buried. As an example, before finding the bodies, it was impossible to estimate even approximately how many Germans had been killed in Villeneuve: Louis Giordano had said there were 14, but he was only eight years old at the time, how could he know? Most witnesses claimed that there were between 20 and 30 dead, while FSSF documents spoke of up to 50 dead.

Finding the exact location of the grave seemed next to impossible, as the area around the Mardaric Creek had changed a lot since 1944. What had once been a field had become a forest overgrown with thorny bramble and weeds. Furthermore, almost none of the witnesses agreed upon exactly where the grave was. However, thanks to the very precise recollections of Antoine Baylet, who was over 90 years old at the time, and of Jean-Pierre Batteli, I was able to suspect quite precisely where the grave was. Some old aerial photos of the area also showed what the field used to look like before becoming overgrown with trees.

In October 2006, I organized an exhumation in collaboration with Julien Hauser of the *Volksbund*. He was willing to let me perform the exhumation, as long as it was done fast (in two or three days). Since it was planned that the exhumation would be done by hand and with no budget, I enlisted several of my friends to help, including amateur archeologist Pascal Boucard, Lionel Alberti, Vincent Meyer (medical student), Ivana Ključarić (medical student), Nicolas Baudier, and Damien Leblanc. We started digging late October 17, 2006, with October 18th being the offical day of the exhumation.

We discovered that the original grave the bodies had been buried in was a rectangle approximately five meters long, 1.8 meters wide, and one meter deep. Fourteen bodies were found within the grave, buried in all directions and all positions, indicating that they had been placed in the grave with little care. We will start by describing the most important characteristics of each of the 14 bodies and will then draw some more general conclusions about the mass grave. Because the bones were in a bad state of preservation, only the larger bones, such as the skull and the limb bones, could be properly examined. The ribs and other small bones were too fragile to be properly exhumed in our rather primitive work conditions, so any possible trauma on these bones went unnoticed. In this report, the term "notable artifact" implies anything other than buttons, coins, or cartridges of which large quantities were found without their location of discovery being noted.

Body number 1: The only notable artifact found on this body was an identification tag, positioned in the region of the thorax. The upper half of the tag had been pierced by a bullet with a trajectory coming from in front and slightly above. This bullet is probably what killed the soldier, though the ribs were in too poor condition to be able to visualize any damage. A callus from an old healed fracture was present mid-high of the right femur. The tag enabled the body to be identified as that of 23-year-old ***Grenadier* Franz Gnielczyk**, born in Jasten (now Jasiona, Poland), of the 7th Company of *Reserve Grenadier Bataillon 372*.

One of Franz Gnielczyk's sisters was located in Poland and was able to provide the following information about him: Franz Gnielczyk had been a coal miner and had broken his hip in a mining accident in 1943. He was drafted into the army in January 1944 and left for France two months later. The fact that Franz was a miner, a job considered essential to the war effort, probably explains why he had not been drafted into the army earlier at age 18. In September 1944, the family received news that Franz was missing in action, and they never heard anything else until I contacted them in 2012. Franz's sister was relieved to finally find out the truth about her brother's death.

Body number 2: This soldier was found still wearing his belt with almost full ammunition pouches, a bayonet sheath with bayonet removed, a gas mask in its box, "Y straps," and a canteen. Although no wounds were visible on the bones, the canteen, as well as some of the cartridges in the ammunition pouches, had been gashed by shrapnel, making the probable cause of death shrapnel wounds. In the absence of any identification tag, the body remained unidentified.

October 18, 2006, the bodies of the German soldiers killed at Villeneuve-Loubet in August 1944 are exhumed by a team of volunteers under the supervision of the Volksbund. Julien Hauser, of the Volksbund, speaks to reporters, while Lionel Alberti, Nicolas Baudier, Vincent Meyer, and Pascal Boucard work in the grave. Author's Collection.

An artist's representation of the grave, with each body numbered and letters assigned to the four helmets that could not be associated with any of the bodies. The bones that are not represented were either not identified properly because of commingling, or were not drawn so as not to overload the drawing. Author's Collection.

Pascal Boucard discovers Franz Gnielczyk's (Body number 1) identification tag, still on his thorax where it was supposed to be worn. The investigators were stunned when they saw that Gnielczyk had been shot right through the middle of his identification tag. Author's Collection.

Grenadier Franz Gnielczyk, of the 7th Company of Bataillon 372, was killed by a bullet that was shot through his identification tag at Villeneuve-Loubet, August 26, 1944. He was 23 years old at the time and had worked in a coal mine in Zabrze before being drafted into the army. Anna Łuszczyńska Collection.

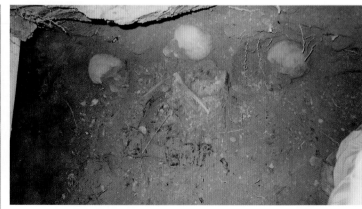

Bodies 1, 2, and 3, and the shrapnel-damaged canteen that was found under body number 2. Author's Collection.

Body number 3: No wounds were found on this body, and the only notable artifact present was a gold crown on the upper left incisor. It was noted that this crown seemed damaged, possibly because somebody had tried to remove it? The body was not identified.

Body number 4: The skull of this body was broken into multiple pieces. The only notable artifact found on the body was an identification tag recovered on the thorax. A helmet (Helmet E) with a large shrapnel hole was, however, buried in proximity to the body. A fragment had penetrated the right side of the helmet and exited on the left side, leaving holes roughly three centimeters in diameter on each side. A second, very small fragment penetrated the rear of the helmet without exiting. The manner in which the steel of the helmet had been bent by the shrapnel provided a graphic illustration of how powerful and devastating the effects of a single shrapnel fragment can be.

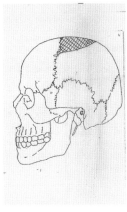

All the skull fragments were carefully washed and glued back together in order to reconstruct the skull. It was found that a large portion of the upper skull was missing, with characteristics of a funneled entry wound being present on the right side. Comparison showed that the damage to the skull matched the damage to the helmet almost perfectly, and furthermore, that the damaged helmet matched no other skulls found in the grave. Everything therefore indicates that the damaged helmet had been on this soldier's head when he was killed. The cause of death was determined to be multiple shrapnel wounds, most likely from a shell that exploded very near the soldier.

The identification tag enabled the soldier to be identified as 22-year-old **Grenadier Otto Mertin**, born in Lentzberg (now Rybnik, Poland), of the 7th Company of *Reserve Grenadier Bataillon 372*. After contacting his relatives, it was found that Otto Mertin had a twin brother and a younger sister who were still alive in Poland, as well as an elder brother who had been killed during the war and whose body had only recently been recovered in Poland. The surviving siblings had known that their brother was killed in action in 1944, but were relieved to find out that his body had finally been found, and that he had died a quick and painless death. Just like Franz Gnielczyk, Otto Mertin had worked as a coal miner before being drafted into the army.

Body number 5: This soldier was found still wearing his helmet, his belt with almost full ammunition pouches, an empty bayonet sheath, an empty pistol holster, and his canteen with Bakelite canteen cup. His identification tag and a Wound Badge in Black (*Verwundetenabzeichen in Scharz*, indicating a previous combat wound) were found on his chest, and a pocket watch and pocket knife were found in the area of his pelvis. The helmet he was wearing had been pierced by two shrapnel fragments coming from the rear, and his canteen and canteen cup had also both been hit by very small fragments. Both the soldier's tibias had comminuted fractures in their upper portions and the right femur was also severely fractured in its lower portion. This damage to the legs seemed to have been inflicted by at least three separate shrapnel fragments and

The helmet and skull of 22-year-old Grenadier Otto Mertin, which tragically illustrates the devastating effect a single shrapnel fragment can have. Author's Collection.

Otto Mertin and his twin brother Georg, who survived the war. Mertin Family Collection.

The first photo of Otto Mertin was taken in 1942 when he was a civilian, while the second one is the last photo of him alive, taken in 1944 in southern France. Shocking changes have occurred to his face over these two years. Some would call it a "thousand yard stare," but an otorhinolaryngologist put it more scientifically: "Even though the photos are not of the same quality, there are several noticeable differences: 1) He has lost a large amount of hair in frontotemporal region. 2) On his forehead there are noticeable wrinkles. 3) Deep wrinkles have formed between the eyebrows. 4) The eyelids are positioned about five mm lower. 5) The lower eyelids are loose and laxity can be seen. 6) The midface area has lost a large amount of subcutaneous fat compared to the fullness of the earlier photo. 7) The nasolabial folds are deep. 8) All facial musculature has lost tonicity, which can especially be seen in the region of the mandible." Mertin Family Collection.

had caused the lower legs to be grotesquely bent out of shape. The cause of death was determined to be multiple shrapnel wounds, probably from a shell exploding at a very close distance behind the soldier.

The identification tag indicated this soldier was 34-year-old **Gefreiter Franz Ficker** (known as Franz Guder), born in Grünborn (now Zelenka, Czech Republic), of the 7th Company of *Reserve Grenadier Bataillon 372*. Both Franz Guder's son and daughter were contacted in Germany. They were very thankful that their father's fate had finally been clarified, and the son came to France to visit his father's grave and the location where his body was found. The son also provided photos of his father where he can be seen wearing a black wound badge and a pistol holster: only one specimen of each of these items had been recovered during the exhumation, both on Franz Guder's body. An Infantry Assault Badge was also visible in the period photos, but had not been found in the grave. This badge was presumably pilfered from the body. The son still had a letter that Franz Guder's wife received in 1944 announcing her husband's death. This letter confirmed that Franz

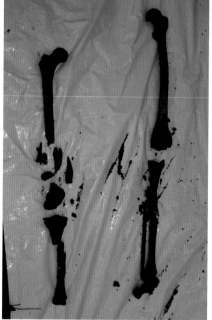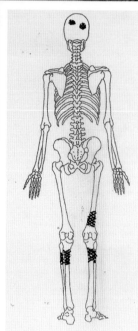

The shrapnel-damaged helmet and severely fractured shins of 34-year-old Gefreiter Franz Guder. There were probably numerous other shrapnel wounds present that were not noted because they had only caused damage to his soft tissues without affecting his bones. Author's Collection.

Guder had been killed by a shell burst occurring at close distance, as had been concluded during the exhumation:

In the field, September 2, 1944.
Miss Sophi Guder

I am herewith fulfilling the sad duty of informing you of the hero's death of your husband, Franz Guder, during the battle at Villeneuve-Loubet, in the region of Nice, on August 26, 1944. Your husband fell for our fatherland, killed by a direct hit from a shell, and death occurred on the spot. Your husband, Franz Guder, was a zealous soldier, a model comrade, and an effective leader, who we had learned to treasure, and who we remember with proud sadness and honor.

I would like to tell you and your loved ones, in the name of all the comrades in the unit, what a great loss this is, and present our sincere condolences.

Truly yours.

Erich Heß *Oberleutnant und Kompanieführer*[48]

This letter shows that, despite the heavy losses suffered by the Germans in Villeneuve, both in prisoners and in dead, the German officers and the military administration remained surprisingly well informed of the fate of their soldiers (there were, however, limits to the quality of this information, as will be seen further on with Alois Wühr's story).

Body number 6: This body was still wearing a helmet and belt, as well as an identification tag on its thorax. The belt had neither ammunition pouches nor bayonet sheath on it. What appeared to be a shrapnel fragment was found in the abdominal area, and a second projectile, apparently a shrapnel fragment, had pierced the back of the helmet without exiting. The cause of death was therefore determined to be multiple shrapnel wounds. The identification tag showed that this was the body of 19-year-old *Grenadier* **Josef Krzyzowski**, age 19, born in Wyrow (now Wyry, Poland), of the 14th *Infanterie Panzerjäger Kompanie* of *Reserve Infanterie Regiment 239*. Josef Krzyzowski is the only man in the grave to have been identified as belonging to this antitank company, and we can assume that he was a crewmember of one of the two 75mm cannons that were destroyed by the forcemen on the road near the castle. He being a crewman of one of the cannons would explain why he was wearing a belt with no ammunition pouches or other utensils attached to it.

Body number 7: This soldier was still wearing his helmet, as well as his shoes. This is notable, as he was the only body out of the 14 still wearing shoes. His wallet was also found, and an X-ray of it showed that it contained a crucifix, several religious medallions, and some coins. No wounds or means of identification were found. One spent and damaged American .30 caliber bullet was found in the area of bodies 7 and 8, and although it was clear that the bullet had participated in killing of one of the two soldiers, it could not be determined which one. Only the posterior part of the bullet's copper jacket remained, its condition being consistent with that often observed on rifle bullets retained within a body after a high-speed impact.

Body number 8: This soldier was still wearing his helmet, his belt with completely empty ammunition pouches, and his empty bayonet sheath. His identification tag was found under his face,

Less than one year after the exhumation, Franz Guder's son visits the location where his father's body was found. Franz Guder Collection.

19-year-old Grenadier Josef Krzyzowski, wearing a helmet that was pierced by a projectile, apparently a shrapnel fragment, as well as a belt. Author's Collection.

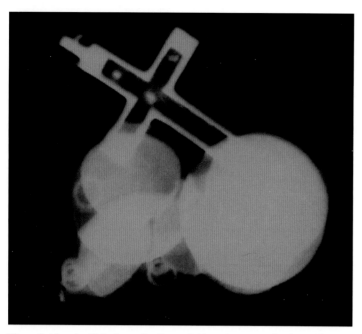

The wallet found with body number 7 revealed its sad contents after it was X-rayed. Author's Collection.

damage. The skull, although intact, was almost incarcerated within the helmet. The identification tag showed that the body was that of 17-year-old **Grenadier** Hubert Pilch, born in Kattowitz (now Katowice, Poland), of the 7th Company of *Reserve Grenadier Bataillon 372*. Hubert Pilch would have turned 18 on August 27, 1944, the day after his death. Some of his distant relatives were located in Katowice and a niece was located in Germany.

Body number 11: This soldier was still wearing his helmet, but no wounds nor means of identification were found on him.

Body number 12: Most of the bones of this body could not clearly be identified or were commingled with the bones of body number 13, so nothing specific could be concluded, except that his skull was intact.

Body number 13: Most of the bones of this body could not clearly be identified or were commingled with the bones of body number 12. However, a helmet was still present on the skull, which was fractured, apparently due to trauma in the facial region. This body was the only one to have a wound that is consistent with the wound

The severely deformed remains of the copper jacket of an American .30 caliber bullet found in the area of bodies 7 and 8. Author's Collection.

Body number 9, lying on its stomach with no helmet, shoes, or any equipment, except for a pocket knife in the area of the right hip pocket. Damien Leblanc Collection.

From top to bottom, the identification tags of bodies 4, 10, 5, and 8. The first tag is made of zinc, while the next three are made of aluminum that has sometimes severely corroded, making interpretation difficult. Thankfully, all the tags pictured here could still be deciphered, revealing the identities of Otto Mertin, Hubert Pilch, Franz Guder, and Otto Forberger. Author's Collection.

which may be explained by the fact that he was lying face down. This identification tag revealed the body to be that of 19-year-old *Grenadier* **Otto Forberger**, born in Kukele (now Kukle, Czech Republic), of the 5th Company of *Reserve Grenadier Bataillon 372*.

Body number 9: No wounds or means of identification were found on this body, and the only artifact present was a pocketknife in the area of the right hip pocket.

Body number 10: This soldier was still wearing his helmet and his identification tag in the area of the thorax. The opening of the helmet was severely crushed, without any particular impact points being visible, and it was not determined what may have caused this

visible on the dead German soldier photographed near the tunnel by the forcemen in August 1944. It therefore seems probable that the body visible in the photo is that of body number 13. The cause of death was determined to be trauma in the facial region.

Body number 14: The skull of this body was fractured into multiples pieces and a callus from an old healed fracture was observed at mid-height of the right femur. It is notable that this was already the second man found in the grave to have previously suffered a broken femur. No artifacts were found on this body. However, a helmet (Helmet D) pierced by a bullet coming from behind and above was found in the grave relatively close to the body, and by elimination, it was determined that this helmet most likely belonged to body

Grenadier Hubert Pilch, who would have turned 18 the day after he was killed. Pilch Family Collection.

Body number 11 still wearing its helmet. Vincent Meyer Collection.

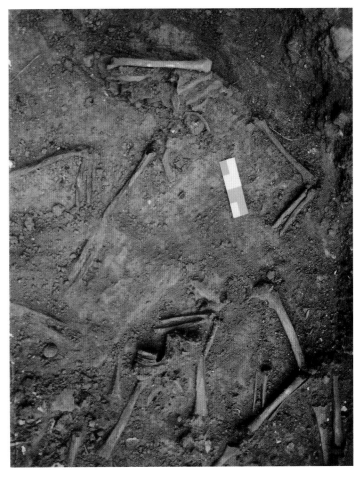

Body number 14 lying among the intermingled bones of several other soldiers. His skull was severely fractured, and by deduction it was found that helmet D, found near the body in the grave, could only belong to it. Pascal Boucard Collection. Author's Collection.

number 14. The cause of death was therefore determined to be a gunshot wound to the head, coming from behind and above.

As the German authorities (*Deutsche Dienststelle*) were identifying these bodies, they discovered that two more soldiers of the 7th Company of *Reserve Grenadier Bataillon 372* were reported as having been killed in action in Villeneuve August 26, 1944. The *Deutsche Dienststelle* therefore decided that two of the unidentified bodies found in the grave would be considered as being the following two soldiers:

- *Grenadier* **Gerhard Foks**, 17 years old, born in Kutschau (now Kuczow, Poland).
- *Grenadier* **Josef Lössl**, 35 years old, born in Komotau (now Chomutov, Czech Republic).

Many more artifacts were found in the grave without them attributable to a specific body. The most notable of these were three undamaged helmets, two belts, one pair of shoes, an identification tag, two rings, a spent .45 caliber bullet, and several shell fragments. One belt had been cut in half with a sharp object, presumably by somebody who wanted to take the bayonet and ammunition pouches that were attached to it. The other belt still had empty ammunition pouches and an empty bayonet sheath attached to it. The pair of shoes seemed to have been damaged by shrapnel; this may explain why somebody took the trouble of removing them from a body, only to throw them away in the end after realizing they were beyond repair. The .45 caliber bullet was probably responsible for the death of a soldier, but it could not be determined which one, as it was found in the pile of dirt produced during the exhumation and not in its original position. The identification tag was severely oxidized and its inscriptions could not be read.

The cut belt, the missing shoes, and the many empty bayonet sheaths and ammunition pouches all gave clear evidence that the bodies had been pilfered. Interestingly, the son of one of the men who had helped bury the bodies was found to have a bayonet with no sheath in his possession. Useful objects such as shoes had been heavily pilfered, while rather useless items, such as helmets, were usually been left on the bodies. The only two canteens that were left over had been pierced by shrapnel, rendering them useless.

Additionally, a large number of German uniform buttons (approximately 100 tunic buttons and 50 trouser buttons) and coins were found during the exhumation. This showed that most of the bodies were still wearing their uniforms when they were buried. Only a few shelter quarter buttons were found, indicating that shelter quarters had not been used to transport or wrap the bodies, unlike in the case of the bodies buried at St Vallier, which was described in chapter four. All seven identification tags that were found were complete; in other words, both the upper and lower portions of the tag were present.

Conclusion: The mass grave found at Villeneuve-Loubet in 2006 contained the bodies of 14 German soldiers. As several witnesses had indicated, the bodies had been pilfered of most useful items and of all their weapons, including bayonets, before being buried in the grave at random. Probable causes of death were found for eight cases: half of these were caused by shrapnel wounds and the other half by bullet wounds. All eight of the identified soldiers came from territories that are no longer part of Germany today, and most were aged over 30, or were approximately 18. This corroborates what the FSSF prisoner of war interrogators concluded at the time: "Prisoners of war state 80-90% of the personnel are non-German in this battalion. Ages average from 17-19 years old and 35-45 years

Grenadier Gerhard Foks, aged 17, was a member of the 7th Company of Bataillon 372 and was reported as having been killed in Villeneuve August 26, 1944. His body was probably among the unidentified bodies recovered in 2006, though it could not be identified specifically, as his identification tag was not found. Foks Family Collection, courtesy Wincenty Balbierz.

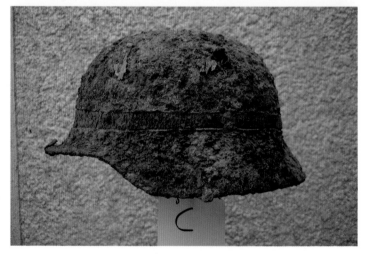

Helmets A and C, both bearing the remains of irregularly cut red rubber bands that were probably made from an old inner tube. Such handmade rubber bands were extremely common in the German army and were used for camouflage purposes. Author's Collection.

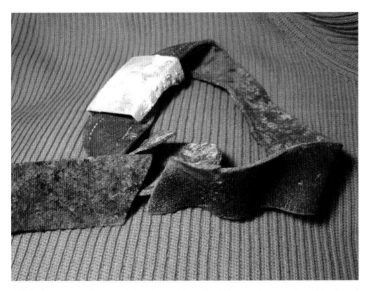

A belt that was cut in two with a sharp object. Such damage is strongly indicative of pilfering. The two halves of the belt were found several meters apart from each other in the grave. Author's Collection.

A ring still on a finger bone that was found in the grave once all the bodies had been removed. Author's Collection.

Combs, a fountain pen, and the handle of a razor that were found in the grave. All these plastic items suffered almost no damage during their stay underground, though several of the combs bear the tattle tale deformations that appear when they are buried with a body. Author's Collection.

A small but emotional find shown before and after cleaning. It is with the help of a metal detector that this medallion was found in the dirt pile produced during the digging. Although many archaeologists seem to have an unexplainable and strong aversion to metal detectors, it is highly advisable to use one during such exhumations, otherwise small but significant items, such as bullet fragments, can easily be missed, as they can be virtually unrecognizable even when held in hand. Author's Collection.

Various shrapnel fragments that were found during the exhumation, as well as one .30 caliber and one .45 Caliber bullet, visible at right. Author's Collection.

old."[49] All but one of the identified bodies belonged to the 5th or 7th Companies of *Reserve Grenadier Bataillon 372*, the exact units that were present in Villeneuve August 26th according to FSSF sources, proving that *Bataillon 372* was still functioning as a relatively well organized and cohesive unit during the battle.

Apart from the number of bodies present, the findings made during the exhumation of the grave were, for the most part, highly consistent with the information about the battle and burial that were available from the various witnesses and documentary sources. All 14 bodies were reburied in the German Military Cemetery at Berneuil, France, June 23, 2007.

Grenadier Alois Wühr

One of the German soldiers of the 7th Company of *Reserve Grenadier Bataillon 372* who had fought at Villeneuve-Loubet was 17-year-old *Grenadier* Alois Wühr. In the weeks after the battle, his grandmother, living in Frathau, received a letter from the company commander, *Oberleutnant* Erich Heß, dated September 2nd, explaining that her grandson had been killed on the spot by a direct hit by a shell during the fighting at Villeneuve-Loubet

Reburial of the 14 bodies in a common grave in the German Military Cemetery in Berneuil, France, in June 2007. EETAA 722 Collection, courtesy Aspirant Cédric Perreuse.

on August 26th. In fact, apart from adaptations to provide for the difference in rank and family relation, the letter was identical to the one *Oberleutnant* Heß had sent to *Gefreiter* Franz Guder's wife.

As was explained previously, it was found during the exhumation at Villeneuve in 2006 that Franz Guder had indeed been killed by multiple shrapnel fragments that inflicted severe wounds to his head and legs. Thankfully, the "death" of young Alois Wühr was to have a much happier ending. Indeed, on September 28, 1944, at roughly the same time Alois Wühr's grandmother received the terrible letter, a U.S. Army Signal Corps photographer was snapping pictures of German prisoners being unloaded from ships at Newport News, Virginia. He took one photo of a young German prisoner that he captioned:

> *Grenadier* (Pvt.) Alois Wuhr, home, Frathau, near Austria, German Prisoner of War, is shown on Pier 6. *Grenadier* Wuhr was captured in Southern France by Americans near Nice, 27 August 1944. He is 17 years old. This shipment of Prisoners included a large number of boys 18 years of age. They and this prisoner are indicative of the type of immature soldiers being used by the German Army.

Evidently, *Oberleutnant* Heß had been given a false report about Alois Wühr being killed by a shell at Villeneuve. Wühr's grandmother had a death announcement published for her grandson, only finding out the good news of his survival at a later date. Alois Wühr came back to Germany in 1946, but then returned to the U.S. after marrying, started a family, and died in 1993 at the age of 67. Unfortunately, it was not possible to interview Alois Wühr about his memories of the battle of Villeneuve; however, his son was able to provide a partial explanation as to why Wühr had been listed as killed in action:

> Alois Wuehr was my father, but he never spoke much about the war. I do know that the reason he wasn't killed is because his friend was wounded and my father carried him away from the platoon. Just as they got away the platoon was killed. My father and his friend were captured and sent to California via Africa and New York. From New York, they were put on a bus and transported across the country to California. His friend was given medical attention, but my father never knew what happened to him.

The Bunker on Route Nationale 7 at Villeneuve-Loubet Plage

The southern part of Villeneuve is in contact with the coast and is known as Villeneuve-Loubet Plage, *plage* meaning beach. The RN7 highway passes through this southern area of Villeneuve, and the Germans had left a small force to defend this important roadway. Villeneuve-Loubet Plage was not in the zone of action of the FSSF, so on August 26th, as the battle raged in the village further north, it was a patrol of the 509th Parachute Infantry Battalion coming from the Brague River that liberated the RN7. The main German strongpoint in the area consisted of a bunker on the northern side of the road, overlooking a roadblock built on a small bridge on the RN7. The entire area of the bunker and roadblock was known as les Deux Rives, and was itself overlooked by a farm belonging to *Monsieur* Aicardi. Numerous local youths were working in this farm and were able to observe the events occurring on the road below them. One of these witnesses was **Joseph Lammli**:

> In those days, the Route Nationale 7, before reaching the Loup River and Cagnes sur Mer, went through a small

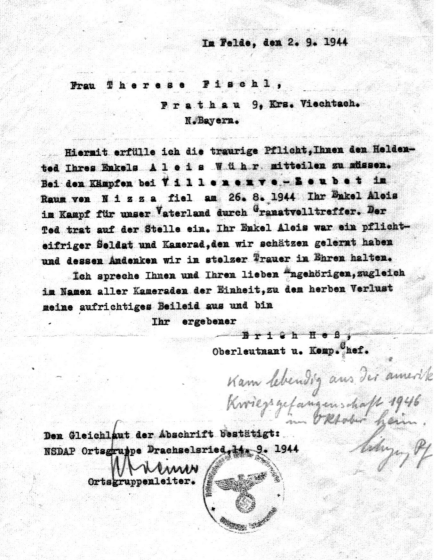

hill by a narrow pass a few meters deep. The Germans had built cement bunkers in the vertical walls on both sides of this pass. Between Cagnes and the pass, they had also built an enormous bunker housing numerous soldiers. The N7 was bordered on either side by minefields and the land between the N7 and the sea was a forbidden zone.

In one of the bunkers at the pass, the Germans had installed tanks remote controlled with wires. At the bottom of the hill leading to the pass was a road block intercepting traffic coming from Antibes. During the summer of '44, I was working at the Aicardi farm with quite a few young people who were avoiding the STO.

The Goliath tank was one of the German "secret weapons" developed late in the war. It was a small remote controlled tank packed with explosives, measuring approximately 1.2 meters long and weighing 100 kilograms.[50] It was meant to be driven towards a target of value and then detonated, hopefully destroying the target as it self destructed. Allied soldiers usually made fun of the Goliath, as in most cases they did not function properly, had their wires cut, or were destroyed before reaching their target. **Barthélémy Tomatis** was a local FTP working on the Aicardi farm, and he tells us more about the Goliaths at Villeneuve Plage:

The Germans dug a cave in the clay at the pass, and there were two Goliaths in there. We saw them being delivered; we were at Aicardi's farm and could see everything from up there. We were working, and at the same time we would observe what was going on. They would often take out the Goliath to test it. We would see it, and it looked like a little pig, a wild boar on the road, walking around. We called it "the Pig," and between ourselves we didn't talk about "the Goliath," we talked about "the Pig." They would close the road down and nobody could go by anymore. The Goliath would go and stop, and they would restart it and make it turn. Facing this cave was a bunker with a Czechoslovakian sergeant.

Joseph Lammli describes the atmosphere at the Aicardi farm as of the moment the Allies landed:

Noisily awakened the morning of August 15th, we spent the day digging a trench on the hill above the farm. We had cut trees to cover our trench and made it into a shelter that was used by all the local inhabitants during the shelling and fighting from August 15th to August 26th or 27th.

August 15th, the bunkers at the pass and the big one further away were already fired on by naval artillery. Unfortunately, the N7 being parallel to the sea, the bunkers were well protected from shells coming from offshore. The Germans, installed in a house above the road, observed the whole area and fired tracer bullets at anything that moved, particularly at night. During the day, we

Grenadier Alois Wühr's death announcement and the letter written by his company commander, Oberleutnant Erich Heß, explaining how Wühr had been killed on the spot by a direct hit with a shell at Villeneuve-Loubet August 26, 1944. The Frathau priest made the following handwritten annotation at the bottom of the letter: "Returned home from American captivity alive in October 1946." Erwin Wuehr Collection. Hödl Collection, Courtesy Maria Krieger.

Grenadier Alois Wühr disembarking from a prisoner of war transport ship at Newport News, Virginia, September 28, 1944, slightly over one month after his "death" at Villeneuve-Loubet. NARA.

ever able to explain what happened. He left with his motorcycle and got to the road block. "Trrrrrrrrr! There! Liquidated! Machine gunned!" The Germans killed him. A guy from Antibes, 27 or 28 years old. The Germans probably carried him away, because we never found his body. Or else they threw it in the ditch by the road!

The nearby presence of the Allied forces provided motivation for the Germans to contact the resistance in order to desert. The FTP group that **Barthélémy Tomatis** was a member of was contacted by some Germans:

We were in contact with the German soldiers; they came along and said: "Kamerad, we want to surrender." So we said: "How many of you are there?" "Well, 10, 12…" So we organized a rendezvous with them at the *Ginestières*. This was a few days before the liberation. The German command post was up there at Maréchal Pétain's house [Maréchal Pétain had a secondary residence in Villeneuve-Loubet], and a rumor started that they were going to attack us. We were outnumbered, there were only four of us: my brother, Dominique Baling, and Marius Melani. We were up there, with one rifle each, and Marius Melani said: "Shit, the patrol is coming to attack us," and that idiot ran away. He got shot in the stomach, but he didn't die. Where the bullet went, it didn't touch any organs. They kept him at Maréchal Pétain's for a day or two, time for the liberation to occur, then he was send up to Grasse. Afterwards, the Germans surrendered: "Kamerad, Kamerad, I surrender, I surrender." So we brought maybe 30, 40, or 50 over to the Brague River. And at the Brague there were the FTPs and the Americans, lots of them.

There were no Germans left here, except in the bunker, and up there only the Czechoslovakian sergeant remained. He was all alone.

would roam around the farm, where there was livestock to be tended to, and at night we remained in our shelter.

August 24th, the 509th PIB reached the Brague River (see Chapters 6 and 7), increasing the amount of German and resistance activity. **Joseph Lammli** continues:

Resistance fighters made several attempts to force their way through the road block. We couldn't warn them because we were too far from the road, and all of them were stopped by machine gun fire before or after passing the road block. The Germans would come down and throw the bodies into the ditch. The Germans made one or two sorties down *Route Nationale* 7 in single file. I remember one group that must have been intercepted by the Allied troops near Antibes.

In fact, only one resistance man was killed at the road block. His name was **Marenda**, and he was killed August 25th, as **Barthélémy Tomatis** remembers:

One FTP whose name I can never remember, a nutcase from Antibes, had a motorcycle, and he decided: "I am going to see what's going on." Afterwards, people said it had something to do with preventing the bridge over the Loup from being blown up, but in fact, nobody was

The Americans were apparently under the impression that all the Germans had left or surrendered, and on August 26, 1944, Company A of the 509th PIB sent a patrol down the RN7, accompanied by Antibes area resistance men. Nine-year-old **César Acchiardi** was standing next to the RN7 with his father when the first U.S. vehicle arrived in the vicinity of the still-defended bunker (Note that César Acchiardi uses the word "little tank" both for the Goliath and for the American vehicle):

I was there looking at what the Resistance men were doing. There were five or six of them, with hunting rifles. They didn't attempt anything, what could they have done? Everybody was afraid, but then the Americans came along with their tanks and everything. They were the vanguard and wanted to go to Nice, but the resistance men stopped them, saying: "No, you can't go any further, the bunker up there is blocking the road," so they stopped.

The first Americans who arrived, four or five of them, had been stopping in the houses on the way and drinking a glass of wine here and a glass of wine there, and they were drunk out of their minds. Even though I was just a kid, I saw they were drunk. I don't remember if they were paratroopers or what, but you could see that they were real tough guys.

They said: "Where are the Germans?" The resistance guys told them to go directly with the tanks, because the Germans were in the bunker with their cannon. There was a little river there in the middle where the Germans had built a roadblock, and with the big tank, the Americans couldn't go through. So they came along with a little tank with four or five guys on it that could pass the road block. They went up with their small tank, and when they got to the roadblock, the Germans sent out a little tank [the Goliath], no bigger than a baby carriage, a little tank with wires. The Germans already had something like that back then!

When the Americans saw that little tank coming down, they knew it was going to explode, but they couldn't back up, because they were engaged in the road block, so they all quickly jumped into the little creek. That is what saved them, because then the little tank arrived and everything exploded. That little tank blew into forty thousand pieces. The Americans were drunk, but they didn't get killed, they managed to pull through. Then they came back and the resistance fighters were there: Tomatis, Marro, and Baling. One *maquisard* asked: "How are we going to get the Germans out of there?" and an American said: "I will get them out, show me how to get up there from behind." A resistance man went with them around through Aicardi's field and they got to the bunker from behind. In bunkers, there are ventilation pipes that go up like chimneys, so they actually climbed up onto the bunker and they dropped a grenade down that hole. Oh! The Germans came out fast! They hadn't seen the Americans coming from behind, and they came out and surrendered. They caught three or four of them, and there was even one killed. He didn't want to surrender and tried to act smart. All he had to do was surrender and he wouldn't have been killed.

This is one of the rather rare cases in which a Goliath tank succeeded in destroying its target. FTP fighter **Barthélémy Tomatis** has a different version of these events, slightly more humiliating for the Americans and glorifying for the Frenchmen:

When the Americans saw that Goliath come out, they took off and beat the world sprint record. At Aicardi's place, there was a pumping station for watering his property, and of course, every day someone went down to the pumping station to do his poo. The Americans dived into the creek and they fell into shit. When they got up to Aicardi's farm they were covered in shit!

Thomas and Dominique had German stick grenades that they had taken from the prisoners, and they said: "Well, what are we going to do?" "Hey, how about bringing two grenades up there each?" The bunker was open because of the remote controls for the Goliath, so they threw in grenades, and that's how they killed the Czechoslovakian sergeant. We found a letter on him that he had written to his wife in Czechoslovakia where he said: "these are the worst days of the war." He had been on the Russian front and had stuffed boots, worth a fortune back then. One guy who lived at les Baumettes wanted to take them, and my friend, Dominique Baling, said: "Hey Merlot, if you touch those boots, you are dead. The bullet is in the barrel, and there is a full loader behind it." "Yeah, but…" "You leave that alone, it's not yours. It will go to the Town Hall, and they will do what they want with them." Unfortunately, we took the German soldier and brought him down so that they would pick him up, but in the end he was buried there, between the bunker and the road block. They dug a hole and they buried him in it.

The soldier who had been killed was 31-year-old *Obergefreiter* **Gerhard Rotter**, from Frankstadt (now located in Czech Republic), of the 5th Company of *Reserve Grenadier Bataillon 372*. At the time of his death, Gerhard Rotter's wife was eight months pregnant with their first child. There are not direct witness accounts of the Goliath event on the American side, though **Lt Justin McArthey**, of C Company of the 509th PIB, did hear about it:

I wasn't there, but somebody told me about that. It was on one of the coastal roads down there. They said that they were in a jeep, and they saw this tank approaching. They got out of the jeep, and they said that thing came up to the jeep and exploded and blew the jeep to hell.

The 509th PIB's period report simply stated:

FFI agents brought word of an enemy-held pillbox north of the Brague River. On 26 August, an "A" Company patrol crossed the river and attacked the pillbox. The patrol returned with 8 prisoners.[51]

The FFI from Biot were also present in the action, serving as guides to the 509'rs, and suffered one wounded. **Commandant Verine**, in Antibes, reported:

On August 26th, [Berrone and Guenno's group] attacks the bunker at les Deux Rives with a few Americans. Together they capture it and capture 25 prisoners, as well as an important stock of equipment and ammunition. During this engagement, only young Roger Petit is wounded in the armpit by a bullet. He is 18 years old.[52]

Lt Mike Reuter, of B Company of the 509th PIB, poses with a Goliath tank found abandoned in the area of la Gaude. The Germans successfully used a similar tank at Villeneuve-Loubet, destroying an American vehicle. Mike Reuter Collection.

Although many claims were made about who had taken *Obergefreiter* Rotter's boots, he may have actually ended up being buried with them, as **Louis Fanti** remembers:

One guy died in a hole at the Deux Rives and remained in the hole. I remember, because I lived at Antibes at the time, and when we walked by there, we could always see the boot sticking out of the hole. He wasn't buried deep, he was in one of those foxholes that they dug.

Another local resident remembers a gruesome detail concerning this improvised grave:

There was a bunker and two or three foxholes that had been dug by the men requisitioned by the Germans. During the Liberation, some Germans were killed and

they threw one of them in a hole and covered him with earth, and instead of compressing itself, the earth was rising up. The guy must have been swelling, and there was hardly any earth on him. I heard that one day a guy over there said: "We have to do something to let all that stuff out, otherwise it will poison us!" He took a pointed iron bar and tried to pierce the body. It let out a smell! It was unbearable! Can you imagine that? He said: "Even dead, this one is still a pain in the ass."

Conclusion

The most violent fighting on the Loup River defensive line occurred at the village of Villeneuve-Loubet, where the 2nd Regiment of the First Special Service Force battled with the 5th and 7th Companies of *Reserve Grenadier Bataillon 372*. The fighting started in the early morning, when the forcemen managed to capture Villeneuve Castle without firing a shot. The Germans offered more resistance in the village, but it was also quickly captured. The Germans then unsuccessfully counterattacked the castle during the rest of the day and part of the night. At least 14 Germans were killed, as well as two Canadian forcemen and one American soldier of the 887th Airborne Engineer Company. On the coast at Villeneuve, a patrol of the 509th Parachute Infantry Battalion, accompanied by resistance men, captured a German bunker, killing one of its occupants. With the use of an ultra-modern Goliath remote controlled tank at the coast and a battle occurring in a medieval castle in the village, the fighting at Villeneuve had definitely not been what could be considered standard.

At la Colle, the 1st Regiment of the FSSF also encountered strong resistance, but it did not attempt to cross the Loup River in force until August 27th, by which time the Germans of 6th Company of *Bataillon 372* had already pulled out on their own. There had been two killed on either side. The artillery duels also caused the death of one or two Germans at Vence, as well as the death of at least seven civilians in Vence, Cagnes, la Colle, and Roquefort. At Pont du Loup, to the north, the 517th Parachute Infantry Regiment had managed to cross the Loup River against little resistance, and they then proceeded north into the mountains, ignoring the small German garrison at Tourrette sur Loup. There were no Germans present in the mountains, so the 517th PIR managed to reach the Var River August 26th, while the FSSF and 509th PIB were still battling at the Loup.

The morning of August 27th, the Loup River was at last firmly in Allied hands. The FSSF, 509th, and 551st were now ready to advance to the next line of German resistance at the Var River.

Obergefreiter Gerhard Rotter, 31 years old, of the 5th Company of Bataillon 372, was killed at the Deux Rives bunker in Villeneuve-Loubet August 26, 1944, a few weeks before the birth of his first child. In the second photo, taken in 1937, Rotter is seen wearing a uniform of the Czechoslovakian army, once again illustrating the troubled life stories of many of the members of Reserve Division 148 and explaining why he was known to the local French residents as "the Czechoslovakian sergeant." Hermann Rotter Collection.

The railroad bridge over the Loup River between Villeneuve-Loubet and Cagnes sur Mer that was blown by the Germans as they retreated, suffering the same fate as almost every other bridge of the French Riviera. Ferdinand Moscone Collection.

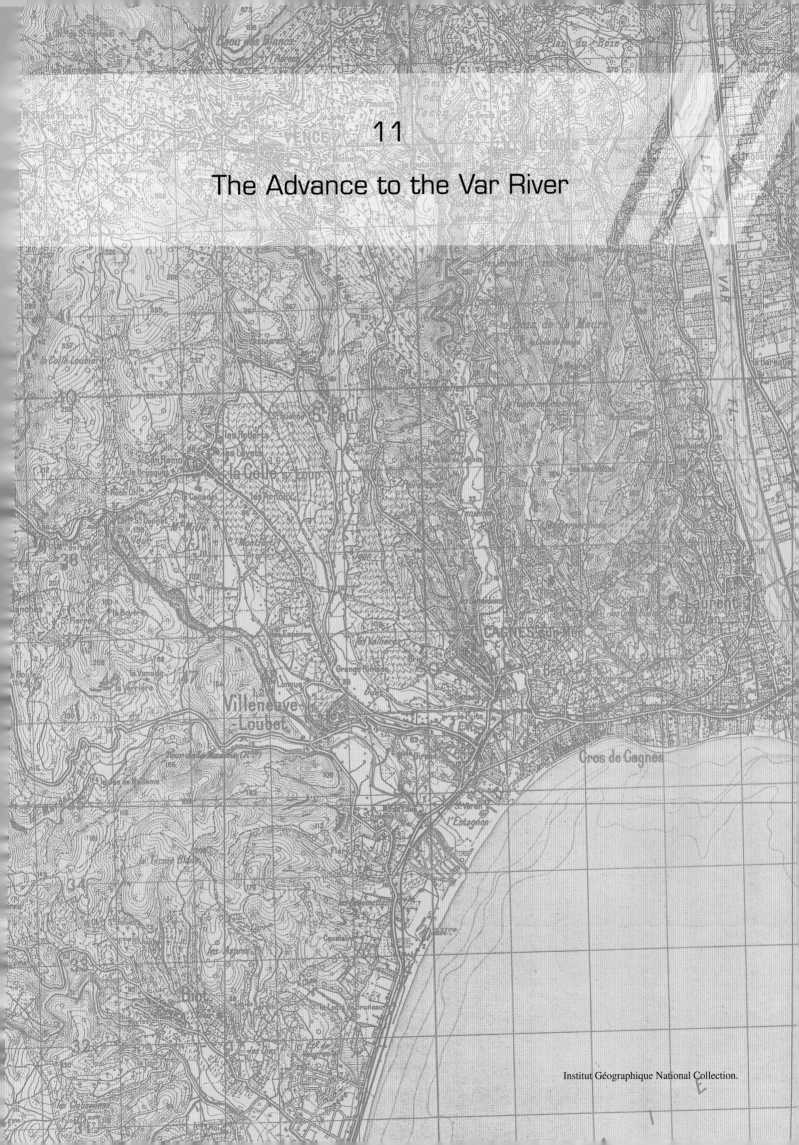

11

The Advance to the Var River

By the morning of August 27th, the entire Loup River line was in the hands of the First Airborne Task Force. Their next major objective was the Var River, where the Germans were expected to put up strong resistance. The 517th Parachute Infantry Regiment had already reached the Var at Carros, in the northern sector of the front, on August 26th. (We will speak more about the 517th in the next chapter.) August 27th, the First Special Service Force would now also push out towards the Var from its newly-gained positions on the Loup River line.

The Liberation of Cagnes sur Mer and Saint Laurent du Var

The afternoon of August 27th, a detachment of the Cannon Company of the First Special Service Force, accompanied by FSSF infantry and tank destroyers of the 645th Tank Destroyer Battalion, was sent on a reconnaissance patrol towards St Laurent du Var. The following report of Cannon Company's actions was written:

At 12:15 on the 27th of August, 1944, we started from the town of Valbonne, France, on an armored reconnaissance to contact the enemy and find out exactly what type of opposition to expect from them. Our primary mission, however, was to make a reconnaissance of main roads and bridges in the area which the FSSF was expected to pass through. Our reconnaissance party consisted of two half tracks with 75mm rifles on them and two half tracks (personnel carriers) carrying one platoon of FSSF men. In addition were attached two M-10 tank destroyers. Our first objective was the town of la Colle; we entered the town and met no opposition, so then pushed on to our second objective, which was the town of St Paul.

We met no opposition there either, but were informed by the civilians the enemy (about 30 strong) had left just a short while before, and that we could expect opposition from them on ahead. Our third objective was the bridge located at (462719). When we gained this objective, we found the enemy had destroyed it by demolitions. But by fording the stream at another point without encountering mines we were able to continue on to our next objective, which was a road crossing at (464793). We were informed by civilians there that the road leading up to the crossing would probably be mined, but we proceeded and found there were no mines, and that the road crossing was in fairly good condition. This information we then radioed back to the FSSF CP and proceeded on to our fifth objective, the town of Villeneuve-Loubet. This objective was also gained without meeting any enemy opposition, so we located at [Cagnes sur Mer].

At this time we received a new mission by radio from Colonel Walker. He informed us there was an enemy armored column reported proceeding down the beach road from the town of St Laurent to Cagnes. We then loaded a full company of FSSF men on all our vehicles and advanced to meet the enemy. We gained the town of Cagnes, where we deposited all but one platoon of infantry to hold the town and protect our rear, then continued on towards the Var River. Here we met enemy opposition in the form of deadly cross fire from three enemy machine guns. One gun was firing from our right front and the other two enemy guns were firing from our left flank. Immediately, our radio peep dropped back and radioed the FSSF advanced CP, giving them the location and the type of opposition encountered. This opposition consisted of

A tank destroyer of the 645th TDB in the Béal district of Cagnes sur Mer. The shot was apparently taken August 27, 1944. Paule Monacelli Collection.

three light machine guns manned by twelve to fifteen men. In the meantime, our two personnel tracks stopped and the platoon of infantry deployed in a skirmish line facing the enemy on our left flank, taking advantage of protective cover behind the railroad bridge and embankment on the left of the road, firing their small arms at the machine gun positions until the second half track backed into firing position and destroyed them. In coordination with this, the lead track engaged the machine gun on the right front, making them retreat to safety from our cannon fire. From there, we continued on our way to St Laurent (…). There we joined forces with a party of French Partisans. They informed us of another machine gun strongpoint further up the road. Due to the enemy behind us, we at this point left the two M-10s to protect our rear and then proceeded up the road with the section of Cannon Company and the section of Infantry, plus a few French partisans. We had gone but a short distance when we came under fire from this enemy machine gun, and also from the party of enemy demolition men from the rear which we had driven from the bridge they had hoped to blow up outside Cagnes. At that time, we did not know they were in the vicinity. This group of enemy we estimated to be six or seven strong, and we did not return their fire; however, we managed to destroy the machine gun in front of us, which during the brief encounter had succeeded in killing one and wounding one of the French Partisans.[1]

The locals of St Laurent have a rather different version of this encounter with a German machine gun in St Laurent. In fact, two Frenchmen were shot and killed, and the culprit German machine gun was not destroyed. **Honoré Oddo** recalls the arrival of the first FSSF half track in town:

> In the afternoon, it must have been 4 o'clock, I went for a walk in the vines that bordered the *Départementale* 209 [Road] (…) and the Boulevard de Provence. (…) Suddenly, I heard the sound of an engine coming from behind my house, along the 209. Instinctively, I lied down on the embankment alongside the road, and I almost immediately see a half track preceded from quite a distance by four Frenchmen on bicycles. They were in civilian clothes, but two of them were carrying rifles and a large French flag. The tragedy unfolded in a few seconds. We later found out that the Germans had set up a machine gun at the foot of the war memorial. There were very few houses, and from the shelter of the small embankment that they had built the Germans could enfilade the road. Additionally, they were clever and only showed themselves at the last moment to fire. Two cyclists – one of them being Mr Ravet, the mayor – had time to see them and lay down on the right side of the road. I also spotted the Germans and didn't move. It was already too late for the two other cyclists anyway. One burst and they both fell to the left side of the road, killed on the spot. Then the Germans ran away towards the Var with their machine gun, and it was over. The half track that had stayed behind did not even have time to strike back. I remember that a man joined me on the road. We were asked to evacuate the two bodies, so I quickly returned home and took a cart that we loaded the bodies on to while the half track kept on going, still preceded by Mr Ravet and the fourth cyclist. The other man and I went up the 209

until we met other military vehicles. They were Canadians who were going to finish up the Liberation of St Laurent. The two killed were **Gabriel Abonnel** and **Jean-Clément Ledieu**, from les Vespins. I will never forget them.[2]

After reaching St Laurent, the FSSF patrol turned back towards St Paul, drawing the following conclusion:

> Not contacting the reported enemy armored column, we were now deep into enemy territory, approximately 15 or more kilometers. We had completely destroyed three enemy machine gun strongpoints, prevented the enemy from demolishing important bridges, and killed or wounded an unknown number of enemy personnel. During the day's operations we had covered approximately 40 kilometers of road in front of the FSSF advance positions. We were in need of fuel, ammunition, and medical attention for the partisans who were wounded, so at this point we returned to FSSF CP, which was located at St Paul.[3]

It would actually seem that no Germans were killed by this patrol whatsoever. In any case, no corresponding victims exist in the database of the *Volksbund*, nor are any remembered by the local inhabitants. Although the FSSF half tracks patrolled into St Laurent August 27th, they then pulled out, and the Allied forces would only return in strength the next day. Cagnes sur Mer, on the other hand, had been liberated for good on the 27th; in fact, one of the crew members of a Cannon Company half track, Bill Ketchens, met a local girl in there that he would later marry and bring back to the United States after the war. **Madame Ozenda**, a resident of Cagnes, remembers a rather comical and typical confrontation that occurred when the town was liberated:

> The day the Americans arrived, somebody came and told us: "Supposedly, they put the Communist flag on the balcony of the town hall." So one guy, I can't remember who, said: "Oh yeah!? Well, we are quickly going to get rid of that one." So we all followed him to see what would happen, but when he got there he shut his trap and left the flag where it was, because another guy was on the balcony and he said: "Yes? Well then come and take the flag down if you have the balls to do so. Come and get it, since you are such a tough guy." He didn't go and remove it because he was afraid of that man, who was a desperado.

Since the Germans had retreated to the other side of the Var, there were no big confrontations with them on the west bank of the river. Only a handful of outposts, as well as a few stragglers and deserters remained behind. The forcemen captured one Polish soldier who, as many others that surrendered, sabotaged future German defense plans by willingly giving all the precious information he knew to his Allied interrogators. The FSSF noted on the 27th:

> One Polish deserter, an officer's orderly who had worked in 3rd Battalion headquarters, 8th Grenadier Regiment [In other words, *Bataillon 164.*], revealed considerable information concerning the 148th Division's future plans. The soldier, a very intelligent man, was frequently used as a recording clerk in staff officer conferences. The division will fight parallel delaying actions along the line Levens - Swiss border – Brenner and Nice – Menton – North Brenner Pass.[4]

An American jeep crosses yet another blown bridge in Cagnes sur Mer. Paule Monacelli Collection.

August 28th, 1st Regiment of the FSSF moved east from Cagnes towards St Laurent du Var, liberating St Laurent for good this time. It captured a few more prisoners in the Cagnes area and concluded:

> Five prisoners of war were captured in the afternoon (…) in Cagnes. Prisoners of war were stragglers and generally confused about the situation. Conflicting statements were made regarding strength and identification of units.[5]

1st Regiment continued on to St Laurent du Var, taking up positions overlooking the Var River during the afternoon. **Louisette Daniel** lived on the main road heading north out of St Laurent and remembers her reaction when she first heard of the arrival of Allied soldiers:

> Suddenly people said: "The Americans are at Cagnes, the Americans are coming!" My God, if we could be liberated! *Monsieur* Nerascu told my husband: "Marius, the Americans are coming, we have to go down and help them." So my husband told him: "But *Monsieur* Nerascu, I have a small child. I don't want to get myself killed," and I told him: "Marius, don't go, they are Germans disguised as Americans." You know, when you are scared, you are scared, and so I had the idea that the Germans had disguised themselves as Americans and that if my husband went down there they would kill him. In the end, it really was the Americans, and they gave us cans with little sausages inside. It is only when I saw they were really Americans that I relaxed, but before that I was so frightened.

Further north, on the road between St Laurent and la Gaude, a small outpost of German soldiers remained, positioned between the road and the Var River. Some resistance men from St Laurent decided to attack these Germans on their own on the 28th, without waiting for the Allies to arrive. **Louisette Daniel** continues:

> We saw a bunch of young people going up: some on bikes, some on carts, some in old trucks. We thought: "My God, but when they get up there they are going to get killed!" Indeed, when they got up there, there were

supposedly 11 Polish soldiers and one German between the road and the Var. When the young people got up there, the German gave the order to open fire on them, but the Poles were sick of it all and they shot and killed the German. Lucky thing, because if they had all been Germans, they would have killed all those young FFIs from St Laurent. The young people brought all the Poles down to our house, into the shade of a fig tree. They disarmed them, took their weapons, and stripped them of everything they had. *Monsieur* Nerascu came and took all the weapons and brought them home, and we never found out what he did with them. The Americans arrived as the Poles were being searched. The Poles were happy to be safe.

> The dead man stayed on the ground, and three of four days later, the FFI put him on a cart. They were stopping at every foxhole they saw, wanting to bury him in one; but there were houses and the people didn't want them to, so they shouted: "No, we don't want him! We don't want that dead man here!" Finally, they reached a hole that was only surrounded by reeds and they buried him in there. We always knew he was there and he wasn't bothering us, since nobody ever went into the reeds. Then one day we saw three or four people with shovels, digging to find that body, but they didn't manage to find it.

In the chapter about Villeneuve-Loubet and la Colle, we mentioned two cases of Polish soldiers being fired at by Germans; this time, the Poles had taken the initiative. Another local resident confirms Louisette Daniel's story:

> At the Liberation, the young people from the district noticed that there was a group of Germans in the Var, so the district got together, they were all armed, and they took off to exterminate the Germans. I think there were 12 of them, one German and 11 Poles. The German, who was the chief, did not want to surrender, and one Pole turned around and shot him in the head. Then they surrendered, and the killed German remained in the Var for three days, as far as I heard. After three days of course the people said: "We have to go and bury him." They went over there with a mule and a cart and loaded him on, wanting to bring him to the cemetery. But it smelled so bad and there were so many flies that they re-dug a foxhole that the Germans had dug at the side of the road and they threw him into it and buried him. That was in '44, and in '50 or '51, Roblot [A French funeral home.] came for two days and started digging trenches, but nothing was found, probably because he was quite deep, and that is why everyone abandoned the search.

This surprising small-scale mutiny is also mentioned in the FSSF reports. Late on the 28th they noted:

> Patrol reports from French patriots disclose that approximately 150 enemy were contacted by patriots (…) at 16:00. Enemy had two machine guns but no artillery. Patriots captured 10 prisoners of war.[6]

The next day, the 29th, a 3rd Regiment patrol crossed the Var, reaching St Isidore, where the French handed over captured Germans from the area to them. More evidence of the mutiny was found:

> Total count on prisoners of war here is 32, all turned over by FFI at St Isidore. (…) One Pole was of a group that shot and killed their NCO because he ordered them to turn their MGs on the French civilians yesterday.[7]

The FSSF wrote a detailed interrogation report of one of the NCOs who had been captured by the French on the west bank of the Var River, just like the group of rebellious Poles. In the report, the German soldier explains what his mission was, as well as the general situation of his unit:

> Name: Otto Helmut. *Unteroffizier.*
> Unit: 10th Company, [*Bataillon 444*] 239th Regiment, 148th Division.
> Captured by: French patriots on 11:00 28 August 1944, 4 kilometers of ford, on the west bank of the Var River.
> Unit strength: 56 (originally 140 men). (…)
> Unit organization: 10th Company had one platoon of 56 enlisted men and one officer.
> Unit location: prisoner of war states that the 10th Company is in position along east bank of the Var River.(…)
> Casualties: 10th Company had one dead and one wounded. (…)
> Non-German: 10th Company had 70% non-German.
> Supplies: 10th Company had not received new supplies, rations, and ammunition in past 10 days. (…)
>
> Intentions: prisoner of war does not know mission of 10th Company. Prisoner of war's own mission was to man an outpost together with seven men four kilometers north of ford on west bank of Var River. In case of contact with American troops, outpost was to fall back to east bank of river and rejoin 10th Company.[8]

The group of Poles who had killed their NCO at St Laurent on the 28th were presumably fulfilling a similar mission. It is important to note that it was only late on August 28th that FSSF troops occupied the west bank of the Var in the St Laurent area. The Resistance had set off an insurrection in Nice early on the 28th, and the claim has often been made that Allied troops were already present on the Var River at that time, but that they were waiting passively on the west bank, instead of intervening to help the Resistance. These false allegations are unfortunately typical of local French sources that all too often attempt to minimize the role the Allied forces played in the Liberation of the Maritime Alps, while exaggerating that played by the Resistance. On the 28th, when the insurrection started in Nice, neither the FSSF nor the 551st Parachute Infantry Battalion had even reached the Var River yet, so they were obviously not in any position to offer help in Nice. Even on the 29th, the FSSF had not yet completely occupied the west bank of the Var River, as it was still performing patrols and contacting the 517th Parachute Infantry Regiment further to the north at St Jeannet. As for the 551st PIB, it only advanced from Biot to the mouth of the Var River the morning of August 29th.[9] The FSSF and 551st PIB would finally cross over the Var River into Nice on 30 August (only patrols had ventured into Nice on the 29th), long after the Resistance had taken control of the town and the last German soldier had retreated, surrendered, or been killed. All this will be discussed in detail in Chapter 13.

Before ending the section on Cagnes sur Mer and St Laurent du Var, we will briefly mention some more "typical" incidents that occurred following the Liberation, in this case in Cagnes: the shaving of the hair of "horizontal collaborators." **Madame Ozenda** remembers:

> At that time, I was very involved with the [French] prisoners of war, because my husband was a prisoner himself. So somebody came to get me: "Mme Ozenda, come and see, come and see. They are going to shave five women, two of which are wives of prisoners." I leaped up, saying: "What!? They are going to shave those women when their husbands are suffering?" I left angrily with a bunch of other people who wanted to help me, particularly some prisoners of war who had returned, to basically go up against the Resistance. So I went and made a speech and opposed myself to the shaving of those women, so as not to shame their husbands, because the husband who had suffered for five years did not need the additional shame of his wife having slept with the Germans when he returned to Cagnes!
>
> Everybody insulted me, even Rossi, who asked me: "What? You Madame Ozenda, who are a woman of honor, you are defending these women?" So I replied: "No, I am not defending them. What they did was wrong, but their husbands should not have to blush because of them when they return." I managed quite well, and Petitjean said: "In the end she is right, we will not shave them." The first three were shaved, but they promised me they wouldn't shave the last two.

Félix Petitjean was the real name of a local resistance leader who had adopted the *nom de guerre* "Ginette." (This was the female nickname he had given to his car, which also ended up being given to him by extension.) **Petitjean** had been in the *maquis* north of Grasse during the Liberation period (as we will see in Chapter 14), and when he returned to Cagnes, he was not pleased with what he saw, particularly concerning the local "resistance":

A shattered family: 18-year-old Grenadier Hermann Zipperer, of the 1st Company of Reserve Grenadier Bataillon 327, died in the German field hospital in Cimiez August 27th, after having received a severe head wound in undetermined circumstances. Presumably, he was wounded somewhere on the west bank of the Var in the preceding hours or days. His brother and only sibling Georg had already been killed in action in Russia just a few months earlier. Stadtverwaltung Waldmünchen Collection, courtesy Hansjörg Schneider.

"Stew in the making," by SSgt Elvis B. McCullough. Mike Reuter Collection.

These photos showing troopers of the 509th PIB living like forest men were reportedly taken in Cagnes sur Mer by Lt Mike Reuter, of B Company. They were presumably shot August 28th or 29th, when the 509th was taking it easy while the FSSF advanced to the Var River. From left to right: Sgt Jim Nunn, Edward Lejkowski, and Pvt James R. Knopp. Kneeling: PFC Howard J. Maxwell. Mike Reuter Collection.

Pvt Gene Neil, Billy Hamilton, Pvt Harold Q. Ofsthun, and Pvt James R. Knopp. Mike Reuter Collection.

Cagnes is liberated. Joy. Flags blossom on the balconies and windows. But there is a rumor: the *Boches* are coming back. Amazement and panic, the flags disappear, the people hide.

False alert. It was only a civilian, dressed in grey, coming down the street on a bike! Funny episode. You can't blame those people who had lived under terror for years. (...)

In Cagnes it is madness. Armbands are blooming everywhere. It seems to me like these excited Sten toting warriors are very numerous. They have rediscovered their courage, now that the danger is gone. A courage that was coming out of a deep lethargy. On the roundabout at the town hall I questioned several of them, three of which went down the stairs on their bottoms. As I returned to my area, other groups occupied the town hall, distributing posts. But we knew that our task was not over yet.[10]

Petitjean, though he himself was a very dubious character (as we will see in Chapter 14), joined the regular French army and was involved in the fighting that continued raging in the mountains of the Maritime Alps until May 1945. Too many "resistance fighters" had only appeared once the Germans had left, and instead of then joining the army to fight the remaining enemy troops, they stayed in their hometowns to fight for their own personal postwar interests.

The Liberation of St Paul de Vence

3rd Regiment of the FSSF, which had been in reserve at Biot since August 24th, set out towards St Paul and Vence on the 27th, reaching the town of St Paul first. The Liberation of St Paul was rather unremarkable, since the Germans had pulled out on their own, as Cannon Company of the FSSF had reported during their previously-mentioned patrol. However, even this "unremarkable" liberation is made interesting by the account that was later written of it by **Marius Issert**, an inhabitant and future mayor of St Paul:

It is mostly on August 25th and 26th that the Germans stationed in St Paul and its surroundings organized the resistance against the imminent arrival of the Americans. On the evening of August 26th, the Germans made my entire family evacuate the hotel. (...) They had installed a few cannons in front of our garage, and they had cut a few orange and mandarin trees in order to better see the Americans arriving from le Pilon. With my father, sister, and brother, we figured that if the Germans fired a single shot, the Americans would strike back in such a manner that our hotel would be destroyed. Lucky thing the Germans pulled out, leaving towards Vence and blowing up the nice Malvan Bridge. (...)

At dawn, the Americans at la Colle and Villeneuve fired at the Germans in the Cayrons, in Vence, who fired back. A shell landed at the corner of the south ramparts, near the cemetery, without doing much damage. The Germans retreated.

The first American jeep arrived in the town square on the morning of August 27th, carrying a Colonel of the First Special. I was one of the first to come and applaud the American Colonel, since I was on my terrace just across the street. Then my father and P.R. arrived, each bringing a bottle of whiskey that they had kept hidden in order to offer it to the first American that they saw. The Colonel thanked them, and then simply gave these bottles to his orderly, as he probably did at each stopover.

The St Paul residents then started flowing in, and the square was quickly full. (…) The Colonel then asked for the mayor. In our enthusiasm we had not noticed his absence. One of us went to get him. When he presented himself to the Colonel, the Colonel did not hide his surprise (or indignation) to not have seen him amongst the first people. He was speaking English, of course, and it was not necessary to understand the language to know that the Colonel was reprimanding him curtly. The mayor excused himself: "He hadn't heard anything, he lives outside the village…." And he returned home. He was a good man, well liked by the population. (…) The Colonel's jeeps left for Vence and some troops arrived, cheered for and covered with gifts. (…)

It is then that an event that I still cannot explain occurred. We saw about 30 young men from St Paul arrive in the town square, all wearing armbands with the French colors and the inscriptions FFI or FTP. Where had they got those armbands? Some even had rifles. Most of them had never showed themselves a few hours earlier. One group that I knew best came searching for me in order to bring a wreath to the war memorial. I was so surprised by their unexpected appearance that I declined the invitation, considering it inappropriate in the presence of the Americans, or at least untimely. Stripes started blossoming on forearms: Captains, Lieutenants, etc.

As soon as the Americans left in pursuit of the Germans, things in St Paul degenerated, just like everywhere else. Though some regrettable incidents did occur, we must admit that St Paul did not live through what certain other towns in the area did: acts of violence, imprisonments, executions… It must be said that no cases in St Paul deserved such punishments.

However, it is difficult to pardon certain people who stole jewels and money, but especially food from some inhabitants of St Paul, just because they had Italian names. The worst was to have cut the hair of five St Paul women, simply because they might have been with Italian or German soldiers. (…)

It was a sort of collective folly, a show of inappropriate authority. As soon as the Americans were gone, the political parties in the area armed and indoctrinated all these youths, who were persuaded that they had a role to play.[11]

This account shows the deep rift that usually existed between the real Resistance, the "last hour resistance," and the general population. The Liberation left bittersweet souvenirs in the minds of most French of the period because of the acts committed by some self-appointed justice makers, whose "activity" after the Liberation often became inversely proportional to what it had been during the Occupation.

The Liberation of Vence

The liberation of Vence sadly occurred with much more loss of life than the liberation of its neighboring towns, even though the Germans retreated before the arrival of the FSSF. We will start our study August 23rd, with the notes that **Henri Einesy**, the mayor of Vence, took as the German troops, including *Generalleutnant* Otto Fretter-Pico, retreated from Grasse:

> Large numbers of German troops are passing through Vence, but in small groups, making the question of billeting extremely difficult to resolve.
>
> We witness the seizure of bicycles, trailers, mules, horses, and horse carriages. They distribute requisition receipts with prices that are clearly insufficient: 20 Marks at the most for a bicycle, 200 Marks for a mule. This pillaging of our last transportation resources is catastrophic and compromises the last chances that we had to survive. I have asked for a hearing with General Fretter-Pico, commander of the Infantry Division coming from Grasse, to demand a reduction of these burdens that are becoming overwhelming.
>
> A liberated prisoner of war from Vence has been arrested by soldiers because of something to do with the requisition of a horse, and I do not know where they brought him.[12]

This missing man, as well as three others, were found dead August 24th and 25th, as **Henri Einesy** wrote on the 25th:

> The population has been appalled by four summary executions that occurred. These crimes were discovered yesterday (three people, of which two are identified) and one this morning. (Identified as Mr Chérico, whom I had reported missing yesterday and before yesterday.)
>
> The headquarters of the division and some of the troops left Vence last night, after having abandoned unusable or untransportable equipment, and after having proceeded to a massive requisition of cars, horses, donkeys, mules, horse carts, and bicycles. Few of the requisition receipts that were given were complete, readable, or regular. Many requisitions were made pistol in hand.
>
> The Germans left Vence, leaving an impression of brutality and cruelty that will be difficult to forget.[13]

The next day, **Henri Einesy** was able to give more details about who the victims of the executions were and why they had been shot:

> Only a very small number of Germans remain in Vence. On the roads and in the villages they do not check any identification papers. Most of the Germans that were garrisoned in Vence or were crossing through the town have left. They abandoned large quantities of ammunition, clothes, and military equipment. All weapons have been taken away or destroyed.
>
> The Germans have killed four men in Vence. Three bodies were found on 24.8.44. They are those of **Nario Joseph**, 34 years of age, Italian, farmer in Vence, and two other unidentified bodies. (We suspect that they are Italian deserters.) People are telling the following version of events: two Italian deserters asked *Monsieur* Nario to bring them to the mountains so that they could hide. On the way they met a German patrol, who after interrogating

32-year-old Joseph Cherico, who was executed by German soldiers in Vence. According to his daughter, the Germans shot him after finding a Lorraine Cross, the symbol of the French resistance, in his tobacco pouch. Author's Collection.

them, killed them with two bullets to the head. The fourth body was discovered 25.8.44. It is that of *Monsieur* **Cherico Joseph**, 33 years old, butcher in Vence, arrested by the Germans 22.8.44 for not having obeyed a German requisition. Cherico Joseph was a repatriated prisoner. He was killed on the 24th or the 25th by two bullets to the head. The trace of a violent blow was present under his left eye.

These executions have only increased the hatred of the population towards the Germans.[14]

August 26th, as fighting raged in Villeneuve, German batteries south of Vence fired at the Allies on the Loup line. The counter-battery fire caused the death of one or two Germans (**Alfons Wiesniewski** and also perhaps **Richard Kamussella**, though his exact date of death is not known), and of local teenager **August Mario**, as mentioned in the previous chapter. One inhabitant remembered:

They have installed two cannons in a farm at the Cayrons. When the boats start appearing off the coast, the Germans fire in their direction. The entire district shakes with each cannon shot. One morning, Allied shells started raining down upon us. One shell lands on the Demaria farm and another lands on a truck that explodes. August Mario's lungs are perforated by a shell fragment and he doesn't survive his wounds.[15]

Another inhabitant remembered the departure of the German artillerymen, leaving the body of Alfons Wiesniewski buried in a field:

One morning, they opened fire at the Americans who were advancing. They retaliated, adjusting their fire with the help of an observation Piper Cub. In the end the Germans take off, leaving a dead man buried under a rosebush at les Vallières with a Polish flag made from bits of cloth and his name written on the cross.[16]

The actual liberation of Vence was done peacefully. The Germans pulled out and the FSSF jeeps drove into town in the afternoon of the 27th. Before departing, however, the Germans had blown and heavily mined the road between Vence and Coursegoules, perhaps as a response to the presence of the 517th PIR in Coursegoules as of the 25th. These mines would cause terrible casualties over the next days. **Jeanette Vola Zimmer**, a child

staying with a *Monsieur* and *Madame* Simon at the time, explains what happened to her family members:

We were in the Free Zone, but when the Germans came down here and started bombing Toulon, one of my aunts decided to come to Vence with three of her children. The eldest, José, was 14 years old, and then there were two small ones who were four and two years old.

August 27th the bells were ringing in the whole town, because we knew the Americans were coming. In the afternoon at about 1 or 2 o'clock, with Mr and Ms Simon, I came to the town hall square, where all the people were. When we got there, Mr Simon saw my other aunt (there were three sisters) crying in a corner. So he went up to her and my aunt said something to him in tears, then he came back and said: "Come Jeanette, I will bring you to the church, I have something important to tell you." He brought me to the church, and during a prayer, he told me what had happened. I took it like a small girl: "Oh, really?" I was surprised and started crying, but didn't really realize.

This is what had happened. My aunt from Toulon had come to live with my younger aunt, who was 26 years old, married but with no children, and who lived in an old house behind Château St Martin. My uncle had hidden two French flags in a box in the shed so that if ever the Germans came to the house they wouldn't find them. At 11 o'clock, when they heard the bells ringing, they set out to get the flags. Both my aunts left with my 14-year-old cousin and a young friend of his. The road was cratered and they suspected it may be mined, so they were very careful; they walked on the side of the road and they got the flags. I am saying that because people later found the shredded flags, so it is on the way back that my 26-year-old aunt stepped on a mine. We knew it was her because her body was the most damaged; she was blown into the olive trees right and left of the road. They found pieces all over the place. I remember a peasant saying: "We found Marcelle's legs in the olive trees." She is the one who put her foot on a mine and when she blew up, my other aunt, who was beside her, and my cousin also exploded. My cousin's young friend had remained 10 or 15 meters behind and he was also blown off his feet, but he didn't die, he only broke his arm.

The three hapless victims were 14-year-old **Joseph Caparros**, his aunt, 26-year-old **Marcelle Zimmer Voisin,** and his mother, 31-year-old **Jeanne Zimmer Caparros**. This tragic death of two young women and a teenager should have served as a warning to all others in the vicinity of Vence. However, the very next day, resistance men coming down from the mountains were killed at the exact same spot. Local resistance leader **Félix "Ginette" Petitjean** explains what happened to his men:

In spite of my efforts, the notion of discipline was very relative with such a mixed crowd. It was hard to get these defectors of civilian life to strictly observe the rules that we had imposed upon ourselves. I had forbidden anybody from leaving la Becassière without my permission. Alas! One night Kosma, Briquet, my companion from Gourdon, and Gazagnaire, from Tourrettes sur Loup, decided to go to Vence. The road had been blown above the city. Only a narrow path against the embankment remained, which my comrades followed.

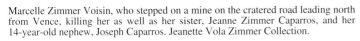

Marcelle Zimmer Voisin, who stepped on a mine on the cratered road leading north from Vence, killing her as well as her sister, Jeanne Zimmer Caparros, and her 14-year-old nephew, Joseph Caparros. Jeanette Vola Zimmer Collection.

30-year-old resistance fighter Marcel Briquet, who was also killed while trying to pass the mined crater north of Vence. Anne Verots Guilbaud Collection.

They didn't go far, for the path had been mined. Briquet and Gazagnaire paid for their carelessness with their lives. Kosma was wounded and found himself in hospital. [Joseph Kosma was a music composer and the future author of *Autumn Leaves*.][17]

Roger Gazagnaire and **Marcel Briquet** were 25 and 30 years old. If these *maquisards* had been better trained, they would have known that the Germans normally mined cratered areas heavily in order to prevent people from bypassing them on foot. Because of all the mines, the locals left the bodies where they were, being rightfully afraid to approach them. August 28th, a new unit, A Company of the 40th Engineer Regiment, was attached to the First Airborne Task Force. On the 29th, a group of these engineers was sent to Vence, where they found the cratered road and the bodies of the victims of the previous days. **Sergeant Sidney Oxman** was one of the engineers present and wrote in his diary:

About 1:20 I was called to take my squad on a demolition job. We went north for many miles and found bridge after bridge blown out. We were past St Paul and in territory that was just taken last night. One high bridge was blown out. There was at least a hundred and fifty foot drop and no way we could build a bypass. We turned back and found a side road leading still further north. We were pretty close to Nice and it hadn't been taken yet. We came up a black top road and ran into a crater in the road about 12 feet deep. At the bottom lay two dead Frenchmen and three other bodies that were blown all over the place.

We put our mine detectors to work and just on the rim of the crater we detected mines. We also picked up several S mines. I thought it strange that S mines were intact after the crater was blown once. I figured the Germans came back and reset these mines. We cleared what we saw. All was well. Mines are nothing to play around with, so we figured

we'd set a charge at the edge of the crater and blow up what mines remained. The father of one of the French boys who lay at the bottom of the crater wanted the body. The other body was an awful looking sight. I can take a lot of stuff, but this sort of thing gets me. Anyway, we managed to get a rope on one of the bodies and pull him out.

Sgt Rose, my platoon sergeant, went down into the crater and tied a rope to the other body. By that time several of our men were at the scene. Normally we only keep two or three men around just for safety. Rose stood at the top of the crater. Kaastad was there, too, Green was there, Gram was there, and Cpl Timm and myself and three other Frenchmen and Lt Monroe. As we pulled the body to the top, all I know was that I was rolling down the road from the blast. Four Tellermines went off. I was 15 feet from the crater. I was hit by shrapnel and gravel, mostly in the side of my head and left arm.

I guess I rolled 50 feet before I got up and ran down the road toward our trucks. Pescoppia [spelling uncertain] slapped a bandage around my head. I knew what happened. I was conscious all the time. Timm came down the road, his face full of blood and his chest, too. Our jeep driver went for an ambulance so we went along. In a small town a few miles away we found a French aid station. There were two doctors. I bled quite a bit, but not enough to warrant plasma. The doctor picked some shrapnel out of my ear and neck. I thought I lost my eye there for a while. It was just swollen, and the brow dropped over my lid where gravel hit me. I haven't seen my ear yet, but they tell me it's pretty well chewed up. The French fixed me up as best they could. Timm was alright. He got hit in both eyes.

A while later they started bringing in our other boys. Gram was in bad shape; he was five feet from Rose. Rose was killed and Green, too. Gram had shrapnel through his legs, chest, and face, had a broken finger and his nose. Kaastad

"Sgt Rose, my platoon sergeant, went down into the crater and tied a rope to the body." 27-year-old SSgt Burnell Rose and 22-year-old PFC Louis F. Green, who were both killed on the spot when the body they were pulling out of the crater caused several German mines to explode. Author's Collection, courtesy Debra Holloman. Joy Baughman Collection.

The mine blast wounded 35-year-old Pvt Olav Kaastad in the torso, head, and left arm. Officially, he died the next day in the 51st Evacuation Hospital in Draguignan. Kaastad was a Norwegian, born in Tysnes, south of Bergen, who had left home to be a sailor as a teenager. He had then lived in the U.S. in Minnesota for numerous years. His family repatriated his body after the war, burying it in the Flatraker Cemetery, near Tysnes. Kaastad Family Collection.

Maquisards August Baron, Jean-Marie Boursac, and Constant Naso, who were also killed by the mines in Vence. Anne Verots Guilbaud Collection.

died from stomach wounds after they brought him in. Two Frenchmen died. One was the father of the boy who lay there before him. He was crying before it all happened to him. I heard his wife scream. It was an awful mess. We left the aid station in a jeep. I was the least injured of the gang of them. We rode to Grasse, where there was an American aid station. From there, they took us by ambulance to a town the other side of St Maxime. It was a long and miserable ride. We arrived at an evacuation hospital at 9:30 A.M. I wasn't there long before they had me in surgery. I was put to sleep and the next thing I knew it was morning. They sewed my ear up. I guess I lost part of it. Timm was fixed up, too. His eyes were still covered. One is scratched and the other has a hole in it. Gram is pretty well marked up, but will be all right in time. They both left for Naples by plane today, which is Sunday, September 3. (…) So I am the only one left to return to the company.[18]

The two engineers who had been killed on the spot were 27-year-old **SSgt Burnell Rose** and 22-year-old **PFC Louis Green**, while

Norwegian-born 35-year-old **Pvt Olav Kaastad** died of his wounds the next day. Cpl Marvin Timm lost his right eye in the incident. Sgt Oxman was told incorrect information about the Frenchmen, as none of the victims were father and son. However, three more *maquisards* that we did not previously mention also died on the mines in unclear circumstances. **August Baron**, aged 25, and **Jean-Marie Boursac**, aged 24, both died on the 28th, perhaps while accompanying Ginette's men. **Constant Naso**, aged 30, died on the 29th, probably with the American engineers. The mines in Vence had thus caused the deaths of 11 people and wounded several more in at least three separate incidents! **Pvt Doug Rockenbach** had just been assigned to A Company of the 40th Engineers on the day of the accident and remembers:

I had been in the infantry and was in the replacement depot, and this other fellow and I joined the 40th Engineers. We pulled in there just a few days after the invasion; it was probably 4 o'clock or so in the afternoon. They were bivouacked down in a valley, and we pitched our pup tents up on the side of a hill and went down and ate, and they said: "We will fix you up in the morning with what you're gonna do." Then the sergeant came up and he said: "I want one person for a detail." My friend was in front of me, so he jumped up. I was sort of mad at him, I wanted to get up there, but obviously it was a good thing I didn't, because several hours later they came back and a guy came up the hill and said: "I am sorry to hear that your friend got hurt very badly. I want you to pack up his duffle bag and everything." I said: "What happened?" He told me that they had these Tellermines, which usually you pick up one at a time, but they tied a rope to them, and they got behind the truck to pull the mines. But when they pulled the mines, where they were standing it was booby trapped, and they got blown up. That's the story I got from the people there. I got the impression that they were very unhappy that somebody didn't follow procedure, but they didn't go into detail with me and I can understand that, because I was a 19-year-old kid that just got there six hours before. I didn't know anything about engineering, I was all by myself, and my buddy got hit. I don't even know if he was killed. All I know is they took him away, and of course he never came back. That was the first day we were with the outfit.

In his account, Sidney Oxman gives the impression that the mines blew up because the body they were trying to remove from the crater happened to drag over a mine. This information is precious, as he is one of the very few people who actually witnessed the explosion first hand, unlike Doug Rockenbach, who heard a altered version of the story. Not surprisingly, the exact circumstances of the explosion quickly became clouded, with the unlikely claim being made that the bodies of the dead Frenchmen had in fact been booby trapped by German soldiers who had returned to the scene. Of course, this was a good chance to accuse the German troops of immoral behavior and **Félix "Ginette" Petitjean** finished the story about his killed resistance comrades with these explanations:

> During the night, the Germans mined the bodies of our unfortunate friends. When the Americans tried bringing them back onto the road, they also fell victim to Teutonic Machiavellianism, that respect for the dead had not touched on.[19]

This rumor of the bodies having been mined seems to have spread like wildfire at the time, since even the FABTF units were warned on August 30th:

> Road from Vence to Coursegoules heavily mined. Area (…) along road about two miles mined and cratered. Shoulder mined as far back as 100 feet. "S" Mines, Shuemines, and double Tellermines found. Many with anti-personnel devices attached. Dead bodies booby trapped. Mines along shoulder of road every four or five feet. Many mines put in at night after the shoulders have been cleared during the day.[20]

August 31st, two more warning messages were sent:

> Local police in Vence report mines have been laid last night by Germans who fired upon patriots patrolling at les Templiers. They have laid other mines at Quartier Ara and Calvarie, as far down as Malvan Valley. Patrols are at your disposal to guide any soldiers you may desire to send through mined areas. (…)
> Engineer officer reports cases of German and partisan dead booby trapped. Request your command to be advised of this. Many anti-tank mines found to be activated with anti-personnel devices (…).[21]

The memorial commemorating all the mine victims that now stands by the road between Vence and Coursegoules. Author's Collection.

Logic, as well as Sgt Sidney Oxman's account, seem to indicate that all these events that occurred long after the departure of the last German were in fact probably due to the paranoia of trigger happy resistance men. Mines were heavy and bulky to transport, and were normally only laid by trained engineer troops; therefore, laying large numbers of mines in a preexisting minefield during the night, apart from being suicidal, was also beyond the capacity of small groups of German stragglers.

Apart from the demonic minefield, the liberation of the area around Vence was quite uneventful. After liberating Vence the afternoon of the 27th, 3rd Regiment of the FSSF advanced to positions overlooking the Var River on the 28th, just like their colleagues from 1st Regiment were doing further south at St Laurent. The first patrols of 3rd Regiment reached la Gaude the morning of the 28th, reporting:

> Patrol to la Gaude reports it clear. Approximately 20 enemy left yesterday morning. Their morale was very low. At the point of crying. All were very young, according to partisan reports.[22]

Once again, we note that the FSSF only reached high ground overlooking the Var River during the day of August 28th, therefore after the French resistance had started its insurrection in Nice in the early morning the same day.

Conclusion

The liberation of the general area of Vence and St Laurent du Var was made with minimal losses, as virtually all the German forces had pulled back to the east side of the Var after the fighting at the Loup River. Only two civilians and one German were killed in gunfights at St Laurent. There was no fighting in Vence, but four men were summarily executed by the Germans for petty offenses. Allied shelling killed one civilian and one or two Germans. The worst occurred when five resistance men, three civilians, and three American Engineers were killed in a minefield north of Vence. The First Special Service Force was able to take up positions overlooking the Var River late on August 28th. As for the 551st Parachute Infantry Battalion, it only advanced from Biot to the mouth of the Var on the 29th. We will now see what was occurring further north, in the area of action of the 517th Parachute Infantry Regiment.

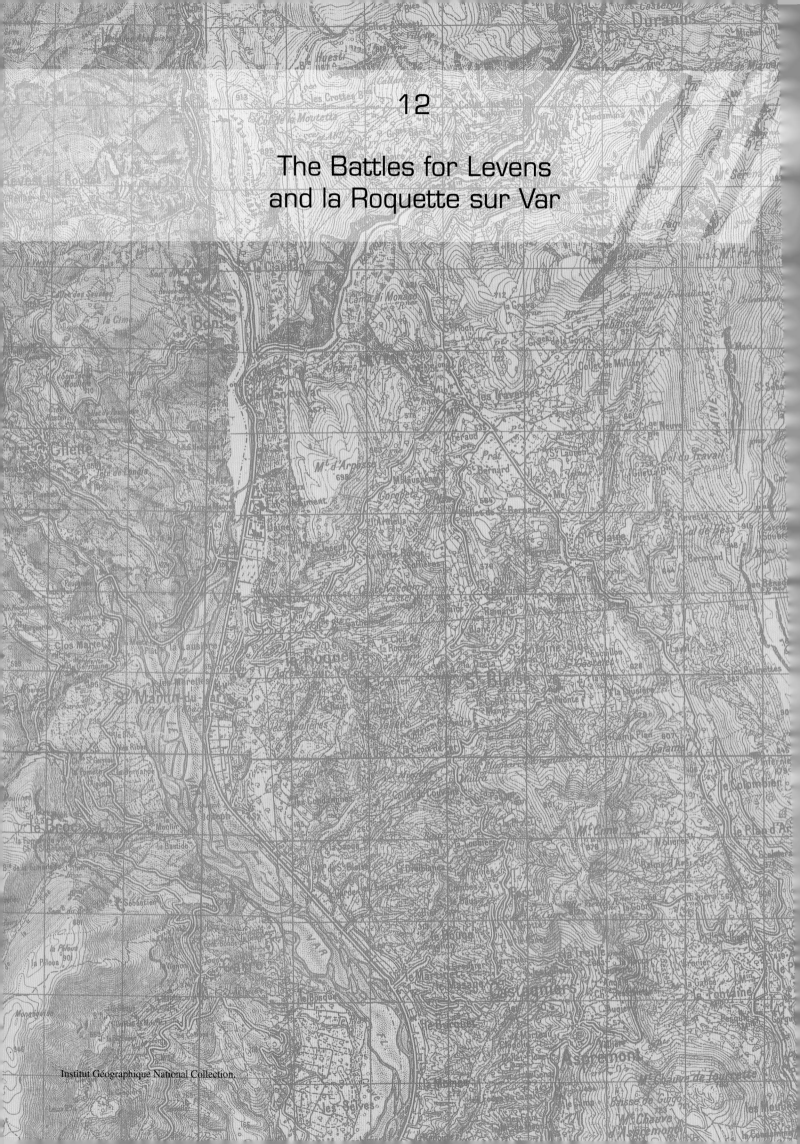

12

The Battles for Levens
and la Roquette sur Var

The story of the liberation of the Levens and its surroundings will bring us back to August 15th, the day of the Allied landing. It is a rather complicated history, involving a series of attacks and counterattacks by the Resistance forces and the Germans before the final American attack. The reason why the Levens area so interested the belligerents is double: first, it overlooked several strategic roads and bridges; and second, the area is a formidable defensive position for attacks coming from the west.

The villages that will be mentioned most in this chapter will be Levens, la Roquette sur Var, St Martin du Var, and Plan du Var, and the reader should therefore familiarize himself with the locations of these towns on the map. The main geographic feature of the region is the Var River, flowing roughly north to south. Its river bed is 200 meters wide, and since it is usually almost dry in summer time, it could be forded rather easily, though the Germans had laid large numbers of mines in it. The smaller Vésubie river flows into the Var at Plan du Var, coming from the northeast. Because of the mountainous nature of the surroundings, the main roads follow the riverbeds and valleys. *Route Nationale 202* (RN 202) was an important highway following the Var and leading to Entrevaux and Digne. A less important road followed the Vésubie into the mountains to la Bollène and onto St Martin Vésubie. A bridge at Plan du Var, the Pont Durandy (Durandy Bridge), controlled both the RN 202 and the Vésubie road. A bit further south, between Plan du Var and St Martin du Var, the Pont Charles Albert (Charles Albert Bridge) crossed over the Var River. Anybody controlling Plan du Var and St Martin du Var could therefore control two important bridges and two important roads and cut off all traffic along the Var and Vésubie Valleys. Plan du Var and St Martin du Var were themselves overlooked by Levens and la Roquette sur Var.

On either side of the Var, which is almost at sea level, the ground rises up extremely steeply, immediately reaching altitudes of over 600 meters. The Arpasse Mountain rises up on the east side of the Var, at the angle formed by the Var and Vésubie Rivers. La Roquette is built on a steep peak in the southern part of the Arpasse. From la Roquette, the Var River and RN 202 highway can be observed towards the south for many kilometers, and the Charles Albert bridge is also clearly visible to the north. La Roquette, being surrounded on three sides by steep valleys or even cliffs, is a virtually ideal defensive position. Levens is located on the northeastern side of the Arpasse, nestled between the Arpasse and the Férion mountains. Though it did not offer as good a vantage point as la Roquette, it did overlook Plan du Var and its bridge over the Vésubie, as well as the Vésubie road. A road leaving Levens to the southeast leads to Tourrette-Levens, then to Nice, providing an excellent escape route.

Describing geography with words is always a delicate task, so the reader should study the associated photos and maps of these areas in order to get a proper feel of what the terrain looks like. To make things simple, the villages of la Roquette and Levens were built in difficult mountainous terrain, accessible only by a few twisting roads or footpaths. They overlooked all the important roads, bridges, and rivers in the area, and were therefore highly strategic positions.

During the Occupation, Levens formed the northern limit of the area under effective German control; in fact, several *maquis* camps had been set up near Levens, la Roquette, and Aspremont. North of Levens were only few roads and villages, and apart from a few main roads and towns, these steep and unwelcoming mountains were under Resistance control.

The Death of Commander Gérôme

When the Allies landed, the Resistance immediately became active, trying to capture the small and isolated German garrisons that were stationed in the villages around Levens. Before getting into the thick of the subject, we will read about a rather strange event that occurred in the village of Aspremont, south of Levens. August 15th, an attempt by the local resistance leader, *Commandant* Marcel Gérôme, to convince the German garrison to surrender turned sour. Resistance newspaper *l'Ergot* later wrote a very detailed article about the incident, and though it may not be the best example of impartiality, it at least gives an idea what happened and of the atmosphere that prevailed when news of the landing reached the *maquis*:

A view of the Var Valley, looking north, as seen from la Roquette sur Var. The RN 202 Highway is visible running along the Var River. The Charles Albert Bridge, in the lower left part of the photo, became the cause of multiple attacks and counterattacks in late August 1944. Author's Collection.

"During the night of August 14th to 15th," explains Lt Lafarge, with soft and simple words that reveal his goodness of heart, "in our camp at the Mont Cima, we intercept the messages announcing the Allied landing in Provence. (…) Around 4:30 we hear cannon fire. Myself and Gérôme had been waiting for this moment for so long!

"Immediately, filled with nervous enthusiasm and accompanied by a few men, we go down towards Aspremont, which is closely guarded by the *Boche*. Going down with us there are Max Ferrara, Maxie Ciampoli, and young Séassau, whose house, which is close to the commander's house, we use as our headquarters. The last one to have joined our camp is also present: the famous Captain 'Charly' Michenon, about whom we have some serious concerns.

"On the way, we tore down all the German signposts and capture two *Boches* that we immediately bring to the commander's house. I want to keep them there and disarm them. But Gérôme sees bigger, as usual. He wants to manage a daring move; he wants to disarm the entire garrison of Aspremont. With the rudiments of the German language that remain from his studies in Nancy, where he was born, he interrogates the two prisoners, judges them, sizes them up, turns them around, penetrates them, and probably also convinces them. He is sure of that, for he lets them go, telling us that they must each return with a comrade that we will capture.

"We are in admiration of Gérôme, at these instants, all the qualities of a great leader exude from him: control and daring. His eyes are shining with a flame in which victory dances.

"It is then that I must leave him. I have to return to the camp where hundreds of men are waiting for me, as well as elders and children who have come to seek our protection." (…)

Once Henry Lafarge left, Commander Gérôme and his wife and Charly Michenon and his wife had gone to eat lunch at Séassau's. In the early afternoon, the men met up in the village. Max Ferrara then explains:

"We were to capture two Germans at the moment when they would come to get water at the wash house. When they appeared, the 'boss' called them over, inviting them for a drink. They followed us without any difficulties. 'Whatever you do,' recommended Gérôme, 'do not move. I order you not to show your weapons. No gunshots.'

- "It was about 3:45," adds Séassau, who had a meeting at 4 o'clock that day.

They are thus all sitting around a table on the terrace of the Trastour restaurant, facing glasses of beer and white wine.

There are eight of them under the arbor. The two Germans have laid down their rifles and are sitting side by side. Facing them, also sitting, are Marcel Gérôme and Charly Michenon, at the right side of the commander. Henri Séassau is standing to the right of Michenon, then there is Max Ferrara, who is sitting with Maxie Ciampoli standing behind him. Further on in a doorway is Max Ferrara's father, observing the whole scene from behind the Germans. Outside, the town square is deserted.

Max Ferrara continues his story: "Gérôme had started speaking with the Germans. After five minutes, I saw Michenon showing the two revolvers he had in his hands above the table, contrary to what the 'boss' had ordered. He puts them back under the table straight away without the Germans noticing anything. But soon afterwards, Michenon repeats his careless gesture. This time the Germans see him and they grab their weapons. Then a gunshot is fired."

Where is it fired from?
- "From my left," claims Henri Séassau.
Who fired?
"Not the Germans," says Mr Ferrara senior, adding: "I saw Michenon firing on them with both hands as the Commander shouted: 'No! No!'"

But it was too late. A shot had been fired, causing a confused firefight.

"I didn't really realize what happened around me," declares Max Ferrara. "What I know is that as for myself, I immediately pulled out the revolver that I was hiding under my shirt, on my chest. I shot the German who was on my right and who was taking aim at Michenon. He was killed on the spot. Then I emptied the rest of my magazine

Le Commandant Gérôme portant barbe et lunettes pour tromper la Gestapo

"Mes enfants, there is a bastard among us…" 47-year-old resistance commander Marcel Gérôme, who was shot and mortally wounded in bizarre circumstances August 15th in Aspremont. L'Ergot/MRA Collection.

in his companion, who was already wounded in the chest, and who held onto the Commander as he fell."

When calm returned and the smoke and powder had cleared, the Commander murmured: "I am hit in the liver." We saw that he was wounded, but in the thigh. We thought it was nothing serious, in spite of what he had just said, and all the more so because he didn't seem to be suffering. He remained standing, worrying about our withdrawal. He had put a clip in his gun and was giving orders.

To preserve the population from reprisals, we carried the two Germans, one of which was still breathing, into the St Claude chapel. The Commander helped us. Now we could see he was in pain, but he clenched his teeth and kept repeating: "Marche ou crève [March or die]." He made us get into position. He fought against pain for 20 minutes, then we saw him stagger. Henri Séassau and myself rushed to him. He leaned on our shoulders. It is then that he told us: "Mes enfants [My children], there is a bastard amongst us…"

And Henri Séassau adds: "He also said: 'Lucky thing you are here… It is a Frenchman who has killed me.'"

Since he was starting to moan, they laid him down on a stretcher and brought him to Séassau's house. They now knew that he had not only been wounded in the thigh.

And here is the rest of Lt Lafarge's account: "I had just finished a meal when a runner reached the Mont Cima camp, bringing us the atrocious news that filled our hearts with consternation and sorrow: the chief was mortally wounded. He was asking for me."

"I left with about 20 men. We went down the little path very fast that day.

"I reached the Séassau's house. Gérôme is lying in Madame Séassau's room. He is writhing on his bed. The pain is atrocious. As soon as he sees me, he quenches it. His hands clench mine, his eyes look into mine: 'Henri, my little Henri… I am going to die… A French bullet… It is a Frenchman who killed me…' Gérôme cries, more wounded in his heart than in his flesh.

"We set out in search of a doctor. There is none in Aspremont. The one in Colomars refuses to come at first. But two of our men go and fetch him by force. As we wait, all the Séassau family, the poor Madame Gérôme, who is strong in her bereavement – a real hero's wife – all of us are there, aghast. We give our treatment, trying to relieve his pain with morphine, supporting the heart with camphor.

"However, Gérôme knows that the game must go on without him. He lets me go. I dispose my men around the house; the *Boches* will pay an expensive price if they try to approach us.

"Then we venture into the village. Everything is calm, silent, empty. An abandoned village! But I perk my ears. A rale is heard, coming from the church. 'It is the wounded German,' says Ferrara.

"We decide to evacuate him. After having buried the dead German in the cemetery, I load the wounded one onto my shoulders. Later on, after I had laid him down in the small chapel next to Séassau's house, he tells me: 'Me not shoot… Me not want to kill… Me Christian…' When he found out he was there near him, Gérôme, that other great Christian who hated killing even his worst enemies, even 'bastards,' told me: 'You have to save him.'

"Hans Muller died in the Levens hospital 10 days later, but not without having intervened to save the lives of 15 of our wounded who had fallen into the hands of the Boche.

"The sun is declining. Time is running out. I need a volunteer to get an ambulance in Nice. I find him in the shape of a small humble but hardy man, worthy of Gerome: Louis Delachaussée.

"Will he succeed in his perilous mission? Will he ever come back? There are so many road blocks to be passed! Yes, he succeeded, after 24 hours the ambulance is in Aspremont.

"Gérôme is exhausted. As we take him out of the small house that was the spirit of our *maquis*, as we follow the path that is bringing our venerated chief away from the Mont Cima forever, 20 men, eyes red, give military honors.

"Before leaving us, he told me: 'Make sure I am avenged Henri… You need to fight and join up with the other companies…' That's all. And then the black car left… I still wonder how it escaped detection by the Germans?

"From far off we followed Gérôme's agony. His image was constantly among us. It stimulated us in the battles we fought. News was reaching us from the clinic in Nice where our beloved wounded had been operated. Hope was living in our hearts. Maybe he would be saved in spite of how late the surgical procedure had been done?

"Alas! Brutally, one day the dreadful news reached us: the boss had left at the dawn of victory. (…)

"It is a French bullet that killed Commander Gérôme. He said so himself. This bullet has disappeared, but Henri Séassau managed to identify it first.

"On the other hand, the Germans did not fire. Mr Ferrara senior affirms it. And better than his affirmations, the proof is that the barrels of the German rifles contained neither cartridges nor casings when Henri Séassau took them apart.

"Mr Ferrara senior and Maxie were armed with Colts; Max Ferrara and Henri Séassau had 92s; Charly Michenon had a 6.35 and a 7.65; Commander Gerome had a 7.65."[1]

The deadly bullet was found in Gérôme's clothes when he was undressed, and according to Henri Séassau, it was a 6.35, so the shooter must have been Charly Michenon. *L'Ergot* further went on to claim that Michenon had shot Gérôme purposefully, in order to take command of his *maquis*. The German soldier who had been killed in the shooting and then buried in Aspremont was 27-year-old **Pionier Ernst Richter**. His wounded comrade's name is not known, unless the name "Hans Müller," which was quoted in the *Ergot* article, was actually real. Other sources claim that this soldier did not die, but was evacuated by the Germans when they

reoccupied Levens (as we will see later). An unidentified body was buried in the Levens cemetery at a later date, but nothing indicates that this was "Hans Müller."

The Occupation of St Martin du Var and of the Levens Region by the Resistance

In the mountains north of Aspremont and Commander Gérôme, the *maquis* were more successful convincing the Germans to surrender. Within three days, the small garrisons at Puget-Théniers, St Martin, Vésubie, and Bancairon had surrendered. The entire area north of the Levens-St Vallier line thus fell into *maquis* control, except in the zone near the Italian border, which the Germans held onto firmly, as the border was where they planned to set up a definite line of resistance after their retreat from the Riviera. August 16th, the day after the landing, the 8th and 27th FTPF companies descended from the mountains and occupied Plan du Var and Levens, finding no opposition. (This is when wounded "Hans Müller" was brought from Aspremont to Levens.) **Sous-Lieutenant Cavenago**, one of the ORA resistance fighters who descended from Ilonse, in the mountains, towards St Martin du Var, later wrote:

> The morning of August 15th, I was at the fountain above the hamlet when a fighter plane flew over Ilonse at low altitude with red, white, and blue roundels; it was British. Joy! Joy! I rush to the old radio that we had to find out about the Allied landing at le Muy and St Tropez. It is not necessary to describe the noisy joyfulness of all our men.
>
> The messages announcing the landing in Provence were: "La burette coule" and "Nancy a le torticolis." ("The oilcan is dripping' and "Nancy has torticolis.") We did not hear them, but it doesn't matter, the landing occurred.
>
> Malherbe's order reaches us very fast: descend to Plan du Var, St Martin du Var, and Pont Saint Blaise with the mission of:
>
> - Strongly holding Plan du Var to block the access to the confluence region (Var, Tinée, Vésubie Rivers).
> - Mounting ambushes on the RN 202 south of Moulin St Blaise.
> - Pushing as far south as possible to help the FFIs in Nice.
>
> Dubeau decides to leave as soon as possible. (…) At 20:00 on August 16th, we leave Ilonse in a long procession of heavily laden men. (…) We cannot take the Tinée Valley road, which is still blocked by the Germans in the Bancairon electricity factory. During the night, following mountains paths, we reach the Col de la Sinne, Pradastier, and Touët du Var.
>
> There, we leave the group to Sous-Lieutenant Fougère. Foncet and I "requisition" a tandem bicycle that was lying in front of the doorway of a house, and that is how we reach the Hotel du Lyon at Plan du Var at 10 o'clock on August 17th.
>
> Great disorder was reigning there. We found the main characters of the FFI general staff, Melin (…), Roubert (…) representing the CDL [Liberation committee], and Jamme (…), chief of the FTPs in the department. They are returning from a meeting at the CP in Valberg and are trying to get back to Nice. After the congratulations that the situation imposes, Dubeau and I try to get things under control.
>
> At Plan du Var, I find Lorrain (…) with his company and Lieutenant Silve and his group. They are also trying to get things under control. I am with Dubeau in the dining

room, where Sedan [**Henri Sedan Miegemolle**], a young doctor from the *Compagnie Lorrain*, is manipulating a Gammon grenade, explaining that as long as the cap is not unscrewed and the string surrounding the neck is not unraveled, the percussion pin cannot function, and one can thus knock it around at will.

I am just telling him: "Beware Doc, one shouldn't fool around with those things…" when Lorrain comes to ask me to help him carry some fuel drums. We leave in a car and have hardly reached the Pont Durandi a few hundred meters away from the hotel when a violent explosion resounds. We turn back immediately.

The spectacle at the hotel is atrocious, there is blood everywhere, and the doctor is torn to shreds! Dubeau and Melin are wounded and evacuated to the Puget Théniers hospital, as well as Imbert and Bacle. I am the only remaining person in charge of the Tinée and Vésubie.[2]

The inexperience of many of the *maquisards* had once again cost the resistance dearly. Also on August 17th, the FTPs of the 8th and 27th Companies advanced out of Plan du Var, down the RN202 towards St Martin du Var. AS member **Joseph "Chambéry" Martin** was with them:

We were coming from Plan du Var with a truck, with a flag, of course. At one point at St Martin, we found ourselves face to face with a German truck coming up. They got out and went into the forest, and so did we. They opened up on us but didn't hit any of us. Supposedly, we killed one of them when they were getting back in their truck to pull out. Bertrand had stayed on our truck with a machine gun and bang bang bang! Apparently when they left, some of the Germans were bleeding.

Laurent Pasquier, of the 27th FTPF Company, was also present at the shooting, and noted in his diary:

August 16th. (...) We go down from Utelle to Plan du Var, where we take up position.

August 17th. We leave [Plan du Var] to occupy St Martin du Var. At the Pont Charles Albert, we have a skirmish with a truck full of *Boches*. The fight lasts two hours. The *Fritzes* pull out, taking at least two wounded with them and abandoning a Mauser that is allocated to me. At noon, we occupy St Martin du Var. I am responsible for occupying the post office and take possession of the telephone and telegraph.[3]

St Martin du Var was now in the hands of the *maquisards*. The resistance would not advance any further south on the eastern bank of the Var, probably because of the presence of German troops in the St Blaise and Aspremont area. The Germans also did not mount any serious counterattacks against the *résistants* at first, their main concern being to fight the Allied invasion near Cannes. However, the *maquisards* only stayed in St Martin for one day before pulling out, probably because St Martin was a very bad defensive position, being located at the bottom of a valley. The inhabitants of the town were at first joyful to have been liberated on the 17th, but the behavior of certain *maquisards* quickly tempered them, as was noted by **Monsieur Fernand**, a member of the Liberation Committee:

I had received instructions about overthrowing the town council, even without the arrival of the FTPs. August 17th, I informed the mayor that he was to withdraw in order to make room for the resistance organizations. The town council was summoned to an extraordinary session for its collective resignation and its replacement by the local National Liberation Committee, which had been formed beforehand.

At 11:00, the FTPs, who had not warned us of their arrival, appeared. They occupied the town hall and asked for the local representative of the National Liberation Movement. I introduced myself, and the commanding officer of the 8th Company asked me to assemble the Committee. This was done on the spot.

The commanding officer of the 8th Company, as well as the chiefs of the Rodez and Pedro detachments, were present at the meeting. Energetic decisions were taken during the 15:00 session, particularly concerning supplies.

Enthusiasm prevailed in the village. At 14:00, the "Marseillaise" was passionately sung at the raising of the colors ceremony. Everything would have occurred satisfactorily if the detachments stationed in the village had adopted a more correct attitude. The storekeepers were visited and their merchandise was demanded without any requisition sheets delivered by the Committee being given, as the commanding officer had prescribed. The door of the Veran factory shop was broken in without any requests having been made to deliver the coal. Mr Ferreri, a St Martin du Var shopkeeper, was required by the AS as well as the FTPs to give 49 hectos of wine without any requisition sheets.

In the school where our FTPs were quartered, a frame containing the picture of the traitor Pétain was smashed with rifle butts, although they could have removed the photo without damaging the frame, which could later have been used for someone else's photo.

In the village, it is rumored that the FTPs are putting three pieces of sugar in their coffee when searches in our shops have found only 80 kilograms of sugar for a population of 1,200 inhabitants.

In short, there seemed to be no discipline in these detachments. The entire population that had been enthusiastic at first started being disgusted by them.

The FTPs stood guard to protect us from the Germans, who were three kilometers away from the village. Following orders, a legal FTP went to ask the *Boches* at the Pont de St Blaise to surrender. This was August 17th, at about 9 o'clock. August 18th, the FTPs left, leaving the village defenseless. Some of them left with their fists held up. The population saw the influence of the [Communist] Party in all this.

On the 18th and 19th, the Germans came closer to the village and opened fire. Comrade **Angelin Zecchini** was killed during one shelling.

The worst impression was when the Germans approached the undefended village August 18th; the members of the Liberation Committee who were in the village all left, except for myself and another member, who is not affiliated with the Communist Party. Almost all the legal FTPs also fled. It was a catastrophe. I myself heard the following remarks: "Look and try to find the people in charge. They have fled like chickens."[4]

It would seem that the only consequence of the brief occupation of St Martin du Var by the Resistance was the death of Angelin Zecchini, who was killed by a mortar shell "while pulling potatoes from his field" August 19th,[5] leaving behind two young daughters. The poor behavior of the *maquisard*s may have been due to the fact that since the Allied landing, the number of volunteers for the Resistance, some with less than noble intentions, had suddenly exploded, as **Marceau Raynaud**, of the 8th FTPF Company, remembers:

> When August 15th came, we saw a bunch of guys come along who wanted to join up. But they arrived at the last minute and they all had armbands and everything. But we took all of them because we thought: "All these men can be useful to us."

Joseph Garnero, also of the 8th Company, recalls a particularly stunning example:

> When we got to Levens and then to Nice, we were submerged. There was a flow of men, including people from the *Gestapo*, people who were coming to take refuge with us so as not to be bothered. Yeah, there were quite a few cases like that. We were in the Westminster Hotel in Nice and one of the new men was standing guard. Then one guy called me, saying: "Chief, come down quick, there is a woman who jumped onto the sentry like a lunatic!" I went down with my submachine gun and asked: "Madame, what is going on?" She told me: "This guy got all my family deported! He killed my entire family!" And in the end, it was true. I don't know what happened to him. Bad things happened on both sides: some people got killed for no reason. Some people joined us at the last moment and then, in the name of the Resistance, went to execute people with which they had personal matters to settle. But when we caught those people, there was no tomorrow for them.

In Levens, the FTPs were holding a dozen German prisoners who had been captured in the area when the partisans had initially seized the town August 16th. One of the *maquisard* remembers them:

> We had 12 prisoners. They were afraid of us terrorists, because they knew that they did not forgive us and killed us, and that we did the same to them. It was normally out of the question to take prisoners, but because they surrendered at a calm moment, we said: "Come on, let's go," with two kicks in the ass, and they followed. They told us: "We would have surrendered already but our warrant officer didn't want to." "Oh, really?" They weren't acting proud, because they saw we were not soldiers and were in civilian clothes. They must have been thinking: "This is it, they are going to kill us." One of them showed us his papers and jabbered: "I am not German, look, I am born in Warsaw." Yeah, maybe, but he was still with the Germans.
>
> We kept them for the day, then said: "Now a truck will come and get you to bring you to the prison camp in Beuille." We had transformed the small barracks in Beuille into a German prisoner of war place. When we got the interpreter to tell them that, they felt a bit better. We loaded them into the truck, and when they left they shouted: "Vive le France," because they were happy that we hadn't killed them. They didn't even say "Vive la France," but "Vive le France."

The Resistance usually could not afford to take prisoners, but with the arrival of the Allies now imminent, and several dozen Germans having surrendered in mountain villages, such as Puget-Théniers, the Resistance took appropriate measures and treated its captives as prisoners of war. However, the NCO who had been in command of the group of prisoners at Levens was not so lucky:

> When they surrendered, the sergeant flatly told us they had wanted to surrender the previous day, but that the warrant officer had not wanted to. They betrayed him in a way; and he supposedly also said: "You have not won the war yet, we still have the secret weapon." He had been in Russia, since he had the ribbon for the Russian campaign.

It was somehow decided that this unfortunate culprit was to be executed:

> He had been a bit of a nuisance to us, so we took him and made him dig his own grave. That was dirty of us, but it was wartime, don't trick yourself. In war, people do bad things regardless of the side they are on. We lectured him a bit, and told him it was over for him. Then the guy said: "I have five kids." "We don't give a damn about your five kids. For us, a Frenchman who has no kids is worth more than you." We made a bit of a ceremony; I was not part of it, but I was there watching. There were six guys in the execution squad. They had their rifles loaded and the guy commanding them was about to say: "Take aim. Fire." But at the moment when they were going to lift their rifles, Cobra, a little 18-year-old Parisian who was not part of the execution squad, discreetly went off to the side, took his Colt, and bang! He shot the German right in the head before the others had time to fire. Cobra said: "I have taken revenge, I have avenged my father." The others also shot the German anyway. He took a lot of bullets, because he fell down and they shot at him again. He didn't suffer as they say, but still... Little Cobra said: "They killed my father like that in Paris. Now I am happy, I have avenged him."

Another *maquisard* who was also present has a quite different recollection of the exact circumstances of the execution:

> We had quite a few prisoners in Levens, and one of my friends said: "I am going to take revenge. My father was deported." He took a sergeant who was a prisoner and said: "We are going to make him dance." We brought him up into the forest in front of Levens, with the excuse that he was going to show us a good position for setting up a machine gun, but the prisoner didn't believe us: he showed us pictures of his children, of his wife, all that stuff... So I told my friend: "Come on, we aren't going to kill him. The Americans are going to arrive and we will hand over all those prisoners." He said: "I want to take revenge, I want to take revenge." "But you shouldn't... He is a prisoner." He was saying: "Your father hasn't been deported, you don't know what it feels like." I told him: "Yes, I can understand you, but even so, it's not a good reason. He is a father and has a family; maybe he was forced to join the army, like so many others. You have to see things the way they are." But he didn't want to and said: "Let him walk in front." He pulled out his Colt and killed the prisoner with two bullets to the back of the head. Then we had to bury the German. We didn't have a shovel or anything, so we found an olive tree that had been uprooted, leaving a hole in the ground. We put him in there and we put some earth on him and that was it. We didn't put a cross or anything,

we didn't take his identification tag. I suspect they must have found him latter on. It was a period when a man's life wasn't worth much, because he had told us that he had a family, that he had children, and all that stuff. It was war, and that's the way it was. Hatred spawns hatred.

The body of the executed prisoner was recovered after the war in the Fondemel district of Levens, but he could not be identified as his identification tag was not found. The *maquisards* were now in control of Levens, la Roquette, and Plan du Var, where they would remain unmolested by the Germans for the next several days.

Sapin's Patrol to Plan du Var

August 16th, Colonel Jacques "Sapin" Lécuyer, the commanding officer of the Resistance of the R2 region of southeastern France, met up with Major General Frederick, commander of the First Airborne Task Force, in Fréjus. Knowing that all the mountains north of Fayence, Grasse, and Levens were in the hands of the resistance, Sapin tried to convince Frederick to make a large flanking movement to the north, in order to come down the Var Valley, behind the German defenses, and attack the Germans from behind.[6] However, Major General Frederick was not particularly interested in this plan, probably because:

- At that point, the FABTF was disorganized and had barely fulfilled its initial mission of securing the le Muy area. Its future missions were not known.
- The FABTF did not have enough vehicles to carry a large body of men through the mountains.
- The FABTF could not afford to weaken the right wing of the Allied invasion front, leaving the landing beaches open to German counterattack.
- The mountain roads that would have been used in such a maneuver could be blocked by the Germans very easily if they realized what was going on, and they were in fact well aware of how exposed their flank was. (The flanking threat is specifically mentioned in the orders *Reserve Division 148* received August 20th, quoted in Chapter 6 and in Otto Fretter-Pico's Knights Cross citation quoted in Chapter 16.)
- The liberation of the Maritime Alps was not a priority for the Allies, so there was no reason for them to try anything risky or "fancy."

According to Colonel Sapin, Major General Frederick did let him guide a patrol of jeeps all the way to the Plan du Var area August 17th, where they were "welcomed with bursts from machine guns set up on the heights around Levens."[7] Sapin did not note the nationality of those who opened fire on them, which is particularly interesting, considering that Levens was occupied by the Resistance at the time! The gunfire that "welcomed" the American patrol may well have been fired by Sapin's own men, thinking they were shooting at a German convoy. **Sapin** later described the reaction of the patrol to the gunfire:

> The whole detachment, luckily with no losses, took refuge in the Chaudan tunnel. I told the detachment commander that by driving at full speed, jeep by jeep, we could go up the Vésubie Valley, reach an old bridge (we had stupidly blown the Pont Durandy), quickly find ourselves in a blind spot from the gunfire, and come back to the Var Valley to get even nearer to Nice.
>
> He asked me how far we were from Nice, and I answered: "A good 20 kilometers." He then told me: "You

told the general that we could reach an area 20 kilometers from Nice without firing a shot. It is true, but now we are being shot at: I will report by radio and turn back."[8]

It is understandable that the American commanding the jeep patrol was not excited by the prospect of driving even nearer to Nice, when his small force was already 50 kilometers behind the front lines and under fire. If they had attempted to go further down the Var Valley, the patrol would undoubtedly have run into serious German resistance and trouble. I have been unable to find any trace of Sapin's patrol in any FABTF sources of information, including in the FABTF daily reports of activity. The jeep patrol may not have belonged to a unit of the FABTF.

On the Western Bank of the Var River

On the eastern bank of the Var River, the Resistance had only reached Plan du Var in its drive south. This Liberation was not necessarily popular among the inhabitants, as we saw, and there was no serious fighting with the Germans for the first week of the *maquis* occupation of the Levens area. On the western side of the Var, the resistance was able to advance much further south, reaching the hills around Carros. From there, it could threaten the important road connecting Vence to the Var Valley, which was being heavily used by German troops retreating from the Allied invasion front. The men participating in these actions were for the most part FFIs belonging to the *Groupe Combat*, but some FTPs were also present. As often, there was a fair amount of tension between the two groups, as **Primo Elisei**, of the *Groupe Combat*, remembers:

> When the landing occurred, we went and occupied Bouyon, and the FTPs arrived at the same time. People were giving us food and stuff. I understood that the *maquis* were already fighting with each other. One of our chiefs said: "If any of you passes over to the FTPs, he will be shot." I heard those words in the town square.

It is unlikely that the FFI leader would actually have followed through with this threat. The *maquisards* then moved south towards Carros, where a first engagement occurred August 18th, the French Gendarmes noting the next day:

> August 18, 1944, an engagement occurred yesterday afternoon near Carros, between a group of FFIs and a convoy of German soldiers made up of three trucks. The "*maquisards*" are said to have blown up the first of these vehicles. There were losses on both sides. We do not know what the outcome of this ambush was.[9]

No FFIs died, but 18-year-old **Soldat Josef Uschold**, of the 3rd Company of *Pionier Bataillon 8*, was reported by the Germans as having been killed "near Carras, 15 kilometers north of Nice." He was then buried in Caucade Cemetery in Nice. This encounter near Carros was followed by a series of small fire fights over the following days. A young inhabitant of Nice named Louis Fiori had been involved with the FTPs in Nice before the Allied landing. Not wanting to miss out on the action after the landing, **Louis Fiori** joined the FFIs under the command of Lt Latruffe near Carros August 19th:

> The morning of the 19th, I am in le Broc with a "Combat" group that has a *maquis* above the village. We are supposed to leave for an operation in Gattières. I am in the village square with a German rifle that had been taken

from a sentry in Gattières. The German had been standing guard, so there were five cartridges in it. I have fun messing around with it, because it is the first time I have a rifle in my hands. I practice taking aim, but it is out of the question to fire a shot and waste a cartridge, since we are going to battle. There is another guy with a German rifle beside me and he suddenly asks: "How many cartridges do you have?" I say: "I have five, why?" He says: "Because I have 25, so we will share like brothers." He gave me 10 cartridges, so both of us went to battle with 15 cartridges. That was typical of the spirit we were in at the time, not selfishness where you say: "I have to save myself, too bad for the others." It wasn't like that at all.

We get into a bus from the Nice-Bouyon line. We are advancing slowly with the windows down, with rifles and submachine guns pointing out. Then a guy from Carros, Jean-Pierre Judelin, arrives on a motorcycle at full speed and says: "The Germans are in Carros!" So we expect them to come towards us. We give the order to stop the bus and all get out and take up positions on either side of the road, above and below it. We set up a machine gun because we can see very far, up to the St Sébastien curve two kilometers away. We have a view that will enable us to see the Germans approaching if they followed the road. But then nothing happens, false alerts. That also happened in those days.

In the evening, we eat and get back in the bus and leave. We go through Carros, take the old road, and stop in a hamlet between Gattières and Carros called la Clapière. We take up positions for the night with the machine gun on one side. In the morning, we realize that if there had been an alert, we would have fired at the machine gun that was posted on the other side of the road! I find myself with two old hands from Marseille who are veterans from the 1939-1940 war: Jo Escudero and Tave Ferlat. So we spend the night in those rocks without any blankets or anything, and it is cold. At one point, I feel an urgent need to urinate, and I get up and see a friend who is standing guard with his back to me. I move off a bit and he doesn't notice me. I can hear detonations in the distance, at night there is always gunfire somewhere, the Liberation is getting nearer. When I come back I heard a shout: "Who goes there?" What? Is there an alert? "Who goes there? I have pulled the pin on a grenade." I lift my head and see the friend facing me. "Hey Joe, I say, it's me!" "Get over here you idiot, and help me put the pin back in this grenade." That was the beginning.

Sunday, August 20th, the group stays down in la Clapière, and we are sent a bit further up. I was only calibrating the bullets. I would take the belts of ammunition out of their metal boxes and calibrate them so that we would not risk jamming the machine gun. Jo Escudero was the gunner. We are in position up there when a German truck rounds the curve two or three kilometers away, coming into the line of fire of the machine gun. The friend lets it come nearer, then he opens fire. The truck stops and the guys jump out on the sides of the road. He fires. Some of them try to hide under the trees, and he tells me: "Look, they are under the olive trees, thinking they are protected." But the foliage of olive trees is transparent when seen from above. He says: "You will see." He fires a burst, bang, the guy down there falls down. He says: "That one won't move anymore. I fire in bursts because if I would fire long series of bullets, the barrel would heat up." So he was a good shooter, he knew how to do it, with the elevation and

An artist's impression of the night spent at la Clapière. Unknown Collection, courtesy Louis Fiori.

everything he takes aim and then fires. I am getting my first lesson on machine guns. Finally the Germans retreat, dragging one or two guys that must have been wounded and throwing them in the back, then the truck drives away in reverse and disappears at the curve. It is the only alert that occurred that day.

We spend the night up there without eating anything. At nightfall, we heard a guy calling; we thought he was probably one of us, but didn't know what he wanted. The next morning, the Lieutenant tells me: "Go down to the farm to get some chow," since we hadn't eaten anything. I take my rifle and go down and find a wash boiler on the side of the path with thick congealed soup in it that is covered with red ants. I scrape off the surface with my drinking cup and throw it away and then eat two or three mouthfuls from below. Then I go down to the hamlet and say: "I am coming for food, because we didn't eat anything last night." A friend says: "There is a water tank over there." I say: "A water tank! There is a unique chance of having a bath!" So we go towards the tank, and just when we were reaching it we hear machine gun and submachine gun fire. One friend says: "That is German gunfire." Now it is out of the question to take a bath or take food. I run off, thinking of my friends who are up there at the machine gun and who risk being outflanked, so I need to take my place in the fight.

I run up towards our positions with my heart pounding. When I get there, Lt Latruffe, a St Cyr graduate, tells me: "Go in front of the positions because they are climbing up towards us, fire on the men coming up." We stopped firing with the machine gun because the hill was so steep that you had to almost be vertical to fire, in other words, offering a good target. So I take up a position a bit below the crest and fire at the Germans who are coming forwards, running along the stone walls and leaping from one terrace to the next. I look out and see a helmet sticking out, bang, I fire. Then there is another head on the other side, maybe the same one, so I fire again, of course without seeing the result, since I am also trying not to expose myself too much. I see guys getting through and jumping from one terrace to the next, so I think: "If we don't shoot them, they will get all the way through to us!"

Then the Lieutenant comes to see me and says: "We are going to stop firing now and wait for them with grenades. You go and find the group that is higher up on the hill and bring them back so that they can help us pull back with all the equipment." So I take my rifle and zigzag up the hill. I reach a flat spot and suddenly hear a burst of gunfire and bullets whistling. I rush through the clearing and throw myself behind a rock. That was a narrow escape! I look at an oak tree beside me and see a piece of bark being shot off, and that is when I figure that they were shooting at me, that I had been spotted and targeted. So I stay hidden behind the rock, with my rifle in front of me to at least be able to shoot anybody coming from ahead. The gunfire continues for a while, then stops, but I don't stick my head out to see what is going on. I stay there, with beating heart, waiting, watching. At one point, I hear noise behind me and say to myself: "This is it, they are going to outflank me." I turn around to face the danger and see guys in civilian clothes with weapons, so I understand that they are *résistants*. It was a group of FTPs under the command of Labbé. They were in the Carros area and had been attracted by the noise. People would do that; there was fighting, so you would go towards the fighting.

I stand up and advance towards them with my rifle over my shoulder and my hands up. I am in shorts, bare chested, with a pair of slippers that my father, who was a tailor, had made for me. They ask me: "Where are you coming from? Who are you? What are you doing?" I explain to them that I am with the "Combat" group down there. It seems strange to them and there is no more gunfire now. I tell them: "The lieutenant asked us to cease firing and to wait for them with grenades." "We can't hear any grenades." "Yeah, well, what can I say to you? The Germans must have stopped their advance, they were down below us."

The Germans did not have the mission of clearing out the area around Carros, Gattières, and le Broc. We thought they were going to climb all the way to our positions, but they didn't. Their mission was not to destroy the group of *résistants* that was there, it was only to cover the retreat of the troops coming to St Jeannet and going down from la Gaude to la Baronne to ford the Var. I ask the FTPs to come and help us pull out. They say: "You go first." I walk about 15 steps, then turn around: nobody had moved. So I continued, very slowly, and turned around again: one guy had separated himself from the group and started following me. I thought: "Good, they are spacing each other out, that is the way it should be done, they are coming." Then before getting back I thought: "What if the first one they see when we get back is the German, Josef [Josef Soppelsa was a German deserter who had joined the FFIs]? Then the two of us will be done for!" Because that German had a side cap and really German features! But then I saw Vincent, a young guy from Marseille, come out. Was I happy to see him!

It was now August 21st, and the *maquisards* pulled out from the Carros area into the hills to the north. Before leaving, however, one mixed group of FFIs from the *Groupe Combat* and FTPs from the 24th FTPF Company prepared to face the Germans again, possibly to cover the retreat of the main body of men. 19-year-old **Marcel Coche**, from Combat, was among them. His account starts the early morning of the 21st, as he had been on a special mission far ahead of the main group:

August 21st, Latruffe brought us together and said: "I need 12 men to go and attack the German garrison of St Laurent and Gattières. They are Polish, so you have nothing to be worried about. We need to get their weapons." We went there at 5 o'clock in the morning and really got a beating. None of us were killed, but we were running away and the Germans were shooting at us. So from five in the morning, we went from St Laurent to Gattières and Latruffe brought us to a place called la Clapière, where we met up with 60, 70, or 80 other guys. They had only been there since eight in the morning, but we were exhausted, because we had performed that attack on the Germans at St Laurent. We were bare chested because it was very hot and we were told: "Beware, after what we have done, the Germans will come after us." Indeed, an hour later we started hearing gunfire, so Latruffe said: "I need 12 men again. Who will come with me?" So we said: "Let's go." Jean Moute, myself, and some other young guys whose names I didn't know went. There was also a small hunchback called Labbé who was the commander of the FTPs. The small hunchback told us: "I will take six with me, come on!" and he brought us to some terraces between Gattières and la Clapière. 50 meters below us there was a sort of old bread oven and an old Roman path, and the Germans were coming from that direction. In the morning, when we escaped from the attack, I had noticed that the Germans had iron heels on their shoes like horses, and I saw traces like that on the ground at the path and said: "The *Fritzes* have been here." Labbé told us: "Get into a skirmish line behind the trees, we will wait for them to come up and then fire." And so we waited. There was Tonin Barbi, an FTP, another FTP further on, and my friend Jean Moute to my left. We were in a line of skirmishers over 100 meters, each 20 or 30 meters apart.

Suddenly we heard gunshots. I could see Latruffe leaving and I saw Natale [**Jean Natale**] stand up, fire, and "bang," he got shot right through the forehead and fell down, so Antonin said: "Get down, they got Tunis." I looked up to see and saw a German coming out from behind the bread oven. I took my submachine gun, fired a burst, and got back down. Tonin told me: "You must have hit him, because he went down." Like an idiot, I looked out from behind the tree, and bang, I got shot in the head. Since I am left handed, the bullet entered beside the left eye, broke the zygomatic bone, and exited behind the ear. I fell down unconscious.

Then I heard bang, bang, bang, bang. There was shooting going on all over the place and a twig from an olive tree fell onto me, waking me up. I got up and started walking like a madman, and I was later told that I was shouting: "Bastards! Dirty *Boches*! Vive la France!" Stupid, childish things. The others all started leaving, so Tonin and Jean Moute carried me and hid me in a little brook. After my friends left two Germans came. At that point, I must have been in a semi-coma. I felt that somebody kicked me, but I had the reflex not to move and heard "Kaputt, kaput." Apparently their presence saved

"The bullet entered beside the left eye, broke the zygomatic bone, and exited behind the ear." Marcel Coche in 2011, with a scar still faintly visible on the left side of his face. Author's Collection.

me, because further on they met a guy from Carros and told him: "Kaputt, Kamerad kaput," so the people figured: "There must be one over there."

I was shot around half past noon, and at 4 o'clock in the afternoon, some peasants and two holiday makers came to get me. I was completely out by then and only know what happened from what other people told me. They brought me to Dr Barbary, who along with two nurses cleaned my wound and provided initial treatment. Jean went to see the doctor, who said: "You have to get out of here fast because the Germans are coming." They took a mattress from the baker and lay me down on it. Jean had requisitioned a truck, and I was loaded onto it with the mattress and then driven away under fire, because the Germans were looking for us. Jean Moute saved my life twice.

Jean brought me to Coursegoules, and I was put on the table of the bar that was at the entrance of the town. They went to get an otorinolaryngologist who was on vacation named Dr Butruille-Mignon. When he saw my state he said: "We can't leave him with his face hanging open like that, we have to do something." I was stitched up with a mending needle and sewing thread. I still have facial paralysis, which is why I don't have any wrinkles on my left forehead. That is how I saved myself.

When I was laying on the table in the bar, three or four people were around me, and suddenly one person bent down and said: "But it's Coche! Would you like a priest to come?" For me, a priest meant that I would die. That caused a reaction in me and I almost insulted him. I said: "I don't want to die! What will the priest be for? I don't want to die!" He was shocked. He was Jean Onimus, my philosophy teacher from Lycée Massena, who was on vacation with his family. The people from Cousegoules hid me in some straw in a sheep barn. For 10 days I was fed milk and honey through a straw, and then the Americans arrived and took care of me.

Marcel Coche returned home a few days later, once Nice had been liberated:

My stepmother opened the door: "But what are you doing here? We received a telegram saying you were dead." Dr Barbary's daughters had sent a telegram to my family, but they didn't receive it. My father had taken a neighbor, Pierre Miquel, and with my elder brother, a fireman, and a car, they had left to try to retrieve my body, thinking I was dead.

After the German attack on their positions on the 21st and the death of Jean Natale, the *maquisard*s pulled out of the Carros area, took refuge in the mountains further north, and made no more attempts to attack down the Var Valley. American soldiers of the 517th Parachute Regimental Combat Team would reach Carros the 26th, liberating the town for good.

The Germans Counterattack at Levens

We saw previously that the FTPs had occupied Levens August 16th, and that the Germans had tolerated their presence without reacting for several days, probably because they already had enough on their hands with the Allied invasion. The German troops in St Blaise simply held their ground, without attempting to push the *maquisard*s back into the mountains. This stalemate lasted until August 24th, by which time the tactical situation compared to that of August 15th had changed drastically for the Germans. The Allied troops were now nearing the Var River very fast, making the control of the Var River and of the Pont Charles Albert a top priority. German troops that had been holding the front lines in the landing zone had now retreated and become available for other duties. *Reserve Grenadier Bataillon 164*, which had previously been engaged in the Cannes area, received the mission of retaking Levens and the Pont Charles Albert. On the 24th (or perhaps on the 23rd, as this date is also mentioned as being the date of the attack by several period documents), *Bataillon 164* attacked Levens from the directions of St Blaise and Tourrette-Levens, surprising the poorly-armed and disorganized FTP outposts. **Raymond Bolini**, who was only 14 years old at the time, had acted as a messenger for the FTPs during the Occupation and was now with the *Groupe Balzac* of the 8th FTPF Company in their advanced position in St Claire, on the road between Levens and Tourrette-Levens. He detailed the circumstances of the German attack in a letter he sent to the family of one of the FTP casualties shortly afterwards:

11 o'clock in the morning. The little camp that our group forms is preparing to welcome the lunch that two comrades, Jean Roux and another, have gone to fetch in Levens, which is one kilometer away. Each one of us is preparing a spot to eat peacefully; nobody pays attention to the weapons, which are either stacked or leaning in a corner.

Suddenly a car appears, then another, with trucks following. "Les *Boches*" screams somebody with the effect of a lightning strike. Everybody shouts, gesticulates, and runs for the weapons. Some fire, others hide or escape. On the way, I grab a rifle and hand it to someone. Somebody yells: "Don't leave, you cowards, we will hold them back!" I recognize him, it is Mauvignant (called Médel in the Underground), and he starts firing, showing by example. He shouts: "To the machine gun." Bonne Aventure rushes forth, but doesn't know his weapon. Everyone screams: "Fire for God's sake, fire!" He finds the trigger, presses it, and shots go off. He pulverizes a side car with a machine gun and kills three *Boches*.

The Germans deploy on the hill facing us. They have set up three mortars and four 37mm cannons. The cannons are on the road, with the *Boches* below. There are about 200 of them, four trucks full, and cars and motorcycles. There are only 24 *maquisards*, half of whom are not firing. The Germans start coming up, throwing grenades.

I try to escape, running straight ahead into the forest, but soon find myself facing a bare clearing with no cover, so I hide in a hole. I look up, and a bit lower down I spot Médel, who is leaning against a terrace, seeming to be suffering horribly from his stomach. A German arrives and points his rifle at him, saying: "Get up." At that moment, Médel pulls a gun out from behind him and fires point blank. A flame, a detonation, and the *Boche* collapses with his black face covered in blood. Hearing the noise, a second German approaches, but he keeps his distance.

Further on, a *maquisard* (Barbier) is captured, as am I soon afterwards. The *Boche* ordered us to take Médel and bring him to the road. On the way he kept telling us: "Leave me be, can't you see that it is over, it is useless." His wound looked like a gaping mouth with lips that hung horribly. His blood runs onto my leg.

We have now reached the path and we delicately put him down against a tree. A German asks him: "For what do terrorist? Now kaput." He answered proudly: "Me kaput. Yes! But I killed one!" He points out a weapon that a German is holding. I recognize it, it is a chromed pistol with pearly handles. He goes on: "The Americans are not very far off anymore, they are going to come and you will get a battering dirty *Boches*." At that moment, they made us move slightly further on. I hear a gunshot. Médel collapses and slowly roles into the ditch, his head folded against his knees, his fists on his face, his back uncovered. That is how I saw Médel for the last time. We were kept as prisoners in a house in Nice.[10]

It would seem that Raymond Bolini romanced the St Claire attack in this letter, as it was meant to console Max Mauvignant's family. He mentions the death of four Germans, when no trace of a single German casualty can actually be found for this time frame and area. Raymond Bolini himself gave what is probably a more realistic version of events years later, also explaining what happened to himself and some of the other FTPs after their capture. The differences in the two versions of **Raymond Bolini**'s story prove how difficult it is to attempt to objectively find out what occurred in such combat situations, as even the same witness tells a different story:

I was captured under Levens in a district called St Claire. There were seven or eight of us, including an Italian deserter who couldn't speak French and always spoke in Italian. We were all captured because it was a bad position, with our backs against a hill. When the Germans arrived, gunfire erupted all over the place. They were firing so much with what was probably a machine gun that we were pinned down. I got down into a deep hole and didn't see anything. I didn't have a weapon or anything, and at my age I couldn't do anything anyway. Then somebody came and tapped me on the shoulder and we were all brought together.

When there have been exchanges of gunfire and things, it is always quite nervous. The atmosphere is so tense that a gesture or a word can make a catastrophe happen. It is very hard to control, your state of mind is altered. Mauvignant and Barbier were killed immediately. The Germans had taken all the weapons, but at one point

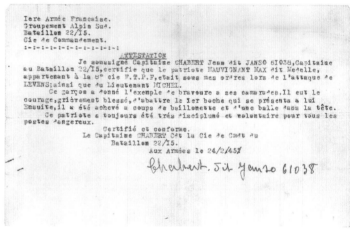

23-year-old FTP Max Mauvignant, who was captured by the Germans at St Claire August 24th and immediately executed at the side of the road because of his insolent behavior. Mauvignant Family Collection.

Barbier lifted up his arms and they noticed that he had a grenade in his belt, so they killed him. As for Mauvignant, he had a very nervous character, and he was insulting them and saying all sorts of things. It angered them, so they immediately took him, killed him, and threw him into the ditch, the soldiers shouting: "Raus!" They were pushing us around, and it bothered them enormously to have to go back down to Nice. I even thought they would kill all of us on the side of the road and continue on, but since there were eight or ten of us there, it was a big problem.

We were brought down to St André on foot, then up to Cimiez, where we were locked in the basement of a villa called "Les Arénas." There were hooks on the wall, and they took chains and padlocks and chained us up. We were all stuck in there and we didn't speak to each other or anything, we were in sort of a state of shock. We couldn't sit down, we could only bend our knees and hang by our wrists. I had chain marks on my wrists for three or four months afterwards.

The next morning, the guys were interrogated. We had not eaten or drank, and they came to interrogate us one by one. That is when people started disappearing. A soldier would open the locks, take them up to be interrogated, and then they would disappear. I was among the two or three first ones to be taken up. I went up to the ground floor with a soldier accompanying me with a rifle. Then an officer walked by and told the soldier to come with him, so he told me to wait. It was the day of the Liberation, so it was full of soldiers and vehicles and things like that, and there was a toilet, a hole that had been dug in the ground by the soldiers. Since I had not gone in two or three days, I entered the toilet and did what I had to do. I was perched up on some pieces of wood, with branches isolating me from the villa, so I climbed onto the pieces of wood and looked at what was on the other side of the wall. I saw the next villa was empty, so I jumped over the wall and escaped. There was gunfire in the streets of Nice and I had to go to Mont Alban. Since I hadn't eaten or drank or anything, I was completely exhausted when I got home. My mother made me some mashed potatoes with a bit of olive oil and I ate that and vomited. I couldn't eat, my stomach was all tensed up and I went to bed. I was extremely tired.

I was later used as a witness, because I am the last one to have seen many people alive. Since he wasn't from our region, I am sure that nobody in the world will ever know what happened to the Italian soldier who was with us. I can still see his face, though it happened 50 years ago. He was small stocky guy, very friendly, a bit shy, with his hair parted on the side. He must have been from southern Italy, so when he deserted, he decided to join us in the *maquis* instead of crossing all through Italy. I am the last one to have seen that guy. He disappeared completely, and he probably had relatives that never found out what happened to him. That is the big problem in those circumstances, it is one of the most miserable aspects of war.

Because the real identity of many *maquisards* was not even known by their own comrades, it was indeed sometimes impossible to establish what had happened to whom. The semi-official conclusion about the attack on St Claire on August 24, 1944, is that 23-year-old **Max Mauvignant** was killed and that 19-year-old **Roger Barbier** was reported missing. Although Raymond Bolini claims that Barbier was shot immediately, another witness, l'Abbé Belckx, told Barbier's family that Barbier had also been brought back to Nice and that he was killed at a later date. Roger Barbier's brother Casimir had already been reported missing in Cannes a few days earlier, and no

trace of either brother has ever been found since. The fact that Roger Barbier's body was not found at St Claire seems to indicate that Abbé Belckx's version of his death is the correct one.

Although it is known that several other *maquisards* were captured by the Germans at St Claire (FTP Laurent Pasquier mentions four prisoners in his diary) and probably later killed, their names are not mentioned on any monuments or official documents. At the same time as they attacked at St Claire, the Germans also attacked towards Levens from St Blaise, once again surprising the FTPs guarding the area, as **Joseph Garnero**, of the 8th FTPF Company, remembers:

> Around noon, the Germans arrived from the Route de St Blaise. We were on a curve and they surprised us. I personally was barefoot and washing my feet because we had been walking a lot. The Germans arrived with armored cars and everything. At first, I wasn't even able to fight back because my rifle was a bit further on. **René Antoniucci** fell down beside me immediately. Unfortunately, we were on terraces and he fell and rolled over the wall. There was shooting going on, but two of us tried to get him and pull him up, but it was impossible, because we needed to face the Germans and fight. Then the Germans submerged us and we were forced to pull back. Claude Rivolta and Edouard Bremont were still firing at them from above, they still had bullets left. I didn't have any cartridges or anything. I even threw away my rifle. The Germans killed Antoniucci there, we saw them hitting him in the face and finishing him off with rifle butts.
>
> When we had left for the *maquis*, Antoniucci was supposed to come with us. But he was an only son and he told us: "I am not coming because my mother doesn't want me to." When the Germans halted us in Levens, a truck driver from the Pont Charles Albert took his truck and drove down into the valley to recruit as many young people as he could to help us. He came back with Antonocchi and he was put in my group. He was dead one hour after reaching us. I don't think he had even been given a weapon yet.

The surviving *maquisards* retreating from the St Claire and St Blaise outposts were able to warn the main force in Levens of the imminent German attacks. **Primo Calzoni**, one of the commanders of the 8th FTPF Company, explains how the German attack was halted before they reached Levens:

> At Levens on the 23rd, the guys thought that because we were occupying the village, everything was over. Nobody was on guard duty. Some were washing in the water tank when the German convoy arrived. We had one or two killed and some wounded. An Italian had his arm cut off. (…) I myself arrived along the road while the guys were retreating. Lucky thing, because some guys were stuck in the water tank under German fire. I covered them with my American rifle, firing on the crew of a small cannon that the Germans were setting up. One German fell and the others disappeared.
>
> I was with Marengo and Denis, and we ran and sometimes crawled all along the meadow. At the Gendarmerie we took up positions again. That is where we saw the Poles who were with Morgan stopping the German progression with their machine guns.[11]

23- and 19-year-old brothers Casimir and Roger Barbier. Roger was captured by the Germans in Levens August 24th, as Casimir had been a few days before in Cannes. Both are reported as missing ever since. Hélène Ghintran Collection.

Antoine Caviglia, who was accompanying Calzoni in these moments, tells us a bit more about the wounded Italian *maquisard* and Morgan's Poles:

> I saw an Italian comrade with a crushed elbow whose arm was dangling. The inhabitants gave us sheets to bandage him. One part of our group, with Pedro, was positioned at the edge of the meadow to fire on the flank of the Germans coming up from St Claire. There were two Poles belonging to the *Compagnie* Morgan. With a machine gun, they stopped the German advance.[12]

We will get back to the wounded Italian a bit later, but first we will see how the attack was halted according to **Norbert Jamme**, known as *Commandant* Job, who was second in command of the Resistance forces in the Levens area. He later wrote:

> We were in the middle of a conference with Jeanseau, Las, and Chabert, who commanded the 8th and 27th FTPF Companies, as well as with a few old *maquisard*s who were supposed to supervise the new men: Denis, Mathe, Labbé, and Rodez. Suddenly, a comrade who was rather panicked arrived, shouting: "The *Boches* are coming!" Indeed, one of the three forward scouts of the Route de St André had just arrived. His two friends had been killed. We would find them the next day: "Le Parisien" had been riddled with bullets, while the other, Antoniucci, from St Martin du Var, a good looking boy, had been pierced with bayonets and the Nazi barbarians had gouged his eyes out.
>
> Decisions were immediately discussed and taken to prevent the *Boches* from entering Levens. The following plan was quickly decided on and executed. Captain Albertini (Commanding the 27th Company), with two machine guns and supported by all the weapons of the section, would take position along a little wall at the foot of the hill that rises on the right side of the road towards the first houses of the village.
>
> With the two heavy machine guns of *Groupe* Charly (AS) that I went to fetch in the middle of the village and all the available small arms, I took position almost facing the road, slightly to the left; not on the summit of the hill nor on the slope, as any professional strategist would have done in my place, but in the little ditch at the foot of the hill, just under the straw that flanked the left side of the road for 300 meters after exciting a forest before the entrance of the village. Lying down like that, we were absolutely invisible from 30 steps away. Only the barrels of our weapons emerged from the thick straw.
>
> I was behind two Polish deserters from the German army who were manning the heavy machine guns taken from the Germans. Only they knew how they functioned. My trust in them was limited, and I clenched my pistol in my hand a bit too nervously. We were waiting for the *Boches*. The wait was short, very short.
>
> Having probably placed their mortars at the edge of the forest, they were advancing through the straw along the road in a line of skirmishers. I was jubilant. Albertini was only to open fire after our first shot. I waited until the extreme limit. Behind and around me I could feel the comrades, who were as tense as ropes: "But what is he waiting for, good God?!"
>
> They were perhaps 50 meters away when, in German, I murmured *"Feuer"* to my two Poles, for whom Lt Berard was acting as ammunition server. At once a hellfire was released. All the weapons fired, not leaving a chance to the Germans, even those who lay down on the ground. For our enemies it was a surprise, a complete rout, and a general escape.
>
> On his side, Las (Albertini) had taken the Germans under flanking fire with his machine guns, and the *Boches* who still could ran breathlessly towards the small forest. A few comrades chased after them, picking up numerous machine guns and rifles left behind by the escapees, wounded, and the many dead.
>
> Knowing that the *Boches* in the forest were going to set off deadly mortar fire and that we were unable to respond to it, I ordered to retreat along the little ditch, as we had decided beforehand. Indeed, a few instants later, mortars fired their rockets onto the slopes and summit of the hill. But nobody was left on the hill, nor around the village. Our war trick had worked perfectly and entirely. The enemy had been completely surprised and our fire had cut him down just as the good peasants had scythed their wheat a few days earlier. The first battle of Levens was won for the FFI of the Maritime Alps against the *Boches*, who had been hit hard, and did not try to enter the village that day.[13]

The Germans had indeed temporarily been repulsed, but the reader must be warned that everything indicates that Jamme's much publicized account of his own exploit is grossly exaggerated to say the least, to the point that it could be considered a source of misinformation. In another version of his text, he even went as far as to claim that the Germans had suffered 200 casualties in the attack! In fact, no trace of a single German killed can be clearly attributed to the events in Levens August 24th! No corresponding dead were buried anywhere in the area, except one man who died at the German field hospital in Cimiez, most likely after having been wounded elsewhere, as he was not a member of *Bataillon 164*. No other period witnesses (such as Calzoni and Caviglia, whose accounts were shown previously) or documents mention such a glorious and successful ambush, nor do any period documents mention that Antoniucci's eyes were gouged out. The local religious community who buried Antoniucci, as well as Dr Flavier, the local doctor, both left written accounts about the fighting, and neither mentions any such abuse to his body.

Dr Flavier did, on the other hand, describe the precarious conditions in which he had to treat *maquisard*s who had been wounded in the fighting, including the Italian, whose severe elbow wound was previously mentioned by Calzoni and Caviglia. **Dr Flavier** worked on them in a hospice that had become a makeshift hospital in Levens, where the wounded (Such as German "Hans Müller," wounded in the *Commandant* Gérôme shooting.) had been brought since August 15th:

> I must briefly explain how the wounded were hospitalized. At night, or at nightfall, they were brought with honking horns, first to my house, then to the hospital if I was unable to treat them at home. Two cases come back to memory. At nightfall, I see a young 20-year-old man with a bullet wound; I suspected it was a gastric perforation.
>
> Knowing that my friend C. was at the Hotel de T.L. [sic], I send him a message, asking him to come to help out at the earliest. He didn't have any instruments and I barely had anything more. Nevertheless, we manage to find a scalpel, some tweezers, some sewing thread for hemostasis, and white horsehair from the tail of the mule belonging to the old doctor of R. [sic] to sew up the gastric wall.

A puff of ether to the patient; ironed towels were used to make an operating field, a bit of iodine on the skin, and off we go. We open the poor kid's abdomen, turn the stomach around on all its sides: impossible to find the bullet's exit hole. We close him back up, and in spite of his bad general condition and a more than doubtful (so as not to say absent) asepsis, we put the almost-dead man to bed. The next day, surprise: he is still alive. The prayers of the nuns were surely more effective than our surgical exploits. After several adventures, at the end of the "funny war," this victim came back to ask for a certificate mentioning his passage at the Levens Hospital.

This leads me to a second very interesting case: it concerns an Italian individual coming from who knows where. He had received a projectile that had shattered his, I think, left elbow, causing a serious hemorrhage bringing him to the brink of death. We needed to act fast.

After having found a tube of catgut, after a good cleaning of the wound and after having stopped the hemorrhage with a decent hemostasis, the humerus needed to be sawed off. Four or five young people from the AS were there to help me, but since they were fainting I asked one of them to quickly fetch the butcher's saw and to clean it carefully. The cutting of the humerus: I was lucky to be assisted by Dr H. Duplay, who is currently a professor in Nice University Hospital. There were no major post operative incidents.

All these "clients," German, Italian, and French, needed to be fed. We didn't have anything, so it was the triumph of the rectal drop by drop. The two or three ampoules of physiological fluid were replaced by boiled water salted at about seven per thousand.

The amputee, as did the stomach case, later came to get a certificate reporting his passage in Levens. He was alive and seemed relatively happy with his fate, as he was going to receive a pension.[14]

16-year-old **Yvette Septembre** was one of the young volunteers who helped Dr Flavier in the hospice. She remembers the German, so-called "Hans Müller," who had been wounded in the August 15th *Commandant* Gérôme shooting, particularly well:

There was a German who had been wounded by the partisans, and they brought him up to the hospice in Levens, where he was treated by Dr Flavier, who was a country doctor and who was also a member of the Resistance. There were four or five of us, including a young doctor who was still studying medicine, and at night we went to keep watch over the German, who by the way was a very handsome man. He was in a sorry state. He had been shot in the spine and was completely paralyzed. We had to feed him.

The summer of '44 was very, very hot, and at night he was moaning because of the heat, because he couldn't move. I remember we needed to sponge him. But we all acted very humanely, in spite of our opinions. In any case, I think that in the face of disease and pain, people forget about many things. But he moaned quite a bit because he was suffering, and on top of that, he couldn't express himself, not knowing the language and not being able to make himself understood. So we had called the Belgian priest [Father Warrant] who could speak German to come and talk with him.

According to Yvette Septembre, and contrary to what was later reported in the *l'Ergot* article about the *Commandant* Gérôme

incident, this German soldier did not die, but was later evacuated by the Germans. Considering her direct involvement with the wounded man, Yvette Septembre's version seems more credible.

The Germans Recapture Levens

We have now seen how *Reserve Grenadier Bataillon 164* launched a serious counterattack towards Levens August 24th, surprising the partisans and inflicting casualties on them, but without managing to push on into Levens itself. The next day, August 25th, *Bataillon 164* repeated its attack, this time successfully retaking Levens, as well as la Roquette. It would seem that the FTPs, well aware of their inferiority after the first day of fighting, decided to pull out on their own once they realized that the Germans' intentions were serious. This was in the normal spirit of guerilla warfare, the point not being to hold a line or resist to the last, but to harass the enemy, then disappear when the enemy reacts.

In the early morning of August 25th, a group of men of the 10th Company of *Bataillon 164* were sent out along the RN 202 towards the Pont Charles Albert, on what was apparently supposed to be a reconnaissance patrol to determine the location of the Resistance outposts. A group of *maquisard*s was guarding the bridge as the Germans approached, however. **FFI** *Sous-Lieutenant* **Silve**, a career officer, was present and later wrote:

August 23rd [Frequently when the Resistance is concerned, there are mistakes in the exact dates]. With the good team of Ben, Robert, Loulou, Gendarme Domoy, Casimir, and a few others, we go rummaging around the

This photo of the Pont Charles Albert being bombed by the American Air Force was taken in the months before the invasion. The RN 202 Highway is clearly visible to the right of the photo, flanking the Var River. August 25, 1944, the maquisards were in position in the bomb craters near the bridge when they noticed a German bicycle patrol coming towards them from the direction of St Martin du Var, at the bottom of this photo. NARA.

Charles Albert Bridge, the only passage over the lower valley of the river. It is early, at daybreak, and a bit misty.

Suddenly, in front of us, on the road some 200 meters away, is a platoon of cyclists dressed completely in black. We have not been spotted. Domoy sets up his machine gun, and the others spread out into the bushes to the left of the road. Fire! The surprise is complete: like a flight of sparrows, some collapse on the road, while the others abandon their bicycles and leap under cover. Others on foot appear further on and disappear into the undergrowth.

Intense exchanges of gunfire, and we can't see further then 10 meters. But the bushes seem to be coming alive on our left; the second German wave is maneuvering to outflank us. We need to pull out, as there are only a handful of us, perhaps a dozen. Casimir the Pole, a former jokey and legionnaire of the REC [Foreign Legion Cavalry Regiment], tells me: "Chief, we have to bluff them and make them believe that there are many of us, otherwise we are done for."

So, to put on airs, we fire with all our weapons and with Casimir yelling: "Kompanie, Vorwärts," and we make a leap forward. Things don't drag on; we pick up two young *Waffen-SS* soldiers, then turn right towards the road, where seven bodies are lying. We quickly recover some bicycles, packs, a few weapons… and we return, running or pedaling, to Plan du Var with our two rascals.[15]

Local FFI volunteer **René Miquelis** was also involved in this fire fight and describes a slightly different version of the story, including a rather unmilitary detail:

Around August 20th, I am in one of the craters dug by Allied bombs in the RN 202 beside the Pont Charles Albert. [The bridge had been bombed several times over the previous months.] There are 12 to 15 of us there, with an experienced Pole serving as our commander… The sentry alerts us: a German cyclist detachment is at the end of the straightaway… We open fire (we would find two dead later on), and the Germans disappear… With two comrades, I receive the mission of going towards the wooded slopes [to the east of the road] and to fire as much as possible, because we needed to make believe that there were large numbers of us. Our Pole shouts: "First compagnie, feuier, zecond compagnie, feuier…" and we fire each time.

Our bluff apparently succeeds, because we are firing from all over: from the side of the mountain and from the road. Even if we can't see anybody, we fire into locations where they could be. There are houses, so we fire into the windows of the houses to make it look like there are large numbers of us. The Germans retreat when they realize that there is gunfire coming from everywhere. They are in a state of uncertainty, because they don't know what our strength is.

I almost get killed, because my resistance chief, Captain Benoit, had been an armored officer, and when I left for the *maquis*, he had given me his tanker's helmet. But I am the only one who has a helmet, so in the forest, when a friend who has gone off to one side sees a helmet in the bushes, he shoots at it. It was me. He had mistaken me for a German, but luckily he misses me.

Amongst us there is a Gendarme from Villars who had joined the *maquis*… When we send him to get water, he discovers the stockroom of what must have been a bar facing the bridge. The water he found was good, but so were the liquors and alcohols… A runner from the CP arrives. When

he sees the state we are in, he immediately returns to the CP to tell them what he saw… We were quickly relieved…

Later in the day, the Resistance was obliged to abandon its positions at the Charles Albert Bridge because the Germans had captured the terrain overlooking the bridge from the east, as we will soon see. Regarding the German casualties of the gunfight, **René Miquelis** added:

The two dead were buried in the fields below the road and they remained there for a very long time. It was unfortunate, because we figured they must have been a company of veterans, since they were on bicycles. I was a *maquisard*, I fought against the Germans and we had suffered from them, but when I later drove by there, I thought: "It is terrible, here are two poor guys who must have had families and who came to die here, next to the road, in an unknown country." War really isn't a nice thing.

As often, the truth about the German casualties became highly deformed in the memories of the witnesses. In the two preceding accounts, *Sous-Lieutenant* Silve claims that seven bodies of German *Waffen-SS* dressed in black were left behind after the shooting, while René Miquelis remembers that only two elder "veterans" were killed. It is interesting to note that there were of course no SS troops in the order of battle of *Reserve Division 148*, and that, in any case, *Waffen-SS* infantrymen did not wear black uniforms! The postwar exhumation reports enable us to sweep away these inconsistencies: in fact, only one German soldier was killed in the shooting at the Pont Charles Albert August 25th. He was neither an SS soldier nor an elderly veteran, but a regular 18-year-old recruit named **Johann Schmidt**, of the 10th Company of *Bataillon 164*. In the following weeks, Johann Schmidt's father received the following letter from the company commander, **Lt Buchmann**, announcing his son's death:

In the field, September 4, 1944.
Dear Mr Schmidt!

I have the sad duty of having to inform you that your son, *Grenadier* Johann Schmidt, born June 2, 1926, was killed by a gunshot to the femoral artery August 25, 1944. He was buried for his last rest next to the road north of St Martin du Vor [sic].

With the death of your son, the company loses one of its best soldiers, as well a company runner who was brave and bold at all times. Because of his friendliness and always helpful manner, he was liked and valued by all the members of the company.

The company knows that you, dear Mr Schmidt, as well as your wife, have suffered a heavy blow due to the loss of your son. May it bring you a bit of comfort in these hours to know that your son gave his young life for the existence of our *Grossdeutsches Reich* and for a better future. (…)

With my deepest sympathies, I greet you with
Heil Hitler!

Buchmann
Lieutenant and Company Commander.[16]

Repulsing the German patrol at the bridge was the last success the Resistance forces would have in the Levens area. In the early afternoon, *Bataillon 164* attacked towards Levens from

18-year-old Grenadier Johann Schmidt, of the 10th Company of Bataillon 164, who was shot and killed when the Germans probed the Resistance positions at the Pont Charles Albert the morning of August 25, 1944. He was apparently the only casualty of the attack, contrary to exaggerated claims made by some of the maquisards, and was buried in a field next to the RN 202 highway. Schmidt Family Collection.

the Tourrette-Levens area, like it had the previous day. This time, the partisans retreated and the Germans seized Levens. The local religious community wrote a small text resuming what occurred August 25th and in the preceding days:

August 23rd, around eleven in the morning, [the Germans] attack with a cannon and a mortar. The Férion pine forest catches fire. (…) The Patriots strike back courageously. Bullets whistle and shells burst. We huddle in the rooms and pray zealously. The battle continues on the 24th. The Patriots have had two killed [Antoniucci and Mauvignant], whom we bury in the noise of battle. Reinforced by the FFI (…), they contain the Germans until the morning of August 25th.

One incident that could have had grave consequences deserves to be mentioned. At the moment when the Germans were assaulting up the hill, a wounded Patriot came asking for us to help him. Several of his comrades follow him through the half-open door. Soon German silhouettes appear beside the war monument. Will the house, that is full of children, become the scene of an atrocious struggle? Luckily, such is not the case and the Patriots move away without being spotted by their adversaries. The divine protection over our house is manifest.

August 25th, the Patriots pull out of Levens, but they continue firing from the sides of Mount Férion, and we are still in the midst of the struggle, for the Germans have set up a cannon at the roundabout and a mortar in the ruins of the castle and the battle goes on fiercely.[17]

Laurent Pasquier, of the 27th FTPF Company, also described the battle of August 24th and the next day's retreat in his diary:

August 24th. The runner warns us that the *Fritzes* have attacked Levens. The chief asks for six volunteers to go and neutralize the cannon that is at the end of the air strip and firing at our buddies. I leave with the volunteers. After a difficult and perilous march, we arrive just as the fight was over, and the *Boches* retreat with casualties. On the FTP side, we have had two killed, three wounded, and four prisoners.

In the evening, I volunteer again with four buddies and a machine gun to go and occupy the bridge at the fork in the roads going to Tourrette-Levens and Contes. In the meantime, the company pulls back to St Jean la Rivière and forgets about us. Around three in the morning, we hear the Germans talking just below us. A truck finally comes to fetch us and we leave in silence, for the *Fritzes* have taken up positions 300 meters away.

August 24th. We go back to Levens to take up positions at "La Pologne." Everything goes well until 13:00, when "The Corsican" and I get baptized by mortar shells. The two first shells land 20 meters from where we are lying. Around 15:00, *Commandant* Jeansau orders us to evacuate the area. With a thousand difficulties, we pull back towards Duranus and St Jean la Rivière, on foot and loaded down. We reach St Jean around 23:00, where we gladly swallow some bad soup; we hadn't eaten anything since the night before.[18]

Local civilian **Louis Maurel**, who was 16 years old at the time, remembers some of the less flattering details of the behavior of certain *maquisard*s as they departed:

> I remember what happened August 25th. My father was the town hall secretary, and every morning he opened the town hall at nine. We lived five kilometers away from the village on the Route de Duranus, and that morning I accompanied my father, because I knew that the village was occupied by the *résistants*, in other words, the FTP, *Armée Secrète*, and FFI— several different groups. Around ten in the morning, bullets started whistling through the village. Around noon, my father came out of the town hall with some of the resistance men. We left down the Route de Duranus, where we met all those *résistants* who were escaping towards Duranus. I saw some who were removing their armbands and hiding them between the stones in the walls. They were afraid the Germans would arrest them and were being cautious. Where I was with my family, we saw such a confusion of *Armée Secrète*, FFI, and FTP… they were almost in opposition with each other, instead of being together and coordinated. When the Germans reached Levens, they didn't go any further than the Route de Duranus because they were scared stiff of the *résistants*, the terrorists, as they called them.

Behind them, the *maquisard*s left 23-year-old **Joseph Bailet**, who was killed in Levens. A second resistance fighter was also apparently killed near the Pont de Fer, though it has not been able to determine who he was. **Louis Maurel** saw the body of this second casualty as he walked out of town towards Duranus:

> He was probably a *résistant*. We never found out who he was. He was killed the afternoon of the 25th, and when my father and I walked by we saw the fresh blood. He had been buried, but we could still almost see his arm protruding from the ground.

A search of the exact location where the body had been buried and later exhumed revealed a French military button marked "Equipement Militaire," seeming to confirm that the body that had been buried there was that of a *maquisard* who had been equipped with old French army issue items. With the *maquisard*s now gone into the mountains, *Reserve Grenadier Bataillon 164* entered Levens and occupied the village. **Yvette Septembre** remembers the very unpleasant circumstances of the arrival of the Germans:

> We were told: "The Germans are coming," so most of the population escaped into the mountains, into the Férion. But we decided to stay, saying: "We will see what happens." At home, I remember we had resistance papers that were compromising for my father, so we burned everything with my mother and one of my sisters.
>
> We saw the Germans arriving in their cars and trucks. They got out and immediately came and knocked at our houses to make us come outside. That is when it was the hardest. The men over 18 and under 60 were locked into the small chapel, and we, the women and children, were lined up in the town square with submachine guns pointed at our stomachs. We thought they were going to shoot us. I can honestly say that I was praying. I was dying of fear. Some people tell you that they aren't afraid, but I was. I was very afraid and that's all, because when you see guys like that with a machine gun pointed at you, you don't feel braver than anybody else.

> We had a priest [Abbé Warrant] who was Belgian, and who could speak German fluently, and he spoke with the Germans for a long time, first in the church, then in the town square. After standing there for three hours, the Germans let us go. We all thought that it was thanks to Dr Flavier, who had treated that wounded German, and thanks to that priest, that they did not kill us or burn down the village.

15-year-old **Roger Bovis**, who lived below Levens, was among the men who were locked in the chapel:

> I remember, they arrived and came to my place and interrogated my father, then they interrogated me and took all my identification papers. In the afternoon, the order came for all the men to go to the town square. I went with my father and elder brother, and my younger brother stayed behind with my mother. All the men from the village were there, except those who had escaped. There were at least 150 or 200 of us.
>
> They locked us in the chapel and we stayed there all night. Everybody was standing up, because it was a small chapel. There was a cannon in the square facing us that was pointed towards the chapel, ready to fire. People's spirits weren't high, but I wasn't in contact with them, because I had climbed under the roof with a friend of mine who lived in Levens and who said: "Don't worry, we are safe. If something happens down there, we will get out of here, I know all the roofs in Levens."
>
> We had a priest who came to the town square and spoke with the German officers all night. Maybe he protected us, who knows, because it was said that the Germans were supposed to burn the village down.

The men were forced to spend all the following nights in the chapel as well, until the final departure of the Germans. The presence of the Germans in Levens forced the *résistants* to evacuate the area of the Pont Charles Albert that they had managed to defend that morning, and to retreat to the right bank of the Vésubie River, north of the Pont Durandy. By late in the day August 25th, the Germans had managed to regain virtually all the strategic territory that the Resistance had seized August 15th and 16th. The 12th Company of *Bataillon 164* now occupied Levens and prepared to defend the area against possible attacks from both the Resistance and the Americans. Some Germans took up quarters in **Yvette Septembre**'s house. She was rather puzzled by their behavior, after her initial experience of having been held on the town square at gunpoint:

> The Germans moved into our apartment because there was a good view on Bonson, a village on the other side of the Var that overlooks the Pont Durandi. So from there, with their devices, they had a good view to see what the Americans were doing. At night we were forced to leave and sleep elsewhere, but during the day we were next to the Germans, and they always behaved in the most correct manner, I have to admit. In our house there were lots of things, including precious items that friends had left with us, thinking our place was safe: they didn't touch a thing! We even received a 50 Franc bill from the German officer with a note to excuse himself because his men had dared take a bottle of wine and so he was reimbursing us.

The Germans Capture la Roquette sur Var

As soon as Levens was taken August 25th, the 9th Company of *Bataillon 164* advanced south from Levens to capture the strategic village la Roquette sur Var, which commanded the Var valley for miles to the south. On their way towards la Roquette, the Germans were ambushed by the Resistance. Young **Adèle Tacconi** lived in an isolated farm at the foot of Arpasse Mountain that overlooked the road from Levens to la Roquette at the location of the ambush. Although she was only seven years old at the time, the events of that day left a lasting impression on her:

In the morning, the *résistants* had come to see us, telling us that the main German force was in Levens, so we should not panic if we saw them coming. One of the resistance chiefs, Captain Roger, told my mother: "If you don't want to see your sons die in front of your eyes, they have to come with us, because the Germans are coming." So my brothers immediately left with them into the forest.

We had closed everything up and were hiding behind the shutters in my parents' room, but the shutters were old and there was a space beneath them. We were looking through that space down onto the road and indeed, at one point, I think it was 10 in the morning, we saw six Germans on bicycles arrive on the road below us, singing and whistling. At that moment, the *résistants*, who were probably hiding in the forest behind our house, opened fire on them, and with my father we saw the Germans toppling off their bikes and falling.

They killed quite a few, but I think one German wasn't killed; he must have only been wounded in the legs and he understood that the gunfire was coming from up above, so he rolled himself over the others and up to the little road parapet; that way he was under cover and could not be seen from up above. Later on, when the main body of the Germans arrived, he must have told them that the attack had come from our house, when in fact it had come from behind us, on the hill. So they started firing at the house until about 1 o'clock in the afternoon. We took shelter in the basement; lucky thing the house was solid, otherwise it would have collapsed.

Then the Germans came up to our house and searched all over the place for the terrorists, but they saw that there were no *résistants* in the house and that they must have been in the forest. My father, who was already old, said: "No, no, it didn't come from our place, we don't know." So then they searched the hill and found **Second Rossi**, one of the *résistants* from la Roquette, who had been killed in the fighting. I remember that we had no drinking water, we only had a well, and my mother was washing some cabbages. When the Germans arrived, they were so thirsty that they drank the water that she was washing the cabbages in.

The dead were buried immediately. They had crosses that I think were pre-made, because they weren't just made with any old pieces of wood; they were well made boards, and they put the helmet on them, then marked the name and date of birth: it was burned into the wood. One young guy was buried at the foot of an olive tree near the fountain on the path that led to our house. He was 17 years old, and I remember that my mother always said he was still just a kid.

One or two soldiers of the 9th Company of *Bataillon 164* had been killed in the attack: 17-year-old *Grenadier* **Johann Meyer** and 18-year-old *Grenadier* **Xaver Erhardt**. Johann Meyer was the one mentioned by Adèle Tacconi, who was buried beneath an olive tree, while Xaver Erhardt was buried slightly further down the road. Although the attack occurred August 25th, Meyer's official date of death is August 26th, so either there is a small mistake in his exact date of death, or his death is actually not linked to the ambush. After this first gunfight, the 9th company of *Bataillon 164* pushed down the road to seize la Roquette, which was occupied by a handful of *maquisards*. The inhabitants who were present at la Roquette when the Germans arrived would remember the date August 25, 1944, for the rest of their lives. **Bruno Municchi**, who was 10 years old at the time, was hiding in the basement of his house near the entrance of the village:

In the morning, the *maquisards* had seen the Germans down on the RN 202 and had fired at them with their machine gun. When the Germans heard that they figured: "The *maquisards* are up there." In the afternoon, around 3 o'clock, the Germans went through Levens, then came here. But if the *maquisards* hadn't fired, the Germans wouldn't have come. When there is a group like that, without enough people, they should have stayed quiet. There were only about 30 *maquisards*, and when they saw the Germans advancing they couldn't hold them back, it wasn't possible. The Germans had a machine gun and were firing, and the bullets were coming one after another as if it was raining. So the poor *maquisards* had to escape as best they could.

Bruno Municchi's 14-year-old brother **François Municchi** was hiding in the same basement, until he was called outside by a *maquisard*:

The Germans arrived from Levens. Before reaching the village they shelled

This photo shows the road that the German soldiers passed on with their bicycles August 25th, with Adèle Tacconi's house and Arpasse Mountain visible in the background. Author's Collection.

18-year-old Grenadier Xaver Erhardt, of the 9th Company of Bataillon 164, who was killed in the ambush the maquisards sprung on the Germans on the road between Levens and la Roquette August 25th. His body was buried at the side of the road. Erhardt Family Collection.

17-year-old Grenadier Johann Meyer, who was also apparently killed in the ambush, though his official date of death is August 26th. Meyer Family Collection, courtesy Dr. Hartmut Pöhlmann.

it, setting the forest all around the village on fire. I was at home at the entrance of the village with my father, mother, my brothers Léon and Bruno, and the neighbors, *Monsieur* and *Madame* Bovis. Because of the shelling, we all took shelter in the stable under the house. At one point *Monsieur* Bovis went outside, then came back to the basement and told my father: "You know *Monsieur* Municchi, the Germans are not far off. They are coming down beside the cemetery."

At the entrance of la Roquette the FFIs had a machine gun, but when the Germans came there were perhaps 600

of them, so the *maquisard*s were forced to leave and cross the Var River, otherwise they would have been killed. I left the basement because Antoine Raynaud—we called him "Being"—came and said: "François, come down and help me carry up some ammunition because the Germans aren't far away," and so he gave me a bag of cartridges. The Germans were already starting to enter the village. There was shooting going on all over and we could hear bullets hitting the walls. When we reached the village, I gave the bag of cartridges to Raynaud and said: "I am leaving you here and getting out of here," because we could hear bullets whistling all over the place.

In the village, I met my neighbors Prosper Bovis and César Baudoin, who were sitting at a table with César's parents, drinking a bottle of white wine. I told them: "But what are you doing? The Germans are coming! Go and hide!" "Oh," they replied, "we will stay here." I said: "We have always stayed together. All the others are in the Sainte Baume [A cave under the village]." But they told me: "No, we will stay here at home." I always remember that bottle of white wine they had on the table.

I turned back and went to the viewpoint at le Portalet [Le Portalet is a viewpoint in la Roquette that overlooks all the surrounding countryside.]. Clément Aguillon, who was a WWI veteran, was there and said: "What are you doing here? Look, the Germans are all around us and Francis and Jean are crossing the Var." Even the *maquisard*s who remained were escaping. So I returned to the Place du Château, and there a woman named Pauline Toche saw me from her window and said: "François, come in quickly, the Germans are coming!" She could see them from her window, but from the Place I couldn't, and then "bangbangbang," they fired and even broke the flower pots in front of her door. That is when she saved me; I went into her basement, where her husband and my brother Antoine were. There were five of us in there. After I entered we closed the door and then the Germans arrived. Madame Toche said: "Be careful, don't speak, the Germans are here."

The Germans were furious when they entered the village. They opened all the doors with rifle butts, then fired all over the place. I don't know if one of their men had been killed, but they were ferocious. It was incredible. They killed and killed. They were savages, real savages. A dog was barking and they shot it. They even killed the dog! They fired at anything that moved. And their faces! Oh! They were frightening. "Raus!" and they were shouting. We were in the basement, waiting. They broke down all the doors except the one to the basement. If they had touched it, all of us would have died.

The Germans started looking around, and all of a sudden they saw **Prosper Bovis** and **César Baudoin** and took the two of them. We were looking through the keyhole of the basement door and suddenly we saw Prosper and César with their hands up, with Germans pushing them forward with fixed bayonets. They made them climb an alley, then cross the Place du Château, then go down the other side. César was a guy that didn't speak, but Prosper was saying: "No, me nicht terrorist! No, me nicht terrorist!" and the Germans pushed them on: "Raus, raus!" We heard that, and I said: "Look, it's Prosper's voice." We recognized him because we were friends from la Roquette." I will always remember Prosper saying: "Me nicht terrorist!" and César's parents were following behind

In 2005, François Municchi shows Pauline Toche's house and the window from which she shouted to him to take refuge in her basement. The basement door is visible to the lower left of the photo. Author's Collection.

César Baudoin, aged 23, who was shot by the Germans because they assumed he was a partisan, though this was not actually the case. Charlotte Cruciani Collection.

saying: "No César, don't go, don't go, they are going to kill you! Come back home César!" and then they killed both of them in the alley just after the Place du Château. When the mother saw her dead son, she lay down on top of him. A German saw that she was crying over her son and lifted her up, saying: "Clear off, this is war." It was horrible. At that time, the Germans really wouldn't do you any favors. They were savages. They killed everything they saw. They took them out of the house and shot them in the alley like dogs.

Madame Toche said: "We heard gunshots, they have killed César and Prosper." In those old houses there are water tanks to collect rainwater, and after that she told us: "Get into the water tank, it will be better if ever they come in." The tank had a manhole to go into it and she said: "Get in this hole." We went in and Madame Toche hid the opening with pieces of wood so that they couldn't see it. There were four of us in the tank, and my brother Antoine was in an oil barrel with the cover on it. He was in pain because he was a *maquisard* and had been wounded in the calf by a shell fragment.

The Germans were opening all the doors, "bangbangbang," and then they saw Madame Toche on her doorstep: "You hiding terrorists! Terrorists!" "No, no, no. No terrorists." "Light! Turn on light!" But there was no more light because all the wires had been torn down by the shelling. She said: "No light. See the wires? Everything broken." They came back a moment later: "You hiding

terrorists!" "No, no terrorists, look, there is nothing" "OK. Ja, ja," and they left. If ever they had touched the wood hiding the opening to the tank and had seen it, they would have thrown a grenade or looked in with a flashlight. It was a miracle we didn't die, because we weren't meant to die. Our time hadn't come. They left and I was cold, because even in August it is cool in those tanks, so Madame Toche came and she gave me a tarpaulin that we used to pick up olives to cover me, then she said: "Tell François whatever he does, not to speak!"

François Municchi mentioned that his brother Antoine, who was part of the Resistance, had been wounded in the calf. **Bruno Municchi** tells us more about how he was wounded:

My brother Antoine was in the *maquis*. He was behind a small window down at the tip of the village with a friend of his from St Sauveur. The Germans had rifle grenades and they fired one, and it just happened to go through the window. My brother was wounded in the calf and the other guy was severely hit. To save the other guy, they brought him to the Cercle [The village club.], but a German opened the window and they threw a grenade in and finished him off.

François Municchi continues:

The *maquisard*s who were able to leave took off, but two were not able to. They were both from St Sauveur and one

19- and 37-year-old maquisards Alfred Agnese and Charles Puons were killed in the street fighting that occurred when the Germans captured la Roquette sur Var August 25th. Both men were inhabitants of the small mountain village of St Sauveur sur Tinée. Author's Collection.

was killed in the Cercle, the other behind the château. They were not able to escape because the Germans were coming. One was wounded and they brought him to the Cercle, put him under the pool table and closed the door. But he was shouting, he was wounded all over, and when the Germans arrived, opening all the doors, they threw a grenade in and that is how they killed him. The pool table was blown to pieces and we could see blood on the ceiling. It was terrible.

The two *maquisards* who had been killed in the Cercle and on a nearby street were 19-year-old **Alfred Agnese** and 37-year-old **Joseph Puons**. As for the civilians, **César Baudoin** and **Prosper Bovis**, they were aged 23 and 36. César Baudoin's niece, **Charlotte Cruciani**, was only five years old when the Germans entered la Roquette, but she remained traumatized by their behavior for the rest of her life:

The event that really struck me was when they came into our house. Instead of knocking on the door, they broke the door down with bayonets. My brother, mother, and I were standing against the wall, terrorized with fear. They went straight through the kitchen to the balcony, where they also broke down the door, then they left. When they walked back past us they jabbered a couple word; they were asking if there was a man. They were searching for my father, who was hiding in a sort of cave under the village. It all happened within two or three minutes. The Germans were furious; it even seemed like they had been drugged or that they were drunk.

In another house the Germans found several men hiding, and they may well have also executed them, were it not for the fact that one of the Frenchmen, Jean Verola, had previously worked for the Germans as a cook in Nice. **Jacques Saussine**, who was 18 at the time, explains how Jean Verola managed to break the tension:

There were five that the Germans had found, including a Jew, though they didn't know that he was Jewish. They had made them all lie down with their hands over their heads. Jean Verola's teeth were chattering with fear, the fear of dying, but he had the presence of mind to signal to the Germans with his left hand to look in his pocket. "Papier!" They took out his wallet, and when they saw "German

Kommandantur" and all that, the German made them stand up and gave each of them a cigarette. That is an amazing souvenir, the German gave a cigarette to each one of them! They were going to shoot, but that document saved them all.

In the meantime, **Bruno Municchi** and his family had remained in the basement of their house at the entrance of town:

When the Germans arrived, I was in the stable with my father, mother, brother, and my aunt and some friends. The Germans entered the basement: "Terrorists?" "No." So they made us all get out and line up against the wall. We didn't move or say anything. They then made us go back into the stable and then brought us back out again. A German who could speak a bit of French said: "Go to the cemetery." I didn't want to go there and said: "They will kill us up there," but then a Germans told me: "No, no, not afraid, not afraid."

The first ones who had arrived had wire netting on their helmets with plane tree leaves hanging from the helmets. You could see their helmets but not their faces. The ones that arrived later had nothing, but those first ones were really frightening. One of them had froth on his mouth like a horse; he must have been drinking, because the other ones were normal.

After helping the Germans put a cannon into position, Bruno Municchi and his family were permitted to return to their house. **François Municchi** explains what happened next:

Beside the house we had a barn to store hay to feed the horse and cow that we had. When the Germans saw the hay, they figured: "There are terrorists in there," and they set it on fire. They burned our house down; there was nothing left of it, only the four walls. We had a mule, a goat, and a cow downstairs: they all burned. There was a big water tank that we used for watering and my elder brother Léon asked: "I would like to extinguish the fire in our house, to take a pail…" A German slapped him, saying: "There is a war on! It is burning, let it burn." We didn't have anything left. We were like worms, with no clothes, nothing. That was terrible. I will always remember: I had short pants, a white shirt, and I was in barefoot.

All the inhabitants of la Roquette were then ordered to regroup in front of the church, in the center of the village. This is when **Bruno Municchi** and his family saw the first dead:

There was a German accompanying us, and we were going up towards the village by the washhouse to get to the Place du Château. I was first in line, and on the way up I saw blood running down the path and the gamekeeper was sweeping it up. Then I saw two guys lying on the ground [Prosper Bovis and César Baudoin]. They were already dead, and it happened to be Prosper Bovis' father and mother following behind me. When the mother saw her son on the ground, she lay down on top of him and was covered in blood. The Germans said: "Go on, go on." So I stepped over them and we didn't say anything. When we reached the square in front of the church, everybody else was there already. They put the mother whose son had been killed and who was crying into Madame Milau's house. One German went in there and said: "That is what war is like" and made her understand that there were also people crying in Germany.

Once all the villagers had regrouped in front of the church, all the men, including **Jacques Saussine**, were ordered inside:

> I had the devil's fear, but my mother told me: "Listen, everybody is going to the town square, you also have to go." I said: "I don't feel like it." "Go!" So I went to the square. In the village, there were electric wires and stones lying on the ground. It was a dead village. The Germans weren't happy. I was the last one to reach the square and I was afraid, I was shaking. The whole village was grouped in front of the church, and there were about forty of us. There were two plane trees in front of the church and the Germans were lined up there, a dozen on one side and a dozen on the other, and we had to walk between them. Their helmets were covered with leaves, olive tree twigs, pine branches, and all that for camouflage. It gave us a terrible impression and a terrible fear to know that we would have to pass between those rows of Germans. One of them spat on *Monsieur* Depot and he let it dribble down his chin; he didn't try to wipe it off because he was too afraid to move. The interpreter could speak French quite well and said: "If a single gunshot is fired against us tonight, we will burn the village down tomorrow morning." Imagine how everybody was shaking, because the *francs-tireurs* were in the surrounding countryside.

François Municchi, who had been hiding in Madame Toche's basement, was also forced into the church, though he was only 14 years old (his 10-year-old brother Bruno was left free, however):

> The Germans took the gamekeeper, Henri Audibert, and asked him, with the help of his trumpet, to tell everybody who was still hiding to go to the church, otherwise they would burn the village down. So Madame Toche told me: "You have to go." I went outside and reached the square. There were Germans everywhere, and at the phone booth in front of the church there was a German phoning. I can still see him, he had a helmet with leaves on it. The deputy mayor, Charles Martin, was at a window and he called out to me: "Don't move François, I am coming down." I wondered what he wanted. He limped up to the church and said: "Get in there, then we will see what will happen." The Germans asked the deputy to count us, then to close the door. I was the last one to go into the church, then he locked us in. It was about 6 o'clock, and it was a nice day in August. There were 75 of us inside. All of us got in except the women.

Jacques Saussine goes on :

> They locked and bolted us into the church, and believe me, it was not a pretty scene. The whole village was in there except the women. We were all lying on the ground on the marble tiles, waiting. Some people's teeth were chattering from fear. "What are they going to do to us tomorrow? What are they going to do to us tomorrow morning?" We figured maybe they were going to shoot all of us, that is what we were thinking about. The church was never so prayed for. Some people were crying, some were holding their hands together in prayer. But since I was young, I didn't realize things that way. It's true, when you are young, you don't realize. But what I do know is that I was cold, because those marble tiles in the church were freezing cold, even in summer time.

Monsieur Jean Depot was terribly frightened and said: "Let's hope that the patriots don't open fire." During the night they didn't fire a single shot, nor the next morning, either. Lucky thing, because they are the ones who caused the whole mess in the first place: the patriots, the so-called patriots.

The woman tried to help as they could, as **François Municchi** explains:

> There was a window in the church, and the women were passing us bottles of water to drink every now and then, or if they found a piece of bread or an apple or something else, they passed it on to us and we would eat it. The night lasted very long; we couldn't sleep because we were always saying: "What is going to happen tomorrow morning? They are going to shoot us." We spoke to each other a bit: "What is going to happen?" I thought: "Let's leave, climb up to the steeple and go on the roofs to hide. But no… If ever anybody is missing, they will kill us all, because they counted us." Those were very bad moments to live through.
>
> We were released the next morning at 10 o'clock. As we stepped out, we saw a group of Germans on the square with foliage on their helmets and machine guns set on tripods. They made us line up against the wall: "Now line up here, and in silence!" Somebody, I can't remember who, said: "Our last hour has come, it is all over."
>
> But no, they didn't kill us. There was an interpreter who could speak a bit of French and he said: "If you

The St Pierre Church, in the center of la Roquette sur Var, in which the male inhabitants of the town were imprisoned during the night of August 25 to 26, 1944. Author's Collection.

wander away from the village more than 100 meters, we will shoot you and kill you. Now go and pick up the dead and bring them to the village cemetery." So we took a cart and went to collect the dead. There was a *maquisard* in the Cercle, and another one leaning against a wall. When we lifted him up to put him on the cart he was stiff. And then there were the two others, César and Prosper. There were four dead, and we brought them to the cemetery, where we dug a hole to bury them, always under guard of Germans with submachine guns. Then we returned to the village.

Jacques Saussine also remembers the moment when the men were released from the church:

In the morning, they finally let us out. When they opened the church door, we heard the lock going "crack, crack." We went out meekly; we really thought that they were going to kill us. We were terribly frightened! A straw wouldn't have fit through where I am thinking of. Then they told us to assemble all the vehicles, bicycles, and rifles. What a relief when they told us to assemble all that. My uncle brought his good rifle that was almost new. Then things happened quietly.

Although the previous day had been full of tragedies and brutality for la Roquette, the inhabitants quickly realized that the German soldiers of *Bataillon 164* were humans just like them, and that many did not even consider themselves German. **Bruno Municchi**, whose house had been burned down by the Germans and who had lost two brothers during the war, remembers:

At the start, the Germans were really scary. I was still too young to be locked into the church, so I went home. The next day, when I came out, the Germans were beside us, and they were speaking to me as if nothing had happened. One German told me: "War not good. Not good, not good." I will always remember that: "It's not good. I want go home."

Every time we saw a German he would say: "We are Polish. We aren't Germans. We are Polish, but we can't help it, we do what the chief tells us to. We are Poles, we don't do any harm." They managed to make us understand. I will tell you frankly, there was a German who had biscuits, and we had nothing to eat, so he went over there and took a package of biscuits for us, since we were hungry.

Bruno's brother **François Municchi** confirms:

The next morning, I was going down to see our burned house and there was a group of Germans in a garage. With his finger, one German signaled me to come over. He knew that we were hungry and that there was nothing left for us to eat. We were really cut off from the world, because there was fighting occurring all over and we couldn't leave the village. The German took a bag of biscuits and gave one package to me! He said: "Here, take it and go and eat." Then, do you know what the German told me, and that I will remember forever: "Us not mean Germans. Us Polish, not German." Because they weren't in agreement with the Germans. Then I brought the biscuits to my parents, saying: "Well, look what the Germans gave me."

Jacques Saussine also spent a friendly moment with one of the "Germans":

They had occupied the village, but there were only Poles left over. They were constantly telling us: "Ich Polak, ich Polak, ich Polak," as if to say: "Don't do us any harm," and yet they had their rifles and everything.

One of them told Charles Aguillon: "Ich Polak, ich Polak." He was friendly! Charles Aguillon told him: "Komm, komm hier. Venez, my house, house." He took a bottle of good rosé wine from his own harvest and served him a glass. The German was happy: "Gut, gut, gut. Wein gut," and I drank a glass with them. The German was called Leon; it's funny I remember the name. "Me, Leon," he said. He told us that he didn't like Hitler, "Hitler no good," so that comforted us a bit, it made us feel good. He was funny, it's true! We didn't realize that we were young and that we were making friends. He kept saying: "Ich Polak, ich Polak." He must have been 20 years old. They were forced to do that, to fight the war. We finished the bottle that day, I remember.

Further up the road towards Levens, Adèle Tacconi was also living in close proximity with the Germans. After the ambush against their cyclists, the Germans had taken up positions on Arpasse Mountain, overlooking the Var River and using **Adèle Tacconi**'s house as their rear base:

After the fighting, the Germans stayed in the house for quite a while. They camped in the house and we slept in the basement. There was an old chapel on our property and

François Municchi holds the iron heel of a boot that was apparently lost by a German soldier and that he found in the streets of la Roquette after the fighting. Author's Collection.

they also slept in the chapel. I don't know what they did during the day, but at nightfall they assembled at our place to eat and everything. We had plenty of fruits in the chapel: pears, apples, and everything because we had an orchard. They ate those because they had no fresh foods. What they mostly took was fresh vegetables in the garden. They took cabbages and cut them into thin slices and ate them raw.

On the other hand, I have to say that when they were distributing bread at nightfall, they always gave a slice to me and my two sisters. It was black bread with rye. They also gave us some kind of black biscuits that were extremely hard, but we took them and said thank you. "For the baby," they would say. They called us kids babies, but we weren't babies anymore. They also had candies that they gave us, but we didn't eat them because we were a bit backward at the time, and we thought: "We shouldn't eat them because there might be poison inside." But think of it, they were distributing the bread to their soldiers, we ate that bread and it wasn't poisoned. But it was wartime, so we were careful: they were the enemy.

The body of Second Rossi, who had been killed by the Germans on Arpasse Montain August 25th at the time of the bicycle ambush, was brought back to la Roquette. Being a carpenter, **Jacques Saussine** was asked to make a coffin for his body:

Rossi was from la Roquette and was married to Germaine Revel, a girl from the village. He was trying to get away and climbed all the way up to the top of the

The cenotaph in la Roquette, listing the names of the five men killed August 25th, as well as the Barbier brothers, who are both reported as missing since August 1944, one in Cannes and the other in Levens, as mentioned previously. Author's Collection.

mountain, but then he got killed and fell into the ravine with his feet sticking up in the air. When they went to get him afterwards he was completely rotten, and it smelled so bad they had to wear handkerchiefs over their mouths to bring him back. It is terrible, it is frightening to think about all that. I made the coffin with old boards, but I still made it in the shape of a coffin, diamond shaped with a cover and everything. They walked past poor Germaine with the coffin and told her: "It's your husband who is in there." When she found out it was him, she cried for two nights, she almost lost her mind. I can still picture the scene, it was terrible, you can't talk about such things.

The Resistance Counterattacks Levens

August 25th, the German soldiers of *Bataillon 164* had successfully attacked Levens and la Roquette, retaking control of all the strategically important positions that the Resistance had seized in the days following the Allied landing August 15th. The Germans prepared to defend the area against the Allied troops that they knew would soon reach the Var River. The 12th Company of *Bataillon 164* occupied Levens, while the 9th and 10th Companies occupied la Roquette, and probably also Arpasse Mountain. (The 11th Company of *Bataillon 164* was apparently not present in the area, as it was still assigned to guarding the coast at the Var Bridge, as it had been before the Allied landing. See Josef Kirsner account in Chapters 1 and 13.)

The Resistance, though it had been pushed back, was still present in strength in the mountains immediately north of Levens, and on the northern bank of the Vésubie River. An FFI messenger from the *Réseau Tartane* had crossed the lines from Grasse and reached Fréjus August 22nd, where he met First Airborne Task Force intelligence officers Capt Geoffrey Jones and Lt Col William Blythe. Jones and Blythe ordered the messenger to cross back through the lines with the mission of informing the French Resistance that they were to hinder the German retreat towards Italy in any manner possible. To give him credibility, the messenger was given a letter signed by Jones and Blythe that simply stated that the bearer of the letter was responsible for conveying orders. What these orders were was of course not stated in the letter, as a precaution in case the messenger was captured. Furthermore, the letter was printed on extremely thin paper that could quickly be destroyed or even eaten in case of danger. The *Réseau Tartane* messenger explains the logic behind the orders Jones and Blythe gave him, and what he found upon contacting the Resistance at Puget-Théniers at the time of their defeat in Levens:

The Germans were deliberately falling back in order to pass into Italy. I suspect the Americans didn't want all those troops to go and reinforce the German Army that was in Italy, so I received a mission. I was to meet with the *maquis* in Thorenc and transmit the American orders, which were that the French Resistance was to try to slow down the German retreat as much as possible by blowing up bridges and by any other means so as to block the German retreat towards the Italian border so that the Americans could take as many prisoners as possible. The Resistance had to act as soon as possible because the Germans were leaving.

The Americans brought me to Thorenc in a car, and there I met a man called Lt Cavaleri. There were two or three men there, as well as two English airmen who must have been shot down by the Germans and had taken refuge there, and who must then have left with my American

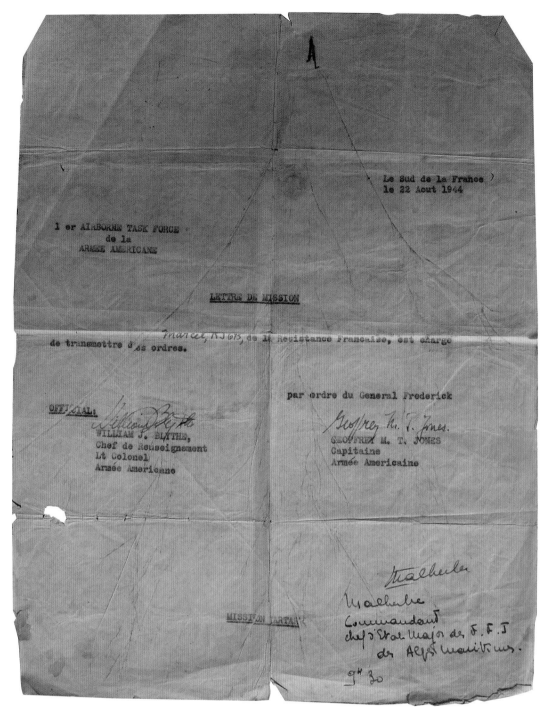

Le Sud de la France
le 22 Aout 1944

1 er AIRBORNE TASK FORCE
de la
ARMÉE AMÉRICANE

LETTRE DE MISSION

de transmettre des ordres.

OFFICIAL:

WILLIAM J. BLYTHE,
Chef de Renseignement
Lt Colonel
Armée Americane

par ordre du General Frederick

GEOFFREY M. T. JONES
Capitaine
Armée Americaine

Malherbe
Commandant
chef d'Etat Major de F.F.I
des Alpes maritimes.

MISSION TARTANE

The letter that Lt Col Blythe and Capt Jones gave to a Réseau Tartane messenger in Fréjus August 22nd, for him to be able to prove that he really was the bearer of orders given by the American command. The letter was typed on very fragile paper that could easily be destroyed, and the actual orders were not included in the letter as a precaution in case of capture. Commander Malherbe signed the lower right corner of the letter to indicate that the messenger had indeed fulfilled his mission and transmitted the orders to him. Private Collection.

driver, I suspect. Lt Cavaleri told me: "Listen, everybody left for Puget-Théniers. If you want to contact the *maquis*, you have to go to Puget-Théniers." I went to a farm to ask if anybody wanted to bring me to Puget-Théniers. Nobody was there, but there was a motorcycle. I took the motorcycle and ended up in Puget-Théniers. There I found an officer, commander Malherbe, who told me: "We regret, but we cannot intervene. My men are just returning from Levens, where we were hit hard, and I cannot ask them to go back into action immediately." Indeed, there were a bunch of wounded sitting against the plane trees, and they looked quite beat up. So I told Malherbe: "Then give me a release saying that I fulfilled my mission."

Although they were in no condition to return to Levens on the same day, Captain Jones' orders may have had an influence on Malherbe, as on August 26th, the very day after losing Levens, the Resistance mounted a *"Grande Attaque"* on Levens from the Férion, the mountainous mass facing Levens from the north. The FFIs joined forces with the FTP companies for this attack, and the *Groupe Combat*, *Groupe Morgan*, the AS, and the 8th and 27th FTPF Companies converged towards the area. **Joseph "Chambery" Martin**, the veteran of the 1940 campaign who had joined the AS, only to then be sent off to spy on the FTPs, participated in the August 26th attack as a member of the 27th FTP Company:

The village of Levens, with Férion Mountain in the background, from which a coalition of FFI and FTP resistance forces attempted to attack the town August 26, 1944. Wikipedia.org.

At that moment, all the French Forces of the Interior that were in the region were put under command of Colonel Sapin and other members of the headquarters to surround Levens. There were large numbers of us: *Groupe Morgan*, the 8th and 27th FTP Companies, and other guys all around. The Morgan Company was supposed to take Levens from above, coming from the swimming pool. My company was to occupy the hills dominating Levens from the north, and there were other people on our right flank. We were on the extreme left flank and the furthest away from Levens, in the direction of St Claire. It was more or less coordinated so that we would all attack simultaneously.

We arrived very early in the morning and took up positions. At that time we had an American machine gun, and not many people knew how to use it, so I said: "OK, I will take it." So I set up the machine gun, but I hadn't chosen the position and did not like it. I had the knowledge and had said: "It would be better to put the machine gun over there," but I had to respect my orders. I had ammunition bearers bringing me little boxes of .30 caliber ammunition belts. I must have had about 2,500 rounds, since the boxes contained belts of 250 cartridges and I had at least a dozen. So we were ready with the machine gun and everything. It was said that the signal to open fire would be three shots being fired.

We were in position, waiting for the signal, and we stayed there for more than an hour, observing without shooting. The Germans must not have suspected that we were there, so we tried to show ourselves as little as possible and looked out, trying to find the ideal spot to be able to advance if necessary. I could see Germans down there in a field who must have been taking a nap. From time to time one would stand up and leave. I counted them: there were 12 of them, but then only 11, one left, then 10. I was looking at them and thinking: "In a moment when I cut loose, I am going to clear you guys out of there."

At one point the signal was given so we went into action: bangbangbang! Pow! Here we go! The *Fritzes* really got some. Right at the start I opened fire on the Germans in the field, dropping several of them, some of which were probably killed, because they didn't move anymore after that. Then a machine gun fired at us from the square beside the Levens town hall. We could see the flames and the smoke, so that is where I fired afterwards; the machine gun was my primary target.

We had two Polish soldiers from the German army who had deserted that were beside us with an MG 34. You could tell that those guys were soldiers, like myself, because when I would fire, they would stop and observe in order to spot the weapon that was firing on us. I was doing the same thing, not firing when they were firing, and then I would look out and that is how I spotted where the machine gun next to the town hall was. There is a wall, and the machine gun was there. Behind the machine gun there was a square, and curious civilians were coming forth and standing in the middle to see who was shooting and preventing me from firing back at the machine gun. I had to be careful not to shoot them because we had been told: "Beware not to kill anybody in Levens." But after a while I blasted away, thinking: "Those assholes are going to get out of the way!" I didn't see any civilians after that; the bullets must have whistled past them and the guys got out of the way.

Then suddenly vrroomm, vromm, a motorcyclist drove down out of Levens. The loader beside me said: "Look, a motorcyclist leaving!" I immediately fired at him. I had tracer bullets and could see I wasn't hitting far from him, but from where I was positioned he had the advantage of being partly hidden by the parapet of the road. I could see my bullets going down and hitting approximately where he was, but he lay down on the motorcycle and I didn't hit him. We saw him disappear down the road towards St Claire. In those cases, it's not like on the firing range. You don't hold your breath, you aim roughly then fire, because in the meantime, the other guys fire back. So the motorcyclist got away and he was able to bring the orders down to St Claire, explaining where we were.

Jean Maicon, a resident of Levens who had been inducted into the 27th FTP Company a few days earlier when the FTPs had first liberated the town, also saw the German motorcyclist:

I was up on the hill and we were firing at the Germans. There was a German motorcyclist driving by. I aimed at him, but I didn't get him because the shot didn't go off. My Italian carbine jammed.

Albert Cresp, an FFI who was attached to the *Groupe Combat*, remembers how some of his buddies got wounded:

When we went to set up our ambush, the Germans were already in position and they started firing at us. We hid behind some rocks, but I saw one or two friends get wounded. In the mountains it's hard to get hit, but they had been curious: they wanted to lift their heads up from behind the rocks and that's how some bullets got them.

The resistance fighters were soon forced to retreat, as **Corrado Marcucci**, the commander of the 27th FTP Company, explains:

The fire fight starts and will last three hours. Our Browning machine guns jam and we find ourselves under a hail of mortar shells and machine gun tracer bullets. Incendiary shells start a fire in the pine trees and bushes behind us. For three hours, we hold our positions that become untenable. The order to fall back on Duranus and Utelle is given.[19]

Laurent Pasquier, of the 27th FTP Company, gave a few more details about the battle in his diary:

August 26th. For the third time, we return to Levens. The Rodez Detachment, that I am part of, is ordered to occupy the extreme left flank of the hill, in the area called les Bassins. It is calm until 15:00. At 15:30, we open fire on the *Boches* who are in the village. The encounter is very fierce from the start, and we are masters of the situation for two hours. I have a tally of at least four Germans shot, confirmed by Pierre Motoni, who is watching with binoculars at my side.

At 18:00, the Germans receive reinforcements and the whole detachment is sprayed with mortars. In less than an hour the forest is in flames, and the shells are landing closer and closer to our positions. A moment later, the German artillery (105 mm batteries) that must be in the area of Aspremont open fire in turn. A retreat order is given, but it is very difficult to follow, because the Germans now occupy all the high ground. At one point at least 15 shells bracket me, and since Marengo doesn't see me moving he reports me as dead, along with Chambéry [Joseph Martin's *nom de guerre*], Rodez, and Le Corse.

I remain in position with a few buddies to cover the retreat of our group, then we manage to disengage and cross through the burning forest. When I get to the road, I find a few buddies who are bustling around our five wounded, the dead body [**Aimé Bovis**] having been abandoned at the very spot where he was mortally hit by a shell. I manage to reach St Jean la Rivière after walking for six hours. I am so tired that I lie down directly on the St Jean bridge and fall into a deep sleep.[20]

In the face of strong German resistance at Levens, accompanied by mortar and artillery fire that set the forest on fire, the *maquisard*s were forced to retreat. However, the retreat order never reached several of the men in the advanced positions, who suddenly found themselves all alone on the Férion. Several were reported as killed or missing, as Laurent Pasquier mentioned. **Marceau Raynaud**, of the 8th FTP Company, was among those left behind:

We were brought to the hill facing Levens and the Germans were on the other side. They were shooting at us and we were shooting at them: the law of war. There were quite a few wounded and killed there. I was with a friend from Puget-Théniers who was manning a machine gun and there were two of us loaders. We were told: "You guys go down there with the machine gun." A bit above us there were two Poles who had deserted from the German army. They had German helmets and had painted American stars on them. The Poles had a German machine gun and were firing constantly, whereas we had an old machine gun from the First World War and it jammed. Maybe that was actually a good thing, because then the Germans didn't spot us.

We had American semi-automatic rifles and we tried to hit the Germans with them. We could clearly see the German dispatch riders driving by on motorcycles and giving orders to the soldiers in their guttural German voices. We fired at them, but it was a bit far off for rifles and we missed them, particularly because we were not seasoned soldiers, we were novices. We fired a lot and we missed them a lot. The problem is that then you get spotted and they fire a mortar at you, and with the rifle you can't fire back, so we stopped firing and waited. The Poles were firing constantly and they got spotted, so a mortar came in and blew both of them up, killing them. We were lower down in a sort of bush and it was harder to see us, and since we weren't moving, they didn't fire at us.

Since we couldn't fire, we stayed in our hole, waiting for somebody to say something to us. After a while things quieted down, we couldn't hear anything anymore, so we stuck our noses out and looked around. We saw that the mortars had set the forest on fire and that the rest of the company had retreated and forgotten us. There were only three of us left; we advanced and found the two Poles who were with us dead at their machine gun, so we took off for Duranus, and at Duranus we found the rest of the company. When we got there they said: "Oh, you are here? We were already going to report you as missing." "Yes, yes. We are here with our weapons."

Joseph "Chambéry" Martin, of the 27th FTP Company, was also left behind with his American .30 caliber machine gun when the main resistance force retreated. Being on the extreme left flank of the attack, and nearest to St Claire, he was in a highly exposed position:

At one point, it must have been in the late afternoon, they started firing mortars. I had all my guys all around me and we heard two detonations: "pof pof." One guy asked me: "What's that? It sounds like a hunting rifle." I said: "Beware! Lie down and stay down!" Feeuuww… Bang! Bang! It was starting to get hot. I said: "A simple hole is enough to shelter you from those. Lie down nice and flat and you will be safe." Mortar shells aren't like artillery shells: the fragments skim the ground. The mortars kept coming and coming, and they set the forest behind us on fire.

Then the Germans started advancing from our left, coming from St Claire. That is where the danger was, because that is where none of our men were, since we were the unit on the extreme left flank of the attack. That is how I got flanked and surrounded by the Germans while the others retreated without saying a thing, leaving me alone up there. I had two ammunition bearers with me, a teacher and a Corsican. We were in a bad position: instead of being on the crest of the hill, we were lower down in front of the crest, meaning that there were 20 dangerous meters to be made to get back up, during which the Germans could see us well. The machine gun was in a hole, and we had put a few stones in front and camouflaged it, so we were good; but leaving was going to be difficult.

I told the first ammunition bearer, the teacher: "OK, you go back. Make sure to crawl when you leave because they can see you from over there. Then make a leap, follow the path, and tell the others up there to fire so that we can pull back with the machine gun." Indeed, when he moved: bang bang! So he crawled a bit, then when he was behind the crest he was able to stand up. The guy left, but then he didn't respond anymore. "Shit!" So I sent the second guy, the Corsican. I told him: "Now you go up there and see what is going on. Crawl up and warn them that they need to send someone down or give me covering fire, so that I can at least bring up the machine gun. Never mind the tripod, we will leave it here." The guy left and didn't come back and I found myself all alone. So I said: "Here we go, they have left me all alone up here like an idiot."

Former FFI Joseph Martin points to the position where he and his crew had set up an American .30 caliber machine gun on Férion Mountain August 26, 1944. Author's Collection.

I am there, so I blast away and I get down to one belt of ammunition. I fired some more and I was out of bullets, so I moved a bit, but from the square in Levens the Germans could see me: bang, bang, bang! I figured: "I have to play dead. I don't have any ammunition left anyway, so I won't move." Behind me there was a fire started by the mortar shells. I managed to remove the bolt from the machine gun so that it couldn't be used anymore. That's what you do in those situations. There was no more noise around me, no more gunfire except for a few shells falling every now and then, and then it stopped. When I stopped firing the Germans thought: "OK, now they are gone or they are all dead," so they ceased firing. I stayed in my hole and started hearing people speaking German.

I looked and said: "There is nobody left up there, no noise, nothing. Oh shit! Now I am in a tight spot." Then I heard some stones falling in front of me. I still had a Colt, that was a good gun, and I wondered what was going on. Suddenly, what did I see? Less than 10 meters in front of me I saw a helmet coming up, then a head. I can still see the guy now and can say that he had a moustache. When I saw his chest, no hesitation, "bang," I fired and got him right in the face. Then I looked to the left, and there were more stones falling, and I saw some Germans coming with submachine guns. "Bang," one fired, so I played dead and stopped moving. The guy must have thought he had got me, but I thought: "Now I am trapped, I have guys in front of me, I have guys on my left, and there is a fire behind me. I am done for!"

At that moment I saw I was surrounded and thought I was going to die. I am not ashamed to say that I had a moment of fear. Things were going very bad, I was losing my faculties. That is when I saw the *Madone des Fenêstres* [The *Madone des Fenestres* was the local appearance of the Virgin Mary that was venerated in Joseph Martin's hometown of St Martin Vésubie.] and my father and mother. I saw them there and suddenly I thought: "Listen, you are shaking, but don't let yourself down. Afraid or not, in any case they will kill me if they catch me." We knew that if the Germans captured us they would kill us because we weren't wearing uniforms yet. So dead for dead, I did the same thing a rabbit does: when you try to catch him,

he escapes. I got hold of myself and said: "Oh coquin de Dieu! Before I get killed, I am going to kill some, too!" I took the pistol and said: "Now I am going."

I knew they were on my left, and behind me there was the fire. The only way out was the right side, but I thought: "That is no good, because they aren't any more stupid than I am and they probably went off to that side to wait for me." So I played dead some more, I didn't move, then I looked and said: "Now I have to get out of here, so too bad, fire or no fire, I will go through the fire." And I ran off! Lucky thing I wasn't fat, because two of them fired at me with their submachine guns, but they missed me. I know why they missed, it is because they didn't shoulder their weapons; they fired from the hip, and when you do that the submachine gun does its own thing. If they had fired from the shoulder they would have gotten me. But they did get me a bit: I had a grenade in my pocket and a bullet sliced my pocket and the grenade fell out. My clothes were hit by three or four bullets that didn't touch my skin. I was lucky… because they didn't fire properly.

After that, I threw myself into the fire; but what was the fire? It was grass and bushes that were burning, making flames that were a meter or a meter and a half high, but not over a wide area. Further up it had already burned and there were ashes. I did burn my eyebrows, but I had a French helmet that I had picked up and that protected me a bit. I burned my feet and shoes (there were embers in some places), but I found myself in the ashes, with the fire all around me that kept on advancing and producing smoke. Instead of going out of the fire across from where I had gone in I turned left, in other words west, because I thought: "If I go in from the south and exit from the north, they will be waiting for me." So I turned left and went out over there. The fire saved my life. Without the fire they would have gotten me, because all I had left was a pistol.

I found a dead guy, but I didn't have time to take care of him. I looked if he had a rifle or not, since I only had a Colt, then I ran as fast as I could. At one place there was a cliff that I couldn't go across, so I went down to the road and what did I see? Two guys on the road, and I didn't know whether they were German or French. I thought they were Germans, so I was being careful. There were two of them: one with his back to me and the other one facing me. I was trying to walk where there was grass so as not to make any noise. I knew the area well and knew that if I could get past them, then there was a curve in the road and I would be safe. The danger was before, so I thought I would shoot the two guys and then get out of there; but there might be more of them. I took out the clip from my pistol: there was only one cartridge left! Where were the others? I don't know. When I had realized that I was left all alone and got discouraged I may have fired at the Germans, I don't know. Since I only had one round left, I couldn't kill both guys. I got to within 10 meters of them, and it seemed to me that they were speaking German. In fact, they were speaking French, but I mistook it for German, because I was convinced they were Germans. The one facing me said: "Eh oui, capit" in Patois. So I suddenly shouted: "Don't shoot, don't shoot!" They looked at me coming, holding me back with their submachine guns. They asked me: "Where are you coming from, we were told there was nobody left? But you are French."

Believe it or not, but when he said: "You are French," I realized I was saved. Then suddenly I felt that I was aching all over. I had been tumbling down when I was running through the rocks and my elbows were hurting, my back was hurting, I was aching all over. I asked: "But where did the others go?" "They have left, they are in Duranus." So I walked to Duranus, and when I got there the last truck was leaving: "Hey Chambéry, where are you coming from?" "I am coming back from the blaze." "Come on, hop aboard." We retreated to St Jean la Rivière and I found my friends there. The captain showed me his notebook and said: "Look, see where it says Chambéry? I had already made a cross."

The number of casualties caused by this *Grande Attaque* on Levens was surprisingly small. No trace can be found of the killed Polish deserters in any documents, and the only *maquisard* who seems to have died is 19-year-old **Aimé Bovis**, who is said to have fallen victim to a German mortar shell and is officially listed as having died August 27th. As for the Germans, it would seem that none of their men were killed, despite the claims made by several *maquisard*s. Maybe these "killed" Germans were in fact only wounded, or simply took cover after they heard a bullet whip past them? In any case, neither the *Volksbund* archives nor the residents of Levens indicate that any German soldiers died. Aimé Bovis is therefore the only person confirmed to have been killed in the fighting at Levens August 26th (if it is assumed that his official date of death is wrong by one day).

To finish the discussion about the *Grande Attaque*, we will read the account of *Sous-Lieutenant* Betemps, who was a member of the AS under *Capitaine* François. Contrary to the other *maquis* forces, his group did not participate in the attack from the direction of the Férion to the north, but was instead positioned south of Levens, somewhere on the Arpasse, overlooking the road to la Roquette. ***Sous-Lieutenant* Betemps** explains why he was on the Arpasse and what happened to he and his men:

I don't know who had the idea of making columns of *maquisard*s from different organizations march down concentrically towards Levens, with no possible coordination once the attack was launched. Levens, perched up on its hill, was well defended! Captain François had smelled the can of worms and had only accepted to prevent the arrival of German reinforcements from the road coming from St Martin du Var and la Roquette. We got into position at first light in a location that was suitable for an ambush. From our emplacement, we could see Levens and were able to follow the events of this failed attack. We moved out around noon. The entire morning, no enemies had presented themselves in front of our rifles. Our withdrawal was spotted by some Germans. Although we had spent the morning unnoticed, without being shot at a single time, our retreat was followed by rather weak 81mm mortar fire. But our surprise became very big and very unpleasant when we reached the crest that dominated the road we had been watching. We had been outflanked by a strong German detachment [These were probably the Germans who had taken position on the Arpasse and that were previously described by Adèle Tacconi.], and a fire fight broke out, brutal and blind in the thick undergrowth. From hunters we had become hunted. Our *Corps Franc* then disintegrated. It did what would later surprise us so much in Indochina: it melted into the countryside just like the Viets would melt into the coconut plantations. We had made a big mistake, we had not left any "alarms" behind us or on the high ground. (…)

Our successful dispersion was certainly not the consequence of clever training, but a reflex action caused by complete surprise, as well as a good dose of fear and luck. We tore straight forward, in small groups, in thick, bushy vegetation, while the Germans coming from our right tried to cut us off and generously sprayed the countryside with MP and MG fire. Bottin, Ernest, and I had followed a small ravine that was easy at first, but soon became so steep that we were stopped in our "escape forward." To continue down carefully while watching our step would mean to get shot like rabbits. To go back up… the Germans were behind us. We leaped into a very dense copse of shrubbery and thorny bramble. All three of us had the same thought: "We are done for." We could hear the Germans very near us, firing and shouting. They were probably going to search the area! We would defend ourselves (we had a machine gun, two Stens, a Colt, and some Mills'), but we would not survive. It was too unequal, they were everywhere and we were stupidly hiding in the bramble, trapped.

A few minutes passed, then 15 minutes, then half an hour. The Germans were no longer firing or shouting. We could hear them speaking, and they were still very near us, but a faint glimmer of hope was born in us that faded then increased, depending on the noises that "they" were making or no longer making. One hour, two hours, three hours: things no longer seemed as hopeless. Why would they search the terrain now if they had not done so in the heat of the action? And yet they were still there. They had even brought two mortars, 81s according to their sound, firing down somewhere in the valley… on Plan du Var perhaps? We started to whisper. Bottin, with his Alsacian accent, promised a candle "this big" to the Holy Mother if we managed to survive. Thirst was gnawing at us. We hadn't drank anything since the morning coffee, and the sun, in this August afternoon, was crushing us in our shrub.

Our plan was to leave our hideout at nightfall, to walk back over the crest, cross the road that we had watched that morning, go down into the ravine that it dominated and follow it, cross the Var, and reach Gillette, where Bottin knew "somebody." With nightfall came silence. Had the Germans pulled out, or were they bivouacking around their mortar positions? We had no idea. We departed around 10 o'clock, crawling, as careful as Siouxs not to make any noise. (…) We stopped often to listen to the noises of the night, and the path and time it took us to get to the crest seemed long.

Once we had passed the crest we stood up, and in single file and bent down, we followed the slope towards the road. We crossed a vineyard, the grapes were very round… and very green. Biting into the bunches of raisins was horribly sour, but it was the first drip of fluid that reached our cotton tongues. Once we crossed the road, we were in cultivated fields… and we quickly located the sound of running water: a little piece of pipe pouring into a cement basin. We drank like horses in a trough. It took five more minutes to get out of the cultivated zone and into the cover of the pines, where we slept for a few hours.

In the early morning, we made out a farmhouse 300 meters from our emplacement. I went there on reconnaissance, navigating as best I could to avoid any areas that were too open. The farmer hurried me in, warning me that the Germans were still in Levens and that they were using the road 100 meters above the farm quite a bit. He offered me a bowl of barley coffee [Real coffee was a luxury in occupied France.] and some bread and cheese. I told him that I had two sidekicks nearby who were as hungry as I was. His wife, who had arrived in the meantime, cooked some hard boiled eggs that she stuffed into a haversack with some bread, cheese, and tomatoes. I asked him for two bottles of water, and he added a third one of wine! I indicated the direction of our hiding place to him. He wanted to be able to warn us if necessary. On the other hand, he asked me not to come back to the farm. Around noon and at nightfall, his daughter would drop off a basket at the corner of his vineyard.

I was welcomed back with my haversack of supplies. We would stick around for the day, then continue on at night. At noon, we saw our Red Riding Hood coming along. Her basket did not contain a biscuit and a pot of butter for grandma, but a copious tomato and potato salad for three hungry boys. In the late afternoon, a series of whines – noise that we had never heard yet – went over our heads. They were followed by explosions in the Levens area. We were under some artillery trajectories, but luckily far away from the targets. [Unbeknownst to Betemps, the 517th PRCT had now reached the west side of the Var River and the 460th PFAB had opened fire at the German positions.] Forest fires started immediately, and with the help of the drought they quickly developed; they reached and blocked off the ravine that we were supposed to follow. We decided to wait for the next morning… and for the evening Red Riding Hood, faithful to her rendezvous. The shelling stopped at night, leaving the fires as a backdrop to the countryside.

When we departed in the morning, the ravine was still smoldering and an abandoned mill was finishing to burn up. In front of us, where the path followed the little brook, we could see fresh traces of German boots, with their characteristic metallic heel; somebody had walked there recently. But one on his own, even armed, was not too serious! We reached the *Route Nationale* that followed the Var. When we asked a woman in her garden if any Germans were in the area, she answered: "The Americans have gone by." She invited us in, offered us drinks, and made us… a tomato salad... yet another one. It is true that it was the full season.

We reached Plan du Var in a truck that drove by. The *Corp Franc* was there, as well as *Capitaine* François, who a few hours earlier had been looking for our bodies in the area of the fire fight! Tralala, the WWI veteran, had also returned a few hours before us. The German footprints were his! He had solitarily lived through the same adventures as we and followed an identical itinerary to ours. Everybody was there, safe and sound and with their weapons. Led by our captain, we went to dance, drink, and celebrate the Liberation in Puget-Théniers.[21]

Betemps' account has brought us all the way to August 28th, the date which, as he mentioned, the Americans crossed the Var. We will now return to August 26, 1944, which was not only the day of the *Grande Attaque* by the Resistance against Levens, but also the day when the first elements of the 517th Parachute Infantry Regiment reached the Var River.

First to the Var River

The 517th Parachute Infantry Regiment had reached the Loup River August 24th, and had then turned north and cut through the mountains above Vence. Because the Germans had no troops

defending this area, the 517th was able to advance much faster than the rest of the First Airborne Task Force, thus becoming the first unit to reach the Var River at Carros August 26th. The local bridge, the Pont de la Manda, had been damaged by the Germans, but two men from C Company, pretending to be French workmen, were able to cross it on foot. **Cpl Leslie Perkins** was one of the two men who volunteered to cross the bridge:

> The S-2 wanted to know what there was across the river, so they came after a volunteer to see what was there. I volunteered to go across with Jim Norris. They set up a good perimeter: they had some of those machine gun people, mortars, and they had infantry behind us. We took off our shirts, and all we wore was a pair of pants; we happened to find a little push cart. It wasn't planned, but we saw that pushing the cart across the bridge would be a good way to do it. We got over and they had a guard there. We got to him, took him out, and then looked around to see what other people were around. Then they began opening fire on us, so we came back across the bridge. We fired back a little, but it was mainly dodge back and forth and get out of there.

No trace of any German having been killed at the Manda Bridge exists in the archives. The story may have been embellished, or perhaps the German sentry was only wounded. However, on the 26th, one German soldier, 17-year-old *Grenadier* **Karl Nuntschitsch**, was killed on the west bank of the Var River, a few kilometers south of the Pont de la Manda. Nuntschitsch was born in Zagreb, Croatia, and his name was clearly a Germanized version of the name Nunčič. Two other German casualties occurred in Gattières in undetermined circumstance on the 25th: they were 17-year-old **Johann Chwaszczynski** and 18-year-old **Johann Rösch**, of the 2nd Company of *Feld Ersatz Bataillon 148*.

The 517th Parachute Infantry Regiment Attacks la Roquette sur Var

After reaching Carros August 26th, elements of the 2nd Battalion of the 517th PIR advanced to le Broc, on the opposite side of the Var River from la Roquette, early on the 27th. Fortunately, **1st Lt Walter Irving**, of the HQ Company of the 2nd Battalion, later wrote a highly detailed report of the operations that followed:

> Second Battalion situation, 27 August 1944
>
> The 2nd Battalion 517th RCT moved along the highway Bézaudun les Alpes - le Broc and approached the Var River opposite the town of la Roquette, which was situated on the eastern bank and commanded the only available bridge [The Pont Charles Albert.] across the Var in this zone. This bridge was as yet undamaged.
>
> The battalion CP was established in the town of le Broc by the Battalion C.O., Lt Colonel R. J. Seitz, by mid-morning 27 August.
>
> Battalion had received orders that the bridge in this area would be secured intact if at all possible, for a supply route to be used by the supporting units on the advance to the east.
>
> A combat patrol consisting of a reinforced platoon had been sent to this bridge location early on the morning of the 27th, and had surprised the enemy security force charged with the holding or demolition of the structure. As the battalion moved into the vicinity of le Broc, the patrol was finding a most determined enemy making successive attempts to

demolish the structure, which had been previously mined for demolition. Enemy forces would lay down a tremendous concentration of machine gun and mortar fire, and under the protection of this would send patrols to attempt the destruction, but each time these were driven back by a just as determined patrol from the battalion.

It was felt by the battalion CO that if a force could effect a crossing on this bridge and neutralize the demolitions, they could establish a bridgehead sufficient to allow the remainder of the regiment to advance.

Company F, reinforced with a section of light machine guns from the Battalion Headquarters Company, was given this mission. Attempts were made to force a crossing near the bridge site, but it was found that due to the nearly perfect defensive terrain on the east bank of the river and the excellent observation, to cross was not worth the cost in casualties.

This view of la Roquette, which can be seen on the crest of the hill in the center of the picture, demonstrates what a superb defensive position the village was, overlooking the Var Valley, the Charles Albert Bridge, and miles of surrounding terrain. Author's Collection.

Enemy machine gun and mortar fire effectively discouraged all attempts to send even small patrols across during daylight hours. This situation, however, worked as well for both forces. The mortar, machine gun, and supporting artillery fire of Company F denied the enemy any success in their numerous attempts to destroy the structure. [The body of an unidentified German engineer soldier was later found next to the Pont Charles Albert, as we will see further on.]

Reconnaissance patrols were dispatched to find possible crossing sites, but in each case of a likely crossing site the area was well covered by well-directed automatic small arms and mortar fire.

Attempts by the attached engineer platoon of the 596 Airborne Engineers to clear a path through the extensive minefield proved unsuccessful due to enemy fire and the very nature of the emplaced mines. Six-foot wooden poles had been set in the riverbed approximately 25 feet apart. From the tops of these wire had been strung to connect each pole, and suspended from between each of these poles, hanging nose down, approximately eight inches from the ground was an activated 170mm high explosive projectile with quick fuse. To stumble into the wire or molest it so that the projectile would touch the ground would cause the projectile to explode. To make matters more difficult, anti-personnel mines had been sprinkled throughout the area.

It was apparent that a force must be sent across the river at some other location to seize the town of la Roquette and the hill mass [the Arpasse] to permit the Battalion to advance and seize the bridge intact.

Second Battalion Intelligence Situation

Weather at this season of the year was extremely warm during daylight hours, but was disagreeably chilly during darkness. It had not rained in the area for some weeks, making the scattered scrub growth dry and highly inflammable.

Terrain in this area consisted of a series of jagged, rock-studded, scrub-covered mountain ridges rising to a high of some fifteen hundred meters at the crests, with the Var River cutting a course running generally north-south through the terrain mass. The mountains extended to the banks of the Var and dropped abruptly down to the river's edge.

This being the dry season of the year, the river was approximately 150 to 200 yards in width, with a reported average depth of three to five feet. The bridge across the Var River in this area was made of concrete construction, two lanes in width, pier supported, and approximately 300 yards in length. Mountain ridge due east of the bridge site rises to a height of 600 meters and commands the approaches on either bank.

Highway number 202 parallels the east bank of the river southward to Nice.

Enemy in area was estimated to be a reinforced battalion of infantry, with positions on ridge line situated east of and paralleling the Var River. Approximately one company was estimated to be in the area of la Roquette. Enemy was well dug in and had prepared positions in the area to command all approaches to the bridge, and had organized all key terrain features along the east bank of the river. Extensive anti-personnel minefields were located in the river bed in the area of the bridge and extended approximately one mile north and south. Wire barriers had been erected on all likely avenues of approach to the east defenses. Travelling patrols moved along Highway 202 during hours of darkness. Support was in the form of an unknown number of mortars (80mm and 120mm) and a few pieces of small caliber mountain artillery. No tanks were reported in the area.

By 1200 hours 27 August, the battalion situation was stagnant. Company F was undergoing no intense hardship, as forward movement had ceased, but the engagement thus far could be called a checkmate.

A most welcome visitor was ushered in to see the battalion CO at approximately 1200 hours, name unknown to members of the command, but later known as "Louie." He proved to be a member of the well organized FFI Forces in the area and was volunteering his services and knowledge of the terrain. After verification of his status from Task Force Headquarters, "Louie" stated that down river, approximately one mile, the channel was shallow and that the area was now unguarded, and further, the FFI had a schedule of all enemy travelling patrols on Highway 202.

Map study and reports from the Intelligence and Reconnaissance Section and the Field Artillery Aerial Observer indicated this could be true.

To preclude any hint of a crossing in this area, all patrol activity in this area was withdrawn until darkness. Thus, with the stage set the Battalion Commander issued his order.

The 2nd Battalion would attack 1700 hours, 28 August 1944, seize the bridge across the Var River, the hill mass east of the bridge, and the town of la Roquette. On order, they would advance to next objective of Levens. Support would be given by 460 Parachute Field Artillery Battalion and Battalion Headquarters Company 81mm mortar platoon. Company F would continue pressure on bridge until H hour; Company D would move to area generally to the west and south of Company F and support the crossing by fire, and would be committed on battalion order. H hour, Company F would force a bridge crossing and seize the high ground east of the bridge. Company D would, on order, advance rapidly to the vicinity of la Roquette and assist Company E should it be needed. Company E, reinforced, was given the mission of making a river crossing, by stealth, 0200 28 August, moving to the rock-bound ridge in the rear of la Roquette, cut the la Roquette - Levens Highway at 1600 hours, and attack the town of la Roquette from the rear at 1630 hours. Artillery liaison would be with Company E and would place fire on enemy positions, firing on bridge site commencing 1530 hours.[22]

The real identity of "Louie" is not known. However, the commanding officer of the FFI forces in the area, **Pierre Gautier**, known as Malherbe, wrote briefly about this cooperation with the 517th PIR:

During the night of the 25th to the 26th [These dates are incorrect, being 24 hours early.], the American forward troops reached the Var. I immediately went to the headquarters of the tactical group, and the situation was quickly explained and understood. The American command notes that we hold Plan du Var and are in contact on the east bank. The artillery is put at my disposal and carries out precise bombardments on the German positions.[23]

Lt Walter Irving continues:

Upon receipt of the battalion order activity increased in Company E area. While the Company Commander and the attached officers discussed a plan of action, the company busied itself preparing for the operation. This was not an unusual undertaking to the men, as training in night operations and participations in numerous night movements had instilled the necessity of thorough preparation of men, weapons, ammunition, and plans. The attached Headquarter Company machine gun section, rocket section, and demolitions personnel were absorbed in the scheme of events and preparations forged ahead. All weapons were oiled, checked, and further prepared for the river crossing. Ammunition was issued to all participating personnel. Machine gun ammunition boxes were submerged in water to assure the gunner that the lid seals did not leak, and extra cardboard was inserted to prevent the belted ammunition from making any noise. All loose metal was either taped, tied, or discarded; 60mm mortars were reduced to two and extra ammunition was carried by the surplus crews; personnel were instructed to carry the very minimum of equipment and were issued grenade bags and extra white phosphorus and fragmentation grenades; 2/3 K rations would be carried and a hot meal fed before departure, the first since leaving Italy.

The attack plan of Company E was simple in nature. Company E (plus) would depart le Broc 0130 hours, 28 August 1944, in order of 1st Platoon, Command Group, 2nd Platoon, Weapons, and 3rd Platoon bringing up the rear and securing the tail. Company would cross the Var at the indicated ford, move to a position 600 yards in rear of la Roquette, and would remain until 1600 hours, at which time would cut the la Roquette - Levens Highway and attack the town from the rear at 1630.[24]

Cpl Eugene Brissey was one of the men of E Company who was to cross the river. He describes the rapid advance of the 517th until its arrival at the Var, then the reaction that the enlisted men had upon being told of their mission. They were of course not as enthusiastic as Lt Irving:

We moved fast, often hungry, thirsty, and sleepy. On one occasion we had to restrain some troops from eating sugar beets. These are not good to eat, but I never found out whether they would kill a human or even make him sick, for that matter. Our only concern was for the paratroopers, who aren't really human... sugar beets would probably make them at least a little ill. On one particular rush through the farm lands of France we came to a river. We were on one side, the Germans on the other. We had no way to cross, so we stopped and waited for the food trucks to catch up. When they did, they brought only field rations. This cold stuff kept us going and was appreciated.

On this occasion the trucks brought candy, gum, and extra smokes for those who wanted them. This time, as usual, the goodies were few, so we carefully split them among the men. Several times while in the field I split candy bars and broke sticks of gum into two pieces to assure that each man in my squad had at least a small share. The guys would sit there like little children and watch with anticipation. A person's feelings at a time like that cannot be described in words, so I'll just drop the subject.

As we sat there on our side of the river, we welcomed the rest and looked forward to a good sleep. This was not to be. Our company was selected to cross the river under cover of darkness. We were to find out what the Germans had on the other side. This was the most dangerous mission assigned to any of the 517th up to that time. We were not at all happy about this, and some even called it a suicide mission. We were expected to get clobbered. Naturally, we ate all our candy... just in case we didn't make it. Didn't want to leave any of that good stuff for anyone who might find our bodies later. We said a sad goodbye to those who were to stay behind. They gave us their best wishes and left us to prepare for the crossing.[25]

Before continuing with E Company's "suicide mission," more must be said about the local French Resistance men. The evening of August 27th, while the paratroopers were preparing to cross the Var, a group of four FFI messengers was sent out from le Broc towards Plan du Var. Their mission was to meet Malherbe and the resistance commanders on the far side of the Var River, probably in order to inform them of the impending American operation so that the Resistance could coordinate their own operations with the American attack. Two of the messengers turned back before crossing the Pont de Gabre, while the remaining two continued on and were then captured by the Germans. The fate of the two who were captured (37-year-old **Marcellin Richier** and 31-year-old **Jean Garente**) was later reconstructed thanks to declarations made by witnesses, one of which was messenger **Hilaire Mallaussène**, who had turned back at the Pont de Gabre:

> On the evening of Sunday, August 27, 1944, I was at my friend Marcellin Richier's house when Mr Aristide Fouques, President of the le Broc Liberation Committee and Chief of the FFIs, came to ask us to join two other FFIs [Jean Garente and Léon Bertola] to accomplish a night mission at Plan du Var for Commander Malherbe. Four of us left around 21:00. Before reaching the Pont des Gabres, as I was going over a wall, I felt dizzy and was not able to cross over or go any further. My comrades went on their way and I returned alone. [In fact, Léon Bertola also turned back.]
>
> I heard the noise of a violent explosion around 2 o'clock in the morning and hoped that my comrades had had time to cross. I realized that the Pont des Gabres had just been blown.[26]

31- and 37-year-old FFI messengers Jean Garente and Marcelin Richier, who were captured by the Germans in the vicinity of Levens during the night of August 27 to 28, 1944, and who were executed the next morning. Garente Family Collection.

What exactly happened to messengers Richier and Garente after that is not known, until they were seen in the hands of the German soldiers of the 12th Company of *Bataillon 164* in front of the town hall of Levens in the early hours of August 28th. Levens **Gendarme Hughes Rasser** was one of the rare witnesses of the tragic scene, as the male population of Levens was still being forced to sleep in the chapel at the time:

> I, as well as my Brigade Chief, were held back in Levens by the Germans after they had occupied the village. We were responsible for the population. Here are the exact events that preceded the martyrdom of the two le Broc residents:
>
> During the night of August 27 to 28, 1944, between four and five in the morning, I was awakened by the cries and wails of a man. Suspecting reprisals against the men of Levens who were locked up in the chapel, I immediately went to the Place de la République. There I noticed a greater number of sentries than usual and made out two human shapes lying along the wall, almost in front of the entrance of the park. Having identified myself with the sentries, they invited me in to see if I could recognize the two men as inhabitants of Levens. One of the two wailed and cried and called "Mother." Under the light of a match, I was able to ascertain that both men were completely unknown to me. I took advantage of this chance to talk to them, and speaking to the one who was wailing, I was not able to get any response other than: "May they kill me but may they not let me suffer like this." Speaking to the other, who seemed calmer, I was able to get their names and addresses: he was Jean Garente, of Le Broc, and the second was Richier (pronounced Riquier) Joseph, also from le Broc.
>
> He was not able to indicate to me the area where they had been arrested, because they had been transported in a truck, making him lose his sense of direction. His comrade Richier had been found carrying a revolver. Mr Garente

did not trust me and revealed neither his mission nor any secrets. Obviously my presence at night amongst the German troops must have seemed suspicious to him, hence his silence. Later on I was forced to move away. However, once daylight came I washed at the fountain near the two poor men. I set down my tunic next to Jean Garente, but I did not notice any sign or gesture from him.[27]

In response to the question: "What ill treatment did they suffer from?" **Hughes Rasser** answered:

> Apart from the suffering they were enduring of having their feet bound, and their hands bound behind their heads and attached to their feet, lying face down, no ill treatment was inflicted on them in my presence. A German aid man even showed some humanity by laying them on their backs so that they could breathe better. (…) [Marcel Richier] seemed oblivious of what was around him, because he seemed to be suffering enormously from being tied up in such a fashion. His fists and face were starting to turn purple. In fact, I was not able to speak to him since he was crying, wailing, and calling "mother."[28]

The anguish of the two messengers ended in the morning when they were executed by the Germans. **Aristide Fouques**, the mayor of le Broc, wrote in a declaration:

> Three days later (...), I found out that two men from le Broc had been shot by the Germans. I went to Levens. The gamekeeper, Lucien Dalmas, told me what happened. The gamekeeper and Mr Bovis, a farmer, declared that the two executed men were named Richier and Garente and that they had been beaten, bound, and tormented in the Town Hall Square by the soldiers of the 148th Division, 12th *Grenadier* Company. They saw them with their hands tied behind their necks being brought down to Mr Bovis' field. Soon thereafter, Mr Bovis heard several gunshots. After the departure of the Germans, he went to his field and saw the place where they had been buried. It was August 28, 1944, between eight and nine o'clock in the morning. September 5th I returned to Levens and helped by Mr Bovis, I exhumed the two FFIs, who I found thrown in

one on top of the other. In the grave I also found the rope that had been used to tie them up.[29]

Let us now return to the men of E Company of the 517th PRCT, who in the meantime were preparing to cross the Var River, unaware of the tragedy that was befalling the two FFI messengers a few kilometers away. **1st Lt Walter Irving** continued his report:

> The weather at 0130 hours, 28 August was clear, with a sliver of a moon. None of the usual fog had fallen, and the bed of the river could be felt by the damp chill rising from the stream.
>
> At 0130 hours, Company passed through the security detachments of le Broc in single file, led by "Louie" and Intelligence and Reconnaissance Section guides, and followed the tortuous path down the mountain side to the river crossing site.
>
> One can well imagine the difficulty of moving a group of men in the dark of night on flat terrain, then increase this some hundredfold and the picture will equal the column of men moving down the side of the mountain, with equipment, over a rock-strewn path.
>
> Progress was slow and control difficult. As radio silence would be observed, this necessitated the passage of orders verbally along the column. This resulted in some confusion as to the original intent of the message, but did not seriously impede progress down the mountain. Further difficulty was encountered in low hanging bushes slapping each person in turn and catching on items of equipment, causing no end of uncomplimentary ejaculations from the men.
>
> Another situation caused some concern, as the path became more precipitous. Loose rocks would become dislodged by the passage of men and would roll several yards down the steep slope, causing what seemed to be a young avalanche. Orders were passed back along the column and urged the selection of proper footholds, and in addition, the rate of descent was slowed considerably. This corrected the major portion of these incidents and possibly eliminated the detection of the Company's advance to the water's edge.
>
> For some 45 minutes the column slipped, slid, and grunted its way to the floor of the riverbed and emerged on the narrow west bank of the Var River.
>
> The river fog caused the river to assume the appearance of some gigantic snake lazily moving to an unknown destination, but the peaceful appearing stream nearly cost the lives of five men with its swift undercurrent.

The River Crossing

> After a 15-minute rest halt, the column moved downstream for some 600 yards to the so-called ford known to "Louie" and the Intelligence and Reconnaissance Section guides.
>
> All personnel were instructed to make a last minute check of equipment and were told to form a human chain upon entering the water by holding to the back of the person's harness to their front. Individual arms were to be held out of water insofar as possible to assure their ability to function should the need arise in the immediate future.
>
> It had been decided to cross two columns each in single file to expedite the company reorganization on the eastern edge of the water, and the company was being so organized for the crossing.
>
> The water at this point was reported to be at low stage due to lack of rain, and 75 to 150 feet in width. The personnel of the company had been told to expect water to a depth of not more than three feet.
>
> A reconnaissance and security patrol was sent across to determine the best crossing and secure the eastern edge of the water to allow the main body of the company to cross. The patrol crossed, and by pointing chins to the sky managed to keep from drowning. The patrol leader sent two of the tallest of his patrol back to the Company Commander to inform him of this fact. Coupled with this unexpected depth was the fact that the river at this point was flowing some five to six miles per hour, which was to be a dangerous undertaking for foot troops with no safety ropes.
>
> The Intelligence and Reconnaissance Section guides, together with "Louie," were accosted with this fact and asked if there could possibly be a mistake in the location of the crossing site. Company Commander was assured that this was the intended site, however, it was found that the Intelligence and Reconnaissance Section, who had been charged with determining the depth, width, and velocity earlier in the evening, had failed to make a physical reconnaissance and had relied upon the word of the French FFI guide. "Louie," when asked specifically if he had actual personal knowledge of the crossing said that he personally had never crossed at this particular spot, but had been told by the FFI Commander of this area that it was shallow and easily fordable.
>
> The men were informed of this development and instructed as to the depth, width, and velocity. Squad leaders were told to make certain that all short men would be behind a tall person in the crossing column. To guard against losing the heavier loaded weapons crews, two columns were to be used as before, but the weapons group would now cross two to three yards upstream from the riflemen. This would give some protection to the crewmen should they lose footing and be carried downstream by the swift current.
>
> Both columns entered the river and had advanced approximately three quarters of the distance across without mishap when a crew member of a 60mm squad, carrying a tube and extra ammunition, lost his footing and was swept downstream. In an effort to save the man, the person next in the column had hung on to the man's harness and was jerked from his feet. In a like manner, the next three were jerked from their feet and carried downstream. Fortunately the riflemen, with a firm grip and not as heavily loaded, grabbed, or was grabbed, by a passing body. All persons were saved, but individual weapons of four of the riflemen were lost in the stream. The column moved without further incident to the eastern edge of the water.
>
> Water soaked and gasping for breath, the column moved some fifty feet east of the water and halted to reorganize.
>
> The security patrol leader reported that he had encountered no mines and that he had advanced some 100 yards to the east, and had heard no sound that would indicate that the area was physically occupied or patrolled. "Louie" assured the commander that no German patrols were due to pass this general area for some 30 minutes.
>
> The column was quickly organized into the original single column for control and prepared to move to the eastern bank of the riverbed.[30]

Cpl Eugene Brissey described the crossing in more colorful terms:

> A Frenchman had been found who would lead us down the steep and dangerous cliff and across the river. We were

This photo of the Var River was taken in the months following the Liberation. The village of le Broc, from which E Company of the 517th PIR started its crossing, is very faintly visible on the crest in the center of the picture. The river bed is covered in small piles of stones built by the Germans to prevent glider landings. Mike Reuter Collection.

told that the water would be about up to our armpits in spots. This wasn't so bad. At about 2:00 A.M., we started down the cliff toward the river. The trail was suitable for mountain goats, but somehow that Frenchman led us to the water during total darkness. The guy, whoever he was, who said the water was only up to the armpit, evidently didn't check where we crossed, or else he was at least seven feet tall. We hadn't gone far when we were in over our heads. We lost a gun or two but made it to more shallow water. Every moment we expected to receive a welcome from the German guns. We were ignored, because the Kraut knew anyone with any brains at all would never try to cross that river at night. They were not aware of the fact that we were paratroopers, thus not very bright. We sneaked in behind the German lines and hid for a while to get organized. A French family brought us a big pot of stew, which was just about the best stuff we had in France.[31]

Once they were on the east side, E Company of the 517th had to cross the RN 202 highway and infiltrate itself onto the hill behind la Roquette. **1st Lt Walter Irving** wrote on:

The next checkpoint on the night movement was a large culvert some six to eight feet in diameter located some 200 to 300 yards to the east of the present position. This culvert allowed a small stream to flow under highway 202, paralleling the Var River.

The FFI guide and a careful study of the terrain from the west bank during the daylight hours had indicated that this pipe was free of any wire or other man-made obstacles, and due to this had been tentatively selected as a possible crossing into the enemy positions.

Reconnaissance proved this to be false, and other places of entry through the concertina and barbed wire had to be found. "Louie" vowed that though he had been wrong on the ford and the culvert, that of a certainty he knew of a breach in the wire on the east bank. For the first time since the beginning of the operation, the FFI produced positive intelligence. The breach proved to be clear of mines and completely through the wire barrier.

The column approached the gap and security elements were sent both up and down the road to prevent enemy patrols from arriving at the time the column would be crossing the road. The FFI guide had assured the Company Commander that patrols were not due in this area for some time, but due to his wrong information on two previous occasions, it was felt that he could be wrong again.

No noise was made as the column moved across the roadway and moved as rapidly as possible away from the roadway. The guide had chosen an evidently little-used trail through one of the small fields bordering the river. This was evidenced by the sticks, stones, and various other obstacles that caused the column to stumble and mutter as it proceeded to its objective.

There was no evidence that the movement had been sensed or discovered by the enemy, as no shots or illuminating shells had been fired. The only noise in the night was an occasional spatter of artillery or mortar fire and the stuttering rip of a German M-42 [MG 42] and the answering heavy pounding of an American machine gun. From the noise, it was apparent that the bridge was still an undecided issue.

From this point to the ridge where the company would spend the day in hiding was strictly enemy territory. This particular section of terrain had been screened from view from the far bank, and it was now up to "Louie," a careful map study, and a great deal of prayer that someone would not kick a trip-flare and expose the maneuver to the enemy.

It was now 0330 hours 28 August, with the company still approximately one mile from the ridge and daylight at 0445. The FFI guide continued to lead off in the right direction with a supposed knowledge of the course he was following.

After marching for some 20 uneventful minutes, the Artillery Forward Observer, Captain James Lantz, remarked that a small wooden foot bridge the column was then crossing looked strangely familiar, and indeed it was. "Louie" had become lost and had wandered in a circle.

At this time, the Command Group oriented themselves with the aid of a covered map and informed "Louie" that he was free to leave and complete his secondary mission of coordinating the FFI Forces in a harassing mission in the rear areas. Needless to relate, his services had not been appreciated.[32]

Lt Irving's judgment of "Louie" seems rather harsh, particularly in light of what was happening to FFI messengers Garente and Richier a few miles further north. "Louie" had taken serious risks to try and help the Americans, when he could very well have just stayed at home. Thankfully, some of the other American officers held "Louie" in higher esteem, such as E Company's commander, **Captain Robert Newberry**:

Colonel Seitz ordered E company to cross the river below the bridge and seize la Roquette. We waded across the river. It was a little deeper and a little swifter than they thought it was and we lost a few weapons crossing it. We had a few French *maquis* with us. It helped us out, and there were supposed to be some on the other side of the river to join us, but they never did join us. [Perhaps this was linked to the interception of Garente and Richier?]

Lt Col Richard Seitz, the commander of the 2ⁿᵈ Battalion of the 517ᵗʰ, was also grateful for "Louie's" help, despite his deficiencies:

I wish I knew his name, because he did help us find a good place to cross the river, and that was very important. But after we got across the river, I am told that he sort of faded out; he was not in on the attack of la Roquette. But he played a very important role in guiding E Company down to the point of crossing the Var River. That was very important.

E Company now proceeded to the hill behind la Roquette without "Louie." **1ˢᵗ Lt Walter Irving** continued:

Guided by an azimuth and dead reckoning, the column moved out for the ridge. For some 30 minutes the column wound upwards, and at 0420, the head of the column could see the outline of the ridge top ahead. Patrols were dispatched to secure the area and the column moved into the selected area.

With the fear of being exposed by the dawn, the platoons were hurriedly given an area among the boulders, last minute instructions were given on security, and the long wait began.

Dawn found the exhausted company securely nestled among the granite boulders on the ridge top, and to all appearances in a position that was impenetrable, except to heavy artillery concentrations or direct air strikes.

With the coming of first light, it was found that the town of la Roquette could be seen situated some 600 yards to the north and west, enthroned on the very top of an extension of the ridge line on which the company was located. A hog-back, or saddle, could be seen connecting the town's ridge top with that of the company's, fairly open, minus any large boulders, and offering an approach directly to the rear gateway to the town. There was a difference of some 100 feet in elevation between the town and the company's location, which gave an additional advantage of being able to partially see into the interior of the town proper.

To the rear (east) of the position, at a range of some 2,000 yards, was another ridge line, slightly higher and extending as far as the eye could see. It was hoped that the enemy did not have this terrain occupied, as observation from this vantage point could permit a keen eye to notice an attack forming the coming afternoon.

To the south was a canyon up which the company had advanced the night before.

To the north was the hill mass [The Arpasse.] overlooking the bridge. The enemy had this mass occupied in force, and from the present position, a fairly accurate location was made of some of the automatic weapon locations causing no end of trouble to the forces still on the west bank of the river.

The morning serenade of mortar and light artillery opened up on the bridge site. It was noticed that at least one large caliber mortar was firing from within the town. Although a portion of the town could be seen, the gun could not be accurately located, but was marked down as a number one objective in the town.

As yet, no definite orders had been issued to the platoon's leaders in regard to specific objectives within the town proper. Up until this time no plan had been formulated due to lack of knowledge of the interior of the walled town. The FFI guide "Louie" had provided a crude map of the town layout, but after his other mistakes, no one was willing to take anything that he had dealings with as gospel.

Observation into the town from this vantage point revealed that the town was divided by two streets, each approximately two hundred yards in length, with the stone houses side by side with no alley room. Width of the street appeared to be some 15 to 20 feet. Two gates led into the town, one from the east and one from the north, each capable of passing an automobile. [This description of la Roquette is largely inaccurate; the town actually has no gates, and there is only one street that spirals around, then into the town.]

From this position visual reconnaissance was carried out down to the assault squad leaders, but was restricted in movement to prevent possible detection of movement by the enemy.

Based on this visual reconnaissance orders were issued to the company. Two platoons would be used in the assault. One platoon would remain initially in reserve to the east of the town on the ridge and be prepared to enter the town and advance down either of the two streets. Weapons, both machine gun and mortar, would go into position in rear of the ridge and cover the advance of the assault platoons. Rally point would be in the town square. Each squad leader was informed that if his squad became lost or separated due to heavy fighting or darkness, that he would take one house, clear it, and remain until the company could extract his unit or direct it to the main body.

The second platoon was elected to be the right street unit and the third platoon would be left. To each was attached two rocket launchers for breaching stone walls. First platoon, minus the road block squad, would be in support and would remain in position on the ridge. Due to the hour of the attack, it was felt that with the coming of darkness the entire company would be brought into the section of town that had been cleared and would remain as a compact unit until the town was either captured, cleared, or the company forced to retire.[33]

As was perfectly understood by 1ˢᵗ Lt Irving, it was vitally important that E Company not be spotted by the Germans until the moment of the attack. However, not all the enlisted men seemed to have realized this! **Cpl Eugene Brissey** wrote in his memoirs:

We made our way nearer the town, la Roquette I think, and dug in on a hill, still not knowing where the Germans were, nor how many there were of them. In mid-afternoon I had to go to the bathroom... of course, there was no bathroom on the battlefields of France, but that was a way of life in combat. At any rate, I had to go, and as I went or was going or whatever... I heard some more familiar thuds. The next thing I knew bullets were flying under my feet. The expression "caught with my pants down" is the best way I know to express my plight. This didn't slow me down much. In a couple seconds I was back in the slit trench with my bare knees sticking up and bullets bouncing all over the place. I wiggled back into my pants and yelled, "Let's get out of here." We started running up the hill, and I dropped my tommy gun. I scrambled back for it and finally made it over the hill in a hail of bullets. Obviously the Germans were a long way off, because they missed us and we could not hear their guns fire.

La Roquette sur Var, as seen from the hill behind the German lines on which E Company of the 517th PIR was hiding August 28th. Vincent Meyer Collection.

Though we could not hear their guns, we knew where they were. They were in this small town, which was situated on a cliff overlooking the river. A beautiful place to be. Unfortunately for the Germans, we were behind them, and even though they had fired at us, they didn't seem to realize the fact that we were there. They might have thought we were French.[34]

All the soldiers of E Company were in later years convinced that the Germans had been completely unaware of their presence behind la Roquette. However, the inhabitants of la Roquette told a different story. **Jacques Saussine**, who was at the Place du Portalet, the viewpoint of la Roquette, remembered:

A tall German, who measured at least 1.8 meters, told me: "Amerikaner hier!" I didn't understand or know what he wanted to say. "Amerikaner hier! Amerikaner!" He repeated it two or three times. I was saying: "Ja, ja, ja!" It was the only thing I knew to say: "Ja, ja." Finally, I indeed saw men on the hill opposite us. I could see a whole column coming up, it looked like caterpillars, and indeed, it was the Americans. The Germans had seen them, and they were afraid and hiding in the basements. They must have been afraid, because they didn't fire at them.

The fact that the Germans had spotted the Americans is confirmed by another inhabitant, as we will see further on. Why exactly did the Germans not react to the American presence? Did the Polish soldiers withhold the information from their officers? Did they not realize how many Americans there were? Since no German sources regarding this action have been found, these questions cannot be answered. With the hour of the attack nearing, the Americans started firing artillery on the German positions, as **1st Lt Walter Irving** described:

At 1530 hours the radio silence, imposed for security reasons, was lifted. The artillery liaison officer, Captain

James Lantz, was immediately occupied with directing very accurate artillery fire on the plotted automatic weapons position and other suspected enemy targets. The accuracy of this fire was evidenced by the fact that the enemy could be seen moving away from the hill mass [The Arpasse.] and a considerable lessening of the automatic weapons fire on the bridge site. Enemy movement of an estimated company strength was noticed some fifteen hundred yards to the east, moving in the direction of Levens. These were immediately taken under fire by the artillery, directed by the forward observer in the grandstand seat, as far as observation was concerned.[35]

Adèle Tacconi remembers the German retreat off Arpasse Mountain and into her parents' farm:

The Germans were dispersed on the hill, and at night they would come back to sleep in our house. The day the Americans arrived, we heard cannon fire coming from the other side of the river. Suddenly, we saw the Germans all coming down the hill wearing their gas masks. [The intense white smoke produced by phosphorus shells was probably the reason the Germans were wearing their gas masks.] That scared me and my sister, because we didn't know what a gas mask was. My father asked: "What is going on now? Why are you fighting again?" and the Germans said: "It's not us, it's Amerikaner." Supposedly, the Americans were on the other side of the Var, and from there they saw the Germans in the forest with their binoculars and they started firing at our house. We went back down into the basement again, and the Germans all rushed into the house.

A bit further north, in Levens, the American artillery fire took deadly effect, as was noted by **Dr Flavier**:

On Monday after lunch - bang! A shell explodes in front of the hospital - some shouts, one child is killed and

A battery of the 460ᵗʰ PFAB in position near Bouyon fires on targets probably located in the vicinity of la Roquette and Levens in late August 1944. Merle McMorrow Collection.

9-year-old Joseph Riquier, who was killed by American artillery fire in Levens August 28, 1944. The same fire also killed three German soldiers in Levens. Author's Collection.

two others are wounded. Soon after, three Germans are killed and two wounded. One of the gun crew members of the piece that was firing from the Château brings me the wounded, trembling like a leaf. "What is it?" "The Americans," he replies - I breathed with relief.[36]

The local child who was killed was nine-year-old **Joseph Riquier**. Dr Flavier noted that the shell had "cut him in two pieces lengthwise." The three Germans who were killed belonged to the 12ᵗʰ Company of *Bataillon 164*, they were: 18-year-old *Grenadier* **Albert Frank**, 19-year-old *Grenadier* **Alois Kruschynski**, and 35-year-old *Gernadier* **Paul Cellary**. These dead were buried in the Levens cemetery. According to **Jacques Saussine**, at least two Germans were also killed by the American artillery within la Roquette:

One German was killed by a cannon, or maybe a mortar, in *Madame* Alfrossi's garage. There was a window about one meter wide and one and a half meters high, and the shell came through the window and killed the German on the spot. One shell also hit a little wall at the Place du Portalet and a German soldier was torn to pieces. There was a leg on one side, one arm ripped off, the head smashed, the body riddled. They put all those pieces in a blanket: a piece of leg, the head, all that. It wasn't a pretty sight!

It may have been hard for the American soldiers in the "grandstand seat" to imagine the effects the artillery they had called in was having. **1ˢᵗ Lt Walter Irving** continues his description of the preparations for the attack:

At 1545 hours, a reinforced squad, under the command of Staff Sergeant Craig, moved under cover along the east slope of the ridge to establish a road block on the Levens - la Roquette Highway. His orders were specific. He would

establish a block and prevent any enemy from either entering or escaping the town of la Roquette. He would remain in this position until relieved or ordered to return to the Company.[37]

A hapless pair of German motorcyclists drove down the road from Levens shortly afterwards. **Bruno Municchi** describes the scene:

The Americans were up there at the curve where the garage is. One motorcycle came with two Germans, and as they took the curve, the Americans shot the first one, who was driving the motorcycle. He fell down, but the second one jumped off the motorcycle and tried to escape and hide behind the barn, but he didn't make it and they shot him anyway.

Jacques Saussine adds a few extra details about the motorcyclists, as he later examined their bodies:

The Americans crossed the Var and climbed up here, and six of them had taken up position above the cemetery. They had dug holes to hide in and be able to fire at the road. A German went up on a motorcycle, but he didn't get far. Unfortunately, at the curve, the poor guy was shot right between the eyes. Bang, he fell to the ground beside the motorcycle. I saw the motorcyclist on the ground, and what struck me the most was his bag. He had a huge leather bag that supposedly contained a very important dispatch that he was to bring to the *Kommandantur* in Levens.

In fact, the motorcycle had been coming from Levens, not going to Levens; however, in his report, **1ˢᵗ Lt Walter Irving** confirms the importance of the dispatch the motorcyclists were carrying:

The only action encountered was a motorcycle that they had been forced to shoot to stop. Papers found in a dispatch case on the driver ordered the troops on the hill mass, east of the bridge, and the company in la Roquette to withdraw to Levens, effective 2130 hours, after demolition of the bridge at all cost.[38]

Some of the American soldiers later wondered why the shooting of the two motorcyclists had still not alerted the Germans in la Roquette of their presence. Once again, according to the local inhabitants, the Germans, or at least some of them, were well aware that the Americans were behind them and had decided to surrender at the first chance. **Bruno Municchi** explains:

I will always remember, from down there where the Germans had burned our house, we could see the motorcycle on the ground at the curve. It stayed there for a good while, and then an American came down and took it and brought it up. We saw him and said: "Hey, he is taking the motorcycle." Even the Germans could see the motorcycle. Then they were frightened and one German told me: "Here, my rifle. Americans, Americans here. Us, finished, kaput! Home, home." I felt sorry for him. Some of the soldiers weren't mean. He made me understand that they couldn't do anything now, so they figured: "Now we will be prisoners, let's keep quiet. Let's not do anything stupid or else we are done for." So they kept quiet and they didn't fire or do anything. The big heads had all left, they had gotten out of the way and left the simple soldiers behind.

Company E now closed in for the kill. **1st Lt Walter Irving** wrote:

At 1600 hours, the company moved along the eastern slope of the ridge to a position in rear of the town. Machine guns and 60mm mortars were set up and prepared to cover the riflemen's advance to the gate in the town's wall. At this point, it was discovered that two of the ammunition bearers had discarded half their ammunition (one box of 250 rounds, belted), their explanation being that during the night movement to the ridge they were just so tired that they couldn't carry it any longer!

A last minute visual reconnaissance of the town now revealed that instead of two streets, there appeared to be three. This last being more of an alleyway between the wall and the rear of one row of buildings than a street, but nevertheless, it was a thoroughfare that must be cleared. To this task the first platoon was assigned, and a reserve was constituted from among the various ammunition bearers of the weapons section.

At 1625 hours, the artillery preparation for the company attacking the bridge began and the leading elements of the Company E platoons moved under cover and advanced toward the town. Up until this time, it is believed that the enemy was totally unaware that any force could possibly be in his rear areas, however, at this time he took notice and began to fire on the advancing troops with small arms and mortar.[39]

The first shots of the battle were apparently shot by **Sgt William Myers**, who had managed to advance all the way to the entrance of la Roquette unnoticed:

I was a sergeant, and I was responsible for a squad of 12 men and an officer, Lt Quigley. We waded across the Var River in the middle of the night and then we got up on the hilltop overlooking la Roquette. At daybreak, we went ahead and explored the area and we made contact with the Germans. I was hiding on one of the terraces overlooking the entrance to the town, and there was a platoon of Germans marching into la Roquette. They were not aware of us being present, and as they went past me, I could have reached out and taken the hat off of one of them. But we just watched them, we didn't do any gunfire, and they went on into la Roquette.

Then, not to long after that, this German came down the terraces by himself to go into la Roquette, and he just stumbled into us. We were about two terraces apart and he saw me, and I saw him. He dropped to the ground and threw a grenade at me. I laid down and concealed myself as best I could and the grenade went off real close to me. I felt around my back, expecting to see some blood, but evidently it was a concussion grenade, so when it went off no shrapnel got me. After that, he fired at one of my guys that was about 100 feet off to my right. Then he saw me moving around again. I had an M1 rifle and a .45 pistol, and I was going to use the .45, but I was nervous and shaking and realized that I couldn't make a good shot. So I picked up my M1 rifle and I exposed myself to get a shot at him. He was just bolting his rifle and getting ready to fire at me and I was a little quicker than him, so I got him first. He was lying down on his stomach, and then he slumped to the ground and that was it. I didn't spend any time looking him over, but some of the guys went through his paperwork and then they were telling me too much information about him. I said: "I just don't want to know it." I felt real bad about having to shoot him and I just closed my mind.

William Myers was awarded a Bronze Star for this action. About the attack of la Roquette, **Cpl Eugene Brissey** wrote:

"This German came down the terraces by himself to go into la Roquette, and he just stumbled into us." William Myers stands where the German soldier he shot was standing during a postwar visit to la Roquette. William Myers Collection.

"Some of the guys went through his paperwork." This photo was, according to William Myers' son, found on the body of the German soldier shot by William Myers at la Roquette, though the passage of time has made it impossible to verify this fact with certainty. Note the bullet hole in the lower right corner. William Myers Collection.

During a postwar visit, Eugene Brissey stands in what he described as the "courtyard," in fact a field just outside la Roquette. Eugene Brissey Collection.

We sneaked in behind the Germans and from cover of trees and grapevines we watched them milling around the town. As we watched, more of their troops marched into town with their hob-nailed boots. They assembled in the courtyard, and some were lying around on the grass, unaware of our presence when we opened fire with all the guns we had. Those Germans were in panic. Some fought, some ran inside buildings, and some jumped over the cliff. One of their mortar shells landed in our squad.

The shell fragments flew in all directions, hitting Ray Helms and Cecil Duncan. Ray was the squad leader and I was the assistant. We did what we could for Ray and Private Duncan and continued toward the city.

The fighting was wild, but we seemed to have profited by the element of surprise. Dick Jones heard a noise in a room and was going to throw a grenade in but heard a child crying. He looked inside and found a woman with two young children. Of course he remembered this until his death.[40]

Sgt Ray Helms explains how he was wounded by one of the German mortar shells:

We stayed behind la Roquette until morning, and then we started to move into the village that the Germans had occupied. We got a portion of the way down the hill towards the village when a mortar shell was fired in our group and all of us hit the ground. One shell fell maybe 20 or 30 feet behind us and then another shell fell just about that distance in front of us. Knowing how a mortar works, we expected the next shell to be right on us, which is what happened.

We had hit the ground. I had the butt of my rifle on my right side and the shell hit on my right side. A pretty good portion of the shell hit me in the right shoulder and it lodged just short of my lung. I was stunned, and it appeared that everybody that passed by me gave me a shot of morphine. I wasn't feeling much pain at all after that. The piece of

shrapnel is still there in my chest real close to the lungs and it's never given me any trouble. On an X-ray it looks like a star. My group continued to go on into la Roquette, and they came out with a number of prisoners; they had given up. I faintly remember when the German prisoners were marched through the area where I was laying. I could hear them walking on the pavement, and that was just sort of a dream, but it was really happening.

Most of the Germans who were killed in the fighting were shot in the fields at the entrance of la Roquette. (What Eugene Brissey referred to as the "courtyard.") **Col Rupert Graves**, the Commanding Officer of the 517th PRCT, later explained how this happened:

As the company advanced into the town after an artillery preparation, some of the Germans made a break for it across an open field. They were cut down by rifle and light machine gun fire.[41]

From the area of his house, **Bruno Municchi** had a good view of the fields at the entrance of town and he apparently witnessed the departure of the Germans who "made a break for it":

When the Americans arrived, the German chief said: "Everybody up there! The Americans are arriving and we have to hold them back up there before they reach the village!" But how could they be held back? There were too many Americans! So as the Germans went up through the olive trees, the Americans were shooting them from up above. I could see the Germans going up from my house, then I got out of there, because you never know, you could get hit by a stray bullet.

One German was in front of the pigeon house and a bullet hit his rifle, and I don't know how, but it ricocheted off the rifle and killed him. My brother Léon later had the rifle and showed me where the bullet had hit.

Pvt Federico Martinez, of E Company, remembers the attack:

We crossed the river, walking across it. There was a lot of water in there, but we made it. There was sort of a little winding road, and there were two Germans coming on their motorcycle around a bend in the road. I think they were going to go tell the rest of the Germans that we were coming and we shot them.

I remember, we were at the little village there and I think the Germans were surprised, because when we were approaching the first house that we saw there, there was a German that came out the door. I guess he had to wash his hands or something; he went to throw water out the door, and then he saw us and he ran back inside and alerted everybody else. We fired at them and then they came out with their hands up and we captured them. There were just a few in there and they never really fired back.

Then we went into the little town, and there were a lot of Germans there, and they were hiding in the basement in some buildings, so we got them, we captured them. By the end of the day they had surrendered, or they had been killed, whatever. I don't think they really tried to fight.

1ˢᵗ Lt Walter Irving's report describes the battle within the village in great detail—perhaps slightly exaggerated detail:

> Fortunately for the attacking force, a large caliber mortar is not effective at a range of some 250 yards and little damage was done to the troops by the scattered small arms fire. The weapons crews on the ridge did not fare quite so well. A mortar round fell near one of the 60mm mortar positions and seriously wounded one of the crewmen, but the weapons continued to fire to cover the advance.
>
> Under the cover of supporting fires, and by the use of marching fire, the assault platoons rushed into the gate of the town and sped towards their assigned streets. Muted rifle reports, the sharp reports of grenades, and the billow of white phosphorus smoke marked the beginning of the clearing of the houses. Excellent progress was made by assault platoons for the first few houses, but by this time the enemy had recovered from his surprise at being assaulted from the rear and had turned his attention on the company. The platoons' advances began to slow, halted, and carried on only by the sheer powers of leadership and profanity of the platoon leaders. However, a later investigation proved that the personnel of the platoons had not been to blame. In the case of both the major assault platoons, no teams organized had been assigned for the house fighting that should have been an SOP [standard operation procedure] order from the platoon leaders (teams support each other from opposite sides of the street, one team clears a house, signals, and covers the advance of its sister team on the opposite side of the street).
>
> Another obstacle was encountered in the fact that squads were not fully clearing the houses. In the case of the third platoon, the clearing squads neglected to clear the upper story of some two or three houses, with a result that the enemy dropped concussion grenades on the platoon leader and the support squad, causing several temporary casualties. Due to these neglected instructions, the advance of the company was held up some 20 to 30 minutes while readjustments could be made, and this time, of course, was used to good advantage by the enemy, who succeeded in moving his scattered forces to a more centralized position in the town.
>
> The first platoon on the northern portion of the town had succeeded in clearing the houses along its street by 1745 hours and radioed the command group that it was now on the western end of the town with approximately 15 prisoners. It was instructed to hold fast and prepare to assist the advance of the remainder of the company if this could be done without firing into each other.
>
> The weapons section was ordered into the town and displaced without incident to the east gate. Mortars were set up and told to be prepared to fire on order of the Company Commander only.
>
> The two major assault platoons (second and third) now radioed that their grenade supply was nearly depleted and asked for help in clearing the buildings. The only remaining fire power of the company was in the four light machine guns, which were now out of action and had displaced into the eastern edge of the town. This section, together with members of the 60mm mortar squads, was formed into a provisional platoon and given the mission of aiding the advance of the third (left) platoon. Machine guns were formed into two teams: two would work down each side of the street; the mortar crewmen and machine gun ammunition bearers, though armed with carbines, would be the assault riflemen and clear the houses after the machine guns had sprayed the inside.
>
> Upon arrival at the third platoon area, it was found that the platoon leader was suffering from a slight concussion from a grenade dropped from an upstairs window, and the platoon well scattered throughout several houses, mostly ones that had been previously cleared.
>
> The provisional platoon moved forward, and by a series of literally spraying the doorway and windows with machine gun fire from a hip-held position, allowing the carbine carrying personnel to enter, it was making a rather rapid advance. At this time the rifle platoon was reformed, and with the combined force the attack swept swiftly along to the tune of numerous "Kamerad" shouted from the enemy.
>
> The enemy Company Commander, a captain, was captured at approximately 1830 hours and informed that he would send out the order for all his personnel to surrender by 1900 or a systematic annihilation of those who refused would follow as the battalion closed into the area. This he did, and by 1930 hours only those that were wounded or dead remained in the area.[42]

Col Rupert Graves briefly mentioned the German Captain in his writings:

> A few white phosphorus grenades tossed into occupied buildings encouraged the remaining Germans to surrender, together with the garrison commander. The latter was a very surly Nazi who would not deign to say anything, except that Germany was going to win the war.[43]

Sgt William Myers also remembered encountering the German captain, as he was regrouped with other prisoners on the Place du Château, meters away from where Prosper Bovis and César Baudoin had been executed three days earlier:

> We decided we would take the sidewalk that was available and go into town. We started into town, and all of a sudden, a group of Germans waved a white flag and they surrendered to us. I think there were about 50 of them, and we were about 12. So that was frustrating, 12 of us trying to handle 50 Germans, and they were turning in their weapons and all. It was just getting dark a little bit, and the German captain was surrendering and had his hands up in the air, and I noticed he had a watch, and I didn't have a watch at that time. So I told him to take it off and give it to me. We waited for him to take it off, then I just put my

hand out and he gave it to me. I think he complained, but I told him to "be glad you're alive and I need the watch." That was the end of the conversation.

Cpl Eugene Brissey remembers the anguish of some of the prisoners:

Within an hour we had cleaned out the town. Several enemy were dead and about one hundred were captured. I was placed in charge of the prisoners, many of whom were very young, even compared to my 19 years. The prisoners thought we were going to kill them, I suppose, because some of them begged us not to shoot them. Others offered us money. We assured them that they would be treated properly. They were lucky and apparently happy at this point, but I think we were the lucky ones, because we had only the two wounded and no deaths.[44]

In the group of prisoners at the Place du Château, **Jacques Saussine** recognized Leon, the friendly Polish soldier he had drunk wine with, as well as the tall German who had informed him of the arrival of the Americans from the Place du Portalet:

There were about 30 Germans left. When the Americans arrived, they brought them to the Place du Château with their hands up. I looked them in the eyes, but they didn't seem mean. The ones who were left weren't even Germans, they were all Poles who had been conscripted into the German army. I saw Leon with the others. I remember, he was smiling at me and I wondered: but why do we have wars? Why do we kill each other? He was smiling, he was a nice guy.

At the entrance of town, a paratrooper was guarding a lone German soldier. **Saussine** continues:

The American had his rifle behind the German's back, but his hands were up, he wasn't going to kill him. The Americans were more reasonable. Then an FFI tried to take the German to punch him or something and the American said: "Get out of here! It's my prisoner, not your prisoner!" I remember that very well, and the Frenchman shut his mouth. The American had made the German prisoner, and the patriot who had been hiding tried to take command!

Still traumatized by the behavior of the Germans when they had invaded la Roquette three days earlier, some of its inhabitants

In 2004, Jacques Saussine poses with an American helmet liner that was given to him by an American soldier at the liberation of la Roquette. Unfortunately, the helmet has no characteristics enabling us to link it to the 517th PIR with any certainty, such as a name or remains of camouflage. Author's Collection.

Captured German Captain and Takes His Wrist Watch

Sgt. Wm. Myers Home on a 28-day Leave From Hospital

Sgt. Wm. R. Myers, a paratrooper in the Armed Forces, who saw service in Belgium, arrived here last week on a 28-day leave from the General Hospital at Camp Carson, Col., where he has been hospitalized taking treatments for frozen feet which he suffered while fighting in Belgium.

Sgt. Myers related some of his experiences in landing back of the enemy lines when a whole regiment of 1500 men would land from parachutes from the gliders that rushed the troops into the enemy area. Once he captured a German captain, and after some argument induced him to take off his German made wrist watch and turned it over to Sgt. Myers. He also took a camera from another German soldier. German make of watches and cameras are of the finest quality. He said that after stripping the prisoners of such articles suitable for keepsakes the prisoners are taken back to prison camps and later sent to interment camps, some coming to the United States. Sgt. Myers said it was not the practice of the American soldiers to take any money or

The German military watch that Sgt William Myers "liberated" from a surrendering German officer in la Roquette. William Myers Collection.

mistook their American liberators for yet more Germans. **François Municchi** remembers one such tragicomic case:

> When he saw that there was firing going on again, Mr Aguillon took cover down in a basement. But the Americans did the same thing as the Germans; they didn't shoot like them, but they were opening all the doors to see if there were any Germans hiding. He went: "No! Don't shoot! Me not terrorist!" "Yeah! We are Americans." But he didn't understand. Then some others came and told him: "Auguste, these are the Americans, we are liberated by the Americans."

Young **Bruno Municchi** was also worried, but his fears quickly turned to joy:

> The Americans told us: "Come on French, come out! Come out!" Yeah but "come out"; we didn't know them! They were tall, you had to see that. They could break somebody into pieces. We hugged them. One American took me in his arms: "How are you doing? Here, some chewing gum." Then we were happy. But at first we were scared.

What some of the soldiers from E Company had feared would be a suicide mission had turned into "the most exciting and the most successful battle that we encountered during the war," as Cpl Eugene Brissey put it. **Lt Col Richard Seitz**, the Commanding Officer of the 2nd Battalion of the 517th PIR, fully agreed:

> La Roquette probably was one of the most significant battles of the 517th. The reason I say the most significant is because the natural barrier of the Var River provided the Germans with a very fine defensive position. The Germans had planned to make a defensive stand there, and E Company of the 2nd Battalion of the 517th, commanded by Robert Newberry, made a brilliant night move across the Var River. To this day, I am amazed at how successful it was.

1st Lt Walter Irving concluded:

> In a summary of this operation, Company E had succeeded in accomplishing its assigned mission, and in doing so had allowed the battalion to secure an undestroyed bridge, which furthered, by some days, the Allied advance to the east. Had the company failed in this mission, casualties could have been extremely heavy in any attempts to secure the bridge by direct assault.
> The company and its attachments were complimented for a job well done by the Regimental Commander, Colonel Rupert D. Graves, and by the First Airborne Task Force commander, Major General Robert Frederick.
> Enemy losses were 26 killed and 81 captured in the town of la Roquette. Company E losses were none killed, 10 wounded. An unknown number of enemy had been killed or wounded by the well-directed artillery fire on the hill mass overlooking the bridge.[45]

All other American sources, other than 1st Lt Irving's report, actually indicate that only two Americans were wounded, not ten. As often, the German body count was also exaggerated. 1st Lt Irving claimed (basing himself on the citation he received for his conduct during the battle) that 26 had been killed. 517th PIR historian Clark Archer was closer to the mark when he claimed in his book

Paratroopers Odyssey that 15 Germans had been killed and 77 captured. In fact, 11 German soldiers of the 9th and 10th Companies of *Bataillon 164* had been killed at the village of la Roquette itself, and one German engineer was found dead near the Pont Charles Albert. We will get back to the fate of these dead soldiers later. For the moment, they remained on the ground where they had fallen, while the paratroopers prepared to spend the night in their newly-won position. In spite of the extraordinary success of their attack, they remained a small force, isolated in enemy territory. **1st Lt Walter Irving** wrote:

> Radio contact was established with battalion and they were informed that the town was clear. The battalion ordered a contact patrol sent down the road to meet the advancing units who had succeeded in forcing their way across the bridge with a minimum of casualties.
> The attack on the town of la Roquette from the rear had caused what troops remained on the hill mass east of the bridge to withdraw, as was later corroborated by prisoner of war reports.
> It was now dark, and any movement outside the town to the east was immediately challenged. Although the German commander had stated that his force was to be the last to withdraw after destruction of the bridge, it was felt that some enemy force might attempt a spite attack before withdrawing to the next defensive line.[46]

Cpl Eugene Brissey describes the night of August 28th to 29th:

> I replaced Ray [Helms] as squad leader. There was no thrill in this for me, because Ray was my best friend and his injury was rather serious. To make things worse, we could not get him out to a doctor. We were still behind enemy lines. Help did not come until the next day, when our troops on the other side of the river were able to cross and find us.
> After the battle we were hungry, but had no food. There was no way of getting any either, until the other troops got through to us. Should have saved some of that candy we had eaten the night before. I'll never forget that night. I was so hungry. The only thing I had which was even remotely associated with food was a package of lemonade powder. A German prisoner gave me some "hard tack" type stuff. This was somewhat like little rocks, but might have been some sort of bread. I mixed the lemonade powder with some stale water and drank it to help melt the German hard tack. Under the circumstances, I believe this tasted better than the stew the French family had given us in the morning. We remained near the town that night, keeping a sharp look-out for more Germans. As luck would have it, none came. During the night, as usual on guard duty, one or two men would watch a small area for an hour, then wake someone else who watched for an hour, and on and on through the night. One of our troops had finished his hour of guard duty and tried to wake a guy to take his turn. The guy would not respond. After a slight hassle, our troop discovered with some surprise that he had been trying to wake a dead German.
> It was a welcome sight the next day when our troops arrived from across the river with food and a jeep to carry Ray and the other wounded man back to safety and medical attention. I know we all wondered who really were the lucky ones. I think most of us would have traded

Troopers of D Company, 517th PIR, pose on Arpasse Mountain, between Levens and la Roquette. The Var Valley is visible in the background, as well as the village of Bonson to the left. From left to right, the troopers have been identified as (though there is some controversy): Charles L. Twibell, Orvil G. Cyrus, Frank S. Wayda, Clifton D. Duggan, Joseph J. Hanes, Roger W. Goodsell, and Joseph A. LaRochelle. Note that all the men seem to have already have gotten rid of their camouflaged jump suits. Because F Company and E Company had been involved in the fighting at the Charles Albert Bridge and in la Roquette, it was apparently D Company that was given the task of advancing on to Levens. Mike Kane Collection.

places with Ray. It was often said that the real lucky ones got shot early... of course, a nice clean wound had to be part of the deal. So there we were, the "unlucky ones" on the march again.[47]

When the rest of the 517th crossed the Var River, it found the body of a German engineer who had been killed on the east side of the Charles Albert Bridge, presumably while trying to approach the bridge in order to blow it on the 27th. **PFC Paul Harris**, of E Company's mortar squad, received the task of "burying" this body, and he remembered:

We were on a cliff above the river, and we were successful in shooting down a couple enemies at the end of the bridge, on the other side. We really burned them up with the mortar, and when we went across the bridge we met very little resistance. There was a dead German right at the end of the bridge, on the road which ran parallel with the river. He was right on that pavement and three of us had to bury him, but we couldn't dig a grave because we didn't have anything to dig it with. So we pulled him over to the side, and all we did was put some paper or something over him and covered him with dirt to keep the flies off of him until whomever was in charge of the burial could come and take care of him. We took his tags and turned them in to the proper people, and later on they came

back and gave him a formal burial. I think he was not a true German, I think he was Polish. I took his belt buckle and he had a picture of a French girl in his pocket with a name and address. One day, when I went on a pass, I had this picture and I showed it to a woman in a bar. She said: "Don't make any contact with the young girl," and I said: "I won't." So I gave her the picture. I never did make contact, it was none of my business.

The body was later buried in one of the numerous bomb holes near the bridge, and it's identification tag placed on a cross. However, when the *Volksbund* came to retrieve the body in 1958, the cross and identification tag had in the meantime disappeared. Only an incomplete transcription of the tag remained, which was unfortunately not enough to identify the body, though it did indicate its owner had been a member of an engineer unit.

After la Roquette had fallen, the Germans evacuated the Levens area quietly and for good the next morning, August 29, 1944. As we will see in the following chapter, they were in grave danger of being cut off from the rest of *Reserve Division 148* and completely surrounded, as an FFI insurrection had broken out in Nice on the 28th. Adèle Tacconi remembers the departure of the Germans and the arrival of the first Americans at her house on the Arpasse Mountain. A large group of Germans had taken cover in the house during the afternoon of the 28th, forcing **Adèle Tacconi** and her family into their basement:

During the night, my mother went upstairs to get a pillow or a blanket. The Germans were piled in the kitchen and sprawled in the hallway and all the other rooms. When she went back up the next morning they were all gone, and we hadn't heard them leaving.

We stayed hidden because we didn't know what was going on. Then, on the afternoon of the same day, we heard loud knocking on the door. My mother always went first, because since my father was a man he would get guns pointed at him every time. So she opened the door and saw two big guys, including one black one. We had never seen a Black before; we knew they existed, but had never seen any. My mother asked: "What do you want now, what is going on?" and they said: "We are American." We were happy, it was the Liberation.

There was still one German who must have stayed behind, and we saw him sitting on the stairs of the chapel in front of the house. He had thrown away his weapons and everything and he made the sign of the cross, then said: "To the grace of God" or something. He surrendered to the Americans.

Not knowing that the Germans had evacuated Levens, the American artillery briefly opened fire on the town again on the 29th, luckily not for long, and without causing any casualties this time. **Dr Flavier** wrote:

The sheath of an American combat knife found in the woods in the vicinity of Levens after the Liberation with the initials W.E.K. carved into it. On the roster of the 517th PIR dating from Christmas 1944, only one soldier with the initials W.E.K. is listed: Woody E. Kennamer, of D Company. Woody furnished us with a sample of his handwriting; the comparison looks quite convincing, though the opinion of a graphologist has not been sought so far. Private Collection.

More D Company troopers pose near Levens. From left to right, standing: Frank S. Faiola, Jack D. Gettman, Radford G. Lewis, John C. Bonner, and James H. Olsen. Kneeling: Benjamin B. Shankman, George F. Geary, McDade, and Fred P. Canziani. Mike Kane Collection. Author's Collection.

Medic paratrooper helmet that was found in Levens. Private Collection.

During the night of Monday to Tuesday, after setting fire to what the patriots had left behind and to the objects that they had stolen, the last [German] detachment left by the Route de Nice (…) after blowing the bridge. On Tuesday morning, we can't believe our eyes, we are still worried, when a salvo of four shells lands on Levens. Here we go, [the Americans] are being pigs… So an Italian takes a French flag and plants it on the hill. Seeing it, the American reconnaissance aircraft orders the fire to be stopped. At five in the evening, a detachment of Americans airdropped in le Muy entered Levens.[48]

Late on August 29th, the 2nd Battalion of the 517th PIR had thus completely taken control of the Levens area. The same day, a few German holdouts were found hiding in a water tank under a house in la Roquette, much like some civilians had hidden from the Germans only a few days earlier.

The German Dead in la Roquette sur Var

During the attack on la Roquette by the American paratroopers, 11 German soldiers of the 9th and 10th Companies of *Reserve Grenadier Bataillon 164* had been killed in and around the village (this number does not include the unidentified engineer who was found down at the Charles Albert Bridge). As several of the French and American witnesses had noted, almost all these casualties were only 17 or 18 years old:

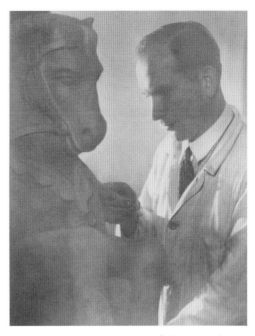

38-year-old Gefreiter Gottfried Mücke, of the 9th Company of Bataillon 164. He is the only known soldier to have been killed at la Roquette who was older than 18. Mücke was an artist in peacetime and had refused officer's training, as he did not want to be responsible for sending soldiers to their deaths. He left behind a daughter and a son whom he never saw. One of Gottfried's brothers, Willibald Mücke, became a collaborator of Chancellor Konrad Adenauer after the war. This information was misinterpreted by some local historians, causing them to claim that a nephew of Adenauer had been killed and buried in la Roquette or Levens, which is untrue. Barbara Exner-Eckert Collection.

Surname	Name	Rank	Age	Date of death	Unit
Fischer	Kasper	Gren	18	28.08.1944	10./Res. Gren.Btl.164
Koffen	Günter	Gren	18	28.08.1944	
Mücke	Gottfried	Gefr	38	28.08.1944	9./Res.Gren. Btl.164
Nordhof	Paul		17	28.08.1944	
Rappold	Georg	Gren	18	28.08.1944	
Seubert	Johann	Gren	18	28.08.1944	9./Res.Gren. Btl.164
Sputek	Leo	Gren	18	28.08.1944	9./Res.Gren. Btl.164
Unknown				28.08.1944	
Unknown				28.08.1944	
Unknown				28.08.1944	
Unknown				28.08.1944	

At first, the bodies of the dead Germans were left where they had been killed. As usual, curious French civilians went to examine and plunder them. One of the locals remembered:

There were a dozen Germans killed, poor guys, and most of them were young. [In the fields near the entrance of the town] there was a dead officer, and we went to look at him with a friend. Of his head only the cheeks, forehead, and ears remained, everything else was gone. There was

no brain or hair or anything left. The head was dug out as if somebody had scraped the inside with a spoon. He must have been hit by a grenade or a shell or something. Where the big garage is, there was a motorcycle and a German on the ground. My friend saw that, and he saw his nice tapering pants and his boots. He took both the pants and the boots. He took all that off, and on the inside the pants were all made of leather.

Behind the pigeon house, I myself saw two feet sticking up. "Oh," I thought, "another German dead…" Without looking too much, because I didn't enjoy it, I untied his shoelaces, as the shoes were intact. Nice shoes! And they were French shoes! I put them on and they fit me very well. I was happy, thinking: "At least I have some shoes." It was wartime and it was difficult to get shoes. I was glad to have them, and plus, they were my size!

The 11 bodies were then buried in a field by some German prisoners. They dug a single hole measuring approximately two meters by two meters and simply piled the bodies inside, without even taking half the identification tags. As we saw in previous chapters, even in the chaos of the Allied invasion, most German families received surprisingly precise information regarding the fate of their loved ones when a soldier was killed. In the battle for la Roquette, however, *Reserve Grenadier Bataillon 164* had lost so many men so abruptly that the unit headquarters had no way of knowing who had been killed as opposed to who had only been captured. The families of the dead were thus left in very painful uncertainty, as is proven by the two following letters (We can assume that all the other relatives of killed or missing men of the 9th and 10th Companies of *Bataillon 164* probably received identical copies of these letters with only the name being changed). The first letter, written by **Leutnant Schultz**, was sent to the father of 18-year-old Johann Seubert, of the 9th Company of *Bataillon 164*:

October 5, 1944
Dear Mr Seubert!

Your son, *Grenadier* Johann Seubert, is reported missing since the battle near La Roquette on 28.8.1944.

It is possible that your son may have fallen into the hands of the enemy during this battle that mostly took place in the forest. I hope that you will soon receive information about him through the "International Red Cross."

In case any facts emerge regarding the location of your son, would you please notify me, as his company commander. I will also immediately do the same if any news about your son reaches the company.

Heil Hitler
Schultz
Leutnant and Company Commander[49]

Meanwhile, the father of 18-year-old Kaspar Fischer, of the 10th Company of *Bataillon 164*, received a more detailed letter written by *Leutnant* **Buchmann**:

September 30, 1944
Dear Mr Fischer!

Today I must disclose the sad news to you that your son, *Grenadier* Kaspar Fischer, born 11.4.1926, is reported missing in the southern France invasion battles, in the area of la Roquette (on the Var) since 28.8.1944. Your son, who was assigned to securing the location of la Roquette with a platoon of the company, did not come back to the company after the successful attack of the location by American troops. Because of the situation, it was not possible to bring any outside help to those who were surrounded. It must be assumed that the entire garrison of la Roquette has fallen into American captivity. The company can give you no further details about the whereabouts of your son, as no witnesses are available.

If the company were to find out anything else about the whereabouts of your son and the fate of the surrounded, you will be, dear Mr Fischer, told about it immediately. If you were to receive a sign of life from your son in the meantime, you are prayed to pass this information on to the company.

The company greatly regrets the loss of your son and so loses a valued and dear comrade.

For the enquiry, you are requested to get in touch with the "International Red Cross." Information about this and other related matters will be given to you by every regional army bureau.

In the hope that the company will be able to tell you something more about the fate of your son, I salute you with Heil Hitler!

Yours truly
Buchmann
Leutnant and Company Commander[50]

In fact, after receiving these letters, most families never heard any additional news for the next 14 years, when the bodies were finally exhumed in 1958! The next of kin of those who were identified were informed, providing closure; however, four bodies were never identified. A curious **François Municchi** went to see the bodies being dug up by the *Volksbund* workers in 1958:

18-year-old Grenadier Johann Seubert, of the 9th Company of Bataillon 164. His brother had already been killed in Italy in 1943, and he himself was to be reported missing in la Roquette until 1958, when his body was finally exhumed from the mass grave near the town and identified thanks to his identification tag. Note that Lt Schultz only signed the letter, but did not write it himself, probably because several dozen identical letters needed to be handwritten after so many men from the 9th Company were reported missing in la Roquette. Hermann Popp Collection.

Long after the war, relatives of Johann Seubert visit his grave in the Dagneux German Military Cemetery, near Lyon. Hermann Popp Collection.

The 11 Germans were buried outside the village. They dug holes and buried them, then put a cross on top. We saw them when they dug them up later on. There were two workers and one specialist. They were digging, and when they saw the skeletons, the specialist came and looked for the bodies with a brush. Only the bones remained. We saw that when they took a head there was still a helmet on it, and they took the helmet off the dead man's head. We were watching that and nobody said anything to us. Then they put all those skeletons in numbered bags that were sealed and then brought to the town hall.

Because of the random manner in which the bodies had been buried, some of the remains could no longer be individualized, as was the case for those buried at St Cézaire, so they were reburied in a common grave.

La Roquette sur Var Battlefield Investigation

After exhuming the bodies from the mass grave at la Roquette, the *Volksbund* carried away the bones and identification tags of the soldiers, but abandoned most of the other artifacts found with the bodies at the site of the exhumation. These artifacts were later recovered, and their analysis gives us worthwhile forensic archaeological information about the soldiers and circumstances surrounding their deaths. The following items were recovered at the former grave site in la Roquette:

- One complete identification tag belonging to a soldier named Alois Gallus. The investigation to find out whether Alois Gallus

Dienststelle Fp.Nr. 25 639 C.   O.U. 30.September 1944

Sehr geehrter Herr Fischer !

      Ich muss Ihnen heute die traurige Mitteilung machen, dass Ihr
Sohn, der Grenadier Kaspar F i s c h e r , geb. 11.4.1926 bei den
Invasionskämpfen in Südfrankreich im Abschnitt La Roquette (am Var)
seit dem 28.8.1944 vermisst wird. Ihr Sohn, welcher mit einem Zuge der
Komp. zur Sicherung des Ortes La Roquette eingesetzt war, ist nach
erfolgtem Angriff auf den Ort durch amerikanische Truppen von dort
nicht mehr zur Komp. zurückgekehrt. Auf Grund der Feindlage war es
nicht möglich, den Eingeschlossenen von aussen Hilfe zu bringen. Es
muss angenommen werden, dass die gesamte Besatzung des Ortes La
Roquette in amerikanische Gefangenschaft geraten ist. Nähere Einzel-
heiten über den Verbleibe Ihres Sohnen kann Ihnen die Komp. nicht
mitteilen, da Augenzeugen nicht vorhanden sind.

      Sobald die Komp. doch noch etwas Näheres über den Verbleib Ihres
Sohnes und das Schicksal der Eingeschlossenen erfahren sollte,
werden Sie, sehr geehrter Herr Fischer, von hier aus umgehend da-
rüber in Kenntnis gesetzt. Sollten Sie aber inzwischen ein Lebens-
zeichen von Ihrem Sohn erhalten, so werden Sie gebeten, dies umgehend
der Komp.mitzuteilen.

      Die Komp. bedauert den Verlust Ihres Sohnes sehr, verliert sie
doch hierdurch einen bewährten und lieben Kameraden.

      Betreffend Nachforschung werden Sie gebeten, sich mit dem " Inter-
nationalen Roten Kreuz " in Verbindung zu setzen. Auskunft in dieser
Hinsicht und über sämtliche Versorgungsangelegenheiten wird Ihnen
von jedem Wehrbezirkskommando erteilt.

      In der Hoffnung, dass Ihnen die Komp. baldmöglichst etwas Näheres
über das Schicksal Ihres Sohnes mitteilen kann, grüsse ich Sie mit

                                    Heil Hitler !

                                          Ihr

                                    B u c h m a n n
                                    Leutnant und Komp.Führer

Abschrift :

18-year-old Grenadier Kaspar Fischer, of the 10th Company of Bataillon 164, who was also killed in la Roquette and was reported missing in action until 1958. Note that Lt Buchmann had access to a typewriter to write his letters, contrary to his colleague, Lt Schultz, of the 9th Company. Fischer Family Collection, courtesy Monika Reiser.

An identification tag belonging to Alois Gallus that was found at the grave site. The ID tag is made of zinc, which preserved quite well. The markings of Bataillon 164 and Gallus' blood group (B) and personal number are still clearly readable. At the time of publication, the German authorities were still investigating to determine whether or not Alois Gallus was actually killed in la Roquette. Private Collection.

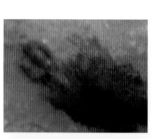

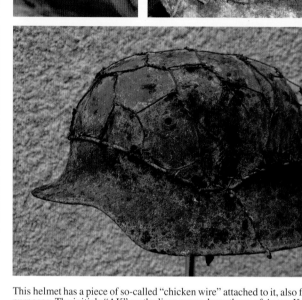

This helmet has a piece of so-called "chicken wire" attached to it, also for camouflage purposes. The initials "AK" on the liner are perhaps those of Anton Kavan, of the 9ᵗʰ Company of Bataillon 164, who is reported as missing in action in la Roquette since August 1944. Private Collection.

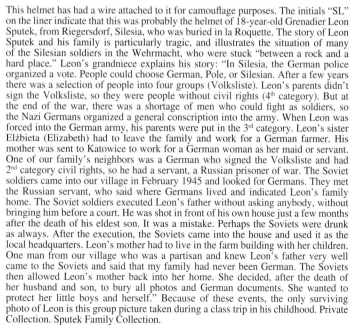

This helmet has had a wire attached to it for camouflage purposes. The initials "SL" on the liner indicate that this was probably the helmet of 18-year-old Grenadier Leon Sputek, from Riegersdorf, Silesia, who was buried in la Roquette. The story of Leon Sputek and his family is particularly tragic, and illustrates the situation of many of the Silesian soldiers in the Wehrmacht, who were stuck "between a rock and a hard place." Leon's grandniece explains his story: "In Silesia, the German police organized a vote. People could choose German, Pole, or Silesian. After a few years there was a selection of people into four groups (Volksliste). Leon's parents didn't sign the Volksliste, so they were people without civil rights (4ᵗʰ category). But at the end of the war, there was a shortage of men who could fight as soldiers, so the Nazi Germans organized a general conscription into the army. When Leon was forced into the German army, his parents were put in the 3ʳᵈ category. Leon's sister Elżbieta (Elizabeth) had to leave the family and work for a German farmer. His mother was sent to Katowice to work for a German woman as her maid or servant. One of our family's neighbors was a German who signed the Volksliste and had 2ⁿᵈ category civil rights, so he had a servant, a Russian prisoner of war. The Soviet soldiers came into our village in February 1945 and looked for Germans. They met the Russian servant, who said where Germans lived and indicated Leon's family home. The Soviet soldiers executed Leon's father without asking anybody, without bringing him before a court. He was shot in front of his own house just a few months after the death of his eldest son. It was a mistake. Perhaps the Soviets were drunk as always. After the execution, the Soviets came into the house and used it as the local headquarters. Leon's mother had to live in the farm building with her children. One man from our village who was a partisan and knew Leon's father very well came to the Soviets and said that my family had never been German. The Soviets then allowed Leon's mother back into her home. She decided, after the death of her husband and son, to bury all photos and German documents. She wanted to protect her little boys and herself." Because of these events, the only surviving photo of Leon is this group picture taken during a class trip in his childhood. Private Collection. Sputek Family Collection.

German bayonets and bayonet sheaths, including one that has been nicked by a bullet, providing useful information on the cause of death of the soldiers in the grave. Private Collection.

was actually killed at la Roquette is still ongoing at the time this book is going to print.

- Four helmets, including three with metallic wires or meshes attached to them for camouflage purposes, as was described by several inhabitants of la Roquette. Two of the helmets had initials written on their liners: one the initials "SL" and the other the initials "AK." When comparing these initials with the list of the 11 German dead who were found in the grave, it seems probable that the helmet with the initials "SL" belonged to soldier Leon Sputek. On the other hand, none of the identified dead had the initials AK, so this helmet may have belonged to one of the four unidentified soldiers. This information was sent to the WASt in Berlin, and it was found that 18-year-old *Grenadier* Anton Kavan, of the 9ᵗʰ Company of *Bataillon* 164, is reported as missing in action at the northern exit of la Roquette since August 28, 1944. It is possible that this helmet may have belonged to Anton Kavan, however, the evidence was not strong enough for the WASt to be able to draw any conclusions on Anton Kavan's fate.

- Four belt buckles, three bayonets, four bayonet sheaths, and remains of ammunition pouches.

- Some German 7.92mm and 9mm ammunition and the remains of several German "egg" concussion grenades. (These remind us of Sgt William Myers' close escape after such a grenade was thrown at him.) One American .45 caliber cartridge was also found. We could imagine that it may have been lost by a resistance fighter in Levens or la Roquette and then picked up by a German soldier as a souvenir.

- Remains of only one pair of shoes were found, corroborating the accounts of many pairs of shoes having been taken from the bodies by civilians.

- Some personal items, such as a watch, a lighter, two religious medallions, a pendent, a pocket knife, a cigarette case, a key, a piece of what appears to be personal jewelry made of aluminum in the shape of the letter "M," remains of two wallets, and pieces of three combs.

- One Hitler Youth proficiency badge.

- Five first aid dressings, seven condoms, and five small glass tubes containing unknown fluid.

- A small military shovel with handmade saw teeth carved into one side, a small wrench, two small light bulbs, and the remains of batteries.

- Approximately 30 coins, all of the recognizable ones being French wartime or prewar coins.

- Approximately 80 German tunic buttons, almost all with metallic hooks on them, indicating they come from light summer uniforms. Also approximately 50 German trouser buttons.

- A large number of various buckles from German military equipment, indicating that some of the soldiers were buried with items such as Y straps, bread bags, etc.

- Remains of six fired U.S. .30 caliber bullets and the tail of one U.S. rifle grenade were also found in the grave. These projectiles or projectile fragments clearly participated in killing or wounding the German soldiers buried in the grave. The presence of such a large number of bullets seems to indicate that most of the soldiers were killed by gunfire, as opposed to artillery. The presence of a rifle grenade fragment is indicative of combat occurring at relatively close quarters.

Because of their large size and the importance of the organ they protect, helmets found with bodies are often battle damaged. However, this was not the case for any of the four helmets found in la Roquette. On the other hand, three much smaller items were found to be battle damaged. A bayonet sheath and a German tunic button were found to have been grazed by bullets. Two French one Franc coins were found to have been damaged by a minuscule iron fragment

Some personal items found at the grave site, including Alois Gallus' ID tag, combs, wallets, a pocket watch, a lighter, religious medallions, jewelry, and the severely damaged remains of a Hitler Youth proficiency badge. Private Collection.

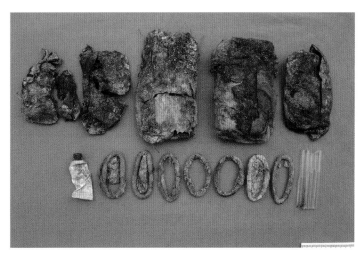

"Medical" items, including first aid dressings and several condoms. The good condition of the condoms may seem surprising, but rubber usually survives very well when buried, though it becomes hard and brittle. Private Collection.

French coins and a cigarette case. Not a single German coin was found at the grave site. Private Collection.

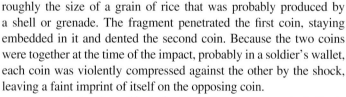

Remains of projectiles that killed the German soldiers at la Roquette and were found in their grave, including the remains of six .30 caliber bullets and the tail of a U.S. rifle grenade. All the bullets have four rifling grooves to the right, corresponding to the four grooves that were present in the American Garand rifle and .30 caliber Browning machine gun. The bullets are also deformed and damaged, as is normally the case for high velocity rifle bullets that strike their human target. The bullet in the center has broken into two pieces that can be matched up, while the bullet on the right is a tracer (recognizable by the location of the crimp, which is positioned much higher on the body of the bullet), indicating that it was probably fired from a machine gun. Note that the patina on the bullet to the right (brown color) is very different from that of the other bullets (green color); this is a sign that it may have ended up being buried by chance after impacting into the earth beside the grave, and that it was in fact not contained within the bodies of one of the killed soldiers. Items buried with bodies typically become much more damaged than items simply buried in the earth. Private Collection.

Extraordinary artifacts found in the grave: a button from a German summer uniform that has been grazed by a bullet, and French Vichy government coins that have been damaged by a miniscule shrapnel fragment that stayed embedded in the right hand coin. The impact caused each coin to faintly imprint its image on the opposite coin. Private Collection.

roughly the size of a grain of rice that was probably produced by a shell or grenade. The fragment penetrated the first coin, staying embedded in it and dented the second coin. Because the two coins were together at the time of the impact, probably in a soldier's wallet, each coin was violently compressed against the other by the shock, leaving a faint imprint of itself on the opposing coin.

To conclude, the artifacts found in the grave seem to indicate that most of the soldiers were killed by rifle or machine gun fire, but that at least one had been killed by a rifle grenade, and probably one other by a grenade or shell. This corroborates the accounts of the witnesses of the battle, according to whom most of the Germans were shot in the fields just outside la Roquette, though at least two are also said to have been killed by shell fire in the town itself.

Demining the Var River

The 517th PRCT, by its daring nighttime crossing of the Var River, had managed to capture the entire Levens area without having one single man killed, while inflicting a serious defeat and heavy losses to the soldiers of *Reserve Grenadier Bataillon 164*. In the aftermath of the attack, the paratroopers of the 596th Parachute Combat Engineer Company were given the mission of clearing some of the mines from the Var River bed. Unfortunately, three engineers were to die August 30, 1944, while fulfilling this much less glamorous essential mission. Their names were:

Surname	Name	Rank	Unit	Age	Date of death
Coffelt	Ernest R.	PFC	596 PCEC	21	30.8.1944
Jaynes	Howard D. Jr.	Sgt	596 PCEC	22	30.8.1944
Mathis	Leonard	Pvt	596 PCEC	22	30.8.1944

All three were awarded a posthumous Silver Star, the citations of which were almost identical. **Howard Jaynes'** was slightly more detailed because of his Sergeant rank and read:

After Sergeant Jaynes and his squad had successfully cleared a path through an enemy anti-airborne minefield which consisted of booby-trapped enemy one hundred fifty-five millimeter artillery shells, Sergeant Jaynes, together with two other soldiers, requested permission to remove the remainder of the booby-trapped shells in the area. Thinking that by doing so he could prevent injury or death to military or civilian personnel who might wander from the cleared path, Sergeant Jaynes removed sixteen of the booby-trapped shells under conditions requiring great skill and the coolest of nerves, as detonation would result in death to all. Although Sergeant Jaynes was mortally wounded while removing a seventeenth mine, his unselfish act was an inspiration to all with whom he served. His actions bespeak of the highest traditions of the American soldier.[51]

Sgt Allan Goodman, of the 596th PCEC, tells us how the three men died and of the gruesome scene that ensued:

Howard Jaynes and I were battle promoted to sergeant together and given squads to lead. When I heard of Howie, Coffelt, and Mathis' death, I immediately went to the site where it happened. What I observed was unbelievable… they had been dismantled while disarming an anti-airborne asparagus. 155 mm shells were hung from wires stretched between poles. It was a very delicate job, as any disturbance would release the tension on the hang wires and the shell would explode! These shells were about five feet above ground level, hanging from the nose attached to a detonator. The three men were clearing a path across the dry riverbed – the Var River, I believe it was – to make a passage for vehicles to cross safely. The procedure was

that one would "embrace" the shell and raise it a fraction of an inch while a second would reach up and insert the safety pin in the detonator, then the third trooper knelt to help catch the shell's weight after the first man cut the hang wire. Mathis was probably the one kneeling, and he was decapitated! Howie was holding the shell I think… his upper torso was missing. Coffelt was inserting the safety pin and only his legs were left. I stayed with the remains of my buddies… alone… for several hours until the Grave Registration team arrived. Only Mathis still had dog tags. Howie was my closest personal friend.[52]

Two days after the tragic death of the engineers, on September 1st, another American soldier, **Pvt James L. Walton**, of the 2nd Battalion Headquarters of the 517th PIR, was killed near Levens when he was accidently shot through the head. The exact details of the incident are not known, but the army ruled his death as being "non-battle." Such accidents were unfortunately quite common, as we will see in the conclusion chapter of this book.

Conclusion

Upon hearing of the Allied invasion, the Resistance descended from the mountains and took control of the area of Levens and its strategic roads and bridges August 16th. The German forces at first did not attempt any serious actions to retake the area. However, as the Allied troops approached, it became increasingly important for the Germans to defend the Var River and blow the remaining bridges. August 24th, *Reserve Grenadier Bataillon 164* reached the Levens area and launched a counterattack against the town. Though it was briefly repelled, by late August 25th, *Bataillon 164* had retaken all the lost ground, killing several resistance fighters and civilians in the process while losing only three men. August 26th, the Resistance unsuccessfully counterattacked Levens from the north. The same day, the 517th Parachute Regimental Combat Team reached the western bank of the Var River at Carros. During the night of August 27th to the 28th, the 517th launched a daring attack against la Roquette, capturing the town along with the Pont Charles Albert, which the Germans had not managed to blow. *Bataillon 164* suffered heavily from the attack, losing roughly 100 prisoners and 14 dead in a single day. With their defense line seriously compromised and their retreat route threatened by the resistance forces in Nice, *Bataillon 164* pulled out of Levens early on the 29th. The entire region of Levens was now liberated for good. The Americans lost three men while demining the Var riverbed August 30th, and a fourth man was accidentally shot near Levens September 1st. These are the only Allied casualties to have occurred in the whole Levens, Aspremont, and Carros region. Between August 15th and September 1st in the same region, the Germans had suffered at least 25 killed, while the French had suffered at least 18 dead, including four civilians, the others having been involved with the Resistance.

PFC Ernest R. Coffelt and Sgt Howard D. Jaynes, Jr., of the 596th PCEC, who were both killed while demining the Var River bed at St Martin du Var, along with Pvt Leonard Mathis. Live Oak Public Libraries Collection, Courtesy Sharen Lee. Chicago History Museum Collection.

13

The Resistance Rises Up in Nice

In the previous two chapters, we have seen how the Allied forces were posing a serious threat to the Germans in Nice by late August 28, 1944, after having reached the Var River and crossing it at la Roquette. However, long before the First Airborne Task Force had time to make any plans to move into Nice, the Resistance took matters into its own hands, starting an insurrection to kick the Germans out of their town early in the morning of the 28th. But before getting into the insurrection of August 28th in Nice, we must first backtrack to the day of the Allied landing, August 15th, to put events back into context.

The Ariane Massacre

When news of the Allied landing reached the *Gestapo* in the Maritime Alps August 15, 1944, it would seem that it caused a sort of panic among these "policemen", and that an order was given to liquidate all prisoners being held by the *Gestapo* in preparation for a hasty departure. In Chapter 7 we saw what happened at Cannes, where eight prisoners were shot in the basement of Villa Montfleury. In Nice, in the Ariane district, it was no less than 23 prisoners of the *Gestapo* that were executed the afternoon of August 15th. Unlike the execution in Cannes, there were no survivors, and few witness accounts exist. However, one witness later reported to the *l'Ergot* newspaper:

> Around 16:20 I see a truck full of civilians escorted by German soldiers passing in front of my factory, driving towards one of the properties I own at l'Ariane. I know that there have already been two executions of patriots and I have the feeling that another tragedy is in preparation.
>
> I rush to my desk, grab my binoculars, and climb to the fifth story of the factory. Through the window, I see two groups forming behind the truck. There are eight people in the first group. They go down the embankment (…). The second group now descends, headed by a priest, immediately followed by three women, with the rest of the hapless crowd a bit further on. At the same moment, four German soldiers armed with submachine guns open fire, cutting down the patriots with bursts. The priest falls face down with his arms spread out… Panicked, some try to climb back up the embankment to save themselves. They are machine gunned in the back and the bodies fall one on top of the other. Those who are still breathing or moaning are finished off.[1]

The official police report written by **Joseph Cape**, the police superintendent of the 3rd District of Nice, tells the rest of the tragic story:

August 15, 1944, at 17:50, the day of the Allied landing in the Mediterranean, we were notified by the German Police that 23 people had just been shot in a vacant lot of the Ariane district, and that the bodies were to be removed urgently. We immediately went to the scene, assisted by Police Secretary André Dupouy, Officer Pluss, and a team of police officers.

In a vacant lot of the Ariane district, near the Domaine de la Porcherie, we noted that 23 corpses (three women and twenty men) were lying one on top of the other, all with their faces mutilated by gunshots fired at point blank range. Each corpse bore the traces of two, three, or four gunshots. Submachine gun bullet casings were strewn on the ground. At our arrival, the bodies were under the guard of two German soldiers who declared to us that they had not participated in this shooting, without however wanting to give us any extra details. We at once summoned Dr Raymond, civil status doctor, who certified the twenty-three deaths, and concluded that in every case death had occurred instantaneously. We got the bodies transported to the morgue of Caucada Cemetery after having notified *Monsieur* le Préfet, *Monsieur* le Procureur de la République, and our direct superiors.

Later on in the Ariane district, we were able to find out that gunfire had been heard around 15:00; in other words, two and a half hours before the telephone call made to us by the Germans. No inhabitant of the district witnessed the shooting. Ten corpses were identified the same day, while the thirteen others, photographed and measured, were recognized by the families following announcements made in the press. During our investigation, we also found out that one part of the

French collaborators Ange Fancellu and Etienne Glasser, who were executed at l'Ariane along with the 21 résistants. Apparently, they had fallen out of favor with the Germans for having impersonated German policemen. Private Collection, courtesy Alain Endinger.

20 of the 21 resistance members, including one priest and three women, were executed by the Germans in the Ariane district of Nice August 15, 1944. Private Collection, courtesy Alain Endinger.

387

victims had been extracted from the German Quarter of the Nice Prison, while the other part had been handed over by the German Services of the Hotel Excelsior in Nice. We were not able to identify the perpetrator or perpetrators of this shooting, who in our opinion can only be members of the Nice *Gestapo*. (…)

Of the 23 victims (…), 21 were members of the resistance, and the two remaining ones, Fancellu Ange and Glasser Etienne, were known to our services as being auxiliary agents of the German Police, having committed false policeman robberies.[2]

It is interesting to note that the Germans took advantage of the execution of their resistance prisoners to rid themselves of two of their former collaborators who had fallen out of favor with them. The 23 victims of this mass execution were:

Surname	Name	Age	Date of death	Location of death
Bocchiardo	Victor	19	15.8.1944	Nice Ariane
Bodo	Joseph	24	15.8.1944	Nice Ariane
Borghni	René	25	15.8.1944	Nice Ariane
Chabaud	Hubert	26	15.8.1944	Nice Ariane
De Lattre	Robert	50	15.8.1944	Nice Ariane
Dunan	Edmond	18	15.8.1944	Nice Ariane
Fancellu	Ange	24	15.8.1944	Nice Ariane
Flandin	Maurice	18	15.8.1944	Nice Ariane
Glasser	Etienne	23	15.8.1944	Nice Ariane
Guillevin	Paul	29	15.8.1944	Nice Ariane
Harang	Victor	43	15.8.1944	Nice Ariane
Hugues	Victorin	18	15.8.1944	Nice Ariane
Kraemer	André	17	15.8.1944	Nice Ariane
Luquet	Laurent	17	15.8.1944	Nice Ariane
Maccagno	Louis	34	15.8.1944	Nice Ariane
Malaussena	Jean Baptiste	45	15.8.1944	Nice Ariane
Poggio	Esther	31	15.8.1944	Nice Ariane
Renard	Jean Jacques	30	15.8.1944	Nice Ariane
Reschkomski Marcus	Marie Ruth	53	15.8.1944	Nice Ariane
Robineau	André		15.8.1944	Nice Ariane
Roux	August	23	15.8.1944	Nice Ariane
Tardieu	Gaston	57	15.8.1944	Nice Ariane
Vagliano	Hélène	35	15.8.1944	Nice Ariane

A Volatile Climate

Feldkommandantur 994 in Nice was commanded by 51-year-old *Generalmajor* Hellmuth Nickelmann, who was a good example of the type of German officer that was present in Nice at the sides of the Silesian conscripts of *Reserve Division 148*. Although he was no longer fit for service on the Eastern front due to the sequella of five wounds suffered during the First World War, he was a highly experienced combat soldier, and his personal officer's file noted that he had an "irreproachable national socialist attitude."[3] *Generalmajor* Nickelmann held a journal of the activities of *Feldkommandantur 994* that gives us precious information on how the Germans were perceiving the situation in the Maritime Alps at the time of the Liberation. (For this book, only the French translation available at the *Musée de la Résistance Azuréenne* was consulted, not the original German text, which caused a few issues with some of the technical terms.) Nickelmann's journal shows that the Germans were well aware that as the Allies approached Nice, the French would seize any opportunity they were given to hinder the German war effort, or even start an outright insurrection. August 16th, as the German units around Nice were making efforts to move west towards the front lines at la Napoule and Fayence, **Generalmajor Nickelmann** noted the volatile climate that prevailed in Nice:

We are encountering enormous difficulties with the use of vehicles. We have no drivers for driving wood burning vehicles. No drivers are available among the troops. The French drivers escape when given requisition orders. (…) The 148th Reserve Division is holding the line Fayence-Brignoles-Cap Roux. Southwest of Fayence it is fighting against terrorists.[4]

This reminds us of the events described in Chapter 4, and of what Karl Cyron experienced as he approached the front in a bus driven by a Frenchman in Chapter 6. In an attempt to keep the French under tight control, the Germans imposed strict new curfew rules. On August 17th, the *Eclaireur de Nice* newspaper published the following regulations, several of which clearly demonstrate that the Germans were expecting to be subject to "terrorist"-style attacks in the near future:

51-year-old Generalmajor Hellmuth Nickelmann, commander of Feldkommandantur 994 in Nice, who wrote a detailed description of the day of August 28, 1944, in Nice as seen from the German side. NARA.

As of now, the following special prescriptions apply in the *département*.

1- From sunset to sunrise, it is forbidden for the population to go about in the streets.

2- Until further notice, it is forbidden to use vehicles or bicycles, to form crowds of more than three people in the streets, or to unite inside or outside of closed buildings, with the exception of the home or the workplace.

3- Local military authorities can provide exemptions to paragraphs 1 and 2.

4- Places of pleasure and public places must be closed. The sale of alcohol is forbidden until further notice.

5- During the entire duration of the day and night, the doors of all buildings must neither be locked nor bolted shut; windows must be kept shut from sunset to sunrise. No one is to loiter near the windows or doors.

6- It is forbidden for the population of towns located in the zone of military operations to go about in the streets, even during the day. The population must remain within buildings, or if necessary in basements. Windows and doors must remain closed during military operations, even during daylight hours; however, doors are not to be locked nor bolted shut.

7- Any transmission of information to the enemy will be considered as espionage.

8- Any civilian, who in any manner, will participate in military operations or give assistance to the enemy will be treated as a *franc-tireur*.

9- The troops have been given the order to use their weapons in cases of violations of the present announcement.[5]

Over the next days the curfew was made even more strict, with specific hours being given during which the population was authorized to be in the streets. One inhabitant of Nice who was 12 years old at the time describes the atmosphere in town in the days following the landing:

Since the beginning of July, Nice had been under a certain amount of tension because of the hanging of Torrin and Grassi and the massacre of young high school boys at St Julien de Verdon [see Chapter 2], and because of the ever-increasing restrictions. As of August 15th, we started hearing the sounds of the naval guns that were shelling the coast in the Var to accompany the landing. The Germans started being rather nervous, and quite an important phenomenon affected the population: the ghost plane. The ghost plane was a small plane that would come out every night and fly over the town at low altitude to drop small bombs, probably at random, on different spots every night. We found out after the Liberation that it was probably an Italian Black Shirt, a Fascist, who had a small aircraft and who used that strategy to terrorize the population. But one night he dropped a much larger bomb that tore open a five or six-story building in which at least five people were killed.

We also found out, although there was no TV and the radio was cut off, that about 20 men and women had been executed at l'Ariane. All this traumatized the population, which had had enough. Then there were the restrictions: the gas was cut off, we were told that the water could be poisoned by the Germans to take revenge on the population, and there was no more bread. We had unfortunately gotten used to restrictions, but that really topped it off.

Many people stopped going to work, which led to a gradual paralysis of life in the city. As the Allied forces approached, the Germans simultaneously prepared to evacuate and to defend the town, as it was part of the temporary defensive line that they planned to form on the Var River. These mixed intensions of both defense and retreat, as well as the certainty of an insurrection, were clearly formulated by **Generalmajor Nickelmann** as early as August 24th, when he wrote:

The *Feldkommandantur* will remain in Nice to counter the insurrectional movement. General Fretter-Pico indicates that as soon as the troops will be on the Var defense line, the order to transport the *Feldkommandantur* will be given with the code word "Hindenburg." Its first retreat location will be Menton.[6]

August 27th, the day before the resistance uprising, **Generalmajor Nickelmann** met with *Generalleutnant* Fretter-Pico, who had just evacuated his temporary headquarters in the Colombe d'Or Hotel in St Paul in the face of the Allied advance:

We receive the visit of General Fretter-Pico, who informs us of the situation; he agrees that the *Feldkommandantur* is efficiently contributing to maintain order amongst the civilian population, thanks to the reputation of General Nickelmann. In spite of this, the transfer of the *Feldkommandantur* to Menton should occur on August 28th or 29th."[7]

As in several other locations mentioned in the previous chapters, a sort of equilibrium was reached between the belligerents, with the Allied and resistance forces usually attacking roughly at the same time as the Germans pulled out. Unbeknownst to Nickelmann, as he was being told on the 27th that he was to retreat within the next day or two, FTP resistance leaders were meeting in Nice and were deciding that the insurrection was to start the next day, early in the morning of August 28, 1944. **Pierre "Georges" Durand** was one of the men present at the meeting:

We discuss the situation. The Americans do not seem to want to cross the Var at the moment. The *maquisard*s are fighting with the Germans in the nearby back country, and we can expect their arrival. [In fact, the Americans were preparing to cross the Var at la Roquette, whereas the Resistance had suffered only setbacks in the past days at Levens.] In town, the strikes launched by the CGT [A workers union] are followed at TNL [an industrial depot in Nice], the gas factory, the train tracks, and in metallurgy and construction. The garbage is no longer being picked up, and the *Eclaireur* and the *Petit Niçois* are only being printed with permission of the personnel. The armed fighters are anxious to put an end to the Occupation. The population is favorable, and contacts have been made with the Police and part of the Gendarmerie. The firemen are part of the Resistance.

We believe we can count on the other combat groups that are in town to join the battle. The enemy troops, confined to the heights of town, through which they only move during daytime, can efficiently be fought in the streets where the MOI and a few teams of FTPs are already in action.

The decision is taken: we will attack together tomorrow at 6 o'clock. Each person knows what he has to do. We separate to transmit the order to all our leaders.[8]

The Start of the Insurrection

There were often heated debates after the war to determine which resistance groups had done what and had been more instrumental in fighting the Germans. This was also the case for the insurrection of Nice, where bitter disputes occurred about who exactly decided the date of the uprising and who had been present at the meeting where this was discussed. In this chapter, however, we will completely ignore these debates, and will simply try to reconstruct the military events that occurred with the historical accounts that are available, regardless of the branch of the resistance that the witness was a member of.

Because of the size of the town of Nice and the chaotic nature of street fighting, it will not be possible to reconstruct events is as minute detail as in many of the smaller villages that have been studied in the previous chapters. We will therefore concentrate on the more important events and try to proceed by theme rather than by precise chronological order. The archives of the *Musée de la Résistance Azuréenne* in Nice were the main source of information for this chapter, as they have preserved most of the documents written by the participants of the insurrection. The majority of the accounts used in the rest of this chapter were written on resistance leader Norbert Jamme's initiative in the weeks following the battle. They were thus put down on paper when memories were still fresh and precise.

The Préfecture

One of the resistance men with the most delicate roles to play during the uprising was FTP leader René Canta, who was to occupy the *Préfecture*, which would act as the central nervous system of the resistance during the insurrection. In the report **René Canta** later wrote, he described the mission given to him and the specially trained group of men that he had formed to accomplish it. They were to take control of key positions in town and manage and lead other resistance groups that they may encounter along the way:

Finally, on August 27, 1944, I receive the order from the Front National to attack the next day, the 28th, at 5:50. The targets that are assigned to my *Group Franc* are the following:

1- The *Préfecture*
2- The Town Hall
3- The central post office
4- The boy's high school, where the police forces are stationed
5- The Regional Police Management
6- The main Police Station, in rue Gioffredo.
7- The Gendarmerie *Départementale*
8- The headquarters of the Gendarmerie
9- The headquarters of the PPF
10- The editing rooms of the *Eclaireur* newspaper
11- The headquarters of the Legion, Avenue de la Victoire
12- The water company
13- The TNL depots.
14- Pasteur Hospital
15- St Roch Hospital (…)
16- The Secours National at 2 rue Maccarani
17- The road from St Isidore to Caucade
18- The level crossing at Boulevard Gambetta
19- St Roman de Bellet and Ventabrun (…)
20- Furthermore, certain Police elements belonging to my group had received the job of occupying, cleansing, and if necessary organizing attack and defense measures at:

21- The Wilson post office
22- The *Petit Niçois* newspaper

A 23rd group was to operate under my orders from the Place St François and the Old Town. I was personally to take and hold the *Préfecture* at the head of a few of my men and organize it, with the help of my external groups in the Old Town, into a starting point for attacks and harassment operations. (…)

At last it was time to go. I left my command post at Pasteur at the head of my *Groupe Franc*, leaving behind a group of four patriots to manage and lead the resistance group of [Pasteur Hospital] into the fight and to assure the immediate liberation of political prisoners that were still in ward G5 at the disposal of the *Gestapo*. Along the way, a second team detaches itself to execute its mission at the Gendarmerie. We continue on, making a detour to avoid two machine gun positions, with the sole purpose of not provoking any incidents before the planned time. The group, minus the few detachments that have already departed for their missions, arrives at the high school, where I had mobilized all my Police members the night before. We immediately occupy the grounds that, as of that moment, will serve as a base for the launching of other missions.

Along with my chosen men, I then proceed towards the *Préfecture*, where I had gotten the chief of my Police groups to double the number of Police staff. On the way I occupy the Town Hall and leave all the necessary instructions there for the group who was responsible for that target. As soon as we reach the *Préfecture*, my policemen recognize me and let me in. As a precaution we exchange the agreed passwords, then burst into the building, where we are forced to set up our automatic weapons because, I do not know why, a certain amount of resistance seems to be stemming from the numerous civilians who are present. I immediately send patriots off to various particularly important points, such as the telephone switchboard (…), where I order all communications coming from the outside to be recorded, while absolutely forbidding any broadcasts.

I then leave the building and send a group composed of firemen to the Legion headquarters, 16 Avenue de la Victoire, to support the action of my group that has already been sent there. The chief of the detachment coming from the Bourse du Travail, Place St François, is here with his entire group to receive instructions. They are very poorly armed, and I assign him the task of first hiding his men in safe spots and from there, with the few men who are armed, to attack small groups of German soldiers or isolated soldiers and to start by amassing a serious amount of weapons. Then, as soon as the sufficiently armed patriots would be capable of undertaking organized guerilla warfare, to spread into all the small streets of the old town and the houses well known to them and stop all *Wehrmacht* circulation on the Boulevard des Italiens on the one hand and the Place Garibaldi on the other. The main goal, I told him, was all out and continuous harassment of the Germans; we must demoralize them by attacking them everywhere at once. I add that in case the situation was to become critical, to immediately take support from the *Préfecture*, which must remain the main base from where all the operations in this vast area will start from; and if it was necessary, to not hesitate to withdraw all his men into it.

I return to the *Préfecture*, where my very energetic men are evacuating all those whose presence they consider unnecessary. I place two armed patriots on the inside of the entrance door, that I order to shut, just like all the other exits, which are to be guarded by partisans. From the top to the bottom of the building, each man is wisely positioned at his combat post. (…) A wave of hostility seems to manifest itself in the Préfet's office when Mr Lauvel, my deputy, and myself informed the personalities of the *Préfecture* of our decision in polite but energetic terms. I am even forced to take my gun in hand again to better remind these gentlemen that as of now, the Vichy *Préfecture* is in the hands of the patriots. There were then a long series of pleas asking us to leave the *Préfecture*. Among those who make them, it is with regret that I notice certain people who I may not permit myself to name here, but of whom I have taken careful note. Among them, Mr Lauvel [The Secretary General of the *Préfecture*.] and especially Mr Ravard [The Chief of Cabinet of the Préfet.], seem particularly disturbed, maybe even frightened by our presence, because, they claim, we had come 48 hours too early. We will continue hearing these words later on from certain very popular people, including FFIs. I will refrain from making any comment, but the observation is very significant as to who is willing to understand it. In the face of these petty reproaches of being freed too early, I cut all these useless conversations short by immediately passing on to the order of the day.[9]

The Level Crossing

While René Canta had been taking control of the *Préfecture*, fighting had broken out in town. The first shots are claimed to have been fired in the area of the level crossing (There is only one major level crossing in Nice.) which controlled Boulevard Cessol, one of the major roads in the northwest part of town leading to Aspremont and Colomars, where German troops were still present. The level crossing and its surroundings were to become one of the most hotly contested and deadly positions in Nice, with sporadic fighting lasting until the early hours of August 29th. One of the FFI officers in command was **Captain Paul Cavenago**, who reported:

The attack: 6:40.

Our men are all at their posts. A first *Boche* car is reported, mounted by German officers, coming from the Place Gambetta by rue Joseph Garnier. It is knocked out by a grenade at the corner of rue August Raynaud: three dead and one *Fritz* commander wounded and taken prisoner, whom I suspect died later.

This brings us two Mausers, three pistols, and a few grenades; very interesting, since we have almost no weapons, so this is a first success for us.[10]

FTP Louis Sana, who was also present, adds an important detail about what apparently was the same German vehicle:

The car was coming from boulevard Gambetta and was immobilized at the level crossing. I seize the wounded commander's bag. It contains important documents on the projects of the German command.[11]

This captured German "commander" was almost certainly *Oberstleutnant* Hans Niedlich, the commanding officer of *Reserve Grenadier Regiment 8*. We will come back to him in much more details further on; in the meantime, we return to **Captain Paul Cavenago**'s report:

7:12. The *Fritzes* are alerted and send men and equipment on a truck with a trailer. They come by Joseph Garnier, and

the first truck is knocked out with a grenade at the level crossing. Conclusion: some *Fritzes* killed, wounded, and captured. This earns us a heavy machine gun, ammunition, and Mausers. The trucks will be used to form a second line road block on rue Cessole.

We fortify our first road block at the level crossing. The gun is in position with a field of fire on Joseph Garnier and Gambetta.

A second truck is reported and suffers the same fate as the first one at the same place as the first one. It brings us a few rifles, ammunition, and prisoners. Things are going well, very well, in fact! Now if they come back, they will have to pay the "copper tax."

8:30. At last, the first encounters. The *Fritzes* come by Gambetta, staying close to the trees. This slows our fire. I give the order to only fire at 30 meters, in short, slow bursts, to spare ammunition and to only fire on certain targets. Our men are full of ardor, they are superb, but too daring. Alas, three severely wounded men die. This only increases the men's fighting spirit; bullets whistle down Cessole and ricochet at the angles of the streets. The *Fritzes* fall; our gunner aims carefully, his machine gun is successful, and the submachine guns as well, without forgetting the Mausers that fire at long range.[12]

FFI member **Lieutenant Mathis** had not been informed of the start of the insurrection because of the competition between the different resistance groups, but as soon as he realized it had started, he joined the fight north of the level crossing:

Normally, nothing seemed to indicate that the attack was to start this early, for we had received no precise orders on the topic. But as early as Sunday [August 27th] night, we had heard that the FTPFs were preparing to attack out of their own initiative. Since similar orders had already been given in the preceding days we didn't know how serious they were. Nonetheless, on Monday at five in the morning, *Capitaine* Cavenago, who I am in touch with, contacts *Commandant* Parent (our direct superior commanding the CFL) to find out to what point the rumors are true. Around six o'clock I hear a few gunshots and go down. (…)

I climb boulevard Cessole. (…) When I reach rue Castellane, I meet a few FTPs in combat positions who announce to me that the fight has indeed started. Just then I see two Germans in avenue Castellane, whom I summon to stop. They escape and I chase after them. Once they are cornered in a house they surrender, though not without difficulty. Result: since I was only in possession of a 6.35, it is with pleasure that I take a Mauser and a belt with full ammunition pouches. Considering the urgency of the situation, and seeing a few groups at the corner of avenue Cyrnos and boulevard Cessole who, without any directives, do not know what to do, I take command and organize a first resistance fort in the "Les Pipistrelles" villa, which is a marvelous observation and attack post right in the middle of boulevard Cessol, and from which I dominate the upper and lower portion of the boulevard, as well as avenue Castellane located in front. The owner puts herself entirely at our disposal, showing a spirit of self sacrifice and devotion. At that moment there are only five or six of us. (…) We still do not have a single automatic weapon.

We are informed that the Germans are patrolling in the superior part of the pine forest. I send three men out on

Some of the resistance men who fought at the level crossing. This photo was probably taken August 29th, the day after the fighting. MRA Collection.

reconnaissance and 10 minutes later find myself surrounded by 15 Germans armed with submachine guns, who have found out that the two prisoners we have captured are somewhere in these whereabouts (Indeed, these two prisoners are in the "Les Pipistrelles" villa.); but finding nothing in front of them, they retreat back to the heights. At that moment, large groups of Fortune's men (FTP) and a few of Olivari's men come up; we have two automatic weapons. I place one in "Les Pipistrelles," guarding the upper boulevard, and the other, along with a few *Grenadiers*, in the property of the Compte de Cessole, guarding the lower boulevard and protecting the much larger groups of the Captain [Cavenago] who are at the level crossing. It is about 8 o'clock, and our position is fortified enough to resist a large-scale attack.

The *Boches* are coming down from the two avenues. In front of the Castellane school and at the corner of avenue Cyrnos, I order the quick construction of two makeshift redoubts. In the meantime, a group with a third submachine gun that I had sent after the Germans who had surrounded us returns after having killed several *Boches* and captured a few prisoners. Result: several Mausers that I distribute to the men who are lacking weapons. At that point, we are sure of being able to resist against the *Boches*, who continue to carefully come down the boulevard, but whose forces are accumulating, coming from St Pancrace, Las Planas, and St Barthélemy. With several Mausers, I get behind one of our redoubts and manage, after intense fire, to stop the *Boche* progression 200 meters away, dispersing them. At that moment I have approximately 30 men under my command. To cover our rear, I send a MOI group, which has come under my command with a submachine gun and five men, to take position in the pine trees to prevent the "Les Pipistrelles" villa from being flanked [13]

The Death of Leutnant Wilhelm Hansen

Following the example of the level crossing, fighting gradually broke out in the other districts of Nice. FTP Barbev Odadjian, alias "Robert," was part of the group whose mission was to "visit" several key positions mentioned earlier by René Canta, before occupying the print shop of the collaborationist *l'Eclaireur* newspaper. **Barbev Odadjian** reported:

We depart from our camp at five in the morning, towards the Gendarmerie. The Gendarmerie was occupied without incident. We went to the boys' high school in Nice, reaching it at 6:40 without any incidents occurring. On the way we met a German car that turned away 200 meters from us without showing any hostility.

Continuing my mission, I then went to Rue Dalpozzo to the PPF headquarters with all my comrades. We occupied said building, as well as the surrounding buildings in the area from rue de la Buffa to Rue Marechal Joffre. The buildings were occupied by men armed with submachine guns forbidding access in or out of the [PPF] building, which also had a machine gun trained on it. I entered the building with one of my comrades and seized all the documents that we could find. We searched the whole building without meeting any resistance. Not a single PPF was found inside.

Around the end of the operation, a German car containing two officers, including a captain, reached our road block. It was immediately taken under the fire of our submachine guns and the two occupants were killed. We put the car out of order and recovered a Bergam [sic] submachine gun and a 7.65 caliber pistol. The attack of the car occurred at 8:30. (…) In addition to the weapons mentioned above, we also recovered six German grenades.

Following orders, we then retreated in order to the *Eclaireur*, which we reached at 8:45. No incidents occurred on the way, although the Germans had immediately surrounded the area of the shooting. Having reached the *Eclaireur*, we occupied the place and set up defenses (submachine guns and machine guns), in order to be able to face any possible attacks from the Germans. We then printed 10,000 copies of the pamphlet, the text of which had been given to us by the high command.[14]

The German "captain" who died in the car was 30-year-old *Leutnant* **Wilhelm Hansen**, an only son whose father had been killed during WWI when he was a few months old.

Telephone Games

We will now read what *Generalmajor* Nickelmann wrote in the *Feldkommandantur's* journal to get an impression of how the start of the Resistance uprising was being perceived by the German forces. When reading Nickelmann's text, one must remember that the *Préfecture*, its telephones, and its Chief of Cabinet Ravard had all fallen under control of the Resistance and René Canta in the early morning. During the morning, Nickelmann contacted Ravard by telephone several times, not seeming to realize that Ravard had been "turned" by the Resistance and that all the information he was feeding *Generalmajor* **Nickelmann** was entirely false. On this occasion, the Resistance masterfully managed to trick the Germans and delay their reaction to the insurrection:

Monday the 28th.

8:15. Lieutenant Kauert, of *Flak Bataillon 875*, informs us that *Leutnant* Hansen and an NCO of the flak battalion commanded by Michelis have been killed by terrorists at the corner of Rue Dalpozzo and Rue de la Buffa as they drove by in a car around 7:30. General Fretter-Pico is aware of this affair. (…)

9:00. Lieutenant Scholz, of *Reserve Grenadier Regiment 8*, tells us that he has been informed by the commander of the Port of Nice that, according to civilian witness accounts, the *Préfecture* has probably been occupied by terrorists. Dr Koechling immediately contacts Ravard, who is in the *Préfecture*. He is told that around 7:00, a group of 30 terrorists had indeed attempted an attack against the *Préfecture*, but that they had been pushed back by the French Police and Gendarmerie, who still have the situation firmly under control. Koechling asks for Police patrols to be reinforced. In return, Ravard asks the German troops not to fire during the next three hours and not to attempt an attack until noon, because at that time he will be master of the situation. Ravard is advised to imperatively keep order in the streets of Nice and to stay in constant connection with the *Feldkommandantur*.

9:20. We receive another phone call from Ravard, asking that our troops not attempt anything until noon. He gives us all guarantees that he is able to reestablish order.

9:30. Major Schulz calls us to give his agreement to Ravard's propositions.

9:40. The French Police has fired at *Leutnant* Kauert, of the flak battalion, who was in Place Massena.

9:45. Ravard informs us about these incidents and asks once again that our troops not open fire. He will immediately send reinforced Police patrols.

9:50. Major Schulz is once again informed about the situation in Nice. The *Feldkommandantur* informs Ravard that if at noon calm and order have not been reestablished, it will ask the troops to intervene sharply. Ravard would like a police car equipped with loudspeakers to circulate to announce the following message: "In agreement with the French authorities, the French uniformed Police and the Gendarmerie must be able to move about freely in order to reestablish calm and order. No other person must be in the streets. The German troops will not attempt any offensive action."

10:08. Ravard informs us that a radio car has left the *Préfecture*.

10:13. Ravard tells us that the troops have opened fire on the radio car in the area of the Town Hall.

10:16. *Oberleutnant* Bergemann, of *Regiment 8*, will issue an order that the troops not fire at the radio car. He also informs us that *Oberstleutnant* Niedlich, the commander of the *Regiment 239* [he in fact commanded the 8th Regiment], is said to have been ambushed on the way back to his regiment. Supposedly he is in the hands of the terrorists.[15]

The Capture of Oberstleutnant Hans Niedlich

The capture of *Oberstleutnant* Hans Niedlich and of the freshly issued field orders that he was transporting became one of the better known exploits of the Nice insurrection. However, like many legendary stories, it has become distorted over time and been told inaccurately. Most authors, historians, and period witnesses who have written about Niedlich have "killed" him, and they have sometimes also self-servingly exaggerated the importance of the capture of the orders found on him. The surviving accounts about Niedlich's documents differ from each other so much, it is sometimes difficult to recognize that they are referring to the same event, to the point that one could question the credibility of some of the witnesses. The documents presented below should help set the story of Niedlich's capture straight.

Oberstleutnant Niedlich was the commanding officer of *Reserve Grenadier Regiment 8*, which included *Reserve Grenadier Bataillons 7* and *164* as well as *Reserve Jäger Bataillon 28*. Niedlich was captured in the area of the level crossing in the early morning, and it is almost certainly he who was being referred to in the previous accounts

of Louis Sana and Paul Cavenago, who wrote about a high-ranking German officer on whom important documents had been found. Other sources confirm their claim, as we will see later. Contrary to what has been written and claimed on numerous occasions, *Oberstleutnant* **Hans Niedlich** was not killed when his car was ambushed. In fact, he was able to explain the circumstances of his capture himself in the following days when he was being interrogated by First Airborne Task Force intelligence officer Lt Col William Blythe, who wrote in his prisoner of war interrogation report:

> Name: Niedlich Hans Lieutenant Colonel.
> Unit: Commanding Officer 8th Reserve Regiment, 148th Division.
> Captured by: French partisans in Nice at 0900 hours 28 August 1944. (…)
> Prisoner of war states that he received 148th Division field orders August 28, 1944, and immediately departed from his command post in Nice for a conference with the Commanding Officer of 239th Regiment. During this trip he was ambushed by French partisans. His driver was killed and he was taken prisoner. Prisoner of war states he did not issue any orders to 8th Regiment in connection with the 148th division field orders prior to his departure for conference with Commanding Officer of the 239th Regiment. Prisoner of war states that he believes that the 148th Division field order is being carried out and did not know who would assume command [in his place]. Prisoner of war does not believe that West Alp positions can be held by Germans without considerable reinforcements of men and material.[16]

Furthermore, *Oberstleutnant* **Niedlich** seems to have fully collaborated with his interrogator, telling him everything he knew about his unit and the planned retreat to the mountains at the Italian border. Lt Col Blythe's interrogation report therefore constitutes a short unit history of *Reserve Grenadier Regiment 8*:

> Unit strength: 1,000 men (Originally 1,900 men).

> Unit organization: 8th Regiment has three rifle battalions: one 13th Company, the Cannon Company, one 14th Company, and the Anti-Tank Company. Each battalion has three rifle companies and one Machine Gun Company. (…)

> Unit history: 8th Regiment was formed at the outset of war as a training regiment in Silesia. Moved to Lorraine in May 1941. Moved to central France September 1942. Moved to vicinity of Toulouse May 1943. Moved into vicinity of Nice to take over defense of coast in December 1943.

> Non-Germans: Prisoner of war stated 8th Regiment has 60% non-Germans.

> Defenses: French defenses on Italian border face generally West [sic]; prisoner of war states that largest gun found in emplacements are 75mm howitzers with little ammunition available for these guns. Prisoner of war states that Italian emplacements facing French border are built elaborately but are not entirely occupied.

> Supplies: Prisoner of war states that transportation of 8th Regiment was sufficient only while Regiment was stationary. The regiment still has ample supply. Huge quantities of supplies were stored in the vicinity of Nice prior

to invasion. Supply roads Nice to Sospel and from Sospel to Italian border have been bombed frequently, but with very little effect due to the rocky foundation of the roads.

Casualties: 8th regiment had approximately 900 casualties (including prisoners of war).

Other units: Prisoner of war states that the 239th Regiment had approximately 2,000 men when invasion started. Believes that 239th Regiment had approximately 1,200 men at present.[17]

As explained above, Niedlich was carrying freshly issued field orders when he was captured at the level crossing early on August 28th. The resistance men grasped the importance of these documents, and by that night they had been brought all the way to Grasse to the FABTF's Intelligence Officer, Captain Geoffrey Jones. Resistance man Pierre Escot was acting as Jones' "Chef de Bureau," and though he was not present in Nice at the time, it is through him and his men that the documents reached Captain Jones. **Pierre Escot** remembered:

As the *Wehrmacht* retreated to Menton, two of my guys found themselves in Nice, on Boulevard Gambetta, face to face with a car driven by a German Lieutenant beside which a captain was sitting with a large briefcase on his knees. They fired on sight, killed the two occupants of the car, ripped the briefcase out of the captain's hands, quickly crossed the Var, and found me on the very same night in Grasse, where I had gone to see Captain Jones, the chief of intelligence of the American paratrooper division commanded by General Frederick, which had jumped in near Draguignan.

I opened the briefcase, and what did I find inside? A file with 28 maps, all annotated, that was called in German: "Defensive use of the Western Alps and new front on the coast – 17 August 1944. 18:00." At the top of the maps was a note: "To be transmitted urgently, considering the necessities of the operations of the 34th Division."

When Captain Jones saw that, he hugged all three of us, my two men and myself, and he went to fetch the general, who congratulated us. A real stroke of luck![18]

As can be seen, there are mistakes in Pierre Escot's version, the most blatant of which is the date. He claims the documents were dated August 17th, and were seen by Jones and Frederick in Grasse on the same day; in other words, a week before Grasse was even liberated from the Germans! One could suspect that Escot may in fact be talking about another set of documents, but such is not the case. Escot's mistake in the dates is caused by Geoffrey Jones' version (that we will see below) of the Niedlich story that was included in the book *The Champagne Campaign*, and that the authors misdated the event as having occurred August 17th instead of 28th. (This being one of only many similar mistakes and misrepresented accounts printed in the book.) Jones made sure to give his former collaborators a copy of *The Champagne Campaign* after the war, and Escot's copy no doubt led him to become confused about the exact date of Niedlich's capture.

Any possible confusion about some August 17th documents with August 28th documents can be eliminated by the fact that Jones kept one of Niedlich's maps in his personal collection (although this was against FABTF orders): Jones himself dated the map August 28th, and the map shows the planned German positions of August 29th. Furthermore, Jones wrote a detailed after action report covering his activities between August 5 and 18, 1944,[19] and no maps nor documents are mentioned August 17th, nor any of the other days. These long explanations about a date prove how damaging false claims or mistakes made by historians can be to the proper interpretation of historical events.

One resistance man of the *Réseau Tartane* who was in Jones' office in Grasse at the moment Niedlich's captured documents were brought in gives a very different and much darker version of the handover than described by Pierre Escot:

I was in the office with Captain Jones and two Monegasques came in and said: "We have important documents." They had incredible luck. I think it was on the Lower or Middle Corniche, there was a German car in a ditch with a driver and two German officers who were dead. So they seized their bag, and in the bag were the retreat plans for the German army in northern Italy. They started negotiating with Captain Jones and they wanted to be paid for the information, or else they weren't giving anything up. So I told Captain Jones: "But all you have to do is arrest them or shoot them. What bastards, to want to be paid like that!" Jones said: "No, no, there is no need for that. We will pay, then we will have the documents, that is simpler." He spoke in American with several people who were there, and no problem, they paid.

They paid 80,000 Francs, I think. It was quite a large sum of money, so those two people went to party at the Perroquet, a sort of restaurant on Boulevard Thiers that was run by Bartolozi, who was responsible for veterans affairs in Grasse. And can you imagine, they lost the money that Captain Jones had given them during the meal? They came back perhaps 15 minutes later and they even held up Bartolozi: "Where is our wallet?" So they returned to the table where they had taken their meal and they found the wallet with all the money under the table. They left, and I never saw them again.

We were volunteers, and to see those two guys wanted to negotiate the information that they were bringing in had

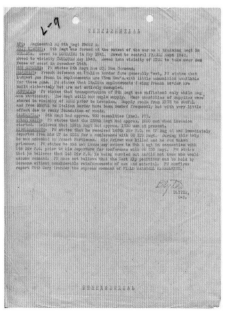

OberstLeutnant Hans Niedlich's prisoner of war interrogation report, dated for the period 1 to 2 September 1944. NARA.

revolted me at the time. It was unacceptable! For me, they were unforgivable for what they had done. But during the Liberation, the Americans were printing money, so I suppose they couldn't care less if they paid."

Emile Litschgy, another of Jones' local French agents, remembered that Niedlich's documents were traded for seven jerry cans of fuel. The truth about the transaction will clearly never be known... We will now read **Captain Geoffrey Jones'** version of events as reported in *The Champagne Campaign*. His account contains at least as much disinformation as information, but this is where part of its interest lies. Indeed, Jones' story shows how far facts can be twisted and inaccurately remembered and told, even by the Intelligence Officer of a division; the very type of person who wrote regimental histories and after action reports, highlighting the importance for historians not to take such official reports as gospel:

> We had been getting these reports concerning active German movement... that they were shifting things and units around, making all kinds of deployments in various directions, but we could never get a serious clue as to what was actually going on. All the Germans were moving, but we didn't know if they were moving forward, backward, or sideways.[20]

This is absolutely inaccurate, for as we have seen in the previous chapters, the German intensions to retreat had been known since a German radio communication was intercepted around August 20th, ordering a withdrawal to the Italian border. These intensions had been confirmed constantly in the following days by the many German prisoners, by reports made by civilians, and by every other available source of information. But let us read the rest of **Captain Jones'** story without further interruption:

> At this point, a group that I had behind the lines near Nice came back that night and told me they had ambushed a German command car. With all due respect to them, I really think that they mostly shot up the car because they just wanted to shoot up any German group they could lay their hands on. But one of them had the presence of mind to pick up a knapsack that was around one of the dead officers in the car and bring it back to me.
>
> We began to look through this thing, and by one of those great coincidences in life, we had an English officer with us who had just come from the beachhead where Patch had landed. He spoke fluent German and I didn't. He began to look over the knapsack's contents and he gasped, "My God! This is a Field Order... it was written this afternoon!"
>
> So we began to translate this material. We put everyone on it who had any expertise at all in German documents. It was voluminous: maps, overlays, and all sorts of other pertinent combat material. The man killed had obviously been the G-3 of the commanding general's staff. He had about four or five of these Field Orders in his knapsack, and we soon realized that the Field Order under examination was one that showed the plan of retreat for the whole German Army in the south of France for the next three days!
>
> We really wouldn't have known what we had, except for this Englishman. And he reacted as if he had spent his whole life waiting for this night. We had no lights, so we worked by candles.
>
> Of course, it wasn't an easy job. Many of the papers were still wet with blood because again, with due respect to my boys, by the time they had decided to bring the knapsack back

to me, they had probably finished taking off the wristwatches and looking for money, medals, or anything else they could pull off the dead Germans. I wouldn't be surprised if they had just brought the knapsack back as an afterthought.

> Anyhow, about four or five o'clock in the morning, the captured orders began to fall into a pattern. We knew where the German units were going, where they wanted their headquarters moved... not only for that night, but where it would be for the next three nights. They were obviously all set to fall back to prepared positions that the Italians had created to protect themselves in case of a French attack. In effect, they had prepared an orderly retreat to positions that they could occupy for the rest of the war.
>
> It was about an hour before daybreak when we finished translating the whole plan. We all felt the same way you do when you open an old drawer and unexpectedly find a pile of money... you don't believe it's there, you think it must be a mistake.
>
> General Frederick had left orders that he was not to be awakened by anybody because he hadn't gotten a night's sleep for quite a while, so they turned me away when I went over to his quarters. From there I went right over to Colonel Blythe [The one who was to interrogate Niedlich a few days later.], and when I showed him what I had he agreed that orders or no orders, Frederick had to see these documents right away.
>
> Of course, Frederick showed no annoyance at all at being awakened for this kind of reason. He quickly glanced through the file and then said, in a very quiet voice, for me to take his plane and fly down to the beach to show it to Sandy Patch.
>
> I took off in his little L-5 plane at dawn, and by the time I got to the beach the sun was up. When I got there, I refused to show the report to anyone but General Patch. I'm sure his staff thought I was a nut, because I really looked like a bum in the first place. I don't remember if I was wearing any insignia or had anything else to identify me because I just hadn't been thinking about those things in the excitement of the night and the flight. You know, I had this leg wound with my left trouser leg cut away so as not to interfere with the dirty cloth I had been using as a bandage for it. Anyhow, I got in to see General Patch and handed over my papers.
>
> I've had other people tell me, and I'm convinced, too, that Patch's use of this file helped him go up the Rhone Valley a hell of a lot faster then he would have if he hadn't been so damned certain of what he needed to protect his right flank. You see, by knowing the German defense plan, he now knew exactly what force he had to use to keep them from interfering or slowing down his advance. He knew just what his opposition would be.
>
> Another thing: since the plan pinpointed the locations of German headquarters, troop movement schedules, and bivouac areas, our headquarters was able to inform Vice Admiral Hewitt of the most advantageous targets for his fleet artillery, which was a great help, since we didn't have very many big guns in the early stages. Hewitt had his gunners plastering every key position in the area. The Germans couldn't move; no matter where they'd go, or how well camouflaged they were, the shells would come in on them within a few minutes after they got there. I guess they had no idea what was going on.
>
> I am certain that when the First Airborne Task Force was finally committed to protect the Seventh Army's right flank, it was as a result of the information that came out of this captured Field Order.[21]

Though Captain Jones' recollection makes for an entertaining read, it vastly exaggerates the supposed consequences of "his" find! Patch's race up north (with the famous Task Force Butler) to cut off the retreating German troops in the Rhone valley had started 10 days earlier, and the FABTF had already been guarding the right flank of the invasion front for a week by the time the field order reached him! The field order could obviously not have had any influence on decisions that had been made 10 days before it was captured! As for the Germans, they knew very well "what was going on." They were aware within hours that *Oberstleutnant* Niedlich had been captured, as is proven by Nickelmann's statement, and they probably assumed immediately that under these circumstances, all of the information known to Niedlich would soon be known by the Allies. Furthermore, the parts of the captured field order that have survived to this day show that it only contained very general information. Though it did give good hints of possible targets, there were no "pinpointed" German headquarters locations, "troop movement schedules," or "bivouac areas" for the Allied artillery to exploit. As we will see in the next chapters, the Germans barely lost any soldiers in the days after the liberation of Nice (see the list of killed German soldiers buried in the Maritime Alps shown in the annex), and

there was no sudden increase in the deadliness of Allied artillery. In fact, quite the opposite was true, as after Nice was liberated, there was a lull in the fighting for several days, with losses decreasing sharply for all the forces involved. Jones' account is a textbook example of the way history becomes distorted when a war event is investigated from the point of view of one of the belligerents only. But then again, what sells better: a good story or a true story?

In fact, Niedlich's documents only confirmed the German retreat intensions that had already been known to the Allied command since at least August 20th (see *Reserve Division 148* orders quoted in Chapter 6), and that had been reconfirmed regularly by all available sources of intelligence after that date. In spite of Jones' exaggerations, it of course remains true that the information contained in the captured documents was very informative to the Allies. Here we present one of the captured maps that Jones kept as a souvenir, showing the new defense line the Germans were planning to hold as of August 29th, and below is a translation of part of the field order. These seem to be the only parts of the field order that have survived, and one can suspect that there may not have been much other relevant information contained in the field order in the first place. It must be noted that the version provided below is a translation made from a French translation presented in Pierre-Emmanuel Klingbeil's *Le front oublié des Alpes-Maritimes*. A fair number of inconsistencies can be expected because of this "double translation," the original German text not having been consulted. Although these orders may seem rather long and tedious to read and understand, they also provide a rare glimpse of an original period document of *Reserve Division 148*:

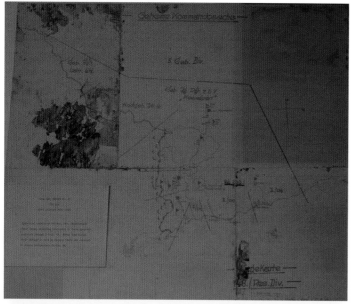
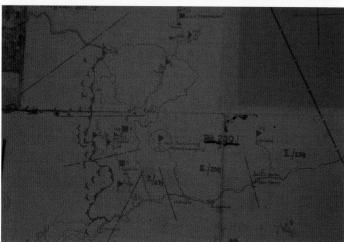

One of the maps captured by the resistance along with OberstLeutnant Hans Niedlich the morning of August 28th in Nice. The stains on the upper left corner are presumably blood from Niedlich's unlucky driver. The map shows the positions on the la Turbie-Col de Braus line to which Reserve Division 148 was already planning to retreat to early on the 28th. In the next chapters, we will see that the Germans did indeed defend these positions over the next days and weeks. The map was kept as a souvenir by Captain Geoffrey Jones. Though keeping such documents as souvenirs was strictly against FABTF orders, Jones' action thankfully enabled the map to survive and be available to us today. Kenneth W. Rendell, Museum of World War II.

Field order concerning the use of the defense of positions in the western Alps and on the new coastal front

Enemy intensions: The enemy will try to cross the passes leading into northern Italy. The action of the partisans seems to prove it. The enemy has advanced slowly, but he could suddenly seize the entire Var.

Defense Plan
The LXXVth army corps will prepare its defense on the Franco-Italian border and on the Ligurian coast up to San Lorenzo al Mare included.

The units of this army corps will be deployed in the following manner:

On the right: 157th Reserve Mountain Division
In the center: 5th (Mountain) Division
On the left: 148th Reserve Division
The 5th Mountain Division will occupy the area of: L'Aiguillette, Enchastrayes, Bagni (15 km southeast of Col de l'Arche), Mont Matto (3.087m), and Limone (20 km south of Cuneo). Lieb's corps will occupy the coast up to San Remo.

Mission: The troops will pull back as slowly as possible, while avoiding to the maximum any costly battles, and in a first step, will go to their positions on the western Alps. On the Alpine positions, the *Meeralpen* (4th High Mountain Infantry Battalion and Special Mountain Teaching Battalion) will defend the southern flank of the corps in the various resistance centers of:

a) Col de Turini – La Calmetta
b) On the Nice – Sospel – Breil Road and Col de Braus
c) On the Nice – Vintimille road, the Mont Agel and

Roquebrune
The Ligurian coast of Saint Roman (northeast of Monte Carlo) is also to be defended.

Detailed retreat order
a) 239th Reinforced Infantry Reserve Regiment, to which the division's *Füsillier* Battalion is attached (CP, 2 km from St André) executes its retreat order immediately.

1) The 1st Battalion of the 239th will retreat if it is under threat of being cut off by the enemy around Saint Isidore, then pulls back in small detachments towards the region north of Menton (Roquebrune excluded) and relieves the 80th Infantry Regiment and the 80th Reserve Infantry Regiment.
2) The 2nd Battalion of the 239th retreats from the High Cornice towards Mortola at nightfall, then directs itself towards the zone north of San Remo.
3) The 3rd Battalion of the 239th, while fighting rear guard actions, retreats along the Upper and Middle Cornices and goes to the area west of Roquebrune. The battalion will avoid Nice, which is infested with partisans.

b) 8th Reserve Infantry Regiment. The 1st and 2nd Battalions of the 8th retreat on the road from Contes to l'Escarène and the Col de Braus, while leaving behind one company to block the road until the 3rd Battalion of the 8th passes through. [The 3rd Battalion was *Bataillon 164*, which on August 28th was fighting in la Roquette and Levens.] The 3rd Battalion will pull back while harassing the enemy on the road from Châteauneuf de Contes to l'Escarène and will then go to Moulinet. The regiment will defend itself at this point.

c) The Replacement Battalion [Probably *Feld Ersatz Battaillon 148*], reinforced with the Hako Nizza [Hako standing for *Haffen Kommando*, or Port Commando], will be displaced to the rear of this area to cooperate closely with the 239th Regiment, where it will retreat as soon as it will receive the order and will reassemble in the region of Mortola to then proceed towards Bajardo and Ceriana.

d) The 26th *Meeralpen* Mountain Reconnaissance Regiment will fulfill the mission that will be assigned to it by the 90th *Panzer Grenadier* Division and will rapidly move in order to be in immediate reserve in the zone determined by the LXXV army corps and by the 90th *Panzer Grenadier* Division.

e) The division's *Füsillier* Battalion, under the command of the 239th, will take position on the line Pointe de Contes, la Trinité, Mont Vinaigrier, where it will establish road blocks. It will make contact with the enemy at Contes, then will pull back without engaging any serious fighting towards Roquebrune, then Airole and Fanghetto.

f) The Hako Nizza will retreat towards San Remo, while the 8th Reserve Infantry Regiment will pull back from the coast, leaving behind commandos to make the enemy believe that the coast defenses will resist. These will pull back as soon as the main force will have passed by them.

Artillery
Must take up new positions in order for a group to be able to take action in the western area of the Alps and the rest on the coast. The main area to defend will be that at the limit of the *Meeralpen* and of the 8th Reserve Infantry Regiment. The 239th Regiment will be supported by most of the artillery.

Engineers
Destruction of the roads on the line Saint Martin Vésubie, Utelle, Nice.

Recommendations
Partisans, avoid Nice. Move in groups and be armed. One company of the Nice port and one platoon of the 1048th Military Police will protect a roadway in Nice.

Division dressing stations
San Remo, Menton, Breil-sur-Roya

Supplies
G-4 in Sospel, then Tende until August 31st. Distribution at Fontan and San Remo.

Division PC G-3 Sospel, August 28, 1944, at 20:00."[22]

These orders issued in the early morning of the 28th, when the insurrection had hardly started, already clearly prove that the German intensions were to evacuate Nice by the end of the day: the retreat was to occur "immediately," "by nightfall," etc. The insurrection therefore mainly served the purpose of hindering and disorganizing the retreating Germans, while also inflicting costly casualties among the German troops, damaging their morale, and preventing them from blowing certain strategic structures.

Following Niedlich's capture, it was Major Zwirner, the commander of *Reserve Grenadier Bataillon 164*, who took his place as commanding officer of *Reserve Grenadier Regiment 8*. Hopefully this section will have cleared up most of the mystery and misinformation that has surrounded *Oberstleutnant* Nieldlich's capture and the true nature of the documents that he was transporting. It is surprising that over the years no resistance groups nor Allied units have ever clearly claimed the responsibility of the capture of this important officer.

The Insurrection Spreads

The detailed explanation of *Oberstleutnant* Hans Niedlich has momentarily carried us off our main topic: the Nice insurrection. Let us now return to the town, where as the morning wore on, the fighting spread and became more and more intensive. Though *Generalmajor* Nickelmann was still communicating with Ravard by telephone, without realizing that Ravard was now under control of the Resistance, it was becoming more and more clear to the Germans that Ravard and the French Police were not about to restore "calm and order" anytime soon, and that more drastic measures needed to be taken to ensure the safety of the retreating German troops. As the violence escalated, *Generalmajor* **Nickelmann** wrote in the *Feldkommandantur's* journal:

10:25. Ravard informs us that the *Feldgendarmerie Leutnant* has fallen into an ambush at Place Massena. Of the 10 German soldiers standing guard in this square, one has been shot and several wounded. (…)
10:55. We receive the following phone dispatch from General Fretter-Pico! "During the retreats, all units must take hostages in the town of Nice, or in suspicious locations, that they are to keep on their vehicles to prevent terrorist fire. Weapons must be held ready to fire and you must not

let yourself be intimidated by the words of intoxication that these hostages may tell you."

11:00. The Grenadier Regiment 8 informs us that it will immediately clean up Place Massena with a commando armed with heavy weapons. Furthermore, *Regiment 239* will supply one battalion for the cleansing operation of the town of Nice.

11:25. Ravard asks us not to occupy the public buildings.

11:35. Major Schulz informs us that two of our soldiers have been wounded by French Policemen close to the *Feldkommandantur*. The toll in the area of the *Feldkommandantur* is one soldier killed and three wounded. Major Schulz gives the order to disarm the French Police, and in case of resistance, to make use of weapons.

Order from *Infanterie Division 148*: Captain Burkhardt will be the new commander of the area of Nice; he will be given all powers and will be entitled to apply martial law. He has just started out towards Nice with a battalion on board five buses, and his mission is to occupy the *Préfecture* and the Town Hall. On the way, he must liberate the west-east roadway that is being held by the terrorists by any means possible. Furthermore, a special commando with heavy weapons is on its way for the clearing up of Place Massena.

12:55. Ravard informs us that five buses containing German troops are present near the *Préfecture* and asks if we have the intention of occupying the *Préfecture*. We reply that we do not know.

13:15. Ravard informs us that German soldiers have fired at the *Préfecture* with machine guns. It has been established that a patrol under the orders of *Leutnant* Pico pushing a flak cannon has been shot at in the area of the *Préfecture*. When fire was returned, a stray bullet hit the *Préfecture* building.

13:50. Orders of the Division to *Reserve Grenadier Regiment 239*:

1) martial law is immediately applicable for the town of Nice;

2) command is placed in the hands of Captain Burkhardt, commanding the 1st Battalion of *Regiment 239*. [This may be the very same Captain Burkhardt who had previously been in command of *Ost Bataillon 661*, though there seems to be a discrepancy in the exact spelling of his name. He was presumably put in command of *Reserve Grenadier Bataillon 327* after the Allied landing, when *Ost Bataillon 661* rapidly disintegrated and Major Tornow, the former commander of *Bataillon 327*, surrendered to Captain Hanna in Fayence (See Chapter 4).]. He has the power of applying martial law. The civilian population must be removed from the streets and must stay within the houses; any person found in the streets will be executed;

3) the command post of the 1st Battalion will establish itself at the *Feldkommandantur*; the *Préfecture* and the Town Hall are to be occupied by one company;

4) in case of resistance, apply orders with no consideration for anybody; greatest possible firmness must be established.

Signed: Schulz[23]

The patience of the Germans had now run thin. *Generalmajor* Nickelmann gave the first indication that he no longer trusted Ravard at 12:55, when he pretended not to know that the *Préfecture* was to be occupied by German troops during a phone conversation with Ravard. Nickelmann made no further mention of Ravard after 13:15, having

probably finally realized that he had been tricked the whole morning and that all the information given to him by Ravard was meant to earn precious time for the Resistance. Nickelmann presumably understood this without a doubt when the troops on the ground ran into heavy gunfire from the *Préfecture* as they attempted to occupy it. After this, it was all-out war in the town.

Interestingly, although they were now aware that the Resistance was on the other end of the line at the *Préfecture*, the Germans kept on communicating with them by telephone throughout the afternoon in order to attempt various negotiations. They even tried to convince the Resistance to hand back *Oberstleutnant* Niedlich, probably fearing for his life. In its report about the actions of the telephone workers during the insurrection, the **FFI *Groupe* Bernard** mentioned one such telephone conversation that occurred around two in the afternoon:

Telephone negotiations are being made with the *Kommandantur*. The Germans are asking for a high ranking officer who disappeared in the morning. This officer has been arrested by a group of FFIs at Cessole. (…) The Germans threaten to "crush" a district of the town if the officer is not returned to them. They direct light mortar fire at the *Préfecture*; the roof is hit by several shells, as are the surrounding houses. A bastard is enfilading the Rue de la *Préfecture* and a nurse who goes outside is wounded in the shoulder and arm.[24]

Within the *Préfecture*, FTP René Canta not only had to deal with the German attacks, but also with the sometimes even more serious threat posed by men from other resistance movements who were jealous of his position of authority and wanted to take his place. **René Canta** mentioned both in his report:

During a lull in the late morning, an FFI chief arrives with two of his men. I ignore what their goal is because I am too busy. At first I exchange a few words with them, then decide not to afford any interest to the reason of their visit. But in the face of an increase of the enemy fire and fearing for the life of my men, and also to find out about the degree of mobilization of his groups, I asked him if by any chance it may be possible for him to send a few reserve men into the houses facing the *Préfecture*. He answers that it is physically impossible for him to help me because he had not at all expected the insurrection at this date, and that consequently, he finds himself cut off from his groups. Although he has no forces to back him at this historical moment, the few men who had infiltrated after him seem to be carrying out propaganda in order for their chief to take control of the operations. Without paying any interest to these backstage negotiations, I kept on giving orders to my men in order to hold the *Préfecture* at all costs, as at that very moment it was the subject of concentric attacks. In spite of this, I did not let my guard down for a single second; I did not want to serve as a toy in a "diplomatic" surprise, which are always possible in such cases. For about 15 minutes, a reciprocal distribution of powers was made in the *Préfecture*, to which I accorded no credit whatsoever. It vanished on its own in the face of the only fact that counts in such cases and that had just been neglected: that of having men in hand.

The intensity of the battle was increasing, for the Germans were tightening their grip on us, particularly on the side facing Cours Saleya, as we had protected the Rue de la *Préfecture* with damaged vehicles to protect the main entrance, which was also covered by the fire of our automatic weapons. Big armored cars, protecting three cars transporting soldiers, were advancing from the Cours Saleya towards the entrance gate of the *Préfecture*. I gave the order to let them come closer, in spite of the intensity of the fire from the armored cars, and then, when the vehicles were within about 15 meters of the entrance gate, I gave the order to fire. From all the windows, the automatic weapons, carbines, and even hunting rifles took the Germans under an infernal fire. Strings of grenades being thrown from all about efficiently supported this counterattack. The panicked Nazis tried to escape, but at the same instant, a young 16-year-old partisan, posted in the right spot, also took them under intensive fire with his machine gun. Those who could, and there were not many, pulled back, and during the rest of the day they never dared try another frontal attack. (…)

Meantime, in the offices, the gentlemen of the *Préfecture* were becoming more pale every instant. As soon as they saw me, they once again begged me to cease fire, blaming me for being responsible for reprisals the Germans would take. I had to mention that patrols from the *Préfecture* had gone to arrest a few traitors who could have bothered us. They were incarcerated in the basements of the *Préfecture*. Prefect Lauvel and his Chief of Cabinet Ravard, who had also been temporarily put under arrest, were put under guard in their offices.

Next to all this, from time to time we had a little conversation with the *Feldkommandantur*, who was sending us ultimatums every half hour or so, summoning us to immediately cease fire in town under threat of severe reprisals, such as: the shelling and destruction of Nice, surrounding the *Préfecture*, executing 10 hostages per German soldier killed, etc… However, in one of them, they asked us for a two hour armistice. I agreed to this rather illusory armistice under the sole condition that they allow the circulation of ambulances displaying Red Cross flags and of police cars with white flags in order to pick up the wounded in the various parts of town and transport them to the hospitals and clinics.

I took advantage of this truce to reorganize, resupply, and give instructions to my various groups holding positions in Nice, of course using the said cars. I also seized this unique opportunity to send a police loudspeaker car into town, in order to broadcast a message aiming to inform all the population and fighters of this first capitulation that taking the form of an armistice was the undeniable forerunning sign of impending defeat. I also took advantage of the armistice to send out a reconnaissance patrol that, having eliminated all its occupants, captured a half track full of ammunition that was immediately transferred to the *Préfecture*.

Of course, this armistice was not respected by either side, particularly not by our positions, as the patriots occupying the windows overlooking the Rue de la *Préfecture* were constantly involved in a difficult battle with two light machine guns that were constantly firing at us from the houses across the street. The armistice, however, did enable us, thanks to a relative lull, to save some wounded and accomplish certain missions.

More ultimatums reach us, to which I do not even respond, and the battle goes on. It is then that from the Place Massena on one side and from the Château on the other side, we are taken under crossfire of heavy machine guns, cannons, and mortars. It wasn't really possible for us to take effective action against the Château guns (…). As for the cannon firing from Place Massena, I at once considered the

possibility of silencing it. I phone the chief of my men who were holding the Town Hall, asking him to eradicate the crew of this cannon, which was also firing at them, at all cost. They brilliantly accomplished their mission, exterminating them almost immediately by shooting at them from the rooftops.

Inside the building the dividing maneuvers continue, but in vain, as my group is united and determined; only my orders count for it. In fact, a patrol is constantly circulating through the stories of the building to prevent any possible attempt to sabotage our work. Our firm and energetic attitude seems to have discouraged the discontented, who thus resort to using the most hypocritical and cowardly methods possible. Indeed,

some of the positions occupied by my men receive false orders signed "René." One of them, "Pensée," the mission chief at TNL, smelling a trap, was forced to come and see me, moving under fire, to ask confirmation of seemingly impossible orders that he had just received in a note signed "René," but that did not originate from me at all. Numerous witnesses who were present, including a member of the Liberation Committee, were able to note this with outrage.

But now a new ultimatum from the *Feldkommandantur* reaches the *Préfecture*, informing me that if we do not evacuate the building, we would be annihilated with shells. My opinion was already made up since the bitter defeat that we had inflicted on them a few hours earlier, and I do not take the threat seriously; however, I do take measures just in case they would execute it. A few moments later, the artillery in the Château sprays us with small caliber shells that will continue to shake the building until the evening. Fearing the destruction of the *Préfecture*, I order the construction of a primitive Morse code signal light with the means available that I install in the middle of the rubble under the roof. Through an open skylight, we send signals to a vessel of the fleet that is cruising out at sea about 15km from the coast. They only seemed to be understood in the evening, when the ship finally opened fire on the Château, reducing it to silence for good.

It became necessary for me to know why the Allies were not intervening, when their presence had been reported on the Var 24 hours earlier. Taking advantage of a lull, I sent a runner out, who returned with the news that the Americans were in fact only in Cagnes, and that only a few weak parachute troops had not yet crossed the Var.[25]

René Canta is one of the few resistance men who seemed to be aware that the Allies had barely even reached the southern portion of the Var River at that time. Because they were misinformed, or

Urban warfare: these photos were apparently taken during the insurrection of Nice August 28th and show silhouettes of armed men running and taking cover at the corners of deserted streets. MRA Collection.

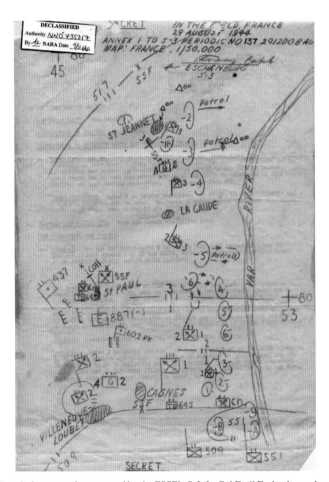

A period map overlay prepared by the FSSF's S-3, Lt Col Emil Eschenburg, showing the positions of the Allied troops August 29, 1944. As can be seen, even the day after the Nice insurrection, many of the most advanced Allied elements had not even reached the Var River yet, contrary to claims made by certain French Resistance members, according to whom the Allies had lazily spent the day of August 28th relaxing on the West bank of the Var. NARA.

perhaps for more insidious political reasons, many resistance men later claimed that during the insurrection the Allied troops, who had, according to them, reached the Var days ago, had simply waited inactively on the western bank of the river while the Resistance was fighting in town. The chief of the FTPs of the Maritime Alps, Philippe "Souny" Giovannini, went as far as to claim that the Americans had been waiting on the west bank of the Var since August 23rd,[26] a date at which the Allies had not even reached Cannes and Grasse! Why would such a high-ranking FTP officer spread such blatant disinformation? Possibly to exaggerate the importance of the FTP (and Communist party) actions, while minimizing the role of the Allied forces, who may just as well have stayed safely at home in America if this was the only credit they were going to be given.

In reality, as detailed in Chapter 11, the First Special Service Force only reached the high ground overlooking the Var River from the west during the day of August 28th, and it was not until the 29th that the FSSF took firm control of the west bank of the Var. (A map of the FSSF positions at 12:00 on the 29th shows that several areas of the west bank were still just being explored by patrols at that time.) As for the 551st Parachute Infantry Battalion, it only advanced from Biot to the mouth of the Var the morning of the 29th. The only unit that actually reached the Var River before August 28th was the 517th Parachute Infantry Regiment, which had occupied the west bank of the river north of Gattières on the 26th and 27th. The 517th PIR had not waited for news of the insurrection in Nice to take action, as it had crossed the river in a very daring operation at la Roquette during the night of August 27th to 28th; but this was much too far to the north to be of direct assistance to the partisans in Nice.

Urban Warfare in Nice

Up until now, we have mostly concentrated on the events occurring at the *Préfecture* and the level crossing. However, this must not lead the reader to believe that these were the only areas where fighting was occurring. Quite the opposite; after the first shots had been fired at the level crossing in the early morning, the insurrection had quickly spread to numerous other districts of Nice. We will now read through accounts that will give an idea of the chaotic street fighting that occurred in town throughout the day of August 28, 1944. Many men had not been informed of the revolt, but when the gunfire started, volunteers flowed into the streets, as **Alfred Gambassi** noted at the level crossing:

> At the first sound of submachine gun fire, groups of men of all ages descended into the streets, asking for weapons. We told them to wait a bit: "You will get some." Any vehicle that was isolated or in a small convoy was captured, the booty increasing constantly, as did the number of fighters in an indescribable enthusiasm.[27]

In some cases, captured "German" soldiers even volunteered to help the partisans. FTP **"Pensée" Martini** wrote:

> At the TNL depots, the Polish soldiers on guard duty that we capture immediately decide to fight with us against the Germans. At the sensitive spots of the depot, we build "bunkers" with sandbags. I give the order to attack all trucks or all Germans moving in our district. Several are killed and others are wounded. In the morning, we are forced to defend ourselves, as we are surrounded. François Suarez falls dead at my side with a bullet in the head.[28]

Starting the battle with few weapons, the resistance men took advantage of the poor motivation of some of the foreign German

soldiers to quickly build up a more deadly arsenal that they put to good use against the more motivated Germans. This is the method that FTP leader **Louis** and his small group of fighters used throughout the day:

> August 28, 1944, at 6:30 in the morning, I went to the previously designated emplacement, the crossroads at Primerose - St Pierre de Féric, accompanied by the following men of my group: Debuissy, Faust, Adrien, and Bastien. No weapons having been distributed to us, we were only armed with our personal weapons: a 7.65 pistol, two 6.35 pistols, and one dagger. As planned, we first proceeded to block the road with felled trees.
>
> Around 11 o'clock, we spotted a group of three German soldiers coming down the St Pierre de Féric road towards us. After calling out to them, we captured them without a fight and seized their weapons, complimenting our armament with three rifles with ammunition and 15 grenades. After a brief interrogation, these soldiers declared that one was Polish and the other two were Czech, and they were all 17 or 18 years old. We immediately handed them over to our leaders. (…)
>
> In the afternoon, around 15:00, at the same crossroads, we surprised five German soldiers who were coming up Avenue Primerose, carrying their supplies. After challenging them, we engaged in a fight: one was killed with a bullet in the forehead by Faust, and two others were wounded, but managed to escape with the remaining two. We recovered the following weapons: one rifle with ammunition, three grenades, and one bag of biscuits. There were no killed or wounded on our side.
>
> We then left the Primerose - St Pierre de Féric crossroads and went to Madeleine hill, in order to observe the German batteries at St Pierre de Féric. Around 17:00, we spotted two German soldiers on the side of the hill facing us, fixing telephone lines. At the same time, we saw a group of FTPFs climbing up the same hill, our comrades not realizing that they were going straight towards the Germans. Considering the danger our comrades were in, we decided to immediately open fire on the Germans: one was hit in the right hand and would later be captured by our now-alert comrades, while the other must have been wounded in the chest, considering his attitude as he escaped. He did, however, manage to return to his battery.[29]

Among the German soldiers who were probably attacked in the St Pierre de Féric area was a four-man telephone line repair party of the 2nd Battery of *Reserve Artillerie Regiment 8*. One of these artillery men, **Erich Baltanz**, described what happened to the four of them in a letter he wrote in 1949 to the wife of his comrade Richart Tönnissen, who was reported missing August 28th:

> Dear Ms Tönnissen!
>
> I have received your letter from February 17th and thank you for it. In order to be able to partially lift the veil covering the fate of your husband, my dear comrade, I will now tell you what happened. This was not possible from captivity for various reasons. I will give you the absolute and unvarnished truth, that will, I hope, be better than eternal and racking uncertainty, or than meaningless and weak information.
>
> Our unit was, as you maybe know, posted in the south of France, namely in the vicinity of Antibes. Our strongpoint, which was under never-ending construction in the depths of a

mountain, was originally supposed to be defended till the last shell. As the invasion in the south occurred very differently from what our leadership had planned, we had to, I think it was on August 22nd, evacuate our strongpoint and march off in the direction of Nice during the night. A few days later, we reached our new positions in the mountains in front of Nice during a march performed in complete darkness.

These exact mountains, with their numerous ravines, caves, crumbling shacks, etc., were infamous to our *Wehrmacht*, as a well organized little war was underway against us from there, and the French freedom fighters could find hiding places and hideouts everywhere. Here we started functioning as a telephone outpost. We laid a five-kilometer telephone line without any incident. The next day, we already had to fix two minor cuts. Then came the so-fateful day of August 28th. At nine o'clock in the morning, the connection on one line was suddenly lost, so the failure search team had to be put into action. This search party was doubled due to the aforementioned dangers, and consequently four men were set out. These four men were: your husband [Richart Tönnissen], Radje [Max Rathje], Mlaker, and myself. After a long climb and search we found the cut. Over 200 meters of cable had been cut out of the line.

As we only had 100 meters of replacement cable on us, two men had to return to the battery to fetch some more from there. Nobody wanted to do so, as the climb in the summer heat had already tired us out. Young Mlaker complained of a headache and your husband had problems with his varicose veins. In the end, Radje and I went to get the missing 100 meters of cable and repaired the line. After this, we wanted to return to the unit. At a house approximately one kilometer from our battery we decided to make a short break. We wanted to drink water, and an old lady came out of the house and brought us a watermelon, which of course was welcome. We shared the watermelon like brothers and were eating when all at once the small hills next to the house suddenly became full of life. We scattered, each quickly looking for cover.

Already, the first shots crackled from rifles and submachine guns. 20 to 25 men had waited for us in ambush. I just managed to crawl into a small field of pole beans, and there I heard that our pursuers were nearby and were looking for a fourth man. I wanted to crawl out of the beans to attempt to break through from the flank and get help from the battery. In doing so, I ran straight into four men, who pointed their firearms at me. To oppose resistance under these circumstances was pointless, and so I entered captivity. The whole ambush had only lasted seconds and everything was over.

Now two men took hold of me, and at a fast tempo and with many detours we went to a house at the top of a mountain where I was interrogated, then led further on again after a short time. In doing so, I found out from one of the men who had participated in the ambush that out of my three comrades, two men were dead and the third had been shot through the stomach. Who this was I was not able to find out, as the information was only given in French, which I was not good in at the time. Where we were I did not attempt to ask, as everybody was excited, especially as our troops were still in the area. That was also the reason why I was quickly moved away.

As of that time, the long period of captivity started for me. So that you will not think that my enquiries about the fate of my comrades ended there, I want to tell you more about it. After being in various camps, in the middle of January 1945 I arrived at the main camp in Nice, where all the prisoners from the zone within 100 kilometers of Nice were being collected and registered. Among the approximately 1,800 prisoners who were in the main camp at the time, I searched frantically for other members of our battery, at first without any success, until after three weeks I suddenly found two comrades from our unit. After a talk with them, I found out the following: these two comrades, along with a noncommissioned officer, had been given an order, and while fulfilling it, they were likewise ambushed by French freedom fighters, with the result that not a trace could be found of the noncommissioned officer and the two comrades were taken to the hospital with severe wounds. After their convalescence, they were immediately sent to the main camp. Neither of them could give me the name of the place where our position was.[30]

Erich Baltanz then made an enquiry about whether either Tönnissen, Rathje, or Mlaker were registered in the prison camp, hoping that the "third man" may have survived his wounds. Upon finding out that neither of his three comrades was registered, **Erich Baltanz** concluded:

It can unfortunately be assumed that my third comrade also died. What could corroborate the assumption is the following: as I already said, we were attacked by freedom fighters, not by regular soldiers, who were in part equipped very primitively: along with highly modern submachine guns, they were armed with grandfather's hunting rifles. The medical equipment available was obviously not comparable with that with which *Wehrmacht* medics are equipped. Even under normal circumstances, with quick and careful

Max Rathje and Richart Tönnisen, aged 37 and 36, of the 2nd Battery of Reserve Artillerie Regiment 8, are both reported missing in the Nice area since August 28, 1944. Both were reportedly shot and killed or mortally wounded in the vicinity of St Pierre de Féric after being ambushed by resistance fighters. They were presumably buried in Caucade Cemetery as unidentified German soldiers in the following days. Karl Heinz Butenschön Collection. Samtgemeindearchiv Jesteburg Collection, courtesy Hans-Heinrich Wolfes.

transportation and an immediate operation, a gunshot to the stomach is a life threatening wound.[31]

Both **Richart Tönnissen** and **Max Rathje** are reported missing to this day. In the days following the insurrection, two unidentified bodies were recovered in the Damiano property, on Boulevard de la Madeleine, in the vicinity of St Pierre de Féric, and buried in Caucade Cemetery. It seems very likely that these two bodies were those of the two men on the wire party who had been immediately killed during the ambush.

In several of the above accounts, the partisans clearly demonstrated a certain amount of respect for human life; when possible, German soldiers were summoned to surrender and their wounded were tended to. This was, however, unfortunately not always the case, and some less professional resistance fighters sometimes shot nonthreatening Germans in order to be able to brag about having "killed a German." One young man remembered:

At Place Gambetta there was a nice old German soldier who was probably Polish or Austrian sitting on a bench. Two young resistance men were so sick of the Germans that they shot him without him having done anything. That shocked my mother, but after everything we had been through, it almost seemed normal.

Luckily, such exactions were the exception and not the rule, as is proven by the fact that after the fighting, the resistance handed a significant number of German prisoners over to the Allied forces. Many resistance men took any weapons they could find in order to participate in the battle, but this sometimes led to unpleasant surprises, as was the case for **Paul Granier**. He had been working in the kitchens of the Filley police station, preparing meals for hungry *maquisard*s, when he was interrupted by gunfire outside:

I was organizing my work in the kitchens when the fighting started around 11:30, some *Boches* being reported

around the station. I went down to make a reconnaissance at Rue Cassini along with several other FFI comrades. The *Boche* submachine guns started spitting, but we were able to get back to the station without suffering any losses. I was positioning myself at the service entrance of the building when I spotted two *Boches*, an NCO and a soldier. At once I tried to fire with my hunting shotgun, but unfortunately the shotgun (I was to notice this later) was a 12 gauge, whereas the cartridges were 16 gauge. I seized my revolver and fired. I saw the sergeant fold up, but I was not able to see what followed, because the other *Boche* had spotted me and was firing at me with his Mauser. There were 350 to 400, and I set to work immediately with my assistant, Louis Sibon, and we prepared the meals in the midst of the fire fight.[30]

The French Police were in a bit of a delicate position, as they had been representatives of the Vichy government for the past few years. However, some of them had been members of resistance movements, and when the insurrection started, many joined the battle wholeheartedly, even if they had not been forewarned. As well-trained policemen, they later wrote reports of what they had done, thus leaving a good trace of their activity. We will now read several of these reports, starting with the one written by Policeman **Georges Damiot**, who was a member of the *Combat* organization:

Monday, August 28th, around six in the morning, as I was finishing my duty, the brigadier announced to us that we were to be confined to the police station to wait for orders from higher up. But around seven o'clock we heard gunshots, and it was only around eight that a brigadier took the responsibility of going to get orders at the *Préfecture*, selecting three of my comrades to accompany him. Seeing that I wasn't chosen, I asked him if I could follow them anyway. When we reached Boulevard Mac Mahon (…), we spotted a *Boche* half track. I got into combat position

38-year-old Soldat Johann Piesiur (in fact Jan Piesiur in Polish) was killed in Nice August 28th, leaving behind three children and a pregnant wife, all of whom remained in Poland after the war. Before being conscripted into the army, Johann Piesiur had been a railroad worker, the uniform of which he is wearing in this photo. Piesiur Family Collection.

17-year-old Grenadier (or Gefreiter, according to the rank visible in the picture) Friedrich Gorinschek, of the 1st Company of Feld Ersatz Bataillon 148, who was apparently mortally wounded in the fighting and died in St Roch Hospital in Nice. Friedrich Gorinschek was Slovenian, his name being a Germanized form of the name "Gorinšek." His remaining family still resides in Slovenia. Gorinšek Family Collection.

18-year-old Grenadier Anton Rodoschek, who was killed during the fighting in Nice. Anton Rodoschek was also Slovenian, his name being a Germanized form of the name "Rodošek." His remaining family also still resides in Slovenia. Rodošek Family Collection.

18-year-old year old Grenadier Eduard Raab, of the 3rd Company of Bataillon 327, who was wounded in Nice and died in the field hospital in Menton the next day. Raab Family Collection.

with one of my comrades and the Germans escaped. With the help of a few patriots we brought the truck to Place du Palais. We then took up positions in the Boulevard des Italiens (…). With the help of three or four patriots we scared off the occupants of three German trucks, recovering the equipment.

In the afternoon I joined a group at Place Garibaldi. This group was attacked by two machine gun nests. During the fight a convoy of six German trucks happened to drive by. We were under the arches and the Germans, having seen us, opened fire on us. We fired back, and it was then that I had the joy of shooting three Germans, but we lost two FFI comrades in the battle. In the evening, we managed to force the crews of the machine gun nests to escape.[33]

George Damiot finished his report with an interesting note, talking about the days after the Liberation: "On Wednesday and Tuesday I made 10 arrests of members of the *Gestapo* and *Milice*, but I did not do enough, I would have liked to arrest more." **Policeman Téobaldi** was with Damiot during the attack of the German half track:

At about 10:00, a Nazi tracked car presents itself. We attack it at once, but the *Boches* do not oppose any resistance and escape, abandoning the half track. We seize it immediately and bring it to the *Préfecture*, where we leave it in the hands of our patriot comrades (…) Around 11:30 a light car is reported to us, coming from Massena and going towards Garibaldi. I post myself behind a plane tree with an FFI comrade and we wait. Shortly afterwards the car arrives. There is an exchange of fire and my FFI comrade collapses, wounded in the ear by a Nazi bullet. The car escapes. Then the area remains calm until 15:00. A civilian reports the presence of two trucks with trailers (…). We proceed to attack; the *Boches* are frightened and escape, bringing a wounded with them in the direction of Garibaldi and abandoning their material.[34]

Policeman Bovis' report gives a good impression of random street fighting that was occurring throughout the town:

Around 12:30 at Place Garibaldi (…), we received the order to fire on all German cars, regardless of their category. We took up positions at the windows at several stories of the building located over the Perfume shop. Hostilities started up again a few minutes later and lasted until the night.

We immobilized a German truck loaded with military bread for about three hours after having wounded the drivers. [One of these may have been 29-year-old **Werner Rudat**, of the *Bäckerei* (Bakery) *Kompanie 1048*, who died of wounds at the German field hospital in Menton two days later.] This act caused us to be spotted and machine gunned, without any losses occurring. During this operation, a convoy of German military trucks transporting troops drove by. We opened fire on said convoy. The infantrymen at the corner of Rues République and Barla opened fire with a barrage from a 25mm cannon and machine guns. An FFI who was at number 1 Place Garibaldi was hit by a blast of machine gun fire. The body was removed by an ambulance. The convoy passed by in spite of our resistance and the barrage fire ceased at once.

A Simca car containing German officers was bothered by various gunfire from the streets and came and parked under our window (…). I fired in its direction, emptying

my clip and wounding the first two in the stomach. My weapon having jammed, the men in my group then machine gunned a German motorcyclist who, abandoning his bike, took refuge behind the ice cream booth of Place Garibaldi, near the public toilets. He shot at us without hitting us and managed to escape on foot in spite of our fire.

We noticed that a certain number of German military officers and soldiers were hiding in the Red Cross ambulances that were passing below our windows. I gave the order to fire on these vehicles that were driving by at very high speed.[35]

As René Canta admitted in his report, the resistance also used Red Cross vehicles to move about the town on certain occasions. **Police Inspector Rossi**, for example, who was at the *Préfecture*, wrote:

Using an ambulance, I went to the [Filley] Police Station with a few policemen and FFIs, where I received about 40 rifles and corresponding cartridges. I then distributed them.[36]

The Resistance admitted having used ambulances and police cars bearing white flags for military purposes, and some witnesses claimed that the Germans were also using ambulances to evacuate armed men. The result is seen here: an ambulance and police car riddled with shrapnel. MRA Collection. Frédéric Brega Collection.

Surprisingly, several *miliciens* and Black Shirts joined the fight and opened fire on resistance men during the day, though it was obvious that their action was near suicidal. **Police Brigadier Louis Pernot** reported the case of one such desperado who was lucky to survive (at least temporarily):

> A service was being provided at the 3rd District Police Station to treat the wounded or fire at the Germans where they are reported to us. At the first gunshots, we pick up some wounded. Shortly thereafter, gunshots are fired from the top story of number 12 Rue Lamartine. Sous-Brigadier Richard, along with a few of us, put a *milicien* who was firing at us from a balcony out of action. In spite of our disgust we arranged his transport to St Roch hospital.[37]

Stefan Jagla, aged 19, was one of the Polish conscripts of *Reserve Division 148* who was in Nice that day. He was a member of an artillery unit positioned on a hill near Nice and was supposed to go down into town August 28th for a dentist appointment, but the insurrection upset these plans. **Stefan Jagla** describes what he remembers of the day:

> Some kind of uprising started in Nice near the train station. There were no American troops then, they said it was the partisans. 30 or 40 of us got the order to drive down there in two lorries. We arrived at the top of the main street right near the train station and the partisans opened fire at us from the houses. Along the main road there were quite a lot of trees, so we hid behind the trees. Of course, we had to defend ourselves and shoot as well. The lorry was passing by us with ammunition. I was on the left hand side of the street and there was a house on the other side of the road. The window was open, a women was inside, and I think she was pointing a revolver at me. I turned around and tried to shoot but she closed the shutter. I had a hand grenade, but if I threw the grenade and missed the window, it would bounce back two or three meters and I would be wounded by the shrapnel, so I didn't throw it. We stayed there for a bit and had four or five wounded. Two of us were behind each tree, and I saw one man getting wounded at the second tree; they had to take him away.
>
> The sergeant said: "The rest of us go back now because we can't stay here." They said it was no use, because there were no American troops. We managed to get into our lorries and were glad to get out of there. When we passed the main road, there must have been some resistance fighters waiting for us. Somebody had brought some sardines, so when we passed them we threw the sardines. They thought it was a hand grenade or something, so we quickly got away. We went back to our unit on top of the mountain, and we got the order to pack up and go. We only had one lorry to pull one of the guns, so we had to blow the other ones up. Then we went past Monaco to Menton. The next day we went to Ventimiglia and stopped in a big garden there.

Though he had no motivation to fight for the Germans, Stefan Jagla was forced, as he said, to "defend himself." He later deserted the German army in Italy and joined a group of Italian partisans.

Meanwhile, the fighting had also continued at the level crossing and around the Villa "Les Pipistrelles," which FFI **Lieutenant Mathis** had changed into a strongpoint:

> From 10 to 12, I continue sending patrols into the hills and a few skirmishes occur on my left, to the great

Stefan Jagla, a Pole who participated in the fighting in Nice as a member of the German army. He later deserted, joining the free Polish Army, the uniform of which he is wearing in this photo. Wojciech Zmyslony Collection.

disadvantage of the Germans, who, not knowing how many of us they are up against, break contact as soon as we make it. Gunshots ring out all over the place. Time speeds by. In the meantime, I find out that the level crossing has acquired a heavy machine gun that has already done some good work. The Germans have been informed of its capture, and knowing that the level crossing represents a formidable point of resistance, they don't hesitate to put their Austrian 88s as well as their long 155s in action at about 12:30.[38]

FFI **Captain Paul Cavenago** was at the level crossing when the Germans started trying to dislodge the resistance men with artillery fire instead of infantry assaults:

> 13:30. The gunfire had almost ceased everywhere. What is the significance of this? We will soon find out: first a whistling sound, and a shell lands at the level crossing, then some more land. Will we be able to hold the position? There are no more *Fritzes* on Gambetta; this is the preparation, the barrage fire that always precedes an attack. A decision must be taken quickly. There is no other solution than to evacuate the level crossing and to concentrate on the Cessol heights.[39]

The artillery fire was enough to severely damage the enthusiasm of some people, as **FTP Pierre Durand** remembered:

> This artillery fire lasted for about one hour, which we spent in the shelter of the entrance hall of a building where numerous inhabitants had also taken refuge. With our FTP armbands, we are indirectly attacked by a few people who wonder out loud: "We are going to be massacred by the Germans, this revolt is dangerous and useless." The majority remain silent. We protest and explain. In our hearts, we believe that crowds are volatile and unpredictable and therefore dangerous. They are non-combatants, however; if this difficult situation had lasted, we would have been under threat of a change of mind. Enthusiasm in the morning, hesitation at noon, and euphoria in the evening.[40]

Lieutenant Mathis wrote on:

The shells keep on falling without interruption, and Captain Paul's groups, as well as those he has assembled under his command, in other words all the fighters at the level crossing, methodically retreat to our positions. (…) The shells constantly spray the level crossing, which is severely damaged. The *Boches* would have managed to reduce the resistance at the level crossing to nothing, had Captain Paul not taken the wise precaution of falling back on our positions (…). The *Boches* are waiting to see the results of their artillery fire, probably in order to start a large scale offensive. (…)

The artillery ceases for a certain time, then starts up again intermittently before finally stopping. The *Boches* do not show themselves. After sending out a patrol, Captain Paul returns to the level crossing positions which, no longer being under the fire of the Austrian 88s, can be reorganized a bit more powerfully.

Three o'clock. The *Boches*, powerfully armed with submachine guns, come down Boulevard Cessol, 50 on the left, 50 on the right. There are still about 30 of us, but we only have a few Mausers available. I send Captain Paul the information on our situation and tell him that it is becoming quite critical for us. Meanwhile, I go down to our redoubts with the few Mausers we have and open fire on the two descending columns. The fights lasts about 15 to 20 minutes. The *Boches*, worried by our high rate of fire and still not knowing how many of us are facing them, stop their progression and retreat. (…) It was a very close call that made sweat pearl on our foreheads.

In the meantime, two other submachine guns have joined us and I put them in position behind the forts that have been abandoned by Captain Paul's machine gun and heavy machine gun, which have returned to their positions in front of Rue Henrie de Cessol.

There is the sound of an engine in the distance. A German car comes down; we let it drive past us intentionally, and I take it under fire from behind with two submachine guns at the Compte de Cessol and the Pipistrelles, and under the fire of several grenades thrown by our men. This car is caught between two fires, with Captain Paul's men firing at it from in front, and it crashes into a tree, with its four occupants dead or grievously wounded.[41]

11-year-old **George Zuntini** lived in one of the streets near the level crossing, and tells of his memories of that day, including the destruction of the German car just mentioned by Lt Mathis:

The young people who were a bit older than me had taken a cart and were using it to go and fetch earth to fill up sandbags to make shelters for the machine guns. At one point, they were forced to take cover under the cart because somebody was shooting at them from the top of the hill. There were Polish prisoners who were helping the *résistants*, because supposedly, the Poles were forcefully conscripted into the German army. They were bringing boxes of grenades that they had found somewhere and were carrying the wounded.

At the corner of the Rue du Grand Pin there was a shelter, and when there was shelling the *résistants* and civilians would hide in that shelter. At one point, a young German soldier was running down Boulevard Cessol in a panic. The guy didn't know what was going on. Mr Pascalis, a plumber who lived on Avenue du Grand Pin, grabbed him by the arm and told him: "Come in and hide, come in and hide." He would have made him a prisoner, but the German didn't want to, he was frightened, and he continued running down towards the level crossing, panicked and all alone, the poor guy. He must have gotten killed lower down.

When shooting erupted, the resistance would tell us kids: "Go back home, don't stay here!" So we would stay in the Rue du Grand Pin, where we were protected. One time, there was a burst of machine gun fire from the small machine that was firing towards the heights of Cessol and a German car crashed into an acacia tree. When the gunfire stopped, I went down to see what had happened. When I was able to see the car everything was over; the *résistants* had emptied it and the wounded had been evacuated. I don't know if there were any dead. It was a civilian car,

Georges Zuntini with souvenirs of the Liberation, including a German backpack and Michelin road map with German army stamps that he found in the area of the level crossing. The backpack bears the name Rademacher; perhaps this man was among those captured, wounded, or killed in the fighting? Author's Collection.

an Opel, but painted khaki. Being curious, I rushed over because I wanted a helmet. I could see the resistance men with German helmets with a blue, white, nad red flag on them, and I wanted a helmet. So I went to the car and saw a helmet in it, but when I turned it over, I saw it was full of blood so I didn't dare take it. Afterwards I found a road map and a knapsack.

All this fighting at the level crossing led to the death of many men, as **FTP Noël Lanzi** explains:

Fighting went on for the whole day at the level crossing. Our toll is heavy, with twelve dead. For the FTPs: **Jean Ballestra**, **Roger Boyer**, **Lucien Chervin**, **August Gouirand**, and **Alphonse Cornil**. For *Groupe Gérôme*: **August Bognot**. For *Groupe Lorraine*: **René Barralis**, then **Raymond Carmine**, **Jean Autheman**, and **Aristakès Arnomamian**. On the other hand, we are proud of our results: 40 prisoners (that we keep in a garage on Rue George Doublet), five trucks and trailers, cars and vans, machine guns and various weapons, large amounts of ammunition…[42]

The *résistants* who had been killed in combat could almost consider themselves lucky compared to their comrades who had fallen into the hands of the Germans. 19-year-old **Roger Simon** was captured and killed. Gendarme **Emil Krieger** was also captured and deported to a concentration camp, where he later died. **Henri Cauvin** was caught by the Germans, but was saved by a remarkable stroke of luck:

We live on the Pessicard heights, in the "La Paix [Peace]" Villa. The morning of August 28th, hearing gunfire coming up from town, we hoist the French flag onto the roof of the house. In the afternoon, my comrade Jacques Garland and I decide to go into town armed with our pistols. The sight of the Germans at the crossroads near Righi forces us back, but then we find that another German patrol is blocking the road higher up. We quickly seek refuge in a house. The occupants let us in, hiding our pistols under a bed, but we have been spotted. The door opens, and in comes a menacing German officer with his submachine gun pointed at us. We

are caught. Jacques and I are led onto the road, facing the wall. The Germans discover our pistols in the house: "Terrorists!" I tell Galand: "We are done for." A young woman who is there sees us and goes down towards the town.

The Germans lead us away. They are young soldiers who are afraid (as much as we are). Walking in a column on each side of the road, with us in the middle, they fire into the windows of houses. We slowly advance down Avenue Cyrnos. The officer makes us take a shortcut down towards Boulevard Cessol. Suddenly gunshots burst out, fired from above and below by FFIs. Some Germans fall. I run down the slope as fast as I can, reach the boulevard, which I run across, and hide in the entrance of a building. Outside gunshots crackle, then stop. The Germans are dead or wounded. The officer is dead, and the FFI fighters are in control of the area.[43]

By heading towards Boulevard Cessol and the level crossing, the German patrol had unknowingly walked straight into one of the most dangerous parts of town. **Lieutenant Mathis** and his men were responsible for the action that liberated Henri Cauvin:

One of the two submachine guns that we have is set up at the top of the hills, where runners report that a group of *Boches* are descending. With three or four men and the second submachine gun we go to the top of Cyrnos, where we were told that a German group with a machine gun has made two FFIs, as well as a woman prisoner. We end up reaching it, and after a short but hard fight, we annihilate this group (All killed, as well as an officer.). We seize the German machine gun and place it in the middle of Boulevard de Cessol.[44]

Albert Piccardo was another resistance man who was captured by the Germans who also managed to survive the ordeal, though in much more tragic circumstances than those we have just mentioned:

August 15th, the day of the landing arrives. Things speed up; the Allies liberate Cannes, Antibes, and continue their advance towards Nice. I join them and find myself at St Laurent du Var with several other civilians. Having found out that the patriots in Nice had started fighting against the Germans since the morning, and knowing that the comrades from our group did not have any weapons, I decided to cross the Var, because I had a few pistols at my house. Three civilians who were also members of various resistance groups joined me. Hardly had we crossed the Var when we were arrested by a German patrol that immediately brought us to their headquarters in the Fabron heights, where we were interrogated one after another.

Around 21:30, the orderly came to get one of my comrades. Ten minutes later it was my turn. I was made to take about 30 steps in the property, and an officer who had joined me coldly shot me from point blank range, the bullet passing through my right shoulder and clavicle. Still fully conscious, I fell heavily to the ground and played dead. A few minutes later I was witnessed an awful sight: the barbarous execution of my two comrades, who, moaning, had their throats slit with a knife.

Losing lots of blood, and feeling numbness overcoming me, I crawled through the barbed wire. Then, having spotted a path, I followed it, and after having walked, crawled, jumped, and fallen down a ditch, I ended up reaching a road, where I asked the inhabitants of the "Le Refuge" villa for

Joseph GIUGE

38 ans, concierge à la mairie de Nice, tombé victime de son dévouement! en ravitaillant, en vivres et armes, des groupes de combat F.F.I. pendant la journée du 28 août dernier. Laisse une veuve et son vieux père âgé de 86 ans.

Jean GORDOLON

21 ans, étudiant en droit, avait fourni au 2ᵉ bureau des renseignements importants d'ordre militaire ; est tombé glorieusement, le 28 août 1944, à Nice, en assurant, sous le feu de l'ennemi, la liaison de son groupe avec le groupe Lenoir à la mairie de Nice.

38-year-old Joseph Giuge and 21-year-old Jean Gordolon, two of the resistance men who were killed in Nice August 28th during the fighting. L'Ergot/MRA Collection.

help. They refused to do so, but at least had the delicacy of telling me where I was. Marvelous luck, I was 100 meters away from the Fabron restaurant belonging to Mr Guido Cordellini, who had been arrested by the *Gestapo* the same day as I. [Albert Piccardo is referring to a previous arrest that had occurred June 16, 1944.] As soon as I reached my destination, I knocked on the door and he was very surprised to see me covered in blood. Having laid me down on a deck chair in his apartment, he and two of his comrades gave me the most urgent care that my state required. Since I had a fever, he watched over me until the morning of August 29th, when the FFIs from Fabron came to get me in the firemen's ambulance and brought me to St Roch hospital.[45]

Albert Piccardo had been lucky to survive his execution. His two companions who were not as fortunate were **Lucien Corbé** and **Joseph Arena**.

The Germans Evacuate Nice

As was described in the section on Niedlich's capture, the German forces in the area of Nice had received orders the morning of August 28th to retreat, or to prepare for an imminent retreat towards the Italian border. The definitive order to evacuate Nice was finally given in the late afternoon, as *Generalmajor* **Nickelmann** wrote in the *Feldkommandantur* journal:

> 17:00. Major Schultz informs the *Feldkommandantur* that it is to join the retreat movement of the troops that will occur between 20:00 and 21:00.
> 18:30. The *Feldkommandantur* reports to General Fretter Pico that it is preparing its departure; it will first pull out to Breil sur Roya, then to Cuneo. Lt Pacher is in charge of organizing the departure.
> 18:40. We telephone Commander Pomader, commander of the garrison in Menton: "Our *Feldkommandantur 994* will reach Monte Carlo around 19:45, and we demand that Captain Hilgenstock be ready to depart; we are planning on reaching Menton around 20:30."[46]

Before leaving, it would seem that the *Feldkommandantur* attempted to outdo the *résistants* in the *Préfecture* at their own game, providing them with threatening information over the phone to better hide the fact that they were actually preparing to retreat out of Nice. FTP **René Canta**, who was still in command in the *Préfecture*, later wrote:

> Around 20:15, while searching for Mr Ravard, who should never have left his office without our permission, I enter Mr Lauvel's office, finding him still talking over the telephone with the *Feldkommandantur*, who was sending us another ultimatum, so conceived: "If the partisans do not immediately pull out and if the doors of the *Préfecture* are not left open, we will put Nice to fire and sword." Mr Lauvel, with an extremely discouraged look, informs me of it. I am already highly excited by Mr Ravard's disappearance, I leap onto the phone and answer very energetically in the following terms, that are perhaps a bit vulgar, but the authenticity of which I would not like to alter: "Here are the partisans. Leave us in peace once and for all, and if you do not evacuate Nice immediately, we will come out of the *Préfecture* and out of everywhere else to kick you out, and fast." Then, after abruptly hanging up, I remain thoughtful for an instant in the face of the responsibility I have just

endorsed, perhaps a bit boldly, I admit, but consciously and in full knowledge of the situation. I trusted my understanding. I was sure that the *Boches* would never have waited so long to throw a large-scale attack against us if they could have, and would especially not have tried to negotiate. Finally, around 21:10, the chief of my detachment occupying the Thiers Post Office informs me by telephone that the Germans are evacuating Nice. I send two runners out on reconnaissance at once who would soon return, confirming the good news.[47]

We will let *Generalmajor* **Nickelmann** describe the retreat (or "departure," as he preferred to call it) out of Nice as he experienced it:

> 19:15. The Nice *Feldkommandantur 994*, after having received the departure order, sends out a call to the commanders of all the dispersed units to come to the *Feldkommandantur* with their baggage. After assembling, a column of seven trucks and 14 cars is formed. A machine gun is mounted on each truck, and the soldiers dispose of 15 submachine guns and 80 rifles per truck.
> 19:50. The column sets off and runs into the first enemy fire coming from the police station located 500 meters away from the *Feldkommandantur*. The Germans retaliate with all their weapons, firing at the police station, but also at all the windows of the houses that border the street. Thanks to its firepower, the column manages to reach the exit of town without suffering any losses. It is to be noted that the fire coming from the houses was very weak. The vehicle of the chief of the *Feldgendarmerie* received four minor hits.
> 19:50. We reach Monte Carlo.
> 20:40. We reach Menton.(…)
> Tuesday 29th. 0:50. We reach Breil without any losses.[48]

It is to be noted that *Generalmajor* Nickelmann was not very impressed by the effectiveness of the resistance gunfire, and that during night hours his group was able to move about the road network all the way to Breil extremely fast and effectively. A similar impression can be found in the account of *Grenadier* **Josef Kirsner**, of the 11th Company of *Reserve Grenadier Bataillon 164*, who up until August 28th had been on guard duty on the Var Bridge (see Chapter 1):

> The night before the landing, we suddenly heard colossal noise during the entire night. We found out a day or two later that the Americans had landed with hundreds of ships all along the coast in the direction of Toulon. We could see the ships going there day and night. We thought: "God, hopefully they won't land where we are!" The front slowly advanced along the coast. My unit was not involved in any of the fighting.
> August 30th [In fact August 28th.], at nine or ten at night, we were told: "Pack everything up, we are leaving!" We didn't know where we were going or anything. We had no more vehicles left. Only the kitchen left by truck, the rest of us had to go on foot with all our equipment and ammunition. A lot of people stole bicycles from the French. We walked through Nice, and there was already a bit of fighting going on there. It wasn't the Americans, but the partisans, the French resistance fighters. They fired at us from the windows of houses. We ran off without shooting back, but there was a four-barrel flak cannon with us that fired back into the houses. It was nothing big, and in my unit we had no casualties.
> We followed the coastal road through Monaco to Menton. When we arrived in Menton, the whole company

A small calibre cannon that the Germans abandoned in Nice. MRA Collection.

23-year-old Raymond Albin, who was shot and killed late on the 28th by a bullet fired by the retreating Germans. MRA Collection.

regrouped. At least 40 or 50 of the Silesians, the Poles—in other words almost half the company—had disappeared during our retreat. I am not sure of it, but I suspect that they had connections with the resistance, with the French, who had told them: "When things go bad, come to us." In any case, they were gone. A couple kilometers off the coast of Menton, there was an American cruiser or battleship or something. In daytime, we could look at it and see men strolling on deck. When a car or something came down the coastal road, they immediately shot at it with their cannons. There were also *Jabos* that shot at anything that moved. We Germans had nothing left.

As often with *Reserve Division 148*, the losses due to desertion were greater than those caused by enemy action. **FTP César Martini** witnessed the type of retreat that has just been described by Nickelmann and Kirsner, but from the French side:

We quickly notice that the German soldiers are going down Rue Barla by foot or by car, coming from downtown and going towards the Middle Cornice. They are under fire from our comrades, who are throwing grenades and firing at them with hunting shotguns from the rooftops and windows. The retreating Germans, harassed and frightened, fire bursts of automatic fire from intersections towards the perpendicular streets. That is how a bullet, after having just missed myself and my brother, strikes **Raymond Albin** in the stomach: we carry him into the shelter under the Place Arson, but he dies shortly afterwards.[49]

The Germans had prepared a few routes that they could follow in relative safety, as FTP **Edouard Bertrand** noted:

During the whole afternoon, we see German soldiers going along Boulevard Impératrice de Russie on foot or in trucks. They are following the itinerary lined with the bunkers

of the Place Riquier and the Place Saluzzo, towards the port and the Route de Villefranche. Some of them fire at us when they spot us. Around 19:00, powerful explosions shake the district; tThe Germans are blowing up the docks in the port.[50]

In his report on the telephone workers who had joined the insurrection, **FFI Bernard** also described some interesting details about the retreat:

Fabron finds itself in a difficult situation because of a strong German force that is trying to pass by, announcing that an agreement has been reached between the *Kommandantur* and the FFIs, according to which the German forces' retreat route is to be left open. We order Fabron to hold the Germans at a distance and only fire in case of a direct attack. (…)
Around 1:30 on the 29th, the Germans who are retreating down Avenue Thiers get stuck in the barbed wire. In their panic, they fire heavily on the Thiers Post Office. The FFIs take cover without firing back, waiting for the attack, only having very small quantities of ammunition and not wanting to waste them. The Germans pull out.[51]

The night was fairly calm, though more skirmishes occurred at the level crossing, probably involving groups of Germans who were descending from the hills north of town and who, after finding resistance at the level crossing, went back up into the hills, bypassing Nice and completing their retreat towards Italy. **Captain Paul Cavenago** was still in command in the level crossing area, though the crossing itself was no longer occupied by the *résistants* out of fear of another artillery attack:

We didn't expect to spend such a calm night, and all our men are now in place. Around midnight, I advise that a bit of rest should be taken in turns. The men are tired, but still valiant and ready to leap up. I do not know what will happen tomorrow and must therefore spare my forces, for

I have understood: we can only and will only be able to count on ourselves. I don't know about the other areas. Have they been successful? No liaison has been established and it is physically impossible to do so without taking too great a risk. Our area is also very tricky because it can be approached from all sides, and this calm does not bode well.

Finally the first patrols return, reporting that *Fritzes* at the level crossing are taking up positions behind our barricade at Rue Cessol. On the left and right some *Fritzes* are also spotted. We are being surrounded; it seems to be becoming serious, but this time we have weapons and tomorrow morning we will see. The patrolling continues, and a few gunshots ring out in the night; people must be trying out weapons. To the right, the left, and behind we are at our posts. All we have left to do is wait for the attack that will come at dawn.

It is 5:45, still nothing. Everybody is ready, we are waiting. Suddenly, some shadows come out from under the trucks at the Rue Cessol barrage. Are they French or *Fritz*? It is still dark, though dawn is breaking. The shadows advance, coming up the left. I hesitate, the situation is serious. Too bad… Fire… The machine gun fires, the shadows collapse. We surge forward together, and the left wing under the command of Lieutenant Mathis performs a flaking movement that is wonderfully successful. The *Fritzes* are surprised, and a few are killed and the rest surrender.[52]

We will let **Lieutenant Mathis** pick up the story from here:

It is 5 o'clock in the morning. Dawn will come soon. We spot three indistinct shadows crawling towards us that we are not able to identify. After challenging them with no effect, the machine gun opens fire and the shadows collapse. It is impossible to know whether they are civilians or Germans. I sent one of my men out to check: it is indeed three *Boches* who have passed from life to death.

Not knowing how many Germans are present at Boulevard Cessol, I form a group of three submachine guns. I send one around the level crossing by Avenue Bellevue, the second by St Marguerite Clinic, and the third one and I go down, staying close to the walls. Bursts of automatic fire ring out and the two submachine guns on the left and right come to my assistance on the boulevard. We find ourselves in front of a group of about thirty *Boches* on which we open fire at once, and who surrender almost immediately.

The resistance of the *Boches* at the level crossing is over. We lead the prisoners to the garage at Rue de Cessol, after having distributed the weapons they were carrying to our men, who after a day and a half of combat were still insufficiently armed.[53]

The three "shadows" were probably the last German soldiers to be killed in Nice. However, even once they had left Nice the Germans were subject to a few more attacks, with one soldier being killed in the vicinity of Eze, for example.. **André Cane**, who lived in Villefranche, described the German columns that passed through his town after evacuating Nice:

Survivors of the fighting at the level crossing pose for the camera August 29th. MRA Collection.

Resistance men proudly pose with a stock of captured German ammunition in the aftermath of the fighting. MRA Collection.

1944, August 28th. The fleet that is offshore is stubbornly targeting Cap Ferrat. From hour to hour, the proximity of the Allied troops is accelerating the departure of the Germans, who are ebbing back from the northwest and west. For several days already, it is with real relief that the population has been watching the escape of the hounded enemy, who is hurrying towards Italy. During the entire day, following the three main roads of our coast, an uninterrupted flow of trucks carries away armed troops and pulls heavy artillery pieces. But the escapees also pile the most random objects onto their vehicles, looted who knows where, and that they will in any case be forced to abandon soon. As they go by, we see higgledy-piggledy: refrigerators, radios, sewing machines, mattresses, coal, flower, etc. The cars and their loads are cleverly camouflaged with foliage.

During the entire night, horse-drawn convoys slowly make their way towards the border. The temporary masters of most of Europe are already hopelessly beaten and this obvious fact devastates them. This march in the thick shadow of the night that has been deserted by any trace of local life is all but gloomy. The complete darkness, only pierced by the feeble light of the lanterns that sway at the rear of each car, is hardly livened up by the sharp and metallic rhythm of the hooves hitting the ground, to which is sometimes added the brief and guttural order of a *Feldwebel*. But let us return to that memorable evening of August 28th, which marks the departure of the last Hitlerian elements. In fact, the night is frightening, as it does not cease to be filled by the deafening crash of explosions that produce huge glimmers to all sides. Indeed, the occupiers destroy the ammunition depots, the military structures that they have erected in Beaulieu and St Jean. But alas, their destructions are not limited to that. Our bridges and certain sections of road are partially or totally demolished. The Darse Port and certain adjoining structures are severely damaged, while boats are sunk to the bottom of the sea and block the ports of Villefranche and St Jean.

The Cap Ferrat lighthouse, a magnificent and historical work of art, does not escape their destructive rage. Powerful explosive charges will not leave a stone standing.

1944, August 29th. The very last elements of the German army leave our territory. At the Col des Caire they are attacked by brave patriots of the French Forces of the Interior. Two young inhabitants of Villefranche fall to their bullets, but the disorganized enemy abandons their material and escapes into the mountains.[54]

The Execution of Civilians in Menton

In this chapter, we have seen that although the battle in Nice opposed partisans and German troops—in other words "terrorists" and "*Boches*", as they called each other at the time—the fighting remained relatively clean, and it seems that the Germans did not take any hostages, as *Generalleutnant* Fretter-Pico had suggested, nor attempted any reprisals against the civilian population. However, when the retreating Germans and some of their Fascist Italian allies reached Menton August 29th, several serious incidents occurred due to the frustration of the soldiers of being attacked by irregular forces, and due to tensions between the various nationalities present amongst the Axis forces. An article later written in *l'Ergot* newspaper describes these incidents. Apart from the "patriotic" and mocking style in which it is written, the story appears to be mostly accurate and is confirmed by other sources, such as a Gendarmerie reports and witness accounts:

Monday, August 28th. The German troops pull out of their defense line in the hills bordering the left bank of the Var River, evacuating Nice under the rifle and grenade fire of its heroic children (…). By the three Cornices, the *Boches* flow back towards Menton, blowing up bridges and viaducts behind them.

Tuesday, August 29th. The main German force has reached Menton. They meet up with the "Nizza" Black Shirt battalion, who, under the orders of Commander Maldi, escaped [Nice] much faster than the soldiers of the Reich. The small amount of combat that they witnessed in Nice was enough both to terrorize the Fascists and put them in a state of fury bordering dementia. The militiamen of the "Nizza" Battalion were able to see the Nice Police firing on the Axis troops and effectively cooperating with the Nice FFIs during the liberation of Nice. And, still breathless from the mad dash that brought them from the banks of the Paillon to those of the Borigo at a stretch, the "Camicie Nere" have a single idea in mind: to take revenge on the Menton Police of the humiliation that was inflicted on them and the fear that was inspired in them by the Nice policemen.

The militiamen go to the central Police Station, arrest the police chief, inspectors, and the policemen, disarm them, and announce that they will shoot them! Luckily, a German Colonel arrives, attracted by the racket produced by the loudmouthed bully boys.

"What are you meddling with?" He asks the Fascist militiamen. "You didn't fight in Nice and you escaped towards Menton without having received any retreat order!"

And turning to the Menton policemen he tells them: "We would probably have executed you ourselves, but since these individuals claim to want to do so, you are free!"

And he got them released. The Black Shirts then spread through the town, looting open houses and threatening their inhabitants.

German troops are bivouacking everywhere in Menton, exhausted, irritated, and still stunned from having, in so few days, passed from the status of victors installed as masters in a conquered land to that of the vanquished, obliged to escape in haste. Under the *feldgrau* uniform there are many non-Germans. Bent under the Nazi discipline up until this point, they hardly dared express their true feelings. The defeat is now releasing their tongues. They ironically comment on the situation without sparing the pure-blooded Huns with their jibes and sarcasms. Quarrels break out between Prussians, Bavarians, Austrians, Czechs, and Poles, who are all assembled under the same uniform.

At about six in the evening at Impasse Mayen, in the district of the train station in Menton, one of these arguments degenerates into a brawl between the *feldgrau* of various nationalities. Gunshots are fired. Officers rush over.

"What is going on?"

"Some terrorists fired at us!" explain the soldiers at fault, suddenly taken aback by discipline and, in the fear of severe sanctions, each inventing more details than the next in order to cover each other. How would the German officers, who had only the day before escaped the bullets of the Nice FFIs, not be under the dread of a *maquisard* firing from a window?

"Terrorists? So be it. We will show them what the German army is made of!"

Orders are given at once. Armed platoons arrive from all directions. According to the soldiers at fault, the gunshots were fired from "Casa Isabella," located on Avenue Edouard VII, some of the windows of which overlook the Impasse Mayen.

The German platoons deploy, surrounding the block of houses that includes "Casa Isabella." On Avenue Edouard VII, in front of this "Casa Isabella," a peaceful inhabitant of Menton, Mr Robert Marze, born January 6, 1897, in Menton, married with no children, is chatting at the door of his religious bookstore with a neighbor, Mr Pierre Bonardi, born January 1, 1899, married, father of two, working as a mason and living at 61 Avenue Edouard VII. The Germans pounce on them, hit them with rifle butts, and leave them unconscious on the road, bathing in their own blood.

Then the boors enter "Casa Isabella" and ransack all the apartments with submachine guns and grenades. In one of the second floor apartments they discover the owner of the building, Mr François Taglioni, born May 1, 1910, in Roquebrune Cap Martin, married, without children, and working as a hotel keeper in Menton. Mr Taglioni has barely gotten home, and doesn't understand anything of the infernal racket that is surrounding him. He is seized and dragged into the street. With machine guns and even a 100mm [sic] cannon that they brought to Avenue Edouard VII, the *Boches* fire at the facades of all the houses on the block.

Menton Policeman Sous-Brigadier Carpi and agents Gaudo, Rieux, and Robert have just reached the scene. Submachine guns are pointed at them.

"You will come with us into the basements of 'Casa Isabella," a German officer tells them. "If we find any 'terrorists' there, you will be executed with them!"

At German gunpoint the agents obey. Along with the *Boches*, they descend into the basements of the building. The Germans search the basements with rage, but of course don't find anybody there. Furious, they announce to the Menton policemen that they will execute them anyway. They are already preparing to put them up against the wall when a *Fritz* exclaims: "A prisoner has vanished!"

Indeed, although Robert Marze is still lying there on the ground in pitiful condition, although François Taglioni is still in the hands of the soldiers who captured him, Pierre Bonardi has disappeared. Assisted by his wife, who ran to his aid, the poor man managed to drag himself to his home at 61 Avenue Edouard VII. The rage of the Germans turns onto him. They abandon the policemen and rush towards 61 Avenue Edouard VII. They grab Bonardi and bring him back in front of "Casa Isabella." His face almost beaten to a pulp with rifle butts, the unfortunate man is nothing but a bloody wreck.

It is 7:30. For more than an hour, the German soldiers have, in a sadistic frenzy, been "cleaning up" the block of houses of Avenue Edouard VII. Their fury has now reached its climax. They drag **Pierre Bonardi**, **Robert Marze**, and **François Taglioni** into the Impasse Mayen, put them against the wall, and shoot them with rifles and submachine guns, leaving the bodies where they fall and rushing back to the buildings of the tragic block.

The adjoining building to "Casa Isabella" is the Villa Delmas. In a corner of the garden of this villa is a hangar that is used as a wine cellar by the elderly couple that inhabits the villa: Mr **Jean Rambert**, born June 13, 1973, at Saint Etienne de Tinée, and his wife, born as **Antoinette Pastore**, who is 68 years old. Terror stricken, Mr and Ms Rambert have taken refuge in this hangar. The Germans find them there and kill them on the spot with rifles and grenades. After having committed this cowardly assassination, their nerves slightly calmed, the Teutonic brutes leave the area. In the end, they have not discovered a single terrorist in the entire block of buildings.

"We have killed innocent people!" A German officer who was slightly more honest than the others would admit a bit later to the Chief of Police of Menton.[55]

24-year-old **Henri Moreau** was a medical student who decided of his own accord to identify the bodies of the executed victims and get them transported to the morgue. He later wrote about the conditions of the bodies in a letter to the editor of *Ergot*:

We were stopped by the Germans. After the usual challenges, they brought us, with our hands up, to the scene of the massacre, in order to see if we knew the terrorists and if we were perhaps their accomplices. (...) After long negotiations and after showing our Red Cross papers multiple times, we were finally authorized to identify the martyrs and certify their deaths. Mr Marze and Mr Taglioni were the first, seven meters after the entrance of Impasse Mayen, (…) one next to the other, Marze on the left and

The memorial plaque dedicated to the five civilians in Menton who were mindlessly killed by German troops. Author's Collection.

Taglioni on the right. Marze had been killed by submachine gun bullets that hit him in the abdomen and chest. Taglioni was horribly mutilated. His skull had burst and bloody shreds of brain matter were protruding through the smashed temporal bone. As for Bonardi, who was a bit further on behind Marze, his head was riddled with bullets.[56]

As Henri Moreau went to fetch coffins for the bodies, yet another person was being killed, this time by the Black Shirts, as the *Ergot* article further explained:

The news of the massacre has spread through all Menton. The French, pale with rage, are clenching their fists. The Italians exult, and so as not to be outdone by the *feldgraus*, a large group of roaring Black Shirts invade the Menton gendarmerie barracks at 4 Avenue du Colonel Leclerc. In the yard, they find *Maréchal des Logis* **André Deparday**, born July 15, 1905, in la Chapelle Saint Messin (Loiret), married, without children.

Maréchal des Logis Deparday is in his barracks outfit. He has no weapon. Upon seeing the fascist Italian militiamen barging in armed to the teeth, he spontaneously lifts up his hands. With no discussion, with no excuse, he is shot dead by the "camicie nere." Then these revolting lowlifes invade and sack the barracks.[57]

Capitaine Bidet, the commander of the gendarmerie, later wrote more details about Deparday's death in his official report:

At 20:30, 50 fascist militiamen (Black Shirts) armed with rifles and submachine guns, who had arrived in Menton 48 hours earlier and who were quartered in the Hotel des Britaniques, surrounded and assaulted the barracks of the territorial brigade of Menton. During this forceful act that was legitimized by nothing, *Maréchal des Logis* Chef Deparday was shot with no warning as he was crossing the yard. Receiving several bullets in the back of the head, he died on the spot.

39-year-old Maréchal des Logis Chef André Deparday's wedding photo, taken a few months before he was murdered by Italian Black Shirts in Menton August 29th. Deparday Family Collection.

To the protest of the adjudant commanding the brigade, the militiamen, who were in a state of extreme excitement, replied: "The police fired at us, we want to take revenge." They then required all the occupants of the barracks to assemble in the yard, and once this was done, they demanded, with threatening submachine guns, that all the weapons still in the hands of the brigade be turned over to them. They then looted all the apartments, offices, garages, and adjoining constructions, breaking the doors of apartments that were locked and furniture.[58]

André Deparday's widow, **Reine Deparday**, still living in Menton 67 years later, simply remembered:

My husband was in the yard, and at that moment the Black Shirts, who had been driven out of Nice, surrounded the barracks and entered the yard like furies, breaking down the gate and everything. They killed my husband at once like you slaughter an animal; they shot him in the back.

The Casualties of the Nice Insurrection

Because of the size of Nice and the circumstances of the battle, it is difficult to establish an exact list of French Resistance casualties, with the difference between a resistant and a civilian, or between a combat death and "collateral damage," sometimes being blurred. According to the various monuments in the town, the period reports, and research made by the historians of the *Musée de la Résistance Azuréenne*, at least 34 resistance fighters were killed in Nice, died of their wounds, or died in consequence of their involvment in the insurrection (such as Emil Krieger, who died in a concentration camp after being captured). An analysis of the number of funerals occurring at the Caucade cemetery in the days following August 28th shows a slight mortality peak, seeming to indicate that at least a dozen civilians also died in the fighting. One victim from Eze and six more from Menton can be added to the number of dead related to the insurrection. Below is a list of resistance victims or execution victims compiled from the various sources mentioned above. Civilian victims of so-called "collateral damage" are excluded from the list.

Surname	Name	Age	Date of death	Location of death	Type of death
Albin	Raymond	23	28.8.1944	Nice, Rue Barla	Combat
Alentchenko	Eugène	20	28.8.1944	Nice, Rue Defly	Combat
Aréna	Joseph	45	28.8.1944	Nice, Fabron sup	Execution
Arnaudo	Auguste	21	28.8.1944	Nice, Place du Palais	Combat
Arzoumanian	Arisdakesse	37	28.8.1944	Nice, Place Gambetta	Combat
Autheman	Jean	30	28.8.1944	Nice, level crossing	Combat
Badino	Jean	48	28.8.1944	Nice, Place Palais de Justice	Combat
Ballestra	Jean	20	28.8.1944	Nice, level crossing	Combat
Barralis	René	22	28.8.1944	Nice, level crossing	Combat
Bernardo	Sauveur	25	29.8.1944	Nice, St Roch train depot	Murder
Bobichon	Jean	21	28.8.1944	Nice, Old Town	Combat
Bogniot	August	34	28.8.1944	Nice, Place Gambetta	Combat
Boscarollo	Vincent	36	28.8.1944	Nice, Place Garibaldi	Combat
Boyer	Roger	33	28.8.1944	Nice, level crossing	Combat
Cantergiani	Venance	40	28.8.1944	Nice, St Marguerite	Combat
Carmine	Raymond	20	28.8.1944	Nice, level crossing	Combat
Chervin	Lucien	44	28.8.1944	Nice, level crossing	Combat
Codaccioni	Antoine	43	DOW 1.9.1944	Nice	Combat
Corbé	Lucien	58	28.8.1944	Nice, Fabron sup	Execution
Cornil	Alphonse	64	28.8.1944	Nice, level crossing	Combat
Fantino	Marius	43	DOW 29.8.1944	Nice, Pasteur hospital	Combat

Surname	Name	Age	Date of death	Location of death	Type of death
Franzini	Guillaume	54/57	DOW 1947	Nice	Combat
Genouillac	Antoine	42	29.8.1944	Nice, Rue de la République	Combat
Gironne	Jean	22	28.8.1944	Nice, Rue Niel	Combat
Giuge	Joseph	38	28.8.1944	Nice, Old Town	Combat
Gordolon	Jean	21	DOW 30.8.1944	Nice, Old Town	Combat
Gouirand	August	42	28.8.1944	Nice, level crossing	Combat
Krieger	Emile	54	Died in captivity	Nice, Cimiez	Concentration camp
Morales	Juan	50	28.8.1944	Nice, *préfecture*	Combat
Rossi	Basile	17	28.8.1944	Nice, Ave Bornala	Combat
Simon	Roger	19	28.8.1944	Nice, Ave Californie	Execution
Suarez	François	39	28.8.1944	Nice, TNL depot	Combat
Vallaghé	Paul	24	28.8.1944	Nice, Place Garibaldi	Combat
Vial	Verdun	27	DOW 2.9.1944	Nice, *préfecture*	Combat
Gianton	François	32	29.8.1944	Eze	Execution
Deparday	André	39	29.8.1944	Menton	Execution
Bonardi	Pierre	45	29.8.1944	Menton	Execution
Marze	Robert	47	29.8.1944	Menton	Execution
Rambert	Antoinette	68	29.8.1944	Menton	Execution
Rambert	Jean	71	29.8.1944	Menton	Execution
Taglioni	François	34	29.8.1944	Menton	Execution

August 28, 1944, and in the following few days, 22 German soldiers were buried in the Caucade Cemetery in Nice, all of which apparently died in the fighting of August 28th and 29th. Three soldiers listed as having died on the 28th were also buried in the St Maurice district of Nice, and one other was buried in the Château de Barla, where the Germans had set up a dressing station. Three soldiers who were also killed in Nice on the 28th were buried in Menton and Drap. One soldier was killed at Eze and another was mortally wounded in Villefranche on the 29th, when the Resistance attacked the columns of retreating Germans. Furthermore, in a field hospital set up in Menton, three soldiers died on August 29th, two on August 30th, and one on September 1st. Most of these men who died in Menton had probably been wounded in the fighting in Nice. Three Germans from *Bataillon 372* were also buried in the St Antoine district of Nice by the Germans themselves, their official date of death being August 27th. The circumstance of death of these last three men is not known, but considering their unit, it is possible that they were actually killed or wounded during the fighting at Villeneuve-Loubet and la Colle sur Loup. Finally, a soldier named Joseph Ginczek, who according to a comrade was killed in Nice on August 28th, is listed in the Volksbund databases as having died in Nice on September 10, 1944. We can suspect that this date may be incorrect, or that he died of wounds after the fighting. All these facts show that it is difficult, if not impossible, to pinpoint the exact number of German dead related to the insurrection. Below we list 41 Germans, the majority of whose deaths are clearly linked to the insurrection of Nice. (The names of previously mentioned Max Rathje and Richart Tönissen have been included in this list, though their bodies were never identified.)

Surname	Name	Rank	Age	Date of death	Location of burial	Unit
Bartsch	Max	Uffz	35	28.8.1944	Caucade	Res.Gren. Rgt.239
Eickelmeier	Anton	Gefr	32	28.8.1944	Caucade	
Gorinschek	Friedrich	Gren	17	28.8.1944	Caucade	1./Feld.Ers. Btl.148
Hansen	Wilhelm	Lt	30	28.8.1944	Caucade	Flak?
Janas	Josef	Gren	37	29.8.1944	Caucade	
Jank	Ulrich	Sold	20	28.8.1944	Caucade	
Kreissl	Johann	Gefr	18	28.8.1944	Caucade	
Krugls	Johann	Sold	24	28.8.1944	Caucade	Res.Pi.Btl.8?
Künz	Reinhold	Sold	31	28.8.1944	Caucade	
Oblak	Johann	Gren	17	28.8.1944	Caucade	Res.Gren. Rgt.8
Piesiur	Johann	Sold	38	28.8.1944	Caucade	

Surname	Name	Rank	Age	Date of death	Location of burial	Unit
Rathje	Max	Kan	37	28.8.1944	Caucade (MIA)	2./Res.Art. Rgt.8
Rodoschek	Anton	Gren	18	28.8.1944	Caucade	
Steinhäuser	Helmut	Pio	18	28.8.1944	Caucade	3./Res. Pi.Btl.8
Tischlerei		Sold		28.8.1944	Caucade	
Tönissen	Richart	Kan	36	28.8.1944	Caucade (MIA)	2./Res.Art. Rgt.8
Unknown				28.8.1944	Caucade	
Unknown				28.8.1944	Caucade	
Unknown				28.8.1944	Caucade	
Unknown				28.8.1944	Caucade	
Unknown				28.8.1944	Caucade	
Unknown				28.8.1944	Caucade	
Bromer	Anton	Gren	18	28.8.1944	Château Barla Nice	
Zeichen	Jakob		18	28.8.1944?	Drap (Nice)	
Unknown				29.8.1944	Eze	
Herrmann	Franz	Gren	24	29.8.1944	La Crau (Villefranche)	1./Feld.Ers. Btl.148
Beyer	Michael	Uffz	33	28.8.1944	Menton (Nice)	3./Heeres. Art. Abt.1196
Stroba	Emil	Kan	18	28.8.1944	Menton (Nice)	3./Res.Art. Rgt.8
Grolik	Theodor	Gren	36	29.8.1944	Menton HVPl	4./Feld.Ers. Btl.148
Raab	Eduard	Gren	18	29.8.1944	Menton HVPl	3./Res.Gren. Btl.327
Schönberger	Adolf	Sold	18	29.9.1944	Menton HVPl	3./Res. Pi.Btl.8
Rudat	Werner	Uffz	29	30.8.1944	Menton HVPl	9 Bäckerei Kp 1048
Urbanski	Wilhelm	Fwb	29	30.8.1944	Menton HVPl	6./Res.Gren. Btl.372
Gonsior	Alois	Gren	18	1.9.1944	Menton HVPl	1./Res.Gren. Btl.327
Granz	Gottfried	Gren	18	27.8.1944	St Antoine	
Waber	Gustav	Uffz	32	27.8.1944	St Antoine	8./Res.Gren. Btl.372
Zimonczyk	Victor	Gren	25	27.8.1944	St Antoine	Res.Gren. Btl.372
Stobbe	Franz	Gefr	33	28.8.1944	St Maurice	
Unknown				28.8.1944	St Maurice	
Unknown				28.8.1944	St Maurice	
Ginczek	Joseph		38	10.9.1944	Undetermined	

The aforementioned casualties may seem small for a 24-hour insurrection in a major city. However, in the area and time frame of study of this book, the Nice insurrection is the engagement that caused the largest number of dead in a single day, with roughly 30 to 40 Germans and resistance men dying. The deadliest battlefield in total number of casualties remains the Cannes-la Napoule-Théoule area, where the fighting lasted nine days (August 15th to 24th) and caused the deaths of roughly 80 Germans and 60 Americans.

The losses suffered by the various French and Italian militiamen and collaborators must also be added to the casualties of the Nice insurrection. Several of these men were killed in combat August 28th and several more were executed over the following days, but the accounting of them is beyond the scope of this book. However, to give an impression of what kind of events took place just after the Liberation, we will quote the Gendarmerie report of **Adjudant-Chef Maurice**:

On Tuesday, August 29, 1944, around 10 o'clock, a resistance group composed of a few young men killed four men with pistols:
- Two were executed along the train tracks of the Ligne du Sud near the Avenue de Villars level crossing. They were about 20 and 50 years old and are not known from the inhabitants of the level crossing district.
- The two others, who are also not known, were shot near the tunnel of the southern train station.
- The bodies of these four men were removed by the group that had executed them. No one was able to say where they were transported to.
- The identity of the executed remains unknown.[59]

Many similar cases would follow, and it is quite obvious that the efforts of the police to solve them remained very limited.

The Arrival of the Allies

The First Special Service Force and the 551st Parachute Infantry Battalion, which had reached the west bank of the Var River on the 28th and 29th, had not played any direct role in the insurrection, though their mere presence was obviously one of the main reasons the Germans pulled out of Nice. August 29th, however, many small groups of soldiers, mostly men of the 551st PIB, ventured into the city on their own, or with patrol missions. Each of these groups later claimed to be the first Americans in town, and virtually none seemed to realize that a battle had occurred just the day before! Regardless of who was really the first American (or Canadian) in town, we will now

Zum frommen Gedenken im Gebete an

Herrn Michael Beyer

Uffz.

geboren am 6. Oktober 1910
gefallen am 28. August 1944 in Nizza (Südfr.)
Nach 16 Jahren wurde uns sein Tod nun zur
Gewißheit. Die Umbettung erfolgte in den
Soldatenfriedhof Dagneux.

Auferstehung ist unser Glaube,
Wiedersehn unsere Hoffnung,
Frommes Andenken unsere Liebe.

Vater unser — Ave Maria
Mein Jesus, Barmherzigkeit!

Uffz Michael Beyer, aged 33, of the 3rd Battery of Heeres Artillerie Abteilung 1196, was buried in Menton after having been killed in Nice August 28, 1944. It was only 16 years later, when the Volksbund exhumed his body in 1958, that his death was confirmed to his family. Robert Beyer Collection.

Maquisards coming down from Levens pose victoriously in Nice August 29th. They are equipped with airdropped British weapons and captured German weapons, including an MG 34 machine gun. MRA Collection.

A false German armored car, made of wood and armed with stove pipes, that the Germans abandoned in Nice. MRA Collection.

An example of the fierce popular justice that took place in the aftermath of the Liberation: a militiaman or collaborator lies dead in a pool of blood. Note that his shoes have been removed. MRA Collection.

read a few accounts about these men and the welcome they received. **FTP Pierre Durand** was at the level crossing on the 29th when an American patrol came to fetch the German prisoners that had been captured the day before. His account is one of the few that describes the conditions that the German prisoners were kept in:

I return to the level crossing and to the garage in which our German prisoners are being held. It is there in the late morning that I see a snappy looking lieutenant in fine form wearing FFL badges being escorted by a few fighters from the district. His mission, he tells me, is to get in touch with me. He has a radio available with which he can communicate with the Allied troops on the other side of the Var. I tell him, among other things, of the problem posed by the German prisoners. Our men, who have been present for 36 hours, are tired and can no longer provide proper guard duty, even with the help of the interpreter (…). Furthermore, supplies are starting to run low, in spite of the kind help of the local inhabitants. The prisoners are not SS men, and few of them have German origins. They surrendered quite fast and must be treated according to international rules. Since our FTPF companies have not entered Nice yet, and in the absence of gendarmes, we are not able, with our limited means, to ensure the minimum amount of food and hygiene. I therefore ask this officer to solve these problems as soon as possible by mentioning them to the Allies. He promises to report this to them.

Indeed, in the late afternoon, this officer returns accompanied by a Lieutenant of the American Army accompanied by two GIs. They take responsibility of the prisoners of war, to the great satisfaction of the prisoners and of myself. (…) The GIs who are in charge of this transfer are the first to have entered Nice in the afternoon of August 29th, and return by Boulevard Gambetta, under the cheers and hugs of the population. They appear as liberators, whereas our tired fighters, who are the first heroes, are abandoned. This is the first feeling of injustice of the after-liberation! There will be more to follow.[60]

Although the resistance men could be rightfully proud of the role they had played in the liberation of their town, they all too often seemed to forget that the Allied troops had been, and still would be, involved in much more fighting than they, and that it was the Allied invasion, not the Resistance, that was responsible for the collapse of the German army. The same can also be said of the Allied soldiers, who were most often oblivious to losses the Resistance had suffered and of the role it had played in weakening and hindering the German forces. As an example of the surprising ignorance of the American soldiers regarding the Resistance and the important role it played, in his history of the 551st PIB, Dan Morgan wrote: "The Battalion remained across the Var River from the city for at least two days, probably to allow Free French military and civil dignitaries time to arrive and make plans for a triumphal entry – a very 'French' touch."[61] The full news of the insurrection in Nice had clearly not reached all the Allied soldiers on the west bank of the Var!

Lt Dick Durkee, of A Company of the 551st PIB, was sent on a patrol into town August 29th, to check the FFI reports of it being cleared. His patrol later became reputed among the men of the 551st to have been the first into Nice:

The S-2 called me in and directed me to take a patrol and find out if Nice was occupied by Germans. I was to go to the edge of the city, report back by radio, and then return. When I got to the outskirts of Nice I didn't see any Germans, and the city was quiet and appeared deserted, so I said to myself, "Damned if I'm going to go back. We'll just go on in." So we just kept going, right down the main street.

Well, the first thing that happened was that a little girl came out of one of the houses, and she was standing there with her finger in her mouth; she was about five years old. She was just looking at me, so I said: "Americains!" Then she ran in the house crying: "Americanes! Americaines! [sic]" Then people started shouting and screaming. They came running out of all the houses by the hundreds. What had been a ghost town as we started in soon changed into a circus. We were joined by some FFIs and some local policemen, and then we found a Frenchman who could speak English and asked him where the best hotel in town was, and then we just moved in. That night the mayor came, and a band came and was playing in the street. They played our National Anthem and we all stood out on the balcony and took the cheers of the crowd. Boy, they

brought us wine and champagne, flowers, you can't imagine. Well, I finally called up our S-2 and reported in, and the next day the Battalion marched in. Our Battalion was the first to enter Nice, and my patrol was the first American unit.[62]

The men of the S-2 section, most likely not wanting to miss out on the fun, also entered town on the 29th, meeting up with **FTP René Canta** in the *Préfecture*, as he reported:

I would like to mention that the officer commanding the American detachment nearest Nice on August 29, 1944, Mr Hartmann, of the S-2 of the 551, came to see me at the *Préfecture*, to warmly congratulate the courage of our men and at the same time to ask for military intelligence that was necessary to him for the continuation of operations.[63]

American paratroopers wearing camouflage painted jump suits venture across the partially destroyed Var River Bridge into Nice in the aftermath of the insurrection. MRA Collection.

An American paratrooper is paraded around town by some resistance men. This photo was mostly likely taken August 29th. Karl Wickstrom Collection.

Jeeps from the 509th PIB cross the Var River into Nice. Note the presence of poles with white bands attached, marking a safe passage from which mines have been removed. Mike Reuter Collection.

The Americans who visited René Canta had a slightly more "colorful" and less military recollection of the event. **Technical Sergeant Ralph Wenthold**, of the 551st Battalion S-2 Section, later remembered:

Lt Hartman and I and about the whole S-2 Section went across the river and walked all the way into Nice and into Messina [sic] Square, in the center of town. When we finally got there the town was going wild. They were giving us drinks and we weren't wasting any of it. One old Englishman came by and said he had been waiting years for this and gave us a bottle of Johnnie Walker Red Label. We were drinking whiskey and wine and cognac. One guy drank up a cup of stuff somebody handed him and it was calvados. It about killed him. They took our pictures, we got carried up the steps of City Hall, and toasts were being drunk on all sides.

Finally we decided to go on back, and by that time we had a snoot-full. The French were going to haul us back in some old Citroens they had, so we started out driving along the waterfront. I was in the back seat and had my rifle butt resting on the floor with the barrel pointing up, and I guess Hartman was in the front seat. Well, we got down the road

a bit, and the driver was snookered, and then I noticed that one guy who was riding on the front-right fender just sort of rolled off the car onto the road, and just at that moment we ran square into a big lamppost. The French driver was looking back at us and talking the whole time and never even saw the post. We sort of piled out of there, and we were wearing our jump suits and I guess some FFI who were on the rooftops mistook us for Germans and began firing at us. That stopped after a while, and we finally got out of there. When we hit that lamppost my front sight split my forehead open and I was bleeding all down my front.[64]

Robert Poindexter, of the HQ Company of the 509th PIB, was also one of those who made his way into Nice August 29th with the impression of being the first American in town:

We were probably about 10 kilometers out of Nice, and they told us that there was a bridge out along the road a few miles ahead. My platoon leader and about five or six of us of the demolition platoon went down to this bridge to see what we could. While we were there, I will always remember this, a Red Cross lady came driving out from towards Nice, and she told us, this bunch that I was with, that the Germans had left Nice, cleared out. She spoke English, and she said that she would take us back to Nice. Well there hadn't been any Americans in Nice, but she said: "It's all clear." So we boarded up on her truck and we went into Nice; the first Americans in there. We were met with joyous people and all of that, and they got our Lieutenant up on one of the buildings on a platform, kind of making a speech. Of course, the drinks were flowing free, and I don't remember getting back with our outfit that night. But we stayed in Nice, got pretty well liquored up, and the next day, when the battalion was going to go into Nice, I was still about under the weather from the day before, but I was in the bunch that marched into Nice with the whole battalion.

Apart from the 551st and the 509th, the FSSF was also positioned outside Nice on the west bank of the Var, and it also sent men into town. **Peter Cottingham**, a Canadian member of the HQ Detachment of 2nd Battalion, 1st Regiment of the FSSF, was one of those sent across the Var on reconnaissance:

On approaching the Var River, our headquarters group joined up with Colonel Jack Akehurst, our regimental commander. He asked our reconnaissance Sergeant, Luther Tilley, and I to accompany him for the entry into Nice. Through radio contact he had learned that Nice was then pretty well in the hands of the FFI, (…) mostly volunteer civilians who were able to show their stuff when the Allies were at the gates of their towns and cities.

The Var flows down from the Alps and into the sea just west of the Nice airport. As we approached the river, we saw that the main bridge leading into the city had been partially destroyed by the retreating enemy. One span of it was sagging into the water. We picked our way across on the roadway, which was still hanging together by the steel reinforcements in it, but about 10 yards of it was under a foot or two of water. We were met on the east side by a delegation of city officials who had brought a very official looking black open car in which they proposed to drive us into their city.

Paratroopers of the 509th PIB are warmly welcomed by overjoyed local inhabitants as they reach downtown Nice. Mike Reuter Collection

Colonel Akehurst sat in the front seat beside the driver and Tilley and I perched on the front fenders with our submachine guns. There didn't seem to be any danger of enemy action at the time, but it was prudent to keep our eyes on roof tops as we did going into Rome. The French certainly had everything under control. The streets were lined with crowds of flag waving people, some of them offering flowers and others wine. We were treated to accolades, which were more deserved by our many friends who had been killed or wounded on their journey of liberation. It was a humbling yet fantastic experience I shall never forget.[65]

Place Massena, August 30, 1944: Allied troops enter Nice en masse to the wild cheers of the inhabitants of the town. Mike Reuter Collection. MRA Collection.

Interestingly, none of the men on these "advanced patrols" into Nice seem to have noticed the presence of other similar groups of Allied soldiers from their own or other units! The next day, August 30, 1944, the 509th and 551st PIBs and the FSSF finally forded the Var River and entered Nice in force, making a triumphant parade through the town. **Lt Paul Hoch**, Battalion Adjutant of the 551st, remembered:

They all lined up for us at Nice, flowers, cheering, kissing us and all. One family invited two of us in for a drink, so I went in and they handed me a glass. It was clear liquid, and it looked like there were three cherries in the bottom of the glass. Well, I thought I could drink anything, but it was like raw gasoline. It was rough. So I put the glass down and they came and filled it again. Then I drank a little more, but every time I put that glass down they would refill it and hand it back to me. We finally staggered out of there.[66]

A truck belonging to the 2nd Chemical Battalion enters Nice, followed by one from the 602nd Pack Field Artillery Battalion. The soldiers in the first vehicle are, from left to right: Erwing Kanowsky, Walzek, and James Hipskind. Walter Eldredge Collection.

2nd Chemical Battalion men Lt Walt Parrot, Willi Martin, Douglas Morrison, and Andy Oravec enter Nice. Note the vertical bar on the front of their jeep, designed to cut booby-trap wires. Walter Eldredge Collection.

An interesting view of the overjoyed French locals, as seen by the Allies from their vehicles. Walter Eldredge Collection.

A half-track of the Cannon Company of the FSSF crosses Place Massena. Theodor Flesser Collection.

Captain Jud Chalkley, the 551st Battalion's Second Surgeon, was also served unreasonable amounts of alcohol by an overexcited local:

We entered Nice in the late afternoon. The FFI were shooting at anything that looked German. We were passing by a corner bar and decided to go in. The proprietor brought out a bottle of cognac and he said: "Viva la America! [sic]" So I said: "Vive la France!" Then he smashed his glass against the wall, so I did, too. Then he said: "Avec moi." So I followed him to the back of the place where he lived, and he moved a table and a rug and there was a trap door. Steps led down to an earth cellar.

I followed him down, and then we got down on our hands and knees and started crawling. About that time I started wondering what I had got myself into. Well, he had a little flashlight, and pretty soon we came to a spot and he started digging into the loose dirt with his hands and soon came up with a bottle of five-year-old cognac. We sat right there in the tunnel and drank up that whole bottle; it was his prize bottle of cognac that he had saved all through the war.[67]

The intense joy and celebration was also closely followed by a popular backlash against those who had collaborated with the Germans during the occupation. The Allied troops were usually very shocked by the way "horizontal collaborators" were treated by freshly self-proclaimed "resistance fighters," who found it easier to attack defenseless women than German soldiers. **Captain Tim Quinn**, of C Company of the 551st PIB, remembers:

They put me in the car with the mayor and we rode around town. I watched them beat up on the female collaborators and shave their hair. They started ripping their clothes off and I stopped them, and the mayor said I shouldn't do that, but I said yes I should, because we came to help them and not to watch them brutalize the women.[68]

Peter Cottingham, of the FSSF, managed to solve one such situation using a bit of diplomacy:

Tilley and I were dispatched to seek out battalion headquarters. They had followed us on foot. We soon located Major McFadden and our people, and we all made our way to our allotted sector, which was the north flank of the city up in the high-priced real estate area. We pulled into an imposing looking villa that perched on a hill overlooking a well-treed orchard. We parked our jeep in the courtyard and were welcomed into the house by a middle-aged lady who spoke perfect English. It turned out she was a widow who had lived in California until she and her late husband moved to Nice just prior to the war. She was most hospitable, and welcomed us to use her beds and bathrooms as we saw fit. We enjoyed an evening meal with our rations and her wine while sitting at her dining room table.

The next morning, I went out to get my shaving gear from the jeep and was met in the courtyard by an unkempt looking bunch of "freedom fighters." I would classify them as a bunch of bandit opportunists after listening to a tirade from their leader. He stepped up to me and, pounding his chest,

Some of the more unpleasant aspects of the Liberation: women suspected of having collaborated with the Germans are shaved in the streets, while a man is paraded around wearing a sign reading: "Has sold 23 patriots to the Gestapo." (Which referred to the mass execution at l'Ariane August 15th.) Frédéric Brega Collection.

demanded that we hand over the woman who owned the villa to him and his band. He stated that she had collaborated with the officers of the German occupation by entertaining them in her home. I knew by now that what they had in mind was the treatment given many of the women who had fraternized with the Germans. They would strip her naked and shave her head and lead her down the streets with a rope around her neck to show everyone what a poor Frenchwoman she was.

I looked around and noted that there were about ten or twelve men in this group. A couple of them had a machine gun set up and aimed at her back door from down in the orchard. Summoning most of the French I had learned in high school, I suggested that they were indeed a brave bunch of Frenchmen. I asked if it took so many armed men to subdue one little old lady. I also suggested that there were "Beaucoup des Allemands dans les Montagnes [Many Germans in the mountains]." They looked around at each other, had a pow-wow, and decided to take off for greener pastures. I really sweated that one out. We never saw those guys again, but I ran across the woman at a later date. I spotted her sitting at a sidewalk café in Nice about a month later. She had learned what I had done for her that morning and asked me to join her for a drink. I congratulated her on still having her hair.[69]

Conclusion

It has often been claimed by some inhabitants of Nice that "Nice liberated itself on its own, without help from the Americans." Although it is technically correct that the Allied troops provided no help on the specific day of August 28, 1944, claiming that Nice liberated itself conveniently ignores the fact that if the insurrection was able to occur at all, it was obviously thanks to the Allied invasion, which had severely mauled *Reserve Division 148* and forced it to retreat at the price of many lives. Fortunately, many French, including **Colonel Jacques "Sapin" Lécuyer**, the commander of the FFI forces of the "R2 zone" of southeast of France, did not share such a narrow self-serving vision of events. In his memoirs, he wrote a very balanced description of the situation in Nice:

Some people thought that the Germans had already decided to abandon Nice and that setting off the insurrection was therefore useless. It is true that the Germans, who were probably rightfully worried about the arrival of the Americans and also perhaps fearing to be cut off from their rear echelon by the *maquisards*, had decided to evacuate Nice. But they

had also decided to perform large-scale destruction aimed at key points, such as the electricity factory, water factory, gas factory, the train tracks, etc., etc. And that is what the action of the urban *résistants* managed to avoid.

In any case, we can say that the liberation of Nice is an example – perhaps the only one – of the combination of three actions – more or less purposefully coordinated – (urban insurrection, very close threat of regular Allied troops, worrisome *maquis*!), even if this combination was both the fruit of will and of chance.[70]

The battle in Nice must indeed be viewed in the greater context of the military situation in the Maritime Alps, and not as an isolated event. If the Germans in Nice were preparing to retreat, it was not because of the Resistance, but because the First Airborne Task Force was slowly but surely closing in on them. The insurrection was simply the final straw that triggered and accelerated an already planned retreat.

Having said this, the courage of the Frenchmen who launched the insurrection must be saluted and the usefulness of their action confirmed. The insurrection caused the death of up to 41 German soldiers and the capture of many more: probably at least 100, including one regimental commander. The insurrection undoubtedly damaged German morale, forcing them to abandon the city, leaving equipment behind and without having performed all the damage to its infrastructures that they may have wanted to inflict. It enabled the Allies to capture the largest city in the Maritime Alps without losing one single soldier. Perhaps most importantly, the insurrection showed that the fighting spirit of the local population was intact, and that they were ready to play an active role in the liberation of their land, even at the cost of their own lives.

The only Allied death that occurred in Nice on August 30th was caused by a dispute between two Forcemen, leading to the death of one soldier. Forceman Peter Cottingham described this tragedy in his book *Once upon a wartime*. August 31st, the units of the FABTF started fanning out to the north and east of Nice, in pursuit of the Germans. However, before getting onto this, we will first backtrack a few days to examine some events that had been occurring in the mountains that were under control of the Resistance, to the north of the sector the FABTF had been operating in.

The famous Promenade des Anglais in Nice as it appeared shortly after the Liberation. Bruce Broudy Collection.

14

In Resistance-Controlled Territory

We saw in several of the previous chapters that the zone of action of the First Airborne Task Force and *Reserve Division 148* was confined to the coastal region of the Maritime Alps. The mountainous areas north of the towns of Fayence, St Vallier, and Levens had already been under heavy *maquis* influence before the Allied invasion, and as soon as the landing finally occurred, the Resistance easily took control, capturing the few small German garrisons at Puget-Théniers, St Martin Vésubie, and Bancairon with almost no loss of life. It is sometimes said that the Resistance liberated 90% of the territory of the Maritime Alps on their own, with the Allies liberating only 10%. While this is pretty much true, it should be added that the 90% liberated by the Resistance was virtually unoccupied in the first place, while the 10% of the territory liberated by the Allies was occupied by over 90% of the German forces and contained all the major cities of the Maritime Alps. Having said this, the role of the Resistance should not be minimized, as it certainly had important consequences for the strategic situation of the Germans. We will let **Colonel Jacques "Sapin" Lécuyer**, the commander of the Resistance in the R2 region of southeastern France, describe the capture of some of the small German mountain garrisons:

August 15th, we went down to Puget-Théniers with a bad truck. The small German garrison of the town had been liquidated by François (Mazier) at dawn. (…)

1-St Martin Vésubie.
August 17th, the small German garrison at St Martin Vésubie surrendered to *Groupe Morgan* (Foatta), which had been harassing them for several days. Morgan left it to the "locals" to hold the town and returned to Lantosque with his prisoners (…).The reinforcing of the border by the Germans took the form of large patrols, one of which reoccupied Saint Martin on the 21st; it was pushed back out on the 22nd (or 23rd) by *Groupe Hochcorn* (Dormoy) (…), which later repulsed all the other patrols that the Germans sent down from their positions at the Madone des Fenestres.

2-Le Bancairon.
That is the name of a hydroelectric plant on the Tinée River. It is quite a large complex of buildings. All the small German garrisons and outposts of the valley had assembled there out of caution as the *maquis* pressure increased. August 16th, the Morgan, Rodolphe (Captain de Lestang-Labrousse), and François (FFI Captain Mazier) groups had surrounded the factory by taking up position on the heights on either side of the valley and were harassing the garrison.

A French Gendarme had been taken, more or less as a hostage, by the Germans. The telephone connection between the factory and the outside had not been cut, and by this means – and through the Gendarme – François had gotten in touch with the commander of the German unit, trying to persuade him that any resistance was now in vain. Francois sent me a messenger to inform me of this situation. I was back in Puget-Théniers after the escapade in the armored jeeps [see Chapter 12]. I was still in *maquisard* uniform. (Since it was impossible to dress all our combatants as "soldiers," none of us – members of the military – wore a uniform, which could have avoided being considered as *franc-tireurs*, for we did not want to let it be imagined that we were trying to take less risks then the others.) With a set of khaki trousers and shirt (every now and then we received some clothing in the parachute drops) I got a sort of uniform made for myself, with a forage cap, rank insignia (…) on the cap, and shoulder boards, and a belt with a magnificent Colt given to me by General Frederick.

I entered the factory on the 19th, got the garrison to assemble and put down their weapons, and set the conditions of the surrender. They were of course accepted. The garrison walked out in order. After the first curve, our "troops" and vehicles came into view! Seeing them, the German commander recoiled and said: "You tricked me." I answered: "No! I am really an officer, from the St Cyr school, I landed slightly over three years ago, and you will be treated as prisoners of war according to the rules of war." The next day they were sent to Beuil, where they joined the prisoners from Puget-Théniers and St Martin Vésubie. (Later on, they were all handed over to the 1st Army.)[1]

It should be noted that these large groups of German prisoners were not executed or maltreated, despite the legends that "the maquis never took any prisoners." On August 16th, three isolated Germans soldiers who were passing through Roquebillière, slightly south of St Martin Vésubie, were not as lucky, however. Realizing that the valley was controlled by the maquis, they decided to surrender to two local residents. Unfortunately for them, a truck of maquisards turned up shortly afterwards and the three men were executed in Lantosque; the local priest, Abbé Bessano, noting:

Three German soldiers, who were captured near Vieux Roquebillière and whose identities were not revealed, were shot with submachine guns in the courtyard of the barracks and buried in a civil manner, under a chestnut tree at the Quartier du Seuil. [2]

After their surrender, the soldiers of the small German garrison of Puget-Théniers sit on the ground awaiting their fate, surrounded by maquisards and curious local civilians. MRA Collection.

These three executed men were apparently named Emil Claus, Rudolf Babel, and Ernst Schafer; however, their identities were never confirmed and all three were later reburied as unknown soldiers. Later on the same day, two motorcycles with sidecars were intercepted at Roquebillière and their crews were shot as they rode into town. Three Germans were killed and one wounded.[3] The three dead were:

Surame	Name	Rank	Age	Date of death	Buried in
Kapler	Gottlieb	Hilfzoll	46	16.8.1944	Roquebillière
Lachmann	Karl	Zollsek	47	16.8.1944	Roquebillière
Wittmann	Albert	Zollsek	40	16.8.1944	Roquebillière

Only in the area of the Italian border, where the Germans were planning to set up their long-term defense line, did they send in troops to take control of the strategic mountain passes, forts, roads, and villages, as Sapin indicates occurred at St Martin Vésubie. All the mountains west of the Var River were left in the hands of the *maquis*. The Germans had no reason to venture into these badlands and they carefully avoided entering them. Local FFI commander Félix Petitjean, known as Lieutenant Ginette, along with his gang of men, was in control of the sector north of Vence and Grasse. In his autobiography *Le Temps des Fauves*, Ginette described one group of Germans who had probably been sent out on reconnaissance to check if the *Route*

Napoleon (so named because it had been used by Napoleon over a century earlier when he had returned from Elba) could be used by them in their retreat. Had the *Route Napoleon* been clear, it could have been a very useful evacuation route for the Germans. However, it was firmly in the hands of the *maquisard*s, the first of which were **Ginette**'s men, guarding a strategic bridge on the road north of St Vallier:

> It was reasonable to think that the Germans would try to use this road to evacuate their troops from the coast. Indeed, after the landings in Provence, an enemy column appeared at the tip of the long straightaway that precedes the bridge. We took it under the fire of our machine gun, inflicting some casualties that were probably light – we only saw a few men fall – but the column didn't insist and turned back towards St Vallier.
>
> With the small forces we disposed of, we would not have been able to resist a proper attack, but the *Boches* understood that the *Route Napoleon* was under control of the *maquisard*s. With a bit of luck and lots of casualties, they could probably have reached Castellane, but beyond that, they would have been doomed to complete destruction.[4]

After this, only a few small groups of Germans who had become lost or isolated in the confusion of the invasion had the bad idea of trying to retreat through the resistance-controlled mountains. We will describe what happened to some of them further on. Though the Germans left the mountains to the Resistance, they did, however, make sure to prevent it from descending down into the strategic coastal zone. In Chapter 12, we saw that the attempt of the resistance to move south in the Var Valley was stopped in the Carros and Levens area. We also saw in Chapter 11 how the Germans blew and heavily mined the road north of Vence, causing multiple casualties and preventing it from being used. The Loup Valley was similarly guarded at Gourdon.

Gourdon

Gourdon is a small eagle's nest type village that overlooks the entire area between Nice and the Estérel Mountains to the south, as well as the Loup River Valley and its road to the east. The Germans had an advanced outpost in Gourdon, probably because it was such an excellent observation point, and also in order to keep the Loup Valley under tight control. The local resistance, which had become too cocky after their recent success in the mountains, was to suffer severely when it attempted to approach Gourdon August 21, 1944, not knowing that it was occupied by the Germans. (According to some, the *maquisard*s approached the town waving a French flag.) **Lt Ginette** described the circumstances and how his team of *maquisard*s was called to the rescue in his autobiography:

> I take position in Gréolières. In the homes of collaborators or enemy sympathizers, we requisition sheets in exchange for legitimate requisition bonds. We get seamstresses from Cannes who have taken refuge in the village to make shorts and shirts for our men. That way we had look-alike uniforms.
>
> August 15th [Actually August 21st.], we were warned that a *maquisard* car had been intercepted by the Germans at Gourdon and that there was fighting going on at the tavern. We rush off with eight men. We go up the hairpin road. A single burst of machine gun fire would be enough to eliminate us. At the last curve before Gourdon, we creep into the underbrush and take position behind a large oak tree.
>
> From our observation point, we can see silhouettes on the road. It is impossible to distinguish whether they are

Germans or *maquisard*s. Not a noise, not a shot. We think that our comrades are besieged in the tavern. I decide to go and see. I bring Briquet, from Tourette sur Loup, with me. [This same Briquet was killed by the mines in Vence a few days later.] I advise the rest of the team not to move and to keep their eyes open. We crawl from bush to bush, getting closer to the tavern. We have some difficulties moving, as Briquet and I aren't exactly dragonflies. We then clearly spot German uniforms.

It is indeed the *Boches* who are occupying the tavern. We turn back. We need to take the same precautions as on the way there. The village, which can be accessed by a single road, must be strongly held and fortified (…). As we were only a hundred meters away from our oak tree, bursts of machine gun fire hit the stones of the terraced walls above us and to our left. It isn't possible, we are not the ones being shot at. We cannot be seen.

We get back to our shelter. Sad tragedy. Several of our comrades, alas oblivious of the danger, waited for a while, but then, the wait prolonging itself, they lost patience. They got up, took a few steps, then got out of the cover of the trees and advanced on the terraces facing the village perched at the top of the crest. They could not be seen from the tavern, but the SS who were holding the town could not miss noticing them. They were **Georges Pagliusa** and **Leclerc**, ages 17 and 18, and **Martini**, from Tourette. The Germans let them advance and opened fire once they were nicely exposed. All of them were mercilessly cut down.

We rejoin our comrades and collapse breathless. Convinced that there is no one left, a group of *Boches* goes down to the cemetery. They observe the bushes, but look too far to the left. They slowly expose themselves, offering us a prime target. Ulysse loads an ammunition belt into our old German machine gun and Jean Sauvageot takes careful aim. In spite of our impatience we wait longer, and when all the chances of success are met, I give the order to open fire. The device jumps and jolts, the belts empty themselves. A sort of rage seizes us, and we fire with all our weapons. From the top of the village, the *Boches* have spotted us and the plants around us are cut down. We can see the position of the enemy machine gun very well, but we cease fire because, oh surprise, the inhabitants of the village are coming and going on the road as if they thought they were at a fairground

shooting competition. We saw *Boches* falling near the cemetery. We later found out that there were two killed and three wounded who were immediately evacuated to Grasse.

What had happened? A *maquisard* vehicle had indeed been intercepted by the *Boches* near the tavern. Two had managed to escape; the third, nicknamed "La Guêpe" ["The Wasp," whose real name was **Raymond Baille**.], had been captured in the morning and left wounded in the town square under the burning sun. The *Boches* had threatened to shoot a woman who wanted to bring him something to drink. La Guêpe was to die during the night. We swear to avenge him and to avenge our comrades who will not get to see the rise of the dawn of victory.

It was out of the question to attack Gourdon, it would have been suicidal. The position was impregnable, even with more manpower. With sad hearts, we fall back.[5]

In total, five *maquisard*s had been killed in this botched and apparently pointless operation. If they had used a minimum amount of caution, all these lives could have been spared. Ginette mentions two German dead, but no traces of them are to be found in the *Volksbund* archives. They were neither buried in Grasse, nor in the Caucade Cemetery, nor next to the Cimiez field hospital. The five French casualties were (note that the ages are slightly different than what Ginette recalled):

Surname	Name	Age	Date of death	Location of death
Baille	Raymond	17	22.8.1944	Gourdon
Leclere	Marcel	20	21.8.1944	Gourdon
Martini	Vincent	33	21.8.1944	Gourdon
Pagliuzza	Georges	20	21.8.1944	Gourdon
Pilastre	Henri	25	21.8.1944	Gourdon

On his way back from Gourdon, **Lt Ginette** decided to apply some of the harsh popular justice that would later cause much controversy:

We stop in the town square of a small village. We had been told that its mayor had denounced a shot-down American aviator who had been hiding in the village. I ask a woman near a cart of straw.

"Can you tell me where the mayor is?"

"What for?"

"Probably to shoot him."

The woman drops her pitchfork and is unwell. She was the mayor's wife. Her husband admits the accusations. He had indeed turned in the aviator, but was compelled and forced to by an Italian who was aware of his presence in the village. It was an attenuating circumstance, but the cowardice remained. The interrogation of the Italian was worth its weight in gold.

"I was afraid, yes, I was afraid to be shot by the Germans if they found out that we were hiding an American. I am not like you," he told me, "I am not a lion."

We return to Greolières and make arrangements to avoid a surprise attack, that in any case is highly unlikely. I was not a lion, no, but I had become a wild beast, and he got the punishment he deserved.[6]

Lt Ginette had a strong character and a natural dislike for authority. He despised the lack of courage that most of the population

The memorial plaque for the maquisards killed in Gourdon. Author's Collection.

displayed during the Occupation. During the war, his hatred of the Germans and their collaborators had grown beyond what even his fellow *maquisards* could consider reasonable, as he would prove at Thorenc August 24, 1944, three days after the Gourdon shooting. That day, a dozen German soldiers of the 3rd Battery of *Heeres Pak Abteilung 1038* (this unit was not part of *Reserve Division 148*) who had been sent into battle at Puget le Muy August 16th and become isolated, had the bad idea of venturing into the mountains, probably hoping to somehow get back to their own lines. **Lt Ginette** and his men were called over to deal with the small group of Germans:

> We leave for the Logis du Pin, where groups of Germans are reported to us. We spot one and open fire. From hunted, we had become the hunters. They strike back. The heel of my shoe is shot off. I believe I am wounded, but such is not the case. My right foot takes a nice dark blue tint.
>
> One of our comrades calls out to the Germans in their own language. They refuse to surrender. They want to give themselves up to the Americans. They are afraid of reprisals, and in fact they are right. We tighten our circle around them and start firing again. They finally surrender, and are very worried… There were twelve of them. After having exchanged their boots for our bad shoes, we pile them into our vehicles. I order the column to stop, pull out a German, and shoot him. I want to exterminate all of them. One would have had to have a short memory to forget La Guêpe and his agony. It had happened only 48 hours earlier. All my comrades leap onto me.
>
> "Don't do that, Ginette, don't do that. Maybe they weren't in Gourdon. They aren't responsible for what happened."
>
> They prevent me from shooting. I am in a mad rage.
>
> Before reaching Thorenc, we order the prisoners to goose step, then enter the village where the people are crying with joy. A women rushes to me and tells me: "You are a hero sir, a hero," and she sobs.
>
> Strange hero, more like a savage beast that dreamt only of blood, death, and revenge. At the CP, the ranking German tells me in impeccable French: "Why did you kill our comrade? We had surrendered, we were prisoners of war."
>
> I burst out: "You bastards, did you take many prisoners of war with us? You despicably tortured and killed all those that you captured. You are not in any position to invoke the rules of war. It is to you that we owe it if we have become savages. You respect nothing, neither women, nor children, nor elders. For several months we have been members of the regular army, soldiers without uniforms, but formalized by the wearing of an armband with the Lorrain Cross. Before yesterday, three of my men were killed in battle in Gourdon. That is one thing, and such is the law of war. But you wounded and captured a 16-year-old kid. You left him in the town square under the blazing sun, you did not take pity of his sufferings or his prayers or his cries of pain. You refused for him to be given anything to drink. Are those methods worthy of soldiers? All those that fall into your hands are shot on the spot after having been mutilated or tortured. No one will be tortured here, but we will apply Lex Talionis to you. Such will be our line of conduct since you have shown it to us."
>
> "I understand," said the NCO, "and I thank God to still be alive, but let me tell you that we are not coming from Gourdon, and I give you my word that I have never shot nor tortured one of yours."
>
> I did not believe him. A *Boche* will always remain a *Boche*. In other words, a being with the primitive and savage instincts of a beast. It is in the blood, in the race, it is atavistic.[7]

At least Félix "Ginette" Petitjean had the honesty of not trying to hide or minimize his actions. His account gives a chilling glimpse into the depths of the hatred that filled the hearts of all too many who lived through the war, but that few would later care to admit or even remember. In Ginette's case, however, the problem may have run much deeper than simple hatred related to the war: indeed, the French police would later suspect him of being linked to numerous illegal activities and several unjustified assassinations, including that of his own wife.[8]

The German soldier he had killed was 19-year-old **Gefreiter Johann Prasch**, of *Heeres Pak Abteilung 1038*, which, as said previously, was retreating from the Draguignan area and had nothing to do with the encounter in Gourdon. Johann Prasch was buried by his fellow prisoners. When he was exhumed years later, the *Volksbund* workers noted that his belt buckle had been pierced by a bullet.

Tourette du Château

Toudon and Tourette du Château are two villages located to the west of Levens and the Var Valley, in a remote mountainous area far removed from any strategic military features. Since the Allied landing, no German or Allied troops had even approached the villages, and it seems that no *maquisards* were in the immediate vicinity either. After the liberation of Nice and la Roquette August 28, 1944, the two villages found themselves far behind Allied lines, and their inhabitants assumed that they could now consider themselves liberated. In Tourette, a French flag was raised on the steeple of the church, but other than that, the inhabitants went on with their daily lives.

August 30th, however, a group of six lost German soldiers were spotted near Toudon, marching east. At least three of the men belonged to the HQ Company of *Grenadier Regiment 932*, which was not even part of *Reserve Division 148*, but of *Infanterie Division 244*, which was stationed in Marseille. Presumably, just like Johann Prasch's group, these six soldiers had gotten isolated during the fighting around Draguignan and had decided to try to rejoin the German lines by crossing through the mountains. **René Marks**, a local teenager, seems to be the first to have noticed the group of Germans as they reached the road east of Toudon:

> Every morning I would go to the farm where there were goats and rabbits. We took care of the animals and then went

19-year-old Gefreiter Johann Prasch, of Heeres Pak Abteilung 1038, who was shot and killed by FFI leader Ginette after surrendering a few kilometers east of Thorenc. Prasch Family Collection.

The village of Tourette du Château, over which a French flag was flying August 30, 1944, when a group of isolated Germans approached the town. Author's Collection.

The seemingly peaceful streambed that the Germans followed in their attempt to avoid the village of Tourette, but that led them straight into an ambush set up by local hunters. Author's Collection.

back home. So I was walking back home at about eleven in the morning, and when I got to the curve in the road at St Jean, where there is a fountain, I heard foreign voices, meaning Germans. There were eight or ten of them. I stopped and listened to their conversation. They were refreshing themselves and drinking water, then two of them came up onto the road that is just above the fountain. One German saw me, but he completely ignored me – I was starting to get a bit frightened at that point – then, with another guy, they pulled out a map, and they were studying it and pointing towards Tourette. They were surely looking for a way to go up and down into the next valley. They stayed at least ten or fifteen minutes, talking to each other, then the ones that had been refreshing themselves also climbed up onto the road and they all left in the direction of Tourette.

At that point I also took off and I arrived in Toudon. I went to where my dad was working and I told him: "I saw Germans down at the St Jean curve. They were at the fountain talking."

My dad asked: "Were they armed?"

"Yes, they were armed, all of them. Well armed actually."

"Oh? And how many of them were there?"

"I don't know. Eight or ten, more or less. Some were down by the fountain, some were sitting down, some were standing up…"

So then my dad told me: "OK, you don't move, you stay here!"

I answered: "Me? Yes… Wait, hem… No, I won't move."

My father was from Alsace, so he could speak German fluently, and he went to see the priest, Tischer, who was from Lorraine and could also speak German fluently. They decided to go and stop the Germans. They took two other guys from Toudon with them: François Cagnol and Félix Alziari, and then another guy, Joseph Cires, but he had a limp, so I think he never actually got up there. But whatever: they left. They only had hunting rifles with buckshot.

But I was a bit curious… so I followed them, but from a distance, because they had left on bikes. When they arrived at the path that goes up to le Gandalet they left the bikes, climbed up on foot, and they got the Germans from behind.

Although no resistance was in town, the local hunters and mavericks had decided to take matters into their own hands. Meanwhile, a few kilometers further east, 14-year-old **Roger Monti**

was working on a hill overlooking the road between Toudon and Tourette, exactly where the Germans were headed:

It was about 7:30 or 8:00 in the morning, and with my father we were plowing a field that overlooks the road. There were no cars at that time – there wasn't much of anything, actually, except a few animals with bells – and we heard footsteps ringing out on the road. So we observed in that direction, and suddenly we saw a group of men appear. As they got nearer, we made out uniforms and rifles and we said: "It's the Germans." As of that moment: beware!

There were six soldiers with weapons and they were advancing towards us, but we were about 100 meters above them. At that moment, an airplane went by quite high above in the sky, but the Germans immediately jumped into the ditch. We could tell that they were very frightened. Once the plane had gone they got back up, went on their way, walked past us, and came into sight of Tourette. When they caught sight of the French flag on the church steeple, they probably panicked, thinking: "This is it, there are partisans here." So what did they do? They came back, but instead of following the road, they took a path and they followed the path, coming nearer to us.

At that moment, above us, we saw some silhouettes that were of course familiar to us, and we recognized some guys from Toudon. There were five or six of them, with rifles glinting. Along with my father, we immediately understood that something was going to happen. My father had already stopped his team of steer so as not to attract attention. We were hiding and observing the scene. At that point, we saw the Germans step off the path and go up into a stream bed. We then said: "Oh là là, now they are in a trap!" It was not hoped for, because the Germans really put themselves into a death trap. Even nowadays we use that stream bed for hunting wild boar. When the guys from Toudon saw that they set an ambush up, and when the Germans arrived at good shooting range, they shot them like rabbits.

We heard 10, 15, or 20 gunshots go off almost at the same time. We said: "That's it, the people have killed them." There was then a long silence, and then we heard a stampede, and we saw a German, probably the commander, running back down the stream bed towards the road. *Monsieur* Marks, who was an Alsatian who could speak German, was shouting at him in German to stop, to surrender. Then he fired two more shots at the German as he was crossing the road. We saw the soldier tumble down into a corn field and we said: "He got him!" But three or four seconds later he stood back up and kept on running. Later on, I realized that he had not been hit: there were two rows of barbed wire to prevent animals from going into that field, and he had simply tangled himself in them, then gotten back up and escaped towards the south.

My grandmother was further down in the valley, watering her garden, and saw that man going down in the rocks, at a place where people don't usually go because it is quite dangerous. At noon, when she came back, she said: "I don't know what that man was doing, going down there. Couldn't he take the path just like everybody else?" Then we told her it was a German. She had seen him, so he was indeed safe and sound, and she saw him take a path that went towards the Var front.

René Marks, the teenager from Toudon who had first spotted the Germans, heard his father and the other men who had set up the ambush describe the shooting many times after the war, including details that Roger Monti had not been able to observe from where he was positioned:

The Germans climbed up into that stream bed, and at the top there are quite a few rocks. They went to the place where they should not have gone. With a hunting rifle, you can't shoot 100 meters away; they have to be at 10 or 15 meters, no more. So they let the Germans get as close as possible, and at that moment my dad, who could speak German fluently, stood up and summoned the Germans twice. He asked them to stop and surrender, saying that if they surrendered and gave up their weapons, nothing would happen to them. Then Father Tischer came out with his robe, thinking that if the Germans saw a priest they would be reassured and understand that nothing would happen to them.

But no; according to what my father told me, one young German soldier shouldered his rifle to fire, but he didn't have time to. Félix was behind a rock, and when he saw the young German lift his rifle he fired and gunned him down. They were waiting, whereas the Germans were not. Those who were there fired, including the priest. He had a 16 caliber and the others had 12 calibers. They were all hunters, so when they fired a bullet it would strike home. The hunting rifles dominated the situation, and they shot all the Germans except one, who took off, running back to where he had come from. With a hunting rifle it was out of the question to fire on him, because as of a range of 30 or 40 meters you can't do anything anymore, so my father picked up a rifle from one of the killed Germans and he shouldered it, but by that time the German was back down the road. My father fired, and according to what they saw he hit him. Supposedly that German was later captured at Puget-Théniers. There were resistance fighters everywhere, including men from Toudon, and they found out later on that German had been hit in the heel.

René Marks continues, giving more details of the scene where the soldiers were shot:

One of the Germans was not hit mortally and could still speak. My father asked him if he would surrender, saying he would be looked after. But he didn't want to surrender, he shouted "Heil Hitler" and moved his hand towards his belt and took his pistol. So then Félix eliminated him. It ended there; nothing else happened, they were all dead. Two

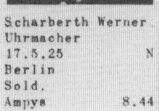

Four of the five German soldiers who were gunned down, then hastily buried by local hunters in Tourette when they refused to surrender. From left to right: 22-year-old Obergefreiter Kurt Fiedler of Grenadier Regiment 932, 19-year-old Funker Franz Mehlis, 19-year-old Grenadier Werner Scharberth of Grenadier Regiment 932, and 18-year-old Soldat Alfred Schütte, also of Grenadier Regiment 932. Deutsches Rote Kreutz and Mehlis Family Collections.

or three of them were quite young. According to my father, the one who had wanted to open fire was 19 years old. The others were between 20 and 30. They took their weapons, one or two took some pairs of boots, and that was it.

When they went up, my dad had thought that the Germans would surrender, and so did Father Tischer. But if Félix hadn't seen that kid prepare his rifle, maybe one of them, my dad or Tischer, would have been shot.

Roger Monti, who had watched the scene from the field with his father, tells us the events that followed from the point of view of the inhabitants of Tourette. They were particularly worried because of the soldier who had managed to escape:

My father immediately told me: "You should go down to the village and warn the people, because that man is armed and may want to take revenge since we killed all his friends." So I went down to Tourette and went to see Mr Gustave Gastaud, who was in fact the president of the Liberation Committee. We warned a few people, and they took out some old rifles that they had hidden in some straw to be able to defend themselves if ever that man came back. We observed the area he had disappeared in, but couldn't see anything. Then, in the afternoon around 4:00 or 4:30, we said: "We should go and bury the bodies."

We arrived up there with picks, shovels, and a few rifles, and we found the bodies lying here and there. Of course, those people had been robbed of everything good they had on them. When we got there, the people who had killed them had taken their weapons, maybe some shoes or whatever. They took all the good stuff and all we got was the trouble of burying them. We also noticed that the Germans were mostly young guys: we could see that their cheeks were practically beardless. We said: "They are all young, 18 and 19 years old, something like that.

We dug at a place where the ground was favorable, not far from where we found them, of course. We dragged them to where it was possible to make a deep hole. I didn't participate in the digging. I was given a rifle. My father was digging, making the hole, but for the younger guys like myself, they said: "You have good eyes and good ears, so take rifles and stand guard all around so that you can warn us in case of trouble." In the meantime, the others were working. They dug the hole and they took the identification tags that the soldiers had. They were brought to the town hall and Mr Gustave Gastaud, who was acting as mayor, took care of dispatching those tags. We spent the afternoon until night time burying the bodies, let's say, decently. About 10 years later, the Germans came to get the remains.

The inhabitants had buried half the tags with the bodies, while the other halves and the information about the existence of the grave were passed down to local authorities in Nice. The town hall of Toudon wrote the following brief report of the incident, confirming Marks' and Monti's accounts:

> August 30, 1944, six armed Germans trying to escape to Italy through the mountains were chased. Summoned to surrender, they refused, and fire was opened, killing five of them. They are buried on the territory of Tourette du Château.[9]

The names of the five soldiers were:

Surname	Name	Rank	Age	Date of death	Location of death	Unit
Fiedler	Kurt	Ogefr	22	30.08.1944	Tourette du Château	Gren.Rgt.932
Mehlis	Franz	Funk	19	30.08.1944	Tourette du Château	
Scharberth	Werner	Gren	19	30.08.1944	Tourette du Château	Gren.Rgt.932
Schütte	Alfred	Sold	18	30.08.1944	Tourette du Château	Gren.Rgt.932
Stange	Werner	Kan	18	30.08.1944	Tourette du Château	

Roger Monti shows the hole in which he helped to bury the five killed German soldiers. Author's Collection.

Three of these men were included by their families on the missing in action lists that were compiled by the German Red Cross after the war. The information provided by the families shows that the German army was very puzzled about what had happened to the soldiers, as two were listed as missing in action in Marseille and one in "Ampys!"

In 1958, the *Volksbund* came to Tourette to exhume the bodies. At the site of the killing the grave was found, measuring approximately two meters by two meters and containing five bodies buried in two layers. Three men had been laid side by side, then the last two men had been added on top, in the opposite direction, with their heads lying on the feet of the men under them. All the bodies were individualized without any problems because they had been buried so neatly, and all were identified thanks to the identification tags that the inhabitants of Tourette had carefully left in place after removing the lower halves of them 14 years earlier. As often, some artifacts were left behind at the location of the grave after the exhumation, and a search made at a later date revealed the following items:

- A fragment of wallet containing coins.
- Approximately 20 German tunic buttons with metal hooks, indicating they came from summer uniforms. All the buttons were found in the grave or downhill from it, except one that was also slightly bent and missing its loop. This suggested the button may have been damaged at the time of the shooting, but the damage was not characteristic enough to be able to determine with certainty that it had been caused by a projectile.
- Approximately 30 German trouser and equipment buttons, including one French military button that a German soldier had probably used to replace a lost German button.
- Approximately 20 German and French wartime and prewar coins.
- A few German trouser or equipment buckles.

Some buckshot pellets were also found in and around the grave, but because the area had been used for hunting so often, it was not possible to determine if these pellets were related to the killed soldiers or not. Unfortunately, none of the items found presented any battle damage that could be used to identify what types of weapons had been used to kill the soldiers.

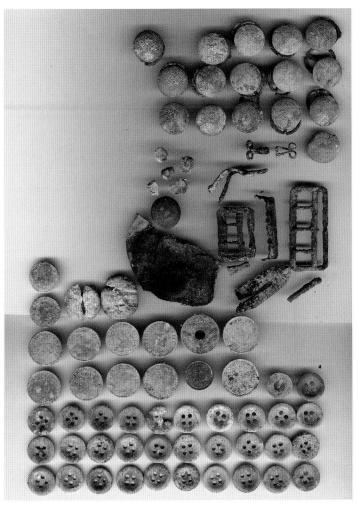

It would seem that the hunters had removed almost everything from the bodies except their uniforms before burying them. Private Collection.

Conclusion

The Resistance took control of the mountains north of the French Riviera very effectively as soon as the Allied invasion occurred, preventing any large-scale German maneuvers or retreats in the area. The resistance made several small German garrisons prisoner and captured or eliminated at least two groups of isolated German soldiers who were attempting to cross back through the lines. It is interesting to note that these two groups of isolated but motivated Germans were not members of *Reserve Division 148*, but members of non-reserve units who had gotten lost within *Reserve Division 148*'s zone. The six men who were killed (one in Thorenc and five in Tourette du Château) were all born in Germany proper, unlike many of the men of *Reserve Division 148*, who were born in Silesia or the Sudetenland. The contrast between the actions of these *Reichsdeutscher* who were willing to fight their way back to their lines and the *Volksdeutscher* of *Reserve Division 148*, who often surrendered in large numbers, is striking!

Advancing to the Italian Border

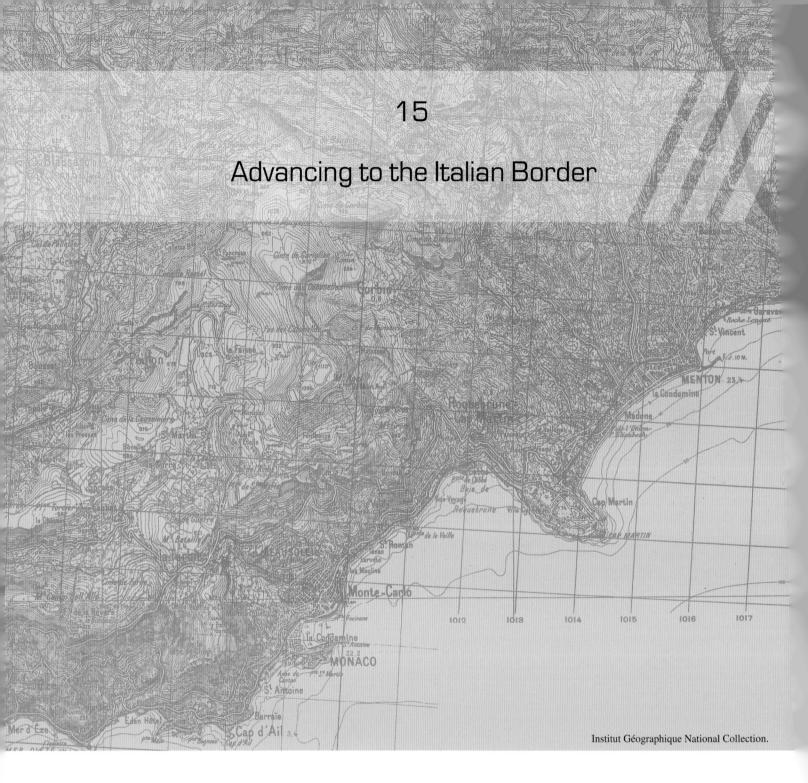

Institut Géographique National Collection.

We have now examined the Allied advance from the landing zones to Nice and Levens, as well as what occurred to the immediate north of the Allied front, in the zone under control of the Resistance. There remained one last stretch to be covered before reaching Menton and the Italian border. This last area to be liberated presented several characteristics that made it uninteresting to the Allied troops: it contained few strategic structures, it was dotted with dozens of Maginot Line forts built by the French to defend themselves from the Italians, and it was very mountainous, even along the coast, where the mountains rise steeply straight out of the sea. For several days, the First Airborne Task Force was therefore told to hold its positions and only send patrols forward before finally being ordered to advance to the Italian border.

This final advance will be more difficult to describe in an orderly manner than the previous advances, because it was made over a one week period, with the various FABTF and resistance units often operating in the same areas at different dates, making exact dates and zones of responsibility difficult to establish. Furthermore, we

will not be able to describe the advance till the end, because except at Menton, the FABTF and the units that later replaced it would not actually reach the Italian border for several more weeks, or even months. Indeed, the Italian border would only be entirely secured in late April 1945, more than seven months later. We are thus reaching the limits of the theme and the geographical area that this book is meant to cover: the rapid advance that liberated the French Riviera between August 15 and September 7, 1944. We will, however, do our best in the following chapter to describe what happened between these dates in the area included within the triangle formed by Nice, Menton, and Turini.

The Peille Insurrection

Before getting to the late August advance of the FABTF, we must first go back in time to mention a Resistance action that occurred in Peille long before the Allied troops reached Nice. Indeed, upon hearing of the Allied invasion August 15th, the local resistance triggered what would later be known as the "Peille Insurrection." Peille is a small and isolated mountain village located north of Monaco. The town itself was not a very strategic position, but it could be used for launching attacks against important nearby roads and structures, such as the High Corniche or the Mont Agel Fort. Resistance fighter **André Laugier** wrote a detailed description of the insurrection, which lasted from August 15th to 20th, that gives interesting insight into the relations and dynamics that were at play between the civilians, *maquisard*s, Gendarmes, and the Germans and the Poles:

Maquisard Jean Miol, who was accidentally shot and mortally wounded in Peille August 16, 1944. In his arms he holds Marcel Brocart, the child of one of his friends. Marcel Brocart Collection.

The sound of intense and continuous shelling far away to the west lets us suspect that an Allied landing operation has occurred. Indeed, it was the Dramont landing. (…) In addition, echoes were reaching us: searches and arrests were being performed, men were being executed, as happened on that very day at l'Ariane. We thought: "We cannot remain inactive, we can wait no longer." (…)

It was thus on the afternoon of August 15th. To the great surprise of the villagers and of the holiday makers, who were very numerous at that time, the weapons and ammunition hidden in the village were pulled out of their dark hiding spots. This operation, which was instinctive to us, proved to be of severe consequence in the following hours; we had thrown away our masks in plain view of everyone. But the reaction of the population was that we expected. It joined us with enthusiasm. It made our spontaneous decisions its own, and our responsibilities, that were thus shared, were lighter for us to bear. What will follow is the description of a daring undertaking containing numerous risks. It was the open battle with the occupants, but also the fight of the clay pot against the iron pot. With the insight of time, we have realized the grave consequences that it could have had, but we will not dwell on that, as others have done so for us. What in our eyes was magnificent, and that deserves to be dwelled on, was the patriotic spirit that animated such an action. It was almost a saga; it was an entire village that wanted to contribute to the cause we were defending and that they had accepted, the liberation of France. (…)

First, combat groups were formed, and instructors were appointed to teach the working of foreign weapons, rifles, and submachine guns, and the use of grenades. It is during one of these teaching sessions that a terrible accident occurred. 25-year-old **Jean Miol** was in one group with his comrades, following the course at the Castellet district. August 16th, one of his comrades was manipulating a loaded weapon and the shot went off, hitting Miol in the abdomen. He was urgently transported to the Monaco Hospital, where he died August 20th. (…)

About 130 men were committed at Peille. The front to defend extended from the Col des Banquettes to the Col St Pancrace, separated from each other by about 10 kilometers, facing the German troops on the coast (Menton) and in the Mont Agel Fort. (…) Let us see one of the most daring and spectacular feats performed by one of our groups, made up of only five men: the attack of the cable car outpost servicing Mont Agel, in the Lacs district. The goal of this attack was to:
- sabotage the cable car
- capture the men on guard
- seize the stocks of food and material
- trigger the rebellion of the fort.

This rebellion was to occur on the very same day.

Indeed, the Mont Agel Fort was for a large part out-posted by Polish soldiers with whom a liaison had been established by two female agents. The rebellion had been prepared and the fort was to give itself up on the same day. In fact, eight Polish deserters had voluntarily come to the camp to help out.

Thus, on August 16th, four patriots from Peille under the command of Gendarme Muntzer, from la Turbie, who was a *maquisard*, and the Peille truck driver who put his vehicle at our disposal, reached the cable car outpost by truck, armed with rifles and grenades. Gendarme Muntzer (…), who speaks Polish, approaches the men on guard duty (three Poles), who let themselves be disarmed without any trouble. The supplies, weapons, and clothing are loaded into the truck at once. As the operation is ending, a truck of German soldiers unexpectedly arrives from la Turbie and causes our operation to fail. The Poles hesitate and don't move and our men open fire on the disoriented Germans, enabling our driver to start his truck while all manage to climb on. The Germans now also open fire, but the truck is already long gone. They hit neither our men nor the truck in any vital spots. Our men put three Germans out of action. August 16th, around 23:00, the Mont Agel Fort opens fire on Peille, shelling the village and the surrounding hilltops. In the face of the continuous shelling, the chiefs decide to evacuate the civilians out of the village, and they find shelter for the night in the houses in the surrounding countryside. (…)

As of then, the Germans will try to enter Peille with ever increasing numbers of men during the four following days: August 17th, 18th, 19th, and 20th. The chiefs in the village decide to stop them and ask for help from the Ongrand *maquis*. (…) August 17th, the Ongrand *maquis*, which has been reinforced by the Sospel Gendarmerie Brigade and its commander, Adjudant Bertrem, left its campground to come and join us. We then felt stronger, our hearts united, each of us engaged in this uniformless army with a single goal: to hit the already staggering enemy hard. Yet others came to join us, holiday makers, external elements who had heard about our undertaking, the whole population was giving us assistance. (…) The combat positions and observation outposts had been well chosen and they accomplished their mission day and night. In the afternoon of August 17th, a German patrol coming towards our village appeared at Col St Pancrace. It had the honor of receiving the bursts of our machine guns positioned at la Tour and at le Castelet. It was saved only by the presence of the nearby tunnel.

These events clearly showed that the fight was going to intensify, and with it our responsibilities and needs. In particular, we needed milk for the kids and the elders in the hospice. Luckily, a few farmers could furnish it to us. One of our men was tasked with picking up milk every morning. One day, a serious adventure happened to him. As he was picking up the milk in the Lacs district, he was arrested by the Germans and brought to the *Kommandantur* in Menton. He was questioned and interrogated, then released the next day at la Turbie, carrying a message from the Germans that he was to pass onto us and that can be resumed in the following way: German troops would attempt to enter Peille the morning of August 19th. If a German soldier was killed, the village would be shelled and destroyed. It was serious and very important, but the messenger, frightened by the interrogation he had undergone and by the way events were turning out, panicked and did not immediately transfer the message to us. He only passed it on to us the next afternoon, through another person. We were not able to judge the seriousness of the situation at once, and had not been able to discuss what decisions should be taken. It was too late, and the events that followed proved so.

Indeed, following the *Kommandantur's* plan, on August 19th, about 40 Germans appeared in a skirmish line in the St Pancrace district. Our outpost pointed its machine guns, and with heavy fire that was answered by the enemy, forced them to turn back, bringing their wounded with them. The action had comforted our valorous fighters, but the Germans held their promise, and following the decision that they had transmitted to us, half an hour later, they sprayed our village with a few shells from the Mont Agel Fort. (…) Following this shelling, the few people who had not evacuated the village in spite of our orders were forced to do so. This decision was a mortal wound that struck us right in the heart, but safety compelled it, and it needed to be obeyed. (…) The night thus ended with the complete evacuation of the village. Only our headquarters and the men who were fulfilling important tasks stayed behind. (…)

August 20th, we found out that the Col des Banquettes, which was held by the Ongrand *maquisards*, was being attacked in force. This offensive seemed to combine with the one that was profiling itself at St Pancrace, and we were worried that the enemy might also appear at Col de la Madone. A threat of encirclement was taking shape. The outpost at les Banquettes, commanded by Camp Chief Albert, was thus attacked first around five o'clock in the morning. He opened fire at the Germans, but the machine gun unfortunately jammed, enabling the enemy to momentarily reduce our resistance. One of our men, Gendarme **Henri Drevon**, and another fighter were wounded. Considering the length of the front, no group was able to go to the help of the threatened outpost, but Camp Chief Albert, who was commanding the defense of the position, directed the retreat of his men with admirable coolness and asked for reinforcements from Peille. With the help of Italian Captain Gino, who was a member of the camp, he prevented the Germans from forcing their way

along the road leading to Peille. Around noon, a reinforcement of six men arrived and a new resistance position was set up. It must be noted that the retreat order did not reach this group, which held its position the whole night and part of the morning of August 21st. This shows their tenacity and their will to resist to the end. The morning of the 21st, Camp Chief Albert discovered the horribly wounded body of Gendarme Drevon [Drevon had been wounded in the jaw].

Also on August 20th, around 12:30, the St Pancrace outpost was attacked in force. It was only after having used up its ammunition and having inflicted casualties on the attackers, and in the face of the numerical superiority of the enemy, who disposed of armored vehicles, that this outpost commanded by Gendarme Yves was obliged to retreat to Peille. (…) At 13:00, the infiltration of numerous groups of Germans continued in the direction of Peille. The shelling of our positions and of the village by the Mont Agel Fort continued and intensified. It became clear to our command that the fight was disproportionate and that the sacrifice of our men would be vain.

The retreat order was thus given at 15:00. It was to be made in the direction of the *maquisard's* camp, but since it had been spotted and shelled by the Mont Agel Fort, it was decided to continue the retreat through the mountains towards Peira Cava. Since some elements had gotten lost, we were only able to regroup completely in the following days. Our last men had thus left after having loaded the equipment and documents of our command post onto a small truck. They were driving towards the Route des Banquettes when they were surprised by gunfire coming from Col St Pancrace. During the fire fight, one of our main leaders, François Ricuort, was grievously wounded in the thigh by a bullet. We had left the village, our brave adventure was ending. It had lasted five days.[1]

The Germans were then able to enter the village without further incident. In total, two *maquisards* had been killed, including one who was accidentally shot by his friends: they were Jean Miol and Henri Drevon, age 25 and 26. A third *maquisard*, Gendarme **Jean Desclair**, age 33, was reported missing in unclear circumstances

The Peillon Bridge, which the Resistance fighters blew before leaving in order to hinder the Germans in their future retreat. It has remained untouched since the war. Author's Collection.

and was probably also killed. The Germans do not seem to have lost any men, as no corresponding bodies were buried anywhere nearby, including at the Caucade Cemetery in Nice. Although the term "insurrection" slightly exaggerates the actual importance that the *maquisard* action had, it did undoubtedly hinder the Germans and showed that the French had not lost their fighting spirit and were ready to take huge risks to help the Allied cause. The symbolic value of this operation was perhaps more important than its military value.

The Allied Advance from August 31 to September 7, 1944

We now return to August 30th, when the First Airborne Task Force troops victoriously entered Nice after the town's insurrection had successfully driven the last German soldiers out. The next day, August 31st, the FABTF sent its troops out towards the east and northeast in order to secure the newly captured ground on the east side of the Var, then it ceased advancing for several days, with the following order being issued:

> Establish main defensive position on line now held. Maintain contact with enemy by aggressive patrol action. Establish outposts well forward of main defensive position to prevent enemy movement in our direction.[2]

There was thus a lull in the fighting between approximately September 1st and September 5th, during which time the action consisted mainly of patrols, artillery duels, and laying or clearing minefields. The events of this period are complicated by the fact that on September 3rd, the areas of responsibility assigned to each of units of the FABTF were changed. Since August 20th, the 509th and 551st Parachute Infantry Battalions had been on the right flank

of the FABTF, following the coast; the First Special Service Force had been in the center; and the 517th Parachute Regimental Combat Team had been on the left flank. September 3rd, the 509th and 551st were ordered to move far into the mountains to the north of Nice to the Italian border area, where the Germans and partisans had been skirmishing for several days. The FSSF was to move south to fill in the gap left by these units at the coast, and the 517th was to fill in the gap left in the northern FSSF sector. The FSSF thus found itself on the right flank, the 517th in the center, and the 509th and 551st on the left. This caused some confusion (and had some serious consequences) at the time and will do the same in this text.

We will first examine the advance along the coast, all the way to the Italian border and Menton. Then we will describe the advance into the mountains towards Turini, and we will finish the chapter with the advance towards Col de Braus, a strategic mountain pass overlooking Sospel from the west.

The 551st Parachute Infantry Battalion's Patrol to la Turbie

August 31st, A Company of the 551st PIB sent a small patrol down the Grand Corniche towards the town of la Turbie, located on the top of a crest between Peille and Monaco. La Turbie was occupied by German soldiers of *Reserve Grenadier Bataillon 7*, as was planned in the August 28th orders that *Oberstleutnant* Niedlich had been captured with in Nice. **Cpl Joe Cicchinelli**, who was acting as a scout, would remember this patrol for the rest of his life:

> Just before we got to the la Turbie area there was this fortress you could see up on the mountain. [This was Fort de le Tête de Chien, in la Turbie, which overlooked Monaco and the surrounding coast.] At this time I was on the road; we were a seven man patrol and I was the scout. Sgt Anderson was also on that patrol, and Bud Hook, Virgil Dorr, and Lou Waters. I called back to Lt Luenning for the binoculars so I could get a better look at that fortress, and I got them and was looking up there, and damned if I don't see this German up there looking down at me through his binoculars. Then he starts running back up the side of the fort, so I shouted at the men to get off the road.[3]
>
> Soon after the enemy started to shell us along the hillside with artillery fire. We continued on towards la

"Champagne Campaign": shortly after the Liberation of Nice, men of the 602nd PFAB relax and swim in the luxurious Château de Crémat, in the hills north of town. Art Helmers Collection.

A rare period color photo of la Turbie, taken from the road on which the patrol of paratroopers of the 551st PIB approached the town. The Germans had prepared a small machine gun nest overlooking the road on the hill visible at the extreme left of this picture. The Tête de Chien Fort mentioned by Joe Cicchinelli was built on the hill to the right of the picture. Ted Rulison Collection.

Turbie. I came upon a house. The area was very quiet. I knocked on the door of the house very hard with my rifle butt. This Frenchman came to the door. He was very startled to see me, for he did not know who I was and I did not look like a Nazi. I told this Frenchman, who was Charles Calori, that I was an American, and that my mother and father were Italian and we Americans were here for information on the Nazis. In the house with Charles were his mother, father, and two children. We were invited into the house. Our mission to la Turbie was to first gather information on the German soldiers (how many), where were all emplacements, artillery, machine guns, and any information we could locate on how strong the Nazis were in la Turbie. All six men were in and out of the house of Calori, looking over the area of la Turbie. Calori's home was on the side of a hill, from which we could look down onto la Turbie. Lt Luenning, Sgt Anderson, and the rest of us were quietly listening to Charles Calori. Charles was telling us there were many installations that Nazis were at. Also, on the hill facing Charles' home, looking towards the city of la Turbie, was a machine gun nest with German soldiers looking over the valley toward the road to Nice. (…) We asked Lt Luenning to let us go and get the machine gun and put the gun and Nazis out of action. He said no: "We have enough information now to return back to Nice and report our information to our headquarters." Charles Calori gave us some wine and again, we asked Lt Luenning to let us go and machine gun the Nazis. We were tired and angry at the Germans for bombing and shelling us and we wanted to get even with the Germans. The Lieutenant then said: "OK, let's go." This brave man, Charles Calori, then led our patrol down the hill to la Turbie and then up the mountain side.[4]

PFC Lou Waters was also on the patrol and later wrote in a letter to Cicchinelli:

We moved in over the hills west of town and came up behind the Frenchman's house, a big stucco and stone building that, along with the shrubbery and trees, effectively concealed our approach from the Krauts. When we were inside, the Frenchman, who was a young, small man in plain white shirt and pants, told us the town was crawling with Krauts and all the local citizens had been warned to stay inside and keep out of sight. There were two old people and two young kids in the house with him. They were his mother and dad, and the kids were his. His wife was in Nice and couldn't get back home because of the German curfew law or something like that.

Anyway, we all proceeded to get half-tanked on the *vino* he served, and when he told us he knew where the Krauts had set up a machine gun nest, Lt Luenning decided to check it out. The Frenchman leading the way (like a white flag waving in a coal yard to my mind), we sneaked along in single file behind the houses lining the road and approached the town. Andy (Sgt Anderson) led. I followed him, and I had a grenade launcher on my M-1 and a grenade already on it, with the pin in. I was the only man in the squad with a launcher. Meyers and O'Dell didn't have their machine gun, and nobody had any ammunition for one anyway.[5]

We will now see the arrival of the paratroopers from **Charles Calori**'s point of view:

The Fort de la Tête de Chien was a French-built Maginot Line fort that was taken over and occupied by the Germans. Mike Reuter Collection.

1944, my family and myself were in no man's land, in other words, between the Americans and the Germans who were holding the village of la Turbie. We had taken refuge in the basement of my parents' villa and had heard some footsteps outside. I went up, opened the shutters of my terrace, and found myself facing a soldier, who told me: "Rome, Rome, I am American soldier. I am, my name is Cicchinelli." That is how I met Cicchinelli. He brought in his five comrades, so there were six of them altogether, and we installed ourselves in the back of the house for a while, because we were receiving fire from the Germans at the Tête de Chien Fort. The lieutenant wanted to go back to Nice, but the others said: "No, no, we absolutely have to see what is going on in the village," because they considered that the Germans had disrespected them or something like that. At that moment they asked me if I wanted to accompany them, which I accepted.

We left the house and went down. To advance, we used the holes that had been dug along the road by the German troops, which were about 50 meters apart from each other. I was in the lead with the six paratroopers behind me. We jumped from one hole to the next, and extraordinarily, we managed to get past the intersection of the Laghet to la Trinité road without being spotted. I never understood: the Germans should have shot at us, because the view from their position was absolutely perfect, but they didn't shoot. At that point, we took the path that goes up to the top of the hill where the German soldiers were outposted. We had to walk about 350 meters up the hill, and we reached a wall that was about five meters high. The Germans didn't see us;

they were calm and didn't hear that we were there, flattened against the wall. I don't know what was going on. Where they sleeping? That is also possible. Then the Americans threw some grenades and killed three Germans. The guys were totally surprised in an extraordinary manner.

Lou Waters wrote on in his letter to Cicchinelli:

The moment we confronted the Krauts at that emplacement (…) is etched on my mind in blood and fire. I can never forget it, mainly I suppose because it was our so-called "baptism of fire," our first face to face encounter. Suddenly, my mind was jarred back to reality from the hypnotic effect of watching Andy's butt move in front of me, by a scrabbling sound and a flash of white bobbing off to my left, like the white tail of a flushed rabbit. It was the Frenchman diving off to the side, seeking cover. At the same time, Sgt Andy, who had just hauled himself up a terrace and was struggling to his feet on top, let out a bellow like a wounded buffalo: "Here they are!" He raised his rifle up over his head with one hand, pointing excitedly with the other, and he looked just like a statue of a WWI hero in a park in my home town.

I got my head above the embankment just in time to see Andy pump all eight rounds from his clip into a Kraut standing open-mouthed not more than seven or eight yards in front of him. The Kraut was unarmed, and it looked to me like he was trying to raise his hands in surrender. Another Kraut was high-tailing it around that ramshackle little hut they were using for concealment. It was so close that if I had fired my grenade at the hut I'm certain it would have killed Andy. I pulled the pin and got ready to fire, but by that time Andy had shoved a new clip in his gun (I can still hear the "ping" as his first one ejected) and was charging forward, followed by Meyers and the others of the squad who had charged past me, all yelling like banshees from hell!

I couldn't fire that grenade without doing more harm to us than to the Krauts, so I ripped it off my launcher and hurled it as far down the hill as I could. Then I joined the charging squad going up just behind Lt Luenning. (…) I withheld fire, not having any targets to shoot at, and the patrol was running around the shack like Indians, firing into it and, I suppose, after the fleeing Krauts. You [Cicchinelli] were just getting ready to go in the door of the shack, screaming like a mad lion, when I grabbed your arm and (recalling basic training) yelled that we should throw in some grenades. You and I then both proceeded to pull our grenade pins, you screamed (and I screamed) "Hold your fire!" to the guys shooting into the shack, and you drew back your foot and kicked the door open. We dropped down and rolled those grenades into the shack, you rolling yours to the left and I rolling mine to the right, and bit dirt, waiting for them to go off.

No sooner had we rolled them in, however, than Sgt Andy came tearing up and was going to charge right in after them. (…) We yelled: "Grenades! Grenades! Get down!" and reached up and hauled him down by his belt and the seat of his pants. I heard somebody swear and yell: "Grenades! Get down!" on the other side of the shack. At the same time as Andy's butt hit the ground, both those grenades went off, not more than ten or twelve feet from us. You and I went tearing in there, firing from the hip as we

The last terrace before reaching the French Army hut that the German machine gunners were quartered in. Author's Collection.

went. The guys outside (our guys) must have thought there were Krauts inside firing at them, so some of them started firing into the shack again.

There was a flimsy partition down the middle inside, I think the whole thing must have been put together out of packing boxes. As I recall, there was a Kraut on your side that had been killed by the grenades and he looked like a bloody pile of old rags. On my side of the partition there was nobody, but I went in firing from the hip and came damn near to fainting dead away when, after my first round, the bolt on my M-1 jammed open. It was that damned M-3 rifle grenade cartridge, it had jammed my bolt open and I stood there pulling the trigger and nothing was happening. I had ball ammo in my clip under the M-3 cartridge, and finally, in sheer desperation, I set the butt down on the floor and kicked the activation rod with my foot to free it.

Then I noticed a window at the back. I knocked it out some, stepped back, and ran right through it, landing outside on the back of a dying Kraut machine gunner. Andy or someone had filled him full of lead and his blood was flowing out of him and running down a little rain ditch the Krauts had dug around the place. There was an air-cooled Kraut machine gun there, and to this day I can't think of a good reason why we didn't take it with us.

The Kraut had a P-38 pistol in a holster on his belt so I confiscated that, shoved it inside my shirt and ran back around the front of the shack. By this time I had heard Lt Luenning hollering "Cease Fire!" and the shooting had died away to a few scattered "pops." When it stopped, we all gathered in a group and sat down in front of the shack. Reaction was setting in, and we were all either red faced or white faced and puffing like steam engines from the effort and excitement. I can still see Sgt Andy dancing up and down like a little boy and grinning from ear to ear. He kept saying: "I got two of 'em!"

I gave Andy the P-38 I had taken from the Kraut gunner. I felt guilty as hell for not having killed any Krauts myself. We were all just sitting there, trying to put together what had happened, when a Kraut mortar round landed up on the next terrace just behind us. Someone said: "Let's get the hell out of here," and we all went bounding down the terraces like so many scattered quail, with Luenning yelling and trying to restore order. That's when Hook caught his foot in a grape vine and pitched down a terrace, badly spraining his knee and ankle. Would you believe it? Out of all that shooting, out of and through that flimsy old shack, no one got hit, even with the grenades.[6]

It must be remembered that the 551st PIB was a "green" unit, having only been in combat since the afternoon of August 15, 1944. **Joe Cicchinelli** also wrote a very detailed account of the gunfight (parts of which may have been influenced by Lou Waters' letter to him):

High on the hill, Sgt Anderson then spotted the Nazi at the house with the machine gun. The sergeant hollered: "Here they are" and started shooting. All of us surrounded the house and were shooting. Lou Waters and I were then at the front door of the house. I kicked in the front door and Lou threw a grenade on the right side. I threw a grenade at the left side. Just then the sergeant, seeing the door open, started to go in the house. I grabbed the sergeant by the back of his trousers and pulled him back and closed the door. The grenade then exploded. Lou rushed inside the house and started shooting on the right and I rushed inside and started shooting on the left side. Then we went out and around the building, and I shot a German in the back of the house. Lou's rifle then jammed. Behind the house there were three dead Nazis. Lou said there were two more dead Nazis inside the house that we had gotten with our hand grenades.[7]

In fact, only three Germans had been killed, not five. In another account made at a later date, **Joe Cicchinelli** added a grisly detail that he had preferred not to mention previously:

Behind the house there were three Germans: two were dead and another was seriously wounded. Part of his brain was coming out of his skull, but he was still breathing. I shot a bullet into his heart, probably to spare him too much suffering. I searched the pockets of their uniforms. In one of them I found a small folding knife that I kept and sent home.[8]

When searching the dead Germans, Joe Cicchinelli also found three identity photos that he kept as souvenirs for the rest of his life. Though this may seem shockingly morbid to some, it was actually common for soldiers to keep personal items of enemy soldiers that they had killed. Furthermore, these photos provide precious information about the Germans who had been killed, as we will see later. **Charles Calori** remembers the aftermath of the fire fight:

The Americans went around the house and climbed a bit further up the hill to see if any Germans had gotten away, but it wasn't possible. In fact, they picked up the photos of the three guys that had been killed. I don't know if they were even Germans; I wonder if they may have been Czech or something like that.

At that moment the Germans at the Tête de Chien started reacting and opened fire on us. We waited for nightfall to go back down. We crossed through the yards of the houses, cutting through the fences with big wire cutters. The Americans came with me back to my parents' house. They left two soldiers for security, because they were afraid

of a German reprisal. So we stayed with the two American soldiers the whole night, and I asked that my parents be taken down to Nice to avoid any trouble. I stayed there with the Americans, who kept on firing at la Turbie.

Joe Cicchinelli remembered a slightly different version of the retreat off the hill:

Now we were all very tired. Then, a German shell exploded just behind the house where we were at and I hollered: "Let's get the hell out of here." The Germans didn't even know whether their men were alive or dead, and already they were shelling us at their own machine gun emplacement. We all started jumping down the terraces, which were six to seven feet high. (…) I thought we would never get to the bottom of the hillside. It was a good thing we were young and in very good physical health. (…) The Germans were shooting and shelling us. Lt Luenning was wounded across his knee and one man, Pvt Hook, caught his leg in a grape vine and twisted his ankle and knee. At the bottom of the hill we found some relief and cover from the shelling. This was early in the afternoon. We could go no further, for the shooting and shelling were too much for us. We then had to wait until night time and darkness before we could try and escape back to Nice and our 551st Parachute Infantry Battalion and headquarters. (…) The firing had quieted down and the Germans could not see us. It was now dark, maybe 10 or 11 p.m. Lt Luenning, Sgt Anderson, Pvt Dorr, and I had started to sneak out of la Turbie and return to Nice. Pvt Hook and Pvt Waters, with Charles Calori, stayed behind because Pvt Hook's ankle and knee were in bad shape and he could not walk. We had to leave Waters, Hook, and Calori behind. Pvt Waters volunteered to stay with Hook. We could now return back to Nice with all the information we had gathered. (…) The following morning, after daybreak, Waters and Hook returned to Nice and our Company A, 551st Parachute Infantry Battalion.[9]

The three German soldiers (all of whom were born in Silesia) of *Reserve Grenadier Bataillon 7* who had been killed in this encounter in la Turbie on August 31st were:

Surname	Name	Rank	Age	Date of death	Location of death	Unit
Hoffmann	Gerhard	Gren	17	31.08.1944	La Turbie	
Weidlich	Herbert	Uffz	29	31.08.1944	La Turbie	1./Res.Gren. Btl.7
Wittig	Eberhard	Gren	17	31.08.1944	La Turbie	4./Res.Gren. Btl.7

It is a bit surprising that these three men were on their own on the hill outside la Turbie with no backup nearby, but such seems to have been the case. Their position was probably considered to be an advanced outpost, and it would seem that no German troops even returned to the location of the fight to investigate what had happened to them (probably because they were too frightened), as all three men were later listed as missing in action. It was only when the bodies were exhumed in 1958 that their deaths could be confirmed to their families. In the meantime, the names of all three men had been included in the German Red Cross list of missing in action

Three identity pictures that Joe Cicchinelli found on the bodies of the German soldiers that were killed above la Turbie. Gerhard Hoffmann is recognizable on the left, as is Eberhard Wittig in the center. It is not known who the third soldier is, but he apparently was not killed at la Turbie. Perhaps he was a friend or family member of one of the other two? Joe Cicchinelli Collection, courtesy Pascal Hainaut.

17-year-old Grenadiers Gerhard Hoffmann and Eberhard Wittig, of Bataillon 7, who were both killed by the paratroopers at la Turbie, along with Unteroffizier Herbert Weidlich. Hoffmann Family Collection. Deutches Rote Kreutz Collection.

A few days after the deadly ambush, French army photographers took this shot showing Charles Calori at the Col d'Eze, guiding a group of paratroopers towards la Turbie. ECPAD/France/Jacques Belin. Author's Collection.

soldiers, as well as a photo of Eberhard Wittig. When this picture is compared with the tree photos that Joe Cicchinelli picked off the bodies, Eberhard Wittig can be recognized in the center picture, looking a bit older then in his photo as a civilian from the Red Cross list. A photo of Gerhard Hoffmann provided by his family enables us to recognize him on the left in Cicchinelli's photos. It is not known who is in Cicchinelli's third photo; it does not seem to be 29-year-old Herbert Weidlich, as the man in the picture appears to be much too young. Perhaps the third picture shows a family member of either Wittig or Hoffmann?

The three pictures that Joe Cicchinelli took from the bodies and preserved provide a powerful and chilling link between the gung ho recollections of the American patrol members and the tragic destiny of three German soldiers whose fate remained unknown to their families for 15 years. Joe Cicchinelli returned to la Turbie many times after the war to meet Charles Calori and the thankful inhabitants of the town. The patrol had been one of the founding events of Joe Cicchinelli's wartime experiences.

Although the Allied commanders had decided not to advance for a few days, the relatively "green" troops of the 551st were eager to become as battle hardened as their brothers of the 509th, as Cicchinelli's patrol had been. **SSgt Joe Kosowski**, of B Company of the 551st, remembered:

Joe Cicchinelli visits la Turbie in 2010. His guide and friend Charles Calori stands near him, holding the folded American flag. Author's Collection.

1st Sgt Tom Thornton was wanting to get into some action, so Capt Evans gave him permission to take a patrol out, but no rifle fire. He was just supposed to locate the enemy and report back. So the whole platoon went out, 20 odd men. I think Thornton had it in mind that he was going to get into a fire fight somewhere along the line. We were walking along this trail above Monte-Carlo and there was this hairpin turn, and as we came around the point we were facing a German field piece. They could have wiped us out if they wanted to, but there were no German officers present and the soldiers wanted to surrender. They were on and around the gun and waving their white flag, so we came up there and spiked the gun. They then showed us where their officers were and there were some grenades tossed, and I think that's when Tom got hit. We cleaned house, went back and blew up the gun with a demolition charge that was right on it, and took three or four prisoners. Tom was happy, he had gotten into a fire fight.[10]

About such prisoners, the unit history noted: "Prisoners were still predominantly of Polish extraction, their morale very low, desertion rate very high, and supplies quite limited."[11] Meanwhile, slightly north of the 551st sector, the FSSF and its supporting units were patrolling in the vicinity of Peille. The low-scale patrol warfare that was going on led to some unexpected encounters, as soldiers from each side ventured through vast expanses of deserted mountains. Such was the case of **Lt George Parnell**, of the 887th Airborne Engineer Company, on September 2nd, who wrote in a letter home September 5th:

Trying to keep a division moving really takes one's imagination and endurance. So far I've managed to stay right with the forward elements – often ahead of them. I went out on a road reconnaissance far ahead of our front lines, and as I sailed blissfully but apprehensively along the highway I rounded a turn and ran smack into two German pillboxes – one on either side of the road. It was only about 20 feet from where I stopped. Mines were stretched across the road between the concrete emplacements. Fortunately we took the Germans completely by surprise. The way they had demolished the roads and bridges – they never expected a vehicle. Three Germans came out from behind the emplacements and the surprised look on their faces was funny to behold – now. We opened up with all we had

(a 30 cal. machine gun and rifle), and at the same time, I slammed poor little Beatrice [Lt Parnell's jeep, which he had named after his wife.] into reverse and she took off like a frightened rabbit.[12]

September 3rd, a patrol from the 551st found that the Germans had evacuated la Turbie of their own will, and the town was thus occupied by members of both the 551st and 509th. Presumably, the Germans had been ordered to retreat back to the Italian border, which was to become their definite line of resistance. The next morning, both parachute battalions were relieved by the FSSF following the

At the Tête de Chien Fort, SSgt Elvis B. McCullough and PFC Howard J. Maxwell have found a more solid roof than their usual hand-dug foxholes. Mike Reuter Collection.

After the German retreat out of la Turbie, paratroopers of B Company of the 509th occupy the Fort de la Tête de Chien. Standing in front of a German swastika symbol that has been sprayed with bullets are Sgt Jim Nunn, Pvt H. Steele, and Pvt Robert N. Powell. Mike Reuter Collection.

Cpl Nick Nagurne. Mike Reuter Collection.

change of zones of responsibilities ordered by FABTF headquarters. Neither unit had suffered any dead while operating in the coastal area east of Nice.

Monaco and Its Surroundings

While the 551st PIB and some of the 509th PIB had been active in the la Turbie and Grande Corniche area, C Company of the 509th had occupied Beaulieu, and from there had patrolled along the seaside and Lower Corniche. Here the situation was complicated by the fact that Monaco was a neutral country, and that the Allied troops

Privates Clifton R. Mullen and Justus F. Patrick dress up in an oversized pair of woman's panties that were reportedly found in the quarters of the German commander of the Tête de Chien Fort. Mike Reuter Collection.

were therefore not to enter it. There was little action, though the Allied navy made life miserable for the Germans. Local 16-year-old **Joseph Vivalda**, from Beausoleil, remembered:

There was a cruiser, the *Emil Bertin*, that was shelling the Hotel Vistaero, where there was a German mortar position. They fired and pounded, making fireworks. Later they found a dead German [*Grenadier* **Joseph Eckmeier**] in the hotel and that was it. The Mont Agel Fort fired back at the ship, and the ship would hide under a cloud of artificial smoke to escape.

September 3rd, a C Company patrol under Captain Walls finally pushed forward towards Monaco in retaliation to some German shelling. The patrol was accompanied by the resistance men of *Companie Cyrano* and ended up advancing much further than planned, as **Captain Jessie Walls** remembered:

In Cap d'Ail my plan was to follow the orders of Lt Col William P. Yarborough. When the problem of mortar casualties occurred in the 2nd Platoon, I planned to drive the German forces back out of observation of activities in the rear area of the company. When Company C was fully committed, I still planned to stop the advance west of the Monaco border. But there were no boundary markers on the frontier and so no manner to determine exactly where we were. After some time, once the German defenses in Cap d'Ail were broken, it was obvious to me that we had driven the German forces inside Monaco, but by then there was no way we could break contact and withdraw. We could either disengage and retire, hold where we were, or continue the attack. We were doing well with the attack, with the assistance of Company Cyrano and the British cruiser offshore.

With the information supplied by Company Cyrano, the attack picked up speed. Meanwhile, there had been practically no injuries to civilians in the zone. I had exceeded the orders I had been given, so I decided to continue the attack and drive the Germans out of Monaco. Events proved in the end that I was correct in this judgment. Company C experienced only light casualties during the operation, thanks to the enemy information supplied by Company Cyrano and the support of the British cruiser. (…) Then we started to wonder how I was going to clear

September 3, 1944, the 509th and 551st PIBs are pulled off the front in order to be redeployed in the mountains north of Levens. Here men from B Company of the 509th await their transportation. Mike Reuter Collection.

This photo snapped secretly by Raymond Gastaud at 15:00 on September 2nd shows a German truck evacuating Monaco. Raymond Gastaud Collection, courtesy Serge Klarsfeld, all rights reserved.

American paratroopers of the 509th PIB "retreat" out of Monaco, which was considered a neutral state. Raymond Gastaud Collection, courtesy Serge Klarsfeld, all rights reserved.

myself with Colonel Yarborough, since I was obviously in a place I wasn't supposed to be in.[13]

According to Captain Walls, he then requested and was given a letter by Prince Louis II of Monaco in order to clear himself in the eyes of his superior. No paratroopers of the 509th had been killed during this period. Beausoleil teenager **Joseph Vivalda** describes the atmosphere in the Monaco area September 3rd or 4th:

On that day, we were waiting for the Americans. They were coming and coming, but never arriving! I took my things and left down *Route Nationale 7* and reached Cap d'Ail. It was mined everywhere, anti-tank mines this big. I was walking on the edge of the sidewalk: mines, mines, mines everywhere and the death head: "Achtung Minen." The houses were all half smashed because the English warships had fired during the night. In front of the Cap d'Ail church there was a human foot, naked and purple, but with no blood.

Then I climbed up towards Cap d'Ail, and there was an American on the sidewalk. That is when I fell in love! He was beautiful! He had the Canada-U.S. badge, and he was a Canadian paratrooper in the American Army. Damn, when he walked, the shoes didn't make any noise. He came and offered me a cigarette, a Camel. Oh! And chewing gum and candies! So I said: "I am going up." He made me understand to be careful because of the mines and I went to Villa Edmond. There was a parking lot there that was full of paratroopers. Two German prisoners of war with a stretcher were carrying an old lady who was smashed up and a paratrooper was following them. They must have been going to a dressing station. That was the Liberation and the first American.

Maybe one or two hours earlier, the Beausoleil *maquisard*s had blown up on a mine on the Moyenne Corniche. They were all in a car, and just like me, were going to see the Americans. They drove over the mine, blew up, and were all killed. And on the same day, at St

Roman, at the border between Monaco and Roquebrune, a guy with a pick axe wanted to defuse something and there were 11 killed! One woman who was killed was called Madame Fassone and she was pregnant. She blew up with a whole crowd. I saw the coffins that they were bringing to the Monaco morgue and there was still blood dribbling out of the wooden boxes.

One woman named **Anna Bosio** was killed by a shell at Beausoleil the same day. Eight men had died in the car that drove over a mine on the Moyenne Corniche at Beausoleil, they were:

Surname	Name	Age	Date of death	Location of Death	Cause of death
Ardisson	Marcel	39	3.9.1944	Beausoleil	Mine
Ferrua	Maurice	30	3.9.1944	Beausoleil	Mine
Panza	Jean	27	3.9.1944	Beausoleil	Mine
Ruppe	Emil	36	3.9.1944	Beausoleil	Mine
Selvetti	Armand	31	3.9.1944	Beausoleil	Mine
Scorpioni	Italo	20	3.9.1944	Beausoleil	Mine
Vada	Paul	22	3.9.1944	Beausoleil	Mine
Zelioli	Joseph	27	3.9.1944	Beausoleil	Mine

During the fighting, three Germans had also been killed in the vicinity of Monaco before the 509th PIB was relieved by the FSSF the morning of September 4th. These three German casualties were:

Surname	Name	Rank	Age	Date of death	Location of burial	Unit
Fluder	Eduard	Gren	17	2.9.1944	Cap d'Ail	
Goletz	Stefan	Gren	23	2.9.1944	Cap d'Ail	Res.Inf.Pz.Jag. Kp.Reg.8
Grohmann	Ottokar	Gren	18	2.9.1944	Roquebrune	

The Mont Agel Fort and the Final Advance to Menton

By September 3rd, the 551st and 509th PIBs had advanced to la Turbie and Monaco. There had been little fighting, and the main trigger of their advance seems to have been the German retreat. Now, however, both units were ordered to move to the Puget-Théniers area, in the northern Var Valley. They left September 4th, and would later take up positions in the small mountain villages near the Italian border in the northern Maritime Alps. The void left by the departure of these units at the coast was filled by the FSSF. Several towns were thus "reliberated" by the FSSF, leading to some postwar disputes between veterans of the various units about who had liberated what towns. It would seem that once the rearrangement of the FABTF units was made, they were ordered to advance to the Italian border, and not just to send out patrols as previously.

The confusion caused by the interchanging of the Allied units, as well as their reluctance to advance during the period, gave a chance for resistance units to "show their stuff." This was particularly the case at the Mont Agel Fort. Though the 551st PIB had occupied the village of la Turbie on September 3rd, it had not ventured into the impressive

Mont Agel Fort that dominated the town, as well as the entire French Riviera. The paratroopers only noted before being relieved that, "It was definitely established that the fort was held by only a very small force, probably not exceeding a platoon."[14] During the first days of September, the *maquisard*s thus sent several patrols up the steep hill to the fort to see what was going on. One of these patrols was performed by *Groupe Hochcorn*, which mostly consisted of Marseille firemen and of all the fit males of a village named Montclar that had been mobilized by an energetic resistance leader. **Louis Fiori**, who had previously fought around Carros, was on the patrol and later wrote:

It happened at the very beginning of September, on the 1st or 2nd, I believe [Actually September 5th]. With *Groupe Hochcorn*, we had reached la Turbie, which had just been liberated during the night. Mont Agel and Roquebrune Cap Martin were still occupied by the Germans, and we were to make a reconnaissance towards Mont Agel.

At sunrise, after having followed the *Route Nationale* for a while, we take a quite steep path, in single file, avoiding to make any rocks roll downhill. In silence, we pursue our climb until reaching a flat area, on which we discover a small house. While the group halts to catch its breath under the cliffs bordering the field, Tave Ferla and Jo Escudero (…) go to the house to speak with those living in it, who claim that there are no more Germans left in the area.

For more safety, the group leader designates a colleague and I to continue up the path in order to have a better view from higher up and be able to face any threats. My comrade, who has a pair of binoculars, takes the lead, and I follow him from about 20 meters back. He stops, observes the countryside, and suddenly comes back down towards me, saying: "The Germans are coming. I am quickly going to warn the others."

I climb up to where he had been, and at first sight do not notice anything abnormal. Lower down, I see that Tave has opened his bag and is handing a package of cigarettes to the man he was speaking to. Suddenly, gunfire bursts out and everything goes very fast. Tave is wounded and collapses. Jo drags him to a foxhole that the Germans had the habit of digging, and quickly going down the cliffs, rejoins the group that is down below. I later found out that he had told Tave: "Don't worry, we will come back to get you." But Tave, aware of the danger that his friends were risking to come and retrieve him, for the fire fight was continuing, decided after a few minutes that were as long as hours to come out of his hole. I see him stand up with difficulty and stagger towards the cliff. At that moment I notice that the back of his shirt is red with blood.

Tave lets himself slip and tumbles down to where the group is. Jo takes him on his shoulders, and with the help of Foli Mario (Vésubie) starts downhill. He advances carefully, slightly hunched down, and presents a formidable target. Some friends cover him and I am closing the march, with my eyes turned towards the skyline on the crest, where I cannot make out the silhouettes of any soldiers. So when I halt, I fire with rage on all the bushes up there that could be hiding somebody. We are soon out of reach of enemy fire for a terrain feature is hiding us, and we can walk faster. Other volunteers replace Jo, and when we reach la Turbie, Tave is transported to a hospital in Nice, still accompanied by Jo.[15]

Tave was back on foot soon enough and rejoined his resistance comrades, who in the meantime had become part of the regular

The Mont Agel Fort, which dominates the entire the French Riviera. Photo credit expansite.com.

French army. FFI **Captain Tilly** was in *Groupe Hochcorn* and wrote about what was apparently the very same patrol on Mont Agel:

September 5, 1944, the battalion is in la Turbie. The Germans are still holding Mont Agel, a huge barren wart that, with its fort at 1,100 meters, dominates the Monaco Principality (…). The entire battalion, flanked at its top by the Italian company of Captain Sorrentino, climbs up the sides of the mountain, at first against no resistance. My "Montclar draftees," apart from a young 18-year-old, refused to follow me. They say it is too dangerous! I still have my firemen with me. We find a few booby traps. Then shooting breaks out. Ferry's brother François is killed. There are two wounded and the battalion, which is not battle hardened, retreats in disorder. I try to cover this retreat, but do not see any enemy. Had we perhaps been trigger happy? We count each other once we get back. The young guy from Montclar is no longer with us! All my "Montclar enlistees" thus organize their own patrol to look for him, and in the end find their comrade!

On the night of September 5th, we must follow the Corniche road to Roquebrune and check if the Germans are still there. I participate in a large nighttime patrol that detects an antitank cannon in the sharp curve before Roquebrune. One of ours is a priest. We can see a peaceful German within firearm range. The priest whispers to me: "I will give him absolution, then I will shoot him." I dissuade him from doing so, telling him that the goal is only to bring back information. He is heartbroken!

Our pressure was not useless, as the next day the Germans evacuate Mont Agel and Roquebrune.[16]

Indeed, the Germans pulled out of Roquebrune and Menton the next day (though the "pressure" from the resistance probably had nothing to do with their retreat), and patrols from 2nd Regiment of the FSSF would find both towns deserted. September 6th, **Lt Bill Story**, of 4-2 of the FSSF, was ordered on another patrol up to Mont Agel Fort to check out what the situation there was. He set out in the late afternoon, later writing:

We were beginning to run into young French men with the *Maquis* or the FFI who were attaching themselves to us. I learned from John Dawson, a friend from 6-2, that several Forcemen were sent along with a large patrol of partisans to probe the defenses of Mt Agel. The partisans attacked and the entire group was greeted with mortar fire from the big border fort, which towered over Monte-Carlo.

It was evident the Germans, who had been back-peddling, had made a stop at Agel. Pat Harrison of 5th Company, 3rd Regiment, was ordered to take a look at Mt Agel and report back. He found the Germans had sewn the pathways with "shoe mines" (Shu-Minen) or "bouncing bettys." He lost his right hand aid to the mines.

I received orders to go up Mt Agel by an existing path which was visible on the map, but was not the main road up. So I assembled the platoon, told them we were going up to this big fort, and named Sgt Arthur Peaslee to be point. I don't suppose we had been on our way up more than ten minutes when Peaslee came running back toward me and asked to be relieved. Again, I had assumed the platoon members were more experienced than I was in conducting patrols. I was wrong. "Oh for Christ's sake," I said, "let's get going before we lose the light." Well, we made it to the path without incident. But the sun had gone down. We glanced into the fort's courtyard, with its gun ports. The gate was ajar. I was concerned that it might be booby-trapped. We had been sent up to see if the Germans had really left. I decided not to put the platoon in danger, but to see if we could get in the fort another way. Creeping alongside the wall, I noted that our shelling from the supporting naval vessels had knocked the wall down and that it had been rebuilt, but not cemented in place, leaving interstices between the rocks. I passed an order to the men to remove their bayonets so that we could use them as places to step upwards, and to unhook their rifle slings and make a "rope" of them. Then the most agile, it might have been Kures, the "Mad Russian," along with one other, took a supply of bayonets and the slings and stepped up the wall, hugging the stones until they got to the top. Then individual men followed up with the help of their own bayonets and the "sling" rope. All was quiet until Dewey's helmet cover fell off and went clatter bang down the slope. We waited. No sound. If anyone was in the fort, they hadn't heard us. We put the slings quietly back on the rifles, recovered what bayonets we could, and moved forward: 1st Section on the right, 2nd Section on the left.

We then proceeded until we came to the moat that separated the new fort from the old fort, and we were stymied. My sergeant, Daddy Bier, and I were wondering what the heck to do next, and then one of the fellows spotted a wooden footbridge across into the old fort. So we quickly took that and got in, and there wasn't anybody there. Not a soul. The Germans had pulled out the night before. I was concerned about that open gate that looked very inviting being booby-trapped, and sure enough, it was booby-trapped.

So then we stayed there 24 hours, and we exhausted our rations. We found some onions, and some other things, and the guys had fixed them up and added them to their rations. But before we got out, just as we were getting ready, somebody said: "Hey Lieutenant, Lieutenant, there is something down in the fort, the old fort." So I went over and listened, and sure enough, it sounded like a platoon of German soldiers were marching slowly up the ramp. There was a sergeant of mine getting more excited all the time, saying: "Alright, come on up you bastards, I have got you covered, I have got you covered!" And around the corner came an old swayback horse. No Germans. We did pick up two Polish deserters. They were hidden in the fort. They came out, and I wasn't going to be bothered being encumbered with them, I just sent them back down the hill and told them to find the first American or British or whomever, and surrender to them, because we had to go on.[17]

September 7th, **Lt Bill Story**'s patrol reported back to its headquarters, then continued on towards Menton, which had been occupied by other units of the 2nd Regiment of the FSSF during the night of the 6th to the 7th:

We made our way down to the road and were walking along there, and we noticed that the Germans had blown the bridges, but there were still trucks coming up. The corps of engineers had put up bailey bridges. A truck came up and I hailed him and stopped him and got the platoon on board, but the driver said: "Well, you know, I am not supposed to take you because the bridges aren't strong enough to support this." So I said: "Fine, you go up to the bridge, we will stop, I will get the guys off, you cross safely, we will get on again and go." And that way we went all the way into Menton. There wasn't any resistance, nobody was firing anything at us. We frankly weren't concerned, because those Germans were second-grade Germans. They were retreating fast, stumbling over themselves to get out.

I was busy watching the wire; you knew you were on the main line because of the telephone wire, which was always to the left. I was busy talking with the driver, and all of a sudden I looked at the side of the road and the wire had disappeared. By then we were around a corner, and we were exposed in the lagoon there, so I turned to the driver and said: "Let's get out of here!" We turned around and hightailed it out just as an 88 fired from right up on the customs point between Italy and France."

Forcemen and French policemen take cover at the Italian border at Menton in early September 1944. The front would remain stable here for the next several months, as the FABTF had been ordered to stop its advance east. Archives Municipales de Menton. 6 Num 20.

After reaching Menton and the Italian border, the FABTF was ordered not to advance any further, apparently because it was expected that the Allied attacks on the Italian front would force the Germans to pull out on their own. The Allies had no plans to mount any costly assaults through the mountains that formed the border. The front was therefore to remain where Bill Story's truck had turned back on September 7th until April 1945. The Liberation of the coastal strip of the Maritime Alps was now over.

September 5th, two Frenchmen (**Charles Cravi** and **Honoré Vial**) had been shot and killed by the Germans in Roquebrune while apparently trying to cross the lines to bring information to the Allied troops. Between August 31st and September 7th, eight additional German soldiers who have not been mentioned in any of the previous sections were killed and buried in the vicinity of Monte-Carlo and Menton. The circumstances of their deaths are not known, but presumably, they were for the most part killed by the Allied artillery and the skirmishes that occurred with the patrols of paratroopers and forcemen. These eight German dead were (In the case of Johann Hahn, he was reported as having been killed in Monte-Carlo September 5, 1944, but his body was never recovered after the war. However, an unidentified body was found in neighboring Roquebrune, so the possibly false assumption is made here that this unidentified body was that of Hahn.):

Surame	Name	Rank	Age	Date of death	Location of burial	Unit
Czarnoski	Waldemar	Gren	23	2.9.1944	Castillon	
Eckmeier	Josef	Gren	19	5.9.1944	Roquebrune (Hotel Vistaero)	3./Div.Füs. Btl.148
Hahn	Johann		18	5.9.1944	Roquebrune?	
Krotofil	Paul	Gren	18	31.18.1944	St Agnès	
Kasprowitz	Heinrich	Gren	18	1.9.1944	St Agnès	
Witt	Josef	Gren	18	1.9.1944	St Agnès	
Meider	Ernst	Pio	18	5.9.1944	Menton	
Schleicher	Josef	Pio	18	5.9.1944	HVPl Ventimiglia	

Gebets- † Andenken
an unseren lieben unvergeßlichen
Sohn und Bruder

Johann Hahn
von Bergham

geb. am 12. Januar 1926
gefallen am 5. September 1944
bei Monte Carlo (Südfrankreich).

Du warst so jung, Du starbst so
früh, wer Dich gekannt,
vergißt Dich nie!

18-year-old Johann Hahn was killed by a gunshot wound to the abdomen in the Monte-Carlo area September 5, 1944. After the war, no body wearing his identification tag was found, though one unidentified body that may have been his was exhumed in nearby Roquebrune. Stadtverwaltung Nittenau Collection.

Allied loses in the same area had in the meantime been very light. One soldier of the Medical Detachment of the 602nd PFAB, 34-year-old **Pvt Frank J. Keefe**, was killed in Nice September 3rd, when a German grenade he was examining unexpectedly detonated in his hands. Apart from this casualty, the Allies had so far managed not to lose a single soldier during the advance from Nice to Menton. However, on September 6th, their luck turned when three forward observers of A Company of the 602nd PFAB were killed while participating in a patrol between Peille and St Agnès. **Peter Cottingham**, of the HQ Detachment of 2nd Battalion, 1st Regiment of the FSSF, was on the patrol and described the circumstances of the artillery men's death in his autobiography:

We had moved out as far as the village of Drap, just a few miles east of Nice. We spent the night there, and the next morning, Major McFadden organized a patrol to proceed eastward into the mountains. The patrol consisted of one of our armored half-tracks with the 75mm gun and a section of men to ride in its truck-like back. I and my driver were to follow the half-track in our jeep. I think my driver's name was Hoskins. I called him "Switchback" because of the way he managed the many sharp curves we encountered in crossing the south of France.

After a brief breakfast of hard rations and coffee we mounted up and set off up a gravel road into the mountains, the armored vehicle leading. Little did we know that three of the men we had enjoyed our brief breakfast with would not live to have lunch. They were the enlisted men in Lt Gettinger's artillery forward observer group of the 607 Pack Artillery Regiment. [In fact, the 602nd Pack Field Artillery Battalion.] We had gone about five or six miles when we rounded a hill and were facing a concrete bunker about a half mile ahead of us to one side of the road where it went through the pass. Sgt Cain, the commander of the half-track, ordered his gunners to zero in on the bunker with one round of high explosive. They fired point blank and hit it right in the gun port. When the dust had settled we proceeded cautiously up the road towards it. As there was no answering fire, we assumed it was either empty or that the round we had sent their way had put them out of action.

We rushed up the road and stopped short of the bunker. We were on a gravel road, so there was a good chance that it would be mined in a location like the pass. Sgt Cain had his men dismount, and with their bayonets they probed the gravel with great care. They were able to locate and dig out about eight or ten Teller mines, each of which contained enough explosive to disable a tank. Being satisfied that there were no more mines in the road, we proceeded eastward.

If it is possible to describe a combat patrol as exciting and extremely interesting from a tourist's point of view, that one certainly qualified. The scenery was enchanting, to say the least. Our road took us through a couple fairly short tunnels and along some narrow ledges with a great view of valleys many feet below. We eventually rounded a bend that exposed a scene right out of fairy tales. We hadn't yet caught up with any of the fleeing enemy so we could enjoy the scenery. There ahead of us, in stark relief, against a panorama of morning mists, stood the picturesque village of St Agnès. It was perched near the top of a small mountain about half a mile distant. (…)

"The scenery was enchanting, to say the least." The road between the villages of Peille and St Agnes that Peter Cottingham's patrol followed September 6th. Author's Collection.

26-year-old SSgt Louis P. Lesmeister, one of the three forward observers of A Battery of the 602nd PFAB who was killed when their jeep drove over a Tellermine at Col de la Madone. Lesmeister Family Collection.

As we raced towards the village, someone spotted a column of German soldiers fleeing down the valley on the road south of St Agnès which leads to Menton, a city on the coast. Our patrol stopped and we commenced firing our small arms (rifles and submachine guns) at the enemy column. They proved to be a difficult target, as they were too far away for our firepower to be effective. The crew on our 75mm could not depress the gun sufficiently to zero in on them, as they were several hundred feet below us.

After a hasty discussion we decided to press on into the village to see if any of the enemy remained there. We were soon inside the village and surprised a German sergeant who was trying to destroy some papers from his office. We took him prisoner and loaded him into our jeep. With our prisoner, "Switchback" and I sped back down the road we had just come up, hoping to find Lt Gettinger and his party so that we could get some howitzer fire directed at the fleeing column below. Howitzers had the ability to lob shells over a mountain and land on targets that flat trajectory guns couldn't reach.

We received a terrible shock when we reached the place where we had cleared the mines from the road. There was a huge crater in the road near the bunker and the only thing recognizable near the crater was the twisted front bumper of a jeep bearing the markings of our 607 Pack Artillery. The remains of the jeep and its crew were scattered about among the rocks and bushes on both sides of the road. We had begun meeting troops on foot by then, and they pointed back down the road to an ambulance which was heading back towards our base at Drap.

They had learned that the only survivor of the explosion was the officer. We were later to learn that he, seeing the mines that were stacked beside the road, had stopped his jeep and told his crew to wait while he double checked the road for mines. It's entirely possible that they may have backed up over a mine we had missed. Their weight added to ours may have been all it took to sever the copper wire in its trigger mechanism. It bothered me for weeks afterwards that on such a fragile thread as the thickness of a copper wire my life may have depended.

We drove through the crater and continued to carry our prisoner back down the road to someone we could hand him over to for interrogation. After driving a couple miles we caught up with the ambulance. As we closed on it we could see the bandaged head of Lt Gettinger staring out the rear windows of the vehicle. He had been wounded by the explosion that killed his three men. As the ambulance pulled in to the base established at Drap we drove in right behind it. I realized too late that we should have bypassed the ambulance and taken our prisoner further back than the aid post at Drap. The rear doors of the ambulance flew open and out charged a very distraught man who had just seen his three best friends blown to bits in front of his eyes.

Before we could react he had our prisoner by the throat and would have killed him with his bare hands except for the intervention of several of us, including Major Jerry McFadden. We managed to hustle the prisoner to another venue before anything further happened to him. We never saw Gettinger again. The poor man had a lot of grief to overcome, as his group was a closely knit bunch who had been together throughout the war.

As a postscript to that episode I must relate the following: my wife Muriel and I have visited the scene of that mine incident twice since the war ended. I guess there was something about it that has touched me more deeply than most of the close calls that I had during the war. It is almost as if I had been given these added years for a purpose ordained by a power beyond our understanding. The first time I was back there was during a motor coach tour of Europe in 1987. We had a two-day stopover in Beaulieu, a town between Nice and Monte-Carlo. During our stay there we took a train to Menton and hired a taxi to take us up the mountain to St Agnès.

We then drove west on the road towards Drap, which is now paved, so we were not worried about mines. We found a spot at which the French had built a small shrine constructed of a large calibre rusted artillery shell and other bits of rusted military hardware which, I assumed, was in honor of the three American lads who were killed there. We took some pictures and had our driver take a picture of us, as well.

"The French had built a small shrine constructed of a large caliber rusted artillery shell and other bits of rusted military hardware." The small monument at Col de la Madone. Apparently some pieces that were identifiable as coming from the U.S. jeep have been vandalized since Peter Cottingham's visit. Author's Collection.

Lt George Parnell's wound tag from September 6th, signed by Major Neeseman of the FSSF. Marion Parnell Collection.

When we returned to the same spot in a car we had rented in Paris in 1994 we had more time to examine everything in detail. The Col de la Madone, as it is known, appears to be a popular picnic area for the locals. I met some of them and explained what really happened there fifty years earlier. The inscription welded on a plate on the cairn indicated that the jeep was destroyed by an artillery shell. Anyone not knowing the details as I had witnessed them could very easily have come to that conclusion. Upon examining the cairn and statuary more closely then on my previous visit, it struck me forcefully that the Madonna and Child depicted by the rusty hardware was composed of pieces of a destroyed jeep. I realized with an emotional shock that it may well have been made of the remains of my own jeep had fate so chosen.[18]

The three men killed by the antitank mine at Col de la Madone September 6, 1944, were:

Surname	Name	Rank	Unit	Age
Green	Louis	Cpl	A Bat 602 FAB	29
Lesmeister	Louis P	SSgt	A Bat 602 FAB	26
Lupone	Arthur J	T4	A Bat 602 FAB	23

In the afternoon of the same day, **Lt George Parnell**, of the 887th AEC, narrowly escaped death when he was ordered to clear some mines in the same vicinity and came under German machine gun fire. He was shot through the right foot and wrote home to his wife Beatrice a few days later:

I could see the machine gun bullets walking down the road towards me and they didn't bother me a bit. I was facing down the road on my stomach and watched them – they came right by my ear and down my side and one caught my foot – on the third burst I rolled off the road and down a steep hill and then played hide and seek with the machine gun and sniper for about an hour and a half, trying to work my way back out of sight and range. The injured foot did not hurt at all. The actual hit felt like someone had tied a rope on my foot and given the rope a short tug. They shelled me at the same time, but fortunately I found a culvert running under the road which protected me from the shelling, and also provided a means of escape. I crawled through it under the road and kept to the ravine it led into up and over the mountain. (…) Yes, Beatrice, I do like it here. Right now I'm doing something more important than I've ever done before in my life. I like it and I'm proud of it, and have every intention of doing it until either it or myself is finished – my little life is so unimportant and I really do realize and believe that – by the way – there are atheists in fox-holes – I am one. My only thought was that son of a bitch couldn't hit the barn door at 50 feet.[19]

By September 7th, the FSSF had occupied Castellar, a mountain village very near the border with Italy. It also expected to be able to occupy Castillon, on the Menton Sospel road, without any trouble, with the 3rd Regiment reporting in the afternoon of the 7th: "Troops are tired and I do not desire to take town [Castillon] tonight."[20] Little could 3rd Regiment's commander imagine he would have to be battling with the Germans in Castillon until October 1944, when they finally decided to evacuate the town of their own accord! In the coastal region of the Maritime Alps, the FABTF had now reached a line of advance that would remain stable for the next month, and would barely change until the end of the war.

Gun crews of the 602nd PFAB pose with their 75mm guns in the Nice hinterland. These photos were presumably taken in early September 1944. Art Helmers Collection.

Shells land near the village of Castellar. The peaks visible in the background form the border between France and Italy, where the FSSF would fight a patrol war for the next months. Note the dried leaves visible at left in the foreground, which were probably used to camouflage the position the photo was taken from. Art Helmers Collection.

The Allied Advance Towards Turini

We will now study the final advances of the FABTF further north, starting with the mountains northeast of Levens. The 517th PIR had captured Levens on the 29th, and its 1st Battalion had then taken up positions in St Jean la Rivière and Lantosque. August 31st, *Groupe Morgan*, reinforced by ORA forces, decided to capture the nearby and strategic Turini Pass. The *maquisards* probably expected an easy victory, without realizing that the Turini Pass was part of the definitive German defense line, and would therefore be strongly defended. The attack was a complete failure: six resistance men were killed and the survivors were forced to retreat. Those killed were: **Xavier Blanc**, **Jean Bertrand**, **Jacques Bloch**, **Nicolas Cornu**, **Gabriel Elleboode**, and **Marius Pisano**. Furthermore, 12 resistance men and shepherds found roaming in the area were executed by the Germans.

August 31st, a jeep patrol of the 1st Battalion of the 517th PIR, accompanied and driven by Nisei soldiers of the 442nd Antitank Company, was also sent towards Turini, apparently completely oblivious of what had happened (or was happening) to the *maquisards*. As often, there was a deep misunderstanding between the resistance men and the Allied soldiers, and **SSgt Hoyt Kelley** thus remembered the jeep patrol in the following manner:

A few words about the French Freedom Fighters, or FFE, as they preferred to call themselves – we found them to be complete frauds. They would drive their old trucks up to the front lines and bum gas from us, and as soon as we gave them any they would head back to Nice with a machine gun on top of their truck and have a parade. I am not aware of them doing any actual fighting. We did once turn over a hill we controlled to them, as their "Captain" assured us that his men would hold it while we went over to the other side of the valley. The next morning I sent a jeep with five of my men up to check on the hill and they were ambushed by Germans. The French Captain later said the men got tired and there was a party in town, so they decided to leave the hill and go back to the city.

I went with three men to try to get our men out. They were about four miles up a steep road that wound around the wooded hills. We thought that the Germans would probably not fire on us if they knew we were merely trying to get out our wounded men. We crawled up the side of the road, keeping in the cover of the small trees and bushes, until we reached the spot where the jeep was. There was an old French truck there that appeared to be operable and the jeep was shot to pieces. Two of the men were still alive. The other three were dead. They said they had no warning, and had just driven up there thinking that the French were still holding the hill. We dragged the one man we could reach off the side of the road, and although he was shot in the leg and stomach, we were able to get him down around the turn of the road and out of sight of the Germans. His name was Steele and he was from Reno, Nevada. (He later recovered and took a battlefield commission when it was offered to him. In the Bulge he lost a leg and ended up in Bushnell Hospital in Utah, where my Mother nursed him.) We could not see the Germans, but we heard them talking. We finally decided to load the other man in the back of the truck and try to get him out that way, hoping that the Germans would not fire on us if we did not have our guns with us. Two of us carried him to the truck, which was already pointed downhill, and we loaded him into the

truck. He was seriously wounded, and I don't think he knew what was going on. I hollered for Steele to get in the truck and I removed a rock from the wheel and tried to push it. It slowly moved, very slowly, down the hill, but just as we got to the corner, and within moments of safety around the bend, the Germans opened up, spraying the truck with machine gun fire. We stopped around the corner, but the fellow was dead with several wounds. I don't remember his name. I recall he was from Michigan, I believe. Having loaded Steele in the truck along with the dead paratrooper, we rolled down the hill about two miles, to where we had left the jeep. The truck never started. I think we tried to start it to get out of there, but it just coasted. The French FFE stayed clear of us after that.[21]

Needless to say, Hoyt Kelley's interpretation of the actions of the *maquisards* was severely distorted. However, this kind of misinterpretation is actually what many of the Allied soldiers believed at the time, and kept on believing after the war! Mishaps happening to one unit are often blamed on the incompetence of neighboring units in any army, and this mechanism was magnified with the disorganized and non-English speaking *maquisard* units. Hoyt Kelley also seems to have confused Robert Steele with another soldier. **PFC Robert Steele**, of the HQ Company of the 1st Battalion of the 517th PIR, was in the action, but was apparently not wounded, as he was awarded a Silver Star, the citation of which read:

While proceeding on a mounted reconnaissance patrol, the vehicle in front of the one in which Technician Steele [He had since been promoted.] was ridding was ambushed by the enemy and all occupants wounded. Although the ambushed vehicle was continuously under heavy machine gun fire, Technician Steele and another soldier, disregarding their own safety, left their vehicle, which was in a protected position, and crawled along the road to the ambushed vehicle. Of the five wounded soldiers, two were able to crawl to a point of safety, from whence they were later taken to an aid station. The other three soldiers were badly wounded and could not move without some assistance. The enemy evidently believed that all occupants of the vehicle had been killed, for they ceased firing. Moving as fast as circumstances would permit, Technician Steele, assisted by the other soldier, succeeded in evacuating two of the wounded; the third wounded soldier, still in the vehicle, made it necessary for the rescue party to stand up in plain view of the enemy to lift the wounded man out. The wounded soldier had just been raised when the enemy again opened fire upon the vehicle, causing the men to take cover. The machine gun fire continued intermittently for thirty minutes, sweeping the area and preventing the men from moving. The enemy then laid a concentration of mortar fire in their vicinity, and two of the rounds hit the vehicle, forcing Technician Steele and the other soldier to dash eighty yards from their exposed position to the rear of a stone wall. Realizing that their comrade was then beyond the need of medical aid, the men withdrew to their unit and reported the enemy location and type of weapons. Technician Steele's splendid example of courage, devotion to duty, and utter disregard for his own safety when going to the aid of his wounded comrades was a great inspiration to the members of his unit. His courage and devotion to duty are in keeping with the highest traditions of the military service.[22]

The other soldier mentioned in the citation was Pvt James Marshall, who was also awarded a Silver Star with the same citation as Steele's. **Captain Don Fraser**, of the 1st Battalion HQ, was also involved in the jeep patrol and remembered (Note that unlike Hoyt Kelley, he does not put the blame of the ambush on the resistance fighters.):

> We got some bad information on where the Germans were. A jeep from the Antitank Company of the 442nd Combat Team, attached to the 517th, with Lt R.L. Emmons and three GIs rounded a bend on a mountain road. German fire knocked them out. Emmons and one man managed to crawl back to me. I was coming up on foot.
>
> I inched forward along the edge of the road to the disabled jeep, but machine gun fire pinned us down so much we couldn't raise our heads off the road. (...) Just about then I heard the cough of a mortar and one round landed just below us in the ravine. I knew the next one would drop on us. Trying to drag one badly wounded trooper around the bend, we had pushed him to a place beside the back of the jeep. The mortar banged once more and the round struck right on that wounded trooper; that was the end of him.
>
> A Frenchman had come up over the ridge top and started a truck up the road, behind the cover of trees. He let the truck coast quietly around the bend above us, and before the Germans realized it, he was rolling by us, heading for the cover round the next curve. As he passed us, we threw the one wounded man who was still alive on the truck and ran alongside it around the bend.[23]

Captain Fraser (who in the meantime had been promoted to the rank of Major) was awarded a Silver Star for this action, the citation of which read:

> For gallantry in action near la Bollène Vésubie, France, 31 August 1944. During a motorized reconnaissance patrol, consisting of one officer and four men, the patrol was ambushed by an enemy road block, wounding all of the personnel and disabling the vehicle. The officer and one man able to walk made their way back to the unit, reporting the situation to Major Fraser. Immediately going to the scene of ambush over the only available route, which was under constant enemy observation and intense machine gun and twenty millimeter gun fire, Major Fraser, without regard for his own safety, succeeded in removing two of the injured men to safety before an intense mortar barrage made it impossible for him to continue. Major Fraser's disregard for his own safety and gallant actions served as an inspiration to the men of his unit and undoubtedly saved the lives of two wounded soldiers.[24]

The Nisei soldier who had been driving the ambushed jeep, **Pvt Mitsugi Nakahara**, from Hawaii, was also awarded a well deserved Silver Star (It is very interesting to note that in his citation, neither the date nor the name of the location are the same as in Captain Fraser's citation, once again highlighting the prudence with which historical documents need to be interpreted):

> For gallantry in action near Baraquements, France, on 30 August 1944. Private Nakahara was driving a vehicle occupied by four other soldiers, whose mission was to patrol a forward area. While proceeding on the mission, their vehicle was suddenly ambushed by the enemy. The intense fire from enemy machine guns and twenty millimeter guns wounded all occupants of the vehicle. During the action, one of the wounded soldiers succeeded in escaping and crawled to the rear, where he reported the ambush to the occupants of another vehicle. For a moment the enemy ceased firing, and Private Nakahara, who had received a leg wound, got back in the vehicle and turned it around to attempt to evacuate his wounded comrades. Seeing this, the enemy again opened fire, wounding Private Nakahara for the second time and puncturing the tires of the vehicle. The fire continued for about ten minutes and again ceased. Private Nakahara, assisted by another soldier, loaded the wounded, and again tried to drive the vehicle to a point of safety. Again the enemy opened fire, hitting Private Nakahara in the back, causing the third wound. During the action, the wounded managed to find cover, and when all firing ceased, two soldiers from the rear vehicle crawled forward to aid the wounded. The rescuers reached Private Nakahara, who refused aid and insisted that the other wounded soldiers be cared for first. Realizing the seriousness of Private Nakahara's wounds, the rescue party, despite his protests, succeeded in sliding him on a blanket and removing him to the rear. Private Nakahara's courage under enemy fire, and his consideration for the welfare of his wounded comrades, reflects great credit upon him as a soldier.[25]

The soldier who was killed by a mortar at the scene of the ambush was **Pvt Joseph F. Van Ness**, of B Company of the 517th PIR. A second soldier, **Cpl Richard A. Jamme** of A Company, died of his wounds the same day. Mitsugi Nakahara survived his multiple wounds. Because of the circumstances of the ambush, Joseph Van Ness' body needed to be left behind at the scene, so he was officially reported as missing in action until his body was retrieved by the graves registration personnel several weeks later. By then his body was mostly reduced to skeletal remains, and since no identification tags were found on it, **Lt Emmons** was called to identify it, writing the following statement:

> 1. I, the undersigned, do certify that the remains which I have **personally viewed** and which are (…) at the Military

26-year-old Pvt Joseph F. Van Ness, of B Company of the 517th PIR, was wounded by German machine gun fire before being killed by a mortar shell. His comrades were forced to abandon his body at the site of the ambush. This caused him to be temporarily listed as missing, as the U.S. Army refused to classify its men as killed until their death had been confirmed beyond doubt. Van Ness had been a pathfinder on the night of the invasion. Van Ness Family Collection.

Cemetery, Draguignan, France, are those of: Joseph F. Van Ness, Pvt., 6273776, 517 P.I.R., Co "B".

2. My identification is based on personal acquaintance covering a period of six months.

3. Remarks: Pvt Van Ness was with me at the place and time he was hit. He was killed by enemy machine-gun and mortar fire. I certify that the remains are those of Pvt. Van Ness.[26]

As for the Germans, they do not seem to have lost any men in either the FFI attack nor the American patrol. However, the German funeral archives are very incomplete for the men they lost in the mountains, as some graves were later pilfered or remain to be found, meaning that the men in them are not included in the *Volksbund* grave lists. The Germans remained in control of the Turini pass, and the front was to remain almost stable in the area until late April 1945. ***Grenadier* Joseph Kirsner**, of *Reserve Grenadier Bataillon 164*, was sent to Turini after evacuating Nice, as was planned in the Niedlich documents. He remembered the march to Turini and some shooting that may have been the FFI attack of August 31st:

We could only move during the night. During the day, it wasn't possible until we got into the mountains. We arrived at the Turini Pass September 4th. [This date is probably late by a few days, as are several dates Josef Kirsner recorded in his diary.] On the way there, there was a bit of shooting, probably from the resistance, but they were forced to retreat. We were in the middle of the forest, and had an observation point two or three kilometers from our camp. We could see the road a few kilometers away with tanks driving on it. We lay there observing with binoculars, counting how many cars and how many tanks drove by on the road. The Americans only advanced on the roads and didn't care about anything else. We were not involved in any fighting. We stayed there from September 4th until September 16th, and then we were replaced by older men who were coming back from Russia. Later on we found out that when the Americans and French attacked, they were almost all killed. September 20th, we moved back into Italy. It took us three days, through the tunnel at the Tenda Pass to Cuneo. Later on we went to Genoa, where we guarded a big railroad bridge.

The men mentioned by Joseph Kirsner were the soldiers of *Infanterie Division 34*, who relieved *Reserve Division 148* in mid-September and would later indeed face the French attack of late April 1945 that became known as the Authion battle (however, its losses were not at all as heavy as Kirsner was told). In the meantime, specialized German mountain units had already come to the rescue of *Reserve Division 148* in late August to hold the Italian border and the area north of Turini, as was indicated in the August 28th Niedlich orders. In the period before September 7, 1944, two men of these units were killed and buried in the Maritime Alps as they battled with the partisans to retake control of the Italian border zone. These two casualties were:

23-year-old OberGefreiter Xaver Paulsteiner, from Gebirgsjäger Regiment 100, who was shot and killed near Isola September 2nd in an ambush set by partisans. Paulsteiner Family Collection.

Several more soldiers from these mountain units were probably killed along the border, but their bodies were brought back and buried in Italy, the burial grounds of which have not been studied for this book. The letter that was sent home to the parents of Xaver Paulsteiner after his death at Isola on September 2nd contains interesting information about the type of warfare that was being waged at the border between the Germans and the partisans before the 509th and 551st PIBs reached the area. Xaver Paulsteiner's company commander, *Oberleutnant* **Erich Niederl**, wrote:

Dear Mr Paulsteiner!

I have the sad duty of making you aware of a blow from destiny that, along with the company, also greatly concerns your family. Your son, *Obergefreiter* Xaver Paulsteiner, fell during a reconnaissance patrol. Your son was appointed to a reconnaissance squad that was sent to Isola (France). Shortly before reaching Isola, the reconnaissance squad was surrounded and taken under very heavy fire by partisans. The reconnaissance squad immediately made its way back, and that is where you son fell. According to the reconnaissance squad commander, your son threw his arms up and fell head first a few meters down the hill. It is likely that your son was killed by a head shot. Because of the strong fire and the pressure from the partisans, it was not possible to retrieve your son. The next day, a stronger combat group was sent out to look for your son. He was no longer to be found and the partisans may have taken him with them. With him, the company now deplores five dead and a string of wounded. Your son was very well liked because of his constant and active will to serve. With him, the entire company is losing a good, loyal, and devoted comrade. All the members

Surname	Name	Rank	Age	Date of death	Location of burial	Unit
Maier	Johann	Ogefr	21	28.8.1944	Belvedere	1./Hoch.Geb. Jäg.Btl.4
Paulsteiner	Xaver	Ogefr	23	2.9.1944	Isola	Geb.Jäg. Reg.100

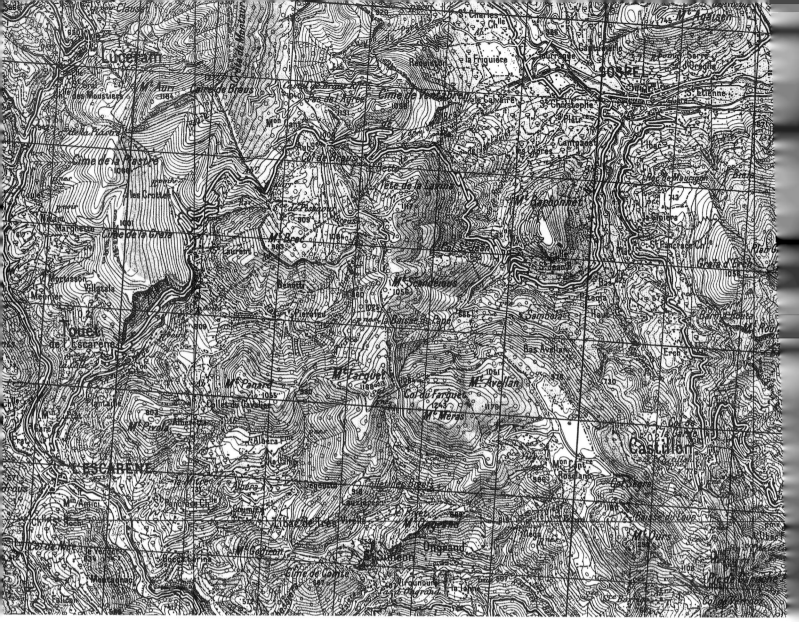

of the company will keep him in their minds at all times. May you and your family, as the company, find comfort in the fact that your son fell for his country, thereby giving the utmost to Germany.[27]

Two Italian resistance fighters had also been killed in the encounter: **Luigi Bertone** and **Guerci Arrigo**. A few days later, a detachment of the 551st PIB reached Isola, where a patrol war similar to that described in the letter would go on until the end of the war.

The Advance to Col de Braus

In the previous pages, we have described the advance of the FABTF towards Menton to the south and towards Turini to the north. We will now study the advance that took place at the center of the front, in the direction of the Col de Braus and Sospel, between August 30 and September 7, 1944. Col de Braus is a mountain pass with an altitude of 1,002 meters that acts as a gate to Sospel, overlooking the town and the road running between Sospel and Castillon. It was therefore a highly strategic area for the Germans to keep control of, and the defense of Col de Braus was assigned to *Reserve Jäger Bataillon 28*. *Batallion 28* was the only *Jäger* unit within *Reserve Division 148*, and it seems to have been considered the most trustworthy unit of the division.

Following the Nice insurrection, the German forces pulled back to Col de Braus on their own, after having blown two craters in the road leading to the pass, and after, as usual, having blown almost all the bridges in the area. The village closest to Col de Braus to the west was Touët de l'Escarène, which was directly connected to Sospel by a railroad tunnel that crossed under the mountain. These particularities caused several encounters to occur in the vicinity of Touët. Charles Erbetta lived in Touët de l'Escarène and, along with several other locals, formed a makeshift resistance group. August 30th, after seeing the departure of the last Germans, Charles Erbetta went to examine the two craters that the Germans had blown in the road between Touët and Col de Braus. The location of the craters had been very well chosen, with a vertical cliff on one side and a deep ravine on the other. Like in Vence, a large number of mines had been laid around the craters to deter people from attempting to bypass them. We will let **Charles Erbetta** describe what happened next:

When the Germans retreated, they blew up the road and then laid mines. We had gone up to see if it was possible to go past the craters, and a woman with a child, the young **Jean Cavallero**, came up behind us, wanting to get to Sospel. I told that woman: "You cannot go by, the road is blown and is mined. Don't go off the road, there are mines all around." In the meantime, the kid felt like

450

The cratered road between Touët de l'Escarène and Col de Braus as it appeared in early September 1944, when it was being repaired by troops of the 596th PCEC. Courtesy Michel de Trez.

10-year-old Jean Cavallero, who was killed by a mine near the craters on the road leading from l'Escarène to Col de Braus August 30, 1944. Author's Collection.

The cratered road after it had been repaired in the following weeks. 517 Parachute Combat Team booklet, courtesy Frédéric Brega.

The village of Touët de l'Escarène as it appears today. The Col de Braus area is visible in the background of the photo. Author's Collection.

going to the toilet, he said: "I want to do a pee, I want to do a poo." The poor kid was frightened. I told him: "If you want to do a pee, there is lots of room here. Do your pee in the middle of the road, it's OK." But he wanted to go to the side of the road. I said: "Don't go there!" but there was nothing I could do. He just got to the side of the road and he stepped on a mine and was killed. It was horrendous to see that. He died 15 meters away from me. It was an atrocious sight. Afterwards I couldn't stand the sight of a drop of blood.

The woman wanted to get to Sospel. Later we found out that she wanted to escape and go with the Germans. Supposedly she went to Austria.

On the road leading to the craters, **Charles Erbetta** and his colleagues had found an abandoned German vehicle containing weapons. They added these to their already existing arsenal of weapons retrieved after the Italian retreat of 1943. Later on in the day of August 30th, the *résistants* ran into a German patrol that had ventured down from Col de Braus:

We were on reconnaissance and captured nine Germans on the path under the craters in the road. André Duneli and Firmin Sereto were on the opposite hill, following the Germans with binoculars, shooting at them and telling us where they were. The Germans were obliged to come towards us, because they knew they were being stalked from the opposite side. We had them trapped; they could neither go forwards nor backwards, and they realized that they were caught between two fires so they surrendered.

At first the Germans had their rifles pointed towards us, which was normal. Our chief, François Cauvin, was an excellent marksman. He was as huge as a door, and was a veteran of the Legion who had been in Africa and Morocco and had then come back home. He knew the tune, and with a pistol he shot at the Germans from at least 50 meters away. The bullet hit a German in the eye at a grazing angle. It tore his eye out and came out the other side. And bad luck: it was a Polish soldier. He was badly wounded, but we helped him anyway. We called the doctor and he treated him on the Place de l'Ecole. Then they brought him to Pasteur Hospital in Nice.

We had captured seven enlisted men, but the two NCOs who were accompanying them escaped because they were afraid we would execute them. We caught up to them between St Laurent and Touët. From up above, Duneli and Sereto told us where they had gone to. Honoré Cauvin, Eugène Cauvin, and I went to get them. They could have shot us because they were still armed, but we were lucky.

As Allied troops were still nowhere in sight, the patriots used an old-fashioned but effective method to make sure the Germans would not escape, as explained by **Albert Bareli**, a child in l'Escarène who remembered seeing the prisoners being evacuated down towards Nice:

The 11 had been captured by a single guy, Cauvin, who was a bit of a nutcase, and they were being accompanied by two or three armed men from l'Escarène. They had taken the Germans' shoelaces and their suspenders or belts, so they had to hold their pants in order not to fall down and they couldn't run because otherwise they would lose their shoes.

Before being sent to Nice, the German prisoners had warned the *résistants* that a patrol would probably be sent out to look for them. Indeed, shortly after the local *maquisards* noticed that some Germans had come through the railway tunnel all the way from Sospel, and that they were now occupying the small but well designed fortifications that had been built into the mouth of the tunnel when it was constructed (In fact, these Germans had probably been sent to make sure no enemy troops would come through the tunnel, not to look for the missing patrol as the *résistants* thought). **Charles Erbetta** explains the events that followed:

We quickly sent the prisoners to Nice for safety reasons and stood guard at the tunnel. There were three centimeter thick armored doors on either side of the tunnel, and since we saw that they were closed, we understood the Germans were there. So we posted three men on the little bridge facing the tunnel, and five of us were further back to cover them in Mr Cairou's house, the last house of the village, because from there the entrance of the tunnel can be observed well. We had set up the machine gun that we had taken from the Germans. Another one of our teams was holding the area of the train station, and during the night we all held our positions. There were only about 15 of us left in Touët because all the villagers had escaped, knowing that the Germans were supposed to come back.

Just before we had gotten into position, *Monsieur* **Antoine Barbera**, an old man [He was 76 years old.] from here, went over to his orchard. When he returned, he was passing over the little bridge that crosses the train tracks, and the Germans shot him in the head from the tunnel. *Madame* **Marie-Louise Pèbre** lived in the mill, and we had advised her to leave because the Germans were going to come and that they would kill her if they went to the mill. So she left, of course, but she was obliged to pass in front of the tunnel. The Germans had already killed Antoine Barbera, and when Marie-Louise Pèbre appeared they fired a bullet at her. It hit her right in the chest and exited from behind. Without falling, she turned around to escape and was hit by a second bullet in the back that exited from her front, tearing off one of her breasts. If you had seen that… It was awful. When the Americans arrived, they put her on a stretcher and drove her down to la Fontone Hospital in Antibes on a jeep, but she didn't survive. She had two hideous wounds.

Another local woman, *Madame* Angèle Verani, wanted to go and see *Madame* Marie-Louise, but Marie-Louise had already been severely wounded. We told her, but she didn't want to listen to anything. She was going down to see if Marie-Louise was coming back, and she was shot in the thigh at the same place, but she survived. She was very lucky, the bullet went in and out of her thigh without causing too much damage.

While this shooting of civilians was tragic, the Germans were understandably extremely nervous after having had several dozen men killed and hundreds more wounded or captured by *résistants* in civilian dress during the previous days. **Charles Erbetta** goes on:

During the night, almost nothing happened. We had to get Antoine Barbera, who was still lying on the bridge. Then at daybreak, the Germans tried to come out of the tunnel and opened fire on the three guards who were on the small

The railroad tunnel leading from Touët de l'Escarène to Sospel as it appears today. Fortifications were built in either side of the tunnel mouth, and at the time the tunnel was also closed by thick metal doors. Author's Collection.

The small bridge on which 76-year-old Antoine Barbera was shot through the head by a German soldier, as seen from within the tunnel fortification in which the Germans were positioned. Author's Collection.

bridge. They wounded one in the arm and the others were forced to flee, retreating to our position. At that moment our chief, François Cauvin, came, telling us: "Pull back urgently, we will retreat to l'Escarène." So we all scattered, because of course we had to avoid all being captured together. We scattered, and Honoré Cauvin and I crossed through the mountains to the l'Escarène train station.

Below the train station we went to see Honoré Cauvin's uncle, who told us: "Don't worry, the Canadians are said to have reached Contes, and we sent out a messenger on a motorcycle to ask them to come to your rescue at Touët." It was Maurice Maurel, who was one of ours, who had left on a motorbike, and indeed, a quarter of an hour later, a patrol of Canadians arrived. So we went down to the road because we needed to show them the only path that they could take, since the main bridge in l'Escarène had been blown. A team of Canadians came, and there was an Indian with them. They asked us if we could bring them to Touët through the mountains, and that is exactly what Cauvin and I did.

These "Canadians" who first reached l'Escarène August 31, 1944' were members of 3-3 of the FSSF. Their regiment radioed back to FSSF headquarters at 17:47: "Believe contact close. Town ahead reported surrounded by enemy. Recon out now."[28] **Charles Erbetta** was guiding this "recon" group and continues:

The lieutenant who was in command could speak French, so he was asking us for the itinerary. We were out in front with the Indian and were telling him where to go. We stayed away from them because they were in uniform, whereas we were in civilian clothes. We had to keep our ears and eyes well open, because when you are on a patrol like that, you never know if anybody is going to show up in front of you. The Indian knew that very well and listened to us. He was a battle hardened guy, not a choirboy. He had no weapon except for a dagger on his boot, and was as agile as a gazelle. His hair was long and he wasn't wearing a helmet or anything, except a thing to hold his hair. He was a real Indian.

From l'Escarène we went around through the mountain. It took us over two hours to cover two kilometers, and we

returned to Mr Cairou's house at the exit of the village. The Canadians set up two .50 caliber machine guns there: one at the foot of the olive tree and the other in the garden. There was a reconnaissance aircraft in the sky that was communicating with the Canadian's captain and they immediately sent a half-track, because the aircraft had given the information that the Germans were in the tunnel. The half-track passed over the one and only bridge that the Germans had forgotten to blow and it arrived with a rapid-fire 75mm cannon.

This was one of the four half-tracks of the FSSF's Cannon Company, which had already been responsible for the destruction of the German 88mm cannon outside Peymeinade August 22nd (see Chapter 9). 3rd Regiment reported on the situation in Touët at 18:35: "Enemy in tunnel. Can't estimate strength. Am launching attack, platoon strength, supported by French as feelers."[29] **Charles Erbetta**:

They fired about 60 shells into the tunnel. The first shell hit the top of the entrance to the tunnel; the fire wasn't properly adjusted. Then they lowered their fire and the shells were entering the tunnel. There was even one German killed inside. But one Canadian officer got wounded in the leg. He was beside the half-track directing its fire, but the Germans fired back; they didn't let themselves get pushed around just like that. The truth is that they were hard nuts to crack. The officer was hit badly, I think it must have been an explosive bullet that got him. It wasn't a pretty sight.

A detailed description of the tunnel attack by 3-3 was later written by the FSSF:

It was learned at Touët de l'Escarène that a sudden surprise attack with heavy fire power on a more or less

Charles Erbetta, who participated in the resistance actions at Touët and helped guide the first FSSF troops to the village. Charles Erbetta Collection.

Shrapnel damage caused by the FSSF halftrack's 75mm shells is still visible on the metal doors of the fortifications inside the tunnel mouth. Author's Collection.

impregnable position may result in the abandonment of the position, even though it cannot be captured at the time. In this case, the objective was a narrow railway tunnel entrance with two blockhouses built into its construction. A 77mm gun lay in the entrance and at least two MGs were firing from the blockhouse. The tunnel mouth was set deep in a ravine, with sheer cliffs on either side. The blockhouse had side ports. The only approach was down the railroad track itself or over a twenty foot drop in front of the side ports. The position, as long as it could be manned, was for all intent and purposes impregnable to infantry attack.

The attack was launched by a platoon of Third Regiment supported by a 75mm cannon mounted in a half-track. The approach had been made swiftly and under cover, so that good surprise was achieved, although the enemy were already alerted and firing on French Patriots. The cannon was run into position 150 yards from the tunnel mouth and some 90 rounds were fired into the tunnel and the blockhouse ports. During the fire all platoon weapons engaged the same targets. When fire was lifted and the platoon closed in, the cries of the enemy wounded could be heard. However, as the leading elements reached the entrance one enemy machine gun opened fire at point blank range and light casualties were suffered. Although heavy machine gun fire was once more brought to bear on the blockhouse, the enemy MG could not be silenced and the attack was abandoned for eight hours. On reconnaissance at this time it was found that the enemy had abandoned the position—an extremely important one, as it was his escape route to Sospel.[30]

The importance of the tunnel was exaggerated by the writer, as all the Germans needing to escape the area had already done so. The identity of the German who was killed in the tunnel is not known. He was initially buried in the cemetery of Touët, but his body was not found when the *Volksbund* later came to retrieve it. It is likely that he was exhumed after a few years and put into the cemetery ossuary. This is common practice in southern France, where cemetery space is scarce and expensive. **Charles Erbetta** explains what happened in the village once the fighting was over:

Things went well in the end. We all went to the Place de l'Ecole with the Canadians. The half-track stood guard at the tunnel and the Germans never came out. The Canadians arrived and took care of everything. Everybody was happy, well, reasonably happy, because those two people had been killed; three with the kid. But the population was still happy. One Canadian asked me: "Is it OK now?" I said: "Yes, perfect, you are here. But there is just one thing…" and I signaled to him that our stomachs were empty. "Oh! But you should have said so." Two of them went to get things to eat. They brought us cans of bacon with eggs, cans of concentrated milk, bread, biscuits, and various victuals.

I will tell you what happened to me. He gave me a can of bacon and opened it for me, and with a knife I gobbled it up like a greedy pig. I won't hide it from you, I was young and I was hungry. In those days, it wasn't a dishonor to be hungry. I ate that can at full speed, I drank the can of concentrated milk on top of it and a good piece of bread or biscuit, something like that. Do you know how long I kept it in? One hour, then it all came back out. It was instantaneous. Oh, and I was sick like a dog the entire afternoon.

In June, July, August, and September, we didn't see any bread. And the term bread was just a figure of speech.

They put all kinds of stuff in it, it was inedible. When you cut the bread, the soft inside of the bread would stay stuck to the knife, so nobody ate it, not even the animals. Sometimes my mother would dip a piece of bread and give it to the chickens; they refused to eat it. It seemed as if the animals could feel that something wasn't normal in it.

A patrol from the 1st Platoon of F Company of the 517th PIR also happened to be in the vicinity of Touët during the battle for the tunnel. The sound of gunfire attracted the paratroopers, as **Pvt Myrle Traver**, who was on the patrol, remembered:

There was a railroad tunnel that went through the mountain there to Sospel, and from where we had our lines set up, we heard firing, so we went down to investigate. The Special Service troops there had a half-track and an artillery gun on it and they were firing into this tunnel because they had some Germans bottled up in there. Actually, they were having a lot of fun just firing round after round into that thing. You could hear the Germans yelling and screaming way back in there, and then finally they retreated on back through the tunnel into Sospel, if I remember right.

We got talking to the Special Service troops and they had been in Alaska earlier during the war, and then they were in on the invasion of southern France, too. I bought this parka from one of the guys. I gave him 20 bucks for it, and I used it until I got captured and put in a prison camp. It was a lot better than an overcoat.

The reversible winter parka was part of the special equipment that the FSSF was outfitted with, along with the legendary V-42 combat knife. It would seem that the F Company patrol had come from the Mont Férion area near Levens. The next day, September 1, 1944, the small patrol pushed north up the road from l'Escarène, entering the nearby village of Lucéram. **Pvt Myrle Traver** tells of the entry into Lucéram:

The Sospel exit of the tunnel after being blown by the Germans. *The Gregg and Michelle Philipson Collection.*

We got to Lucéram. It was a mountainous area with just houses on each side of the road going through the village, on up to Peira Cava. We had just got there and were sitting in a little restaurant, and of course, the French were all giving us wine and something to eat. We told the people there that we wanted to go over to Sospel, but they said: "You can't go to Sospel and take it, there are a couple divisions of Germans over there!" And so we didn't want to go down there, just 12 guys.

We had a 300 radio and we radioed back, and about that time three Germans came down to get water in their buckets. They took off running when they saw us and a couple guys shot two of them. They killed one, and the other one was wounded bad and he died. But the third one took off and went back to his outpost, wherever he was from up in the mountains. We don't know what happened to him, but we were very worried, because here we were, 20 some miles from our outfit, and we had killed those two Germans, and the third one got away, and here we are by ourselves out here. So we radioed back real fast with the 300 radio and told our battalion about it. They said they would head that way as fast as they could, and just sit tight and try to keep from getting killed out there. We didn't have any other Germans until our outfit got up there.

According to the Intelligence Report for September 1st, four Germans of the 8th Company of *Reserve Jäger Bataillon 28* were also captured by the patrol in Lucéram. The l'Escarène area was now firmly in Allied hands; however, their advance would now stop for a few days, for as we saw previously, the FABTF had been momentarily ordered to hold its positions and to only send out strong patrols to the east in order to maintain contact with the Germans. Patrolling was the specialty of the FSSF, and over the next days its 3rd Regiment was able to effortlessly penetrate the German defenses being held by *Bataillon 28* at Col de Braus. In the period September 1st to 2nd, for example, the unit reported: "3rd Regiment patrols towards Sospel and Castillon attacked and cleared Tête de la Lavina."[31] It would later cost the 517th PIR 12 days of fighting and numerous casualties to retake Tête de la Lavina, as we will see further on.

It is much more difficult to reconstruct the events of mountain warfare then those of urban warfare, as the terrain is rather featureless, making it difficult for the soldiers to remember where they fought, and there are no (or very few) local civilians to note where and when the soldiers arrived. The exact chain of events that occurred at Col de Braus between September 1st and September 4th can therefore not be described in an orderly manner. However, we will use Rex Atwell's memories of that period as an example of the type of warfare that occurred. Rex Atwell, of 2-3 of the FSSF, was a battle hardened veteran who seemed to enjoy taking risks, rather than attempting to avoid them. It was such men who gave the FABTF the upper hand over the poorly motivated men of German *Reserve Division 148*. **Rex Atwell** participated in at least two patrols in the area of Col de Braus in early September:

The Italian border and the French Maginot line were just a few miles ahead. We stopped overnight with a steep cliff protecting us. I continued to patrol alone for the purpose of determining whether friend or foe was nearby. (…) Climbing up a ridge above the road, I viewed a large green pasture. Its saucer-like shape had to be 50 acres. Beyond the center were three horses without saddles and three Germans without helmets. With binoculars, I watched in prone position for twenty minutes. The Germans were

wrapping the horses' hooves. Then I returned to my group with this information to report.

Lt Woodard sent out scouts to gather our full company for a plan of attack that very night. When darkness fell, a hundred of us gathered just below the position from which I observed the horses and Germans. 1st Lt George A. Piercy, platoon commander, was to lead. Heretofore, I had no respect, only disdain, for anyone who had fear or fright, or obvious hesitation going into combat. I had participated in well over one-hundred such instances in the previous twelve months of such conditions at night. This circumstance caused me fear! I simply sat down and watched my people move out. All of a sudden I realized what my people had been feeling. Fear had overcome me, too! The evening went well for the Force. The three Germans were long gone, together with their three mules, which I had reported were horses.[32]

Rex Atwell's fears did not last, as soon afterwards he went out on a second, long range and very risky patrol. This second patrol departed towards Col de Braus September 3rd and seems to have gone as far as Cime de Ventabren or Tête de la Lavina:

During a temporary base and orientation somewhere in these Maritime Alps, Dick Hilton, Canadian Sergeant, was appointed to lead a five-man patrol in the general direction of Sospel, France. Dick Hilton then asked me if I would join him. I agreed, and that included my number one, Colin D'Entremont. We headed in a north, northeast direction at 3 p.m. The route was relatively easy. We did not climb significantly, more of a slight grade.

As darkness closed in, we had traveled more than 10 miles. Suddenly I heard a distinct metal sound of a machine gun ammunition container. It sounded to me like a machine gun bunker was closing down for the night. We were in a broad open area, with nothing for protection. The sound

The Col de Braus pass that the FSSF patrol led by Rex Atwell found virtually undefended the night of September 3 to 4, 1944. The Germans would considerably reinforce the position in the next days, causing Col de Braus to become a major battlefield. Author's Collection.

emanated from some trees a hundred feet from us. I hand signaled to Dick Hilton and my man, Colin D'Entremont. I motioned to them to spread out to the right, keep separate, and move forward. I would move in behind the enemy site. I no sooner had reached that position when a figure moved quickly toward me as if he were escaping. I dropped him to the ground with a round from my Tommy gun. The balance of the Germans stood up with their hands held high. There were six of them standing, but they were not Germans! They were mixed nationalities from countries occupied by the Germans and forced into the German army. What to do now? I bid our leader, Dick Hilton, to take our prisoners back to our Force base. I said Colin and I were going on for the time being. I could find no wires or wireless communication equipment in the bunker. We said goodbye to Dick Hilton and his crew.[33]

It took very intrepid soldiers indeed to voluntarily decide to separate from each other far behind enemy lines in the dark and pursue the patrol, when their achievements were already enough for them to return to their base with heads high! The soldier Rex Atwell shot may have been 17-year-old *Jäger* **Josef Walz**, who was buried approximately one kilometer southwest of Col de Braus after being reported killed September 4th. The mix of nationalities that Rex Atwell noted among the prisoners was as we know typical of *Reserve Division 148*. September 4th, at 05:50, once the prisoners and their escort had returned to their lines, 3rd Regiment made a report confirming Rex Atwell's story:

> The seven prisoners of war identified as 5th Company, 28th Battalion, Reserve Regiment. Captured (…) at approximately 24:00. Stated they were on outpost duty. Six men were sleeping, other was working. No resistance offered. Captured by patrol from 1st Battalion. One man from patrol returned with prisoners of war; remainder of patrol still out.[34]

We will now let **Rex Atwell** describe the rest of the patrol:

> Colin and I then continued on until Sospel! A small town well spread out. Sometime after midnight, Colin and I stretched out to sleep. We stayed out of sight of the roadway. A motorcycle with a sidecar awakened us. It was coming from below with a driver and officer. They would

soon learn the loss of their gun crew. It crossed my mind to capture the motorcycle twosome, but I decided against it. Several ambulances crisscrossed the roads in the town below us. I told Colin I would love to drive back in one of those ambulances.

Below and off to our left there was considerable enemy activity. Maintaining our elevation, we made our way toward the German lines. The Germans had five small-bore cannons with limited range. However, they had been harassing us during the last few days. Bushes and trees became good cover for us as we worked our way closer to the cannon site. They were wheeled and designed to be towed. They sat side by side with their barrels almost vertical. As we sat and watched, the enemy seemed to disappear. Colin and my other patrol member usually carried two high explosive hand grenades, as I did. Colin never ever questioned my decisions. I asked him for two grenades and told him to wait for me.

Between we and the cannons was only bush and a steep grade. I worked my way toward them slowly and carefully, but never saw a soul. I pulled the safety pins and dropped a grenade into four barrels. The detonation was muffled. In no time I was back with Colin. We gave a wide berth to our former approach. Topping the surrounding grade, it became downhill all the way home. Less than an hour later, after reaching level terrain, we observed a German cutting wood. He was 300 yards to our right. We stopped and looked at each other. Colin frowned for a moment. Let him live! Our Tommy gun could not reach him anyway. This was a first for me to experience.

Although we were – that is, Colin and I – just a full day and night out of touch, Dick Hilton was facing court-martial for leaving us in enemy territory. After all, it was Dick Hilton's patrol! Our safe return canceled the punishment. Dick Hilton has never forgotten how close he came to being in big trouble.[35]

It would seem that both the Allied and German command had temporarily neglected the strategic importance of the Col de Braus area. The Germans were guilty of not having defended it more fiercely,

Jäger Josef Walz, aged 17, who was killed in action near Col de Braus September 4, 1944. The date and location seem to coincide with the patrol that Rex Atwell, of 2-3 of the FSSF, was on, during which Atwell shot and killed one German soldier. Huber Haas Collection.

 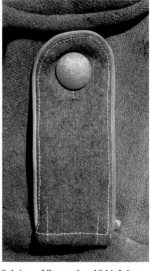

Greatcoat recovered from Col de Braus after the fighting of September 1944. It bears shoulder boards with the green corps color of the Jägers, indicating that it was lost by a soldier of Reserve Jäger Bataillon 28, the unit that indeed was involved in most of the fighting in the area until it was relieved by troops from Grenadier Regiment 80 of Infanterie Division 34. Private Collection.

while the Allies were guilty of not having firmly taken control of it, although they could have done so with minimal losses. However, the Germans would soon correct their mistake. Indeed, on September 4th, when the FABTF units' areas of responsibility were changed, the FSSF moved to the south, handing over Touët to the 2nd Battalion of the 517th PIR and leaving the Col de Braus area unguarded. The Germans took advantage of this situation and reinforced their positions at Col de Braus before the 517th PIR had time to move in. It would now cost the 517th PIR direly to capture the terrain that the FSSF had managed to penetrate without losing a single man.

A sign of increased German aggressiveness came after the first paratroopers of the 517th PIR relieved the FSSF in Touët. Literally from his doorstep, **Charles Erbetta** witnessed the arrival of a German patrol into town:

Two days [In fact, probably four days.] after the tunnel events, the Canadians were relieved by the Americans, and a column of tanks was parked on the Grand Place of l'Escarène. The Americans didn't realize it, but from up on Col de Braus, the Germans could see them down there, so they sent out two saboteurs, to sabotage the tanks. Just across the street from our gate there is an olive tree, and two Americans with submachine guns were at the foot of the olive tree. At that moment we heard the rhythmic steps of the Germans, because we could hear that iron on their shoes. They reached the gate and the American said: "Halt!" but they continued. After a second "Halt" they still continued, so he let off a burst with his Thompson and both the Germans fell down. One was killed in front of the gate, but the other got hold of himself, and although he was severely wounded he made it another 50 meters and died in front of the fountain.

They had come down to do sabotage work, since they had explosives and incendiary grenades in their musette bags. But they didn't have any luck. Actually, they committed suicide to say the truth; they should have answered the American's challenges. They knew very well that the Americans were here, since they were being sent for the tanks.

This shooting probably occurred during the night of September 4th to 5th. It is not known what became of the bodies of the two killed Germans. The sabotage mission is only Charles Erbetta's interpretation, and in fact seems unlikely. A second sign of increased German aggressiveness came at daybreak September 5th, as A Battery of the 460th PFAB moved into new positions around the railway embankment near the l'Escarène train station. **Ignatius Bail** explains what happened:

We set up our guns right away in position, and then dug our fox holes and sighted in our weapons and got everything set up. Then we had a few minutes to wait around until we had a fire mission. It wasn't more than 15 or 20 minutes after that we heard one round come in short. Then another round went over, and by then we knew that the next round was going to come in pretty close, so we all ran for our foxholes. When I got to my foxhole, Ramsey was in it already, so I got in there with him. The third shell hit our howitzer and blew it up, and at the same time it wounded nine of the men and killed **Robert Brown**, who was one of my best buddies. Two or three seconds later Ramsey raised his head up and started screaming. He had blood coming out of his neck and he panicked and jumped up and ran down the bank. I got up and ran after him. I thought there was something wrong with him, so I wanted to catch him before he got in trouble.

He ran to the bottom of the bank to the tunnel where the CP was located, and I asked: "Where is Ramsey? He was bleeding and he ran in, we need a medic." They said: "We are taking care of him right now. It looks to me like you are hit, too." I looked at my back and I was hit in the back. I didn't even feel it. They said: "It looks like you are both going to have to go to the hospital." So they put me in a jeep and they put my buddy Brown in the back of the jeep, and they drove us to the hospital. When I got there, the doctor told me that he took eight pieces out of my back and upper shoulder. They took Brown away. He was killed, and I didn't see him anymore after that because they just took him and put him with the rest of the fellows that had been shot.

19-year-old PFC Robert Brown, of A Battery of the 460th PAFB, was the first Allied soldier to be killed in the battle for Col de Braus. Unfortunately, he was soon to be followed by many more, as we will see. Later the same day, September 5th, a platoon of D Company of

Camouflaged 517th PRCT modified helmet recovered from the area between Nice and l'Escarène. Frédéric Brega Collection.

19-year-old PFC Robert W. Brown, of A Battery of the 460th PFAB, who was killed by German artillery fire near the l'Escarène train station September 5th. 517prct.org. Courtesy Ignatius Bail and Nicolas Arnulf.

the 517ᵗʰ PIR left Touët, heading for Col de Braus. It was only now that the paratroopers would realize the catastrophic consequences that not taking total control of the Col de Braus in the previous days would have. The best description of the events that followed was made by **Clark Archer** in his history of the 517ᵗʰ PRCT:

Lieutenant Starkey selected a platoon, checked the tunnel and found nothing, and headed up the hairpin bends for Col de Braus. The road had been extensively blown, cratered, and mined. It was impassable for trucks and dangerous on foot. Starkey had been told that Col de Braus was unoccupied, but when a sniper opened fire he began to suspect that he had been misinformed. The platoon halted briefly, resumed the march, and came under fire again. Another resumption of the march was met by machine gun fire, and feeling that "he'd be damned if one lousy sniper was going to stop him," Starkey led his troops off the road to the northeast.

Circling left, the platoon moved for a mile or so up steep slopes, finally arriving at a 30-foot sheer rock wall. Continuing to the left would put them far off course. They had to go up the wall. Lieutenant Starkey moved forward with two scouts, watching the top of the cliff for signs of enemy. He stumbled over a tripwire and a stunning explosion occurred. One scout was wounded and Starkey was dazed and deafened.

This would have been more than enough to stop most men, but not "muscles" Starkey. A little further on he found a place with foot and hand holes leading to the top of the wall. The platoon came forward and Lieutenant Starkey led the climb up, pausing halfway to observe, "Ain't this a hell of a way to make a living?" One by one the troopers followed him to the crest.

The ridge was occupied by a platoon-sized German force. They had apparently relied upon the mined cliff for security, and were taken completely by surprise. Seven enemy were killed and eleven captured.

More Germans arrived and began a series of counterattacks, supported by mortar and artillery fire. The troopers formed a semi-circle at the cliff's edge, placing the wounded and prisoners in the center. As the shelling grew heavier and the attacks came deeper around his flanks, Lieutenant Starkey decided to bring up more men.

After dark platoon runner Felix Povinelli made his way through German patrols back to the Battalion position. Next morning, the balance of the Company arrived with machine gun and mortar attachments from Battalion. Lieutenant Leonard Cooper's platoon reinforced Starkey just as the Germans began another counterattack.[36]

The paratroopers had managed to surprise the Germans on Caire de Braus, a peak overlooking Col de Braus itself. Both **Pvt Felix Povinelli** and **Lt Leonard Cooper** were awarded Silver Stars for their actions on September 5ᵗʰ and 6ᵗʰ, the citations of which read:

The platoon to which Private Povinelli was attached as runner was to advance a distance of three miles, seize the high ground, and cover the movement of the remainder of the company into position. Private Povinelli traveled for three miles under heavy mortar and artillery fire and, upon reaching the objective, aided in repelling a fierce counterattack. He then volunteered and was sent for medical aid and reinforcements, as it was impossible to

The famous switchbacks in the road leading to Col de Braus as they appeared at the time once the area had been secured, and as they appear today. Mike Kane Collection. Author's Collection.

evacuate the wounded due to the numerical superiority of the enemy. Although harassed constantly by sniper fire, he reached the company safely and delivered the request for aid. An hour later, the company moved out with Private Povinelli as guide. By constantly pointing out enemy positions and minefields, and leading the company around them, the forward position was reached without casualties. Shortly after reaching the forward position the enemy attacked in force. Private Povinelli had made it possible to repel this counterattack by effecting the timely arrival of reinforcements. His demonstration of physical endurance and coolness under fire, against tremendous odds, reflect high credit upon himself and his unit.

Lieutenant Cooper, leading his platoon, moved into position on high ground while positions for defense were being reconnoitered. To prevent his taking up this position, the enemy attacked in force, surprising the position held by his platoon. With great speed and efficiency, Lieutenant Cooper took command of the situation and directed his men in meeting the attack. Then, leading his men forward in the face of small arms, mortar, and artillery fire, he drove the enemy from their position with hand grenades, after his own weapon had been destroyed by shrapnel. Immediately thereafter, Lieutenant Cooper rushed thirty yards through heavy rifle and machine gun fire to the aid of one of his men who had been wounded. Lieutenant Cooper's courage and daring inspired his men to repel the counterattack of the enemy and to inflict heavy casualties upon them. His actions also enabled his company to maintain its objective.[37]

Pvt Woodie Kennamer was one of the D Company men who was sent up to reinforce the position held by Lt Starkey on Caire de Braus during the night of September 5 to 6, 1944 (It is to be noted that the name Caire de Braus is not known to any of the 517th veterans, who instead usually refer to it wrongly as Hill 1098, or even some other combinations of numbers, as below.):

We had to come up to help a fellow by the name of Starkey, a Lieutenant. So we marched all night and came to this place, which was Hill 238, I think it was, and the Germans were just beating the heck out of D Company. Tom Latimer was our sergeant, and he said: "Woody, you take the left over there, and Chuck Thompson, you take the right." So we separated about 20 yards from each other and Chuck says: "Woody, there's no damn Germans here. I am going to suggest that you take the first nap, I will take the first watch, and we will rotate that way." And he had no more then said that, and there was a whole bunch of Germans coming right toward us, right in the open field. I don't know how they didn't know that we were there. I was looking eyeball to eyeball at one guy not over 20 yards away. I almost froze in my tracks and I said: "Chuck, they are coming right at us." I took dead aim at this one guy, and that was an awesome feeling. I had shot at Germans before, plenty, but I was always with four or five others who were shooting at the same guy. But here we were just him and myself. The time he saw me to raise his gun, why, I got him. Then all hell broke loose. The Germans started to run, and some of them were Polish, and the German officer was shooting them because they were trying to get out of the way of fire. Then of course he got hit and we took the hill back. We had quite a few lost, I don't remember how many.

I said to Sgt Tom Latimer: "Tom, you better get behind those rocks," and he said: "Well, I have got rocks here, jump over, they are not firing this way right now." Then he made the statement of the day. I asked: "What are you looking at?" He says: "See those gray squirrels? They are flying from tree to tree. I haven't seen that since I was hunting in Tennessee." Even with people getting killed all around him, he still brings that up.

Cpl Robert Cooper, of D Company of the 517th PIR, was also among the men who were sent up to Caire de Braus the night of September 5th to 6th:

Our 1st Platoon was under Lt Starkey, and he was atop Hill 1098 and they got attacked. He was able to get a runner down to the other two platoons in the company, the 2nd and the 3rd platoon. The runner got down there to alert us just before dark. We had just been issued mail and hadn't had time to read it, but we started climbing right at dusk. We climbed all night, and we got up to the top of Hill 1098 and reinforced our 1st platoon up there.

I was a scout and had picked my spot out from behind a great big tree. It was just getting daylight, and I got my mail out and was starting to read my mail when the Germans started firing at us; but they were firing high, you couldn't tell where they were coming from. I rolled over and watched up in the trees, and I could see bullets raking the leaves high up in the trees. I rolled back over when I could see some movement out in the distance and I started firing. I had tracer bullets in my rifle because I was a scout, and of course you know the old infantry saying: "Tracer bullets work both ways," which they did. I took a lot of fire, but I was well covered behind the big tree.

The men started to fan out and fire at the attacking Germans. **Anthony Fabrik**, my machine gunner, came running up to my left. He was a little guy, but he carried the tripod. Well he got hit with two burp gun bullets right in his stomach. I got to him a little bit later. I rolled him over and I took his pulse and I knew he was dead. He never knew what hit him. **Sgt Thorng** got killed up there at the same time.

Evidently, the Germans didn't realize that we had reinforced the position, because we hadn't made any noise, and after their first assault with some burp guns the infantry tried to move up. But we got them and captured a couple Germans and killed two or three others. Then they backed off and whenever they back off, they know where they have been and then they start shelling. That night we stayed there, and then we went down off of there the next day. We were relieved.

Pvt Robert Boese, of D Company, was awarded a Silver Star for his role during the battles. The citation read:

For gallantry in action near Col de Braus, France, September 6th 1944. As Private Boese's company moved to a

23-year-old Pvt LaVerne LaBar, Jr., 21-year-old PFC Travis V. McDonald, and 24-year-old Pvt William Thorng, of D Company of the 517th PIR, who were all killed during the fighting at Caire de Braus September 6 and 7, 1944. LaBar Family Collection. McDonald Family Collection. National WWII Memorial Collection.

ridge which would afford better cover from enemy mortar and artillery fire, Private Boese, the leading scout, moved down the ridge and spotted an enemy machine gun nest. Realizing that this machine gun would impede his company's progress and probably result in death or injury to his comrades, Private Boese, armed only with a carbine, closed to within seventy-five yards of the enemy. He then stood erect and advanced fearlessly towards the enemy. Firing steadily as he advanced, he killed one, wounded one, and captured three of the enemy, and in three minutes silenced the enemy position. Private Boese's skill and courage prevented his company from being ambushed and insured his uninterrupted advance. His gallantry was an inspiration to his comrades and reflects much credit upon himself and his unit.[38]

September 7th, D Company was relieved by G Company of the 517th, and the prisoners and casualties were evacuated from the hill. Seven men of the 2nd Battalion had been killed in the fighting of September 5th to 7th, they were:

Surname	Name	Rank	Unit	Age	Official date of death
York	Joe I.	PFC	HQ 2 517 PIR	20	6.9.1944
Fabrick	Anthony	PFC	D Co 517 PIR		6.9.1944
LaBar	LaVerne Jr	Pvt	D Co 517 PIR	23	6.9.1944
Lopez	Daniel T.	Pvt	D Co 517 PIR	19	6.9.1944
McDonald	Travis V.	PFC	D Co 517 PIR	21	7.9.1944
Thorng	William	Pvt	D Co 517 PIR	24	7.9.1944
Arredonds	James M.	Cpl	F Co 517 PIR		6.9.1944

When Col de Braus had been left with only light defenses, the FABTF had refused to seize it, but on September 6th, now that it was too late and heavy fighting had erupted, the FABTF was not only ordered to capture the pass, but also the town of Sospel. It would seem, however, that the Germans had in the meantime grasped how important the control of Col de Braus was for the defense of Sospel, and they had made a determined attempt to regain total control of the pass and its surroundings. Early September 6th, they had not only attacked D Company's positions on Caire de Braus, but had also simultaneously attacked Mont Méras and Cime de Baudon (Hill 1264), south of Col de Braus, which were held by the 3rd and 1st Regiments of the FSSF. Some of the German soldiers performing these attacks acted in an unusually aggressive manner, as one forceman was even stabbed to death! Extracts of the messages received at FSSF headquarters September 6th give an idea of the events of that day in the FSSF's sector:

07:25. (…) 1st Regiment reports one prisoner of war captured during night. They also had two casualties vicinity Hill 1264 (…) one stabbed and one wounded by pistol fire. (…)

Calling in regard to situation. Informed that during night one man shot by patrol. One man killed – stabbed vicinity east of saddle Hill 1264. (…)

08:15. (…) From 3rd Regiment to Commanding Officer FSSF: Having some trouble on Mont Méras. Enemy infiltrated in on left flank last night. Having a fire fight. Sent another company to reinforce them. Have had a few casualties. Communications bad. (…)

09:03. (…) **Lt Moore** has been killed. Enemy strength not over 50-60 on Mont Méras. Withdrawing a platoon from Mont Méras. (…)

21:30. 3rd Regiment. During night 5/6 September, enemy infiltrated and attacked our positions on Mont Méras at dawn. Strength of attacking forces one company. Our troops forced to withdraw. At 06:10, two companies 3rd Regiment counterattacked and regained their positions, taking eight prisoners of war and consolidating their positions. Our casualties were light.[39]

These were some of the actual communications passed September 6th, explaining that 3rd Regiment had to retreat in the face

Dear Mrs. McDonald,

I am sending you some pictures that (Mac) Travis had. He left these in my bag and I'm sending them to you. I am ashamed that I haven't wrote you sooner, but I'm not much at writing sympathy letters. I sympathize with all the family over the loss of your son Travis. He was just like a brother to me. It hurt me just as much as my own brother's death did, because it had been three years since I saw my only brother, and Travis and I had been together the last year and a half. The army censors won't let us write to any of the casaultie's folks until after they notify them. That is the reason I haven't written sooner.

Travis was shot by a 37 mm anti-tank gun Sept. 6th. The kid lived awhile after being hit, but the shock and loss of blood was too much. He was smiling all during those hours he was dying. He smiled until the morphine put him to sleep. He was the best friend and best soldier I ever met or ever want to meet. He and I planned to meet at his house the first Christmas after we got home. If you don't mind, I would still love to keep that promise.

Forever a friend,
Pvt. S.D. Moxon 38530630
Co. D 517th Prcht. Inf.P.T.R.
A.P.O. 758 C/o P.M.
N.Y., N.Y.

P.f.c. Travis V. McDonald
Killed in action Sept. 6, 1944
Southern France, Colde Brause, France
Purple Heart Hill

McDonald Family Collection.

20-year-old Pvt Joe I. York, of the HQ Company, 2nd Battalion, 517th PIR, who was killed September 6th, presumably in the area between l'Escarène and Col de Braus. Crawford Historical Society Collection, courtesy Diana Watson.

LIEUT. JAMES MOORE.

22-year-old Lt James D. Moore and 19-year-old Pvt Emmett J. Reed, of 4-3 of the FSSF, who were killed on Mont Méras in the early hours of September 6th. Lt Moore left a young wife and a daughter he had never seen. Emmett Reed had gotten married a month before and had just joined the unit. Hastings Pioneer Room Collection, courtesy Cindy Thury Smith. Reed Family Collection.

The German losses in the general area of Col de Braus between September 1st and September 7th cannot be evaluated with any precision, because it would seem that many of the bodies of those killed were never recovered, and are thus not listed in the archives of the *Volksbund*. Indeed, most of the dead were buried where they were killed; in other words, often in the forest. Some of these graves were never found, and others were plundered years later by souvenir seekers. Furthermore, some soldiers were simply never buried at all and their bones were scattered by wild animals. For the period we are concerned with, only the following men were recovered by the *Volksbund* when they visited Col de Braus in 1958 (some bodies were also found at later dates, but the data about them was not located when doing the research for this book):

Pte. S.E. Dainard Killed in Italy

Private Stanley E. Dainard, son of Mr. and Mrs. E. J. Dainard, 29 St. Paul Street, has been killed in action in Italy according to official notification received by the family.

Private Dainard, a member of the original first battalion of the Hastings and Prince Edward Regiment, enlisted in 1939 and trained with his unit in Picton. He went overseas in December of the same year.

A brother Fred, is overseas with the armed services and another, George, is at home. Mrs. Gordon Burrell (Jennie) is a sister.

The obituary of Canadian forceman Pvt Stanley E. Dainard. Note that it mistakenly lists his location of death as Italy, evidence of how poorly informed families of Allied casualties were. Community Archives of Belleville Collection, courtesy Sharon White.

Surname	Name	Rank	Age	Date of death	Location of burial	Unit
Sauermann	Hans	Uffz	25	1.9.1944	Lucéram	8./Res.Jäg. Btl.28
Linert	Berthold	Gren	36	2.9.1944	Mont Méras	
Walz	Josef	*Jäger*	17	4.9.1944	Col de Braus	Res.Jäg. Btl.28
Czora	Gerhard	*Jäger*	17	5.9.1944	US Draguignan	Res.Jäg. Btl.28
Gallitzschke	Erich		35	5.9.1944	Peira Cava	
Gutmann	Wilhelm	Gren	18	5.9.1944	Peira Cava	7./Res.Gren. Btl.372
Marciniak	Josef	*Jäger*	18	5.9.1944	Lucéram	
Gruber	Georg	Pio	18	6.9.1944	Col de Braus	Res.Pi.Btl.8?
Locateli	Bastian				Col de Braus	
Schönle	Walter	Pio	18	6.9.1944	Col de Braus	3./Res. Pi.Btl.8
Unknown					Col de Braus	
Tomanek	Rudolf	Jäger	27	6.9.1944	US Draguignan	
Skowronski	Heinrich	*Jäger*	18	6.9.1944	MIA Lucéram	
Glowania	Roman	Kan	20	7.9.1944	Breil cemetery	2./Res.Art. Abt.8
Winkler	Richard	*Jäger*	34	7.9.1944	Pas de l'Agrée	Res.Jäg. Btl.28
Hau	Richard	Schütze	18	7.9.1944	Lucéram	

of the German attack before counterattacking later in the day. Interestingly, these events were twisted beyond recognition in the FSSF daily report, which claimed: "3rd Regiment moved east to occupy new positions; ambushed 30-man enemy patrol (...), killing eight. At 06:10 assaulted Mont Méras, inflicting casualties on enemy."[40] This report conveniently changed what had been a retreat into an ambush! Proof, once again, that military reports are to be interpreted with a grain of salt.

The FSSF suffered four killed during these German attacks and patrols, who were:

Surname	Name	Rank	Unit	Age	Date of death	Location of death
Dainard	Stanley E.	Pvt	3-1 FSSF	24	6.9.1944	Hill 1264
Mann	Rex C.	Pvt	1-1 FSSF	19	6.9.1944	Hill 1264
Moore	James D.	2Lt	4-3 FSSF	22	6.9.1944	Mt Méras
Reed	Emmett U.	Pvt	4-3 FSSF	18	6.9.1944	Mt Méras

It is noteworthy that the German troops that performed the aggressive attacks of September 6th were still men of *Reserve Division 148*, and not men of the much better quality *Infanterie Division 34* that was to replace them shortly afterwards.

Too Much to Bear

September 7th, the 517th PIR's 3rd Battalion was given the task of taking over the Col de Braus area. G Company therefore relieved D Company at Caire de Braus and I Company took up position at Mont Scandéious, south of Col de Braus. That evening, I Company sent a small patrol out towards Tête de la Lavina, which I Company's **Guy Carr** later described in his memoirs:

The remains of a German grave in the vicinity of Col de Braus in the 1980s after it has been visited by unscrupulous relic hunters looking for militaria. Private Collection.

Sgt Wilbur G. Hymbaugh, who was severely wounded in the stomach on the patrol during which Sgt Robert J. Miller was killed. Hymbaugh Family Collection.

Two sergeants and another trooper left on a patrol to seek the layout of the enemy positions on the hill. They had advanced about halfway up the hill when they came face to face with a pill box. The Germans opened up with burp guns. One sergeant got his belly completely riddled with bullets. The other sergeant [**Sgt Robert J. Miller**] was hit with a Potato Masher (German grenade) which killed him instantly. The trooper who went with them hit the dirt and rolled off the road, not hit. He started running back toward our lines and looked around and saw the sergeant following, holding his midsection together with his hands.

They finally made it back to our lines, but I'll never know how the sergeant made it with his stomach torn up as much as it was. He was sent back to a field hospital. That episode was too much for the trooper who was not hit, and he went berserk that evening and was also sent back. Earlier that morning, that trooper and I had been talking over a cup of "so-called" coffee, and he appeared to be in complete command of his faculties. When he returned from that ordeal he was very shook up. He just seemed to sit there in a daze, when all at once he jumped up, ran, and threw himself to the ground and literally ripped off all his fingernails. His mind was completely gone, and I had to knock him out to keep him from killing himself. Episodes such as this made you wonder just how much more anyone could endure.[41]

Guy Carr's platoon buddy, **Pvt Marvin Moles**, remembered a few extra details about Sergeant Robert Miller's death:

We had some battles in there, I didn't think we were going to live to get through them. Three of them went out on a patrol and a German threw one of those potato masher hand grenades, hit Miller in the head and blew his head off. There was another guy with him, his name was Bailey. He must have seen Miller when the German hit him with that grenade. I guess it was just more than he could handle, for he was just about 17 or 18 years old. Of course, at two or three o'clock that morning, he had come running back, him and two other guys. He must have had a nervous breakdown, he started screaming and trying to dig a hole in the ground with his bare hands. He tore the blood out of his fingers. One of the sergeants had to knock him out. They carried him out, and I never did hear or see from him

anymore. The other two guys, they just hung on in there. We found Miller the next day when we went out to take the place where the Germans had been, and of course they had taken his boots.

The battle for the Col de Braus area had now started in earnest, and many more soldiers were to die in the next days. Because he had been left behind, Sgt Robert Miller was listed as missing in action until his body was finally recovered September 18th, when the 3rd Battalion of the 517th PIR captured Tête de la Lavina for good. However, the rest of this battle is beyond the scope of our study.

Conclusion

After entering Nice, the First Airborne Task Force units were initially ordered to halt their advance, and to only send patrols to the east. September 4th, the 509th and 551st Parachute Infantry Battalions were removed from the front, while the remaining First Special Service Force and 517th Parachute Infantry Regiment filled in the void and were ordered to resume the advance towards Italy. Along the coast, the First Special Service Force managed to reach Menton and the Italian border without any difficulties. The FSSF patrols had also initially managed to reach Col de Braus and Tête de la Lavina without any losses. However, when the 517th PIR relieved the FSSF in this area, the Germans took advantage of the lull to retake possession of the important Col de Braus mountain pass. Since the FABTF had crossed the Var August 30th, losses had been minimal. However, as the 517th PIR and FSSF attempted to take control of the Col de Braus area September 5th, 6th, and 7th, 13 Allied soldiers were killed. The battle of Col de Braus had begun and many more casualties were to follow.

20-year-old Sgt. Robert J. Miller of I Company, 517th PIR, who was reportedly killed by a grenade in the Col de Braus area on September 7, 1944. His body was only recovered several days later when the 517th PIR finally captured the area. Garrett Culhane Collection, courtesy Tony Ventura.

16

Conclusion and a Few More Stories

Conclusion about the Allied advance from August 15 to September 7, 1944

The aim of this book was to study the battle movement that the First Airborne Task Force (as well as the 141st Infantry Regiment and the *Groupe Naval d'Assaut de Corse*) and *Reserve Division 148* were involved in between August 15 and September 7, 1944. We have therefore now reached the term of this study. After September 7th, the rapid advance of the FABTF was halted, both by the strong resistance the Germans put up and by the FABTF orders that were to not advance beyond the Italian border. From September 7, 1944, until the end of the war May 8, 1945, the front would remain virtually unchanged. The 517th Parachute Infantry Regiment did advance a few kilometers in September and October. It was able to capture Col de Braus after a successful and well planned attack, but when it finally took Sospel in late October, it was only because the Germans had decided to evacuate the town of their own accord in order to shorten their lines. The major change in the front came in the very last days of the war, in late April 1945, when Free French Forces, which were by then holding most of the Maritime Alps front, launched a large-scale and costly offensive that captured the Authion forts and pushed the Germans into Italy. As the French troops pursued the retreating Germans into Italy, the war finally came to an end.

It is a little-known fact that the German army resisted in the Maritime Alps until the last days of the war. While the Red Army was storming into Berlin, German soldiers were still bitterly defending barren and isolated mountains located in the hinterland of the French Riviera!

The Liberation of the French Riviera later became known as the "Champagne Campaign." However, this name is misleading, since as we have seen, the Allied advance was marked by several episodes of violent fighting and hundreds of deaths. In the period and area of our study (the general area between Agay, Seillans, Turini, and Menton from August 15th to September 7th), at least 127 Allied and over 300 German soldiers died over a three-week period. Approximately 150 resistance men and women (in the broad sense of the word) were also killed or executed in the same time frame. The number of civilian deaths is difficult to evaluate, but is at least equal to 100. More than 600 dead in three weeks may be little compared to certain other battles of WWII, but it was still a great many dead,

particularly by modern standards. As an example, the FABTF was suffering more killed per day (approximately seven) during its first month in southern France than the total of the deployed U.S. forces during Operation Iraqi Freedom and Operation Enduring Freedom combined.[1] (Approximately three killed per day in 2007, the most deadly year of these operations.) The 509th PIB alone lost no less than 48 killed (out of approximately 700 men) in the ten-day period from August 15th to August 24th, including the Battalion Executive Officer, one Battalion Surgeon, one Company Commander, and one Intelligence Officer. It had not been a Champagne Campaign for them! In total, the FABTF suffered at least 302 dead during its operations in southern France between August and November 1944 (this count does not include the 15 glider pilots who were killed the day of the landing), of which over 200 died during the first month of combat.

The fighting remained relatively clean, with the Geneva Convention usually being respected. Although a large number of French men and women were executed by the German troops, sometimes in despicable circumstances, they actually were members of the Resistance in the vast majority of cases, and not innocent civilians. I have only found three clear cut cases of German soldiers being executed by the Resistance during the period (at Levens, Thorenc and Lantosque), and one case involving American troops (the German sniper with wooden bullets at Théoule). Though there were probably several more cases that remain to be brought to light, there were definitely no large-scale massacres of captured German soldiers. The Resistance played a very important role during the campaign (though many Allied soldiers may not have realized it), as it constantly guided and informed Allied troops, and in several cases launched relatively large-scale attacks on the Germans. Of the more than 300 German dead, at least 60, or approximately 20%, were killed during Resistance operations, particularly in Nice, Montauroux, Levens, and Tourette du Château.

The Allied high command had little interest in liberating the French Riviera, as it presented no strategic value to it. However, once the campaign got underway, it was quite successful for the Allied forces. They systematically managed to inflict much greater casualties on the Germans than the Germans managed to inflict on them. This is mainly because the Allies had superior artillery, air forces, and navies, and because the Allied units consisted of particularly highly motivated and well trained soldiers. The German

Although it quickly bogged down, the "Champagne Campaign" did continue to offer some outlandish aspects. Masato Doi of the 442nd Anti-Tank Company: "I think it was the third platoon of the Anti-Tank Company that captured and caught a one-man submarine off the coast at Menton. They at first thought it was a big fish, and when they waded out to get to it, this one German popped out of the submarine. I guess he was surprised to see Japanese soldiers as American soldiers." From left to right: Akira Fujiki, unidentified, Yoshio Hikichi, and Yugo Okubo. Courtesy Masato Doi.

The so-called "Champagne Campaign" quickly turned into static warfare fought on barren and isolated mountains. Here a paratrooper from the 517th PIR is apparently reduced to melting snow to have something to drink, while a forward observer from the 602nd PFAB observes the German lines on an inhospitable and frozen mountain top. Mike Kane Collection. Art Helmers Collection.

forces were just the opposite, many of the soldiers not having finished their training and wishing only to desert at the first chance. *Reserve Division 148* suffered mostly due to this weakness: the majority of its losses were caused by desertion and surrender. The number of *Reserve Division 148* men captured in August 1944 is probably somewhere around 2,000. On the Allied side, there seem to have been only two cases of surrender in our study area (excluding all the paratroopers who were captured but soon re-liberated the morning of the invasion), neither of which involved the FABTF. The first was the mass surrender of the *Groupe Naval d'Assaut de Corse*, which was forced to give up, as it was trapped in the open in a minefield and had suffered approximately 50% casualties. The second case was that of Lt Walter Taylor, USMC, who was captured after having being wounded and knocked unconscious by a grenade at St Cézaire. The contrast with the numerous mass German surrenders is striking!

Although they suffered very heavy losses, the campaign can be considered a partial success for the Germans, as well. The orders received by *Reserve Division 148* were to slowly retreat to the Italian border, and to organize the main line of resistance there. The division did exactly this, and if it had not been for the cases of mass surrender and desertion, its losses would not have been that much greater than those of the Allied forces. The Germans performed their retreat skillfully, setting up their temporary resistance lines at the most strategically appropriate spots and systematically blowing and mining bridges and roads before departing. Many of the FABTF soldiers felt that they were getting the short end of the stick during the advance, as it was the Germans who decided where and how the fight would occur, always choosing the best locations to strike at the advancing Allies.

The German retreat from the French Riviera has often been presented as a "run for your life" massive failure. Such was not the case at all, in reality. As we have seen chapter after chapter, the German units, although plagued by desertion, remained well organized and cohesive during the retreat. In fact, *Generalleutnant* Otto Fretter-Pico, the commander of *Reserve Division 148*, was awarded the Knight's Cross, Germany's highest award, for his role in skillfully organizing the retreat to the Italian border! The following article about the reasons for which *Generalleutnant* Fretter-Pico was awarded the Knight's Cross also explains the retreat of *Reserve Division 148* as seen through the eyes of the German propaganda:

> How *Generalleutnant* Fretter-Pico earned the Knight's Cross.
>
> The reserve division led by *Generalleutnant* Fretter-Pico cordoned off the front in the Estérel Mountains, west of the Grasse-Cannes line, over several days of intense fighting. But its right flank remained open and the enemy could use his numerical superiority in a flanking movement at any time. With indications of the flanking risk being very strong, the division received the order to quickly withdraw to the Var River. But since only parts of the division were mobile, this meant that some of the heavy weapons and the supplies would have to be left behind and destroyed.
>
> Therefore, and because of his good knowledge of the enemy positions that he had acquired during his numerous visits to the front, *Generalleutnant* Fretter-Pico decided, under his own responsibility, to retreat slowly and in several steps, so that the entire movement to the Var lasted about one week. Because the division commander visited his troops down to the level of the company command posts daily in the heaviest enemy artillery and mortar fire, and was thus able to picture the situation as it really was (…), the difficult operation succeeded smoothly and according to plan. It not only succeeded in enabling the division to pull back without any loss of weapons and equipment, in other words, in full combat strength, but also in transporting back all the supplies. It was thanks to the responsible and independent decision of *Generalleutnant* Fretter-Pico that it was possible to build a strong and stable defense line in the Maritime Alps with the entire strength of the division, on which the enemy attack was halted.
>
> The brave and determined division commander, who has already earned the German Cross in Gold in December 1941, was awarded the Knight's Cross of the Iron Cross for this performance.[2]

Although the article is clearly exaggerated, particularly in its claim that *Reserve Division 148* remained in full combat strength, it is true that the division had managed to retreat in order, and that the final defense line it set up did momentarily stop the Allied advance, most notably at Col de Braus.

A Few More Stories

During my research, I came across a large number of interesting accounts or facts regarding the war in the Maritime Alps that did not fit the theme covered by this book, but were nonetheless particularly interesting and worthy of publishing. We will thus end this book by going through a few of these stories.

"What can I say?"

At the end of the previous chapter, we told the story of the small battle D Company of the 517th PIR fought as it reached the Col de Braus area late September 5th. On the 7th, it was relieved by G Company, having lost five men killed. September 9th, G Company's 2nd Platoon, under the leadership of 1st Lt Arthur Ridler and 2nd Lt Richard Spencer, was sent on an aggressive patrol (or was it an attack?) up the hill laying to their front. The hill would later become known as Bloody Stump as a consequence of the patrol. G Company's **Private Ralph Nelson** remembered:

Generalleutnant Otto Fretter-Pico, commanding officer of Reserve Division 148, was awarded the Knight's Cross of the Iron Cross he is seen wearing here for having skillfully organized the retreat of Reserve Division 148 from the French Riviera. Author's Collection.

Lt Spencer and I, and about three or four other guys were going up the hill. It was pretty steep, but not too long and we got about halfway up. A couple Germans were laying down, watching us, but we couldn't see them, they were on top. They waited until we were halfway up, then all of a sudden they stood up and each threw a potato masher grenade at us. Of course, you could see them up in the air, but there was nothing you could do and we had to quickly get back down. One guy got hit in the face with the grenades and I don't know what happened to him, but then we got down in the woods.

Lt Spencer called in the artillery but he screwed up. You have got to tell the artillery people where you are and the height and distance of where you want the shots to go. What they do is they throw one round, and then you have to call back and tell them to come higher or lower. Well, that one round landed right on top of us, and that is where **Staat** got killed: by our own artillery. He was sitting down in a little hollow, cleaning his fingernails, and he got killed right then and there. He was a nice looking young blond fellow, my age. He was the only one that even got hit there, and then, of course, they told them: "Raise up, raise up the artillery, you're on top of us!" and they did.

21-year-old Pvt John A. Staat, of G Company of the 517th PIR, who was killed by friendly artillery fire at Col de Braus. Staat Family Collection.

A photo taken on "Bloody Stump" in September 2010, 66 years after Lt Ridler's patrol. Author's Collection.

Lt Spencer himself had been wounded by the German grenades. Despite this setback, the 2nd Platoon returned back up the hill, led by Lt Ridler, as **Private William Bowers** later wrote:

September 9, 1944, Maritime Alps near Sospel, a ridge called "Bloody Stump" (1000-1300 hours), 3rd Battalion, G Company, 2nd Platoon, 1st Squadron [sic], Lieutenant Ridler leader. In the morning, we climbed the hill before us. All was serene until we were in an area of unstable footing. All at once the sky was full of potato masher grenades, accompanied by rifle and machine gun fire. There were casualties before we were able to extract ourselves.

(1500-1800 hours) After resting, regrouping, and reorganizing, we started up the hill again, aware that they were waiting for us this time. We had gone some distance when I spotted a telephone wire angling down from the left. I cut the wire and threw the two ends in opposite directions, then followed it to the top of the ridge while the others continued straight up the hill. When I reached the top of the ridge, the wire crossed over and downward out of sight. I started to follow the wire, but changed my mind. Later, I realized that I had been practically standing on top of their observation post.

As I was trying to decide what to do, what seemed to be an endless column of Germans was quietly going past an opening, one at a time, below me and to my right, not more than 20 feet away. We were being encircled; however, I did not read it that way at the moment. I was some distance to the left of the others, and I signaled Lt Ridler to send somebody over to me. When the fellow arrived and saw the Germans passing by, the jerk said much too loudly: "Do you want to get killed!" I told him I was going to pop one, but would wait until he got back to Ridler. (His visit obviously alerted the couple in the observation post.) I decided to shoot one of them as he crossed the opening.

I got my timing as the Germans were crossing the opening below me and was squeezing the trigger when a voice said: "Who do you think you are - God?" I stopped squeezing the trigger, stood up, and looked around to see who had said that, but I saw no one. I stood there trying to figure it out. I knew I was not God, but I was a soldier who would kill or be killed! Now what do I do? Finally, I compromised, which was a mistake, and squatted down again to keep my shadow from falling across the Germans when I was standing. I reestablished my timing, closed my eyes, and fired as the next German was in the middle of the crossover space. Up to this moment in our second time up the hill, not a shot had been fired by anyone.

I fired and immediately heard voices behind me, but did not understand the language. I whirled around in a half crouch but saw no one. I said to myself: "You're dead." As I started to turn to my right to get out of there, my unseen adversary let me have it with a burp gun. My face just exploded, but I was still standing, as the whole ridge just seemed to blow apart. I decided that I had better get down, and fortunately I got down into a shallow depression.

The character who shot me must have been really upset, for he kept trying to finish me off. The bullets were kicking up the dirt in front of my face, much as you see dirt jumping up in the movies from machine gun fire. He also threw a couple grenades my way. I don't believe I was hit beyond the first burst of fire, but then it is doubtful I would have felt anything if I had been hit again.

I laid there for a short time, then decided to get back to the others, and I did, with bullets flying all over the place. As I got back to the others I was greeted by: "Hey, fellow, what outfit are you from?" I thought: "My God, I must be a mess." Our medic saw me and called me to him. He told me to lie down and gave me a 4x4 gauze to cover the wound on the left side of my lower jaw. The bullet had lodged in the shattered bone on the right side. My lower jaw was broken from both hinges. Then I was told to remove my backpack, which contained rifle grenades. As I struggled to get my backpack off, my head began spinning and I was about to pass out, so I laid back down, waited a few minutes, and tried again. this time succeeding with the medic's help. After that, Doc started messing around on the right side of my back. Until then, I was not aware of any wounds in my chest area. As Doc was working on me, I was hearing some others getting hit.

Somebody decided that we had better move back down the hill. Since I now knew that my wounds were serious, I was not going to stay where I was and went with them. Partway down the hill we entered an abandoned pillbox. Sometime later it was decided that the wounded would be left with a person not wounded or armed, because the wounded would probably be captured, and without anyone armed there would be no excuse to kill them.

Again, I felt certain that to survive I had to get back to our own doctors, so I got up and took off with those leaving. God obviously had Staff Sergeant Jerome V. Callahan and Corporal Allan H. Douglas go with me to make sure I made it. I went as far as I could and my legs just turned to rubber and down I went, unable to move. I think I was nearly out of blood. Douglas picked me up on his shoulder, but I couldn't breathe, so he put me down. Callahan said they would get a stretcher and be back.

They had not been gone long until I heard firing from a German MG and M-1s. Soon all was quiet and I thought that was it. Sometime later I heard somebody walking through the brush but no talking. I decided to play dead. They walked right up to me and stood there for a bit without a word. Finally somebody said: "Is he dead?" It was English, so I grunted to let them know I was alive.

They put me on a stretcher and started off, and it was only now and then that I was aware of anything. As they started up the road, we were observed by Germans on another mountain, and bless their hearts, they tried to get us with their 88s, which they really knew how to use.

I vaguely remember being put in a jeep, but none of the ride to the next point. When I next became aware of things, I was on my back and a doctor was gently wiping around my right eye, which had no vision. Suddenly my eye popped open and I could see. Blood had pooled and dried over my eye as I lay on the stretcher on my right side. The doctor gave me a shot and I next awoke on an operating table as they dug out of my body much of the metal that did not belong there.

As I awoke, I was on my back and I heard what sounded like pebbles dropping into a metal dish pan. Finally I realized it was pieces of bullets being pulled out of my chest, then I was gone again.

As I came to again, I thought I was screaming, as I had tremendous pain across my stomach. I indicated I needed a support under my buttocks and as soon as a support was in place, I passed out.

One again I awoke, and this time a doctor was trying to remove a bullet from the right inside of my lower jaw with forceps, but they kept slipping off the bullet. He asked if I would mind his cutting through from the outside to extract the bullet. I said: "Go ahead" and passed out.

Each time I regained consciousness, it seemed as if I was rising from a pit to the surface of awareness. The next time I awoke I was on a cot, on my back at a field hospital, and as I slowly came to my senses, there were three or four nurses standing around me and someone said: "But he's so

The day of September 9, 1944, on Bloody Stump as it was later described with a certain amount of journalistic exaggeration. 517prct.org Collection.

young." They seemed to be crying, but for what reason I still do not know, and out I went again.

The issue of my survival was in doubt for some time, humanly speaking, but today I am remarkably healthy, yet I sense that I am very vulnerable. During my 14½ months of hospitalization, three different times I was told that medically I should never have lived. As many can tell you, it does humble one to have survived through some of the first-hand experiences of combat. America and freedom are worth the cost and we must never forget that.[3]

Meanwhile, the main body of the patrol had not fared any better than Bowers, and had fallen into an ambush. **Henry Filipczak**, also of G Company's 2nd Platoon, remembered:

I recall that September 9th was a beautiful Saturday. Shortly after noon, our squad from 2nd Platoon were told to report to Lt Ridler. He advised us to get ready to go on patrol to basically establish where the German front line was. He said: "Filip, bring the machine gun along." As always, Lt Ridler took the lead. We probably walked a mile when we approached a very large wooded hill a first time, pretty much in single file because of the trees, and the Germans chased us down. They had a lot of machine guns and stuff like that, but we were far enough away that we were able to get down safely.

At that point, I really honest to God thought that we were going to go back, because we found out where they were. Well, that Lt Ridler, he was a soldier's soldier or whatever; he decided that we were going to follow him around down the side of this mountain about half a mile, then go back up again. Why did we do this? I thought we had accomplished our mission, but apparently Lt Ridler didn't feel that we did, so we went up and followed him. I remember being right behind him as we came across a plateau. Ridler kept going, even though it was a pretty open area. We had barely started when we had a hail of machine gun and rifle fire, maybe even some grenades.

We hit the ground, and there was still considerable German firing when I saw a crater in front of me and I crawled in. My body was pretty much covered, but my legs were exposed. I felt my leg go up into the air and down and felt a severe burning sensation and realized I was hit. Shortly thereafter I heard someone say to go back down the hill. Even though Ridler was quite close, I never heard a word from him. I started to crawl, knowing full well that the Germans would never take a wounded soldier prisoner. I was in the open and the Germans could have easily killed me, but nothing happened, so I kept crawling down the hill.

Near the bottom of the hill I heard a voice, and words can't describe the feeling when I recognized it was Cpl Allan Douglas, who said: "Filip, how are you doing?" knowing I was wounded. He had stayed back just to see if everyone was able to get back down. I had a live grenade in my hand with the pin pulled, thinking I would throw it if attacked. Douglas got rid of it safely and said: "We can't stay here, so I'm going to carry you." He did this until he was exhausted and would put me down and I would crawl until I was exhausted. This went on several times until, unbelievably, a soldier from 1st Battalion came along and helped carry me until we were close to our lines and others came out and met us. A jeep was dispatched and I was taken to the evacuation hospital. I later found out that Lt Ridler had been killed and several others were wounded.

The hill was finally named Bloody Ridge because Lt Ridler was killed, and I think four of us out of 12 were wounded. When they picked up Ridler's body two days later, they determined that a bullet went through his forehead, right out the back of his head, and literally blew the back of his head off, so he was killed in an instant. He didn't suffer, from what I understand. He obviously lifted up his head to see what was going on and the shot entered his head and went out the back. There was never a sound from him, never.

I have always, in the back of my mind, thought that Lt Ridler just wanted to accomplish more than what we were intended to do and it cost him his life. But he was a tough cookie. He wasn't afraid of anything; he was, in a way, a fearless guy, because he was always in front of us and stuff like that. He was married and I understand had kids, but when it came to being a gung-ho guy, he was gung-ho. He was looking for action.

I was flown Stateside, and after several operations advised to have an amputation. The small bones in my foot were so shattered that I would always have extreme difficulty walking. I was fortunate that the surgeon was familiar with Syme's amputations, where the foot was removed at the ankle joint, and I have a prosthetic foot. It worked out great for me.

I owe my life to Cpl Allan Douglas and have tried unsuccessfully to contact him or a family member to extend heartfelt gratitude to him. I believe he was from the Atlanta area originally, but that has not helped me.

Ralph Nelson was one of the lucky ones who escaped unscathed:

We got to the top of the hill and then it was level ground, and we started going east. Elmer Carlson was first, I was second, Filipczak was third, then Lt Ridler, and then Carroll Eckert was number five. We all made a little right turn there, and Lieutenant Ridler, he was still in the middle of the aisle there and they had a good bead on him, and he got shot right below his nose. They are told: "If you can shoot at an officer," they think they are more important, so maybe they let us go and got the lieutenant instead, I don't know for sure. He got killed right there, and this Carroll was 5 or 10 feet behind him, and he got shot there pretty bad but he didn't get killed.

Filipczak had the machine gun, I had the tripod, and I said: "Can you bring the gun up?" "I can't," he said, "I am shot." I said: "No you're not!" I didn't know it right away, but a couple guys helped him down. We were overwhelmed there; the Germans were behind a big rock formation and we couldn't get near it. We withdrew and got down to the bottom of the hill and called for artillery.

Carroll Eckert was told when we left: "We can't take you with us." It sounds bad, but we were told: "If one of us is shot, don't stop and help him, because if you do, then you're a sitting duck and you can get shot too, and that's a couple of rifles out of commission." We were taught: "Don't try to help anybody," so he lay there, and the next day we found out that he had crawled back a mile or so in the dark.

Lt Arthur Ridler was posthumously awarded a Silver Star for this action. His citation is particularly interesting, in that the action is described so differently from what is remembered by Filipczak, Nelson, and Bowers, that it is no longer recognizable:

For gallantry in action near Col de Braus, France, 9 September 1944. Lieutenant Ridler was leading his platoon in an attack on high ground whose wooded approach made it necessary to move his troops up a rocky, precipitous limestone formation to reach the top of the hill. The enemy was well dug in and occupied permanent type pill boxes and gun emplacements. Lieutenant Ridler, although outnumbered, led his platoon through strongpoint after strongpoint with great intrepidity. When advance became impossible and grenades proved ineffective, he called for artillery fire, which lasted for six hours, enabling them to move higher up the hill. As he neared the top of the hill, enemy snipers harassed this advance and inflicted many casualties upon his men. Lieutenant Ridler, noting this, moved forward to fire upon the snipers, and while so doing was himself mortally wounded. Lieutenant Ridler's gallant actions and bold indifference to enemy fire inspired the men of his platoon to continue the attack with rapid success and to destroy all enemy resistance in the area.[4]

Despite the optimism of the citation, the mission had in fact been a disastrous failure, the Americans being forced to retreat, leaving two dead and several wounded behind, while the Germans remained in firm control of Bloody Stump! Furthermore, two additional men of G Company had also been killed further back, behind the American lines, in circumstances recalled by **Ralph Nelson**:

> We were running out of water, so they sent two guys back down to get some. They had these big canvas bags, about five gallons of drinking water in each one, and they didn't come back! A couple hours later, we found them in an open field. Germans were in the woods there and they shot them both in the back and killed them. Their names were Buk and Bell. The Germans who did it took off right away, because they didn't take their rifles or the water.

September 9th at Col de Braus had thus cost the lives of four men of G Company of the 517th PIR: **PFC Marvin C. Bell**, **PFC William Buk**, **1st Lt Arthur W. Ridler**, and **Pvt John A. Staat**. Several other men had been seriously wounded. The death of his friend Arthur Ridler inspired **Lt Richard Spencer** to write the following poem, that is put bluntly into context by the previous accounts:

What can I say?

When I return from over the sea,
I hope fate spares these sights from me.
A baby bubbling with childish prattle,
Whose father I saw killed in battle.
Those tear-stained eyes of a sweet, young bride,
Whose husband I talked to the day he died.
What can I say when they want to know
Just how it happened… How did he go…?
Was it over quickly… Did he feel much pain?
Before he passed on… Did he call my name?
She shows me his picture; it gives me a chill…
That's not how he looked that night on the hill!
Can't tell what I saw… So I go on lying
But it doesn't help much, she's softly crying.
The God of the battlefield is doubly unkind…
The ones hurt the deepest are those left behind.

Lt Richard Spencer.[5]

The German Sniper at Col de Braus

At roughly the same period as Lt Ridler was killed, German soldier **Egon Fergg**, of *Reserve Pionier Bataillon 8*, was also

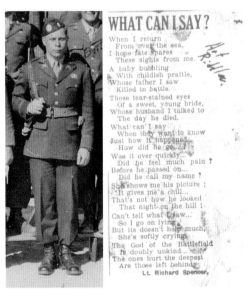

Lt Arthur W. Ridler.
517prct.org Collection.

present at Col de Braus, but on the opposite side of the lines, where he made the following encounter:

> We were staying in a wood beside Col de Braus. I was sent to bring the departure order to our position in the mountains. From Sospel, which was being heavily shelled by U.S. ships, I climbed up to Col de Braus. In my pockets I had the departure order, some mail, one bottle of cognac, and two bottles of whiskey. I climbed up through the pine trees until I came upon a well camouflaged sniper lying in a bush with leaves on his helmet. The soldier told me in a low voice that I couldn't go any further because the Americans were already at the pass. He had an unarmed and bareheaded GI in his sights, who was wandering through a clearing peacefully, as if he had been walking down Broadway. It was a peaceful and fascinating picture. I told the sniper that he had to stop aiming at the American soldier. He lay down his rifle. It was not without danger for me, because as a soldier, I was not to do that; but I had a Christian education, and for me religion had priority over the orders of my commanders. I was a peaceful soldier. Then at last I found my comrades and told them: "Come down, we have the order to go to Italy."

With a bit of imagination, one could think that this very sniper may have been responsible for the deaths of some of the G Company men. In mid September, as mentioned by Egon Fergg, *Reserve Division 148* troops were replaced by troops of the veteran *Infanterie Division 34*, which had previously been resting in Italy after being involved in heavy fighting on the Russian Front.

Hill 1098

In early September 1944, the 517th PIR was trying to fulfill its hardest mission yet: to capture Col de Braus. In the previous pages, we have seen what D and G Companies experienced upon reaching the battle zone. **Clark Archer** made a good description of the plight of the 517th in the unit history he wrote:

> A week of trying to capture the Col de Braus - Tête de la Lavina area had cost 147 casualties, including 21 dead, 123 wounded, and three captured – the equivalent of a rifle company. It was clear that continued piecemeal attacks would only play into the enemy's hands and produce longer casualty lists. The key to the area was Tête de la Lavina, and a major effort was going to be required to take it. Colonel Graves directed the next five or six days to be spent in preparation for a full-scale assault with massive fire support.
>
> North of Col de Braus, the 2nd Battalion had worked around the back trail from Lucéram, cleared Plan Constant, and was pushing to gain Hill 1098 (Cime de Ventabren). This was an east-west cliff with vertical sides and a knob at each end that overlooked Col de Braus and provided excellent observation into Sospel. Lieutenant John Lissner's F Company held the western knoll and the Germans clung to the one on the east, a few hundred yards away. With only enough room to deploy a platoon, each attack had to be head-on because of the sheer cliffs on the flanks. Company F attacked Hill 1098 once on September 13th, twice on the 14th, and once more on the 15th. The first three tries they were beaten back. On the fourth attack, the Germans gave up the eastern knob, but launched an immediate counterattack; F Company was forced back once more. Hill 1098 became another objective for the

planned big attack and was titled "Lissner's Folly," in honor of the redoubtable F Company commander.[6]

Hill 1098 was in a particularly exposed position, with a French Maginot line fort placed at the summit of the hill immediately to its east able to cover Hill 1098 with artillery fire. However, Hill 1098 also provided excellent observation on Sospel and the road between Sospel and Castillon, where the Germans were still fighting back the FSSF, and it was therefore an important objective for the paratroopers. **Private Myrle Traver**, of the 1st Platoon of F Company of the 517th PIR, remembered the multiple attacks his company took part in on Hill 1098:

All our platoons took turns taking it. We would beat the Germans back and they would leave us there a few hours, and then they would open up from the fort across the valley that had big guns in it and they would knock us off it. We would retreat and get off it, and then a few days later the Germans would occupy it. They sometimes even towed up some little artillery pieces and started firing on our area. Then we would take it again. It was no big fighting, no big amounts of men. It would usually just be a platoon or something like that. There was a dirt road winding up and going up to it, and then a flat top on it that they were using for outposts. Everybody, every platoon had to take turns taking that, because they wanted to try and hold it, but they just finally gave up on it. We had a couple guys killed and several wounded in our F Company.

PFC Gene Frice was also on Hill 1098 with F Company of the 517th PIR:

Even our own people say: "Well 1098 was just a pushover and nobody got hit up there." Well I differ with that, we probably lost five or six killed and probably about 25 wounded, and it was a daily battle to take the top of 1098 back, because it was about the easiest and the neatest observation point, looking down the valley and overseeing Sospel. We had to observe and they had to observe, and we had our daily disagreement with the Germans about that. We would take it every night, and then we would be up there in the morning until the artillery would fight us off, and then they would occupy it for the day, and we would take it again the next night.

Jim Pacey was killed up there, and I think Thomas Sherman, who was a medic. Gary Davis and Lt Ridle were wounded up there. We probably had at least a dozen that were wounded. We didn't get somebody killed every day, but we generally had somebody wounded every day, not necessarily in a fire fight, but from the fort. Once we got on the top and the Germans had pulled off, the fort would blow us off the top of the mountain. That's how Pacey was killed – shrapnel – and he was in a substantial foxhole. It was relatively deep and surrounded by all those rocks that are all over that hilltop. A shell lit outside, close to the foxhole but away from it, and a very small sliver of shrapnel came through the rock pile, ricocheted through it, and hit him in the forehead.

PFC Mel Dahlberg, another member of F Company, remembered another casualty that occurred on Hill 1098:

We fought for over two weeks for that hill. The Germans would come up and be on top of the hill, but that is as far as they got, they never advanced down to our side. It was just mortars and mortars back and forth. I know that from my experience, I shouldn't be here today; a mortar came over and landed about four to five feet away from me and covered me with dirt, but it didn't go off. So I am thankful for that. Then, towards the end of our battle there, I remember I got the duty of trying to retrieve some of our people that got killed up on the top of 1098. I know one of

Hill 1098 as it appeared to the men from F Company, 517th PIR, in 1944, and as it appears today. Mike Kane Collection. Author's Collection.

The German occupied Fort du Barbonnet, positioned right across from Hill 1098, could take the American positions under fire with its reinforced gun turrets that were impervious to return fire. Joe Broudy Collection.

my sergeants, Arnold Ridout, was up there for well over a week, and we knew he was dead because he never returned. I had to retrieve his body, and that was quite an experience.

He must have met the Germans. He was against a tree, so obviously he was trying to cover himself. It's hard to tell, but he still had his helmet on, so I know it had to be rifle fire that got him. If it was a mortar, it would have blasted it off of him. He had a beautiful head of hair, all red. When I got to his body his face was all gone, it was all obliterated, but I knew it was him because of the red hair. He was tough to bring back to our lines, the dead weight was really something. In fact, I just dragged his body back.

Then there was another, a 2nd Platoon guy, his name was John Pacey. He had put rocks all around him to protect him from the enemy, and believe it or not, a piece of shrapnel went through a little crack and got him in the head and killed him. He lay right there in his foxhole.

The Germans managed to hold on to the hill despite the repetitive attacks. As of approximately September 12th, Hill 1098 had been held by soldiers of *Infanterie Division 34*, probably explaining why it had been so well defended. These were not Silesian recruits, but real and fully-trained German soldiers who had previously fought in Russia and were battle hardened veterans. One particular diehard, *Feldwebel* Wilhelm Zimmermann of 6th Company of *Grenadier Regiment 80*, had been sent up to Hill 1098, where he was responsible for organizing the bitter resistance that

"Arnold Ridout was up there for well over a week and we knew he was dead because he never returned." SSgt Arnold C. Ridout, aged 20, who was killed on Hill 1098. Ridout Family Collection.

471

"Believe it or not, a piece of shrapnel went through a little crack and got him in the head and killed him." PFC James "Jim" Pacey, aged 19, who died on Hill 1098. Catherine Pacey Zonaras Collection.

Feldwebel Wilhelm Zimmermann, of the 6th Company of Grenadier Regiment 80 of Infanterie Division 34, shows off his numerous awards, including the Knight's Cross he has recently earned on Hill 1098. Frode Steine Collection.

the Germans put up. He was awarded the Knights Cross of the Iron Cross for successfully holding onto the hill despite the repeated assaults by F Company. The following period newspaper article tells the tale of the fighting on Hill 1098 in a version enhanced by the German propaganda, but highly informative nonetheless (Zimmermann had since been promoted to *Oberfeldwebel*):

One from the brave infantry
Knight's Cross bestowal to *Oberfeldwebel* Zimmermann, from Kausen

The Führer has awarded the Knight's Cross of the Iron Cross to *Oberfeldwebel* Wilhelm Zimmermann, who was born in Stuttgart March 3, 1920, who recently got married in Kausen, and who is still on leave for the moment. The brave young soldier has been in the *Wehrmacht* since 1940 and has already proven himself at many hot spots in the east with his dashing spirit of attack. Cool, decisive acts brought him the Iron Cross 2nd Class and 1st Class in 1942. He also wears the Infantry Assault Badge, the Close Combat Clasp, and the Wound Badge in Gold.

The following article from his division's newspaper bears witness to *Oberfeldwebel* Zimmermann's raciness that has now won him the Knight's Cross:

Whoever has seen Hill 1098, which lies two kilometers west of S. [Sospel, censored for security reasons], knows how important it is. Whomever controls 1098 controls S., and all the roads leading into it. As *Oberfeldwebel* Zimmermann's company reached the area, the enemy, with his strong infantry forces and his masses of bunkers, was occupying this hill. In full knowledge that the defense of S. could not be continued if the enemy remained in control of Hill 1098, the battalion commander made the decision to take the hill. This mission was given to Zimmermann's platoon.

On the way up, the platoon was already noticed by an enemy patrol and taken under artillery and mortar fire shortly afterwards. Radio connection with the battalion was lost. The platoon's positions could not be held due to casualties, because they were located on the forward slope and were already well known to the enemy. Under these conditions, Zimmermann took the decision on his own and under his responsibility to flank the hill from the north and attack it without any reconnaissance or reinforcements. Without being noticed by the enemy, he brought his platoon over an impassable ridge into striking distance and broke into the enemy positions. The enemy resisted desperately. His huge materiel superiority was of no use to him. The fight was now man against man. As the soldiers of the platoon started rolling up the positions, the enemy cleared the area in panic, abandoning the bulk of his equipment. An enemy at least four times superior in numbers had not withstood the attack.

At the crack of dawn the next day, the enemy opened fire on Hill 1098 with all his weapons. An artillery barrage started at nine o'clock. Within an hour the hill was reduced to a field of debris by mortars, antitank guns, and artillery. Believing that no living being could remain on the hill, the enemy, in battalion strength, attacked from three sides at 11 o'clock, surrounding the platoon. In spite of heavy casualties, the platoon let the enemy approach to within 50 meters of its position before suddenly opening fire with MGs and rifle grenades. The enemy retreated with heavy losses. For the rest of the day, the hill constantly remained under the fire of his heavy artillery. At 18:00 hours, the fire increased to the level of a barrage. At 19:00 hours, the enemy again moved in to attack. In the meantime, Zimmermann's platoon had suffered such heavy casualties that only two NCOs and nine men remained.

The enemy broke into the position and split into two parts, each of which he completely surrounded. The survivors replied to an enemy demand for surrender with the same demand. With the four men who were surrounded with him, Zimmermann then decided to break through to the rest of his platoon. With hand grenades and light machine guns, he penetrated the enemy ring, destroying everything in front of him. The troops were reunited. With all the soldiers and three MGs, he pushed into the enemy positions, firing on the way. All the enemy groups immediately withdrew under the cover of a smoke screen.

Hill 1098 was in our hands. 60 dead were evacuated by the enemy. Over the following days, the efforts of the enemy to completely eliminate the hill with fire remained unsuccessful. Three more consecutive attacks were beaten back. This brave feat that was led by *Oberfeldwebel* Zimmermann enabled a gap in the front to be closed and the defense of S. to be continued.

We congratulate the successful *Grenadier* for receiving the high decoration and wish him more soldier's luck for the future.[7]

In reality, F Company of the 517th PIR had only lost three men on Hill 1098 between September 12th and 18th: **PFC James Pacey** on the 12th, **SSgt Arnold Ridout** on the 13th, and **Cpl Arthur Sherman** on the 18th. Additionally, on September 12th, one artillery observer had been killed on hill 1098, as well as perhaps three men from the HQ Company of the 2nd Battalion. The total number of American killed during the battle was therefore seven at the very most, a far cry from the 60 dead claimed by the German article. This alone gives a good hint as to just how exaggerated the German article was! Despite the bravery displayed by *Feldwebel* Zimmermann and his men, the German success was short lived. Hill 1098, along with the rest of Col de Braus, was captured by the American paratroopers of the 517th PIR for good September 18th 1944… in spite of which the Germans were still able to hold onto Sospel and Castillon for more than a month.

Friendly Fire

Not all the Allied soldiers killed overseas died in circumstances that their family members back home could have imagined. Some deaths occurred in accidents that could easily have been avoided, but soldiers who had cheated death so many times on the battlefield often failed to use basic safety precautions when off the lines. Joseph Tully, of the 512th Signals Company, was killed when he fell off a telephone pole August 24th. Frank Keefe, of the 602nd FAB, was killed September 3rd by a German grenade he was manipulating. September 18th, five men of the 596th PCEC were killed when a truck full of mines they had cleared from the Nice airport blew up. It was said that the men had been seen passing mines to each other by throwing them before the explosion occurred! The violence of the blast mangled three of the troopers so badly that they had to be buried in a common grave. At least two paratroopers were killed in car accidents in September and October 1944. The first was **Pvt Patrick Michael**s, of the 596th PCEC. His friend **Allan Johnson** recalls the circumstances:

> September 14th, we were off line and we were not doing anything for several days. At that point, a friend of mine was teaching me to drive and I was in the peculiar position of having to find how to use the clutch and the pedal and so forth without knowing what I was doing, and the jeep rolled backwards over an incline and turned over. I broke my foot and my friend was killed. That was the worst thing that happened to me personally in the war. He was a good friend, and his name was Patrick Michaels,

The ground at Col de Braus is littered with shell fragments to this day, bearing testimony to the hard fighting that occurred there in September 1944. Here three rusty pieces of shrapnel are visible. Author's Collection.

from Pennsylvania. They sent me down to wherever the hospital ship was, and they took us down to Naples.

Lt Rushton Peabody, of the 551st PIB, also died in a vehicle accident, though since he was alone at the time, the circumstances were not as clear. The doctors who examined his body simply reported: "He was dead on arrival, apparently from fracture of cervical vertebra sustained in a jeep wreck at about 0030 hours 2 October 1944."[8] There were also cases of suicide. One man of the HQ Company of the 3rd Battalion of the 517th PIR shot himself in Berre les Alpes. The case of the wounded German soldier who blew himself up with a grenade in St Cézaire remembered by Frank Dallas also comes to mind.

Finally, shockingly large numbers of soldiers were killed in so-called "friendly fire" incidents, in which the deadly projectile was fired by one of the soldier's own countrymen, or in which explosive devices of the soldier's own side were accidentally detonated. A study performed by the U.S. Army Medical Department in New Guinea and Burma concluded that up to 17.9% of American casualties were caused by American fire or weapons![9] Throughout this book we have already mentioned several such cases:

- Lt Paul Mckee, of the 636th TDB, was killed when friendly aircraft strafed his vehicle August 18th south of Callian.
- Lt Henry Apperman and Sgt Joseph Gabrus, of the 141st IR, were both killed by friendly artillery near le Tremblant August 20th.
- Joseph Hernandez, of the 509th PIB, was wounded by his own grenade near la Napoule August 21st.

- Pvt Louis Tenute, of the 551st PIB, was mortally wounded by friendly mortar fire near le Tremblant August 21st.
- 1st Sgt Thomas Crane, of the 509th PIB, was killed by friendly mortar fire near la Napoule August 22nd.
- A Canadian soldier of the FSSF was shot and killed by one of his buddies in Nice during a brawl in late August.
- Pvt James L. Walton, of the 517th PIR, was killed by an accidental gunshot to the head near Levens September 1st.
- Pvt John Staat, of the 517th PIR, was killed by friendly artillery fire near Col de Braus September 9th.

More cases were probably not reported, or were never discovered in the first place. On the German side, we noted that at least three soldiers were killed by their own mines at St Cézaire and Biot, while another accidentally killed himself with his own grenade at Callian. We also noted several reports of Polish soldiers being shot at by their own officers, or *vice versa*, though these do not really fit into the definition of friendly fire.

Once the FABTF reached the mountains at the Italian border, at least four more paratroopers of the 517th PIR, one officer of the FSSF, and one soldier of the 460th PFAB fell victim to friendly fire. **T5 Casimer Szczech** was shot by a machine gunner at nightfall, **PFC Anthony Celli** stepped on an American mine while hunting squirrels, **PFC Marvin Oliver** was shot in the head with a .45 caliber pistol by a guard one morning, **Sgt Kenneth Mattice** was killed by American artillery fire, and **2nd Lt Kenneth McDougall** was shot in the head by one of his own men, who mistook him for an enemy when returning from a patrol. The victim of the 460th PFAB will be mentioned further down. **PFC Warren Boehmke**, of the 509th PIB, reported yet another case, though the identity and unit of the victim are not known:

> We moved up through the mountains and made a couple moves, then we were relieved by I think the 517th, but I am not sure [Warren Boehmke is clearly confusing the 517th with another unit.], and they were real rookies, fresh from the States. They had just come over, and we had been over there a couple of years by that time. I was left behind the first night to get them oriented and then our company pulled out. So that night I went out to check the lines and see where everybody was, and all these guys were crawled into bed in sleeping bags, with shoes off. Nobody was watching! Nobody was on guard! The Germans could have come there and wiped the whole outfit out.
>
> The next day they were going to go out on patrol, and they had a jeep there with a 50 caliber machine gun mounted on it and two guys sitting in the back of the jeep. The sergeant walked around in front and somebody tripped the trigger on the machine gun and one shot went off and hit the sergeant in the neck, piercing both arteries. He just lay there and bled to death in about one minute. And then the funny thing was somebody tried to put a tourniquet around the guy's neck to stop the bleeding. I said: "Just take it off. There is nothing you can do, you can't stop the bleeding, he punctured two main arteries in his neck." I was glad to get out of there.

Although many such cases can be found being reported in war literature, it is only very rarely that the soldiers responsible for killing one of their friends come to terms with themselves and find the courage to talk about their unfortunate experience. **Merle McMorrow**, of C Battery of the 460th PFAB, was one of these men, writing in his autobiography:

> We were in a fairly stationary position in October. The position had a trail to the end of the valley and the area would appear as a horseshoe on a map. A 75mm howitzer was positioned at the closed end of the horseshoe. Bill Houston was on outpost at one end of the arms and I was across the valley on the outpost at the end of the other arm. We were probably 100 yards apart. That night a tragic accident happened. I, along with a detail of three other men, manned the outpost in shifts. The accident happened during a period when I wasn't on duty and was sleeping. During a dream, which still seems so real today, I shot one of the men of our battery. I was dreaming I was walking on guard duty and I could hear a noise in the background. In my semi-conscious state, I was actually hearing someone moving around, but it was a member of our detail. I reached for my rifle, and in my dream I challenged the person. When I got no response, I fired. The fellow then began calling for the medics. His yelling in English probably brought me back to a conscious state.
>
> It was a terrible memory to carry with me, and I felt as though I was the only person in the service that had such an experience. As time passed, I discovered there were thousands of lives lost through accidents and misinformation. For instance, the U.S. Navy shot down 27 planeloads of 82nd airborne paratroopers and damaged many others on their way to Sicily from North Africa. There were 10 to 16 troopers in each plane. This does not minimize my actions, but it helped me to realize that accidents do occur under unusual circumstances. A number of times, our Army Air Corps dropped bomb loads short and killed hundreds of Americans. On other occasions, friendly units would be firing on each other because of lack of communication or other foul-ups. Many lives were lost during the war due to actions other than those relating directly to the enemy. It was referred to as being killed by "friendly fire."
>
> Under the 104th Article of War I was court-martialed, found guilty, fined one dollar, given a carton of cigarettes, and transferred to the 463rd Field Artillery Battalion. This procedure was followed for two reasons: (1) a person could never be tried again for the same crime in civilian life, and (2) if the accident victim had some real strong friends, it eliminated the possibility of these friends having the opportunity to avenge the loss of their friend.[10]

SSgt Hoyt Kelley, of HQ Company of the 1st Battalion of the 517th, wrote about how the constant stress of the battlefield led some men to lose their sanity, leading to at least one friendly fire incident:

> The constant time under fire was very hard on our men and several cracked up mentally. One man, whose brother was killed in the Pacific, killed a whole truck load of German prisoners we were taking to Nice by shooting them with his automatic Tommy Gun. One of my men, who lost a brother in the armored division, turned up missing from our outfit, and I went out to find him. I found him boiling the head of a German in his helmet over a fire. He cleaned all the flesh off the skull and carried it in his duffel bag until three months later we shipped him back to the States during the Battle of the Bulge. Another man in our outfit, while at Peira Cava, went crazy and ran down the road shooting his rifle at everyone. He was killed by one of our men. I always thought they could have shot him

in the legs, but they didn't. I was not there; although he was assigned to me (…) and he was one of the men who went on patrols with me. He was a good guy.[11]

The Champagne Campaign

The Maritime Alps Theater of Operations had one stunning characteristic that was probably not equated by anything similar on any other front. A mere few miles away from the front lines lay a world of festive luxury, seemingly oblivious of the war that was still raging nearby. Many of the soldiers were country boys who had never known the joys and vices of large cities, let alone coastal tourist resorts, such as those of the Riviera, the morals of which had further been corrupted by the war. The soldiers could literally be drinking at a terrace in Nice with some local *demoiselles* during the day and find themselves patrolling the front lines the very same night. In Monaco, from where the front lines could actually be seen in the distance, the contrast between the battle zones and principality life were so great that they could have been considered indecent. **Marvin McRoberts**, an enlisted man of the 602nd FAB, related his surreal visit to Monaco in his wartime memoir:

> At this point, I have to tell you about my experience in Monaco / Monte Carlo. A GI could not go into the Province of Monaco, it was declared off limits. It was a separate, neutral country. The town that surrounded the area was called Beausoleil.
>
> As the front lines were stable at this time, there seemed to be no big build up on either side. We were allowed to have leave for a few hours, as long as we had a full crew on duty. A 6x6 truck, as we called them, would pick us up and deliver us to Beausoleil. Later, it would pick us up at a certain time and place. The town had a large hall that was open for us GIs, with the local girls coming there to dance. I was able to attend a few of these. If you stayed too long you would miss the truck, and then had to walk back up the hill to our gun position. One night, I spotted a young girl that I had danced with on a previous night. I asked her if she wanted to dance with me again. She spoke very good English. Halfway through the dance, she asked me to come with her to meet her mother. Her mother was sitting in a chair next to the wall of the dance floor. She also spoke English. She asked me a few questions about my hometown and where I was born, etc. She then asked if I would come with them to meet her husband, the girl's father. Being a California boy, and having not travelled much, I could still sense something was up. I went with them, but as we walked a few blocks, I was certain we were in Monte Carlo, this area being off limits to GIs. I was led into a complex that turned out to be a very large apartment. The girl was not saying much, but the mother grabbed my hand, saying, "Come with me." She led me into another room with a male sitting next to a radio that he called a wireless. He didn't seem happy to see us, as he was still trying to listen to the radio. He and the mother spoke French and I could only pick up a word now and then. He then turned to me, asking in English all kinds of questions about my name, my family, where I lived at home, and where I was born. He even asked about my religion.
>
> All of a sudden, he started talking in French really loud. It sounded to me like he was angry. He made the mother and daughter cry. The mother grabbed my hand again, showing me the door, then telling me to leave. Before leaving, I asked what this was all about. Her answer was:

Howard Prichard and Art Helmers, of the 602nd PFAB, play golf near their gun positions in the vicinity of la Turbie September 10, 1944. Such blunt contrasts between war and luxury were common for the men of the FABTF during their stay in the Maritime Alps. Art Helmers Collection.

Mike Reuter Collection.

"I was hoping you would marry my daughter. That you would send her to California, where she would divorce you. From there, she then would go to Jerusalem. Then, at a later date, she would send for her family." I asked her why they wanted to go to Jerusalem. She said: "It would be easier for her to go there from the United States than from where we are now." I asked her again: "Why would you want to go to Jerusalem?" She looked at me, with a straight face: "We are Jewish." Besides, they would pay me. How much I don't remember, but seems to me it was a lot of money. The father came out of his room and was yelling at them, then he turned to me, speaking in English. He told me to leave, or he would have someone throw me out and hand me over to the MPs. I didn't know that they didn't have much of a police force at that time, but our MPs did come in and pick up GIs. As I left the apartment, I could hear all three of them yelling at each other.

Weary looking officers of the 509th PIB pose in front of the main door of the famous and luxurious Negresco Hotel in Nice. From left to right are Lt Orval W. Webb, Lt Ferris Knight, Capt Jesse Walls, Lt O'Brien, and Lt Justin T. McCarthy. Mike Reuter Collection.

I started walking, but didn't know the way back to the dance hall. I figured the truck had already come and gone without me. I knew that I would have to walk all the way back to the gun. While making up my mind on what was the best way back to the gun, I saw a large building that had people coming and going from it. I looked inside and realized it was one of their gambling casinos. I made my way inside, trying to make myself and my GI clothing as inconspicuous as possible. I made my way across the room to a far wall, where I stood by a tall window with very heavy curtains. I was enjoying the action, watching the civilians laugh and talk. After a while, a gentleman came up to me, smiled, and talking in English, asked me how I was. He then asked me if I smoked. When he found out that I did smoke, he asked for an American cigarette. I gave him one and lit it for him. He thanked me, saying he wished me luck, then walked away. I watched him go. I wondered if the good luck was for me if I gambled. I was thinking of maybe trying.

Before I did anything, another person came up beside me. I thought that he might also want a cigarette; instead, he pointed to the fellow I had been talking to. He asked if I knew who he was. I said: "No." He then took a coin out of his pocket, pointing again at the man now standing and talking with someone else, his right profile toward us. This person said: "Look at the coin and at him, he's the Prince of Monaco." After looking at it a couple times, you could see his profile was very similar to the image on the coin. I didn't know anything about the prince at this time, but was impressed that his profile was on a coin. He then said: "You just gave the Prince of Monaco a cigarette." Handing me the coin: "As a favor, I will escort you out of the area or you will be paying him fifty dollars from your next pay check." As we walked, he seemed to know that I came from the dance hall. He then went on to tell me that all GIs caught in the Province of Monaco are turned over to the MPs. "Your next pay check will be fifty dollars short, as the Province is a neutral country, even when the Germans were here, this rule was in effect." When we were close enough to see the hall, he shook my hand, then wished me luck. I had to walk all the way back to the gun. I crawled into my sleeping bag for about thirty minutes before I had to wake up to go on duty at the gun. I kept that coin until I was getting ready to come home on a boat in December 1945. Someone had gone through my duffel bag and removed some of my souvenir items, and the coin was one of them.[12]

While the Allied troops had fun in the towns surrounding Monaco, some local youths took advantage of the situation, the wealth of the Allied soldiers being too great a temptation for them after the bleak years of occupation. One of the 16-year-olds from Beausoleil remembered:

Every night, with my friends, we would steal from the jeeps. We even stole a 22 caliber carbine and grenades! On the night before Christmas, we had prepared a small banquet at a friend's house at the Rue des Ecoles, but before the banquet we all made one round. There were a whole bunch of jeeps at the border between Beausoleil and Monaco. There was a night club full of Americans who were dancing.

We went out spotting, and there were plenty of tin cans. "Take them, take them!" Each one of us was taking some and I had a coat that was heavier than myself with everything I had stolen. Suddenly, I saw a big tough guy come out of the darkness and start running towards me. I escaped as I could; I was so weighted down that I threw everything on the ground because I wanted to get away. But the American ran so fast that he caught me. When he grabbed me, I pissed myself. I can still feel the warm piss dribbling down, I couldn't hold it back.

Then we went back down and he made me pick up everything I had stolen, and then he said: "Now I am bringing you to the cops. Police, come on, police!" I said: "No, no, no!" and I started to cry. "My father is dead," I said, "my mother is in the hospital and my brothers...." And I am actually an only son [Both his parents were actually alive and well]! I said: "Let me go, let me go!" He called me all kinds of things: "Fucking boy!" I said: "Moment" and I put my hand in my pocket as if to say: "I will pay you, leave me be, leave me be." He thought I was getting a weapon and he pulled out his Colt and put it on my temple. So I said: "Moment please" and I made the sign of the cross. He kicked me in the ass and said: "Get out of here!"

When I got back to the banquet, the others were already all at the table eating. I said "You bunch of bastards! I got myself caught, but you don't seem to care much about me!" And then it continued, every night we went and raided the jeeps."

Patroling at Peira Cava

Meanwhile, in the mountains, the "Champaign Campaign" continued under the form of nerve wracking artillery duels and long patrols through mined terrain. **Lt Howard Hensleigh**, of the 3rd Battalion of the 517th PIR, participated in one particularly eventful patrol at Tête du Pin, near Peira Cava, on October 2, 1944, which is worth mentioning:

One bright fall morning of 1944, Lt. Col. Paxton [3rd Battalion commander] decided to take his command group, which meant the company commanders, all of his battalion staff, his artillery liaison officer, etc., on a tactical walk out into no man's land, where I patrolled three or four times a week. There must have been 15 or maybe 20 of us. Everybody that ran the battalion was involved. If the Germans would have killed us all or captured us, it would have been a real disaster for the battalion.

I usually led patrols, but I decided the best part of valor on this one was to bring up the rear with Woody Woodhull, artillery observer. We went forth on a four foot wide hiker's path, which was a "no no" for me, and these guys made a lot of noise. Paxton was leading the bunch, and at a critical juncture, he halted the group and allowed two enlisted men to go on forward. They went ahead and were mowed down by German small arms fire, so everybody took off, running as fast as they could back towards Peira Cava. Woody and I hit the dirt off the trail to see if there is anything we might possibly do. The German machine guns were firing right up the trail; the fire was above our heads and several tree branches were cut off and fell on us. Woody turned to me and said: "Henze, it looks like they have this path pretty well covered." There was nothing we could do in the face of that fire and we were sure the two scouts were dead.

The paratroopers had just fallen into a German ambush laid by men of the 7th Company of *Grenadier Regiment 107*, of *Infanterie Division 34*. The two American soldiers who had been killed were **PFC Jack Whitfield** and **Pvt Julius J. Richmond**, of the HQ Company of the 3rd Battalion and of the Regimental HQ, respectively. Unbeknownst to Howard Hensleigh, a third soldier, Pvt John P. Gannon, of the Regimental HQ, had been shot through the arm and captured by the Germans, becoming one of the very few paratroopers to be captured in the Maritime Alps. Though John Gannon passed away long before the making of this book, his daughter **Marie McGuire** was able to provide the following information:

Pvt Julius "Jimmy" Richmond, of the Regimental HQ Company of the 517th, was gunned down by a machine gun manned by German soldier Gerhart Höfig during a patrol at Peira Cava October 2, 1944. He is seen here with his young wife, Elizabeth Richmond, who had given birth to their daughter Barbara three weeks before his death. Jimmy Flynn Collection.

My father never talked about the war and what happened to him. The only thing I remember him saying was that he was on an "advance" patrol with a few other soldiers that day, and they had stopped to take a cigarette break. When the others got up to leave, my dad, who was not done smoking his cigarette, said: "Go on, I will catch up with you in a minute." And so the men got up to leave, and minutes later (maybe sooner) were shot and killed. My father was shot in the left arm and was taken prisoner by the Germans. He said that the Germans saved his arm. He spent the next six months, approximately, in a German prison camp until the war ended. My mother always said he told her that the Russians liberated the prisoners when the war ended. When he was shot, the U.S. Army classified him as missing in action (MIA). His family took him for dead. Then one day, months later, there came word through the Red Cross that he was alive.

In the meantime, the rest of the patrol returned to Peira Cava. As soon as they got back the Americans prepared their revenge. **Lt Howard Hensleigh** continues:

When we got back to the battalion, Paxton had rounded up Fuller's I Company platoon to go back up the trail and attack these Germans who had killed the two enlisted men. Later, one of my friends told me that when Paxton counted noses and found me gone, he said: "It looks like Hensleigh has taken one chance too many." Apparently he did not miss Woody. I told Paxton that I thought it was a good idea for Woody and I to accompany Fuller's platoon. Paxton agreed. After we were out of sight on the trail, I told Fuller we should cross over the ridge until we were past the ambush, then hit them from the rear. We did that and designated a sharpshooting sergeant to fire the first shot. When I was sure we had gone far enough, we re-crossed the ridge, put the platoon "as skirmishers" and started to close in. The Germans were all facing the other way, eating lunch out of sardine cans and so forth. We got within fifty to a hundred yards from them before the sergeant took his first shot. The fire fight was tense and must have lasted at least a half hour. When the fire came from many angles, all the Germans but one realized the jig was up. We could hear people groaning and one thing and other, and we had no casualties at all, so I yelled: "Handen hoch [Hands up]," and all the Germans but one came up with their hands up.

But then there was a German non-com in a bush that had a machine gun, and he would start firing at us and the other Germans would hit the dirt. This happened two or three times. I told Woodhull: "Woody, somebody's got to knock that guy off," and so he and I crawled forward to get the die-hard. When the German non-com was shooting his machine gun, I could see the leaves of the bush vibrating, so I knew pretty much right where he was. But they had smokeless ammunition, which we didn't, so I knew I had to get the guy with one clip of ammunition, because there wouldn't be a second chance. I put a whole M-1 clip into the bush and I did kill him. Then I yelled: "Handen hoch" and "Kamerad," and all these Germans got up and we took them prisoner. We had killed several of the ambush and took over twenty prisoners. I searched the non-com and found pictures in his backpack, including the guy's wedding picture. It is a shame we couldn't have met in different circumstances; he was a brave guy, we might have been friends.

Also found on the body of the NCO who had been shot through the head was a diary, the last ominous entry in it being: "Oct. 2: One prisoner, two dead Americans, Tête du Pin."[13] While the diary was handed over to Intelligence Officer Lt Neiler, Lt Hensleigh preserved the photos he had found on the killed German NCO for the rest of his life. A strange bond is often created amid the chaos of battle between the killers and their victims, and many soldiers (like Joe Cicchinelli in the previous chapter) thus kept photos, ID booklets, or other mementos from their fallen enemies.

Three Germans from the 7th Company of *Grenadier Regiment 107* had been killed in the fire fight: 27-year-old *Feldwebel* **Georg Rieck**, 32-year-old *Unteroffizier* **Martin Janostik**, and 19-year-old *Gefreiter* **Hans Jantzen**. According to the 517th PIR Intelligence Report of October 3rd, three Germans had also been captured (one of which died shortly afterwards and who may well be one of the previously mentioned three dead).[14] It was only years later, in 2012, that Lt Hensleigh would find out that the German NCO he had killed and whose wedding photos he had found was named Georg Rieck. In a unique turn of events, Georg Rieck's grandson and Howard Hensleigh exchanged several emails about the ambush, and peace was made between Hensleigh and the Rieck family 68 years after Hensleigh had killed Georg Rieck. Georg Rieck's family was also able to provide some outstanding information on the ambush as it had been seen from the German side. Indeed, *Gefreiter* **Gerhart Höfig**, the German soldier who had been manning the machine gun that had killed Jack Whitfield and Julius Richmond during the initial ambush, wrote a letter to the Rieck family, explaining the circumstances of the ambush and of *Feldwebel* Rieck's death:

Dear Rieck Family,

(...) When I now recall October 2, 1944, it was the darkest day that the company had to experience since it had been in the south. It was the responsibility of the Janostik section, that I was also a member of, to defend the "Tete du Pin" strongpoint.

The wedding pictures that Lt Howard Hensleigh found on the German NCO he shot and killed near Peira Cava. Note that two of the pictures are stamped to a photo studio in Ellwangen an der Jagst. A subsequent investigation in Ellwangen led to the discovery that the man in the pictures is 27-year-old Feldwebel Georg Rieck, whose young wife was approximately five months pregnant at the time he was shot and killed by Lt Hensleigh. Howard Hensleigh Collection.

478

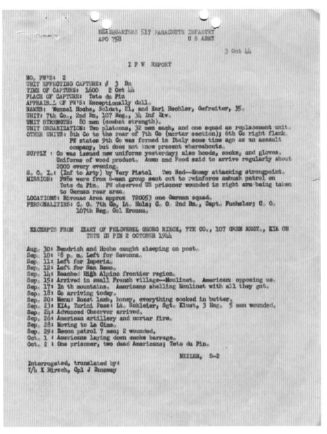

The prisoner of war interrogation report prepared by Lt John Neiler after the October 2nd action at Tête du Pin. Also included is a partial translation of the diary found on Feldwebel Georg Rieck's body. NARA.

In spite of the very mountainous terrain, the hill was heavily wooded with spruce trees. Our main priority was to cut off a path that crossed through there, as it was used by enemy patrols. Everything had gone well so far, until another enemy patrol came along the path on October 2nd at 12:00.

At that moment, I was on guard duty and I opened fire from a short distance. The effect was devastating; one enemy prisoner and some dead were left behind. We successfully smashed the enemy patrol without suffering any casualties of our own.

Hereupon, *Herr Feldwebel* [*Feldwebel* Georg Rieck] appeared amongst us immediately and enquired about what had happened. He was very pleased that a section from his platoon had once again chalked up a proud success.

He now arranged to have another section come up the hill. A few more hours passed. The other section arrived between four and five o'clock. Just as *Herr Feldwebel* was briefing the section, the enemy attack took place. We fought back at once and opened fire. A tough encounter developed, and that is where I was put out of action by a twist of fate. I was wounded in the buttocks by a bullet. I kept on firing, and at one point *Herr Feldwebel* appeared to my right. I shouted out to him that I was wounded; he immediately came to me and took the MG from me.

The battle nonetheless didn't lose any of its intensity. *Herr Feldwebel* continued firing on and on with the MG, allowing me to move back in order to get bandaged up. Words cannot describe how greatly thankful and in debt I am to *Herr Feldwebel*. I can still see *Herr Feldwebel*'s ghost in front of me, taking the MG from me and resuming the battle.

Up until now I could describe to you what I personally saw, I am writing the rest to you based on what I was told by my comrades.

After changing positions with the MG numerous times, his sad fate reached him in a bush he was firing from. He met his hero's death with a head shot that killed him immediately. In the tough battle for the strongpoint, the company lost three men, the best in the company. Three other men were wounded.

With the hero's death of *Herr Feldwebel*, the company is losing its best platoon leader, who in the past had rightfully assessed and solved so many tough situations. *Herr Feldwebel* was also my leader and my comrade, which can be confirmed by all of us comrades from his platoon. We have only really learned to appreciate this now that *Herr Feldwebel* is no longer among us.

After you will have received this terrible news, I can assure you that I share your pain and present my most heartfelt condolences to you. Words are too weak to provide comfort. May God stand at your side in these though times. In the hope of having been of some use to you, I will close.

With German greetings

Gehart Höfig[15]

Georg Rieck's family was also sent a glorified description of the encounter, similar to the Zimmermann article about the Hill 1098 fighting, that was written by the Commander of the 2nd Battalion of *Grenadier Regiment 107*:

Battalion order of the day:

On 2.10.1944, the strongpoint on the "Tete du Pin" (Hill 1674) under the command of *Feldwebel* Rieck, 7./G.R. 107, was defended heroically several times.

After pushing back an enemy patrol that caused the opponent to leave three dead in front of our positions as well as a lightly wounded prisoner in our hands, the enemy attacked the strongpoint again two hours later with some 60 men, coming from three sides. The enemy's invitations to surrender were answered on the spot with a determined volley of fire from the two light machine guns and all the riflemen. After the volley of fire, *Feldwebel* Rieck rushed forth through the heavy machine gun, submachine gun, and rifle fire of the attackers towards the point of the attack. The entire strongpoint followed him like a single man.

During this counterattack, *Feldwebel* Rieck, *Unteroffizier* Janostik, and *Gefreiter* Jantzen heroically and bravely met the soldier's death. *Stabsgefreiter* Altpeter and *Grenadier* Kessler were severely wounded, while *Gefreiter* Höfig was lightly wounded. The strongpoint defended its position to the last cartridge.

Taking away all the weapons and the wounded, the "Tête du Pin" was given up in order to avoid capture.

I present my congratulations to the "Tête du Pin" strongpoint for its exemplary battle and to the 7th Company for its excellent spirit.

My *Grenadier*s, the battle of our fallen and the blood of our wounded must serve as an example and debt to us for all time. We will not forget them and will remember them in days of hard battle.

Heil my *Grenadier*s![16]

After all this, Georg Rieck's grandson was still left wondering: "He must have known that the war was lost. Why didn't he give up? Nobody will answer that at last."

The last photo of Feldwebel Georg Rieck alive, apparently taken in Moulinet in the days preceding his death as he enjoys grapes with a comrade. This photo was included in Gerhart Höfig's letter to the Rieck family. Georg Rieck Collection.

Feldwebel Georg Rieck's grave in the German soldier's cemetery in Breil sur Roya. Georg Rieck Collection.

Mines

After the Allied advance ground to a halt in the region of the Italian border, both the Germans and Allies planted thousands of mines in any area likely to attract the enemy, such as footpaths, water points, houses, and pretty much any landmark. I often asked veterans how they dealt with mines. The answer was that they didn't do anything; they just looked where they stepped and tried to avoid any areas that were likely to be mined. The result, of course, is that mines caused a large number of casualties. PFC Guy Carr, of I Company of the 517th PIR, was involved in several ever more dangerous patrols at Peira Cava in which mines were the main threat. **Guy Carr**'s description (though the dates he quotes all seem to be incorrect) gives a very good impression of the hell that frontline soldiers had to endure on a daily basis during the so-called "Champaign Campaign":

Each day and night our troopers were sent out on patrol, down the mountain, to try to locate the enemy weak spots and the source of their supply lines. Every patrol maimed or took the lives of many troopers because the enemy also had their patrols out. Most of the ground throughout that area was either booby-trapped or mined. It was very treacherous just walking around in the dark, trying to miss those personnel mines and booby-traps.

One of our patrols departed our artillery observation outpost just after dark. Their route down the mountain was very dangerous, as we had all that area mined. They had to grasp a wire that was strung down between the mines and feel their way down. About an hour later we heard mines going off way below us. The patrol had run into an enemy minefield, and that area was also covered by mortars. The patrol was really trapped. Four of us started down the mountainside to try to help.

By the time we got down the mountain, most of the patrol had gotten out of the mined area. They were all torn up real bad. One fellow was completely blind and another had lost both legs. Another one lost one leg; however, the one who lost both legs never made it. He died while we were carrying him back up the mountain. It took us nearly all the rest of the night to bring the remainder of the patrol back to our lines.

Corporal John Rupczyk, also of I Company, actually removed two of the wounded men from the minefield in this particular incident, which occurred September 25th:

There were some French howitzers up on some mountain that we could see if we looked at them through

480

After the Liberation, thousands upon thousands of mines and other explosive devises needed to be found and neutralized in the Maritime Alps. Much of this dangerous work was performed by German prisoners, who often had no previous experience with mines, which led to the death of several dozen, if not hundred, men. This eloquent badge of the "Section de Déminage Département Alpes Maritimes" (Demining Group of the Maritime Alps Departement) was apparently locally made for the French soldiers accompanying the groups of German mine clearers. This example was found in the Col de Braus area. The letters PPN stand for "Priez pour nous" (Pray for us). Private Collection.

IT WAS NO **CHAMPAGNE CAMPAIGN** FOR THIS MAN

According to the recollections of Sgt Frank Dallas, this photo illustrates some of the remains of Private Stanley Radon, of I Company of the 517th, who was killed and severely mangled by a Tellermine. 517 Parachute Combat Team booklet, courtesy Frédéric Brega.

field glasses. We were going to go and blow them up. There must have been ten or twelve of us, and we went up in the woods at Peira Cava, then down towards Moulinet. It was just about dusk when we got there, so we waited until it got dark, and my platoon sergeant took three guys with him and they left. We laid there, and all of a sudden we heard explosions up where they were, and before long my sergeant came running down, hollering for me, and he says "the guys stepped on some mines up there." So we ran up and there were three guys in the minefield. One came out, and there were two more in there who were hurt bad. I don't know why I did it, but I got down on my belly and I crawled down there and, heck, this one guy weighed about 240 pounds, he was big. I got to him and I couldn't lift him, so I laid on the ground and rolled him over on me, then I backed up with my back to the ground. I got him up to where the guys were and they took him, and then I went and got the other guy. His name was Shumaker [**PFC Harold I. Shumaker**], and he must have stepped on the mine, because he was blown to pieces. His hands were blown off and all and he wanted us to shoot him, but nobody could do that. He died about an hour later. We left his body down at the bottom of the hill, and they went there about a month later and picked him up and buried him. The big guy, his name was Bagan, and I think they had to cut one part of his leg off. They said he was awful mad for the rest of his life.

John Rupczyk was awarded a Bronze Star for this action. A few days later, **Guy Carr** was sent on a similar patrol towards Moulinet:

It was now the first week of October 1944, and the weather was becoming much colder. We were not equipped for any cold weather and that, plus the nerve-wracking patrols, were beginning to thin our ranks more and more. Every patrol took the life of another trooper. I had been on two or three patrols myself, and to this day I still wonder how any of us returned. Early on the morning of 10 October 1944, eight of us were "volunteered" to go on a special patrol. This patrol was to be led by a Lieutenant (a new recruit). We were all given maps of the area and shown the terrain, enemy emplacements, and our logical lines of approach to such emplacements.

We began our journey at daybreak and proceeded down the mountain toward the villages of Moulinet and Sospel.

We arrived at the foot of the mountain without encountering much resistance. We then proceeded toward "X" objective, which consisted of mortar and machine gun emplacements. They were located near the top of a wooded hill. We had not gone far when the forward scout stepped on a personnel mine and was completely disintegrated [This was **Pvt Stanley E. Radon**]. I must mention here that I was probably within 20 feet of him when this happened. We had to stay off the trails as much as possible thereafter to avoid the mines.

We finally approached "X" hill and crawled to higher ground just to the right of our objective. From that position we could look down on the enemy emplacement. We had a rocket launcher "bazooka" with us and launched about three rounds into the emplacement, then we began our attack. We moved down the hill through a lot of timber and moved to the rear of the enemy. We then crawled forward until we came to a road which ran parallel to the upper slopes of the hill. The road was well covered by enemy weapons, so we positioned ourselves in the brush just below the road and waited to see what might happen next.

All at once, my sergeant [Frank Dallas] stood up and made a fast break across the road. He had a submachine gun, and he never stopped until he was at the enemy emplacements. He let go with his submachine gun and cleaned house damn quick. This objective was taken about noon, and we then proceeded towards "Y" objective. We did not know just what that objective was; however, we knew where it was located. We spent some three hours infiltrating enemy outposts, and our nerves were becoming more and more tense. Just before sundown, we arrived at our objective. We crawled in as close as we dared and saw a large 170mm gun emplacement. It was protected by about a company of goose-steppers. This was one of the emplacements that was playing havoc with our lines back at Peira Cava. We noted the position of the gun on our maps and withdrew to a safer position. It would have been a foolish move for us to try to take it.

It was now getting dark, and we were very far from Peira Cava. We moved about one mile back from the enemy gun emplacement and lay down for the night. Not much sleep was had, as all through the night German soldiers walked through the area, sometimes so close we could have reached out and touched them. This was another time I'll never know why they failed to spot, capture, or shoot us. About four o'clock the next morning, we started back towards our lines above Peira Cava. We had given up the thoughts of proceeding to objective "Z," as it was located beyond the big gun located at objective "Y". We all knew it would be suicide to attempt a move in that direction.

Our former training really came to good use on patrols such as this. We had been thoroughly trained to infiltrate and guide ourselves through enemy lines during nighttime or daytime. A paratroop outfit spent much of its time either within or behind enemy lines; therefore, they knew the art of behind enemy lines combat. Further, a paratrooper had to outguess, outthink, and outmaneuver any known enemy.

About noon on 11 October, we arrived back at our own lines, very tired and hungry, but we were really relieved. The next few days were spent under bitter enemy shell fire. Enemy patrols were more numerous, and their burp guns and 88mm and 170mm guns kept our slower firing machine guns, mortars, rifles, etc., pinned down most of the time.[17]

Frank Dallas was involved in the same patrol, and was the sergeant mentioned by Guy Carr in his story. **Frank Dallas** remembered:

We were on a combat patrol. We were about four or five miles behind the lines. We were going down a path and my first scout, Radon, stepped on a Tellermine. Fortunately, he was way ahead of us. I went back to recover his body three months later with the graves registration, and all that was left from him was from his chest up. All I got left of his was one of those small army bibles, and that was all black from the explosion. I took it home and sent it to his mother.

The first night we were out, we bivouacked behind a battalion of German artillery. We had two Germans who were coming from town drunk. They walked right through our bivouac area, and luckily, nobody shot or tried to do anything; they went right on through. We got up and moved out of there that night.

In fact, Stanley Radon's shredded body was only recovered from the battlefield in August 1945, almost one year after his death. A few days after this, **PFC Guy Carr** was sent on yet another memorable patrol that would also be his last. He wrote on in his memoirs:

The morning of 14 October 1944, our Captain and Lieutenant volunteered six of us to go on a patrol up the road north of Peira Cava. This area had not been penetrated by any of

us before. An army half-track had been giving us one hell of a pasting from that area, and our observers surmised that it was located at a house near the far end of a clearing. For some reason, that morning I left my billfold and all other personal effects with the fellows at Peira Cava. Deep down inside I felt that this day was my time.

About noon, our patrol moved out of Peira Cava and headed northward up the road. We followed the road for a short distance, then left the road and proceeded through the trees and brush to bypass any personnel mines. So many of the troopers had been put out of action by mines that we had become very leery of them.

We moved slowly through the timber and brush, as this was also an area where you could be ambushed. Finally, at about 1400 hours, we came to the clearing and stopped. The house was located at the far end, and our only approach was through that clearing. I remember taking out my canteen and gulping a big drink of water, all the time wishing we were across that clearing and back. We were fortunate that the enemy had not originally spotted our patrol, as we were perfect targets while approaching the house. There was no sign of enemy activity, so we checked all around the house and grounds and noticed that the half-track had been there. It had departed for reasons unknown to us.

We used a rifle butt to break open the door. No one was in the house, but I found a salt and pepper shaker on the table and looked them over. They looked very antique to me, so I pocketed them and headed for the door. Meanwhile, the other fellows, had already started back across the clearing. I had taken no more than ten steps from the house, when all at once I was blown straight up into the air, end over end. I hit the ground very hard and tried to get up and run. I could barely see or hear, and my body was completely numbed. I looked down and saw that my left leg was gone. Most of my clothing had been blown off, and the rifle I was carrying (a 1903 type with a grenade launcher mounted on the barrel) was completely splintered. There were hand grenades and rifle grenades in all my pockets, and I'll never know why they failed to detonate. I guess I was just a lucky "GUY." (I must make

Paratroopers of I Company of the 517th PIR stand in the yard of the French barracks in Peira Cava. From left to right are: Marvin D. Moles, Dewey, Thomas L. Patterson, and Guy E. Carr. Marvin Moles Collection.

a footnote here that I never did know where that salt and pepper shaker set disappeared to.)

The other fellows thought that a mortar shell had landed, because they hit the ground fast and lay there. I called out to them that I was hit bad, and then they crawled out there to help me. They had to use plenty of caution, as it was very likely that more than one mine existed in that clearing. They finally crawled out to me and administered what first aid they could by giving me a syrette of morphine and using my belt as a tourniquet. They then helped me to the edge of the clearing. I remember that I had a terrible urge for water, and I drank nearly a canteen, which caused me severe chills. My whole body would go into spasms.

At first I tried to hop between two other fellows, but my right leg and foot had been damaged, also. They fashioned a stretcher out of two rifles and field jackets, and by this method and carrying me on their backs, we slowly proceeded back towards Peira Cava. The route back was very hazardous, as we had to go down over rocks, through trees and brush. The fellows would tie me to their belts and slide me over the rocks to the next ledge.

I cannot remember too much of the trip back, but one fellow later told me that I kept telling him to "Please cut it off." Darkness was approaching fast as we neared Peira Cava. The initial shock was beginning to wear off, and I was not feeling too much pain. We arrived back at our lines, and all my buddies came to see me. They brought my wallet and all other personal items they could find. I was put on a stretcher and laid across the hood of a jeep. Everyone said their goodbyes, and I started my last journey out of the Alps. I was very lucky, as many of those fellows never had a chance to make that trip.

I was operated on that same night in a clearance hospital located in Nice, France. Later I was informed that, had it not been for the transfer of blood from a German prisoner, which went directly into my veins, I could not possibly have survived. The next morning, I partially came out of my shock, only to find Alex Capitan [This was a Russian member of the German army who had "joined" the 517th PIR after they captured him in the days following the invasion.] sitting beside my bed. He had somehow journeyed from Peira Cava to Nice, which must have been around forty kilometers, during the night. He grabbed my arm and squeezed it, then, with a satisfied smile, arose and departed. He had been on the patrol with us when I was clobbered, and he had made that long trek out of the Alps just to see that I was all right. I'll never forget that man as long as I live. Further, I will never forget or stop thanking all the others who saved my life on that patrol. A more loyal and true group of friends, to this day, could never have been found.[18]

Pvt Marvin Moles was also on the patrol, and describes the conditions under which they evacuated Guy Carr:

Me and about four of us, I guess, went on patrol to see if we could find where the Germans were dug in or something. We got right at the top of the hill and Guy Carr stepped on a mine. I guess it was just a regular personnel mine. It blew his foot off, cutting it off just as smooth as if you had taken a razor right through the ankle joint. Of course, then I volunteered to go back out through the minefields to find us a place to get back, because we had to cross over some piano wire things down where we first came in to get on the patrol. As we started back, the Germans let off with a volley of machine gun and rifle fire.

We got back down to where the wires were, and I had to roll up my sleeves so I could put my hands down next to the ground and hold them so when I got to one of the wires I could feel it. Then I would stand there, they would come and lift Carr across, and then I would get over and I would go to the next one and do the same thing. I think it was four or five wires, but then we got him out and got him back down to that village. They had a first aid station there and we got him to that. They did what they could for him and then sent him back to the hospital. I guess he went to England then from there back to the States.

For his brave actions to help evacuate Guy Carr, **Marvin Moles** was awarded the Silver Star, the citation of which read:

For gallantry in action near Pierra Cava [sic], France, 18 October 1944. While returning from a mission behind enemy lines, the lead scout of a reconnaissance patrol stepped on an enemy mine which blew off the scout's foot. Private Moles, 2nd scout, rushed to his wounded comrade's aid and applied a tourniquet. Although the shortest possible evacuation route was across a minefield, Private Moles, noting the grave condition of the casualty, volunteered to lead the patrol across. The enemy, alerted by the exploding mine, swept the area with intense rifle and machine gun fire. Despite this, Private Moles probed his way until he found a path, along which the patrol, carrying the injured man, crawled to safety. Private Moles' action was instrumental in saving his comrade's life. His daring and coolness under fire conform with the highest traditions of the military service.[19]

Marvin Moles had been ready to take the risks of crossing the minefield to save a friend. The situation could be very different in cases when the victim was not a comrade, as **Lt William Story**, of 4-2 of the FSSF, explains:

There was somebody who came through from the Italian side and who stumbled into the German minefield. We never found out whether he was a refugee, deserter, or whatever. He must have walked on a mine. He lay out there the whole day, dying, and we could hear him plead for help: "Please come and help." My guys wanted to go out, but I ordered them to stay put. I wasn't going to risk anybody in a minefield. It was a tough thing to go through and let him expire there, but there was no other way.

The demining teams that cleaned up the battlefields once the war was over sometimes discovered human skeletons that had been left in the minefields for months or more. The German army was very experienced with mines and had developed numerous models that could be fitted with several types of detonators designed for various battlefield scenarios. During both WWI and WWII, the German army had performed pre-planned retreats, abandoning vast expanses of land to the enemy. The German engineer troops had developed a number of perverse techniques to render life as miserable as possible for the troops that would take over the evacuated areas. The men of D Company of the 517th PIR discovered this to their expense when they entered Sospel, out of which the Germans executed a pre-planned retreat October 27th 1944. The paratroopers that took over the town found a large nice-looking empty house and decided to take up quarters in it. Unbeknownst to them, the Germans had anticipated that the Americans, and hopefully their officers, would be attracted by the house, so they had booby-trapped it with a large explosive charge. **Pvt Alexander Sierra**, of D Company, was one of those who entered the house:

When we came down from the mountains, we occupied the town that the Germans had left and we moved into this nice home. There were quite a few of us, and a lot of us ended up in the basement. We were drinking wine that we found there, and just relaxing. We had been up there quite a while, steady, without any relief. But anyway, we went down to this house the first night and the Lieutenant came down there and said: "Some of you guys have to get out of here, there's too many of you." There was a house right behind there, maybe 20 or 30 yards apart, and he said: "Mortar squad go out there." I was in the mortar squad, and we really raised hell, because we didn't want to go. We were playing cards and dice with the guys, and just plain old drinking and shooting the bull about home and girls and everything. So regretfully we moved out to the other house at two o'clock in the morning.

The Lieutenant's order may have saved his life, as shortly afterwards, the house suddenly blew up. **Alexander Sierra** continues:

We were half drunk, and the next thing I remember, some guy slammed the door open and this guy was in his brown horrible army overcoat we used to have, and that's all he had: he was naked and he had cuts all over him. He had been in this explosion, but we weren't, we were safe because we were 20 or 30 yards apart. So I remember that, and we all got up and Jesus, the house was a mess. Digging for friends and buddies, some of the guys who were alive. We would set them aside so the rest of the guys could evacuate them. I wasn't actually digging, because there was so many of us that it was just like chaos. It was just didn't know where to start, didn't know where to look, except we were hearing noises.

PFC Mel Dahlberg and Pvt Myrle Traver, of F Company, also had a narrow escape:

Myrle Traver and I were chosen to lead D Company and parts of E Company of the 2nd Battalion down into the valley of Sospel because we had made patrols down in there. We took off about midnight, and we worked our way up to the German command post, which was a chalet. That was their headquarters and they had abandoned it. We got in there early morning and looked over the whole chalet to make sure that they didn't have any time bombs in there, and so forth. We found none. The rest of my own company was coming into Sospel from another direction, we didn't know just where or when, so we stayed overnight in one room. Then Myrle Traver and I got up in the morning, as we needed to go to meet our company. We got a block away and the chalet blew up! She went up in a cloud of smoke. We had missed whatever they had in there to blow the place up. I suppose it was a time bomb, and it killed a number of people. I remember running back, and in that confusion we could see the bodies of the poor guys that had been blown up. There were at least four or five that

were killed; I remember a grand piano being on top of one of the guys. Oh, it was terrible.

When you capture something, you have got to be very careful about having set traps. But I remember looking in every nook and cranny of that place, along with officers of D Company. We just missed it! We don't know how it was done, but it was a good blast.

Pvt Erwin Scott, of D Company, was actually in the house when it exploded and was one of the lucky ones to escape unscathed. In an interview from 2002, he explained the perverse and almost artful cleverness with which the German engineers had hidden the bomb in the house, according to him:

[The house] had been cleared by the engineers as being safe. It killed seven of my buddies and scratched up three of us. I didn't even get enough scratch out of it for the Purple Heart. It was a booby-trap, and a damn good one, too. The only reason [the house] wasn't full of officers is because they hadn't seen it. The engineers had been there and cleared it. The Germans had taken and dug out, down in the cellar. There were some potatoes down there, but it was dirty. Didn't look like anything had been done to it for 50 years. (…) They estimated later that there was 500 pounds of TNT under the floor. They poured a new concrete floor, made it look old, and dumped the potatoes on it. I don't know when they set the timer. I guess they allowed a full day after they left, because it blew at 2:00 in the morning. I do believe that the Colonel and the Battalion tops would have been in the house if they'd seen it. It was that nice a house. I was in one of the rooms, but it was closer to the outside of the house. I got a few scratches and a lot of dust up my nose. My ears rang for quite a while.[20]

A more official version of the story can be found in the citation for the Silver Star that **T5 Ernest Engle** was awarded for helping dig the casualties out of the ruined house:

For heroism not involving action with the enemy, on 4 November 1944, near Sospel, France. Due to inclement weather, Technician Engle and his unit were living in an abandoned house. All precautions had been taken to see that the house was free of booby-traps, explosives, or other devices left by the enemy. In spite of these precautions, a time bomb exploded in the house in which fifteen men were asleep. The building was completely demolished and resulted

Robert Cooper, of D Company of the 517th PIR, poses in the ruins of the house in Sospel, in which five of his comrades were killed when a German time bomb exploded November 4, 1944. Floyd Polk Collection. The Gregg and Michelle Philipson Collection.

in the death of five men, five wounded, and five badly shaken. Technician Engle, pinned down by a steel girder and his legs buried, saw the structure was a mass of debris, ten to twelve feet deep, with men and equipment buried in the wreckage. Freeing himself, he first revived his platoon leader, then searched until he found the medical supplies and proceeded to dig out one man after another, giving them necessary first aid. Finding one man buried to his neck in the wreckage, his mouth and nose full of pulverized concrete, Technician Engle instantly realized the man was choking to death. Removing the dust and dirt from the soldier's nose and mouth with his fingers, he was able to restore his normal breathing, thus saving his life. He then continued to search for other men who were in need of immediate aid, saving many from further suffering. Technician Engle, himself suffering from shock, working unassisted, saved one man's life and greatly aided in preventing the disaster from causing additional deaths. Technician Engle's prompt and voluntary aid and outstanding courage reflect much credit upon himself and his unit.[21]

A total of five men of D Company were killed in the blast. They were: **Pvt Alton Allen**, **T4 Homer Beaver**, **Pvt John Fouts**, **PFC Daniel Ogniewski**, and **Pvt Walter Vanderpool**. Five others were injured, including one, Floyd Polk, who lost a leg.

A Single Death on the Battlefield

Although casualties were rather light during the long period of static mountain warfare that started in mid-September 1944 and lasted until April 1945, the face of war never became any prettier. **Sgt John Cooley**, of A Company of 509th PIB, which was holding the front lines to the north of the 517th PIR, tells of how horrendous the effects of one single casualty could be on those around him:

It took many years before I could even talk about what happened to me, and it took several days to type it out, because it brought back some of the most horrible days and nights of my entire life.

The 509th PIB was to dig in on a hill that was facing the Germans located on the opposite side of the valley. Late one evening, I was ordered to dig a two-man foxhole with a new replacement. The guy smoked a lot and I told him several times to stop, because some German might spot our position and drop some mortar shells in on us. He was very nervous and kept hunching down in the lowest part of the hole we were busy digging and lighting up another smoke. We dug almost all night because of the rocks and roots. We never dug it deep enough or wide enough, but thought we could finish it the next day. Our platoon was either pulling patrons or staying in their foxholes, watching the front. I was sitting at the bottom of the foxhole, trying to catch some sleep. The fog had just started lifting as daylight set in. I suddenly heard a loud splash and was instantly covered in blood, brains, and hair… this new replacement had been hit by a sniper and a large part of his head was missing! The trooper was on top of me, and I knew that if I tried to push his body out of the foxhole, the sniper would know that someone else was still in the foxhole… he'd know for sure I was there. Every once in a while, the German would shoot at the hole, just to let me know he had zeroed in on it and that I wasn't going any place. I couldn't stick my head out long enough to even find out where he was so I could shoot back. I had to stay in the hole all day and just wait for it

T4 Homer C. Beaver, Pvt John "Jack" Fouts, and PFC Daniel L. Ogniewski, three of the five troopers of D Company of the 517th PIR who were killed in the booby-trapped house in Sospel. Beaver's brother had been killed in action six months earlier, while Fouts' father, who was part Cherokee, died of a heart attack less than a month after finding out about his son's death. Franklin County Genealogical Society Collection, courtesy Pamela Barrett. Ron Watkins Collection. Mayes County Historical Society Collection, courtesy Leslie Trogdon. National WWII Memorial Collection.

to get dark again. I never wanted to look at the trooper's exposed brain… but I couldn't help myself, I had to look, and when I did, I passed out and fainted. When I awoke, my entire body was covered with ants. Flies were there by the hundreds, together with many small gnats. The insects were after the blood, and it was everywhere. I almost went crazy itching and scratching all over my body and couldn't stop. I couldn't get the dead trooper's body off me, there just wasn't any room. I don't know how many times I blacked out, but every time I came to, the nauseous smell of his body parts was almost unbearable. I had lost control of my body functions and was shaking from head to toe. I had thrown up, defecated in my pants, and urinated as well, and didn't even remember doing it. I knew that I did not want to die and was more scared than I had ever been in my whole life. I was also in constant fear of a mortar shell landing in my hole.

Even now, after all these years, sometimes I will get a whiff of a certain smell and instantly throw up. Sometimes even the sight of blood will make my body itch all over, and I will scratch myself feverishly and I can't keep myself from doing it. There were many more experiences such as this, and the war never got any easier because of the bad experiences. Our Southern France mission was supposed to be only a three-day war, and we were then supposed to be relieved. We were in combat for as long as 99 days and 100 nights before being relieved! Someone called the Southern France invasion the Champagne Campaign; that might sound like having a good time, but I was twice the sole survivor of my platoon. Does that tell you anything?[22]

The Puerto Ricans and their Colonel at Peira Cava

In mid-November 1944, the FABTF was removed from the Maritime Alps front, where it was replaced by several American units, one of which was the 3rd Battalion of the 65th Infantry Regiment, which took up positions around Peira Cava December 12th. The interesting characteristic about the 65th Infantry Regiment was that it consisted of Puerto Rican soldiers, and being at Peira Cava was their very first experience of front line duty. December 14th, the newly-appointed regimental commander, 41-year-old West Pointer **Colonel George A. Ford**, reached Peira Cava. The next day he wrote home to his wife and three children:

> I arrived at my CP yesterday afternoon. I found it in a tiny hamlet 5,000 feet up in the Maritime Alps. It is a jewel of a setting, the most gorgeously magnificent scenery I have ever encountered. It is futile to attempt to describe it, a tumbled sea of mountains all around, rugged grey masses dusted with snow and snow-covered ranges interspersed. A belt of spruce trees here, all feathered with snow, and at this elevation the ground snow covered. The morning and evening light on the mountains is lovely beyond description, and each turn of the road reveals a new and fascinating vista. (...) Altogether I am so darned happy over the situation that I am likely to burst into a song at any moment. My surroundings are such that it is a shame to take the taxpayer's money for being here. To have my own command again, and in the combat zone, doing work that I love and can be enthusiastic over again, and with a unit which appears basically excellent but in need of lots of work – it is just perfect. Or would be if you were here, too. Short of that, I have been so very lucky and after the last miserable six months, too, that I can hardly keep down to earth. Nor need you have the least concern for my safety – it is a nice quiet little war we have here, and my only risk is of bumping my head against a cloud. A merry, merry Christmas to the best and sweetest wife and family ever.[23]

Although the snow may have looked beautiful, it wreaked heavy havoc on the morale of the Puerto Rican soldiers, who were used to living in a tropical climate and not in freezing cold foxholes. Two weeks later, **Colonel George Ford**, whose enthusiasm had in the meantime been tempered, wrote home:

> I have a major operation in personnel shake-up to be performed. I called in all my officers today, that is all I could safely take out of positions, and laid down the law. Last night, I relieved my second in command and sent him to the brigade commander with a letter to the effect that I never again wanted to see him. It will cause some surprises in view of the fact that my predecessor recommended him to take command. I gather that (as usual) I am regarded as a very mean old ----. I do not mind that in the slightest, but I hate to think of the long hard job I have to do. It is difficult to change people's way of thought and to lift them bodily out of a really deep rut.[24]

This American helmet was found in the vicinity of Peira Cava in the early 2000s. A Malta Cross, the symbol of the Puerto Rican 65th Infantry Regiment, is carved into the paint on the front of the helmet. The 65th Infantry Regiment arrived in Peira Cava in December 1944, after the FABTF had been removed from the Maritime Alps front. Private Collection.

January 4, 1945, only five days after writing these lines, Colonel Ford decided to personally lead a 12-man patrol out to the German lines that were held by *Infanterie Division 34*. This bold display of leadership and aggressiveness was undoubtedly meant to serve as an inspiration to his men and as a boost to their morale. The patrol advanced east towards a cable house held by the Germans, halting shortly before their objective. **SSgt Jose Robles, Jr.** picks up the story from here:

> When we got to the rifle pit, Colonel Ford gave a signal to stop, which I did. He walked up to me and told me that we were close to the enemy positions. I continued with my patrol to the left of the ridge. He also told me that he would continue to the right, with Capt Logan behind. I warned the Colonel twice that he was exposed. I told that to the Colonel because I had been there before and he grinned. Then I continued with my patrol to the position that he told me to take. He kept going with Capt Logan until he reached a place about 25 yards from the cable house. I could see the Colonel standing up, observing through field glasses.[25]

Captain Daniel B. Logan, who was accompanying Colonel Ford, continues:

> There was a double tree. I put my rifle between the tree and put it to my shoulder, aiming at the house. The Colonel stepped out from behind the tree to the left and advanced in the direction of the house. He took about three or four steps, slightly crouching, when there was one single shot fired from the direction of the cable house. After the shot I heard the Colonel's carbine hit the ground. I looked in his direction and saw him lying down on the ground on his back, in the axis of his movement, his head towards the cable house. I asked the Colonel: "Where were you hit, Colonel?" He replied: "Logan, I am hit in the back." Right after he said that he drew his knees up and stretched out and quivered. I could see blood was flowing from his

mouth. After that I called at the Colonel: "Colonel, come to me," and there was no answer. I remained in my position about a minute, and before I left I took another look at him, and he looked to me like he was dead.

Immediately after the first shot was fired, the one that hit the Colonel, a machine gun opened up from the direction of the right side of the house. I withdrew to the rear about five yards and then to the left, where I knew the patrol was. As I was withdrawing to the left, I withdrew into the right flank of the patrol, and it began to give way when I came in sight. When I reached the cover of a large tree and counted the men there were five. By this time mortar fire was falling in our immediate vicinity. I called for the sergeant and he answered. I went to him and told him that the Colonel was hit, that we had to get him. I asked him what the best way to do it was. We arrived at no conclusion, and I told the sergeant to go ahead towards the house, which he did. I then discovered that one man in front of me was badly wounded, which left only three riflemen, not counting the sergeant. I dispatched the one on the right to go to higher ground to our right to protect the flank. I told the man in the center to cover straight ahead and the man on the left to cover our left. At that time, I started to move up along the sergeant's right, towards the higher ground from which I had come. I moved up about one bound of about 15 yards and motioned for the center and the left riflemen to also move forward. I seemed to be unable to convey my intensions to them. I then went back to them and pointed out the bound which I wanted them to take. At that time they took their designated bound.[26]

In the meantime, **SSgt Jose Robles** was trying to retrieve Colonel Ford's body:

[Capt Logan] told me to go up there and get the Colonel and I started on my mission. Before leaving, I noticed Capt Logan posting some men to guard my flanks. When I reached near the top of the ridge, I saw one German behind the small house and he fired at me, so I returned the fire. I saw four enemies run out from behind the little house, and before I had a chance to fire at them, they hit the ground close to the position where the Captain told me the Colonel was. They were about 25 yards from me, but after they hit the ground I could not see them. I never saw the Colonel while I was up there. The four enemies were Germans, I could tell this by their uniforms; they were not wearing helmets. I looked back towards Capt Logan and he signaled me to come back, which I did. He asked me what was going on up the hill and I told him what I had observed.[27]

The experienced soldiers of *Infanterie Division 34* were preparing to surround the small patrol, as **Captain Logan** explains:

The rifleman who had been sent to the top of the ridge to cover our right came back at about this time and motioned to me to come to him, which I did. He reported that an enemy patrol was moving so as to envelope our right flank. At this time, I decided that we would withdraw. Before we withdrew, I checked the wounded man's pulse and found him dead. I said to the men "let's go." We withdrew down the hill about 50 yards, at which place I checked with the sergeant to see if everyone was accounted for. He counted them and said they were.[28]

Colonel George A. Ford, commander of the Puerto Rican 65th Infantry Regiment, 41 years old and father of three, who was shot and killed while leading a patrol northeast of Peira Cava January 4, 1945. Ann Ford Collection.

The patrol was forced to withdraw, leaving the bodies of their regimental commander and of one enlisted man behind. The patrol had not gone at all as planned. Instead, the 65th IR had suffered a huge setback and the Germans had proven once again that the war was far from over by killing and capturing the body of the highest ranking American officer to be killed on the Maritime Alps front. Since his death could at first not be confirmed with certainty, Colonel Ford was listed as missing in action, and it was not until after the war that his body was found buried in a shallow grave near the scene of his death. Because no identification tags were found on his body, it needed to be identified with a dental chart. It was a tragic fate for Colonel George Ford; only one day before his death, on January 3, 1945, his wife and children had received his letter, wishing them a merry Christmas and assuring them: "it is a nice quiet little war we have here and my only risk is of bumping my head against a cloud."

The Fate of the Wounded

Throughout this book we have read many accounts of Allied soldiers describing the circumstances in which they were wounded, but without going into details of how the medical service was organized. Each combat unit of the FABTF contained medical personnel in the form of doctors and aid men who were to give first aid to the wounded and evacuate them out of the immediate combat zone. This was not without risk, and several aid men, as well as one doctor of the FABTF, were killed while operating in southern France (See Dr Roy Baze and medics Victor Osborn, Clarence Bergeman and Lee Polson in Chapter 6, as well as several of the FSSF soldiers killed in Tanneron in Chapter 5). The 676th Medical Collecting Company (as well as the 638th Medical Clearing Company as of August 28th) then had the mission of transporting the wounded back to the field hospitals and treating them during transit. The units in charge of the field hospitals and the locations of these field hospitals changed with time, so I will not even attempt to list them. However, in the days following the invasion, for example, the 11th and 51st Evacuation Hospitals had taken quarters in Draguignan, working under tents and in a former German military hospital in town. In the field hospitals, conditions remained primitive and only temporary treatment could be given to the more severely wounded, who then needed to be shipped back, first to Naples and then to the U.S. for definitive treatment. The lightly wounded could remain in the field hospitals near the front and then return to their units once their wounds had healed. **William E. Johnston** was an enlisted man in the 676th Medical Collecting Company. He had no medical experience before joining the military and tells us what daily life was like for the men in his unit after landing in France by glider August 15th:

We went down through Grasse, Antibes, and Cannes, and we wound up in Nice. We stayed in Drap for about six months. We ran a little two-car hospital train out of Nice. We would go up to Monte-Carlo, Cap Ferrat, Menton, and then come back to Nice, and then we would go north, up in the mountains. There was a big tunnel up there and we stayed in the tunnel at night.

I was just an aid man. When I went into service they put me in that, I didn't have a choice. We had learned to make temporary splints, bandage, administer drugs, and things like that. We had doctors that did all the serious stuff. All we did was get the patients ready for the doctor. We had four medical doctors in my company. We would give the patients morphine and at that time they had a sulpha drug powder that you would put on the wound. You would put tourniquets on and things like that and stabilize them, and then get them down to where they could be transferred to a field hospital. The wounded would come in, we would have no history, you know, how bad it was, or anything like that. We would just go ahead and check and make sure it wasn't bleeding. If it had a tourniquet, we would loosen the tourniquet, then tighten it back up and mov him on to the field hospital or to our doctor as quick as we could.

When you got a patient that was shell shocked or something like that, you would have to more or less tie him where he couldn't hurt himself or you and go from there. We had a few that would come in, and to them you are an enemy and they don't trust you. I can remember one case where this soldier, I would say he was 40 or 45 years old, he got in a corner and he just scrounged up in the corner and put his face in the corner where you couldn't see it. We would try to get him out, and then he would just act like you were going to cut his head off or something like that. He was just frightened. For people like that, all we would do is just give them a couple of shots of morphine and that kind of quieted them down a little bit. Some of them came out of it after they found out that they weren't going to get hurt, but they would still have those shakes. I have seen them wake up hollering from a deep sleep, just wake up and you would have to hold them down until they got control of themselves.

You learned a lot. You learned you could eat sitting beside a dead man, or you could eat with a guy dying beside you. You learned that life goes on regardless of what happens around you. Sometimes it's hard to take, but life goes on. It was a big shock. A big shock, but you learned pretty quick that you couldn't carry it around with you. You had to do the best you could and then forget it.

It was very hard, I will put it that way. I had one that died in my arms at night, and he was calling for his mother all night long. All I could do was keep him from tearing his bandage off. He was shot in the stomach, about half of his stomach was torn out, and he kept trying to pull the bandage off and I sat there and held him all night long. Something like that… you don't forget it. I am 82 years old now and I was 19 then, and it was like it happened yesterday. You don't forget it. You don't forget the good things that happened, either, like when a woman delivered a child, or something like that. You bandaged kids up that got hurt and put them on their way.

In Chapter 11, we read about how several men of A Company of the 40th Engineer Regiment were killed or wounded while attempting to remove bodies from a minefield north of Vence. **Sgt Sidney Oxman** was wounded in this incident, and while his more severely wounded buddies got evacuated back to Naples, he remained in the field hospital in Draguignan, where he was able to observe the functioning of the hospital, which he wrote about it in his diary:

Sept 3. (…) I thank God that I came out of this alive. I've been looked after all the time and the war is nearly over, and I now I know I'll get back to my darling. There are German, Russian, and Polish here being treated. Yesterday, a German was brought in very badly injured. They worked on him for 24 hours straight. He died when his fever went up to 108°. We hope our boys are being helped, too. (…)

Tues Sept 5. (…) There are still a few Germans here. Last night a gang had one talking. He spoke perfect English. He still thinks Germany will win. The damn fools. You've got to kill them before they'll believe they're through. The first night I came here, there was a German on the cots each side of me. After that happened I was ready to kill them. I couldn't stand that German lingo and I made them know it. I'd have killed them if I had a gun that night. One moaned all night because his arm hurt. He wasn't badly hurt. The yellow skunks. I cooled down by morning, but it still got my goat having them in the same ward. (…)

The installations of the 51st Evacuation Hospital in Draguignan. Ted Rulison Collection.

Friday Sept 8. (…) Tonight I helped around the ward. I fed a paratrooper his supper. He has a brain concussion and an arm in a cast. When I see some of the cases brought in this hospital, I look back to the night I came in. My injuries were scratches compared to some brought in. Boys without an arm or leg, or so badly burned and shot up you don't make out their features, yet they pull through. The doctors perform miracles. The surgery is busy from morning till night. (…)

Sat, Sept 9. This morning, after feeding a bed patient I shaved and wrote letters. No one slept very much last night. They brought in a five-year-old French boy. He was hit by a bomb fragment. They operated, but it looks like he won't pull through. There's a hole in his head and part of his brain is exposed. They're working every minute to save him. Then this afternoon, while I was sitting in my cot, one of the boys from the company walked in. He was brought down from the Swiss border, where the third platoon is. He's gone a little off his mind. I didn't know what to make of it at first, then I checked up another one of our boys from there (…). He gave me the whole story. It seems they were under heavy shell fire and he just cracked under the strain. (…)

Monday, Sept 11. (…) Casualties come and go. Some are bad and others just minor cases. In the ward there are mostly head injuries. Just before supper, a Capt was brought in. He was got by a mine. Concussion of the brain and body injuries. He came to and started ripping the bandage off his head and tried getting out of bed. I watched over him for a while to help out around here. There's plenty to do for the nurses and ward boys. I am glad to be able to help out a bit by feeding a patient his meal or see that he keeps in bed. Some just don't know what's going on. (…)

Tues, Sept 12. This morning I helped feed patients again. We've got a couple of violent ones now. They don't know what hit them. They get out of bed, talk out of the head. They have to be watched at all times. (…) This morning they operated on the little five-year-old French boy. They cut part of his brain away. There can't much hope for him. It's a pity to see the father and mother stand over him. He'll be an imbecile if he does live.[29]

Where Have All The Flowers Gone?

In the region of study of this book (the area between Agay, Seillans, Col de Turini, and Menton), a total of at least 127 Allied (American, French, and Canadian) and over 300 German soldiers died between August 15 and September 7, 1944. In the famous song about the cycle of life and death of soldiers, the flowers go to young girls, the young girls go to young men, the young men become soldiers, the soldiers go to graveyards, and the graveyards then become covered with flowers that young girls pick. The reality of the battlefields in southern France comprised a few notable differences. First, many of the soldiers, particularly the Germans, were so young that they had never been with any girls yet. Second, not all the killed soldiers had the luck of ending up buried in a graveyard: some, like Captain Miller and his men of the 509th PIB, were never found. Others, mainly Germans in the mountain areas, were never buried, and their bones were scattered by animals and time. Finally, there don't seem to be many flowers growing on the graves in the American, German, and Commonwealth war cemeteries in Draguignan, Dagneux, and Mazargues... and very few young girls ever seem to visit the young men buried there.

The body of a dead German soldier that was discovered by troopers of the 551st PIB. The remains are contained within a German shelter quarter, giving the impression that this soldier's comrades first tried to evacuate his body before being forced to abandon it in the wilderness; presumably with several hours of walking through difficult terrain left between them and their base. When exposed to the elements, insects, and animals, a few weeks are sufficient for a body to become partially skeletonized like this. Charles Fairlamb Collection, courtesy Michel de Trez.

Throughout the book, what happed to the bodies of killed German soldiers has been described several times. It would seem that as of August 15, 1944, an order was issued not to transport the dead back to Caucade Cemetery in Nice as during the Occupation, but instead, to bury the dead in the vicinity of where they had been killed. This was often done by the Germans within a few meters of where death had occurred. Other times the dead were regrouped in makeshift cemeteries or in local civilian cemeteries. As we saw, because the Germans were retreating, their dead were also often simply abandoned on the battlefield and would then be buried by the French civilians. The German bodies were later recovered by the *Volksbund*, mostly in 1958, and were reburied in a German military cemetery in Dagneux, near Lyon. The families were not given the choice of retrieving the bodies, so all of them are still buried in Dagneux today.

So far, we have not said much about the Allied dead. This is because they were usually promptly removed from the battlefield and transported to Draguignan, so neither the fellow soldiers of the dead nor the local civilians therefore had much of a chance to see or come into contact with the bodies. A makeshift cemetery had been opened to bury the dead Allied troops next to the civilian cemetery of the town of Draguignan within a day or two of the invasion. Local doctor Angelin German buried the first killed paratroopers there on about August 16th.[30] This improvisation was then made official by the chaplain of the 36th Infantry Division, Colonel Herbert E. MacCombie, with the permission of the mayor of Draguignan. The location that had initially been chosen to be used as a burial ground for the 36th Infantry Division proved unsuitable, causing **Colonel Herbert MacCombie** to search for a new burial ground, as he later explained in his wartime autobiography:

> August 17th, I went back to the cemetery to conduct religious services for the dead. I found that not even one grave had been opened. They were digging in shale rock and waiting for TNT to blast open graves.
>
> I told the officer in charge that we couldn't have a cemetery there. Regulations provided that graves must have proper drainage. We had quite a discussion. Fortunately, Lieutenant Colonel Clifton C. Carter, the Division Quartermaster, came by. We agreed to ask for help from the French officials in the selection of a cemetery site.

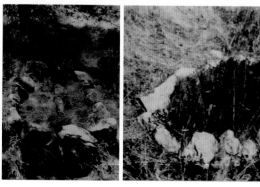

Examples of some of the miserable cemeteries and graves that remained in the mountains of the Maritime Alps after the German defeat. Most of these graves remained untouched until 1958, when they were finally excavated and the bodies transferred to Dagneux cemetery. Volksbund Bildarchiv.

A local Frenchman leads members of a postwar German search party to an isolated forest grave. Volksbund Bildarchiv.

We decided to go to Draguignan, the capital of Var. It was reported that our troops were fighting in the town that morning, but we thought they would have the Germans driven out by afternoon. We were correct.

When we reached Draguignan, everyone was rejoicing in the eviction of the enemy. We went to the office of the Mayor and told him we needed land for a cemetery for our dead. He suggested that we use their cemetery. It would be an honor for the American dead to be buried with French soldiers.

I told him, "There are too many dead for us to use your present cemetery."

"C'est dommage! (It is a pity)," he exclaimed.

He assigned his secretary to help us find an appropriate spot. The young man was delighted to accompany us in our jeep. As we rode along, he waved to all his friends. They cheered him.

He took us to a beautiful field. The digging would be easy. Some trees could be left in place. We agreed that it would be a suitable area. Colonel Carter agreed to come

The Draguignan Cemetery as it appeared in late 1944. Griffitts Family Collection. Author' Collection.

A comparative view showing the Draguignan Cemetery in 1944 and today. The cemetery was initially used to bury American, Commonwealth, and German dead. Nowadays, however, the cemetery is purely American and all the non-American bodies have been exhumed and transferred to other cemeteries. Author's Collection.

back the next day with the necessary papers to purchase the land. When we arrived the next day with the necessary papers for the purchase, we found that local people had taken up a collection to buy the land and present it to the American army.

We made arrangements with the Airborne Division to bury their dead in our cemetery. Later on, I had to return to the cemetery many times to conduct religious services for our dead. Every time I came there were fresh flowers on the graves. They had been placed there by the local people. No one could be more appreciative of the sacrifices of these men than were the French people of Var.

After the war, the cemetery at Draguignan was made a permanent American cemetery. I visited the cemetery in 1961 and found it very well maintained. Appropriate buildings had been erected. Walls bore the names of all the honored dead. Proper recognition was given to the 36th Infantry Division. I visited the graves of some of the men whom I had known personally and offered prayers in the Chapel for all the men of the 36th Division who are buried there.[31]

By August 19th, the Draguignan cemetery was taken over by the American 46th Quartermaster Graves Registration Company (and later the 48th QMGRC as of September), and it became the official cemetery for the American and Commonwealth forces participating in Operation Dragoon. Over the following weeks and months, the 46th and 48th QMGRCs even exhumed some bodies that had been buried near the landing beaches and drop zones to transfer them to Draguignan. Thus, with a few notable exceptions, such as bodies that were left between the lines (For example, the Joseph Van Ness case in Chapter 15, or the Shumaker and Radon cases mentioned above), or in cases when very numerous casualties had occurred (As at Théoule and la Napoule in Chapter 6), the bodies of killed Allied soldiers were brought to Draguignan and buried there within two or three days of dying on the battlefield. The Americans were buried in one plot, Commonwealth soldiers in another plot, and there was even one plot reserved for German soldiers.

It was thus American Graves Registration Companies that were responsible for the Draguignan cemetery, and because of their remarkable organization, very few Allied soldiers remained unidentified. We will now see what happened to Allied casualties from the battlefield to their final resting place.

When a soldier was killed, his body was normally brought back to the nearest aid station by the medics. One French civilian whose garage was used to stock American soldiers' duffel bags remembered that some supply soldiers had set up a system to take advantage of the deaths:

When the jeeps came down with wounded, or even, unfortunately, dead soldiers, they immediately went to look, because the doctor was just across the street. They went to see who it was, then they went to get the duffel bag, because each bag had the name written on it. Since the bags were closed with a padlock, they would cut it open with a knife and then they would go down to Nice to sell everything inside it. Shirts, pants, and shoes were highly sought after; even boxers. They would throw away whatever wasn't interesting. There was all kinds of stuff in the bags, because they had already landed in Italy and brought things back from over there. There was some plundering going on, because they weren't all choir boys. There was all kinds of stuff, even money and jewels and things like that.

Under such circumstances, it is not surprising that some items went missing, with families later enquiring on their whereabouts. As an example, one letter received by the Quartermaster depot where the belongings of killed soldiers were shipped stated:

Mrs XXX (...) was in our office recently and was wondering if anything further had ever been found of her son's. In May 1945 she received a camera, but nothing has come

FOR THE CAUSE OF
FREEDOM

A casualty of the 517th PRCT is evacuated from the battlefield, to be buried in the Draguignan Cemetery. 517 Parachute Combat Team booklet, courtesy Frédéric Brega.

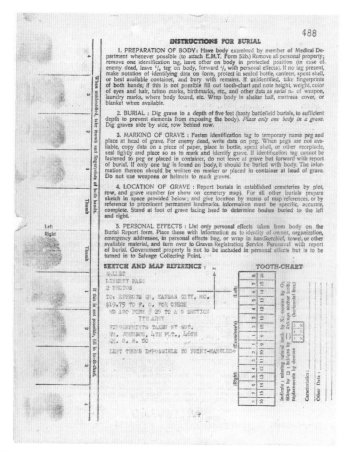

The instructions to be followed by U.S. Army graves registration teams as printed on the reverse side of Report of Burial sheets. In this particular case, the body was found with no identification tags, so it needed to be fingerprinted, leading to a grisly detail noted by Sgt Johnson, of the 46th Quartermaster Graves Registration Company: "Left thumb impossible to print - mangled." U.S. Army Human Resources Command.

since then. She knows he had a billfold with several hundred dollars in it that she never received. I would appreciate if you would advise her if anything further has been found.

From the aid stations, the bodies were then driven to the American Cemetery in Draguignan, where they were unloaded and taken over by the soldiers of the 46th or 48th QMGRC. Here, the bodies were searched for personal items and identified, the primary means of identification being identification tags; but only if they were found being worn around the neck, and not elsewhere, for example in a pocket. A "Report of Burial" had to be filled in for every casualty, and if a body was not wearing identification tags, then fingerprints or a tooth chart were systematically taken, assuming there were still fingers or teeth to be examined, which was not always the case. Indeed, the following notes were found written in the Reports of Burial of some of the casualties mentioned in this book: "Hands mutilated and burned, fingerprinting impossible. Face and head blown to pieces, tooth chart not possible"; "Body was taken out of water, head and hands missing"; or "Legs blown off at knees, head crushed, both arms crushed." In such extreme cases, the identification had to be made with secondary evidence, such as witness testimony, documents found on the body, and laundry marks, consisting of initials and partial serial numbers found written on the insides of items of clothing.

As an example of how complex the identification procedure could become in cases where no identification tags were found with the body, we will study the details of the identification process of Pvt Raymond F. Thompson, of H Company of the 517th PIR, who was killed in action September 8, 1944. When a body that was apparently his was recovered without any identification tags in late September, his squad sergeant, **Richard Robb**, was asked to describe the circumstances of Thompson's death and to state his opinion on the identity of the body:

8 September 1944, I was a squad sergeant in Private Thompson's platoon. Our platoon mission was to contact Company I on our right. We reached a road south of Col de Braus and sent two four-man patrols: one to the top of the ridge, and the other, with myself in charge, to the building at the Col de Braus (pass). The ridge patrol started out first, and as my patrol got a few yards down the road, we heard firing near the top of the ridge.

Shortly thereafter, three of the four men returned. Sergeant Kenneth Erickson, the non-commissioned officer in charge, informed me that Private Thompson had been shot; that he fell and did not move or emit a cry. Sergeant Erickson believe that he killed the German that fired on Private Thompson.

Enemy fire, both machine gun and rifle, forced our platoon to withdraw to our own lines. Upon our return, Sergeant Erickson reported Private Thompson missing in action because his death was not definite.

Two days later, our company took the ridge south of Col de Braus, but because of extensive enemy shelling, a thorough search could not be instituted for Private Thompson's body. Heavy fighting continued for almost a week, until our company was relieved from the ridge. That day, a private from another company, who knew Private Thompson well, mentioned the fact that he had found the body. I asked him to direct me to the spot. I further verified the position by the body of a German soldier close by, as had been described by Sergeant Erickson. The body of the American soldier had blonde hair and wore one piece coveralls. Private Thompson, at that time, was the only man in the battalion wearing such a garment. The body was badly decomposed, but at that time still recognizable. I looked at the face, and knowing Private Thompson personally as I did, am positive the body was that of Private Thompson. The man with me was equally as positive.

I feel that he died almost instantly from the bullet wound received on the patrol, as the bullet entered just above the left eye and came out the back of the head.

Because of a counterattack during relief troop movements on the ridge and the confusion in our company in the process of moving to another sector, I did not notify the company commander of my discovery until several days later.

Soon after, a new company commander took the company, and not knowing of my discovery, sent another man to the Graves Registrations officer. The man was unable to positively identify the body because of further decomposition.

To this day, however, there is not the slightest doubt in my mind that the body I found south of Col de Braus was that of Private Thompson. The man with me, however, has since been killed in action.[32]

Lt Warren Caulfield, who had been acting as the 517th PIR's graves registrations officer at the time, also submitted a report on the discovery of the body:

8 September 1944, I was Graves Registrations Officer for the 517th Parachute Infantry, and approximately that date I received word that Private Thompson of Company H was missing in action, in the area south of Col de Braus, but I could not search the area, because our unit was still engaged with the enemy.

Approximately two weeks later, after Company H had changed areas and the sector south of Col de Braus was partially cleared, we searched for Private Thompson and we found an American soldier clothed in a one-piece coverall uniform without any identification on his person, in the same area that Private Thompson was said to be hit and shot down; the body was within ten feet of a dead German. The body we found, in my opinion, was beyond recognition, caused by the wound in the head and decomposition caused by the excessive heat.

I then went to the company commander of H Company and asked for someone to identify the body. He gave me a Private Johnson of his company, who at the present time is missing in action since the Belgian break through. This Private Johnson was unable to identify the body because of the decomposition.

I then brought the body to the Graves Registration Collecting Station, which was attached to the 1st Airborne Task Force. At this station I was told that at the cemetery, which was located at Draguignan, France, they would try to take fingerprints and make the report of findings to the War Department.

Being that I did not know Private Thompson personally, but that the body I found was approximately in the same area that Private Thompson was said to be shot down, I believe that it was the body of Private Thompson.[33]

One can only guess how the men felt when recovering and seeing the body of their friend in such condition, particularly when any of them could himself end up in a similar state in the very near future, and as at least one of those mentioned in these reports did. At the Draguignan cemetery, Sgt Paul E. Pander, of the 48th QMGRC, reported that it was not possible to fingerprint the body, as the fingers were "dried, shriveled and hardened." To further complicate matters, no identification tags, nor any other personal belongings were found on the body. However, on the tongues of the paratrooper boots the body was wearing, the graves registration team found a name and serial number written, though they were not those they were expecting. Instead of bearing Raymond Thompson's name, the boots were named to an Elza Watkins, 37530485. A tooth chart was taken, though several teeth were already missing. Considering the uncertainty as to the body's identity, it was buried as an unknown, under the code X-88.[34]

It was not until 1947 that the investigation was concluded. First, Elza Watkins, who was alive and well, was contacted in late 1946 and asked if he had any knowledge of the possible identity of the body who was found wearing his boots. **Elza Watkins** replied:

In regards to your letter about the parachute boots having my name and serial number. When we were in camp near Roma, Italy, my friend Thomas and I traded boots. I am very sorry, but I do not know his first name.[35]

The only big discrepancy was therefore explained, as it was confirmed that the boots with Watkins' name in them had been given to a "Thomas." In 1947, the body was then disinterred and a tooth chart taken once again, better than the initial chart that had been taken in haste in 1944. It was found that X-88's teeth matched those of Raymond Thompson, and that all the other information: height, weight, color of hair, type of boots found, and date and location of death, all corresponded favorably with Raymond Thompson's case. It was therefore concluded that the body was indeed that of Private Raymond F. Thompson, and his mother was finally informed March 1948 that her son was no longer missing in action, but was identified and buried at Draguignan Cemetery.

Thompson's case and the multiple witnesses and procedures it involved is an excellent example of the high quality standards of work and professionalism followed by the American Graves Registrations during WWII. Enemy dead, when they were buried in American cemeteries, were handled with the same care, and were also fingerprinted if necessary. It would, however, seem that the postwar German administration was so overwhelmed by the huge number of casualties that Germany had suffered, that it was not able to make any use of highly specific information, such as fingerprints, in the vast majority of cases.

After the bodies had been searched for identification tags and personal belongings, they were then buried with one identification tag, or with a sheet of paper placed in a sealed container in the cases where identification tags were missing. The second tag was attached to the cross on the grave. Detailed instructions on the procedure to be followed when burying a body were printed on the reverse side of the Report of Burial, in case a burial had to be performed by non-qualified personnel. **Lt Joseph Reek**, of the 46th QMGRC, who signed the burial forms of many of the soldiers mentioned in this book, explains what he remembers about the search and identification process:

The division people had personnel that did some preliminary IDing and then they would collect and bring the deceased to where we had established a cemetery. We had medics who were appointed to examine remains and determine what the cause of death was and others working with the medics would search the bodies for personal effects. They would have to make the decision whether

Lieutenant Joseph Reek, of the 46ᵗʰ Quartermaster Graves Registration Company, who along with his colleague, Lt Vandermoor Van Utt, was responsible for the burial of most of the Allied casualties mentioned in this book. Reek Family Collection.

The tragic face of war: German bodies wrapped in bloodstained mattress covers await burial at Draguignan Cemetery. Raymond Zaciek Collection.

the personal effects should be forwarded on to an archives place where it would go back to the family of the deceased. We would find on some occasions pornographic type things, which we would destroy, but personal jewelry or money was sacked with the name. They also searched the deceased for his dog tags, because the procedure was all soldiers should have two tags, and if they were deceased, one tag would remain with the corpse and the other tag would be put into the bag with the other personal effects. Then there were some times the deceased either didn't wear his dog tags like he should have, or he lost them, then we would have problems identifying who this person was. There was a form, and part of it had a section for fingerprinting and the medics would do that. The condition of some bodies was indescribable. They were so torn up with injuries that it was hard to even look at them. But you could also see where they were killed instantly so they didn't know what was going on. The people that were involved in doing that became pretty used to the idea. They tried to handle it as best they could. I would say that part of what we were doing classified as pretty distasteful.

Technical Sergeant Donald Hagvall, of the 48ᵗʰ QRGMC, later made a description of this "distasteful" work that would

become famous. Though he was not talking specifically about Draguignan Cemetery in the following quote, his words paint a gruesome picture of what the men of the graves registrations had to deal with on a daily basis:

> You know what a direct hit by a shell does to a guy. Or a mine, or a solid hit with a grenade even. Sometimes all we have is a leg or a hunk of arm. The ones that stink the worst are the guys who got internal wounds and are dead about three weeks, with the blood staying inside and rotting, and when you move the body the blood comes out of the nose and mouth.
>
> Then some of them bloat up in the sun; they bloat up so big that they bust the buttons and then they get blue and the skin peels. They don't all get blue, some of them get black. But they all stunk. There's only one stink and that's it. You never get used to it, either. As long as you live, you never get used to it. And after a while, the stink gets in your clothes and you can taste it in your mouth. You know what I think? I think maybe if every civilian in the world could smell this stink, then maybe we wouldn't have any more wars.[36]

The personal items that were found on the bodies were sent

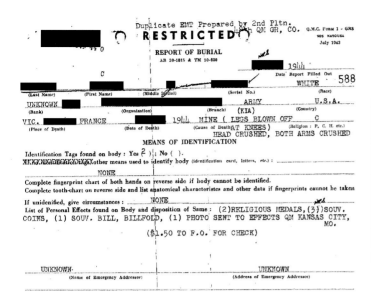

Local civilians work in Draguignan Cemetery in late 1944. Author's Collection.

"The condition of some bodies was indescribable. They were so torn up with injuries that it was hard to even look at them." Example of a burial report for a soldier killed by a mine that had inflicted horrendous wounds. U.S. Army Human Resources Command.

back to a Quartermaster Corps depot in Kansas City, and eventually back to the next of kin. The bodies were then buried roughly by the chronological order in which they had been brought to the cemetery, regardless of the unit and rank of the casualty. Many local men in Draguignan were enlisted to help dig the graves, and the daughter of one of these men remembered:

> My father was recruited, and when he would come back at night he would be sick because they made him touch all those corpses. It wasn't his domain. My father was a lumberjack and a hard worker, but doing that work made him sick. He would say: "I can't wait for the work to be finished," because it gave him the impression that he was burying his own children. It was all young Americans who were dying. They were wrapped in a special sheet and then had to be put into coffins. It was an abomination. It was really pitiful. Pitiful.

In fact, the bodies were initially not even buried in coffins, but in simple shrouds or mattress covers. Whereas we have previously seen that German families were usually sent a letter by the victim's company commander, with precise details about the circumstances of the death, American families were only sent a very brief telegram from the Adjutant General that contained no information other than the country of death, the date of death, and the type of death (killed in action, died of wounds, etc.). The telegram reached the family approximately one month after the soldier had died and was always worded in almost exactly the same manner:

> The Secretary of War desires me to express his deep regret that your son [rank and name] was killed in action on [date] in [name of country] letter follows.
> J.A.Ulio The Adj. General

The effect of this telegram was usually devastating, of course. **Robert Reginato**, the brother of Pvt Joseph Reginato, of E Company of the 517th, who was shot and killed during a patrol at Peira Cava September 9, 1944, tells of the day when such a telegram reached his home:

I remember the day that my mother received the telegram. I was not there. I was nine years old when he was killed, and I remember coming home from elementary school and walking up the driveway. I heard my mother crying, she was in the back yard, and I walked around there and my sister was holding her, and she just couldn't control herself at all. I didn't know what had happened, and then when they told me, I just couldn't comprehend it, because even though he was 10 years older than me, I remember vividly that he and I had a lot of fun together. That's what I remember on that particular day. Now as a sideline, my mother belonged to the Gold Star mothers. When your son or daughter would go off to war, they hung a little flag inside the front room window with a blue star in the middle, and if that person was killed, it was replaced with a little flag with a gold star on it. My mother was a member of that Gold Star thing forever. She never, ever got over her son being killed. Never. She would never talk about it, ever.

Gloria Klinner, the young niece of PFC William Rogge, of A Company of the 509th PIB, who was killed near Cannes August 23, 1944, also remembers the day the fateful telegram arrived at her grandmother's house:

I remember Billy. I have a picture of him holding me when I was a baby. I was born August 4, 1940. When he was home on leave, we had a picnic. I remember when he put on his gas mask and scared me. I wish I could remember more about him. I do remember a sad time when our mail man (Mr Baer, we called him) came to the front door. I answered and he asked for my grandma. I heard him say: "I'm sorry Frieda," and then I saw her on the davenport, crying hard. It seared me. I was four. Other family came from upstairs to help. I'll never forget that day till I die. She lost one son Bobby at 19 from a ruptured appendix and another son three months old of pneumonia. All that remained was my mom Dorothy and her sister Lorraine.

The letter that the Adjutant General sent as a follow up to the telegram was just as impersonal and did not contain any more actual information about the soldier's death. Only the luckier families received letters sent by the unit officers or buddies who had personally known the casualty and who actually knew about the events in which he had been killed. Families that asked the Adjutant General for additional details were simply given the

Pvt Joseph Reginato, E Company 517th PIR, who was killed at Peira Cava September 9, 1944. Robert Reginato Collection.

Details Unknown Of Paratrooper's Death

Details surrounding the death of Pfc. Travis V. McDonald, paratrooper, who paid the supreme sacrifice in action in France on the 7th of September, are still unknown.

A letter received by his parents, Mr. and Mrs. Claude McDonald of Northfield, from Major General J. A. Ulio, dated October 4, only confirmed the message as relayed earlier in a telegram, and expressed the sympathy of the war department at their loss. "Unfortunately, reports of this nature contain only the briefest details as they are prepared under battle conditions and the means of transmission are limited", General Ulio's letter stated.

Travis V. McDonald was born at Northfield, Texas, May 11, 1923 and was 21 years, 3 months and 26 days old at his death. He attended Matador High School and following graduation in 1942, attended Texas A. & M. College in the fall of that year. He entered the armed service April 19, 1943 and trained at Camp McCall, N. C., and Ft. Benning, Ga., receiving his final training in Tennessee.

Following a furlough visit at his home at Northfield in April, he was sent overseas and landed in Italy. He was in the invasion in Southern France the 15th of August, he advised his parents in a letter written just a few days prior to his death.

Survivors are his parents, one sister, Mrs. Dorothy Carnes, and one brother, Foy McDonald. His paternal grandmother, Mrs. Ella McDonald also survives and is a resident of Glen Allen, Alabama, and his maternal grandfather, B. F. Simpson, of Northfield, is a pioneer resident of this county.

The obituary of PFC Travis V. McDonald, in which the unsettling lack of information given to the family is mentioned. McDonald Family Collection.

name of the town where the soldier had died and a brief description of the wounds that had caused death; for example, "multiple fragment wounds to the back." Many were unsatisfied and sent multiple letters complaining about the lack of information, as well as the long delays before the personal items of the casualty were sent back. January 11, 1945, for example, **Murrell Rose**, the wife of Sgt Burnell Rose, who had been killed by the mines in Vence, wrote:

> Concerning my husband's death August 29, 1944, in France. (...) I wrote his Captain E.J. Mullay for information, as I haven't had any from War Dept. telling me how it happened and he told me to write to this address. Could you please give me any information as to the cause of his death?
>
> Also, I haven't received any of his personal things, and why haven't I? I've known others to get them. Would appreciate any information. Thank you.[37]

The authorities apparently did not realize how much anguish was caused to the next of kin by the lack of personalized information. However, this anguish can clearly be felt in letters such as the following that **Olive Gates**, the mother of Pvt William Gates, killed on Hill 105 August 21, 1944, sent in January 1949, over four years after her son's death:

> Gentlemen: thank you so much for the flag sent me from the burial of my son in France. (…) One other request I would like to make. We have not read or heard an account of the battle or campaign in which he gave his life in southern France? Everything was so secret when last he wrote that we do not know whom to ask.
>
> Were all the paratroopers killed in that invasion? Has no account been written of their part in the invasion? If there has been please tell me where it can be obtained. Three times my son refused the officers training because

he felt it would keep him here in this country. There seems to be no one left who can tell us anything.[38]

These letters seem to indicate that the German system, in which people who knew the casualty personally had the responsibility of informing the next of kin, was more appropriate for answering the expectations and needs of a bereaved family. Relying on a bureaucratic institution such as the War Department to inform the families only caused delays, paperwork, and dissatisfaction.

After the war, the bodies of the Commonwealth soldiers who had been buried in Draguignan were exhumed and reburied in the Commonwealth Cemetery at Mazargues, near Marseille. The families were not given any say in what happened to the body, and all of them are therefore still buried in Mazargues today. The Americans, on the other hand, contacted the next of kin in 1947, giving them the choice of either leaving the body in the U.S. Military Cemetery at Draguignan or having the body repatriated to the USA at the expense of the government. Approximately 60 percent of the families opted to reclaim the body, while the remaining 40 percent preferred to leave the bodies in Draguignan, buried next to their comrades in arms. This consideration of the U.S. government (that was not shared by the Canadian or German governments) for the wishes of the family concerning the final burial location partly made up for the clumsy manner with which the death announcements had been handled. We will provide some examples of letters sent by next of kin as illustrations of what could motivate the family's choice. **Martha Dirkson**, the mother of PFC Vernon Dirkson, of H Company of the 517th PIR, who on August 28, 1944, died of wounds received shortly after the invasion, wrote:

> I wish to thank you for information regarding the burial location of my beloved son (…). It is my great desire to have his remains returned to this country as soon as this is possible.[39]

The family of Pvt William Gates initially made the same choice, but after Gates' father passed away, his mother **Olive Gates** decided to reverse the choice:

> Prior to my husband's death, he completed burial forms for our son (...). At that time, it was his request that the body of our son be returned to the United States for reinterment.
>
> At the time of my husband's burial, members of the family were gathered together, and the above subject was thoroughly discussed. It was decided at that time, that it would be best to have my son's body retained overseas in the cemetery in which he is now interred. We do not wish his body returned to the United States for burial, we feel that he would want to be buried with his comrades.[40]

For Ms **Jesse Parks** (formerly known as Ms August Bednarz), the mother of Richard Bednarz, a 517th PIR trooper who was killed September 21, 1944, there was no hesitation whatsoever. She wrote:

> It is a wonderful thing that is being done, and from the bottom of my heart I wish to thank you for myself and my son. But I do not wish to have my son's body disturbed. It was his wish that should something happen he should remain with his fallen comrades and that is my wish, also. To me he is not far across the sea. I lived very close to my son, and even though God saw fit to take his soul, I still feel that he is now and ever will be close to us.[41]

As one of the witnesses said, not all the soldiers were "choir boys," and the same held true for their families. The death of a soldier was unfortunately often a cause for dispute between family members, such as war brides that the casualty had barely known, and the parents, some of which were themselves estranged from the casualty. Who was to get his pension and decide where he would be buried? Wives had priority, as long as they had not remarried since the death, and fathers were next in line, followed by mothers and then elder brothers and sisters. This system, of

The body of PFC Willard E. Meek, of L Company of the 141st IR, who was killed in the Estérel Mountains August 16, 1944, is reburied in his hometown of Newcomerstown, Ohio, in 1948. Meek Family Collection, courtesy William Casteel of the Newcomerstown Historical Society.

Sgt. Gerald K. Tilney's Body Will Arrive in City Friday

The body of Sgt. Gerald Kenneth Tilney, Crawfordsville paratrooper who was killed in action Aug. 25, 1944, near Nice, France, is scheduled to arrive in this city at 5:54 o'clock (CDT) Friday, according to word received Tuesday by his mother, Mrs. Tom Hartley, 1004 Darlington avenue.

Funeral services for Sgt. Tilney will be conducted at o'clock Monday afternoon from the Proffitt and Sons mortuary in charge of Rev. Paul Million. Burial will be made in the Masonic cemetery.

The body will be taken directly from the train to the mother's residence, where friends may pay their respects until time for it to be removed to the funeral home Monday afternoon.

Sgt. Tilney

trenched. The brush surroun the hill was infested with er snipers who were inflicting ca ties and successfully harassing advancing troops. One platoo the company fought its way to top of the hill only to be de complete possession of their jective by sniper fire. Sgt. T volunteered to locate and e nate the snipers in order tha platoon could complete its sion. Knowing that he could locate the snipers by attra their fire, Sgt. Tilney with plete disregard for his own s advanced from bush to bush his tommy-gun at every spot ly to conceal an enemy. The my snipers were forced to firing on the platoon, and co trate their fire on Sgt. T While the sniper fire was dir on him, Sgt. Tilney's platoon, ing the diversion of the fire able to move and eliminate enemy activity in the area. though Sgt. Tilney was f wounded as a result of this a his unselfish act served as a

Crawfordsville District Public Library Collection, courtesy Diane Moore.

PFC J.B. Hampton, who was killed during the attack of the 517th PIR on St Cézaire August 22, 1944, is reburied in Trenton, Tennessee, in 1948. Hampton Family Collection, courtesy Tony Burriss and Catherine Edwards.

course, did not always give satisfaction to all parties, and some did not hesitate to declare that one of the higher priority parties was deceased or otherwise undeserving. One particularly striking example of apparent injustice is given by the letter below, written by an employee of the local veterans service office in the name of the soldier's mother (The names have been changed for confidentiality purposes.):

Lena X., mother of the above deceased, called at this office, stating that she has been informed that Frank Z., alleged father of the deceased, has received a communication from your office in regard to the disposition of the body of Joseph Z. I have had a lot to do with filing claims in behalf of the mother as the dependent parent of Joseph Z. And it is the opinion of this office, as well as that of the Indian Department, that the said Frank Z. has no rights concerning the disposition of the body of Joseph Z. We base these opinions on the following facts:

1. Frank Z. only lived with Lena X. a couple months and left her long before Joseph Z. was born.
2. They were never legally married, nor were they ever considered married by Indian custom or by a common law marriage.
3. Frank Z. never contributed to the support of Joseph Z.
4. Further, Frank Z., on two separate occasions, when filing claims with the U.S. Government, denied having any children.
5. School records show that Lena X. raised and supported Joseph Z.
6. Numerous affidavits have been submitted to the Veterans Administration, both from private individuals and the County Welfare Board, verifying the fact that as far as any of them knew, Lena X. solely raised and supported Joseph Z.

It is the wish of the mother, Lena X., who is also the recipient of the deceased's National Service Life Insurance, that her son's, Joseph Z., body be interred in a military cemetery overseas in the area where he was killed.

In this particular case, the body was repatriated in spite of the mother's complaints. Once the families had made their choice, all the bodies were exhumed from the Draguignan cemetery in 1948, including those who were to remain at Draguignan, so that they could be put into coffins and reburied in an esthetically pleasing pattern at the center of the cemetery grounds. This displacement of the bodies within the cemetery was enough to confuse some families, who noticed that the references of the plot number of their loved one's grave had changed. The bodies that were returned to the United States were reburied all over the country in whichever cemetery had been chosen by the family. Some of the boys were finally back home.

We will end this book with a short story written by **Willa Ward Parks**, the sister of Pvt Leon Parks, of the 551st PIB, who was killed in the Hill 105 area August 21, 1944:

I could never say that I had any intuition or foreboding about how that day would turn out. I walked into our house after the school bus had let me off at the end of our road, and I had no idea what was waiting for me. I remember that it was the best time of the year, one of those golden days, summer almost gone, fall coming

Willa Ward Parks, with her brother Leon Parks, of the 551st PIB, who was killed outside la Napoule August 21, 1944. Jeanne Ward Collection.

on fast. The leaves on the trees were just beginning to turn color, getting ready for their vivid swan song before we moved on to the sombre season ahead.

It was 1944, and I was just beginning my sophomore year in high school. My mother and I were alone most of the time out in the country in the old house that had been left to our family by my father's parents. Our few acres were in the midst of dairy farms in upstate New York. My father worked on the Barge Canal and could get home only on weekends, partly because of the distance involved, but also because of the strict gas rationing that was in effect. My brother, who had signed up to become a paratrooper immediately after graduating from high school, had been shipped overseas in March of that year. His letters to us were from North Africa, but they hinted that he would be moving on soon.

As I walked into the house through the kitchen, there were signs of activity that had been interrupted. Wisps of steam rose from a big kettle on the cook stove, and a dish towel laid out on the table held empty canning jars lined up and waiting to be filled. Other tools of the trade, knives and ladles and funnels, were strewn about the kitchen. A box that held the red rubber rings used to seal the jars had been opened. Some of the rings had spilled out onto the table. It was as if all action in the room had been halted just an instant before. Why was everything so quiet? Where was my mother? She always met me in the kitchen when I came home. As I started through the house to look for her, I remember noticing a shaft of brilliant afternoon sun striking a basket of tomatoes. They glowed red.

Our dining room was on the north side of the house and was always dark. In the gloom, I saw a creased yellow paper lying on the table, and in one terrible moment everything became clear to me. Written on the paper were the most dreaded words of those wartime years, "We regret to inform you. . ."[42]

As Lt Spencer had written in his poem about Arthur Ridler's death: "The God of the battlefield is doubly unkind… The ones hurt the deepest are those left behind."

"The ones hurt the deepest are those left behind." (Left) The mother of James "Jim" Pacey, who was killed by a sliver of shrapnel on Hill 1098, and (right) the parents of Johann Meyer, shot on the road between la Roquette and Levens, visit their sons' graves long after the war at the Draguignan and Dagneux military cemeteries. Catherine Pacey Zonaras Collection/Hartmut Pöhlmann Collection.

Appendices

1) Honor roll of 127 Allied soldiers (110 American, 11 French and six Canadian) who died the Maritime Alps and eastern Var between August 15 and September 7, 1944. The region covered by this list is contained between the locations of Agay, Seillans, Col de Turini and Menton (A total of at least 314 Germans died in the same region over the same period of time, their names can be found in Var and Maritime Alps German casualty lists presented below). Classification by date of death, then by unit. For soldiers who died of wounds, the date of actual death is indicated in between brackets if it is known and different than the date of wounding. The following references were helpful in establishin the following Allied casualty lists: 509 PIBthgeronimo.org, insigne.org, ww2-airborne.us and *The Black Devil's Brigade*, by Joseph Springer.

Surname	Name	Rank	Unit	Age	Date of death	Location of death
Gruwell	Robert R.	Pvt	G Co 517 PIR	21	15.8.1944	Callian
Arzallier	Marius	Sgt Chf Inf Col	71 BGC	29	15.8.1944	Théoule
Braconnier	Henri	Matl Can	GNA	20	15.8.1944	Théoule
Cacaud	René	Qrt Mtr Mnvr	GNA	24	15.8.1944	Théoule
Corlou	Albert	2 Mtr Fsl	GNA	23	15.8.1944	Théoule
Dourous	Pierre	Matl Fsl	GNA	20	15.8.1944	Théoule
Fichefeux	Pierre	2 Mtr Mnvr	GNA	33	15.8.1944	Théoule
Guidoni	Jacques	Qrt Mtr Can	GNA	28	15.8.1944	Théoule
Guilcher	Henri	Matl Gbr	GNA	28	15.8.1944	Théoule
Marche	Gérard	Capt Corvette	GNA	23	15.8.1944	Théoule
Mignot	Georges	Matl Fsl	GNA	22	15.8.1944	Théoule
Servel	Pierre	Ensgn Vaisseau	GNA	24	15.8.1944	Théoule
Chesunas	Charles	PFC	AT Co 141 IR	32	15.8.1944	
Foster	Albert S.	PFC	HQ1 141 IR	26	15.8.1944	Anthéor
Griffitts	William C.	Sgt	C Co 141 IR	26	15.8.1944	Anthéor
Hillerson	Sayre	Pvt	C Co 141 IR		15.8.1944	Anthéor
Benter	William C.	Pvt	D Co 141 IR	24	15.8.1944	Anthéor
Hessong	Arthur J.	PFC	E Co 141 IR	24	15.8.1944	Agay?

500

Surname	Name	Rank	Unit	Age	Date of death	Location of death
Petras	Adolph	T/Sgt	K Co 141 IR	25	15.8.1944	Agay?
Brookshier	Vivian F.	PFC	A Co 141 IR	22	16.8.1944	Théoule
Carvalho	Joseph	PFC	A Co 141 IR	30	16.8.1944	Théoule
Cross	Roderick S.	PFC	A Co 141 IR	28	16.8.1944	Théoule
Henderson	William B.	PFC	A Co 141 IR		16.8.1944	Théoule
Strassburg	Alton W.	PFC	A Co 141 IR	20	16.8.1944	Théoule
Beeman	Edgar F.	PFC	C Co 141 IR	22	16(19).8.1944	Théoule
Dorschel	Carl H.	1Lt	C Co 141 IR	31	16.8.1944	Théoule
Obenrader	Eugene E.	PFC	E Co 141 IR	19	16.8.1944	La Napoule RN7
Edwards	Thurman H.	PFC	L Co 141 IR		16.8.1944	Théoule
Meek	Willard E.	PFC	L Co 141 IR	23	16.8.1944	Théoule
Braff	Samuel	Pvt	A Co 141 IR	29	17.8.1944	Théoule
Hosey	Carl O.	PFC	A Co 141 IR	24	17.8.1944	Théoule
Nichols	William E.	PFC	A Co 141 IR		17.8.1944	Théoule
Dunlap	George H. IV	Pvt	141 IR	32	17.8.1944	
Sheehan	Thomas L.	Pvt	L Co 141 IR	19	17.8.1944	Théoule
McKee	Paul R.	1Lt	Rec Co 636TD	33	18.8.1944	Callian
Hudson	Dudley W.	SSgt	I Co 141 IR	23	19(22).8.1944	Callian
Dodson	Robert L.	1Lt	B Co 636TD	23	19.8.1944	Callian
Apperman	Henry-Heinrich	2Lt	G Co 141 IR	29	20.8.1944	La Napoule
Gabrus	Joseph	Sgt	G Co 141 IR	29	20.8.1944	La Napoule
Ellis	Perry I.	Sgt	HQ 551 PIB	25	20(10.9.)1944	La Napoule
Gates	William H.	Pvt	HQ 551 PIB	24	20.8.1944	La Napoule
Lawson	William C.	PFC	HQ 551 PIB	23	20.8.1944	La Napoule
Osburn	Victor A.	T5 Med	HQ 509 PIB	25	21.8.1944	La Napoule
Sweetitz	Frank J.	Pvt	HQ 509 PIB	31	21.8.1944	La Napoule
Bloyd	David G.	Pvt	A Co 509 PIB	20	21.8.1944	Théoule
Ducote	Larry J.	Pvt	B Co 509 PIB	32	21.8.1944	Théoule
Hemsworth	George P.	PFC	B Co 509 PIB	23	21.8.1944	La Napoule
Hirales	Ralph V.	PFC	B Co 509 PIB	24	21.8.1944	La Napoule
Kaplar	Joseph J.	Pvt	B Co 509 PIB	20	21.8.1944	La Napoule
Knapp	Burl J.	Cpl	B Co 509 PIB	22	21.8.1944	La Napoule
Lundquist	Arthur E.	PFC	B Co 509 PIB	19	21.8.1944	La Napoule
David	Roy W.	Sgt	C Co 509 PIB	23	21.8.1944	La Napoule
Haller	Leonard R.	Pvt	C Co 509 PIB	21	21.8.1944	La Napoule
Tilney	Gerald K.	Sgt	C Co 509 PIB	28	21.8.1944	La Napoule
Zadlo	Joseph L.	PFC	C Co 509 PIB		21.8.1944	La Napoule
Yellowrobe	Alvin J.	PFC	A Co 551 PIB	19	21.8.1944	La Napoule
Billman	Lewis R.	T5	B Co 551 PIB	23	21.8.1944	La Napoule
Deming	James W.	T5	B Co 551 PIB	21	21.8.1944	La Napoule
Dennis	William E.	PFC	B Co 551 PIB	22	21.8.1944	La Napoule
Fields	Warren B.	Pvt	B Co 551 PIB	29	21.8.1944	La Napoule
Parks	Leon W.	Pvt	B Co 551 PIB	19	21.8.1944	La Napoule

Surname	Name	Rank	Unit	Age	Date of death	Location of death
Sepulveda	Ramon M.	Pvt	B Co 551 PIB	25	21.8.1944	La Napoule
Tenute	Louis J.	Pvt	B Co 551 PIB	21	21(22).8.1944	La Napoule
Williams	Max G.	Cpl	B Co 551 PIB	26	21.8.1944	La Napoule
Wright	William J.	Pvt	B Co 551 PIB	20	21.8.1944	La Napoule
Granger	Renaldo	Sgt	5-3 FSSF	25	22.8.1944	Les Veyans
Apperson	John N.	Maj	HQ 509 PIB	39	22.8.1944	La Napoule
Fiander	Hubert J.	1Lt	HQ 509 PIB	23	22.8.1944	La Napoule
Crane	Thomas J.	1Sgt	A Co 509 PIB	23	22.8.1944	La Napoule
Davison	Robert E.	Pvt	A Co 509 PIB		22.8.1944	La Napoule
Colo	Hector H.	PFC	G Co 517 PIR	19	22.8.1944	St Cézaire
Goswick	Jesse O.	PFC	G Co 517 PIR		22.8.1944	St Cézaire
Hampton	J B	PFC	G Co 517 PIR	20	22.8.1944	St Cézaire
Stanford	Charles F.	PFC	G Co 517 PIR	31	22.8.1944	St Cézaire
Sailor	Richard	Pvt	I Co 517 PIR	23	22.8.1944	St Cézaire
Webb	Lee M.	1Lt	2680 Intel Co	31	22.8.1944	La Napoule
Brown	Frank S. Jr	Pvt	1-3 FSSF	20	23.8.1944	Les Veyans
Bowden	Foster V.	Pvt	Sv Co FSSF		23.8.1944	Tanneron
Duarte	Toney F.	Pvt	Sv Co FSSF		23.8.1944	Tanneron
Durham	George E.	MSgt	Sv Co FSSF		23(3.9).8.1944	Tanneron
Starr	Hugh R.	T5	Sv Co FSSF	30	23(24).8.1944	Tanneron
Ruell	George P.	PFC	D Bat 463 PFAB	20	23.8.1944	La Napoule
Hay	John J.	Pvt	D Bat 463 PFAB	30	23.8.1944	La Napoule
Bergeman	Clarence	PFC	HQ 509 PIB	21	23.8.1944	La Napoule
Cooper	William C.	Cpl	HQ 509 PIB	26	23.8.1944	La Napoule
Crosby	James H.	Pvt	HQ 509 PIB	24	23.8.1944	La Napoule
Polson	Lee W.	T5 Med	HQ 509 PIB	23	23.8.1944	La Napoule
Beatham	Stanley Jr	Sgt	A Co 509 PIB	28	23(25).8.1944	La Napoule
Griffin	Donald F.	Pvt	A Co 509 PIB	23	23.8.1944	La Napoule
Rogge	William A.	PFC	A Co 509 PIB	21	23.8.1944	La Napoule
White	James E.	Pvt	A Co 509 PIB	20	23.8.1944	La Napoule
Baze	Roy E.	Capt	HQ 509 PIB	34	24.8.1944	La Napoule
Tully	Joseph J.	Pvt	512 Ab Signal Co	22	24.8.1944	
Bartow	Clifford H.	PFC	2-1 FSSF	32	25.8.1944	La Colle
Ladd	Walter L.	T4	1-1 FSSF		26.8.1944	La Colle
Samuel	Ross L.	Lt	4-2 FSSF	22	26(27).8.1944	Villeneuve
Schmidt	Floyd S.	Sgt	6-2 FSSF	24	26.8.1944	Villeneuve
Fitzgerald	Cecil M.	PFC	887 Co	31	26.8.1944	Villeneuve
Tierno	James J.	Pvt	FABTF	-	29.8.1944	-
Green	Louis F.	PFC	A Co 40 ER	22	29.8.1944	Vence
Kaastad	Olav	Pvt	A Co 40 ER	35	29.8.1944	Vence
Rose	Burnell	SSgt	A Co 40 ER	27	29.8.1944	Vence
Pollender	Paul E. M.	Pvt	5-1 FSSF	25	30.8.1944	Nice
Coffelt	Ernest R.	PFC	596 PCEC	21	30.8.1944	St Martin du Var
Jaynes	Howard D. Jr	Sgt	596 PCEC	22	30.8.1944	St Martin du Var

Surname	Name	Rank	Unit	Age	Date of death	Location of death
Mathis	Leonard	Pvt	596 PCEC	22	30.8.1944	St Martin du Var
Jamme	Richard A.	Cpl	A Co 517 PIR	21	31.8.1944	La Bollène
Van Ness	Joseph F.	Pvt	B Co 517 PIR	26	31.8.1944	La Bollène
Walton	James L.	Pvt	HQ2 517 PIR	19	1.9.1944	Levens
Ratajczak	Carl R. Jr	Pvt	334 QM		2.9.1944	
Keefe	Frank J.	Pvt	Med 602 FAB	34	3.9.1944	Nice
Brown	Robert W.	PFC	A Bat 460 PFAB	19	5.9.1944	L'Escarène
Dainard	Stanley E.	Pvt	3-1 FSSF	24	6.9.1944	Hill 1264
Mann	Rexford C.	Pvt	1-1 FSSF	19	6.9.1944	Hill 1264
Moore	James D.	2Lt	4-3 FSSF	22	6.9.1944	Mt Méras
Reed	Emmett J.	Pvt	4-3 FSSF	18	6.9.1944	Mt Méras
Arredonds	James M.	Cpl	F Co 517 PIR		6.9.1944	Col de Braus
Fabrick	Anthony	PFC	D Co 517 PIR		6.9.1944	Col de Braus
LaBar	LaVerne Jr	Pvt	D Co 517 PIR	23	6.9.1944	Col de Braus
Lopez	Daniel T.	Pvt	D Co 517 PIR	19	6.9.1944	Col de Braus
McDonald	Travis V.	PFC	D Co 517 PIR	21	6.9.1944	Col de Braus
Thorng	William	Pvt	D Co 517 PIR	24	6.9.1944	Col de Braus
York	Joe E.	PFC	HQ 2 517 PIR	20	6.9.1944	Col de Braus?
Green	Louis	Cpl	A Bat 602 FAB	29	6.9.1944	Col de la Madonne
Lesmeister	Louis P.	SSgt	A Bat 602 FAB	26	6.9.1944	Col de la Madonne
Lupone	Arthur J.	T4	A Bat 602 FAB	23	6.9.1944	Col de la Madonne
Miller	Robert J.	Sgt	I Co 517 PIR	20	7.9.1944	Col de Braus

2) Honor roll of 302 Allied soldiers (262 Americans, 20 British, 19 Canadians and one French) of the First Airborne Task Force who died between August 15 and November 30, 1944. Classification by unit, then by name between August 15th and August 19th. Classification by date of death, then by unit, as of August 20th.

Surname	Name	Rank	Unit	Date of death
Calvert	Ernest	Lnc Cpl	4th Bn	15.8.1944
Dowie	Benjamin	Pvt	4th Bn	15.8.1944
Newell	Harry	Pvt	4th Bn	15.8.1944
O'Flaherty	Patrick	Pvt	4th Bn	15.8.1944
Rodger	Robert G.	Pvt	4th Bn	15.8.1944
Stewart	Arthur C.	Lt	4th Bn	15.8.1944
Burns	Gavin P.	Pvt	5th Bn Scott	15.8.1944
Brierley	Levi	Pvt	5th Bn Scott	17.8.1944
Davis	Charles R.	Cpl	5th Bn Scott	17.8.1944
Fouracre	Robert G.	Pvt	5th Bn Scott	17.8.1944
Jones	Davy J.	Pvt	5th Bn Scott	17.8.1944
Rodgers	Herbert	Lnc Sjt	5th Bn Scott	17.8.1944
Thomas	Gwilym J.	Cpl	6th Bn Welch	15.8.1944
Williams	John	Cpl	6th Bn Welch	15.8.1944
Stevenson	Leonard	Pvt	6th Bn Welch	17.8.1944
Morley	Eric A.	Pvt	23rd Ind Para Bn	15.8.1944
Birtles	Joseph H.	Pvt	127 Para Field Amb	15.8.1944

503

Surname	Name	Rank	Unit	Date of death
Cox	Francis E.	Pvt	127 Para Field Amb	15.8.1944
Patterson	James F.	Pvt	127 Para Field Amb	15.8.1944
Booley	Thomas F.	Bmb	165th Field Reg	15.8.1944
Debray	Jacques G.F.		1er Bat de Choc	15.8.1944
Kennamer	Philip M.	PFC	C Bat 460 PFAB	15.8.1944
Moore	Harry F.	2Lt	C Bat 460 PFAB	15.8.1944
Hulshier	Allen H.	Pvt	HQ 463 PFAB	15.8.1944
Jozefski	Chester B.	Pvt	HQ 463 PFAB	15.8.1944
Legg	Theodor N.	PFC	D Bat 463 PFAB	15.8.1944
Beckner	Eugene	T 4	B Co 509 PIB	15.8.1944
Butler	Ira J.	Pvt	B Co 509 PIB	15.8.1944
Campos	Frank	PFC	B Co 509 PIB	15.8.1944
Crevelling	Oscar F.	Sgt	B Co 509 PIB	15.8.1944
David	Robert B.	S Sgt	B Co 509 PIB	15.8.1944
Dawson	Albert T.	T 5	B Co 509 PIB	15.8.1944
Dorsa	Anthony J.	1 Sgt	B Co 509 PIB	15.8.1944
Ford/Fort	Johnnie C.	PFC	B Co 509 PIB	15.8.1944
Garcia	Julius	Pvt	B Co 509 PIB	15.8.1944
Gillman	Marvin N.	T 4	B Co 509 PIB	15.8.1944
Lynch	George R.	PFC	B Co 509 PIB	15.8.1944
Miller	Ralph R. Jr	Capt	B Co 509 PIB	15.8.1944
Pennebaker	Thomas W.	Pvt	B Co 509 PIB	15.8.1944
Pipino	Alfred Jr	Pvt	B Co 509 PIB	15.8.1944
Potter	Leon V.	Pfc	B Co 509 PIB	15.8.1944
Reid	George W.	T 5	B Co 509 PIB	15.8.1944
Sutherland	William A.	Sgt	B Co 509 PIB	15.8.1944
Buchanan	Joseph	Sgt	C Co 509 PIB	15(21).8.1944

Surname	Name	Rank	Unit	Date of death
Moore	Stanley W.	Pvt	B Co 509 PIB	15.8.1944
Kobel	Harold L.	Pvt	509 PIB	18.8.1944
Metzger	Harold D.	Cpl	C Co 509 PIB	19.8.1944
Sexton	Rex D.	PFC	509 PIB	19.8.1944
Anderson	Elmer J.	Pvt	HQ 517 PIR	15.8.1944
Baldwin	William F.	T5	HQ 1 517 PIR	16.8.1944
Campbell	John J.	Pvt	H Co 517 PIR	18.8.1944
Ciner	Henry A.	PFC	HQ 517 PIR	15.8.1944
Clark	John W.	Pvt	HQ2 517 PIR	15.8.1944
Cross	Lynwood W.	Pvt	HQ1 517 PIR	WIA 17.8.1944
Dirkson	Vernon D.	Pvt	H Co 517 PIR	18(28).8.1944
Ernst	Albert J.	Pvt	A Co 517 PIR	16.8.1944
Fisher	Daniel A.	Cpl	HQ1 517 PIR	15.8.1944
Freeman	Harold M.	2Lt	H Co 517 PIR	16.8.1944
Gaunce	John E.	1Sgt	H Co 517 PIR	16.8.1944
Gruwell	Robert	Pvt	G Co 517 PIR	15.8.1944
Hathorn	Robert R.	Pvt	B Co 517 PIR	16.8.1944
Henderson	Lowell Jr.	PFC	C Co 517 PIR	17.8.1944
John	Frederick M.	Pvt	D Co 517 PIR	15.8.1944
Lemen	Charles C.	Pvt	E Co 517 PIR	15.8.1944
Miley	Maurice J.	2Lt	HQ2 517 PIR	15.8.1944
Montgomery	Walace A.	Pvt	B Co 517 PIR	16.8.1944
O'Brien	Joseph E.	Pvt	F Co 517 PIR	15.8.1944
Robinson	Albert M.	2Lt	HQ2 517 PIR	17.8.1944
Salmon	Carl G.	Pvt	C Co 517 PIR	17.8.1944
Scecina	George J.	Pvt	A Co 517 PIR	16.8.1944
Shaneyfelt	Alton L.	T4	F Co 517 PIR	15.8.1944
Blair	Charles P.	PFC	550 GIB	18.8.1944

Surname	Name	Rank	Unit	Date of death
Dunbar	Vernon E.	PFC	550 GIB	15.8.1944
Florent	John L.	Pvt	550 GIB	15.8.1944
Klausen	Albert J.	PFC	550 GIB	15.8.1944
Legros	Joseph	PFC	550 GIB	15.8.1944
Paplatario	Anthony	1Sgt	550 GIB	16.8.1944
Sharpe	George W.	1Lt	550 GIB	15.8.1944
Tappen	Jerome F.	T5	550 GIB	15.8.1944
Yulo	Basil	PFC	550 GIB	15.8.1944
Funk	Jack D.	Pvt	B Co 551 PIB	16.8.1944
Wikins(ki)	Henry	Pvt	596 PCEC	15.8.1944
Collinson	Thomas	Pvt	A Bat 602 FAB	16.8.1944
Lencer	Rudolph M.	Sgt	A Bat 602 FAB	18.8.1944
Barnhurst	Ira	Pvt	887 AEC	19.8.1944
Brown	Douglas	Cpl	887 AEC	15.8.1944
Tobiassen	Reidar	Pvt	887 AEC	15.8.1944
Unknown				15/16.8.1944
Ellis	Perry I.	Sgt	HQ 551 PIB	20(10.9.)1944
Gates	William H.	Pvt	HQ 551 PIB	20.8.1944
Lawson	William C.	Pfc	HQ 551 PIB	20.8.1944
Osburn	Victor A.	T5 Med	HQ 509 PIB	21.8.1944
Sweetitz	Frank J.	Pvt	HQ 509 PIB	21.8.1944
Bloyd	David G.	Pvt	A Co 509 PIB	21.8.1944
Ducote	Larry J.	Pvt	B Co 509 PIB	21.8.1944
Hemsworth	George P.	PFC	B Co 509 PIB	21.8.1944
Hirales	Ralph V.	PFC	B Co 509 PIB	21.8.1944
Kaplar	Joseph J.	Pvt	B Co 509 PIB	21.8.1944
Knapp	Burl J.	Cpl	B Co 509 PIB	21.8.1944
Lundquist	Arthur E.	PFC	B Co 509 PIB	21.8.1944
David	Roy W.	Sgt	C Co 509 PIB	21.8.1944
Haller	Leonard R.	Pvt	C Co 509 PIB	21.8.1944
Tilney	Gerald K.	Sgt	C Co 509 PIB	21.8.1944
Zadlo	Joseph L.	PFC	C Co 509 PIB	21.8.1944

Surname	Name	Rank	Unit	Date of death
Yellowrobe	Alvin J.	PFC	A Co 551 PIB	21.8.1944
Billman	Lewis R.	T5	B Co 551 PIB	21.8.1944
Deming	James W.	T5	B Co 551 PIB	21.8.1944
Dennis	William E.	PFC	B Co 551 PIB	21.8.1944
Fields	Warren B.	Pvt	B Co 551 PIB	21.8.1944
Parks	Leon W.	Pvt	B Co 551 PIB	21.8.1944
Sepulveda	Ramon M.	Pvt	B Co 551 PIB	21.8.1944
Tenute	Louis J.	Pvt	B Co 551 PIB	21(22).8.1944
Williams	Max G.	Cpl	B Co 551 PIB	21.8.1944
Wright	William J.	Pvt	B Co 551 PIB	21.8.1944
Granger	Renaldo	Sgt	5-3 FSSF	22.8.1944
Apperson	John N.	Maj	HQ 509 PIB	22.8.1944
Fiander	Hubert J.	1Lt	HQ 509 PIB	22.8.1944
Crane	Thomas J.	1Sgt	A Co 509 PIB	22.8.1944
Davison	Robert E.	Pvt	A Co 509 PIB	22.8.1944
Colo	Hector H.	PFC	G Co 517 PIR	22.8.1944
Goswick	Jesse O.	PFC	G Co 517 PIR	22.8.1944
Hampton	JB	PFC	G Co 517 PIR	22.8.1944
Stanford	Charles F.	PFC	G Co 517 PIR	22.8.1944
Sailor	Richard	Pvt	I Co 517 PIR	22.8.1944
Webb	Lee M.	1Lt	2680 Intel Co	22.8.1944
Brown	Frank S. Jr	Pvt	1-3 FSSF	23.8.1944
Bowden	Foster V.	Pvt	Sv Co FSSF	23.8.1944
Duarte	Toney F.	Pvt	Sv Co FSSF	23.8.1944
Durham	George E.	MSgt	Sv Co FSSF	23(3.9).8.1944
Starr	Hugh R.	T5	Sv Co FSSF	23(24).8.1944
Hay	John J.	Pvt	D Bat 463 PFAB	23.8.1944
Ruell	George P.	Pfc	D Bat 463 PFAB	23.8.1944

Surname	Name	Rank	Unit	Date of death
Bergeman	Clarence	PFC	HQ 509 PIB	23.8.1944
Cooper	William C.	PFC	HQ 509 PIB	23.8.1944
Crosby	James H.	Pvt	HQ 509 PIB	23.8.1944
Polson	Lee W.	T5 Med	HQ 509 PIB	23.8.1944
Beatham	Stanley Jr	Sgt	A Co 509 PIB	23(25).8.1944
Griffin	Donald F.	Pvt	A Co 509 PIB	23.8.1944
Rogge	William A.	PFC	A Co 509 PIB	23.8.1944
White	James E.	Pvt	A Co 509 PIB	23.8.1944
Baze	Roy E.	Capt	HQ 509 PIB	24.8.1944
Tully	Joseph J.	Pvt	512 Ab Signal Co	24.8.1944
Bartow	Clifford H.	PFC	2-1 FSSF	25.8.1944
Ladd	Walter L.	T4	1-1 FSSF	26.8.1944
Samuel	Ross L.	Lt	4-2 FSSF	26(27).8.1944
Schmidt	Floyd S.	Sgt	6-2 FSSF	26.8.1944
Fitzgerald	Cecil M.	PFC	887 AEC	26.8.1944
Tierno	James J.	Pvt	FABTF	29.8.1944
Green	Louis F.	PFC	A Co 40 ER	29.8.1944
Kaastad	Olav	Pvt	A Co 40 ER	29(30).8.1944
Rose	Burnell	SSgt	A Co 40 ER	29.8.1944
Pollender	Paul E.M.	Pvt	5-1 FSSF	30.8.1944
Coffelt	Ernest R.	PFC	596 PCEC	30.8.1944
Jaynes	Howard D. Jr	Sgt	596 PCEC	30.8.1944
Mathis	Leonard	Pvt	596 PCEC	30.8.1944
Jamme	Richard A.	Cpl	A Co 517 PIR	31.8.1944
Van Ness	Joseph F.	Pvt	B Co 517 PIR	31.8.1944
Walton	James L.	Pvt	HQ2 517 PIR	1.9.1944
Ratajczak	Carl R. Jr	Pvt	334 QM	2.9.1944
Keefe	Frank J.	Pvt	Med 602 FAB	3.9.1944
Brown	Robert W.	PFC	A Bat 460 PFAB	5.9.1944
Mann	Rexford C.	Pvt	1-1 FSSF	6(7).9.1944
Dainard	Stanley E.	Pvt	3-1 FSSF	6.9.1944
Moore	James D.	2Lt	4-3 FSSF	6.9.1944
Reed	Emmett J.	Pvt	4-3 FSSF	6.9.1944

Surname	Name	Rank	Unit	Date of death
York	Joe E.	PFC	HQ 2 517 PIR	6.9.1944
Fabrick	Anthony	PFC	D Co 517 PIR	6.9.1944
LaBar	LaVerne Jr	Pvt	D Co 517 PIR	6.9.1944
Lopez	Daniel T.	Pvt	D Co 517 PIR	6.9.1944
McDonald	Travis V.	PFC	D Co 517 PIR	6.9.1944
Thorng	William	Pvt	D Co 517 PIR	6.9.1944
Arredonds	James M.	Cpl	F Co 517 PIR	6.9.1944
Green	Louis	Cpl	A Bat 602 FAB	6.9.1944
Lesmeister	Louis P.	SSgt	A Bat 602 FAB	6.9.1944
Lupone	Arthur J.	T4	A Bat 602 FAB	6.9.1944
Miller	Robert J.	Sgt	I Co 517 PIR	7.9.1944
DeCamilla	Bernard J.	Pvt	6-1 FSSF	8.9.1944
Farrell	Charles S.	PFC	6-2 FSSF	8.9.1944
LaPorte	Paul G.	Lt	6-2 FSSF	8(9).9.1944
Thompson	Raymond F.	Pvt	H Co 517 PIR	8.9.1944
McDonald	Theodore M.	Pvt	4-1 FSSF	9.9.1944
McLey	Melvin W.	PFC	A Co 517 PIR	9.9.1944
Reginato	Joseph J.	Pvt	E Co 517 PIR	9.9.1944
Bell	Marvin C.	PFC	G Co 517 PIR	9.9.1944
Buk	William	PFC	G Co 517 PIR	9.9.1944
Richards	William	PFC	H Co 517 PIR	9.9.1944
Ridler	Arthur W.	1Lt	G Co 517 PIR	9.9.1944
Statt	John A.	Pvt	G Co 517 PIR	9.9.1944
Luksis	Albert V.	PFC	B co 509 PIB	10.9.1944
McGeever	Joseph T.	Capt	HQ 3 517 PIR	11.9.1944
Woodcock	Willis A.	Pvt	I Co 517 PIR	11.9.1944
Juve	Walter H. Jr	Pvt	1-2 FSSF	12.9.1944
Rader	Sam L.	T4	1-2 FSSF	12.9.1944
Biblowitz	Solomon	SSgt	2-3 FSSF	12.9.1944

Surname	Name	Rank	Unit	Date of death
Baggett	Al D.	Pvt	HQ 2 517 PIR	12.9.1944
Burnside	Don N.	PFC	HQ 2 517 PIR	12.9.1944
Lewis	Harold J.	PFC	HQ2 517 PIR	12.9.1944
Pacey	James J.	PFC	F Co 517 PIR	12.9.1944
Smith	Duane L.	2Lt	A Bat 460 PFAB	12.9.1944
Daley	Richard R.	PFC	B Bat 460 PFAB	12.9.1944
Tatro	Charles H.	Pvt	C Bat 460 PFAB	12.9.1944
Arsennek	Arthur A.	Sgt	1-1 FSSF	DOW 13.9.1944
Painton	Robert J.	Lt	2-1 FSSF	13.9.1944
Wright	Stephen J.	Pvt	2-1 FSSF	13.9.1944
Anderson	Robert C.	Pvt	1-2 FSSF	13.9.1944
Ridout	Arnold C.	SSgt	F Co 517 PIR	13.9.1944
Michaels	Patrick L.	Pvt	596 PCEC	14.9.1944
McDougall	Kenneth D.	2Lt	3-1 FSSF	15.9.1944
Barbeau	Melvin E.	Pvt	1-2 FSSF	16.9.1944
Gallardo	Jesus M.	Cpl	1-2 FSSF	16.9.1944
Armatta	Edward A.	SSgt	1-3 FSSF	16.9.1944
Belanger	Joseph	Sgt	1-3 FSSF	16.9.1944
Cutmore	William C.	Pvt	1-3 FSSF	16.9.1944
Crane	Oakley H.	SSgt	1-1 FSSF	17.9.1944
Buckley	Robert S.	Pvt	1-3 FSSF	18.9.1944
Sherman	Arthur E.	Cpl	F Co 517 PIR	18.9.1944
Thomas	Hillard B.	2Lt	H Co 517 PIR	18.9.1944
Boggan	William F.	PFC	596 PCEC	18.9.1944
Englert	Wallace P.	Sgt	596 PCEC	18.9.1944
McLamb	Herbert B.	PFC	596 PCEC	18.9.1944
Miller	Harold H.	Pvt	596 PCEC	18.9.1944
Siewierski	Alois J.	PFC	596 PCEC	18.9.1944
Bednarz	Richard B.	Pvt	HQ 517 PIR	20.9.1944
Carlson	Elmer J.	Pvt	G Co 517 PIR	20.9.1944
Hofsommer	Walter M.	Pvt	G Co 517 PIR	20.9.1944
Smith	David W.	Sgt	B Co 551 PIB	23(24).9.1944
Shumaker	Harold I.	PFC	I Co 517 PIR	25.9.1944

Surname	Name	Rank	Unit	Date of death
Camden	Charles H.	Pvt	2-2 FSSF	26.9.1944
Stewart	Joseph M.	Cpl	A Co 517 PIR	26.9.1944
Naylor	Thomas A.	Pvt	Med 517 PIR	26.9.1944?
Attebery	Edgar R. Jr	Sgt	D Co 517 PIR	27.9.1944
Radon	Stanley E.	Pvt	I Co 517 PIR	27.9.1944
Haight	David B.	PFC	Med 517 PIR	27.9.1944
Grodin	Morrie	SSgt	602 FAB	27.9.1944
Begue	Arthur C.	Pvt	B Bat 602 FAB	29.9.1944
Gregory	Burton M.	Pvt	B Bat 602 FAB	29.9.1944
Everett	William E.	Pvt	B Bat 602 FAB	29.9.1944
Houck	Robert M.	Pvt	2-2 FSSF	30.9.1944
Peabody	Rushton D.	1Lt	A Co 551 PIB	1.10.1944
Olson	Clarence B.	PFC	B Bat 602 FAB	1.10.1944
Richmond	Julius J.	Pvt	HQ 517 PIR	2.10.1944
Whitfield	Jack	PFC	HQ 3 517 PIR	2.10.1944
Jensen	George W.	PFC	551 PIB	2.10.1944
Guynup	Clarence N.	Pvt	4-2 FSSF	3.10.1944
Jones	Raymond L.	PFC	887 AEC	2(4).10.1944
Palmer	Melvin R.	Pvt	D Bat 460 PFAB	5.10.1944
Patenaude	Eugene F.	T4	HQ3 FSSF	6.10.1944
Blais	Joseph A.	Pvt	1-3 FSSF	6.10.1944
Driscoll	John A. Jr	Pvt	1-3 FSSF	6.10.1944
Kuehl	Orrin F.	Pvt	1-3 FSSF	6.10.1944
Swank	Glenn W.	Pvt	Sv Co FSSF	6.10.1944
Vickers	Charles E.	T4	6-2 FSSF	7.10.1944
Sadlo	Charles J.	2Lt	A Co 517 PIR	8.10.1944
White	Harley L.	T5	FSSF	9.10.1944
Collins	James T.	PFC	4-1 FSSF	DOW 10.10.1944
Lee	Calvin R.	PFC	550 GIB	11.10.1944
Rigby	Don A.	Pvt	1-3 FSSF	DOW 12.10.1944
Lucas	Vestal R.	Pvt	596 PCEC	DOW 12.10.1944

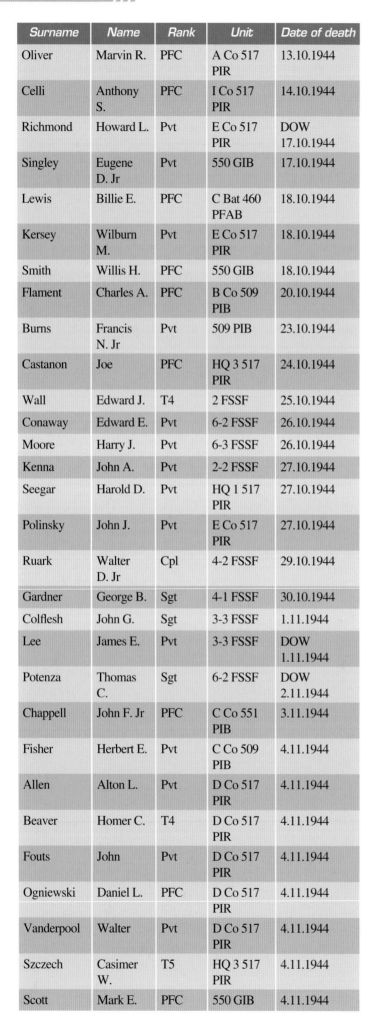

Surname	Name	Rank	Unit	Date of death
Oliver	Marvin R.	PFC	A Co 517 PIR	13.10.1944
Celli	Anthony S.	PFC	I Co 517 PIR	14.10.1944
Richmond	Howard L.	Pvt	E Co 517 PIR	DOW 17.10.1944
Singley	Eugene D. Jr	Pvt	550 GIB	17.10.1944
Lewis	Billie E.	PFC	C Bat 460 PFAB	18.10.1944
Kersey	Wilburn M.	Pvt	E Co 517 PIR	18.10.1944
Smith	Willis H.	PFC	550 GIB	18.10.1944
Flament	Charles A.	PFC	B Co 509 PIB	20.10.1944
Burns	Francis N. Jr	Pvt	509 PIB	23.10.1944
Castanon	Joe	PFC	HQ 3 517 PIR	24.10.1944
Wall	Edward J.	T4	2 FSSF	25.10.1944
Conaway	Edward E.	Pvt	6-2 FSSF	26.10.1944
Moore	Harry J.	Pvt	6-3 FSSF	26.10.1944
Kenna	John A.	Pvt	2-2 FSSF	27.10.1944
Seegar	Harold D.	Pvt	HQ 1 517 PIR	27.10.1944
Polinsky	John J.	Pvt	E Co 517 PIR	27.10.1944
Ruark	Walter D. Jr	Cpl	4-2 FSSF	29.10.1944
Gardner	George B.	Sgt	4-1 FSSF	30.10.1944
Colflesh	John G.	Sgt	3-3 FSSF	1.11.1944
Lee	James E.	Pvt	3-3 FSSF	DOW 1.11.1944
Potenza	Thomas C.	Sgt	6-2 FSSF	DOW 2.11.1944
Chappell	John F. Jr	PFC	C Co 551 PIB	3.11.1944
Fisher	Herbert E.	Pvt	C Co 509 PIB	4.11.1944
Allen	Alton L.	Pvt	D Co 517 PIR	4.11.1944
Beaver	Homer C.	T4	D Co 517 PIR	4.11.1944
Fouts	John	Pvt	D Co 517 PIR	4.11.1944
Ogniewski	Daniel L.	PFC	D Co 517 PIR	4.11.1944
Vanderpool	Walter	Pvt	D Co 517 PIR	4.11.1944
Szczech	Casimer W.	T5	HQ 3 517 PIR	4.11.1944
Scott	Mark E.	PFC	550 GIB	4.11.1944

Surname	Name	Rank	Unit	Date of death
Edgerly	Joseph A.	PFC	B Co 551 PIB	4.11.1944
Rowe	Joe G.	Pvt	C Co 551 PIB	4.11.1944
Davis	James M.	T4	1-1 FSSF	6.11.1944
Pinciak	John A.	Pvt	4-3 FSSF	6.11.1944
Mattice	Kenneth R	Sgt	I Co 517 PIR	6.11.1944
Flynn	Leo L. Jr	Pvt	A Co 551 PIB	10.11.1944
Waddle	Ernest	2Lt	550 GIB	DOW 14.11.1944
Adams	Marion L.	Pvt	C Bat 460 PFAB	28.11.1944
Cook	Moffet C.	Pvt	C Bat 460 PFAB	30.11.1944
Dohner	Sigurd L.	Pvt	509 PIB	
Lindsey	Lewis N.	Pvt	509 PIB	
Buechler	Paul H.	PFC	550 GIB	
Beauchaine	Arthur E.	Sgt	Sv Co 551 PIB	
Hughes	Felix J.	Pvt	A Co 551 PIB	

3) Honor role of 221 German army soldiers who were buried after August 14, 1944, in the eastern Var département; in the area including and east of the towns of Agay, Roquebrune sur Argens, les Arcs and Lorgues (Fréjus and Vidauban not being included). Classification by location of burial, then by name.

Surname	Name	Rank	Age	Date of death	Location of burial	Unit
Klann	Erich	Gren	18	14.8.1944	Agay	
Reiniger	Heinz	Gefr	24	14.8.1944	Agay	
Unknown	8.1944	Agay	20	15.8.1944	Théoule	
Unknown	8.1944	Agay	24	15.8.1944	Théoule	
Unknown	8.1944	Anthéor	23	15.8.1944	Théoule	
Unknown	8.1944	Anthéor	20	15.8.1944	Théoule	
Unknown	15.8.1944	Anthéor	33	15.8.1944	Théoule	
Unknown	15.8.1944	Anthéor	28	15.8.1944	Théoule	
Bock	Jakob	Ogefr	44	9.1944	Bagnols	
Ehrig	Martin	Ofwb	29	21.11.1944	Bagnols	
Cziolek	Simon	Uffz	25	17.8.1944	Callas	Leicht Art.Ers.Abt.8
Unknown				17.8.1944	Callas	
Unknown				17.8.1944	Callas	
Unknown				17.8.1944	Callas	
Unknown				17.8.1944	Callas	
Unknown				17.8.1944	Callas	
Bittner	Georg	Gren	20	19.8.1944	Callian	Res.Inf.Pz.Jäg.Kp.Reg.8
Fröse	Walter	Kan	20	21.8.1944	Callian	
Hörl	Herbert	Gren	18	21.8.1944	Callian	
Plöchl	Johann	Pio	18	19.8.1944	Callian	
Poppe	Robert	Lt	31	18.8.1944	Callian	Stab.Res.Div.148
Stedherm				19.8.1944	Callian	
Völker	Franz	Uffz	31	21.8.1944	Callian	3./Inf.Rgt.417
Zebisch	Josef	Gefr	31	21.8.1944	Callian	
Unknown				8.1944	Callian	
Unknown				8.1944	Callian	
Baum	Arthur	Uffz	40	14.8.1944	Draguignan	
Filipowski	Josef	Gefr	38	8.1944	Draguignan	
Lepperhoff	Friedhelm	Flg	17	8.1944	Draguignan	
Pötzinger					Draguignan	
Scheuerling	Alfred	Uffz	24	15.8.1944	Draguignan	
Schroeter	Arthur	Hptm	53	15.8.1944	Draguignan	
Wanielik	Wilhelm	Ogefr	39	14.8.1944	Draguignan	
Weber	Paul		17	14.8.1944	Draguignan	
Weise	Richard	Soldat	38	13.8.1944	Draguignan	

Surname	Name	Rank	Age	Date of death	Location of burial	Unit
Unknown					Draguignan	
Unknown				15.8.1944	Draguignan	
Unknown		Officer		16.8.1944	Draguignan	
Adams	Martin	Gefr	31	16.8.1944	US Draguignan	
Busch	Franz		19	15.8.1944	US Draguignan	
Chojnacki	Julian	Schütze	40	15.8.1944	US Draguignan	
Dehnel	Gotthard	Gefr	23	15.8.1944	US Draguignan	
Demmel	Johann	Ogefr	36	15.8.1944	Drag. (Le Muy)	
Dietl	Josef	Uffz	27	15.8.1944	Drag. (Le Muy)	
Dirnberger	Josef	Gefr	39	17.8.1944	US Draguignan	
Döhre	Franz	Gefr	22	18.8.1944	US Draguignan	
Ferstl	Paul		39	17.8.1944	US Draguignan	
Gröbner	Karl	Ogefr	42	17.8.1944	US Draguignan	
Grüne	Walter	Hptm	48	15.8.1944	US Draguignan	
Grunwald	Karl	Owchmst	29	15.8.1944	US Draguignan	
Hörnig	Horst	Ogefr	24	18.8.1944	US Draguignan	
Huth	Franz	Ogefr	45	15.8.1944	US Draguignan	
Jörg	Friedrich	Gren	17	16.8.1944	US Draguignan	
Kempf	Ferdinand		36	15.8.1944	Drag. (Le Muy)	
Kniep	Adolf		37	17.8.1944	US Draguignan	
Koch	Wilhelm	Uffz	42	15.8.1944	US Draguignan	
König	Eduard	Ogefr	36	17.8.1944	US Draguignan	
Kramer	Johannes	Olt	40	18.8.1944	US Draguignan	
Lackinger	Michael	Gren	32	15.8.1944	Drag. (Le Muy)	
Loibl	Georg	Funker	18	18.8.1944	US Draguignan	
Lukossek	Adolf	Ogren	18	15.8.1944	US Draguignan	
Maibach	Adolf	Ogefr	33	17.8.1944	Drag. (Les Arcs)	
Merkel	Leonhard	Gren	30	17.8.1944	US Draguignan	
Messemer	Walter	Uffz	31	18.8.1944	US Draguignan	
Naujoks	Otto	Soldat	45	18.8.1944	US Draguignan	
Nieper	Wolfgang	Oberst	49	18.8.1944	US Draguignan	
Pahl	Otto	Uffz	43	15.8.1944	Drag. (Le Muy)	
Pirkl	Johann		17	18.8.1944	US Draguignan	
Puin	Kurt	Fwb	28	15.8.1944	Drag. (Le Muy)	
Röhsle	Josef	Stbwachmst	46	17.8.1944	US Draguignan	
Rychta	Adalbert	Gefr	35	15.8.1944	Drag. (Le Muy)	
Städtler	Ludwig	Gefr	42	15.8.1944	Drag. (Le Muy)	
Strauch	Heinrich	Gefr	40	18.8.1944	US Draguignan	
Summerer	Anton	Uffz	30	17.8.1944	US Draguignan	
Tosch	Johann	Gren	37	16.8.1944	US Draguignan	
Trojza	Edmund	Ogefr	17	17.8.1944	US Draguignan	
Valent	Josef	Sold	20	16.8.1944	US Draguignan	
Walter	Ludwig	Gefr	43	15.8.1944	Drag. (Les Arcs)	

Surname	Name	Rank	Age	Date of death	Location of burial	Unit
Weipert	Gregor	Gefr	34	15.8.1944	Le Muy	
Wittkamp	Willi	Gefr	39	15.8.1944	Le Muy	
Bahns	Johannes	Ogefr	32	15-20.8.1944	Fayence	
Maier	Hans Georg	Lt	35	8.1944	Fayence	See Kommandant Franzosische Riviera
Müller	Albrecht		38	15-20.8.1944	Fayence	
Schwalbe	Walter	Ogefr	32	21.8.1944	Fayence	
Unknown				8.1944	Fayence	
Unknown				15-20.8.1944	Fayence	
Burghardt	Johann	Gefr	19	17.8.1944	Flayosc	
Förster	Romanus	Ogefr	42	15.8.1944	La Motte	
Haug	Friedrich	Uffz	42	15.8.1944	La Motte	
Riebs	Jakob	Gefr	42	15.8.1944	La Motte	
Rittmann	Wilhelm	Gefr	45	15.8.1944	La Motte	
Brandt	Valentin	Gefr	35	15.8.1944	Le Muy	
Dauser	Karl	Olt	36	15.8.1944	Le Muy	Pz.Jäg.Kp.1048
Eckl	Martin	Gefr	31	14.8.1944	Le Muy	
Ehrig?	Martin			15.8.1944	Le Muy	
Häfele	Wilhelm	Gefr	40	15.8.1944	Le Muy	
Hübner	Willi	Gefr	38	15.8.1944	Le Muy	
Kokott	Alfons	Soldat	31	21.8.1944	Le Muy	
Konradt	Willi	Gefr	21	16.8.1944	Le Muy	
Körber	Georg	Pio	18	15.8.1944	Le Muy	3./Res.Pi.Btl.8
Krakowski	Teophiel	Gefr	33	8.1944	Le Muy	Aufkl.Schw.1048
Kusserow	Paul		37	8.1944	Le Muy	
Mehltreter	Max	Gefr	32	18.8.1944	Le Muy	Stab.Aufkl.Schw.1048
Neumann	Herbert	Ogefr	31	8.1944	Le Muy	2./Res.Pi.Btl.8
Ott	Anton	Gefr	40	16.8.1944	Le Muy	
Schwenk	Johannes	Ogefr	37	15.8.1944	Le Muy	
Sciskala	Rudolf		39	8.1944	Le Muy	
Sobschak	Willi	Gren	40	8.1944	Le Muy	
Steiner	Johann		37	8.1944	Le Muy	
Stempfle	Lorenz	Schütze	43	8.1944	Le Muy	
Striegl	Franz	Gefr	20	16.8.1944	Le Muy	
Witzigmann	Paul	Uffz	38	16.8.1944	Le Muy	
Unknown				8.1944	Le Muy	
Unknown				8.1944	Le Muy	
Unknown				8.1944	Le Muy	
Unknown				8.1944	Le Muy	
Unknown				8.1944	Le Muy	
Unknown				8.1944	Le Muy	
Unknown				8.1944	Le Muy	
Unknown				8.1944	Le Muy	
Krassa	Georg	Uffz	38	16.8.1944	Le Trayas	

Surname	Name	Rank	Age	Date of death	Location of burial	Unit
Krumpill	Roman		18	16.8.1944	Le Trayas	
Nemoikin	Iwan		23	8.1944	Le Trayas	Ost.Btl.661
Pollin	Kurt	Fwb	22	16.8.1944	Le Trayas	
Unknown				16/17.8.1944	Le Trayas	
Unknown				15.8.1944	Le Trayas	
Kritner	Erich	Sold		18.8.1944	Les Adrets (Fréjus)	
Ludwig	Ernst	Uffz	31	8.1944	Les Adrets (Fréjus)	10./Res.Gren.Btl.444
Weber	Fritz	Jäg	31	18.8.1944	Les Adrets (Fréjus)	7./Res.Jäg.Btl.28
Unknown				8.1944	Les Adrets (Fréjus)	
Unknown				8.1944	Les Adrets (Fréjus)	
Frings	Josef	Ogefr	37	8.1944	Les Arcs	
Ganswindt	Franz	Uffz	31	14.8.1944	Les Arcs	
Gatermann	Heinrich	Uffz	30	16.8.1944	Les Arcs	11./Gren.Rgt.932
Lapok	Josef	Soldat	24	8.1944	Les Arcs	
Lindner	Rudi	Gefr	19	21.9.1944	Les Arcs	
Löscher	Johannes	Soldat	19	8.1944	Les Arcs	
Marschner	Martin	Uffz	31	16.8.1944	Les Arcs	
Neurath	Jakob	Ogefr	38	14.8.1944	Les Arcs	
Prokop	Gregor	Soldat	20	8.1944	Les Arcs	
Schneider	Ludwig	Ogefr	25	16.8.1944	Les Arcs	
Trenne	Heinrich	Lt	30	16.8.1944	Les Arcs	
Unknown				8.1944	Les Arcs	
Unknown				8.1944	Les Arcs	
Unknown				8.1944	Les Arcs	
Unknown				8.1944	Les Arcs	
Unknown				8.1944	Les Arcs	
Unknown				8.1944	Les Arcs	
Unknown				8.1944	Les Arcs	
Unknown				8.1944	Les Arcs	
Unknown				8.1944	Les Arcs	
Unknown		Ofwb		8.1944	Les Arcs	
Unknown				8.1944	Les Arcs	
Unknown				8.1944	Les Arcs	
Unknown				8.1944	Les Arcs	
Unknown				8.1944	Les Arcs	
Unknown				8.1944	Les Arcs	
Unknown				8.1944	Les Arcs	
Unknown				8.1944	Les Arcs	
Unknown				8.1944	Les Arcs	
Unknown		Hptm		8.1944	Les Arcs	
Unknown				8.1944	Les Arcs	

Surname	Name	Rank	Age	Date of death	Location of burial	Unit
Unknown				8.1944	Les Arcs	
Vocke	Max		31	15.8.1944	Lorgues	
Stockl	Soldat			8.1944	Montauroux	
Unknown				8.1944	Montauroux	
Unknown				8.1944	Montauroux	
Unknown				8.1944	Montauroux	
Unknown				8.1944	Montauroux	
Unknown				8.1944	Montauroux	
Unknown				8.1944	Montauroux	
Unknown				8.1944	Montauroux	
Unknown				8.1944	Montauroux	
Unknown				8.1944	Montauroux	
Unknown				8.1944	Montauroux	
Unknown				8.1944	Montauroux	
Unknown				8.1944	Montauroux	
Damschke	Artur	Gefr	42	14.8.1946	Puget sur Argens	
Hanke	Ulrich	Gefr	39	16.8.1944	Puget sur Argens	
Marquardt	Kurt	Ogefr	36	16.9.1945	Puget sur Argens	
Rehfeldt	Wilhelm	Sold	35	16.8.1944	Puget sur Argens	
Dahlhaus	Friedrich		38	16.8.1944	Roquebrune	
Gläser	Werner	Gren	19	16.8.1944	Roquebrune	
Hamburger	Fridolin		34	17.8.1944	Roquebrune	
Ketelsen	Thomas	Stbgefr	29	16.8.1944	Roquebrune	
Mysuna	Tomasz	Soldat	38	16.8.1944	Roquebrune	
Nadolny	Emil	Sold		15.8.1944	Roquebrune	
Pettke	Edmund	Soldat	33	16.8.1944	Roquebrune	
Petzi	Fritz	Uffz	36	15.8.1944	Roquebrune	
Reith	Paul	Gefr	18	14.8.1944	Roquebrune	
Saling	Heinrich	Lt	41	16.8.1944	Roquebrune	
Spillmann	Theodor	Ogren	19	16.8.1944	Roquebrune	
Winkler	Fritz	Uffz	37	16.8.1944	Roquebrune	
Unknown				8.1944	Roquebrune	
Unknown				8.1944	Roquebrune	
Unknown				8.1944	Roquebrune	
Unknown				8.1944	Roquebrune	
Unknown				8.1944	Roquebrune	
Unknown				16.8.1944	Roquebrune	
Unknown				16.8.1944	Roquebrune	
Unknown				16.8.1944	Roquebrune	
Unknown				16.8.1944	Roquebrune	
Knödlseder	Josef	Kan	18	22.8.1944	Tanneron	4./Res.Art.Regt.8
Kroliczek	Georg	Gren	20	17.8.1944	Tanneron	10./Res.Gren.Btl.444
Kuhnert?	Lt			22.8.1944	Tanneron	

Surname	Name	Rank	Age	Date of death	Location of burial	Unit
Vogl	Georg	Sold	17	17.8.1944?	Tanneron	1./Res.Art.Abt.44
Unknown					Tanneron	
Unknown				22.8.1944	Tanneron	
Unknown				22.8.1944	Tanneron	
Undetermined					Trans en Provence	
Undetermined					Trans en Provence	
Undetermined					Trans en Provence	
Undetermined					Trans en Provence	
Undetermined					Trans en Provence	
Undetermined					Trans en Provence	
Undetermined					Trans en Provence	
Undetermined					Trans en Provence	
Unknown					Trans en Provence	
Unknown					Trans en Provence	

4) Honor role of 996 German army soldiers who were buried in the Maritime Alps during and after World War II or who were buried in Draguignan after having been killed or mortally wounded in the Maritime Alps. Soldiers who were apparently prisoners of war at the time of their death (of which there are approximately 229) are listed at the end. Classification by date of death, then by location of burial. This list should not be considered to be a complete register for the Maritime Alps front, as it does not include any soldiers buried in Italy, not to mention the soldiers whose bodies were never recovered.

Surname	Name	Rank	Age	Date of death	Location of burial	Unit
Klemenschitz	Robert	Kan	29	19.4.1943	Menton	
Widmer	Hans	Schütz	21	21.7.1943	Mandelieu Capitou	11./Gren.Rgt.578
Burkhardt	Erich	Ogren	19	13.8.1943	Antibes	
Kiefer	Willi	Kan	19	18.8.1943	Nice Caucade	11./Art.Rgt.305
Brandt	Franz	Hauptmann	49	8.9.1943	Nice Caucade	Frontleistelle Nice
Abel	Kurt	Fwb	23	8.9.1943	Nice Caucade	Stab III.Btl.I.R.178?
Krüger	Ernst	RB Inspektor	28	8.9.1943	Nice Caucade	Deutsche RB H.V.D. Paris
Stocker	Josef	Gef	23	16.9.1943	Nice Caucade	1./Pi.Btl.(mot.) Feldhernhalle
Armbruster	Ernst	Ogefr	24	17.9.1943	Cannes	
Gassauer	Kurt	Gef	21	17.9.1943	Nice Caucade	2./Füs.Rgt. Feldhernhalle
Renner	Johann	Uffz	27	18.9.1943	Nice Caucade	Eisenbahnpanzerzug N°25
Gartner	Albert	Fwb	29	19.9.1943	Cannes	
Burchardt	Erwin	Gef	21	19.9.1943	Nice Caucade	9./Füs.Rgt. Feldherrnhalle
Schütz	Artur	SS Scharführer	31	21.9.1943	Nice Caucade	Sicherheitspolizei Nizza

Surname	Name	Rank	Age	Date of death	Location of burial	Unit
Wilde	Horst	Okan	19	23.9.1943	Nice Caucade	Stabs-Battr.H.Flak-Abt. Feldherrnhalle
Möser	Heinrich	Uffz	24	23.9.1943	Nice Caucade	2./Pi.Btl.(mot) Feldherrnhalle
Fischer	Franz	Uffz	26	27.9.1943	Nice Caucade	Stabskp. Pz.Feldherrnhalle
Wagner	Siegfried	Gef	19	27.9.1943	Nice Caucade	Stabskp. Pz.Feldherrnhalle
Royal	Soldat			3.10.1943	Nice Caucade	Callian
Klipingat	Arthur	Gef	21	4.10.1943	Nice Caucade	8./Füs.Rgt. Feldherrnhalle
Puttkammer	Günther	Ogef	23	7.10.1943	Nice Caucade	2./SF.Art.Rgt. Feldherrnhalle
Meiborg	Georg	Uffz	33	13.10.1943	Nice Caucade	
Maciewski	Bruno	Pio	18	16.10.1943	Nice Caucade	3./Pi.Btl.(mot) Feldherrnhalle
Beyer	Helmut	Gren	20	19.10.1943	Nice Caucade	2./Gren.Rgt.(mot) Feldherrnhalle
Seisler	Hermann	Ogef	24	27.10.1943	Nice Caucade	2./Wachbtl.Wiesbaden
Eberle	Henrich	Gef	34	7.11.1943	Nice Caucade	5./Gren.Rgt.725
Schneider	Herbert	Gef	27	11.11.1943	Nice Caucade	12./Res.Gren.Btl.444
Makiola	Paul	Soldat	42	11.11.1943	Nice Caucade	Einheit Hunke
Reck	Franz	Gren	36	15.11.1943	Nice Caucade	6./Res.Gren.Btl.372
Glieden	Nikolaus	Ogef	30	16.11.1943	Nice Caucade	2./Wachtbatl.Wiesbaden
Wilde	Eduard	Ogef	35	25.11.1943	Nice Caucade	7./Gren.Rgt.735
Losert	Alfred	Uffz	25	2.12.1943	Nice Caucade	Res.Inf.Pi.Kp.148
Keilmann	Valentin	Matr Ogef	35	14.12.1943	Nice Caucade	Franz.SüdKüste der Nesperrflotille West
Scholl	Hermann	Matr Gef	20	14.12.1943	Nice Caucade	Franz.SüdKüste der Nesperrflotille West
Frommelt	Horst	Gren	18	21.12.1943	Nice Caucade	4./MG.Kp.Res.Gren. Btl.7
Kammandel	Karl	Uffz	26	26.12.1943	Nice Caucade	Eisenbahn Pi.Kp.100
Ackermann	Hermann	Ogef	23	26.12.1943	Nice Caucade	7.Funkmess
Bunke	Gerhard	Gefr	20	28.12.1943	Nice Caucade	H-S.Gruppe Cannes
Biedermann	Anton	Gren	37	28.12.1943	Nice Caucade	Res.Gren.Rgt.8.Nachr. Kp.
Pfaffendorf	Walter	Gef	38	1.1.1944	Nice Caucade	HKP Grasse
Maroschek	Stanislaus	Gren	28	2.1.1944	Nice Caucade	Res.Gren.Btl.164
Sokoll	Johann	Gren	42	2.1.1944	Nice Caucade	Res.Gren.Btl.164
Richter	Franz	Gef	18	14.1.1944	Nice Caucade	2./Res.Gren.Btl.327
Liebers	Joachim	Gren	18	16.1.1944	Nice Caucade	14./Res.Gren.Rgt.8
Wuthenow	Herbert	Ogef	22	27.1.1944	Nice Caucade	Stabs-Kp.Gren.Rgt.735
Langer	Josef	Fwb	29	30.1.1944	Nice Caucade	1./Res.Pi.Btl.8
Glaser	Erwin	Gef	18	30.1.1944	Nice Caucade	1./Res.Pi.Btl.8
Krumm	Friedrich	Gef	37	30.1.1944	Nice Caucade	14./Res.Gren.Rgt.8
Weber	Otto	Matr Gef	19	31.1.1944	Nice Caucade	Mar.Bordflak.Abt.
Wrobel	Gerhard	Gren	27	31.1.1944?	Nice Caucade	14./Res.Gren.Rgt.8
Scholz	Hans	Gren	25	4.2.1944	Nice Caucade	2./Res.Gren.Btl.7

Surname	Name	Rank	Age	Date of death	Location of burial	Unit
Brachmann	Paul	Gren	18	10.2.1944	Nice Caucade	Res.Inf.Pi.Kp.148
Löhr	Siegfried	Ogef	32	16.2.1944	Nice Caucade	15./Res.Inf.Nachr. Kp.239
Fröhlich	Alfons	Pio	36	19.2.1944	Nice Caucade	3./Res.Pi.Btl.8
Neubauer	Hugo	Matrose	20	20.2.1944	Nice Caucade	Kriegsmarine
Borstel	Joachim	MatrOgef	20	20.2.1944	Nice Caucade	Kriegsmarine
Berghof	Günter	Matr Ogef	19	20.2.1944	Nice Caucade	Kriegsmarine
Rosen	Adolf	Matr Gef	20	20.2.1944	Nice Caucade	Kriegsmarine
Wendisch	Johannes	Uffz	19	20.2.1944	Nice Caucade	Kriegsmarine
Herbolzheimer	Albrecht	Uffz	25	21.2.1944	Nice Caucade	Jagdlehrergruppe 1.Staffel
Faber	Josef	Uffz	25	2.3.1944	Nice Caucade	1./Res.Pi.Btl.8
Cremer	Wilhelm	RB Sekretär	52	3.3.1944	Nice Caucade	Reichsbahn
Ofiera	Otto	Uffz	30	4.3.1944	Nice Caucade	1./Res.Pi.Btl.8
Drescher	Kurt	Gren	18	6.3.1944	Nice Caucade	Res.Inf.Nachr.Kp.239
Weber	Johannes	Hauptmann	52	8.3.1944	Nice Caucade	
Haselhuhn	Walter	Gren	37	11.3.1944	Belvédère	
Priefert	Otto	OT Man	55	11.3.1944	Nice Caucade	Todt
Kunadt	Hans	Uffz	24	17.3.1944	Nice Caucade	
Slonka	Josef	Jäg	20	24.3.1944	Nice Caucade	Res.Jäg.Btl.28
Dubiel	Paul	Pio	34	25.3.1944	Nice Caucade	Res.Pi.Btl.8?
Schawrow	Gregorj	Soldat	46	1.4.1944	Nice Caucade	Ost.Btl.661?
Paul	Franz	Ogef	20	3.4.1944	Nice Caucade	
Friedauer	Josef	Jäg	17	3.4.1944	Nice Caucade	Res.Jäg.Btl.28
Barth	Johann	Maat	21	4.4.1944	Nice Caucade	Kriegsmarine
Schmidt	Arthur	Uffz	30	8.4.1944	Nice Caucade	
Polok	Josef	Gren	18	11.4.1944	Nice Caucade	
Bijok	Josef	Gren	32	12.4.1944	Nice Caucade	11./Kp.Res.Gren. Btl.164
Kondziolka	Theophil	Gren	29	12.4.1944	Nice Caucade	11./Kp.Res.Gren. Btl.164
Kotzur	Alois	Gren	27	12.4.1944	Nice Caucade	11./Kp.Res.Gren. Btl.164
Schulz	Josef	Gren	28	12.4.1944	Nice Caucade	11./Kp.Res.Gren. Btl.164
Neumann	Kurt	Uffz	23	12.4.1944	Nice Caucade	
Janulek	Ernst	Gren	29	15.4.1944	Nice Caucade	
Artel	Georg	Opio	34	18.4.1944	Nice Caucade	Res.Pi.Btl.8?
Kotzur	Anton	Gren	19	18.4.1944	Nice Caucade	
Schmidpeter	Johann	Gren	18	19.4.1944	Nice Caucade	
Teuner	Ferdinand	Gren	31	25.4.1944	Nice Caucade	
Miadowicz	Josef	Gren	19	26.4.1944	Nice Caucade	
Beresitzky	Serge	Dolmetscher	28	3.5.1944	Nice Caucade	SS
Neber	Berhard	SS Hauptscharführer	36	3.5.1944	Nice Caucade	SS
Brychczy	Mieczyslaus	Gren	20	3.5.1944	Nice Caucade	Res.Inf.Gesch.Kp.8
Mjasejedow	Wladimir		31	4.5.1944	Nice Caucade	Ost.Btl.661?

Surname	Name	Rank	Age	Date of death	Location of burial	Unit
Schmidt	Emil	Uffz	31	7.5.1944	Nice Caucade	4./MG.Kp.Res.Gren. Btl.7
Mlotek	Alois	Gren	19	8.5.1944	Nice Caucade	4./MG.Kp.Res.Gren. Btl.7
Schmegner	Siegfried	Gren	34	12.5.1944	Nice Caucade	1./Kampfmarsch. Btl.1021
Hübner	Karl	Matr Gef	19	14.5.1944	Nice Caucade	Hako-Stabkp
Kraudzun	Herbert	Gef	23	17.5.1944	Nice Caucade	12./Heeresküsten Art. Rgt.1291
Romich	Georg	Gren	18	20.5.1944	Nice Caucade	3./Res.Gren.Btl.7
Tainschek	Anton	Gren	18	21.5.1944	Nice Caucade	Res.Gren.Btl.164
Saczawa	Josef	Gren	18	21.5.1944	Nice Caucade	Res.Inf.Gesch.Kp.8
Stasser	Kasper	Gren	17	21.5.1944	Nice Caucade	4./MG.Kp.Res.Gren. Btl.7
Kaske	Willy	Ogef	28	21.5.1944	Nice Caucade	Marine Kraftfahrabteilung
Sachatsch	Makar	Gren	26	23.5.1944	Nice Caucade	4./Ost.Btl.661
Zolisz	Thaddäus	Gren	18	23.5.1944	Nice Caucade	3./Res.Gren.Btl.327
Glotow	Konstantin	Soldat	30	26.5.1944	Nice Caucade	4./Ost.Btl.661
Walla	Alois	Gren	17	26.5.1944	Nice Caucade	Res.Gren.Btl.164
Ullrich	Otto	Gren	36	26.5.1944	Nice Caucade	Res.Gren.Btl.164
Mayer	Karl	Lokomotivführer	36	26.5.1944	Nice Caucade	Reichsbahn
Hessenauer	Walter	Ogef	39	26.5.1944	Nice Caucade	
Friedrich	Karl	Gren	28	28.5.1944	Nice Caucade	Res.Gren.Btl.164
Kulesza	Alfons	Kan	21	28.5.1944	Nice Caucade	12./Heeresküsten Art. Rgt.1291
Karpowich	Nikolas	Soldat		28.5.1944	Nice Caucade	Ost.Btl.661
Gorczyk	Ewald	Uffz	27	30.5.1944	Nice Caucade	3./Res.Art.Rgt.8
Egger	Johann	Gren	18	30.5.1944	Nice Caucade	Res.Gren.Btl.164
Schlünz	Wilhelm	Gren	22	3.6.1944	Nice Caucade	3./Res.Gren.Btl.327
Stokowy	Paul	Gren	22	5.6.1944	Nice Caucade	Res.Inf.Gesch.Kp.239
Von Sarporski	Edgar	Hauptmann	29	6.6.1944	Nice Caucade	
Cieply	Ludwig	Gren	19	7.6.1944	Nice Caucade	14./Res.Inf.Pz.Jg. Kp.239
Tomcyl	Stanislaw			8.6.1944	Cannes	
Thoma	Vinzenz	Uffz	27	8.6.1944	Nice Caucade	8./Res.Jäg.Btl.28
Majewski	Joseph			9.6.1944	Cannes	
Erbs	Alfons	Uffz	32	10.6.1944	Nice Caucade	14./Res.Inf.Pz.Jg. Kp.239
Zwirner	Josef	Gren	18	11.6.1944	Nice Caucade	Stab.148.Res.Div.
Steger	Fritz	Matr Ogef	44	12.6.1944	Nice Caucade	6.Sich.Flottille Marseille Hafenwach
Walach	Karl	Gren	22	12.6.1944	Nice Caucade	3./Res.Gren.Btl.7
Heiderski	Georg	Gren	17	14.6.1944	Nice Caucade	11./Res.Gren.Btl.444
Miehling	Josef	Gren	18	14.6.1944	Nice Caucade	5./Res.Gren.Btl.372
Moscha	Bruno	Uffz	30	14.6.1944	Nice Caucade	5./Res.Gren.Btl.372
Prange	Walter	Ogef	21	15.6.1944	Nice Caucade	Kriegsmarine

Surname	Name	Rank	Age	Date of death	Location of burial	Unit
Stark	Franz	Ogef	22	15.6.1944	Nice Caucade	Torpedoboots Flotille TA 307
Witt	Ernst	Ogef	22	15.6.1944	Nice Caucade	Kriegsmarine
Unknown				15.6.1944	Nice Caucade	Kriegsmarine
Unknown				15.6.1944	Nice Caucade	Kriegsmarine
Unknown				15.6.1944	Nice Caucade	Kriegsmarine
Unknown				15.6.1944	Nice Caucade	Kriegsmarine
Wolka	Alfred	Gefr	17	15.6.1944	Nice Caucade	Torpedoboots Flotille TA 307
Weidisch	Wilhelm	Ogef	22	15.6.1944	Nice Caucade	Kriegsmarine
Lipus	Walter	Matrose	18	15.6.1944	Nice Caucade	Kriegsmarine
Kolodzig	Konrad	Gren	22	19.6.1944	Nice Caucade	
Baron	Ignaz	Pio	31	19.6.1944	Nice Caucade	
Kutz	August	Gren	17	20.6.1944	Nice Caucade	Res.Inf.Gesch.Kp.239
Porada	Josef	Ofwb	28	21.6.1944	Nice Caucade	2./Res.Gren.Btl.7
Sturow	Nikita	Freiwll	19	21.6.1944	Nice Caucade	2./Ost.Btl.661
Otzik	Josef	Ojäg	27	23.6.1944	Nice Caucade	5./Res.Jäg.Btl.28
Kossyk	Johann	Ogef	31	26.6.1944	Nice Caucade	9./Res.Gren.Btl.164
Hoffmann	Kurt	Fwb	29	28.6.1944	Nice Caucade	10./Res.Gren.Btl.164
Olejok	Ernst	Gren	19	28.6.1944	Nice Caucade	
Ochmann	Ernst	Gren	17	28.6.1944	Nice Caucade	
Huber	Otto			28.6.1944	Nice Caucade	Reichsbahn
Haas	Johann			28.6.1944	Nice Caucade	Reichsbahn
Poenitz	Helmut			30.6.1944	Nice Caucade	
Kahleyß	Wilhelm	Stabartzt	44	30.6.1944	Nice Caucade	
Rutschia	Paul			2.7.1944	Nice Caucade	
Kositza	Helmut	Gren	17	2.7.1944	Nice Caucade	
Rieger	Johann	Gren	17	2.7.1944	Nice Caucade	
Schulz	Albert	Fwb	31	5.7.1944	Nice Caucade	
Olbrich	Günther	Uffz	24	5.7.1944	Nice Caucade	
Dahlhaus	Karl	Uffz	25	5.7.1944	Nice Caucade	
Löblein	Hugo	Gren	19	8.7.1944	Nice Caucade	
Wieczorek	Kazimierz	Jäg	18	11.7.1944	Nice Caucade	
Schnurr	Gustav	San.Uffz	40	11.7.1944	Nice Caucade	Sani
Jaworek	Franz	Gren	31	14.7.1944	Nice Caucade	
Wagner	Johann	Gren	17	16.7.1944	Nice Caucade	
Jendreiek	Karl	Lt	27	16.7.1944	Nice Caucade	3./Heeres.Art.Abt.1196
Jessel	Alfons	Gren	17	16.7.1944	Nice Caucade	
Marscholik	Anton	Jäg	18	18.7.1944	Nice Caucade	Res.Jäg.Btl.28
Hoffmann	Fritz	Uffz	24	18.7.1944	Nice Caucade	
Hansel	Heinrich	Fwb	29	18.7.1944	Nice Caucade	
Schmohel	Erich	Jäg	19	18.7.1944	Nice Caucade	Res.Jäg.Btl.28
Schmidt	Paul	Jäg	18	18.7.1944	Nice Caucade	Res.Jäg.Btl.28
Gutzmann	Joachim	Ogef	21	18.7.1944	Nice Caucade	Kriegsmarine
Kausch	Paul	Uffz	43	18.7.1944	Nice Caucade	

Surname	Name	Rank	Age	Date of death	Location of burial	Unit
Zädow	Horst	Olt	25	18.7.1944	Nice Caucade	2./Res.Gren.Btl.327
Mansky	Rudolf	Gren	17	18.7.1944	Nice Caucade	
Horak	Othmar	Gef	18	18.7.1944	Nice Caucade	
Schindler	Franz	Gren	17	18.7.1944	Nice Caucade	
Fietz	Karl	Gren	17	18.7.1944	Nice Caucade	
Voit	Edgar	Gren	17	18.7.1944	Nice Caucade	
Planer	Karl	Gren	17	18.7.1944	Nice Caucade	
Altmeier	Anton	Uffz	21	18.7.1944	Nice Caucade	
Pluczok	Victor	Gren	18	18.7.1944	Nice Caucade	2./Res.Gren.Btl.327
Blasytza	Richard	Jäg	17	19.7.1944	Nice Caucade	Res.Jäg.Btl.28
Steinhauer	Otto	Gren	17	20.7.1944	Nice Caucade	
Kruse	Heinrich	Hilfszollass	42	25.7.1944	Nice Caucade	Zoll
Berensdorf	Erich	Ogef	23	27.7.1944	Nice Caucade	Kriegsmarine
Schneider	Willi	Ogef	20	27.7.1944	Nice Caucade	Kriegsmarine
Schochmantiw	Tachir	Sold		27.7.1944	Nice Caucade	Ost.Btl.661
Zierl	Wilhelm	Gren	37	28.7.1944	Nice Caucade	
Undetermined				7.1944?	Cannes Hespérides	
Undetermined				7.1944?	Cannes Hespérides	
Undetermined				7.1944?	Cannes Hespérides	
Nemitz	Herbert	Ogef	21	1.8.1944	Nice Caucade	
Eckert	Herbert	Ogef	23	2.8.1944	Nice Caucade	
Ledwon	Ludwig	Gren	35	2.8.1944	Nice Caucade	
Schultes	Alfred	Pio	18	2.8.1944	Nice Caucade	Res.Pi.Btl.8?
Erhard	Siegfried	Pio	18	2.8.1944	Nice Caucade	Res.Pi.Btl.8?
Brand	Karl	Uffz	23	2.8.1944	Nice Caucade	
Reissig	Felix	Uffz	33	2.8.1944	Nice Caucade	
Kirilow	Michail	Soldat	34	3.8.1944	Nice Caucade	
John	Theodor	Uffz	31	3.8.1944	Nice Caucade	1./Res.Gren.Btl.327
Sokolow		Sold		4.8.1944	Nice Caucade	Ost.Btl.661?
Sikora	Josef	Jäg	20	4.8.1944	Nice Caucade	Res.Jäg.Btl.28
Dyga	Franz	Pio	18	4.8.1944	Nice Caucade	Res.Pi.Btl.8?
Rosenblatt	Georg	Fwb	29	4.8.1944	Nice Caucade	
Kobiela	Ludwig	Gren	19	6.8.1944	Nice Caucade	
Wypior	Josef	Gren	29	6.8.1944	Nice Caucade	
Krüger	Herbert	Soldat		8.8.1944	Nice Caucade	
Richter	Rudolf	Gren	37	9.8.1944	Nice Caucade	
Amann	Heinz	Ogef	19	12.8.1944	Nice Caucade	
Schiller	Josef	Fwb	30	12.8.1944	Nice Caucade	
Steinwedel	Günther	Gren		12.8.1944	Nice Caucade	
Habicht	Alfred	Uffz	29	15.8.1944	Antibes	7./Alarm Flak 308
Friede	Walter	Gefr	18	15.8.1944	Antibes	7./Alarm Flak 308
Richter	Ernst	Pio	27	15.8.1944	Aspremont	
Dürr	Willi	Stbs Gefr	29	15.8.1944	Nice Caucade	
Peschen	Kaspar	Ogefr	22	15.8.1944	Nice Caucade	2./Flak.Abt.391

Surname	Name	Rank	Age	Date of death	Location of burial	Unit
Griesberger	Adolf	Uffz	37	15.8.1944	Drag. (La Napoule)	
Ingold	Friedrich	Ogefr	24	15.8.1944	Drag. (La Napoule)	
Karwatzski	Alfred	Fwb	34	15.8.1944	Drag. (La Napoule)	
Jeck	Andreas	Gefr	42	15.8.1944	Grasse	1./Fest.Pi-Stab 14
Metzger	Georg	Jäger	18	15.8.1944	La Napoule	Res.Jäg.Btl.28
Neuwirth	Franz	Gren	18	15.8.1944	Le Cannet	12./Res.Gren.Btl.444
Rodoschek	Anton	Gren	18	15.8.1944	Le Cannet	12./Res.Gren.Btl.444
Sowka	Gerhard	Pio	17	15.8.1944	Pegomas	
Fuchs	Josef	Gren	18	15.8.1944	St Vallier	1./Res.Gren.Btl.327
Jeschke	Willi	Gefr	40	15.8.1944	St Vallier	1./Res.Gren.Btl.327
Schneider	Paul	Gren	32	15.8.1944	St Vallier	1./Res.Gren.Btl.327
Schwarz	Michael	Gren	17	15.8.1944	St Vallier	1./Res.Gren.Btl.327
Synczek	Josef	Gren	21	15.8.1944	St Vallier	2./Res.Gren.Btl.327
Fleischer	Paul	Gren	17	15.8.1944	St Vallier	2./Res.Gren.Btl.327
Pollak	Richard		18	15.8.1944	St Vallier	2./Res.Gren.Btl.327
Steinke	Franz	O Gefr	35	15.8.1944	St Vallier	2./Res.Gren.Btl.327
Bilko	Paul	Krftfahrer	21	15.8.1944	St Vallier	Kr.K.Zug 1048
Unknown				15.8.1944	St Vallier	
Heckelmann	Lorenz	Gren	18	16.8.1944	Antibes	7./Res.Gren.Btl.372
Bohl	Paul	OT Mann	39	16.8.1944	Nice Caucade	Todt
Seidel	Georg	O Lt	43	16.8.1944	Nice Caucade	7./Res.Jäg.Btl.28
Tkocz	Reinhold		19	16.8.1944	Drag. (La Napoule)	
Hümmer	Otto	Schütze	21	16.8.1944	Drag. (Le Trayas)	
Oelschlegel	Hans	Stbs Gefr	45	16.8.1944	Grasse	Stab.Res.Div.148
Czech	Erich	Jäger	28	16.8.1944	La Napoule	Res.Jäg.Btl.28
Falkus	Eduard	Jäger	17	16.8.1944	La Napoule	Res.Jäg.Btl.28
Lingansch	Paul	Fwb	27	16.8.1944	La Napoule	Res.Jäg.Btl.28
Niesporek	Franz	Jäger	17	16.8.1944	La Napoule	Res.Jäg.Btl.28
Claus?	Emil			16.8.1944?	Lantosque	
Babel?	Rudolf			16.8.1944?	Lantosque	
Schafer?	Ernst			16.8.1944?	Lantosque	
Styppa	Konrad	Gren	28	16/17.8.1944	Le Cannet	10/12.Res.Gren.Btl.444
Kube	Paul	Okan	37	16.8.1944	Les Termes Cannes	
Kapler	Gottlieb	Hilfzoll	46	16.8.1944	Roquebillière	Zoll
Lachman	Karl	Zollsek	47	16.8.1944	Roquebillière	Zoll
Wittmann	Albert	Zollsek	40	16.8.1944	Roquebillière	Zoll
Bergmann	Karl	Lt	33	17.8.1944	Cannes	
Döring	Edwin	Ogefr	37	17.8.1944	Cannes	
Klöditz	Willy	Uffz	23	17.8.1944	Cannes	13./Heeresküsten Art. Rgt.1291
Drischel	Helmuth	Gren	17	17.8.1944	La Napoule	
Götz	Reinhold	Jäger	27	17.8.1944	La Napoule	Res.Jäg.Btl.28
Janus	Josef	Jäger	18	17.8.1944	La Napoule	5./Res.Jäg.Btl.28
Ritzka	Josef	Jäger	18	17.8.1944	La Napoule	5./Res.Jäg.Btl.28

Surname	Name	Rank	Age	Date of death	Location of burial	Unit
Unknown				8.1944	Levens	
Kluge	Werner	O Gren	34	17.8.1944	St Vallier	14./Res.Pz.Jäg.Kp.239
Ammer	Alfred	Zollass	50	18.8.1944	Cannes	Zoll
Aurmer	Kurt			18.8.1944	Cannes	
Korte	Josef	Stbs Gefr	27	18.8.1944	Nice Caucade	1./Flak.Abt.391
Uschold	Josef	Sold	18	18.8.1944	Nice Caucade	3./Res.Pi.Btl.8
Pattloch	Günter	O Pio	31	18.8.1944	Grasse	Stab.Res.Pi.Btl.8
Janise	Franz	Gren	17	18.8.1944	La Napoule	Res.Inf.Gesch.Kp.239
Helms	Wilhelm	O Gefr	39	18.8.1944	St Vallier	2.M.K.Abt.28
Liebetanz	Herbert	O Kan	19	18.8.1944	St Vallier	Art?
Drzisga	Otto	Gren	18	18.8.1944	Valbonne	1./Res.Art.Abt.44
Scheffczyk	Viktor	Gefr	34	19.8.1944	Cannes	HAKA Cannes
Herold	Richard	O Fwb	30	19.8.1944	Nice Caucade	Fest.Pi.Abschn.Gr.II/44
Jahn	Johann	Ob Gefr	30	19.8.1944	Nice Caucade	21 Flugmelde Res. West Frankr.
Manietzki	Johann	Gren	18	19.8.1944	Nice Caucade	10./Res.Gren.Btl.164
Jasper	Theodor	Ob Gefr	31	20.8.1944	Cimiez	Stab.Res.Gren.Rgt.239
Sikora	Zdenko	Jäger	18	20.8.1944	Cimiez	6./Res.Jäg.Btl.28
Graca	August	Jäger	18	20.8.1944	La Napoule	7./Res.Jäg.Btl.28
Poller	Franz	Gren	17	20.8.1944	La Napoule	10./Res.Gren.Btl.164
Oczko	Herbert	Uffz	24	20.8.1944	La Napoule	10./Res.Gren.Btl.164
Thieme	Hans	Uffz	34	20.8.1944	La Napoule	10./Res.Gren.Btl.164
Cinader	Johann	Gren?	17	20.8.1944	Valbonne	7./Res.Jäg.Btl.28
Gerhold	Heinz	Ogefr	20	21.8.1944	Cannes (sea)	22.U-Jagdflottille
Wegen	Willi	Hauptgefr	23	21.8.1944	Cannes (sea)	22.U-Jagdflottille
Römmen	Matthias	Ogefr	24	21.8.1944	Cimiez	8./Res.Jäg.Btl.28
Cisek	Johann	Jäger	18	21.8.1944	La Napoule	Res.Jäg.Btl.28
Link	Lothar	Jäger	18	21.8.1944	La Napoule	5./Res.Jäg.Btl.28
Wrodarczyk	Viktor	Jäger	17	21.8.1944	La Napoule	5./Res.Jäg.Btl.28
Schiffhorst	Gerhard	Uffz	30	21.8.1944	La Napoule	5./Res.Jäg.Btl.28
Olschenka	Erich	Jäger	17	21.8.1944	La Napoule	6./Res.Jäg.Btl.28
Wall	Arthur	Jäger	18	21.8.1944	La Napoule	6./Res.Jäg.Btl.28
Weimann	Paul	O Gefr	26	21.8.1944	La Napoule	6./Res.Jäg.Btl.28
Nowrotek	Alois	Jäger	27	21.8.1944	La Napoule	7./Res.Jäg.Btl.28
Schuster	Leopold	Jäger	20	21.8.1944	La Napoule	Res.Jäg.Btl.28
Skrzydolski	Adam	Jäger	18	21.8.1944	La Napoule	Res.Jäg.Btl.28
Strzoda	Herbert	Jäger	18	21.8.1944	La Napoule	Res.Jäg.Btl.28
Härtel	Ernst	Ogefr	31	21.8.1944	St Cézaire	1./Res.Gren.Btl.7
Büddemann	Friedrich	O Gefr	24	21.8.1944	Vallauris	22.U-Jagdflotille
Dahmen	Heinrich	Ogefr	20	22.8.1944	Cimiez	22.U-Jagdflottille
Meyer-Detring	Klaus	O Lt	35	22.8.1944	Cimiez	7./Res.Jäg.Btl.28
Temel	Johann	Gren	18	22.8.1944	Grasse	4./Res.Gren.Btl.7
Bartsch	Heinz	Uffz	25	22.8.1944	La Napoule	
Konsek	August	Gren	18	28.8.1944	La Napoule	

Surname	Name	Rank	Age	Date of death	Location of burial	Unit
Böhm	Gustav	Jäger	17	8.1944	La Napoule	Res.Jäg.Btl.28
Fischer	Herbert	Jäger	18	8.1944	La Napoule	Res.Jäg.Btl.28
Glomb	Alfred	O Gren	24	8.1944	La Napoule	
Gübler?			18	8.1944	La Napoule	
Niergond	Anton		18	8.1944	La Napoule	
Seifert	Rudolf		35	8.1944	La Napoule	
Unknown				8.1944	La Napoule	
Unknown				8.1944	La Napoule	
Unknown				8.1944	La Napoule	
Unknown				8.1944	La Napoule	
Unknown				8.1944	La Napoule	
Unknown				8.1944	La Napoule	
Unknown				8.1944	La Napoule	
Unknown				8.1944	La Napoule	
Häusig	Karl	Uffz	28	22.8.1944	Mouans Sartoux	Stab.Res.Gren.Btl.327
Flögel	Alfred	Uffz	18	20.8.1944	St Cézaire	1./Res.Gren.Btl.7
Feldkamp	Klemens	Gren	17	22.8.1944	St Cézaire	1./Res.Gren.Btl.7
Matlok	Alois	Gren	33	22.8.1944	St Cézaire	1./Res.Gren.Btl.7
Stumpe	Helmut	Gren	17	22.8.1944	St Cézaire	2./Res.Gren.Btl.7
Himmel	Heinrich	Gren	18	22.8.1944	St Cézaire	Res.Gren.Btl.7?
Peukert	Fritz	Gren	18	22.8.1944	St Cézaire	Res.Gren.Btl.7?
Raschke	Gerhard	Gren	17	22.8.1944	St Cézaire	Res.Gren.Btl.7?
Unknown				22.8.1944	St Cézaire	Res.Gren.Btl.7?
Unknown				22.8.1944	St Cézaire	Res.Gren.Btl.7?
Kubitzky	Günter		18	23.8.1944	Cannes	
Medwed	Anton	Gren	17	23.8.1944	Cannes	
Novok	Eduard	Gren	17	23.8.1944	Cannes	9./Res.Gren.Btl.444
Unknown				23.8.1944	Cannes	
Knirsch	Franz	Uffz	36	23.8.1944	Nice Caucade	Res.Gren.Btl.444
Kuchenmeister	Max	Ogefr	22	23.8.1944	Cimiez	Kriegsmarine
Podbarschek	Franz	Sold	18	23.8.1944	Cimiez	2./Res.Pi.Btl.8
Szafranek	Richard	Jäger	18	23.8.1944	Cimiez	5./Res.Jäg.Btl.28
Münzel	Hermann	Wachtmeister	31	23.8.1944	Grasse	3./Flak.Abt.391
Krautschneider	Josef	Jäger	18	23.8.1944	Mougin	6./Res.Jäg.Btl.28
Siegert	Lothar	Jäger	18	23.8.1944	Mougin	Res.Jäg.Btl.28
Woznicka	Stefan	Jäger	17	23.8.1944	Mougin	5./Res.Jäg.Btl.28
Foitzik	Vincent	Ogefr	23	23.8.1944	Peymeinade	Flak
Rein	Josef	Gren	19	23.8.1944	Peymeinade	St Kp Btl 61?
Strunk	Johann	Ogefr	37	23.8.1944	Peymeinade	Hafenkapitän San Remo
Unknown				23.8.1944	Peymeinade	Flak
Unknown				23.8.1944	Peymeinade	
Fiedler	Hubert	Jäger	18	23.8.1944	Valbonne	8./Res.Jäg.Btl.28
Buffen	Lars			24.8.1944	Antibes	
Krapp	Willy			24.8.1944	Antibes	

Surname	Name	Rank	Age	Date of death	Location of burial	Unit
Kirchner	Hermann	Kan	36	24.8.1944	Biot	Art
Laske	Robert	Stbs Gefr	30	24.8.1944	Biot	Res.Art.Abt.44
Muschiol	Anton	Gren	29	24.8.1944	Cimiez	12./Res.Gren.Btl.444
Kadrmann	Karl	Gefr	33	24.8.1944	La Colle	8./Res.Gren.Btl.372
Prasch	Johann	Gefr	19	24.8.1944	Thorenc	3./Heeres.Pak.Abt.1038
Lesch	Helmut	Gren	17	24.8.1944	Valbonne	Inf.Pz.Jg.Ers.Kp.
Rauch	Hans	Sold	18	24.8.1944	Valbonne	
Chwaszczynski	Johann	Gren	17	25.8.1944	Gattières	
Rösch	Johann	Gren	18	25.8.1944	Gattières	2./Feld.Ers.Btl.148
Maizen	Vinzent	Gren	18	25.8.1944	La Colle	6./Res.Gren.Btl.372
Erhardt	Xaver	Gren	18	25.8.1944	La Roquette Var	9./Res.Gren.Btl.164
Schmidt	Johann	Gren	18	25.8.1944	La Roquette Var	10./Res.Gren.Btl.164
Nuntschitsch	Karl	Gren	17	26.8.1944	La Gaude	
Meyer	Johann	Gren	17	26.08.1944	Levens	9./Res.Gren.Btl.164
Kamussella	Richard		37	8.1944	Vence	
Wiesniewski	Alfons	Kan	34	26.8.1944	Vence	Art
Forberger	Otto	Gren	19	26.8.1944	Villeneuve	5./Res.Gren.Btl.372
Ficker	Franz	Ogefr	34	26.8.1944	Villeneuve	7./Res.Gren.Btl.372
Foks	Gerhard	Gren	17	26.8.1944	Villeneuve	7./Res.Gren.Btl.372
Gnielczyk	Franz	Gren	23	26.8.1944	Villeneuve	7./Res.Gren.Btl.372
Lössl	Josef	Gren	35	26.8.1944	Villeneuve	7./Res.Gren.Btl.372
Mertin	Otto	Gren	22	26.8.1944	Villeneuve	7./Res.Gren.Btl.372
Pilch	Hubert	Gren	17	26.8.1944	Villeneuve	7./Res.Gren.Btl.372
Krzyzowski	Josef	Gren	19	26.8.1944	Villeneuve	14./Inf.Pz.Jäg.Kp.239
Unknown				26.8.1944	Villeneuve	Res.Gren.Btl.372?
Unknown				26.8.1944	Villeneuve	Res.Gren.Btl.372?
Unknown				26.8.1944	Villeneuve	Res.Gren.Btl.372?
Unknown				26.8.1944	Villeneuve	Res.Gren.Btl.372?
Unknown				26.8.1944	Villeneuve	Res.Gren.Btl.372?
Unknown				26.8.1944	Villeneuve	Res.Gren.Btl.372?
Rotter	Gerhard	Ogefr	31	26.8.1944	Villeneuve Plage	5./Res.Gren.Btl.372
Swobodnik	Reinhard	Gren	18	27.8.1944	Castillon	7./Res.Gren.Btl.372
Reh Dr.	Fritz	Lt	34	27.8.1944	Cimiez	Heeres.Art.Abt.1191
Zipperer	Hermann	Gren	18	27.8.1944	Cimiez	1./Res.Gren.Btl.327
Granz	Gottfried	Gren	18	27.8.1944	St Antoine (Nice)	
Waber	Gustav	Uffz	32	27.8.1944	St Antoine (Nice)	8./Res.Gren.Btl.372
Zimonczyk	Victor	Gren	25	27.8.1944	St Antoine (Nice)	Res.Gren.Btl.372
Unknown				27.8.1944	St Laurent du Var	
Maier	Johann	Ogefr	21	28.8.1944	Belvédère	1./Hoch.Geb.Jäg.Btl.4
Bartsch	Max	Uffz	35	28.8.1944	Nice Caucade	Res.Gren.Rgt.239
Eickelmeier	Anton	Gefr	32	28.8.1944	Nice Caucade	
Gorinschek	Friedrich	Gren	17	28.8.1944	Nice Caucade	1./Feld.Ers.Btl.148.Res. Div.
Hansen	Wilhelm	Lt	30	28.8.1944	Nice Caucade	Flak

Surname	Name	Rank	Age	Date of death	Location of burial	Unit
Janas	Josef	Gren	37	28.8.1944	Nice Caucade	
Jank	Ulrich	Sold	20	28.8.1944	Nice Caucade	
Kreissl	Johann	Gefr	18	28.8.1944	Nice Caucade	
Krugls	Johann	Sold	24	28.8.1944	Nice Caucade	Pi.Btl.8?
Künz	Reinhold	Soldat	31	28.8.1944	Nice Caucade	
Oblak	Johann	Gren	17	28.8.1944	Nice Caucade	Res.Gren.Rgt.8
Piesiur	Johann	Sold	38	28.8.1944	Nice Caucade	
Rathje	Max	Kan	37	28.8.1944	Nice Caucade	2./Res.Art.Rgt.8
Rodoschek	Anton	Gren	18	28.8.1944	Nice Caucade	
Steinhäuser	Helmut	Pio	18	28.8.1944	Nice Caucade	3./Res.Pi.Btl.8
Tischlerei	Soldat			28.8.1944	Nice Caucade	
Tönissen	Richart	Kan	36	28.8.1944	Nice Caucade	2./Res.Art.Rgt.8
Unknown				28.8.1944	Nice Caucade	
Unknown				28.8.1944	Nice Caucade	
Unknown				28.8.1944	Nice Caucade	
Unknown				28.8.1944	Nice Caucade	
Unknown				28.8.1944	Nice Caucade	
Unknown				28.8.1944	Nice Caucade	
Zeichen	Jakob		18	28.8.1944	Drap	
Unknown				8.1944	La Roquette Var	
Mücke	Gottfried	Gefr	38	28.8.1944	La Roquette Var	9./Res.Gren.Btl.164
Seubert	Johann	Gren	18	28.8.1944	La Roquette Var	9./Res.Gren.Btl.164
Sputek	Leo	Gren	18	28.8.1944	La Roquette Var	9./Res.Gren.Btl.164
Fischer	Kaspar	Gren	18	28.8.1944	La Roquette Var	10./Res.Gren.Btl.164
Koffen	Günter	Gren	18	28.8.1944	La Roquette Var	Res.Gren.Btl.164?
Nordhof	Paul		17	28.8.1944	La Roquette Var	Res.Gren.Btl.164?
Rappold	Georg	Gren	18	28.8.1944	La Roquette Var	Res.Gren.Btl.164?
Unknown				28.8.1944	La Roquette Var	Res.Gren.Btl.164?
Unknown				28.8.1944	La Roquette Var	Res.Gren.Btl.164?
Unknown				28.8.1944	La Roquette Var	Res.Gren.Btl.164?
Unknown				28.8.1944	La Roquette Var	Res.Gren.Btl.164?
Cellary	Paul	Gren	35	28.8.1944	Levens	12./Res.Gren.Btl.164
Frank	Albert	Gren	18	28.8.1944	Levens	12./Res.Gren.Btl.164?
Kruschynski	Alois	Gren	19	28.8.1944	Levens	12./Res.Gren.Btl.164?
Stroba	Emil	Kan	18	28.8.1944	Menton	3./Res.Art.Rgt.8
Beyer	Michael	Uffz	33	28.8.1944	Menton	3./Heeres.Art.Abt.1196
Bromer	Anton	Gren	18	28.8.1944	Nice Cht Barla	
Stobbe	Franz	Gefr	33	28.8.1944	St Maurice (Nice)	
Unknown				28.8.1944	St Maurice (Nice)	
Unknown				28.8.1944	St Maurice (Nice)	
Unknown				29.8.1944	Eze	Heer
Herrmann	Franz	Gren	24	29.8.1944	Villefranche	1./Feld.Ers.Btl.148.Res. Div.
Grolik	Theodor	Gren	36	29.8.1944	Menton	4.Feld.Ers.Btl.148.Res. Div.

Surname	Name	Rank	Age	Date of death	Location of burial	Unit
Raab	Eduard	Gren	18	29.8.1944	Menton	3./Res.Gren.Btl.327
Schönberger	Adolf	Soldat	18	29.9.1944	Menton	3./Res.Pi.Btl.8
Rudat	Werner	Uffz	29	30.8.1944	Menton	9./Bäckerei.Kp.1048
Urbanski	Wilhelm	Fwb	29	30.8.1944	Menton	6./Res.Gren.Btl.372
Fiedler	Kurt	Ogefr	22	30.8.1944	Tourette Cht	Gren.Rgt.932
Mehlis	Franz	Funk	19	30.8.1944	Tourette Cht	
Scharberth	Werner	Gren	19	30.8.1944	Tourette Cht	Gren.Rgt.932
Schütte	Alfred	Sold	18	30.8.1944	Tourette Cht	Gren.Rgt.932
Stange	Werner	Kan	18	30.8.1944	Tourette Cht	SAEuAA 59
Hoffmann	Gerhard	Gren	17	31.8.1944	La Turbie	Res.Gren.Btl.7?
Weidlich	Herbert	Uffz	29	31.8.1944	La Turbie	1./Res.Gren.Btl.7
Wittig	Eberhard	Gren	17	31.8.1944	La Turbie	4./Res.Gren.Btl.7
Krotofil	Paul	Gren	18	31.8.1944	St Agnes	
Unknown				8.1944	Levens	
Sauermann	Hans	Uffz	25	1.9.1944	Lucéram	8./Res.Jäg.Btl.28
Gonsior	Alois	Gren	18	1.9.1944	Menton	1./Res.Gren.Btl.327
Kasprowitz	Heinrich	Gren	18	1.9.1944	St Agnes	
Witt	Josef	Gren	18	1.9.1944	St Agnes	
Fluder	Eduard	Gren	17	2.9.1944	Cap d'Ail	
Goletz	Stefan	Gren	23	2.9.1944	Cap d'Ail	Res.Inf.Pz.Jäg.Kp.Reg.8
Paulsteiner	Xaver	Ogefr	23	2.9.1944	Isola	Geb.Jäg.Rgt.100
Linert	Berthold	Gren	36	2.9.1944	Lucéram	
Grohmann	Ottokar	Gren	18	2.9.1944	Roquebrune	
Czarnowski	Waldemar	Gren	23	2.9.1944	Sospel	
Walz	Josef	Jäger	17	4.9.1944	Lucéram	Res.Jäg.Btl.28
Czora	Gerhard	Jäger	17	5.9.1944	US Draguignan	Res.Jäg.Btl.28
Schleicher	Josef	Pio	18	5.9.1944	Drag. (Ventimiglia)	
Gallitzschke	Erich		35	5.9.1944	Lucéram	
Gutmann	Wilhelm	Gren	18	5.9.1944	Lucéram	7./Res.Gren.Btl.372
Marciniak	Josef	Jäger	18	5.9.1944	Lucéram	
Meider	Ernst	Pio	18	5.9.1944	Menton	
Eckmeier	Josef	Gren	19	5.9.1944	Roquebrune	3./Div.Füs.Btl.148
Hahn	Johann		18	5.9.1944	Roquebrune?	
Tomanek	Rudolf	Jäger	27	6.9.1944	Drag. (Col de Braus)	
Sliwiek	Robert	Gefr	18	6.9.1944	Drag. (Vic. Nice)	
Gruber	Georg	Pio	18	6.9.1944	Lucéram	Res.Pi.Btl.8?
Locateli	Bastian			6.6.1944?	Lucéram	
Schönle	Walter	Pio	18	6.9.1944	Lucéram	3./Res.Pi.Btl.8
Unknown					Lucéram	
Schiche	Walter	Ogefr	33	6.9.1944	Sospel	
Glowania	Roman	Kan	20	7.9.1944	Breil	2./Res.Art.Abt.8
Bock	Karl	Jäger	36	7.9.1944	US Draguignan	Res.Jäg.Btl.28
Winkler	Richard	Jäger	34	7.9.1944	Lucéram	
Hau	Richard	Schütz	18	7.9.1944	Lucéram	

Surname	Name	Rank	Age	Date of death	Location of burial	Unit
Tieman	Theodor	Uffz	32	8.9.1944	Breil	2./Res.Pi.Btl.8
Borys	Karl	Jäger	17	8.9.1944	Breil	
Liboschik	Karl	Hptfwb	30	8.9.1944	Sospel	8./Res.Jäg.Btl.28
Renner	Alfred	Gren	18	8.9.1944	Sospel	
Novak	Franz		18	8.9.1944	St Agnes	
Malek	Georg	Uffz	25	9.9.1944	Belvédère	7./Inf.Rgt.525
Loy	Josef	Jäger	35	9.9.1944	Breil	13./Res.Gren.Rgt.8
Krossmeyer	Walter	Jäger	18	9.9.1944	Breil	
Melzer	Franz	Jäger	18	9.9.1944	Drag. (Col de Braus)	
Lorenz	Alois	Gren	17	9.9.1944	Lucéram	
Walfest?	Willi			9.9.1944	Menton	
Tasler	Josef	Gren	17	9.9.1944	Menton	
Adler	Josef	Uffz	31	9.9.1944	Menton	
Deubel	Rudolf	Uffz	24	9.9.1944	Menton	
Mientus	Konrad	Wachtmeister	28	9.9.1944	Menton	
Wolf	Franz	Stbfwb	43	9.9.1944	Sospel	3./Füs.Btl.148
Wittwer	Berhard	Fwb	30	9.9.1944	Sospel	2./Res.Art.Rgt.8
Täufer	Georg	Ogefr	20	9.9.1944	Sospel	
Maly	Friedrich	Uffz	36	9.9.1944	Sospel	6./Res.Gren.Btl.372
Rogalski	Edmund	Gren	17	9.9.1944	Sospel	
Ziermann	Johann	Pio	17	9.9.1944	Sospel	
Faltermeier	Ludwig	Gren	17	9.9.1944	Sospel	
Leber	Alois	Gren	18	9.9.1944	Sospel	
Kulawik	Erich	Gren	17	9.9.1944	Sospel	
Adamiec	Gustav	Gren	18	9.9.1944	Sospel	
Gross	Johann	Gren	18	9.9.1944	Sospel	
Hartenfels	Stephan	Kan	19	10.9.1944	Breil	3./Heeres.Art.Abt.1197
Meier	Alfons	Ogref	36	10.9.1944	Moulinet	
Altmeyer	Martin	Gefr	21	10.9.1944	Sospel	Stab.I.Gren.Rgt.8
Gryschnik	Vinzenz	Füs	18	10.9.1944	Sospel	3./Füs.Btl.148
Ginczek	Joseph	Ogefr	38	10.9.1944	(Nice)	
Krzonkalla	Siegfried	Pio	17	11.9.1944	Breil	Pi.Kp.Res.Gren.Rgt.239
Schaustin	Alfons	Gefr	33	11.9.1944	Castellar	I.E.B. 80
Preuss	Werner	Ogefr	22	11.9.1944	Drag. (Ventimiglia)	
Schindler	Friedrich	Gren	19	11.9.1944	Drag. (Sospel)	
Ring	Johann	Gren	18	11.9.1944	Sospel	1./Res.Gren.Btl.7
Mesch	Ludwig	Gren	18	11.9.1944	Sospel	1./Res.Gren.Btl.7
Blasius	Karl	Gren	17	11.9.1944	Sospel	1./Res.Gren.Btl.7
Ulrich	Bruno	Ogefr	31	11.9.1944	Sospel	
Tenschert	Alois	Gefr	17	11.9.1944	Sospel	
Spick	Alois	Gren	18	11.9.1944	Sospel	
Iblitz	Willi	Uffz	30	12.9.1944	Breil	7./Gren.Rgt.80
Gottwald	Paul	Ogref	30	12.9.1944	Breil	3./Res.Gren.Btl.7
Schweizer	Heinz	Fwb	31	12.9.1944	Breil	4./Gren.Rgt.80

Surname	Name	Rank	Age	Date of death	Location of burial	Unit
Strobel	Enno	Gren	19	12.9.1944	Drag. (Scandeious)	3./Res.Gren.Btl.7
Kau	Josef	Gefr	18	12.9.1944	Drag. (Sospel)	
Seebacher	Georg	Ogefr	42	12.9.1944	Drag. (Sospel)	
Starosta	Berhard		18	12.9.1944	Menton	
Kreutzer	Alfons	Gren	21	12.9.1944	Sospel	3./Gren.Rgt.80
Schulz	Josef	Ogefr	30	12.9.1944	Sospel	
Hanel	Karl	Gren	18	12.9.1944	Sospel	2./Res.Gren.Btl.7
Radwainski	Peter	Gren	18	12.9.1944	Sospel	
Rüggeberg	Walter	Gefr	33	12.9.1944	Sospel	
Juraske	Heinrich	Ogefr	32	12.9.1944	Sospel	2./Res.Art.Rgt.8
Mooser	Karl	Gren	18	12.9.1944	Sospel	2./Gren.Rgt.Schlesien
Pieper	Ferdinant	Ogefr	23	12.9.1944	Sospel	
Raabe	Alfred	Ogefr	36	12.9.1944	Sospel	
Lukassek	Robert		18	12.9.1944	Sospel	
Bahrmann	Carl	Gefr	20	12.9.1944	Sospel	
Grossberger	Richard	Gefr	18	12.9.1944	Sospel	
Stellmach	Rudolf	Gren	17	12.9.1944	Sospel	
Jakubek	Gerhard	Gren	18	12.9.1944	Sospel	
Kowatschetz	Johann	Gren	17	12.9.1944	Sospel	
Müller	Albert	Uffz	25	13.9.1944	Breil	6./Gren.Rgt.80
Franke	Ernst	Ogefr	44	13.9.1944	Breil	4./Res.Btl.I 183?
Zogota	Josef	Gefr	20	13.9.1944	Breil	7./Gren.Rgt.80
Sistig	Alfons	Uffz	24	13.9.1944	Sospel	2./Gren.Rgt.80
Lubetzki	Viktor	Jäger	18	13.9.1944	Sospel	
Sippl	Johann	Gren	18	13.9.1944	Sospel	
Timte	Josef	Uffz	23	14.9.1944	Breil	14./Gren.Rgt.80
Heismann	Adam	Fwb	27	14.9.1944	Breil	8./Gren.Rgt.80
Heger	Alois	Gren	17	14.9.1944	US Draguignan	
Zimmermann	Kurt	Gren	17	14.9.1944	Sospel	1./Res.Gren.Btl.7
Musil	Georg	Gren	34	14.9.1944	Sospel	
Rzehak	Adolf	Gren	36	14.9.1944	Sospel	
Seifer	Hubert	Ofwb	30	15.9.1944	Breil	2./San.Kp.34
Back	Bertold	Ogefr	23	15.9.1944	Castillon	
Laux	Bernhard	Stfwb	37	15.9.1944	US Draguignan	
Kueter	Franz		34	15.9.1944	Moulinet	
Kruse	Georg	Owachtmst	29	16.9.1944	Sospel	
Pewetz	Franz	Gren	18	16.9.1944	Sospel	
Sievert	Paul	Ogefr	21	16.9.1944	Sospel	
Mederer	Michael	Pio	18	17.9.1944	Breil	3./Res.Pi.Btl.8
Petry	Karl	Fwb	30	17.9.1944	Breil	7./Gren.Rgt.80
Schu	Mathias	Uffz	29	17.9.1944	Breil	3./Gren.Rgt.107
Schneider	Josef	Gefr	32	17.9.1944	Moulinet	2./Res.Pi.Btl.8
Klesen	Herbert	Gefr	19	17.9.1944	Sospel	1./Gren.Rgt.107
Bettner	Ernst	Uffz	30	17.9.1944	Sospel	1./Gren.Rgt.107

Surname	Name	Rank	Age	Date of death	Location of burial	Unit
Riedel	Wilhelm		26	17.9.1944	Sospel	
Altrichter	Mathias	Jäger	18	17.9.1944	Sospel	6./Res.Jäg.Btl.28
Mzyk	Konrad	Jäger	18	17.9.1944	Sospel	6./Res.Jäg.Btl.28
Kreher	Franz	Ogefr	24	18.9.1944	Breil	14./Gren.Rgt.80
Ziegler	Hans Ulrich	Uffz	20	18.9.1944	Sospel	1./Gren.Rgt.107
Schon	Ernst	Schütze	20	18.9.1944	Sospel	1./Gren.Rgt.107
Von Appen	Wilhelm	Uffz	23	18.9.1944	Sospel	2./Gren.Rgt.107
Schäfer	Anton	Gefr	23	18.9.1944	Sospel	2./Gren.Rgt.107
Reineke	Theodor	Uffz	30	18.9.1944	Sospel	8./Gren.Rgt.107
Weber	August	Gefr	37	18.9.1944	Sospel	8./Gren.Rgt.107
Jertz	Philipp	Ogefr	35	18.9.1944	Sospel	2./Gren.Rgt.107
Ringbeck	Anton	Ogefr	23	19.9.1944	Breil	5./Gren.Rgt.107
Birtel	Theodor	Gren	32	19.9.1944	Breil	14./Gren.Rgt.80
Junk?				19.9.1944?	Sospel	
Ritz	Peter	Ogren	20	19.9.1944	Sospel	1./Gren.Regt.80
Borst	Werner	Stgefr	27	20.9.1944	Breil	Stab. II.Gren.Rgt.80
Herbst	Gerhard	Ogefr	36	20.9.1944	Breil	1./Pi.Btl.34
Tretter	Jakob	Gefr	35	20.9.1944	Breil	1./Pi.Btl.34
Juchemich	Edwin	Fwb	27	20.9.1944	Breil	1./Pi.Btl.34
Hohn	Gottfried	Uffz	38	20.9.1944	Breil	1./Pi.Btl.34
Irmer	Friedrich	Gefr	20	20.9.1944	Breil	1./Pi.Btl.34
Kubiak	Edmund	Füs	17	20.9.1944	Sospel	2./Füs.Btl.148
Wenke	Friedrich	Füs	18	20.9.1944	Sospel	3./Füs.Btl.148
Wlotzka	Josef	Füs	17	20.9.1944	Sospel	3./Füs.Btl.148
Nowak	Josef	Füs	18	20.9.1944	Sospel	2./Füs.Btl.148
Wurzer	Michael	Füs	18	20.9.1944	Sospel	2./Füs.Btl.148
Richter	Franz	Ogefr	32	20.9.1944	Sospel	
Kächele	Georg	Ogefr	24	21.9.1944	Breil	7./Gren.Rgt.80
Becking	Herbert	Gefr	22	21.9.1944	Breil	7./Gren.Rgt.80
Garbunow	Agathi	Hilfsw	17	21.9.1944	Breil	7./Gren.Rgt.80
Litko	Miklos	Hiwi	43	21.9.1944	Breil	2./Gren.Rgt.107
Walter	Heinrich	Ogefr	23	22.9.1944	Breil	Stab.Bat.Art.Rgt.34
Klust	Martin	Fwb	22	22.9.1944	Breil	5./Gren.Rgt.107
Wild	Fritz	Ogefr	33	22.9.1944	Breil	St.Kp.Gren.Rgt.107
Schmitt	Nikolaus	Stgefr	27	22.9.1944	Breil	St.Kp.Gren.Rgt.107
Fischer	Karl Heinz	Gefr	21	22.9.1944	Breil	St.Kp.Gren.Rgt.107
Schleyer	Walter	Lt	23	22.9.1944	Breil	St.Kp.Gren.Rgt.107
Bohlig	Johann	Gren	19	22.9.1944	Sospel	
Wallach	Erich	Gren	18	23.9.1944	Sospel	
Kukowetz	Lorenz	Gren	25	23.9.1944	Sospel	3./Res.Gren.Btl.7
Becker	Alphons	Ogefr	34	24.9.1944	Breil	8./Gren.Rgt.80
Gerhards	Johann	Gefr	35	24.9.1944	Breil	2./Gren.Rgt.80
Grones	Albert	Stgefr	25	24.9.1944	Breil	6./Gren.Rgt.80
Benesch	Karl	Gren	17	24.9.1944	Sospel	

Surname	Name	Rank	Age	Date of death	Location of burial	Unit
Mayer	Johann	Gren	20	25.9.1944	Sospel	
Wolf	Hermann	Uffz	25	28.9.1944	Breil	Stab.Bat.Art.Rgt.34
Stoecker	Karl	Fwb	31	29.9.1944	Breil	10./Fest.St.Abt.AOK19
Bogisch	Arnold	Gren	18	29.9.1944	Breil	3./Gren.Rgt.80
Herrmann	Horst		21	9.1944?	Sospel	
Pawlik	Bernhard	Sold	33	9.1944?	Sospel	
Unknown				9.1944?	Sospel	
Unknown				9.1944?	Sospel	
Unknown				9.1944?	Sospel	
Ernst	Friedrich			9.1944?	Sospel	
Unknown				9.1944?	Sospel	
Barucha	Konrad		18	9.1944?	Sospel	
Undetermined					Sospel	
Undetermined					Sospel	
Undetermined					Sospel	
Unknown					St Agnes	
Unknown					St Agnes	
Hildebrand	Gerhard	Ogefr	21	2.10.1944	Breil	2./Gren.Rgt.80
Rieck	Georg	Fwb	27	2.10.1944	Breil	7./Gren.Rgt.107
Janostik	Martin	Uffz	32	2.10.1944	Breil	7./Gren.Rgt.107
Jantzen	Hans	Gefr	20	2.10.1944	Breil	7./Gren.Rgt.107
Wallach	Stefan	Jäger	18	2.10.1944?	Drag. (Col de Braus)	
Geilker	Herbert	Lt	22	5.10.1944	St Etienne Tinée	
Jürs	Hermann	Olt	34	7.10.1944	Breil	5./Gren.Rgt.107
Fischer	Heinrich	Ogefr	36	12.10.1944	Breil	1./Gren.Regt.80
Wehmann	Johann	Gefr	36	13.10.1944	Breil	8./Gren.Rgt.107
Mund	Kurt	Ofwb	28	13.10.1944	Breil	1./Pz.Jäg.Abt.34
Heftrich	Rudolf	Uffz	20	18.10.1944	Breil	2./Gren.Rgt.107
Wester	Andreas	Gefr	19	19.10.1944	Breil	L/FEB 34 ?
Weinand	Richard	Ogefr	24	19.10.1944	Castillon	
Hofmann	Friedrich	Lt	30	19.10.1944	Castillon	
Bersch	Phillip	Ogefr	27	19.10.1944	Castillon	2./Feldausbildungs-Btl.34
Schuh	Nikolaus	Ogefr	31	19.10.1944	Castillon	Feldausbildungs-Btl.34
Deutsch	Herbert	Gren	18	21.10.1944	Breil	1./Gren.Regt.80
Schmid	Eugen	Ogefr	32	22.10.1944	Breil	14./Gren.Rgt.107
Kötter	Alfred	Ogefr	35	22.10.1944	Sospel	
Stadler	Anton	Gefr	21	23.10.1944	Breil	3./Gren.Rgt.80
Fett	Erwin	Ogefr	21	23.10.1944	Breil	3./Gren.Rgt.80
Müller	Ludwig	Uffz	21	23.10.1944	Breil	3./Gren.Rgt.80
Wilhelm	August	Ogefr	32	23.10.1944	Breil	3./Gren.Rgt.80
Morgenschweiss	Arthur	Stgefr	27	23.10.1944	Breil	3./Gren.Rgt.80
Johannes	Josef	Uffz	31	23.10.1944	Breil	3./Gren.Rgt.80
Kraus	Paul	Uffz	33	23.10.1944	Breil	3./Gren.Rgt.80

Surname	Name	Rank	Age	Date of death	Location of burial	Unit
Beinhauer	Gustav	Gefr	20	23.10.1944	US Draguignan	
Spitzl	Hermann	Gefr	19	24.10.1944	Breil	3./Gren.Rgt.80
Wohlbold	Paul	Ogefr	19	24.10.1944	Breil	3./Gren.Rgt.80
Träger	Josef	Stgefr	36	25.10.1944	Breil	Feldzeug Kp.34
Kuesters	Aloys	Uffz	19	25.10.1944	Breil	3./Gren.Rgt.80
Vogl	Johann	Gefr	19	26.10.1944	Breil	2./Gren.Rgt.80
Bohndorf	Wilhelm	Uffz	28	27.10.1944	Moulinet	
Bessel	Karl				Castellar	
Klinnert	Wilhelm	Ojäg	30	10.1944	Sospel	
Unknown				9-10.1944?	Sospel	
Unknown				9-10.1944?	Sospel	
Unknown				9-10.1944?	Sospel	Heeres.Art.Abt.1196
Unknown				9-10.1944?	Sospel	
Probst	Hermann	Ogefr	34	10.1944	Sospel	
Frassek	Wolf-Dieter	Sold	17	9-10.1944	Sospel	
Engert	Emil	Pio	18	10.1944	US Draguignan	
Riehl	Erich	Gefr	36	1.11.1944	St Dalmas	6./Gren.Rgt.107
Gratzer	Hermann	Gefr	20	8.11.1944	St Dalmas	GAR 95?
Duismann	Adolf	Uffz	22	8.11.1944	St Dalmas	6./Gren.Rgt.107
Heppelmann	Theodor	Ogefr	36	8.11.1944	St Dalmas	6./Gren.Rgt.107
Zilske	Karl	Gefr	21	10.11.1944	US Draguignan	5./Gren.Rgt.253
Brüggemann	Wilhelm	Gefr	20	13.11.1944	Sospel	
Kloep	Matthias	Gefr	19	16.11.1944	St Dalmas	6./Gren.Rgt.107
Ihben	Meino	Gefr	20	16.11.1944	St Dalmas	6./Gren.Rgt.107
Werling	Willi	Olt	24	20.11.1944	St Dalmas	8./Gren.Rgt.107?
Awater	Rudolf	Matrose	19	29.11.1944	Nice Caucade	KM?
Reuther	Helmuth	Gefr	38	29.11.1944	St Dalmas	Gren.Rgt.107
Becker	Wilhelm	Fwb	30	30.11.1944	St Dalmas	V Feldin?
Ochs	Hans	Ogefr	21	7.12.1944	St Dalmas	2/H.A.A.(mot)45I?
Nosick	Nikolei		20	9.12.1944	St Dalmas	8./Gren.Rgt.107
Fimpler	Heinz	Matrose	18	10.12.1944	Cannes sea	10 M.A.S.
Wiegelmann	Jakob	Ogefr	25	19.1.1945	St Dalmas	14./Gren.Rgt.107
Möller	Konstantin	Ogefr	22	28.1.1945	St Dalmas	9./Gren.Rgt.107
Hulle	Herbert	Gefr	20	29.1.1945	St Dalmas	9./Gren.Rgt.107
Meyer	Joseph		31	6.2.1945	MIA Breil	
Pietsch	Max	Ogefr	22	6.2.1945	Cannes	Kriegsmarine?
Köhler	Wilhelm	Olt	26	7.2.1945	St Dalmas	
Voigt	Alfred	Ogefr	37	9.2.1945	St Dalmas	1./Gren.Rgt.107
Schmidt	Oswald	Stbs Int	46	14.2.1945	St Dalmas	III/AR 2 Littorio
Strübing	Karl	Ogefr	35	2.3.1945	St Dalmas	2./Gren.Rgt.107
Rodenstein	Helmut	Ogefr	23	4.3.1945	Cannes	Kriegsmarine
Schadde	Wilhelm	Hptgefr	36	4.3.1945	Cannes	Kriegsmarine?
Wolf	Konrad	Stgefr	33	4.3.1945	St Dalmas	Stab.Gren.Rgt.107
Pfaffmann	Friedrich	Olt	27	10.3.1945	St Dalmas	6./Gren.Rgt.107

Surname	Name	Rank	Age	Date of death	Location of burial	Unit
Neumann	Georg	Gefr	29	15.3.1945	St Dalmas	St.Kp.Gren.Rgt.107
Sarnes	Oskar	Maat	25	18.3.1945	Cannes	Kriegsmarine ?
Rensch	Walter	Ogefr	20	24.3.1945	St Dalmas	DUK 18?
Ketterer	Max	Gefr	35/36	3.1945	Moulinet	
Winkler	Adolf	Sold	25	1.4.1945	St Dalmas	1./Gren.Rgt.107
Klump	Kurt		22	2.4.1945	Beaulieu	Kriegsmarine
Fuckner	Alfred	Ogefr	26	5.4.1945	St Dalmas	8./Gren.Rgt.107
Daub	Leopold	Gefr	37	5.4.1945	St Dalmas	8./Gren.Rgt.107
Schilling	Georg	Gefr	38	5.4.1945	St Dalmas	8./Gren.Rgt.107
Palm	Alfred	Ogefr	31	5.4.1945	St Dalmas	8./Gren.Rgt.107
Unknown				6.4.1945	Sospel	
Hüpschle	Konrad		25	9.4.1945	St Dalmas	
Burbach	Karl	Ogefr	31	10.4.1945	St Dalmas	
Haffner	Ludwig	Lt	24	10.4.1945	St Dalmas	4./Gren.Rgt.107
Hinn	Josef	Ogefr	24	11.4.1945	Moulinet	
Reisbitzer	Wilhelm	Gefr	32	11.4.1945	Moulinet	
Mitsch	Josef	Ogefr	25	11.4.1945	St Dalmas	
Titz	Erich	Ogefr	21	13.4.1945	St Dalmas	
Bürger	Georg	Gefr	29	15.4.1945	St Dalmas	
Bauer	Philipp	Ogefr	24	17.4.1945	Saorge	
Krüger	Günther	Gren	17	17.4.1945	Saorge	
Brümmer	Werner	Schütz	21	17.4.1945	Saorge	
Seib	Peter	Gefr	21	17.4.1945	Saorge	
Wittorf	Hans	Uffz	33	17.4.1945	St Dalmas	
Boden	Lorenz	Ogefr	29	17.4.1945	St Dalmas	14./Gren.Rgt.107
Hammer	Wolfgang	Ogefr	37	18.4.1945	Fontan	
Gwizdala	Johann	Ogefr	28	18.4.1945	Fontan	1./Gren.Rgt.107
Rumpelsberger	Johann	Gefr	25	19.4.1945		
Perego?	A.		23	20.4.1945?	Cannes	Kriegsmarine
Schramm	Kurt	Uffz	32	20.4.1945	St Dalmas	2./Gren.Rgt.107
Czieselsky	Günter	Gefr	21	20.4.1945	St Dalmas	2./Gren.Rgt.107
Blumm/Biova	Edgar	Olt		20.4.1945?	St Dalmas	
Roschkar	Johann	Gefr	23	20.4.1945	St Dalmas	2./Gren.Rgt.107
Ertel	Martin	Gefr	25	20.4.1945	St Dalmas	
Krämer	Karl	Ogefr	32	20.4.1945	St Dalmas	
Frank	Matthias	Uffz	23	20.4.1945	St Dalmas	2./Gren.Rgt.107
Menton	Ernst	Gefr	39	20.4.1945	St Dalmas	2./Gren.Rgt.107
Eiden	Ernst		20	20.4.1945	St Dalmas	4./Gren.Rgt.107
Gimnich	Hermann	Gefr	34	20.4.1945	St Dalmas	4./Gren.Rgt.107
Köppe	Herbert	Ogefr	21	4.1945	Moulinet	
Hoffmann	Otto		19	4.1945	Moulinet	
Bredlow	Herbert	Jäger	17	4.1945	Saorge	2Kp III J.E.B.34
Unknown				4.1945?	Saorge	
Unknown				4.1945?	Saorge	

Surname	Name	Rank	Age	Date of death	Location of burial	Unit
Braun	Herbert		18	4.1945	Saorge	
Unknown	Fwb			4.1945	Sospel	
Massarczyk	Erich	Gren	21	4.1945		
Stürze	Rudolf	Gefr	18	5.1945	Cagnes	Kriegsmarine
Unknown					Belvédère	
Unknown					Biot	
Richter					Menton	
Unknown					Menton	
Unknown					Menton	
Unknown					Menton	
Unknown					Menton	
Unknown					Menton	
Unknown					Moulinet	
Unknown					Moulinet	GJ
Czerner	Viktor	Gefr	21		Moulinet	
Unknown					Moulinet	
Unknown					Moulinet	
Unknown					Moulinet	
Unknown					Moulinet	
Unknown					Sospel	
Unknown					Sospel	
Unknown					Sospel	
Unknown					Sospel	
Unknown					Sospel	
Unknown					Sospel	
Undetermined					St Dalmas	
Jager?	Herbert				St Jean Cap Ferrat	Kriegsmarine
Unknown					St Martin Vésubie	
Unknown					Valdeblore	
Unknown					Valdeblore	
Jolowiscki	Heinrich		17	1.9.1944	Cannes	POW?
Wahl		OT-Man		14.9.1944	Cannes	POW?
Unknown				b.16.9.1944	Cannes	POW?
Unknown				30.9.1944	Mougins	
Warzecha	Georg	Soldat	18	12.10.1944	Nice Caucade	POW
Eichhorn	Karl	Gefr	36	13.10.1944	Nice Est	POW?
Schütz	Arnold	Arbeitsmann	18	17.10.1944	Nice Est	POW?
Schalinski	Hans	Hilfszollass	48	8.11.1944	Nice Caucade	POW
Klein	Robert	Ogefr	38	17.11.1944	Nice Caucade	POW
Iser	Johann	Hilfszollass	42	19.11.1944	Nice Caucade	POW
Böhm	Wilhelm	Hilfszollbetriebassistent	45	20.11.1944	Nice Caucade	POW 338 055
Rössler	Philipp	Arbeitsman	17	24.11.1944	Nice Caucade	POW
Schrezenmeier	Josef	Ogefr	39	24.11.1944	Nice Caucade	POW
Totzke	Walter	Zollass	40	26.11.1944	Nice Caucade	POW

Surname	Name	Rank	Age	Date of death	Location of burial	Unit
Rothe	Paul	Zollass	48	4.12.1944	Nice Caucade	POW
Döhmann	Heinz	Gefr	18	6.12.1944	Nice Caucade	POW
Michels	Hermann	Arbeitsman	18	14.12.1944	Antibes	POW?
Beyer	Herbert	Gefr	20	14.12.1944	Antibes	POW?
Gruhl	Gerhardt	Uffz	30	18.12.1944	Cagnes	POW
Höhl	Alfred	AM	18	18.12.1944	Cagnes	POW
Jegodtka	Hans	Gefr	20	18.12.1944	Cagnes	POW
Merle	Heinrich	Gren	18	18.12.1944	Cagnes	POW
Friebertshäuser	Hans	HVM	19	18.12.1944	Cagnes	POW
Bittner	Leo	Uffz	36	20.12.1944	Cannes	POW
Haase	Alfons	Arbeitsman	18	22.12.1944	Antibes	POW
Kotte	Rudolf	Untertruppfü	18	22.12.1944	Antibes	POW
Schunack	Walter	Hilfszollass	43	24.12.1944	Nice Caucade	POW
Theobald	Lothar	Arbeitsman	18	25.12.1944	Nice Caucade	POW
Sippel	Heinrich	Arbeitsman	18	28.12.1944	Nice Caucade	POW
Heuer	Bernhard	Hilfszollass	40	28.12.1944	Nice Caucade	POW
Dach	Hans	Arbeitsman	18	3.1.1945	Nice Caucade	POW
Böttcher	Joachim	Ogefr	18	6.1.1945	Antibes	POW
Metzler	Georg	Hilfzollass	49	11.1.1945	Antibes	POW
Bäumer	Engelbert	Matrose	18	12.1.1945	Nice Caucade	POW
Mühlbauer	Franz	Hilfzollass	43	24.1.1945	Antibes	POW
Rehbein	Walter	Stabsgefr	30	24.1.1945	Nice Caucade	POW
Schiedler	Albert	Hilfszollass	48	31.1.1945	Nice Caucade	POW
Zinn	Hugo	Soldat	18	1.2.1945	Antibes	POW
Heinrichs	Richard	Hilfszollass	46	5.2.1945	Nice Caucade	POW
Behm	Johannes	Ogefr	25	5.2.1945	Nice Caucade	POW
Husen	Willy	Zollass	40	29.12.1944/6.2.1945	Nice Caucade	POW 338 442
Benediex	Erich	Obervorman	19	6.2.1945	Nice Caucade	POW
Kurth	Alfred	Ogefr	31	12.2.1945	Nice Caucade	POW
Schönrock	Siegfried	Matrose	19	12.2.1945	Nice Caucade	POW
Thies	August	Gefr	39	14.2.1945	Nice Caucade	POW
Bienert	Georg	Ogefr	43	14.2.1945	Nice Caucade	POW
Lehnert	Gotthard	Gefr	54	16.2.1945	Nice Caucade	POW
Baumann	Johann	Hauptzollass	40	17.2.1945	Nice Caucade	POW
Edlfurtner	Josef	Gefr	41	18.2.1945	Nice Caucade	POW
Felten	Johann	Ogefr	42	21.2.1945	Nice Caucade	POW
Papenfuß	Franz	Gefr	37	21.2.1945	Nice Caucade	POW
Peters	Heinz	Gefr	22	24.2.1945	Nice Caucade	POW
Nakel	Heinrich	Matrose	46	24.2.1945	Nice Caucade	POW
Nirschl	Michael	Ogefr	43	27.2.1945	Nice Caucade	POW
Herzberg	Karl	Gefr	38	27.2.1945	Nice Caucade	POW
Krieger	Konrad	Gefr	37	1.3.1945	Nice Caucade	POW
Wipper	Franz	Ogefr	38	3.3.1945	Nice Caucade	POW
Freitag	Wilhelm	Ogefr	35	6.3.1945	Nice Caucade	POW

Surname	Name	Rank	Age	Date of death	Location of burial	Unit
Hein	Reinhold	Arbeitsman	19	12.3.1945	Cannes	POW?
Wahl	Heinz	Artillerist	21	12.3.1945	Cannes	POW?
Jordan	Heinz	Gefr	19	20.3.1945	Cannes	POW?
Schäfer	Heinz	Ogefr	20	20.3.1945	Cannes	POW?
Häupel	Josef	Hilfszollsekretär	43	30.3.1945	Nice Caucade	POW
Schmidt	Walter		35	15.4.1945	Beaulieu	POW
Affeldt	Alfons	Gefr	19	16.4.1945	Cannes	POW?
Leistikow	Günter	Ogren	18	16.4.1945	Cannes	POW?
Rostkovius	Karl	Kan	21	16.4.1945	Cannes	POW?
Hansen	Heinz	Arbeitsman	18	16.4.1945	Cannes	POW?
Hollweg	Karl	Uffz	31	17.4.1945	Nice Caucade	POW
Reckholder	Wilhelm	Gefr	22	20.4.1945	Antibes	POW?
Hechelsberger	Theo	Ogefr	21	24.4.1945	Antibes	POW
Combecher	Conrad	Hilfszollass	50	24.4.1945	Nice Caucade	POW
Götzke	Paul	Hilfszollass	48	28.4.1945	Nice Caucade	POW
Arndt	Helmuth	Gefr	20	1.5.1945	Nice Caucade	POW
Lenz	Walter	Lt	23	8.5.1945	Nice Caucade	POW
Thiemann	Heinrich	Ogefr	36	13.5.1945	Nice Caucade	POW
Streckfuss	Karl	Arbeitsman	19	23.5.1945	Antibes	POW
Gaiser	Robert	Ogefr	20	23.5.1945	Antibes	POW
Reimann	Franz	Gefr	22	23.5.1945	Cannes	POW
Frischbier	Leo	Arbeitsmann		24.5.1945	Monaco	POW
Polutta	Josef	Gren	19	30.5.1945	Nice Caucade	POW
Gliemroth	Erich	Arbeitsman	18	4.6.1945	Menton	POW
Neumann	Lothar	Uffz	44	7.6.1945	Nice Caucade	POW
Krumm	Helmut	Arbeitsmann	19	12.6.1945	Nice Caucade	POW
Schwarze	Anton	Vormann	18	14.6.1945	Menton	POW
Berthold	Andreas	Uffz	27	15.6.1945	Breil	POW Flak Abt.3/355
Pfeiffer	Hans	Gren	18	15.6.1945	Menton	POW
Scholz	Adolf	Ogefr	32	17.6.1945	Antibes	POW
Walter	Franz	Soldat	35	17.6.1945	Nice Caucade	POW
Brunke	Heinz	Gefr	24	19.6.1945	Cannes	POW
Dreissig	Friedrich	Uffz	30	22.6.1945	Menton	POW
Rauckmann	Friedrich	Ogefr	22	24.6.1945	Nice Caucade	POW
Bisslich	Gerhard	Uffz	46	26.6.1945	Nice Caucade	POW
Daniel	Wedelin	Soldat	41	27.6.1945	Nice Caucade	POW
Weber	Karl	Hilfszollass	42	27.6.1945	Nice Caucade	POW
Ahrens	Werner	Obermat	24	6.1945	Menton	
Clorius	Georg	Uffz	40	1.7.1945	Nice Caucade	POW
Vogg	Josef	Schütze	39	1.7.1945	Nice Caucade	POW
Grauduschus	Kurt	Gefr	22	4.7.1945	Antibes	POW
Odehnal	Kurt	Gefr	19	7.7.1945	Antibes	POW
Niendorf	Otto	Gefr	26	12.7.1945	Nice Caucade	POW
Kunert	Gerhard	Gefr	20	18.7.1945	Valdeblore	POW

Surname	Name	Rank	Age	Date of death	Location of burial	Unit
Quenzer	August	Gefr	45	20.7.1945	Nice Caucade	POW
Muus	Hans	Uffz	22	22.7.1945	Nice Caucade	POW
Fluche	Bernhard	Gefr	41	25.7.1945	Menton	POW
Nohr	Rudolf	Gren	32	27.7.1945	Antibes	POW
Kowalke	Heinz	Gefr	35	30.7.1945	Antibes	POW
Biehl	Heinrich	Ogefr	21	30.7.1945	Antibes	POW
Kellerer	Josef	Gefr	30	30.7.1945	Antibes	POW
Kirsch	Rolf	Gren	18	31.7.1945	Antibes	POW
Förster	Helmut	Gefr	23	3.8.1945	Nice Caucade	POW
Hahn	Adam	Gefr	39	5.8.1945	Nice Caucade	POW
Weber	Paul	Gefr	20	7.8.1945	Nice Caucade	POW
Becker	Franz	Arbeitsman	19	7.8.1945	Le Cannet	POW
Schmidt	Hans	Gefr	20	7.8.1945	Le Cannet	POW
John	Fritz	Gefr	23	7.8.1945	Le Cannet	POW
Braun	Heinz-Walter	Gefr	21	7.8.1945	Menton	
Werrbach	Siegfried	Ogefr	32	18.8.1945	La Bolène	POW
Böhmann	Heinrich	Stbgefr	30	19.8.1945	La Bolène	POW
Bettendorf	Anton	Arbeitsman	19	21.8.1945	Antibes	POW
Ernst	Erich	Soldat	29	21.8.1945	Antibes	POW
Erb	Ewald	Gefr	39	21.8.1945	Nice Caucade	POW
Erkelenz	Alois	Ogefr	31	21.8.1945	Nice Caucade	POW
Kist	Gustav	Volksturmmann	53	21.8.1945	Nice Caucade	POW
Mader	Horst	Zivilist	17	21.8.1945	Nice Caucade	POW
Koch	Erich	Gren	33	21.8.1945	Nice Caucade	POW
Rittmeyer	Egon	Gefr	19	21.8.1945	Nice Caucade	POW
Voss	Otto	Soldat	34	21.8.1945	Nice Caucade	POW
Womann	Hermann	Stabsgefr	38	21.8.1945	Nice Caucade	POW
Zyla	Rudolf	Soldat	17	21.8.1945	Nice Caucade	POW
Langer	Gerhard	Flieger	20	21.8.1945	Menton	POW
Weiland	Alexander	Stbgefr	31	23.8.1945	Antibes	POW
Brodersen	Johannes	Gefr	45	27.8.1945	Nice Caucade	POW
Glueck	Ernst	Gefr	38	27.8.1945	Nice Caucade	POW
Kittel	Rudolf	Ogefr	36	28.8.1945	Antibes	POW
Anselmann	Georg	Fwb	45	2.9.1945	Nice Caucade	POW
Scholl	Emil	Gren	27	3.9.1945	Nice Caucade	POW
Rüger	Max	Ogefr	23	6.9.1945	Menton	POW
Schaaf	Josef	Ogefr	30	9.9.1945	Nice Caucade	POW
Götzel	Arno Otto		46	9.9.1945	Nice Caucade	POW
Scherf	Edmund	Gefr	19	10.9.1945	Nice Caucade	POW
Stauss	Gustav	Gefr	46	10.9.1945	Nice Caucade	POW
Berke	Walter	Ogefr	40	10.9.1945	Vence	POW
Winterlich	Helmut	Ogefr	21	12.9.1945	Menton	POW
Grimm	Adolf	Ogefr	37	12.9.1945	Nice Est	POW

Surname	Name	Rank	Age	Date of death	Location of burial	Unit
Waidmann	Josef		43	17.9.1945	Nice Est	POW
Grasnick	Wilhelm	Ogefr	44	18.9.1945	Nice Est	POW
Wolff	Erich	Gefr	23	22.9.1945	Nice Est	POW
Felske	Erich	Uffz	48	24.9.1945	Nice Est	POW
Dennerlein	Johann	Hptgefr	51	25.9.1945	Nice Est	POW
Geisler	Otto	Uffz	45	26.9.1945	Nice Est	POW
Horner	Eduard	Gefr	41	27.9.1945	Nice Est	POW
Jarosch	Hans	Ogefr	33	29.9.1945	Nice Est	POW
Scharschinger	Alois	Soldat	41	29.9.1945	Nice Est	POW
Herre	Anton	Fwb	48	30.9.1945	Nice Est	POW
Stiegmann	Wilhelm	Ogefr	46	30.9.1945	Nice Est	POW
Schühle	Walter	Gefr	33	19.9.1945	Antibes	POW
Kappel	Paul	Gefr	38	1.10.1945	Nice Est	POW
Luniak	Ernst	Ogefr	42	2.10.1945	Nice Est	POW
Ihlbrock	Hermann	Gefr	41	3.10.1945	Nice Est	POW
Von Husen	Wilhelm	Flieger	41	3.10.1945	Nice Est	POW
Jünger	Karl	Uffz	49	4.10.1945	Nice Est	POW
Heinicke	Wilhelm	Gefr	44	4.10.1945	Nice Est	POW
Kastler	Peter	Gren	41	5.10.1945	Nice Est	POW
Schillo	Alois	Volksturmmann	40	7.10.1945	Nice Est	POW
Hentzer	Kurt	Ogefr	22	10.10.1945	Mougins	POW
Claus	Heinrich	Arbeitsmann	19	11.10.1945	Nice Est	POW
Gentner	Erwin	Gefr	48	13.10.1945	Nice Est	POW
Schnittker	Franz	Ogefr	41	15.10.1945	Antibes	POW
David	Wilhelm	Ogefr	36	15.10.1945	Nice Est	POW
Hansemann	Berhard	Gefr	19	16.10.1945	Antibes	POW
Bittokleid	Heinz	Arbeitsm	19	16.10.1945	Sospel	POW
Umann	Rudolf	Ogefr	41	17.10.1945	Nice Est	POW
Jöcks	Hermann	Ogefr	44	18.10.1945	Nice Est	POW
Janko	Karl		44	23.10.1945	Nice Est	POW
Deutsch	Jakob	Volksturmmann	44	23.10.1945	Nice Est	POW
Schmidt	Hermann	Ogefr	39	27.10.1945	Nice Est	POW
Jäckel	Kurt	Gefr	43	27.10.1945	Peille	POW
Hübner	Franz	Funker	44	31.10.1945	Nice Est	POW
Bröske	Otto	Uffz	48	4.11.1945	Nice Est	POW
Schaan	Leo	Soldat	38	5.11.1945	Nice Est	POW
Seidler	Hans	Fwb	46	9.11.1945	Nice Est	POW
Bösch	Hans	Sold	18	16.11.1945	Nice Est	POW
Höhne	Kurt	Ogefr	25	19.11.1945	Menton	POW
Weixler	Hugo	Uffz	38	19.11.1945	Nice Est	POW
Hartmann	Wilhelm	Vormann	19	20.11.1945	Menton	POW
Grunow	Ernst	Ogefr	41	22.11.1945	Nice Est	POW
Pröhl	Arthur	Ogefr	39	24.11.1945	Biot	POW
Kuberg	Heinrich	Gefr	39	26.11.1945	Nice Est	POW

Surname	Name	Rank	Age	Date of death	Location of burial	Unit
Schwenk	Rudolf	Wachtmeister	26	2.12.1945	Nice Est	POW
Gerstmeier	Michael	Stbgefr	42	7.12.1945	Nice Est	POW
Mauckisch	Kurt	Soldat	17	23.12.1945	Nice Est	POW
Pfau	Alfons	Uffz	34	25.12.1945	Nice Est	POW
Grünh	Karl	Ogefr	48	8.1.1946	Nice Est	POW
Fritz	Emil	Soldat	37	9.1.1946	Nice Est	POW
Kress	Walter	Arbeitsmann	18	10.1.1946	Nice Est	POW
Rudolph	Werner	Ogefr	31	22.1.1946	Menton	POW
Klos	Franz	Hauptgefr	36	25.1.1946	Menton	POW
Glös	Erich	Ogefr	25	2.2.1946	Nice Est	POW
Jung	Peter	Hilfzoll	41	25.2.1946	Nice Est	POW
Sandvoss	Erich	Schütze	40	16.3.1946	Menton	POW
Manstein	Hermann	Soldat	20	12.4.1946	Nice Est	POW
Körner	Hermann	Gren	19	23.4.1946	Nice Est	POW
Thalheim	Herbert	Uffz	35	23.4.1946	St Martin du Var	POW
Messmann	Richard	Fwb	31	14.5.1946	St Martin Vésubie	POW
Apel	Wilhelm	Mat Ogefr	40	22.5.1946	Grasse	POW
Peters	Ernst	Uffz	35	9.6.1946	St Laurent du Var	POW
Jurgait	Harry	Ogefr	20	9.6.1946	St Laurent du Var	POW
Rossgoderer	Johann	Gefr	23	21.6.1946	Moulinet	POW
Funke	Helmut	Vormann	20	6.7.1946	Menton	POW
Pfeil	Josef	Uffz	37	24.7.1946	Nice Est	POW
Schmitz	Hans	Soldat	45	9.8.1946	Nice Est	POW
Poppe	Alfred	Ogefr	38	24.8.1946	Cannes	POW
Votteler	Gustav	Gefr	21	28.8.1946	Menton	POW
Gänger	Oskar	Arbeitsmann	20	3.10.1946	Breil	POW
Wendler	Otto	Stbgefr	31	5.10.1946	Levens	POW
Hergert	Alfred		21	9.10.1946	Sospel	POW
Heid	August	Soldat	19	13.11.1946	Grasse	POW
Brecht	Hans	Gefr	20	24.11.1946	Nice Est	POW
Dietrich	Kurt	Uffz	28	12.3.1947	Nice Est	POW
Tengler	Bruno	Stabsgefr	36	20.4.1947	Cannes	POW
Elbert	Ernst	Fwb	28	20.6.1947	Nice Est	POW
Kafka	Rudolf	Ogefr	41	27.8.1947	Nice Est	POW
Jarmer	Franz	Ogefr	39	3.10.1947	Sospel	POW
Rosenberger	Emil	Gren	20	31.12.1947	Nice Est	POW
Plöcker	Karl	Gefr	30	1.4.1948	Nice Est	POW
Hobelmann	Georg	Gefr	22	17.6.1948	Mougins	POW
Speller?	Bernhard				St Jean Cap Ferrat	POW?

5) Honor role of 73 German army soldiers who were buried in the towns of Cuneo, Sanremo and Vinadio, Italy. This list can only be considered as a partial and incomplete list of German army soldiers killed on the Maritime Alps front and buried in Italy. Classification by date of death.

Surname	Name	Rank	Age	Date of death	Location of burial	Unit
Haese	Anton	Gefr	35	22.10.1943	Sanremo	
Sconoscineje?	Mandelieu	Capitou	21	21.7.1943	Sanremo	11./Gren.Rgt.578
Wermar?	Antibes		19	13.8.1943	Sanremo	
Knuppertz	Leo	Gefr		27.12.1943	Cuneo	11./Art.Rgt.305
Graaf	Hans	Gefr		31.12.1943	Cuneo	Frontleistelle Nice
Schütze	Alfred	Uffz	38	18.5.1944	Sanremo	
Scholten?	Bernhard			18.5.1944?	Sanremo	Deutsche RB H.V.D. Paris
Androsch	Karl	Gefr	19	3.6.1944	Sanremo	
Nitzeninsk?	Kristof		22	6.1944	Sanremo	
De la Porte?	Albert Ernst		49	6.1944	Sanremo	
Schillei	Hugo			6.1944	Sanremo	
Wagner	Maximillian	Gefr	21	27.6.1944	Sanremo	
Graf	Hans-Horst	Hptm	30	5.7.1944	Cuneo	
Dill	Alexander			29.7.1944	Cuneo	
Hammer	Ernst	Pio	19	29.7.1944	Sanremo	
Wegner	Kurt	Uffz		13.8.1944	Sanremo	
Abasan?	Abas	Leg		16.8.1944?	Sanremo	Ost.Btl.661?
Undetermined	Ost	Ogefr		16.8.1944?	Sanremo	Ost.Btl.661?
Egle	Paul	Lt	30	16.8.1944	Sanremo	
Zangerl	Josef	Jäg	36	16.8.1944	Sanremo	
Walbaum	Wilhelm	Owchtmster	28	20.8.1944	Cuneo	
Fischer	Leopold	Hauptgefr		23.8.1944	Sanremo	
Zihrnel?	Jean			8.1944	Sanremo	
Undetermined				8.1944	Sanremo	
Selbach	Alfred	Uffz	20	25.8.1944	Cuneo	
Blomenkamp	Jobst Wilhelm	Lt Zur See	21	29.8.1944	Sanremo	Kriegsmarine
Honisch	Josef	Jäg	34	30.8.1944	Sanremo	
Drese	Hermann	Ogefr		31.8.1944	Cuneo	
Roge	Hermann	Uffz	22	2.9.1944	Cuneo	
Harth	Adolf	Ogefr	32	2.9.1944	Sanremo	
Ziegler	Max	Ogefr	21	2.9.1944	Sanremo	
Wipper	Hans Georg	Uffz	26	7.9.1944	Cuneo	
Strzodka	Berhard	Gren	24	7.9.1944	Sanremo	
Undetermined				9.1944	Sanremo	
Richart?	Julio			9.1944	Sanremo	
Böhm	Leopold	Gren	18	11.9.1944	Sanremo	

Surname	Name	Rank	Age	Date of death	Location of burial	Unit
Köller	Florenz	Gren	33	11.9.1944	Undetermined	
Pieper	Helmut	Ogefr	21	13.9.1944	Cuneo	
Segitz	Hermann	Kan	18	13.9.1944	Cuneo	
Smilowski	Erich	Kan		16.9.1944	Sanremo	
Ksienzyk	Walter	Uffz	31	17.9.1944	Undetermined	5./Gren.Rgt.253
Undetermined				9.1944	Sanremo	
Robert?	Bootsman			9.1944	Sanremo	
Bauer	Josef	Ogefr	20	17.9.1944	Sanremo	
Stutnitz?	Karl Ludwig			9.1944	Sanremo	
Kümpel?				9.1944	Sanremo	
Klukuski?				9.1944	Sanremo	
Peisalour?	Gerhard			9.1944	Sanremo	
Visseco	Hans			22.9.1944	Sanremo	
Hammer	Ludwig	Uffz	19	26.9.1944	Undetermined	5./Gren.Rgt.253
Buchholz	Ernst	Oberst	49	19.11.1944	Sanremo	Inf.Div.34
Brülh	Paul	Hptm	43	19.11.1944	Sanremo	Inf.Div.34
Stark	Helmut	Uffz	24	19.11.1944	Sanremo	
Schulz?	Heinz Gerhard			11.1944	Sanremo	
Schramm	Anton	Ogefr	30	22.11.1944	Sanremo	
Kuch	Ernst	Uffz	31	1.12.1944	Sanremo	
Chutkin	Grigori	Hilfsw	52	4.12.1944	Sanremo	
Dorn	Jakob	Gefr	24	8.2.1945	Cuneo	
Jakoby	Erich	Uffz	25	15.2.1945	Undetermined	5./Gren.Rgt.253
Schmitt	Wilhelm	Ogefr	20	17.4.1945	San Remo	Stab.Gren.Rgt.253
Schork	Adolf	Uffz	42	18.4.1945	Cuneo	
Pretz	Heinrich	Stabsgfr	27	26.4.1945	Cuneo	
Caliebe	Hans-Otto	Lt	25	26.4.1945	Cuneo	
Hägele	Hermann	Ogefr	25	28.4.1945	Cuneo	
Unknown				4.1945?	Cuneo	
Kohler?	Werner				Cuneo	
Kluge?	Hans				Cuneo	
Mayer?	Karl-Heinz				Cuneo	
Klein?	Hans Diederich				Cuneo	
Trautwein?	August				Cuneo	
Schreiber?	Walter				Cuneo	
Undetermined					Vinadio	
Undetermined					Vinadio	

6) Honor role of 154 French resistance fighters, gendarmes, and civilians, executed by the Germans or reputed as having being killed while performing patriotic activities, between August 15 and September 7, 1944, in the area contained between the locations of Agay, Seillans, Col de Turini and Menton. Classification by location of death, then by name. This list is not to be considered as complete.

Surname	Name	Date of death	Location of death
Gérôme	Marcel	15.8.1944	Aspremont
Ardisson	Marcel	3.9.1944	Beausoleil
Ferrua	Maurice	3.9.1944	Beausoleil
Panza	Jean	3.9.1944	Beausoleil
Ruppe	Emil	3.9.1944	Beausoleil
Selvetti	Armand	3.9.1944	Beausoleil
Scorpioni	Italo	3.9.1944	Beausoleil
Vada	Paul	3.9.1944	Beausoleil
Zelioli	Joseph	3.9.1944	Beausoleil
Albert	Marius	24.8.1944	Biot Pont de Brague
Daver	Joseph-Charles	24.8.1944	Biot Pont de Brague
Cabasson	Jean	16.8.1944	Callas Pont de l'Estoc
Chevalier	Henri	16.8.1944	Callas Pont de l'Estoc
Ollivier	Marius	16.8.1944	Callas Pont de l'Estoc
Ricard	Emmanuel	17.8.1944	Callas
Astier	Maurice	17.8.1944	Callian
Albertini	Jean	15.8.1944	Cannes Montfleury
Bianca	Conchita	15.8.1944	Cannes Montfleury
Biny	Gustave	15.8.1944	Cannes Montfleury
Chalmette	Pierre	15.8.1944	Cannes Montfleury
Froidurot	Alfred	15.8.1944	Cannes Montfleury
Krengel	Georges	15.8.1944	Cannes Montfleury
Martini	Marius	15.8.1944	Cannes Montfleury
Séguran	Hippolyte	15.8.1944	Cannes Montfleury
Berrone	Gabriel	18.8.1944	Cannes
Costa	Charles/Clément	18.8.1944	Cannes
Barbier	Casimir	18.8.1944?	Cannes
Bergia	Henri	23.8.1944	Cannes St Cassien
Passero	Janvier	23.8.1944	Cannes St Cassien
Tonner	Francis	23.8.1944	Cannes St Cassien
Cogno	Jules	24.8.1944	Cannes
Natale	Jean	21.8.1944	Carros Clapière
Kireeff	Georges	17.8.1944	Fayence Prafagous
Baille	Raymond	22.8.1944	Gourdon

Surname	Name	Date of death	Location of death
Leclere	Marcel	21.8.1944	Gourdon
Martini	Vincent	21.8.1944	Gourdon
Pagliuzza	Georges	21.8.1944	Gourdon
Pilastre	Henri	21.8.1944	Gourdon
Gianton	François	29.8.1944	Eze
Arrigo	Guerci	2.9.1944	Isola
Bertone	Luigi	2.9.1944	Isola
Pallanca	Joseph	22.8.1944	La Roquette sur Siagne
Thomas	Jose	22.8.1944	La Roquette sur Siagne
Agnese	Alfred	25.8.1944	La Roquette sur Var
Baudoin	Cesar	25.8.1944	La Roquette sur Var
Bovis	Prosper	25.8.1944	La Roquette sur Var
Puons	Joseph	25.8.1944	La Roquette sur Var
Rossi	Second	25.8.1944	La Roquette sur Var
Antoniucci	René	24.8.1944	Levens
Barbier	Roger	24.8.1944	Levens
Mauvignant	Max	24.8.1944	Levens
Bailet	Joseph	25.8.1944	Levens
Unknown		25.8.1944	Levens Pont de Fer
Bovis	Aimé Marcel	27.8.1944	Levens
Garente	Jean Joseph	28.8.1944	Levens
Richier	Marcelin	28.8.1944	Levens
Thibaud	Roland	21.8.1944	Magagnosc
Deparday	André	29.8.1944	Menton
Bonardi	Pierre	29.8.1944	Menton
Marze	Robert	29.8.1944	Menton
Rambert	Antoinette	29.8.1944	Menton
Rambert	Jean	29.8.1944	Menton
Taglioni	François	29.8.1944	Menton
Bono	Jean	31.8.1944	Monaco
Perrimond	August	15.8.1944	Montauroux
Ramonda	Justin	15.8.1944	Montauroux
Bocchiardo	Victor	15.8.1944	Nice Ariane
Bodo	Joseph	15.8.1944	Nice Ariane
Borghni	René	15.8.1944	Nice Ariane
Chabaud	Hubert	15.8.1944	Nice Ariane

Surname	Name	Date of death	Location of death
De Lattre	Robert	15.8.1944	Nice Ariane
Dunan	Edmond	15.8.1944	Nice Ariane
Flandin	Maurice	15.8.1944	Nice Ariane
Guillevin	Paul	15.8.1944	Nice Ariane
Harang	Victor	15.8.1944	Nice Ariane
Hugues	Victorin	15.8.1944	Nice Ariane
Kraemer	André	15.8.1944	Nice Ariane
Luquet	Laurent	15.8.1944	Nice Ariane
Maccagno	Louis	15.8.1944	Nice Ariane
Malaussena	Jean Baptiste	15.8.1944	Nice Ariane
Poggio	Esther	15.8.1944	Nice Ariane
Renard	Jean Jacques	15.8.1944	Nice Ariane
Reschkomski Marcus	Marie Ruth	15.8.1944	Nice Ariane
Robineau	André	15.8.1944	Nice Ariane
Roux	August	15.8.1944	Nice Ariane
Tardieu	Gaston	15.8.1944	Nice Ariane
Vagliano	Hélène	15.8.1944	Nice Ariane
Albin	Raymond	28.8.1944	Nice
Alentchenko	Eugène	28.8.1944	Nice
Aréna	Joseph	28.8.1944	Nice
Arzoumanian	Arisdakesse	28.8.1944	Nice
Arnaudo	Auguste	28.8.1944	Nice
Autheman	Jean	28.8.1944	Nice
Badino	Jean	28.8.1944	Nice
Ballestra	Jean	28.8.1944	Nice
Barralis	René	28.8.1944	Nice
Bernardo	Sauveur	28(29).8.1944	Nice
Bobichon	Jean	28.8.1944	Nice
Bogniot	August	28.8.1944	Nice
Boscarollo	Vincent	28.8.1944	Nice
Boyer	Roger	28.8.1944	Nice
Cantergiani	Venance	28.8.1944	Nice
Carmine	Raymond	28.8.1944	Nice
Chervin	Lucien	28.8.1944	Nice
Codaccioni	Antoine	28.8(1.9).1944	Nice
Corbé	Lucien	28.8.1944	Nice
Cornil	Alphonse	28.8.1944	Nice
Fantino	Marius	28(29).8.1944	Nice
Franzini	Guillaume	28.8.1944(1947)	Nice
Genouillac	Antoine	28(29).8.1944	Nice
Gironne	Jean	28.8.1944	Nice
Giuge	Joseph	28.8.1944	Nice
Gordolon	Jean	28(30).8.1944	Nice

Surname	Name	Date of death	Location of death
Gouirand	August	28.8.1944	Nice
Krieger	Emile	Dachau	Nice
Morales	Juan	28.8.1944	Nice
Rossi	Basile	28.8.1944	Nice
Simon	Roger	29.8.1944	Nice
Suarez	Francois	28.8.1944	Nice
Vallaghe	Paul	28.8.1944	Nice
Vial	Verdun	28.8(2.9).1944	Nice
Desclair	Jean	25.8.1944	Peille
Drevon	Henri	20.8.1944	Peille
Miol	Jean	16(20).8.1944	Peille
Van Schoorisse	Antoine	23.8.1944	Peymeinade
Sedan-Miegemolle	Henri	17.8.1944	Plan du Var
Cravi	Charles	5.9.1944	Roquebrune
Vial	Honoré	5.9.1944	Roquebrune
Roux	Léon	21.8.1944	St Cezaire
Colmars	Antoine	28.8.1944	St Cezaire
Koblatz	Ferdinand	28.8.1944	St Cezaire
Roux	Edmond	28.8.1944	St Cezaire
Abonnel	Gabriel	27.8.1944	St Laurent du Var
Ledieu	Jean-Clément	27.8.1944	St Laurent du Var
Giraud	Joseph Fleury	16.8.1944	Tourrettes (Var)
Bertrand	Jean	31.8.1944	Turini
Blanc	Xavier	31.8.1944	Turini
Bloch	Jacques	31.8.1944	Turini
Cornu	Nicolas	31.8.1944	Turini
Elleboode	Gabriel	31.8.1944	Turini
Pisano	Marius	31.8.1944	Turini
Chierico	Joseph	23-24.8.1944	Vence
Nario	Joseph	19.8.1944?	Vence
Unk italian deserter		19.8.1944?	Vence
Unk italian deserter		19.8.1944?	Vence
Caparros	Joseph	27.8.1944	Vence
Zimmer Caparros	Jeanne	27.8.1944	Vence
Zimmer Voisen	Marcelle	27.8.1944	Vence
Baron	August	28.8.1944	Vence
Boursac	Jean-Marie	28.8.1944	Vence
Briquet	Marcel	28.8.1944	Vence
Gazagnaire	Roger	28.8.1944	Vence
Naso	Constant	28.8.1944	Vence
Marenda		25.8.1944	Villeneuve plage

Glossary and List of
Abbreviations and Translations

ADAM: Archives *Départementales des Alpes Maritimes* (Maritime Alps Departement Archives).

AS: *Armée Secrète* (Secret Army), a Gaulist resistance movement, containing a large number of former officers and NCO's of the regular French army.

Austrian 88: a nickname given to an unknown type of German shell by French troops during World War I. There is no evidence that these shells were Austrian, nor that they had an 88mm caliber.

Bakelite: a primitive type of plastic that the German army used abundantly during World War II. Like other plastics, it remains in excellent condition over time, even when buried.

BAR: Browning Automatic Rifle, a machine gun used by the American army, that was fed by a magazine and could be operated by a single soldier.

Brandenburg Division: a German unit specializing in unconventional warfare techniques such as infiltrating behind enemy lines wearing enemy uniforms, etc.

Boche: the most widely used derogatory nickname the French used for the Germans.

Burp gun: a nickname given by American troops to the German MP 40 submachine gun.

Camicie Nere: black shirts, a Fascist Italian paramilitary organization.

CDL: *Comité de Libération* (Liberation Committee), a makeshift council of resistance members and other influential locals that was put up in many French towns shortly after the Liberation.

Château: meaning castle in French, can be used to name anything from an actual castle to a large house.

Chemin: means path in French.

Cime: term used to describe an elongated peak or crest of a mountain in French.

CO: Commanding officer

Colt: the nickname given to the Colt 1911 pistol by Allied troops and French civilians.

Corps Franc: a French term that literally translates as 'free unit', meaning something in the lines of 'commando group' or 'storm trooper unit'.

CP: Command Post.

Département: the administrative areas that France is divided into. There are 100 *départements* in France.

DRK: *Deutsches Rotte Kreutz*, or German Red Cross.

Eclaireur: a local French newspaper in Nice that disappeared after the war because of accusations of collaboration with the Germans.

Epuration: a French word literally translating as 'purification' or 'purge'. In the context of the Liberation it referred to the witch hunt that the French performed to punish all those responsible of collaborating with the Germans.

FABTF: First Airborne Task Force, the Allied Airborne Division that landed in southern France on August 15, 1944. See chapter 3 for more details.

FFE: an Anglo-Saxon way of misspelling the term FFI.

FFI: *Forces Françaises de l'Intérieur* (French Forces of the Interior). This abbreviation can be used to refer to any resistance movements within France; or to refer to Gaullist resistance movements only, in opposition to the term FTP.

FFL: *Forces Françaises Libres* (Free French Forces). This abbreviation referred to all French forces that were fighting with the Allied troops as regular soldiers, such as the French forces fighting in Italy. This is not to be confused with the Anglo-Saxon abbreviation for the French Foreign Legion.

Feldgendarme: German Military Police.

Feldgrau: means 'field grey' in German. It was the theoretical color of German military uniforms.

Feldwebel: German NCO rank roughly equivalent to that of sergeant.

Flak: abbreviation of the German term *Flieger Abwehr Kanone*, or anti-aircraft cannon; that was adopted in English to refer to anti aircraft fire and even regular shrapnel.

Forceman: a soldier of the 1st Special Service Force, or FSSF.

Franc-tireur: a French term that literally translates as 'free shooter', meaning 'partisans' or 'civilian snipers'.

Front National: a communist tendency resistance movement.

FSSF: First Special Service Force, a mixed American and Canadian unit. See chapter 3 for more details.

FTP: See FTPF.

FTPF: *Francs Tireurs Partisans Français* (French Free Shooters and Partisans), an umbrella term referring to the communist tendency French resistance movements.

G-1: branch of the US military responsible for discipline and personal services.

G-2: branch of the US military responsible for intelligence and security.

G-3: branch of the US military responsible for training and staff duties.

Garde champêtre: a French term literally translating as 'field guard', with a role similar to that of a game keeper.

Gendarme: a member of the Gendarmerie.

Gendarmerie: a specialized branch of the French military that acts as a police force in non-urban areas of France, the French Police only having jurisdiction in larger towns.

Gestapo: an abbreviation of the term *Geheim Staatspolizei*, the German Secret State Police. French civilians and Allied soldiers often used the name 'Gestapo' as an umbrella term for all other German police and security services.

Grenadier: equivalent to the rank of private in German *Grenadier* units.

Groupe Franc: a French term that literally translates as 'free group', meaning something in the lines of 'commando group' or 'storm trooper unit'.

HBT: Herringbone Twill, a type of fabric that was used for German summer uniforms, as well as for many American uniforms.

HQ: headquarters.

IDPF: Individual Personnel Deceased File. This is a file preserved by the US Army containing funerary information about each American soldier killed during World War II.

IR: Infantry Regiment.

Impasse: the French term for a dead end street.

Jabo: an abbreviation of the German term *Jäger-Bomber* (fighter bomber), used by German soldiers to refer to the deadly and ever present Allied fighter bombers.

Jäger: equivalent to the rank of private in German *Jäger* (light infantry) units.

JU 88: Junkers Ju, a type of German twin engined bomber.

Kampfgruppe: German term literally meaning 'combat group'.

Kanonier: equivalent to the rank of private in German artillery units.

Krf: abreviation of the German term *Kraftfahrer* (truck driver), equivalent to the rank of private in German trucking units.

Kriegsmarine: the German navy.

Légal: a French slang term referring to members of the France Resistance who in appearance kept on living their normal daily lives, as opposed to men who lived clandestinely in hiding or in *maquisard* groups.

Légaux: plural form of the word *légal*.

Legion: the shortened term used to refer to the *Légion des Volontaires Français Contre le Bolchévisme* (Legion of French Volunteers Against Bolshevism), a French militia that collaborated with the Germans and fought on the Eastern Front. Not to be confused with the Foreign Legion.

Lorraine Cross: the symbol of the Free French Forces and French Resistance during WWII.

Lt: Lieutenant.

Luftwaffe: the German Air Force.

Mae West: nick name given to inflatable life jackets by Allied soldier's because of the large volume is gave to their breast area, making them resemble famous actress.

Maquis: the name given to French Resistance groups living clandestinely in the country. The name was inspired by the thick vegetation called *maquis* that grows in dry areas of southern France and Corsica.

Maquisard: a French Resistance fighter.

Maman: 'mother' in French.

Marseillaise: the French national anthem. This song dates back to the period of the French revolution and its bloodthirsty lyrics were particularly well suited to the circumstances of World War II.

Mauser: term used to refer to the German model 1898 Mauser rifle.

MG: 'machine gun' in English or *Machinen Gewehr* (machine gun) in German.

MG 34: abbreviated named of the German *Machinen Gewehr 1934*, a well designed 7.92mm machine gun firing up to 15 rounds per second.

MG 42: abbreviated named of the German *Machinen Gewehr 1942*, an improved version of the MG 34 capable of firing over 20 rounds per second.

Milice: a collaborationist French paramilitary force that was created by the Vichy government tin early 1943 to help hunt down Resistants.

Milicien: a member of the Milice.

Mills: a type of British fragmentation grenade that was often used by the Resistance.

MOI: *Main d'Oeuvre Immigrée* (Immigrated work force), one of the sub-movements of the FTP resistance forces.

MP: abbreviation of *Machinen Pistol*, or submachine gun.

MRA: *Musée de la Résitance Azuréenne* (Museum of the French Riviera Resistance), a museum in Nice that preserves a large number of documents related to the Maritimes Alps.

Mutter: 'mother' in German.

NARA: National Archives and Records Administration.

Oberleutnant: German rank roughly equivalent to that of an American First Lieutenant.

Oblt: abbreviation of the German word *Oberleutnant*.

ORA: *Organisation de Résistance de l'Armée*, the French Army Gaullist tendency resistance organization.

OSS: 'Office of Strategic Services', an American intelligence agency that was later to become the CIA.

Pak: abbreviation of the German term *Panzer Abwehr Kanone*, or anti-tank cannon.

Panzerjäger: German anti-tank troops.

PCEC: Parachute Combat Engineer Company.

PFAB: Parachute Field Artillery Battalion.

PFC: Private First Class.

PIB: Parachute Infantry Battalion.

PIR: Parachute Infantry Regiment.

Place: the French term for square, as in 'town square'.

Pont: the French word for bridge.

POW: prisoner of war.

PPF: *Partie Populaire Français* (Popular French Party), a French Fascist party that was created in 1936 and that became collaborationist after the German invasion.

Préfecture: the government building in which the administration of a French *département* (including the 'préfet') takes its headquarters.

Préfet: the administrative officer that is placed at the head of each French *département*.

Provencal: a local dialect spoken in the Provence region of France.

Purple Heart: a medal awarded to members of the US Army for being killed or wounded by enemy fire.

Pvt: Private.

PW: prisoner of war.

QMGRC: Quartermaster Graves Registration Company

Rafle: the French term for 'roundup', as in when German soldiers rounded up random civilians on the street to be checked or deported.

Réfractaire: the name given to French civilians who preferred to go into hiding then to be sent to Germany to work as forced labor under the STO.

Reichsdeutche: a word whose meaning is highly dependent on the exact context, but in the case of this book meaning a true German.

Resistant: a member of the French Resistance.

Rue: the French word for street.

S-2: the intelligence officer, or intelligence section within American military units.

S-mine: abbreviated name for the German *Springmine* (jumping mine). A particularly deadly German mine that was filled with ball bearings and that, after being stepped on, only exploded after being projected approximately one meter up from the ground.

Saint Cyr: the Military School that forms French military officers, equivalent to West Point or Sandhurst.

SAP: *Section Aterrissages Parachutages*, meaning 'landing and parachuting sections', groups of *maquisard*s specialized in organizing and receiving Allied airdrops of material.

SD: *Sicherheit Dienst* one branch of the German state Police, often lumped together with the *Gestapo* in the minds the WWII generation.

Secours National: a French charity that aimed to bring help to French soldiers and civilian victims of the war. It gradually turned into a collaborationist organization during the Occupation.

Sgt: Sergeant.

Silver Star: the third highest American military decoration awarded for valor in the face of the enemy.

Stab: German word for headquarters.

Sten: a cheap and low quality 9mm British submachine gun, that was often used by members of the French Resistance.

STO: *Service du Travail Obligatoire* (Compulsory Work Service), a mandatory work service established by the Vichy government. It enlisted unemployed Frenchmen to be sent to work in Germany.

Stockmine: meaning 'stake mine' in German, a type of mine that was on a stake.

Stützpunkt: a German word basically meaning 'support point' or 'resistance point'.

Tellermine: a large German anti-tank mine, *Teller* meaning plate in German.

Thompson: an American submachine gun firing .45 caliber bullets.

Uffz: abbreviation of the German word *Unteroffizier*.

Unteroffizier: German rank roughly equivalent to that of an American Sergeant.

Villa: the name given to larger and more luxurious French houses.

Volksdeutsch: a word whose meaning is highly dependent on the exact context, but in the case of this book meaning a person finding himself living within the borders of Germany and having German citizenship, though he does not feel any attachment to Germany.

Wehrpass: a German soldier's military ID booklet.

Zug: the German word for platoon.

Zugführer: The German word for platoon leader.

Endnotes

Chapter 1

1. Caucade cemetery register, Nice, France. 1944.
2. *Generalleutnant* Otto Fretter-Pico. "148 *Infanterie*-Division Mai-September 1944." Foreign Military Studies B Series (RG 338). 1950. NARA.
3. Various POW interrogations. 509th PIB G-3 files. August-September 1944. NARA.
4. Uffz Rodolf Danjek POW interrogation. 509th PIB G-3 files. 9-10 September 1944. NARA.
5. Alain Chazette. *L'Armée Allemande Sur la Côte Méditerranéenne, A.O.K.19 Mittelmeerküstenfront, volume 1*, Paris: Editions Histoire & collection, 2004. Lt Col Hans Niedlich POW interrogation. 509th PIB G-3 files. 1-2 September 1944. NARA.
6. Lt Col Hans Niedlich POW interrogation. 509th PIB G-3 files. 1-2 September 1944. NARA.
7. *Generalleutnant* Otto Fretter-Pico. "148 *Infanterie*-Division Mai-September 1944." Foreign Military Studies B Series (RG 338). 1950. NARA.
8. Mempel Werner. POW interrogation report. CSDIC West M.857. 3 September 1944. NARA.
9. Soldatenzeit Leopold Bohne. Bohne family Collection.
10. Ivan Samorkin and Piotr Tichanow. POW interrogation report. CSDIC West M.829. 25 August 1944. NARA.
11. "Bombardement du 26 mai 1944." http://fr.wikipedia.org/wiki/Bombardement_du_26_mai_1944
12. Marcel Perez, quoted in *Saint Laurent du Var 1940-1944*. (St Laurent du Var : Le souvenir Français, 1994)
13. Caucade cemetery register, Nice, France. 1944.
14. Alpes Maritimes file. VDK Archives, Kassel.
15. Richard Held interrogation by Cannes Police. 616w259. ADAM.
16. Richard Held interrogation by Cannes Police. 616w259. ADAM.
17. Richard Held interrogation by Cannes Police. 616w259. ADAM.
18. "L'homme nu de la Mescla déchiqueté par deux charges d'explosif." *L'Ergot*. MRA.
19. Lorenz Rhode. "Schneewittchen in Monte Carlo." *Mitteilunggen der Gemeinschaft ehemaliger Angehöriger der 148 ID*. September 1967.

Chapter 2

1. Documents in file 0308 W 0016. ADAM.
2. Louis Tenerini, quoted in *Les 8ème et 27ème Compagnies FTPF dans le Résistance dans les Alpes-Maritimes*. Louis Tenerini ed. (Louis Tenerini, 1999) pg. 41.
3. Corrado Marcucci, quoted in *Les 8ème et 27ème Compagnies FTPF dans le Résistance dans les Alpes-Maritimes*. Louis Tenerini ed. (Louis Tenerini, 1999) pg. 18.
4. Caucade cemetery register, Nice, France. 1944.
5. Primo Calzoni, quoted in *Les 8ème et 27ème Compagnies FTPF dans le Résistance dans les Alpes-Maritimes*. Louis Tenerini ed. (Louis Tenerini, 1999) pg. 31-32.
6. Sapin (Jacques Lécuyer). *Méfiez Vous du Toréador*. (Editeur AGPM, 1987) pg. 61.
7. Most likely the chorus of the German marching song "Ein Heller und ein Batzen."
8. Meurtre de deux soldats allemands à Nice (A.M.). Police report. ADAM, courtesy Alain Endinger.
9. *Le Petit Niçois*. MRA.
10. Caucade cemetery register, Nice, France. 1944.
11. Caucade cemetery register, Nice, France. 1944.
12. Document in file 616W259. ADAM.
13. "A Sospel, quinze *maquisard*s Italiens antifascistes torturés et fusillés." *L'Ergot*. MRA.
14. Caucade cemetery register, Nice, France. 1944.
15. Friedrich Baumgaertel. POW interrogation report. CSDIC West M.874. September 13 1944. NARA.

Chapter 3

1. The information provided in this section comes from a large number of sources, such as the official unit histories available at NARA, interviews with veterans, and the Wikipedia.org website.
2. FABTF Operations Report. August 1944. NARA.
3. FABTF Operations Report. August 1944. NARA.
4. FSSF Journal. August 1944. NARA.
5. Guy E. Carr. *The Champaign campaign*. Unpublished manuscript.
6. Harland L. 'Bud' Curtiss. Letter to his mother dated August 22, 1944. 517prct.org Collection.
7. Danniel A. Fischer IDPF. US Army Human Resources Command, Fort Knox, Kentucky.
8. Hoyt Kelley. Email to 517prct.org. Mail Call 2075. Oct 2011. 517prct.org Collection.
9. Howard Hensleigh hand annotated casualty list of the 517th PRCT. Howard Hensleigh Collection.
10. Erwin W. Scott Jr. interview. The National Museum of the Pacific War. Fredericksburg, Texas. Transcribed by Mary Dru Burns. 6 April 2002. Scott Atkinson and 517thprct.org Collections.
11. Clark Archer account of the Mercedes Incident. 517prct.org Collection.
12. Thomas J. Higgins. "The Truth About Tulsa's Kennamer-Gorrel Case." *The Master Detective*. Vol. 12. Number 6. August 1935. Walter Kennamer Collection.
13. *The Milwaukee Sentinel*. February 16, 1935.
14. Milton Rogers. *How I saw it*. Unpublished manuscript. 517prct.org Collection.
15. Milton Rogers. *How I saw it*. Unpublished manuscript. 517prct.org Collection.
16. Woody Anderson Kelley. *The Kennemer Book: A Great American Family*. (Gurley, AL: Concept Inc., 1982), pg 97. Courtesy Walter Kennamer.
17. Generalmajor Ludwig Bieringer. "Die Invasion in Suedfrankriech am 15/16 Aug vom Feldkdt 800 in Draguignan aus gesehen." Foreign Military Studies B Series (RG 338). 1951. NARA.
18. Generalmajor Ludwig Bieringer. "Die Invasion in Suedfrankriech am 15/16 Aug vom Feldkdt 800 in Draguignan aus gesehen." Foreign Military Studies B Series (RG 338). 1951. NARA.
19. Generalmajor Ludwig Bieringer. "Die Invasion in Suedfrankriech am 15/16 Aug vom Feldkdt 800 in Draguignan aus gesehen." Foreign Military Studies B Series (RG 338). 1951. NARA.
20. Generalmajor Ludwig Bieringer. "Die Invasion in Suedfrankriech am 15/16 Aug vom Feldkdt 800 in Draguignan aus gesehen." Foreign Military Studies B Series (RG 338). 1951. NARA.
21. Generalmajor Ludwig Bieringer. "Die Invasion in Suedfrankriech am 15/16 Aug vom Feldkdt 800 in Draguignan aus gesehen." Foreign Military Studies B Series (RG 338). 1951. NARA.
22. Art Helmers. *One soldier's view*. Unpublished manuscript.
23. Milton Dank. *The Glider Gang*. (J.B. Lippincott Company,1977) pg. 151.
24. Marvin McRoberts. Unpublished manuscript. Available online from http://community-2.webtv.net/masterofneon4/602dFieldArtillery/index.html
25. Dan Morgan. *The Left Corner of my Heart*. (Alder Enterprises, 1984) pg.173.
26. Richard Fisco. *Your Lives Will be Beautiful*. (Ramsey, NJ: Arbor Books, 2008) pg. 55-56.
27. Harvey Sutherland quoted in Charles H. Doyle, Terrell Stewart. *Stand in the Door*. (Williamstown, NJ: Phillipps Publications, 1988) pg. 263.

Chapter 4

1. Guy E. Carr. *The Champaign campaign*. Unpublished manuscript.
2. Richard Bigler, in Operation Dragoon After Action Report. 517prct.org Collection.
3. Dr. Wagner letter to Emma Hessert. August 23, 1944. Otto Hessert Family Collection.
4. Olt Puche letter to Emma Hessert. September 12, 1944.Otto Hessert Familly collection.
5. Raymond Carbonel. *La libération à Montauroux telle que je l'ai vécue*. 1993, quoted in Charles Gandiglio. *La Libération de Montauroux à Peymeinade*.
6. 141st IR Regimental Journal. August 1944. NARA.
7. Grant Hooper, in Operation Dragoon After Action Report. 517prct.org Collection.
8. Alpes Maritimes and Var files. VDK archives. Kassel.
9. Walter Plassman, quoted in Gerald Astor. *Battling Buzzards*. (NY, NY, Dell Publishing, 1993) pg. 181-182.

10. Letter from Walter Plassman to Clark Archer. Date unknown. Mail call number 161, 517prct.org.

11. 141st IR Regimental Journal. August 1944. NARA.

12. 141st IR Regimental Journal. August 1944. NARA.

13. Martin Fastia, in Operation Dragoon After Action Report. 517th PIR, Aug 1944. NARA.

14. *Generalleutnant* Otto Fretter-Pico. "148 *Infanterie*-Division Mai-September 1944." Foreign Military Studies B Series (RG 338). 1950. NARA.

15. Louis Holzworth Silver Star Citation. Holzworth Family Collection.

16. 141st IR Regimental Journal. August 1944. NARA.

17. Richard Bigler, in Operation Dragoon After Action Report. 517prct.org Collection.

18. Raymond Carbonel. *La libération à Montauroux telle que je l'ai vécue.* 1993, quoted in Charles Gandiglio. *La Libération de Montauroux à Peymeinade.*

19. Grant Hooper, in Operation Dragoon After Action Report. 517prct.org Collection.

20. Raymond Carbonel. *La libération à Montauroux telle que je l'ai vécue.* 1993, quoted in Charles Gandiglio. *La Libération de Montauroux à Peymeinade.*

21. La Crau cemetery register. Mairie de La Crau Collection, Var, France.

22. 636th TDB Journal. August 1944. NARA.

23. Raymond Carbonel. *La libération à Montauroux telle que je l'ai vécue.* 1993, quoted in Charles Gandiglio. *La Libération de Montauroux à Peymeinade.*

24. 141st IR Regimental Journal. August 1944. NARA.

25. 636th TDB Journal. August 1944. NARA.

26. Raymond Carbonel. *La libération à Montauroux telle que je l'ai vécue.* 1993, quoted in Charles Gandiglio. *La Libération de Montauroux à Peymeinade.*

27. 141st IR Regimental Journal. August 1944. NARA.

28. 141st IR Regimental Journal. August 1944. NARA.

29. 141st IR Regimental Journal. August 1944. NARA.

30. FABTF General Orders. August 1944. NARA.

31. 141st IR Regimental Journal. August 1944. NARA.

32. Clark Archer. *Paratroopers' Odyssey. A History of the 517th Parachute Combat Team* (Hudson, FL: 517th PRCT Association, 1985) Chap IV.

33. FABTF General Orders. August 1944. NARA.

34. FABTF General Orders. August 1944. NARA.

35. Angelin German. *Les Chemins de la Mémoire.* (Draguignan, France: Imprimerie Bonnaud) pg. 85-88.

36. OSS Team Sceptre report. August 1944. NARA.

37. OSS Team Sceptre report. August 1944. NARA.

38. OSS Team Sceptre report. August 1944. NARA.

39. OSS Team Sceptre report. August 1944. NARA.

40. Albert Deshayes letter to Clark Archer. 1984. Deshayes Family Collection.

41. Clark Archer. *Paratroopers' Odyssey. A History of the 517th Parachute Combat Team* (Hudson, FL: 517th PRCT Association, 1985) Chap IV.

Chapter 5

1. Charles Petty, quoted in Michel de Trez. *First Airborne Task Force : Pictorial History of the Allied Paratroopers in the Invasion of Southern France* (Wesembeek-Oppem, Belgium: D-Day Publishing, 1998) pg. 14.

2. Charles Petty, quoted in Michel de Trez. *First Airborne Task Force : Pictorial History of the Allied Paratroopers in the Invasion of Southern France* (Wesembeek-Oppem, Belgium: D-Day Publishing, 1998) pg. 15.

3. Charles Petty, quoted in Michel de Trez. *First Airborne Task Force : Pictorial History of the Allied Paratroopers in the Invasion of Southern France* (Wesembeek-Oppem, Belgium: D-Day Publishing, 1998) pg. 15.

4. FSSF Summary of enemy operations. August 1944. NARA.

5. FSSF journal. August 1944. NARA.

6. FSSF Summary of enemy operations. August 1944. NARA.

7. Bosler Walter. POW interrogation report. CSDIC West M.888. 10 Sept 1944. NARA.

8. Bosler Walter. POW interrogation report. CSDIC West M.888. 10 Sept 1944. NARA.

9. FSSF journal. August 1944. NARA.

Chapter 6

1. Capitaine de Frégate Sériot. Compte rendu d'opérations du Capitaine de Frégate Sériot au Commandant de l'Armée B. 30 Aout 1944. Jean Campana Collection.

2. Lucien Chaffiotte. Unknown article in *Cols Bleus*. 1955. Courtesy Denise Bernard.

3. Capitaine de Frégate Sériot. Compte rendu d'opérations du Capitaine de Frégate Sériot au Commandant de l'Armée B. 30 Aout 1944. Jean Campana Collection.

4. Jack Wilson. Unpublished manuscript.

5. Carl Strom. Unpublished manuscript.

6. Carl Strom. Unpublished manuscript.

7. Lt L.E. Gilbert. Report of loss of LST 282. September 2, 1944. Available online from http://www.landingship.com/282/

8. Excerpt by Hans E. Bergner. Reprinted by permission, from Paul Stillwell, Editor, *Assault on Normandy: First Person Accounts from the Sea Services* (Annapolis, Md:

Naval Institute Press: © 1994).

9. 141st IR Regimental Journal. August 1944. NARA.

10. Jack Wilson. Unpublished manuscript.

11. Jack Wilson. Unpublished manuscript.

12. 141st IR Regimental Journal. August 1944. NARA.

13. 141st IR Regimental Journal. August 1944. NARA.

14. Olt Börner. 22 U.Jagdflottille war diary. August 1944. Bundesarchiv/ Militärarchiv Freiburg/Breisgau. RM 74. Courtesy Manfred Krellenberg

15. FABTF Summary of our Operations. August 1944. NARA

16. Arthur L. Funk. *Hidden Ally*. (New York : Greenwood Press, 1992)

17. Arthur L. Funk. *Hidden Ally*. (New York : Greenwood Press, 1992)

18. *Generalleutnant* Otto Fretter-Pico. "148 *Infanterie*-Division Mai-September 1944." Foreign Military Studies B Series (RG 338). 1950. NARA.

19. Ray Donavan. Unpublished manuscript.

20. Gerald K. Tilney Silver Star Citation. FABTF General Orders. Awards. Late 1944. NARA.

21. Richard Fisco. *Your lives will be beautiful.* (Ramsey, NJ: Arbor Books, 2008) pg. 55-56

22. Victor Osborn Silver Star Citation. FABTF General Orders. Awards. Late 1944. NARA.

23. John Frazier, quoted in Charles H. Doyle, Terrell Stewart. *Stand in the Door.* (Williamstown, NJ: Phillipps Publications, 1988) pg. 281.

24. 509th PIB Unit History. August 1944. NARA.

25. FSSF Journal. August 1944. NARA.

26. John Frazier, quoted in Charles H. Doyle, Terrell Stewart. *Stand in the Door.* (Williamstown, NJ: Phillipps Publications, 1988) pg. 281.

27. Capt Roy E. Baze letter to his father. August 22nd 1944. Baze Family Collection.

28. Leonard Haller IDPF. US Army Human Resources Command, Fort Knox, Kentucky.

29. Charlie Fairlamb, quoted in Dan Morgan. *The Left Corner of my Heart.* (Alder Enterprises, 1984) pg. 231.

30. Jim Aikman, quoted in Dan Morgan. *The Left Corner of my Heart.* (Alder Enterprises, 1984) pg. 33.

31. Charlie Fairlamb, quoted in Dan Morgan. *The Left Corner of my Heart.* (Alder Enterprises, 1984) pg. 228.

32. Don Garriges, quoted in Dan Morgan. *The Left Corner of my Heart.* (Alder Enterprises, 1984) pg. 227-228.

33. Jim Aikman, quoted in Dan Morgan. *The Left Corner of my Heart.* (Alder Enterprises, 1984) pg. 228.

34. Leo Urban, quoted in Dan Morgan. *The Left Corner of my Heart.* (Alder Enterprises, 1984) pg. 225.

35. 551st PIB unit history. August 1944. NARA.

36. Don Thompson, quoted in Dan Morgan. *The Left Corner of my Heart.* (Alder Enterprises, 1984) pg. 220-222.

37. 551st PIB unit history. August 1944. NARA.

38. 551st PIB unit history. August 1944. NARA.

39. Martin Kangas, quoted in Dan Morgan. *The Left Corner of my Heart.* (Alder Enterprises, 1984) pg. 226.

40. George Kane, quoted in Dan Morgan. *The Left Corner of my Heart.* (Alder Enterprises, 1984) pg. 228-229

41. Joe Kosowski, quoted in Dan Morgan. *The Left Corner of my Heart.* (Alder Enterprises, 1984) pg. 226.

42. Emory Albritton, quoted in Dan Morgan. *The Left Corner of my Heart.* (Alder Enterprises, 1984) pg. 224-225.

43. Jud Chalkley, quoted in Dan Morgan. *The Left Corner of my Heart.* (Alder Enterprises, 1984) pg. 229.

44. 551st PIB unit history. August 1944. NARA.

45. Dick Durkee, quoted in Dan Morgan. *The Left Corner of my Heart.* (Alder Enterprises, 1984) pg. 234.

46. Don Garriges, quoted in Dan Morgan. *The Left Corner of my Heart.* (Alder Enterprises, 1984) pg. 228.

47. FABTF Orders. POW report. 22 August 1944. NARA.

48. POW Interrogation Report. 2 September 1944. 517th PIR Summary of Operations. September 1944.

49. Olt Johann Bönsch letter to Olt Klaus Meyer-Detring wife. 17 September 1944. Meyer-Detring Family Collection.

50. Joseph Bartsch letter to Gerhard Schiffhorst wife. 15 July 1962. Schiffhorst Family Collection.

51. 551st PIB unit history. August 1944. NARA.

52. John Frazier, quoted in Charles H. Doyle, Terrell Stewart. *Stand in the Door.* (Williamstown, NJ: Phillipps Publications, 1988) pg. 282.

53. Lt Lieber, quoted in Charles H. Doyle, Terrell Stewart. *Stand in the Door.* (Williamstown, NJ: Phillipps Publications, 1988) pg. 283.

54. Orthelle Cherry letter to Lorraine Schwebke. Late 1944. Gloria Klinner Collection.

55. Lt Shaker Silver Star citation. FABTF General Orders. Late 1944. NARA.

56. Jack Darden and Henry Klisiewicz Silver Star citations. FABTF General Orders. Late 1944. NARA.

57. Hyman Perlo Silver Star citation. FABTF General Orders. Late 1944. NARA.

58. Capt Roy E. Baze Silver Star Citation. Baze Family Collection.

59. Walter Lindenthal letter to Franz Knirsch wife. 17 December 1944. Knirsch Family Collection.

60. 509th PIR Unit History. August 1944. NARA.

61. Jud Chalkley, quoted in Dan Morgan. *The Left Corner of my Heart*. (Alder Enterprises, 1984) pg. 229.

62. Capt Alfred J. Kelly letter to Capt Roy E. Baze wife. 17 October 1944. Baze Family Collection.

63. 509th PIR Unit History. August 1944. NARA.

64. Dick Spencer, quoted in George Adleman, Robert Walton. *The Champagne Campaign*. (Little, Brown and Company, 1969) pg. 192.

Chapter 7

1. M.A. Vidal. "L'opération de la Force Rosie. Les résistants du Groupe Tonner libèrent 11 marins. " *Le Patriote Côte d'Azur*. Late August 1969.

2. Richard Held interrogation by Cannes Police. 616w259. ADAM.

3. Richard Held interrogation by Cannes Police. 616w259. ADAM.

4. Louis Balesi. "Le drame de la Villa Montfeury. Comment j'ai été assassiné par les Allemands." *L'Ergot*. MRA.

5. Dely Renaud. "Mort de Paul Malaguti, un fidèle de Le Pen". *Libération*. 26 october 1996. Liberation.fr.

6. Honoré Isnard. *Les derniers jours de l'Occupation et la Libération du port et de la ville de Cannes*. (Cannes : Imprimerie Devay, 1950)

7. Alexandre Carini. "Squelettes découverts à Cannes : "C'est peut-être notre frère ! "" *Nice-Matin*. 19 April 2009.

8. Amélie Mougins diary. Geneviève Mougins de Bustos Collection.

9. Ferdinand Moscone Diary. Moscone Family Collection.

10. Franck Boulingez. Article about José Thomas. Service des Archives de Mouans Sartoux Colletion.

11. Amélie Mougins diary. Geneviève Mougins de Bustos Collection.

12. Commandant A. Vérine. *Historique de la Libération d'Antibes*. Unpublished manuscript. MRA.

13. Commandant A. Vérine. *Historique de la Libération d'Antibes*. Unpublished manuscript. MRA.

14. Ferdinand Moscone Diary. Moscone Family Collection.

Chapter 8

1. Grant Hooper, in Operation Dragoon After Action Report. 517prct.org Collection.

2. Robert C. Euler. Walter Willard Taylor Jr. obituary. Society for American Archeology bulletin 15(4).

3. Walter W. Taylor. Letter to Head, Historical Branch Headquarters, U.S. Marine Corps. 31 May 1966. Marine Corps Historical Center Archives.

4. Col Rupert D. Graves. "Combat Team." *Blue Book Magazine*. Dec 1947. pg. 60. 517prct.org Collection.

5. Hector Colo IDPF. US Army Human Resources Command, Fort Knox, Kentucky.

6. Nello Arterburn letter to his wife. 22 May 1945. Arterburn Family Collection. Courtesy 517prct.org.

7. William M. Bowers Jr. *Don't Ever Give Up*. 1997

8. Milton Rogers. *How I saw it*. Unpublished manuscript. 517prct.org Collection.

9. Maj Forrest Paxton Silver Star citation. FABTF General Orders. NARA.

10. Guy E. Carr. *The Champaign campaign*. Unpublished manuscript.

11. Col Rupert D. Graves. "Combat Team." *Blue Book Magazine*. Dec 1947. pg. 60.

12. Col Rupert D. Graves. "Combat Team." *Blue Book Magazine*. Dec 1947. pg. 60.

13. Richard Sailor IDPF. US Army Human Resources Command, Fort Knox, Kentucky.

14. Richard Sailor IDPF. US Army Human Resources Command, Fort Knox, Kentucky.

15. Richard Sailor IDPF. US Army Human Resources Command, Fort Knox, Kentucky.

16. M. Laugier letter to Volksbund. Alpes Maritimes File. Volksbund Archives. Kassel.

17. Karl-Ernst Schimdt. "Ernstes und Heiteres aus meiner Zeit bei der 148 I.D." *Mitteilunggen der Gemeinschaft ehemaliger Angehöriger der 148 ID*. Nr 24. November 1977.

Chapter 9

1. FSSF Summary of enemy operations. August 1944. NARA.

2. FSSF journal. Aug 1944. NARA.

3. Capt Robert I. Smith letter to Thos A. Best. 2 July 1945. Deanna Petri Collection.

4. Olt Georg Weis letter to Johann Strunk wife. 31 August 1944. Strunk Family Collection.

5. FSSF Summary of enemy operations. August 1944. NARA.

6. FSSF journal. August 1944. NARA.

7. Roe Rapp Silver Star citation. FABTF General Orders. NARA.

8. FSSF journal. August 1944. NARA.

9. FSSF journal. August 1944. NARA.

10. René Ghio. *Mes Années de Guerre*, quoted in : Actes du Colloque du 2? Novembre 2007, Devoir de mémoire. L'Occupation, la Résistance et la Libération à Grasse et en pays de Grasse, Association Historique du Pays de Grasse.

11. Art Helmers. *One soldier's view*. Unpublished manuscript.

Chapter 10

1. Elisabeth de Vanssay (de Panisse Passis). *Le Siège de Villeneuve*. Unpublished manuscript. 1944. Nadèje le Lédan Collection.

2. FSSF daily reports. August 1944. NARA.

3. FSSF daily reports. August 1944. NARA.

4. René Ghio. *Mes Années de Guerre*, quoted in : Actes du Colloque du 27 Novembre 2007, Devoir de mémoire. L'Occupation, la Résistance et la Libération à Grasse et en pays de Grasse, Association Historique du Pays de Grasse.

5. Elisabeth de Vanssay (de Panisse Passis). *Le Siège de Villeneuve*. Unpublished manuscript. 1944. Nadèje le Lédan Collection.

6. Adna H. Underhill. *The Force*. (Tucson, AZ: Arizona Monographs, 1994) pg. 291.

7. Raymond Giraud. *L'enfer du Vallon de Cireuil*. Villeneuve-Loubet Town Hall Collection.

8. Art Helmers. *One soldier's view*. Unpublished manuscript.

9. FSSF journal. August 1944. NARA.

10. Capt Larry Piette Silver Star citation. Piette Family Collection.

11. Elisabeth de Vanssay (de Panisse Passis). *Le Siège de Villeneuve*. Unpublished manuscript. 1944. Nadèje le Lédan Collection.

12. Larry Piette, quoted in Joseph A. Springer. *The Black Devil's Brigade*. (Pacifica, CA: Pacifica Military History, 2001)

13. John Dawson, quoted in George Adleman, Robert Walton. *The Champagne Campaign*. (Little, Brown and Company, 1969) pg. 220.

14. Capt Larry Piette Silver Star citation. Piette Family Collection.

15. Capt Larry Piette Silver Star citation. Piette Family Collection.

16. Ross Orr Distinguished Service Star citation. Orr Family Collection.

17. Lt George Parnell letter to his wife. 26 August 1944. Marion Parnell Collection.

18. Elisabeth de Vanssay (de Panisse Passis). *Le Siège de Villeneuve*. Unpublished manuscript. 1944. Nadèje le Lédan Collection.

19. Lt George Parnell letter to his wife. 26 August 1944. Marion Parnell Collection.

20. FSSF journal. August 1944. NARA.

21. Art Helmers. *One soldier's view*. Unpublished manuscript.

22. FSSF Summary of enemy operations. August 1944. NARA.

23. FABTF consolidated POW report. 27 August 1944. NARA.

24. Elisabeth de Vanssay (de Panisse Passis). *Le Siège de Villeneuve*. Unpublished manuscript. 1944. Nadèje le Lédan Collection.

25. Elisabeth de Vanssay (de Panisse Passis). *Le Siège de Villeneuve*. Unpublished manuscript. 1944. Nadèje le Lédan Collection.

26. Henry Blackman Silver Star ciation. FABTF General Orders. Late 1944. NARA.

27. Ross Orr Distinguished Service Star citation. Orr Family Collection.

28. FSSF Summary of enemy operations. August 1944. NARA.

29. 509th PIB documents. POW interrogation reports. August 1944. NARA.

30. 937th FAB history. POW interrogation reports. August 1944. NARA.

31. Elisabeth de Vanssay (de Panisse Passis). *Le Siège de Villeneuve*. Unpublished manuscript. 1944. Nadèje le Lédan Collection.

32. FSSF journal. August 1944. NARA.

33. 937th FAB history. August 1944. NARA.

34. John Dawson, quoted in George Adleman, Robert Walton. *The Champagne Campaign*. (Little, Brown and Company, 1969) pg. 220-221.

35. HQ FABTF 7th Army. Field order number 1 for Operation Dragoon. 5 August 1944. NARA.

36. Elisabeth de Vanssay (de Panisse Passis). *Le Siège de Villeneuve*. Unpublished manuscript. 1944. Nadèje le Lédan Collection.

37. FSSF journal. August 1944. NARA.

38. FSSF journal. August 1944. NARA.

39. FSSF journal. August 1944. NARA.

40. 937th FAB history. August 1944. NARA.

41. René Ghio. *Mes Années de Guerre*, quoted in : Actes du Colloque du 27 Novembre 2007, Devoir de mémoire. L'Occupation, la Résistance et la Libération à Grasse et en pays de Grasse, Association Historique du Pays de Grasse.

42. 512th Airborne Signal Company Historical Record. August 1944. NARA.

43. FSSF journal. August 1944. NARA.

44. FSSF Summary of enemy operations; and FABTF POW interrogation reports from late August 1944. To be found in the August files of the 937th FAB, 509th PIB and FABTF. NARA.

45. Elisabeth de Vanssay (de Panisse Passis). *Le Siège de Villeneuve*. Unpublished manuscript. 1944. Nadèje le Lédan Collection.

46. Elisabeth de Vanssay (de Panisse Passis). *Le Siège de Villeneuve*. Unpublished manuscript. 1944. Nadèje le Lédan Collection.

47. FSSF journal. August 1944. NARA.

48. Olt Erich Hehs, letter to Sophie Ficker. 2 September 1944. Franz Guder Collection.

49. FABTF consolidated POW report. 27 August 1944. NARA.

50. "Goliath tracked mine." http://en.wikipedia.org/wiki/Goliath_tracked_mine

51. 509th PIB Unit History. August 1944. NARA.

52. Commandant A. Vérine. *Historique de la Libération d'Antibes.* Unpublished manuscript. MRA.

Chapter 11

1. FSSF Operations of small units. September 1944. NARA.

2. *Saint Laurent du Var 1940-1944.* (St Laurent du Var : Le souvenir Français, 1994)

3. FSSF Operations of small units. September 1944. NARA.

4. FSSF Summary of enemy operations. August 1944. NARA.

5. FSSF Summary of enemy operations. August 1944. NARA.

6. FSSF journal. August 1944. NARA.

7. FSSF journal. August 1944. NARA.

8. 509th PIB Unit History. August 1944. NARA.

9. 551st PIB unit history. August 1944. NARA.

10. Ginette (Félix Petitjean). *Le Temps des Fauves.* (Paris: La Pensée Universelle, 1972) pg. 64.

11. Marius Issert. *Souvenirs d'un maire.* 1945-1995. (St Paul: Editions de la Commune de St Paul, 2000) pg. 27-31.

12. Henry Einesy. Notes from late August 1944. Archives Municipales de Vence.

13. Henry Einesy. Notes from late August 1944. Archives Municipales de Vence.

14. Document from unknown ADAM file. Courtesy Alain Endinger.

15. Anne Verots-Guibaud. *Chronique de la Vie Vencoise. 1930-1975.* (A. Verots-Guilbaud, 1999)

16. Anne Verots-Guibaud. *Chronique de la Vie Vencoise. 1930-1975.* (A. Verots-Guilbaud, 1999)

17. Ginette (Félix Petitjean). *Le Temps des Fauves.* (Paris: La Pensée Universelle, 1972) pg. 78-79.

18. Sidney Oxman diary. 1944. Oxman Family Collection.

19. Ginette (Félix Petitjean). *Le Temps des Fauves.* (Paris: La Pensée Universelle, 1972) pg. 79.

20. 550th GIB journal. August 1944. NARA.

21. 550th GIB journal. August 1944. NARA.

22. FSSF journal. August 1944. NARA.

Chapter 12

1. "Qui a Tué, le 15 Août 1944, à Aspremont, le Commandant Gérôme." *L'Ergot.* 19 August 1945. ADAM. Courtesy Alain Endinger.

2. Sous Lieutenant Cavenago, quoted in Sapin (Jacques Lécuyer). *Méfiez Vous du Toréador.* (Editeur AGPM, 1987) pg. 349-350.

3. Laurent Pasquier. *Journal de Marche d'un Maquisard des Alpes Maritimes.* Unpublished manuscript. MRA.

4. Fernand. Rapport du Responsable Local du Comité de Libération Nationale. 20 August 1944. Archives Communales de St Martin du Var. ADAM.

5. Letter to Monsieur le Délégué Régional du Service de Recherches des Crimes de Guerre. Archives Communales de St Martin du Var. ADAM.

6. Sapin (Jacques Lécuyer). *Méfiez Vous du Toréador.* (Editeur AGPM, 1987) pg. 70.

7. Sapin (Jacques Lécuyer). *Méfiez Vous du Toréador.* (Editeur AGPM, 1987) pg. 71.

8. Sapin (Jacques Lécuyer). *Méfiez Vous du Toréador.* (Editeur AGPM, 1987) pg. 71.

9. Gendarmerie. Note de Renseignement numéro 3804. 19 August 1944. ADAM. Courtesy Alain Endinger.

10. Raymond Bolini. Letter to Max Mauvignant's mother. Undated. Max Joulin Collection.

11. Primo Calzoni, quoted in *Les 8ème et 27ème Compagnies FTPF dans le Résistance dans les Alpes-Maritimes.* Louis Tenerini ed. (Louis Tenerini, 1999) pg. 34-36.

12. Antoine Caviglia, quoted in *Les 8ème et 27ème Compagnies FTPF dans le Résistance dans les Alpes-Maritimes.* Louis Tenerini ed. (Louis Tenerini, 1999) pg. 80.

13. Norbert Jamme, quoted in *Les 8ème et 27ème Compagnies FTPF dans le Résistance dans les Alpes-Maritimes.* (Louis Tenerini, 1999) pg. 99-101.

14. Dr Flavier. Unpublished manuscript. Flavier Family Collection.

15. Sapin (Jacques Lécuyer). *Méfiez Vous du Toréador.* (Editeur AGPM, 1987) pg. 364.

16. Lt Buchmann letter to Johann Schmidt's father. 4 September 1944. Schmidt Family Collection.

17. Œuvre de Saint-Pierre-d'Arène. Levens. August 1944. Flavier Family Collection.

18. Laurent Pasquier. *Journal de Marche d'un Maquisard des Alpes Maritimes.* Unpublished manuscript. MRA.

19. Corrado Marcucci, quoted in *Les 8ème et 27ème Compagnies FTPF dans le Résistance dans les Alpes-Maritimes.* Louis Tenerini ed. (Louis Tenerini, 1999) pg. 25.

20. Laurent Pasquier. *Journal de Marche d'un Maquisard des Alpes Maritimes.* Unpublished manuscript. MRA.

21. Sous-Lt Betemps, quoted in Sapin (Jacques Lécuyer). *Méfiez Vous du Toréador.* (Editeur AGPM, 1987) pg. 285 and 358-360.

22. Walter G. Irving. *The Operation of Company E, 517th Parachute Infantry Combat Team, In a River Crossing and Attack at La Roquette, France, 27-28 Aug 1944.* Staff Department, The Infantry School, Fort Benning, Georgia. 1946-1950. 517prct.org Collection.

23. Pierre Gautier, quoted in Sapin (Jacques Lécuyer). *Méfiez Vous du Toréador.* (Editeur AGPM, 1987) pg. 133.

24. Walter G. Irving. *The Operation of Company E, 517th Parachute Infantry Combat Team, in a River Crossing and Attack at La Roquette, France, 27-28 Aug 1944.* Staff Department, The Infantry School, Fort Benning, Georgia. 1946-1950. 517prct.org Collection.

25. Eugene L. Brissey. *What did you do in the war, Daddy ?* Unpublished manuscript. 517prct.org Collection.

26. Hilaire Mallaussène declaration on Marcellin Richier and Jean Garente deaths. Garente Familly Collection.

27. Gendarme Hughes Rasser declaration on Marcellin Richier and Jean Garente deaths. Garente Familly Collection.

28. Gendarme Hughes Rasser declaration on Marcellin Richier and Jean Garente deaths. Garente Familly Collection.

29. Aristide Fouques declaration on Marcellin Richier and Jean Garente deaths. Garente Familly Collection.

30. Walter G. Irving. *The Operation of Company E, 517th Parachute Infantry Combat Team, in a River Crossing and Attack at La Roquette, France, 27-28 Aug 1944.* Staff Department, The Infantry School, Fort Benning, Georgia. 1946-1950. 517prct.org Collection.

31. Eugene L. Brissey. *What did you do in the war, Daddy ?* Unpublished manuscript. 517prct.org Collection.

32. Walter G. Irving. *The Operation of Company E, 517th Parachute Infantry Combat Team, in a River Crossing and Attack at La Roquette, France, 27-28 Aug 1944.* Staff Department, The Infantry School, Fort Benning, Georgia. 1946-1950. 517prct.org Collection.

33. Walter G. Irving. *The Operation of Company E, 517th Parachute Infantry Combat Team, in a River Crossing and Attack at La Roquette, France, 27-28 Aug 1944.* Staff Department, The Infantry School, Fort Benning, Georgia. 1946-1950. 517prct.org Collection.

34. Eugene L. Brissey. *What did you do in the war, Daddy ?* Unpublished manuscript. 517prct.org Collection.

35. Walter G. Irving. *The Operation of Company E, 517th Parachute Infantry Combat Team, in a River Crossing and Attack at La Roquette, France, 27-28 Aug 1944.* Staff Department, The Infantry School, Fort Benning, Georgie. 1946-1950. 517prct.org Collection.

36. Dr Flavier letter to his parents. Undated. Flavier Family Collection.

37. Walter G. Irving. *The Operation of Company E, 517th Parachute Infantry Combat Team, in a River Crossing and Attack at La Roquette, France, 27-28 Aug 1944.* Staff Department, The Infantry School, Fort Benning, Georgia. 1946-1950. 517prct.org Collection.

38. Walter G. Irving. *The Operation of Company E, 517th Parachute Infantry Combat Team, in a River Crossing and Attack at La Roquette, France, 27-28 Aug 1944.* Staff Department, The Infantry School, Fort Benning, Georgia. 1946-1950. 517prct.org Collection.

39. Walter G. Irving. *The Operation of Company E, 517th Parachute Infantry Combat Team, in a River Crossing and Attack at La Roquette, France, 27-28 Aug 1944.* Staff Department, The Infantry School, Fort Benning, Georgia. 1946-1950. 517prct.org Collection.

40. Eugene L. Brissey. *What did you do in the war, Daddy ?* Unpublished manuscript. 517prct.org Collection.

41. Col Rupert D. Graves. "Combat Team." *Blue Book Magazine.* January 1948. pg. 58. 517prct.org Collection.

42. Walter G. Irving. *The Operation of Company E, 517th Parachute Infantry Combat Team, in a River Crossing and Attack at La Roquette, France, 27-28 Aug 1944.* Staff Department, The Infantry School, Fort Benning, Georgia. 1946-1950. 517prct.org Collection.

43. Col Rupert D. Graves. "Combat Team." *Blue Book Magazine.* January 1948. pg. 58. 517prct.org Collection.

44. Eugene L. Brissey. *What did you do in the war, Daddy ?* Unpublished manuscript. 517prct.org Collection.

45. Walter G. Irving. *The Operation of Company E, 517th Parachute Infantry Combat Team, in a River Crossing and Attack at La Roquette, France, 27-28 Aug 1944.* Staff Department, The Infantry School, Fort Benning, Georgia. 1946-1950. 517prct.org Collection.

46. Walter G. Irving. *The Operation of Company E, 517th Parachute Infantry Combat Team, in a River Crossing and Attack at La Roquette, France, 27-28 Aug 1944*. Staff Department, The Infantry School, Fort Benning, Georgia. 1946-1950. 517prct.org Collection.

47. Eugene L. Brissey. *What did you do in the war, Daddy ?* Unpublished manuscript. 517prct.org Collection.

48. Dr Flavier letter to his parents. Undated. Flavier Family Collection.

49. Lt Schultz letter to the parents of Johann Seubert. 5 October 1944. Seubert Family Collection, courtesy Herman Popp.

50. Lt Buchmann letter to the parents of Kaspar Fischer. 30 September 1944. Fischer Family Collection.

51. Howard Jaynes Silver Star citation. FABTF General Orders. Awards. Late 1944. NARA.

52. Allan Goodman, quoted in Michel de Trez. *First Airborne Task Force : Pictorial History of the Allied Paratroopers in the Invasion of Southern France* (Wesembeek-Oppem, Belgium: D-Day Publishing, 1998)

Chapter 13

1. "Livre Noir… Livre d'Or de la Résistance. L'Ariane." *L'Ergot.* MRA.

2. Joseph Cape. Liste des Crimes de Guerre Corporels Commis par les Allemands sur le Térritoire de la Commune de Nice. 616 W 259. ADAM.

3. Generalmajor Hellmuth Nickelmann personal file. NARA.

4. Hellmuth Nickelmann, quoted in "La Libération de Nice vue par les Autorités Allemandes." *Documents, Témoignages, Recherches* no 26. MRA.

5. Hellmuth Nickelmann, quoted in "La Libération de Nice vue par les Autorités Allemandes." *Documents, Témoignages, Recherches* no 26. MRA.

6. Hellmuth Nickelmann, quoted in "La Libération de Nice vue par les Autorités Allemandes." *Documents, Témoignages, Recherches* no 26. MRA.

7. Hellmuth Nickelmann, quoted in "La Libération de Nice vue par les Autorités Allemandes." *Documents, Témoignages, Recherches* no 26. MRA.

8. Pierre Durand, quoted in : "Nice, 28 août 1944. L'insurrection racontée par les insurgés." *Documents, Témoignages, Recherches* no 9. MRA.

9. René Canta. "FFI. FTPF. Reseau BADG 131 – Groupe René." 8 September 1944. MRA.

10. Capitaine Paul Cavenago report. MRA.

11. Louis Sana, quoted in : "Nice, 28 août 1944. L'insurrection racontée par les insurgés." *Documents, Témoignages, Recherches* no 9. MRA.

12. Capitaine Paul Cavenago report. MRA.

13. Mathis. "Rapport du Lieutenant Mathis." MRA

14. Robert. "Rapport d'activité du 27 aout inclus." MRA.

15. Hellmuth Nickelmann, quoted in "La Libération de Nice vue par les Autorités Allemandes." *Documents, Témoignages, Recherches* no 26. MRA.

16. 509th PIB G-3 reports. IPW report. 1 to 2 September 1944. NARA.

17. 509th PIB G-3 reports. IPW report. 1 to 2 September 1944. NARA.

18. "Résistance en Provence: Missions Spéciales sur le "Front des Alpes" par Remy." Extract of an unknown publication, preserved at the MRA in the file of Joseph le Fou. MRA.

19. Report on Operation Rabelais. Late 1944. NARA.

20. Geoffey Jones, quoted in George Adleman, Robert Walton. *The Champagne Campaign.* (Little, Brown and Company, 1969) pg. 155.

21. Geoffey Jones, quoted in George Adleman, Robert Walton. *The Champagne Campaign.* (Little, Brown and Company, 1969) pg. 155-160.

22. Service Historique de l'Armée de Terre. 10 P 188, E.-M., Armée B, 3ème bureau, 31 août 1944. Published in: Pierre-Emmanuel Klingbeil. *Le Front Oublié des Alpes Maritimes.* (Serre Editeur, 2005) pg. 424-426.

23. Hellmuth Nickelmann, quoted in "La Libération de Nice vue par les Autorités Allemandes." *Documents, Témoignages, Recherches* no 26. MRA.

24. Bernard. "Rapport du chef de groupe Bernard, adjoint CFL." MRA.

25. René Canta. "FFI. FTPF. Reseau BADG 131 – Groupe René." 8 September 1944. MRA.

26. Philippe Giovannini. "La Libération de Nice – 28 août 1944." Unpublished manuscript. pg. 3 and 10. MRA.

27. Alfred Gambassi. "Les Résistants Etrangers dans la Ribération de Nice." MRA.

28. 'Pensée' Martini, quoted in : "Nice, 28 août 1944. L'insurrection racontée par les insurgés." *Documents, Témoignages, Recherches* no 9. MRA.

29. Louis, matricule 62459. "Rapport sur la journée du 28 août 1944." MRA.

30. Erich Baltanz, letter written to the wife of Richart Tönnissen on 25 February 1949. Karl-Heinz Butenschön Collection.

31. Erich Baltanz, letter written to the wife of Richart Tönnissen on 25 February 1949. Karl-Heinz Butenschön Collection.

32. Paul Granier. "A Monsieur Brunetti." MRA.

33. Georges Damiot. "Rapport d'activité du 28 août au 3 septembre." MRA.

34. A. Téobaldi. "Rapport du Gardien de la Paix Téobaldi A. du Groupe Combat, concernant la journée du 28 août 1944." MRA.

35. Bovis. "Rapport. Participation aux opérations de nettoyage du 28 août 1944." MRA.

36. Inspecteur Rossi. "A Monsieur le Commandant Parent, chef des Corps Francs de la Libération des A.M. Nice." MRA.

37. Brigadier Louis Pernot. "A Monsieur le Commandant des FFI Section Combat." MRA.

38. Mathis. "Rapport du Lieutenant Mathis." MRA

39. Capitaine Paul Cavenago report. MRA.

40. Pierre Durand. *Nice Libérée. De Sacco et Vanzetti à la Libération.* Unpublished manuscript. MRA.

41. Mathis. "Rapport du Lieutenant Mathis." MRA

42. Noël Lanzi, quoted in: "Nice, 28 août 1944. L'insurrection racontée par les insurgés." *Documents, Témoignages, Recherches* no 9. MRA.

43. Henri Cauvin, quoted in: "Nice, 28 août 1944. L'insurrection racontée par les insurgés." *Documents, Témoignages, Recherches* no 9. MRA.

44. Mathis. "Rapport du Lieutenant Mathis." MRA

45. Albert Piccardo. Albert Piccardo file. MRA.

46. Hellmuth Nickelmann, quoted in "La Libération de Nice vue par les Autorités Allemandes." *Documents, Témoignages, Recherches* no 26. MRA.

47. René Canta. "FFI. FTPF. Reseau BADG 131 – Groupe René. 8 September 1944." MRA.

48. Hellmuth Nickelmann, quoted in "La Libération de Nice vue par les Autorités Allemandes." *Documents, Témoignages, Recherches* no 26. MRA.

49. César Martini, quoted in: "Nice, 28 août 1944. L'insurrection racontée par les insurgés." *Documents, Témoignages, Recherches* no 9. MRA.

50. Edouard Bertrand, quoted in: "Nice, 28 août 1944. L'insurrection racontée par les insurgés." *Documents, Témoignages, Recherches* no 9. MRA.

51. Bernard. "Rapport du chef de groupe Bernard, adjoint CFL." MRA.

52. Capitaine Paul Cavenago report. MRA.

53. Mathis. "Rapport du Lieutenant Mathis." MRA

54. André Cane. *Histoire de Villefranche sur Mer et de ses Anciens Hameaux de Beaulieu et de Saint Jean.* (Beaulieu sur Mer: André Cane, 1960) pg. 103.

55. "Tandis que les Allemands pris de furie dévastent un quartier et massacrent cinq civils les Chemises Noirs assassinent un sous officier français." *L'Ergot.* 29 december 1944. MRA.

56. "L'étudiant en médecine qui alla relever les cadavres des cinq suppliciés failli être fusillé lui aussi." *L'Ergot.* MRA.

57. "Tandis que les Allemands pris de furie dévastent un quartier et massacrent cinq civils les Chemises Noirs assassinent un sous officier français." *L'Ergot.* 29 december 1944. MRA.

58. Capitaine Bidet. "Rapport sur la physionomie de la circonscription pendant la période du 28/2 au 11/9/1944." 616 W 259. ADAM.

59. Adjudant Chef Maurice. "Rapport de l'Adjudant Chef Maurice commandant la brigade sur l'exécution de 4 personnes." ADAM.

60. Pierre Durand. *Nice Libérée. De Sacco et Vanzetti à la Libération.* Unpublished manuscript. MRA.

61. Dan Morgan. *The Left Corner of my Heart.* (Alder Enterprises, 1984) pg. 242.

62. Dick Durkee, quoted in Dan Morgan. *The Left Corner of my Heart.* (Alder Enterprises, 1984) pg. 244.

63. René Canta. "FFI. FTPF. Reseau BADG 131 – Groupe René. 8 September 1944." MRA.

64. Ralph Wenthold, quoted in Dan Morgan. *The Left Corner of my Heart.* (Alder Enterprises, 1984) pg. 245-247.

65. Peter L. Cottingham. *Once Upon a Wartime.* (Brandon, Manitoba: Leech Printing, 1996) pg. 164-165.

66. Paul Hoch, quoted in Dan Morgan. *The Left Corner of my Heart.* (Alder Enterprises, 1984) pg. 252.

67. Jud Chalkley, quoted in Dan Morgan. *The Left Corner of my Heart.* (Alder Enterprises, 1984) pg. 244-245.

68. Tim Quinn, quoted in Dan Morgan. *The Left Corner of my Heart.* (Alder Enterprises, 1984) pg. 244.

69. Peter L. Cottingham. *Once Upon a Wartime.* (Brandon, Manitoba: Leech Printing, 1996) pg. 165-166.

70. Sapin (Jacques Lécuyer). *Méfiez Vous du Toréador.* (Editeur AGPM, 1987) pg. 76-77.

Chapter 14

1. Sapin (Jacques Lécuyer). *Méfiez Vous du Toréador.* (Editeur AGPM, 1987) pg. 69-74.

2. Ginette (Félix Petitjean). *Le Temps des Fauves.* (Paris : La Pensée Universelle, 1972) pg. 54.

3. Alain Otho. Libération de la vallée de la Vésubie. 15 août-30 août 1944. Pays Vésubien. n°7/2006. p 240. Courtesy Alain Endinger.

4. Alain Otho. Libération de la vallée de la Vésubie. 15 août-30 août 1944. Pays Vésubien. n°7/2006. p 240. Courtesy Alain Endinger.

5. Ginette (Félix Petitjean). *Le Temps des Fauves.* (Paris : La Pensée Universelle, 1972) pg. 65-67.

6. Ginette (Félix Petitjean). *Le Temps des Fauves.* (Paris : La Pensée Universelle,

1972) pg. 67-68.

7. Ginette (Félix Petitjean). *Le Temps des Fauves*. (Paris : La Pensée Universelle, 1972) pg. 68-70.

8. Jules Pivot. *Vous avez dit Résistance ? Dans la police des Alpes-Maritimes. L'Épuration. Guerre 1939 - 1945*. Octobre 1987. www.michel-elbaze.fr

9. Questionaire sur l'Occupation envoyé aux mairies; Toudon. 169 W 003. ADAM.

Chapter 15

1. André Laugier. *L'Insurrection de Peille*. MRA.

2. FSSF journal. September 1944. NARA.

3. Joe Chicchinelli, quoted in Dan Morgan. *The Left Corner of my Heart*. (Alder Enterprises, 1984) pg. 264.

4. Joe Cicchinelli. *The Liberation of la Turbie*. Joe Chicchinelli Collection.

5. Lou Waters, quoted in Dan Morgan. *The Left Corner of my Heart*. (Alder Enterprises, 1984) pg. 265-266.

6. Joe Chicchinelli, quoted in Dan Morgan. *The Left Corner of my Heart*. (Alder Enterprises, 1984) pg. 266.

7. Joe Cicchinelli. *The Liberation of la Turbie*. Joe Chicchinelli Collection.

8. Pascal Hainaut. *Sur les Pas d'Un Parachutiste Américain*. (Houffalize, France: Pascal Hainaut, 2006) pg. 54.

9. Joe Cicchinelli. *The Liberation of la Turbie*. Joe Chicchinelli Collection.

10. Joe Kosowski, quoted in Dan Morgan. *The Left Corner of my Heart*. (Alder Enterprises, 1984) pg. 252-253.

11. 551st PIB unit history. September 1944. NARA.

12. Lt George Parnell letter to his wife. 5 September 1944. Marion Parnell Collection.

13. Capt Walls, quoted in Charles H. Doyle, Terrell Stewart. *Stand in the Door*. (Williamstown, NJ: Phillipps Publications, 1988) pg. 294-295.

14. 551st PIB unit history. September 1944. NARA.

15. Louis Fiori. *Les Cahiers du Musée de la Résistance Azuréenne*. No 68. February 2011. pg 11-12. MRA

16. Capitaine Tilly, quoted in Sapin (Jacques Lécuyer). *Méfiez Vous du Toréador*. (Editeur AGPM, 1987) pg. 235-236.

17. William Story. Unpublished manuscript.

18. Peter L. Cottingham. *Once Upon a Wartime*. (Brandon, Manitoba: Leech Printing, 1996) pg. 168-171.

19. Lt George Parnell letter to his wife. 9 September 1944. Marion Parnell Collection.

20. FSSF journal. September 1944. NARA.

21. Hoyt Kelley. *World War II Journal Hoyt Frank Kelley 1943-1945*. Unpublished manuscript. pg. 43. 517prct.org Collection.

22. Robert Steel Silver Star citation. FABTF General Orders. Late 1944. NARA.

23. Don Fraser, quoted in Gerald Astor. *Battling Buzzards*. (NY, NY, Dell Publishing, 1993) pg. 220-221.

24. Don Fraser Silver Star citation. FABTF General Orders. Late 1944. NARA.

25. Mitsugi Nakahara Silver Star citation. FABTF General Orders. Late 1944. NARA.

26. Joseph Van Ness IDPF. US Army Human Resources Command, Fort Knox, Kentucky.

27. Olt Erich Niederl letter to Xaver Paulsteiner's father. 9 September 1944. Paulsteiner Family Collection.

28. FSSF journal. August 1944. NARA.

29. FSSF journal. August 1944. NARA.

30. FSSF. Operations of small units. September 1944. NARA.

31. FSSF. Summary of our operations. September 1944. NARA.

32. Rex Attwel. Unpublished manuscript.

33. Rex Attwel. Unpublished manuscript.

34. FSSF journal. September 1944. NARA.

35. Rex Attwel. Unpublished manuscript.

36. Clark Archer. *Paratroopers' Odyssey. A History of the 517th Parachute Combat Team* (Hudson, FL: 517th PRCT Association, 1985) Chap IV.

37. Felix Povinelli and Leonard Cooper Silver Star citations. FABTF General Orders. NARA.

38. Rober Boese Silver Star citations. FABTF General Orders. NARA.

39. FSSF journal. September 1944. NARA.

40. FSSF. Summary of our operations. September 1944. NARA.

41. Guy E. Carr. *The Champaign campaign*. Unpublished manuscript.

Chapter 16

1. Iraq and Afghanistan Coalition Military Fatalities By Year. http://icasualties.org/

2. Period newspaper clipping from an unknown source. Author's Collection.

3. William M. Bowers Jr. *Don't Ever Give Up*. 1997

4. Arthur Ridler Silver Star citation. FABTF General Orders. Late 1944. NARA.

5. Dick Spencer. "What can I say?" *The Thunderbolt*. Late 1944. Howard Hensleigh Collection.

6. Clark Archer. *Paratroopers' Odyssey. A History of the 517th Parachute Combat Team* (Hudson, FL: 517th PRCT Association, 1985) Chap IV.

7. "Einer von der tapferen *Infanterie*." *Nationalblatt, ausgabe Neuwied*. 13

November 1944. Frode Steine Collection.

8. Historical report HQ First Airborne Task Force for October 1944. NARA.

9. James E. T. Hopkins, M.D. "Casualty Survey-New Georgia and Burma Campaigns," in *Wound ballistics*. Edited by Leonard D. Heaton, James Boyd Coates Jr, James C. Beyer. (Washington D.C.: Office of the Surgeon General Department of the Army. 1962) pg. 277.

10. Merle McMorrow. *From Breckenridge to Bastogne*. 2nd Edition. (Fargo, ND: Richman's Press Club, 2004) pg. 119-121.

11. Hoyt Kelley. *World War II Journal Hoyt Frank Kelley 1943-1945*. Unpublished manuscript. pg. 43. 517prct.org Collection.

12. Marvin McRoberts. Unpublished manuscript. Available online at: http://community-2.webtv.net/masterofneon4/602dFieldArtillery/

13. John Neiler. 3 October 1944 POW report. 517th PIR files. NARA

14. Ruppert Graves. 517th PIR S-3 Periodic Report. 3 October 1944. 517th PIR files. NARA.

15. Gerhard Höfig letter to Georg Rieck family. 28 January 1945. Rieck Family Collection.

16. Order of the day. 2nd Battalion 107th *Grenadier* Regiment. 2 October 1944. Rieck Family Collection.

17. Guy E. Carr. *The Champaign campaign*. Unpublished manuscript.

18. Guy E. Carr. *The Champaign campaign*. Unpublished manuscript.

19. Marvin Moles Silver Star citation. Marvin Moles Collection.

20. Erwin W. Scott Jr. interview. The National Museum of the Pacific War. Fredericksburg, Texas. Transcribed by Mary Dru Burns. 6 April 2002. Scott Atkinson and 517thprct.org Collections.

21. Ernest Engle Silver Star citation. FABTF General Orders. Late 1944. NARA.

22. John C. Cooley in Michel de Trez. *First Airborne Task Force : Pictorial History of the Allied Paratroopers in the Invasion of Southern France* (Wesembeek-Oppem, Belgium: D-Day Publishing, 1998) pg. 108.

23. George A. Ford, letter to his wife dated December 15, 1944. Ann Ford Collection.

24. George A. Ford, letter to his wife dated December 30, 1944. Ann Ford Collection.

25. Jose Robles Jr., statement dated January 6, 1945. Ann Ford Collection.

26. Daniel B. Logan, statement. Ann Ford Collection.

27. Jose Robles Jr., statement dated January 6, 1945. Ann Ford Collection.

28. Daniel B. Logan, statement. Ann Ford Collection.

29. Sidney Oxman diary. 1944. Oxman Family Collection.

30. Angelin German. *Les Chemins de la Mémoire*. (Draguignan, France: Imprimerie Bonnaud) pg. 77

31. Herbert E. MacCombie. *Chaplains of the 36th Infantry Division*. Mary MacCombie Fietsam Collection.

32. Raymond Thompson IDPF. US Army Human Resources Command, Fort Knox, Kentucky.

33. Raymond Thompson IDPF. US Army Human Resources Command, Fort Knox, Kentucky.

34. Raymond Thompson IDPF. US Army Human Resources Command, Fort Knox, Kentucky.

35. Raymond Thompson IDPF. US Army Human Resources Command, Fort Knox, Kentucky.

36. Donald Hagvall, quoted in Purnell's History of the Second World War.

37. Burnell Rose IDPF. US Army Human Resources Command, Fort Knox, Kentucky.

38. William Gates IDPF. US Army Human Resources Command, Fort Knox, Kentucky.

39. Vernon Dirkson IDPF. US Army Human Resources Command, Fort Knox, Kentucky.

40. William Gates IDPF. US Army Human Resources Command, Fort Knox, Kentucky.

41. Richard Bednarz IDPF. US Army Human Resources Command, Fort Knox, Kentucky.

42. Willa Parks Ward. "One Autumn Afternoon." 2001. Available online from the National Public Radio 'National Story Project' at http://www.npr.org/programs/watc/storyproject/

Allied sources

Adleman George, Robert Walton. *The Champagne Campaign,* Little, Brown and Company, 1969.

Anderson Kelley Woody. *The Kennemer Book: A Great American Family*, Gurley, Alabama: Concept Inc., 1982.

Archer Clark. *Paratroopers' Odyssey. A History of the 517th Parachute Combat Team*, Hudson, FL: 517th PRCT Association, 1985.

Astor Gerald. *Battling Buzzards*, NY, NY, Dell Publishing, 1993.

Attwell Rex. Unpublished manuscript.

Banks Herbert C. II., ed., *517th Parachute Regimental Combat Team*, Padukah, KY: Turner Publishing Company, 1998.

Bowers William M. Jr. *Don't Ever Give Up.* Manuscript. 1998.

Brissey Eugene L. *What did you do in the war, Daddy?* Unpublished manuscript. Available at 517prct.org

Burhans Robert D. *The First Special Service Force. A War History of the North Americans. 1942-1944*. Washington, D.C.: Washington Infantry Journal Press, 1947.

Carr Guy E. *The Champaign campaign.* Unpublished manuscript.

Cottingham Peter L. *Once Upon a Wartime*, Brandon, Manitoba: Leech Printing, 1996.

Dank Milton. *The Glider Gang*, J.B. Lippincott Company,1977.

De Trez Michel. *First Airborne Task Force : Pictorial History of the Allied Paratroopers in the Invasion of Southern France*, Wesembeek-Oppem, Belgium: D-Day Publishing, 1998.

Donavan Ray. Unpublished manuscript.

Doyle Charles H., Terrell Stewart. *Stand in the Door*, Williamstown, NJ: Phillipps Publications, 1988.

Fisco Richard. *Your Lives Will be Beautiful,* Ramsey, NJ: Arbor Books, 2008.

Funk Arthur L. *Hidden Ally*, New York : Greenwood Press, 1992.

Graves Rupert D. "Combat Team." *Blue Book Magazine.* December 1947 and January 1948. Available at 517prct.org

Hainaut Pascal. *Sur les Pas d'un Parachutiste Américain*, Houffalize, France: Pascal Hainaut, 2006.

Heaton Leonard D., Ed. *Wound Ballistics,* Washington D.C.: Office of the Surgeon General, Department of the Army, 1962.

Helmers Art. *One soldier's view*. Unpublished manuscript.

Higgins Thomas J.. "The Truth About Tulsa's Kennamer-Gorrel Case." *The Master Detective*. Vol. 12. Number 6. August 1935.

Irving Walter G. *The Operation of Company E, 517th Parachute Infantry Combat Team, in a River Crossing and Attack at La Roquette, France, 27-28 Aug 1944.* Staff Department, The Infantry School, Fort Benning, Georgia. 1946-1950. Available at 517prct.org

Jansen Clarence R. *Clarence R. Jansen and World War II.* Unpublished manuscript.

Kelley Hoyt. *World War II Journal Hoyt Frank Kelley. 1943-1945.* Unpublished manuscript.

MacCombie Herbert E. *Chaplains of the 36th Infantry Division.* Unpublished manuscript. Available at: http://www.texasmilitaryforcesmuseum.org

McMorrow Merle. *From Breckenridge to Bastogne.* 2nd Edition, Fargo, ND: Richman's Press Club, 2004.

McRoberts Marvin. Unpublished manuscript.

Morgan Dan. *The Left Corner of my Heart,* Alder Enterprises, 1984.

Oxman Sidney. Unpublished diary.

Parks Ward Willa."One Autumn Afternoon." 2001. Available online from the National Public Radio 'National Story Project' at http://www.npr.org/programs/watc/storyproject/

Rogers Milton. *How I saw it.* Unpublished manuscript. Available at 517prct.org

Scott Erwin W. Jr. interview. The National Museum of the Pacific War. Fredericksburg, Texas. Transcribed by Mary Dru Burns. 6 April 2002. Available at 517prct.org

Springer Joseph. *The Black Devil's Brigade*, Pacifica, CA: Pacifica Military History, 2001.

Stillwell Paul, ed. *Assault on Normandy: First Person Accounts from the Sea Services* (Annapolis, Md: Naval Institute Press: © 1994).

Story William. Unpublished manuscript.

Strom Carl. Unpublished manuscript.

Underhill Adna H. *The Force*, Tucson, AZ: Arizona Monographs, 1994.

Wilson Jack. Unpublished manuscript.

French sources

Boulingez Franck. Article about José Thomas. Service des Archives de Mouans Sartoux Colletion.

Cane André. *Histoire de Villefranche sur Mer et de ses Anciens Hameaux de Beaulieu et de Saint Jean*, Beaulieu sur Mer: André Cane, 1960.

Chazette Alain. *L'Armée Allemande Sur la Côte Méditerréenne, A.O.K.19 Mittelmeerküstenfront, volume 1*, Paris: Editions Histoire & collection, 2004.

De Vanssay Elisabeth (de Panisse Passis). *Le Siège de Villeneuve.* Unpublished manuscript. Nadèje le Lédan Collection.

Gandiglio Charles. *La Libération de Montauroux à Peymeinade.*

Garino Pierre-Robert. *La Roquette-Saint Martin. Crounica dei Rouquetan e San Martinenc.* Serre Editeur, 1994.

German Angelin. *Les Chemins de la Mémoire,* Draguignan, France: Imprimerie Bonnaud.

Ghio René. *Mes Années de Guerre*, quoted in : Actes du Colloque du 27 Novembre 2007, Devoir de mémoire. L'Occupation, la Résistance et la Libération à Grasse et en pays de Grasse, Association Historique du Pays de Grasse.

Ginette (Félix Petitjean). *Le Temps des Fauves*, Paris : La Pensée Universelle, 1972.

Giraud Raymond. "L'Enfer du Vallon de Cireuil." Villeneuve-Loubet town hall publication. Unknown date.

Isnard Honoré. *Les Derniers Jours de l'Occupation et la Libération du Port et de la Ville de Cannes*, Cannes: Imprimerie Devay, 1950.

Issert Marius. *Souvenirs d'un maire*. 1945-1995, St Paul: Editions de la Commune de St Paul, 2000.

Klingbeil Pierre-Emmanuel. *Le Front Oublié des Alpes Maritimes.* Serre Editeur, 2005.

Le souvenir Français. *Saint Laurent du Var 1940-1944*, St Laurent du Var: Le souvenir Français, 1994.

Moscone Ferdinand. *La Libération d'Antibes.* Unpublished manuscript.

Mougins Amélie. Unpublished diary.

Musée de la Résistance Azuréenne. "Nice, 28 août 1944. L'Insurrection Racontée par les Insurgés." *Documents, Témoignages, Recherches* no 9.

Œuvre de Saint Pierre d'Arène. Levens. August. 1944.

Otho Alain. Libération de la vallée de la Vésubie. 15 août-30 août 1944. Pays Vésubien. n°7/2006. p 240.

Panicacci Jean-Louis. *Les Alpes-Maritimes de 1939 à 1945 - Un département dans la tourmente*. Nice : Éditions Serre, 1996.

Pivot Jules. *Vous avez dit Résistance ? Dans la police des Alpes-Maritimes. L'Épuration. Guerre 1939 - 1945*. Octobre 1987. www.michel-elbaze.fr

Robichon Jacques. *Le Débarquement de Provence*, Presse de la Cité, 1982.

Sapin (Jacques Lécuyer). *Méfiez Vous du Toréador*, Editeur AGPM, 1987.

Tenerini Louis ed. *Les 8ème et 27ème Compagnies FTPF dans le Résistance dans les Alpes-Maritimes*, Louis Tenerini, 1999.

Torel Denis, F. Detaille. *Monaco Sous les Barbelés*, Editions Serge Klarfeld, 1996.

Verots-Guibaud Anne. *Chronique de la Vie Vencoise. 1930-1975*, A. Verots-Guilbaud, 1999.

German Sources

Bieringer Ludwig. "Die Invasion in Suedfrankriech am 15/16 Aug vom Feldkdt 800 in Draguignan aus gesehen." Foreign Military Studies B Series (RG 338). 1951. NARA.

Fretter-Pico Otto. "148 *Infanterie*-Division Mai-September 1944." Foreign Military Studies B Series (RG 338). 1950. NARA.

Nickelmann Hellmuth, quoted in "La Libération de Nice vue par les Autorités Allemandes." *Documents, Témoignages, Recherches* no 26. MRA.

Rohde Lorenz. "Schneewittchen in Monte Carlo." *Mitteilunggen der Gemeinschaft ehemaliger Angehöriger der 148 ID.* September 1967.

Schimdt Karl-Ernst. "Ernstes und Heiteres aus meiner Zeit bei der 148 I.D." *Mitteilunggen der Gemeinschaft ehemaliger Angehöriger der 148 ID.* Nr 24. November 1977.

Sources of research documents

Archives Départementales des Alpes Maritimes. Nice, France.

Musée de la Résistance Azuréenne. Nice, France.

National Archives and Records Administration. Washington D.C. USA.

U.S. Army Human Resources Command. Fort Knox, Kentucky, USA.

Volksbund Deutsches Kriegsgräberfürsorge. Kassel, Germany.

Index

551

Index of people